Voyages in World History

Valerie Hansen
YALE UNIVERSITY

Kenneth R. Curtis
CALIFORNIA STATE UNIVERSITY LONG BEACH

WADSWORTH
CENGAGE Learning

Australia • Brazil • Japan • Korea • Mexico • Singapore • Spain • United Kingdom • United States

Voyages in World History
Valerie Hansen and Kenneth R. Curtis

Senior Publisher: Suzanne Jeans

Senior Acquisitions Editor: Nancy Blaine

Senior Development Editor: Jennifer E. Sutherland

Consultant Development Editor: Jean L. Woy

Associate Editor: Adrienne Zicht

Senior Marketing Manager: Katherine Bates

Marketing Coordinator: Loreen Pelletier

Marketing Communications Manager: Christine Dobberpuhl

Senior Content Project Manager: Christina M. Horn

Senior Media Editor: Lisa Ciccolo

Art Director: Jill Haber

Print Buyer: Arethea Thomas

Permissions Editor: Terri Hampton

Text Designer: Henry Rachlin

Art Editor: Charlotte Miller/Janet Theurer

Photo Researcher: Linda Sykes

Copyeditor: Susan Zorn

Cover Designer: Faith Brosnan

Cover Image: A ship of the Turkish merchant navy from a 16th-century manuscript, *Codex Cicogna*. Photo: Museo Correr, Venice/Cameraphoto Arte, Venice/Art Resource, NY.

Title Page Photo: *Universale descrittione di tutta la terra conoscivta fin qui*, by Paolo Forlani, 1565. From the Rosenwald Collection, Library of Congress, no. 1304.

Compositor: NK Graphics

Library of Congress Control Number: 2008938670

ISBN-13: 978-0-495-90053-5

ISBN-10: 0-495-90053-2

Wadsworth
25 Thomson Place
Boston, MA 02110-1202
USA

Cengage Learning products are represented in Canada by Nelson Education, Ltd.

For your course and learning solutions, visit **www.cengage.com.**

Purchase any of our products at your local college store or at our preferred online store **www.ichapters.com.**

Printed in the United States of America
1 2 3 4 5 6 7 12 11 10 09

Brief Contents

CONTENTS

CHAPTER 1   **The Peopling of the World, to 4000 B.C.E.**   2

TRAVELER: Kennewick Man

CHAPTER 2   **The First Complex Societies in the Eastern
Mediterranean, ca. 4000–550 B.C.E.**   28

TRAVELER: Gilgamesh

Note: All images are copyrighted. For full photo credit information, please see each chapter opener
page.

CHAPTER **3**

Ancient India and the Rise of Buddhism, 2600 B.C.E.–100 C.E.
60

TRAVELER: Ashoka

CHAPTER **4**

Blueprint for Empire: China, 1200 B.C.E.–220 C.E.
88

TRAVELER: First Emperor of the Qin Dynasty

CHAPTER 5

The Americas and the Islands of the Pacific, to 1200 C.E.

114

TRAVELER: Yax K'uk Mo'

CHAPTER 6

New Empires in Iran and Greece, 2000 B.C.E.–651 C.E.

144

TRAVELER: Herodotus

CHAPTER 7

The Roman Empire and the Rise of Christianity, 509 B.C.E.–476 C.E.   174

TRAVELER: Polybius

CHAPTER 8

Hindu and Buddhist States and Societies in Asia, 100–1000   208

TRAVELER: Xuanzang

CHAPTER **9**

Islamic Empires of Western Asia and Africa, 600–1258

238

TRAVELER: Khaizuran

CHAPTER **10**

The Multiple Centers of Europe, 500–1000

268

TRAVELERS: Gudrid and Thorfinn Karlsefni

CHAPTER **11**

Expanding Trade Networks in Africa and India, 1000–1500

300

TRAVELER: Ibn Battuta

CHAPTER **12**

China's Commercial Revolution, ca. 900–1276

328

TRAVELER: Li Qingzhao

CHAPTER **13**

Europe's Commercial Revolution, 1000–1400

356

TRAVELERS: **Peter Abelard and Heloise**

CHAPTER **16**

Maritime Expansion in Afro-Eurasia, 1500–1700
450

TRAVELER: Matteo Ricci

CHAPTER **17**

Religion, Politics, and the Balance of Power in Western Eurasia, 1500–1750
480

TRAVELER: Jean de Chardin

CHAPTER 20

Empires in Early Modern Asia, 1650–1818

568

TRAVELER: Xie Qinggao

CHAPTER 21

European Science and the Foundations of Modern Imperialism, 1600–1820

598

TRAVELER: Joseph Banks

CHAPTER 27

War, Revolution, and Global Uncertainty, 1905–1928

782

TRAVELER: Louise Bryant

CHAPTER 28

Responses to Global Crisis, 1920–1939

812

TRAVELER: Halide Edib

MAPS

VISUAL EVIDENCE

MOVEMENT OF IDEAS

WORLD HISTORY IN TODAY'S WORLD

PREFACE

What makes this book different from other world history textbooks?

- Each chapter opens with a narrative about a traveler that grabs the reader's attention.
- Shorter than most world history textbooks, this survey still covers all of the major topics required in a world history course.
- The book's theme of "movement" highlights cultural contact.
- A single authorial voice makes many comparisons among different societies, reinforcing what students have learned in previous chapters.
- Innovative, reader-friendly maps show the travelers' routes while inviting students to think analytically about geography and its role in world history.
- A beautiful, open, student-friendly design—with chapter outlines, bold key terms, and an on-page glossary and pronunciation guide—helps students learn better.
- Chapter-opening focus questions and chapter summaries (which can be downloaded to an MP3) help students grasp the main ideas of the chapters.

This world history textbook will, we hope, be enjoyable for students to read and for instructors to teach. We have focused on thirty-two different people and the journeys they took, starting ten thousand years ago with Kennewick Man (Chapter 1) and concluding in the twenty-first century with the film director Mira Nair. Each of the thirty-two chapters (one for each week of the school year) introduces multiple themes. First, the travelers' narratives introduce the home society and the new civilizations they visited. This demonstrates the movement of people, ideas, trade goods, and artistic motifs. We introduce other evidence, often drawn from primary sources, to help students reason like historians. Each chapter also covers the effects of increasing contact and trade among civilizations, changes in political structure, spread of world religions, and finally, the prevailing social structure and gender.

These chapter-opening narratives enhance the scope and depth of the topics covered. The travelers take us to Mesopotamia with Gilgamesh, to Africa with the hajj pilgrim Ibn Battuta, to Peru with the cross-dressing soldier and adventurer Catalina de Erauso, to the Americas with the African Olaudah Equiano, and to Britain during the Industrial Revolution with the Russian socialist Alexander Herzen. They wrote vivid accounts, often important sources about these long ago events that shaped our world.

Chapter 12, for example, tells the story of the Chinese poet Li Qingzhao. She lived during the Song dynasty (960–1275) and experienced firsthand China's commercial revolution and calamitous warfare. Her eyewitness account of her husband's death brings this pivotal period in Chinese history to life. Students also learn about the contacts between China and Japan, Korea, and Vietnam during this time of economic growth. In Chapter 24, the focus is on the great Japanese reformer Fukuzawa Yûkichi, an influential participant in the revolutionary changes that accompanied his country's Meiji Restoration (1868).

Students new to world history, or to history in general, will find it easier, we hope, to focus on the experience of thirty-two individuals before focusing on the broader themes of a new society each week. Instead of a canned list of dates, each chapter covers the important topics at a sensible and careful pace, without compromising coverage or historical rigor. Students compare the traveler's perceptions with alternative sources, and so awaken their interest in the larger developments. Our goal was to select the most compelling topics and engaging illustrations from the entire record of human civilization, presented in a clear spatial and temporal framework, to counter the view of history as an interminable compendium of geographical place names and facts.

We have chosen a range of travelers, both male and female, from all over the world. Many travelers were well-born and well-educated, and many were not. The Scandinavian explorers Thorfinn and Gudrid

Karlsefni (Chapter 10) and the blind Chinese sailor Xie Qinggao (Chapter 20) were born into ordinary families. These individuals help cast our world history in a truly global format, avoiding the Eurocentrism that prompted the introduction of world history courses in the first place.

The book originated at a meeting in 1998 that reviewed twenty or so of the most important world history textbooks on the market. Most of the books seemed similar and all felt encyclopedic. They were crammed with facts, big as phone books, and hard to read. Everything about these books was sacrificed for the sake of comprehensiveness. Few of these texts conveyed the excitement—or pleasure—of studying history.

When we asked Ken Curtis to join the project, he responded very cautiously to the idea of co-authoring a traditional world history textbook. But eventually the chance to write a different type of book, one focusing on the experience of individual travelers, one that worked toward making students enthusiastic about world history, won him over.

Achieving the right balance between the traveler's experience and the course material has certainly been a challenge. After circulating draft chapters to over 120 instructors of the course, we have found that most agree on the basic topics to be covered. The long process of revision resulted in our giving less space to the traveler and more to the basic themes of the book. We realized that we had achieved the right balance when the reviewers asked for more information about the travelers.

In this way, our book is self-contained but open-ended, should instructors or their students wish to do more reading. Some instructors may decide to devote some time in their lectures to the travelers, who are indeed fascinating; students, we hope, will naturally be inclined to write term papers about them. Almost all of these travel accounts are available in English translation, listed in the suggested readings at the end of each chapter. If instructors assign readings in addition to the textbook, they can assign those travel accounts from the world area with which they are most familiar. Where a Europeanist might assign additional readings from Herodotus, for example, an Asianist might prefer to assign the narratives of the Buddhist pilgrim Xuanzang.

We aspire to answer many of the unmet needs of professors and students in world history. Because our book is not encyclopedic, and because each chapter begins with a narrative of a trip, our book is more readable than its competitors, which strain for all-inclusive coverage. They pack so many names and facts into their text that they leave little time to introduce beginning students to historical method. Because our book gives students a chance to read primary sources in depth, particularly in the Movement of Ideas feature (described below), instructors can spend class time teaching students how to reason historically—not just imparting the details of a given national history. Each chapter includes discussion questions that make it easier for instructors new to world history to facilitate interactive learning. Each chapter closes with answers to those questions: a feature in response to student views as expressed in focus groups.

Our approach particularly suits the needs of young professors who have been trained in only one geographic area of history. Our book does not presuppose that instructors already have broad familiarity with the history of each important world civilization.

Volume 1, which covers material from the first hominids to 1500, introduces students to the important regions and societies of the world: ancient Africa and the Americas (Chapter 1), Mesopotamia and Egypt (Chapter 2), India (Chapter 3), China (Chapter 4), and the Americas again (Chapter 5). The next section of the book emphasizes the rise of world religions: Zoroastrianism in the Persian empire (Chapter 6); Rome's adoption of Christianity (Chapter 7); the spread of Buddhism and Hinduism in East, South, and Southeast Asia (Chapter 8); and the rise of Islam (Chapter 9). The final third of Volume 1 focuses on the parallel commercial revolutions in Europe and China (Chapters 12 and 13) and the gradual increase in knowledge about other societies resulting from the Vikings' voyages to Iceland, Greenland, and Newfoundland (Chapter 10); Ibn Battuta's trips in North, Central, and East Africa (Chapter 11); the Mongol conquest (Chapter 14); and the Spanish and Portuguese voyages to the Americas (Chapter 15). Because many of the people who traveled long distances in the premodern world did so for religious reasons, many of the travelers in Volume 1 were pilgrims. Their experiences help to reinforce student's understanding of the traditions of different world religions.

Volume 2 explores the development of the increasingly interconnected modern world, with the rise and fall of empires a persistent theme. We explore the new maritime trade routes that connected Europe to Asia

(Chapter 16) and the relationship between religion and politics in both the Christian and Muslim empires of western Eurasia (Chapter 17). The analysis of the colonial Americas (Chapter 18) is expanded by Chapter 19's discussion of Africa and the Atlantic slave trade. The expansion of Asian empires (Chapter 20) is complemented by an analysis of the relationship between science and empire in the Pacific Ocean and around the world (Chapter 21). The role of revolutions in modern history is addressed in Chapters 22 and 23. Chapters 24 through 26 address the global impact of the Industrial Revolution in Asia, the Americas, Africa, and Southeast Asia. The twentieth century is explored (Chapters 27–31) with an emphasis on the common experiences of globalized humanity through world wars, economic upheavals, and the bitter divisions of the Cold War. Though we cannot properly assess twenty-first century conditions using the historian's tools, Chapter 32 attempts to lay out some of the main challenges and opportunities we face today.

Themes

Our book has four themes: (1) increasing contact; (2) changing political structures of empire; (3) religion; (4) and social structure. The first is linked to our overall theme of movement, but the other three—the changing political structures of empire, religion, and social structure—form the backbone of all world history classes. The book develops these themes in each chapter.

Movement is the key theme of world history because world historians focus on connections among the different societies of the past. The movement of people, whether in voluntary migrations or forced slavery, has been of the most fruitful topics for world historians, as are the experience of individual travelers like Ibn Battuta or Simón Bolívar. Their reactions to the people they met on their long journeys reveal much about their home societies as well as about the societies they visited.

Theme 1: The Effects of Increasing Contact

Our focus on individual travelers leads naturally to the first major theme of the book: the increasing ease of contact among different civilizations with the passage of time. This theme highlights the developments that resulted from improved communications, travel among different places, the movement of trade goods, and the mixing of peoples: the movement of world religions, mass migrations, and the spread of diseases like the plague. The book shows how travel has changed over time—how the distance covered by travelers has increased at the same time that the duration of trips has decreased. As a result, more and more people have been able to go to societies distant from their own.

The book examines the different reasons for travel over the centuries. While some people were captured in battle and forced to go to new places, others visited different societies to teach or to learn the beliefs of a new religion like Buddhism, Christianity, and Islam. This theme, of necessity, treats questions about the environment: how far and over what terrain did early man travel? How did sailors learn to use monsoon winds to their advantage? What were the effects of technological breakthroughs like steamships, trains, and airplanes—and the use of fossil fuels to power them? Because students can link the experience of individual travelers to this theme, movement provides a memorable organizing principle for the book.

Theme 2: Changing Political Structures of Empire

Our second theme, the changing structure of empire, introduces students to political history. This theme permits students to compare the different empires under consideration and to understand that empires became increasingly complex over time, especially as central governments took advantage of new technologies to register and to control their subjects. Students need not commit long lists of rulers' names to memory: instead they focus on those leaders who created innovative political structures. After an opening chapter on the peopling of the world, the book begins with the very ancient empires (like Mesopotamia and Egypt) that did not control large swathes of territory and progress to those that did—like Qin dynasty China, Achaemenid Persia, and ancient Rome. It examines the political structures of empire: What was the relationship of the central government to the provinces? How were taxes collected and spent? How were officials recruited? Such questions remained remarkably persistent into the modern period, when societies around the world had to contend with rising Western empires.

The focus on the structure of empire helps students to remember the different civilizations they have studied, to explore the borrowing that occurred among various empires, and to understand how the empires were structured differently. This theme fits well with travel because the different travelers were able to make certain journeys because of the political situation at the time. For example, William of Rubruck was able to travel across all of Eurasia because of the unification brought by the Mongol empire, while Jean de Chardin's tavels from France to Iran were facilitated by the size and strength of the Ottoman Empire.

Theme 3: Religion

Our third theme, religion, follows naturally from the second because many rulers patronized religions to increase their control over the people they ruled. Students of world history must grasp the teachings of the major world religions, and, more important, they must have some understanding of how originally regional or national religions moved across political borders to become world religions. Volume 1 introduces the religions of Judaism (Chapter 2), Buddhism (Chapters 3 and 9), Confucianism (Chapter 4), Christianity (Chapters 6 and 10), Hinduism (Chapter 8), and Islam (Chapter 9). Volume 2 provides context for today's complex interplay of religion and politics (Chapter 17) and the complex cultural outcomes that occurred when such religions expanded into new world regions (Chapters 16 and 18). The renewed contemporary focus on religion, as seen in the rise of fundamentalist movements in various parts of the world, is analyzed in the two final chapters.

The theme of religion fits well with our focus on travelers. Some chapters examine the experience of religious travelers—such as the Chinese monk Xuanzang who journeyed to India and Matteo Ricci who hoped to convert the Chinese emperor to Christianity. Other travelers did not travel for religious reasons, but they had their own religious beliefs, encountered the religious traditions of the peoples they conquered, and sparked religious exchanges. Because the different chapters of the book pay close attention to the religious traditions of diverse societies, students gain a familiarity with the primary religious traditions of the world.

Theme 4: Social Structure

Our final theme is social structure. Students of world history need to understand how societies have been structured and how these ways of organizing society have changed over the past five thousand years. Abandoning the egalitarian structures of the distant past, Sumerian and Egyptian civilizations and their successors developed more hierarchical societies. Between 500 and 1500 both Europe and China moved from land-based aristocracies toward bureaucracy, but European and Chinese governments conceived of bureaucracy very differently. Some societies had extensive slavery; others did not.

Because the travelers were acutely aware of the differences between their own societies and those they visited, they provide crucial comparisons, although their observations were not always correct. For example, in the early seventh century the Chinese pilgrim Xuanzang described the Indian caste system as though it were rigidly structured, but he was not aware of groups who had changed the status of their caste.

The topic of gender falls under social structure, and each chapter devotes extensive space to the experience of women. Because in many societies literacy among women was severely limited, especially in the premodern era, we have included as many women travelers as possible: the slave girl and eventual wife of the caliph, Khaizuran (Chapter 9), Leif Eriksson's sister-in-law Gudrid (Chapter 10), the Chinese poet Li Qingzhao (Chapter 12), Heloise (Chapter 13), Catalina de Erauso (Chapter 18), Pauline Johnson-Tekahionwake (Chapter 25), Louise Bryant (Chapter 27), Halide Edib (Chapter 28), Nancy Wake (Chapter 29), and Mira Nair (Chapter 32). In addition, each chapter provides extensive coverage of gender so that students can grasp the experience of ordinary women.

Features

We see the features of this book as an opportunity to help students to understand the main text better. Each chapter opens with a map feature about the route of the chapter's traveler and then presents—not always in the same order—World History in Today's World, Movement of Ideas, and Visual Evidence.

Chapter Opening Map

At the beginning of each chapter is a map illustrating the route of the traveler. With their imaginative graphics, these chapter-opening maps look more like the maps in a travel book than the usual textbook maps. This section provides a biographical sketch for each traveler, a portrait, and extended passage from his or her writings (or, if not available, an extended passage about the individual). The goal of this feature is to capture the student's attention at the outset of each chapter. Although many students do not bother to read the beginning of each chapter, we hope that shifting smoothly from the traveler to the focus questions encourages them to do so.

World History in Today's World

This brief feature (no longer than 400 words, more often around 250) picks one element of modern life that originated in the period under study. We have made every effort to find things interesting to students ("The World's First Beer," "Japanese Baseball," and "The Coffeehouse in World History") and to highlight their relationship to the past. This feature should provide material to trigger discussion and help instructors explain why world history matters since so often students simply have no sense that the past has anything to do with their own lives.

Movement of Ideas

This feature offers an introduction, an extensive excerpt from one or more primary sources, and discussion questions. The chosen passages emphasize the movement of ideas, usually by contrasting two different explanations of the same idea. This feature aims to develop the core historical skill of analyzing original sources. Topics include "Doing What Is Right in *The Avesta* and the Bible" and "Fascism and Youth."

Visual Evidence

The goal of this feature is to train students to examine either an artifact, a work of art, or a photograph and to glean historical information from them. These features are illustrated with pictures or photographs to explain the importance of the find or the artwork. A close-up photograph of the Chinese terracotta warriors, for example, shows students how the figurines were mass-produced yet have individual features. Potraits of George Washington and Napoleon Bonaparte lead students to analyze the symbolism they contain to view the portraits as *representations* of political power. Discussion questions help students analyze the information presented.

Ancillaries

A wide array of supplements accompany this text to help students better master the material and to help instructors teach from the book:

- *Student Website*
- *Instructor Website*
- *CL Testing CD-ROM (powered by Diploma)*
- *Online Instructor's Resource Manual*

- *PowerPoint maps, images, and lecture outlines*
- *PowerPoint questions for personal response systems*
- *Blackboard™ and WebCT™ course cartridges*
- *Interactive ebook*
- *HistoryFinder*

The Student Website is a companion website for students, which features a wide array of resources to help students master the subject matter. The website, prepared by Mark Seidl, includes material such as learning objectives, chapter outlines, and pre-class quizzes for a student to consult before going to class; review material like interactive flashcards, chronological ordering exercises, primary sources, and interactive map exercises; and our successful ACE brand of practice tests as well as other self-testing materials. Students can also find additional text resources such as an online glossary, audio MP3 files of chapter summaries, and material on how to study more effectively in the "General Resources" section. Throughout the text, icons direct students to relevant exercises and self-testing material located on the Student Website.

The Instructor Website is a companion website for instructors. It features all of the material on the Student Website plus additional password-protected resources that help instructors teach the course, such as an electronic version of the *Instructor's Resource Manual* and *PowerPoint* slides. Access both the Student and Instructor Websites for this text by visiting **www.cengage.com/history/hansen/voyages1e.**

The *Instructor's Resource Manual,* prepared by Candace Gregory-Abbott of California State University, Sacramento, contains instructional objectives, chapter outlines, lecture topics and suggestions for discussion, classroom activities and writing assignments, analyzing primary sources, activities for the traveler feature, map activities, geography questions, audiovisual bibliographies, suggested readings, and Internet resources.

CL Testing (powered by *Diploma*) offers instructors a flexible and powerful tool for test generation and test management. Now supported by the Brownstone Research Group's market-leading *Diploma* software, this new version of *CL Testing* significantly improves on functionality and ease of use by offering all the tools needed to create, author, deliver, and customize multiple types of tests. Diploma is currently in use at thousands of college and university campuses throughout the United States and Canada. The *CL Testing* content for this text was developed by Dolores Grapsas of New River Community College and offers multiple-choice questions (with page references to the correct response), key term identification, geography questions (with blank outline maps provided), and essay questions (with guidelines for how to effectively write the essay).

We are pleased to offer a collection of World Civilization *PowerPoint* lecture outlines, maps, and images for use in classroom presentations. Detailed lecture outlines correspond to the book's chapters and make it easier for instructors to cover the major topics in class. The art collection includes all of the photos and maps in the text. *PowerPoint* questions and answers for use with personal response system software are also offered to adopters free of charge.

A variety of assignable homework and testing material has been developed to work with the *Blackboard™* and *WebCT™* course management systems. *Blackboard™* and *WebCT™* are web-based online learning environments that provide instructors with a gradebook and communication capabilities, such as synchronous and asynchronous chats and announcement postings. They offer access to assignments such as more than 650 gradable homework exercises, writing assignments, interactive maps with questions, primary sources, discussion questions for online discussion boards, and tests, which all come ready-to-use. Instructors can choose to use the content as is, modify it, or even add their own. They even contain an interactive ebook, which contains in-text links to interactive maps, primary sources, and audio pronunciation files, as well as review and self-testing material for students.

HistoryFinder, a new Cengage Learning technology initiative, helps instructors create rich and exciting classroom presentations. This online tool offers thousands of online resources, including art, photographs, maps, primary sources, multimedia content, Associated Press interactive modules, and ready-made *PowerPoint* slides. *HistoryFinder*'s assets can easily be searched by keyword or browsed from pull-down menus by topic, media type, or by textbook. Instructors can then browse, preview, and download resources straight from the website.

Acknowledgments

It is a pleasure to thank the many instructors who read and critiqued the manuscript through its development:

Wayne Ackerson, Salisbury University; Sanjam Ahluwalia, Northern Arizona University; Mark A. Allee, Loyola University, Chicago; Michael Thad Allen, Georgia Institute of Technology; Patricia Ali, Morris College; Ali Al-Taie, Shaw University; Melanie A. Bailey, South Dakota State University; William P. Bakken, Rochester Community and Technical College; Brett A. Berliner, Morgan State University; Corinne Blake, Rowan University; Stanley E. Blake, Ohio State University; Wayne Bowen, Ouachita Baptist University; Connie Brand, Meridian Community College; Michael Burger, Mississippi University for Women; Suzanne E. Cahill, University of California, San Diego; Michael Cassella-Blackburn, Peninsula College; Leslie G. Cecil, Baylor University; Robert Chisholm, Columbia Basin College; William Clay Poe, Sonoma State University; Paul R. Clementi, Immaculata University; Robert Cliver, Humboldt State University; Christine A. Colin, Mercyhurst College; Theron Corse, Tennessee State University; Scott Cotton, University of Texas, Dallas; Eric Cunningham, Gonzaga University; Jennifer Kolpacoff Deane, University of Minnesota, Morris; Hilde De Weerdt, University of Tennessee, Knoxville; Timothy C. Dowling, Virginia Military Institute; Mark Dupuy, Edith Cowan University; Elizabeth Endicott, Middlebury College; Krista Feinberg, Lakeland College; Kyle Fingerson, UW Rock County; Eve Fisher, South Dakota State University; David Flaten, Tompkins Cortland Community College; Monica Fleming, Edgecombe Community College; Hal Friedman, Henry Ford Community College; Erik Gilbert, Arkansas State University; Dolores Grapsas, New River Community College; Robert Greene, University of Montana; Candace Gregory-Abbott, California State University, Sacramento; Sumit Guha, Brown University; Jim Halverson, Judson University; Jason Hardgrave, University of Southern Indiana; David Head, Jon Tyler Community College; James Heitzman, University of California, Davis; Henry Heller, University of Manitoba; Craig Hendricks, Long Beach City College; Gerald Herman, Northeastern University; Lisa R. Holliday, Appalachian State University; Tamara L. Hunt, University of Southern Indiana; Raymond P. Hylton, Virginia Union University; Matthew Jacobs, University of Florida; Effie Jones, Crichton College; David M. Kalivas, Middlesex Community College; Joy Kammerling, Eastern Illinois University; Frank Karpiel, College of Charleston; Robert L. Kelly, University of Wyoming; Steven King, Valley City State University; Michael Krenn, Appalachian State University; Michael Kulikowski, University of Tennessee; Scott Levi, University of Louisville; Marilyn Levine, Lewis-Clark State College; Michael Lewis, Salisbury University; Ann Livschiz, IPFW; Christine E. Lovasz-Kaiser, University of Southern Indiana; Norman D. Love, El Paso Community College; Lynn MacKay, Brandon University; Moira Maguire, University of Arkansas, Little Rock; Fred McDonald, Cecil College; Patrick F. McDevitt, University at Buffalo SUNY; Mark McLeod, University of Delaware; Brendan McManus, Bemidji State University; John T. McNay, University of Cincinnati, RWC campus; Eben Miller, Southern Maine Community College; Garold Mills; Tim Myers, Butler Community College; Ken Orosz, University of Maine at Farmington; Donald Ostrowski, Harvard University Extension School; John Pinheiro, Aquinas College; Margaret Power, Illinois Institute of Technology; Richard Reiman, South Georgia College; Robert Reinert, Our Lady of the Lake University; Len Rose, Myers University; Ivancica Schrunk, University of St. Thomas; Jane Scimeca, Brookdale Community College; Bruce Scott, Northeastern Junior College; Jonathan Seitz, Drexel University; Courtney Shah, Lower Columbia University; Colonel Rose Mary Sheldon, Virginia Military Institute; David Simonelli, Youngstown State University; Paul D. Steeves, Stetson University; Forrest Studebaker, Clinton Community College; Steve Tamari, Southern Illinois University, Edwardsville; Loyd Uglow, Southwestern Assemblies of God University; David J. Ulbrich, Ball State University; Michael G. Vann, California State University, Sacramento; Dr. Maria Vecchio, Felician College; Tommy Walter, Jacksonville University; Charles Wheeler, University of California, Irvine; Gregory R. Witkowski, Ball State University; William Wood, Point Loma Nazarene University; Aharon Zorea, University of Wisconsin; and Alex Zukas, National University, San Diego.

Valerie Hansen would also like to thank the following for their guidance on specific chapters: Benjamin Foster, Yale University; Karen Foster, Yale University; Stephen Colvin, London University; Phyllis Granoff,

Yale University; Stanley Insler, Yale University; Mridu Rai, Yale University; Thomas R. H. Havens, Northeastern University; Charles Wheeler, University of California, Irvine; Haydon Cherry, Yale University; Marcello A. Canuto, Yale University; William Fash, Harvard University; Stephen Houston, Brown University; Mary Miller, Yale University; Stephen Colvin, University of London; Frank Turner, Yale University; Kevin van Bladel, University of Southern California; Anders Winroth, Yale University; Paul Freedman, Yale University; Frederick S. Paxton, Connecticut College; Francesca Trivellato, Yale University; Stuart Schwartz, Yale University; and Koichi Shinohara, Yale University.

The study of world history is indeed a voyage, and Kenneth Curtis would like to thank the following for helping identify guideposts along the way. First, thanks to colleagues in the World History Association and the Advanced Placement World History program, especially Ross Dunn, San Diego State University; Patrick Manning, University of Pittsburgh; Peter Stearns, George Mason University; Jerry Bentley, University of Hawai'i; Merry Wiesner-Hanks, University of Wisconsin–Milwaukee; Alan Karras, University of California, Berkeley; Omar Ali, Vanderbilt University; Heather Streets, Washington State University; Laura Mitchell, University of California, Irvine; Anand Yang, University of Washington; Heidi Roupp, Ane Lintvedt, Sharon Cohen, Jay Harmon, Anton Striegl, Michelle Foreman, Chris Wolf, Saroja Ringo, Esther Adams, Linda Black, and Bill Ziegler. He would also like to acknowledge the support of his colleagues in the history department at California State University Long Beach, especially those who aided with sources, translations, or interpretive guidance: Houri Berberian, Timothy Keirn, Craig Hendricks, Margaret Kuo, Andrew Jenks, Ali Igmen, Sharlene Sayegh, and Donald Schwartz. He also benefited from the feedback of the students who read early drafts of the modern history chapters and gave valuable feedback, with a special nod to those graduate students—Charlie Dodson, Patrick Giloogly, Daniel Lynch—who brought their passion for world history teaching in the public schools to the seminar table, and to Colin Rutherford for his help with the pedagogy.

The authors would also like to thank the many publishing professionals at Houghton Mifflin and Wadsworth/Cengage Learning who facilitated the publication of this book, in particular: Nancy Blaine, for guiding us through the entire process from proposal to finished textbook; Jean Woy, for her extraordinary historical judgment; Jennifer Sutherland, for paying attention to everything from the smallest detail to the largest conceptual questions; Jan Fitter, for elegant and perceptive readings of many chapters; Adrienne Zicht, for an excellent ancillary package to accompany the text; Linda Sykes, for her extraordinary photo research that has made this book so beautiful to look at; and Christina Horn, for shepherding the book through the final, chaotic pre-publication process.

In closing, Valerie would like to thank Brian Vivier for doing so much work on Volume 1; the title of "research assistant" does not convey even a fraction of what he did, always punctually and cheerfully. She dedicates this book to her children, Lydia, Claire, and Bret Hansen Stepanek, and their future educations.

Kenneth Curtis would like to thank Francine Curtis for her frontline editing skills and belief in the project, and his mother Elizabeth J. Curtis and siblings Jane, Sara, Margaret, Jim, Steve, and Ron for their love and support. In recognition of his father's precious gift of curiosity, Ken dedicates this book to the memory of James Gavin Curtis.

About the Authors

Valerie Hansen

Since her graduate work in premodern Chinese history at the University of Pennsylvania, Valerie Hansen has used nontraditional sources to capture the experience of ordinary people. Professor of History at Yale, she teaches the history of premodern China, the Silk Road, and the world. *Changing Gods in Medieval China* drew on temple inscriptions and ghost stories to shed light on popular religious practice in the Song dynasty (1127–1276), while *Negotiating Daily Life in Traditional China* used contracts to probe Chinese understandings of the law both in this world and the next. Her textbook *The Open Empire: China to 1600* draws on archaeological finds, literature, and art to explore Chinese interactions with the outside world. With grants from the National Endowment for the Humanities and the Fulbright Association, she has traveled to China to collect materials for her current research project: a new history of the Silk Road.

Kenneth R. Curtis

Kenneth R. Curtis received his Ph.D. from the University of Wisconsin–Madison in African and Comparative World History. His research focuses on colonial to post-colonial transitions in East Africa, with a particular focus on the coffee economy of Tanzania. He is Professor of History and Liberal Studies at California State University Long Beach, where he has taught world history at the introductory level, in special courses designed for future middle and high school teachers, and in graduate seminars. He has worked to advance the teaching of world history at the collegiate and secondary levels in collaboration with the World History Association, the California History/Social Science Project, and the College Board's Advanced Placement World History course.

Note on Spelling

Students taking world history will encounter many new names of people, terms, and places. We have retained only the most important of these. The most difficult, of course, are those from languages that use either different alphabets or no alphabet at all (like Chinese) and that have multiple variant spellings in English. As a rule, we have opted to give names in the native language of whom we are writing, not in other languages. In addition, we have kept accents and diacritic marks to a minimum, using them only when absolutely necessary. For example, we give the name of the world's first city (in Turkey) as Catalhoyuk, not Çatalhüyük.

In sum, our goal has been to avoid confusing the reader, even if specific decisions may not make sense to expert readers. To help readers, we provide a pronunciation guide on the first appearance of any term or name whose pronunciation is not obvious from the spelling. There is also an audio pronunciation guide on the text's accompanying website. A few explanations for specific regions follow.

The Americas

The peoples living in the Americas before 1492 had no common language and no shared identity. Only after 1492 with the arrival of Columbus and his men did outsiders label the original residents of the Americas as a single group. For this reason, any word for the inhabitants of North and South America is inaccurate. We try to refer to individual peoples whenever possible. When speaking in general terms, we use the word "Amerindian" because it has no pejorative overtones and is not confusing.

Many place names in Spanish-speaking regions have a form in both Spanish and in the language of the indigenous peoples; whenever possible we have opted for the indigenous word. For example, we write about the Tiwanaku culture in the Andes, not Tiahuanaco. In some cases, we choose the more familiar term, such as Inca and Cuzco, rather than the less-familiar spellings Inka and Cusco. We retain the accents for modern place names.

East Asia

For Chinese, we have used the pinyin system of Romanization, not the older Wade-Giles version. Students and instructors may wish to consult an online pinyin/Wade-Giles conversion program if they want to check a spelling. We use the pinyin throughout but, on the first appearance of a name, alert readers to nonstandard spellings, such as Chiang Kai-shek and Sun Yat-sen, that have already entered English.

For other Asian languages, we have used the most common romanization systems (McCune-Reischauer for Korean, Hepburn for Japanese) and have dropped diacritical marks. Because we prefer to use the names that people called themselves, we use Chinggis Khan, for the ruler of the Mongols (not Genghis Khan, which is Persian) and the Turkish Timur the Lame (rather than Tamerlane, his English name).

West Asia and North Africa

Many romanization systems for Arabic and related languages like Ottoman Turkish or Persian use an apostrophe to indicate specific consonants (*ain* and *hamza*). Because it is difficult for a native speaker of English to hear these differences, we have omitted these apostrophes. For this reason, we use Quran (not Qur'an).

Voyages in
World History

The Peopling of the World, to 4000 B.C.E.

From the earliest moments of human history our ancestors were on the move. Archaeologists continue to debate when and how our earliest forebears moved out of Africa, where humankind originated millions of years ago, and how it populated the rest of the world. One of the last places people reached—probably around 16,000 years ago—was the Americas. For this reason, archaeologists are particularly interested in any human remains that date from this early period.

On Saturday, July 28, 1996, two college students found this skull in the riverbed of the Columbia River, near the town of Kennewick in Washington State. The students called the police, who the next day contacted Chatters to determine if the bones were those of a murder victim. At the find-spot, Chatters collected an additional 350 bones and determined that the man had lived between 7580 and 7330 B.C.E. (As is common among world historians, this book uses B.C.E. [Before Common Era] and C.E. [Common Era] rather than B.C. [Before Christ] and A.D. [Anno Domini, In the Year of Our Lord].) Here James C. Chatters, a forensic anthropologist, describes what he learned by examining the skull of the skeleton now known as **Kennewick Man**:

KENNEWICK MAN

I looked down at the first piece, the braincase, viewing it from the top. Removing it from the bag, I was immediately struck by its long, narrow shape and the marked constriction of the forehead behind a well-developed brow ridge. The bridge of the nose was very high and prominent. My first thought was that this skull belonged to someone of European descent. . . .

I turned the bone to inspect the underside, and what I saw seemed at first to be at odds with the rest of the picture. The teeth were worn flat, and worn severely. This is a characteristic of American Indian skeletons, especially in the interior Pacific Northwest, where the people ate stone-ground fish, roots,

 This icon will direct you to interactive activities and study materials on the *Voyages* website: **www.cengage.com/history/hansen/voyages1e**

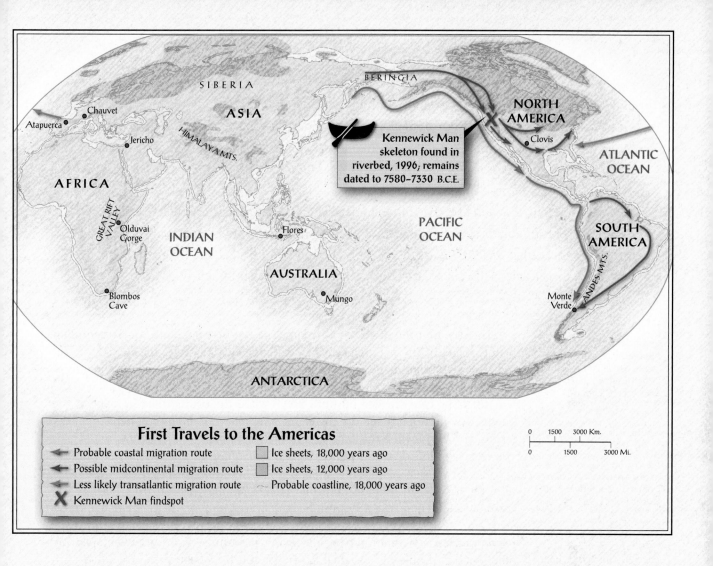

SIBERIA

ASIA

BERINGIA

NORTH
AMERICA

Clovis

ATLANTIC
OCEAN

Chauvet

Atapuerca

Jericho

HIMALAYA MTS.

Kennewick Man
skeleton found in
riverbed, 1996; remains
dated to 7580–7330 B.C.E.

AFRICA

GREAT RIFT VALLEY

Olduvai
Gorge

INDIAN
OCEAN

Flores

PACIFIC
OCEAN

SOUTH
AMERICA

ANDES MTS.

AUSTRALIA

Monte
Verde

Blombos
Cave

Mungo

ANTARCTICA

First Travels to the Americas

- ← Probable coastal migration route
- ← Possible midcontinental migration route
- ← Less likely transatlantic migration route
- X Kennewick Man findspot

- ☐ Ice sheets, 18,000 years ago
- ☐ Ice sheets, 12,000 years ago
- ⁓ Probable coastline, 18,000 years ago

0   1500   3000 Km.
0   1500   3000 Mi.

	13,000 B.C.E.	12,000	11,000	10,000	9000	8000	7000	6000

Lifetime of Kennewick Man
ca. 7580 7330

AMERICAS

Arrival of first
Americans
16,000–12,000

Clovis culture
11,400   10,000

Early agriculture
in Mesoamerica,
Peruvian Andes
8000

Settlement at Monte Verde
12,600

AFRO-EURASIA

Harvesting of wild
crops in western Asia
12,500

Domestication
of dog
10,000

Natufian settlement
at Jericho
8300   7500

Town of Ain Ghazal
7250

Domestication of plants and animals in
eastern Mediterranean, eastern Sahara
8000

Large settlement
at Catalhoyuk
6000

Note: All dates are approximate.

and berries and lived almost constantly with blowing sand. My mind jumped to something I'd seen when I was fourteen years old, working at an ancient site on the Snake River in Washington. . . . "Paleo-Indian!" came the involuntary thought. "Paleo-Indian" is the label given to the very earliest American immigrants, traditionally presumed to be early versions of today's Native Americans.

No, I thought, that can't be. The inhabitants of the Americas had broad faces, round heads, and presumably brown skin and straight black hair. They had come over from Siberia no more than 13,000 years ago across the Bering Land Bridge and therefore resembled their modern-day Siberian relatives. This was no Paleo-Indian—was it?[1]

• Kennewick Man
Remains of a male found near Kennewick, Washington, dated to between 7580 and 7330 B.C.E.

• hominids Term referring to all humans and their ancestors.

• Homo sapiens sapiens Biological term for modern human beings belonging to the genus *Homo*, species *sapiens*, and subspecies *sapiens*.

The day after the discovery, the Umatilla (oo-mah-TILL-uh), the Amerindian people living in the region, argued that Kennewick Man was their ancestor and the remains should be given to them for reburial. A group of scientists countersued, arguing that the remains were so ancient that they could not be linked to the Umatilla. The case dragged on until 2004, when the courts ruled in favor of the scientists, who hope that studying Kennewick Man's remains can help them determine how and when the Americas were first settled.

The peopling of the Americas was a late phase in the history of humankind. As early as seven million years ago, the earliest **hominids** (HAH-moh-nids), a term referring to all humans and their ancestors, branched off from gorillas and chimpanzees. These early hominids had moved out of Africa by 1.8 million years ago. By 150,000 B.C.E., anatomically modern people, the species ***Homo sapiens sapiens*** (HO-mo SAY-pee-uhnz SAY-pee-uhnz), had fully developed. By 60,000 B.C.E. people had reached Australia, and by 50,000 B.C.E. they had populated Eurasia. However, the Western Hemisphere was probably not settled before 14,000 B.C.E., and Kennewick Man is one of the earliest and most intact skeletons ever found in the Americas. Since none of these early peoples could read and write, no documents survive. But archaeological evidence, including human remains, cave paintings, and ancient tools, allows us to reconstruct the early history of humanity.

Focus Questions

🛶 Who were the first hominids? What were the main stages in their development?

🛶 When and how did hominids leave Africa and settle Eurasia?

🛶 When did ancient hominids become recognizably human?

> How and when did the first people move to the Americas? What was their way of life?
>
> How and where did agriculture first arise? How did its impact vary around the world?

The Origins of Humankind

Paleontologists (pay-lee-on-TAHL-oh-gists), scientists who study ancient life in the distant past, agree that humans and chimpanzees are descended from a species that no longer exists. About seven million years ago in central Africa that lost species gave rise to two separate species. One branch developed into chimpanzees, the other, into hominids. After leaving their homeland in Africa around 1.8 million years ago, hominids continued to develop until anatomically modern people, or *Homo sapiens sapiens*, appeared 150,000 years ago.

The First Hominids: Australopithecines

Biologists use four different subcategories when classifying animals: family, genus (JEAN-uhs) (the Latin word for group or class), species, and subspecies. Modern humans are members of the Primate family, the genus *Homo* ("person" in Latin), the species *sapiens* ("wise" or "intelligent" in Latin), and the subspecies *sapiens,* so the correct term for modern people is *Homo sapiens sapiens.* Members of the same species can reproduce, while members of two different species cannot. The species closest to modern human beings today is the chimpanzee, whose cells contain nuclei with genetic material called deoxyribonucleic acid (DNA) that overlaps with that of humans by 98.4 percent.

Scientists use the concept of **evolution** to explain how all life forms, including modern humans, have come into being. In the nineteenth century Charles Darwin proposed that natural selection is the mechanism underlying evolutionary change. He realized that variations exist within a species (we now know that genetic mutations cause them) and that certain variations increase an individual's chances of survival. All variations, beneficial or not, are passed along to offspring. Because those individuals with beneficial traits—perhaps a bigger brain or more upright posture—are more likely to survive, they will have more offspring. And, because traits are inherited, these offspring will also possess the beneficial traits. Individuals lacking those traits will have few or no offspring. As new mutations occur within a population, its characteristics will change and a new species can develop from an earlier one, typically over many thousands or even millions of years.

The process of natural selection caused the early hominids to diverge from other primates, especially in their manner of walking. Our very earliest ancestors did not belong to the genus *Homo* but to the genus ***Australopithecus*** ("southern ape"), whose habitat was also Africa. The defining characteristic of australopithecines (au-stral-oh-PITH-uh-seens) was bipedalism (buy-PEH-dahl-izm), the ability to walk on two feet, whereas chimpanzees and gorillas knuckle-walked on all four limbs.

● **evolution** Model proposed by Charles Darwin to explain the development of new species. In each generation, genetic mutations cause variation among members of a species, eventually changing the characteristics of that population into new, distinct species.

● ***Australopithecus*** Hominid species, dating to 3.5 million years ago, who walked on two feet (adjectival form: australopithecine).

Paleontologists have found australopithecine remains in different regions of Africa, including Malawi, Chad, South Africa, and most importantly northern Tanzania in the Olduvai (OHL-doo-vaye) Gorge, which lies in the Great Rift Valley. Located along a crack in the earth's crust where two giant tectonic plates are slowly moving apart, the Great Rift Valley runs for 2,000 miles (3,600 km) from the Red Sea to Tanzania. Now 25 to 50 miles (40–80 km) wide, it exposes many earlier layers of human occupation. In the 1960s and 1970s, Richard and Mary Leakey found in this valley australopithecine skulls, jawbones, teeth, and even footprints, the first tangible evidence of the australopithecine ability to walk.

Since early hominids could walk, they were able to leave the cover of forests and hunt in the open grasslands. Scientists believe that millions of years ago grasslands began to replace forests. At that time the African continent, then much wetter than it is today, began to dry up. As grassy savannah replaced rainforest, walking upright conferred an important advantage over those species that walked on four limbs. Upright walking also used fewer calories than knuckle-walking.

One of the most complete sets of australopithecine remains comes from a female known as Lucy. She was named for "Lucy in the Sky with Diamonds," a Beatles song playing on a tape recorder when, in 1974, archaeologists found her remains in Ethiopia. She stood 39 inches (1 m) tall and lived 3.5 million years ago. Her face was shaped like an ape, with a small brain like a chimpanzee, and she made no tools of her own. But the remains of Lucy's knee showed that she walked upright.

Homo Erectus and the First Migrations Outside of Africa, 2.5–1.8 Million Years Ago

One can easily get the impression that our ancestors evolved in a logical progression, with ancient tiny hominids growing taller and more human-like, but the reality was more complex. Fossil evidence suggests that a number of species came into existence, flourished for a time, and then died out. Some of these had more human characteristics, while others had more in common with chimpanzees and gorillas.

Recent finds suggest that four different groups of human ancestors coexisted 2.5 million years ago, or one million years after Lucy was alive. These different human ancestors all shared two important characteristics that set them apart from the australopithecines: they had bigger brains and made tools of their own by chipping off stone flakes from cores. This innovation marked the beginning of the **Paleolithic** (pay-lee-oh-LITH-uhk) period, or Old Stone Age (2.5 million years ago–8000 B.C.E.). The earliest tools were sharp enough to cut through animal hides and to scrape meat off bones. Over the long course of the Paleolithic period, protohumans made tools of increasing complexity.

These early hominids belonged to the same genus, but not the same species, as modern people: they are called *Homo habilis* (HO-mo hah-BEEL-uhs) ("handy human"). Standing erect, *Homo habilis* weighed less than 100 pounds and measured under 5 feet tall. They ate whatever fruits and vegetables grew wild and competed with other scavengers, such as hyenas, to get scraps of meat left behind by lions and tigers.

The species that evolved into modern humans—***Homo erectus*** (HO-mo-ee-RECT-oos) ("upright human")—appeared about 1.9 million years ago. *Homo erectus*

• **Paleolithic** The "Old Stone Age" period, from 2.5 million years ago to 8000 B.C.E.

• ***Homo erectus*** Hominid species, appearing 1.9 million years ago, who left Africa and populated Eurasia.

had a brain double the size of earlier hominid brains, about the same size as that of modern humans, as well as far greater mobility than any earlier human ancestor. Armed with hand axes, and perhaps even simple boats (evidence of which does not survive), *Homo erectus* left Africa and migrated to Asia.

Two main routes connect Africa with Eurasia: one leads across the Strait of Gibraltar into Spain, and the other crosses the Sinai Peninsula into western Asia. The earliest hominid remains found outside of Africa date to 1.8 million years ago in Dmanisi, Georgia (in the Caucasus Mountains) and in Ubeidiya, Israel, from 1.4 million years ago. The distribution of the few *Homo erectus* finds in Eurasia shows that the route into western Asia was more heavily traveled than the route across the Mediterranean at the Strait of Gibraltar.

These early species did not move quickly from western Asia to Europe, perhaps because the cold climate there was not inviting. They entered Europe by crossing the Bosporus strait in modern Turkey and then walking along the northern shore of the Mediterranean. The earliest evidence that our ancestors lived in Europe, from Atapuerca (ah-TAH-poo-air-kah), Spain, dates to 1.1 million years ago.

It seems likely that *Homo erectus* learned how to control fire at this time. One early find, dating to 1.4 million years ago, at the site of Chesowanja (chuh-SOH-wahn-juh), Kenya, included lumps of burnt clay alongside animal bones and stone tools, but many think a natural fire might have occurred. A more convincing find, from northern Israel, dates to 790,000 years ago. There archaeologists found fragments of flint next to charred remains of wood in different layers of earth, an indication that the site's occupants passed the knowledge of fire making to their descendants. To keep a fire going requires planning far ahead, an ability that earlier hominids lacked.

Following the discovery of fire, our ancestors began to eat more meat, which resulted in a larger brain size. By 500,000 years ago, they had settled many sites throughout Europe and Asia. At this time, *Homo erectus* began to evolve into archaic *Homo sapiens*.

The Emergence of *Homo Sapiens Sapiens*, 2 Million–150,000 Years Ago

One of the fiercest debates currently raging among paleontologists concerns the development of humankind between about 1.9 million years ago, when *Homo erectus* was alive, and the appearance of *Homo sapiens sapiens*, or anatomically modern people, about 150,000 years ago. The "regional continuity" school holds that, after *Homo erectus* settled the Eastern Hemisphere about two million years ago, different hominids from different regions gradually merged to form modern people. The "single origin" school posits a very different history for humankind. It agrees with the regional continuity school that *Homo erectus* settled the Eastern Hemisphere starting 1.9 million years ago, but it suggests that a second wave of migration out of Africa—of *Homo sapiens sapiens* between 100,000 and 50,000 years ago—supplanted all pre-existing human species.

The "single origin" school cites DNA evidence in support of its position. The DNA in the nucleus of every cell in our bodies contains about 100,000 genes, an inherited mix of one's father's and mother's DNA. In addition, all of our cells contain structures outside the nucleus called mitochondria (my-toe-CON-dree-uh). Each of these mitochondria contains a single DNA strand that is inherited only from the egg cell of the mother. If one examines mitochondrial DNA from different populations around the world, statistical analysis of minute differences points toward an ancestral female population that lived somewhere in Africa about 100,000 years ago, an indication that the descendants of an "African Eve" replaced all other human populations after a second migration out of Africa.

The "regional continuity" scholars argue that different regional populations could have mixed with the second wave of migrants from Africa and that they did not necessarily die out. Everyone agrees, though, that the earliest hominids originated in Africa and that *Homo erectus* left Africa about 1.9 million years ago.

⬤ How Modern Humans Populated Eurasia and Australia

When anatomically modern humans (*Homo sapiens sapiens*) first appeared in central and southern Africa some 150,000 years ago, their bodies and braincases were about the same size as ours. They lived side by side with other animals and other hominid species. But in important respects they were totally different from their neighbors, for they had learned to change their environment with radically new tools and skills. Carrying their supplies themselves since they had no domesticated animals, they moved out of Africa into Eurasia after 150,000 B.C.E. By 60,000 B.C.E. they were using simple rafts or boats to travel over water to Australia.

The First Anatomically Modern Humans Leave Africa

Paleontologists have found very few human remains dating to the time when *Homo sapiens sapiens* first arose in Africa, but in 2003 they were extremely pleased to find three skulls (from two adults and one child) dating to 160,000 B.C.E. in Ethiopia. Of the same shape and dimensions as modern human skulls, these skulls show that the *Homo sapiens sapiens* species arose first in Africa. Concluding that all modern people are descended from this group, one of the excavating archaeologists commented: "In this sense, we are all African."[2]

Starting in 150,000 B.C.E., *Homo sapiens sapiens* began to migrate out of Africa to populate Eurasia. By 100,000 B.C.E. they had reached North Africa and crossed the Sinai Peninsula into modern-day Israel in western Asia. As they migrated, they encountered groups of pre-modern humans called **Neanderthals** (knee-AHN-dehr-thalls) in Israel and then western Europe. Named for the site in West Germany where their remains were first found, Neanderthals were shaped differently from modern humans: their skulls were longer and lower, their faces protruded, and their bones were bigger and heavier. Neanderthal tools included longer stone flakes, which they chipped off larger stone cores. They painted themselves, their dwellings, and their graves with clumps of pigment such as ocher (OH-kerh), a naturally occurring mineral that can be mixed with water to make a red paint. The Neanderthals used fire to cook large animals that they had caught.

To be able to migrate out of Africa and displace existing populations in Asia and Europe, modern humans had to behave differently from their forebears. They showed a capacity for symbolic thinking, evident in the creation of the world's

⬤ Neanderthals
Group of pre-modern humans who lived between 100,000 and 25,000 B.C.E. in western Asia and Europe, eventually replaced by *Homo sapiens sapiens*.

first art, as well as an ability to plan far ahead. (See the feature "Visual Evidence: The First Art Objects in the World.") Archaeologists believe that these characteristics indicate a new stage in human development, when humans became recognizably human.

The earliest evidence of religion comes from sites dating to 100,000 B.C.E. The defining characteristic of **religion** is the belief in a divine power or powers that control or influence the environment and people's lives. The most reliable evidence is a written text demonstrating religious beliefs, but early humans did not write. They did, however, bury their dead. In 100,000 B.C.E., anatomically modern humans who had migrated to western Asia interred three people in the Qafseh (KAHF-seh) cave near Nazareth, Israel, most likely because they believed in an afterlife, a major component of many religious belief systems.

● **religion** Belief system that holds that divine powers control the environment and people's futures.

Modern humans had larynxes starting around 150,000 B.C.E., but many suspect that they did not begin to speak until sometime between 100,000 and 50,000 B.C.E. We cannot know exactly because the act of speaking produces no lasting evidence in the archaeological record.

The Settling of Australia, ca. 60,000 B.C.E.

Homo sapiens sapiens of the Upper Paleolithic Era were sufficiently versatile that they could adjust to new, even cold, habitats far removed from their original home in central Africa, and their improved hunting skills allowed them to move to new places. The farthest they traveled was to Australia. One of the most isolated places on earth, this continent provides a rich environment for animals, such as kangaroos, that are found nowhere else in the world. No animals from Eurasia, except for rodents and modern humans, managed to reach Australia.

How *Homo sapiens sapiens* traveled to Australia is still a mystery. Oceans then lay about 250 feet (76 m) below modern levels, and the body of water dividing Australia from the Asian landmass was at least 40 miles (65 km) across, suggesting that this species knew how to cover short distances by raft. Yet no watercraft from this time have been found, possibly because any remains would have disintegrated.

Once they reached Australia, the early settlers did not stay on the coast but moved inland rapidly, reaching the site of Mungo (muhn-GO), in southeast Australia, by 60,000 years ago. There archaeologists found a burial in which a male skeleton (known as Mungo Man) was placed in the ground and sprinkled with red ocher powder. Nearby was a woman (Mungo Woman), whose burnt remains constitute the earliest known example of human cremation. Since many later peoples cremated the dead in the hope that their souls could proceed safely to the next world, the human settlers of Australia may have had similar beliefs.

The Settling of Eurasia, 50,000–30,000 B.C.E.

The settlers of Europe continued to refine the advanced hunting technologies of their African forbears, who had formed large, organized hunting parties that killed big game with sharp-pointed spears. In addition to hunting, the migrants also gathered wild plants. Starting around 50,000 B.C.E. the humans living in Europe began to organize hunts of migrating animals in the fall to provide meat during the winter. The Paleolithic period entered its final phase, the Upper Paleolithic, or the late Stone Age, around 38,000 B.C.E. The rise of agriculture around 10,000 B.C.E. (see page 21) marks the end of this period.

THE FIRST ART OBJECTS IN THE WORLD

One site in Africa—Blombos Cave in South Africa—has produced some of the earliest art objects in the world. The Blombos Cave site, near Stilbai about 186 miles (300 km) from Cape Town, dates to 75,000 B.C.E. The surface of this chunk of ocher (opposite) bears a geometric design of triangles between three parallel lines. This pure design, with no functional purpose, points to the capacity for abstract thinking.

The occupants of Blombos Cave fished and hunted and made sets of fine bone tools, all of the same size. First they cut bone with stone tools and then polished it with leather and abrasive powder. The excavating archaeologist explains the significance of these tools: "Why so finely polished? It's actually unnecessary for projectile points to be so carefully made. It suggests to us that this is an expression of symbolic thinking. The people said 'Let's make a really beautiful object.'"*

At Blombos archaeologists found nineteen snail shells, about the size of a kernel of corn, each with a hole through it (see opposite, bottom). Traces of wear at the ends of the shell indicate that they were originally strung together to make a strand of beads, worn perhaps on the wrist or at the neck. The beads also show traces of ocher. The beads, archaeologists speculate, may have functioned at Blombos as they do among the Ju/'hoansi people who live in the Kalahari Desert in Botswana and who are sometimes called Bushmen. Speakers of a language with many click sounds, the Ju/'hoansi present ostrich shell beads to other groups with whom they hope to form alliances.

The scientist who discovered these shells argued convincingly that these are very early signs of human creativity. A recent discovery suggests that they may be more. In 2007, archaeologists excavating the Pigeon Cave site in Morocco have found similar shells dated between 91,000 and 74,000 years ago. These beads also have holes, abrasion marks at the ends where they were strung together, and traces of ocher. They are not from exactly the same species of snail as those from Blombos Cave, but the two species of snail look identical to the naked eye (one can see the differences between them only with a microscope). Other undated finds of similar shells in Israel and Algeria suggest that a trading network that spanned Africa and Israel may have existed as early as 82,000 years ago.

The chunk of ocher, the bone tools, and the beads from Blombos reveal that their makers were able to produce beautiful objects because they had the time and energy left over after meeting basic subsistence needs. These early objects clearly display the artistic impulses of their makers and suggest that *Homo sapiens sapiens* engaged in the recognizably human activity of making art objects as early as 75,000 B.C.E. and possibly even before.

---

*Interview with Christopher Henshilwood in "When Humans Became Human," *New York Times,* February 26, 2002, p. F5.

QUESTIONS FOR ANALYSIS

 Which evidence from the archaeological record (including, but not limited to, the objects discussed above) do you find most convincing as the earliest indication of people becoming recognizably human? Why?

This is a block of red ocher, a pigment made from iron oxide. Now the color of rust, the surface would have originally been a vivid blood red. This block, 2.5 inches (6 cm) long, formed a small crayon that was used, perhaps, to decorate the body.

These abstract triangle markings may be purely decorative or may represent a way to count something, perhaps the passage of days.

This object was found in Blombos Cave, some 186 miles (300 km) from Cape Town, where the cave's occupants hunted and fished around 75,000 B.C.E.

The humans living in Europe during the Upper Paleolithic period are called Cro Magnon (CROW MAG-nahn), after the site where their remains were first found. Their methods of food acquisition show that they were better able to think about the future, not just the present. Cro Magnon bands traveled to rivers and coasts to catch fish. As they moved in search of more game and fish, they built new types of houses and developed better clothes.

These humans also produced the extraordinary cave paintings of Chauvet (SHOW-vay) in southern France (dated to 30,000 B.C.E.), which show the different animals hunted by the local peoples: mammoths (various types of extinct elephants), lions, and rhinoceroses. Some are decorated with patterns of dots or human handprints. Other cave sites, such as the well-known Lascaux (las-KOH) (15,000 B.C.E.) site in southwestern France, show horses, bison, and ibex, suggesting that ancient hunters targeted different animals during different seasons. (See the feature "Movement of Ideas: The Worship of Goddesses?")

Most experts thought that by 25,000 B.C.E. *Homo sapiens sapiens* was the only human species on earth, since all other species, including the Neanderthals, had died out. But a discovery announced in October 2004 has forced everyone to reconsider this view. Archaeologists working on the island of Flores in western Indonesia announced that they had discovered bones from a previously unknown

■ **An Ancient Artist at the Chauvet Caves of France** Traces of charcoal from the battling woolly rhinoceros (*lower right*) have been dated to about 30,000 B.C.E., making this one of the earliest cave paintings found anywhere in the world. The panel also portrays the same horse in four different poses, rare sketches done by an individual artist. Many of the paintings in the Chauvet caves display this artist's distinctive style. (AP/Wide World Photos)

human species they called *Homo floresiensis* (HO-mo flor-ehs-ee-EHN-suhs) ("Human from Flores"). The remains date from 95,000 to 13,000 B.C.E. The most complete skeleton, intact except for missing arms, came from a female who stood only 3 feet (.9 m) tall and whose brain was as small as the australopithecine Lucy's. The excavating archaeologists propose that the new species was a descendant of either the australopithecines or *Homo erectus*. Because other pygmy animals, such as pygmy elephants, developed on the island, these scientists suggest that the process of island-dwarfing could also have produced smaller-than-usual *Homo erectus*. The island is currently home to a group of human pygmies, who could be the descendants of the earlier population.[3]

Yet some scientists have loudly voiced their skepticism, largely because the stone tools found at the site are much more sophisticated than any associated with australopithecines or *Homo erectus*. They suggest, instead, that the skeleton may be that of a small *Homo sapiens sapiens* afflicted with a disorder called microcephaly (my-cro-SEPH-uh-lee) that results in a shrunken brain and other deformities. This controversial find shows how a single discovery can prompt radical revision of the scientific consensus on human evolution.

●The Settling of the Americas

*H*omo sapiens sapiens reached the Americas much later than they did any other landmass. The earliest confirmed human occupation in the Western Hemisphere dates to about 10,500 B.C.E., some forty thousand years after the settling of the Eurasian landmass and Australia. Accordingly, all human remains found so far in the Americas belong to the *Homo sapiens* species.

We know, however, much less about the settlement of the Americas than we do about the other continents. Scholars are not certain which routes the early settlers took, when they came, or if they traveled over land or by water. Far fewer human burials have been found in the Americas, and the few that have been found were excavated with much less scientific care than in Eurasia and Africa. Many sites had been disturbed so that the original layers of earth, so valuable to archaeologists, are no longer intact. Many early sites contain no human remains at all. For this reason, even skeletons like Kennewick Man are of great interest to those studying early migration to the Americas.

Beringia: The Land Bridge from Siberia to the Americas

One theory is that humans reached America on a land bridge from Siberia. **Beringia** (bear-in-JEE-uh) is the landmass, now below water, that connected the tip of Siberia in Russia with the northeastern corner of Alaska. Today Beringia is covered by a 50-mile-wide (80-km-wide) stretch of the Bering Sea. The water in this part of the Bering Sea is shallow, consistently less than 600 feet deep (182 m). As the earth experienced different periods of extended coldness, called Ice Ages, ocean water froze and covered such northern landmasses with ice. During these periods the ocean level declined and the ancient Beringia landmass emerged to form a land bridge between Russia and America. It was a large land bridge, measuring over 600 miles (1000 km) from north to south.

● **Beringia** Landmass now submerged below water that connected the tip of Siberia with the northeastern corner of Alaska.

The Worship of Goddesses?

What were the religious beliefs of the residents of Europe between 26,000 and 23,000 B.C.E.? Over twenty female figurines have been found at sites in Austria, Italy, Ukraine, Malta, the Czech Republic, and most often France. Made from mammoth ivory tusk, soapstone, and clay, the figurines range in size from 2 inches (5 cm) to a foot (30 cm) tall. The wide distribution of the figurines poses an interesting problem: Did different groups learn independently to make similar objects, or did one group first craft a model, which was then diffused to other places? Modern archaeologists require striking similarities before they can be persuaded of diffusion. It seems likely in this case that people in different places crafted women according to their own conceptions and that diffusion did not necessarily take place.

Some of the women are shown with extremely wide hips and pendulous breasts. Almost none have feet. They may have been placed upright in dirt or on a post. Their facial features remain vague, a suggestion that they are not portraits of particular individuals. Some appear to be pregnant, others not. Some have pubic hair, and one, from Monpazier, France, has an explicitly rendered vulva.

Some have suggested that the figurines are fertility icons made by men or women who hoped to have children. Others propose that the images are self-portraits because no mirrors existed at this early time. If women portrayed their own bodies as they looked to themselves, they would have shown themselves with pendulous breasts and wide hips. Still other archaeologists take these figurines as a sign of a matriarchal society, in which women served as leaders, or a matrilineal society, in which people traced descent through their mother (as opposed to a patriarchal society, in which descent is traced through the father). Since most of these figurines were found in the nineteenth century and were taken to museums or private collections, we do not know their original context and cannot conclude more about their function.

The one exception is a cave site at Laussel in the Dordogne region of France, where five different two-dimensional pictures were carved onto the cave walls and could not be easily removed. One picture, Woman with a Horn, was carved into the face of a block of stone. This two-dimensional rendering has the large breasts and wide hips of the smaller freestanding figurines, but her right hand is unusual in that it holds a horn, perhaps from a bison.

The Laussel cave had other pictures of a similar woman, a younger man in profile, a deer, and a horse. One design showing a woman on top and another figure below has been interpreted alternatively as two people copulating or a woman giving birth to a child. Several vulvas and phalluses were shown in the same cave. The conjunction of these different images strongly suggests that the Woman with a Horn was worshiped, along with the other images and sexual body parts, probably to facilitate conception or easy childbirth.

QUESTIONS FOR ANALYSIS

▸ How do archaeologists determine if an idea or motif diffused from one place to another or developed independently?

▸ What constitutes evidence of religious belief among preliterate peoples?

▸ How have scholars interpreted female figurines found across Europe between 26,000 and 23,000 B.C.E.?

Woman with a Horn, Laussel Cave, Dordogne River Valley, France. An Ancient Pregnancy? Standing 17.5 inches (44 cm) high, this block of stone, along with five others, came from a rock shelter occupied by people between 25,000 and 21,000 B.C.E. Similar carvings of women with wide hips and pendulous breasts have been found throughout the Dordogne River Valley region in France, but only this woman holds a bison horn. Interpreting the markings on the horn as calendrical records (perhaps of moon sightings), some analysts propose that her hand on her stomach indicates that she may be pregnant. (Musée d'Aquitaine, Bordeaux, France/Erich Lessing/Art Resource, NY)

Being covered with ice, sometimes very deep, Beringia would not have been an easy route for humans to cross. Yet we know that people had already migrated as far south as the site of Monte Verde (MAHN-tay VEHR-day), Chile, in South America at a time when Beringia was covered with ice. So how did humans get there?

Core samples of the ocean floor, drilled into what used to be Beringia, have yielded the remains of animal, insect, and plant life that reveal the extent of glaciation. The most intense phase of the late Wisconsin Ice Age was in 16,000 B.C.E., a time when the sea level fell 650 feet, exposing Beringia to its largest extent. The islands of the Bering Sea then stood as giant peaks on the Beringia landmass.

Less ice formed on the Alaskan and Canadian side of Beringia. In fact, cores reveal that small, low shrubs, many of them dwarf birches, shaped a tundra environment.

The first migrations to the New World may have occurred in 14,000 B.C.E. or even earlier, and certainly took place by about 10,500 B.C.E., when ice still covered much of Beringia. Much of North America was covered by sheets of ice over 10,000 feet (3,000 m) thick. Some scientists believe that an ice-free corridor between ice masses allowed movement through today's Canada. Others hypothesize that the ancient settlers hugged the coast, traveling in boats covered by animal skins stretched tight over a wooden pole frame. Boats would have allowed the settlers to proceed down the coast from Beringia to modern Chile, going from ice patch to ice patch. Where no ice had formed, the early settlers could have disembarked to pitch temporary camp.

Monte Verde, Chile: How the First Americans Lived, 10,500 B.C.E.

The best evidence for this first wave of migration comes from far down the west coast of the Americas, from a settlement called **Monte Verde, Chile,** which lies only 9 miles (14 km) away from the Pacific coast, south of the 40th parallel. Monte Verde is the most important ancient site in the Americas for several reasons. First, without a doubt it contains very early remains. Lying under a layer of peat, it also preserves organic materials like wood, skin, and plants that almost never survive. Finally, and most important, professional archaeologists have scrupulously recorded which items were found at each level following the key principle of **stratigraphy.** This is the idea that, at an undisturbed site, materials from lower levels predate those found above them. Using this principle, we can conclude that, at an undisturbed site, any remains found under one layer are earlier than anything from above that layer.

Monte Verde's undisturbed state made it an excellent place from which to collect samples for carbon-14 testing. **Carbon-14** is an isotope of carbon with a known half-life of 5,700 years. A fixed percentage of the carbon atoms in a living organism consists of this isotope, but this percentage declines after death because new carbon no longer enters the organism. Accordingly, one can determine the approximate age of an archaeological sample by analyzing the percentage of carbon-14 in it. Carbon-14 dates always include a plus/minus range because they are not completely accurate: the farther back in time one goes, the less accurate the dating is. (This book gives only one date for ease of presentation.) Carbon-14

• Monte Verde, Chile
Earliest site in the Americas, dating to 12,500 B.C.E., where evidence of human occupation has been found.

• stratigraphy
Archaeological principle that, at an undisturbed site, material from upper layers must be more recent than that from lower layers.

• carbon-14
Isotope of carbon whose presence in organic material can be used to determine the approximate age of archaeological samples.

analysis of evidence from Monte Verde gave an approximate date of 10,500 B.C.E. for the lowest level definitely occupied by humans.

Forming a bony spine running along the western edge of the Americas, the Rocky Mountains and the Andes Mountains formed a barrier that kept the first settlers in the coastal zones west of the mountain chain. Latin America's climate in this early period, like Africa's, is still the subject of intense study. Climatologists concur that the climate was extremely variable: periods of heavy glaciation were much cooler than those when glaciers retreated. In comparison to North America, there was much less ice, except in the southernmost reaches of the continent. Major rivers and lakes had not yet formed.

Although no human remains have been found at Monte Verde so far, the footprints of a child or a young teenager were preserved on the top of a level dated to 10,500 B.C.E. This finding provides indisputable evidence of human occupation. The twenty to thirty residents of Monte Verde lived in a structure about 20 yards (18 m) long that was covered with animal skins; the floor was also covered with skins. The residents used poles to divide the structure into smaller sections, probably for family groups, and heated these sections with fires in clay hearths. There they prepared food that they had gathered: wild berries, fruits, and wild potato tubers. An even lower layer with stone tools has been dated to approximately 31,000 B.C.E., but the evidence for human occupation is less convincing than the human footprints from the higher level.[4] If people lived at the site at this time, then the Americas may have been settled much earlier than the 14,000 B.C.E. date that is widely accepted today.

A separate building, shaped like a wishbone, stood about 100 feet away from the large structure. The residents hardened the floor of this building by mixing sand, gravel, and animal fat to make a place where they could clean bones, produce tools, and finish animal hides. Healers may have treated the ill in this building, too, since the floor contained traces of eighteen different plants, some chewed and then spit out, as though they had been used as medicine.

The unusual preservation of wood at Monte Verde means that we know exactly which tools the first Americans used. The site's residents mounted stone flakes onto wooden sticks, called hafts. They also had a small number of more finely worked spear points. Interestingly, Monte Verde's residents used many round stones, which they could have easily gathered on the beach, for slings or bolos. A bolo consists of a long string made of hide with stones or round beach pebbles tied at both ends. Holding one end, early humans swung the other end around their heads at high speed and then released the string. If on target, the spinning bolo wrapped itself around the neck of a bird or other animal and killed it.

The residents of Monte Verde hunted mastodon, a relative of the modern elephant that became extinct about 9000 B.C.E. They also foraged along the coast for shellfish, which could be eaten raw. In the initial stages of migration, the settlers found a coastal environment much more hospitable than an inland one because they could forage for many different types of food at the beach. Hunting parties could leave for long periods to pursue mastodon and other large game, confident that those left behind had ample food supplies.

The main weapon used to kill large game at Monte Verde and other early sites was the atlatl (AHT-latt-uhl) a word from the Nahuatl (NAH-waht) language spoken in central Mexico. The atlatl was a powerful weapon, capable of piercing thick animal hide, and was used for thousands of years (see the illustration on the next page).

■ A Powerful Ancient Weapon: The Atlatl The residents of the Monte Verde site used the atlatl spear-thrower to kill game. The atlatl had two parts, a long handle with a cup or hook at the end, and a spear tipped with a sharp stone point. The handle served as an extension of the human arm, so that the spear could be thrown farther with much greater force. (Illustration by Eric Parrish from James E. Dixon, *Bones, Boats and Bisons: Archaeology and the First Colonization of Western North America* [Albuquerque, N.M.: University of New Mexico Press, 1999], p. 153, Figure 6-1.)

The Rise of Clovis and Other Regional Traditions, 11,400–10,900 B.C.E.

By 11,000 B.C.E., small bands of people had settled all of the Americas. They used a new weapon in addition to the atlatl: wooden sticks with sharp slivers of rock, called microblades, attached to the shaft. Studies of different sites have determined that while the people in these regions shared many traits in common, different technological traditions also existed in different North American regions. Each left behind distinct artifacts (usually a spear point of a certain type). In contrast, South American sites do not show the same clear signs of regional difference because the residents of different sites mixed and matched different types of tools and spear points.

Like the residents of Monte Verde, these later peoples combined hunting with the gathering of wild fruits and seeds. They lived in an area stretching from Oregon to Texas, with heavy concentration in the Great Plains, and hunted a wide variety of game using atlatl tipped with stone spear points. Archaeologists call these characteristic spear points the **Clovis technological complex.** It takes its name from Clovis, New Mexico, where the first such spear points were found. It is difficult to estimate the number of residents at a given location, but some of the Clovis sites are larger than earlier sites, suggesting that as many as sixty people may have lived together in a single band. The Clovis people ate small animals such as rabbit, ground sloth, and turtle as well as larger animals like deer and bison. They also used tools to grind vegetables, but the types of vegetables have left few traces in the archaeological record.

The Clovis spear points impress all viewers with their beauty: their makers chose glassy rocks of striking colors to craft finely worked stone points. Foraging bands covered large stretches of territory, collecting different types of stone and carrying them far from their areas of origin. The Clovis peoples buried some of these collections in earth colored by ocher, the same mineral element used by the

● **Clovis technological complex** The characteristic stone spear points that were in use ca. 11,000 B.C.E. across much of modern-day America.

ancient peoples of South Africa and Australia. Archaeologists working at later Clovis sites throughout the Great Plains have also found a different type of stone blade lodged in bison bones. It seems that, as mammoth and mastodon became extinct, the residents shifted to hunting bison.

The Oldest Americans?

Who lived at sites like Monte Verde in the Americas in 10,500 B.C.E. or at the different Clovis sites in 9000 B.C.E.? This question would be much easier to answer if archaeologists had found multiple human remains at Monte Verde or at the Clovis sites in the Western Hemisphere. In both North and South America, thirty-six sites predate 9500 B.C.E., but only thirty-eight skeletons older than 9000 B.C.E. have been found.[5] Unfortunately, almost all of these early skeletons were removed from their original location. As a result, archaeologists must study bones divorced from their original context as they reconstruct the patterns of ancient migration to the Americas.

Some scholars of early migration to the Americas have conducted statistical analysis of these early remains in the hope of identifying the ancestors of today's Amerindians. Although we use the concept of race in casual conversation every time that we say someone is white or black, it is impossible to classify people by race scientifically. Many of the world's peoples do not fall into the widely used categories of black, white, or yellow; Australian aborigines have dark skin but light hair color, and Polynesians do not fit any of these categories. Rather than use the problematic category of race, scientists today focus on determining the geographic origin of a given population.

Physical anthropologists use one basic technique for identifying the characteristics of a given population in modern times. They collect measurements of the skull and other body parts for many different people from one place and input all the values into a computer database. Because skulls give the most information, anthropologists measure their shape, eye sockets, and teeth carefully. All provide clues about a given skeleton's background. Skulls and bones from a single place, however, tend to vary widely. A bone or skull may look like those normally associated with one place but may actually belong to an atypical individual from another place.

Once they have finished measuring a skeleton, physical anthropologists use databases containing thousands of data points to assign, however tentatively, a certain skeleton to a given population. The thirty-eight skeletons found in the Americas divide into two groups: individuals with longer heads and those with rounder heads. Those with rounder heads have wider, flatter faces. Their teeth share certain characteristics with modern-day Chinese, Japanese, Siberians, Russians, and Amerindians. They could well be the ancestors of today's Amerindians, who also have rounder, flatter faces and teeth like those of people living in Asia.

Those with the longer heads have small faces that tend to be narrow and noses that jut out. Their teeth have the characteristics of one group whose modern members live in Indonesia and Southeast Asia. Kennewick Man belongs to the group with the longer heads. Examination of his remains showed that he had sustained several injuries, the most obvious being a projectile point lodged in his pelvis. The growth of bone around the wound showed that the injury had occurred long before his death in his 40s. He had broken ribs, a dent on his forehead (perhaps from a wound), and arthritis in his elbows and knees, and he probably did not have full use of his left arm, which was fully grown but less developed than his right arm.

Kennewick Man in Court

For over a century Amerindian skeletons, unlike European skeletons, were kept in storage bins and displayed in museums. In 1990 the U.S. Congress passed the Native American Graves Protection and Repatriation Act, or NAGPRA, which required that all Amerindian skeletal remains that demonstrated cultural affiliation to an existing, federally recognized Amerindian people be offered for repatriation.

The case of Kennewick Man is different from most because of the skeleton's great age. Kennewick Man lived nearly ten thousand years ago, and his bone structure does not resemble that of the Umatilla people living near the Columbia River. One Umatilla leader insisted that they had lived in the region for ten thousand years: "Our oral history goes back 10,000 years. We know how time began and how Indian people were created."* Bruce Babbitt, Secretary of the Interior at the time of the discovery, agreed and ordered the remains of Kennewick Man repatriated to a consortium of five tribes living in the Northwest, including the Umatilla.

A group of scientists led by Robson Bonnichsen, a professor of anthropology at Texas A & M University, sued the government for return of the remains.

The scientists focused on the language of NAGPRA: "Native American means of, or relating to, a tribe, people, or culture that is indigenous to the United States." The act, they contended, required a relationship first to be established between the Umatilla and Kennewick Man before the Umatilla could claim him.

If Kennewick Man belonged to a group that had died out, they argued, then the Umatilla did not have the right to claim his remains. The scientists and their legal team hoped to show that Congress had not considered an exceptional example like Kennewick Man when drafting NAGPRA.

In 2002 a federal magistrate decided that Kennewick Man could not be "related to any identifiable group or culture, and the culture to which he belonged may have died out thousands of years ago."† In 2004 the Ninth Circuit Court of Appeals upheld his ruling, and scientists examined the remains in the summer of 2005.

---

*New York Times, September 30, 1996, Section A, p. 12.
†New York Times, July 19, 2005, Section F; Column 2; Science Desk; p. 4.

Like the other members of the longer-head group, Kennewick Man's head and body measurements did not seem to correspond to those of any Amerindians living in the region today. In fact, those in the long-headed group do not closely resemble *any* modern population. This lack of correspondence suggests that the long-headed group may have become extinct in the past, leaving no descendants today.

Scientists are still grappling with the implications of these finds, and many refuse to speculate further, since the data are so sparse and inconclusive. However, a small number of scientists have proposed a provocative, but tentative, model for the peopling of the Americas: they suggest that, as early as 14,000 B.C.E. and certainly by 10,500 B.C.E., the long-headed peoples came first, perhaps from northeast Asia, and lived along the west coast of the Americas. These settlers may have lived in Monte Verde and other early sites. Several thousand years later, these scientists suggest, a second wave of round-headed settlers came to the Americas, replaced the original settlers, and moved inland. Others dispute this hypothesis vigorously. (See the feature "World History in Today's World: Kennewick Man in Court.")

In sum, many scholars agree that people migrated to the Americas but not on when or in how many waves. Everyone concurs that the age of migrations ended when the world's climate warmed quickly at the end of the Wisconsin Ice Age. Between 8300 and 7000 B.C.E., the sea level (as measured near British Columbia, Canada) rose 400 feet (122 m), from 350 feet (107 m) below today's level to 50 feet (15 m) above it.[6] By 7000 B.C.E., the Bering Strait had filled with water and most of Beringia lay under water once again. The only regions of the world that had not yet been settled were the islands of the Pacific (see Chapter 5). After 7000 B.C.E., the ancestors of modern Amerindians dispersed over North and South America, where they lived in almost total isolation from the rest of the world until 1492.

●The Emergence of Agriculture, 12,500–3000 B.C.E.

The development of **agriculture,** when people planted the first seeds and harvested the resulting crops using domesticated animals, marked a crucial breakthrough in the history of humankind. Before it, all ancient peoples were hunters and gatherers and never established permanent settlements. They were constantly in motion, whether following herds of wild animals or gathering wild berries and plants. Over thousands of years, early peoples in different parts of the globe experimented first by gathering certain plants and hunting selected animals. Eventually they began to plant seeds in specific locations and to raise tame animals that could help them harvest their crops. The cultivation of crops facilitated settled life first in small farming villages and then in towns.

●**agriculture** The planting of seeds and harvesting of crops using domesticated animals.

The Domestication of Plants and Animals, ca. 12,500–7000 B.C.E.

The first people in western Asia, and possibly the world, who learned how to plant seeds, domesticate animals, and cultivate crops were the Natufians (NAH-too-fee-uhnz), who lived in Palestine and southern Syria in 12,500 B.C.E. (see Map 1.1). Hunters and gatherers, they harvested fields of grain, particularly wild barley and emmer wheat, which flourished because the region's climate was warmer and wetter than today. They also picked fruits and nuts and hunted wild cattle, goats, pigs, and deer.

The Natufians used small flint blades mounted on wooden handles to cut down the stands of wild barley and emmer wheat, and they ground the harvested grain in stone mortars with pestles. Because they knew how to make advanced stone tools, archaeologists class them as **Neolithic,** literally "New Stone Age." Unlike Paleolithic peoples, the Natufians and other Neolithic peoples practiced agriculture. Gradually the Natufians began to modify their way of life, possibly to support a growing population.

●**Neolithic** "New Stone Age," the archaeological term for societies that used stone tools and practiced agriculture.

The Natufians at first gathered wild grain where it grew naturally. But wild grains had two flaws: their stems were so weak that their seeds easily fell to the ground, and their thick husks made it difficult to remove the kernels of grain from inside the seeds. The Natufians gradually started to weed these naturally occurring stands of grain and to plant extra seeds in them. The Natufians picked seeds from tall plants, a practice that eventually fostered the growth of wheat with stronger stems. Similarly, as they favored plants whose kernels had thinner husks, the wheat and barley they planted began to diverge from their wild prototypes.

People took thousands of years to master the two major components of farming: taming animals and planting crops. The first step to domesticating wild animals was simply to stop killing young female animals. Then people began to watch over wild herds and kill only those animals that could no longer breed. Eventually,

🌐 **MAP 1.1**

Ancient Southwestern Asia The Natufians, who lived in Palestine and southern Syria, began to practice agriculture around 12,500 B.C.E. and gradually learned how to raise animals and plant crops over the next several thousand years. Agriculture eventually spread beyond the Levant and Mesopotamia to southern Anatolia, where agriculturalists built the world's earliest city at Catalhoyuk.

the Natufians began to feed the herds in their care. The dog was the first animal to be tamed, around 10,000 B.C.E., and its function was to help hunters locate their prey. After several thousand years, villagers had domesticated goats, sheep, and cattle. All these animals produced meat, and sheep produced wool that was woven into cloth.

The size of excavated Natufian sites suggests that groups as large as 150 or 250 people—far larger than the typical hunting and gathering band of 30 or 40—lived together in settlements as large as 10,800 square feet (1000 sq m). Although some analysts have idealized life in ancient society and imagined early peoples sharing their food and clothing with each other, archaeological evidence shows just the opposite: some people, presumably the higher-ranking members of the group, gained control of more resources than others. Burials reveal the greatest differences: some Natufian tombs contain the unadorned corpses of the lower ranked, while corpses decorated with shell, bone, or stone ornaments are clearly those of the more powerful members of the society.

After 8300 B.C.E., possibly because of a sustained period of dryer weather, it became increasingly difficult for the Natufians to continue gathering wild grain as before. Some Natufians returned to a life of hunting undomesticated crops and gathering wild plants, a possible indication that they found the cultivation of crops too difficult. Still others intensified their planting and gathering of wheat and barley.

By 8000 B.C.E. many peoples throughout the eastern Mediterranean, particularly near the Zagros Mountains in modern Turkey, had begun to cultivate wheat and barley (see Map 1.2). Unlike the Natufians, these peoples did not live near pre-existing stands of wild wheat and barley but rather in more difficult living conditions that forced them to experiment with planting seeds and raising crops. Archaeologists have noticed that peoples living in marginal areas, not the most fertile areas with the heaviest rainfall, tended to plant crops because they had to innovate. Once they had begun to cultivate crops, the larger size of their villages forced them to continue farming because agriculture could support a larger population than hunting and gathering.

The First Larger Settlements, 7000–3000 B.C.E.

Between 8300 and 7500 B.C.E., the largest Natufian settlement was Jericho (JEHR-ih-koh), near the Jordan River in the present-day occupied West Bank, where as many as one thousand people may have lived in an area of 8 to 10 acres (.03–.04 sq km).[7] Residing in mud-brick dwellings with stone foundation bases, the residents of Jericho planted barley and wheat, possibly along with figs and lentils, at the same time they continued to hunt wild animals. The more grains they ate, the more their bodies needed salt, which they collected by evaporating water from the Dead Sea.

The residents of Jericho dug a wide ditch and built a wall at least 8 feet (2.5 m) high around their settlement to protect their accumulated resources from wild animals, human enemies, or possibly both. They also built a 28-foot (8.5-m) tower inside the wall that may have served as a lookout post. The ditches, the wall, and the tower all show the ruler's ability to mobilize laborers and supplies for large-scale construction.

Around 7250 B.C.E., more than one thousand people lived at the site of Ain Ghazal (AYN GUH-zahl) near Amman, Jordan, which also covered 10 acres (.04 sq km).

The Earliest Depictions of People? The Plaster Statues of Ain Ghazal, Jordan Dating to 6500 B.C.E., these figures were probably used in rituals and commemorated the dead. Their makers fashioned a core of reeds and grass, covered it with plaster, and then painted clothes and facial features on it. The eyes, made from inlaid shells with painted dots, are particularly haunting. (Photo by John Tsantesi, courtesy Dr. Gary O. Rollefson, Whitman College, Walla Walla, Washington)

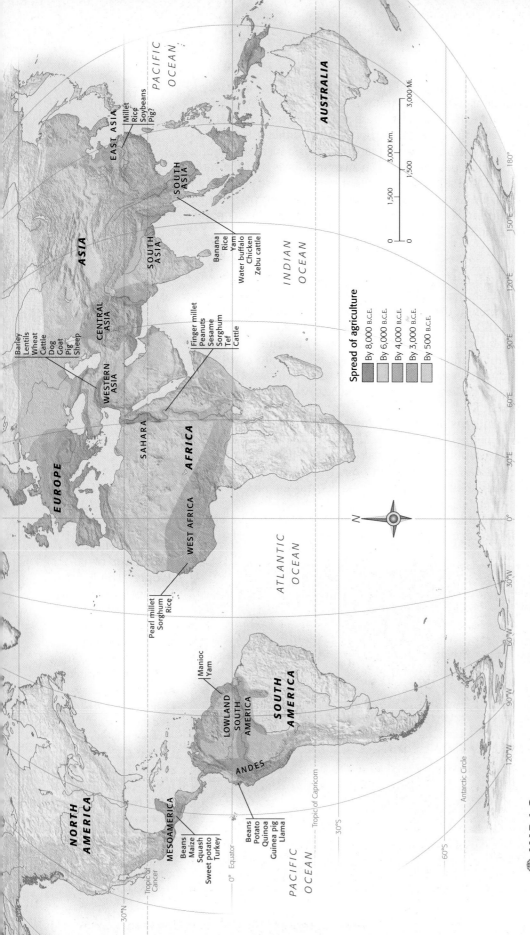

MAP 1.2

Early Agriculture Agriculture developed independently at different times in the different regions of the world. In some places, like western Asia, residents gradually shifted to full-time cultivation of crops and raising domesticated animals, while in others, like New Guinea, they continued to hunt and gather.

 Interactive Map

Spread of agriculture

By 8,000 B.C.E.
By 6,000 B.C.E.
By 4,000 B.C.E.
By 3,000 B.C.E.
By 500 B.C.E.

In 6500 B.C.E., the site had become twice as large, and by 6000 B.C.E. it was three times as large. Like the residents of Jericho, the people of Ain Ghazal planted wheat, barley, and lentils, even as they continued to hunt for wild animals and gather wild plants. They also raised their own domesticated goats. The site is most famous for producing quantities of unusual human figurines, some as tall as 3 feet (.9 m), with distinctive shell eyes.

By 7000 B.C.E. early farmers were living in villages in western Turkey and the region of the Levant (the eastern shore of the Mediterranean in today's Lebanon and Israel). Their residents could depend on rainfall to support their crops, and they continued to hunt and gather as they raised their own herds. By far the largest settlement in the region was at Catalhoyuk (CHAH-tal Her-yerk) in south central Anatolia, where some five thousand people were living in 6000 B.C.E.

Catalhoyuk did not resemble earlier settlements. Unlike Jericho, it had no external wall or surrounding moats. The residents lived in mud-brick dwellings touching each other, and the exteriors of the houses on the perimeter of the village formed a continuous protective wall.

Frequently white-washed, the walls of the Catalhoyuk dwellings depicted animals, hunters, gods, and even the earliest known landscape painting of a volcano exploding. Of the more than one hundred rooms that have been excavated, forty had plaster models of bull or ram heads mounted on the walls or paintings showing women giving birth to rams or bulls. Some archaeologists believe that these rooms served as shrines where residents worshiped bulls and rams; others see them simply as the homes of the wealthy, who worshiped ram and bull deities.

The different types of houses at Catalhoyuk indicate that some residents had more wealth than others. The wealthy buried their dead with jewelry and tools, while the poor interred only their dead bodies. At the same time that they worked in the fields, some families worked bone tools, wove cloth, or made clay pots, which they could trade for other goods, especially obsidian, a naturally occurring volcanic glass. Ancient peoples treasured obsidian because they could use it to make sharp knives and beautiful jewelry.

Archaeologists have found evidence of the independent development of agriculture in a number of regions around the world: in western Asia around 12,500 B.C.E., as we have seen in this chapter (see Map 1.2); in Mesoamerica around 8000 B.C.E.; in the Yangzi Valley of China around 7000 B.C.E.; in the Indus River Valley in today's Pakistan between 6500 and 5000 B.C.E.; in the Peruvian Andes around 8000 B.C.E.; in New Guinea around 5000 B.C.E.; in eastern Sahara around 8000 B.C.E.; and in sub-Saharan Africa around 2000 B.C.E. Many peoples of the world continued to hunt and gather as the major source of their food supply. In the spring hunter-gatherers in New Guinea planted the seeds of a particularly desirable crop, such as bananas, and then returned in the fall to harvest the ripened fruit. Only in a few places in the world did the development of agriculture lead to the rise of a complex society, as we will see in Chapters 2 through 5.

The World's Earliest City: Catalhoyuk, Turkey This artist's reconstruction shows what Catalhoyuk looked like in 6000 B.C.E., when it had a population of around five thousand people. The settlement had no streets, and the houses had no doors at ground level. Instead, residents walked on top of the roofs to get from one place to another. Entering houses through a hole in the roof, they climbed down a ladder to get inside. (From *Vanished Civilization: The Hidden Secrets of Lost Cities and Forgotten People*. Reader's Digest Association, Ltd., London, 2002.)

Chapter Review

KEY TERMS

Kennewick Man (2)

hominids (4)

Homo sapiens sapiens (4)

evolution (5)

Australopithecus (5)

Paleolithic (6)

Homo erectus (6)

Neanderthal (8)

religion (9)

Beringia (13)

Monte Verde, Chile (16)

stratigraphy (16)

carbon-14 (16)

Clovis technological complex (18)

agriculture (21)

Neolithic (21)

Download the MP3 audio file of the Chapter Review and listen to it on the go.

The remains of Kennewick Man shed light on the settlement of the Americas, one of the last phases in the peopling of the world. The movement of peoples from Africa to almost every corner of the globe was a long one, requiring six or seven million years. This complex migration involved many different human ancestors, some closely related to modern people, some less so. One theme is constant: from the very beginning ancient hominids were constantly moving. They followed herds, crossed rivers, traveled by boat, and ultimately covered enormous distances at a time when their most powerful weapon was a stone hand ax and the fastest means of locomotion was running. From their beginnings, early humans were voyagers who traveled the world.

Who were the first hominids? What were the main stages in their development?

The history of humankind began some seven million years ago in Africa, when the first hominids probably broke off from chimpanzees and other primates. By 3.5 million years ago, australopithecines like Lucy stood upright. Around 2.5 million years ago, Homo habilis made the first tools by breaking flakes off stone cores.

When and how did hominids leave Africa and settle Eurasia?

The first human ancestor to move outside of Africa, *Homo erectus*, crossed the Sinai Peninsula and reached modern-day Georgia in the Caucasus Mountains by 1.8 million years ago and Ubeidiya, Israel, 1.4 million years ago. *Homo erectus* could probably control fire but did not settle in northern Eurasia because it was too cold.

When did ancient hominids become recognizably human?

Homo sapiens sapiens, or anatomically modern humans, first arose in central Africa around 150,000 B.C.E. In 100,000 B.C.E. they buried their dead in Israel, a sign that they believed in the afterlife, a major element of most religious systems. In 75,000 B.C.E. they created the world's first art objects, such as the chunk of ocher from Blombos Cave. By 50,000 B.C.E. these humans were planning hunting expeditions in the fall so that they had meat over the winter, and they probably used speech to do so. Their ability to hunt, to build boats and rafts, and to adjust to new environments allowed them to settle Australia by 60,000 B.C.E. and Europe by 50,000 B.C.E.

⛵ How and when did the first people move to the Americas? What was their way of life?

The final phase of the expansion occurred when *Homo sapiens sapiens* moved from Siberia across the Beringian land bridge to the Western Hemisphere about 14,000 B.C.E. The earliest confirmed site with human habitation in the Americas is Monte Verde, Chile, where humans lived in 10,500 B.C.E. Almost all of the residents of the Americas were hunter-gatherers who lived in small bands of about forty members.

⛵ How and where did agriculture first arise? How did its impact vary around the world?

Agriculture arose first in western Asia around 12,500 B.C.E. There, the Natufians and other Neolithic peoples used stone tools to gather wild barley and emmer wheat. By 8,000 B.C.E. different peoples in western Asia had domesticated dogs, goats, sheep, and cattle, and they were planting and harvesting strains of barley and wheat. In some parts people continued to hunt wild animals and gather plants at the same time they cultivated certain crops, while in other parts of the world, including western Asia, agriculture resulted in the rise of complex societies, as we will learn in the next chapter.

WEB RESOURCES

Pronunciation Guide

Interactive Maps

MAP 1.1 Ancient Southwestern Asia

MAP 1.2 Early Agriculture

Chapter Objectives

ACE Multiple-Choice Quiz

Flashcards

For Further Reference

Benedict, Jeff. *No Bone Unturned: The Adventures of a Top Smithsonian Forensic Scientist and the Legal Battle for America's Oldest Skeletons.* New York: HarperCollins, 2003.

Chatters, James. *Ancient Encounters: Kennewick Man and the First Americans.* New York: Simon and Schuster, 2001.

Dillehay, Thomas D. *The Settlement of the Americas: A New Prehistory.* New York: Basic Books, 2000.

Dixon, E. James. *Bones, Boats, and Bison.* Albuquerque: University of New Mexico Press, 1999.

Fagan, Brian M. *The Great Journey: The Peopling of Ancient America.* London: Thames and Hudson, 1987.

Fagan, Brian M., ed., *The Oxford Companion to Archaeology.* New York: Oxford University Press, 1996.

Klein, Richard, with Blake Edgar. *The Dawn of Human Culture.* New York: John Wiley, 2002.

Koppel, Tom. *Lost World: Rewriting Prehistory—How New Science Is Tracing America's Ice Age Mariners.* New York: Atria Books, 2003.

Stiebing, William H. *Ancient Near Eastern History and Culture.* New York: Longman, 2003.

Stringer, Chris, and Peter Andrews. *The Complete World of Human Evolution.* London: Thames & Hudson, 2006.

Wells, Spencer. *The Journey of Man: A Genetic Odyssey.* Princeton: Princeton University Press, 2002.

White, Randall. *Dark Caves, Bright Visions: Life in Ice Age Europe.* New York: American Museum of Natural History in association with W. W. Norton, 1986.

Websites

American Museum of Natural History, History of Human Evolution (http://www.amnh.org/exhibitions/permanent/humanorigins/history/humans5.php).   Virtual, interactive tour of the Museum's Hall of Human Origins.

Northern Clans, Northern Traces (http://www.mnh.si.edu/arctic/html/kennewick_man.html).   James Chatters provides his explanation of the Kennewick man discovery.

Scientific American (http://www.sciam.com).   Excellent source for latest discoveries in human history and archaeology.

The Smithsonian Institution: Human Origins Program (http://anthropology.si.edu/humanorigins/). Comprehensive introduction to the history of all human species.

Films

"Nova: Mystery of the First Americans."

2

The First Complex Societies in the Eastern Mediterranean, ca. 4000–550 B.C.E.

The epic *Gilgamesh* (GIL-ga-mesh), one of the earliest recorded works of literature, captures the experience of the people of Mesopotamia (mess-oh-poh-TAME-ee-ah), who established one of the first complex societies in the world. **Mesopotamia** (Greek for "between the rivers") is the region between the Tigris (TIE-gris) and Euphrates (you-FRAY-teez) Rivers in today's Iraq and eastern Syria. The epic *Gilgamesh* indicates that the people in this region remembered what life was like before the rise of cities. It describes the unlikely friendship between two men: Enkidu (EN-kee-doo), who lives in the wild like an animal, and **Gilgamesh,** the king of the ancient city Uruk (OO-rook), located in modern-day Warka in southern Iraq. Ruler of the walled city between 2700 and 2500 B.C.E., Gilgamesh enjoys the benefits of a complex society: wearing clothing, drinking beer, and eating bread. Early in the epic, when a hunter complains to Gilgamesh that Enkidu is freeing the animals caught in his traps, Gilgamesh sends the woman Shamhat, a priestess at the main temple of Uruk, to introduce Enkidu to the pleasures of complex societies:

Enkidu, born in the uplands,
Who feeds on grass with gazelles,
Who drinks at the water hole with beasts, . . .
Shamhat looked upon him, a human-man,
A barbarous fellow from the midst of the steppe:
Shamhat loosened her garments,

GILGAMESH
KILLING A BULL

Courtesy Schøyen Collection

 This icon will direct you to interactive activities and study materials on the *Voyages* website:
www.cengage.com/history/hansen/voyages1e

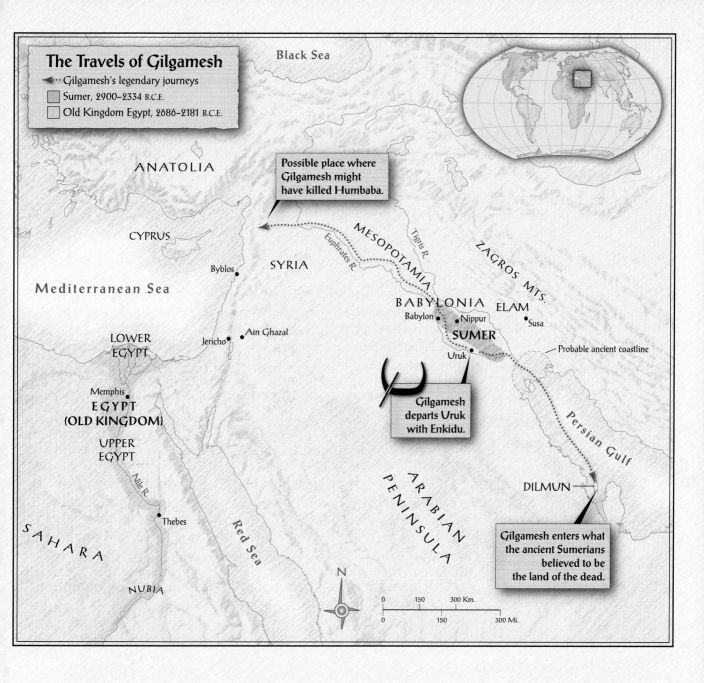

The Travels of Gilgamesh

◄···· Gilgamesh's legendary journeys

▢ Sumer, 2900–2334 B.C.E.

▢ Old Kingdom Egypt, 2686–2181 B.C.E.

Black Sea

ANATOLIA

Possible place where Gilgamesh might have killed Humbaba.

CYPRUS

MESOPOTAMIA

Tigris R.

ZAGROS MTS.

Euphrates R.

Byblos

SYRIA

Mediterranean Sea

BABYLONIA   ELAM

Babylon   Nippur

Ain Ghazal   **SUMER**   Susa

LOWER EGYPT

Jericho

Uruk

— Probable ancient coastline

Memphis

EGYPT (OLD KINGDOM)

Gilgamesh departs Uruk with Enkidu.

UPPER EGYPT

ARABIAN PENINSULA

Persian Gulf

Nile R.

SAHARA

Thebes

Red Sea

DILMUN

Gilgamesh enters what the ancient Sumerians believed to be the land of the dead.

NUBIA

N

0   150   300 Km.

0   150   300 Mi.

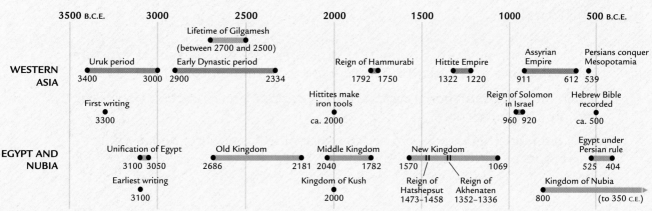

	3500 B.C.E.	3000	2500	2000	1500	1000	500 B.C.E.

Lifetime of Gilgamesh (between 2700 and 2500)

WESTERN ASIA

Uruk period
3400   3000

Early Dynastic period
2900   2334

Reign of Hammurabi
1792 1750

Hittite Empire
1322 1220

Assyrian Empire
911   612

Persians conquer Mesopotamia
539

First writing
3300

Hittites make iron tools
ca. 2000

Reign of Solomon in Israel
960 920

Hebrew Bible recorded
ca. 500

EGYPT AND NUBIA

Unification of Egypt
3100 3050

Old Kingdom
2686   2181

Middle Kingdom
2040   1782

New Kingdom
1570   1069

Egypt under Persian rule
525   404

Earliest writing
3100

Kingdom of Kush
2000

Reign of Hatshepsut
1473–1458

Reign of Akhenaten
1352–1336

Kingdom of Nubia
800   (to 350 C.E.)

> She exposed her loins, he took her charms, . . .
> After he had his fill of her delights,
> He set off towards his beasts.
> When they saw him, Enkidu, the gazelles shied off,
> The wild beasts of the steppe shunned his person. . . .
> Enkidu was too slow, he could not run as before,
> But he had gained reason and expanded his understanding.[1]

CL Primary Source: The Epic of Gilgamesh *Find out how Gilgamesh's friend Enkidu propels him on a quest for immortality, and whether that quest is successful.*

After his encounter with Shamhat, Enkidu immediately adopts the ways of those living in complex societies and becomes Gilgamesh's close friend. First written around 2100 B.C.E., *Gilgamesh* is not a strict chronicle of the historic king's life but the romanticized version of a legendary king's life, complete with appearances by different gods who controlled human fate.

The hero of the epic is constantly in motion. Gilgamesh makes two long journeys, traveling overland by foot and across water on a small boat he guides with a pole. First, he travels with Enkidu to kill the ferocious monster Humbaba, who guards a cedar forest somewhere to the west. Then, after Enkidu dies, Gilgamesh voyages to the land of the dead, where he learns about a flood surprisingly like that described in the Hebrew Bible.

The story of Gilgamesh was written by people living in one of the world's first complex societies. This chapter traces the rise of the first cities, then city-states, then kingdoms, and finally regional powers that interacted in an international system spanning Mesopotamia, Egypt, and the eastern coast of the Mediterranean, including Anatolia (the western section of present-day Turkey), Crete, and Greece in the Aegean Sea. These societies were significantly more complex than those that preceded them. As the centuries passed, an international system developed in which envoys traveled from one ruler to another and merchants transported goods throughout the region.

Focus Questions

- What were the similarities in political structures, religion, and social structure in Mesopotamia and Egypt? What were the main differences?

- When did the international system of the eastern Mediterranean take shape, and how did it function?

- How did monotheism arise among the ancient Hebrews, and under what circumstances did they record their beliefs?

●The Emergence of Complex Society in Mesopotamia, ca. 3100–1590 B.C.E.

As we have seen in the previous chapter, the settlements of the eastern Mediterranean increased in size gradually, reaching some five thousand people living in Catalhoyuk by 6000 B.C.E. Eventually some villages became larger than the surrounding villages and thus became centers. In time these centers grew to become cities of twenty thousand inhabitants or more. By 3100 B.C.E. even larger urban centers had formed in southern Mesopotamia, where the first city of forty or fifty thousand people was located at Uruk. Here complex society took shape for the first time.

Scholars define a **complex society** as a large urban center with a population in the tens of thousands whose residents pursue different occupations, the mark of specialized labor. Some have higher social positions than others, an indication of social stratification. Some earlier definitions of complex society required the presence of a writing system, but today the term also covers urban societies without writing systems. In recent years, analysts have stressed that, unlike Neolithic societies, early complex societies had much larger surpluses—of both material goods and labor—and believed that their rulers, their gods, and their human representatives, the priests, were entitled to a large share of these surpluses.

The shift from a simpler society to a complex one took thousands of years. Complex societies interest historians because they had larger populations than simple societies and their residents often left behind written records that allow historians to study how they changed over time, the major topic of historical writing. The world's first complex societies appeared in Mesopotamia and Egypt at about the same time, before 3000 B.C.E.; this chapter first considers Mesopotamia.

● **Mesopotamia**
Greek "between the rivers": the region between the Tigris and Euphrates Rivers in today's Iraq and eastern Syria.

● **Gilgamesh**   Name of a historic king of Uruk (modern-day Warka, Iraq) who ruled between 2700 and 2500 B.C.E. Also, the name of an epic about him.

● **complex society**
Societies characterized by large urban centers with specialized labor and social stratification, as well as the belief that rulers and deities were entitled to the surpluses these societies produced.

City Life in Ancient Mesopotamia

The first settlers came to southern Mesopotamia from the eastern Mediterranean and western Turkey. They found the environment harsh. Each year not enough rain fell to support farming, and no wild grain grew naturally in the marshlands. In addition, the Tigris and Euphrates Rivers tended to flood in the late summer, when crops were ripening, and the floodwaters often washed away the settlers' homes.

The settlers responded by developing techniques for draining the water. They settled along the shore of the Euphrates, which flowed less rapidly than the Tigris, and dug channels for the floodwater from the Euphrates. They discovered that they could use these channels to move the water to fields far from the river. Using irrigation, these early farmers permanently settled the lower Mesopotamian plain between 6000 and 5000 B.C.E.

Their first villages were small, but by 4000 B.C.E. some villages had grown into walled urban centers of over ten thousand people. The farmland within the walls could not produce enough food for the growing population, so the urban centers came to depend on surplus food grown by the residents of the surrounding villages. The food was stored in temples. Excavations reveal that temples had a main chamber surrounded by multiple rooms for the storage of grain. In turn, the cities provided the villages with military protection from raids by neighboring cities.

● **city-state** A city whose ruler governs both the city center and the surrounding countryside.

Historians use the term **city-state** for a city whose ruler governs both the city center and the surrounding countryside. Kings descended from prominent families, like Gilgamesh, ruled these city-states, often with the support of temple priests and in consultation with other prominent families (see page 36). The first kings were probably successful military leaders who continued to rule in peacetime.

The epic describes Gilgamesh's city of Uruk as the leading city of its time, and ancient texts simply call Uruk "the city," because no other city rivaled Uruk in size or importance between 3400 and 3000 B.C.E., the dates of the Uruk period. One of the most ancient cities to be excavated by archaeologists, Uruk meets the definition of a complex society: its population numbered between forty and fifty thousand, and its inhabitants had specialized occupations and were divided by social level. The surrounding countryside provided a large surplus of grain that the ruler and temple leadership distributed to the residents of the city.

The opening section of *Gilgamesh* provides a vivid description of the region's greatest city:

> Go up, pace out the walls of Uruk,
> Study the foundation terrace and examine the brickwork.
> Is not its masonry of kiln-fired brick?
> And did not seven masters lay its foundations?
> One square mile of city, one square mile of gardens,
> One square mile of clay pits, a half square mile of Ishtar's dwelling,
> Three and a half square miles is the measure of Uruk!

Uruk, then, contained one square mile each of land occupied by residences, farmland, and clay pits, with the remaining half square mile taken by the temple of Ishtar, the city's guardian deity. (The Sumerian mile does not correspond exactly to the modern English mile.)

Dating to 700 B.C.E., the most complete version of the Gilgamesh epic is a retelling of the original story, and historians must use archaeological data to supplement the information it provides about early Uruk. Although the epic claims that the walls were made from fired bricks, the actual walls were made from sundried mud brick. In roughly 3000 B.C.E., the city had a wall 5 miles (9.5 km) long. Enclosing approximately 1,000 acres (400 hectares), it was by far the largest city in the world at the time. Much of it consisted of open farmland.

Farming required year-round labor and constant vigilance. Unlike Neolithic farmers, whose tools were made from bone, wood, or stone, Mesopotamian farmers had much more durable tools made of **bronze,** an alloy of copper and tin. In addition to axes used to cut down trees and clear fields, they used bronze plow blades to dig the furrows and bronze sickles to harvest the grain. Other workers also had bronze tools. Those who smelted metal used hammers and tongs, while carpenters had saws and drills.

● **bronze** An alloy of copper and tin used to make the earliest metal tools.

Archaeologists are not certain where the wheel was first invented. One of the most important tools used by the Mesopotamians, it first appeared sometime around 3500 B.C.E. in a wide area extending from Mesopotamia to the modern European countries of Switzerland, Slovenia, Poland, and Russia. The earliest wheeled vehicles were flat wooden platforms that moved on two logs pulled by laborers. By 3000 B.C.E. the Mesopotamians were using narrow carts, usually with four solid wooden wheels, to move loads, both within city-states and over greater distances. By 2500 B.C.E., they had begun to add spokes to wheels, which moved much faster.

Built in the flood plain of the Euphrates, Uruk had no tall trees suitable for lumber, little stone, and almost no mineral deposits. The epic tells of Gilgamesh and Enkidu's overland journey to the wooded home of the monster Humbaba to obtain lumber, and the real-life inhabitants of Uruk shipped wood in carts or by boat first from the highlands of northern Mesopotamia, near the Zagros (ZAH-groes) Mountains, and later from the forests of Lebanon.

At Uruk, archaeologists have found extensive evidence of occupational diversity and social stratification, both important markers of a complex society. Large quantities of broken pottery found in the same area suggest that potters lived and worked together, as did other craftworkers like weavers and metalsmiths. Because people received more or less compensation for different tasks, some became rich while others stayed poor. Poorer people lived in small houses made of unfired mud bricks and mud plaster, while richer people lived in fired-brick houses of many rooms with kitchens. They hosted guests in large reception rooms in which they served lavish meals washed down with generous quantities of beer. (See the feature "World History in Today's World: The World's First Beer.")

The Beginnings of Writing, 3300 B.C.E.

People living in southern Mesopotamia developed their writing system sometime around 3300 B.C.E., making it the earliest in the world. Scholars call the language of the first documents Sumerian, after **Sumer,** a geographical term referring broadly to the ancient region of southern Mesopotamia. It is not always easy to determine whether a given sign constitutes writing in ancient script. Markings on pottery, for example, look like writing but may be only the sign of the person who made the pot. A sign becomes writing only when someone other than the writer associates a specific word or sound with it.

> **Sumer** A geographical term from Akkadian meaning the ancient region of southern Mesopotamia.

We can track the invention of writing in Mesopotamia because the residents used clay, a material that once baked was virtually indestructible. At first, sometime between 4000 and 3000 B.C.E., the ancient Sumerians used small clay objects of different shapes to keep track of merchandise, probably animals being traded or donated to a temple. Eventually they began to incise lines in these objects to stand for a certain number of items. Later, they placed these small objects in a bag made from a clay sheet and incised these bags, while still soft, on the outside to indicate their contents. These markings did not yet constitute written language because they could be understood in different ways; one had to cut open the clay bag, after it had hardened, to find out what was inside.

The transition to written language came when people drew a picture on a flat writing tablet that represented a specific animal and could not be mistaken for anything else. The first documents in human history, from a level dating to 3300 B.C.E., depict the item being counted with a tally next to it to showing the number of items. Temple accountants needed writing to record increasingly sophisticated transactions, like the number and type of animal or the amount of grain donated on successive days.

By 3300 B.C.E., a full-blown writing system of more than seven hundred different signs had emerged. Some symbols, like an ox-head representing an ox, are clearly pictorial, but many others are not. The word *sheep,* for example, was a circle with an *X* inside it (see Figure 2.1).

Over time, the marks lost their original shapes, and by 700 B.C.E. each symbol represented a certain sound; that is, it had become phonetic. We call this later

					SAG head
					NINDA bread
					GU₇ eat
					AB₂ cow
					APIN plow
					SUHUR carp
ca. 3100 B.C.E. (Uruk IV)	ca. 3000 B.C.E. (Uruk III)	ca. 2500 B.C.E. (Fara)	ca. 2100 B.C.E. (Ur III)	ca. 700 B.C.E. (Neo-Assyrian)	Sumerian reading and meaning

FIGURE 2.1

Cuneiform   The Mesopotamians first made small pictures, or pictographs, to write, but these symbols gradually evolved into combinations of lines that scribes made by pressing a wedge-shaped implement into wet clay. The cuneiform forms from 700 B.C.E. hardly resemble their original pictographic shapes from 3100 B.C.E. (From J. N. Postgate, *Early Mesopotamia: Society and Economy at the Dawn of History* [New York: Routledge, 1992], p. 63. Reprinted with permission of Taylor and Francis Books Ltd.)

●**cuneiform**
The term, meaning "wedge-shaped," for the writing system of Sumer in its late stages, when the script became completely phonetic.

writing **cuneiform** (cue-NAY-i-form), meaning "wedge-shaped," because it was made by a writing implement pressed into clay. These early records, most of them temple accounts, allow us to understand early Sumerian religion and how the ancient Sumerians distributed their surplus wealth.

Sumerian Religion   The people of ancient Sumer believed that various gods managed different aspects of their hostile environment. The most powerful god, the storm-god, could control storms and flooding. Like human beings, the Sumerian gods had families who sometimes lived together in harmony and sometimes did not.

The largest building in Uruk was the temple to Ishtar, the protective deity of Uruk and the storm-god's daughter. Sumerian temple complexes sometimes housed a thousand priests, priestesses, and supporting laborers. The largest structure inside each temple was a ziggurat, a stepped platform made from bricks. Throughout the year both rich and poor participated in different festivals and ceremonies presided over by priests and priestesses. The Warka Vase from Uruk (Warka is the modern name for Uruk) shows the residents of the city-state bringing different offerings to Ishtar (see the illustration on page 36).

The human king played an important role in Sumerian religion because he was believed to be the intermediary between the gods and human beings. The epic describes Gilgamesh as two-thirds divine, one-third human. He was sufficiently attractive that Ishtar proposed marriage to him. He brusquely turned her down, pointing out that each of her previous lovers had come to a bad end.

The World's First Beer

"Enkidu did not know how to eat bread, / Nor had he ever learned to drink beer!"* the author of *Gilgamesh* exclaims. Having grown up in the wild, Enkidu had never tasted the two basic foodstuffs of the Sumerians—bread and beer—both made from barley and wheat.

The usual way to make malt is to add water, allow barley or wheat to germinate partially in a sealed container, and then remove the water before the grain sprouts. Partial germination creates enzymes that produce the malty flavor. The Sumerians used large clay jars with lids for this process. We do not know exactly how they learned to make malt, but perhaps someone tasted a piece of discarded bread that had become wet and then fermented. The Sumerians were the first people in the world to make beer.

Gilgamesh vividly describes Enkidu's first taste:

Enkidu drank seven juglets of the beer.
His mood became relaxed, he was singing joyously,
He felt light-hearted and his features glowed.

The Sumerians drank beer constantly. The rations provided by the king to royal messengers included beer, bread, and onions. Temple-goers offered clay jars full of beer to their gods, and Sumerians regularly gave wedding presents ranging from 5 to 10 gallons (20–40 liters), or one-third or two-thirds of a modern keg of beer.

By the year 2000 B.C.E., the Babylonians had learned to make at least twenty types of beer, some from emmer wheat, some from barley, and some from a mixture of the two. The art of brewing spread throughout the region, and people throughout Egypt and Mesopotamia learned how to make beer.

The main ingredient in beer, even today, is malt extract, which is made from grain that has been allowed to ferment. Home brewers make beer by boiling water mixed with malt extract, adding sugar, combining it with still water, and adding yeast. After one to two weeks, the mixture is drinkable but tastes quite different from commercial beers.

*Quotes from Benjamin R. Foster, *The Epic of Gilgamesh: A Norton Critical Edition* (New York: W. W. Norton, 2001), p. 14.

Ishtar persuaded her father to retaliate by sending the Bull of Heaven to punish Gilgamesh and destroy Uruk. Gilgamesh's friend Enkidu killed the bull, to the delight of Uruk's residents but to the dismay of the gods, who then convened in council. The storm-god decided that Enkidu must die.

Before he died, Enkidu dreamed of the world of the dead:

To the house whence none who enters comes forth,
On the road from which there is no way back,
To the house whose dwellers are deprived of light,
Where dust is their fare and their food is clay.
They are dressed like birds in feather garments,
Yea, they shall see no daylight for they abide in darkness.

This description provides certain evidence—not available for earlier, preliterate societies—that the Sumerians believed in an afterworld.

After Enkidu dies, the heartbroken Gilgamesh resolves to escape death himself and travels a great distance over mountains and desert to reach the entrance to the underworld, believed to be near modern-day Bahrain. At the end of his journey, Gilgamesh meets Utanapishtim (OO-tah-nah-pish-teem), who tells him that a great flood occurred because the storm-god became angry with humankind and that Utanapishtim escaped when another divinity secretly informed him in time to build a boat. Utanapishtim, a human being to whom the gods granted

The Warka Vase: The Earliest Example of Narrative Art in the World?   Found at Uruk, this limestone vase dates to 3200 B.C.E. and stands over 3 feet (1 m) tall. Like a comic book, it tells a story in different panels; the bottom shows crops and sheep on their way to the temple where they will be presented to the gods; the middle, nude priests carrying more offerings; and the top, the deities, who stand on the back of a ram, receiving all the offerings. (Iraq Museum, Baghdad/Art Resource, NY)

immortality, tells Gilgamesh the story of the flood, and Gilgamesh realizes that he, like all human beings, must die, and returns to Uruk to rule the city-state.

Sumerian Government

The ruler of each city-state claimed to rule with the support of the local guardian deity, but an early version of *Gilgamesh* makes clear that he actually ruled in consultation with one or more assemblies. Faced with a demand from a neighboring kingdom to surrender, Gilgamesh consults with two separate assemblies, one of elders, one of younger men. While the elders oppose Gilgamesh's decision to go to war, the younger men support him.

During the Early Dynastic period, between 2900 and 2334 B.C.E., settlers moved out of Uruk to build new city-states closer to supplies of lumber and precious metals. Because transportation was slow and communication difficult, these satellite cities had their own rulers but maintained trade ties with the mother cities. Thirty-five different city-states, each with a temple and its own guardian deity, traded and increasingly warred with one another. Higher city walls, increasing numbers of bronze weapons, and more artistic depictions of battle victories indicate regular warfare among these different city-states.

The first ruler to conquer all the city-states and unify the region was **Sargon of Akkad** (r. 2334–2279 B.C.E.). Sargon (SAHR-gone) and the Akkadians ruled the world's first **empire,** defined as a large territory with subject peoples of different languages and different religious traditions. He and his descendents ruled over southern Mesopotamia for slightly over one hundred years until their empire broke apart. As surviving inscriptions show, Sargon changed the language of administration from Sumerian to Akkadian (uh-KAY-dee-uhn), named for his home city of Akkad (AHK-cad). Akkadian was a Semitic language related to modern Arabic and Hebrew. Sumerian, which was not related to any other language, continued to be used as a religious language, but Akkadian replaced it as the language of daily life in the Mesopotamian region. *Gilgamesh,* like many other literary works originally in Sumerian, was retold and embellished in the Akkadian version.

The Babylonian Empire, 1894–1595 B.C.E.

After the fall of the Akkadian empire, Mesopotamia again broke into several different kingdoms. Sometime around 2200 B.C.E., a new city, Babylon, located north of Uruk on the Euphrates, gained prominence. Babylon was a small city-state ruled by a succession of kings until the great military and legal leader Hammurabi

Documenting the Violence of War: The Standard of Ur Like the Warka vase (opposite), this object tells a story of war in different panels read from bottom to top. Notice the trampled bodies of the enemy under the feet of the donkeys on the bottom frame. The battle continues in the middle, and, on the top, officials present prisoners to a larger-than-lifesize king. (© British Museum, London/Art Resource, NY)

(ham-u-ROB-ee) (r. 1792–1750 B.C.E.) unified much of Mesopotamia. Surviving lists give the king's name and how long he ruled, enabling historians to count backwards to determine the exact dates of a given ruler's reign.

Hammurabi is famous, even today, for the laws that he issued. Many people have heard of a single provision in Hammurabi's law—"an eye for an eye"—but few realize that the original document contained nearly three hundred articles on a host of topics, including the treatment of slaves, divorce, criminal punishments, and interest rates on loans.

Hammurabi's laws were inscribed onto stone tablets over 7 feet (2 m) tall. Although they are often called a "code," the texts of many surviving decisions indicate that judges did not actually consult them. The king carved different legal cases in stone as proof of his divine rule and as model cases for future kings to study.

The laws recognized three different social groups, who received different punishments for the same crime. The most privileged group included the royal family, priests, merchants, and other free men and women who owned land. In the middle were commoners and peasants, and at the bottom were slaves.

The original wording of the famous eye-for-an-eye clause says, "If an awālu [freeman] should blind the eye of another awālu [freeman], they shall blind his eye."[2] At the most basic level this is the law of exact retaliation: if you bring harm to someone else, the identical wound shall be your punishment. It operated only among social equals, however. If a freeman destroyed the eye of a commoner, he paid only a moderate fine. If he destroyed the eye of a slave or broke one of his bones, then he had to pay the owner half of the slave's value, an even lesser amount. The laws stipulated the payment of fines in fixed amounts of silver or grain because coins did not yet exist.

As trade increased in the years after 2000 B.C.E., the Babylonian law codes on regulations governing commerce became more detailed. The main trading partners

CL **Primary Source: The State Regulates Healthcare: Hammurabi's Code and Surgeons** *Consider the various rewards and punishments for surgeons who either succeed or fail at their job in 1800 B.C.E.*

of the Babylonians lay to the southeast and included communities in the Persian Gulf and modern-day Afghanistan, who exported copper, the blue semiprecious mineral lapis lazuli, and other metals and precious stones in exchange for Mesopotamian textiles.

Hammurabi's laws also provide insight into marriage and the roles and status of women. Marriage had to be recorded in a written contract to be legally valid. Women were entitled to a share of their father's and/or mother's property, either as a gift when they married or as a share of the father's wealth upon his death. Punishment for adultery was severe: if a wife was found "lying with" someone other than her husband, she and her lover were tied together and thrown into water to drown; she was permitted to live if her husband allowed it.

At the same time, the law afforded women certain legal rights: if a woman was accused of adultery and denied it (and was not found with a lover), she could take an oath of innocence before a god and return to her husband's house unpunished. A wife could initiate divorce on the grounds that her husband failed to support her or had committed adultery. If the judge found that her husband had taken a lover but she had not, the divorce would be granted.

The tablets reveal only how the king hoped his laws would operate, not how they actually did. One case, recorded shortly before Hammurabi's reign on a clay tablet found at Nippur, shows how the legal system actually functioned. Three men—a barber, a gardener, and a third person whose occupation is not mentioned—killed a temple official named Lu-Inanna. They confessed to the victim's wife, but she, for unstated reasons, failed to report the crime.

Eventually the murderers were apprehended and the case came before the assembly of Nippur. A group of about ten men, including a bird-hunter, a porter, and a gardener, argued against the murderers: "They who have killed a man are not worthy of life. Those three males and that woman [the widow] should be killed in front of the chair of Lu-Inanna." An official and a gardener, whose different social ranks show the mixed composition of the assembly, spoke on the wife's behalf: "Granted that the husband . . . had been killed, but what had the woman done that she should be killed?"[3] The assembly decided that the murderers should be punished but that the wife was innocent.

Hammurabi's dynasty left a permanent imprint on southern Mesopotamia, which came to be known as Babylonia. Yet his dynasty was short-lived. Babylonia reverted to a city-state after his death, and the dynasty officially ended in 1595 B.C.E., when the Hittites (see page 50) sacked the city. Although the pace and extent of trade continued to increase, between 3300 and 1500 B.C.E. Mesopotamia remained politically apart from the other kingdoms of the eastern Mediterranean, as well as from Egypt, its neighbor to the west.

Egypt During the Old and Middle Kingdoms, ca. 3100–1500 B.C.E.

Complex society arose in Egypt at about the same time as in Mesopotamia—3100 B.C.E.—but under much different circumstances. The people of Egypt never lived in city-states but rather in a unified kingdom made possible by the natural geography of the Nile River Valley. Their god-king was called the **pharaoh.** Although Egypt did not have the large cities so characteristic of early complex societies, its society was highly stratified, with great differences between the poor and the rich. Large construction projects, like the building of the pyramids, required the same kind of occupational specialization so visible in Mesopotamian cities. The less tangible aspects of complex societies—the belief that the ruler governed with the support of the gods and that his subjects owed him their surplus—were also present in ancient Egypt.

• **pharaoh** The god-king who ruled the unified kingdom of Egypt since at least 3100 B.C.E.

In certain periods Egypt was unified under strong rulers, while in others someone with the title of pharaoh presided over Egypt but did not actually govern the entire region. Historians call the periods with strong governments "kingdoms" and those with weak governments "intermediate periods." The pharaohs of the Old Kingdom, between 2686 and 2181 B.C.E., ruled the Nile Valley from the Delta to the first impassable rapids; those who ruled during the Middle Kingdom, between 2040 and 1782 B.C.E., controlled an even larger area.

The Central Role of the Nile

The Egyptian climate is mild, and the country is protected by natural barriers: deserts on three sides and the Mediterranean Sea on the fourth. Fed by headwaters coming from Lake Victoria and the Ethiopian highlands, the Nile flows north, and its large delta opens onto the Mediterranean. Along the river are six steep, perilous, unnavigable rapids called cataracts (see Map 2.1). Lying 620 miles (1,000 km) upstream, the First Cataract formed a natural barrier between Egypt and **Nubia,** an ancient kingdom that straddled modern Egypt and Sudan (see page 48). Egypt was divided into three parts: Lower Egypt (the Delta region north of present-day Cairo), Upper Egypt (which ran from the First Cataract to the Delta), and Nubia (sometimes called Kush), south of the First Cataract.

• **Nubia** Region south of the First Cataract on the Nile, in modern-day Egypt and Sudan; was an important trading partner of Egypt.

Because almost no rain falls anywhere along the Nile, farmers must tap the river to irrigate their wheat and barley fields; thus the Nile Valley waters almost all the arable land in Egypt. Two types of soil filled the banks of the Nile: averaging one-quarter mile (.65 sq km) on both sides, "the black land" consisted of very fertile soil, each year renewed by the river's deposits of silt; beyond the black land lay the red land, which was less fertile. Beyond the red land lay uncultivable desert.

The Nile, with its annual summer floods, was a much more reliable source of water than the Tigris and Euphrates in Mesopotamia; thus the Egyptians had no equivalent of the vengeful Mesopotamian storm-god who ordered the flood in *Gilgamesh.* The Egyptians began to cultivate the flood plain of the Nile between 4400 and 4000 B.C.E. Their calendar had three seasons, each 120 days long: "Inundation," "Emergence of the Fields from Waters," and "Drought." During "Emergence," farmers used irrigation to move the Nile waters to their fields and planted seeds, which they harvested during the "Drought" season.

Egyptian Government and Society

Scholars have wondered if the Sumerian invention of writing prompted the Egyptians to develop their own writing system. But the **hieroglyphs** (pictorial and phonetic symbols) of written Egyptian are so different from Sumerian writing that the two societies probably developed writing independently. The Egyptians were writing by 3100 B.C.E., but the surviving record does not explain how writing

• **hieroglyphs** The writing system of ancient Egypt, which consisted of different symbols, some pictorial, some phonetic, used on official inscriptions.

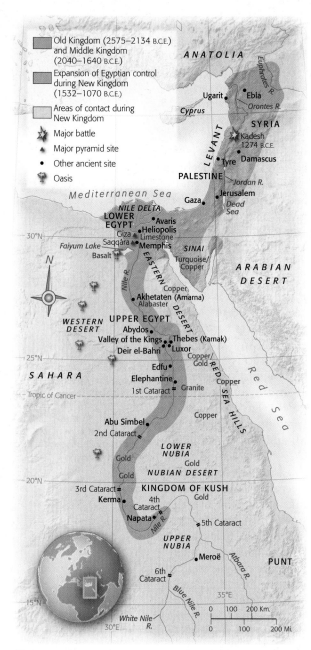

🌐 MAP 2.1

Ancient Egypt and Nubia   The Nile River lay at the heart of ancient Egypt, but one could not sail all the way from its headwaters in Lake Victoria and the Ethiopian highlands to the delta at the Mediterranean. Because no boat could cross the sheer vertical rapids called cataracts, the First Cataract formed a natural barrier between Egypt and the Nubia, the region to the south where many gold fields were.

Ⓒ️ Interactive Map

developed in Egypt because the Egyptians used a perishable writing material, **papyrus.**

Papyrus (pah-PIE-rus) was a reed that grew along the banks of the Nile. After removing the outer stem, the Egyptians layered strips of the inner stem horizontally and vertically. When they placed a weight on the reeds and left them to dry, the fibers bonded to form a lightweight, convenient writing material that was far more fragile than the clay tablets of Mesopotamia. Most of the surviving sources for Egyptian history were carved into stone, which was much more durable than papyrus.

Ancient historians credited the legendary founder of the First Dynasty (3200–3000 B.C.E.), Narmer, with consolidating the entire Nile Valley into a single kingdom, but many scholars today think that Egypt may have been unified as early as 3500–3200 B.C.E. It seems likely that Upper Egypt and Lower Egypt originally formed two separate regions. Over time various rulers of Upper Egypt gradually conquered more of the Delta until they unified Egypt.

The lack of certainty about these basic events shows that important gaps persist in our knowledge of Egypt. In the third century B.C.E., the Egyptian historian Manetho listed thirty separate dynasties without explaining what caused one dynasty to end and another to begin. Even today, after comparing Manetho's list with others, historians do not agree about the dates of individual dynasties. Thus the dates given in this book, although accepted by many, are only approximate.[4]

One of the earliest records, possibly recording the unification of Lower and Upper Egypt, is a piece of slate. At the top is a horizontal catfish (pronounced "nar") suspended above a chisel ("mer"). These hieroglyphs indicate the king's name, Narmer (NAR-mer), and the piece is called the Narmer Palette. (See the feature "Visual Evidence: The Narmer Palette.") In other contexts these hieroglyphs could be used to mean catfish or chisel; one can determine their use only from the context, which makes deciphering hieroglyphs difficult. By 2500 B.C.E., Egyptians were using two writing systems: a pictorial script, called hieroglyphs, and a cursive form, called hieratic ("priestly"). Hieroglyphs were reserved for public writing on monuments and plaques.

Certainly after 3050 B.C.E., and possibly even before then, Egypt was united under the rule of one man, the pharaoh. As a god-king, the pharaoh presided over rituals to the Egyptian gods. In theory, the pharaoh removed the gods' statues from their shrines in each temple, dressed them, fed them, and prayed to them. In the evening he fed them again before returning them to their shrines. In practice, the pharaoh performed these rites in the capital and delegated his duties to priests throughout Egypt.

Egypt was one of the few cultures that did not observe the incest taboo. Since the pharaoh's family members shared his semidivine status, pharaohs often married their closest kin, including their sisters and mothers. They also took multiple wives. The frequency of intermarriage meant that a single woman could simultaneously be the wife of the serving pharaoh, the mother of the future pharaoh, and the daughter of the previous one. For example, the wife of King Tutankhamen (too-tunk-AH-muhn), Ankhesenamen (ON-kays-ah-muhn), was also his half-sister.

The pharaoh's chief adviser, the vizier, was the only person permitted to meet with the pharaoh alone. Since the pharaoh was often occupied with ritual duties, the vizier handled all matters of state. He was assisted by a variety of higher- and lower-ranking officials, many of whom came from the same small group of families.

Egypt was divided into some forty smaller districts, each ruled by a governor with his own smaller establishment of subordinate officials and scribes. Scribes were among the few Egyptians who could read and write. Legendary for its record keeping, the Egyptian government employed a large number of scribes to keep detailed papyrus records of every conceivable item. The demand for scribes was so great that the government often hired people from nonofficial families, and some of these managed to be promoted to higher office, a rare chance for social mobility in Egyptian society.

Craftspeople and farmers formed the illiterate majority of Egyptian society. Slavery was not widespread. Those who worked the land gave a share of their crop to the pharaoh, the owner of all the land in Egypt, and also owed him labor, which they performed at fixed intervals on roads and royal buildings.

> **• papyrus** A convenient but perishable writing material made from a reed that grew naturally along the Nile.

The Old Kingdom and Egyptian Belief in the Afterlife, 2686–2181 B.C.E.

The five hundred years of the Old Kingdom, between 2686 and 2181 B.C.E., marked a period of prosperity and political stability for Egypt. No invasions occurred during this time. The Old Kingdom is also called the Pyramid Age because government officials organized the construction of Egypt's most impressive monuments at this time, an indication of how complex Egyptian society had become.

Egyptians believed that each person had a life-force (*ka*) that survived on energy from the body. When the body died, Egyptians preserved it and surrounded it with food so that the life-force could continue. The Great Pyramid was built between 2589 and 2566 B.C.E. to house the life-force of the pharaoh Khufu (KOO-fu), also called Cheops (KEY-ops).

Covering an area of 571,211 square feet (53,067 sq m), the Great Pyramid stands 480 feet (147 m) tall. It contains an estimated four million stone blocks ranging from 9.3 tons (8,445 kg) to 48.9 pounds (22.2 kg) in weight.[5] By pouring water into channels forming a grid, Egyptian architects managed to construct a base that was perfectly level. They also used a system of ramps and poles to move the large blocks, since they had no system of levers. An estimated fifteen to twenty thousand laborers, both male and female, worked on the pyramids at any single time. None of these laborers were slaves. About five thousand skilled workers and craftsmen worked full-time, while the remaining fifteen thousand unskilled workers

THE NARMER PALETTE

Found buried in a temple in southern Egypt, the Narmer Palette portrays the conquest of Lower and Upper Egypt by the ruler Narmer (ca. 3200–3000 B.C.E.) on a 25-inch-long (63.5-cm-long) piece of slate only half an inch (1.27 cm) thick. The slate is shaped like an ordinary *palette,* the word archaeologists apply to stone dishes that were used to mix ground minerals such as malachite for make-up or medicinal purposes. Palettes were usually about 6 inches (15 cm) long. This palette has a place for mixing minerals on the front face and is much larger than ordinary palettes, an indication that it was used as a ceremonial object.

Although very early, the Narmer Palette employs many artistic conventions familiar to us from later Egyptian art. Narmer, the pharaoh, stands larger than either his servant or his defeated enemies. The artist presents Narmer in a classic pose with his chest facing forward but with his head and legs sideways.

The palette documents the early use of hieroglyphs. Scholars can decipher Narmer's name because they know that *catfish* was pronounced "nar" and *chisel* "mer," but they do not know what the hieroglyph label reading "Wash" on the defeated enemies means. Various proposals have been put forward

This framed box, which resembles a walled palace, holds two hieroglyphs: a catfish (*nar*) and a chisel (*mer*) that together form Narmer's name.

The top frame of the palette, which appears on both the front and back faces, contains two bull's heads with human facial features; these bulls represent Narmer.

Narmer, identifiable by the catfish-and-chisel hieroglyphs to the right of his face, wears the chair-shaped crown used by the ruler of Lower Egypt. Behind him stands a servant; in front of him is an officer leading shorter soldiers. On the right lie ten fallen enemy soldiers in two horizontal rows, with their cut-off heads between their feet.

Two servants hold back the reins connected to the long, serpentine necks of two felines. The circular space between their entwined necks provides the area for the mixing of minerals, indicating that this is the front of the oversized palette.

Here a bull, representing Narmer, knocks down fortified walls and tramples on an enemy.

(Both photos: Egyptian Museum, Cairo/Werner Forman/Art Resource, NY)

about their identity, but no one is certain: Were they the residents of a certain region? Could they have lived outside Egypt?

However, scholars concur on the basic meaning of the palette: Narmer is claiming victory over his enemies. On one face of the palette, he wears the conical crown of Upper Egypt, and on the reverse, the chair-shaped crown of Lower Egypt. Because the palette dates to around 3100 B.C.E. and because historians believe that Egypt was unified at that time, they accept Narmer's claim as put forward by the palette's artist.

The themes of Narmer's palette are exactly those we would expect of a society in the early stages of becoming a complex society. Narmer rules with the support of the deities, including the sky-god, who appears as a falcon. His subjects owe him labor, as represented by his servants and soldiers, and goods, such as papyrus, because he, like a powerful bull, defends them by clubbing, decapitating, castrating, and trampling enemy troops. The ruler's task is exactly that of the two servants who rein in the felines in the central image on the face of the palette: to restrain the forces of disorder.

The largest picture of Narmer shows him wearing the conical crown of the ruler of Upper Egypt. His right hand raises a club to hit his kneeling victim, whose hair he clutches and who is labeled with undeciphered hieroglyphs reading "Wash." Above the victim is a falcon, the symbol of the sky-god protector of kings, who perches on a group of papyrus plants growing from a human body.

These two soldiers beneath Narmer's feet have been defeated. The penis of the figure on the right is visible, while that of the left figure is not, suggesting that he has been castrated. Both men are probably dead.

QUESTION FOR ANALYSIS

How did Egyptian and Mesopotamian artists who made the Narmer Palette and the Warka Vase portray their different understandings of what the ruler owes his subjects and what they owe him in return?

came to the site during the Inundation season to perform their labor service and then returned home, to be replaced by a new group of workers the following year.[6]

The size of his funerary monument provides a tangible measure of each ruler's power. The government had to organize the labor of all the workers and coordinate the shipment of large stones to the site of the pharaoh's tomb. Projects like the building of the Great Pyramid required a level of social organization and occupational specialization characteristic of early complex societies; at the same time, they also contributed to the growing complexity of these ancient societies.

During the Old Kingdom, only the pharaoh and his family could afford to preserve his corpse for eternity, but in later centuries, everyone in Egypt, whether rich or poor, hoped to travel to the next world with his or her body intact. The earliest surviving examples of Egyptian mummification date to 2400 B.C.E., just after the time of the Great Pyramid, yet detailed descriptions date from much later, around 450 B.C.E., when the Greek traveler Herodotus (he-ROD-uh-tuhs) visited Egypt (see Chapter 6).

Embalmers offered their customers three options, Herodotus explained, depending on how much money they could spend. In the most expensive process, embalmers removed the brain through the nose with a hook and pulled out the internal organs through an incision in the abdomen. Then they rinsed the body

◼ Great Pyramid of Khufu (Cheops): How did the Egyptians Do It? The Great Pyramid contains some four million stone blocks, which the builders moved by means of a system of ramps and poles. They managed to construct a perfectly level base by pouring water into a grid of channels, some still visible here. (Photos.com/Jupiter Images)

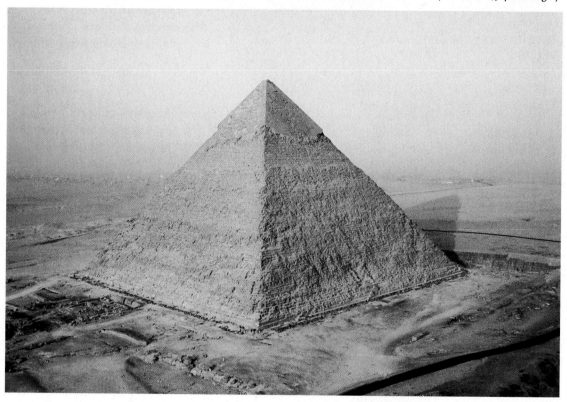

and covered it with natron (NAY-tron), a crystallized form of potassium carbonate that kept the corpse dry. After forty days, bandagers spent two weeks wrapping the body in linen before placing it in a coffin. The earliest surviving mummy, from 2400 B.C.E., happens to be one of the best preserved, with his facial features and even a callus on his foot still visible.

In the less expensive option, the embalmers simply injected the body with cedar oil, which caused the internal organs to decay and to be expelled through the anus. Bandaging and burial followed. The poorest Egyptians could only afford to have the unbandaged corpse prepared and buried.

Egyptians believed that the dead had to appear before Osiris (oh-SIGH-ruhs), the god of the underworld, who determined who could enter the realm of eternal happiness. Compiled in the sixteenth century B.C.E. yet drawing on materials dating back to 2400 B.C.E., the *Book of the Dead* contained detailed instructions for what the deceased should say on meeting Osiris. At the moment of judgment, the deceased should deny having committed any crime:

> I have not committed evil against men.
> I have not mistreated cattle.
> I have not committed sin in the place of truth [that is, a temple
>   or burial ground]
> I have not blasphemed a god. . . .
> I have not made (anyone) sick.
> I have not made (anyone) weep.
> I have not killed. . . .
> I have not held up water in its season [that is, denied floodwaters to others].
> I have not built a dam against running water. . . .[7]

The list reveals the offenses thought most outrageous by the Egyptians: diverting water from the irrigation channels belonging to one's neighbor constituted a major infraction.

During the First Intermediate Period (2180–2040 B.C.E.), Old Kingdom Egypt broke apart into semi-independent regions ruled by rival dynasties. The pharaoh was unable to appoint regional governors because certain families refused to give up government posts they had retained for multiple generations. Nor could the pharaoh collect as much revenue as his predecessors, possibly because sustained drought reduced agricultural yields.

CL **Primary Source:**
The Egyptian Book of the Dead's Declaration of Innocence
Read the number of potential sins that would likely tarnish a journeying spirit and prevent entrance into the realm of the blessed.

Egyptian Expansion During the Middle Kingdom, 2040–1782 B.C.E.

In 2040 B.C.E. the ruler based in Thebes (modern-day Luxor) reunited Egypt and established what became known as the Middle Kingdom (2040–1782 B.C.E.), the second long period of centralized rule. Egypt's trade with other regions increased dramatically. Like Mesopotamia, Egypt had few natural resources and was forced to trade with distant lands to obtain wood, copper, gold, silver, and semiprecious stones. Its main trading partners were modern-day Syria and Lebanon to the north and Nubia to the south. At the height of the Middle Kingdom, the pharaoh sent his armies beyond Egypt for the first time, conquering territory in Palestine and Nubia. Various Middle Kingdom rulers conquered and governed the regions south of the First and Second Cataracts.

Sometime around 2000 B.C.E., Egyptian sources begin to mention the kingdom of Kush, another name for Nubia, whose capital lay south of the Third Cataract.

Since the cataracts of the Nile could not be crossed in a ship, merchants hired bearers to unload goods and carry them to the next stage of the river. During the Middle Kingdom, trade goods coming from sub-Saharan Africa, including panther and other rare animal skins, gold, ivory from elephant tusks, and slaves, traveled through Nubia, overland around the cataracts, and down the Nile to Egypt.

By 1720 B.C.E., the Middle Kingdom had weakened, most likely because a group of immigrants from Syria and Palestine, whom the Egyptians called Hyksos (HICK-sos) (literally "chieftains of foreign lands"), settled in the Delta. Historians call the years between 1782 and 1570 B.C.E. the Second Intermediate Period. The Hyksos had horse-drawn chariots with spoked wheels as well as strong bows made of wood and bone, while the Egyptians had no carts and only wooden bows. The Hyksos formed an alliance with the Nubians and ruled Egypt from 1650 to 1570 B.C.E.

The International System, 1500–1150 B.C.E.

Around 1500 B.C.E., western Asia entered a new stage of increasingly sophisticated material cultures and extensive trade. During the third period of centralized rule in Egypt, the New Kingdom (1570–1069 B.C.E.), Egypt had more dealings with the other kingdoms of the eastern Mediterranean than in previous periods. Pharaohs of the Eighteenth Dynasty (1570–1293 B.C.E.) exchanged diplomatic envoys with rulers in Crete, Cyprus, and Anatolia and brought captured foreigners from the Mediterranean and Nubia to serve in the Egyptian army and to work as slaves.

Egypt's main rivals in the region were the Hittites (see page 50), who were based in Anatolia, Turkey, and Syria (see Map 2.2). Smaller kingdoms also arose in southern and northern Mesopotamia, eastern Iran, the Aegean islands, and Syria and Palestine. Egypt reached its greatest extent at this time, governing a swath of territory that included Palestine, Lebanon, Syria, and Nubia. For five hundred years, the states of the eastern Mediterranean enjoyed a period of relative tranquility as they intensified their trade and diplomatic contacts to form what has been called the first international system.

New Kingdom Egypt and Nubia, 1570–1069 B.C.E. During the New Kingdom period, Egypt continued to expand into Nubia. After eliminating the kingdom of Kush as a rival, Egypt destroyed its capital and extended control all the way to the Fourth Cataract. Nubia's most valuable natural resource was gold, which the pharaohs required in large amounts.

The pharaohs of the Eighteenth Dynasty venerated the sun-god Amun-Ra (AH-muhn–RAH) above all other deities because they believed that he had enabled them to expel the Hyksos from Egypt and establish their dynasty. They built an enormous temple at Karnak to house the image of Amun-Ra. Every day the temple's priests carried the bathed image around the temple, and once a year they sent the main image of Amun-Ra in an elaborate barge along the Nile to the capital at Thebes.

⊕ MAP 2.2

The International System, ca. 1500–1250 B.C.E. Wen-Amun's journey from Egypt to Lebanon and Cyprus in around 1130 B.C.E. shows the ease with which individuals moved in the region of the eastern Mediterranean. International credit networks made it possible for Egyptian merchants to send gold, silver, linen, and papyrus to Lebanon, meaning that Wen-Amun did not have to return to Egypt to collect them.

Ⓒⓛ Interactive Map

The Egyptians believed that the most appropriate offerings to Amun-Ra were made from gold because gold was the color of the sun. Being indestructible, gold also represented immortality. Living people who wore gold became like gods, and the Egyptians buried the dead with multiple gold ornaments in the hope that they would live forever. While Egypt had some gold mines (see Map 2.1), Nubia had many more, and New Kingdom pharaohs were able to exploit these mines to the fullest extent.

After conquering Nubia, the pharaohs of the Eighteenth Dynasty worked to transform Nubia into an Egyptian society: they brought the sons of Nubian chiefs to Egypt, where they studied the Egyptian language, wore Egyptian linen clothing made from the flax plant, received Egyptian names, and worshiped Egyptian deities like Amun-Ra. When they returned home, they served the Egyptians as administrators.

Egypt continued to trade with Nubia and other regions during the reign of Hatshepsut (hat-SHEP-soot) (r. 1473–1458 B.C.E.), the only woman pharaoh of the Eighteenth Dynasty. Older women, whether mothers and aunts, occasionally served as regents when the pharaoh was too young to rule on his own, but Hatshepsut ruled for a full fifteen years as pharaoh. She imported gold, ebony, and cedar to add new rooms at Amun-Ra's temple at Karnak and build a spectacular new temple in the Valley of the Kings, where the New Kingdom pharaohs were buried. She was particularly proud of an expedition that she dispatched to Punt (in modern-day Ethiopia), which brought back to Egypt exotic goods such as monkeys and myrrh trees.

One ruler near the end of the Eighteenth Dynasty, Akhenaten (Ah-ken-AHT-n) (r. 1352–1336 B.C.E.), introduced an important change to Egyptian religion. Rather than accepting Amun-Ra as the supreme deity, he worshiped a different form of the sun-god, whom he called the "living sun-disk," "Aten" (AHT-n) in Egyptian. Artists of his reign portrayed Aten as a circular disk whose rays ended with small human hands extending downward to the pharaoh and his wife. The art of Akhenaten's reign was also new: realistic portraits showed him frontally, with stomach protruding, rather than in profile. In the past analysts erroneously thought Akhenaten worshiped Aten as the only god. In fact, he continued to worship other gods as well, even though Aten clearly ranked highest among them. After Akhenaten's death, Egyptians restored Amun-Ra to his position as the most important deity.

During the New Kingdom period, Egypt established a series of alliances with the various powers in the region and occasionally went to war with them. An extraordinary find of 350 letters concerning diplomatic matters at Amarna, where the pharaoh Akhenaten (see above) established his capital, makes it possible to reconstruct the international system of the time. Akhenaten addressed the rulers of Babylonia, Assyria, and Anatolia, who governed kingdoms as powerful as Egypt, as "brother," an indication that he saw them as his equals, while he reserved the term "servant" for smaller, weaker kingdoms in Syria and Palestine.

Many of the letters concern marriage. Akhenaten tried to persuade other rulers to send their daughters to marry Egyptian men, but he did not ask for their sons because Egyptians would not allow Egyptian women to marry non-Egyptians. Even though the arrangement was unequal, the rulers usually sent their daughters because they wanted gold, and only Egypt had gold (obtained from Nubia).

The Kingdom of Nubia, 800 B.C.E.–350 C.E.

Much weaker after 1293 B.C.E., when the Eighteenth Dynasty ended, Egypt eventually lost control of Nubia. For several centuries no centralized power emerged in Nubia, but around 800 B.C.E. a political center formed at Napata, the administrative center from which the Egyptians had governed Nubia during the New Kingdom.

Seeing themselves as the rightful successors to the pharaohs of the Eighteenth Dynasty, the rulers of Nubia conquered Egypt under King Piye (r. 747–716 B.C.E.). King Taharqo (690–664 B.C.E.) ruled over Nubia at its peak. The builder of an elaborate cult center to Amun-Ra, King Taharqo also revived the building of pyramids, a practice that had long since died out in Egypt. His pyramid was the largest ever built by the Nubians, standing 160 feet (49 m) tall (see the photo opposite).

The Nubians continued to erect pyramids even after 300 B.C.E., when they shifted their capital from Napata to Meroë. Initially the Nubians, like the Egyptians, used hieroglyphs for monuments and hieratic script for less important matters, but by 300 B.C.E. they had developed their own writing system, called Meroitic

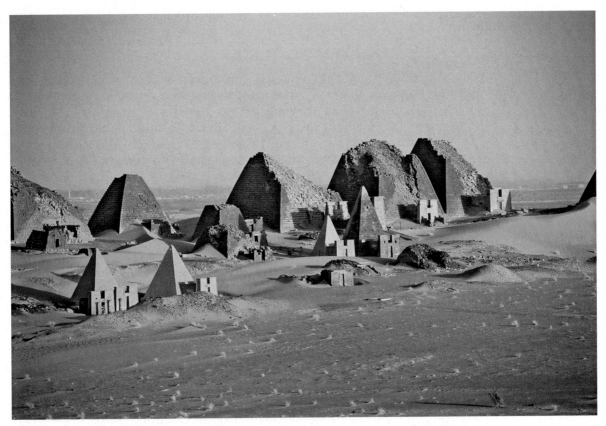

🏴 **Nubia, Land of Pyramids**   Modern Sudan has more pyramids—a total of 223—than Egypt. Modeled on those of Old Kingdom Egypt, the Nubian tombs are steeper and originally had a layer of white plaster on their exterior. Starting in the mid-700s B.C.E. and continuing to 370 C.E., the Nubian rulers of Kush built pyramids over their tombs, which were in the ground—unlike the Egyptian tombs, which were constructed above ground and inside the pyramids (contrast with Cheops' tomb shown on page 44).   (Photograph courtesy of SacredSites.com)

(mer-oh-IT-ick), which combined hieroglyphs with hieratic script. Scholars know how to pronounce the Meroitic script because it is phonetic, but they cannot understand it because it is not related to any living language.

The royal cemetery at Meroë contains the pyramids of thirty kings and eight queens. As was common throughout sub-Saharan Africa, the Nubian dynasties practiced matrilineal succession in which the king was succeeded by his sister's son. (In a patrilineal system, the son succeeds the father.) If the designated successor was too young to rule, the king's sister often ruled in his place. Nubian queens did everything the male kings did, including patronizing temples, engaging in diplomacy, and fighting in battle.

The kingdom of Meroë thrived because it was able to tax the profitable trade between sub-Saharan Africa and the Mediterranean, but it broke apart in the fourth century C.E., possibly because the trade was diverted to other sea routes it did not control. Located south of Egypt, Nubia had little contact with the different states of the eastern Mediterranean to the north of Egypt. Accordingly, it did not actively participate in the system of international alliances that had begun to take shape as early as 1500 B.C.E.

The Hittites, 2000–1200 B.C.E.

During the New Kingdom period, Egypt's rulers frequently wrote to the rulers of a powerful new kingdom based in Anatolia and Syria, the **Hittites.** The language of the Hittites belonged to the Indo-European language family, meaning that its structure resembled that of Latin, Greek, and Sanskrit (see Chapter 3). The Hittites were the first speakers of an Indo-European language to establish a complex society in western Asia.

> **Hittites** A people based in Anatolia, Turkey, and Syria who spoke the Indo-European language of Hittite and learned to work iron around 2000 B.C.E. The Hittite Empire reached its greatest extent between 1322 and 1220 B.C.E. and ended around 1200 B.C.E.

The Hittites were able to do so because, sometime around 2000 B.C.E., they learned how to work iron, which had a much higher melting point (2,786 degrees Fahrenheit, 1,530 degrees Celsius) than other metals, including bronze. The high melting point meant that iron could not be melted and then poured into molds like bronze. Metalsmiths heated iron and hammered it into the shape of the tool or weapon needed, a process that removed impurities in the metal. Much stronger than bronze weapons, the iron weapons of the Hittites were much prized.

The Hittite Empire reached its greatest extent between 1322 and 1220 B.C.E., when the Hittites controlled all of Anatolia and Syria. In the thirteenth century B.C.E. the Hittite ruler wrote to the ruler of the Assyrians to apologize for not sending any unworked iron. Instead he sent a single blade, an indication of iron's value at the time.

The Hittites had another advantage over their enemies: they had mastered the art of chariot warfare. Two horses pulled a chariot that carried three men (a driver and two warriors). While consolidating their rule in Anatolia, the Hittites sent only a small number of chariots into battle. Thus in 1750 B.C.E., the Hittite king commanded only 40 chariots. But by the Battle of Kadesh in 1285 B.C.E., when the Hittites faced the Egyptians, the ruler commanded 2,500 chariots.[8] Egyptian documents claim that the pharaoh Ramesses II (r. 1290–1224 B.C.E.) had triumphed, but Egypt gained no territory, an indication that the Hittite and Egyptian forces were probably evenly matched. After the Battle of Kadesh, Egypt signed a treaty with the Hittites, who sent a Hittite princess to marry Ramesses II.

The Hittite kingdom came to an end in 1200 B.C.E. when their capital fell to outsiders. Historians are not certain who the invaders were, but they note a period around 1200–1150 B.C.E. of prolonged instability throughout western Asia. Egyptian sources mention attacks by "sea peoples," and Egypt lost control of both Syria-Palestine to the north and Nubia to the south.

Wen-Amun's Voyage to Lebanon and Cyprus, 1130 B.C.E.

In the centuries after 1200, Egypt continued to enjoy extensive trade relations with the Mediterranean, as we can see in the earliest detailed account of an actual voyage, recorded on a torn papyrus dating to 1130 B.C.E.[9] In that year, an Egyptian priest named Wen-Amun (one–Ah-muhn) traveled first to Cairo, where he caught a ship across the Mediterranean to Lebanon to buy cedar for the Amun-Ra temple at Karnak, which had so much money and land that it was independent of the pharaoh's authority.

On arriving at a port in modern-day Lebanon, Wen-Amun realized that a shipmate had stolen almost 9 pounds (4 kg) of gold and silver—all the money Wen-

Amun had with him to buy the lumber for the ceremonial boat. Desperate, he sailed to the next port, where he stole some silver. When the victims reported the theft to their king, he refused to allow Wen-Amun to land.

Then something unusual happened. A young boy at court was suddenly afflicted by seizures, and the king's advisers concluded that Amun-Ra was responsible. Their explanation reveals that the Egyptian deity's reputation had spread far beyond Egypt. The local ruler made a proposal: if Wen-Amun sent to his home temple for funds, he would be allowed to depart. The credit network of the local merchants was sufficiently sophisticated that Wen-Amun was able to write home to request that another ship bring him gold, silver, ten linen garments, and five hundred rolls of papyrus to cover the cost of the lumber.

When Wen-Amun set off for home, his ship was blown off course to the island of Cyprus. There he met an Egyptian interpreter, who explained his predicament to the ruler, and Wen-Amun managed somehow to make his way back. Thus even during this time of instability, the international system of the time functioned smoothly enough that people could obtain credit and travel in the eastern Mediterranean.

● Syria-Palestine and New Empires in Western Asia, 1200–500 B.C.E.

Several kingdoms occupied the land along the eastern shore of the Mediterranean where modern-day Palestine, Israel, Lebanon, and Syria are located. They participated in the international system, but always as minor players in a world dominated by kings of larger powers such as Egypt, Assyria, Babylonia, and Anatolia. Around 1000 B.C.E. a smaller complex society arose in the eastern Mediterranean that was notable for its innovation in religion.

This lightly populated and politically weak region was important because it was the homeland of the ancient Hebrews or Israelites. The Hebrews were the first people in the eastern Mediterranean to practice **monotheism,** or belief in only one god, whom they called Yahweh (YAH-way) in Hebrew (God in English). Belief in a single god underlay the religious teachings recorded in the Hebrew Bible (called the Old Testament by Christians). Hebrew monotheism would profoundly shape both Christian and Islamic teachings (see Chapters 7 and 10).

● **monotheism** Belief in only one god.

The History of the Ancient Hebrews According to the Hebrew Bible

Geographers call the region bordering the eastern Mediterranean the Levant (see Map 2.3). The most populated section of the Levant was the strip of land between 30 and 70 miles (50–110 km) wide along the Mediterranean coast. The northern section, between the Orontes River and the Mediterranean, formed Lebanon, while the land west of the Jordan River formed Israel and Palestine. Israel and Palestine stretched only 250 miles (400 km) from north to south, with the southern half consisting almost entirely of desert. Its population around 1000 B.C.E. has been estimated at 150,000, and its largest city, Jerusalem, reached its maximum population of 5,000 in 700 B.C.E.[10]

🌐 **Map 2.3**

The Assyrian and Neo-Babylonian Empires at Their Greatest Extent The rulers of the Assyrian empire were the first in the eastern Mediterranean to resettle subject populations. Their successors, the Neo-Babylonians, continued the practice and resettled many subject peoples, including the Hebrews, in their capital at Babylon.

(CL) Interactive Map

Historians and archaeologists of Israel and Palestine disagree sharply about the value of the Bible as a historical source. Some view everything in the Bible as true, while others do not credit the accounts of the Bible unless they are confirmed by other documentary or archaeological evidence. World historians rarely have as much material for a given society as they have for ancient Israel and Palestine, and they often rely on orally transmitted sources far more recent than the Hebrew Bible, which was written sometime around 700 B.C.E. and whose current text dates to around 500 B.C.E.[11]

The first book of the Hebrew Bible, Genesis, traces the history of the ancient Hebrews from the earth's creation. The Hebrew Bible contains a later version of the flood story that closely resembles that in *Gilgamesh*. After the flood, Yahweh makes a promise, called a covenant, to Noah that he will not bring another flood. The ancient Hebrews, like many of the other peoples of the eastern Mediterranean, believed that certain individuals, whom they respected as prophets, could speak directly with God and also speak for him. Archaeologists have not found evidence of a single flood as described in either *Gilgamesh* or the Hebrew Bible; most think the flood narrative collapses repeated floods in the Tigris and Euphrates into a one-time calamity. (See the feature "Movement of Ideas: The Flood Narrative in the *Epic of Gilgamesh* and the Hebrew Bible.")

The most important event in their history, the ancient Hebrews believed, was God's choice of Abraham to be the leader of his people. Abraham, like his direct ancestor Noah, spoke directly to God and agreed to be the leader of his people. Abraham's father had brought the ancient Hebrews from the city-state of Ur to Haran, Genesis reports, and Abraham then brought them from Haran to Canaan, or modern-day Israel. God, in turn, made Abraham promise that all his descendants would be circumcised.

Although God designated Abraham as the leader of his community, the Hebrew Bible teaches, he and his wife Sarah had no children. God promised that Sarah would give birth to a son, even though Abraham was 100 years old and Sarah 90. When their son Isaac was born, she was overjoyed. Abraham had one son, Ishmael, with Sarah's maid Hagar, but Sarah sent Hagar away after the birth of Isaac.

God then subjected Abraham to the most severe test of all: he asked him to sacrifice his son Isaac as an offering. Abraham led his young son up into the mountains and prepared the sacrificial altar. At the moment when he was about to kill

Isaac, the Bible records, God, speaking through an angel, commanded: "Do not lay your hand on the boy or do anything to him; for now I know that you fear God, since you have not withheld your son, your only son, from me" (Genesis 22:12). Abraham untied Isaac and allowed him to go free.

The Bible's dramatic account of Isaac's rescue reflects a crucial change in Israelite religious observance. In an earlier time, the ancient Hebrews sacrificed animals and perhaps even children to their gods. An inscription dating to the eighth century B.C.E. from modern-day Lebanon records that during a plague the priests advised the local ruler to sacrifice a son or a grandson, in addition to an animal offering, to end the disease.[12] In later times, when the Isaac story was recorded, the Hebrews abandoned child sacrifice. The Bible gives no dates for the events it describes.

After the ancient Hebrews came to Israel, the book of Exodus claims that they went to Egypt and then returned to Israel under the leadership of the patriarch Moses. Since no archaeological evidence confirms that a single migration out of Egypt occurred, many scholars suggest that the Exodus may have been a series of migrations.

The History of the Ancient Hebrews According to Archaeological Evidence

The earliest archaeological evidence of the ancient Hebrews dates to between 1300 and 1100 B.C.E. In 1300 B.C.E. approximately twelve to fifteen thousand people lived in three hundred small villages on previously unoccupied hillsides in the southern Levant; by 1100 B.C.E. the population had mushroomed to seventy-five to eighty thousand.[13] No urban centers existed. Most of the residents had tools made of bronze, flint, and occasionally iron. Archaeologists have analyzed the bones they deposited in refuse pits and found no more than 1 percent are pig, an indication that the taboo on eating pork that is recorded in the Hebrew Bible may already have been in effect.

The few inscriptions found so far reveal that the residents wrote ancient Hebrew, a Semitic language. An Egyptian inscription dated 1210 B.C.E. lists several different defeated peoples living in modern-day Lebanon, one of whom it calls "Israel peoples,"[14] most likely the residents of the hill country.

Although the Bible portrays the ancient Hebrews as practitioners of monotheism from ancient times on, archaeological evidence indicates that they, like all the other peoples of the eastern Mediterranean, worshiped several different deities. The most important were the storm-god, called El or Ba'al (BAHL), and his wife, a fertility goddess. In this early period, some of the Israelites also worshiped a storm-god named Yahweh.

The Bible describes the ancient Hebrews as living under a united monarchy that linked both the north and the south. King David built a shrine to Yahweh in Jerusalem, which his successor Solomon (r. 960–920 B.C.E.) rebuilt and expanded. After Solomon's death the kingdom broke into two parts: Judah in the south with its capital at Jerusalem, and Israel in the north.

Archaeologists have not found evidence of a united kingdom under the rule of either David or Solomon. But a significant change did occur sometime between 1000 and 900 B.C.E., when complex society first took shape in the region. The main evidence, as in Mesopotamia, is the formation of large urban centers with massive walls and impressive gates. At this time what had been a loose tribal confederacy

The Flood Narrative in the *Epic of Gilgamesh* and the Hebrew Bible

The striking similarities in the two versions of the flood story demonstrate that the Hebrew Bible drew on oral traditions circulating throughout Mesopotamia. The most complete version of the *Epic of Gilgamesh* was written in 700 B.C.E., but it drew on written versions dating to at least 2100 B.C.E. and even earlier oral traditions. Like the *Epic of Gilgamesh*, the Bible had a long history of oral transmission before being recorded in its current version around 500 B.C.E. Some of its oldest content may have circulated orally as early as 1200 B.C.E., when the ancient Hebrews first settled what is now modern Israel.

The two accounts of the flood differ most notably in their depiction of the divine. In the *Epic of Gilgamesh,* multiple gods squabble and the god Enki warns Utanapishtim that the storm-god Enlil is sending the flood to destroy his home city of Shuruppak. In the Bible, one god decides to punish all of humanity except for Noah and his family.

Sources: Benjamin R. Foster, *The Epic of Gilgamesh: A Norton Critical Edition* (New York: W. W. Norton, 2001), pp. 85–89; Genesis 6:11–19, Genesis 7:17–18, Genesis 8:1–3, Genesis 8:6–12 (New Revised Standard Version).

The Flood Story in Gilgamesh

Instructions to Utanapishtim for Building the Ark

O Man of Shuruppak, son of Ubar-Tutu,
Wreck house, build boat,
Forsake possessions and seek life,
Belongings reject and life save!
Take aboard the boat seed of all living things.
The boat you shall build,
Let her dimensions be measured out:
Let her width and length be equal,
Roof her over like the watery depths.

The Length of the Flood

Six days and seven nights
The wind continued, the deluge and windstorm leveled the land. . . .
The sea grew calm, the tempest stilled, the deluge ceased.

The End of the Flood

When the seventh day arrived,
I [Utanapishtim] brought out a dove and set it free.

The dove went off and returned,
No landing place came to its view so it turned back.
I bought out a swallow and set it free,
The swallow went off and returned,
No landing place came to its view, so it turned back.
I brought out a raven and set it free,
The raven went off and saw the ebbing of the waters.
It ate, preened, left droppings, did not turn back.
I released all to the four directions,
I brought out an offering and offered it to the four directions.
I set up an incense offering on the summit of the mountain,
I arranged seven and seven cult vessels,
I heaped reeds, cedar, and myrtle in their bowls.

The Flood Story in the Bible

Instructions to Noah for Building the Ark

Now the earth was corrupt in God's sight, and the earth was filled with violence. And God saw that the earth was corrupt; for all flesh had corrupted its ways upon the earth. And God said to Noah, "I have determined to make an end of all flesh, for the earth is filled with violence because of them; now I am going to destroy them along with the earth. Make yourself an ark of cypress wood; make rooms in the ark, and cover it inside and out with pitch. This is how you are to make it: the length of the ark three hundred cubits, its width fifty cubits, and its height thirty cubits•. Make a roof for the ark, and finish it to a cubit above; and put the door of the ark in its side; make it with lower, second, and third decks. For my part, I am going to bring a flood of waters upon the earth, to destroy from under heaven all flesh in which is the breath of life; everything that is on the earth shall die. But I will establish my covenant with you; and you shall come into the ark, you, your sons, your wife, and your sons' wives with you. And of every living thing, of all flesh, you shall bring two of every kind into the ark, to keep them alive with you; they shall be male and female."

The Length of the Flood

The flood continued forty days on the earth; and the waters increased, and bore up the ark, and it rose high above the earth. The waters swelled and increased greatly on the earth; and the ark floated on the face of the waters. . . .

But God remembered Noah and all the wild animals and all the domestic animals that were with him in the ark. And God made a wind blow over the earth, and the waters subsided; the fountains of the deep and the windows of the heavens were closed, the rain from the heavens was restrained, and the waters gradually receded from the earth. At the end of a hundred fifty days the waters had abated.

The End of the Flood

At the end of forty days Noah opened the window of the ark that he had made and sent out the raven; and it went to and fro until the waters were dried up from the earth. Then he sent out the dove from him, to see if the waters had subsided from the face of the ground; but the dove found no place to set its foot, and it returned to him to the ark, for the waters were still on the face of the whole earth. So he put out his hand and took it and brought it into the ark with him. He waited another seven days, and again he sent out the dove from the ark; and the dove came back to him in the evening, and there in its beak was a freshly plucked olive leaf; so Noah knew that the waters had subsided from the earth. Then he waited another seven days, and sent out the dove; and it did not return to him any more.

* **cubit** Approximately 450 feet (137 m) long, 75 feet (23 m) wide, 45 feet (14 m) tall.

QUESTIONS FOR ANALYSIS

▶ **What are the similarities between the two versions of the flood story? What are the differences? Explain why the later version diverges from the original.**

became a small kingdom, complete with a bureaucracy and intermediate-level cities.

The residents of both Judah and Israel worshiped Yahweh, but in the ninth century two distinct groups formed. One, consisting of the rulers and probably most of their subjects, continued to worship Yahweh as one of many gods. The other, called the prophetic school, strongly believed that Yahweh was the most important god.

The Assyrian Empire, 911–612 B.C.E.

The two kingdoms of Israel and Judah remained separate and independent until 721 B.C.E., when the Assyrians, whose homeland was in northern Mesopotamia, conquered southern Mesopotamia, Egypt, and the kingdoms of Israel and Judah. Like the Hittites, the Assyrians had iron weapons. In addition, their cavalry was particularly powerful because it was the first true army on horseback. The cavalry soldiers rode bareback since neither saddles nor stirrups had been invented.

Unlike the various conquerors of the eastern Mediterranean before them, the Assyrians did not simply send in armies and subjugate enemy territory. Because the Assyrian ruler saw himself as the representative of the gods, he asked the rulers of foreign territories to submit voluntarily to him and his deities. Those who surrendered he treated gently, but his troops were infamous for their cruel treatment of those who resisted. Soldiers skinned captives alive, removed their eyes or cut off their hands and feet, and impaled others on stakes. These atrocities served as a warning to those who had not yet been conquered: if they surrendered quickly, they could avoid such barbarities. Such treatment was justified, the Assyrians believed, because the subject populations were resisting the gods, not just a human king.

Once the Assyrians had conquered a given region, they forcibly resettled the conquered rulers and skilled craftsmen to another part of the empire. The original intent in the ninth century was to fill up the lightly populated sections of the empire; later, resettlement was simply a demonstration of the ruler's power. Several hundred thousand people were resettled in this way, including many people from Israel and Judah who were sent to Assyria.

The last Assyrian king, Asshurbanipal (as-shur-BAH-nee-pahl) (r. 668–627 B.C.E.), built one of the world's earliest libraries, which consisted of over 1,500 texts for his own private use. In the 1850s, British excavators found the most complete set of clay tablets of the Gilgamesh epic, and the basis of all modern translations, in the ruins of Asshurbanipal's palace.

The Babylonian Captivity and the Recording of the Bible, 612–539 B.C.E.

The Neo-Babylonians conquered the Assyrians and established their capital at Babylon. Their most powerful ruler was Nebuchadnezzar II (r. 605–562 B.C.E.), who rebuilt the city of Babylon, repaired its temples, and constructed magnificent hanging gardens. They were so beautiful that the second-century B.C.E. compilers of the Seven Wonders of the World included them with the Great Pyramids (the only wonder still standing). Nebuchadnezzar II (nab-oo-kuhd-NEZ-uhr) extended his empire all the way to Syria, Palestine, and Lebanon. He sacked Jerusalem twice, in 597 and 586 B.C.E., and destroyed much of the city. He leveled Solomon's Temple and, like the Assyrians, deported thousands of Hebrews to Babylon, in what is known today as the Babylonian Exile or Babylonian Captivity.

The exiled Hebrews living in Babylon were not allowed to return to Israel, but otherwise they had some freedom of movement, and some seem to have prospered as merchants or farmers. The exiled community reached a new understanding of their past. Many of the tales they told, including those about Noah and Abraham, included episodes in which God punished the ancient Hebrews for failing to follow his instructions, and they interpreted the Assyrian and Neo-Babylonian conquests in the same light. The Israelite community, the prophets explained, had strayed from righteousness, which they defined as ethical behavior.

The Hebrew Bible took shape during these years. Some parts, such as the book of Deuteronomy, already existed in written form, but the exiles recorded the core of the modern Hebrew Bible, from Genesis to 2 Kings. The first five books of the Bible, known either as the Torah in Hebrew or the Pentateuch in Greek, stress that God is the only god and that he will not tolerate the worship of any other gods. This pure monotheism was the product of specific historical circumstances culminating in the Babylonian Exile and the recording of the Bible.

The Neo-Babylonians were the last dynasty to rule from Babylon. In 539 B.C.E. Cyrus the Great, the leader of the Persians, conquered Mesopotamia, and the entire Neo-Babylonian empire came under Persian rule (see Chapter 6). In 538 B.C.E. Cyrus allowed the Hebrews to return to Judah, bringing the Babylonian Captivity to an end, and he ordered the rebuilding of the Temple in Jerusalem. The word "**Jew**," derived from the Hebrew *Yehudhi*, literally means a member of the nation of Judah. After 538 B.C.E., it came to refer to all Hebrews.

● **Jew** A term (derived from Hebrew) that originally meant a member of the nation of Judah and later came to refer to all Hebrews.

The Mesopotamians, along with the Egyptians, were the first people to use writing to record the past. A gulf of several thousand years separates the people of the Mesopotamian city-states and Egypt from the present, yet their literature and documents vividly capture the experience of the world's first peoples in complex societies. The next chapter will contrast their complex society with that of India.

Chapter Review

KEY TERMS

Mesopotamia (28)

Gilgamesh (28)

complex society (31)

city-state (32)

bronze (32)

Sumer (33)

cuneiform (34)

Sargon of Akkad (36)

empire (36)

pharaoh (39)

Nubia (39)

hieroglyphs (39)

papyrus (40)

Hittites (50)

monotheism (51)

Jew (57)

 Download the MP3 audio file of the Chapter Review and listen to it on the go.

Complex society arose in the eastern Mediterranean. Gilgamesh prided himself on the splendors of the city of Uruk. Society at Uruk fulfilled the definition of a complex society: living in a large city, the residents specialized in different types of labor and were socially stratified.

 What were the similarities in political structures, religion, and social structure in Mesopotamia and Egypt? What were the main differences?

In both Mesopotamia and Egypt human kings ruled with the assistance of officials and bureaucrats. Both societies worshiped many different deities and believed a few gods were more powerful than all the others. Both societies had distinct social classes: the ruler and his or her relatives at the top, officials and priests below, and the vast majority of ordinary people at the bottom.

Mesopotamia and Egypt also differed in important ways. The Mesopotamian kings were believed to be intermediaries between their subjects and the gods; the Egyptian pharaohs were thought to be living gods. The Mesopotamians lived first in city-states and then in regional empires after Sargon first unified the region around 2300 B.C.E. Egypt never had city-states, since the first pharaohs ruled both Lower and Upper Egypt.

 When did the international system of the eastern Mediterranean take shape, and how did it function?

Starting around 1500 B.C.E. an international system took shape throughout the eastern Mediterranean that included the New Kingdom in Egypt, the Assyrians in northern Mesopotamia, and the Hittites in Anatolia. The rulers of these kingdoms corresponded with each other frequently, usually to arrange marriages among the different royal families, and also traded goods with one another.

 How did monotheism arise among the ancient Hebrews, and under what circumstances did they record their beliefs?

The ancient Hebrews had worshiped Yahweh as one of many deities since at least 2000 B.C.E. After 1000 B.C.E., one group of ancient Hebrews came to believe that they should worship Yahweh as the most important god. In the sixth century B.C.E. they recorded their monotheistic beliefs in the core of the Hebrew Bible, which took shape in Babylon during the Babylonian Exile and was written down in about 500 B.C.E.

For Further Reference

Andrews, Carol. *Egyptian Mummies.* Cambridge, Mass.: Harvard University Press, 1984.

Brewer, Douglas J., and Emily Teeter. *Egypt and the Egyptians.* New York: Cambridge University Press, 1999.

Casson, Lionel. *Travel in the Ancient World.* Baltimore: Johns Hopkins University Press, 1994.

Dever, William G. *What Did the Biblical Writers Know and When Did They Know It? What Archaeology Can Tell Us About the Reality of Ancient Israel.* Grand Rapids, Mich.: William B. Eerdmans, 2001.

Foster, Benjamin R. *The Epic of Gilgamesh: A Norton Critical Edition.* New York: W. W. Norton, 2001.

Kramer, Samuel Noah. *History Begins at Sumer: Thirty-nine Firsts in Recorded History.* Philadelphia: University of Pennsylvania Press, 1981.

Manzanilla, Linda, ed. *Emergence and Change in Early Urban Societies.* New York: Plenum Press, 1997.

Postgate, J. N. *Early Mesopotamia: Society and Economy at the Dawn of History.* New York: Routledge, 1992.

Richards, Janet, and Mary Van Buren, eds. *Order, Legitimacy, and Wealth in Ancient States.* New York: Cambridge University Press, 2000.

Shaw, Ian. *The Oxford History of Ancient Egypt.* New York: Oxford University Press, 2000.

van de Mieroop, Marc. *A History of the Ancient Near East, ca. 3000–323 B.C.* Malden, Mass.: Blackwell Publishing, 2004.

 WEB RESOURCES

Pronunciation Guide

Interactive Maps

MAP 2.1 Ancient Egypt and Nubia

MAP 2.2 The International System, ca. 1500–1250 B.C.E.

MAP 2.3 The Assyrian and Neo-Babylonian Empires at Their Greatest Extent

Primary Sources

Chapter Objectives

ACE Multiple-Choice Quiz

Flashcards

Websites

The Metropolitan Museum of Art (http://www.metmuseum.org/).   Important collections of Egyptian, Nubian, and Mesopotamian art.

Museum of Fine Arts, Boston (www.mfa.org).   Important collections of Egyptian, Nubian, and Mesopotamian art.

The Nubian Museum in Aswan (http://www.touregypt.net/nubiamuseum.htm). Introduction to the museum with photographs of artifacts.

Ancient India and the Rise of Buddhism, 2600 B.C.E.–100 C.E.

For the first eight years he was king, **Ashoka** (r. 268–232 B.C.E.) led his armies on a series of campaigns in north and central India that culminated in a ferocious struggle in Kalinga (kuh-LING-uh) in modern-day Orissa on India's eastern coast. Victorious at last but appalled by the losses on both sides, Ashoka (uh-SHO-kuh) made a decision that would affect world history long after his Mauryan (MORE-ee-ahn) dynasty (ca. 320–185 B.C.E.) came to an end: he decided to embrace the teachings of Buddhism.

Because the ancient Indians used perishable materials like palm leaves as writing material, we have no written documents before the third century B.C.E. from South Asia (including the modern countries of India, Pakistan, Bangladesh, Nepal, Sri Lanka, Bhutan, and the Maldives). However, throughout his reign, Ashoka had his ideas carved on both large and small stones, called rock edicts, and later on stone pillars. Thus Ashoka's inscriptions provide the fullest record of a single individual's thoughts and movements in South Asia before the modern era. Ashoka explained why in an inscription carved in 260 B.C.E., shortly after conquering Kalinga:

When he had been consecrated eight years the Beloved of the Gods, the king Ashoka, conquered Kalinga. A hundred and fifty thousand people were deported, a hundred thousand were killed and many times that number perished. Afterwards, now that Kalinga was annexed, the Beloved of the Gods very earnestly practiced dharma, desired dharma, and taught dharma. On conquering Kalinga the Beloved of the Gods felt remorse, for, when an independent country is conquered the

ASHOKA AND HIS WIFE DISMOUNTING FROM ELEPHANT

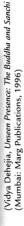

(Vidya Dehejia, *Unseen Presence: The Buddha and Sanchi* (Mumbai: Marg Publications, 1996)

This icon will direct you to interactive activities and study materials on the *Voyages* website: www.cengage.com/history/hansen/voyages1e

60

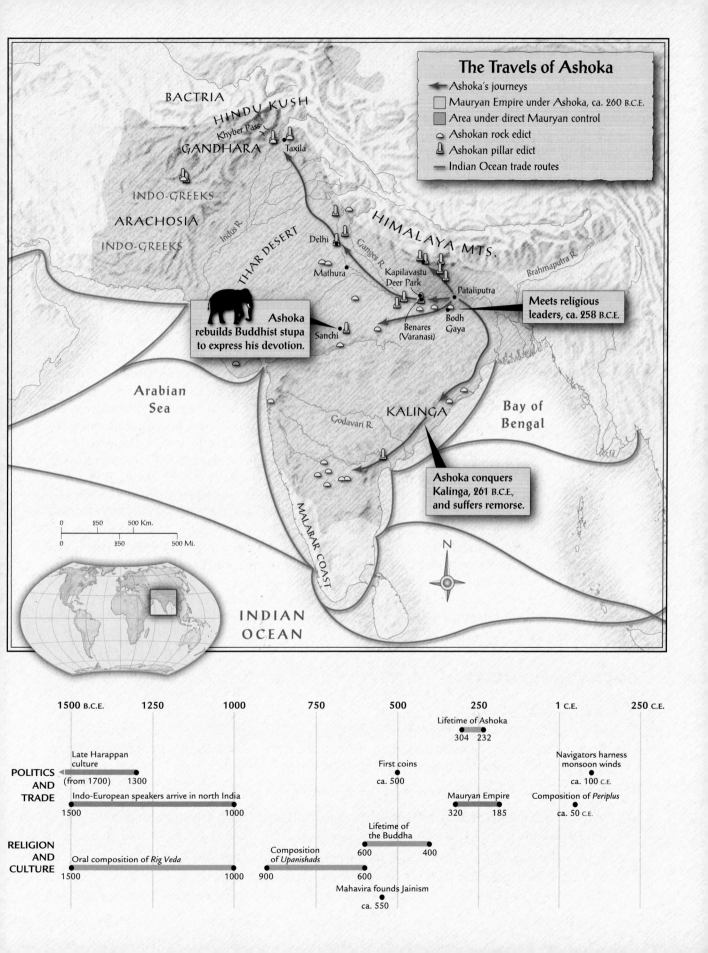

The Travels of Ashoka

→ Ashoka's journeys
▢ Mauryan Empire under Ashoka, ca. 260 B.C.E.
▦ Area under direct Mauryan control
⬮ Ashokan rock edict
🮲 Ashokan pillar edict
— Indian Ocean trade routes

BACTRIA
HINDU KUSH
Khyber Pass
GANDHARA
Taxila
INDO-GREEKS
ARACHOSIA
INDO-GREEKS
Indus R.
THAR DESERT
HIMALAYA MTS.
Delhi
Mathura
Ganges R.
Kapilavastu
Deer Park
Brahmaputra R.
Pataliputra
Sanchi
Benares
(Varanasi)
Bodh
Gaya

Ashoka rebuilds Buddhist stupa to express his devotion.

Meets religious leaders, ca. 258 B.C.E.

Arabian
Sea

KALINGA
Godavari R.
Bay of
Bengal

Ashoka conquers Kalinga, 261 B.C.E., and suffers remorse.

0   250   500 Km.
0   250   500 Mi.

MALABAR COAST

N

INDIAN
OCEAN

	1500 B.C.E.	1250	1000	750	500	250	1 C.E.	250 C.E.
						Lifetime of Ashoka **304 232**		
POLITICS AND TRADE	Late Harappan culture (from 1700) **1300**				First coins ca. **500**		Navigators harness monsoon winds ca. **100 C.E.**	
	Indo-European speakers arrive in north India **1500 1000**					Mauryan Empire **320 185**	Composition of *Periplus* ca. **50 C.E.**	
RELIGION AND CULTURE	Oral composition of *Rig Veda* **1500 1000**			Composition of *Upanishads* **900 600**	Lifetime of the Buddha **600 400**			
					Mahavira founds Jainism ca. **550**			

slaughter, death, and deportation of the people is extremely grievous to the Beloved of the Gods, and weighs heavily on his mind. Today if a hundredth or a thousandth part of those people who were killed or died or were deported when Kalinga was annexed were to suffer similarly, it would weigh heavily on the mind of the Beloved of the Gods.[1]

● **Ashoka** (r. 268–232 B.C.E.) The third king of the Mauryan dynasty (ca. 320–185 B.C.E.), the first Indian ruler to support Buddhism.

● **dharma** A Sanskrit term meaning correct conduct according to law or custom; Buddhists, including Ashoka, used this concept to refer to the teachings of the Buddha.

The concept of dharma occurs repeatedly in Ashoka's inscriptions. The word **dharma** here means the teachings of the Buddha, but more broadly it means correct conduct according to law or custom, which is how many people in South Asia would have understood it. Dharma was also an important concept in Hinduism, the major religion that arose in India after Buddhism declined (see Chapter 8).

Ashoka governed an unusually large area. Riding on an elephant, he traveled along the trunk roads that radiated out like spokes on a bicycle wheel from his capital at Pataliputra (puh-TAH-lee-poo-truh). For much of its history South Asia was divided into separate regions governed by various rulers; only a few dynasties, like the Mauryan, succeeded in uniting the region for brief periods. Although not politically unified, Indians shared a common cultural heritage: living in highly developed cities, many spoke Sanskrit or related languages, used religious texts in those languages, and conceived of society in terms of distinct social ranks.

In contrast to rulers of the city-states of ancient Mesopotamia, the kingdom of ancient Egypt, and the Neo-Assyrian and Neo-Babylonian empires, South Asian rulers exercised much less direct control over their subjects. Instead, leaders like Ashoka ruled by example, often patronizing religion to show what good monarchs they were. Indeed, religion provided one of the major unifying forces in the often-disunited South Asia. This chapter first discusses the ancient Vedic religion of India and then the exciting alternatives that appeared around the fifth century: Buddhism and Jainism (JINE-is-uhm). It concludes by discussing the Indian Ocean trade network.

Focus Questions

 What evidence survives of social stratification at the Indus Valley sites? How did the Indo-Aryans describe the social stratification in their society?

 What were the main teachings of the Buddha?

 Why did Ashoka believe that supporting Buddhism would strengthen the Mauryan state?

 Who were the main actors in the Indian Ocean trade? What types of ships did they use? Along which routes? To trade which commodities?

The Origins of Complex Society in South Asia, 2600–500 B.C.E.

We can glimpse the origins of South Asian social structures and religious traditions from archaeological evidence in the Indus River Valley dating between 2600 and 1700 B.C.E. One of the most important urban sites lies near the modern Pakistan village of Harappa (ha-RAHP-pa). The Harappan culture, with its brick cities, elaborate water systems, fertility deities, and extensive trade, extended over a wide area that included parts of present-day Pakistan, India, and Afghanistan (see Map 3.1). The people of the Indus Valley society used the same script, but, because archaeologists have not deciphered their writing system, we do not know what cultural forces bound them together. We learn more about ancient Indian society from evidence dating to 1500 B.C.E., when people in India, though never politically unified, came to share certain religious beliefs and conceptions of society. The pattern they established at that time held for much of Indian history.

• **monsoon** A term referring both to seasonal winds in South Asia blowing northeast in spring and early summer and southwest in fall and winter, and to the heavy seasonal rains they bring.

Complex Society in the Indus River Valley, 2600–1700 B.C.E.

Long before the continents assumed their current configuration, India was a separate, diamond-shaped island located south of what would become the Eurasian landmass. Over time, the tectonic plate carrying India shifted north until it collided with the Eurasian landmass, forming a massive chain of mountains, the Himalayas. Mount Everest, at 29,028 feet (8,848 m), is the highest mountain in this chain. The South Asian landmass, often called a subcontinent, can be divided into three geographical regions: the high and largely uninhabited mountains to the north, the heavily populated plains of the Indus and Ganga (GUN-ga) Rivers, and the southern peninsula, which is not as densely settled.

The Indian subcontinent has two great rivers: the Indus to the west and the Ganga to the east. The headwaters of both rivers start in the high mountain chain of the Himalayas and drain into the sea, with the Indus flowing into the Arabian Sea and the Ganga into the Bay of Bengal. The earliest farmers planted wheat and barley on the hillsides of what is now western Pakistan. The domestication of plants and animals, sometime between 6500 and 5000 B.C.E., made it possible for the people to create larger settlements in the valley of the Indus River.

India's pattern of rainfall differed from that in Mesopotamia and Egypt. Much of the annual rainfall came in several months in late summer or fall, called the **monsoon** season, and a second period came in the winter months. Indus Valley farmers had to build water storage tanks and measure out the water

🌐 **MAP 3.1**

Indus River Valley Society Between 2600 and 1700 B.C.E., the Indus River Valley society covered a large area in modern-day India and Pakistan. The most important sites were at Mohenjo-daro and Harappa. The region exported carnelian and lapis lazuli to Mesopotamia, to the northeast, and imported shells in return.

[CL] **Interactive Map**

carefully until the next monsoon came. Like the Mesopotamians and the Egyptians, the Indus Valley residents learned to make pottery and to work metal, usually copper and bronze.

In the 1920s British and Indian archaeologists began to excavate huge mounds of brick and debris near the town of Harappa in the **Indus River Valley.** They uncovered the remains of a large urban settlement built from mud brick, complete with walls, drainage systems, open plazas, and avenues several yards (meters) across. Subsequent excavations have revealed that at its height Harappa had an area of over 380 acres (150 hectares) and a population between forty and eighty thousand.[2] Archaeologists have found over fifteen hundred settlements belonging to the Indus River Valley society, the largest complex society of its time on the Indian subcontinent.[3]

Mohenjo-daro (mo-HEN-juh DAH-ro), the second-largest site of the Harappan settlements, was perhaps the most impressive. The city's great bath measured 40 feet (12 m) high and 23 feet (7 m) wide and was "without doubt the earliest public water tank in the ancient world." Although it resembles a swimming pool, complete with staircases at either end, it was actually the source of water for eight bathing rooms in an adjacent building. Unlike other cities of the ancient world, the cities of the Indus River Valley provided drinking water, bathing facilities, and sewer drains to all their residents, not just a privileged few.

We know frustratingly little about the people who occupied the Harappan sites because their script has yet to be deciphered. Seals with the same signs have been found at different sites throughout the Indus River Valley, suggesting that the region shared a common writing system. Archaeologists have identified 400 to 450 signs. But this number is puzzling; 400 signs is more than an alphabet (most alphabets contain fewer than 50 letters) yet fewer than a pictorial writing system (the earliest, simplest phase of Sumerian writing had 700 signs). Scholars wonder whether these mysterious signs stood for an individual word, syllable, or sound.

● **Indus River Valley** Site of the earliest complex society on the Indian subcontinent (2600–1700 B.C.E.), characterized by brick cities, drainage systems, open plazas, and broad avenues.

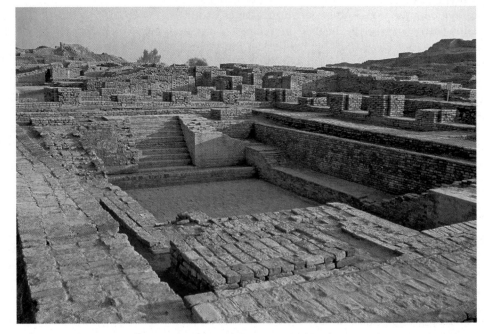

▧ **The "Great Bath" at Mohenjo-daro, Pakistan** One of the most impressive ruins from the Harappan period (2600–1700 B.C.E.), the Great Bath is misnamed. It was a water tank—not a pool or a bathing area. It held water for the ritual use of the city's residents, who bathed in a nearby building. (Borromeo/Art Resource, NY)

Can You Decipher the Harappan Seals of Mohenjo-daro, Pakistan?

These five seals have Indus Valley writing above several figures (*from top left to right, clockwise*): a unicorn, a rhinoceros, an elephant, a water buffalo, and a short-horned bull. A water fountain, possibly with a square sieve on top, stands below the unicorn's mouth; other animals eat from feeding troughs on the ground. No one has yet deciphered the symbols of the Indus Valley writing system.   (Copyright J. M. Kenoyer. Courtesy Department of Museum and Archaeology, Government of Pakistan)

Since no key giving their meaning in another language has yet been found, they are almost impossible to decipher.

A seal made in the Indus River Valley was found at the Mesopotamian city-state of Ur from a level occupied in 2600 B.C.E. The ancient peoples of the Indus River Valley were heavily involved in trade, and the people of Mesopotamia were among their most important trading partners. The residents of ancient Mesopotamia imported carnelian and lapis lazuli from the Indus Valley (see Chapter 2), and shells traveled in the opposite direction (see Map 3.1).

The absence of written documents makes it difficult to reconstruct either the social structure or the religious practices of the residents of the Indus River Valley. As in Mesopotamia, craftsmen who made similar goods seem to have lived in the same residential quarter. There is clear archaeological evidence of social stratification, one of the hallmarks of cities and complex societies. The people who had more possessions than others lived in bigger houses and were buried in graves with more goods.

Beginning in 1900 B.C.E., the large urban sites of the Harappan society become smaller. Archaeologists have different explanations: one possibility is that a slight environmental change adversely affected farmers, who were no longer able to supply urban dwellers with foodstuffs. The characteristic Indus River pottery vessel types give way to new shapes and decorative patterns. Some of the pots have graffiti markings in Indus Valley script, indicating that the script remained in use.

We know too little about the Indus Valley peoples to identify any particular practices that continued in later periods. With incontrovertible evidence of social stratification, occupational specialization, and large urban centers, the Indus River Valley sites certainly meet our definition of a complex society, including a writing system. Although the people were probably not united under a single ruler, they shared a common system of weights and measures, standardized brick size, and urban planning. Shared cultural practices in the absence of political unification characterized later South Asian societies as well.

● **Sanskrit**
A language, such as Latin, Greek, and English, belonging to the Indo-European language family and spoken by Indo-Aryan migrants to north India around 1500–1000 B.C.E.

The Spread of Indo-European Languages

Our understanding of the South Asian past becomes much clearer with the first textual materials in the Indo-European language of **Sanskrit.** Linguists place languages whose vocabulary and grammatical structures are most closely related into the same language family. If you have studied French or Spanish, you know that many words are related to their English counterparts. English, French, and Spanish all belong to the Indo-European language family, as do ancient Greek, Latin, Hittite, and Sanskrit. The Indo-European languages contain many core vocabulary words related to English, such as the words for mother, father, and brother (see Table 3.1). If you study a non-Indo-European language, like Chinese or Arabic, few words will resemble any word in English, and word order may be different.

Sometime in the distant past, thousands of years ago, a group of herding peoples who spoke Indo-European languages began to leave their homeland. The migrations took place long before the introduction of writing, so even today we cannot be certain where the homeland of the Indo-European speakers was or when they left. Horse-drawn carts gave these peoples a technological edge because they could cover far more ground than most of their contemporaries, who did not know how to breed horses or drive wheeled carts.

The distribution of Indo-European languages over Eurasia shows how far these peoples went: Russia, most of Europe, Iran, and north India, but not southern India or East Asia (see Map 3.2). By at least 2000 B.C.E., those going west reached Anatolia, where they spoke Hittite (see Chapter 2); they reached the island of Crete in the Mediterranean Sea at about the same time (see Chapter 6). Those going east passed through Iran and arrived in north India sometime between 1500 and 1000 B.C.E., where they spoke Sanskrit. The modern inhabitants of the region speak a range of Indo-European languages descended from Sanskrit, including Hindi (HIN-dee), while those in south India speak Dravidian (druh-VID-ee-uhn) languages, which belong to a different language family.

Most people living in the northern regions of modern South Asia speak Indo-European languages, including Hindi and Urdu, while those living in the south speak Dravidian languages like Tamil and Telegu. The dominance of Indo-European languages in much of today's Eurasia is the result of migrations occurring over three thousand years ago.

When linguists first discovered the similarities among Latin, Greek, and Sanskrit in the early nineteenth century, they assumed that the speakers of Indo-European languages invaded and wiped out the indigenous peoples. Modern scholars have since proposed variations on the original conquer-and-destroy model. Perhaps, when the Indo-European speakers migrated into a new region, their superior technology convinced the local peoples to adopt the newcomers' language.

Table 3.1	Related Words in Various Indo-European Languages		
English	**Latin**	**Greek**	**Sanskrit**
mother	mater	meter	matar
father	pater	pater	pitar
brother	frater	phrater	bhratar
sister	soror	(unrelated)	svasar
me	me	me	ma
two	duo	duo	duva
six	sex	hex	shat
seven	septem	hepta	sapta

The Indo-European Migrations and Vedic Culture, 1500–1000 B.C.E.

The Indo-European migrants left us the **_Rig Veda_** (RIG-VAY-duh), a collection of 1,028 hymns that were preserved because the priests who sang them passed them down orally from one generation to the next. They date to around 1500 to 1000 B.C.E., the

🌐 MAP 3.2

Distribution of Languages in Modern South Asia   Most people living in the northern regions of modern South Asia speak Indo-European languages, including Hindi and Urdu, while those living in the south speak Dravidian languages like Tamil and Telegu. The dominance of Indo-European languages in much of today's Eurasia is the result of migrations occurring over three thousand years ago.

probable time of the Indo-European migrations to South Asia, yet they were not written down until more than two thousand years later, perhaps in 1000 C.E.[4] The word *hymn* is slightly misleading, since hymns touch on many everyday activities, including sex and gambling. Accordingly, they reveal much about ancient society.

Linguists have concluded that the Sanskrit of the older hymns varies slightly from the later hymns, making it possible to determine the order of their composition. The earlier hymns mention many place names to the west of those included in the later hymns, an indication that the migrants came first to northwest India and later to all of north India.

These migrants sometimes called themselves "Aryan," a Sanskrit word whose meaning is "noble" or "host." While modern researchers think that many and varied peoples spoke Indo-European languages, the propagandists of Nazi Germany wrongly imputed a racial unity to what was a linguistic group. Always mindful that we know nothing of their appearance, it is best to refer to these migrants as Indo-Aryans because their language belonged to the Indo-Aryan branch of the Indo-European language family.

● **Rig Veda**
A collection of 1,028 Sanskrit hymns, composed around 1500 to 1000 B.C.E. yet written down around 1000 C.E. One of the most revealing sources about Indo-Europeans who settled in north India.

• **Vedic religion** Religious belief system of Indo-European migrants to north India; involved animal sacrifice and elaborate ceremonies to ensure that all transitions in the natural world—day to night, or one season to the next—proceeded smoothly.

Scholars have named the religion of the Indo-Aryans Vedic (VAY-dick), from the *Rig Veda*. The roots of Hinduism, a major religion in modern South Asia, lie in **Vedic religion,** but the religious practices of the early Indo-Aryans differed from later Hinduism, which will be discussed in Chapter 8. Many scholars of South Asian religion date the rise of Hinduism to the seventh century C.E., after the decline of Buddhism.[5]

Many Vedic rituals focused on the transition between day and night or between seasons. A priest had to make the correct offering to the appropriate deity to ensure that the sun would rise each day or that at the winter solstice the days would begin to grow longer. The deities mentioned in the *Rig Veda* include the war-god, Indra (IN-druh), who carried a thunderbolt and led large conquering armies, the god of fire, the sun-god, and the god of death, as well as many minor deities. Often the rituals involved fire, thought to be the purest of the elements. Rituals honoring these gods could last several days and involve intricate sequences of steps, including animal sacrifice, and the ritual specialists who performed them, the Brahmin (BRAH-min) priests, were paid handsomely by local rulers. There was no single ruler in Vedic society. Instead a number of kings ruled small territories by collecting taxes from farmers to finance these lavish ceremonies.

• **nomads** A term for people who migrate seasonally from place to place to find grass for their herds. They do not usually farm but tend their herds full-time.

The *Rig Veda* provides a few valuable hints about social organization. The original Indo-European migrants were **nomads** who migrated seasonally from place to place to find grass for their herds. Carrying their tents with them, they usually did not farm but tended their herds full-time. The most important animal in their society was the horse, which pulled the carts that transported their families and possessions across Eurasia. According to some hymns, some people began to cultivate grain after settling in India.

One early hymn, addressed to Indra, gives a clear sense of the diverse occupations of the Indo-European speakers:

> Our thoughts bring us to diverse callings, setting people apart: the carpenter seeks what is broken, the physician a fracture, and the Brahmin priest seeks one who presses Soma.[6]

CL **Primary Source:**
The Rig Veda
Read how Indra, "the thunder-wielder," slew Vritra, "firstborn of dragons," and how Purusha created the universe through an act of ritual sacrifice.

Soma was an intoxicating beverage, possibly made from ephedra (AY-fay-druh) leaves, that was drunk at ceremonies. This poem shows that Vedic society included carpenters, doctors, Brahmin priests, and people who prepared the ritual drink.

The position of women in Vedic society was probably not much lower than that of men. Girls could go out unsupervised in public. Both girls and boys received an education in which they memorized hymns and studied their meaning, yet only male specialists recited hymns in public ceremonies. One hymn instructs educated girls to marry educated husbands. Girls could sometimes even choose their own husbands, provided they had obtained permission from their mother and father. Women could inherit property, and widows could remarry.

• **varna** From the Sanskrit word for "color": the four major social groups of ancient Indian society, ranked in order of purity (not wealth or power): Brahmin priests at the top, then warriors, then farmers and merchants, and finally dependent laborers.

Changes After 1000 B.C.E.

The later hymns, composed perhaps around 1000 B.C.E., indicate that social roles in Vedic society became more fixed, and women's freedom declined, as the former nomads settled down to a life of agriculture. Eventually people came to be classed into four different social groups, called **varna** (VAR-nuh), that were determined by birth. The literal meaning of *varna* is "color," reflected in the modern English word *varnish*. One hymn, "The Hymn of the Primeval Man," explains that when the gods dismembered a cosmic giant, they created each varna from a different part of his body:

When they divided the man, into how many parts did they apportion him? What do they call his mouth, his two arms and thighs and feet?

His mouth became the Brahmin; his arms were made into the Warrior, his thighs the People, and from his feet the Servants were born.

This passage sets out the major social groups of late Vedic society, ranked in order of purity (not wealth or power): Brahmin priests at the top, then warriors, then farmers and merchants ("the People"), and finally dependent laborers. Brahmins were the purest because they conducted Vedic rituals; the warrior category included the kings who sponsored the rituals. The farmers and merchants were supposed to farm the land and tend the herds. The fourth varna of dependent laborers, many of whom were the region's original residents, served all the varna above them. Like all documents, however, this hymn has a distinct point of view: a Brahmin priest composed it, and it is not surprising that he placed Brahmins at the top of the social hierarchy.

India's caste system has changed greatly over the last three thousand years. There is no exact equivalent in Indian languages of the English word *caste,* which comes from the sixteenth- to seventeenth-century Portuguese word *castas,* meaning breed or type of animal or plant. Most Indians would say that the word **jati** (JAH-ti), sometimes translated as "subcaste," comes closest. People in a jati sometimes specialize in a certain occupation, but many jati have members with many different occupations, and some jati have completely given up their traditional occupations in favor of something new. (See the feature "World History in Today's World: The Modern Caste System and Its Ancient Antecedents.")

Different changes took place in the centuries after circa 1000 B.C.E., when the later poems in the *Rig Veda* were composed. Iron came into widespread use, and iron tools proved much more effective at clearing land than bronze or copper ones. Between 1000 and 500 B.C.E. the residents of the lower Ganga Valley cleared much of the forest cover so that they could intensively pursue agriculture there. The sedentary peoples, armed with horses and iron weapons, continuously extended the area of cultivated land. Higher agricultural yields prompted an increase in population and a boom in trade, as shown by the appearance of the first coins around 500 B.C.E., at the same time as in China (see Chapter 4) and the Persian Empire (see Chapter 6).

This time period also saw other challenges to the old order. Composed between 900 and 600 B.C.E., the *Upanishad* (oo-PAHN-ih-shahd) texts claim to be linked to the Vedic tradition but introduce entirely new ideas. These texts turn inward, away from costly sacrificial rituals. One new and exciting idea was that souls transmigrated: according to the doctrine of karma, people's acts in this life determined how they would be reborn in the next. New gods appeared and are still worshiped by Hindus today. Unlike the gods of the *Rig Veda,* these gods intervene actively in human affairs and sometimes assume human form.

The *Mahabharata* (muh-HAH-bah-ruh-tuh) and the *Ramayana* (ruh-MAH-yuh-nuh), the two great Sanskrit epics, began to be composed at this time, although they were recorded only in the fourth century C.E. The *Mahabharata,* over 100,000 verses in length, describes a long-running feud between two clans. Its major theme is dharma, or right conduct. The epic vividly enacts some of the most basic conflicts in the human psyche as the characters struggle to understand what it means to be good and what the consequences of evil actions might be. We see men and women struggling with the question of whether it even matters if a person is

• **jati** A term, sometimes translated as "subcaste," for groups of 5,000 to 15,000 people in modern India. Many, but not all, Indians marry someone from the same jati and share meals on equal footing only with people of the same jati.

The Modern Caste System and Its Ancient Antecedents

If asked to identify their own caste, most South Asians would name their jati first and then perhaps add the varna to which they think they belong. Varna is the general term describing the same four groups as in Vedic times: Brahmin, warrior, farmer or merchant, and dependent laborer. People often disagree about the varna ranking of a given jati; for example, one person may think a given jati belongs to the warrior category, while another may place it within the merchant and farmer varna. These disagreements can result in actual disputes between members of different jati.

Not all jati fit neatly into the four-varna classification. Approximately 15 percent of modern Indians belong to government-listed castes and 7.5 percent to government-listed tribes (two groups previously considered untouchables). Although India's constitution, adopted in 1949, abolishes untouchability and forbids discrimination against untouchables, both groups continue to suffer widespread discrimination. However, today government quotas ensure them a certain number of university places and civil service positions in proportion to their size.

Most outside observers tend to exaggerate the rigidity of caste in modern India. The caste system is most powerful in small communities, such as villages, in which everyone recognizes everyone and people marry people from families they know well. Politicians frequently invoke jati identity to get votes. Of course, as soon as someone enters a large city, no one can tell simply from that person's appearance to which jati or varna he or she belongs. Still, it is possible to make an educated guess because members of lower-ranked jati often continue to practice their traditional occupations, like sweeping, by force of circumstance.

Jati usually range in size from five thousand to fifteen thousand people. Many, but not all, people in modern South Asia find their spouse through arranged marriages with people from the same jati. Because each generation tends to marry within its own jati, the jati have developed into social groups with strong identities. People socialize within their own jati and share meals together. They naturally turn to others in their jati to ask for jobs, loans, and assistance with their problems. Castelike groups exist within other modern societies, too, although we do not realize how many people in non-Indian societies, including the United States, also tend to marry spouses from similar social and economic backgrounds.

actively trying to change the world, or whether perhaps everything is simply fated to be the way it is.

One part of the *Mahabharata,* the *Bhagavad Gita* (bug-GAH-vud GEEH-tuh), was often read as an independent work. Composed around 200 C.E., it tells the story of a battle between two armies. One leader hesitates before the battle: his dharma is to fight, but he will not be able to escape from the cycle of death and rebirth if he kills any of his relatives fighting on the other side. The deity Krishna, in human form as a chariot driver, argues that each person should fulfill his dharma, or his given role, in life. Then Krishna appears as a deity and urges the warrior to devote himself fully to worshiping him. Krishna's teaching later become a key tenet in Hinduism.

The much-shorter *Ramayana* tells of a great king, Rama (RAH-muh), whose wife is abducted by a demon king. Rama fights to get Sita (SEE-tuh) back, but when he defeats the demon king he greets her coldly and explains that he cannot take her back because, although a married woman, she has lived alone with her captors. After ordering a pyre of wood to be built, she jumps into the flames, but the fire-god lifts her from the flames and presents her to Rama. Only then does he accept that she has remained loyal to him. Some have seen this as evidence that widows committed suicide by immolating themselves at their husbands' cremations. (The first detailed evidence of widow immolation, from the early nineteenth century, indicates that the practice was limited to specific regions and small social groups.) In the centuries after their initial composition, both the *Mahabharata* and the *Ramayana* spawned many versions throughout South Asia and even Southeast Asia, and today's television versions captivate millions of viewers.

Different teachers continued to debate new religious concepts in succeeding centuries. Between the sixth and fourth centuries B.C.E., Jainism, an Indian religion with some two million followers today, took shape. Mahavira, the founder of the Jains (JINES), went from place to place for twelve years, testing himself and debating ideas with other ascetics. After thirteen months he stopped wearing even a single garment and wandered naked for eleven years before reaching liberation from the bondage of human life. He died, it is thought, in his seventies after voluntarily renouncing food and water. Jains believe in right faith, right knowledge, and right conduct, and they emphasize the obligation to harm no living beings. They abstain from eating and drinking at night, when it is dark, so that they will not kill any insects by mistake.

The Rise of Buddhism

Also living in this time of religious ferment was the founder of the Buddhist religion, Siddhartha Gautama (sid-DAR-tuh gow-TA-muh), or the Buddha. The word **Buddha** literally means "the enlightened or awakened one." The religion that he founded became one of the most influential in the world, and Ashoka's decision to support Buddhism marked a crucial turning point in the religion's history. Buddhism spread to Sri Lanka, Central Asia, Southeast Asia, and eventually to China and Japan, where it continued to thrive after it declined in its Indian homeland. Today Japan, Tibet, and Thailand have significant Buddhist populations, and growing Buddhist communities live in Europe and North America.

• **Buddha**
The founder of the Buddhist religion, Siddhartha Gautama (ca. 600–400 B.C.E.); also called the Buddha, or the enlightened one.

We know many details about the Buddha's life but cannot be sure which are facts and which myths because all our sources date to several centuries after his death and were recorded by Buddhist monks and nuns. Born at a time when India was not politically unified, the Buddha did not intend to found a religion that would bind Indian society together. His stated goal was to teach people how to break out of the endless cycle of birth, death, and rebirth.

The Life of the Buddha Even the dates of the Buddha's life are uncertain. Born along the southern edge of the Himalaya Mountains in today's Nepal, the Buddha lived to almost eighty. Sri Lankan Buddhist sources point to a death date of 543 B.C.E., while Chinese and Tibetan Buddhist sources suggest either 486 B.C.E. or 370 B.C.E. Scholarly consensus now puts the death of the Buddha closer to 400 B.C.E. than to 500 B.C.E.

The legend of his life, known to all practicing Buddhists, recounts that his mother dreamed of a white elephant with a lotus flower in his trunk. The wise men she consulted explained that she was going to give birth to either a great monarch or a great teacher. One seer predicted that, if he learned about human problems, he would become a teacher, prompting his parents to raise him inside a walled palace precinct so that he would never see any signs of suffering or illness. He grew up, married, and fathered a child.

One day when he was driving inside the palace park with his charioteer, he noticed an extremely elderly man. Later he glimpsed a feverish man who was so ill that his skin was covered with growths. His third encounter with human suffering came when he saw a corpse being taken away to be cremated. The fourth encounter, with a wandering ascetic who wore a simple robe but who looked happy, gave him hope, and he resolved to follow his example. For six years he subjected himself to all kinds of self-mortification. Then he decided to stop starving himself and meditated under a tree, later known as the Tree of Wisdom (also called a bodhi tree), for forty-nine days. He gained enlightenment and explained how he had done so.

The Teachings of the Buddha

According to much later Buddhist tradition, the Buddha preached his first sermon in the Deer Park near Benares (buh-NAR-us) in the Ganga Valley to five followers, who, like him, were seeking enlightenment. First he identified two incorrect routes to knowledge: extreme self-denial and complete self-gratification. The Buddha preached that his listeners should leave family life behind and follow him, and they should live simple lives, avoiding the strenuous fasts and self-mortification advocated by other ascetic groups.

He explained that one could escape from the endless cycle of birth, death, and rebirth by following a clear series of steps, called the Noble Eightfold Path. Like a doctor, the Buddha diagnosed suffering in the First Noble Truth, analyzed its origins in the Second Noble Truth, stated that a cure exists in the Third Truth, and explained that cure in the Fourth Noble Truth: to follow the Noble Eightfold Path. This path consists of right understanding, right resolve, right speech, right action, right livelihood, right effort, right mindfulness, and right meditation. When people follow the Noble Eightfold Path, their suffering will end because they will have escaped from the cycle of life and rebirth by attaining nirvana. The word **nirvana** literally means "extinction," as when the flame on a candle goes out, but in the Buddha's teachings it took on a much broader meaning: those who followed the Eightfold Path and understood the Four Noble Truths would gain true understanding.

Buddhism shared with Jainism much that was new. Both challenged Brahminic authority, denied the authority of the Vedic hymns, and banned animal sacrifices. Vedic religious practice did not address the question of individual liberation; the goal of Vedic ritual was to make sure that the cosmos continued to function in an orderly way. In contrast, the Buddha preached that salvation was entirely the product of an individual's actions. He focused on the individual, outside of his or her family unit and any social group and without regard to his or her varna ranking.

The people who heard the Buddha preach naturally wanted to know how they could attain nirvana. He urged them to leave their families behind so that they could join him as monks in the Buddhist order. Those who followed him went from place to place, begging for their daily food from those who did not join the

CL **Primary Source:**
Setting in Motion the Wheel of Law
Siddhartha's first sermon contains the core teaching of Buddhism: to escape, by following the Middle Path, the suffering caused by desire.

● **nirvana** A Sanskrit word that literally means "extinction," as when the flame on a candle goes out. In Buddhism the term took on broader meaning: those who followed the Eightfold Path and understood the Four Noble Truths would gain true understanding.

order. They lived nowhere permanently except during the monsoon months, when it was not practical to live by begging. The early monastic orders reached decisions by consensus. When the members of the Buddhist order did not agree, they voted, and the leader of the group implemented the decision.

Only those monks who joined the Buddhist order could attain nirvana, the Buddha taught. His first followers were all men, but Buddhist sources record that the Buddha's aunt asked to join the Buddhist order. The Buddha refused her until his star disciple Ananda (uh-NAN-duh) intervened and persuaded him to change his mind. Women did become Buddhist nuns, but they were always subordinate to men.

The Buddha assumed that the people who could not become monks and nuns would donate food and money instead. Those outside the order could not attain nirvana, but they could gain merit by making such donations, the Buddha taught, and many kings and merchants gave large gifts in the hope of improving their lives, either in this world or in future rebirths.

This teaching marked a major departure from the pre-existing Vedic religion. According to the *Rig Veda,* Brahmins stood at the top of the ritual hierarchy, and those who ranked below them could do nothing to change their position. The Buddhists took a radically different view: a merchant, a farmer, or even a laborer who made a donation to the Buddhist order could enhance his or her standing. From its very earliest years, Buddhists attracted merchant support, and communities of Buddhists often lived near cities, where merchants had gathered.

The Buddha forbade his followers from worshiping statues or portraits of him. Instead, they worshiped at the four sites that had been most important during the Buddha's life: where he was born, where he gained enlightenment, where he preached the first sermon, and where he died. Before his death the Buddha had instructed his followers to cremate him and bury his ashes under a bell-shaped monument built over a burial mound, called a stupa (STEW-pah). The first generation of Buddhists divided the Buddha's remains under many different stupas, where they honored him by circling them in a clockwise direction, in a practice called circumambulation (pradaksina) (pra-DUCKSH-ee-nah). To gain merit, they walked with their right arm, thought to be more pure than the left, facing the stupa for a fixed number of times. They also left flowers, incense, and clothing on the stupas, where they lit lamps and played music as an expression of their devotion. (See the feature "Visual Evidence: The Buddhist Stupa at Sanchi.")

The depictions of the Buddha changed in later centuries. Beginning in the first and second centuries C.E., sculptors began to make images of the Buddha himself. One group in north India portrayed the Buddha as a young man, while another, active in the Gandhara (gahn-DAHR-ah) region of modern Pakistan and Afghanistan, was influenced by later copies of Greek statues brought by Alexander the Great and his armies in the fourth century B.C.E. They made statues of the Buddha, often in a sitting position, with noticeably Greek-looking facial features (see photo).

▣ A Mix of Sculptural Traditions from Gandhara, Afghanistan

This Gandharan statue's posture is classically Buddhist: his legs are crossed so that both feet face up, the left hand grasps his robe, and the right makes a gesture meaning to dispel fear. But the facial expression, hair, and overall posture are drawn from Greco-Roman models already familiar to Gandharan sculptors for several centuries. Neither Buddhist nor Greco-Roman, the spokes in the halo behind the Buddha's head probably represent the sun's rays. (The Metropolitan Museum of Art. Gift of Moneichi Nitta, 2003)

THE BUDDHIST STUPA AT SANCHI

The oldest and best-preserved stupa in India is at Sanchi (SAN-chee), near Bhopal, India. The Buddha never visited Sanchi during his lifetime, but Ashoka chose it as the site of a new stupa because it lay on the main route between Pataliputra and the western coastal ports and had frequent visitors. Ashoka ordered the remains of the Buddha removed from their original resting place and placed in a new burial mound. He covered the mound with a layer of sandstone and erected a wooden railing around it. He also placed a pillar edict on the site.

The site today looks the way it did after extensive renovations done during the first century B.C.E. A square stone wall with a central gate on each side surrounds the main burial mound; beautifully carved stone pillars decorate each of the gates (see opposite). In addition to the main stupa, Sanchi contains two other large stupas and hundreds of smaller ones, where monks seeking to share the Buddha's merit were buried. Buddhists believe that visiting a stupa holding someone's remains brings them closer to the deceased.

Built in the first century B.C.E., the Eastern Gate at Sanchi contains three horizontal sections held up by the two main vertical posts. The carvings of people and animals worshiping the Buddha are wonderfully lifelike. The artists carved scenes from the Buddha's life but never the Buddha himself. In his dying instructions, the Buddha forbade his followers to worship representations of him.

The top horizontal scene shows Buddhists standing with hands folded in a position of reverence facing a series of stupas, each of which represented the Buddha. In the middle horizontal scene depicting the Great Departure, when the Buddha left his father's palace, the Sanchi artists showed five riderless horses at increasing distances from the palace, each scene portraying a moment in continuous action. At the right end of the frame, the artists carved a pair of footprints under a parasol, a convention the viewers would have understood to represent the Buddha.

The beautifully carved frieze on the lowest horizontal section depicts an Indian monarch, most likely Ashoka, at a royal procession. Ashoka and his wife have dismounted from a crouching elephant, and they pause to observe musicians. At the center of the scene is a depiction of the Tree of Wisdom under which the Buddha gained enlightenment. A structure protects the base of the tree, where people are praying and making offerings.

After looking at the friezes on the front and back of the gate, worshipers followed the path leading them through an outer wall to the stupa itself, climbing a flight of steps to reach a railed walkway that led all the way around the stupa. The pillars and gates at Sanchi contain hundreds of inscriptions from Ashoka's time and later, recording the names of those making a donation to pay for part of a railing or a frieze in the hope of gaining merit. All those who circumambulated the stupa shared the same goal.

QUESTION FOR ANALYSIS

 How did people of different social ranks—Ashoka, monks, nuns, and ordinary people—express their devotion to Buddhism at different places—the friezes of the gates, the pillars, the walkways, and the stupa itself—at the site of Sanchi?

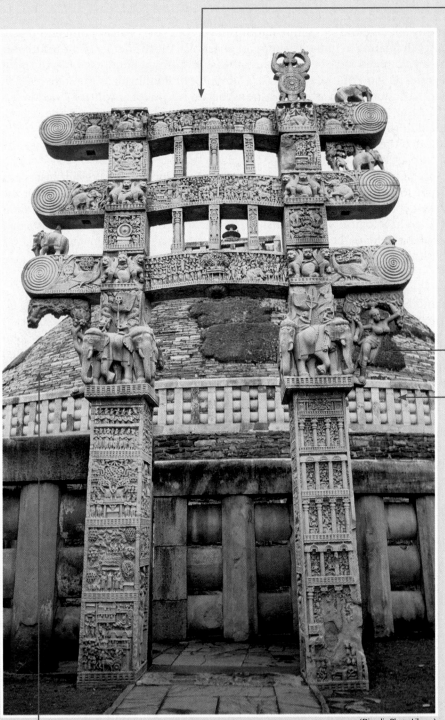

The Eastern Gate was built in the first century B.C.E. The high quality of the carvings makes this one of the greatest surviving monuments of Buddhist art in India, as well as one of the earliest.

This buxom woman beneath a mango tree is a local female deity, credited with the ability to help women conceive and undergo easier childbirth. Buddhist monuments often incorporated local deities in subordinate positions.

This railing surrounds the interior walkway on which worshipers circumambulated the stupa. Individual stones bear the names of contributors—including monks, nuns, and merchants—who made donations to finance the building of the walkway.

(Dinodia Photo Library)

The stupa mound was first built over the remains of the Buddha in the third century B.C.E. and attained its current size—120 feet (36.5 m) in diameter and 54 feet (16.5 m) high—one hundred years later.

●The Mauryan Empire, ca. 320–185 B.C.E.

●Mauryan dynasty
(ca. 320–185 B.C.E.)
A dynasty that unified
much of the Indian
subcontinent. Relying
on trunk roads, it exer-
cised more control in
the cities than in the
countryside.

During the Buddha's lifetime, Buddhism was but one of many different teach-ings circulating in India. The support of Ashoka, the third ruler of the **Mauryan dynasty,** founded by Ashoka's grandfather, transformed Buddhism into the most influential religion of its day. Ashoka's adoption of Buddhism as the state religion promoted cultural unity as well as strengthened his political control. The Maury-ans came to power at a time when trade was increasing throughout the region, and Buddhism was able to succeed because it appealed to merchants. The Maury-ans created the first large state in India, extending over all of north India (see the map on page 61).

Surprisingly few materials about the Mauryans survive. As a result, historians continue to debate the amount of control the Mauryan Empire exercised over the regions it conquered. Local rulers may have retained considerable power. In addi-tion to archaeological excavations, our major sources are the partial report of a Greek ambassador named Megasthenes (ME-gas-thuh-nees), written after 288 B.C.E., and Ashoka's rock edicts.

Life and Society in the Mauryan Dynasty, ca. 300 B.C.E.

In 320 B.C.E. the grandfather of Ashoka, a gen-eral named Chandragupta (chuhn-druh-GOOP-tuh) Maurya (r. ca. 320–297 B.C.E.), defeated another gen-eral and gained control of his territory and his capital Pataliputra (modern-day Patna [PUTT-nuh]), located on the Ganga. After Chan-dragupta Maurya took power, his forces fought those of Seleucus I (321–281 B.C.E.), a general who succeeded Alexander the Great (see Chapter 6) in Mesopotamia. After making peace, Seleucus (seh-LOO-kuhs) sent an ambassador named Me-gasthenes to the Mauryan court at Pataliputra in 302 B.C.E., where he stayed for fourteen years.

Megasthenes wrote a work entitled *Indika* (IN-dick-uh), which provides a de-tailed description of Pataliputra in approximately 300 B.C.E., some thirty years before Ashoka ascended to the throne. Unfortunately, Megasthenes's original work does not survive; we know it only from passages quoted by later Greek and Roman writers.[7]

Pataliputra's size impressed Megasthenes deeply.

> This city stretched in the inhabited quarters to an extreme length on each side of eighty stadia [nearly 10 miles or 16 kilometers], and that its breadth was fifteen stadia [nearly 2 miles or 3.2 kilometers], and that a ditch encompassed it all round, which was six hundred feet in breadth and thirty cubits [45 feet or 14 meters] in depth, and that the wall was crowned with 570 towers and had four-and-sixty gates.

This description of the city's size is plausible. Archaeological excavations early in the twentieth century around Patna revealed clear evidence of large fortification walls, including large reinforcing wooden trusses.

The Mauryans exercised considerable control within the capital. Most of their officials supervised trade and commerce, the major source of Mauryan revenue. Market officials regulated weights and measures to ensure that no one was cheated.

They encouraged merchants to sell only one type of good by charging them twice as much tax as if they sold more, and they levied fines on those merchants who passed off old goods as newly made. The Mauryans concentrated their officials at marketplaces in the capital, where they could regulate measures and prices at the same time that they collected taxes.

The passages that have come down to us take a detached tone: Megasthenes includes no personal anecdotes. His account of the officials who watched over the foreigners comes closest to describing his own life in Pataliputra:

> Those of the second branch attend to the entertainment of foreigners. To these they assign lodgings, and they keep watch over their modes of life by means of those persons whom they give to them for assistants. They escort them on the way when they leave the country, or, in the event of their dying, forward their property to their relatives. They take care of them when they are sick, and if they die bury them.

We may surmise that city officials gave Megasthenes a servant.

According to Megasthenes, the military section of the government was the same size as the urban section: thirty men, divided into six branches, each with its own area of responsibility—navy, supplies, infantry, cavalry, war chariots, and elephants. Elephants fascinated Megasthenes, who devoted many lines to their capture, training, loyalty to their masters, and general care; when on active duty, he reports, they consumed rice wine and large quantities of flowers.

Megasthenes's descriptions of Indian society have long puzzled analysts. He identifies seven ranks within Indian society: (1) philosophers, (2) farmers, (3) herdsmen, (4) artisans, (5) soldiers, (6) spies, and (7) councillors. This overlaps only slightly with the varna scheme described in the *Rig Veda* some seven hundred years earlier (discussed above), with its four ranks of Brahmin, warriors, merchants and farmers, and dependent servants. Three of Megasthenes's groups (herdsmen, artisans, and spies) do not even appear in the varna ranking.

The top-ranking group, according to Megasthenes, was the smallest: the king's advisers, military generals, and treasury officials, who were "the most respected on account of the high character and wisdom of [their] members." Megasthenes's ranking suggests that this was the group he probably encountered directly.

Ranking second were the "philosophers," or religious practitioners. They performed sacrifices and funerals, and Megasthenes explains that the Brahmins among them married and had children but lived simply. Another group of religious practitioners underwent various privations, such as abstaining from sexual intercourse or sitting in one position all day. The Jains would have belonged to this group. Finally, a third group followed the Buddha, "whom they honor as a god on account of his extraordinary sanctity." Although the Buddha had taught his followers not to worship him as a god, Buddhist devotees began to credit him with divine capabilities soon after his death, as we can see from Megasthenes's report. Megasthenes devotes only a few sentences to the Buddhists, an indication that the Buddhists had only a small following in 300 B.C.E.

Conceptions of caste, Megasthenes suggests, were much more fluid than many of our surviving sources, which almost always place Brahmins at the top, would indicate. Megasthenes lists five other groups (farmers, herdsmen, artisans, soldiers, and spies) without ranking them in any way. The farmers, the largest group, were exempt from military service but paid a land tax to the king as well as one-quarter of all their crops. The military was the second-largest group. Megasthenes concludes his list by saying, "No one is allowed to marry out of his own caste, or to exercise any calling or art except his own."

Mauryan Control Outside the Capital

The Mauryans exercised close supervision over the rural areas in the immediate vicinity of the capital, but not over all of north India. Megasthenes reports that the kingdom contained three different types of territory: those ruled directly by the Mauryan king, those territories where the local king was allowed to remain in place with reduced powers, and local republics. This description of the Mauryans suggests an empire quite different from that of the Assyrians (see Chapter 2). Whereas the Mauryans exercised direct rule in only a limited area, the Assyrians sometimes forcibly resettled large groups of people throughout their empire.

The Ashokan inscriptions, written after Megasthenes left India (most likely between 260 and 232 B.C.E.), provide more information about the extent of Mauryan control outside the capital. Some of the inscriptions were written on tall pillars, while others were carved on boulders (shown on the map on page 61). They were placed in the capital, in northwest India in the Punjab (PUHN-juhb) region, on the east and west coasts, and in central India.

Earlier analysts have often assumed that one could connect the different monuments with a line, with the territory inside the line being that of the Mauryan Empire. Recently, however, historians have realized that since not all empires were able to exercise a uniform control over a large area, the Mauryan Empire should be mapped differently. The region about Pataliputra should have the darkest shade to indicate where Mauryan control was greatest. The trade routes linking the capital with outlying trade centers should also be shaded dark because the Mauryans could have dispatched officials to markets to collect sales taxes. But the regions lying in between the trade routes should remain lightly shaded, if at all.

An Ashokan Column from Vaishali, Bihar, India This pillar, made of polished red sandstone, stands 60 feet (18.3 m) high. Capped with a lion, it was visible in all four directions. This and the other stone columns Ashoka commissioned are the first monuments worked in stone anywhere in ancient India. Some scholars have wondered if Ashoka knew of other stone monuments in neighboring regions like Iran. (Dinodia Photo Library)

The Mauryan Empire remained a decentralized one in which local people continued to speak their own languages. Ashoka drafted the texts of his inscriptions in his native language of Magadhi (muh-GUH-dee), a language related to Sanskrit. They were then translated into the different Prakrit (PRAH-krit) vernaculars used in north India, which are all descended from Sanskrit. Some in the northwest were translated into Greek, a European language, and Aramaic, a western Asian language, because the local population spoke both languages.

Ashoka drafted short, medium, and lengthy versions of each edict so that his local officials could decide which one to use. Officials sometimes left out passages from the original to save space, Ashoka realized, and the officials at Kalinga did not even put up the text cited at the beginning of this chapter about Ashoka's bloody conquest of the region, possibly because they did not want to antagonize the local population.

The inscriptions report that Ashoka sent officials to inspect outlying regions every three to five years. He claims to have built new roads, along which his men planted trees and dug wells, and he encouraged his officials to discover new medicinal herbs and plant them where they had not previously been cultivated. Ashoka and the other Mauryan rulers did not mint their own coins; rulers in each locality did.

Ruling by Example: The Ceremonial State

Ashoka was the first major Indian ruler to support Buddhism. The ideal ruler followed Buddhist teachings and made donations to the Buddhist order, which he did not join. Nor did he renounce his family. The Buddhists called such a ruler a *chakravartin* (chuh-kruh-VAR-tin), literally "turner of the wheel," a broad term indicating that the sovereign ruled over a wide territory. Although Ashoka does not use the word, his inscriptions fully express his ideal of ruling by example. Every measure he took had the same goal: to encourage his subjects to follow dharma, which he described in this way:

> There is no gift comparable to the gift of dharma, the praise of dharma, the sharing of dharma, fellowship in dharma. And this is—good behavior towards slaves and servants, obedience to mother and father, generosity towards friends, acquaintances, and relatives and towards shramanas [shrah-MUH-nuhz; Buddhists and other renunciants] and Brahmins, and abstention from killing living beings.[8]

Many subsequent rulers, particularly in South and Southeast Asia, followed Ashoka's example.

Historians call this type of rule a **"ceremonial state"** to contrast it with empires in which rulers exercised more direct control. The ruler of a ceremonial state sponsored religious observances and contributed money for the construction of religious edifices in the hope that his subjects would recognize his generosity and willingly acknowledge him as their leader.

Ashoka's inscriptions permit us to see how his devotion to Buddhism increased over time. Before the battle of Kalinga (discussed at the beginning of the chapter) in 260 B.C.E., he was not yet a Buddhist, and so he was able to lead his armies into battle and kill thousands of enemy soldiers. At the end of the battle the huge number of deaths filled him with remorse and he made a decision to follow the teachings of the Buddha. In the following year he promised to uphold the five most important precepts—not to kill, steal, commit adultery, lie, and drink alcohol—

• ceremonial state
States whose rulers sponsored religious observances and construction of religious edifices in the hope that their subjects would willingly acknowledge them as rulers. Usually contrasted with rulers who depended on sheer force to govern.

The First Sermon of the Buddha and Ashoka's Fourth Major Rock Edict

After gaining enlightenment under the Tree of Wisdom at Bodh Gaya, the Buddha preached his first sermon at the Deer Park at Benares. The Buddha's sermon presented the main teachings of Buddhism in a capsule form that could be translated into other languages when Buddhism spread beyond India to East and Southeast Asia. Because the language is easy to understand, this would have worked well as a spoken sermon, with repetition of important concepts to ensure the comprehension of his five followers, or bhikkhus (BEAK-kooz), whom he addressed. This text was transmitted orally by Buddhists in north India. Hundreds of monks met, first following the Buddha's death and then one hundred years later, to make sure that they were reciting the standard version of the sermon. The text was committed to writing only in the first century B.C.E. by monks in modern-day Sri Lanka, evidence that Buddhism had spread to south India and beyond by that time.

The Fourth Major Rock Edict provides a summary of Ashoka's beliefs. Some overlap with the Buddha's teachings in the First Sermon, while others differ. Although Ashoka himself embraced Buddhism, he reached out to both Buddhist and non-Buddhist subjects by erecting pillar and rock throughout India (see page 78). The location of his edicts provides a rough indication of how far Buddhist teachings reached during his reign.

Sources: Walpola Sri Rahula, *What the Buddha Taught* (New York: Grove Press, 1974), pp. 92–94; Romila Thapar, *Aśoka and the Decline of the Mauryas* (Delhi: Oxford University Press, 1973), pp. 251–252. (Some changes in spelling and capitalization made for the sake of consistency.)

The First Sermon of the Buddha

Thus I have heard. The Blessed One was once living in the Deer Park at Isipatana (the Resort of Seers) near Varanasi (Benares). There he addressed the group of five bhikkhus:

Bhikkhus, these two extremes ought not to be practiced by one who has gone forth from the household life. What are the two? There is devotion to the indulgence of sense-pleasures, which is low, common, the way of ordinary people, unworthy and unprofitable; and there is devotion to self-mortification, which is painful, unworthy and unprofitable.

Avoiding both these extremes, the Tathagatha [the Buddha] has realized the Middle Path: it gives vision, it gives knowledge, and it leads to calm, to insight, to enlightenment, to nirvana. And what is that Middle Path . . . ? It is simply the Noble Eightfold Path, namely, right view, right thought, right speech, right action, right livelihood, right effort, right mindfulness, right concentration. . . .

The Noble Truth of suffering (*dukkha*) is this: Birth is suffering; aging is suffering; sickness is suffering; death is suffering; sorrow and lamentation, pain, grief and despair are suffering; association with the unpleasant is suffering; dissociation from the pleasant is suffering; not to get what one wants is suffering—in brief, the five aggregates of attachment are suffering.

The Noble Truth of the origin of suffering is this: It is this thirst (craving) which produces re-existence and re-becoming, bound up with passionate greed. It finds fresh delight now here and now there, namely, thirst for sense-pleasures; thirst for existence and becoming; and thirst for non-existence (self-annihilation).

The Noble Truth of the cessation of suffering is this: It is the complete cessation of that very thirst, giving it up, renouncing it, emancipating oneself from it, detaching oneself from it.

The Noble Truth of the path leading to the cessation of suffering is this: It is simply the Noble Eightfold Path, namely right view; right thought; right speech, right action; right livelihood; right effort; right mindfulness; right concentration.

"This is the Noble Truth of Suffering (*dukkha*)"; such was the vision, the knowledge, the wisdom, the science, the light, that arose in me with regard to things not heard before. "This suffering, as a noble truth, should be fully understood"; such was the vision, the knowledge, the wisdom, the science, the light, that arose in me with regard to things not heard before. "This suffering, as a noble truth, has been fully understood"; such was the vision, the knowledge, the wisdom, the science, the light, that arose in me with regard to things not heard before. . . .

As long as my vision of true knowledge was not fully clear . . . regarding the Four Noble Truths, I did not claim to have realized the per-

fect Enlightenment that is supreme in the world. . . . But when my vision of true knowledge was fully clear . . . regarding the Four Noble Truths, then I claimed to have the perfect Enlightenment that is supreme in the world. . . . And a vision of true knowledge arose in me thus: My heart's deliverance is unassailable. This is the last birth. Now there is no more re-becoming (rebirth).

This the Blessed One said. The group of five bhikkhus was glad, and they rejoiced at his words.

The Fourth Major Rock Edict

In the past, the killing and injuring of living beings, lack of respect towards relatives, Brahmins and shramanas had increased. But today, thanks to the practice of dharma on the part of the Beloved of the Gods, the king Ashoka, the sound of the drum has become the sound of dharma, showing the people displays of heavenly chariots, elephants, balls of fire, and other divine forms. Through his instruction in dharma abstention from killing and non-injury to living beings, deference to relatives, Brahmins and shramanas, obedience to mother and father, and obedience to elders have all increased as never before for many centuries. These and many other forms of the practice of dharma have increased and will increase.

The Beloved of the Gods, the king Ashoka, his sons, his grandsons and his great grandsons will advance the practice of dharma, until the end of the world and will instruct in the law, standing firm in dharma. For this, the instruction in the law, is the most valuable activity. But there is no practice of dharma without goodness, and in these matters it is good to progress and not to fall back. For this purpose, the inscription has been engraved—that men should make progress in this matter, and not be satisfied with their shortcomings. This was engraved here when the Beloved of the Gods, the king Ashoka, had been consecrated twelve years.

QUESTIONS FOR ANALYSIS

▶ What are the Four Noble Truths taught by the Buddha, and what is the relationship among them?

▶ What are the signs that the First Sermon was transmitted orally?

▶ Which Buddhist teachings did Ashoka think most important? What did he mean by dharma?

and became a lay Buddhist (*upasaka*). Anyone could become a lay Buddhist; one simply had to vow to uphold the five precepts and then continue in one's normal profession while living with one's family. Four distinct groups formed the early Buddhist order: monks and nuns were ordained, while male and female lay Buddhists were not.

In the tenth year of his reign, around 258 B.C.E., Ashoka visited the site at Bodh Gaya where the Buddha had gained enlightenment and decided to increase his devotion to Buddhism even further. Presumably along with learned Buddhists, he conducted a series of meetings with non-Buddhist "ascetics" engaged in different austerities, as well as with Brahmin priests, who continued to sacrifice animals. Ashoka discussed the teachings of the Buddha and gave them gifts to encourage them to convert to Buddhism. He used the same combination of persuasion and gift giving with elderly people and with ordinary people in the countryside. (See the feature "Movement of Ideas: The First Sermon of the Buddha and Ashoka's Fourth Major Rock Edict.")

Ashoka visited the Deer Park in Benares as well as the site of the Buddha's birth in present-day Nepal, where he built a stone fence and erected a stone pillar in memory of the Buddha. Another legend records that, as a sign of his devotion to Buddhism, Ashoka paid for the construction of 84,000 stupas, none of which survive, and later Buddhist rulers often emulated him by building monuments to express their devotion to Buddhism.

Ashoka's style of governing was very personal. One inscription describes how seriously he took the business of ruling and explains that his officials were free to interrupt him with public business no matter what he was doing. "And whatever I may order by word of mouth, whether it concerns a donation or a proclamation, or whatever urgent matter is entrusted to my officers, if there is any dispute or deliberation about it in the Council, it is to be reported to me immediately, at all places and all times." We learn that some officers could speak directly to the king and that there was a council, but not how it functioned.

Ashoka claimed to exercise influence over lands far from north India because of his support for dharma:

> The Beloved of the Gods considers victory by dharma to be the foremost victory. And moreover the Beloved of the Gods has gained this victory on all his frontiers to a distance of six hundred yojanas [about 1,500 miles, or 2400 km], where reigns the Greek king Antiochus [in Syria], and beyond the realm of that Antiochus in the lands of four kings named Ptolemy [in Egypt], Antigonus [in Macedonia], Magas [of Cyrene], and Alexander [of Epirus]; and in the south over the Colas and the Pandyas as far as Ceylon.

This inscription, composed between 256 and 254 B.C.E., claims that Ashoka had brought about "victory by dharma" far beyond his frontiers, as far west as the realms of Greek rulers in Egypt and Greece, and as far south as the island of Ceylon, modern Sri Lanka. Modern scholars concur that he may have sent missionaries, particularly to Sri Lanka, where oral accounts record their names. Otherwise, there is no independent evidence of Buddhism spreading outside the Indian subcontinent in Ashoka's reign.

We must keep in mind that Ashoka wrote his inscriptions and had them carved into huge, dramatic monuments to remind his subjects that he had the right to rule over them. The only external confirmation of their veracity comes from later Buddhist sources, which mention Ashoka's devotion to Buddhism. If

Ashoka had violated his Buddhist vows, or if a certain region had risen up in rebellion during his reign, we can be sure that the inscriptions would not mention it. One recent analysis suggests that the inscriptions not be seen "as solid blocks of historical fact, but as flightier pieces of political propaganda, as the campaign speeches of an incumbent politician who seeks not so much to record events as to present an image of himself and his administration to the world."[9]

After Ashoka's death in 232 B.C.E., the Mauryan Empire began to break apart; the Mauryans lost control of the last remaining section, the Ganga Valley, around 185 B.C.E. Few documents survive from this time. Historians wonder if the central government was unable to raise the funds it needed to support its sizable army, without which it could not control the massive territory that Chandragupta and Ashoka had conquered. A series of regional kingdoms gained control, as was the usual pattern for much of South Asian history.

● South Asia's External Trade

India's geographic proximity to western Asia meant that outsiders came to South Asia in very early times, and, conversely, Indian culture, particularly Buddhist teachings, traveled out from India on the same paths. In ancient times travelers seeking to enter South Asia had a choice of routes. Although the Himalaya Mountains in the north and extensive mountains in the northeast prevented large-scale overland trade, regular cultural contacts and the movement of valuable goods always remained possible. Land routes through the Hindu Kush (HIHN-doo KOOSH) in the northwest, including the Khyber (KAI-ber) Pass, allowed more extensive contacts between South Asia and Central Asia through what is today Afghanistan. These are the routes that allowed the expansion of Indo-European languages and that Megasthenes used when he came to India.

However, the most important mode of communication between South Asia and the rest of the world was by sea. By 100 C.E., if not earlier, mariners from South and Southeast Asia had learned to capture the monsoon winds blowing northeast in the spring and early summer, and southwest in the fall and winter, to carry on regular commerce and cultural interaction with Southwest Asia and Africa. Finds of Harappan artifacts in the archaeological assemblages of early Sumer testify to the importance and age of these ancient sea routes.

Because no written descriptions of the ancient trade exist, archaeologists must reconstruct the trade on the basis of excavated commodities. Natural reserves of the semiprecious blue stone lapis lazuli exist only in the Badakhshan (BAH-duck-shan) region of northern Afghanistan, so we know that, by 2600 B.C.E., if not earlier, trade routes linked Badakhshan with ancient Sumer, where much lapis lazuli has been found. Similarly, the red-orange semiprecious stone carnelian traveled from mines in Gujarat (GOO-juh-ruht), India, to Mesopotamian sites. The presence of Harappan seals and clay pots at Sumer reveals that the trade included manufactured goods as well as minerals. These goods traveled overland or by boat down the Indus River to the Arabian Sea, where they hugged the coast as they traveled west to the Persian Gulf. Ancient sea routes across the Indian Ocean connected India with Mesopotamia, the Arabian Peninsula, and East Africa (see the map on page 61).

● **dhows** Small sailboats used in the Indian Ocean made from teak planks laid edge to edge, fastened together with coconut fiber twine, and caulked to prevent leaking.

The monsoon winds changed direction two times a year, so if one caught them going west on a summer departure, one could return in the following winter as they blew east. They varied enormously in their intensity. Merchants traveling in the Indian Ocean usually sailed in small boats called **dhows.** Dhows (DOWZ) were made from teak planks laid edge to edge, fastened together with coconut fiber twine, and then caulked to prevent leaking. This method of construction gave them greater flexibility during storms than boats made from nailed wooden planks.

We learn much about the Indian Ocean trade during the first century C.E. from an unusual work called the *Periplus* (PAY-rih-plus) (literally "around the globe"), written in colloquial Greek not by a scholar but by an anonymous merchant living in Egypt around 50 C.E. By the first century C.E., navigators from Egypt had learned how to harness the monsoon winds and travel by boat to India. The *Periplus* describes the routes sailors took and the goods they traded at Indian ports.

Written explicitly for merchants, the *Periplus* is organized as a guidebook: port by port, down the East African coast, around the Arabian Peninsula, and then to India. One-quarter of the book describes the trade with East Africa, one-quarter with Arabia, and one-half with India, the most important trading destination. In African and Arabian ports sailors could purchase ivory or gum resins like frankincense and myrrh, which were prized for their fragrance, but India offered far more goods than either Arabia or Africa. The author says almost nothing about social structure and little about government, other than the names of local rulers; he is much more interested in which commodities were for sale.

Analyzed carefully, however, the descriptions in the *Periplus* have much to tell us. For example, it summarizes the import trade on India's southwestern Malabar (MAH-lah-bar) coast. At the markets one could buy a yellow gem called peridot (PAY-ree-doh), clothing and textiles, coral, raw glass, copper, tin, lead, and wine. The author instructs his readers to bring money, and lots of it, to the southwestern coast because there were few opportunities for barter. Thousands of Roman silver and gold coins have been found on the south coast but not farther north, suggesting that the traders could barter in the north but had to pay Roman coins in the south (see Chapter 7, "The Roman Empire and the Rise of Christianity"). The author continues his discussion of the southwest coast by explaining the goods the region exported. Most of the items on the list, like pepper, pearls, ivory, and precious stones, are valuable even today, and nard and malabathron (MAH-la-bath-ruhn) were two indigenous plants used for their fragrance or as ingredients in drugs.

Aimed at non-Indian readers, the *Periplus* gives the misleading impression that the Indian Ocean trade was controlled by foreigners, possibly because its author was a Greek living in Egypt who used Roman coins to purchase Indian goods. In fact, though, Indian merchants played an active role in the Indian Ocean trade.

The author offers much briefer descriptions of the ports on the east coast of South Asia because foreign ships were too big to travel through the shallow channels separating India from Sri Lanka. Greek and Roman geographers exaggerated the size of Sri Lanka for centuries because no one had actually sailed around the island. At the end of the *Periplus,* the author describes one final destination:

> Beyond this region, by now at the northernmost point, where the sea ends somewhere on the outer fringe, there is a very great inland city called Thina from which silk floss, yarn, and cloth are shipped by land . . . and via the

Ganga River. . . . It is not easy to get to this Thina; for rarely do people come from it, and only a few.[10]

Thina? The spelling makes sense when one realizes that ancient Greek had no letter for the sound "ch," so the author had to choose either a "th" or an "s" for the first letter of the place whose name he heard from Indian traders. He opted for Thina. We cannot be sure how the word was pronounced in local ports, but *China* was pronounced "CHEE-na" in Sanskrit (and is the source of our English word *China*).

The author thought Thina was a city, not a country, but he knew that silk was made there and exported in three forms: yarn, floss, and woven cloth. The *Periplus* closes with the admission that China lay at the extreme edge of the world known to the Greeks: "What lies beyond this area, because of extremes of storm, bitter cold, and difficult terrain and also because of some divine power of the gods, has not been explored." The India described in the *Periplus,* then, was a major trade center linking the familiar Roman Empire with the dimly understood China.

Chapter Review

(CL) Download the MP3 audio file of the Chapter Review and listen to it on the go.

Between 2600 B.C.E. and 100 C.E. South Asia was seldom unified, and, even during the rare intervals when a ruler like Ashoka managed to conquer a large amount of territory, their rule was decentralized, granting much authority to local rulers. Yet political disunity did not result in cultural disunity. Different cultural elements, particularly Vedic religion and Buddhism, bound together the people living under various rulers in different regions.

🐘 ### What evidence survives of social stratification at the Indus Valley sites? How did the Indo-Aryans describe the social stratification in their society?

At the time of the Indus Valley society (2600–1700 B.C.E.), people lived in enormous cities with clear evidence of social stratification. The wealthy occupied bigger houses than the poor, and when dead, graves with more goods. Because the Indus Valley writing system is still undeciphered, we do not know exactly how the people conceived of these social differences.

Written evidence survives from one of the great mass migrations of antiquity, sometime between 1500 and 1000, when the Indo-Aryans entered north India. The Indo-Aryans created a forerunner of the modern caste system, ranking different occupational groups. The late hymns of the *Rig Veda*, dating perhaps to 1000 B.C.E., equate four social groups, called varna, with parts of a mythic body: at the top, Brahmins form the mouth; warriors, the arms; farmers and merchants, the

KEY TERMS

Ashoka (60)

dharma (60)

monsoon (63)

Indus River Valley (64)

Sanskrit (66)

Rig Veda (66)

Vedic religion (68)

nomads (68)

varna (68)

jati (69)

Buddha (71)

nirvana (72)

Mauryan dynasty (76)

ceremonial state (79)

dhows (84)

thighs; and servants, the feet. Today, we may not understand all the details of the ancient caste system, but we know that different people, even within South Asia, understood it in various ways and that it evolved over time.

 ### What were the main teachings of the Buddha?

The Buddha founded a religion that challenged the caste system and the primacy of Brahmin priests, who had been so influential in Vedic times. He taught that one could escape the sufferings of this life by adhering to the Four Noble Truths. His new religion welcomed members of all social groups, and merchants found the religion particularly appealing because they could improve their social position by making large donations to the Buddhist order.

 ### Why did Ashoka believe that supporting Buddhism would strengthen the Mauryan state?

Ashoka made extensive donations to the Buddhist order because he wanted to fulfill the Buddhist ideal of the chakravartin ruler. As the ruler of a ceremonial state, Ashoka led by example: he sponsored religious observances and contributed money to build Buddhist structures in the hope that his subjects would support his Mauryan Dynasty. This style of ruling influenced later dynasties.

Ashoka, unlike any South Asian ruler before or since, erected stone pillars bearing his inscriptions through his empire. Uncannily, some forty years later, the founder of the Qin dynasty (r. 221–210 B.C.E.) in China also carved royal pronouncements on gigantic rocks throughout his empire, as we shall see in the next chapter.

 ### Who were the main actors in the Indian Ocean trade? What types of ships did they use? Along which routes? To trade which commodities?

Though separated from the rest of Eurasia by high mountains, India in ancient times traded goods and ideas with people far to the west. Carnelian and lapis lazuli from South Asia have been found all over Mesopotamia and Egypt, evidence of active trade networks linking South Asia to the outside world in at least 2600 B.C.E., and the trade continued long after the collapse of the Mauryans at the end of the second century B.C.E. Traders, both foreign and Indian, sailed to the ports of the Indian Ocean in dhows and purchased semiprecious stones, metals, spices, and textiles. Few traveled beyond India to China.

For Further Reference

Basham, A. L. *The Wonder That Was India: Survey of the Culture of the Indian Sub-continent Before the Coming of the Muslims.* New York: Grove Press, 1959.

Casson, Lionel. *The Periplus Maris Erythraei Text with Introduction, Translation, and Commentary.* Princeton: Princeton University Press, 1989.

Elder, Joe. "India's Caste System." *Education About Asia* 1, no. 2 (1996): 20–22.

Fussman, Gerard. "Central and Provincial Administration in Ancient India: The Problem of the Mauryan Empire." *Indian Historical Review* 14 (1987–1988): 43–72.

Kenoyer, Mark. *Ancient Cities of the Indus Valley Civilization.* Karachi: Oxford University Press, 1998.

Liu, Xinru. *Ancient India and Ancient China: Trade and Religious Exchanges, A.D. 1–600.* Delhi: Oxford University Press, 1988.

O'Flaherty, Wendy Doniger. *The Rig Veda: An Anthology.* New York: Penguin Books, 1981.

Pearson, Michael. *The Indian Ocean.* New York: Routledge, 2003.

Thapar, Romila. *Aśoka and the Decline of the Mauryas.* Delhi: Oxford University Press, 1973.

Thapar, Romila. *Early India: From the Origins to AD 1300.* Berkeley: University of California Press, 2003.

Websites

Homepage of the Wales Professor of Sanskrit, Harvard: Michael Witzel (http://www.people.fas.harvard.edu/~witzel/mwpage.htm). Information on various topics in ancient Indian history, including Harappan society.

An Introduction to Buddhism (http://webspace.ship.edu/cgboer/buddhaintro.html). Detailed information on Buddhism and Buddha from a faculty member at Shippensburg University, Pennsylvania.

Sanchi (Madhya Pradesh) Berger Foundation (http://www.bergerfoundation.ch/wat4/museum1?museum=Sanchi&col=pays&country=Inde&genre=%&cd=7256-3191-2328:7256-3191-2325:7256-3191-2326&cdindex=1). Excellent collection of sharp, clear photographs from Sanchi.

Films

The Little Buddha.

 WEB RESOURCES

Pronunciation Guide

Interactive Maps

MAP 3.1 Indus River Valley Society

MAP 3.2 Distribution of Languages in Modern South Asia

Primary Sources

Chapter Objectives

ACE Multiple-Choice Quiz

Flashcards

Blueprint for Empire: China, 1200 B.C.E.– 220 C.E.

In 221 B.C.E., the **First Emperor of the Qin dynasty** (259–210 B.C.E.) united China for the first time and implemented a blueprint for empire that helped to keep China united for much of the following two thousand years. Born in the Qin (CHIN) territory in the town of Xianyang (SHYEN-yahng) in Shaanxi (SHAHN-shee) province, western China, the future emperor was named Zheng (JUHNG). Prince Zheng's father, one of more than twenty sons of a regional ruler in west China, lived as a hostage in the eastern city of Handan (HAHN-dahn) because it was customary for younger sons to be sent to the courts of allied rulers. Two years after Zheng's birth, during an attack on Handan, his father escaped home, and his mother and the young prince went into hiding. Six years later they returned to Xianyang, and in 246 B.C.E., on the death of his father, Prince Zheng ascended to the Qin throne at the age of 13. For the first nine years he governed with the help of adult advisers until he became ruler in his own right at the age of 22.

During his reign he went on five different expeditions. At the top of each mountain he climbed, he erected a stone tablet describing his many accomplishments and asserting widespread support for his dynasty. One of these tablets read as follows:

FIRST EMPEROR OF THE QIN DYNASTY

(British Library, London/HIP/Art Resource, NY)

In His twenty-sixth year [221 B.C.E.]
He first unified All under Heaven—
There was none who was not respectful and submissive.
He personally tours the distant multitudes,
Ascends this Grand Mountain
And all round surveys the world at the eastern extremity. . . .
May later ages respect and follow the decrees He bequeaths
And forever accept His solemn warnings.[1]

 This icon will direct you to interactive activities and study materials on the *Voyages* website:
www.cengage.com/history/hansen/voyages1e

88

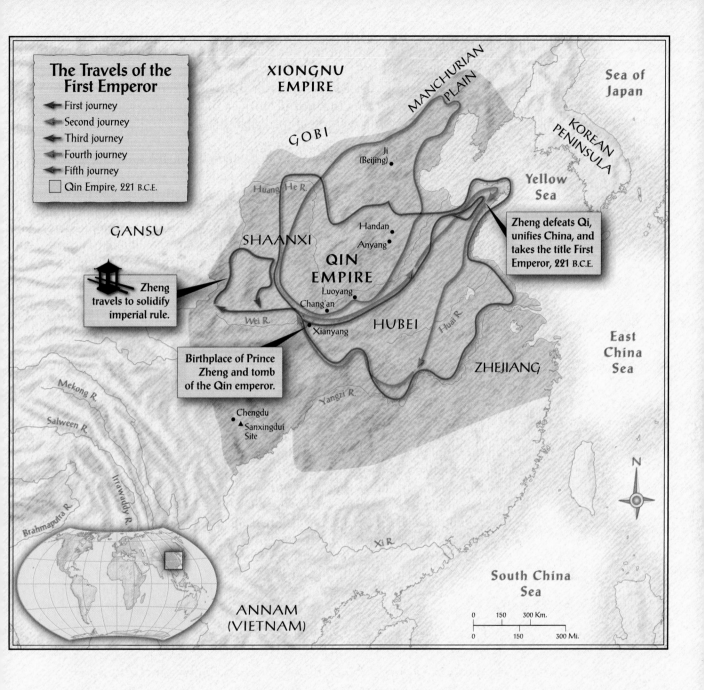

The Travels of the First Emperor

← First journey
← Second journey
← Third journey
← Fourth journey
← Fifth journey
☐ Qin Empire, 221 B.C.E.

XIONGNU EMPIRE

Sea of Japan

GOBI

MANCHURIAN PLAIN

KOREAN PENINSULA

Ji (Beijing)

Huang He R.

Yellow Sea

GANSU

SHAANXI

Handan

Anyang

QIN EMPIRE

Zheng defeats Qi, unifies China, and takes the title First Emperor, 221 B.C.E.

Zheng travels to solidify imperial rule.

Luoyang

Chang'an

Wei R.

Xianyang

HUBEI

Huai R.

ZHEJIANG

East China Sea

Birthplace of Prince Zheng and tomb of the Qin emperor.

Yangzi R.

Mekong R.

Salween R.

Chengdu

▲ Sanxingdui Site

Irrawaddy R.

Brahmaputra R.

Xi R.

N

South China Sea

ANNAM (VIETNAM)

| 0 | 150 | 300 Km. |
| 0 | 150 | 300 Mi. |

| 1200 B.C.E. | ••• 600 | 400 | 200 | 1 C.E. | 200 C.E. |

Lifetime of First Emperor
259 210

Shang dynasty (from 1766)

Zhou dynasty
1045

Wang Mang interregnum

POLITICS AND WAR

Shang Yang's reforms
359

Qin dynasty
221 | 207

256   206

Han dynasty

Reign of Emperor Wu 140–87

9 23

220

Qin legal texts 217

RELIGION AND CULTURE

Earliest surviving writing on oracle bones
1200

Lifetime of Confucius
551   479

First money circulates
ca. 500

Earliest Daoist texts
ca. 300

Invention of paper
ca. 150

Imperial Academy founded
124

Lifetime of Ban Zhao
ca. 45   120

● **First Emperor of the Qin dynasty**
Founder of the Qin dynasty (221–207 B.C.E.) and the first ruler to unify ancient China. Eliminated regional differences by creating a single body of law and standardizing weights and measures.

The new emperor traveled overland in a sedan-chair carried by his servants and along rivers by boat. By the time he finished his last journey, he had criss-crossed much of the territory north of the Yangzi (YAHNG-zuh) River in modern-day China.

His unusual childhood must have affected Prince Zheng, but surviving sources convey little about his personality except to document his single-minded ambition. For the next fifteen years, he led the Qin armies on a series of brilliant military campaigns. They fought with the same weapons as their enemies—crossbows, bronze armor, shields, and daggers—but their army was organized as a meritocracy. A skilled soldier, no matter how low-ranking his parents, could rise to become a general, while the son of a noble family, if not a good fighter, would remain a common foot soldier for life.

The Qin was the first dynasty to vanquish all of its rivals, including six independent kingdoms, and unite China under a single person's rule. The First Emperor eliminated regional differences by creating a single body of law for all his subjects, standardizing all weights and measures, and even mandating a standard axle width for the ox- and horse-drawn carts. He coined a new title, *First Emperor* (*Shi Huangdi*), because he felt that the word *king* did not accurately convey his august position. The First Emperor intentionally stayed remote from his subjects so that they would respect and obey him.

On his deathbed, the First Emperor urged that his descendants rule forever, or "ten thousand years" in Chinese phrasing. Instead, peasant uprisings brought his dynasty to an end in three years. The succeeding dynasty, the Han dynasty (see below), denounced the Qin but used Qin governance to rule for four centuries. Subsequent Chinese rulers who aspired to reunify the empire always looked to the Han as their model. Unlike India, which remained politically disunited for most of its history, the Chinese empire endured for over two thousand years. Whenever it fell apart, a new emperor put it back together.

Focus Questions

 What different elements of Chinese civilization took shape between 1200 and 221 B.C.E.?

 What were the most important measures in the Qin blueprint for empire?

 How did the Han rulers modify the Qin blueprint, particularly regarding administrative structure and the recruitment and promotion of officials?

 Which neighboring peoples in Central, East, and Southeast Asia did the Han dynasty conquer? Why was the impact of Chinese rule limited?

The Origins of Chinese Civilization, 1200–221 B.C.E.

Agriculture developed independently in several different regions in China circa 7000 B.C.E. In each region, as was true elsewhere in the world (see Chapters 2 and 3), people began to harvest seeds on an occasional basis before progressing to full-time agriculture. By 1200 B.C.E., several independent cultural centers had emerged. One, the Shang (SHAHNG) kingdom based in the Yellow River Valley, developed the Chinese writing system. Many elements of Chinese civilization— the writing system, the worship of ancestors, and the Confucian and Daoist systems of belief—developed in the years before China was united in 221 B.C.E.

The First Agriculture, 7000–1200 B.C.E.

North China was particularly suited for early agriculture because a fine layer of yellow dirt, called loess (less), covers the entire Yellow River Valley, and few trees grow there. The Yellow River carries large quantities of loess from the west and deposits new layers each year in the last 500 miles (900 km) before the Pacific Ocean. As a result, the riverbed is constantly rising, often to a level higher than the surrounding fields. Sometimes called "China's River of Sorrow," the Yellow River has exhibited a dangerous tendency to flood throughout recorded history.

Three major climatic zones extend east and west across China (see the map on page 89). Less than 20 inches (50 cm) of rainfall each year falls on the region north of the Huai (HWHY) River; about 40 inches (1 m) per year drops on the middle band along the Yangzi River; and over 80 inches (2 m) a year pours on the southernmost band of China, including Guangzhou (GWAHNG-joe) and Hong Kong. This differential pattern of rainfall is due to the monsoon winds off the ocean: the water-laden winds first cross south China, where they drop much of their water; by the time they reach the north, they are carrying much less water. The climate of the Yellow River was probably hotter and wetter than it is today. Elephants and rhinoceros both lived there as late as 1000 B.C.E.

Agriculture was not limited to the Yellow River Valley. Wheat and millet cultivation extended as far north as Manchuria and as far south as Zhejiang (JEH-jeeahng), near the mouth of China's other great river, the Yangzi. The peoples living farther south raised rice; some hunted and gathered while others depended on agriculture. The different implements found in various regions suggest great cultural diversity within China between 7000 and 2000 B.C.E.

These different peoples evolved from small, egalitarian tribal groups who farmed intermittently to larger settled groups with clearly demarcated social levels living in large urban settlements, demonstrating all the elements of civilization described in Chapter 2. A given people can be identified as Chinese when they use Chinese characters, because only then can archaeologists be certain that they spoke Chinese. Some pots dating to circa 2000 B.C.E. are illustrated with different pictures, but these were probably potters' marks and not written characters (see Chapter 2 about first writing).

Early Chinese Writing in the Shang Dynasty, ca. 1200 B.C.E.

The first identifiable Chinese characters appeared on bones dating to around 1200 B.C.E. The discovery and deciphering of these bones mark one of the great intellectual breakthroughs in twentieth-century China. In 1899 the city of Beijing experienced an outbreak of malaria for which there was no known cure. In desperation the city's residents turned to an untried remedy: so-called dragon bones. When a scholar examined one of these bones, he realized that the scratchy lines on it were not magical symbols but vestiges of writing. The bones came from near the modern city of Anyang (AHN-yahng) in the central Chinese province of Henan (HUH-nahn), the core region of China's first historic dynasty, the **Shang dynasty** (1766–1045 B.C.E.).

Scholars call the excavated bones **"oracle bones"** because the Shang ruler used them to forecast the future. Like many ancient peoples around the world who used oracles to consult higher powers, the Shang placed a heated poker on cattle shoulder blades and turtle shell bottoms, or plastrons, and interpreted the resulting cracks. They then recorded on the bone the name of the ancestor they had consulted, the topic of inquiry, and the outcome. It was an extremely difficult feat, and we still do not know how the ancient Chinese incised characters on these bones with the bronze tools available to them.

◼ The Earliest Records of Chinese Writing

Starting around 1200 B.C.E., ancient Chinese kings used the clavicle bones of cattle (as shown here) and the bottom of turtle shells to ask their ancestors to advise them on the outcomes of future events, including battles, sacrifices, their wives' pregnancies, and even their own toothaches. After applying heat, the fortunetellers interpreted the resulting cracks and wrote their predictions—in the most ancient form of Chinese characters—directly on the bones and turtle shells.   (Lowell Georgia/Corbis)

Since 1900 over 200,000 oracle bones, both whole and fragmented, have been excavated in China. The quantities are immense, with 1,300 oracle bones concerning rainfall in a single king's reign, and their language is grammatically complex, suggesting that the Shang scribes had been writing for some time, possibly on perishable materials like wood. Scholars have deciphered the bones by comparing the texts with one another and with the earliest known characters. Shang dynasty characters, like their modern equivalents, have two elements: a radical, which suggests the broad field of meaning, and a phonetic symbol, which indicates sound. Like Arabic numerals, Chinese characters retain the same meaning even if pronounced differently: 3 means the number "three" even if some readers say "trois" or "drei."

During the Shang dynasty only the king and his scribes could read and write characters. Presenting the world from the king's vantage point, some oracle bones treat affairs of state, like the outcomes of battles, but many more touch on individual matters, such as his wife's pregnancy or his own aching teeth. The major religion of the time was **ancestor worship.** The Shang kings believed that their recently dead ancestors could intercede with the more powerful long-dead on behalf of the living. They conducted frequent rituals in which they offered food and drink to the ancestors in the hope of receiving help.

The Use of Component Parts in Chinese Food

Have you ever wondered how even a small Chinese food stand staffed by a single person quickly turns out so many distinctive dishes? Using a technique developed in at least 1200 B.C.E., if not before, chefs in today's Chinese restaurants combine component parts in various ways to produce a slightly different product each time. They start with a variety of precut meats and vegetables. When a customer gives the order for chicken in peanut sauce, the chef tosses chicken cubes and peppers into a wok, stir-fries them, and adds sauce as the final touch. The chef modifies the same technique to cook precut meat and vegetables in an array of sauces to make a large number of dishes, each with a different name and recognizable taste.

Chinese people eat these dishes with an accompanying starch, usually white rice in south China and noodles, dumplings, or wheat gruel in the north. Since the beginnings of agriculture, people in north China have eaten millet and wheat as their main starches, while those living in south China have almost always eaten rice.

This division between dishes and starch gave Chinese cuisine great flexibility. The poor could eat a single vegetable dish with whatever starch was cheapest, and the Chinese even developed labor-intensive recipes, like boiled almond shells, for normally inedible foods that could be prepared during famines. The rich could eat many dishes made from expensive delicacies with only a small amount of starch. However, even today, the most lavish banquets end with a bowl of plain white rice.

Shang dynasty cooks used many of the same tools as today's cooks—knives, stirring utensils, and bronze cooking pots. However, rather than stir-frying, they steamed and braised food. Those who presided over Shang rituals used chopsticks, one of the hallmarks of East Asian culture, to move food from large serving vessels to smaller plates. People then ate the food with their hands. Ordinary diners began to use chopsticks as eating utensils sometime around 200 B.C.E., the time of the first stir-fried food.

The peoples living in China used two types of vessels: flat bronze vessels for grain (usually wheat or millet) and baskets and wooden and pottery vessels for meat and vegetables. The division between starch and dishes made from cut-up meat and vegetables continues to the present day: Chinese chefs always prepare the starch separately from the meat and vegetable dishes. (See the feature "World History in Today's World: The Use of Component Parts in Chinese Food.")

Historians of China have ingeniously combined the information in oracle bones with careful analysis of Shang archaeological sites to piece together the outlines of early Chinese history. Like the Mesopotamians, the early Chinese lived inside walled cities. They mastered the exacting technology of mixing copper, tin, and lead in differing ratios to cast impressive bronze vessels. The earliest bronze vessels, from circa 2000 B.C.E., predate the first writing, but bronze-casting techniques reached full maturity around 1200 B.C.E. Ancient Chinese bronze casters made ritual vessels, farm implements, mirrors, chariot fittings, and daggers.

● oracle bones The earliest surviving written records in China, scratched onto cattle shoulder blades and turtle shell bottoms, or plastrons. These record the diviners' interpretations of the future.

● ancestor worship The belief in China that dead ancestors could intercede in human affairs on behalf of the living. Marked by frequent rituals in which the living offered food and drink to the ancestors in the hope of receiving help.

Shang Dynasty Relations with Other Peoples

Oracle bones have allowed scholars to understand how Shang government and society functioned between 1200 and 1000 B.C.E. Until then, the main source for early Chinese history was a book entitled *Records of the Grand Historian,* written by **Sima Qian** (SUH-mah CHEE-EN) (145– ca. 90 B.C.E.) in the first century B.C.E. Combining information drawn from several extant chronicles, Sima Qian wrote a history of China from its legendary founding sage emperors through to his lifetime. He gave the founding date of the Shang dynasty as 1766 B.C.E. and listed the names of the Shang kings but provided little detail about them. Setting a pattern for all future historians, Sima Qian believed that there could be only one legitimate ruler of China at any time and omitted any discussion of regional rulers who coexisted with the Shang and other dynasties.

In fact, though, the Shang exercised direct control over a relatively small area, some 125 miles (200 km) from east to west, and the Shang king sometimes traveled as far as 400 miles (650 km) away to fight enemy peoples. Beyond the small area under direct Shang control lived many different non-Shang peoples whose names appear on the oracle bones but about whom little is known. Shang kings did not have a fixed capital but simply moved camp from one place to another to conduct military campaigns against these other peoples.

◼ **Early Chinese Bronze-working** The ancient Chinese combined copper, tin, and lead to make intricate bronze vessels like this wine container, which dates to circa 1050 B.C.E. and was found buried in the hills of Hunan, in southern China. Analysts are not sure of the relationship between the tiger-like beast and the man it embraces. The man's serene face suggests that the beast is communicating some kind of teaching—not devouring him. (Musée Cernuschi, Paris/Scala/Art Resource, NY)

Many oracle bones describe battles between the Shang and their enemies. When the Shang defeated an enemy, they took thousands of captives. The fortunate worked as laborers, and the less fortunate were killed as an offering. One oracle bone asks the ancestors' opinion about the number of human sacrifices necessary—ten? twenty? thirty?—and gives the name of the conquered people.

Shang subjects interred their kings in large tombs with hundreds of sacrificed corpses. Even in death they observed a hierarchy. Placed near the Shang king were those who accompanied him in death, with their own entourages of corpses and lavish grave goods. Royal guards were also buried intact, but the lowest-ranking corpses, most likely prisoners of war, had their heads and limbs severed.

The Shang were but one of many peoples living in China around 1200 B.C.E. Yet, since only the Shang left written records, we know much less about the other peoples. Fortunately an extraordinary archaeological find at the Sanxingdui (SAHN-shing-dway) site near Chengdu (CHUHNG-dew), in Sichuan (SUH-chwan) province, offers a glimpse of one of the peoples contemporary with the Shang. Inside the ancient city walls, archaeologists found two grave pits filled with bronze statues, bronze masks, and elephant tusks that had been burnt and cut into sections. Like the Shang, the people at the Sanxingdui site lived in small walled settlements and cast various bronze tools.

The people of Sanxingdui also made bronze masks more than a yard across with huge protruding eyes, whose significance no one can explain satisfactorily.

■ **Early Bronze-working Outside the Core of Ancient China**   Found in Sanxingdui, Sichuan, over 1,000 miles (1600 km) west of the Shang dynasty heartland, this statue looks completely different from anything made at Anyang, in the Yellow River Valley. This priest (or king or deity?) stands over 6 feet (1.8 m) tall. His enlarged hands originally held some type of round object—an elephant tusk?—and he stands on a base made from four elephant heads. Scholars now recognize that many distinct regional cultures coexisted in China at the same time as the Shang dynasty, in about 1200 B.C.E.   (Sanxingdui Museum, Guanghan, Sichuan Province/Cultural Relics Publishing, Beijing)

Whereas the Shang made no human statues, the most impressive artifact from Sanxingdui is a statue of a man. Unlike the Shang, the people at Sanxingdui do not seem to have practiced human sacrifice, nor do they appear to have had a writing system, although some archaeologists hope in the future to find samples of their writing.

The Zhou Dynasty, 1045–256 B.C.E.

The oracle bones are most plentiful during the period from 1200 to 1000 B.C.E. and diminish in quantity soon after. In 1045 B.C.E. a new dynasty, the **Zhou dynasty,** overthrew the Shang. The Grand Historian Sima Qian wrote the earliest detailed account of the Zhou (JOE) conquest in the first century B.C.E., long after the fact, and historians question his account. Claiming that 48,000 Zhou troops were able to defeat 700,000 Shang troops because the Shang ruler was corrupt and decadent, Sima Qian alleged that the last Shang ruler killed his enemies and roasted them on a rack or cut them into mincemeat before eating them.

Sima Qian's description set a pattern followed by all subsequent historians: vilifying the last emperor of the fallen dynasty and glorifying the founder of the next. According to Sima Qian, the Zhou king was able to overthrow the Shang because he had obtained the **Mandate of Heaven.** A new god, worshiped by the Zhou ruling house but not previously worshiped by the Shang, Heaven represented the generalized forces of the cosmos, rather than the abode of the dead. China's rulers believed that Heaven would send signs—terrible storms, unusual astronomical events, famines, even peasant rebellions—before withdrawing its mandate. But because the recipient of the Mandate of Heaven could only be known after the fact, it often served as a retrospective justification for overthrowing a dynasty by force.

Many other states coexisted with the Zhou dynasty (1045–256 B.C.E.), the most important being the Qin, who first unified China. The long period of Chinese history known as the Zhou dynasty is usually divided into the Western Zhou, 1045–771 B.C.E., when the capital was located in the Wei (WAY) River Valley, and the Eastern Zhou, 771–256 B.C.E., when, after defeat in battle, the Zhou rulers were forced to move east.

Throughout the long years of Zhou rule, the people writing Chinese characters gradually settled more and more territory at the expense of other peoples. Because the final centuries of the Zhou were particularly violent, the period from 481 to 221 B.C.E. is commonly called the Warring States Period. Yet constant warfare brought benefits, such as the diffusion of new technology. Iron tools spread throughout China, and people were able to use iron farm implements to plow the

●**Zhou dynasty** The successor dynasty to the Shang that gained the Mandate of Heaven and the right to rule, Chinese historians later recorded. Although depicted by later generations as an ideal age, the Zhou witnessed considerable conflict.

●**Mandate of Heaven** The Chinese belief that Heaven, the generalized forces of the cosmos (not the abode of the dead), chose the rightful ruler. China's rulers believed that Heaven would send signs before withdrawing its mandate.

land more deeply. Agricultural productivity increased, and the first money—in the shape of knives and spades but not round coins—circulated around 500 B.C.E., at roughly the same time as in India.

Changes in warfare brought massive social change. Since the time of the Shang, battles had been fought with chariots, and only boys who grew up in wealthy households had the time and the resources to learn how to guide a galloping horse pulling a chariot with three men into battle. But in the sixth and fifth centuries B.C.E., as they went farther south, armies began to fight battles in muddy terrain where chariots could not go. Instead, generals began to use large armies of foot soldiers. Some of the most successful generals were not necessarily the sons of powerful families, but those, regardless of family background, who could lead armies of ten thousand soldiers into battle. At this time ambitious young men studied strategy and general comportment with tutors, one of whom became China's most famous teacher, **Confucius** (551–479 B.C.E.).

• **Confucius** (551–479 B.C.E.) The founder of Confucianism, a teacher who made his living by tutoring students. Known only through *The Analects,* the record of conversations with his students that they recorded after his death.

Confucianism

Confucius was born in 551 B.C.E. in Shandong (SHAHN-dohng) province. His family name was Kong (KOHNG); his given name, Qiu (CHEE-OH). (*Confucius* is the English translation of *Kong Fuzi* [FOO-zuh], or Master Kong, but most Chinese refer to him as Kongzi [KOHNG-zuh], which also means Master Kong.) Acutely aware of living in a politically unstable era, Confucius was a professional teacher who lived off fees from his students. They have left us the only record of his thinking, a series of conversations he had with them, which are called *The Analects,* meaning "discussions and conversations." Recently scholars have begun to question the authenticity of the later *Analects* (especially chapters 10–20), but they agree that the first nine chapters probably date to an earlier time, perhaps just after Confucius's death in 479 B.C.E.

Confucianism is the term used for the main tenets of Confucius's thought. The optimistic tone of *The Analects* will strike any reader. Teaching students in one of the most chaotic periods in Chinese history, Confucius did not advocate violence. Instead, he emphasized the need to perform ritual correctly. Ritual is central because it allows the gentleman, the frequent recipient of Confucius's teachings, to express his inner humanity (a quality sometimes translated as "benevolence," "goodness," or "man at his best"). Since Confucius is speaking to his disciples, he rarely explains what kind of rituals he means, but he mentions sacrificing animals, playing music, and performing dances.

• **Confucianism** The term for the main tenets of the thought of Confucius (551–479 B.C.E.), which emphasized the role of ritual in bringing out people's inner humanity (a quality translated variously as "benevolence," "goodness," or "man at his best").

Confucius's teachings do not resemble a religion so much as an ethical system. Filial piety, or respect for one's parents, is its cornerstone. If children obey their parents and the ruler follows Confucian teachings, the country will right itself because an inspiring example will lead people toward the good. (See the feature "Movement of Ideas: *The Analects* and Sima Qian's Letter to Ren An.")

Confucius was also famous for his refusal to comment on either the supernatural or the afterlife:

CL **Primary Source:**
The Book of Documents
Read this Confucian classic to discover how rulers gain or lose the right to rule, an authority known as the Mandate of Heaven.

> Zilu [ZUH-lu; a disciple] asked how to serve the spirits and gods. The Master [Confucius] said: "You are not yet able to serve men, how could you serve the spirits?"
> Zilu said: "May I ask you about death?"
> The Master said: "You do not yet know life, how could you know death?"[2]

If we define religion as the belief in the supernatural, then Confucianism does not seem to qualify. But if we consider religion as the offering of rituals at different turning points in one's life—birth, marriage, and death—then Confucianism can be considered a religion. Confucius's immediate followers made offerings to their ancestors and other gods.

Daoism   Many of Confucius's followers were also familiar with the teachings of **Daoism** (DOW-is-uhm) (alternate spelling Taoism), the other major belief system of China before unification in 221 B.C.E. The earliest Daoist texts excavated so far, dated to 300 B.C.E., were found in tombs alongside Confucian texts, an indication that the deceased did not necessarily think of Daoism and Confucianism as separate religions. Both Confucius and the leading Daoist teachers spoke about the "Way," a concept for which they used the same word, *dao* (DOW).

> **Daoism**   A Chinese belief system dating back to at least 300 B.C.E. that emphasized the "Way," a concept expressed in Chinese as "dao." The Way of the early Daoist teachers included meditation, breathing techniques, and special eating regimes.

For Confucius, the Way denoted using ritual to bring out one's inner humanity. In contrast, the Way of the early Daoist teachers included meditation, breathing techniques, and special eating regimes. They believed that, if one learned to control one's breath or the life-force present in each person, one could attain superhuman powers and possibly immortality. Some said that immortals shed their human bodies much as butterflies cast off pupas. Such people were called Perfect Men. One early Daoist text, *Zhuangzi* (JUAHNG-zuh), named for the author of its teachings, Master Zhuang (JUAHNG), describes such people: "The Perfect Man is godlike. Though the great swamps blaze, they cannot burn him; though the great rivers freeze, they cannot chill him."[3]

Zhuangzi is one of the funniest and most ironic books ever written in China. It describes many paradoxes, including this well-known anecdote:

> Once Zhuang Zhou [Zhuangzi] dreamt he was a butterfly, a butterfly flitting and fluttering around, happy with himself and doing as he pleased. He didn't know he was Zhuang Zhou. Suddenly he woke up and there he was, solid and unmistakable Zhuang Zhou. But he didn't know if he was Zhuang Zhou who had dreamt he was a butterfly, or a butterfly dreaming he was Zhuang Zhou.

The question of knowledge—of how we know what we think we know—permeates *Zhuangzi*.

Zhuangzi often mocks those who fear death because they cannot know what death is actually like; he dreams that a talking skull asks him, "Why would I throw away more happiness than that of a king on a throne and take on the troubles of a human being again?" *Zhuangzi*'s amusing tales underline how profoundly gloomy was the Daoist view of death, which pictured it as a series of underground prisons from which no one could escape.

The other well-known Daoist classic, *The Way and Integrity Classic,* or *Daodejing* (DOW-deh-jing), combines the teachings of several different masters into one volume. It urges rulers to allow things to follow their natural course, or *wuwei* (WOO-way), often misleadingly translated as "nonaction": "Nothing under heaven is softer or weaker than water, and yet nothing is better for attacking what is hard and strong, because of its immutability."[4] In the centuries leading up to 221 B.C.E., no Daoist church had a recognized leader, but many Daoist masters had disciples, and *Zhuangzi* and *The Way and Integrity Classic* offer a glimpse of the wide variety of teachings circulating alongside Confucian teachings in China at that time.

The Analects and Sima Qian's Letter to Ren An

Unlike the first sermon of the Buddha (see Chapter 3), Confucianism has no short text that summarizes its main teachings. Throughout history students read and memorized *The Analects* because it was thought to be the only text that quoted Confucius directly. Each chapter contains ten to twenty short passages, often dialogues between Confucius and a student, and each passage is numbered. The first chapter introduces the most important Confucian teachings, including respect for one's parents, or filial piety.

Living more than three hundred years after Confucius's death, the Grand Historian Sima Qian wrestled with the issue of how to best observe the tenets of filial piety. Convicted of treason because he defended a general who had surrendered to the Xion-gnu, he was offered a choice: he could commit suicide or he could undergo castration. In the excerpts from this letter to his friend Ren An, whom he called Shaoqing, he explains why he chose castration even though it brought shame to his ancestors. According to Confucian teachings, one's body was a gift from one's parents, and each person was obliged to protect his body from any mutilation. But Sima Qian's father had begun *The Records of the Grand Historian,* and he chose physical punishment so that he could complete his father's project.

Sources: The Analects, trans. Simon Leys (New York: W. W. Norton, 1997); Sima Qian, *Records of the Grand Historian: Qin Dynasty,* trans. Burton Watson (New York: A *Renditions*-Columbia University Press Book, 1993), Appendix II: Sima Qian's letter to Ren An, pp. 233, 235.

Chapter One of *The Analects*

1.1. The Master said: "To learn something and then to put it into practice at the right time: is this not a joy? To have friends coming from afar: is this not a delight? Not to be upset when one's merits are ignored: is this not the mark of a gentleman?"

1.2. Master You said: "A man who respects his parents and his elders would hardly be inclined to defy his superiors. A man who is not inclined to defy his superiors will never foment a rebellion. A gentleman works at the root. Once the root is secured, the Way unfolds. To respect parents and elders is the root of humanity."

1.3. The Master said: "Clever talk and affected manners are seldom signs of goodness."

1.4. Master Zeng said: "I examine myself three times a day. When dealing on behalf of others, have I been trustworthy? In intercourse with my friends, have I been faithful? Have I practiced what I was taught?"

1.5. The Master said: "To govern a state of middle size, one must dispatch business with dignity and good faith; be thrifty and love all men; mobilize the people only at the right times."

1.6. The Master said: "At home, a young man must respect his parents; abroad, he must respect his elders. He should talk little, but with good faith; love all people, but associate with the virtuous. Having done this, if he still has energy to spare, let him study literature."

1.7. Zixia said: "A man who values virtue more than good looks, who devotes all his energy to serving his father and mother, who is willing to give his life for his sovereign, who in intercourse with friends is true to his word—even though some may call him uneducated, I still maintain he is an educated man."

1.8. The Master said: "A gentleman who lacks gravity has no authority and his learning will remain shallow. A gentleman puts loyalty and faithfulness foremost; he does not befriend his moral inferiors. When he commits a fault, he is not afraid to amend his ways."

1.9. Master Zeng said: "When the dead are honored and the memory of remote ancestors is kept alive, a people's virtue is at its fullest."

1.10. Ziqing asked Zigong: "When the Master arrives in another country, he always becomes informed about its politics. Does he ask for such information, or is it given him?"

Zigong replied: "The Master obtains it by being cordial, kind, courteous, temperate, and deferential. The Master has a way of enquiring which is quite different from other people's, is it not?"

1.11. The Master said: "When the father is alive, watch the son's aspirations. When the father is dead, watch the son's actions. If three years later, the son has not veered from the father's way, he may be called a dutiful son indeed."

1.12. Master You said: "When practicing the ritual, what matters most is harmony. This is what made the beauty of the way of the ancient kings; it inspired their every move, great or small. Yet they knew where to stop: harmony cannot be sought for its own sake, it must always be subordinated to the ritual; otherwise it would not do."

1.13. Master You said: "If your promises conform to what is right, you will be able to keep your word. If your manners conform to the ritual, you will be able to keep shame and disgrace at bay. The best support is provided by one's own kinsmen."

1.14. The Master said: "A gentleman eats without stuffing his belly; chooses a dwelling without demanding comfort; is diligent in his office and prudent in his speech; seeks the company of the virtuous in order to straighten his own ways. Of such a man, one may truly say that he is fond of learning."

1.15 Zigong said: "'Poor without servility; rich without arrogance.' How is that?"

The Master said: "Not bad, but better still: 'Poor, yet cheerful; rich, yet considerate.'"

Zigong said: "In the *Poems*, it is said: 'Like carving horn, like sculpting ivory, like cutting jade, like polishing stone.' Is this not the same idea?"

The Master said: "Ah, one can really begin to discuss the *Poems* with you! I tell you one thing, and you can figure out the rest."

1.16. The Master said: "Don't worry if people don't recognize your merits; worry that you may not recognize theirs."

Sima Qian's Letter to Ren An

A man has only one death. That death may be as weighty as Mount Tai, or it may be as light as a goose feather. It all depends on the way he uses it. Above all, a man must bring no shame to his forebears. Next he must not shame his person, or be shameful in his countenance, or in his words. Below such a one is he who suffers the shame of being bound, and next he who bears the shame of prison clothing. . . . Lowest of all is the dire penalty of castration, the "punishment of rottenness"! . . .

It is the nature of every man to love life and hate death, to think of his parents and look after his wife and children. Only when he is moved by higher principles is this not so. Then there are things that he must do. Now I have been most unfortunate, for I lost my parents very early. With no brothers or sisters, I have been left alone and orphaned. And you yourself, Shaoqing, have seen me with my wife and child and know I would not let thoughts of them deter me. Yet the brave man does not necessarily die for honor, while even the coward may fulfill his duty. Each takes a different way to exert himself. Though I might be weak and cowardly and seek shamelessly to prolong my life, I know full well the difference between what ought to be followed and what rejected. . . . But the reason I have not refused to bear these ills and have continued to live, dwelling in vileness and disgrace without taking leave, is that I grieve that I have things in my heart that I have not been able to express fully, and I am ashamed to think that after I am gone my writings will not be known to posterity.

QUESTIONS FOR ANALYSIS

▸ According to *The Analects,* how should a gentleman conduct himself? How should a son treat his parents?

▸ According to Sima Qian, how should a virtuous person live? Why does he choose castration over suicide?

⬤ Qin Rulers Unify China, 359–207 B.C.E.

While Confucian and Daoist thinkers were proposing abstract solutions to end the endemic warfare, a third school, the Legalists, took an entirely different approach based on their experience governing the Qin homeland in western China. In 359 B.C.E., the statesman Shang Yang (SHAHNG yahng), the major adviser to the Qin ruler, implemented a series of reforms reorganizing the army and redefining the tax obligations of all citizens. Those reforms made the Qin more powerful than any of the other regional states in China, and it gradually began to conquer its neighbors. The First Emperor implemented Shang Yang's blueprint for rule both as the regional ruler of the Qin and as emperor after the unification of China in 221 B.C.E.

Prime Minister Shang Yang's Reforms, 359–221 B.C.E.

In 359 B.C.E., Prime Minister Shang Yang focused on the territory under direct Qin rule. The government sent officials to register every household in the Qin realm, creating a direct link between each subject and the ruler. Once a boy resident in the Qin region reached the age of 16 or 17 and a height of 5 feet (1.5 m), he had to serve in the military, pay land taxes (a fixed share of the crop), and perform labor service, usually building roads, each year. To encourage people to inform on each other, Shang Yang divided the population into mutual responsibility groups of five and ten: if someone committed a crime but was not apprehended, everyone in the group was punished.

Most people in ancient China took it for granted that the son of a noble was destined to rule and the son of a peasant was not, but the Legalists disagreed. Rejecting the Confucian values of ritual and benevolence and renouncing a special status for "gentlemen," they believed that the ruler should recruit the best men to staff his army and his government. Qin officials recognized no hereditary titles, not even for members of the ruler's family.

Instead the Qin officials introduced a strict meritocracy, which made their army the strongest in China. A newly recruited soldier might start at the lowest rank, but if he succeeded in battle, he could rise in rank and thereby raise the stature of his household. Because Qin rules tolerated no value judgments, which could be biased, a soldier had to present the heads of all those enemy soldiers he had killed before he could advance. The more heads he presented, the higher he rose in the army. This reorganization succeeded brilliantly because each soldier had a strong incentive to fight. Starting in 316 B.C.E., the Qin polity began to conquer neighboring lands and implement Shang Yang's measures in each new region.

Legalist philosophers valued the contributions of the farmer-soldiers most highly because they paid taxes and were the backbone of the army. Accordingly, Legalist thinkers ranked peasants just under government officials, or scholars, who could read and write. Because artisans made objects peasants needed, like baskets and tools, they ranked third, and merchants, who neither worked the land nor manufactured the goods they traded, ranked at the bottom of society.

This ranking reflected how Legalist thinkers thought society should be, not how it actually was. Any Chinese peasant would gladly have changed places with a merchant because merchants did not perform arduous physical labor and could afford better clothes and food. Although the Legalist ranking, like the explanation of varna in the Indian "Hymn of Primeval Man," did not reflect reality, it persisted throughout Chinese history.

The Policies of the First Emperor, 221–210 B.C.E.

In 246 B.C.E., Prince Zheng, the future First Emperor, ascended to the Qin throne and launched a series of military conquests that culminated with the defeat of his final rival, the ruler of Qi (modern-day Shandong) in 221 B.C.E. He then named himself First Emperor. Determining what happened during the Qin founder's eleven-year reign (221–210 B.C.E.) poses great challenges because immediately after his death Sima Qian portrayed him as one of the worst tyrants in Chinese history who murdered his opponents, suppressed all learning, and adamantly opposed Confucian virtues. This view of the First Emperor prevails today, but the evidence *from* his reign (as opposed to that composed *after* it) suggests that the First Emperor conceived of himself as a virtuous ruler.

After 221 B.C.E., the emperor placed stone tablets on high mountaintops that recorded his view of his reign:

> The way of good rule is advanced and enacted;
> The various professions achieve their proper place,
> And all find rule and model.
> His great principle is superb and shining.[5]

Each line invoked Confucian learning. "Superb and shining" is a title used by the first ruler of the Zhou, and the First Emperor adopted it because he, too, hoped to be perceived as the virtuous founder of a new dynasty.

To compose the stone inscriptions, the Qin emperor commissioned a team of scholars who drew on all the classical learning of China's different regions that had taken shape in the previous millennium, including Confucius's teachings. One of their inscriptions claims, "The way of filial piety is brilliantly manifest and shining!" According to Confucian teachings, the ruler's main role was to lead his subjects in ritual, and the Qin emperor assumed this role each time he put up a stone tablet.

The Qin emperor placed these monuments in the far corners of his realm to demonstrate that he directed all of his subjects, both those in the Qin homeland and those recently conquered, in correct ritual observance. Unlike the Ashokan inscriptions in different languages, all the Qin inscriptions were written in Chinese because the Qin enforced linguistic standardization throughout their empire. And whereas Ashoka's inscriptions were phrased colloquially, the Qin inscriptions were rigidly formal, consisting of thirty-six or seventy-two lines, each with exactly four characters. Although Ashoka's inscriptions were completed within the Qin emperor's lifetime, northern India lay some 1,000 miles (1,600 km) from the western edge of the Qin emperor's realm, and no evidence of direct contact between the Mauryan and Qin Empires survives.

The inscriptions use the characteristic Chinese technique of manufacture: their authors placed component parts, or characters, in various combinations to produce a slightly different text for each inscription. Each Qin stone text runs exactly the same length and covers the usual themes, but no two inscriptions are identical.

Qin dynasty sources demonstrate clearly that the First Emperor exercised far more control over his subjects than had his predecessors. Using government registers listing all able-bodied men, the First Emperor initiated several enormous public works projects. Hundreds of thousands of conscripts built 4,000 miles (6,400 km) of roads, roughly as many as the Romans did,[6] as well as long walls of pounded earth, the most readily available building material. (The Great Wall that one sees today was built of stone in the fifteenth through seventeenth centuries C.E. along the foundations of the Qin dirt walls.) The Qin emperor also used conscript labor to build his tomb, where he was buried in 210 B.C.E. (See the feature "Visual Evidence: The Terracotta Warriors of the Qin Founder's Tomb.")

Many Qin subjects left their homes either to perform labor service on these different projects or to serve in the army, which had several hundred thousand conscripts and which traveled as far north to modern-day Mongolia or south to Vietnam (see below). The central government sent supplies overland to its armies on the roads it built, but when the armies traveled too far, it became difficult to sustain their supply lines, and many died far from home in unsuccessful military campaigns.

■ **The Great Wall Then and Now**   Few people realize that the Great Wall that we see today (*right*) was built during the Ming dynasty (1368–1644), not during the Qin dynasty (221–207 B.C.E.). The Qin emperor ordered the construction of the Great Wall by linking together many preexisting dirt walls. The remains of the Qin wall, which was made largely from pounded earth, survive in only a few places in China (*left*).   (left: © Zhao Guangtian/Panorama Media (Beijing) Ltd./Alamy; right: © Graham French/Masterfile)

Legalism and the Laws of the Qin Dynasty

The Qin ruler viewed the establishment of laws as one of his most important accomplishments. According to one inscription, he "created the regulations and illuminated the laws" as soon as he became emperor. Viewing law as a tool for strengthening the realm, the Legalists advocated treating all men identically, regardless of birth, because they believed that only the systematic application of one set of laws could control man's inherently evil nature. Subjects could not use law to challenge their ruler's authority because the only law for Legalists was the law of the ruler. They did not acknowledge the existence of a higher, divine law.

In place for only fourteen years, the **Qin dynasty** (221–207 B.C.E.) did not have time to develop a governmental system for all of China, but it did create a basic framework. The First Emperor appointed a prime minister as the top official in his government. Different departments in the capital administered the emperor's staff, the military, and revenue. The Qin divided the empire into over forty military districts called commanderies, each headed by a governor and a military commander. They in turn were divided into districts, the smallest unit of the Qin government, which were governed by magistrates with the help of clerks. All these officials were charged with carrying out the new laws of the Qin.

• **Qin dynasty** (221–207 B.C.E.) The first dynasty to rule over a unified China; heavily influenced by Legalist teachings that promoted soldiers and officials strictly on the basis of accomplishment, not birth.

Later historians described Qin laws as arbitrary and overly harsh; they were also surprisingly detailed, clearly the product of a government deeply concerned with following legal procedures carefully. Archaeologists working in Shuihudi (SHWAY-who-dee) town, in Hubei (WHO-bay) province, found a partial set of Qin dynasty laws dating to 217 B.C.E. in the tomb of a low-ranking clerk. We know only his last name, Xi.

Clerk Xi was buried with a set of model cases illustrating legal procedures. All were written on bamboo slips preserved in stagnant water, with holes punched into them. They were then sewn together to form sheets that could be rolled up, similar to a modern placemat made from cord and reeds. Some writers used silk, but most used bamboo because silk was ruined if one's brush slipped.

Each model case described in the Shuihudi materials is equally complex, pointing to the existence of established procedures for officials to follow before reaching a judgment. One text begins as follows:

> Report. A, the wife of a commoner of X village, made a denunciation, saying, "I, A, had been pregnant for six months. Yesterday, in the daytime, I fought with the adult woman C of the same village. I, A, and C grabbed each other by the hair. C threw me, A, over and drove me back. A fellow-villager, D, came to the rescue and separated C and me, A. As soon as I, A, had reached my house, I felt ill and my belly hurt; yesterday evening the child miscarried."[7]

The text provides detailed instructions for investigating such a case. The legal clerk, someone like Clerk Xi, had to examine the fetus and consult with the local midwife; he also had to interrogate A and the members of her household to determine her condition.

The Shuihudi tomb also contained sections of the Qin legal code that make fine distinctions: the penalties for manslaughter (inadvertently killing someone) were lighter than those for deliberate murder. Officials had to examine the murder weapon: a determination of manslaughter hinged on whether the assailant had used an object lying at hand or had concealed his weapon, which indicated intent to murder. The fine legal distinctions among different types of murder resemble

THE TERRACOTTA WARRIORS OF THE QIN FOUNDER'S TOMB

The Qin emperor's tomb, sometimes called the eighth wonder of the world, was discovered in 1973 by a farmer digging a well. The enormous tomb is so big that archaeologists have to dig test pits to probe its dimensions. Test pit #1, shown to the right, contains over seven thousand soldiers of four types—foot soldiers, archers, charioteers, and soldiers riding on horseback—who staffed the emperor's terracotta army. Because the Qin emperor expected the afterlife to be exactly the same as his life, his tomb formed a miniaturized world in which he could pursue his usual activities, including commanding his troops in battle.

The terracotta warriors do not resemble the figurines placed in any Chinese tomb before or since, prompting much speculation about the identity of their creators. One intriguing possibility, recently proposed, is that the emperor used his plumbers, because the soldiers' legs greatly resemble clay water pipes found in the ruins of the Qin palace.

Over one thousand soldiers bear labels stamped into the clay by eighty-five foremen, who were presumably responsible for supervising their construction. One estimate suggests that it took eleven years for these foremen, each supervising some ten men, to make the entire army of over seven thousand figures.[*]

How did the Qin craftsmen make so many different soldiers in such a short time? Like chefs in today's Chinese restaurants, they arranged thousands of prefabricated parts in various combinations to make a slightly different product each time. Archaeologists have identified two types of feet, three types of shoes and four types of boots, two types of legs, eight types of torso, and two types of armor used to make the mass-produced soldiers, whose bodies range from 5 feet 11 inches to 6 feet 5 inches (180 to 195 cm) tall.

Once a soldier's body was completed, a craftsman used clay to make his facial features. All the soldiers have individual faces, as if the craftsmen worked from living models. Yet the faces are idealized: no soldier has any wounds or scars. When the soldiers were completed, craftsmen painted them with bright colors, most of which has flaked off on the surrounding dirt.

The core of the tomb, where the Qin emperor himself was buried, has yet to be excavated, but writing one hundred years later, Sima Qian described it: "Artisans were ordered to install mechanically triggered crossbows set to shoot any intruder. With mercury the various waterways of the empire, the Yangzi and Yellow Rivers, and even the great ocean itself were created and made to flow and circulate mechanically."[†] Sima Qian also claimed that the son of the Qin founder ordered that the craftsmen who worked on the tomb be buried alive so that the tomb's exact location would remain secret. Archaeologists have not found human remains, but they continue to announce new discoveries, most recently of clay wrestlers and tumblers who performed for the emperor's pleasure in the next world.

---

[*]Lothar Ledderose, *Ten Thousand Things: Module and Mass Production in Chinese Art* (Princeton: Princeton University Press, 2000), pp. 69–70.

[†]Maxwell K. Hearn, "The Terracotta Army of the First Emperor of Qin," in *The Great Bronze Age of China: An Exhibition from the People's Republic of China*, ed. Wen Fong (New York: Metropolitan Museum of Art, 1980), p. 357.

QUESTION FOR ANALYSIS

 How do the terracotta warriors illustrate the Chinese technique of using prefabricated component parts to mass-produce multiple objects that differ from each other?

This ordinary soldier's head was made by combining molded forms of the front and the back and smoothing them together. Like all Chinese, he did not cut his hair, considered to be a gift from his parents, but bound it in intricate patterns on the back and top of his head.

His headdress indicates that this figure is an officer. This group of nine statues includes at least three officers who stand at the front of their unit so that they can lead their subordinates into battle.

A roof of wooden beams was originally built over the entire army and then covered with mats, a layer of sand and chalk, and finally a layer of dirt.

This missing head reveals how the hollow statues were made. The armor, lower skirt, and legs were made from sheets of clay in a construction technique originally used by palace plumbers for water pipes.

(© Alfo Garozzo/Cuboimages srl/Alamy)

Each Qin soldier wore a uniform consisting of a gown to the knees, leather armor on the upper torso, short pants, leg guards, and a headdress (never a helmet).

This officer's hands originally held weapons, most likely wooden spears or staffs, which have since disintegrated.

those in Hammurabi's laws (see Chapter 2). However, whereas in Babylon an assembly decided whether the murder victim's wife was guilty of killing her husband, in China the presiding official or clerk determined an individual's guilt.

Qin punishments were grisly. One could have one's foot cut off or one's nose severed for various offenses, and many of those sentenced to hard labor were not "complete," meaning that they were missing a limb. But if we consider the punishments in use elsewhere in the world at the time, such as Roman crucifixion, the Qin punishments do not seem unusual.

The Han Empire, 206 B.C.E.–220 C.E.

Han dynasty (206 B.C.E.–220 C.E.)   The immediate successor to the Qin dynasty. Han rulers denounced Legalist governance but adopted much of the Qin blueprint for empire. Because of its long rule, the Han dynasty was a model for all subsequent dynasties.

The Qin dynasty came to a sudden end in 207 B.C.E. with the suicide of the First Emperor's son. The following year, in 206 B.C.E., the new emperor founded the **Han dynasty.** Although the Han founder always depicted the Qin as a brutal dynasty, he drew on many Legalist precedents to create a blueprint that allowed him and his descendants to rule for four hundred years. The Han modified the Qin structure of central and local government, developed a mechanism for recruiting officials, and linked education with bureaucratic advancement for the first time in Chinese history. Starting in 140 B.C.E. and continuing throughout the dynasty, Han emperors encouraged students and future officials to study the Confucian classics. The dynasty's support of learning encouraged the spread of Confucianism throughout the empire. The Confucian emphasis on education was so strong that the Chinese of that era schooled not only their sons but also, when they could, their daughters. Yet because the Han continued many policies of the Qin, we should recognize the Han as a Legalist dynasty with a Confucian exterior, not a genuinely Confucian dynasty.

Han Government and the Imperial Bureaucracy

The Qin forces had conquered an enormous swath of territory, but some regions, sensing weakness at the center, rebelled against the unpopular second Qin emperor and asserted their independence. Gradually one man, formerly a low-ranking official under the Qin named Liu Bang (LEO bahng) (r. 206–195 B.C.E.), emerged as leader of the rebels and founded the Han dynasty in 206 B.C.E. Liu Bang was one of only two emperors (the other founded the Ming dynasty in 1368) to be born as a commoner. When he and his forces entered the Qin capital, he assured the capital's residents:

> You elders have long suffered under the harsh laws of Qin. . . . I make an agreement with you that the law shall consist of only three sections: He who kills others shall die; he who harms others or steals from them shall incur appropriate punishment. For the rest, all other Qin laws shall be abolished.[8]

Like a modern politician's campaign promise, this statement does not provide an accurate description of Han law, which actually retained many provisions of Qin law.

When the Han forces took power, they faced the immediate problem of staffing a government large enough to govern the empire. They adopted the Legalist structure of a central government with the emperor at the head and a prime minister (sometimes called a chancellor) as the top official. Underneath the prime minister were the different sections of the central government, which had three main divisions: collection of taxes, supervision of the military, and recruitment of personnel.

The Han dynasty ruled for four hundred years, with only one interruption by a relative of the empress, named Wang Mang (WAHNG mahng), who founded his own short-lived Xin (SHIN) ("new") dynasty (9–23 C.E.). During the first two hundred years of the Han, the capital was in Chang'an (CHAHNG-ahn); historians refer to this period as the Former Han or the Western Han (206 B.C.E.–9 C.E.). After Wang Mang was deposed, the original ruling family of the Han dynasty continued to govern, but in the new capital of Luoyang (LWAW-yahng). The Later Han (25–220 C.E.) is also called the Eastern Han because Luoyang was some 300 miles (500 km) east of Chang'an.

The Han Empire exercised varying amounts of control over the sixty million people under its rule. The emperor managed to regain control of distant regions through a combination of military conquest and administrative flexibility. Immediately after taking over, the Han founder ceded about half of Qin territory to independent kings. He divided the remaining territory into one hundred commanderies and subdivided them into fifteen hundred prefectures. Each prefecture was headed by a magistrate whose task was to register the population, collect revenues, judge legal disputes, and maintain irrigation works.

To get a government position during the Han dynasty, the first step was to get a referral. Men already serving in the government suggested younger men of good reputation, usually from wealthy families with large landholdings, to staff lower positions in prefectural offices. There they could learn how government functioned.

Not content to recruit men who could read and write and knew how to draft documents, the Han was the first Chinese dynasty to require that officials study classical writings on ritual, history, and poetry, as well as *The Analects*. Although these texts did not teach the nuts-and-bolts workings of local government, which remained Legalist in all but name, officials embraced the Confucian view that knowledge of these classic texts would produce more virtuous, and thus better, officials.

In 124 B.C.E., one of the most powerful Han emperors, Emperor Wu (also known as Han Wudi) (r. 140–87 B.C.E.), established the **Imperial Academy** to encourage the study of Confucian texts. At first the Academy consisted of five scholars, called Academicians, who specialized in the study of a given text, and the fifty students who studied with them. Within one hundred years the number of students at the Academy ballooned to several thousand. Ambitious young men already in the government realized that knowledge of Confucian texts, demonstrated by success in examinations conducted by the Imperial Academy, could advance their careers.

The study of Confucian texts was aided by the invention of paper. The earliest examples of Chinese paper found by archaeologists date to the second century B.C.E. Ragpickers who washed and recycled old fabric left fibers on a screen to dry and accidentally discovered how to make paper. Initially, the Chinese used paper for wrapping fragile items, not as a writing material. But by 200 C.E. paper production had increased so much that people used paper, not bamboo slips, for letter writing and books.

With the adoption of paper as the primary writing material, the culture of learning in China shifted from an oral to a written one. In the early years, Han

● **Imperial Academy**
Established in 124 B.C.E. by the Han emperor, Emperor Wu (r. 140–87 B.C.E.), to encourage the study of Confucian texts. Initially consisted of five scholars, called Academicians, specializing in the study of a given text.

dynasty teachers taught students to memorize texts and recite them orally, but by the end of the dynasty they were reading books. When one poet in the first century B.C.E. submitted a written poem to the court as a gift, the emperor could not imagine that someone would commit a poem to writing without first reciting it in person. By the end of the dynasty, though, writing literary works on paper without reciting them had become commonplace. Paper was one of China's most important inventions; it spread from China to the Islamic world in the eighth century C.E. and finally to Europe only in the eleventh century.

Ban Zhao's *Lessons for Women*

During the first century C.E., the Later Han capital of Luoyang became an important literary center where young men came to study. One of the most famous literary families was that of the poet and historian Ban Biao (BAHN-beeow) (d. 54 C.E.), who had three children: twin boys and a daughter. One of the boys followed in his father's footsteps, while his twin became a successful general. Their sister, **Ban Zhao** (BAHN jow) (ca. 45–120 C.E.), was the most famous woman writer of her day. She is best known for her work *Lessons for Women,* which Chinese girls continued to read for centuries after her death.

Ban Zhao wrote *Lessons for Women* when in her mid-50s. It contained everything she would like to have known when she married at age 14. Ban Zhao's main theme is clear: women exist to serve their husbands and their in-laws, whom they should always obey and with whom they should never quarrel. Yet Ban Zhao's ideal woman was also literate. She began her book by advising her readers to copy down her instructions, sure evidence that they could read and write. She also criticized men who taught only their sons to read:

> Yet only to teach men and not to teach women—is that not ignoring the essential relation between them? . . . It is the rule to begin to teach children to read at the age of eight years. . . . Only why should it not be that girls' education as well as boys' be according to this principle?[9]

This is an eloquent call to teach girls to read at the same age as boys at the age of 7 (8 in Chinese reckoning includes the time in the womb).

We must remember that Ban Zhao differed from her contemporaries in several ways. For one, she had studied with her father the historian and was sufficiently skilled that she completed his manuscript after he died. When married, she bore children, but she was widowed at a young age and became a tutor to the women at the imperial court. When an infant emperor ascended the throne in 106 C.E., his 25-year-old wife became regent, and Ban Zhao advised her on matters of state. A year later, the infant died, but the female regent retained power over the new emperor.

These two women did not have typical careers. Still, their unusual lives show that it was possible for women to take on male roles under certain circumstances. The literacy rate during the first century could not have exceeded 10 percent among men, but *Lessons for Women* was read, and Ban Zhao's ideal of literate women stayed alive in subsequent centuries. Well-off families made every effort to educate their daughters, if only to allow them to study a few years with their brothers' tutors; of course, few laboring people could afford to do so.

• Ban Zhao (45–120 C.E.) A historian and the author of *Lessons for Women,* a book that counseled women to serve men and advocated education for girls starting at the age of 8.

Ⓒ**Primary Source:**

Lessons for Women *Discover what Ban Zhao, the foremost female writer in Han China, had to say about the proper behavior of women.*

Extending Han Rule

As the Qin and Han dynasties left their successors with a blueprint of how to govern the empire, the territories they conquered established boundaries that would define the geographical idea of China for centuries to come. After conquering six independent kingdoms to form their empire (see the map on page 89), the Qin controlled most of the land watered by the Yellow and Yangzi Rivers. If one compares Qin dynasty China with Han dynasty China, the most visible difference is that the Han rulers controlled a narrow stretch of territory in the northwest, now Gansu (GAHN-sue) province and the Xinjiang (SHIN-jyahng) Autonomous Region. Han armies also extended the empire's borders northeast to control much of the Korean peninsula and south to modern-day Vietnam (see Map 4.1).

Han Dynasty Conflict with the Xiongnu Nomads, 201–60 B.C.E.

The Han dynasty gained much of this territory during its wars between 201 and 60 B.C.E. with the **Xiongnu** (SHEE-AWNG-new), a northern nomadic people who moved across modern-day Mongolia in search of grass to feed their sheep and horses. Only the Xiongnu had an army sufficiently powerful to threaten the Han, and they tried to conquer Chinese territory for the first century and a half of Han rule. Their military strength derived from their quick-footed horses and brilliant horsemanship, which enabled them to defeat the Chinese in battle after battle.

The Xiongnu language is completely lost. The Chinese word *Xiongnu* may be a translation of the same word as the Latin word *Hun*. If *Xiongnu* and *Hun* are different forms of the same word (scholars disagree sharply on this point), then the Xiongnu were an earlier, eastern branch of the nomadic peoples who invaded western Europe in the fifth century C.E.

Having formed a confederation of the different tribal peoples living in Mongolia in Qin times, the Xiongnu fought their first battle with the Han soon after the founding of the dynasty. The Xiongnu won. The treaty settling this conflict brought only a temporary peace because the Xiongnu continued to launch military campaigns into China.

In 139 B.C.E. Emperor Wu dispatched an envoy named Zhang Qian (JAHNG chee-en) to Central Asia to persuade the Yuezhi (YOU-EH-juh) people to enter into an alliance against the Xiongnu. Zhang Qian reached the Yuezhi only after being held hostage by the Xiongnu for ten years. When he returned to China, he explained to the emperor that he had been unable to secure an alliance against the Xiongnu, but he had visited local markets. There, to his surprise, he had seen Chinese goods for sale, certain evidence that merchants carrying Chinese goods had preceded him. Today most Chinese regard Zhang Qian as the person who discovered the Silk Road (see Chapter 8).

The Xiongnu supplied the Chinese with animals, hides, and semiprecious gems, particularly jade; in return the Chinese traded silk. The Chinese never succeeded, at least within the Chinese heartland, in breeding horses as strong as those the Xiongnu bred in the Mongolian steppe, probably because they did not have comparable grasslands.

The Xiongnu threat came to a sudden end in 60 B.C.E., not because of any military victory by the Han, but because the huge Xiongnu confederation broke apart

Xiongnu Northern nomadic people who moved across modern-day Mongolia in search of grass for their sheep and horses. Their military strength derived from brilliant horsemanship. Defeated the Han dynasty in battle until 60 B.C.E., when their federation broke apart.

into five warring groups. Much to the relief of the Han emperors, the Xiongnu never again posed a serious threat to their dynasty, but other nomadic peoples living in the grasslands to the north, like the Mongols, intermittently threatened later dynasties.

Han Expansion to the North, Northwest, and South

The Han dynasty ruled China for over four hundred years. In certain periods, it was too weak to conquer new territories, but in other periods, particularly during the long reign of Emperor Wu, the army was so strong that the emperor launched military campaigns into border areas. Once the Han army had conquered a certain region, it established garrisons in the major towns. Chinese officials and merchants in these towns led Chinese-style lives, eating Chinese food and speaking Chinese, while the indigenous peoples largely continued to live as they had before. The officials living in the garrison towns exercised

🌐 **MAP 4.1**

The Han Empire at Its Greatest Extent, ca. 50 B.C.E.   The Han dynasty inherited all the territory of its predecessor, the Qin dynasty, and its powerful armies conquered new territory to the north in the Korean peninsula, to the west in the Taklamakan Desert, and to the south in modern-day Vietnam.

Ⓒ Interactive Map

Legend:
- Boundary of Qin Empire, 210 B.C.E.
- Territory of Han dynasty, ca. 50 B.C.E.
- Other cities of the Han dynasty
- (108 B.C.E.) Date conquered by Han
- Great Wall
- Silk Road
- Sea trade routes
- *YUE* Peoples

only tenuous control over the indigenous peoples, and, if a local army retook a city, Chinese control could end suddenly. Han armies managed to take parts of the Taklamakan Desert, Korea, and Vietnam, but they ruled these borderlands only briefly.

When the Xiongnu confederation collapsed in 60 B.C.E., the Han dynasty briefly took control of its headquarters and established garrisons in some of the oasis kingdoms ringing the Taklamakan Desert. After 127 C.E., Chinese supply lines were unable to reach troops in the northwest, and the Chinese ceded control to a succession of local kingdoms. But a Han garrison remained at the city of Dunhuang (DUHN-hwahng), the staging point for going farther west and the outermost point of Chinese control.

The region south of China, extending from modern-day Fujian (FOO-jee-en) province to Vietnam, differed from the northwest because one could reach it overland or, more easily, by sea. Much like camel caravans visited oases in their voyage west across the Taklamakan Desert, small boats, many propelled by oars, visited ports on the South China Sea, which offered a chance to rest, trade, and buy provisions for the next leg of the journey. Like all the rivers in Vietnam, the most important river, the Red River, drained from the mountains in the west to the South China Sea. High mountain chains separated the different river valleys, making overland transport much more difficult than sea travel.

The Vietnamese language belongs to the Austroasiatic language family, a different family from Chinese. The modern Chinese provinces of Guangdong (GWAHNG-dohng), Guangxi (GWAHNG-shee), and Yunnan (YUHN-nahn) were home to a regional people that the Chinese called Yue (YOU-EH), the ancestors of the Vietnamese. The Yue people had early (about 8000 B.C.E.) developed the cultivation of rice and were also avid sailors.

Yue cultural practices differed significantly from the Chinese. For example, they traced their descent through both their mothers and their fathers (see Chapter 8). Chinese historians writing before the Qin unification called them the people with "tattooed foreheads," a label that later Vietnamese historians thought pejorative because tattooing clearly violated the Confucian teaching that one should not physically alter one's body, a gift from one's parents. The sparse population in these southern regions also prompted Chinese historians to call the region the "Empty Land."

When the Qin armies conquered Vietnam before 207 B.C.E., they established centers of Chinese control in garrison towns. After 207 B.C.E., an independent kingdom also ruled by a Chinese leader, called the Southern Kingdom of Yue (Nam Viet), took over from the Qin. The kingdom was home to fishermen and traders who specialized in unusual goods like ivory tusks, pearls, tortoise shells, and slaves. After several attempts, the Han armies defeated this ruler and established garrison towns in 110 B.C.E., which they retained throughout the Han dynasty.

While Vietnam marked the southern extent of Han territory, Korea marked the northern extent. Korea did not receive as much rainfall as Vietnam, and its climate was much cooler. Large, dense forests covered the region, and most early settlements were along rivers or on the coast, where residents could easily fish. Before 300 B.C.E., the region was home to several tribal confederations; then, during the third century B.C.E., the Old Choson (JOE-sohn) kingdom united much of the Korean peninsula north of the Han River, in what is today's North Korea. Qin armies defeated the Old Choson kingdom, and Han armies again conquered the region in 108 B.C.E., soon after gaining control of China.

Although officially under Han rule, the local people exercised considerable independence. Many local men held positions of authority in the Chinese administration. Officials and merchants lived in a garrison city located in modern-day Pyongyang (BYOHNG-yahng), but the people outside the garrison were much less affected by the Chinese presence. Since no written documents from this period survive, archaeologists must study burials to reconstruct religious practices. Large, wealthy graves suggest that the people living on the Korean peninsula believed that the dead would travel to another realm. In one region they were buried with large bird wings so that they could fly to the next world.

In later periods (see Chapter 8), these three regions—northwest China, Vietnam, and Korea—would all join the Chinese cultural sphere and adopt the Chinese writing system. But during the Qin and Han dynasties Chinese influence was limited because the Chinese presence consisted only of military garrisons.

The most obvious signs of the Qin and the Han legacy are the words used today for "China" and "Chinese." *China* entered English via the Sanskrit word *Chee-na*, the Indian pronunciation of *Qin*. Ask your classmates studying Chinese what the modern Chinese word for the Chinese language is. The answer should not surprise you: *Hanyu*, literally, "the language of the Han." Almost all Chinese say that they are *Han-ren*, "people of the Han." In a sense they are. If the Han dynasty had not modified the First Emperor's blueprint for empire, there might not be a China today.

Chapter Review

KEY TERMS

First Emperor of the Qin dynasty (88)

Shang dynasty (92)

oracle bones (92)

ancestor worship (92)

Sima Qian (93)

Zhou dynasty (95)

Mandate of Heaven (95)

Confucius (96)

Confucianism (96)

Daoism (97)

Qin dynasty (103)

Han dynasty (106)

Imperial Academy (107)

Ban Zhao (108)

Xiongnu (109)

CL Download the MP3 audio file of the Chapter Review and listen to it on the go.

Following the lead of the First Emperor, the Qin and Han dynasties created a blueprint for imperial rule that lasted for two thousand years. In the centuries after the fall of the Han, China was not always unified. But subsequent Chinese rulers always aspired to reunify the empire and conceived of China's physical borders as largely those of the Han dynasty at its largest extent.

What different elements of Chinese civilization took shape between 1200 and 221 B.C.E.?

The culture tying the people of China together had deep roots. Their shared diet, with its division of starch and meat-and-vegetable dishes, dated to at least 1200 B.C.E. That was also the time of the first written characters, whose descendants are still in use today. Around 500 B.C.E., Confucius taught the importance of obeying both one's parents and the ruler, yet since Confucius refused to say anything about the other world, many Chinese turned to Daoist teachings, which offered immortality to a rare few and eternal detention in underground jails to everyone else.

What were the most important measures in the Qin blueprint for empire?

The Qin dynasty introduced a blueprint for empire that tied their subjects to local officials far more tightly than anywhere else in the world. Qin officials recorded the names of all their subjects and assigned them to mutual responsibility groups. They implemented a single law code for their entire empire and standardized the writing system and all weights and measures. They also created a strict meritocracy in both the army and the government that promoted only those who demonstrated success, not those born to powerful families.

 How did the Han rulers modify the Qin blueprint, particularly regarding administrative structure and the recruitment and promotion of officials?

The successors to the First Emperor, including the Han rulers, did not acknowledge the path-breaking role of the Qin dynasty. Yet even as succeeding rulers maligned the First Emperor, they all adopted the Qin title *emperor*. Han emperors created different administrative districts from those in use under the Qin and also recruited officials in a different way, appointing new officials to the lowest ranks on the recommendation of those already in office. After 140 B.C.E., officials could be promoted only after demonstrating knowledge of Confucian texts in written examinations.

 Which neighboring peoples in Central, East, and Southeast Asia did the Han dynasty conquer? Why was the impact of Chinese rule limited?

Han dynasty armies conquered and briefly controlled parts of northwest China, Vietnam, and Korea, but their influence was limited because the Chinese military rarely ventured beyond their garrison towns.

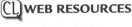
WEB RESOURCES

Pronunciation Guide

Interactive Maps

MAP 4.1 The Han Empire at Its Greatest Extent, ca. 50 B.C.E.

Primary Sources

Chapter Objectives

ACE Multiple-Choice Quiz

Flashcards

For Further Reference

The Analects of Confucius. Translated by Simon Leys. New York: W. W. Norton, 1997.

Eckert, Carter, et al. *Korea Old and New: A History.* Cambridge, Mass.: Harvard University Press, 1990.

Hansen, Valerie. *The Open Empire: A History of China to 1600.* New York: W. W. Norton, 2000.

Keightley, David N. *Sources of Shang History: The Oracle Bone Inscriptions of Bronze Age China.* Berkeley: University of California Press, 1978.

Kern, Martin. *The Stele Inscriptions of Ch'in Shih-huang: Text and Ritual in Early Chinese Imperial Representation.* New Haven: American Oriental Society, 2000.

Ledderose, Lothar. *Ten Thousand Things: Module and Mass Production in Chinese Art.* Princeton: Princeton University Press, 2000.

Schwartz, Benjamin. *The World of Thought in Ancient China.* Cambridge, Mass.: Harvard University Press, 1985.

Swann, Nancy Lee. *Pan Chao: Foremost Woman Scholar of China.* New York: American Historical Association, 1932.

Tao Te Ching: The Classic Book of Integrity and the Way. Translated by Victor Mair. New York: Bantam Books, 1990.

Tarling, Nicholas, ed. *The Cambridge History of Southeast Asia.* Cambridge: Cambridge University Press, 1999.

Twitchett, Denis, and Michael Loewe, eds. *The Cambridge History of China.* Vol. 1, *The Ch'in and Han Empires 221 B.C.–A.D. 220.* New York: Cambridge University Press, 1986.

Websites

Asian Art Museum, San Francisco (http://www.asianart.org/collection.htm).   An introduction to one of America's most important collections of Asian art.

The First Emperor: China's Terracotta Warriors (http://www.britishmuseum.org/whats_on/all_current_exhibitions/the_first_emperor/exhibition_overview .aspx).   A short history of the terracotta warriors including downloadable images.

Metropolitan Museum of Art (http://www.metmuseum.org/TOAH/hd/cgrk/hd_cgrk .htm).   Detailed description of Chinese gardens and collector's rocks. See the museum website for other Asian art.

Films

The First Emperor of China from the Canadian Film Board. USA orders: 800-542-2164.

The Americas and the Islands of the Pacific, to 1200 C.E.

A vast area of the globe—North and South America and the islands of the Pacific—developed in almost total isolation from Eurasia because, after approximately 7000 B.C.E., much of the ice covering the world's surface melted and submerged the Beringia ice bridge linking Alaska to Siberia (see Chapter 1). Since few of the peoples living in this area have left written records, archaeologists and historians have exercised great ingenuity in reconstructing the different paths they took to complex society, each very different from those of Eurasian peoples. Scholars know more about the Maya (MY-ah), a Central American people whose writing system was translated only in the 1970s. Yet because the deciphering of Mayan is ongoing, experts continue to debate the exact meaning of surviving texts, rarely translating word for word. Here one professor paraphrases an inscription describing a 152-day trip a ruler named **Yax K'uk Mo'** (YASH cook moh) took to Copán in what is now Honduras:

(© Kenneth Garrett)

YAX K'UK MO' FROM ALTAR Q

T he top of Altar Q here tells the story of Yax K'uk Mo' really. It begins up here with a date, and it's a date that comes around the early fifth century. And it says that on that particular day in that time, he took the emblems of office, he took the kingship. The place where he took that kingship is recorded in the next glyph, and we've known for a long time that this glyph has some sort of connection to Central Mexico. . . . Then we have his name here, and then the date's three days later. And three days later he leaves that location.

This icon will direct you to interactive activities and study materials on the *Voyages* website: www.cengage.com/history/hansen/voyages1e

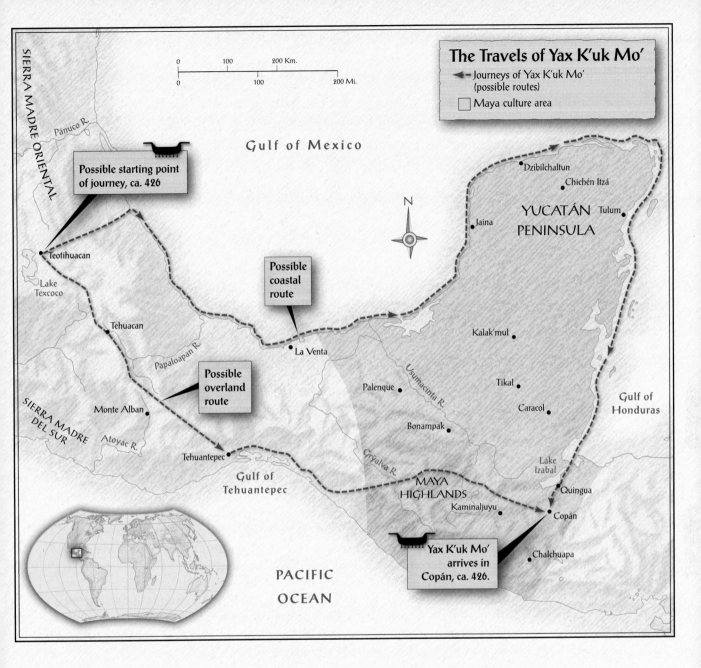

The Travels of Yax K'uk Mo'

◄- - Journeys of Yax K'uk Mo'
(possible routes)

☐ Maya culture area

Gulf of Mexico

SIERRA MADRE ORIENTAL

Pánuco R.

Possible starting point of journey, ca. 426

Teotihuacan

Lake Texcoco

Tehuacan

Papaloapan R.

Possible coastal route

La Venta

SIERRA MADRE DEL SUR

Monte Alban

Possible overland route

Atoyac R.

Tehuantepec

Gulf of Tehuantepec

PACIFIC OCEAN

Dzibilchaltun

Chichén Itzá

YUCATÁN PENINSULA

Tulum

Jaina

Kalak'mul

Usumacinta R.

Palenque

Tikal

Caracol

Gulf of Honduras

Bonampak

Grijalva R.

MAYA HIGHLANDS

Lake Izabal

Kaminaljuyu

Quingua

Copán

Yax K'uk Mo' arrives in Copán, ca. 426.

Chalchuapa

N

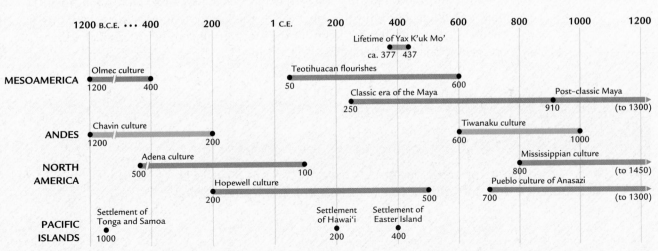

1200 B.C.E. • • • 400	200	1 C.E.	200	400	600	800	1000	1200

Lifetime of Yax K'uk Mo'
ca. 377 — 437

MESOAMERICA

Olmec culture
1200 — 400

Teotihuacan flourishes
50 — 600

Classic era of the Maya
250 — 910 — Post-classic Maya (to 1300)

ANDES

Chavin culture
1200 — 200

Tiwanaku culture
600 — 1000

NORTH AMERICA

Adena culture
500 — 100

Mississippian culture
800 — (to 1450)

Hopewell culture
200 — 500

Pueblo culture of Anasazi
700 — (to 1300)

PACIFIC ISLANDS

Settlement of Tonga and Samoa
1000

Settlement of Hawai'i
200

Settlement of Easter Island
400

The inscription goes on to say something really remarkable. A hundred and fifty-three days after he leaves this place where he's become a king, then, on this day, he "rests his legs," or "rests his feet," and "he is the West Lord." It's a title that Yax K'uk Mo' has throughout his references at Copán. And then finally it says "he arrived" at Copán. So, I think the conclusion from this is that Yax K'uk Mo' came a long way before he arrived at Copán.[1]

• Yax K'uk Mo'   The king of Copán during the classic period of the Maya (250–910 C.E.). Founded a dynasty that lasted at least sixteen generations, until 776 C.E.

Yax K'uk Mo' must have walked or was carried, since the Maya, like all the peoples of Americas and unlike the peoples of Eurasia, did not use the wheel or ride animals. Maya scholars are not certain where Yax K'uk Mo' began his journey. Some feel that he set out from somewhere near modern-day Mexico City, while others contend that he stayed within the territory of the Maya (see the map on page 115)—in the region known as Mesoamerica, which includes much of Mexico and Central America.

Because the Maya developed one of the few writing systems used in the Americas before 1500, they differed from almost every other people of the Americas and the islands of the Pacific. Some earlier peoples living in modern-day Mexico developed notational systems; much later, the Mexica (MAY-shee-kah) people, or the Aztecs, of Mexico used a combination of pictures and visual puns to record events, but their writing system was not fully developed (see Chapter 15).

Complex societies arose in Mexico, the Andes, and the modern-day United States at different times and in different ways than in Eurasia. Because hundreds, sometimes thousands, of years elapsed between agriculture and the rise of cities, archaeologists pay close attention to the American peoples who built large earthworks or stone monuments. Their rulers had the ability to command their subjects to work on large projects. Similarly, although the peoples of the Pacific never built large cities, they crossed the Pacific Ocean, possibly all the way to Chile. The lack of navigational instruments did not prevent them from conducting some of the world's longest ocean voyages. By 1350 they had reached New Zealand, the final place on the globe to be settled by humans.

Since the Maya had a writing system, archaeologists know more about them than any other society in the Americas or the Pacific Islands. Accordingly, this chapter begins with the precursors of the Maya in modern-day Mexico and then proceeds to the Maya themselves.

Focus Questions

How did the development of agriculture and the building of early cities in Mesoamerica differ from that in Mesopotamia, India, and China?

ᴗ **What has the decipherment of the Maya script revealed about Maya governance, society, religion, and warfare?**

ᴗ **What were the similarities between the complex societies of the northern peoples and those of Mesoamerica? What do they suggest about contact?**

ᴗ **How did the history of complex society in the Andes differ from that in Mesoamerica?**

ᴗ **Where did the early settlers of the Pacific Islands come from, and where did they go? What vessels did they use, and how did they navigate?**

⬤ The First Complex Societies of Mesoamerica, 8000 B.C.E.–500 C.E.

Unlike in Mesopotamia, Egypt, India, and China, agriculture in the Americas arose not in river valleys but in a plateau region, the highlands of Mexico. The first planting occurred around 8000 B.C.E., two thousand years after it had in western Asia. The residents of Mexico continued to hunt and gather for thousands of years as they slowly began to cultivate corn, potatoes, cocoa beans, and other crops that grew nowhere else in the world. Large urban centers, one of the markers of complex society, appeared in Mexico around 1200 B.C.E.

The Development of Agriculture, 8000–1500 B.C.E.

The people of Tehuacán (tay-WAH-káhn) in the modern state of Puebla (PWAY-bla), Mexico, initially harvested wild grasses with tiny ears of seeds. Their grinding stones, the first evidence of cultivation in the Americas, date to 8000 B.C.E. Just as the Natufians of western Asia had gradually domesticated wheat by harvesting certain wild plants with desirable characteristics (see Chapter 1), the residents of Tehuacán selected different grasses with more rows of seeds until they eventually developed a domesticated variety of maize sometime around 7000 B.C.E. (Specialists prefer the term *maize* to *corn* because it is more specific.) Unlike the early farmers of western Asia, the people of Tehuacán used no draft animals.

Maize spread from the Tehuacán Valley throughout the region of **Mesoamerica,** which includes the southern two-thirds of modern Mexico, Guatemala, Belize, El Salvador, Honduras, Nicaragua, and Costa Rica. Located between the Atlantic and Pacific Oceans, Mesoamerica is bounded by barren desert north of modern Mexico. More rain falls in the east than in the west; because of the uneven rainfall, residents used irrigation channels to move the water. Maize later spread north to Canada and south to the tip of South America.

Once planted, maize required little tending until the harvest, when the hard husk on each kernel made it very difficult to eat. The dried kernels were ground or boiled and mixed with ground limestone to make a paste, called nixtamal (NISH-ta-mal), that was used to make unleavened cakes. As the proportion of cultivated

● **Mesoamerica** The region that includes the southern two-thirds of modern Mexico, Guatemala, Belize, El Salvador, Honduras, Nicaragua, and Costa Rica.

crops in the diet increased, the Mesoamericans gradually abandoned hunting and gathering. Eating little meat because they raised no animals, they cultivated squash and beans along with maize, three foods that together offered the same nutritional benefits (amino acids and vitamin B12) as meat. The systematized cultivation of maize made it possible to support larger populations. By 2500 B.C.E., the population of Mesoamerica had increased by perhaps twenty-five times; the largest settlements had several hundred residents who both farmed and continued to hunt.

Most of the peoples living in Mesoamerica had given up hunting and gathering and adopted full-time agriculture by 1500 B.C.E., the date of the earliest agricultural villages in the region. If an ancient farmer from anywhere in Mesopotamia, China, or India had visited at this time, he or she would have been amazed to see that no one in Mesoamerica employed the basic tools of farming so familiar to them—the plow, the wheel, or draft animals. Instead of the plow, the Mesoamericans used different types of digging sticks, and they dragged or carried things themselves because they did not have draft animals or the wheel. (The only wheels in the Americas appear on children's toys around 500 C.E.)

● **Olmec** A complex society (1200–400 B.C.E.) that arose on the Gulf of Mexico coast from modern-day Veracruz to Tabasco. Known particularly for the massive colossal heads hewn from basalt.

The Olmecs and Their Successors, 1200–400 B.C.E.

The **Olmec** peoples (1200–400 B.C.E.) built the first larger settlements along a 100-mile (160-km) stretch on the coast of the Gulf of Mexico from Veracruz to Tabasco (see Map 5.1) Raising two maize crops a year, the Olmec produced a large agricultural surplus, and the population may also have increased because of the nutritional benefits of the nixtamel diet.

Surviving colossal heads testify to the Olmec rulers' ability to mobilize their subjects for large labor projects. The Olmecs used stone hammers to hew these heads from basalt. They are 5 to 10 feet (1.5–3 m) tall, and the largest weighs over 40 tons (36 metric tons). The nearest source of basalt lay more than 50 miles (80 km) to the northwest, and archaeologists surmise that Olmec laborers carried the rock overland (they did not have the wheel) and built rafts to transport it along local rivers.

The peoples of Mesoamerica used two methods to count days: one cycle ran 365 days for the solar year, while the ritual cycle lasted 260 days. The solar year had 18 months of 20 days each with 5 extra days at the end of the year; the 260-day ritual cycle had 13 weeks of 20 days each. This complex calendrical system developed after the Olmec urban centers had already begun to decline around 400 B.C.E.

🔲 **Drawing of La Mojarra Stele**   This monument shows a warrior-king who ruled along the coast of Mexico in the second century C.E. He wears an elaborate headdress showing a bird deity. The glyphs, not all of which have yet been deciphered, describe how he became king with the assistance of a ritual specialist. The middle of the inscription uses the telltale bars and dots of the Long Count to give the date of 159 C.E.   (Drawing by George Stuart, from the Boundary End Archaeology Research Center)

MAP 5.1
Complex Societies in the Americas, ca. 1200 B.C.E. Starting around 1200 B.C.E., complex societies arose in two widely separated regions in the Americas. In modern-day Mexico the Olmec hewed giant heads from basalt; in modern-day Peru, the Chavin built large temples decorated with statues combining human and animal body parts.

CL Interactive Map

If one combined the two ways of counting time so that both cycles started on the same day and ran their full course, 18,980 days, or 52 years, would pass before the two cycles converged again. The 52-year cycle had one major drawback: one could not record events occurring more than 52 years earlier without confusion. Accordingly, the peoples of Mesoamerica developed the **Long Count**, a calendar that ran cumulatively, starting from a day far in the mythical past (whose equivalent is August 13, 3114 B.C.E.) and continuing to the present. The Long Count came into use in the fifth and fourth centuries B.C.E., when the successors to the Olmecs built several monuments bearing Long Count dates. The inscriptions use a mix of bars and dots to show the different units of the calendar: 400 years, 200 years, 1 year, 20 days, and 1 day.

These monuments contain texts written in at least three different languages used in Mexico after 400 B.C.E.: one near Oaxaca (WAH-ha-kah), another on the coast in the core Olmec areas, and Mayan in the Yucatán. These difficult texts have been partially deciphered because the local Amerindians speak languages descended from those used in the inscription and because some of the words are the same as in Mayan (see page 121).

• **Long Count** A calendar that ran cumulatively, starting from a day equivalent to August 13, 3114 B.C.E. and continuing to the present. Came into use in the fifth and fourth centuries B.C.E., when inscriptions of bars and dots showed different calendar units.

Teotihuacan, ca. 200 B.C.E.–600 C.E.

At the same time that the peoples along the coast were developing the Long Count and using glyphs, a huge metropolis, covering an area of 8 square miles (20 sq km) arose at **Teotihuacan** (tay-oh-tee-WAH-kahn), some 30 miles (50 km) northeast of modern-day Mexico City. Founded around 200 B.C.E., the city continued to grow until the year 650 C.E. Estimates of its population range between 40,000 and 200,000, certainly enough to qualify as a complex society. Teotihuacan's population made it the largest city in the Americas before 1500 but smaller than contemporary Rome's one million (see Chapter 7) or Luoyang's 500,000 during the Han dynasty (see Chapter 4). (See the feature "Visual Evidence: The Imposing Capital of Teotihuacan.")

On Teotihuacan's neatly gridded streets, ordinary people lived in one-story apartment compounds whose painted white exteriors had no windows and whose interiors were covered with colorful frescoes. Divided among several families, the largest compounds housed over a hundred people; the smallest, about twenty. A plumbing system drained wastewater into underground channels along the street, eventually converging in aboveground canals. The compounds show evidence of craft specializations: for example, one was a pottery workshop.

One residential district in the city has atypical rounded houses instead of the more common apartment compounds and contains pottery similar to that in the Veracruz region. Since this type of dwelling has been found in many sites along the Gulf of Mexico, archaeologists surmise that this was a community of migrant workers from the Veracruz region that continued to make the characteristic pottery of their homeland.

Some monuments in Teotihuacan have glyphs similar to those found elsewhere in Mexico, but scholars have not succeeded in deciphering them. Accordingly, we do not know whether Teotihuacan served as the capital of an empire, but it was definitely a large city-state. Sometime around 600 C.E. a fire, apparently caused by an internal revolt, leveled sections of the city, causing the residents to gradually move away.

● The Classic Age of the Maya, 250–910 C.E.

The **Maya,** like the other peoples of the Americas, differed from the Eurasian empires in that they created a remarkable complex society unaided by the wheel, plow, draft animals, or metal tools. But did the residents of Teotihuacan, the successors to the Olmecs, and the Maya people influence each other or develop separately? Scholars sharply disagree. Some see the Olmecs as a mother culture that gave both the Teotihuacan and Maya peoples their calendar, their writing system, and even their enormous flat-topped stepped pyramids—perhaps temples, perhaps palaces—of limestone and plaster packed with earth fill. These scholars believe that Yax K'uk Mo' traveled to Copán from Teotihuacan and introduced Teotihuacan's ways to the Maya. Others argue that the Olmecs, Teotihuacan, and Maya were neighboring cultures that did not directly influence each other. They think it more likely that Yax K'uk Mo' traveled only within Maya territory. Maya studies is a lively field, made even more exciting by the stream of new discoveries and new decipherments that may some day resolve these ongoing debates.

Some scholars also thought the Maya were a peace-loving people governed by a religious elite, until inscriptions dating between 250 and 910 C.E. were deciphered in the 1970s. The Maya today are seen rather as unrelentingly violent but no different from the Assyrian Empire and Shang dynasty China. Maya victors removed the fingernails of war captives, cut their chests open to remove their hearts, and publicly beheaded them as sacrifices to their deities.

The Deciphering of Maya Writing

One of the great intellectual breakthroughs of the twentieth century was the decipherment of the Mayan script. (Scholars today use the word *Maya* to refer to the people and *Mayan* for the language they spoke.) Mayan glyphs did not look like any of the world's other writing systems. They were so pictorial that many doubted they could represent sounds. In 1952, Yuri Knorosov, a Russian linguist, suggested that the Maya combined phonetic elements in different combinations to form words. Using dictionaries of various dialects spoken in the Maya heartland, he deciphered a few words that resembled their modern forms. His breakthrough meant that scholars were trying to decipher a living language, or at least the ancestor tongue of living languages, and not a dead language. Linguists suddenly wanted to do fieldwork among the 7.5 million living native speakers of Mayan dialects in Mexico and Guatemala.

For twenty years, a group of scholars and devoted amateurs—mostly Americans, but also Russians, Canadians, and Australians—pored over all known Maya ruins, making rubbings and sketching the glyphs they saw, and studying modern Mayan dialects. In 1973 they met at an academic conference held in Mexico, where for ten days they collectively deciphered the Mayan script.

The conference participants realized that one could write a single Mayan word several different ways: entirely phonetically, entirely pictorially, or using a combination of both phonetic sounds and pictures. For example, the artists who made Altar Q wrote the name of Yax K'uk Mo' by using both pictures of the quetzal (KATE-zahl) (*k'uk*) and macaw (*mo'*) birds and syllables representing the sounds "yax" and "k'inich" (*k-ih-niche*). Combined, they spell the name K'inich Yax K'uk Mo', or Great Sun Lord Quetzal Macaw (see the photo on page 114). It is as if one could write *hat* in English by drawing a picture of a hat 👒, or writing h + a + t, h + @ + t, or simply h + @.

Scholars specializing in Maya studies refer to the period from 250 to 910 as the classic age, because there are written inscriptions on monuments, and the period before 250 as the pre-classic age. Recent discoveries of Mayan inscriptions with earlier dates are forcing scholars to reconsider these labels. In the early classic period, between 250 and 550, Teotihuacan may have exerted political influence on various Maya kingdoms, including that of Yax K'uk Mo', before Teotihuacan's prosperity came to a sudden end. In some Maya cities, such as Tikal (TEE-kal), but not in others, such as Copán, construction of monuments and inscriptions stopped between 550 and 600, possibly because of a political or ecological crisis. This half century marks the division between the early classic period (250–550) and late classic period (600–800), when the building of monuments resumed. The latest Maya monument with an inscription is dated 910, marking the end of the terminal classic period (800–910).

THE IMPOSING CAPITAL OF TEOTIHUACAN

The three magnificent pyramids of Teotihuacan, 30 miles (50 km) northeast of Mexico City, impress visitors even today. Lined with smaller pyramids, the broad Avenue of the Dead runs from the Pyramid of the Moon past the Pyramid of the Sun to the Feathered Serpent Pyramid. All of these names, including *Teotihuacan,* which means "the abode of the gods," were given by Nahuatl-speaking settlers from the north after their arrival sometime in the twelfth century (see Chapter 15).

Since we do not know what the original residents of the city called these structures and since no one has deciphered the few glyphs that appear on scattered stones, archaeologists have exercised great ingenuity in trying to understand the city's layout. Teotihuacan is unusual in that none of the city's rulers built monuments to themselves. Because deities of later peoples, like the Maya (see below), were often associated with stars and planets, most concur that the city's orientation must have been astronomical, based on the different phases of Venus, the Morning Star honored by so many peoples in the Americas.

The discovery of more than two hundred skeletons under the Feathered Serpent Pyramid has shed new light on the building's purpose. The group with the most valuable jewelry appears to have the highest social status; another group that wears less valuable shell beads seems to rank lower. A third group of women had even less jewelry, while a fourth group consisted of uniformed men buried with large quantities of projectile points, most likely an army. The people in these groups assume different postures, some with their hands tied behind their backs, as if they had been killed before burial, possibly with the accompanying obsidian knives, blades, and piercing implements. Because looters dug two large trenches in the center of the Feathered Serpent Pyramid, archaeologists cannot be certain who was originally buried there, but the mass burials and valuable grave goods make it likely that this was the ruler's tomb. The dead buried at Teotihuacan, like the terracotta warriors of the Qin founder (see Chapter 4), appear to have served as a sacrificial army for the deceased ruler, who was buried circa 200 C.E. at the time of the pyramid's completion.

The World's Largest Pyramids

Name	Site	Date	Material	Height
Great Pyramid	Giza, Egypt	2580 B.C.E.	stone	480 ft (146 m)
Pyramid of the Sun	Teotihuacan	200 C.E.	volcanic rubble and earth	216 feet (66 m)
Tarharqa's Pyramid	Nuri, Nubia	664 B.C.E.	stone	160 ft (49 m)
Pyramid of the Moon	Teotihuacan	200 C.E.	volcanic rubble and earth	140 feet (43 m)
Pirámide Mayor	Caral	2600 B.C.E.	brick and earth	60 ft (18 m)

QUESTION FOR ANALYSIS

 Compare and contrast the site of Teotihuacan with the urban centers of other early complex societies in the Americas (Caral, Olmec, Maya) and in Eurasia (Sumer, Indus River Valley, Shang dynasty).

With sides over 700 feet (213 m) long at the base, and over twenty stories high, the Pyramid of the Sun is the largest structure in the Americas made before 1500.

The Feathered Serpent Pyramid, also called the Quetzalcoatl Temple, has staircases up the side of the monument with stone facades and elaborate serpent heads dividing the different terraces.

The Citadel, facing the Feathered Serpent Pyramid, was the political center of the city.

(Georg Gerster/Photo Researchers, Inc.)

The Avenue of the Dead, 50 yards (50 m) wide, extends for more than 3 miles (5.2 km) and connects the different pyramids of Teotihuacan.

Laborers made the Pyramid of the Moon in the same way that they made the Pyramid of the Sun: they piled up earth and rubble to form a pyramid shape, leveled off horizontal terraces, and then faced the surface with adobe and stone.

This modern ring road, the Periférico, was built in the 1960s to steer traffic away from the monuments.

123

Since 1973 Mayanists have learned to read about 85 percent of all surviving glyphs. Since inscriptions follow a set format, beginning with the rise of a particular ruler, it is possible to understand inscriptions at ruins throughout the Maya region. So far the focus on the history of royal dynasties unfortunately reveals little about ordinary people. Analysts are trying to bridge that immense information gap by ingeniously combining inscriptions and paintings from the classic period with information from European observers in the sixteenth century (see Chapter 15) and even ethnographic data on Maya peoples alive today.

Maya Government and Society

• **Copán** A typical Maya city-state. At its peak in the eighth century, Copán had a population of eighteen to twenty thousand divided into sharply demarcated groups: the ruling family, the nobility, ordinary people, and slaves.

Copán, where Yax K'uk Mo' founded his dynasty, provides a good example of a typical Maya city-state. At its peak in the eighth century, when the sixteenth king commissioned Altar Q to commemorate his sixteen dynastic predecessors, Copán had a population of eighteen to twenty thousand. The population was divided into sharply demarcated groups: the ruling family, the nobility, ordinary people, and slaves.

As the ruler of Copán and commander of the army, Yax K'uk Mo' ranked higher than everyone else. He decided when to ally with other city-states and when to fight them, as well as how to allocate the different crops and taxes received from the populace. When a ruler died, a council of nobles met to verify that his son or his younger brother was fit to rule. If a ruler died without an heir, the council appointed someone from one of the highest-ranking noble families to succeed him.

We can understand something of Yax K'uk Mo's status from his tomb. (See the feature "World History in Today's World: The World's First Chocolate.") Lying on a stone platform, the body of Yax K'uk Mo' had a jade chest ornament like that shown in his portrait on Altar Q (see page 114). In his Altar Q portrait he wears a shield on his right arm; the shattered right arm of the corpse indicates that he badly wounded this arm, perhaps in battle. Archaeologists have compared the levels of certain unusual isotopes of strontium in his bones with soil samples from different regions and have found that he was a native of neither Teotihuacan nor Copán. He most likely spent time in other Maya cities and Teotihuacan before coming to Copán in 426 near the age of 50.

Archaeologists working at Copán found an even more lavish grave near that of Yax K'uk Mo' that held a tripod vessel painted with a picture of a Teotihuacan-style pyramid and over ten thousand jade beads. They initially assumed that it was another king's tomb, yet analysis of the pelvis indicated that the person was a 50-year-old woman who had given birth to at least one child. Since her tomb contains no glyphs, archaeologists are not certain of her identity, but the grave's central location suggests that she was the wife of Yax K'uk Mo'.

Ranking just below the members of the ruling family, the nobles of Maya society lived in large, spacious houses such as those found in the section of Copán known as the House of the Officials. One typical compound there contains between forty and fifty buildings surrounding eleven courtyards. In judging a man's prominence, the Maya considered all of his relatives on both his father's and mother's side. The Mayan word for "nobles" means "he whose descent is known on both sides."[2]

Literate in a society where few could read or write, scribes came from the highest ranks of the nobility. When the king's armies did well in battle, the scribes

The World's First Chocolate

When scientists tested the residue found on a deer-shaped vessel from Yax K'uk Mo's tomb, they discovered traces of theobromine, a caffeine-like molecule found only in chocolate. They guess that Mesoamericans started preparing drinks made from pounded seeds from the cacao (*ka-ka-wa* in Mayan) tree, perhaps as early as 600 B.C.E. and certainly by the early fifth century, when Yax K'uk Mo' was buried at Copán. The origins of the English word *chocolate* are much disputed; the word probably comes from the combination of the Mayan word for "hot" (*chocol*) with "water" (*atl*) used by the Nahuatl peoples of Mexico.

The Maya did not sweeten the cacao drink but added spices and crushed chile peppers to make a variety of drinks they prized for their foam. When Spaniards introduced chocolate to Europeans in the sixteenth century, they added sugar to the cacao paste and heated it to make it more palatable. The addition of sugar made chocolate irresistible. The annual consumption of chocolate in the United States averages 11.3 pounds (5.13 kg) per person, or 1.5 million tons (1.33 million metric tons).

The Maya believed that cacao could cure a variety of ills, including hemorrhoids and nervous tension. Some Amerindian tribes in Panama have surprisingly low blood pressure, possibly because they consume cacao with every meal. Fresh cacao contains flavonol, a naturally occurring chemical that lowers blood pressure and possibly LDL ("bad cholesterol"). In the past few years, the Mars chocolate bar company and the U.S. National Institutes of Health have cosponsored research to see if they can make either a chocolate beverage or a candy bar that lowers blood pressure. Unfortunately, it is difficult to manufacture a chocolate product with as much flavonol as fresh cacao beans. Some skeptics think the potential benefits in lowered blood pressure or cholesterol, which have yet to be demonstrated conclusively, may be more than offset by the likely weight gain. Although Americans name chocolate as their favorite snack, demand has been flat for the past five years in weight-conscious America.

Sources: New York Times, June 10, 2003, first Science page, p. 2; *New York Times,* February 17, 2004, pp. F5, F10; Sophie D. Coe and Michael D. Coe, *The True History of Chocolate* (New York: Thames and Hudson, 1996).

enjoyed the best treatment that the king could give them. When the king's armies lost, they were often taken prisoner.

Only those scribes with mathematical skills could maintain the elaborate calendar. Having developed the concept of zero, Maya ritual specialists devised an extraordinarily sophisticated numerical system. Astronomers observed the stars and planets so closely that they could predict eclipses. They were particularly skilled in tracking the movements of Venus, which during some seasons appeared first in the evening before any stars, and in others was the last to disappear in the morning. The Maya used their knowledge of celestial bodies to determine auspicious days for inaugurating rulers, conducting elaborate religious ceremonies, or starting wars.

The most prosperous ordinary people became merchants specializing in long-distance trade. Salt was the one necessity the Maya had to import because their diet did not provide enough sodium to prevent a deficiency. They collected salt from the Yucatán beaches and shipped it in canoes along the ocean's shore and on interior rivers until it had to be carried by hand. Some of the items traded were luxury goods like jade, shells, and quetzal bird feathers, which flickered blue, gold, or green in the light.

The craft specialists who transformed these raw materials into finely worked goods lived in the small houses of ordinary people. The Maya first encountered gold around the year 800 and learned to work it, yet they made few items from it. They preferred green jade, which they carved and smoothed with saws made of coated string and different types of sandpaper.

The most important trade good in the Maya world was **obsidian,** a naturally occurring volcanic glass. The best material available to the Maya for making tools, obsidian could be worked into fine art objects, dart tips, and knife blades sharper than modern scalpels. Obsidian shattered easily though, and so the Maya also made tools from chert, a flintlike rock that was more durable.

Outside the city lived the farmers who provided Copán's residents with their food supply, since the urban inhabitants could not raise enough food to feed themselves. Their diet consisted of large amounts of maize and smaller amounts of beans, squash, and chili peppers. City dwellers had fruit gardens and were able occasionally to hunt wild game.

Since the Maya had no draft animals, most cultivators worked land within a day or two's walk from the urban center. Their fields probably marked the limit of each city-state's direct political control. The Maya practiced swidden agriculture (sometimes called slash-and-burn farming), meaning they farmed the same place for only one or two seasons. Once the fertility of a given plot gave out, cultivators moved to a new site, where they cleared fields by cutting down trees. They waited for the felled trees and plants to dry, set fire to the brush, and then planted maize in the fertile ashes. Recently, aerial photographs of the Yucatán, Mexico, and Belize have revealed raised fields dating back to the time of the Maya, which were farmed season after season.

The lowest-ranking people in Maya society were the slaves, who were forced to work in the fields after being taken as prisoners of war. Higher-ranking prisoners of war, drawn from the nobles, were almost always killed in public displays.

The Religious Beliefs of the Maya

Many Maya rituals featured the spilling of royal blood, which the Maya considered sacred. Surviving paintings from throughout the Maya region depict women pulling thorny vines through their tongues and kings sticking either a stingray spine or a pointed bone tool through the tips of their penises. No surviving text explains exactly why the Maya thought blood sacred, but blood offerings clearly played a key role in their belief system.

One of the few Mayan sources that survives, an oral epic named **_Popul Vuh_** (POPE-uhl voo), or "The Council Book," features a series of games in which players on two teams moved the ball by hitting it with their hips and tried to get it past their opponents' end line. The Maya believed that the earth was recreated each time the hip ballgame was played, and the side seen as being tested by the gods, usually prisoners of war, always lost, after which their blood was spilled in an elaborate ceremony. (See the feature "Movement of Ideas: The Ballgame in _Popul Vuh_.")

Recorded nearly one thousand years after the decline of the Maya, the _Popul Vuh_ preserves only a part of their rich legends, but scholars have used it in conjunction with surviving texts to piece together the key elements of the Maya belief system. All Maya gods, the _Popul Vuh_ explains, are descended from a divine pair. The Lizard House, the father, invented the Mayan script and supported all learning, while his wife, Lady Rainbow, was a deity of weaving and medicine who also helped women endure the pain of childbirth. Their descendants, the Maya believed, each

· obsidian A naturally occurring volcanic glass used by different peoples in the Americas to make fine art objects, dart tips, and knife blades sharper than modern scalpels. The most important good traded by the Maya.

· _Popul Vuh_ One of the few surviving sources in the Mayan language, this oral epic features a series of hip ballgames between the gods and humans. Originally written in Mayan glyphs, it was recorded in the Roman alphabet in the 1500s.

presided over a different realm: separate gods existed for merchants, hunters, fishermen, soldiers, and the ruling families. Maya rulers sacrificed their prisoners of war as offerings to these deities.

The Maya communicated with the dead using various techniques. Caves served as portals between the world of the living and the Xibalba (SHE-bal-ba) Underworld described in *Popul Vuh*. One cave is 2,790 feet (850 m) long; its walls are decorated with drawings of the Hero Twins, the ballgame, and sexual acts. The Maya who visited this and other caves employed enemas to intoxicate themselves so they could see the dead. They performed these enemas by attaching bone tubes, found in large quantities at Maya sites, to leather or rubber bags filled with different liquids. Surviving drawings make it impossible to identify the liquids, but anthropologists speculate that the enema bags were filled with wine, chocolate, or hallucinogens made from the peyote cactus.

Watching a Ballgame   Seven contestants play the ballgame in front of an attentive audience seated on all four sides. Spectators lean forward with great interest; mothers watch with their arms draped over their children's shoulders. This clay model was found in a tomb in Nayarit, in western Mexico, and dates to between 100 B.C.E. and 250 C.E., making it one of the earliest representations of the game ever found.   (Yale University Art Gallery)

War, Politics, and the Decline of the Maya

In the past few decades, scholars have devoted considerable energy and ingenuity to sorting out the relationships among the sixty or so Maya city-states. Much hinges on the interpretation of a few key phrases that appear in inscriptions: some rulers are said to be someone else's king, an indication that they accepted another king as their overlord or ruler. It is not clear what ties bound a subordinate ruler to his superior: marriage ties, loyalty oaths, military alliances, or perhaps a mixture of all three.

Because various rulers vied continuously to increase their territory and become each other's lord, the different Maya city-states devoted considerable resources to war. Armies consisted of foot soldiers, commoners who wore light protection made from either animal skins or padded cotton. Their weapons included spears with obsidian points, slingshots, and darts propelled by a spear-thrower. The Maya did not have the bow and arrow, which appeared among the Mississippian peoples to the north around 900 C.E. On the most informal level of conflict, a group of soldiers might steal into enemy territory to take captives, while in formal battles, two opposing armies of infantry faced off and showered each other with darts or stones from slingshots. Traps and ambushes were common, and the fighters used both daggers and spears in hand-to-hand combat.

The goal of all Maya warfare was to obtain captives. Low-born captives were assigned to work in the maize fields of nobles, while prisoners of higher status, particularly those from noble families, were held in captivity for long periods of time, sometimes as much as twenty years. In inscriptions rulers brag about how many captives they held at any one time because they wanted to appear more powerful. Rulers also staged public spectacles in which they tore out the hearts of the defeated prisoners or publicly beheaded them.

The Ballgame in *Popul Vuh*

The detailed narrative of the Maya epic *Popul Vuh* describes the destruction of multiple previous worlds and the creation of a new one. The complicated plot involves two sets of ball-playing twins: after disturbing the gods with their play, one pair go to the Xibalba Underworld (derived from the Mayan word for "fear," "trembling"), where they die at the hands of One and Seven Death, the head lords of Xibalba. The severed head of one of these twins hangs on a tree from which its spittle magically impregnates Lady Blood, who gives birth to the second set of twins, Hunahpu (HOO-nah-pooh) and Xbalanque (sh-bal-on-kay). These Hero Twins, far more skillful than their father and uncle, at first trick the gods of the Underworld repeatedly and then defeat them in the ballgame described in the episode below. Eventually they also die, but because the gods grant them another life, they rise at the end of the narrative to become the sun and the moon, creating the upper world or cosmos.

The earliest archaeological evidence of the game comes from the Olmec site of El Manatí, located 6 miles (10 km) east of San Lorenzo, where a dozen rubber balls dating to around 500 B.C.E. were found. Almost every Maya city-state had a ball court, usually in the shape of L, with walls around it, located near a major temple. The Maya played this soccer-like game with heavy rubber balls measuring 12 or 18 inches (33 or 50 cm) across. The Maya cooked liquid rubber from latex trees and allowed it to cool and solidify into a heavy mass.

Sometimes the ball-makers used a human skull to make a hollow, less lethal, ball. The game spread throughout the Maya core region and as far north as Snaketown near Phoenix, Arizona, the home of an early Anasazi people who had two ball courts and rubber balls.

Since ball courts and balls do not provide enough information to understand how the game was played, anthropologists are closely studying the modern hip ballgames in the few villages near Mazatlán (ma-zát-LAN), Sinaloa (sin-A-loh-a) State in northwestern Mexico, where the game is still played. Two opposing teams of three to five players try to get the ball past the other team's end line. After serving with their hands, they propel the heavy rubber balls with their hips. Although players covered their hips with padding, called a "yoke" below, the hips of modern players develop calluses and often become permanently bruised a deep-black color. We cannot be sure that everyone who played the game knew the story of the Hero Twins, but many players probably understood the game as a contest between two teams, one representing good, life, or the hero twins, and the other evil, death, or Xibalba, which was always victorious.

This passage from the *Popul Vuh* describes the first test the twins must endure.

Source: *Popul Vuh: The Definitive Edition of the Mayan Book of the Dawn of Life and the Glories of Gods and Kings,* trans. Dennis Tedlock (New York: Simon and Schuster, 1996), pp. 119–122.

First they entered Dark House.

And after that, the messenger of One Death brought their torch, burning when it arrived, along with one cigar apiece.

"'Here is their torch,' says the lord. 'They must return the torch in the morning, along with the cigars. They must return them intact,' say the lords," the messenger said when he arrived.

"Very well," they said, but they didn't burn the torch—instead, something that looked like fire was substituted. This was the tail of the macaw, which looked like a torch to the sentries.

And as for the cigars, they just put fireflies at the tips of those cigars, which they kept lit all night.

"We've defeated them," said the sentries, but the torch was not consumed—it just looked that way. And as for the cigars, there wasn't anything burning there—it just looked that way. When these things were taken back to the lords:

"What's happening? Where did they come from? Who begot them and bore them? Our hearts are really hurting, because what they're doing to us is no good. They're different in looks and different in their very being," they said among themselves. And when they had summoned all the lords:

"Let's play ball, boys," the boys were told. And then they were asked by One and Seven Death:

"Where might you have come from? Please name it," Xibalba said to them.

"Well, wherever did we come from? We don't know," was all they said. They didn't name it.

"Very well then, we'll just go play ball, boys," Xibalba told them.

"Good," they said.

"Well, this is the one we should put in play, here's our rubber ball," said the Xibalbans.

"No thanks. This is the one to put in, here's ours," said the boys.

"No it's not. This is the one we should put in," the Xibalbans said again.

"Very well," said the boys.

"After all, it's just a decorated one," said the Xibalbans.

"Oh no it's not. It's just a skull, we say in return," said the boys.

"No it's not," said the Xibalbans.

"Very well," said Hunahpu. When it was sent off by Xibalba, the ball was stopped by Hunahpu's yoke [hip-pad].

And then, while Xibalba watched, the White Dagger came out from inside the ball. It went clattering, twisting all over the floor of the court.

"What's that!" said Hunahpu and Xbalanque. "Death is the only thing you want for us! Wasn't it *you* who sent a summons to us, and wasn't it *your* messenger who went? Truly, take pity on us, or else we'll just leave," the boys told them.

And this is what had been ordained for the boys: that they should have died right away, right there, defeated by that knife. But it wasn't like that. Instead, Xibalba was again defeated by the boys.

"Well, don't go, boys. We can still play ball, but we'll put yours into play," the boys were told.

"Very well," they said, and this was time for their rubber ball, so the ball was dropped in.

And after that, they specified the prize:

"What should our prize be?" asked the Xibalbans.

"It's yours for the asking," was all the boys said.

"We'll just win four bowls of flowers," said the Xibalbans.

"Very well. What kinds of flowers?" the boys asked Xibalba.

"One bowl of red petals, one bowl of white petals, one bowl of yellow petals, and one bowl of whole ones," said the Xibalbans.

"Very well," said the boys, and then their ball was dropped in. The boys were their equals in strength and made many plays, since they only had very good thoughts. Then the boys gave themselves up in defeat, and the Xibalbans were glad when they were defeated:

"We've done well. We've beaten them on the first try," said the Xibalbans. "Where will they go to get the flowers?" they said in their hearts.

"Truly, before the night is over, you must hand over our flowers and our prize," the boys, Hunahpu and Xbalanque, were told by Xibalba.

"Very well. So we're also playing ball at night," they said when they accepted their charge.

And after that, the boys entered Razor House, the second test of Xibalba.

QUESTIONS FOR ANALYSIS

▸ What tricks do the hero twins play on the lords of the Xibalba underworld? How do the Xibalba lords retaliate?

▸ What happens that is unexpected? Why do the twins lose?

■ **Celebrating a Maya Victory in Battle**   This colorful fresco in a Maya tomb in Bonampak, Mexico, commemorates the victory of the ruler, who wears an elaborate headdress and a jacket made from jaguar skin. He relentlessly thrusts his spear downwards and grasps the hair of a prisoner whose outstretched hand implores his captor. These murals, which reveal so much about the lives of the Maya, were suddenly abandoned around 800, a time when work on many other monuments stopped abruptly, marking the end of the classic era.   (© Charles and Josette Lenars/Corbis)

At the peak of Maya power in 750, the population reached eight to ten million. Sometime around the year 800, the Maya city-states entered an era of decline, evident because site after site has produced unfinished monuments abruptly abandoned by stoneworkers. So sudden was the decline that workers at some sites seem to have stopped carving after completing a single face of a square monument.

Archaeologists have different explanations for the Maya decline. In the seventh and eighth centuries, two city-states, Tikal in northern Guatemala and Kalak'mul (KA-lack-muhl) 60 miles (100 km) to the north, formed blocs of allied city-states that engaged in unending warfare. The drain on resources may have depopulated the Maya cities. The fragile agricultural base, with its heavy use of slash-and-burn farming, depleted the nutrients in the fields close to the political centers. In some places, a sustained drought between 800 and 1050 may have dealt the final blow to the ecosystem. Some residents of the different Maya city-states may have relocated to defensible locations in the northern Yucatán after 910.

Maya culture revived during the post-classic period (910–1300), and the city of Chichen Itza (CHEE-chen It-za) in the northern Yucatán, which flourished between 1000 and 1200, combined classic elements of Maya and central Mexican architecture and city planning. The ball court at Chichen Itza measures 545 feet (166 m) by 223 feet (68 m), making it the largest ball court in the Americas. The Maya continued to create monuments, but instead of carving them in stone, they used paint, which has since worn off. Although Maya culture did not die out after 1200, the Maya never again matched the social stratification, specialized occupations, and large urban centers of the classic period.

⬤ The Northern Peoples, 500 B.C.E.–1200 C.E.

Complex society arose north of the Rio Grande, in the area occupied by the modern United States and Canada, relatively late—after the decline of the Maya—and possibly because of contact with Mesoamerica. The North Americans planted maize as the Mesoamericans did, and their cities resembled their Maya counterparts. The first complex societies in North America, both dating to after 700 C.E., were the Mississippian culture in the central United States and the Anasazi (AH-nah-sah-zee) culture in the southwest United States.

Until about 500 B.C.E., the peoples living to the north continued to hunt and gather in small bands of around sixty people, much like the residents of Monte Verde, Chile (see Chapter 1), and, as a result, their communities remained small. A major change occurred when the Adena (uh-DEE-nuh) (500 B.C.E.–100 C.E.) created earthworks along the Ohio River Valley in Ohio and Illinois. Their settlements were not large urban centers, but these earthworks demonstrate that their leaders could organize large-scale labor projects.

The Adena peoples built mounds containing rich burials, most likely of their leaders, a sign of increasing social stratification. Some mounds form perfect circles, while others are in the shape of animals, like the famous 1,300-foot (400-m) Serpent Mound of Ohio that portrays a snake eating an egg. Living in circular houses constructed from tree trunks and bark, the Adena ate a diet of wild animals, fish, and plants they gathered in the forest. They did not farm.

The successors to the Adena, the Hopewell peoples (200 B.C.E.–500 C.E.), built larger earthworks in the valleys of the Ohio, Illinois, and Mississippi Rivers. They occupied a wide region extending from western New York to Kansas and from the Gulf of Mexico to the Great Lakes. Unlike the Adena, the Hopewell peoples cultivated maize, beans, and squash. Taller and more elaborate than the Adena mounds, the Hopewell earthworks formed clusters of circles, rectangles, and polygons linked by dirt causeways. These earthworks also contained graves of their leaders, who were buried with various goods.

Archaeologists have reconstructed the Hopewell trade routes by locating the sources of unusual items, such as alligator teeth and skulls from Florida, mapping the sites where those items appear, and then inferring the trade routes by linking the source with its various destinations. The Hopewell trading networks, more extensive than those of the Adena, extended from the Rocky Mountains to the Atlantic Ocean; with their neighbors to the south in modern-day Mexico, they traded conch shells, shark teeth, and obsidian.

The Mississippian peoples (800–1450) were the first northern people to build the large urban centers that characterize complex society. They occupied over a hundred different sites concentrated in the Mississippi River Valley. Mississippian towns followed a Maya plan, with temples or palaces on earthen mounds around a central plaza. The Mississippian peoples were the first in the Americas to develop the bow and arrow, sometime around 900 C.E.

The largest surviving mound, in the Cahokia (kuh-HOKE-ee-uh) Mounds of Collinsville, Illinois (just east of Saint Louis), is 100 feet (30 m) high and 1,000 feet (300 m) long and was built in fourteen stages. The sheer magnitude of this earthwork testifies to the power the leaders had over their subjects. Cahokia, with a population of thirty thousand, held eighty-four other mounds, some for temples, some for mass burials. One mound contained the corpses of 110 young women, evidence of a sacrificial cult to either a leader or a deity.

The other major complex society of the north appeared in modern-day Colorado, Arizona, Utah, and New Mexico: the Anasazi. Their centers also show signs of contact with the Maya, most notably in the presence of ball courts. During the Pueblo period (700–1300), the Anasazi built two kinds of houses: pit houses carved out of the ground and pueblos made from bricks, mortar, and log roofs. One pueblo structure in Chaco, New Mexico, had eight hundred rooms in five stories, home to one thousand residents. After 1150 the Anasazi began to build their pueblos next to cliff faces, as at Mesa Verde, Colorado. They used irrigation to farm, and their craftspeople made distinctive pottery, cotton and feather clothing, and turquoise jewelry.

These two North American complex societies postdate the Maya, and their many similarities to the Maya suggest extensive contact with them. Like so many other urban centers in the Americas, Cahokia Mounds and Mesa Verde declined suddenly after 1200 C.E., when their populations dispersed, and archaeologists do not know why.

The Peoples of the Andes, 3100 B.C.E.–1000 C.E.

Several complex societies arose, flourished, and collapsed between 3100 B.C.E. and 1000 C.E. in the Andean region, which includes modern-day Peru, Bolivia, Ecuador, Argentina, and Chile in South America. These complex societies predated the first Mesoamerican complex society of the Olmecs by nearly two thousand years, indicating that the two regions developed independently of each other.

All the Andean complex societies built city-states with large urban centers, though never on the scale of Teotihuacan. Archaeologists have identified the largest urban centers and know when they reached their greatest population, but, since there are no documents, they know less about the cities and their relationships to the surrounding villages.

The Andean mountain chain runs up the center of the Andean region, which extends east to the edge of the dense Amazon rainforest and west to the Pacific coast. Although at a higher altitude than Mesoamerica, this region has a similarly uneven distribution of rainfall. In the east, rain falls heavily, while to the west, almost none falls. When agriculture spread from Mexico to these dryer regions, the residents collected rainwater and brought it to their fields by a system of channels.

The main staple of the diet was potatoes, supplemented by squash, chili peppers, beans, and sometimes maize, which could grow only at lower altitudes. The earliest strains of domesticated squash date to about 8000 B.C.E. Sometime around 5000 B.C.E., the Andeans domesticated the llama and the alpaca. Both animals could carry loads of approximately 100 pounds (50 kg) over distances of 10 to 12 miles (16–20 km) a day. The Andeans never rode these animals or raised them to eat. Their main source of animal protein was the domesticated guinea pig.

The earliest large urban settlement in the Americas, at the site of **Caral** (KA-ral) in the Andes, lies some 100 miles (160 km) north of Lima, the capital of modern Peru, and only 14 miles (22 km) from the Pacific coast. People have known about the site since the early twentieth century because its structures are prominent and so clearly visible from the air, but only in 2001 did archaeologists realize that it dated to 3100 B.C.E. Since then they have found more than twenty satellite communities around Caral.

> • **Caral** The earliest complex society (3100–1800 B.C.E.) in the Americas, whose main urban center was located at Caral, in modern-day Peru, in the Andes Mountains.

■ **Latin America's First Civilization at Caral, Peru**   Since 1900 people have known about the Caral site, with its five smaller pyramids and one large central structure, but only recently were archaeologists able to date the site to 3100 B.C.E. Caral was a large city-state, with some twenty smaller communities in the immediate neighborhood. Archaeologists have found clear signs of social stratification: the wealthiest residents lived on the tops of the pyramids while the poorer lived on lower levels or on the outskirts of the town.   (© George Steinmetz)

The Caral site contains five small pyramid-shaped structures and one large one: the Pirámide Mayor (PI-ra-me-day my-your), which stands 60 feet (18 m) tall and covers 5 acres (.02 km) (see the table "The World's Largest Pyramids," included in the feature "Visual Evidence: The Imposing Capital of Teotihuacan"). Inside the pyramid, archaeologists found a set of thirty-two carved flutes made from condor and pelican bone with decorations showing birds and monkeys, possibly deities. The three thousand or so people at the site included wealthy residents living in large dwellings on top of the pyramids, craftsmen in smaller houses at their base, and unskilled laborers in much simpler dwellings located around the perimeters of the town. Caral, like Uruk in Mesopotamia or Harappa in India, showed clear signs of social stratification. It was probably a city-state, not an early empire.

The history of the site reflects the rise-and-fall pattern so common to the early cities of the Americas and also to the Indus Valley (see Chapter 3). Agricultural improvements led to dramatic urban growth, followed by sudden decline. Usually no direct evidence reveals why a given city was abandoned, but drought and over-farming may have caused agricultural productivity to decline and food to run out. Caral was abandoned in 1800 B.C.E.

● **Chavin** Andean complex society (1200–200 B.C.E.) in modern-day Peru. Best known for its temples and large stone sculptures of animals.

In 1200 B.C.E., more than one thousand years after Caral was occupied, a major urban center arose at **Chavin** (cha-VEEN), about 60 miles (100 km) north of Caral (see Map 5.1). Chavin cities have large temples, some in the shape of a U, and impressive stone sculptures. The statues at the temple in Chavin combine elements of different animals such as jaguars, snakes, and eagles with human body parts to create composite human-animal sculptures, possibly of deities.

In 350 B.C.E., during the last years of the Chavin culture, several distinct regional cultures arose on the south coast of Peru that are most famous for the Nazca (NAZ-ka) lines, a series of earthworks near the modern town of Nazca. The Nazca people scraped away the dark surface layer of the desert to reveal a lighter-colored soil beneath; they then used the dark earth to build embankments along the trenches. No one knows how people working on the ground created these designs, which are still visible from the air today. Some of the Nazca lines run 6 miles (10 km) in a straight line through the desert; others form elaborate designs of spiders, whales, and monkeys, which may have been offerings to or depictions of their gods. No large cities of the Nazca people have been found, but the Nazca lines, like the earthworks of the Adena and Hopewell peoples, show that their rulers were able to mobilize large numbers of laborers.

Occupied between 600 and 1000 C.E., the biggest Andean political center was at Tiwanaku (TEE-wan-a-koo), 12 miles (20 km) south of Lake Titicaca (tit-tee-ka-ka), southern Bolivia, at the high altitude of 11,800 feet (3,600 m) above sea level. The rulers of the Tiwanaku city-state, archaeologists surmise, exercised some kind of political control over a large area extending through modern-day Bolivia, Argentina, northern Chile, and southern Peru. At its peak, Tiwanaku was home to some forty thousand people. Its farmers could support such a large population because they used a raised-field system: the irrigation channels they dug around their fields helped to keep the crops from freezing on chilly nights.

Sometime around 700 to 800 C.E., the Andean peoples, alone among the peoples living in the Americas, learned how to work metal intensively. Unlike the Maya, the Andeans discovered how to extract metallic ore from rocks and heat different metals to form alloys. They made bronze both by combining copper with tin, as was common in Eurasia, and also by combining copper with arsenic.

One site in Peru, in continuous use after 700, had draft furnaces in which families melted fuel and metal ore together, producing slag with copper in it, which they extracted and worked into ingots, small sheets, or "ax money"—ax-shaped pieces of metal tied together in bundles and placed in tombs as an offering for the dead.

Andean graves have produced the only metal tools found so far in the Americas. Some are oversized, some unfinished, yet all were clearly designed for display. Most Andean metal was used to make decorations worn by people or was placed on buildings, not for tools or weapons.

The Andean use of metal challenges yet another preconception prompted by the complex societies of Eurasia. In Mesopotamia, Egypt, India, and China, people switched to metal tools—first bronze, then iron—as soon as they learned to mine metal ore and make alloys. But the Andean peoples continued to use their traditional tools of wood and stone and used their new discovery of metal quite differently: for ceremonial and decorative purposes.

The Polynesian Voyages of Exploration, 1000 B.C.E.–1350 C.E.

Almost all the societies of the Americas discussed above, including the Maya, were land-based. Their residents used canoes for trips on inland waterways and for occasional voyages hugging the ocean shore, but they focused their energies on farming and building cities. In contrast, the peoples of the Pacific, who lived on the islands inside the Polynesian Triangle, spent much of their lives on the sea. Like the residents of the Americas, they developed in isolation from Eurasia, and like them, they developed quite differently from the Eurasians. Although their urban centers never became the large cities of complex societies, their societies were stratified and their leaders mobilized large numbers of their subjects for labor projects, often the construction of stone monuments.

Humans had reached Australia in about 60,000 B.C.E. (see Chapter 1), and they ventured into the Pacific sometime after that. Starting around 1000 B.C.E., when the Fiji islands of Tonga and Samoa were first settled, early voyagers crossed the Pacific Ocean using only the stars to navigate and populated most of the islands of the Pacific. Their voyages resulted in one of the longest yet least-documented seaborne migrations in human history. How and why did these ancient voyagers travel so far? These questions have excited a century of lively debate and are far from settled.

The Settlement of the Polynesian Triangle

The islands of the Pacific fall into two groups: those lying off Australia and Indonesia—Micronesia (mike-ro-NEE-zhuh), Melanesia (mel-uh-NEE-zhuh), and New Guinea—and those within the **Polynesian Triangle,** an imaginary triangle with sides 4,000 miles (6,500 km) long linking Hawai'i, Easter Island, and New Zealand (see Map 5.2). With seventy times more water than islands, the Polynesian Triangle contains several thousand islands ranging in size from tiny

• Polynesian Triangle An imaginary triangle with sides 4,000 miles (6,500 km) long linking Hawai'i, Easter Island, and New Zealand and containing several thousand islands.

🌐 **MAP 5.2**
Pacific Migration Routes Before 1500 Starting around 1000 B.C.E., the peoples living in Micronesia and Melanesia began to go to islands lying to the east in the Pacific Ocean. At first, they took canoes to the islands they could see with the naked eye. But later they traveled thousands of miles without navigational instruments, reaching Hawai'i before 300 C.E., Easter Island by 400 C.E., and New Zealand in 1350 C.E.

uninhabited atolls to the largest, New Zealand, with an area of 103,695 square miles (268,570 sq km). The triangle's vast area can hold the continental United States twice over with room to spare.

The islands lying close to Indonesia and Australia were settled first. As the discovery of Mungo Man in Australia, which dates to circa 60,000 B.C.E., showed (see Chapter 1), ancient peoples could go from one island to the next in small crafts. Since the islands of Micronesia and Melanesia were located close together, the next island was always within sight. But as these ancient settlers ventured farther east, the islands became farther apart: between Easter Island and Peru lie 2,250 miles (3,600 km) of open ocean. Sometime before 300 C.E. the first settlers reached Hawai'i, and after the year 400 C.E. they had reached Easter Island, or Rapa Nui (RA-pah nwee). Their final destination, in 1350 C.E., was New Zealand.

All the spoken languages within the Polynesian Triangle belong to the Oceanic language family, a subset of the Eastern Austronesian family. (Western Austronesian languages, including Vietnamese [see Chapter 4], are spoken in Southeast Asia.) Languages within the Oceanic family differ only slightly among themselves; while the Tahitians say, "tabu," meaning "forbidden" or "prohibited," the Hawaiian pronunciation is "kabu." (This word has entered English as *taboo*.)

The most distinctive artifact that reveals the direction of migration in the Pacific is low-fired brown pottery with lines and geometric decorations made with a pointed instrument. This **Lapita pottery** is named for a site in Melanesia. The oldest examples found so far were unearthed on sites in the Bismarck Archipelago, northeast of New Guinea. Since pottery with Lapita (la-PEE-tuh) designs appear first on Melanesia in 1500 B.C.E. and then 500 years later on Tonga and Samoa, archaeologists have reconstructed the ancient route of migration starting from Asia's Pacific coast and traveling east.

Lapita pottery
Named for a site in Melanesia, a low-fired brown pottery with lines and geometric decorations made with a pointed instrument. In use between 1500 and 1000 B.C.E., it reveals the direction of migration into the Pacific.

Polynesian Seafaring Societies

While historians concur on the overall direction of travel, they disagree about almost everything else. Did the settlers intentionally explore the distant islands of the Pacific? Or were these mariners simply blown off course in the easterly direction of the prevailing winds? Since they had no nautical instruments, how did they know where they were going?

Most observers agree that the original settlers must have traveled by canoe. Unlike in a rowboat, rowers in a canoe can face forward and see where they are going. It is not known when canoes first were developed, but once their shape was perfected, it continued to be used for hundreds of years with no major modifications. Different peoples have used various coverings stretched over a light wooden frame: bark in heavily wooded areas like the temperate United States, and skins farther north, where trees were scarce. Today's fiberglass canoes have the same basic design. However, in rough water canoes are not stable and can easily capsize.

Sometime in the first century C.E., the peoples of the Pacific developed a **double canoe,** which consisted of two canoes connected by a wooden frame lashed together with rope. Much more stable than single canoes, double canoes could also carry more cargo on the platform between the two boats. A modern double canoe 50 feet (15 m) long can carry a load weighing 18,000 pounds (8,165 kg). Double canoes were propelled by a sail, an essential requirement for long ocean voyages, and could reach speeds of 100 to 150 miles (160–240 km) per day. Double canoes, however, had drawbacks. Since they had no roofs, mariners would get wet during rainstorms. If one canoe sprang a leak and began to fill with water, it would sink, pushing the other canoe higher and the sinking canoe even lower. In storms the two canoes could easily break apart, resulting in the loss of all the baggage on the platform.

double canoe A sailing vessel made by connecting two canoes with rope to a wooden frame. Used by the ancestors of modern Polynesians for ocean voyages. Capable of speeds of 100 to 150 miles (160–240 km) per day.

The people of Tahiti and Hawai'i were using this type of vessel in the eighteenth century when the Europeans first sketched them. Many historians assume that Polynesian life in earlier centuries resembled that in the early European descriptions of the villages of Tahiti and Hawai'i. The predominantly male chiefs and their kin lived lives of leisure, supported by gifts of food from the lower-ranking populace. Ordinary people tended crops in fields, which were often irrigated, and also hunted wildlife, mostly small birds.

Although some earlier scholars wondered if the settlement of the Pacific was the purely accidental result of boats being blown off course, many modern analysts think it resulted from both deliberate settlement and accidental exploration. They know that the early settlers of both sexes were traveling in boats, because if no women had traveled, the settlers could not have reproduced and the different islands would not have been populated. They also know that the settlers carried dogs and small rats because these animals became the main sources of protein for the settlers on the islands.

A Double Canoe on the Pacific   This painting of masked rowers in the Sandwich Islands is one of the earliest Western paintings of a double canoe, the primary mode of transportation throughout the Pacific. Notice that a wooden frame connected two canoes of identical size. The sail gave the canoes additional speed. (National Library of Australia)

The voyagers also carried plants, most likely in pots, to all the islands they reached. The staple crops of the Polynesian diet, breadfruit and taro, dispersed throughout the Pacific. Breadfruit, a seedless fruit with the texture of bread when baked, can be quite filling; taro is an edible starchy root plant that is pounded before being eaten. The distribution of two other plants points to early contacts between the Polynesian islands and South America: the sweet potato and the coconut. It seems most likely that the sweet potato originated in South America and later spread throughout the Pacific; the coconut, in contrast, appears first in Asia and later in Latin America.

A recent archaeological find provides further evidence that the voyagers traveled all the way to Chile. Bones found at the site of El Arenal (ell AH-ray-nahl) in Chile show that chickens occupied the site between approximately 1304 and 1424. Chickens did not originally live in the Americas. Prior to this find, many scholars believed that European settlers introduced chickens to the Americas in the 1500s (see Chapter 15), but the similarities between the Chilean and Polynesian chickens suggest that American chickens originally came from Polynesia.

The Polynesians may have followed large sea mammals, possibly orca or bottlenose dolphins, as they migrated for long periods of time over great distances. The first European observers were struck by the Polynesians' ability to travel long distances—sometimes up to several hundreds of miles or kilometers—to go deepsea fishing.

Most puzzling to modern observers is how the Polynesians were able to travel such large distances using only the stars for navigation. In 1976, an anthropologist at the University of Hawai'i and several others decided to see if it was possible to sail, without navigational aids, the full distance of 2,400 miles (3,800 km) from Hawai'i to Tahiti. They built a facsimile of a traditional double canoe out of modern materials like fiberglass.

Because no one in Hawai'i knew the traditional method of navigation by the stars, the Polynesian Voyaging Society sought the help of a skilled sailor who lived in Micronesia, "Mau" Pius Piailug (MOW pee-US PEE-eye-luke). Identifying the prevailing winds through careful study of the waves, he used the changing position of the stars each day to determine the boat's position. He guided the boat all the way to Tahiti on a voyage that took thirty-three days to complete and that many Pacific peoples celebrated as evidence of their ancestors' accomplishments. Piailug did not make the return trip home, but in 1980 the Polynesian Voyaging Society sponsored a second voyage, this time piloted by a Hawaiian native, that made the round trip from Hawai'i to Tahiti.

Once navigation by the stars brought boats close to land, observant navigators used other means to pinpoint the exact location of the islands. They became skilled at following the flight routes of migratory birds. Certain birds nest on land and then fly far out to sea each day to look for fish before returning to their nests in the evening. Boobies fly 30 to 50 miles (50–80 km) each day; terns and noddies, 18 to 25 miles (30–40 km). When sighting these birds, ancient sailors knew whether land was nearby and how close it was.

Although the history of the Eastern Hemisphere may suggest that long ocean voyages required large boats and navigational instruments like a compass, the Polynesian Voyaging Society sailings showed that the ancestors of the Polynesians could cross the Pacific in double canoes. They used nonmechanical means of navigation, like observing the movements of birds, ocean currents, and the position of stars. Like the peoples of the Americas who farmed without the wheel, the plow, or draft animals, the Polynesians remind us that the peoples of the Western Hemisphere developed different ways of adapting to their environments than those living in the Eastern Hemisphere, from whom they remained isolated.

The Mystery of Easter Island

These techniques may have sufficed to reach the island chains of Hawai'i and Tahiti, but no one has a good explanation for how the ancestors of the Polynesians reached Easter Island. The easternmost inhabited island in the Pacific, Easter Island lies 1,300 miles (2,100 km) southeast of its nearest neighbor, Pitcairn Island, and 2,250 miles (3,600 km) off the coast of Chile. These distances are less than the 2,400 miles (3,800 km) between Hawai'i and Tahiti, but since Easter Island is a single island only 14 miles (23 km) across at its widest point, not part of an island chain, it would have been extremely difficult for ancient navigators to locate. It was probably settled in 300 C.E. by a small party of Polynesians blown far off their original course. Since linguists believe that the Easter Island language retains many more archaic features than that of its neighbors, the early settlers probably had little contact with the other peoples of Oceania after they arrived on Easter Island.

Easter Island has two names, neither of which is original. Most English speakers refer to it as Easter Island because a Dutch navigator first glimpsed the island on Easter Day, 1722. In the nineteenth century Polynesian sailors named the island Rapa Nui after the Polynesian Island Rapa, 2,400 mi (3,850 km) to the west, the name currently in use by Polynesian speakers.

The people of Easter Island, like those elsewhere in the Pacific, subsisted on a diet of sweet potatoes, taro, and sugarcane supplemented by chicken, their only domesticated animal. Their garbage pits contain bones of dolphin, porpoise, and

● **moai** The name for the 887 statues, probably of ancestral leaders, made from tufa volcanic rock and erected on Easter Island around 1000 C.E. The largest are more than 70 feet (21 m) high and weigh more than 270 tons.

tuna, an indication that they also engaged in deep-sea fishing. With no metal, they had tools of stone, wood, and bone.

All early European visitors to Easter Island noticed the huge statues of volcanic tufa stone, called **moai** (MOH-ai), that dot the island, some taller than 70 feet (21 m). The islanders began to construct the statues during the island's most prosperous period, starting in 1000 C.E., when the population reached some fifteen thousand. The most recent count of the moai statues is 887.[3] Some stand on platforms that hold up to fifteen statues. The average weight is around 10 tons (9 metric tons), but the heaviest weighs a massive 270 tons (245 metric tons) (it was never moved from its quarry). No two statues are identical. Some have designs showing tattoos and loincloths.

🖼 **Moai Figures, Easter Island** The giant stone figures, or moai, of Easter Island portray ancestral leaders. When alive, the leaders commissioned a statue of themselves that remained horizontal. After they died, the statues were placed in an upright position, and eye inlays of coral and other rock were inserted into the eye sockets. The chunk of red stone on the top of this moai represents a headdress. (Andreas M. Gross/Westend 61/Alamy)

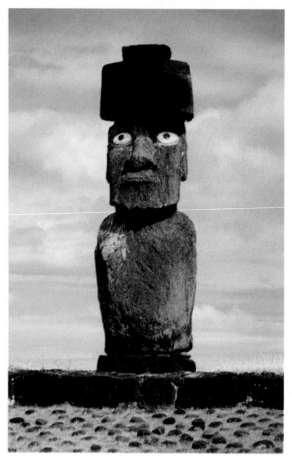

Local oral traditions hold that the statues portray ancestral leaders. When alive, the leaders commissioned a statue of themselves that remained horizontal; after they died, the statues were placed in an upright position and inlays of coral and other rock were inserted into the eye sockets. Many of these faces were topped with a chunk of red stone to represent a headdress or a hat with red feathers. The island was divided into small bands, whose leaders built the monuments as an expression of their power. Competition would account for the variation in height of the monuments; as leaders sought to outbuild one another, they erected ever-higher statues.

How could a Stone Age people with no metal tools make statues of such size and transport them? Earlier analysts proposed that the statues must have been brought by outsiders from South America or even outer space, but modern scholars concur that these statues were built and erected by indigenous peoples with no outside assistance. Sculptors used stone choppers and water to hew each statue's basic shape from the soft volcanic rock.

In 1998, Jo Anne Van Tilburg designed an experiment as innovative as the Polynesian Voyaging Society's sailing from Hawai'i to Tahiti. She found that between fifty and seventy people working five hours a day for a week could move a 12-ton (11-metric-ton) statue 9 miles (14.4 km). Some think that once the stone was at its destination, the Easter Islanders made a series of ramps from dirt, each steeper than the next, to move the statues into a standing position; others think they must have used ropes to hoist the statues into place. Tilburg's findings suggest that the islanders used a wooden frame, giant logs that functioned as rollers, or both to pull the statues from the quarry to their destinations. Although the island has no trees now, it did in the past. One of the largest was a palm tree that grew over 65 feet tall (20 m).

Sometime around 1600 the Easter Islanders stopped making moai. In the end, the different chiefs made war against each other so intensively and for so long, pausing only to create these monuments, that they used up their resources. The activities of the Easter Islanders resulted in the total degradation of their environment: no trees or large animals remained in the eighteenth century. The only large bones available on the island were those of humans, which the islanders worked into fishhooks, and they used human hair to make ropes, textiles, and fishnets, a chilling demonstration of survival with few natural resources.

The Impact of Humans on New Zealand

New Zealand was the final island in the Pacific to be settled by humans. The first artifacts made by humans appear in a layer of volcanic ash dating to circa 1350. Studies of mitochondrial DNA (see Chapter 1) show that the indigenous Maori people of New Zealand were descended from some seventy different female ancestors, indicating a founding population of more than one hundred settlers.

These settlers had a profound effect on the New Zealand environment. Like the Easter Islanders, they demonstrated that environmental damage is not simply a modern development. Within a century after their arrival, twenty different species of birds had died out, and hunters had killed more than 160,000 giant moa birds. Surviving skeletal remains indicate that some twenty different species of moa once flourished on the island; the tallest stood over 10 feet (3 m) tall. After the residents had eliminated the large birds, they preyed on large mammals like seals and sea lions until those populations were also depleted. The hunters then targeted smaller animals. As the supply of wild animals dwindled, the residents became more dependent on slash-and-burn agriculture for their food supply, destroying an estimated 40 percent of the island's forest cover.[4]

We do not know about the social structure of the original settlers because, like all other Polynesian peoples, they had no writing system. When the first Europeans arrived in the seventeenth and eighteenth centuries, they found many small warring bands leading an arduous existence that was the unintended result of their ancestors' overhunting and overfishing.

Chapter Review

[CL] Download the MP3 audio file of the Chapter Review and listen to it on the go.

The experience of the peoples living in the Americas, including Yax K'uk Mo', and the islands of the Pacific repeatedly demonstrates that the path taken to complex society by peoples of the Eastern Hemisphere was not the only possible one. After 7000 B.C.E. the peoples of the Americas and the Pacific Islands lived in almost total isolation from Eurasia. During the long period of separation, they developed very different techniques of adapting to their environments.

KEY TERMS

How did the development of agriculture and the building of early cities in Mesoamerica differ from that in Mesopotamia, India, and China?

The first agriculture in Mesoamerica arose on the high plateau of Mexico, not in river valleys. The first farmers used digging sticks instead of the plow or the wheel so common in Eurasia, and they had no domesticated animals. Even so, they built imposing cities like Teotihuacan and the unusual colossal heads of the Olmecs.

What has the decipherment of the Mayan script revealed about Maya governance, society, religion, and warfare?

The decipherment of the Mayan writing system in the 1970s brought new understanding of the period between 250 and 910 C.E. Rulers like Yax K'uk Mo' stood at the top of social hierarchy; below them were their royal kin, then nobles, ordinary people, and, most pitiable of all, war captives who became either slaves or sacrificial victims. The many Maya rulers were locked in constant warfare, hoping to capture their enemies and dreading capture themselves. Capture might mean having to play the ballgame in an unequal contest: when the captive finally admitted defeat, the triumphant captors would hold a ceremony and spill his blood. The Maya gods played this game as well; the creation of the world, the Popul Vuh narrative reveals, resulted from the defeat of human twins in a cosmic ballgame by the gods of the underworld.

What were the similarities between the complex societies of the northern peoples and those of Mesoamerica? What do they suggest about contact?

Like the Mesoamericans, the northern peoples at Cahokia Mounds and Mesa Verde planted maize, beans, and squash, and their cities contain characteristically Mesoamerican architectural elements, such as a central plaza and ball courts. Later than the Maya, both complex societies may have developed as a result of contacts with Mesoamerica.

How did the history of complex society in the Andes differ from that in Mesoamerica?

Certain striking differences distinguished the Andean complex societies from those in Mesoamerica. The Andean diet was potato-based, and the residents only occasionally ate maize, the Mesoamerican staple, which they grew at lower altitudes. Also unlike the Mesoamericans, the Andeans domesticated animals—the llama and the alpaca—and they knew how to mine metal and make alloys. These differences all suggest that there was little contact between the Andean peoples and those living in Mesoamerica.

Where did the early settlers of the Pacific Islands come from, and where did they go? What vessels did they use, and how did they navigate?

Starting sometime before 1000 B.C.E., the ancestors of the Polynesians departed from mainland Southeast Asia and moved from one island in the Pacific to the next. Traveling in double canoes, navigating by the stars, and observing ocean currents and bird flight patterns, they landed first in Hawai'i and then in Easter Island. The final place in the world to be settled, circa 1350 C.E., was New Zealand, which lay far from any continental landmass. The early settlers of both Easter Island and New Zealand overfished the nearby waters and exterminated many of the large animals on the islands, leaving themselves with seriously depleted food supplies.

The settlement of New Zealand marked the close of the first long chapter in world history: the settlement of all habitable regions of the globe that had begun over a million years earlier with the departure of the earliest hominids from Africa. After 1350, no unoccupied land was left other than Antarctica, where humans can survive only with the help of modern technology. After that date, people migrating from their homeland to anywhere else in the world always encountered indigenous peoples, with conflict almost always being the result.

CL WEB RESOURCES

Pronunciation Guide

Interactive Maps

MAP 5.1 Complex Societies in the Americas, ca. 1200 B.C.E.

MAP 5.2 Pacific Migration Routes Before 1500

Primary Sources

Chapter Objectives

ACE Multiple-Choice Quiz

Flashcards

For Further Reference

Coe, Michael D. *The Maya.* 6th ed. New York: Thames and Hudson, 1999.

Coe, Michael D. *Mexico: From the Olmecs to the Aztecs.* New York: Thames and Hudson, 1984.

Flenley, John, and Paul Bahn. *The Enigmas of Easter Island: Island on the Edge.* New York: Oxford University Press, 2002.

Howe, K. R. *The Quest for Origins: Who First Discovered and Settled the Pacific Islands?* Honolulu: University of Hawai'i Press, 2003.

Jennings, Jesse D., ed. *The Prehistory of Polynesia.* Cambridge, Mass.: Harvard University Press. 1979.

Martin, Simon, and Nikolai Grube. *Chronicle of the Maya Kings and Queens: Deciphering the Dynasties of the Ancient Maya.* New York: Thames and Hudson, 2000.

Oliphant, Margaret. *The Atlas of the Ancient World: Charting the Civilizations of the Past.* New York: Barnes and Noble Books, 1998.

Popol Vuh: The Definitive Edition of the Mayan Book of the Dawn of Life and the Glories of Gods and Kings. Translated by Denis Tedlock. New York: Simon and Schuster, 1996.

Schele, Linda, and Mary Ellen Miller. *The Blood of Kings: Dynasty and Ritual in Maya Art.* Fort Worth: Kimball Art Museum, 1986.

Stuart, George E. "The Timeless Vision of Teotihuacan." *National Geographic* 188, no. 6 (December 1995): 3–38.

Sugiyama, Saburo. *Human Sacrifice, Militarism, and Rulership: Materialization of State Ideology at the Feathered Serpent Pyramid, Teotihuacan.* New York: Cambridge University Press, 2005.

Websites

Foundation for the Advancement of Mesoamerican Studies, Inc. (http://www.famsi.org/research/pohl/pohl_aztec6.html).   A description of the daily life of the Aztecs.

Polynesian Voyage Society (http://pvs.kcc.hawaii.edu/welcome.html).   Introduction to attempts to reconstruct Polynesian sea travel in modern times.

The Sport of Life and Death: The Mesoamerican Ballgame (www.ballgame.org).   Interactive and educational introduction to the Maya ballgame.

Teotihuacan: The City of the Gods (http://archaeology.la.asu.edu/teo/).   Introduction to the site of Teotihuacan.

Films

Nova movie about Easter Island in "Secrets of Lost Empires" series.

"Nova: Lost King of the Maya" (the source of the chapter-opening quote).

New Empires in Iran and Greece, 2000 B.C.E.–651 C.E.

On September 29, 522 B.C.E., **Darius** (r. 522–486 B.C.E.) led six conspirators in a plot to kill the pretender to the throne of Iran, who ruled ancient Persia. Writing nearly one hundred years later, the Greek historian **Herodotus** (ca. 485–425 B.C.E.) recounted a lively discussion among the seven about the best form of government. While one suggested the democracy of the Greek city-state of Athens, another spoke up for rule by a few, or oligarchy (OLL-ih-gahr-key), the governing system of the city-state of Sparta. Darius (duh-RYE-uhs), the future king, vigorously defended rule by one man, or monarchy:

HERODOTUS

Take the three forms of government we are considering—democracy, oligarchy, and monarchy—and suppose each of them to be the best of its kind; I maintain that the third is greatly preferable to the other two. One ruler: it is impossible to improve upon that—provided he is the best. His judgment will be in keeping with his character; his control of the people will be beyond reproach; his measures against enemies and traitors will be kept secret more easily than under other forms of government. . . .

To sum up: where did we get our freedom from, and who gave it us? Is it the result of democracy, or oligarchy, or of monarchy? We were set free by one man, and therefore I propose that we should preserve that form of government, and, further, that we should refrain from changing ancient ways, which have served us well in the past.[1]

(Antikensammlung Staatische Museen zu Berlin, Berlin, Germany/ Bildarchiv Preussischer Kulturbesitz/Art Resource, NY)

(CL) This icon will direct you to interactive activities and study materials on the *Voyages* website: **www.cengage.com/history/hansen/voyages1e**

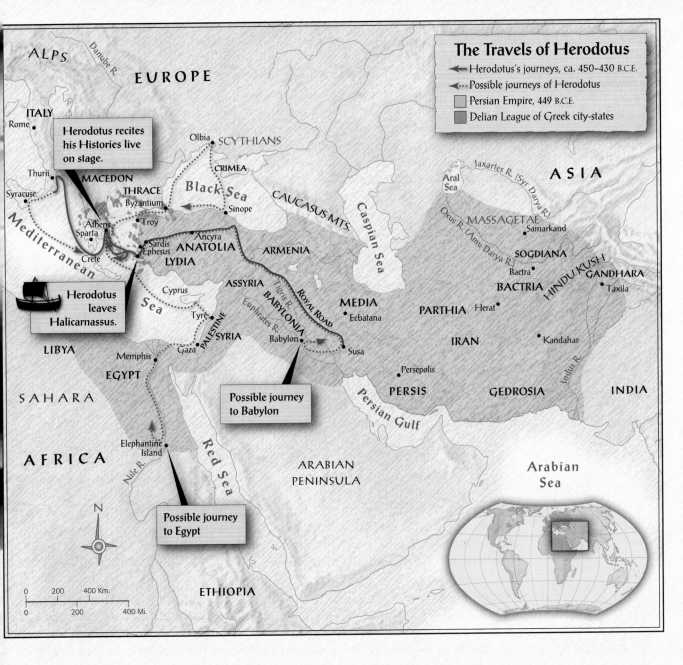

The Travels of Herodotus

← Herodotus's journeys, ca. 450–430 B.C.E.

◄···· Possible journeys of Herodotus

Persian Empire, 449 B.C.E.

Delian League of Greek city-states

ALPS

EUROPE

Danube R.

ITALY

Rome

SCYTHIANS

Olbia

Thurii

Herodotus recites his Histories live on stage.

MACEDON

CRIMEA

Syracuse

THRACE

Black Sea

Byzantium

CAUCASUS MTS.

ASIA

Aral Sea

Jaxartes R. (Syr Darya R.)

MASSAGETAE

Samarkand

Oxus R. (Amu Darya R.)

Sinope

Mediterranean

Athens

Sparta

Troy

Crete

Sardis

Ephesus

ANATOLIA

Ancyra

ARMENIA

Caspian Sea

SOGDIANA

Bactra

HINDU KUSH

GANDHARA

Taxila

BACTRIA

Sea

LYDIA

Herodotus leaves Halicarnassus.

Cyprus

ASSYRIA

Tigris R.

ROYAL ROAD

MEDIA

PARTHIA

Herat

IRAN

Kandahar

Indus R.

Tyre

Euphrates R.

BABYLONIA

Babylon

Ecbatana

Susa

LIBYA

PALESTINE

SYRIA

Gaza

Memphis

Possible journey to Babylon

Persepolis

PERSIS

GEDROSIA

INDIA

EGYPT

Persian Gulf

SAHARA

AFRICA

Red Sea

ARABIAN PENINSULA

Arabian Sea

Elephantine Island

Nile R.

N

Possible journey to Egypt

ETHIOPIA

0   200   400 Km.

0   200   400 Mi.

	800 B.C.E.	700	600	500	400	300	200	100 B.C.E.

Lifetime of Herodotus
ca. 485 — 425

PERSIAN EMPIRE

Medes conquer Assyrian Empire
612

Achaemenid Empire
550 — 330

Parthian Empire
247

Zoroastrianism takes shape
600

Reign of Cyrus 558–530

Reign of Darius 522–486

Reign of Xerxes 486–465

Alexander defeats Achaemenid Empire
331

GREECE

Greeks establish colonies in Mediterranean
800

Peloponnesian War
431   404

Reign of Alexander the Great
336   323

Rome conquers Macedonia
168

Greco-Persian Wars
490–479

Homer
ca. 800

First coins minted at Lydia
ca. 600

Democratic reforms in Athens
508

Athenians adopt oligarchy
322

Solon's reforms in Athens
594

Trial of Socrates
399

Aristotle tutors Alexander
343–340

Many have wondered how Herodotus (heh-ROD-uh-tuhs) could have possibly known what was said in a secret conversation that occurred long before his birth in Persian, a language that he did not speak. Herodotus must, they conclude, have created this dialogue to enliven his narrative. No one doubts, though, that he articulated a question of great interest to his contemporaries and of equal importance to anyone studying history today: what was the most effective form of government for an empire?

Herodotus, a native speaker of Greek, was born to a well-to-do literate family in Halicarnassus (modern Bodrum), a city on the southwest coast of modern-day Turkey. Part of the Persian Empire, Halicarnassus (HAH-lee-kar-nuh-suhs) was home to a large Greek-speaking community that had settled there several centuries earlier. As a young man, Herodotus received a traditional education, and he wrote his life's great work, *The Histories,* in Greek.

The title Herodotus chose, *Historia* (hiss-TOR-ee-uh), means "inquiry" or "investigation," not necessarily about the past; it is the root of the English word *history*. Unlike other historians of his time, Herodotus makes it clear when he is including a hearsay account rather than his own observations and openly expresses doubt about some of the taller tales he presents. For this reason, the Roman orator Cicero (SIS-erh-oh) (106–43 B.C.E.) called Herodotus the father of history, a label he retains to this day.

Not a first-person travel account, *The Histories* presents the history, folklore, geography, plants, and customs of the known world in Herodotus's day. Herodotus went to Athens, where he recited sections of the book before live audiences, who loved to hear poetry, stories, and plays performed aloud. He must have traveled as well along the Aegean coast of Turkey and to Italy, if not as far as Egypt, the Crimean peninsula on the Black Sea, Sicily, Babylon, and North Africa, all places *The Histories* claims that he visited in person (see the map on page 145). Herodotus recorded his book on long rolls of papyrus sometime after 431 B.C.E. and died soon after, most likely around 425 B.C.E.

Herodotus devoted his life to explaining the success of the Persian Empire, easily the largest and certainly the most powerful empire of its time. From 550 to 330 B.C.E. the **Achaemenid** (a-KEY-muh-nid) dynasty of Iran governed the entire region extending from modern-day Egypt and Turkey through Iran and Iraq and as far east as Samarkand. Between thirty and thirty-five million people lived in the Achaemenid Empire.[2] Up to around 500 B.C.E., the greatest western Asian empires—the Akkadians, the Babylonians, the Assyrians—had been based in the Tigris and Euphrates River valleys (see Chapter 2); for more than a thousand years after 500 B.C.E., some of the largest empires were in Iran.

The Greeks were among the few who managed to defeat the powerful Persian army and resist conquest. In Athens, during the sixth and fifth centuries B.C.E., a new political system emerged, a system the Athenians called *democracy,* or rule by the people. Some 30,000 men, but no slaves and no women, made decisions affecting the estimated 300,000 people living in Athens, 1 percent or less of the total population of the Persian Empire.

The Achaemenid rulers developed a flexible type of empire that allowed them to conquer and rule the many different peoples of western Asia for more than two centuries until their defeat in 331 B.C.E. by the Macedonian king Alexander the

Great. When Alexander came to power, democracy in Athens had already failed, and he took over Persian conceptions and structures of kingship intact. Unable to match the Achaemenid feat of governing for two centuries, his empire broke apart after only thirteen years. Many different governments rose and fell in western Asia, but those that ruled the most territory for the longest periods of time—the successor states to Alexander, the Parthians, and the Sasanians—were all monarchies that drew much from the Achaemenid Empire.

Note that many of the answers this chapter proposes must be based on the work of Greek writers, including Herodotus, because so few sources in Persian survive.

Focus Questions

 What military and administrative innovations enabled the Achaemenid dynasty to conquer and rule such a vast empire?

 What were the important accomplishments of the Greek city-states? Consider innovations in politics, intellectual life, fine arts, and science.

 Who was Alexander, and what was his legacy?

 How did the Parthians and the Sasanians modify the Achaemenid model of empire?

The Rise of the Achaemenids in Iran, 1000–330 B.C.E.

After departing from their homeland somewhere in southern Russia (see Chapter 3), the Indo-European migrants broke into different branches, one of which arrived in the region of modern-day Iran in approximately 1000 B.C.E. These tribal people were largely nomads who did not plant crops but moved their sheep and camel flocks from pasture to pasture seeking fresh grass. Their language, Indo-Iranian, belonged to the same language family as Sanskrit, and their caste system resembled that of Vedic India (see Chapter 3) but had only three ranks: priests, rulers or warriors, and ordinary herders or farmers. Their herding way of life took maximum advantage of the high plateau environment of Iran, which had no major river valley comparable to the Nile, the Indus, or the Yellow Rivers. The tall mountains of Iran contain streams that drain into the high plateaus; many end in either salt lakes or trickle out into the desert.

Farming was only possible if farmers dug irrigation channels to collect water, and the first people who did so lived in the region of Persis (the origin of the English word *Persian*) in southwestern Iran. (*Iran* is the name of the larger geographic unit, while *Persia* refers to the smaller region, the heartland, of Persis.)

Starting in 550 B.C.E. the Achaemenids created an empire far larger than any the world had seen before. Their realm contained some of the world's most advanced cities, such as Babylon and Susa, and some of its most barren stretches, like the deserts of Central Asia. The key innovation in Achaemenid rule was the use of **satraps:** after conquering a region, they appointed a local governor, or satrap (SAH-trap), who was responsible for collecting taxes from the defeated and forwarding them to the capital at Susa. This flexible system suited the many different peoples of western Asia far better than the system used by the Qin and Han Empires, which had identical districts all over China (see Chapter 4).

Zoroastrianism

Our best source for understanding the early migrants to Iran is ***The Avesta*** (uh-VEST-uh), a book that contains the core teachings of their religion, **Zoroastrianism** (zo-roe-ASS-tree-uhn-iz-uhm). Zoroastrianism, like Vedic religion, featured hymn singing and the performance of elaborate rituals but also held that the world was governed by two opposing forces: good and evil. Describing pastoral nomads active in eastern Iran, *The Avesta* portrays ancient Iran as having no cities or any political unit larger than a tribe.

Zoroastrianism is named for its founding prophet Zarathustra (za-ra-THOO-stra) (in Persian; Zoroaster in Greek), who lived in the region of Herat, a city in the Iranian highland plateau now located in modern Afghanistan. With only *The Avesta* as their guide, scholars have no way to determine when Zarathustra lived, and informed estimates diverge widely, from 1500 to 700 B.C.E. Sometime around 1000 B.C.E. seems a reasonable compromise. Three thousand years old, Zoroastrianism is one of the world's most ancient religions still practiced today.

Written in an extremely ancient form of Indo-Iranian, *The Avesta*, which means "The Injunction of Zarathustra," contains a group of hymns attributed to the prophet Zarathustra himself, so its earliest contents probably date to circa 1000 B.C.E. The written version was first recorded sometime around 600 C.E., and the earliest surviving manuscript copies date to the thirteenth century C.E. These hymns provide our best guide to Zarathustra's original thought.

Zarathustra believed in a supreme deity, **Ahura Mazda** (ah-HURR-uh MAZZ-duh), the Lord of Truth, who created heaven and earth, day and night, and darkness and light. But Ahura Mazda was not the only spiritual force. He gave birth to twin entities, the good spirit and the evil spirit. Zoroastrianism is dualistic because it posits two equal, opposing entities: a host of good deities and evil demons, all in perpetual conflict.

Each person, whether male or female, Zarathustra taught, had to prepare for the day of judgment when everyone would appear before Ahura Mazda. Zarathustra firmly believed in the ability of human beings to shape their world by choosing between the good and the bad. People who chose the good had to think good thoughts, do good deeds, and tell the truth. Herodotus remarked that young boys were taught to "speak the truth," the fundamental Zoroastrian virtue. Whenever anyone lied or did a bad deed, the evil spirit gained ground.

Much of Zoroastrian ritual involved the worship of fire. The Zoroastrians built three permanent fire altars, each dedicated to a different caste group. At each site, male hereditary priests called Magi (MAH-jai) tended the fire to make sure that it never went out. If it did, an elaborate ritual was performed to relight the fire. Towns had fire altars, as did individual households, and worshipers fed fires five times a day, when they recited prayers.

• satrap The third Achaemenid ruler, Darius, divided his empire into provinces called *satrapies*, each administered by a governor, or satrap. The officials under the satrap were recruited locally, a hallmark of the Persian system.

• *The Avesta* A book, probably dating to circa 1000 B.C.E. and first recorded in writing around 600 C.E., whose title means "The Injunction of Zarathustra." Contains hymns attributed to Zarathustra himself, which provide our best guide to his original thought.

• Zoroastrianism Iranian religion named for its founding prophet Zarathustra (in Persian; Zoroaster in Greek), who may have lived around 1000 B.C.E. He taught that a host of good deities and evil demons, all in perpetual conflict, populate the spiritual world.

• Ahura Mazda The name of the supreme deity of Zoroastrianism, the Lord of Truth, who created heaven and earth, day and night, and darkness and light. On the day of judgment, Zoroastrians believe, Ahura Mazda will judge each person's good and bad deeds.

Zoroastrians also recited prayers at the daily preparation of the intoxicating, sacred potion made from the desert plant ephedra, which was called *haoma* (HOW-muh) in Persian and *soma* in Sanskrit (see Chapter 3). The potion was thought to bring various desired outcomes—victory in battle, wealth, or children, and even immortality. This practice of reciting prayers ensured the transmission of the original wording of the sacred hymns for a full two thousand years before they were written down. (See the feature "Movement of Ideas: Doing What Is Right in *The Avesta* and the Bible.")

The funerary practices of the Zoroastrians differed from those of almost all other ancient peoples. Whereas most peoples buried their dead, Zoroastrians, believing that dead flesh polluted the ground, left corpses outside so that scavenging birds and dogs could eat the flesh; then they collected the cleaned bones and buried them.

The Military Success of the Achaemenid Empire, 550–486 B.C.E.

In the centuries after Zarathustra formulated his teachings, Iran remained a tribal society that had little contact with the neighboring empires of western Asia. In 612 B.C.E., an Iranian tribe called the Medes captured the Assyrian capital and brought Assyrian rule to an end. The Medes began to expand beyond Iran's borders into western Asia. In 550 B.C.E. the leader of a different tribe, **Cyrus** (r. 558–530 B.C.E.), defeated the Medes and founded the Achaemenid dynasty, named for his ancestor Achaemenes. Since Cyrus was from Persis and natives of Persis staffed many of the important positions in the empire, the Achaemenid Empire is often called the Persian Empire. Cyrus employed many Medes in high positions as well.

● **Cyrus** (r. 558–530 B.C.E.) Founder of the Achaemenid dynasty in Iran. A native of Persis, Cyrus staffed his administration with many Persians as well as Medes, the tribe he defeated when he took power.

When Cyrus founded his dynasty, his soldiers from Persis were obliged to serve in the king's army and to provide their own equipment. They served as foot soldiers, cavalrymen, archers, or engineers. They were not paid but were entitled to a share of the spoils from the cities they conquered.

As Cyrus's army conquered new territory, the structure of the military changed. The army of citizen-soldiers became a paid full-time army staffed by Persians and other Iranians, the conquered peoples, and large contingents of Greek mercenaries. The most prestigious unit, the king's bodyguard, was called the "Immortals, because it was invariably kept up to strength," Herodotus explains. "If a man was killed or fell sick, the vacancy he left was at once filled, so that its strength was never more nor less than 10,000." No records of the size of the army survive in Persian; Greek observers, prone to exaggerate, give figures as high as 2.5 million men, but the army certainly numbered in the hundreds of thousands, if not millions.

To bind their empire together physically, the Persians built an extensive network of roads that allowed them to supply the army no matter how far it traveled. The military stored food in designated warehouses where horse-drawn supply carts could be replenished. The Persians were fortunate to inherit a system of roads from earlier dynasties in the region: some were simple caravan tracks through the desert, while others, usually in or just outside the main cities like Babylon, were paved with bricks or rock. The main road, the Royal Road, linked the cities near the Aegean coast with the capital at Susa.

Doing What Is Right in *The Avesta* and the Bible

The ancient core texts of Zoroastrianism are still recited by one of the most active communities of Zoroastrian believers today, the Parsis of modern Bombay, India. The Parsis (also spelled Parsees, which means Persian) left Iran after the Islamic conquest and moved to India sometime between the eighth and tenth centuries C.E. Ever since then they have recited the two prayers of the first selection in the ancient Indo-Iranian language and continued to sing a small group of ancient hymns as they maintain the Zoroastrian tradition of fire worship and truth-telling.

The first prayer stresses that both the Lord of Truth, Ahura Mazda, and his true judgment should be chosen by mankind for the good of the world. These choices result in establishing a worldly sovereignty founded on good thinking that will benefit both "the Wise One" (Ahura Mazda) and "the pastor for the needy dependents" (Zarathustra) in this world. The second prayer focuses on the truth. It simply says that truth is the highest good and that everyone has the ability to follow and promote the truth.

The second selection is a prayer in *The Book of Tobit,* from the Apocrypha. All the Apocryphal texts originally circulated as part of the Hebrew Bible but were not included in certain later versions. Composed in the third or fourth centuries B.C.E., this book tells the story of an ordinary man named Tobit, a Jew who lived in exile in the Assyrian capital of Nineveh. Tobit continued to perform the ritual observances required of Jews, but the Hebrew God subjected him to various trials, including blindness, to test his devotion. Scholars think it likely that the text was written by a Jew in exile who had some knowledge of Zoroastrianism. After going blind, Tobit remembers that he deposited a large sum of money in the town of Rages in Iran, near modern-day Teheran, and sends his son there to retrieve the money. The advice he gives his son clearly reflects the influence of Zoroastrianism.

Source: The translation from *The Avesta* of the prayers in selection 1 is courtesy of Stanley Insler, Edward E. Salisbury Professor of Sanskrit and Comparative Philology at Yale University (email dated September 4, 2002). Second selection from Tobit 4:5–21 (New Revised Standard Version).

The Avesta

(1) Just as the lord in accord with truth must be chosen, so also the judgment in accord with truth. Establish a rule of actions stemming from an existence of good thinking for the sake of the Wise One and for the lord whom they established as pastor for the needy dependents.

(2) Truth exists as the very best good thing. It exists under your will.

Desire the truth for what is the very best truth.

The Book of Tobit

Revere the Lord all your days, my son, and refuse to sin or to transgress his commandments. Live uprightly all the days of your life, and do not walk in the ways of wrongdoing; for those who act in accordance with truth will prosper in all their activities. To all those who practice righteousness, give alms from your possessions, and do not let your eye begrudge the gift when you make it. Do not turn your face away from anyone who is poor, and the face of God will not be turned away from you. If you have many possessions, make your gift from them in proportion; if few, do not be afraid to give according to the little you have. So you will be laying up a good treasure for yourself against the day of necessity. For almsgiving delivers from death and keeps you from going into the Darkness. Indeed, almsgiving, for all who practice it, is an excellent offering in the presence of the Most High.

. . . For in pride there is ruin and great confusion. And in idleness there is loss and dire poverty, because idleness is the mother of famine.

Do not keep over until the next day the wages of those who work for you, but pay them at once. If you serve God you will receive payment. Watch yourself, my son, in everything you do, and discipline yourself in all your conduct. And what you hate, do not do to anyone. Do not drink wine to excess or let drunkenness go with you on your way. Give some of your food to the hungry, and some of your clothing to the naked. Give all your surplus as alms, and do not let your eye begrudge your giving of alms. Place your bread on the grave of the righteous, but give none to sinners. Seek advice from every wise person and do not despise any useful counsel. At all times bless the Lord God, and ask him that your ways may be made straight and that all your paths and plans may prosper. For none of the nations has understanding, but the Lord himself will give them good counsel; but if he chooses otherwise, he casts down to the deepest Hades. So now, my child, remember these commandments, and do not let them be erased from your heart.

And, now my son, let me explain to you that I left ten talents of silver in trust with Gabael son of Gabrias, at Rages in Media. Do not be afraid, my son, because we have become poor. You have great wealth if you fear God and flee from every sin and do what is good in the sight of the Lord your God.

QUESTIONS FOR ANALYSIS

▶ What is the single most important value of the Zoroastrians?

▶ What does Tobit tell his son to do? Which of Tobit's instructions show the influence of Zoroastrianism?

A system of government couriers made excellent use of these roads, as Herodotus remarks:

> There is nothing on earth faster than these couriers. The service is a Persian invention, and it goes like this, according to what I was told. Men and horses are stationed a day's travel apart, a man and a horse for each of the days needed to cover the journey. These men neither snow nor rain nor heat nor gloom of night stay from the swiftest possible completion of their appointed stage.

Traveling at a breathtaking 90 miles (145 km) each day, government couriers could cover the 1,600 miles (2,575 km) of the Royal Road in less than twenty days, and ordinary travelers, also allowed to use the road, could do so in three months.[3] The couriers were crucial to the army's success because generals could communicate easily with one another across large expanses of territory.

The Persian army was responsible for a long string of military conquests. Cyrus began from his base in Persis and headed north to Ecbatana (ek-buh-TAH-nuh) (modern-day Hamadan) in central Iran. In 547–546 B.C.E., his troops then moved north and west into Anatolia (modern-day Turkey), a region called Lydia in ancient times whose capital was Sardis. A busy commercial center in an enormously wealthy region, Sardis became the most important city in the western part of the empire. The riverbeds near Sardis had large deposits of electrum, a naturally occurring alloy of gold and silver. Around 600 B.C.E., the local people gathered the electrum and used it to mint **Lydian coins,** the first metal coins made anywhere in the world.

● **Lydian coins** The first metal coins in the world, dating to ca. 600 B.C.E. Made from electrum, a naturally occurring alloy of gold and silver collected from the riverbeds in Lydia, a region on the Aegean coast of modern-day Turkey.

After a series of successful military campaigns, Cyrus conquered the various Ionian ports on the eastern Aegean, Syria, Palestine, and Babylon. He did not attempt to change their cultures but made offerings to local gods and allowed his subjects to continue to worship as they had before. He allowed the Jews, who had been forcibly deported to Babylon, to return home, ending the sixty-year-long Babylonian Captivity (see Chapter 2). Modern scholarship indicates that the Hebrew concepts of the afterlife and of the Devil arose after the Babylonian Captivity, and some attribute these new ideas to the influence of Zoroastrianism.

The Persian army was not invincible. In 530 B.C.E. it entered the unfamiliar terrain of Central Asia and attacked the Massagetae (mass-uh-GET-aye) peoples east of the Amu Darya River. The Persians, Herodotus reports, were able initially to gain the advantage by offering the Massagetae tribes wine so that they fell drunk, but the fierce Massagetae recovered and defeated the Persians in hand-to-hand combat. Cyrus died while campaigning in Massagetae territory.

Darius's Coup, 522 B.C.E.

Cyrus's son Cambyses (kam-BEE-zuhs) resumed the conquests and conquered Egypt and Ethiopia before dying in 522 B.C.E. A group of Zoroastrian priests kept his death secret, placed a Magi priest named Gaumata (GOW-mah-tah) on the throne, and ruled briefly in Cambyses's name. In the same year Darius I led a group of conspirators who killed the pretender. At the time of the murder the conspirators had not yet agreed on the political system they would implement. Persuaded by Darius that monarchy was the best system (see chapter opener), they agreed to choose the future king by seeing whose horse neighed first after the sun came up. Darius's wily groom made sure that his master's horse did so first, and Darius became *king of kings,* the Persian term for the ruler of the empire.

Darius commemorated his accession to power in an extraordinary inscription at Behistun, the site of a steep cliff. Stone steps led 300 feet (100 m) from the road to the cliff face, but they were removed after the inscription was completed.

■ **Darius's Victory: The Stone Relief at Behistun, Iran**   In 522 B.C.E., Darius ordered this stone relief commemorating his victory over his rivals to be carved over 300 feet (100 m) above the road below. In it, Darius triumphantly places his left foot on the deposed Magi priest Gaumata, who lies dead on his back with his arms pointing vertically upward. The eight tribal leaders that Darius defeated are shown on the right; the larger figure with the pointed hat was added later. Above the human figures floats the winged Ahura Mazda, who looks on approvingly.   (Henry Rawlinson, *The Persian Cuneiform Inscription at Behistun*, 1846)

This large rock relief was 18 feet (5.5 m) long and 10 feet (3 m) tall, with blocks of text in different languages around it bragging of the murder of the imposter-king. At the simplest level, Darius's message was obvious: if you oppose me, this is what will happen to you. Darius justified Gaumata's murder by appealing to a higher authority:

> There was not a man, neither a Persian nor a Mede nor anyone of our family, who could have taken the kingdom from Gaumata the Magian. The people feared him greatly.... There was no one who dared say anything about Gaumata the Magian until I came. Then I prayed to Ahura Mazda. Ahura Mazda bore me aid.... Then I with a few men slew that Gaumata the Magian.... Ahura Mazda bestowed the kingdom upon me.[4]

Darius's inscription differs from those of Ashoka (see Chapter 3) and the Qin founder (Chapter 4), both of whom had inherited the throne from their fathers. Darius, however, had killed the reigning king, and his distant family ties to Cyrus did not entitle him to the throne. He married Artystone (AR-tih-stoe-nay), daughter of Cyrus and half-sister of Cambyses, to bolster his claim to the Achaemenid throne.

Darius's use of languages also differed from that of Ashoka and the Qin founder. The text framing the Behistun relief appears in three languages: Elamite (EE-luhm-ite), the original language of administration of the Achaemenids; Babylonian, the language they adopted as their administrative language; and Old Persian, which

THE PARADE OF NATIONS AT DARIUS'S PALACE AT PERSEPOLIS

To document his accomplishments, Darius built an enormous audience hall in Persepolis in modern-day Iran. The hall held 10,000 people and was 62,500 square feet (5,800 sq m), with a roof supported by columns more than 60 feet (20 m) high. Although the original wooden buildings, which were lavishly decorated with curtains, tiles, and paintings, no longer stand, the surviving stone reliefs show the many different peoples of the Achaemenid Empire coming to pay homage to their ruler.

The stairways leading to the audience hall have been called "perhaps the most perfect flight of stairs ever built."* Alongside the staircases, stone masons carved reliefs of twenty-three distinct peoples bringing gifts to the king to celebrate the coming of spring, one of the most important ritual occasions in the Zoroastrian calendar. On one side of the staircase the masons depicted the peoples of the empire as seen from the left, and on the facing side, as seen from the right. Each view of the procession occupies three tiers stretching 300 feet (92 m) long, making the frieze the largest mirror image in the world.

The top register, now partially destroyed, shows different regiments in the Achaemenid army: the Persians and the Medes have different headdresses. The soldiers lead the king's horse, two empty chariots, a tent, and the throne for the king. The king himself is not shown.

On the lower tiers, trees divide the friezes into frames that show a small group of men from each place, wearing their native dress and led by a Persian or Median envoy. They carry local products as gifts for the king and guide a native animal. The animals reflect the great reach of the empire: horses from Syria, a humped bull and a wild donkey from Pakistan, a two-humped camel from Central Asia, and an antelope and a giraffe from Ethiopia. The animals are more detailed than the people, whose faces are the same and can be distinguished only by their clothing and different hairstyles.

The portraits capture the essence of the Achaemenid Empire. Each subject people occupies the same amount of space in the tableau; tall animals like giraffes are scaled down so that they take as much space as smaller animals like sheep and horses. Each group wears its national dress and offers its own distinctive gifts, while participating in a single procession designed to honor the Persian ruler.

The timing of the monument reveals something important about the Achaemenid concept of empire. Darius began construction in 515 B.C.E., soon after he came to power, and the complex provided vivid testimony of his conquests of many different peoples. Xerxes completed the monument after the 480 B.C.E. defeat at Salamis, but the Achaemenid vision of empire remained unchanged. The omission of certain Greek peoples is the only indication that the expansion of the Persian Empire had come to an end.

The facing page shows a small section of the frieze taken from the left side of the staircase.

---

*R. Ghirshman and E. Herzfeld, *Persepolis: The Achaemenian Capital* (Tehran: Mirdashti Farhangsara, 1999), p. 33.

These Scythians, from the region north of the Black Sea, wear their characteristic pointed hoods and offer a fine horse.

This magnificent two-humped Bactrian camel follows Central Asians bearing cups and other gifts from the region east of the Caspian Sea.

These seven men from the impoverished Assyrian empire, defeated in 612 B.C.E., offer low-cost objects: a pair of rams, animal skins, and bowls.

(© Corbis)

The Ionians, from the Aegean coast of modern-day Turkey, offer folded bolts of cloth, and bowls, most likely of gold.

These trees, like vertical lines in a comic strip, divide the different delegations in the Parade of Nations from one another. Each delegation is led by either a fully robed Mede, as in the bottom panel, or a bare-chested Persian guide, as directly above.

This Armenian groom keeps a close watch on this fine steed, while the countrymen behind him carry bolts of cloth.

155

the royal family spoke at home. All three were written in cuneiform script. The Qin founder used a single language, confident that he could communicate with his subjects in Chinese; Ashoka had the same text translated into the different languages spoken in the various parts of the Mauryan Empire. But Darius ruled a multilingual empire in which people living in the same place spoke different languages. For this reason, Darius had rubbings of the inscription made and distributed translations of it throughout the empire; fragments of an Aramaic translation on papyrus have even been found in Egypt. Most of Darius's subjects were illiterate; even the king had to have the Old Persian text read aloud to him.

When Darius commissioned the Behistun inscription, he had no way of knowing that his dynasty would last. His account largely matches Herodotus's except for a few details (they agree on the names of six of the conspirators, but not the seventh), but Herodotus has the advantage of hindsight: he knew that Darius became one of the most important Achaemenid rulers. During his reign, the empire expanded to include Thrace in northern Greece and the Indus Valley in present-day Pakistan, but not the Scythian peoples living south of the Black Sea or the Greeks in Athens (see page 162).

Achaemenid Administration Fully aware of the challenges of governing his large empire, Darius instituted a series of far-reaching administrative reforms that held the Persian Empire together for the better part of two centuries. He established a flexible administrative and taxation system and implemented a uniform law code for all his subjects.

Seeing himself as transmitting Ahura Mazda's laws to all his subjects, Darius appointed judges for life to administer those laws in his name. Just as on the day of judgment Ahura Mazda would judge each person's good and bad deeds, Persian judges were supposed to examine lawsuits carefully. They were to inquire deeply into the facts of a dispute and to reach a judgment that took into account the previous conduct. Accordingly, a man who had adhered to Zoroastrian teachings and told the truth his entire life was treated more leniently than one who had not.

As they reformed the courts, the Achaemenids also changed the system of taxation. Herodotus explains:

> During the reign of Cyrus and Cambyses there was no fixed tribute at all, the revenue coming from gifts only; and because of his imposition of regular taxes, and other similar measures, the Persians called Darius a huckster, Cambyses a master, and Cyrus a father; the first being out for profit wherever he could get it, the second harsh and arrogant, and the third, merciful and ever working for their well-being.[5]

We must remember that Cyrus had died nearly a century before Herodotus was writing and that Cambyses was reputed to be insane, a judgment with which Herodotus enthusiastically concurred. The view of Darius as a huckster, though, contains an important element of truth: in seeking to put his empire on sound financial footing, Darius revolutionized the way the Persians collected taxes.

Darius divided his empire into provinces called satrapies, each administered by a governor, or satrap. The officials under the satrap were recruited locally, a hallmark of the Persian system. Darius required each satrap to submit a fixed amount of revenue each year, and the taxes due from many of the different regions were assessed in silver. Silver was more convenient because government administrators could use a single system to calculate the empire's revenue and expenses. Darius allowed several regions to pay some of their taxes in other items: Egypt, the empire's breadbasket, was required to forward 120,000 bushels of grain each year. The Indians, Herodotus explains, paid in gold dust, which they collected from riverbeds, while the Ethiopians submitted an annual quota of "two quarts of unrefined gold, two hundred logs of ebony, and twenty elephant tusks."

Archaeologists have found over three thousand baked clay tablets giving the day-to-day accounts of the empire in the ruins of Persepolis (per-SEH-poe-lis), the site of the royal ritual center some 200 miles (360 km) west of Susa. Darius had several wives, but his favorite was Artystone, who possessed her own palace and wielded genuine authority within her own estate. The tablets record her orders to organize banquets and trips, and sometimes the king would even take her with him on military campaigns. Darius frequently gave his wives gifts of food or wine. One such order reads: "King Darius has instructed me: 100 sheep from my property are to be delivered to Queen Artystone."

The friezes at Persepolis illustrate beautifully how Darius ruled over such a diverse empire (see the feature "Visual Evidence: The Parade of Nations at Darius's Palace at Persepolis"). After Darius died in 486 B.C.E., his son Xerxes (ZERK-sees) succeeded him, ruled for twenty years, and completed the complex at Persepolis. But in 465, Xerxes' younger son killed both his father and his elder brother, the designated heir, so that he could succeed to the throne. Royal assassinations occurred frequently over the next one hundred years, and the Achaemenids conquered no new territory, but the administrative structure they originated allowed them to hold on to their empire until 331 B.C.E., when Alexander defeated them (see below).

●Ancient Greece and the Mediterranean World, 2000–334 B.C.E.

A branch of the Indo-European speakers reached the Greek peninsula around 2000 B.C.E., earlier than they arrived in either India (see Chapter 3) or Iran (see above) but the same time as the Hittites reached Anatolia. The Greek speakers, as well as the Phoenicians (FOE-knee-shuns) (see page 158), were active traders in the Mediterranean. Although historians sometimes speak of the Phoenician and Greek "empires," neither people had a centralized administration governing many different peoples. Instead, both lived in scattered city-states, whose residents sailed across the seas to establish new outposts that retained their ties to the mother city-state.

Although we tend to think of Greece as a single Greek-speaking entity, whether in earlier times or today, there was no unified nation called "Greece" in the ancient world. Greek speakers thought of themselves as citizens of Athens, Sparta, or the city-state where they lived. By the year 500 B.C.E. Athens emerged as the largest of over one hundred different Greek city-states, and only Athens had a democracy in which all male citizens, some 10 percent of the city's population, could participate equally. In addition to being a military power, Athens was also a cultural center famous for its drama, art, and philosophy.

Greek Expansion in the Mediterranean, 2000–1200 B.C.E.

When the Indo-European speakers arrived in Greece, they found that the rocky land of the Greek peninsula, the Aegean coast of Turkey, and the islands of the

Mediterranean offered little grass for their herds. No major rivers flowed in these areas. As the Indo-European migrants shifted from herding to farming, they used irrigation channels to distribute water over their fields. They usually planted barley, which was sturdier than wheat, in the lowlands, olive trees in the foothills, and grapes on the hillsides. It required so much labor to terrace the rocky soil and make fields suitable for cultivation that often the most efficient way to obtain new land was to set sail for the nearest land, frequently visible across a body of water.

The earliest trading centers of the Mediterranean have left ample archaeological evidence. Between 2000 and 1500 B.C.E., the Mediterranean island of Crete was home to a civilization with lavish palaces, well-built roads, bronze metallurgy, and a writing system called Linear A, which has not been deciphered. The archaeologist who discovered the site in the early twentieth century named the residents the Minoans (mih-NO-uhns) after the king Minos (mih-NOHS) who, Greek legends recounted, ruled a large empire with many ships. Archaeologists have found pottery made in the Minoan style all over the Mediterranean and western Asia, evidence of a wide-reaching Minoan trade network.

The remains of the Minoan civilization came to an abrupt end in 1500 B.C.E., probably because the Minoans were conquered by the Mycenaeans (1600–1200 B.C.E.), the earliest ancient civilization based on mainland Greece in the city of Mycenae. The Mycenaeans (my-see-NEE-uhns) used Linear B script, which remained undeciphered until 1952. In that year, an architect and amateur cryptographer, Michael Ventris, realized what no one else had: Linear B was a dialect of Greek. He used his high school ancient Greek to decipher four thousand surviving clay tablets, which unfortunately reveal much about the palace accounting system but little about Mycenaean society.

Archaeologists are not certain whether the Trojan Wars between the Greeks and the Trojans living across the Aegean in modern-day Turkey occurred as the poet Homer (ca. 800 B.C.E.) described them centuries later in his epic poems *The Odyssey* and *The Iliad*. If they did, it was during the time of the Mycenaean civilization. When the international system broke down in 1200 B.C.E. (see Chapter 2), Linear B fell into disuse, and the final archaeological evidence of Mycenaean culture dates to no later than 1200 B.C.E.

●**Phoenicians** A seagoing people who, around 900 B.C.E., expanded outward from their base on the Mediterranean coast of modern-day Lebanon. Their alphabet, which used only letters with no pictorial symbols, is the ancestor of the Roman alphabet.

The Phoenicians and the World's First Alphabet

Around this time, another seafaring people, the **Phoenicians,** appeared in the western Mediterranean. The Greeks called this people "red men," *Phoinikes,* or Phoenicians in English, most likely because they produced an extremely rare reddish-purple dye made from the glands of snails. The Phoenicians began to expand outward from their homeland in modern-day Lebanon around 900 B.C.E. They used a new type of writing system: an alphabet of twenty-two letters, each representing a different consonant. Unlike cuneiform, this alphabet had no pictorial symbols and depicted only sounds. Like many other scripts, Phoenician did not record vowels, which most native speakers can readily supply. (Consider the following sentence from a subway advertisement for a secretarial school: f y cn rd ths, thn y cn lrn t wrt qckly.) The phonetic alphabet was surely one of the most influential innovations in the ancient world because it was much faster to learn an alphabet than to memorize a symbolic script like cuneiform.

By 814 B.C.E., the Phoenicians had established one outpost at Carthage (KAR-thudge) (modern-day Tunis in Tunisia) and subsequently built others at different ports along the North African coast as well as the southern coast of modern-day

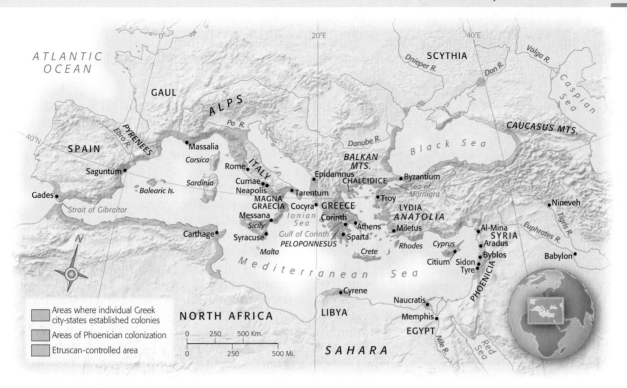

🌐 **MAP 6.1**

Greek and Phoenician Settlement in the Mediterranean   Starting in 900 B.C.E., the Phoenicians expanded westward into the Mediterranean from their base along the eastern shore; they settled on the island of Sardinia and the North African shore. In 800 B.C.E., settlers from different Greek-speaking city-states left their homelands and formed more than 250 city-states in the eastern Mediterranean and Black Seas.

Spain (see Map 6.1). Herodotus credited the Phoenicians with the discovery that Africa was surrounded by water except where it joins Asia. He described a Phoenician voyage circumnavigating Africa sometime around 600 B.C.E.: "Every autumn they [the voyagers] put in where they were on the African coast, sowed a patch of ground, and waited for next year's harvest. Then, having got in their grain, they put to sea again, and after two full years rounded Gibraltar in the course of the third, and returned to Egypt." These early voyagers realized that prevailing winds and currents made sailing clockwise around Africa from the Red Sea much easier than sailing counterclockwise from Gibraltar.

The Phoenicians founded new colonies by sending groups of men and women to coastal towns around the Mediterranean and even beyond.[6] We learn this from a Greek account about the Phoenician explorer Hanno, who set off from Carthage in 500 B.C.E. with sixty vessels and thirty thousand men and women. Hanno passed a river and two large gulfs and then captured three "gorillas," probably chimpanzees or baboons. Then he turned back. The vagueness of the description makes it difficult to know how far the Phoenicians traveled, but they may have reached Sierra Leone.

The veracity of both of these accounts—the Phoenician circumnavigation of Africa and the Phoenician colonization of West Africa—is much debated because of the lack of independent confirmation, but it is certain that the oceangoing Phoenicians transmitted their knowledge of geography along with their alphabet to the Greeks. The Phoenicians retained control of the western and southern

Mediterranean throughout the Achaemenid period until their defeat by ancient Rome in 202 B.C.E. (see Chapter 7).

◼ Woman Temple Priest in Ancient Athens
Women temple priests played a major, if not always documented, role in ancient Greek religion. This amphora, dated to the 500s B.C.E., places a woman priest at the center of the painting because of her crucial role in the ritual being performed. She raises branches and sprinkles water on an altar in preparation for the sacrifice of the bull to the goddess Athena (*right*). This scene may portray an actual sacrifice performed on the Acropolis, where the Parthenon featured a similar giant statue of the goddess carrying a shield.   (Staatliche Museen Antikensammlung 1686. Bildarchiv Preussischer Kulturbsitz/Art Resource, NY)

The Rise of the Greek City-State, 800–500 B.C.E.

Since no materials in ancient Greek survive from between 1200 and 900 B.C.E., there is a gap in our knowledge. A new era in Greek history starts around 800 B.C.E., when various regions—including mainland Greece, the islands of the Aegean and the eastern Mediterranean, and the Aegean coast of Turkey—coalesced into city-states (*polis;* plural, *poleis*). The residents of these different places began to farm more intensively, and the resulting increase in agricultural production permitted a diversification of labor among the growing population: while the vast majority of people farmed the agricultural land around the cities, a tiny minority were able to settle inside walled cities. These cities had both markets for agricultural goods and temples to different gods. Each of these city-states, including the surrounding agricultural area, was small, with a population of between five and ten thousand people, but it was self-sufficient, having its own courts, law code, and army (see Map 6.1).

These city-states each had a guardian deity whose temple was located within the city walls. The Greeks believed in a pantheon of many gods headed by Zeus and his wife Hera. Each god possessed specific traits: Athena, the guardian god of Athens, was a goddess of war and of weaving. The Greeks told many myths about the gods and goddesses, often focusing on their attempts to intervene in the human world.

The citizens of the city-state gathered during festivals to offer animal sacrifices to the gods, with whom they communicated through prayers and oracles. The most famous oracle was at Delphi, on the Gulf of Corinth, where individuals and city-states consulted Apollo's priests to learn what would happen in the future before making any important decisions. People traveled all over the Aegean to pray for medical cures and to participate in temple festivals such as the Olympic games, which were held every four years since 776 B.C.E. at the temple to Zeus at Olympia in the Peloponnese (see the feature "World History in Today's World: The Olympics").

An important breakthrough in shipbuilding occurred around 800 B.C.E. that facilitated such travel. Greek shipbuilders added a partial deck to boats that covered the center but left an open aisle along the sides. (Earlier boats, whether powered by oars or sails, had no decks.) Easily capable of traversing the Mediterranean, these improved boats made it possible for the citizens of the different city-states of Greece to establish more than 250 different city-states along the coasts of the Mediterranean and Black Seas (see Map 6.1).

Like Mesopotamian city-states, the Greek city-states remained linked to the mother city through trade. Ships carried olive oil, wine, and pottery produced by

The Olympics

The Olympic games formally began in 776 B.C.E. (the earliest date that can be verified in ancient Greek history) at the temple to Zeus in Olympia, in the western Peloponnesus. In 720 B.C.E., one competitor started the race wearing some kind of garment but shed it by the end of the race; after his victory, no competitor ever wore clothes again.

At first competitors participated in only a 656-foot-long (200-m) footrace, but the number of events increased quickly. By the year 600 B.C.E., they included the 1,312-foot-long (400-m) footrace, the pentathlon of five different events in one, wrestling, boxing, and chariot races. At their height the games ran for five full days and included the first day, set aside for prayers and oath-taking, and a final day of competition and of feasting and crowning of the winners. Tens of thousands of people who did not participate traveled from all over the Mediterranean to see the races and to enjoy the feasting and drinking.

Only the victor of each event received a prize, always a simple wreath of leaves. Although the award of a wreath makes the Olympics seem an amateur event, most winners also received tangible rewards from their home city-states. Athletes sometimes competed for city-states where they had not been born simply to attain the higher rewards they offered. Winners from Athens were particularly fortunate: the city-state awarded them the equivalent of two years' income, a permanent tax break, and free meals for life.

Cheating did occur, even though it was considered an insult to the gods and was punished severely by fines or beatings. Athletes lied about their age so they could compete in the boys' events, which were less competitive. Wrestlers rubbed oil on their bodies so that their opponents could not get a grip on them.

The Olympic games occurred every four years until 393 C.E., when the Roman emperor forbade the worship of pagan gods (see Chapter 7). Inspired by the success of hundreds of festivals bearing the name *Olympics,* in 1896 a French aristocrat revived the games in Athens with the explicit intention of giving amateur athletes from all over the world a chance to compete. This inclusiveness, though, is new: the ancient games were for Greeks only.

the Greeks to other regions, where they obtained lumber to make more ships. The leaders of the mother city-state appointed a founder to lead the expedition; citizens of the mother city-state were always welcome, as were settlers from other city-states.

During this period of vibrant growth and expansion, the Greeks adopted the twenty-two original consonants of the Phoenicians, created vowels by using leftover Phoenician letters for sounds not present in Greek, and added three new letters. The first inscriptions in the new Greek alphabet date to 730 B.C.E. This new alphabet underlies many modern alphabets, including that of English, because the vowels and consonants of ancient Greek could be used to represent the sounds of other languages.

During the eighth and seventh centuries B.C.E., most Greek city-states were governed by powerful landowning families, but around 600 B.C.E. several city-states enacted reforms. Sparta became one of the first to grant extensive rights to its citizens. Only the descendents of original Spartans could be citizen-soldiers, who fought full-time and were not permitted to farm the land or engage in business. A second group, called "dwellers around," were descended from the first peoples to be conquered by the Spartans; entitled to own land, they also worked as craftsmen and traders but could not vote. The lowest-ranking group, full-time state slaves (Helots), cultivated the land of the citizens. Because their husbands were often away at war, Spartan women ran their estates and had more freedom than women in other city-states, yet they did not vote.

Future Spartan citizens joined the army as young children and received an austere military upbringing; only when successfully completed could they become citizens. Citizens (but not the state slaves) exercised a limited veto over the policies enacted by a council of elders who ruled in conjunction with two kings. This was the government system Herodotus chose as an example of oligarchy (see chapter opener).

It took more than one hundred years for Athens to establish democracy. The most famous reformer, Solon (SOH-luhn), became the civilian head of state of Athens in 594 B.C.E. and launched a reform that abolished the obligation to pay one-sixth of one's crop as tax to the state. He also cancelled debts, which made it possible for former debtors to acquire and farm their own land. Athenian citizens formed four groups, defined by how much property they owned; all citizens could participate in the assembly, the lawmaking body.

In 508 B.C.E., a group of aristocrats extended Solon's reforms further and established direct democracy. All citizens above the age of 20—roughly thirty thousand men, or 10 percent of the population—could join the assembly. Many, however, were too busy to attend the frequent meetings, which occurred as much as forty times a year.

Women, who could not serve as soldiers or become citizens, never participated in the assembly. The women who enjoyed the greatest security were married; only children born to such couples were legitimate. Athenian men had many other sexual partners, both male and female: prostitutes whom they visited occasionally, concubines whom they supported financially, and slaves who could not say no to their owners.

Roughly two-fifths of Athens's population, some 120,000 people, were slaves, who also did not participate in the assembly. Many different types of slaves existed: those who had skills and lived with their masters had less arduous lives than those who worked in the fields or in the silver mines, where working conditions were dangerous.

The Greco-Persian Wars, 490–479 B.C.E.

The Athenian army was particularly effective because it consisted of citizen-soldiers with a powerful commitment to defend their home city-state. Greek soldiers, called hoplites (HAHP-lites), could defeat the Persians in hand-to-hand combat because they had better shields, stronger armor, and more effective formations. The soldiers were divided into units, called phalanxes, eight men deep. If the first row of soldiers was broken, the row behind them pressed forward to meet the attack.

The first important Athenian victory came at the battle of Marathon in 490 B.C.E. The Persian ruler Darius sent a force to punish the Athenians for supporting an uprising against the Persians by the Greeks living on the east coast of the Aegean. The Athenian forces of 11,000 men attacked the Persian army of 25,000 when they were foraging for food and, in a stunning reversal of what every informed person expected, won a decisive victory on the plain of Marathon. (The English word *marathon* comes from a later legend about a messenger running over 20 miles [32 km] from Marathon to Athens to announce the victory.) Herodotus's tally of the casualties underlines the immensity of the Athenian victory: the Athenians lost 192 men; the Persians, 6,400.

After Darius died in 486 B.C.E. (see above), his son Xerxes (r. 486–465 B.C.E.) decided to avenge his father's defeat and gathered a huge army that he hoped would frighten the Greeks into surrendering. But Sparta and Athens for the first time organized a coalition of the Greek city-states that fought the Persians for control of a mountain pass north of Athens at Thermopylae (thuhr-MOP-uh-lie). The Greeks held the Persians off until an informer told the Persians about a secret path around the pass. Realizing that they had been betrayed, many of the Greeks fled, but three hundred Spartans fought to their deaths. The victorious Persians then sacked the deserted city of Athens.

The Greeks regrouped, and the Athenian naval commanders took advantage of their superior knowledge of the local terrain to secure a surprising Greek victory at Salamis. Xerxes fell for a Greek trap: he believed an infiltrator who reported that the Greeks planned to retreat from the narrow bay of Salamis (SAH-lah-miss). Xerxes ordered his men to stay up all night to watch for the Greek withdrawal, with the result that the Persians were exhausted when the naval battle began.

In recounting the battle, an important turning point in the war, Herodotus highlighted the role of **Artemisia** (fl. 480 B.C.E.), the woman ruler of Halicarnassus, Herodotus's hometown, who had become queen on the death of her husband and who, like all conquered peoples in the Persian Empire, fought alongside the Persians. The Persians had a fleet of 1,207 triremes (TRY-reems), three-story boats powered by rowers on each level, of which Artemisia (ar-TEM-ee-zee-uh) commanded 5. "She sailed with the fleet," Herodotus explains, "in spite of the fact that she had a grown-up son and that there was consequently no necessity for her to do so," implying that he would not have found her participation worthy of comment if her son had still been a child. Artemisia fascinated Herodotus because she differed so much from well-off Athenian women, who stayed indoors and devoted themselves to managing their households.

Herodotus employed contrasts to heighten his comparisons between Greeks and non-Greeks. The Athenians enjoyed the benefits of democracy while the Persians suffered under the tyranny of Xerxes. Greek men were strong while Persian men were weak, which is why Xerxes had to depend on Artemisia. In the inverted world of the war, the only Persian commander worthy of mention in Herodotus's eyes is the Greek woman Artemisia.

Contrary to all expectations, the Greeks defeated the Persians. Defeat, however, had little impact on the Persian Empire except to define its western edge. Xerxes returned home to an empire just as large as his father's, and no Achaemenid ruler after Xerxes ever succeeded in adding Greece to his empire.

●**Artemisia** (fl. 480 B.C.E.)   The woman ruler of Halicarnassus, on the Aegean coast of modern-day Turkey, who fought with the Persians against the Greeks at the battle of Salamis.

Politics and Culture in Athens, 480–404 B.C.E.

During the century after the defeat of the Persians, Athens experienced unprecedented cultural growth. The new literary genre of Greek tragedy took shape, and the Athenians constructed the great temple to Athena on the Acropolis (uh-KRAW-poe-lis), the great bluff overlooking the city, as a lasting monument to Greek victory against the Persians.

In 472 B.C.E., the playwright Aeschylus (525–456 B.C.E.) wrote *The Persians*, the earliest Greek tragedy surviving today. Set in the Persian capital at Susa, the play opens with a chorus of elderly men speculating about Xerxes' attempted invasion of Greece because they have had no news for so long. One-quarter of the way through the play, a lone messenger arrives and mournfully announces:

> A single stroke has brought about the ruin of great
> Prosperity, the flower of Persia fallen and gone.
> Oh oh! To be the first to bring bad news is bad;
> But necessity demands the roll of suffering
> Be opened, Persians.[7]

Writing only eight years after the war, Aeschylus (ESS-kih-luhs), himself a veteran, exaggerates the losses to make the audience sympathize with the Persians and emphasize the shared humanity of the Persians and the Greeks. Xerxes' mother, the Queen, struggles to understand why the Persians have lost: they have violated natural law, she eventually realizes, by trying to conquer what did not belong to them. *The Persians* is the first of over one hundred tragedies written during the fifth century B.C.E. by three great playwrights—Aeschylus, Sophocles (sof-uh-KLEEZ) (496–406 B.C.E.), and Euripides (you-RIP-uh-deez) (ca. 485–406 B.C.E.)—that show individuals, both male and female, struggling to understand their fates.

In 478 B.C.E., the Athenians formed the Delian (DEE-lih-yuhn) League, a group of city-states whose stated purpose was to drive the Persians from the Greek world. After several victories in the 470s against the Persians, the Persian threat was eliminated, prompting some of the league's members to withdraw. Athens invaded these cities and forced them to become its subjects. In the 460s a general named Pericles (PER-eh-kleez) (ca. 495–429 B.C.E.) emerged as the most popular leader in the city, and in 454 B.C.E. the Athenians moved the league's treasury to Athens, ending all pretense of an alliance among equals. This was the closest that Athens came to having an empire, but its possessions were all Greek-speaking, and its control was short-lived.

In the early years after the victory at Salamis, the Athenians had vowed never to build anything on the Acropolis so that they would not forget the Persian destruction of their city. But the city's mood changed as the memory of the war receded. In 449 B.C.E., Pericles signed a peace treaty with Persia on behalf of the Delian League and used the league's funds to finance a building campaign to make Athens as physically impressive as it was politically powerful.

The centerpiece of the city's reconstruction, the Parthenon, was both a temple to Athena, the city's guardian deity, and a memorial to those who had died in the wars with Persia. As the many artists and artisans worked together over the course of fifteen years, they developed a collective style that many regard as the pinnacle of Greek artistic achievement. Once completed, the Parthenon expressed the Athenians' desire to be the most advanced people of the ancient world.

The Spartans, however, felt that they, not Athens, should be the leader of the Greeks. Since the 460s, tensions had been growing between the two city-states, and from 431 to 404 B.C.E. Athens and Sparta, and their allied city-states, engaged in the Peloponnesian

The Acropolis: A Massive Construction Project Completed in Only Fifteen Years   Built between 447 and 432 B.C.E., the Parthenon was a two-roomed building surrounded by columns over 34 feet (10 m) tall; one of the interior rooms held a magnificent statue of Athena, now lost. Beautiful friezes inside the roofs and above the columns portrayed the legendary battles of the Trojan War, in which the Greek forces (symbolizing the Athenians and their allies) defeated the Trojans (the ancient counterpart of the Persian enemy), whom the Athenians had only recently defeated.   (Georg Gerster/Photo Researchers, Inc.)

War. Since Athens was a naval power and Sparta a land power, the struggle was protracted, and Sparta, with the help of the Persians, finally defeated Athens in 404 B.C.E. Much as the long wars between the city-states of Tikal and Kalak'mul resulted in the decline of the Maya (see Chapter 5), the long and drawn-out Peloponnesian War wore both Sparta and Athens down, creating an opportunity for the rulers of the northern region of Macedon to conquer Greece (see below).

Athens as a Center for the Study of Philosophy

Even during these years of conflict, Athens was home to several of the most famous philosophers in history: Socrates (469–399 B.C.E.) taught Plato (429–347 B.C.E.), and Plato in turn taught **Aristotle** (384–322 B.C.E.). Their predecessors, the earliest Greek philosophers, were active around 600 B.C.E. in the city-state of Miletus, just north of Halicarnassus on the eastern coast of the Aegean Sea. Members of this school argued that everything in the universe originated in a single element: some proposed water; others, air. Their findings may seem naive, but they were the first to believe in rational explanations rather than crediting everything to divine intervention, and the Athenian philosophers developed this insight further.

One of the most famous Athenian philosophers, Socrates (sock-ruh-TEEZ), wrote nothing down, so we must depend on the accounts of his student Plato (PLAY-toe). He perfected a style of teaching, now known as the Socratic (suh-KRAT-ick) method, in which the instructor asks the student questions without revealing his own views. Many of the dialogues reported by Plato stress the Greek concept of *aretê* (virtue or excellence), which people can attain by doing right. Virtue was the highest good for Socrates, who believed that wisdom allows one to determine the right course of action.

Immediately after Sparta defeated Athens in the Peloponnesian War, a small group of men formed an oligarchy in Athens in 404–403 B.C.E., but they were overthrown by a democratic government. Some of those in the new government suspected Socrates of opposing democracy because he had associated with those in the oligarchy. In 399 B.C.E. they brought him to trial on vague charges of impiety (not believing in the gods) and corrupting the city's youth. Found guilty by a jury numbering in the hundreds, Socrates did not apologize but insisted that he had been right all along. His death in 399 B.C.E. from drinking poisonous hemlock, the traditional means of execution, became one of the most famous infamous executions in history. After his death the Athenians tried to modify their democratic government in various ways, but democratic rule ended in 322 B.C.E.

Plato continued Socrates' method of teaching by asking questions. He founded the Academy, a gymnasium where he could teach students a broad curriculum emphasizing ethics. Gymnasiums had begun simply as an open ground for soldiers to train, but they had evolved into schools for young boys where they engaged in exercise and studied texts. Plato taught that people could choose the just course of action by using reason to reconcile the conflicting demands of spirit and desire. Reason alone determined the individual's best interests. Plato admitted boys to the Academy as well as some girls. Scholars debate the extent of literacy among Greek women; some contend that all well-off women could read and write, while others think that only a small minority could.

Plato's student, Aristotle (AH-riss-tot-uhl) , was not a native of Athens but was born in Macedon, a northern peripheral region. He entered Plato's Academy at the age of 17 in 367 B.C.E. and studied with him for twenty years. He left Athens after the death of Plato in 347 B.C.E. and returned to Macedon, where he later served as

● **Aristotle** (384–322 B.C.E.) Greek philosopher who encouraged his students to observe the natural world and explain logically how they proceeded from their starting assumptions. This system of reasoning shapes how we present written arguments today.

Ⓒ**Primary Source:** Apologia
Learn why Socrates was condemned to death, and why he refused to stop questioning the wisdom of his countrymen.

a tutor to Alexander, the son of the Macedonian ruler Philip (382–336 B.C.E.). Aristotle did not share Socrates' and Plato's optimism that knowledge alone would result in ethical behavior because he did not accept their view that human nature was good. He emphasized, instead, that people had to study hard so that they could gain control over their desires.

Aristotle had a broad view of what constituted a proper education. Observing the round shadow the earth cast on the moon during eclipses, he concluded that the earth was a sphere and lay at the center of the universe. He urged his students to observe live animals in nature and was one of the first to realize that whales and dolphins were mammals, a discovery ignored for nearly two thousand years. Aristotle required that his students identify their starting assumptions and explain logically how they proceeded from one point to the next. This system of reasoning remained influential in the Islamic world and Europe long after his death and continues to shape how we present written arguments today.

Alexander the Great and His Successors, 334 B.C.E.–30 B.C.E.

In the course of his lifetime Aristotle witnessed the decline of Athens, which never recovered from the costs of the Peloponnesian War, and the rise of his native region of Macedon. Philip and his son **Alexander of Macedon** (also called Alexander the Great) were autocrats untouched by the Athenian tradition of democracy: as generals they ordered their professional armies to obey them and governed conquered territory as if the inhabitants were part of their army. Many scholars use the term *Helenization* to describe the process by which societies, peoples, and places during Alexander's rule became more Greek (the Greek word for Greece is *Hellas*). As Alexander's army conquered territory, his Greek-speaking soldiers encountered many different peoples living in West, Central, and South Asia. Some settled in these regions and built communities that resembled those they had left behind in Greece.

Recent historians have questioned this depiction of Alexander as a champion of Greek culture, noting how much he emulated the Persians. After the death of the last Achaemenid ruler, Darius III, Alexander portrayed himself as a defender of the Achaemenid tradition and adopted many Achaemenid practices, sometimes to the dismay of his Greek followers. Newly discovered leather scrolls show that four years after defeating the Achaemenids, Alexander's government issued orders under his name in the same format and language as the Achaemenids.[8] The borders of his empire overlapped almost entirely with those of the Achaemenid Empire, and his army, administration, and tax system were all modeled on those of the Achaemenids. After his death, Alexander's empire broke into three major sections, each ruled by a successor dynasty which followed Achaemenid practice.

Philip and Alexander: From Macedon to Empire, 359–323 B.C.E.

Lying to the north of Greece, Macedon was a peripheral region with no cities and little farming where Greek was spoken. Originally a barren region, it became a powerful kingdom under Philip II (r. 359–336 B.C.E.), who reorganized the army into a professional fighting force of paid soldiers. Philip and Alexander built empires by amassing wealth from the peoples they conquered.

Philip created, and Alexander inherited, an army more powerful than any of its rivals. Philip reorganized his army by training them to use close-packed infantry formations and by arming some of the infantry with pikes 17 feet (5 m) long. Alexander's infantry, who carried the same long pikes, formed two formidable groups on the battlefield. The infantry phalanx had 15,000 men who fought in rows and were almost invincible; 1,800 cavalry aided them by attacking the enemy on either side.

Following his father's assassination, Alexander defeated the Persian forces in 331 B.C.E., and in 330 B.C.E. one of the Persian satraps killed the reigning Achaemenid emperor Darius III (r. 336–330 B.C.E.). This turn of events allowed Alexander to take over the Persian Empire intact; he did not alter the administrative structure of satrapies. A brilliant military strategist, Alexander led his troops over eleven thousand miles in eight years, going as far as Egypt and north India, but did not significantly expand the territory of the Persian Empire (see Map 6.2).

Alexander constantly wrestled with the issue of how to govern. Should he rule as a Macedonian or adopt the Achaemenid model? To the horror of his Macedonian troops, he donned Persian clothing and expected them to prostrate themselves before him as the Achaemenid subjects honored the Persian king. When his senior advisers protested, Alexander made one of many compromises during his thirteen-year reign: he required the Persians, but not the Macedonians, to prostrate themselves. Like the Achaemenids, Alexander married women to cement his political alliances; his wife Roxane was a native of Samarkand, one of the cities that most vigorously resisted his rule.

The farther they traveled from Greece, the more unhappy Alexander's men grew. In 326 B.C.E., when they reached the banks of the Hyphasis River in India, they refused to go on, forcing Alexander to turn back. After a long and difficult march along the northern edge of the Indian Ocean, Alexander and the remnants of his army returned to Babylon, where Alexander died in 323 B.C.E.

The Legacy of Alexander the Great

The aftereffects of Alexander's conquests lasted far longer than his brief thirteen-year reign. Initially the greatest impact came from his soldiers. Thousands traveled with him, but thousands more chose to stay behind in different parts of Asia. Some could not continue at his breakneck pace because of battle wounds or age, and some preferred to live with their local wives. These men were responsible for the spread of Greek culture over a large geographic region.

Archaeologists have unearthed an entire Greek city in the Afghan town of Ai Khanum (aye-EE KAH-nuhm), which had all the usual buildings of a Greek town: a theater, a citadel where the army was stationed, a gymnasium, and temples. The temples built by Alexander's men contained statues of gods made by local artists following Greek prototypes. The population of Ai Khanum and other similar settlements included both the local Iranian peoples and descendants of Alexander's soldiers.

After Alexander's death, his empire broke into three sections, each ruled by one of his generals: Egypt went to Ptolemy (TOHL-uh-mee), Greece and Macedon to Antigonas (an-TIG-uh-nass), and all other territories—including Mesopotamia, the Mediterranean coast, and satrapies all the way to the Indus River Valley—to Seleucus (seh-LOO-kuhs), who sent Megasthenes as his ambassador to the Maurians in 302 B.C.E. (see Chapter 3). Each general founded a regional dynasty named

CL Interactive Map

🌐 **MAP 6.2**

The Empires of Persia and Alexander the Great   The Achaemenids (550–330 B.C.E.), the Parthians (247 B.C.E.–224 C.E.), and the Sasanians (224–651) all formed powerful dynasties in Iran. The largest (shown with a green border) was that of the Achaemenids. After conquering it in 330 B.C.E., Alexander of Macedon enlarged its territory only slightly. Under the Achaemenids, this large region remained united for over two hundred years; under Alexander, for only thirteen. After Alexander's death, the empire split into three.

for himself: the Ptolemies (TOHL-uh-meze), the Antigonids (an-TIG-uh-nidz), and the Seleucids (seh-LOO-sidz). These successor regimes continued to administer their territories using the Achaemenid system of administration.

The city of Alexandria in Egypt, founded by Alexander in 332 B.C.E., became a major center of learning within the territory of the Ptolemies. At Alexandria, the Ptolemies built the Museum, a temple to the Muses (the goddesses of the arts), and they welcomed scholars in many different fields, including mathematics, medicine, astronomy, history, and geography. Archaeologists have found thirteen lecture halls of the same size, each with benches for a lecturer and his audience, an indication of the size of the city's schools. The city's library was particularly impressive because customs officials confiscated all papyrus rolls that travelers brought to Alexandria; the library retained the originals and returned copies to the owners.

In 240 B.C.E. the Greek astronomer Eratosthenes (eh-ruh-TOSS-thih-nees) was appointed librarian. Since Aristotle, the Greeks had believed that the earth was spherical, but they had no idea how big it was. Eratosthenes devised an ingenious experiment. He had heard that, on the day of the solstice, when the sun shone straight above a city named Syene (SIGH-ee-nee) to the south of

Alexandria, it cast no shadow. At high noon on June 21, the day of the solstice, Eratosthenes measured the angle of the sun's shadow in Alexandria at nearly one-fiftieth of a 360-degree circle. He then drew an imaginary triangle connecting Alexandria, Syene, and the center of the earth (see Figure 6.1). He concluded that since Syene was 5,000 stadia (488 miles, 785 km) away from Alexandria, the earth's circumference must be fifty times larger, or 250,000 stadia (24,427 miles, 39,311 km). The actual circumference of the earth is 24,857 miles (40,000 km), meaning that his error was less than 2 percent. Eratosthenes' brilliant experiment taught the Greeks that the known world occupied only a small section of the earth's northern hemisphere.

The Romans defeated the last of the Antigonids in 168 B.C.E. when they conquered Macedonia (see Chapter 7) and won Egypt from the Ptolemies in 30 B.C.E., but they never conquered the Iranian Plateau. A people based in northern Iran, the Parthians, broke off from the Seleucids in 247 B.C.E. and took Iran from the Seleucids by 140 B.C.E.

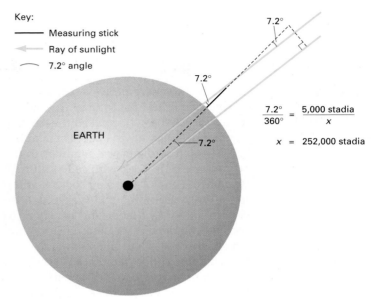

FIGURE 6.1

Eratosthenes' Measurement of the Earth   Eratosthenes knew that, on June 21, a ray of light entering a well at the city of Syene cast no shadow because the sun was directly above. At Alexandria, 5,000 stadia away, also at noon, a parallel sun ray cast a shadow of 7.2 degrees on the ground next to a measuring stick. Using the law of congruent angles, Eratosthenes reasoned that 1/50th of the earth's circumference was 5,000 stadia, and therefore the circumference of the earth was 250,000 stadia. His result (24,427 miles, or 39,311 km) was less than 2 percent from the correct figure of 24,857 miles (40,000 km).   (Illustration by Lydia Stepanek)

The Parthians and the Sasanians, Heirs to the Achaemenids, 247 B.C.E.–651 C.E.

After the defeat of the Seleucids, two dynasties—the **Parthians** (247 B.C.E.–224 C.E.) and the **Sasanians** (224–651 C.E.)—governed Iran for nearly nine hundred years. The two dynasties frequently emulated the Achaemenids; they built monuments like theirs, retained their military and tax structures, and governed the different peoples under them flexibly. The Parthians followed the Achaemenid precedent closely, while the Sasanians experimented more.

The homeland of a seminomadic people who lived near the modern city of Gorgan in northern Iran, Parthia had been a satrapy within both the Achaemenid and Seleucid Empires. In 247 B.C.E., according to a legend, Arsaces I formed a conspiracy to found his own dynasty with six other men. It was no coincidence that he had exactly the number of conspirators that his role model Darius had. Like the Achaemenids, the Parthians were Zoroastrians who worshiped fire, but they allowed their subjects to practice their own religions.

● **Parthians** (247 B.C.E.–224 C.E.)   The ruling dynasty of Iran, who defeated the Seleucids and took over their territory in 140 B.C.E. Famous for their heavily armored cavalry, they posed a continuous problem for the Roman Empire.

• **Sasanians** The ruling dynasty (224–651 C.E.) of Iran who defeated the Parthians and ruled for more than four centuries until the Islamic conquest of Iran. Introduced innovations such as non-satrap royal lands and government support of Zoroastrianism.

The dynastic founder and his successors eventually conquered the Tigris and Euphrates River Valleys and the Iranian Plateau extending up to the Indus River Valley in Pakistan (see Map 6.2). The Parthians were famous for their fine and fast horses, which were heavily coated with armor. Parthian archers tricked the enemy by pretending to retreat and then turning backwards on their mounts to shoot, in a display of archery prowess still known as the Parthian shot. Starting in the first century B.C.E. and continuing through the first and second centuries C.E., the Romans (see Chapter 7) attacked the Parthians at periodic intervals, but the powerful Parthian military always kept them at bay.

Parthian soldiers were retainers to the nobles, for whom they performed military service. The king, who called himself "king of kings" in the Persian tradition, stood at the top of Parthian society, and the upper nobility ranked just below him but above the lower nobility. Though not slaves, the retainers had to perform a certain amount of labor and to pay a fixed amount of goods to the nobles they served. Doctors, artists, singing storytellers, and traders formed a middle level between the nobles and the retainers.

Trade was important because the Parthians occupied the territory between the Greco-Roman world and their Asian trading partners. In times of peace with Rome the Parthians traded spices and textiles for Roman metals and manufactured goods, but during the frequent periods of war, trading routes were blocked and smugglers became active.

The Parthians ruled for nearly five hundred years, far longer than the two-hundred-year reign of the Achaemenids, and their rule came to an end in 224 C.E. when Ardashir, one of their satraps based in the Iranian heartland of Persis, overthrew them and founded the Sasanian empire (named for his ancestor, Sasan). After defeating the Parthians, the Sasanians incorporated the Parthian forces into their army, of which the armored cavalry continued to be the strongest section. The Sasanian rulers led their powerful army to conquer all the territory of the former Parthian empire in addition to Sogdiana, Georgia, and the northeastern Arabian peninsula (see Map 6.2).

Sasanian society remained as hierarchical as in earlier Achaemenid and Parthian times, and the greater number of surviving documents means that we know more about it. The upper nobility was divided into four ranks, with the king's direct relatives ranking highest and those unrelated to the king lowest. Royal women continued to exercise considerable power, as in Achaemenid times; some of the most powerful rulers' mothers were called "queen of queens." Under the upper nobility were a lower group of nobles, some of whom received their lands and positions directly from the king. The middle ranks included craftsmen, traders, doctors, and singers. At the bottom of society were the cultivators, who had to give a share of their crop to the nobles in addition to the taxes they paid.

Once the Sasanians conquered a region, they divided the territory into two types of land: some was reserved for the king, while that portion entrusted to a satrap was divided into smaller districts. Only on the royal lands could the king establish cities, which he populated with deported peoples, most often skilled craftsmen, drawn from prisoners of war. The practice of forcible resettlement had a long history in western Asia going back to the Assyrians and the Babylonians (see Chapter 2). The resettled peoples could not leave their assigned cities, but they were free to marry local women, practice their own religions, and speak their native languages. These skilled craftsmen received high pay for their work as weavers and as builders and engineers who constructed roads and bridges.

The Sasanians realized that many different peoples lived within their empire, and to propagate knowledge they encouraged the translation of certain books from Sanskrit, Greek, and Syriac (the language spoken in Mesopotamia). They appointed officials to supervise Zoroastrian observances in each province at the local level, and the state constructed fire altars all over the empire. These government policies made Sasanian Iran actively Zoroastrian, and the Sasanians had difficulty managing the great religious diversity of their subjects.

By the third century C.E. two new religions, each with sizable followings, appeared in Iran: Christianity (see Chapter 7) and Manichaeism (mah-nih-KEE-iz-uhm). Mani (mah-KNEE) (216–ca. 274) was an Iranian preacher born in Mesopotamia who believed that his Manichaean teachings incorporated all the teachings of earlier prophets, including Zarathustra, the Buddha, and Jesus Christ. He deliberately recorded his teachings in written form so that his followers could translate them into other languages to encourage conversion. Like Zoroastrianism, his was a dualistic system in which the forces of light and dark were engaged in a perpetual struggle. Ordinary people could strengthen the forces of light by supporting the Manichaean clergy, who ate only vegetarian food provided by the laity, lived celibate lives, and conducted Manichaean rituals.

The Sasanians saw both the Christians and the Manichaeans as threats because they had their own religious hierarchy and refused to perform Zoroastrian rituals. Some kings tried to strengthen Zoroastrianism by commissioning a written version of *The Avesta* to rival Manichaean scriptures and the Bible. Other rulers directly persecuted members of the two churches: Manichaeism was banned even before Mani's death, and some Christians, suspected of being allies of the enemy Roman forces, were killed.

The third major religious community, the Jews, fared better under the Sasanians than did the Christians and the Manichaeans. The Sasanians allowed the Jews to govern their own communities as long as the Jews paid their taxes. Yet, whenever the Jews united behind a leader who challenged the legitimacy of Sasanian rule, the Sasanians put down the rebellion.

Adherence to the Achaemenid model of flexible empire allowed the Sasanians to rule for over four centuries. Surviving several military defeats and forfeiting large chunks of their empire, the Sasanians ruled until 651, when their capital at Ctesiphon fell to the Islamic armies of the caliphate (see Chapter 9).

For over a thousand years, the model of a flexible empire based on satrapies was so successful that the Achaemenids, Alexander, the successor states, the Parthians, and the Sasanians all used it to govern their empires. During this time, a very different empire and a powerful military rival to both the Parthians and the Sasanians arose in Rome in modern-day Italy, as the next chapter will explain.

The Sasanian Palace, Ctesiphon, Iran   The ruins of the Sasanian palace at Ctesiphon demonstrate the ingenuity and great skill of the brickmasons, who came from all over the empire and were resettled there by the emperors. The vaulted arch stands 118 feet (36 m) high, making it one of the world's largest brick arches. Its open doorways and fine brickwork inspired Islamic architects who incorporated these same features into early mosques.   (Gerard Degeorge/AKG Images)

Chapter Review

KEY TERMS

Darius (144)

Herodotus (144)

Achaemenids (146)

satrap (148)

The Avesta (148)

Zoroastrianism (148)

Ahura Mazda (148)

Cyrus (149)

Lydian coins (152)

Phoenicians (158)

Artemisia (163)

Aristotle (165)

Alexander of
  Macedon (166)

Parthians (169)

Sasanians (169)

Born in the decade of the most intense fighting between Athens and the Achaemenid Empire, Herodotus devoted his life to understanding the conflict between the two. Indeed, he defined the goal of *The Histories* as "to show why the two peoples fought with each other." Although, as a Greek, Herodotus sympathized with the Athenians, he attributed much of the Persians' success to their monarchical form of government.

 What administrative and military innovations enabled the Achaemenid dynasty to conquer and rule such a vast empire?

The Achaemenids succeeded in conquering the 30 to 35 million people who populated the entire world known to them; they did not conquer Greece or the area south of the Black Sea. The decentralized structure of the Persian Empire, divided into satrapies, allowed for diversity; as long as each region fulfilled its tax obligations to the center, its residents could practice their own religion and speak their own languages. Conquered peoples were recruited into the powerful infantry, cavalry, archers, and engineers of the Achaemenids. Hundreds of thousands of soldiers marched by foot over Eurasia on a fine system of roads whose major artery was the Royal Road.

 What were the important accomplishments of the Greek city-states? Consider innovations in politics, intellectual life, fine arts, and science.

For all their military success, the Persians proved unable to defeat the Athenians and their allied city-states, who were able to outwit and outfight the Persian army and its navy twice in the late fifth century B.C.E. The city's democracy survived for more than two centuries until 322 B.C.E. The city-state's wealth supported an extraordinary group of dramatists who wrote plays, artists and craftsmen who built the Acropolis, and philosophers who debated the importance of reason. The Athenians knew that the world was round, and a later Greek scholar in Alexandria even calculated the world's circumference to within 2 percent of its actual length.

Who was Alexander, and what was his legacy?

Alexander conquered the entire extent of the Persian Empire and completely adopted its administrative structure. He died young after ruling only thirteen years, but thousands of his men stayed behind, building Greek-style cities like Ai Khanum throughout Central Asia. On his death, his empire broke into three smaller Achaemenid-style empires: the Antigonids in Greece, the Ptolemies in Egypt, and the Seleucids in western Asia.

How did the Parthians and the Sasanians modify the Achaemenid model of empire?

Parthia, originally a satrap in northern Iran, overthrew the Seleucids and largely adopted the Achaemenid model of empire. The Parthians and their successors, the Sasanians, broke from the Achaemenid model by creating royal lands on which the king resettled captured skilled craftsmen who built impressive cities. Zoroastrians like the Achaemenids, the Sasanians departed from earlier policies of religious tolerance by occasionally persecuting the Manichaean, Christian, and Jewish communities in their realm.

 WEB RESOURCES

Pronunciation Guide

Interactive Maps

MAP 6.1 Greek and Phoenician Settlement in the Mediterranean

MAP 6.2 The Empires of Persia and Alexander the Great

Primary Sources

Chapter Objectives

ACE Multiple-Choice Quiz

Flashcards

For Further Reference

Casson, Lionel. *Travel in the Ancient World.* Baltimore: Johns Hopkins University Press, 1974.

Harley, J. B., and David Woodward. *The History of Cartography.* Vol. 1, *Cartography in Prehistoric, Ancient, and Medieval Europe.* Chicago: University of Chicago Press, 1987.

Herodotus. *The Histories.* Translated by Aubrey De Sélincourt. Further rev. ed. New York: Penguin Books, 1954, 2003.

Hornblower, Simon, and Antony Spawforth. *The Oxford Companion to Classical Civilization.* New York: Oxford University Press, 1998.

Insler, Stanley. *The Gāthās of Zarathustra.* Leiden: E. J. Brill, 1975.

Markoe, Glenn E. *Peoples of the Past: Phoenicians.* Berkeley: University of California Press, 2000.

Martin, Thomas R. *Ancient Greece from Prehistoric to Hellenistic Times.* New Haven: Yale University Press, 1996.

Nylan, Michael. "Golden Spindles and Axes: Elite Women in the Achaemenid and Han Empires." In *Early China/Ancient Greece: Thinking Through Comparisons,* ed. Steven Shank-

man and Stephen W. Durrant. Albany: State University of New York Press, 2002.

Pollitt, J. J. *Art and Experience in Classical Greece.* Cambridge: Cambridge University Press, 1972.

Wiesehöfer, Josef. *Ancient Persia from 550 BC to 650 AD.* Translated by Azizeh Azodi. New York: I. B. Tauris, 2001.

Websites

Evolution of Alphabets
(http://www.wam.umd.edu/~rfradkin/alphapage.html).   Introduction to the history of many alphabets.

The Parthian Empire
(www.parthia.com).   Introduction to Parthia Empire with excellent maps.

The Perseus Digital Library
(www.perseus.tufts.edu).   A wealth of searchable texts from the classical world in both the original language and English translation.

The Roman Empire and the Rise of Christianity, 509 B.C.E.–476 C.E.

The events of 168 B.C.E. cut short the promising career of a young Greek statesman named **Polybius** (ca. 200–ca. 118 B.C.E.). In that year, after defeating the ruler of Macedon, the Romans demanded that the Greeks send over one thousand hostages to Italy for indefinite detention. Polybius (poh-LIH-bee-us) was deported to Rome, which remained his home even after his sixteen years of detention ended. His one surviving book, *The Rise of the Roman Empire,* explains why he felt that Rome, and not his native Greece, had become the major power of the Mediterranean:

(Alinari/Art Resource, NY)

There can surely be nobody so petty or so apathetic in his outlook that he has no desire to discover by what means and under what system of government the Romans succeeded . . . in bringing under their rule almost the whole of the inhabited world, an achievement which is without parallel in human history. . . .

The arresting character of my subject and the grand spectacle which it presents can best be illustrated if we consider the most celebrated empires of the past which have provided historians with their principal themes, and set them beside the domination of Rome. Those which qualify for such a comparison are the following. The Persians for a certain period exercised their rule and supremacy over a vast territory, but every time that they ventured to pass beyond the limits of Asia they endangered the security not only of their empire but of their existence. . . . The rule of the Macedonians in Europe extended only from the lands bordering the Adriatic to the Danube, which

POLYBIUS

This icon will direct you to interactive activities and study materials on the *Voyages* website: www.cengage.com/history/hansen/voyages1e

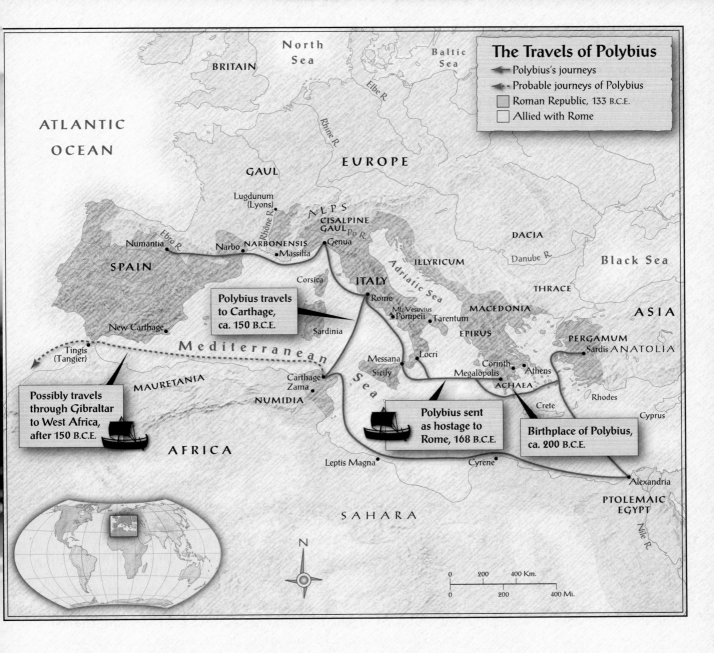

The Travels of Polybius

← Polybius's journeys
◄-- Probable journeys of Polybius
■ Roman Republic, 133 B.C.E.
□ Allied with Rome

ATLANTIC OCEAN

North Sea

Baltic Sea

BRITAIN

EUROPE

GAUL

Lugdunum (Lyons)

Rhône R.

Rhine R.

Elbe R.

ALPS

CISALPINE GAUL

Po R.

DACIA

Danube R.

Black Sea

Numantia

Ebro R.

Narbo

NARBONENSIS

Massilia

Genua

ILLYRICUM

THRACE

SPAIN

Corsica

ITALY

Rome

Adriatic Sea

MACEDONIA

ASIA

New Carthage

Sardinia

Mt. Vesuvius
Pompeii

Tarentum

EPIRUS

PERGAMUM

Sardis ANATOLIA

Mediterranean Sea

Polybius travels to Carthage, ca. 150 B.C.E.

Messana

Sicily

Locri

Corinth
Megalopolis

Athens

ACHAEA

Rhodes

Tingis (Tangier)

Possibly travels through Gibraltar to West Africa, after 150 B.C.E.

MAURETANIA

Carthage
Zama

NUMIDIA

Polybius sent as hostage to Rome, 168 B.C.E.

Crete

Cyprus

Birthplace of Polybius, ca. 200 B.C.E.

AFRICA

Leptis Magna

Cyrene

Alexandria

PTOLEMAIC EGYPT

SAHARA

Nile R.

N

0   200   400 Km.
0   200   400 Mi.

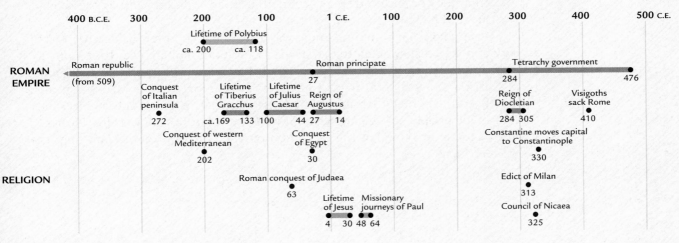

	400 B.C.E.	300	200	100	1 C.E.	100	200	300	400	500 C.E.

Lifetime of Polybius
ca. 200   ca. 118

ROMAN EMPIRE

Roman republic (from 509)

Roman principate

Tetrarchy government

27

284   476

Conquest of Italian peninsula
272

Lifetime of Tiberius Gracchus
ca.169   133

Lifetime of Julius Caesar
100   44

Reign of Augustus
27   14

Reign of Diocletian
284 305

Visigoths sack Rome
410

Conquest of western Mediterranean
202

Conquest of Egypt
30

Constantine moves capital to Constantinople
330

RELIGION

Roman conquest of Judaea
63

Edict of Milan
313

Lifetime of Jesus
4   30

Missionary journeys of Paul
48 64

Council of Nicaea
325

would appear to be no more than a small fraction of the continent. Later, by overthrowing the Persian Empire, they also became the rulers of Asia; but although they were then regarded as having become the masters of a larger number of states and territories than any other people before them, they still left the greater part of the inhabited world in the hands of others. . . . The Romans, on the other hand, have brought not just mere portions but almost the whole of the world under their rule, and have left an empire which far surpasses any that exists today or is likely to succeed it.[1]

● **Polybius** (ca. 200–ca. 118 B.C.E.) A Greek historian who was deported to Rome. Author of *The Rise of the Roman Empire,* a book that explained how Rome acquired its empire. Believed the task of the historian was to distinguish underlying causes of events.

Most historians today would challenge Polybius's decision to rank Alexander of Macedon above the Achaemenids, whose empire he inherited (see Chapter 6). Polybius was also unaware of the Han dynasty in China (see Chapter 4), which probably had as many subjects as the Romans (some fifty-five million). Yet Rome did bring under its rule "almost the whole of the world" if we grant that Polybius meant the entire Mediterranean region, including western Asia, North Africa, and much of Europe. Even after the empire broke apart, the Mediterranean remained a coherent geographical region with shared cultural and linguistic ties forged during the nearly one thousand years of Roman rule.

During his detention, Polybius stayed in the city of Rome, where he lived with the descendants of a prominent general. After 152 B.C.E., when he was freed, Polybius accompanied his host's grandson to modern-day Spain and Carthage in North Africa and sailed down the Atlantic coast of West Africa. (The chapter opening map shows Polybius's travels and the extent of the Roman Empire after the conquests of Greece, Macedonia, and Carthage.) Travel around and across the Mediterranean was much more common in Polybius's lifetime than before, and it became even easier in the centuries after his death. Officials, soldiers, and couriers of the Roman Empire proceeded along a network of straight paved roads that ringed the Mediterranean Sea, the heart of the Roman Empire. Large boats crisscrossed the sea, while smaller vessels hugged its shore. Roman armies protected travelers from attacks, and the Roman navy lessened the threat of piracy.

During Polybius's lifetime Rome was a republic, but after his death, a century of political chaos culminated in the adoption of monarchy as the empire's new political system. In the beginning of the Common Era, the new religion of Christianity spread on roads and waterways throughout the Mediterranean region and eventually became the empire's official religion. The empire, increasingly unable to defend itself from powerful tribes in western Europe, moved to a new capital in the east and ultimately lost control of Rome and its western half.

Focus Questions

- How did Rome, a small settlement in central Italy, expand to conquer and control the entire Mediterranean world of Europe, western Asia, and North Africa?
- How did the political structure of the Roman Empire change as it grew?
- What were the basic teachings of Jesus, and how did Christianity become the major religion of the empire?
- What allowed Rome to retain such a large empire for so long, and what caused the loss of the western half of the empire?

●The Roman Republic, 509–27 B.C.E.

In its early years Rome was but one of many city-states on the Italian peninsula, but one with an unusual policy toward defeated enemies: once a neighboring city-state surrendered to Rome, Rome's leaders offered its citizens a chance to join forces with them. As a result, more and more men joined Rome's army. This policy increased the size of the Roman army and made it almost unstoppable, and by 272 B.C.E. Rome had conquered the Italian peninsula. In 202 B.C.E., after defeating Carthage, it gained dominance in the western Mediterranean, and in 146 B.C.E., after defeating a Greek coalition, it controlled the eastern Mediterranean as well. Those conquests were the crucial first step in the formation of the Mediterranean as a geographical region. After 146 B.C.E., Rome's armies continued to win territory, but the violence and civil wars of the first century B.C.E. brought an end to the republic in 27 B.C.E.

Early Rome to 509 B.C.E. The city of Rome lies in the middle of the boot-shaped peninsula of Italy, which extends into the Mediterranean. One chain of mountains, the Apennines (AP-puh-nines), runs down the spine of Italy, while the Alps form a natural barrier to the north. Italy's volcanic soil is more fertile than Greece's (see Chapter 6), and many different crops flourished in the temperate climate of the Mediterranean. Several large islands, including Sardinia and Corsica, lay to the west of Italy; immediately to the south, the island of Sicily formed a natural steppingstone across the Mediterranean to modern-day Tunisia, Africa, only 100 miles (160 km) away.

Written sources reveal little about Rome's origins. The earliest surviving history of Rome, by Livy, dates to the first century B.C.E., nearly one thousand years after the site of Rome was first settled in 1000 B.C.E. (Polybius's history starts in 264–260 B.C.E., long after the city's founding.) The city's original site lay 16 miles (26 km) from the Tyrrhenian Sea at a point where the shallow Tiber River could be crossed easily. The seven hills surrounding the settlement formed a natural defense, and from the beginning people gathered there to trade.

Romans grew up hearing a myth, also recorded by Livy, about the founding of their city by two twin brothers, Romulus and Remus, grandsons of the rightful king. An evil king who had seized power ordered a servant to kill them, but the servant abandoned them instead. Raised by a wolf, the twins survived, and Romulus went on to found Rome in 753 B.C.E. This legend is not unique to Rome; it is a Romanized version of a western Asian myth. Archaeologists have found that small communities surrounded by walls existed in Rome by the eighth century B.C.E.

During the sixth and fifth centuries B.C.E., when the Persian and the Greek Empires were vying for power, Rome was an obscure backwater (see Chapter 6). Greek colonists had settled in the south of Italy, and their cities were larger and far better planned than Rome. To the north lived the Etruscans (ee-TRUS-kunz), who built impressive fortresses dug into the sides of the hills. The Romans learned city planning, sewage management, and wall construction from their Etruscan neighbors. The Etruscans modified the Greek alphabet to write their own language, which the Romans in turn adopted around 600 B.C.E. to record their first inscriptions in their native Latin, a language in the Indo-European family.

The Early Republic and the Conquest of Italy, 509–272 B.C.E.

The earliest form of government in the Roman city-state was a monarchy. The first kings governed in consultation with an assembly composed of men from Rome's most prominent and wealthiest families, the patricians (puh-TRISH-uhns) who owned large landholdings. The origins of the patricians are unclear, but they formed a propertied, privileged social group distinct from the plebians (pluh-BEE-uhns), or commoners. Each time the king died, the patrician assembly chose his successor, not necessarily his son; the early kings included both Etruscans and Latins.

After overthrowing an Etruscan king, the Romans founded the **Roman Republic** in 509 B.C.E. In a republic, unlike direct democracy, the people choose the officials who govern. The power to rule was entrusted to two elected executives, called consuls, who served a one-year term. The consuls consulted regularly with an advisory body, the **Roman senate,** which was composed entirely of patricians, and less often with the plebian assembly, in which all free men, or citizens, could vote. The Romans never allowed a simple majority to prevail; instead they divided each assembly into smaller groups and reached a decision by counting the votes of the rich more heavily than the poor.

After 400 B.C.E., the republic continuously fought off different mountain peoples from the north who hoped to conquer Rome's fertile agricultural plain. The Celts or Gauls were residents of the Alps region who spoke Celtic, also an Indo-European language. In 387 B.C.E., Rome suffered a crushing military defeat at the hands of the Gauls, who took the city but left after plundering it for seven months.

Rome recovered and began to conquer other city-states. To speakers of Latin among their defeated enemies, the Romans offered all the privileges of citizenship

• Roman Republic
Type of Roman government between 509 B.C.E. and 27 B.C.E. Ruled by two elected executives, called consuls, who served one-year terms. The consuls consulted regularly with the senate, composed entirely of patricians, and less often with the plebian assembly, where all free men could vote.

• Roman senate
Roman governing body, composed largely of appointed patricians. During the years of the republic (509–27 B.C.E.), membership was around three hundred men and grew slightly in later periods, when the senate became an advisory body.

and the accompanying obligations; those who did not speak Latin had to pay taxes and serve as soldiers but could not participate in the political system.

The Romans learned much from the different peoples they conquered; they worshiped Greek gods to whom they gave Roman names (see below), and they adopted elements of Greek law. They also constructed roads linking Rome with their new possessions. This combination of policies provided a winning formula for Roman military success, and by 321 B.C.E. Roman troops had gained control of the entire Italian peninsula except for the south (the toe and heel of the Italian boot), a region where the Greek settlers' presence was so pronounced that the Romans referred to it as Magna Graecia ("Greater Greece"). It took almost fifty years before Rome conquered the final Greek city-state in Italy.

The Conquest of the Mediterranean World, 272–146 B.C.E.

In 272 B.C.E., the year that Rome gained control of the Italian peninsula, six different powers held territory around the coastline of the Mediterranean, and the residents of these different regions had no shared cultural identity. To the east, the three successors to Alexander (see Chapter 6) still occupied territory: the Antigonids in Macedon, the Seleucids in Syria, and the Ptolemies in Egypt. In addition, two separate leagues of city-states controlled the Greek peninsula. **Carthage,** a city originally founded by the Phoenicians (see Chapter 6), prospered by taxing trade. With an oligarchic government, Carthage controlled the north coast of Africa between today's Tunis and Morocco, the

> • **Carthage** A city in modern-day Tunisia originally founded by the Phoenicians. Rome's main rival for control of the Mediterranean. Between 264 and 146 B.C.E., Rome and Carthage fought three Punic Wars, and Rome won all three.

🔲 **A Modern Reconstruction of the Port of Carthage**   The city's most prominent feature was its protected port. During peace, ships used the port behind the sea-wall, but during war, all the ships could retreat behind the city walls into the interior circular harbor, where they were well-protected.   (Museum of Carthage/Gianni Dagli Orti/The Art Archive)

southern half of modern-day Spain, Corsica, Sardinia, and half of Sicily. The only two actively expansionist states among these different powers, Rome and Carthage, collided in 264 B.C.E.

In that year Rome sent troops to support one city-state in Sicily against a different city-state allied with Carthage, triggering the first of the **Punic Wars.** (The Latin word for Phoenicians was *Poeni,* the origin of the English word *Punic* [PYOO-nik].) Whereas Rome had an army of citizens who fought when they were not farming, Carthage's army consisted almost entirely of mercenary troops paid to fight. Previously a land power, Rome built its first navy of sailing ships powered by multiple levels of oarsmen. After more than twenty years of fighting—some on land, some on sea—Rome won control of Sicily in 241 B.C.E., but Carthage continued to dominate the Mediterranean west of Sicily.

Rome and Carthage faced each other again in the Second Punic War (sometimes called the Hannibalic War) from 218 to 202 B.C.E. This war matched two brilliant generals: Carthage's **Hannibal** (ca. 247–ca. 182 B.C.E.) with Rome's Scipio Africanus (236–183 B.C.E.), the grandfather of Polybius's host Scipio Aemilianus (ca. 185–ca. 129 B.C.E.). Writing about events that occurred before he was born, Polybius believed that while an army might use a pretext to attack an enemy and a battle could begin a war, the historian should distinguish the underlying causes of war from both their pretexts and their beginnings. The underlying cause of the Second Punic War, Polybius argued, dated back to Hannibal's childhood and his father's anger at losing the First Punic War. Hannibal probably hoped, too, to cut Rome off from its territories so that Carthage could regain control over Roman territory in Spain. Launching his attack from New Carthage (modern-day Cartagena) in Spain, Hannibal led a force of 50,000 infantry, 9,000 cavalry, and 37 elephants on a five-month march across southern France and then through the Alps.

Polybius believed that the historian had to do on-site research; as he said, "I . . . have personally explored the country, and have crossed the Alps myself to obtain first-hand information and evidence." Hannibal's decision to cross the Alps was audacious: "These conditions were so unusual as to be almost freakish," Polybius learned from interviews with the locals. "The new snow lying on top of the old, which had remained there from the previous winter, gave way easily, both because it was soft, having just fallen, and because it was not yet deep." Many of Hannibal's men froze or starved to death, and Polybius estimated that less than half the original army, and a single elephant, survived the fifteen-day march through the Alps.

Carthage's army included Africans, Spaniards, Celts, Phoenicians, Italians, and Greeks. Although all of Hannibal's soldiers came from the Mediterranean region, Polybius noted that they "had nothing naturally in common, neither in their laws, their customs, their language, nor in any other respect," because the region had not yet become a coherent unit. The varied composition of Hannibal's army intimidated the Romans: "The troops were drawn up in alternate companies, the Celts naked, the Spaniards with their short linen tunics bordered with purple—their national dress—so that the line presented a strange and terrifying appearance."

Polybius attributed much of the Romans' success to the rules governing their army. Like the Qin army in China (see Chapter 4), the Roman commanders enforced a complex policy of rewards and punishments. Men who fought bravely in battle could win a spear, cup, or lance. The punishments for failure to fight were severe. If a group of men deserted, their commander randomly selected one-tenth

● **Punic Wars** The three wars between Rome and Carthage. The First Punic War, fought from 264 to 241 B.C.E., was for control of Sicily. In the second, between 218 and 202 B.C.E., Hannibal was defeated. In the third, in 146 B.C.E., Rome defeated Carthage and ordered all the city's buildings leveled and its residents enslaved.

● **Hannibal** (ca. 247–ca. 182 B.C.E.) The leader of Carthage's armies during the Second Punic War. A brilliant military strategist who led his troops over the Alps into Rome but who was defeated by Rome's superior army in 202 B.C.E.

of the deserters to be beaten to death. "This is carried out as follows," explains Polybius. "The tribune takes a cudgel and lightly touches the condemned man with it, whereupon all the soldiers fall upon him with clubs and stones, and usually kill him in the camp itself." Fear of this punishment kept Roman soldiers at their posts even when defeat was certain.

Diminished as their numbers were by the trip across the Alps, Hannibal's army entered Italy and won several major battles in succession, yet Hannibal never attacked Rome directly. When the two armies finally met in 202 B.C.E. at Zama, on the North African coast, Rome defeated Carthage. In 201 B.C.E., Rome and Carthage signed a peace treaty that imposed heavy fines on Carthage, granted Carthage's holdings in Spain to Rome, and limited the size of its navy to only ten vessels. With the elimination of Carthage as a rival power, the Roman Empire gained control of the entire western Mediterranean.

After the Second Punic War, Roman forces fought a series of battles with the three successor states to Alexander. Fighting in Greece and Anatolia, the Romans defeated the Seleucids in 188 B.C.E. yet allowed them to continue to rule in Syria. After several wars, Rome defeated the Antigonids in 168 B.C.E., the year Polybius came to Rome as a hostage, and brought the Antigonid dynasty to an end. In the same year, Ptolemaic Egypt became a client state of Rome, nominally ruled by a Ptolemy king. Rome secured control of the eastern Mediterranean only in 133 B.C.E. Before that time, Rome's power in the eastern Mediterranean was due to a series of treaties that created dependent and allied states through the region.

In 146 B.C.E. Rome defeated Carthage a third time. After he had taken the city, Scipio Aemilianus (SIP-ee-o ay-mill-YAN-us), the commander in charge of Roman forces, ordered all the buildings in the city leveled and the survivors sent to Rome to be sold as slaves. The Roman senate passed a bill forbidding anyone to rebuild Carthage and in place of Carthage's empire established the province of Africa (the origin of the continent's name), an area of about 5,000 square miles (13,000 sq km) along the North African coast. As we have seen in previous chapters, conquering rulers frequently exacted a high price from the people of a newly subjugated territory, but the order to destroy a city and enslave all its inhabitants marked a new level of brutality.

Each conquest brought new territory to be administered by the Roman Empire. Before the First Punic War, the newly conquered lands usually acquired the same governing structure as the city-state of Rome; in later periods the conquered territories, including Sicily, Sardinia, and Spain, were ruled as military districts by a governor, usually a former consul, appointed by the senate. The residents of these military districts did not receive citizenship.

Like the Achaemenid satraps (see Chapter 6), each Roman governor was in charge of an extremely large area; the district of North Africa stretched across the Mediterranean coastline of the three modern nations of Libya, Tunisia, and Algeria. The governor had a tiny staff: one official to watch over the province's finances, an advisory panel of his friends and high-ranking clients, and a small entourage composed of lower-ranking freedmen or slaves. The low number of officials meant that the governor almost always left the previous governmental structures in place.

The greatest challenge for the provincial governors was the collection of taxes, which their small staffs were supposed to forward to Rome. Unlike the Achaemenid satraps, who retained control over tax collection, the Roman governors delegated tax collection to others. The governors divided their provinces into regions and auctioned off the right to collect taxes in each region to the highest bidder. The **tax farmers,** the businessmen who paid in advance for the right to collect taxes in their territory, agreed to provide the governor with a certain amount of revenue; anything above that was theirs to keep. The residents of provinces suffered because the tax farmers took much more than they were entitled to. Most of the men who applied for the position of tax farmer belonged to a new commercial class of entrepreneurs and businessmen, called equites (EH-kwee-tays) because they were descended from soldiers who rode on horseback.

● **tax farmers**   Under the Roman empire, businessmen who paid in advance for the right to collect taxes in a given territory and who agreed to provide the governor with a fixed amount of revenue. Anything else they collected was theirs to keep.

Roman Society Under the Republic

In 168 B.C.E., the family of the general Scipio Africanus (SIP-ee-o ah-frih-KAHN-us) persuaded the authorities to allow Polybius to stay with them. In *The Rise of the Roman Empire,* Polybius explains how he became acquainted with the grandson of Scipio Africanus, named Scipio Aemilianus. One day Scipio Aemilianus asked Polybius, "Why is it, Polybius, that although my brother and I eat at the same table, you always speak to him, address all your questions and remarks in his direction and leave me out of them?" Polybius responded that it was only natural for him to address the older brother, but he offered to help the 18-year-old Scipio Aemilianus launch his public career: "I do not think you could find anybody more suitable than myself to help you and encourage your efforts."

This conversation illustrates how influential Romans gained clients, or dependents not in their families. The people most likely to become clients were newcomers to a city, traders, or people who wanted to break from their own families. Patrons had the same obligation to help their clients as the head of the family had to help his own family members. They gave their clients food and money or assistance with legal matters, and clients in turn demonstrated loyalty by accompanying their patrons to the Forum, the marketplace where the residents of every Roman town gathered daily to transact business.

Scipio, like most important patrons in Rome, belonged to an eminent patrician family. Both his father and mother were the children of consuls. When he met Polybius, he was living with his adopted father, who was the head of his family, or the **paterfamilias** (pah-tehr-fah-MIL-lee-us). In Roman society only the paterfamilias could own property. He made all decisions affecting his wife, children, and son's wives, including, for example, the decision of whether the family could afford to raise a newborn baby or should deny it food and expose it to the elements. When the head of the family died, the sons might decide to split up the immediate family or to stay together under a new paterfamilias.

● **paterfamilias**   The legal head of the extended family in Rome and the only person who could own property. Made all decisions affecting his wife, children, and son's wives.

The Romans had a marriage ceremony, but most people did not bother with it; a man and a woman simply moved in together. Women were allowed to inherit, own, and pass on property in their own right, but under the stewardship of a male guardian, usually the paterfamilias. Marriage among more prominent families, like the Scipios, required a formal contract stipulating that the father would recognize as heirs any children resulting from the match. Roman men took only one wife, but the shorter life spans of the ancient world meant that remarriage among the widowed was common. Either the husband or wife could initiate divorce, which was accomplished by simple notification; the main legal issue was the settlement of property. Scipio Aemilianus's parents divorced two or three years after his birth, but he remained close to both.

Roman women devoted considerable energy to educating their children, whose marriages they often helped to arrange. The biographer of Cornelia, the widowed aunt of Scipio Aemilianus, praised her for being "proper in her behavior" and "a good and principled mother." She refused to marry the ruler of Ptolemaic Egypt so that she could devote herself to her twelve children, of whom only three survived to adulthood. Late in her life, "she had a wide circle of friends and her hospitality meant that she was never short of dinner guests. She surrounded herself with Greek and Roman scholars, and used to exchange gifts with kings from all over the world. Her guests and visitors used particularly to enjoy the stories she told of the life and habits of her father, Africanus."[2] Cornelia's example shows how Roman women were able to exert considerable influence even though they were formally barred from holding public office.

Well-off Roman households like the Scipios also owned slaves, who were usually captured in military campaigns abroad, brought to Rome, and sold to the highest bidder. Those who worked the fields or inside the homes of their masters were more fortunate than those who toiled in gold and silver mines, where mortality rates were high because the underground tunnels often collapsed. Some estimate that a ratio of three free citizens to one slave prevailed in the republic, one of the highest rates in world history.[3] On the rare occasions when Roman slaves obtained their freedom, they gained the full rights of citizens. However, many more slaves remained slaves for their entire lives, as did their children, because a child born to a slave mother, regardless of the father's status, remained a slave unless freed by the owner.

The Late Republic, 146–27 B.C.E.

Polybius and his contemporaries were well aware of the strains on Roman society that came with the rapid acquisition of so much new territory. During the years of Rome's conquests, the political system of the republic had functioned well. But soon after the victories of 146 B.C.E., the republic proved unable to resolve the tensions that came with the expanded empire.

In the early years of the republic, most Roman soldiers lived on farms, which they left periodically to fight in battles. As the Roman army fought in more distant places, like Carthage, soldiers went abroad for long stretches at a time and often sold off their fields to rich landowners, who invested in large-scale agricultural enterprises that grew fruit or vegetables, pressed olive oil, or produced wine. With few freedmen for hire, the rich landowners turned increasingly to slaves, and privately held estates, called latifundia (lat-uh-FUN-dee-uh), grew larger and larger. The gulf widened between the well-off owners of latifundia estates and the ordinary people who had lost their land. Many of the landless moved to Rome, where they joined the ranks of the city's poor because they had no steady employment.

Cornelia's son Tiberius Gracchus (ty-BEER-ee-us GRAK-us) (ca. 169–133 B.C.E.) was one of the first to propose economic reforms to help the poor. Each time Rome conquered a new region, the government set aside large amounts of public land, much of it controlled by the wealthy landed families of the city. Tiberius wanted to enforce an existing limit on the amount of land any individual family could own and give the remainder to the poor. Such land grants, he hoped, would ease unemployment among the city's poor while increasing the number of landed peasants eligible for military service.

Elected tribune in 133 B.C.E., Tiberius Gracchus brought his proposals before the plebian assembly, not the senate. The bill passed because Tiberius removed the other tribune, who was opposed to the measure. Furious that he did not follow the usual procedures, a gang of senators and their supporters killed him. This was the first time since the founding of the republic that participants in a political dispute used murder as a weapon. Even after his death, calls for agrarian reform persisted. In 123 B.C.E. Tiberius's younger brother Gaius Gracchus (GUY-us GRAK-us) launched an even broader program of reform that urged purchase of grain by the state and guaranteed sale to the poor living in Rome at low cost. He, too, was killed during the violence that broke out between his supporters and their political opponents.

Polybius and his contemporaries were shocked by the sudden violent turn in Roman politics, but the trend grew only more pronounced in the first century B.C.E., when many institutions of the republic ceased to function. In order to raise an army, one general, Marius (157–86 B.C.E.), did the previously unthinkable: he enlisted volunteers from among the working poor in Rome, waiving the traditional requirement that soldiers had to own land. Unlike the traditional farmer-soldiers, these troops had to be paid, and the leader who recruited them was obliged to support them for their entire lives. The troops eagerly looked forward to military campaigns because they received a share of the plunder each time they won a battle. Their loyalties were to the commander who paid them, not the republic.

After Marius died, Sulla, another general with his own private army, came to power. In 81 B.C.E. Sulla was not content to serve only a single year as consul and so arranged for the senate to declare him **dictator,** or temporary commander with full authority for a fixed amount of time. In earlier periods, the senate had the power to name a dictator for a six-month term during a crisis, but Sulla used the position to secure his hold on the government. In the different years after Sulla's death in 78 B.C.E., different generals vied to lead Rome. The senate continued to meet and to elect two consuls, but the generals with their private armies controlled the government, often with the senate's tacit consent.

Large privatized armies staffed by the clients and slaves of generals conquered much new territory for Rome in the first century B.C.E. They defeated the much-weakened Seleucids in 64 B.C.E. in Syria, bringing the dynasty to an end, but they never defeated the powerful Parthian cavalry (see Chapter 6). The most successful Roman commander was **Julius Caesar** (100–44 B.C.E.), who conquered Gaul, a region that included northern Italy and present-day France. Although the Romans looked down on the peoples of Gaul as barbarians, or less civilized people who could not read and write, the Gauls participated actively in trade and had a strong economy. After his term as governor ended in Gaul, Caesar led his armies to Rome, and in 49 B.C.E. the senate appointed Caesar dictator. Between 48 and 44 B.C.E. Caesar continued as dictator and served as consul every other year.

Caesar named himself dictator for life in 44 B.C.E. This move antagonized even his allies, and a group of senators killed him in March that year. Caesar's death, however, did not end Rome's long civil war. In his will, Caesar had adopted as his heir his great-nephew Octavian (63 B.C.E.–14 C.E.), the future Augustus. In 30 B.C.E. Octavian conquered Egypt, bringing the rule of the Ptolemies, the last successor state to Alexander, to an end. Egypt joined the Roman Empire as a province.

With this move Octavian eliminated all his rivals and brought nearly a century of political chaos and civil war to a close. The battles fought in Greece, Macedonia, Egypt, North Africa, and Spain demonstrate that commanders could move their armies easily around and across the Mediterranean in pursuit of their rivals.

• dictator A position given by the Roman senate before the first century B.C.E. to a temporary commander that granted him full authority for a limited amount of time, usually six months.

• Julius Caesar (100–44 B.C.E.) Rome's most successful military commander in the first century B.C.E. Conquered and governed much of Gaul, the region of modern-day France. Named dictator by the senate in 49 B.C.E.

Primary Source: A Man of Unlimited Ambition: Julius Caesar *Find out how Roman attitudes toward kingship led to the assassination of Julius Caesar.*

When the republic came to an end, Octavian had to devise a new political system capable of governing the entire Mediterranean region.

●The Roman Principate, 27 B.C.E.–284 C.E.

In 27 B.C.E. Octavian became the sole ruler of Rome and made all of the important decisions governing the empire. He never named himself emperor. Instead he called himself *"princeps"* (PRIN-keps), or first citizen, even though he made all the important decisions governing the empire. The new political structure he devised, in which he held almost all power, is called the **Roman principate** (PRIN-sih-pate) (government of the princeps). The principate remained in place until 284 C.E. Historians call the period between 27 B.C.E., when Octavian took power, and 180 C.E. the "Pax Romana" (PAHKS ro-MAHN-uh), or Roman Peace, because the entire Mediterranean region benefited from these centuries of stability. People moved easily across the empire, which became even more integrated as a result.

> ●**Roman principate** The system of government in Rome from 27 B.C.E. to 284 C.E., in which the *princeps*, a term meaning "first citizen," ruled the empire as a monarch in all but name.

The Political Structure of the Principate

Octavian wanted to establish a regime that would last beyond his own life. He hoped, too, to prevent a future general from seizing the government, yet he did not want to name himself perpetual dictator or king for fear that he would antagonize the Roman political elite. In 27 B.C.E. the senate awarded him a new title, **Augustus,** meaning "revered," the name by which he is usually known.

Augustus transferred the power to tax and control the army from the senate to the princeps. Fully aware that the armies were dangerously big, Augustus ordered many soldiers demobilized and used his own private funds to buy land for them—some in Italy, some in the provinces. Augustus made sure that the senate approved the measures he enacted. The most important of his changes concerned the provinces; he asserted the right to appoint all military leaders and the governors of the important provinces, thus ensuring that no one could form an army in the provinces and challenge him in Rome.

> ●**Augustus** The name, meaning "revered," that Octavian (63 B.C.E.–14 C.E.) received from the senate when he became princeps, or first citizen, of Rome in 27 B.C.E. and established the monarchy that ruled the empire.

The one issue that Augustus did not resolve was who would succeed him: with no son of his own, he named his wife's son from a previous marriage as his heir, establishing a precedent that a princeps without a son of his own could name his successor. The best solution was the product of chance; since the three princeps who ruled from 98 to 161 C.E. did not have sons, they were able to choose their successors while still in office. The last century of the principate was not as smooth; between 211 and 284 C.E., the empire had thirty-six emperors, of whom nineteen were murdered, were executed, or died in battle with their successors.

The Social Changes of the Principate

Ever since the second century B.C.E., when the government classified Sicily and other new conquests as provinces, the men who had staffed the provincial governments had not received the privileges of citizens. They did not have access to Roman courts, and they could not participate in the political system of Rome. In the first century C.E. Augustus had deliberately increased the number of citizens by awarding Roman citizenship to discharged soldiers. On Augustus's death in

14 C.E. about four million people had become citizens,[4] and the number continued to increase. In 212 C.E. the emperor granted citizenship status to all free men anywhere in the empire, possibly in the hope of increasing tax revenues.

Roman law also changed during the course of the principate. Originally the magistrates and provincial governors who decided judicial cases applied Roman law to citizens and local law to noncitizens. They considered both unwritten laws, or customary practices, and written laws, which included laws passed by the senate or the plebian assembly, edicts from the emperor, and sometimes the writings of learned jurists. Many of the principles they developed still inform the modern practice of law. A person charged with a crime had the right to appear before a judge, who was to consider all the evidence fairly before deciding on the person's guilt. Everyone was innocent until proven guilty.

The Roman justice system did not, however, treat everyone equally. The sharp differences of the republic among patricians, equites, and plebians gradually faded, and, over the course of the principate, as more people gained the rights of citizens, two new social groups subsumed the earlier divisions: the elite *honestiores* (hoh-NEST-ee-or-eez) and the *humiliores* (HUGH-meal-ee-or-eez), or the humble. Membership in these groups did not overlap with citizenship: noncitizen honestiores existed, as did citizen humiliores. Courts tended to treat the two groups very differently, allowing the wealthy to appeal their cases to Rome while sentencing the humble to heavier punishments for the same crime.

The years of the principate also saw some gradual changes in the legal position of women. Most people lived in small families consisting of a couple, their children, and whichever slaves or servants they had. On marriage, women moved in with their husbands but technically remained in their father's families and so retained the right to reclaim their dowries when their husbands died. Dowries were small, often about a year of the father's income, because daughters were entitled to a share of their father's property on his death, which granted them financial independence during the marriage.

Although they had greater control over their property than women in most other societies, Roman women continued to assume a subordinate role in marriage, possibly because many were much younger than their husbands. Men tended to marry in their late twenties and early thirties, women in their teens or early twenties. Most families arranged their children's marriages to form alliances with families of equal or better social standing.

Some marriages turned out to be quite affectionate. One well-known writer in the first century who was also a lawyer, Pliny (PLIH-nee) the Younger (ca. 61–113 C.E.), wrote to his wife's aunt about his wife:

> She is highly intelligent and a careful housewife, and her devotion to me is a sure indication of her virtue. In addition, this love has given her interest in literature: she keeps copies of my works to read again and again and even learn by heart. She is so anxious when she knows that I am going to plead in court, and so happy when all is over! . . .
>
> Please accept our thanks for having given her to me and me to her as if chosen for each other.

Pliny married in his 40s, at the peak of his legal career, while his third wife Calpurnia was still a teenager. Despite their closeness, she must have often deferred to Pliny, who was much older.

House of the Faun, Pompeii, Italy One of the loveliest surviving villas at Pompeii is the House of the Faun, named for the figure in the fountain. The well-off residents of Pompeii, a provincial Roman town, lived in lovely villas like this one with hot and cold running water, lush gardens, and exquisite tiled fountains. (Casa del Faune, Pompeii, Italy/Scala/Art Resource, NY)

Pliny also wrote about the famous eruption from Mount Vesuvius, which he witnessed from his home in the Bay of Naples in the early afternoon on August 24, 79 C.E. He described the cloud of smoke as "white, sometimes blotched and dirty, according to the amount of soil and ashes carried with it."[5] Many of the residents of nearby Pompeii (POMP-ay) did not realize how dangerous the situation was and stayed in town, and Pliny's uncle, Pliny the Elder, actually traveled to the site of the erupting volcano to see if he could rescue anyone.

When Pliny the Elder arrived, "ashes were already falling, hotter and thicker as the ships drew near, followed by bits of pumice [PUH-miss] and blackened stones, charred and cracked by the flames." That evening Pliny the Elder went to bed inside his house; he awoke to find his door blocked. His servants dug him out, and the entire household went outside; even though the sun had come up, the ash-filled sky was "blacker and denser than any ordinary night." The uncle tried to escape by boat, but the waves were too high, and he collapsed. Two days later, when the cloud lifted, Pliny the Elder had died, killed by the poisonous fumes from the volcano. The sites of Pompeii and Herculaneum have afforded historians new understanding of Roman society in a provincial town during the first century C.E. (See the feature "Visual Evidence: Pompeii.")

Travel and Knowledge of the Outside World

While Romans had been traveling for business and pleasure ever since the conquests of the second century B.C.E., travel continued to increase throughout the principate and contributed to the further integration of the Mediterranean

POMPEII

The eruption of Mount Vesuvius in 79 C.E. preserved the entire provincial city of Pompeii—not just an individual building or a tomb—under a layer of ash, where it remained undiscovered until 1748. Pompeii possessed all the important features of a typical Roman city: a theater, temples to Roman and non-Roman gods, baths, a gymnasium, an amphitheater, shops, paved streets, and a forum where the residents met each day and carried out their business transactions.

The city's twenty thousand residents participated in a highly commercialized economy. No one baked bread because it was available fresh from bakeries every day. The bakeries at Pompeii are easily identified by their millstones of volcanic tufa stone, which slaves or draft animals rotated to grind the grain. Other shops also sold pastries and cakes. Farmers sold local products, like onions and herbs, at the markets, where people also purchased wine or *garum*, a sauce made from fermented fish.

One of the most developed industries in the city processed raw wool from sheep into luxurious woolen textiles. After the sheep were sheared, women slaves in many households washed the dirt and oils from the wool and carded it to make thread for spinning. After they wove the spun thread into cloth on looms, householders brought the homespun cloth to workshops to be finished. Workshop employees moistened, heated, and pressed the wool so that it would shrink and thicken. Only then could the cloth be dyed, often bright yellow or deep purple, or bleached with sulphur. The painting on the facing page shows male and female workers processing wool.

This particular wall painting was probably commissioned by the owner of a textile workshop. The residents of Pompeii lived in lavish houses whose walls were filled with frescoes showing scenes of daily life and legendary exploits of the gods. Painted on wet plaster, these frescoes retain their original brilliant pigments, particularly the dark red so characteristic of Pompeii's art.

The large houses of the rich had extensive gardens and stables outside and lavish interior rooms. One tile floor portrayed Alexander the Great defeating Darius III, the last emperor of the Achaemenids (see Chapter 6). Large houses often had a dining room, called the triclinium, with three couches on which diners reclined as they ate. A sophisticated system of pipes supplied these houses with hot and cold running water.

The remains at Pompeii provide a valuable reminder of the high living standards of the Romans, even those living in a provincial town. Few people elsewhere in the world in the first century C.E. had hot running water, large gardens, or exquisite art. True, not everyone in Pompeii occupied such houses; poor people lived crowded together in small apartments without gardens or plumbing. The extraordinary archaeological remains at Pompeii afford a glimpse of exactly how rich and poor lived in 79 C.E., a view unmatched by any other site in the ancient world.

QUESTION FOR ANALYSIS

 What does this fresco reveal about the attire and working conditions of men and women of different social levels in Pompeii?

Craftsmen made this pigment by mixing red-colored minerals with powdered lime, soap, and wax and applying them to the wet plaster, which they polished after it dried.

An owl, the symbol of the Roman goddess Minerva (the Latin name of the Greek Athena), an expert weaver, rides on top of the wicker frame.

(Museo Archeologico Nazionale, Naples, Italy/Scala/Art Resource, NY)

A seated woman—a customer? a supervisor?—examines a piece of cloth shown to her by a young girl worker.

A male textile worker brushes a piece of wool hanging on a wooden frame with a thorned implement to smooth out the tangled threads.

This lightly clad man carries a metal bowl filled with burning sulphur, a bleaching agent, and carries a frame for hanging bleached textiles on his back.

MAP 7.1

The Roman Empire at Its Greatest Extent Some fifty-five million people lived in the 2 million square miles (5 million sq km) of the Roman Empire in the second century C.E. A network of roads and shipping lanes bound the different regions together, as did a unified currency. Two common languages—Latin in the western Mediterranean and Greek in the eastern Mediterranean—helped to integrate the Mediterranean world even more closely.

Legend:
- Roman Empire by death of Augustus, 14 C.E.
- Territory added by death of Hadrian, 138 C.E.
- Territory gained and lost, with dates held
- Parthian Empire, ca. 200 C.E.
- Major battle

CL Interactive Map

world. The empire reached its largest extent in the second century C.E. (see Map 7.1), with an estimated population of fifty-five million people living in an area of 2 million square miles (5 million sq km).[6] Rome controlled not only the entire Mediterranean coast of North Africa, western Asia, and Europe but also large amounts of territory inland from the Mediterranean: modern-day Spain, France, England, Germany west of the Rhine River, the Balkans, and Turkey. Roman roads connected the different parts of the empire, and sea transport, even with its dangers, remained even cheaper. Travelers needed to carry only one type of currency, Roman coins. Just two languages could take them anywhere within the empire: Latin was used throughout the western Mediterranean and in Rome itself, while Greek prevailed in the eastern Mediterranean.

The appearance of new maps and guides testifies to the frequency of travel. Some simply listed each place on a given road and the distance to the next city; others portrayed the information visually. When papyrus was not available, the Romans used parchment, or treated animal skin, for writing material. One of the longest surviving texts on parchment, the Peutinger Map, occupies a piece of

The Peutinger Map: The Roman Equivalent of the Mobil Guide?

This detail from the Peutinger Map shows Jerusalem, where many Christians traveled in the late 300s and 400s. (This is a twelfth- or thirteenth-century copy of a map dating to the 300s). The cartographer devised symbols for the different type of lodging at each stopping place: a square building with a courtyard, for example, indicated the best kind of hotel. Modern guidebooks use exactly the same type of system.   (akg-images)

parchment 13 inches (34 cm) wide and over 22 feet (6.75 m) long. It depicts the full 64,600 English miles (104,000 km) of the empire's road system.

The study of geography flourished throughout the empire and particularly in the city of Alexandria, Egypt, which continued to be a center of learning even after the Roman conquest of Egypt in 30 B.C.E. The geographer Ptolemy (ca. 100–170 C.E.) (not related to the Ptolemy royal family), devoted his life to making a map of all the world's known countries. Ptolemy's data survive in a list of longitudinal and latitudinal coordinates for eight thousand places. We do not know whether he made an actual map, but his work marks the high point of geographic knowledge in the Roman Empire. China and Southeast Asia marked the eastern edge of the world known to the Romans; the Canary Islands in the Atlantic Ocean marked the western end. To the north lay the British Isles and the Scythian region (north of the Black Sea in Russia); to the south, below Ethiopia, lay Africa. Although he made some errors, Ptolemy knew where more places were located on the globe than did any geographer elsewhere in the world. His comprehensive knowledge of geography remained influential in the Islamic world (see Chapter 9) and Europe until 1500 (see Chapters 10 and 13).

● The Rise of Christianity, ca. 30–284 C.E.

During these years, as Rome was consolidating its empire, people and religious teachings moved easily and widely throughout the Mediterranean world as never before. The Romans had their own gods, to whom officials offered regular sacrifices, and they worshiped many deities originating in other parts of the empire. Christianity began as a faith professed by a small group of Jews in the province of Judaea (joo-DAY-uh) and began to spread throughout the Mediterranean in the first and second centuries C.E. The emperor Constantine's decision to support Christianity in 313 proved to be the crucial step in its extension throughout the Mediterranean world.

Roman Religion and Judaism

Throughout the republic and the principate, the state encouraged the worship of many different gods in the Roman polytheistic religion. Most Romans worshiped major deities, like Jupiter, the most powerful of all the gods, or Mars, the god of war, both of which have given their names to the planets. Many of these gods were originally Greek; for example, the Roman Jupiter was the same as the Greek Zeus. Officials frequently spent tax monies in support of public cults, sometimes to a deity and sometimes to the current or former deified princeps.

In addition to their public obligations to state-supported gods, many people privately worshiped mystery cults that drew on the symbolism of fertility deities. A female deity, sometimes with a male partner, disappeared in the fall and had to be coaxed to return in the spring. Mystery cults promised adherents immortality and a closer personal relationship with the divine. Throughout the Mediterranean, believers worshiped deities not originally from Rome, including Isis (EYE-sis), the Egyptian goddess of the dead, thought to have power to cure the sick, and Mithra (MIH-thruh), the Iranian sun-god sent by Ahura Mazda (see Chapter 6) to struggle against evil. Gathering in small groups to sacrifice bulls, the worshipers of Mithra believed that the souls of the dead descended into earth before ascending into heaven.

Unlike almost everyone else in the Roman Empire, Jews were monotheistic (see Chapter 2). Worshiping a single god, whom they never depicted in images or paintings, Jews refused to worship any of the Roman gods or former princeps, a stance that was tolerated by the Roman government. Their center of worship was the Jerusalem Temple, a building that housed their scriptures. After the Babylonians destroyed the First Temple (see Chapter 2), the Jews built the Second Temple under King Cyrus of the Achaemenids (see Chapter 6). The Second Temple survived the Roman conquest of Judaea in 63 B.C.E., when Judaea came under indirect Roman rule.

The Romans initially delegated the task of governing the region to the leadership of the Temple, yet many Jews challenged the authority of the Temple's leaders. One group of reformers, the Pharisees (FAIR-uh-seez), believed that Jews should also obey a body of oral law in addition to the written laws of the Hebrew Bible. Unlike the traditional leaders, the Pharisees did not believe that Jews should exclusively worship in the Temple and encouraged them to worship in separate buildings called synagogues.

The discovery of the Dead Sea Scrolls, a group of texts on leather, papyrus, and copper, has revealed the diversity of beliefs among Jewish groups. The scrolls mention a Teacher of Righteousness, a figure who the authors believed would bring salvation, called a Messiah (muh-SIGH-uh) in Hebrew. Many Jewish groups at the time believed that a Messiah would come, yet they disagreed about how to identify him.

The Life and Teachings of Jesus, ca. 4 B.C.E.–30 C.E.

Almost every surviving record about early Christianity written before 100 C.E., whether about the life of **Jesus** or the early ministry, is written by a Christian believer.[7] The earliest sources, and so the most reliable, are the four gospels of Mark, Matthew, Luke, and John, written between 70 and 110 C.E. Accordingly, historians use the gospels to piece together the chronology of Jesus' life, all the while remembering that, like sources about Zarathustra or the Buddha, they were written by devotees, not outsiders.

The gospels relate that Jesus was born around 4 B.C.E. to a well-off Jewish family near the Sea of Galilee, where residents made a good living fishing. They say little about his life before about 26 C.E., when his cousin John the Baptist baptized him. Jewish tradition held that baptism, or ritual washing with water, could cleanse someone from impurities; converts to Judaism sometimes were baptized, and women bathed to mark the end of their menstrual periods. Invoking this tradition, John claimed to be a prophet and urged Jews to undergo baptism in preparation for the kingdom of God. However, John's message was new because he urged everyone to be baptized.

In 28 and 29 C.E. Jesus began preaching publicly in Galilee and, like John, urged Jews to repent and undergo baptism. Illness was a sign of Satan's presence, Jesus taught, and many of the miracles recorded in the gospels are anecdotes about his curing the sick. Historians, particularly those who do not subscribe to the teachings of a given belief system, are often skeptical about whether the events described in miracle tales actually occurred. But they realize that many religious figures were able to win converts because of them.

Jesus (ca. 4 B.C.E.–30 C.E.) Jewish preacher believed by Christians to be the Messiah, the figure who would bring salvation. The Christian doctrine of atonement holds that God sent Jesus to the world to bring eternal life to all those who believed in him.

As he explained in the Sermon on the Mount, Jesus welcomed the poor and downtrodden: "Blessed are the poor in spirit, for theirs is the kingdom of heaven" (Matthew 5:3). According to the gospels, Jesus' preaching in Galilee culminated in the feeding of five thousand supporters, possibly in the summer of 29 C.E. Jesus summed up his teachings succinctly in response to a Pharisee who asked him what the most important commandment was:

> "'You shall love the Lord your God with all your heart, and with all your soul, and with all your mind.' This is the great and first commandment. And a second is like it: 'You shall love your neighbor as yourself.'" (Matthew 22:36–39)

Jesus also taught his followers that a time of great difficulty was coming and that God would send a Messiah to usher in a new age. *Christos* was the Greek word for Messiah, and Jesus came to be known as Jesus Christ because his followers believed that he was the Messiah. Jesus' teachings attracted converts because the egalitarian religion promised salvation to all, including the poor, and welcomed all to join the new church, regardless of their background.

Jesus also wanted to reform and challenge the abuses he saw. His criticisms provoked the Jewish community leaders, who may also have feared that he would lead the residents of Palestine, where there was already a great deal of unrest, in an uprising against Roman rule. They asked the Roman governor, Pontius Pilate, to convict Jesus on the grounds that he claimed to be king of the Jews and thus posed a political threat to Rome. The gospels portray Pontius Pilate as being hesitant to punish Jesus, who refused to directly answer Pilate's question "Are you the King of the Jews?" Fearful of possible disorder, in 30 C.E. Pilate agreed to crucify Jesus. At the time of his death Jesus had been actively preaching for only three years.

On the third day after he died, Christians believe, several of Jesus' female disciples visited his tomb and found it empty, and some of the disciples then had visions of Jesus. The gospels concur that Jesus was resurrected, or raised from the dead. The gospel of John explains: "For God so loved the world that he gave his only Son, so that everyone who believes in him may not perish but may have eternal life" (John 3:16). This teaching, that Jesus died so that all believers will be able to overcome death, is called atonement, and it became one of the most important teachings of the Christian church.

Paul and the Early Church, 30–284 C.E.

Jesus preached that a new age of salvation would come soon after his death, yet his disciples realized that they had to devise a governing structure for the church no matter how temporary they expected the wait to be. The early church followed the model of Jewish synagogues and established churches in each community where a sufficient number of Christians lived. Bishops headed these districts; below them were deacons and deaconesses, a position of genuine authority for the many women who joined the church.

The teachings of another early Christian leader, Paul, were highly influential. **Paul** (ca. 5–ca. 64 C.E.) was born to a wealthy family of Roman citizens living in Tarsus in modern-day Turkey. Like many Jews living outside Judaea, Paul had grown up in a bilingual household in which both Greek and Hebrew were spoken,

● **Paul** (ca. 5–ca. 64 C.E.) An influential early Christian leader. Born in Tarsus (in modern-day Turkey) and grew up in a Greek-speaking Jewish household. Traveled widely in modern-day Turkey, Cyprus, and Greece to teach about early Christianity.

■ **Picturing the Apostles Peter and Paul**   After the government in 313 permitted Christians to worship openly (see page 200), many Romans began to decorate their stone coffins with Christian images. This is a very early depiction of Peter and Paul, who are identified by name. The symbol between them combines two Greek letters, *chi* and *ro,* the first two letters in the word Greek word for Christ, *Christos,* a symbol used throughout the Christian world.   (Vatican Museums, Vatican State/ Erich Lessing/Art Resource, NY)

but he received a traditional education in Jerusalem, where he studied with the Pharisees.

As described in the book of Acts, the turning point in Paul's life came when Jesus appeared to him in a vision, probably in the year 38 C.E., as he traveled to Damascus. After deciding to become a Christian, Paul was baptized in Damascus. The Christian leadership in Jerusalem, however, never granted that Paul's vision was equal to their own experience of knowing Jesus personally and hearing him teach. Understandably suspicious of him, they sent Paul to preach in his native Tarsus in 48 B.C.E.

Paul initially focused on converting the Jewish communities scattered throughout the eastern half of the Mediterranean, preaching and writing letters in Greek. Written with the sophistication of an educated Roman, his letters carried the teachings of Christianity to many fledgling Christian communities. When he arrived in a new place, he went first to the local synagogue and preached. (See the feature "Movement of Ideas: Early Christianity in the Eastern Provinces.") Whereas Jesus had preached to the poor and to slaves, Paul's potential audience consisted of more prosperous people. He did not call for the abolition of slavery or propose any genuine social reform. Accepting the right of the Roman Empire to exist, he, like Jesus before him, urged his audiences to pay their taxes.

Early Christianity in the Eastern Provinces

What did early Christians believe? The book of Acts in the New Testament contains this very interesting summary of a sermon given by Paul in Pisidian Antioch (in modern-day Turkey), one of the first cities he visited in 46. Local Jews constituted the bulk of his audience, and Paul expected them to be familiar with the predictions about the coming of prophets in the Old Testament, which they read in a Greek translation of the original Hebrew Bible. His sermon concludes with a statement of the important doctrine of atonement: Jesus died so that the sins of everyone who believed in his teachings could be forgiven. He closes with a pointed contrast between the law of Moses, or traditional Jewish teachings, and the teachings of Jesus, which he says offer more benefits.

The second selection is from Pliny the Younger, who was not a Christian. He served as a provincial governor in a region of present-day Turkey, south of the Black Sea, between 111 and 113. In one letter, he wrote to ask the emperor Trajan exactly how he should determine who was a Christian and who deserved punishment. The details in his letter offer a vivid description of the impact of Christianity on local religious practice during a period when it was officially banned. Unlike Pliny, many Roman officials did not persecute the Christians in their districts.

Sources: Acts 13:16–39 (New Revised Standard Version); Betty Radice, *The Letters of the Younger Pliny* (New York: Penguin Books, 1963), pp. 293–295.

Paul's Sermon at Antioch

You Israelites, and others who fear God, listen. The God of this people Israel chose our ancestors and made the people great during their stay in the land of Egypt, and with uplifted arm he led them out of it. . . . Then they asked for a king . . . ; he [God] made David their king. In his testimony about him he said, "I have found David, son of Jesse, to be a man after my heart, who will carry out all my wishes." Of this man's posterity God has brought to Israel a Savior, Jesus, as he promised; before his coming John had already proclaimed a baptism of repentance to all the people of Israel. And as John was finishing his work, he said, "What do you suppose that I am? I am not he. No, but one is coming after me; I am not worthy to untie the thong of the sandals on his feet."

My brothers, you descendants of Abraham's family, and others who fear God, to us the message of this salvation has been sent. Because the residents of Jerusalem and their leaders did not recognize him nor understand the words of the prophets that are read every sabbath, they fulfilled those words by condemning him. Even though they found no cause for a sentence of death, they asked Pilate to have him killed. When they had carried out everything that was written about him, they took him down from the tree, and laid him in a tomb. But God raised him from the dead; and for many days he appeared to those who came up with him from Galilee to Jerusalem, and they are now his witnesses to the people. And we bring you the good news that what God promised to our ancestors, he has fulfilled for us, their children, by raising Jesus; as also it is written in the second psalm,

"You are my son; today I have begotten you."

. . . Let it be known to you therefore, my brothers, that through this man [Jesus] forgiveness of sins is proclaimed to you; by this Jesus everyone who believes is set free from all those sins from which you could not be freed by the law of Moses.

Pliny to Emperor Trajan

I have never been present at an examination of Christians. . . .

For the moment this is the line I have taken with all persons brought before me on the charge of being Christians. I have asked them in person if they are Christians, and if they admit it, I repeat the question a second and third time, with a warning of the punishment awaiting them. If they persist, I order them to be led away for punishment;• for, whatever the nature of their admission, I am convinced that their stubbornness and unshakeable obstinacy ought not to go unpunished. There have been others similarly fanatical who are Roman citizens. I have entered them on the list of persons to be sent to Rome for trial. . . .

Others, whose names were given to me by an informer, first admitted the charge and then denied it; they said that they had ceased to be Christians two or more years previously, and some of them even twenty years ago. They all did reverence to your statue and the images of the gods in the same way as the others, and reviled the name of Christ. They also declared that the sum total of their guilt or error amounted to no more than this: they had met regularly before dawn on a fixed day to chant verses alternately among themselves in honor of Christ as if to a god, and also to bind themselves by oath, not for any criminal purpose, but to abstain from theft, robbery, and adultery, to commit no breach of trust and not to deny a deposit when called upon to restore it. After this ceremony it had been their custom to disperse and reassemble later to take food of an ordinary, harmless kind; but they had in fact given up this practice since my edict, issued on your instructions, which banned all political societies. This made me decide it was all the more necessary to extract the truth by torture from two slave-women, whom they call deaconesses. I found nothing but a degenerate sort of cult carried to extravagant lengths.

I have therefore postponed any further examination and hastened to consult you. The question seems to me to be worthy of your consideration, especially in view of the number of persons endangered; for a great many individuals of every age and class, both men and women, are being brought to trial, and this is likely to continue. It is not only the towns, but villages and rural districts too which are infected with contact with this wretched cult. I think though that it is still possible for it to be checked and directed to better ends, for there is no doubt that people have begun to throng the temples which had been almost entirely deserted for a long time; the sacred rites which had been allowed to lapse are being performed again, and flesh of sacrificial victims is on sale everywhere, though up till recently scarcely anyone could be found to buy it. It is easy to infer from this that a great many people could be reformed if they were given an opportunity to repent.

• The Latin text has *puniri*, which Radice translates as "execute," but "punishment" is more accurate.

QUESTIONS FOR ANALYSIS

▶ How do these descriptions of Christianity by a believer and a nonbeliever differ? Which Jewish teachings and which Christian teachings does Paul present?

▶ Which of Pliny's points support his contention that Christianity can be controlled? Which do not?

🌐 **MAP 7.2**

The Spread of Christianity During his lifetime, Jesus preached in the Roman province of Judaea. After his death, Paul and other missionaries introduced Christian teachings to the eastern Mediterranean. By the late 300s, Christianity had spread throughout the Mediterranean, making it possible for pilgrims like Egeria to travel all the way from Rome to Jerusalem and Egypt, where she visited the earliest Christian monasteries.

Paul took advantage of the ease of travel within the Roman Empire to propagate his views. A list of the cities he visited vividly conveys how much he traveled: Antioch, Iconium, Lystra, Derbe, and Ephesus in modern-day Turkey; Paphos on the island of Cyprus; and Thessalonica, Philippi, and Corinth in Greece. By the time Paul died, circa 64, a Christian community had arisen in each of these cities. In Rome, according to Christian tradition, Jesus' apostle Peter, who died about the same time as Paul, headed the Christian community (see Map 7.2). A Jewish uprising in 66 prompted the Roman authorities to intervene with great brutality: they destroyed the Second Temple in 70, and many Jews fled Jerusalem. After 70, Rome replaced Jerusalem as the center of the Christian church.

In subsequent centuries the Christian church must have expanded, more than the spotty historical record indicates. We see early Christian centers proliferate around the Mediterranean like the tips of icebergs, but surviving sources do not indicate how deep or wide the icebergs were at the base. The church grew steadily during the first, second, and third centuries.

The Decline of the Empire and the Loss of the Western Provinces, 284–476

Although the principate was still nominally the structure of the government, the Pax Romana ended in the third century. In 226 C.E. Rome faced new enemies on its northern borders, as a Germanic tribal people called the Goths launched a series of successful attacks in the region of the Danube River. (In later centuries, the word *Goth* came to mean any social movement, whether Gothic architecture or today's Goth styles, that challenged existing practices.) The attacks by Germanic peoples continued in the following centuries. As a result, different Roman rulers repeatedly restructured the Roman Empire and shifted the capital east. During these same centuries, they lifted the ban on Christianity and increasingly offered government support to the religion, which led to its further spread. Although the Romans lost chunks of their empire and even the city of Rome to barbarian invaders, the region of the Mediterranean remained a cultural unit bound by a common religion—Christianity—and the same two languages—Latin and Greek—that had been in use since the time of the republic.

Political Changes of the Late Empire

The principate came to a formal end early in the reign of Diocletian (r. 284–305). Diocletian (dy-oh-KLEE-shun) increased the size of Rome's armies by a third so that they could fight off their various enemies, including the Goths and the Sasanians, the dynasty established in Iran in 224 (see Chapter 6). In 260, the Sasanians had captured the Roman emperor Valerian and forced him to crouch down so that the Sasanian emperor could step on his back as he mounted his horse. Realizing that the new threats made the empire too large to govern effectively, Diocletian divided the empire into an eastern and western half and named a senior emperor and a junior emperor to govern each half. Diocletian ruled with the assistance of appointed advisers, no longer pretending to consult the senate. He reorganized the empire into twelve units called dioceses. This new structure of government, which replaced the principate, is generally referred to as the tetrarchy (teh-TRAR-kee) because two senior and two junior emperors ruled the empire.

The structure of the tetrarchy did not make it easier to defend the empire. **Constantine** (272–337, r. 312–337), the son of one of the junior emperors named by Diocletian, defeated each of the other emperors in battle until he was the sole ruler of the reunited empire. In 330, to place himself near threatened frontiers, Constantine established a new capital 800 miles (1,300 km) to the east at Byzantium (bizz-AN-tee-um) on the Bosphorus, which he named for himself, Constantinople (modern-day Istanbul, Turkey). At the time the population of Byzantium was around fifty thousand, while that of Rome was over one million. The move was strategic: it was difficult to maintain control of the empire from a base in Rome, and the emperors of the tetrarchy had already established individual capitals outside of Rome. Constantinople, located near the Danube and the Euphrates frontiers, could be defended more easily than Rome.

Constantine (272–337, r. 312–337) May have converted to Christianity late in life. In 313 C.E. issued the Edict of Milan, the first imperial ruling to allow the practice of Christianity. Shifted the capital from Rome to the new city of Constantinople (modern-day Istanbul, Turkey) in 330 C.E.

When Constantine died in 337, he left the empire to his three sons, who immediately began fighting for control. After the last of Constantine's sons died in 364, no ruler succeeded in reuniting the empire for more than a few years at a time. In 395 the emperor formally divided the empire into western and eastern halves.

The fourth century was a time, particularly in the west, of economic decline. Repeated epidemics struck Rome and killed many of those living in the overcrowded city. In addition, armies had difficulty recruiting soldiers to staff their units. The central government, chronically short of revenues, minted devalued coins that contained far less metal than indicated by their face value. People living in regions where the use of coins had been common were forced to barter simply because fewer coins were in use. As the economy contracted, many urban dwellers moved to the countryside to grow their own crops.

During the fourth century, the armies of Germanic-speaking peoples repeatedly defeated the overstretched Roman army. These peoples, including the Vandals (see below), the Visigoths and Ostrogoths (both branches of the Goths), and other tribes (see Map 7.3), lived north and west of the empire and spoke a variety of languages in the Germanic language family (see Chapter 10). Although the residents of the Roman Empire looked down on these preliterate peoples, who lived in simple villages, the Goths and Vandals proved to be highly mobile and ferocious fighters. They had little to defend and so could devote their energies to attacking the long Roman frontier. In 410 the Visigoths sacked Rome for three days and then retreated; this was the first time since the fourth-century B.C.E. attack of the Gauls (see page 178) that foreign armies had entered the city.

Religious Changes of the Late Empire

Diocletian launched the last persecution of Christianity in 303. In addition to ordering that Christian scriptures be destroyed and churches torn down, he called for the punishment of all practicing Christians. Since officials implemented these measures unevenly, the eastern section of the empire, which Diocletian ruled, was more severely affected than the west. The suppression was brief because his successor issued an edict of toleration in 311.

In that year Constantine defeated one of the other claimants to the throne. Initially he claimed to have had a vision of the Roman sun-god Apollo and the Roman numeral for 30, which is written XXX; he interpreted the vision to mean that Apollo chose him to rule for the next thirty years. However, Constantine later began to worship the Christian God alongside other Roman deities, and according to his biographer, a Christian bishop, Constantine had actually seen a Christian cross.

Whatever the precise nature of Constantine's own beliefs, we know for certain that he ended Diocletian's persecution of Christianity in 313. With his co-emperor, Constantine issued the Edict of Milan, which compensated Christians for any property confiscated during Diocletian's persecution and officially allowed the practice of Christianity. This decision proved crucial to Christianity, in the same way as had Ashoka's support for Buddhism and the Achaemenid emperors' support for Zoroastrianism. (See the feature "World History in Today's World: Snapshot of Christianity.") In 380 Christianity was declared the only permissible religion in the empire, the final step to its becoming the official religion of the Roman Empire.

MAP 7.3

The Germanic Migrations   Although the Romans looked down on the pre-literate Germanic peoples living on their borders, the Germanic armies proved surprisingly powerful and launched wave after wave of attack on the empire and Rome itself. In 410, the Visigoths came from the east and sacked Rome. In 430 Augustine (354–430) witnessed 80,000 Vandals attack his home city of Hippo on the north African coast. After his death, the Vandals crossed the Mediterranean and looted Rome for two weeks in 455.

Interactive Map

In 325 Constantine summoned different church leaders to Nicaea (ny-SEE-uh) (modern-day Iznik, Turkey) and encouraged them to reach an agreement about the nature of the Trinity, which consisted of God, Jesus Christ, and the Holy Spirit, often mentioned in the book of Acts in conjunction with healing and exorcism. By the fourth century, many Christians had come to believe that God, Jesus, and the Holy Spirit were equal. Arius (AIR-ee-us), a teacher from Alexandria, Egypt, disagreed. He maintained that God the Father was superior to Jesus and the Holy Ghost because he had created them. The council drew up a basic statement of faith, the Nicene (ny-SEEN) Creed, which was worded specifically to counter the teachings of Arius and to assert that God and Jesus were

Snapshot of Christianity

Of the 6.1 billion people in the world today, 2.1 billion people identify themselves as Christian, making Christianity the world's largest religion. The largest groupings belong to Catholic, Protestant, or Eastern Orthodox churches, while the smaller Christian churches include Jehovah's Witnesses, Quakers, and the Copts of Egypt, among many others. The degree of observance varies enormously: some attend services at least once a week and possibly more often, while others have not been inside a church since being baptized.

The heartland of Christianity has shifted since the early centuries of the religion, when most early Christians lived in the Mediterranean region governed by the Roman Empire. After the seventh century, many people in North Africa and western Asia converted to Islam (see Chapter 9), while the number of Christians in Europe continued to grow. In 1900, 95 percent of Europeans identified themselves as Christian, yet in 2000, only 77 percent did.

The area of greatest growth is unquestionably in Africa, where 45 percent of the population identifies itself as Christian (versus 9 percent in 1900). One of the fastest-growing branches of African Christianity is Pentecostalism, whose ministers perform healings in the name of Jesus. Many Africans are drawn to Christianity because of Christian churches' promise to provide good health, money, and a better standard of living.

In 2000, the world area with the greatest concentration of Christians (93 percent) was Latin America. Yet the percentage of Latin Americans who identify themselves as Christian is shrinking slightly, while the number of Christians in Africa and Asia is growing. In short, fully 60 percent of the world's Christians in 2000 lived in Africa, Latin America, and Asia.

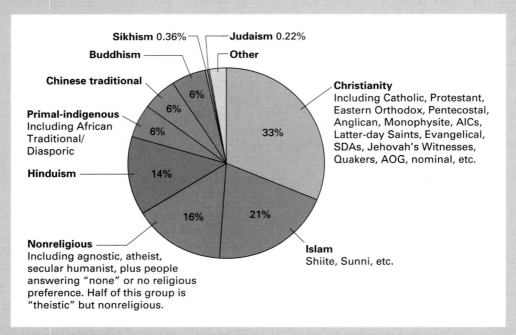

Chart from www.adherents.com. Used by permission.

made of the same substance.[8] When Arius refused to sign the Nicene Creed, which became the basic statement of Christian belief, the Council of Nicaea excommunicated, or expelled, him from the church. In subsequent centuries the church convened many similar meetings to ensure doctrinal agreement among the different Christian branches.

During the third and fourth centuries, church leaders met to decide which books of the Bible, both in the Hebrew Bible (which Christians call the Old Testament) and the New Testament, should be included in the canon and which should be viewed as less reliable, or apocryphal. One of Arius's main opponents, Saint Athanasius (293–373), lived in Alexandria, Egypt, an important Christian center. He was the first person to list the twenty-seven books of the New Testament as canonical, the final step in the formation of the Bible.

As part of his support for the Christian church, Constantine also ordered churches built at sites in Jerusalem that Jesus had visited. Although more difficult than in earlier, more peaceful centuries, travel was still possible in the fourth and fifth centuries, and Christian pilgrimages, often to Jerusalem, became increasingly popular. Travel was safe enough that ordinary women could also make the trip, as we learn from a travel account written by a woman named Egeria, who, sometime between 380 and 400 C.E., traveled all the way from her homeland in Spain to the Holy Land, the Christian name for Judaea. She went to Egypt, the Sinai, Jordan, and modern-day Turkey to visit the important sites of Judaism and early Christianity. After a three-year stay in Jerusalem, Egeria decided to continue her journey before returning home: "by the will of God, I wished to go to Mesopotamia of Syria [modern-day Edessa, Turkey], to visit the holy monks who were said to be numerous there and to be of such exemplary life that it can scarcely be described."[9] The devout Egeria wanted to see monasteries because they were a new institution.

Christianity in North Africa

As we can see from Egeria's itinerary, North Africa had already become an important center of Christianity by the fourth century. An Egyptian Christian, Pachomius (ca. 290–346), had founded the first monastic communities early in the fourth century. Before Pachomius, Christians who wanted to devote themselves full-time to a religious life had lived alone as hermits. Pachomius designed a monastic community whose members worked in the fields and prayed each day. In the centuries after his death, monasteries became so popular that they spread from Egypt to all over the Mediterranean.

One important Christian center lay to the east of Egypt in Aksum, in modern-day Ethiopia, whose rulers converted soon after Constantine issued the Edict of Milan. Their kingdom profited by taxing the trade from Egypt that went via the Red Sea to India. Merchants, who exported ivory from Africa and imported frankincense and myrrh from Arabia, encountered Christians while on trading voyages to the Mediterranean and introduced the religion to their countrymen.

The pre-Christian inscriptions commissioned by the rulers of Aksum mention local deities, including the southern Arabian goddess of the evening star, while the later ones mention the Lord of Heaven. One inscription, in Greek, names the Father, the Son, and the Holy Ghost, a definite indication of the ruler's support for Christianity. The Aksum Christians looked to the Egyptian church for leadership; the first bishop of Aksum and all his successors received their appointments from Egyptian bishops.

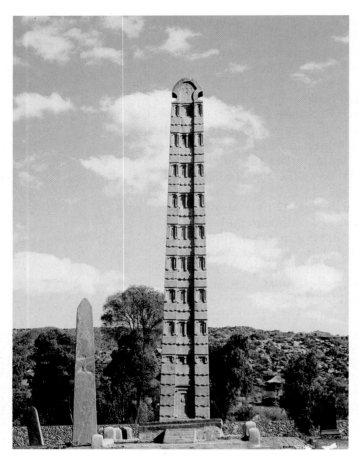

■ **Stone Stele at Axum, Ethiopia**
Supported by a counterweight placed underground, this stone tower stands 67 feet (21 m) tall. It represents a building ten stories high, with closed windows and a door bolted shut. Notice the lock on the ground floor level. Some two hundred stone towers like this were built in the 300s and 400s, when the rulers of Aksum converted to Christianity, but, unlike coins from the same period that show the cross, these towering monuments give no hint that the rulers who built them had converted to Christianity. (Werner Forman/Art Resource, NY)

To the west of Egypt was another Christian center at Hippo, now Annaba, Algeria, home to one of the most important thinkers in early Christianity, Augustine (354–430). Educated in North Africa, Augustine wrote over five million words in his lifetime. His book *The Confessions* detailed his varied experiences, which included fathering a child and belonging to the Manichaean order (see page 171), before he joined the Christian church and became the bishop of Hippo. According to Augustine, God's grace was so great that all, no matter how much they had violated the church's teachings, would be forgiven if they joined the church. Augustine encouraged the practice of confessing one's sins to a member of the clergy, and confession became an important rite in early Christianity.

● **Vandals** A Germanic tribe that attacked North Africa in 430 C.E. and sacked Rome for two weeks in 455 C.E. Their fighting techniques and looting were so brutal that the word *vandal* came to mean any deliberate act of destruction.

[CL] **Primary Source:** Augustine Denounces Paganism and Urges Romans to Enter the City of God *In* The City of God, *Augustine uses sarcasm to condemn the rituals of Rome's pre-Christian religion.*

The Barbarian Invasions: The Fall of Rome

In 430, the last year of Augustine's life, the **Vandals** led a force of eighty thousand men from different Germanic tribes across the Mediterranean and laid siege to Hippo. Augustine witnessed whole cities sacked, country villas razed, their owners killed or scattered as refugees, the churches deprived of their bishops and clergy, and the holy virgins and ascetics dispersed; some tortured to death, some killed outright, others, as prisoners, reduced to losing their integrity, in soul and body, to serve an evil and brutal enemy.[10]

For him, the invasions indicated the breakdown of the Roman Empire and the end of the civilized world.

After taking Hippo, the Vandals went on to conquer all of North Africa and the Mediterranean islands of Sardinia, Corsica, and Sicily. Their fighting techniques and looting were so brutal that the word *vandal* came to mean any deliberate act of destruction. In 455, the Vandals moved north to Italy and sacked Rome for two weeks, exposing again the city's vulnerability.

For the next twenty years different Germanic tribes gained control of the city and placed puppet emperors on the throne. In 476, the final emperor of the western empire was deposed and not replaced. This date marks the end of the western empire, and many earlier historians declared that the Roman Empire fell in 476.

Most recent historians, however, prefer not to speak in these terms. They note that the Eastern Roman Empire, the Byzantine Empire, continued to be governed from Constantinople for another thousand years (see Chapter 10). The cultural center of the Mediterranean world, thoroughly Christianized by this time, had shifted once again—away from the Latin-speaking world centered on Rome to the Greek-speaking world, where it had been before Polybius was deported to Rome in 168 B.C.E.

Three different governments—a republic, a principate, and a tetrarchy—had ruled Rome for nearly one thousand years. During that time the Mediterranean world had taken shape, and, with the support of Rome's rulers, a single religion, Christianity, had spread throughout the Roman Empire. The next chapter will analyze how decisions made by many different rulers led to the spread of two different religions, Buddhism and Hinduism, throughout Asia.

Chapter Review

 Download the MP3 audio file of the Chapter Review and listen to it on the go.

In the second century B.C.E., travel around the Mediterranean was so convenient that Polybius, the client of a Roman general, was able to visit many places in Italy, Spain, Carthage, and North Africa and even to sail down the Atlantic coast of Africa. With each passing century, transportation, both overland and by sea, improved, and even in the last years of the western empire Egeria was able to travel throughout the Holy Land and western Asia. The roads around the Mediterranean and the waterways across it provided wonderfully effective channels for the spread of Christian teachings. With the emperor's support, Christianity became the sole religion of the empire at the end of the fourth century, and the Mediterranean region governed by the Roman Empire became the core area of Christianity.

 How did Rome, a small settlement in central Italy, expand to conquer and control the entire Mediterranean world of Europe, western Asia, and North Africa?

The Roman Republic was gradually able to gain control of the Italian peninsula through a series of conquests; it then granted the victorious citizen-soldiers land, allowed the Latin speakers among the defeated to join the republic on an equal footing with its citizens, and welcomed the defeated soldiers to serve in its army. By 272 B.C.E. Rome had conquered the Italian peninsula. The treaty ending the Second Punic War with Carthage granted Rome control of the western Mediterranean in 201 B.C.E., and Rome's defeat of both the Macedonians and the Greeks brought control of the eastern Mediterranean in 133 B.C.E.

KEY TERMS

Polybius (174)
Roman Republic (178)
Roman senate (178)
Carthage (179)
Punic Wars (180)
Hannibal (180)
tax farmers (182)
paterfamilias (182)
dictator (184)
Julius Caesar (184)
Roman principate (185)
Augustus (185)
Jesus (193)
Paul (194)
Constantine (199)
Vandals (204)

How did the political structure of the Roman Empire change as it grew?

The structure of the republic proved incapable of handling the huge empire. During the first century B.C.E., privatized armies of slaves and clients led by generals plunged the empire into civil war, and peace came only with Augustus's creation of the principate, a monarchy in all but name, in 27 B.C.E. Rome expanded to its widest borders under the principate, and until 180 C.E. it enjoyed nearly two centuries of peace, called the Pax Romana. In 284 C.E. the Romans adopted yet another governmental system, the tetrarchy, which had two senior emperors and two junior emperors.

 ### What were the basic teachings of Jesus, and how did Christianity become the major religion of the empire?

According to the gospels, Jesus distilled his teachings to two major points: everyone should love God, and everyone should love his or her neighbor. His disciple Paul taught that God had sent his son Jesus as the Messiah to atone for the sins of all Christians. Although banned during the principate, Christianity spread throughout the empire, and Emperor Constantine's support for the new religion proved crucial. By the end of the fourth century, when the emperor forbade worship of the different Roman gods, Christianity had become the only permitted religion of the empire.

 ### What allowed Rome to retain such a large empire for so long, and what caused the loss of the western half of the empire?

The empire was able to retain so much territory for so long because of its rulers' willingness to adopt new structures. At the end of the third century, the emperor Diocletian created the tetrarchy, a government headed by two senior and two junior emperors, in the hope of bringing greater order. He also reorganized the provincial structure. Diocletian's successor Constantine established a new capital at Constantinople, a measure that strengthened the empire but left the city of Rome vulnerable. Sustained attacks by different barbarian tribes, including the Visigoths and the Vandals, weakened the western half of the empire so much that in 476 its governing tribes did not even bother to name a puppet emperor. But even after the empire shifted east to the new capital, the Mediterranean remained a coherent region bound by the Christian religion and the common languages of Greek and Latin.

For Further Reference

Boardman, John, Jasper Griffin, and Oswyn Murray. *The Oxford History of the Roman World*. New York: Oxford University Press, 1986.

Casson, Lionel. *Travel in the Ancient World*. Baltimore: Johns Hopkins University Press, 1974.

Etienne, Robert. *Pompeii: The Day a City Died*. New York: Harry N. Abrams, 1992.

Frend, W. H. C. *The Rise of Christianity*. Philadelphia: Fortress Press, 1984.

Garnsey, Peter, and Richard Saller. *The Roman Empire: Economy, Society and Culture*. Berkeley: University of California Press, 1987.

Hornblower, Simon, and Antony Spawforth, eds. *The Oxford Companion to Classical Civilization*. New York: Oxford University Press, 1998.

Kebric, Robert B. *Roman People*. 4th ed. New York: McGraw-Hill, 2005.

Polybius. *The Rise of the Roman Empire*. Translated by Ian Scott-Kilvert. New York: Penguin Books, 1979.

Scarre, Chris. *The Penguin Historical Atlas of Ancient Rome*. New York: Penguin Books, 1995.

Tingay, G. I. F., and J. Badcock. *These Were the Romans*. Chester Springs, Pa.: Dufour Editions, 1989.

Wilken, Robert L. *The Christians as the Romans Saw Them*. New Haven: Yale University Press, 2003.

Websites

In Old Pompeii
(http://edsitement.neh.gov/view-lesson-plan.asp?ID=271). A field trip to ancient Pompeii.

 WEB RESOURCES

Pronunciation Guide

Interactive Maps

MAP 7.1 The Roman Empire at Its Greatest Extent

MAP 7.2 The Spread of Christianity

MAP 7.3 The Germanic Migrations

Primary Sources

Chapter Objectives

ACE Multiple-Choice Quiz

Flashcards

Internet Medieval Sourcebook: End of Rome
(http://www.fordham.edu/halsall/sbook.html). Extremely valuable collection of primary sources about the fifth century C.E. and the "fall" of the Roman Empire.

The Perseus Digital Library
(www.perseus.tufts.edu). A wealth of searchable texts from the classical world in both the original language and English translation.

World Religions
(www.adherents.com). Takes an informed Religious Studies approach to the world's many religions.

Films

A Funny Thing Happened on the Way to the Forum

Gladiator

Spartacus

Hindu and Buddhist States and Societies in Asia, 100–1000

The year was 629, only eleven years after the founding of the Tang dynasty (618–907). Emperor Taizong (TIE-zohng) (r. 626–649) had banned all foreign travel because he had not yet secured control of the Chinese empire. Undeterred, the Chinese monk **Xuanzang** (ca. 596–664) departed on foot from the capital of Chang'an (CHAHNG-ahn) and headed overland for India so that he could obtain the original Sanskrit versions of Buddhist texts. One of his first stops after leaving China was the Central Asian oasis kingdom of Gaochang (GOW-chahng) on the western edge of the Taklamakan Desert, whose rulers—like many others throughout Asia at the time—adopted from Indian and Chinese models to strengthen their governments. At Gaochang, we learn from a biography written decades later by a disciple, the Buddhist king politely requested that Xuanzang (SHUEN-zahng) give up his trip and preach to his subjects. Xuanzang courteously explained that he preferred to go to India. The conversation suddenly turned ugly:

CHINESE BUDDHIST
MONK, TANG DYNASTY

(Musée des Arts Asiatiques-Guimet, Paris, France/
Réunion des Musées Nationaux/Art Resource, NY)

The king's face flushed. He pushed up his sleeves, bared his arms, and shouted, "Your disciple has other ways to deal with you. How can you go on your own? Either you stay or I send you back to your country. Please consider my offer carefully. I think it is better for you to do what I say."

The Master replied, "I have come on my way to seek the Great Dharma and now have encountered an obstacle. Your majesty may detain my body but never my spirit."

This icon will direct you to interactive activities and study materials on the *Voyages* website:
www.cengage.com/history/hansen/voyages1e

The Travels of Xuanzang

→ Xuanzang's journey
⇢ Possible journeys
▨ Tang dynasty, 619–907
▨ Tang conquests, 629–751
▨ Harsha Empire, 606–647
— Silk Road

Goes on hunger strike in Gaochang Kingdom, 630.

Xuanzang arrives in Nālandā on horseback, 631.

Xuanzang leaves Chang'an on foot, 629.

Lake Baikal
Aral Sea
SOGDIANA
Talas
Oxus R.
Jaxartes R.
Iron Gate
PAMIRS
TIAN SHAN
Kucha
GAOCHANG
Dunhuang
TAKLAMAKAN
GOBI
Mt. Wutai
Huang He R.
KOGORYO
SILLA
Yellow Sea
Luoyang
Chang'an
Wei R.
HINDU KUSH
Peshawar
Indus R.
HIMALAYA MTS.
TIBET
Ganges R.
Nālandā
Buddh Gaya
Brahmaputra R.
INDIA
Irrawaddy R.
Salween R.
Yangzi R.
NAN CHAO
Xi R.
Guangzhou
Arabian Sea
DECCAN
Bay of Bengal
PYU
Mekong R.
South China Sea
CHAMPA
FUNAN
0   250   500 Km.
0   250   500 Mi.
N
SRI LANKA

	100 C.E.	200	300	400	500	600	700	800	900	1000

Lifetime of Xuanzang
596   664

CHINA
Six Dynasties
220
Sui dynasty
589 618
Tang dynasty
907

INDIA
Kushan Empire
ca. 100   260
Gupta Empire
320   ca. 600
Chola kingdom in south India
907

SOUTHEAST ASIA
Funan kingdom in Mekong Delta
ca. 75   550
Srivijaya kingdom in Sumatra
350   1000
Angkor kingdom
802

KOREA
Silla kingdom in south Korea
935

JAPAN
Nara period
710   794
Heian period

His sobs made it impossible for him to say more. Even so, the king did not give in but increased the gifts he gave. Every day at mealtimes, the king presented a tray of food to Xuanzang. Since Xuanzang was detained against his will and his plans thwarted, he vowed not to eat so that the king would change his mind. Accordingly, for three days he sat erect and refused all water.

On the fourth day, the king discovered that the Master's breathing had become very faint. Feeling deeply ashamed of himself and afraid, the king bowed with his head touching the ground and apologized: "I will allow you to go to the West. Please eat immediately."[1]

Xuanzang (ca. 596–664) A monk who traveled to Central Asia and India between 629 and 644 to obtain original Buddhist texts.

Xuanzang's three-day hunger strike succeeded. The contrite king offered to provide his travel expenses, and Xuanzang in turn agreed to teach the king's subjects before continuing his journey.

We might wonder why the Gaochang king so desperately wanted a lone monk to remain in his kingdom. As this chapter explains, Xuanzang represented an important element of the revised Chinese blueprint for empire. After reuniting China, the Sui (SWAY) (589–617) and Tang (TAHNG) emperors introduced important additions to the Qin/Han synthesis of Legalist and Confucian policies (see Chapter 4), including civil service examinations, a new system of taxation, and a complex law code. They also aspired to fulfill Ashoka's model of the ideal **chakravartin** king who patronized Buddhism. The Gaochang king applied the new Chinese model to his kingdom in the hope of strengthening his rule. After the hunger strike, he realized that if he could not persuade Xuanzang to stay, at least he could provide him with travel expenses and become known as a generous donor, a key component of being a chakravartin. (Conversely, if Xuanzang had died while staying with him, it would have permanently damaged his reputation as a pious ruler.)

chakravartin Literally "turner of the wheel," a Buddhist term for the ideal ruler who patronized Buddhism but never became a monk.

When Xuanzang returned to China in 644, he had covered over 10,000 miles (16,000 km). The Gaochang kingdom had fallen to the armies of the Tang dynasty, and Emperor Taizong welcomed Xuanzang enthusiastically. He sought both Xuanzang's skills as a translator and the valuable information he brought about distant lands. Historians of India and Central Asia are particularly grateful for Xuanzang's detailed accounts of his trip, which supplement sparse indigenous sources. After he returned, Xuanzang translated over seventy Buddhist texts, many still read today because of their accuracy.

Silk Routes Overland routes through Central Asia connecting China and India, as well as the sea routes around Southeast Asia, along which were transmitted teachings, technologies, and languages.

The overland routes through Central Asia that Xuanzang took to India—and the sea routes around Southeast Asia taken by others—are known today as the **Silk Routes.** These routes were conduits not just for pilgrims like Xuanzang but also for merchants plying their goods, soldiers dispatched to fight in distant lands, and refugees fleeing dangerous areas for safety. These travelers told of powerful rulers in India and China, whose accomplishments inspired chieftains in border areas to imitate them. These Asian leaders introduced new writing systems, law codes, ways of recruiting government officials, and taxation systems, often modifying them to suit their own societies. Some, like the Gaochang king and the rulers of Korea, Japan, and Tibet, patronized Buddhism and adopted Tang policies. Others, particularly in South and Southeast Asia, emulated South Asian monarchs and built temples to deities such as Shiva (SHIH-vah) and Vishnu (VISH-new), the most important deities in the emerging belief system of **Hinduism.**

The individual decisions of these rulers resulted in the religious reorientation of the region. In 100 C.E., a disunited India was predominantly Buddhist, while the unified China of the Han dynasty embraced Legalist, Confucian, and Daoist beliefs. By 1000 C.E., the various kingdoms of India and Southeast Asia had become largely Hindu, while China, Japan, Korea, and Tibet had become Buddhist. This religious shift did not occur because a ruler of an intact empire, such as Constantine in the West (see Chapter 7), recognized a single religion. It was the result of many decisions taken by multiple rulers in different places over the course of centuries.

• **Hinduism** Temple-based religious system that arose between 300 and 700 in India. Hinduism has two dimensions: public worship in temples and daily private worship in the home.

Focus Questions

 How did Buddhism change after the year 100? How did Hinduism displace it within India?

 How did geography, trade, and religion shape the development of states and societies in Southeast Asia?

 How did the Sui and Tang dynasties modify the Qin/Han blueprint for empire?

 Which elements of the revised Chinese blueprint for empire did Korea and Japan borrow intact? Which did they modify?

●Religion and the State in India, 100–1000

By the year 100, India had broken up into different regional kingdoms, all much smaller than the Mauryan Empire ruled by Ashoka (see Chapter 3) but bound by common cultural ties of Buddhism, social hierarchy, and respect for classical Sanskrit learning. Although the Ashokan inscriptions claim that Buddhist missionaries went to other countries to spread the dharma, the first evidence of the spread of Buddhism beyond South Asia dates to the Kushan empire (ca. 50–260 C.E.). The most important Kushan ruler, Kanishka (r. ca. 120–140 C.E.), launched a missionary movement that propelled the new Greater Vehicle teachings of Buddhism (see next page) into Central Asia and China.

Between 100 and 1000 C.E., Buddhism gained many adherents outside India but increasingly lost ground to new deities inside India. When Xuanzang traveled to north India in the early 600s, he noticed Buddhism in decline everywhere, and he recorded, often regretfully, the rise of a new religion taught by Brahmins. We know this religion as Hinduism, a name not used until the nineteenth century, when British scholars of Indian religion coined the term to denote Indians who were not Zoroastrian, Christian, or Muslim.[2] By the year 1000, in many regions in India, particularly south India, the largest religious institutions were temples to Hindu deities such as Vishnu and Shiva, and kings recorded magnificent gifts to Hindu temples in long inscriptions.

The Rise of Greater Vehicle Teachings in Buddhism

Buddhism changed a great deal between Ashoka's time in the third century B.C.E. and Kanishka's reign in the second century C.E. Most importantly, Buddhist teachings no longer required an individual to join the Buddhist order to gain enlightenment. New interpreters of Buddhism referred to their own teachings as the Greater Vehicle (Mahayana) and denigrated those of earlier schools as the Lesser Vehicle (Hinayana). For this reason, scholars sometimes call the earlier schools Theravada, meaning "the Tradition of the Elders."

The Buddha had also taught that he was not a deity and that his followers should not make statues of him. Yet Indians began to worship statues of the Buddha in the first and second centuries C.E. (see Chapter 3). They also began to pray to **bodhisattvas** (BODE-ee-saht-vahz) for easier childbirth or the curing of illness. A bodhisattva—literally, a being headed for Buddhahood—refers to someone on the verge of enlightenment who chooses, because of his or her compassion for others, to stay in this world for this and future lives and help other sentient beings (the Buddhist term for all living creatures, including humans) to attain nirvana.

- **bodhisattva** Buddhist term denoting a being headed for Buddhahood.

The proponents of the Greater Vehicle schools emphasized that Buddhists could transfer merit from one person to another: if someone paid for a Buddhist text to be recited, he or she acquired a certain amount of merit that could be transferred to someone else, perhaps an ill relative. Buddhist inscriptions frequently state that someone gave a gift to the Buddhist order, such as paying for part of a monastery, in someone else's name.

During the early centuries of the Common Era, Buddhist monasteries appeared throughout India. This, too, was a departure from earlier times. The Buddha had wandered from place to place with his followers and had stayed in one place only during the rainy season. Over the centuries, though, most Buddhist monks ceased the daily walk in which they asked for offerings from townspeople and instead moved into permanent monasteries. Since monastic rules forbade the monks from working in the fields, most monasteries hired laborers to do their farming for them. One monastery erected a giant stone begging bowl by its front gate. Rather than feed monks as they had in the past, the monastery's supporters placed large gifts in the stone bowl for the monks and nuns.

King Kanishka certainly supported the Buddhist order, and rich merchants probably did as well. Many Buddhist texts encouraged donors to make gifts of gold, silver, lapis lazuli, crystal, coral, pearls, and agate. These valuable items, often referred to as the Seven Treasures, were traded overland between India and China. The blue mineral lapis lazuli could be mined only in present-day Afghanistan, and one of the world's best sources of pearls was the island of Sri Lanka, just south of India.

The Buddhists, like the Christians at the Council of Nicaea (see Chapter 7), met periodically to discuss their teachings, and Buddhist sources credit Kanishka with organizing the Fourth Buddhist Council, whose primary task was to determine which versions of orally transmitted texts were authoritative. Because the few writing materials available in ancient India, such as leaves and wooden tablets, decayed in India's tropical climate, Buddhist texts were not recorded. Monks specialized in a specific text, or a group of texts, and they transmitted them to their disciples by teaching them to memorize them.

The Kushan dynasty was only one of many regional dynasties in India during the first to third centuries C.E. After 140 C.E., Kanishka's successors fought in various military campaigns, and Chinese sources report the arrival of refugees fleeing the political upheavals of their homeland in north India. The earliest Buddhists to arrive in China in the first and second centuries C.E. were missionaries from the Kushan empire, and their propagation of Buddhist teachings was particularly influential (see below). In 260 C.E. the Sasanians (see Chapter 6) defeated the final Kushan ruler, bringing the dynasty to an end.

The Rise of Hinduism, 300–900

In the centuries after the fall of the Kushan dynasty, various dynasties arose in the different regions of South Asia, which continued to be culturally united even as it was politically divided. One of the most important was the **Gupta dynasty,** which controlled much of north India between 320 and 600. An admirer of the Mauryan dynasty (ca. 320–185 B.C.E.), Chandragupta (r. 319/320–ca. 330), the founder of the Gupta (GOO-ptah) dynasty took the same name as the Mauryan founder and governed from the former capital at Pataliputra (modern-day Patna).

In an important innovation, the Gupta rulers issued land grants to powerful families, Brahmins, monasteries, and even villages. These grants gave the holder the right to collect a share of the harvest from the cultivators who worked his land. Inscriptions on stone and copper record the details of these gifts: the dimensions of the land, the share of the harvest given to the grantee and to village officials, and the names of the accountants responsible for implementing these arrangements. Scribes developed a decimal system that allowed them to record the dimensions of each plot of land. Certainly by 876, and quite possibly during the Gupta reign, they also started to use a small circle to hold empty places; that symbol is the ancestor of the modern zero.[3] On the other side of the globe, the Maya started to use zero at roughly the same time (see page 125).

The Gupta rulers, inscriptions reveal, made many grants of land to Brahmins, members of the highest-ranking varna (see Chapter 3) who conducted rituals honoring Hindu deities like Vishnu and Shiva. The two deities, who appear only briefly in the *Rig Veda* of ancient India, became increasingly important in later times. Both deities took many forms with various names. Worshipers of Vishnu claimed that the Buddha was actually Vishnu in an earlier incarnation.

In 631, when Xuanzang reached Gandhara, which had been a center of Buddhism under Kanishka, he noticed many abandoned monasteries: "On both banks of the Shubhavastu River there were formerly fourteen hundred monasteries with eighteen thousand monks, but now the monasteries were in desolation and the number of monks had decreased."[4] Buddhist monasteries were not as large as they had been in earlier centuries, and the number of Buddhist monks had also declined. (See the feature "World History in Today's World: Snapshot of Hinduism and Buddhism.")

• **Gupta dynasty** (ca. 320–600) Indian dynasty based in north India; emulated the earlier Mauryan dynasty. The Gupta kings pioneered a new type of religious gift: land grants to Brahmin priests and Hindu temples.

Snapshot of Hinduism and Buddhism

Hinduism, with 900 million adherents worldwide, is the world's third-largest religion (after Christianity and Islam); Buddhism, with 350 million believers, is the fourth. Almost all Hindus live in South Asia or are of South Asian descent. The largest group of Hindus, 780 million, resides in India.

Modern India is home to a Buddhist community as well. Indian Buddhists are not the descendants of long-established Buddhist families but members of untouchable groups, as they were called in the British colonial period, who converted to Buddhism at the urging of Dr. Bhimrao Ramji Ambedkar (1891–1956). A member of a jati who traditionally had been sweepers and messengers, Ambedkar became a leader of untouchables after receiving his Ph.D. from Columbia University. In 1935, he announced his decision to stop being a Hindu because he felt that Hinduism reinforced discrimination against members of lower castes.

On October 14, 1956, nine years after India gained independence, Ambedkar took the traditional vows to become a lay Buddhist and composed twenty-two new vows that he administered to nearly 400,000 followers. The nineteenth vow explained: "I renounce Hinduism, which is harmful for humanity and impedes the advancement and development of humanity because it is based on inequality, and adopt Buddhism as my religion."

Ambedker objected to Hindu teachings because they ranked Brahmins as the most pure of all jati.

Only two months later, Ambedkar died. Since then others have organized similar mass conversions. One occurred on October 14, 2006, fifty years after Ambedkar took his vows. The Buddhism movement has been most successful in Ambedkar's home state of Maharashtra and in neighboring Uttar Pradesh. Of the 7.95 million Indians who said that they were Buddhist in the 2001 census, 5.83 million, or 73 percent, lived in Maharashtra.

Many of the world's Buddhists are not as explicit about their religious adherence as are Ambedkar's followers. Several Southeast Asian nations subscribe to Theravada Buddhist teachings, including Thailand, Cambodia, and Sri Lanka. Almost all young Thai men undergo temporary ordination and spend a year or so studying Buddhism at Buddhist monasteries. The largest numbers of Buddhist adherents, however, live in China, with an estimated 100 million Buddhists, or in Japan, with 90 million. While many modern Chinese or Japanese may identify themselves as Buddhists if asked, they visit Buddhist temples only rarely and are much less actively Buddhist than Thais.

Sources: www.adherents.com and www.columbia.edu/itc/mealac/pritchett/00ambedkar/ambedkar_buddha/.

Xuanzang's time in India from 630 to 643 coincided with the long reign of King Harsha (606–647) in Kanauj (KAHN-awj) (modern-day Kanpur), one of the successor dynasties to the Guptas. Remarking on the caste system, which was so different from that in China, he ranked the four varna in the traditional order according to purity: Brahmins, royal caste, merchant class, and agricultural class.[5] Brahmin priests played an important role in Hindu worship, but unlike the Brahmins of Vedic times, who had conducted large public ceremonies with animal sacrifices, the Brahmins of the Gupta era performed offerings to Vishnu and Shiva at temples.

Hindu worship of Shiva and Vishnu had two dimensions: public ceremonies conducted by Brahmins in temples, which allowed local rulers to proclaim their power for all visiting the temple to see, and private worship in the home. In private worship, devotees daily sang songs of love or praise to their deities. This strong personal tie between the devotee and the deity is known as **bhakti.** The main evidence for the rise of bhakti devotionalism is a large corpus of poems

• **bhakti** Literally "personal devotion or love," a term for Hindu poetry or cults that emphasizes a strong personal tie between the deity and a devotee, who did not use priests as intermediaries.

written in regional languages such as Tamil, a language of great antiquity spoken in the southernmost tip of India.

The Beginnings of the Chola Kingdom, ca. 900

The Tamil-speaking Chola (CHOH-la) kings, who established their dynasty in south India in 907, were among the most powerful leaders who patronized Hindu temples. In their capital at Tanjore, they bestowed huge land grants on the Shiva temple in the hope that their subjects would associate the generosity of the royal donors with the power of the deity.

The Tanjore temple to Shiva, like many other Hindu temples, had an innermost chamber, called the womb room, that housed a stone lingam, to which

▨ Brihadeshwara Temple at Tanjore, with Womb Room   Rajaraja I (r. 985–1014) built this imposing temple (*below*) to Shiva at Tanjore. The temple's ornate exterior contrasts sharply with the austere interior. The innermost sanctuary of the Hindu temple, the womb room (*right*), held the lingam, on which devotees placed offerings, like the flowers shown here. A Hindu goddess sits on the peacock on the wall. Many temples allowed only Hindus, sometimes only Hindu priests, to enter the womb room.   (below: Dinodia Photo Library; right: Robert Harding/Jupiter Images)

Hindu priests made ritual offerings. *Lingam* means "sign" or "phallus" in Sanskrit. The lingam was always placed in a womb room because male and female generative power had to be combined. On a concrete level, the lingam symbolized the creative force of human reproduction; on a more abstract level, it stood for all the creative forces in the cosmos.

The Shiva temple lands lay in the agricultural heartland of south India and, when irrigated properly, produced a rich rice harvest whose income supported the thousands of Brahmins who lived in the temple. These Brahmins performed rituals, memorized and transmitted different texts, and taught local boys in temple schools. The Chola kings controlled the immediate vicinity of the capital and possibly the other large cities in their district, but not the many villages surrounding the cities. Many of these villages were self-governing. But since their temples were subordinate to the larger temple in the Chola capital, they also acknowledged the Chola kings as their spiritual overlords.

One of the most successful Chola rulers was Rajaraja (RAH-jah-rah-jah) I (r. 985–1014), who conquered much of south India and sent armies as far as Srivijaya (sree-VEE-jeye-ah) (modern Indonesia, on the southern Malay Peninsula and Sumatra). Although he did not conquer any territory there, the people of Southeast Asia learned of the Chola king's accomplishments from these contacts. As a direct result, local rulers encouraged priests literate in Sanskrit to move to Southeast Asia to build Hindu temples and teach them about Chola governance (see page 218).

● State, Society, and Religion in Southeast Asia, 300–1000

The term *Southeast Asia* encompasses a broad swath of land in subtropical Asia and over twenty thousand islands in the Pacific. In most periods, travel among islands and along the shore was easier than overland travel, which was possible only on some of the region's major rivers like the Irrawaddy and the Salween in modern Myanmar (Burma), the Red River in Vietnam, and the Mekong in Laos, Thailand, Cambodia, and Vietnam. Most of the region's sparse population (an estimated fifteen people per square mile [six people per sq km] in the seventeenth century,[6] and even lower in earlier centuries) lived in isolated groups separated by forests and mountains, but the coastal peoples went on sea voyages as early as 1000 B.C.E.

Like India, Southeast Asia received heavy monsoon rains in the summer; successful agriculture often depended on storing rainwater in tanks for use throughout the year. While people in the lowlands raised rice in paddies, the different highland societies largely practiced slash-and-burn agriculture. Once farmers had exhausted the soil of a given place, they moved on, with the result that few states with fixed borders existed in Southeast Asia.

With no equivalent of caste, the shifting social structure of the region was basically egalitarian. People lived in different groups in the forested mountains without settling permanently in any given spot. From time to time, a leader unified some of the groups, dedicated a temple to either the Buddha or a Hindu deity, and adopted other policies in hopes of strengthening his new state.

Buddhist Kingdoms Along the Trade Routes

Merchants and religious travelers going from India to China (and back) by boat traveled along well-established routes (see Map 8.1). Before 350 C.E., ships usually landed at a port on the Isthmus of Kra, and travelers crossed the 35-mile (56-km) stretch of land dividing the Andaman Sea from the Gulf of Thailand by foot before resuming their sea voyages. This overland route could reduce an often treacherous sea route by 1,600 miles (2,500 km). The Buddhist kingdom of Funan, centered on the Mekong River Delta, arose in this area and thrived between the first and sixth centuries C.E. Surprisingly little is known about Funan; scholars debate its exact location and refer to it by its Chinese name, *Funan,* because they do not know its indigenous name.

Prevailing winds and the types of boat available determined which routes merchants and pilgrims took. During the spring and summer, while the Eurasian landmass heated up, travelers could follow the monsoon winds that blew toward India; during the fall and winter, as the landmass cooled, they could leave India and follow the winds that blew away from the landmass. Most boats had to wait in Southeast Asian ports for the winds to change. The long periods of waiting meant that entire ships—sometimes with several hundred crew and passengers—needed food and shelter for three to five months, and port towns grew up to accommodate their needs. Local rulers discovered that they could tax the travelers, and merchants realized that there was a market for Southeast Asian aromatic woods and spices in both China and India.

Funan declined as a Buddhist center sometime after 350 C.E., when the mariners of Southeast Asia discovered a new route between China and India. Merchants and monks boarded ships at Sri Lanka and traveled all the way to either the Strait of Malacca or the Sunda Strait. They disembarked in the kingdom of Srivijaya in modern-day Indonesia, waited for the winds to shift, and then continued through the South China Sea to China. The main port for the kingdom was located at the modern-day city of Palembang, which has a deep natural harbor. The kingdom traded with many regional kingdoms in central Java, where the world's largest Buddhist monument, at Borobudur (boh-roh-BUH-duhr), provides a powerful example of religious architecture connected with early state formation. (See the feature "Visual Evidence: Borobudur: A Buddhist Monument in Java, Indonesia.")

Srivijaya's ruler welcomed Buddhist travelers and made extensive contributions to local Buddhist monasteries as well as non-Buddhist deities. The Srivijayan kings called themselves "Lord of the Mountains" and "Spirit of the Waters of the Sea," titles from the local religious traditions. The kingdom of Srivijaya flourished between 700 and 1000 C.E.

Buddhist and Hindu Kingdoms of Inland Southeast Asia, 300–1000

Buddhist images made in stone appeared throughout interior Southeast Asia between 300 and 600. In the pre-Buddhist period, all the different societies of the region recognized certain individuals as "men of prowess" who used military skill and intelligence to rise to the leadership of their tribes. They succeeded against other claimants to power because they had more active networks of loyal supporters whom they could lead in times of war. Sometimes a leader was so successful that various tribal leaders acknowledged him as a regional overlord.

CL Interactive Map

🌐 **MAP 8.1**

The Spread of Buddhism and Hinduism to Southeast Asia Sea routes connected Southeast Asia with both India and China, facilitating travel by missionaries to the region and by devotees from the region. The regions closest to China, particularly Vietnam, became predominantly Buddhist, like China, while the rulers of other regions, including Cambodia, patronized both Buddhism and Hinduism, as did most rulers in India.

Most societies in Southeast Asia recognized descent through both the mother and the father. In practice this meant that the son of a man of prowess was not necessarily the leading candidate to succeed him as leader; a nephew, particularly the child of his sister, had the same claim as the son. As a result, no group hung together for very long. People were loyal to a given individual, not to a dynasty, and when he died, they tended to seek a new man of prowess to support. After these men of prowess died, they became honored ancestors.

Burial practices varied widely throughout Southeast Asia. In modern Cambodia alone, archaeologists have found evidence of cremation, burial in the ground, burial by disposal in the ocean, and exposure of the dead above ground. Many people conceived of a natural world populated by different spirits usually thought to inhabit trees, rocks, and other physical features. Specialists conducted rituals that allowed them to communicate with these spirits.

This was the world into which literate outsiders came in the fourth, fifth, and sixth centuries C.E. Most of the visitors, some identified as Brahmins, came from India and knew how to read and write Sanskrit. Southeast Asians also traveled to India, where they studied Sanskrit and returned after they memorized both sacred texts and laws. Inscriptions often refer to men literate in Sanskrit as *purohita*, a Sanskrit word meaning a chief priest, who conducted rituals for leaders and served in their governments as an adviser or administrator. The teachings of devotional Hinduism, or bhakti (see above), encouraged devotees to study with a teacher, or purohita, so that they could get closer to the divinity they worshiped.

Literate teachers, whether native or not, brought different teachings—some we now identify as Buddhist, some as Hindu—to the rulers of Southeast Asia. We can see how they came together in one ruler's mind in the case of Jayavarman II (JAI-ah-var-mahn) (ca. 770–850), who ruled the lower Mekong basin in Cambodia between 802 and 850. (Jayavarman II was named for a seventh-century ruler of the same name.) Before the Mekong River empties into the South China Sea, much of its waters flow into Tonle Sap (the Great Lake). The lake served as a holding tank for the monsoon rains, which were channeled into nearby rice fields.

Historians view Jayavarman II's reign as the beginning of the Angkor period (802–1431), named for the **Angkor dynasty,** whose rulers spoke the Khmer (KMEHR) language. Because Jayavarman II is closely identified with the Hindu deity Shiva, this dynasty is often called a Hindu dynasty. Jayavarman II was a devotee of Shiva, who was believed to preside over the entire universe, with other less powerful deities having smaller realms. Similarly, Jayavarman II presided over the human universe, while the surrounding chieftains had their own smaller, inferior,

● **Angkor dynasty**
Khmer-speaking dynasty in modern-day Cambodia founded by Jayavarman II. His combination of Hindu and Buddhist imagery proved so potent that it was used by all later Angkor kings.

■ **Bayon Gate, Angkor Thom, Cambodia**   In the 1180s and 1190s, the ruler Jayavarman VII built a series of monuments and temples, including this one at Angkor Thom, a fortified city just north of Angkor Wat. The figures on the road leading up to the Bayon Gate are Buddhist guardians: on the left stands a line of warrior deities; on the right, a row of gods. The faces on the four sides of the tower are those of a bodhisattva, but the multiple faces also seem Hindu, in an artful blending of Hindu and Buddhist imagery.   (Gavin Hellier/Robert Harding Picture Library Ltd./Alamy)

BOROBUDUR: A BUDDHIST MONUMENT IN JAVA, INDONESIA

The largest Buddhist monument in the world lies not in the homeland of the Buddha in India but over 1,000 miles (1,600 km) to the southeast at Borobudur on the island of Java in Indonesia. The Shailendra (SHAI-len-drah) kings (ca. 775–860) built the monument out of volcanic rock sometime in the eighth or ninth century, just as they were consolidating their rule. When they moved their capital to a different location in east Java, they abandoned the magnificent complex, and it lay unknown until the early nineteenth century, when Sir Thomas Raffles, founder of Singapore, saw it covered with mold and lichen plants in the middle of a dense forest.

Since no surviving documents explain the meaning of the elements of the monument, analysts must study the different sections of the enormous monument to reconstruct its possible meaning. Rising over 100 feet (31.5 m) above the ground, the monument rests on a large squarish base measuring 400 feet (122 m) on each side. The overall effect resembles the ziggurat temples of Mesopotamia. Staircases at the center of each level lead up to the next, and visitors walk around each level for a total of 3 miles (5 km) until they reach the top.

The lowest level of the monument, originally below ground, depicts an underground hell for those who do not obey Buddhist teachings. The four square terraces above contain over 2,500 panels, most showing scenes from the earlier lives of the Buddha. Monks and guides probably explained the meaning of these scenes to pilgrims. Near the top, the visitor reaches the three terraces holding seventy-two bodhisattvas, each sitting under a bell-shaped stone with holes to look through. At the top of the monument stands an empty stupa, which may have originally held a relic.

Borobudur was a pilgrimage site for people all over Southeast Asia. Pilgrims brought simple clay objects in the shape of stupas and buried them underground at the site. Archaeologists have unearthed 2,397 clay stupas and 252 clay tablets with writing on them. Pilgrims also buried clay pots and sheets of silver covered with written Buddhist charms, either to keep away evil spirits or to bring good health. The many languages on the tablets indicate that people came from great distances to see Borobudur and to make offerings to the Buddha who came to be worshiped so far from his original home.

Most analysts concur that the monument was designed to lead pilgrims from the underworld, shown in the base, up through the five platforms showing human existence, through the world of the seventy-two bodhisattvas to the single Buddha on top who had attained enlightenment. While the content of the different panels is clearly inspired by Buddhism, the design of the monument, with its multiple ascending levels, is distinctly local. No other Buddhist monument is like it.

Borobudur is made of two million separate blocks of yellow-brown andesite, volcanic rock found throughout Java. Each year over 70 inches (2 m) of rain falls on the rocks, creating the perfect environment for moss and lichen to thrive. Between 1973 and 1983, with UNESCO support, workers dismantled the monument, removed and cleaned each of the blocks, and restored the monument for the third time since its rediscovery in the early 1800s.

QUESTION FOR ANALYSIS

 How had Buddhist worship at stupas changed from the first century B.C.E. at Sanchi (see Visual Evidence, Chapter 3) to the eighth and ninth centuries at Borobudur?

These three circular terraces hold seventy-two smaller stupas, each housing an image of a bodhisattva.

This large stupa, 36 feet (11 m) in diameter and 460 feet (43 m) above the ground, is empty. It probably originally held an image of the Buddha.

All of the stones today are grayish-black, but they were originally covered with a layer of white plaster and then painted different eye-catching colors.

The galleries on the four square levels hold 1,460 six-foot-wide stone panels, each showing a different scene from Buddhist songs, poems, sacred texts, and the earlier lives of the Buddha.

The heavy stone monument rests on an unstable core of earth. After construction first started, the monument sagged, prompting a reconfiguration of the subterranean level, which now is surrounded by a terrace to prevent it from slipping even further. Some observers have compared the resulting uneven profile to a cake that did not rise properly.

realms. Jayavarman II did not have to conquer them militarily because they acknowledged him as a bhakti teacher who could provide them with closer access to Shiva.

Devotees of Shiva built temples that incorporated pre-existing local shrines, usually on sites where local spirits were thought to live. If the spirit inhabited a rock, that rock could be worshiped as the lingam of the new Shiva temple. When devotees conducted a Hindu ceremony to request children, they poured a sacred liquid over the lingam, a practice that echoed earlier fertility cults. The largest temple in the kingdom came to be known as Angkor Wat (en-CORE waht). Built in the early twelfth century, it used motifs borrowed from Hinduism to teach its viewers that they were living during a golden age, when peace reigned and the Angkor dynasty controlled much of modern-day Cambodia. Jayavarman II also invoked Buddhist terminology by calling himself a chakravartin ruler. This combination of Hindu and Buddhist imagery proved so potent that all subsequent Angkor kings, and many other Southeast Asian rulers, used it.

With the exception of Vietnam, which remained within the Chinese cultural sphere even when not under direct Chinese rule, Southeast Asia faced toward India, where Buddhism and Hinduism often coexisted. Buddhism and Hinduism came to Southeast Asia not because of conquest but because local rulers aspired to create new states as powerful as those they heard existed in India.

● Buddhism and the Revival of Empire in China, 100–1000

With the fall of the Han dynasty in 220 C.E., China broke up into different regions, each governed by local military leaders. When the first Buddhist missionaries from the Kushan empire arrived in China during the first and second centuries C.E., they faced great difficulties in spreading their religion. Buddhist teachings urged potential converts to abandon family obligations and adopt a celibate lifestyle, yet Confucian China was one of the most family-oriented societies in the world. The chakravartin ideal of the universal Buddhist ruler, though, appealed to leaders of regions no longer united under the Han dynasty. During the Sui dynasty, which reunited China, and its long-lived successor, the Tang dynasty, Chinese emperors introduced important additions to the Qin/Han blueprint for empire, additions that remained integral to Chinese governance until the end of dynastic rule in the early 1900s.

Buddhism in China, 100–589

The first Buddhists in China came to the Han dynasty capitals at Chang'an and Luoyang early in the Common Era, most likely by sea and overland through Central Asia. The first Chinese who worshiped the Buddha did so because they thought him capable of miracles; some sources report that his image shone brightly and could fly through the air. The earliest Chinese document to mention Buddhism, from 65 C.E., tells of a prince worshiping the Buddha alongside the Daoist deity

Laozi, the purported author of *The Way and Integrity Classic* (see Chapter 4), indicating that the Chinese initially thought the Buddha was a Daoist deity.

The Han dynasty ended in 220 C.E. when a general decided to end the fiction of ruling through a puppet emperor and founded a new dynasty. He was never able to unite the entire empire, and no other regional dynasty succeeded in doing so until 589. Historians call this long period of disunity the Six Dynasties (220–589 C.E.).

During the Six Dynasties, Buddhist miracle workers began to win the first converts. Historians of Buddhism treat these miracle accounts in the same way as historians of Christianity do biblical accounts (see Chapter 7). Nonbelievers may be skeptical that the events occurred as described, but people at the time found (and modern devotees continue to find) these tales compelling, and they are crucial to our understanding of how these religions gained their first adherents.

One of the most effective early missionaries was a Central Asian man named **Fotudeng** (d. 349), who claimed that the Buddha had given him the ability to bring rain, cure the sick, and foresee the future. In 310, Fotudeng managed to convert a local ruler named Shi Le (274–333) just as he was about to lead an army into Luoyang, the former Han dynasty capital. Shi Le asked Fotudeng to perform a miracle to demonstrate the power of Buddhism. A later biography explains what happened: "Thereupon he took his begging bowl, filled it with water, burned incense, and said a spell over it. In a moment there sprang up blue lotus flowers whose brightness and color dazzled the eyes."[7] A Buddhist symbol, the lotus is a beautiful flower that grows from a root coming out of a dirty lake bottom; similarly, Fotudeng explained, human beings could free their minds from the impediments of worldly living and attain enlightenment. As usual with miracle tales, we have no way of knowing what actually happened, but Fotudeng's miracle so impressed Shi Le that he granted the Buddhists tax-free land so they could build monasteries in north China.

The son of a Xiongnu (SHEE-awng-new) chieftain (see Chapter 4), Shi Le could never become a good Confucian-style ruler because he spoke but could not read or write Chinese. Buddhism appealed to him precisely because it offered an alternative to Confucianism. He could aspire to be a chakravartin ruler.

Fotudeng tried to persuade ordinary Chinese to join the new monasteries and nunneries, but most people were extremely reluctant to take vows of celibacy. If they did not have children, future generations would not be able to perform ancestor worship for their parents and grandparents. A Buddhist book written in the early sixth century, *The Lives of the Nuns*, portrays the dilemma of would-be converts. When one young woman told her father that she did not want to marry, he replied, "You ought to marry. How can you be like this?" She explained, "I want to free all living beings from suffering. How much more, then, do I want to free my two parents!"[8] But her father was not persuaded by her promise that she could free him from the endless cycle of birth, death, and rebirth. When Fotudeng met the woman's father, he promised: "If you consent to her plan [to become a nun], she indeed shall raise her family to glory and bring you blessings and honor." Deeply impressed, the father agreed to let her enter a nunnery.

Similar encounters between parents and children took place all over China during the Six Dynasties. Many families made a compromise between the demands of Buddhism and Confucianism; they allowed one child to join the Buddhist order and transfer merit to the other children, who married and had children.

Fotudeng (d. 349) Central Asian Buddhist missionary who persuaded the ruler Shi Le to convert to Buddhism; Shi Le's decision to grant tax-free land to Buddhist monasteries was a crucial first step in the establishment of Buddhism in China.

Buddhist missionaries found that they could use miracles to convert uneducated people like Shi Le, but they needed accurate Chinese translations of Buddhist texts to impress China's scholars. Still, the structure and vocabulary of Sanskrit, an Indo-European language, differed greatly from Chinese, and no dictionaries or other translation aids existed. The first understandable translations in Chinese appeared only in the year 400, long after Buddhists had been active in China, when a monk who knew both Chinese and Sanskrit founded a translation bureau with teams of bilingual translators.

Buddhists continued to win converts during the fifth and sixth centuries. They gained support because Buddhist teachings offered more hope about the afterlife than did Confucian and Daoist teachings. Confucius had refused to discuss the afterlife, except to urge his students to mourn their parents, yet many Chinese envisioned an underground prison where the dead languished forever while remaining recognizably themselves.

The original Indian belief in the transmigration of souls as expressed in the *Upanishads* (oo-PAHN-ih-shahdz; see Chapter 3) presumed that someone's soul in this life stayed intact and could be reborn in a different body. But the Buddhists propounded the no-self doctrine, which taught that there is no such thing as a fixed self. Each person is a constantly shifting group of five aggregates—form, feelings, perceptions, karmic constituents, and consciousness—that change from one second to the next. Accordingly, there is no self that can be reborn in the next life. This idea proved extremely difficult for people to grasp and was much debated as a result.

Gradually, Chinese Buddhists abandoned the strict no-self doctrine and began to describe a series of hells, much like the indigenous Chinese concept of the underground prison, where people went when they died. A few people could attain nirvana and ascend to a Buddhist paradise, they taught, but most people went to these hells and awaited their rebirth as one of six different types of being, depending on whether they had accrued good or bad karma in their previous existences. The willingness of Buddhist teachers to modify their original no-self teachings won them many converts. (See the feature "Movement of Ideas: Teaching Buddhism in a Confucian Society.")

By the year 600, Buddhism was firmly implanted in the Chinese countryside. A history of Buddhism written in that year explained that three types of monasteries existed. The largest 47 monasteries were completely financed by the central government; educated monks who lived in them conducted regular Buddhist rituals on behalf of the emperor and his immediate family. In the second tier were 839 monasteries that depended on royal princes and other powerful families for support. The final category included over 30,000 smaller shrines that dotted the Chinese countryside. Dependent on local people for contributions, the monks who worked in these shrines were often uneducated and could recite only a handful of Buddhist texts from memory. Some could not even read and write. The number of monks, educated and not, varied over the centuries, but it never exceeded more than 1 percent of China's total population, which was about fifty million in 600.[9]

• **Tang dynasty**
Dynasty (618–907) that represented a political and cultural high point in Chinese history. The Tang emperors combined elements of the Qin/Han blueprint for empire with new measures to create a model of governance that spread to Tibet, Korea, and Japan.

China Reunified, 589–907

After more than three hundred years of disunity, the founder of the Sui dynasty reunified China in 589. Then, in less than thirty years, the **Tang dynasty** succeeded it. The Sui and Tang emperors embraced the chakravartin ideal, for they hoped Buddhism would help to bind their many subjects together. Tang dynasty China represented a high point in Chinese history; the Tang emperors ruled more territory than any dynasty until the mid-eighteenth century, and Chinese openness to the influences of Central Asia made Tang art and music particularly beautiful.

The Sui founder consciously modeled himself on the great chakravartin ruler Ashoka, whose support for the Buddhist order was well known in China. He gave money for the construction of monasteries all over China and ordered prayers to be chanted in them on the Buddha's birthday. He also built a new capital at Chang'an, the former capital of the Han dynasty, with a gridded street plan (see Figure 8.1). The city housed 120 new Buddhist monasteries. When the emperor turned 60, in 601, he explicitly followed Ashoka's lead and ordered stupas for Buddhist relics to be built throughout the empire.

In 604, when the Sui founder died, his son succeeded him and led his armies on a disastrous campaign in Korea. He was soon overthrown by one of his generals, who went on to found the Tang dynasty. After only eight years of rule, in 626, the Tang founder's son, Emperor Taizong, overthrew his father in a bloody coup in which he killed one brother and ordered an officer to kill another.

In 645, when Xuanzang wrote asking permission to return, the emperor had defeated his domestic opponents, and his brilliant military leadership had succeeded in extending Tang China's borders deep into Central Asia. Taizong was able to fulfill the chakravartin ideal by making generous donations of money and land to Buddhist monasteries and by supporting famous monks like Xuanzang. He built a special brick pagoda where Xuanzang could translate the hundreds of texts he brought from India.

One of Taizong's greatest accomplishments was a comprehensive law code, the *Tang Code,* that was designed to help local magistrates govern and adjudicate disputes, a major part of their job. It taught them, for example, how to distinguish between manslaughter and murder and specified the punishments for each. Tang

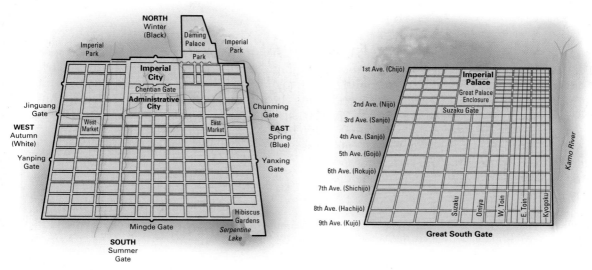

TANG CHANG'AN   **HEIAN (KYOTO)**

FIGURE 8.1
Layout of Chang'an and Heian (Kyoto)   Many rulers in East Asia followed Tang models very closely. Compare the city plans of Chang'an, the Tang capital, and Kyoto, the Heian capital. Both cities had square walls enclosing a gridded street plan, and the imperial palace was located in the north. Unlike Chang'an, Kyoto did not have a city wall or two central markets.

Teaching Buddhism in a Confucian Society

Monks frequently told stories to teach ordinary people the tenets of Buddhism. The story of the Indian monk Maudgalyayana (mowd-GAH-lee-yah-yah-nah) survives in a Sanskrit version, composed between 300 B.C.E. and 300 C.E., and a much longer Chinese version from a manuscript dated 921. This story has enormous appeal in China (it is frequently performed as Chinese opera or on television) because it portrays the dilemma of those who wanted to be good Confucian sons as well as good Buddhists. Maudgalyayana may have been filial, but he was unable to fulfill his Confucian obligations as a son because he did not bear a male heir. The Buddhist narrator takes great pains to argue that he can still be a good son because Confucian offerings have no power in a Buddhist underworld.

In the Sanskrit version, Maudgalyayana, one of the Buddha's disciples, realizes that his mother has been reborn in the real world and asks the Buddha to help her to attain nirvana. Maudgalyayana and the Buddha travel to find the mother, who attains nirvana after hearing the Buddha preach.

In the Chinese version, the protagonist retains his Indian name but acts like a typical Chinese son in every respect. The tale contrasts the behavior of the virtuous, if slightly dim, Maudgalyayana with his mother, who never gave any support to her local monastery and even kept for herself money that her son had asked her to give the monks. As a filial son, he cannot believe her capable of any crime, and he searches through all the different compartments of the Chinese hell to find her. Unrepentant to the very end of the tale, she explains that traditional Confucian offerings to the ancestors have no power in the underworld. Only offerings to the Buddhist order, such as paying monks to copy Buddhist texts, can help to ease her suffering. At the end of the story, the Buddha himself frees her from the underworld, a grim series of hells that do not exist in the Sanskrit original.

Sources: John Strong, "Filial Piety and Buddhism: The Indian Antecedents to a 'Chinese' Problem," in *Traditions in Contact and Change: Selected Proceedings of the XIVth Congress of the International Association for the History of Religions,* ed. Peter Slater and Donald Wiebe (Winnipeg, Man: Wilfrid Laurier University Press, 1980), p. 180; Victor H. Mair, trans., *Tun-huang Popular Narratives* (New York: Cambridge University Press, 1983), pp. 109–110.

Sanskrit Version

From afar, [Maudgalyayana's mother] Bhadrakanya [bud-DRAH-kahn-ee-ya] saw her son, and, as soon as she saw him, she rushed up to him exclaiming, "Ah! At long last I see my little boy!" Thereupon the crowd of people who had assembled said: "He is an aged wandering monk, and she is a young girl—how can she be his mother?" But the Venerable Maha Maudgalyayana replied, "Sirs, these skandhas• of mine were fostered by her; therefore she is my mother."

Then the Blessed One, knowing the disposition, propensity, nature and circumstances of Bhadrakanya, preached a sermon fully penetrating the meaning of the Four Noble Truths. And when Bhadrakanya had heard it, she was brought to the realization of the fruit of entering the stream.

- **skandhas** The five aggregates—form, feelings, perceptions, karmic constituents, and consciousness—which in Buddhism are the basis of the personality.

QUESTIONS FOR ANALYSIS

▶ What are the main differences between the Indian and Chinese versions?

▶ How do they portray the fate of the mother after her death?

▶ What is the Chinese underworld like?

Chinese Version

This is the place where mother and son see each other: . . .

Trickles of blood flowed from the seven openings of her head.

Fierce flames issued from the inside of his mother's mouth,

At every step, metal thorns out of space entered her body;

She clanked and clattered like the sound of five hundred broken-down chariots,

How could her waist and backbone bear up under the strain?

Jailers carrying pitchforks guarded her to the left and the right,

Ox-headed guards holding chains stood on the east and the west;

Stumbling at every other step, she came forward,

Wailing and weeping, Maudgalyayana embraced his mother.

Crying, he said: "It was because I am unfilial,

You, dear mother, were innocently caused to drop into the triple mire of hell;

Families which accumulate goodness have a surplus of blessings,

High Heaven does not destroy in this manner those who are blameless.

In the old days, mother, you were handsomer than Pan An•,

But now you have suddenly become haggard and worn;

I have heard that in hell there is much suffering,

Now, today, I finally realize, 'Ain't it hard, ain't it hard.'

Ever since I met with the misfortune of father's and your deaths,

I have not been remiss in sacrificing daily at your graves;

Mother, I wonder whether or not you have been getting any food to eat,

In such a short time, your appearance has become completely haggard."

Now that Maudgalyayana's mother had heard his words,

"Alas!" She cried, her tears intertwining as she struck and grabbed at herself:

"Only yesterday, my son, I was separated from you by death.

Who could have known that today we would be reunited?

While your mother was alive, she did not cultivate blessings,

But she did commit plenty of all the ten evil crimes•;

Because I didn't take your advice at that time, my son,

My reward is the vastness of this Avici Hell•.

In the old days, I used to live quite extravagantly,

Surrounded by fine silk draperies and embroidered screens;

How shall I be able to endure these hellish torments,

And then to become a hungry ghost for a thousand years?

A thousand times, they pluck the tongue from out of my mouth,

Hundreds of passes are made over my chest with a steel plough;

My bones, joints, tendons, and skin are everywhere broken,

They need not trouble with knives and swords since I fall to pieces by myself.

In the twinkling of an eye, I die a thousand deaths,

But, each time, they shout at me and I come back to life;

Those who enter this hell all suffer the same hardships.

It doesn't matter whether you are rich or poor, lord or servant.

Though you diligently sacrificed to me while you were at home,

It only got you a reputation in the village for being filial;

Granted that you did sprinkle libations of wine upon my grave,

But it would have been better for you to copy a single line of sutra."

• **Pan An** A well-known attractive man.

• **ten evil crimes** The ten worst offenses according to Buddhist teachings.
• **Avici Hell** The lowest Buddhist hell, for those who had committed the worst offences.

dynasty governance continued many Han dynasty innovations, particularly respect for Confucian ideals coupled with Legalist punishments and regulations.

The *Tang Code* also laid out the **equal-field system,** which was the basis of the Tang dynasty tax system. The Tang state adopted the system, named for an ideal agricultural society in the Chinese classics, from a regional dynasty that had ruled in the north during the Six Dynasties period. Under the provisions of the equal-field system, the government conducted a census of all inhabitants and drew up registers listing each household and its members every three years. Dividing households into nine ranks on the basis of wealth, it allocated to each householder a certain amount of land—some for temporary use and some for permanent use. It also fixed the tax obligations of each individual. Historians disagree about whether the equal-field system took effect throughout all of the empire, but they concur that Tang dynasty officials had an unprecedented degree of control over their sixty million subjects.

Emperor Taizong made Confucianism the basis of the educational system. As in the Han dynasty, most officials continued to be appointed on the basis of another official's recommendation, but the Tang recruited some 5 percent of officials by testing their knowledge of the Confucian classics in a written examination. This policy set an important precedent: it reserved the highest posts in the government for those who had passed the exams. Taizong combined the chakravartin ideal with Confucian policies to create a new model of rulership for East Asia.

One Tang emperor extended the chakravartin ideal to specific government measures: **Emperor Wu** (r. 685–705), the only woman to rule China as emperor in her own right. Many English-language books incorrectly refer to her as Empress Wu, even though she called herself emperor and founded a new dynasty, the Zhou, that supplanted the Tang from 690 to 705. Originally the wife of the emperor, she engineered the imperial succession so that she could serve first as regent to a boy emperor and then as emperor herself.

The chakravartin ideal appealed to Emperor Wu because an obscure Buddhist text, *The Great Cloud Sutra,* prophesied that a kingdom ruled by a woman would be transformed into a Buddhist paradise. (The word *sutra* means the words of the Buddha recorded in written form.) Emperor Wu ordered the construction of Buddhist monasteries in each part of China so that *The Great Cloud Sutra* could be read aloud. She issued edicts forbidding the slaughter of animals or the eating of fish, both violations of Greater Vehicle teachings, and in 693 she officially proclaimed herself a chakravartin ruler. In 705 she was overthrown in a palace coup, and the Tang dynasty was restored. Although today we often focus on Emperor Wu's gender, contemporary documents and portrayals do not indicate that she was particularly aware of being female. Like the female pharaoh Hatshepsut (see Chapter 2), Emperor Wu portrayed herself as a legitimate dynastic ruler.

• **equal-field system**
The basis of the Tang dynasty tax system as prescribed in the *Tang Code*. Dividing households into nine ranks on the basis of wealth, officials allocated each householder a certain amount of land.

• **Emperor Wu** (r. 685–705) The sole woman to rule China as emperor in her own right; she called herself emperor and founded a new dynasty, the Zhou (690–705), that replaced the Tang dynasty.

The Long Decline of the Tang Dynasty, 755–907

Historians today divide the Tang dynasty into two halves: 618–755 and 755–907. In the first half, the Tang emperors ruled with great success. They enjoyed extensive military victories in Central Asia, unprecedented control over their subjects through the equal-field system, and great internal stability. The first signs of decline came in the early 700s, when tax officials reported insufficient revenues from the equal-field system. In 751, the Tang sent an army deep into Central Asia to Talas (modern-day Dzhambul, Kazakhstan) to fight an army sent by the Abbasid caliph, ruler of much of the Islamic world (see Chapter 9). The Tang army lost the battle, marking the end of Tang expansion into Central Asia.

The defeat drew little notice in the capital, where all officials were transfixed by the conflict between the emperor and his leading general, who was rumored to be having an affair with the emperor's favorite consort, a court beauty named Precious Consort Yang. In 755 General An Lushan led a mutiny of the army against the emperor. The Tang dynasty suppressed the rebellion in 763, but it never regained full control of the provinces. The equal-field system collapsed, and the dynasty was forced to institute new taxes that produced much less revenue.

In 841, a new emperor, Emperor Huichang, came to the throne. Thinking that he would increase revenues if he could collect taxes from the 300,000 tax-exempt monks and nuns, in 845 he ordered the closure of almost all Buddhist monasteries except for a few large monasteries in major cities. Although severe, Huichang's decrees had few lasting effects. Since the central government controlled little territory outside the capital, the ban was not carried out in the provinces. When a new emperor took the throne two years later, in 847, he rescinded the ban and rebuilt the damaged monasteries.

The eighth and ninth centuries saw the discovery by faithful Buddhists of a new technology that altered the course of world history. Ever since the founding of the religion, Buddhists had encouraged their followers to propagate Buddhist teachings, usually by memorizing a text or paying someone else to recite it. In China, devout Buddhists paid monks to copy texts to generate merit for themselves and their families. Sometime in the eighth century, believers realized that they could make multiple copies of a prayer or picture of a deity if they used **woodblock printing.** The carver made an image in reverse on a block of wood and then pressed the block onto sheets of paper.

At first Buddhists printed multiple copies of single sheets; later they used glue to connect the pages into a long book. The world's earliest surviving printed book, from 868, is a Buddhist text, *The Diamond Sutra*. During the Tang dynasty, almost all printing was religious, but later the Chinese realized that they could use the same technique for nonreligious books as well.

After 755, no Tang emperor managed to solve the problem of dwindling revenues. In 907, when a rebel deposed the last Tang emperor, who had been held prisoner since 885, China broke apart into different regional dynasties and was not reunited until 960 (see Chapter 12).

■ **Woodblock Printing**   This single sheet of paper is slightly larger than a standard sheet of computer paper. With a drawing of a bodhisattva above and the words of prayers below, it demonstrates how believers used woodblock printing to spread Buddhist teachings. The new medium reproduced line drawings and Chinese characters equally well, and printers could make as many copies as they liked simply by inking the woodblock and pressing individual sheets of paper on it. The more copies they made, they believed, the more merit they earned.   (© The Trustees of the British Museum)

● **woodblock printing**   Printing technique developed by the Chinese in which printers made an image in reverse on a block of wood and then pressed the block onto sheets of paper. An efficient way to print texts in Chinese characters.

The Tang dynasty governed by combining support for Buddhist clergy and monasteries with strong armies, clear laws, and civil service examinations. In so doing, it established a high standard of rulership for all subsequent Chinese dynasties and all rulers of neighboring kingdoms.

The Tibetan Empire, ca. 617–ca. 842

The rulers of the Tibetan plateau were among the first to adopt the Tang model of governance. Most of the Tibetan plateau lies within today's People's Republic of China, but historically it was a borderland not always under Chinese control. Located between the Kunlun Mountains to the north and the Himalayan Mountains to the south, the Tibetan plateau is high, ranging between 13,000 and 15,000 feet (4,000 and 5,000 m), and contains extensive grasslands suitable for raising horses and some river valleys where barley can be grown. The inhabitants used knotted cords and tallies to keep records, Chinese sources report, because they had no writing system.

Sometime between 620 and 650, during the early years of the Tang, a ruler named Songtsen Gampo (ca. 617–649/650) unified Tibet for the first time and founded the Yarlung dynasty (ca. 617–ca. 842), named for the valley to the southeast of Lhasa. Hoping to build a strong state, he looked to both India and China for models of governance. In 632, an official he had sent to India to study Buddhism returned and introduced a new alphabet, based on Sanskrit, for writing Tibetan.

Songtsen Gampo learned that the Tang emperor had provided Chinese brides for the leaders of several peoples living in western China and demanded that he be given a Chinese bride as well. At first Emperor Taizong refused, but when a Tibetan army nearly defeated the Tang forces in Sichuan, he sent a bride in 641. Later sources credit this woman, the princess of Wencheng (ONE-chuhng) (d. 684), with introducing Buddhism and call her a bodhisattva because of her compassion for Tibetans.

Songtsen Gampo saw China as more than a source of Buddhist teachings. He requested that the Tang court send men to his court who could read and write, and he dispatched members of his family to Chang'an to study Chinese. He also asked the Chinese to send craftsmen to teach Tibetans how to make silk and paper and how to brew wine. He was the first to record traditional laws on Chinese paper with ink.

The Tibetans took advantage of Tang weakness during the An Lushan rebellion and briefly invaded the capital of Chang'an in 763 before retreating. They conquered territory in western China, in modern-day Xinjiang (SHIN-jyahng) and Gansu provinces, which they ruled for nearly a century until 842, when the confederation of peoples who had supported the Yarlung dynasty suddenly broke apart. The Tibetan experience demonstrates the utility of the Sui/Tang model of governance for a people in the early stages of state formation, and subsequent Tibetan dynasties periodically returned to it.

● State, Society, and Religion in Korea and Japan, to 1000

Because of the Han dynasty military garrisons stationed in Korea, Koreans had some contact with China as early as the Qin and Han dynasties (see Chapter 4), while their neighbors to the east in Japan, who were surrounded by water, did not (see Map 8.2).

In Korea and Japan, as in Tibet, rulers introduced Buddhism to their subjects because they hoped to match the accomplishments, particularly the military success, of the Tang dynasty. By the year 1000, both Korea and Japan had joined a larger East Asian cultural sphere in which people read and wrote Chinese characters, studied Confucian teachings in school, emulated the political institutions of the Tang, and even ate with chopsticks.

Buddhism and Regional Kingdoms in Korea, to 1000

The northern part of the Korean peninsula, around modern-day Pyongyang, North Korea, was easily accessible to Chinese armies and had come under Han dynasty rule in 108 B.C.E. It remained under Chinese dominance until 313 C.E., when the king of the northern Koguryo (KOH-guh-ree-oh) region overthrew the last Chinese ruler. Because the Chinese presence had been limited to military garrisons, there was little lasting influence.

During this time, Korea was divided into different small chiefdoms on the verge of becoming states. The three most important ones were Koguryo (traditionally 37 B.C.E.–668 C.E.), Paekche (traditionally 18 B.C.E.–660 C.E.), and Silla (traditionally 57 B.C.E.–935 C.E.). Historians call these dates "traditional" because they are based on much later legends, not contemporary evidence. Constantly vying with each other for territory and influence, the three kingdoms adopted Buddhism at different times but for the same reason: their rulers hoped to strengthen their dynasties.

Before the adoption of Buddhism, the residents of the Korean peninsula prayed to local deities or nature spirits for good health and good harvests. The vast majority lived in small agricultural villages and grew rice. Most Koreans, particularly the people in the north, had contact with Chinese, from whom they learned about Buddhism. In the 370s and 380s, the ruling families of the Koguryo and Paekche (PECK-jeh) kingdoms adopted Buddhism to strengthen their kingdoms. Believing that Buddhist rituals could bring this-worldly benefits, particularly if performed by trained religious specialists, they welcomed Buddhist missionaries from China, who brought statues of the Buddha and Chinese-language sutras to their kingdoms.

Like Chinese rulers, the Koguryo and Paekche kings combined patronage for Buddhism with support for Confucian education. Koreans used Chinese

🌐 MAP 8.2

Korea and Japan, ca. 550 The Japanese island of Kyushu lies some 150 miles (240 km) from the Korean peninsula, and the island of Tsushima provided a convenient stepping stone to the Japanese archipelago for those fleeing the warfare on the Korean peninsula. The Korean migrants introduced their social structure, with its bone-rank system, and Buddhism to Japan.

CL Interactive Map

characters as their writing system but not always easily, since Chinese word order differed from that of Korean. Accordingly, the Koguryo and Paekche kings established Confucian academies where students could study Chinese characters, Confucian classics, the histories, and different philosophical works in Chinese.

The circumstances accompanying the adoption of Buddhism by the **Silla** (SHE-luh) royal house illustrate how divided many Koreans were about the new religion. King Pophung (r. 514–540), whose name means "King who promoted the Dharma," wanted to patronize Buddhism but feared the opposition of powerful families who had passed laws against it. Sometime between 527 and 529, he persuaded one of his courtiers to build a shrine to the Buddha. However, since such activity was banned, the king had no choice but to order the courtier's beheading. The king and his subject prayed for a miracle. An early history of Korea describes the moment of execution: "Down came the sword on the monk's neck, and up flew his head spouting blood as white as milk." The miracle, we are told, silenced the opposition, and Silla became Buddhist.

By the middle of the sixth century, all three Korean kingdoms had adopted pro-Buddhist policies, and all sent government officials and monks to different regional kingdoms within China. When the delegations returned, they taught their countrymen what they had learned. With the support of the royal family, Buddhist monasteries were built in major cities and in the countryside, but ordinary people continued to worship the same local deities they had in pre-Buddhist times.

The Sui dynasty reunification of China in 589 had repercussions on the Korean peninsula. In 598, the Koguryo king attacked the Sui, and the Sui retaliated by trying to invade but failed because of bad weather and the strength of the Koguryo armies. In 612, in a second attempted invasion, 300,000 Sui dynasty soldiers attacked the Koguryo capital, but only 2,700 Chinese are reported to have survived the defeat. The Sui attacked three more times, each time unsuccessfully, until the Sui dynasty was fatally weakened and fell to the Tang dynasty in 618. Chinese armies did not return to the Korean peninsula again until the 640s, when Emperor Taizong led several attacks against Koguryo. All were defeated. As a result,

● **Silla** Korean kingdom that adopted Buddhism and united with the Tang dynasty in 660 to defeat the Koguryo and Paekche kingdoms, unifying Korea for the first time in 668.

 Miniature Buddhist Pagodas, Korea During the ninth century, Buddhist believers in the Silla kingdom placed this set of ninety-nine tiny clay pagodas inside a stone pagoda. Each pagoda stands 3 inches (7.5 cm) tall and contains a small hole at the base for a small woodblock-printed prayer. Rulers throughout East Asia sponsored similar projects in the hope of generating merit. (Japan Society Catalog, May 2003, *Transmitting the Forms of Divinity*, Gyeongu National Museum)

in the middle of the seventh century, the same three kingdoms—Paekche, Koguryo, and Silla—still ruled a divided Korea.

The Silla kingdom cultivated ties with the Tang dynasty in hopes of defeating the Paekche and Koguryo kingdoms. One of the most influential monks in Silla was Chajang (active 635–650), who studied Buddhism for seven years at the Chinese pilgrimage center of Mount Wutai in Shanxi province from 636 to 643. When he returned to Silla, the king named him to the highest religious post in the government, in charge of overseeing all the monks in the kingdom.

In 660, the Silla kingdom allied with the Tang. The combined Silla-Tang forces defeated first the Paekche and then, in 668, the Koguryo dynasty. The Silla ruler paid lip service to Tang sovereignty by accepting the inferior status of a tributary that sent annual gifts to the Tang emperor, but by 675 the Silla forces had pushed Tang armies back to the northern edges of the Korean peninsula, and the Silla king ruled a united Korea largely on his own.

Silla's rule ushered in a period of stability that lasted for two and a half centuries. Silla kings offered different types of support to Buddhism. Several Silla rulers followed the example of Ashoka and the Sui founder in building pagodas throughout their kingdom. One Chinese Buddhist text that entered Korea offered Buddhist devotees merit if they commissioned sets of identical pagodas that contained small woodblock-printed texts, usually Buddhist charms. A gift of ninety-nine miniature pagodas with texts inside, the text promised, was the spiritual equivalent of building ninety-nine thousand life-size pagodas (see the photo on the facing page). The Koreans adopted the brand-new Chinese innovation of woodblock printing as part of their efforts to learn from China.

The Silla rulers adopted some measures of Tang rule, such as Confucian academies and extensive support for Buddhism, but not the equal-field system or the Confucian examination system, which were not suited to the stratified Korean society of the seventh and eighth centuries. Aristocratic families were quite separate from ordinary peasant families. The **bone-rank system** classed all Korean families into seven different categories. The true-bone classification was reserved for the highest-born aristocratic families, those eligible to be king. Below them were six other ranks in descending order. No one in the true-bone classification could marry anyone outside that group, and the only way to lose true-bone status was to be found guilty of a crime.

The Silla rulers found that they could govern better if they granted entire villages to members of the true-bone families. In turn, these families appointed government officials and paid their salaries. The rigid stratification of the bone-rank system prevented the Silla rulers from attempting to implement civil service examinations.

The Silla kingdom entered a period of decline after 780 with the death of the first Silla king to be assassinated while in office. From that time on, different branches of the royal family fought each other for control of the throne, yet no one managed to rule for long.

● bone-rank system
Korean social ranking system used by the Silla dynasty that divided Korean families into seven different categories, with the "true-bone" rank reserved for the highest-born families.

The Emergence of Japan

Japan is an island chain of four large islands and many smaller ones. Originally connected by a land bridge to the Asian mainland, it was cut off about 15,000 years ago. Like Korea, Japan had no indigenous writing system, so archaeologists must piece together the island's early history from archaeological materials and later sources like the

Chronicle of Japan (*Nihon shoki*) (knee-HOHN SHOW-kee), a year-by-year account written in 720. The royal Yamato (YAH-mah-toe) house, this book claims, was directly descended from the sun-goddess Amaterasu (AH-mah-TAY-rah-soo). The indigenous religion of Japan, called Shinto (SHIN-toe), included the worship of different spirits of trees, streams, and mountains, as well as rulers. Because people believed that the spirit of a deceased chieftain might threaten the living, they buried their chieftains with goods used in daily life and distinctive clay figurines, called haniwa (HAH-knee-wah), a modern term meaning "clay rings."

In the fifth and sixth centuries, many Koreans fled the political instability of the disunited peninsula to settle in the relative peace of Japan only 150 miles (240 km) away. These Korean refugees significantly influenced the inhabitants of the islands. The Yamato kings gave titles modeled on the Korean bone-rank system to powerful Japanese clans. They had the most sustained contact with the Paekche kingdom because the two states had been allied against the Silla kingdom, which was geographically closest and the most threatening to Japan.

Once the Paekche royal house adopted Buddhism, it began to pressure its clients, the Yamato clan, to follow suit. In 538, the Paekche ambassador brought a gift of Buddhist texts and images for the ruler of Japan, but the most powerful Japanese families hesitated to support the new religion. The conflict among supporters and opponents of Buddhism lasted for nearly fifty years, during which the Paekche rulers continued to send the Japanese gifts of Buddhist writings, monks, and nuns.

Two miracles played a key role in persuading the Japanese to adopt Buddhism. The first occurred in 584, when Soga no Umako, the leader of the powerful **Soga family,** which had provided the Yamato clan with many wives, saw a small fragment of bone believed to be from the original Buddha's body. Skeptical of the relic's authenticity, he tried to pulverize it, but his hammer broke, and when he threw the relic into water, it floated up or down on command. As a result, Soga no Umako became an enthusiastic supporter of Buddhism. This miracle tale illustrates the early stages of state formation as the Soga family tried to unify the region through Buddhism. Three years later, in 587, the 13-year-old Soga prince Shotoku (574–622) went into battle against the powerful families opposed to Buddhism. Prince Shotoku vowed that, if the Soga clan won the battle, their government would support Buddhism, an indication of how the new religion helped the Soga family to consolidate its hold on power. The pro-Buddhist forces won.

Because Prince Shotoku was too young to be king, his mother, Queen Suiko (r. 592–628), was named regent, and Soga no Umako became the chief minister. Throughout Queen Suiko's regency, the Japanese court depended on Korean monks to learn about Buddhism. Only in the 630s were there enough knowledgeable Japanese monks at court to conduct Buddhist rituals correctly without Korean guidance.

Queen Suiko's reign coincided with the Sui dynasty and the founding of the Tang, but Chinese forces never threatened Japan as they had Korea. Japan embarked on an ambitious program to learn from China. Between 600 and 614, it sent four missions to China, and then a further fifteen during the Tang dynasty. A large mission could have as many as five hundred participants, including officials, Buddhist monks, students, and translators. Some Japanese stayed in China for as many as thirty years.

In 645, the Fujiwara clan overthrew the Soga family, and the Yamato clan remained the titular rulers of Japan. The Fujiwara continued to introduce Chinese institutions, particularly those laid out in the *Tang Code* like the equal-field

• **Soga family**
Powerful Japanese family that ruled in conjunction with the Yamato clan from 587 to 645; introduced Buddhism to Japan.

Ⓒ **Primary Source:**
Chronicles of Japan
These guidelines for imperial officials show how the Soga clan welcomed Chinese influence in an attempt to increase the authority of the Japanese imperial family.

system. However, they modified the original Chinese rules so that members of powerful families received more land than they would have in China. It is not clear whether the Japanese state was actually able to implement the redistribution of land every three years.

The Fujiwara rulers sponsored Buddhist ceremonies on behalf of the state and the royal family at state-financed monasteries. Like the Chinese, they established a head monastery at their capital with branch temples elsewhere. The Fujiwara clan built their first Chinese-style capital at Fujiwara and the second at Nara in 710, which marked the beginning of the Nara period (710–794). Both were modeled on the gridded street plan of Chang'an. In 794, the start of the Heian (HEY-on) period (794–1185), the Fujiwara shifted their capital to Kyoto, where it remained for nearly one thousand years (see Figure 8.1 on page 225).

Gradually the Fujiwara lessened their efforts to learn from the Chinese. The final official delegation went to China in 838. Some Chinese-style reforms lasted longer than others: for example, educated Japanese continued to study Buddhist and Confucian texts written in Chinese characters. Because Japanese, like Korean, was in a different language family from Chinese, characters did not capture the full meaning of Japanese. In the ninth century, the Japanese developed an alphabet, called kana (KAH-nah), that allowed them to write Japanese words as they were pronounced.

A Japanese woman named Murasaki Shikibu (MOO-rah-sock-ee SHE-key-boo) used only kana to write one of the world's most important works of literature, *The Tale of Genji,* in 1000. Some have called it the world's first novel. The book relates the experiences of a young prince as he grows up in the court. Lady Murasaki spent her entire life at court, and her novel reflects the complex system of etiquette that had developed among the Japanese aristocracy. For example, lovers choose sheets of paper from multiple shades, each with its own significance, before writing notes to each other. While the highest members of Japan's aristocracy could read and write—men using both Chinese characters and kana and women more often only kana—the vast majority of their countrymen remained illiterate.

By 1000, Japan had become part of the East Asian cultural realm. Although its rulers were predominantly Buddhist, they supported Confucian education and used the *Tang Code* as a model of governance. The Fujiwara family modified some Chinese institutions, like the equal-field system, to better suit Japanese society.

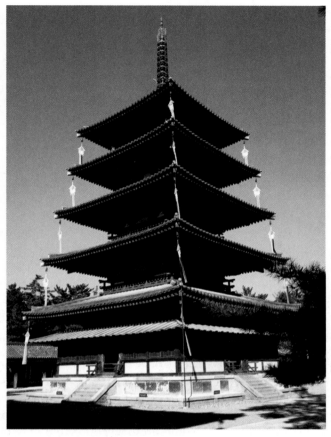

Horyuji Pagoda, Nara, Japan   Built before 794, this five-story pagoda is possibly one of the oldest wooden buildings in the world. Like the stupa at the Indian site of Sanchi, it was built to hold relics of the Buddha. Not certain how the building survived multiple earthquakes without sustaining any damage, architects speculate that the central pillar is not directly connected to the ground below, allowing it to float slightly above the ground.   (Christopher Rennie/Robert Harding Picture Library Ltd./Alamy)

Chapter Review

KEY TERMS

Xuanzang (208)

chakravartin (210)

Silk Routes (210)

Hinduism (211)

bodhisattva (212)

Gupta dynasty (213)

bhakti (214)

Angkor dynasty (219)

Fotudeng (223)

Tang dynasty (224)

equal-field system (228)

Emperor Wu (228)

woodblock printing (229)

Silla (232)

bone-rank system (233)

Soga family (234)

 Download the MP3 audio file of the Chapter Review and listen to it on the go.

India gave two models of royal governance to the world. Ashoka pioneered the Buddhist chakravartin ideal in the third century B.C.E., and the Kushan and Gupta dynasties developed it further. When Xuanzang visited India, he witnessed the decline of this model and the appearance of a new model in which kings patronized Brahmin priests and Hindu temples. Although it died out in India, the chakravartin model traveled to China, where the Sui and Tang rulers added new elements: the equal-field system, civil service examinations, and a legal code. Tibetan, Korean, and Japanese rulers all adopted variations of the Tang model, with the result that, by 1000, East Asia had become a culturally unified region in which rulers patronized Buddhism, which coexisted with local religious beliefs, and subjects studied both Confucian and Buddhist teachings. In South Asia and Southeast Asia, on the other hand, rulers worshiped Hindu deities and supported Sanskrit learning.

How did Buddhism change after the year 100? How did Hinduism displace it within India?

Greater Vehicle teachings, which gradually replaced earlier Theravada teachings, emphasized that everyone—not just monks and nuns—could attain nirvana. They could do so with the help of bodhisattvas who chose not to attain enlightenment themselves but to help all other beings. Indian rulers like Kanishka of the Kushan dynasty supported Buddhism with gifts to monasteries, but between 320 and 500 Gupta rulers pioneered a new type of gift: land grants to Brahmin priests and to Hindu temples. Over time, as more rulers chose to endow temples to Vishnu and Shiva, support for Hinduism increased, and Buddhism declined.

How did geography, trade, and religion shape the development of states and societies in Southeast Asia?

The timing of the monsoon winds meant that all boats traveling between India and China had to stop in Southeast Asia for several months before they could resume their journeys. The rulers of coastal ports such as Funan and Srivijaya taxed the trade brought by these boats and used the revenues to construct Buddhist centers of worship. At the same time, different local rulers—some along the sea route between India and China, some in the forested interior—patronized purohita and built monuments to Buddhist and Hindu deities, all in the hope of strengthening their states as they were taking shape.

How did the Sui and Tang dynasties modify the Qin/Han blueprint for empire?

The emperors of both the Sui and Tang dynasties took over the Qin/Han blueprint for empire with its Legalist and Confucian elements and governed as chakravartin rulers who patronized Buddhism. The Sui founder designed the gridded street plan of his capital at Chang'an, which the Tang retained. Emperor Taizong of the Tang, who welcomed Xuanzang back from India, promulgated the *Tang Code,* which established the equal-field system throughout the empire. In addition, the Tang emperors used the civil service examinations to recruit the highest-ranking 5 percent of officials in the bureaucracy.

 Which elements of the revised Chinese blueprint for empire did Korea and Japan borrow intact? Which did they modify?

Korean and Japanese rulers patronized Buddhism and supported the introduction of Chinese characters and education in the Confucian classics. The Silla rulers tried to introduce civil service examinations and the equal-field system but had no success in the hierarchical bone-rank society of Korea. Similarly, the Fujiwara clan had to modify the equal-field system to suit Japan's aristocratic society. The Fujiwara clan modeled all three of their capitals—at Fujiwara, Nara, and Kyoto—on the gridded street plan of Chang'an.

 WEB RESOURCES

Pronunciation Guide

Interactive Maps

MAP 8.1 The Spread of Buddhism and Hinduism to Southeast Asia

MAP 8.2 Korea and Japan, ca. 550

Primary Sources

Chapter Objectives

ACE Multiple-Choice Quiz

Flashcards

FOR FURTHER REFERENCE

Ebrey, Patricia Buckley, Anne Walthall, and James B. Palais. *East Asia: A Cultural, Social, and Political History.* 2d ed. Boston: Wadsworth/Cengage Learning, 2009.

Hansen, Valerie. *The Open Empire: A History of China to 1600.* New York: Norton, 2000.

Holcombe, Charles. *The Genesis of East Asia, 221 B.C.–A.D. 907.* Honolulu: Association of Asian Studies and the University of Hawai'i Press, 2001.

Kapstein, Matthew. *The Tibetan Assimilation of Buddhism: Conversion, Contestation, and Memory.* New York: Oxford University Press, 2000.

Keown, Damien. *Buddhism: A Very Short Introduction.* New York: Oxford University Press, 1996.

Mair, Victor H. *Tun-huang Popular Narratives.* New York: Cambridge University Press, 1983.

Ray, Himanshu Prabha. "The Axial Age in Asia: The Archaeology of Buddhism (500 BC to AD 500)." In *Archaeology of Asia,* ed. Miriam T. Stark. Malden, Mass.: Blackwell, 2006, pp. 303–323.

Tarling, Nicholas, ed. *The Cambridge History of Southeast Asia.* Vol. I, *From Early Times to c. 1500.* New York: Cambridge University Press, 1992.

Thapar, Romila. *Early India from the Origins to AD 1300.* Berkeley: University of California Press, 2003.

Washizuka, Hiromitsu, et al. *Transmitting the Forms of Divinity: Early Buddhist Art from Korea and Japan.* New York: Japan Society, 2003.

Wolters, O. W. *History, Culture, and Region in Southeast Asian Perspectives.* Singapore: Institute of Southeast Asian Studies, 1982.

Wriggins, Sally Hovey. *Xuanzang: A Buddhist Pilgrim on the Silk Road.* Boulder: Westview Press, 1996.

Websites

Borobudur (http://rubens.anu.edu.au/htdocs/bycountry/ indonesia/borobudur/).   Information on the Borobudur monument in Java, Indonesia.

The Buddha and His Dhamma (http://www.columbia.edu/itc/mealac/pritchett/ 00ambedkar/ambedkar_buddha/).   B. R. Ambedkar's explanation of the Buddha's teachings.

Silk Road Narratives: A Collection of Historical Texts (http://depts.washington.edu/silkroad/texts/texts .html).   A valuable collection of primary sources in translation about the Silk Road, including Xuanzang's *Record of the Western Regions,* which describes the different countries he visited.

Islamic Empires of Western Asia and Africa, 600–1258

K**haizuran** (ca. 739–789) grew up as a slave girl but became the favored wife of the supreme religious and political leader of the Islamic world, the caliph Mahdi (MAH-dee), who reigned from 775 to 785 as the third ruler of the Abbasid (ah-BAHS-sid) caliphate (750–1258). As the wife of Mahdi and the mother of the caliph who succeeded him, Khaizuran (HAY-zuhr-ahn) played an active role in court politics. A slave dealer brought her, while still a teenager, to Mecca, where she met Mahdi's father. He had come to perform the hajj pilgrimage that is the religious obligation of all Muslims. In reply to his asking where she was from, she said:

ABBASID SINGING GIRL

(Los Angeles County Museum of Art, The Nasil M. Heeramaneck Collection, gift of Joan Palefsky. Photograph © 2007 Museum Associates/LACMA)

Born at Mecca and brought up at Jurash (in the Yaman)."[1]

Of course we would like to know more, but she has left no writings of her own. The written record almost always says more about men than about women, and more about the prominent and the literate than about the ordinary and the illiterate. To understand the experience of everyone in a society, historians must exercise great ingenuity in using the evidence at hand. Khaizuran provides a rare opportunity to study the life of an ordinary Muslim woman who rose to become a leader in her own right.

In its support for Islam, the Abbasid dynasty (see page 250) played a role in world history similar to that of the Roman Empire, which patronized Christianity (see Chapter 7), and the Tang dynasty in China, which supported Buddhism (see Chapter 8). Under the Abbasids, Islam was a world religion with millions of

 This icon will direct you to interactive activities and study materials on the *Voyages* website:
www.cengage.com/history/hansen/voyages1e

238

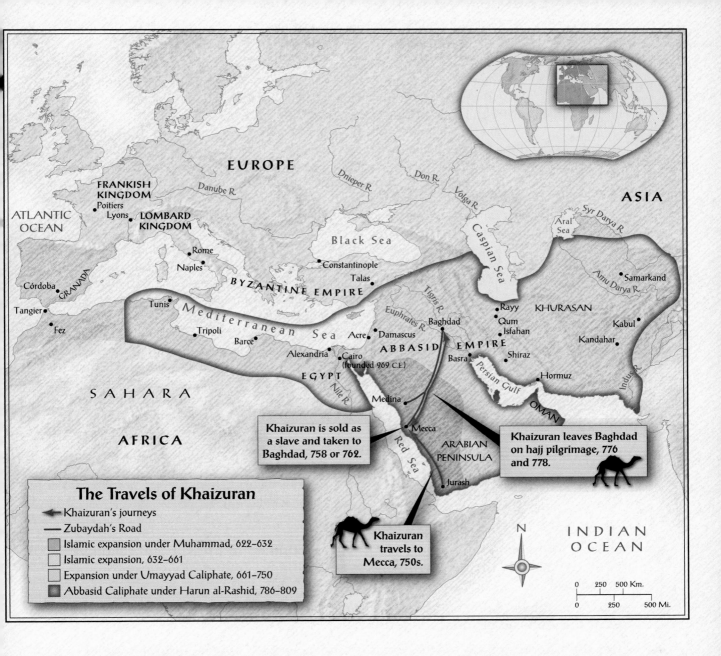

The Travels of Khaizuran

Khaizuran is sold as a slave and taken to Baghdad, 758 or 762.

Khaizuran leaves Baghdad on hajj pilgrimage, 776 and 778.

Khaizuran travels to Mecca, 750s.

← Khaizuran's journeys
— Zubaydah's Road
Islamic expansion under Muhammad, 622–632
Islamic expansion, 632–661
Expansion under Umayyad Caliphate, 661–750
Abbasid Caliphate under Harun al-Rashid, 786–809

EUROPE

FRANKISH KINGDOM
Poitiers
Lyons
LOMBARD KINGDOM
Rome
Naples
Córdoba
GRANADA
Tangier
Fez
Tunis
Tripoli
Barce
ATLANTIC OCEAN
Danube R.
Dnieper R.
Don R.
Black Sea
Constantinople
Talas
BYZANTINE EMPIRE
Mediterranean Sea
Acre
Damascus
Alexandria
Cairo (founded 969 C.E.)
EGYPT
Nile R.
SAHARA
AFRICA
Medina
Red Sea
Mecca
Jurash
ARABIAN PENINSULA
Caspian Sea
Volga R.
Aral Sea
Syr Darya R.
ASIA
Amu Darya R.
Samarkand
KHURASAN
Tigris R.
Euphrates R.
Baghdad
Rayy
Qum
Isfahan
Kabul
Kandahar
ABBASID EMPIRE
Basra
Shiraz
Persian Gulf
Hormuz
OMAN
Indus R.
N
INDIAN OCEAN

0 250 500 Km.
0 250 500 Mi.

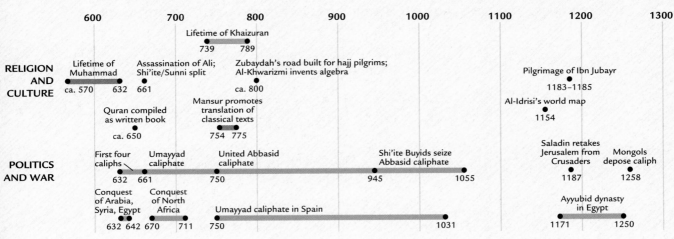

	600	700	800	900	1000	1100	1200	1300

Lifetime of Khaizuran
739 789

RELIGION AND CULTURE

Lifetime of Muhammad
ca. 570   632

Assassination of Ali; Shi'ite/Sunni split
661

Zubaydah's road built for hajj pilgrims; Al-Khwarizmi invents algebra
ca. 800

Pilgrimage of Ibn Jubayr
1183–1185

Al-Idrisi's world map
1154

Quran compiled as written book
ca. 650

Mansur promotes translation of classical texts
754 775

POLITICS AND WAR

First four caliphs
632 661

Umayyad caliphate
661

United Abbasid caliphate
750

Shi'ite Buyids seize Abbasid caliphate
945   1055

Saladin retakes Jerusalem from Crusaders
1187

Mongols depose caliph
1258

Conquest of Arabia, Syria, Egypt
632 642

Conquest of North Africa
670 711

Umayyad caliphate in Spain
750   1031

Ayyubid dynasty in Egypt
1171   1250

• **Khaizuran** Slave girl (ca. 739–789) who became the wife of the caliph Mahdi (r. 775–785), the third ruler of the Abbasid caliphate. Khaizuran played an active role in court politics.

adherents in Africa, Europe, and Asia. At the peak of their power, around the year 800, the Abbasids governed over thirty-five or forty million people living in North Africa and Southwest Asia.[2]

But the Abbasid Empire differed in a crucial way from either the Roman or the Tang Empire. When the Roman emperor Constantine issued the Edict of Milan in 313 (see Chapter 7), he recognized a religion already popular among his subjects. And when the early Tang emperors supported Buddhism, they did so because many Chinese had come to embrace Buddhism since its entry into China in the first century C.E. Yet the Roman and Tang emperors could withdraw their support for these religions, and they sometimes did.

• **Muhammad** (ca. 570–632) Believed by Muslims to be the last prophet who received God's revelations directly from the angel Gabriel. The first leader of the Muslim community.

In contrast, the Abbasid rulers were religious leaders who claimed a familial relationship with the prophet **Muhammad** (ca. 570–632) through his uncle Abbas (ah-BAHS). They could not withdraw their support from the Islamic religious community because they led that very religious community. At the same time, they were also political leaders; the founder of the Abassid dynasty seized power from the Umayyad (oo-MY-uhd) dynasty in 750. Even when it became no longer possible for the Abbasid caliphs to serve as political leaders, the caliphs retained their religious role. Others could be king, but the Abbasids had a unique claim to being caliph.

This chapter will examine the history of Islam, from the first revelations received by Muhammad to the final collapse of the Abbasid Empire in 1258.

Focus Questions

🐪 Who was the prophet Muhammad, and what were his main teachings?

🐪 Between Muhammad's death in 632 and the founding of the Abbasid caliphate in 750, what were the different ways that the Islamic community chose the new caliph?

🐪 Which economic, political, and social forces held the many peoples and territories of the Abbasid caliphate together?

🐪 After the fragmentation of the Abbasid Empire in 945, which cultural practices, technologies, and customs held Islamic believers in different regions together?

The Origins of Islam and the First Caliphs, 610–750

Muhammad began to preach sometime around 613 and won a large following among the residents of the Arabian peninsula before his death in 632. The man who succeeded to the leadership of the Islamic religious community was called the caliph, literally "successor." The caliph exercised political authority because the Muslim religious community was also a state, complete with its own government and a powerful army that conquered many neighboring regions. The first four caliphs were chosen from different clans on the basis of their ties to Muhammad, but after 661 all the caliphs came from a single clan, or dynasty, the Umayyads, who governed until 750.

The Life and Teachings of Muhammad, ca. 570–632

Muhammad was born into a family of merchants sometime around 570 in Mecca, a trading community in the Arabian peninsula far from any major urban center. At the time of his birth, the two major powers of the Mediterranean world were the Byzantine Empire (see Chapter 10) and the Sasanian Empire of the Persians (see Chapter 6).

On the southern edge of the two empires lay the Arabian peninsula, which consisted largely of desert punctuated by small oases. Traders traveling from Syria to Yemen frequently stopped at the few urban settlements, including Mecca and Medina, near the coast of the Red Sea. The local peoples spoke Arabic, a Semitic language related to Hebrew that was written with an alphabet.

The population was divided between urban residents and the nomadic residents of the desert, called Bedouins (BED-dwins). The Bedouins moved from place to place, tending their flocks of sheep, horses, and camels, and were divided into different clans. Even though they no longer followed a nomadic way of life, many city people maintained a strong clan identity.

All Arabs, whether nomadic or urban, belonged to clans who worshiped protective deities that resided in an individual tree, a group of trees, or sometimes a rock with an unusual shape. One of the most revered objects was a large black rock in a cube-shaped shrine, called the Kaaba (KAH-buh) at Mecca. Above these tribal deities stood a creator deity named Allah (AH-luh). (The Arabic word *allah* means "the god" and, by extension, "God.") When, at certain times of the year, members of different clans gathered to worship individual tribal deities, they pledged to stop all feuding. During these pilgrimages to Mecca, merchants like Muhammad bought and sold their wares. Extensive trade networks connected the Arabian peninsula with Palestine and Syria, and both Jews and Christians lived in its urban centers.

While in his forties and already a wealthy merchant, Muhammad had a series of visions in which he saw a figure. Muslims believe that God spoke to Muhammad through the angel Gabriel, after which Muhammad called on everyone to submit to God. The religion founded on belief in this event is called Islam, meaning "submission" or "surrender." Muslims do not call Muhammad the founder of Islam because God's teachings, they believe, are timeless. Muhammad taught that his predecessors included all the Hebrew prophets from the Hebrew Bible as well as Jesus and his disciples. Muslims consider Muhammad the last messenger of

God, however, and historians place the beginning date for Islam in the 610s because no one thought of himself or herself as Muslim before Muhammad received his revelations. Muhammad's earliest followers came from his immediate family: his wife Khadijah (kah-DEE-juh) and his cousin Ali, whom he had raised since early childhood.

Unlike the existing religion of Arabia, but like Christianity and Judaism, Islam was monotheistic; Muhammad preached that his followers should worship only one God. He also stressed the role of individual choice: each person had the power to decide to worship God or to turn away from God. Those who submitted to God became the first Muslims. Men who converted to Islam had to undergo circumcision, a practice already widespread throughout the Arabian peninsula.

Islam developed within the context of Bedouin society, in which men were charged with protecting the honor of their wives and daughters. Accordingly, women often assumed a subordinate role in Islam. In Bedouin society, a man could repudiate his wife by saying "I divorce you" three times. Although women could not repudiate their husbands in the same way, they could divorce an impotent man.

(CL) Primary Source:
The Quran: Muslim Devotion to God
This excerpt articulates the Muslim faith in a heavenly reward for believers and a hellish punishment for unbelievers.

Certificate of Pilgrimage to Mecca Islamic artists often ornamented manuscripts, tiles, and paintings with passages from the Quran. This document, written on paper, testifies that the bearer completed the pilgrimage to Mecca in 1207 and thus fulfilled the Fifth Pillar of Islam. Arabic reads from right to left; the red lines and dots guide the reader's pronunciation. (Turkish and Islamic Art Museum, Istanbul/Alfredo Dagli Orti/The Art Archive)

Although Muhammad recognized the traditional right of men to repudiate their wives, he introduced several measures aimed at improving the status of women. For example, he limited the number of wives a man could take to four. His supporters explained that Islamic marriage offered the secondary wives far more legal protection than if they had simply been the unrecognized mistresses of a married man, as they were before Muhammad's teachings. He also banned the Bedouin practice of female infanticide. Finally, he instructed his female relatives to veil themselves when receiving visitors. Although many in the modern world think the veiling of women an exclusively Islamic practice, women in various societies in the ancient world, including Greeks, Mesopotamians, and Arabs, wore veils as a sign of high station.

Feuding among different clans was a constant problem in Bedouin society. In 620, a group of nonkinsmen from Medina, a city 215 miles (346 km) to the north, pledged to follow Muhammad's teachings in hopes of ending the feuding. Because certain clan leaders of Mecca had become increasingly hostile to Islam, even threatening to kill Muhammad, in 622 Muhammad and his followers moved to Medina. Everyone who submitted to God and accepted Muhammad as his messenger became a member of the umma (UM-muh), the community of Islamic believers.

The Kaaba, Mecca   This photograph, taken in 2006, shows hajj pilgrims circumambulating the cube-shaped shrine of the Kaaba, which means "cube" in Arabic. Muhammad instructed all Muslims who could afford the trip to make the pilgrimage to Mecca. Today some two million pilgrims perform the hajj each year. (Interfoto Pressebildagentur/Alamy)

This migration, called the *hijrah* (HIJ-ruh), marked a major turning point in Islam. All dates in the Islamic calendar are calculated in the year of the hijrah (Anno Hegirae, a Latin term usually abbreviated A.H.). (Because of the differences in the calendars, Islamic years often straddle two Common Era years. For example, 165 A.H. = 781–782 C.E.) The Islamic calendar calculated each year as twelve lunar months of 29.5 days each, with no adjustment for the remaining days (each solar year has 365.25 days). As a result, each day falls at a slightly different time each year. For example, the first day of the month of Ramadan, when Muslims fast during daytime, falls ten or eleven days earlier than it did the previous year.

Muhammad began life as a merchant, became a religious prophet in middle age, and assumed the duties of a general at the end of his life. In 624, Muhammad and his followers fought their first battle against the residents of Mecca. Muhammad said that he had received revelations that holy war, whose object was the expansion of Islam—or its defense—was justified. He used the word **jihad** (GEE-hahd), whose root in Arabic means "striving or effort," to mean struggle or fight in military campaigns against non-Muslims. (In addition to its basic meaning of holy war, modern Muslims use the term in a more spiritual or moral sense to indicate an individual's striving to fulfill all the teachings of Islam.)

In 630, Muhammad's troops conquered Mecca and removed all tribal images from the pilgrimage center at the Kaaba. Muhammad became ruler of the region and exercised his authority by adjudicating among feuding clans. The clans, Muhammad explained, had forgotten that the Kaaba had originally been a shrine to God dedicated by the prophet Abraham (Ibrahim in Arabic) and his son Ishmael. Muslims do not accept the version of Abraham's sacrifice given in the Old Testament, in which the elderly couple, Abraham and Sarah, have a son, Isaac, whom Abraham spares at God's command. In contrast, Muslims believe that Abraham offered God another of his sons: Ishmael, whose mother was the slave woman Hajar (Hagar in Hebrew). The pilgrimage to Mecca, or **hajj** (HAHJ), commemorates that moment when Abraham freed Ishmael and sacrificed a sheep in his place. Later, Muslims believe, Ishmael fathered his own children, the ancestors of the clans of Arabia.

The First Caliphs and the Sunni-Shi'ite Split, 632–661

Muhammad preached his last sermon from Mount Arafat outside Mecca and then died in 632. He left no male heirs, only four daughters, and did not designate a successor, or **caliph** (KAY-lif). Clan leaders consulted with each other and chose Abu Bakr (ah-boo BAHK-uhr) (ca. 573–634), an early convert and the father of Muhammad's second wife, to lead their community. Because Abu Bakr could not receive divine revelations, he had to govern on the basis of what he and his advisers remembered of Muhammad's teachings. Although not a prophet, he held political and religious authority and also led the Islamic armies. Under Abu Bakr's skilled leadership, Islamic troops conquered all of the Arabian peninsula and pushed into present-day Syria and Iraq.

When Abu Bakr died only two years after becoming caliph, the Islamic community again had to determine a successor. This time the umma chose Umar ibn al-Khattab (oo-MAHR ibn al-HAT-tuhb) (586?–644), the father of Muhammad's third wife. Muslims brought their disputes to Umar, as they had to Muhammad. As the number of cases increased, the caliph appointed jurists (*qadi* in Arabic), who listened to the aggrieved parties often after the close of Friday prayers in the Islamic house of worship, or mosque.

CL **Primary Source:**
The Quran: Call for Jihad
Discover what the Quran says about the duty of Muslims to defend themselves from their enemies.

• **jihad** (Arabic root for "striving" or "effort"). A struggle or fight against non-Muslims. In addition to its basic meaning of holy war, modern Muslims use the term in a spiritual or moral sense to indicate an individual's striving to fulfill all the teachings of Islam.

• **hajj** The pilgrimage to Mecca, required of all Muslims who can afford the trip. The pilgrimage commemorates that moment when, just as he was about to sacrifice him, Abraham freed Ishmael and sacrificed a sheep in his place.

• **caliph** Literally "successor." Before 945, the caliph was the successor to Muhammad and the supreme political and religious leader of the Islamic world. After 945, the caliph had no political power but served as the religious leader of all Muslims.

During Muhammad's lifetime, a group of Muslims had committed all of his teachings to memory, and soon after his death they began to compile them as the **Quran** (also spelled Koran), which Muslims believe is the direct word of God as revealed to Muhammad. In addition, early Muslims recorded testimony from Muhammad's friends and associates about his speech and actions. These reports, called **hadith** (HAH-deet) in Arabic, formed an integral part of the Islamic textual tradition, second in importance only to the Quran (kuh-RAHN).

Umar reported witnessing an encounter between Muhammad and the angel Gabriel in which Muhammad listed the primary obligations of each Muslim, which have since come to be known as the **Five Pillars of Islam:** (1) to bear witness to Allah as the sole god and to accept Muhammad as his messenger, (2) to pray five times a day in the direction of Mecca, (3) to pay a fixed share of one's income to the state in support of the poor and needy, (4) to refrain from eating, drinking, and sexual activity during the daytime hours of the month of Ramadan, and, (5) provided one has the necessary resources, to do the hajj pilgrimage to Mecca. (See the feature "Movement of Ideas: The Five Pillars of Islam.")

When Umar died in 644, the umma chose Uthman to succeed him. Unlike earlier caliphs, Uthman was not perceived as impartial. He gave all the top positions to members of his own Umayyad clan, which angered many. In 656, a group of soldiers mutinied and killed Uthman. With their support, Muhammad's cousin Ali, who was also the husband of his daughter Fatima, became the fourth caliph. Ali was unable to reconcile the different feuding groups, and in 661 he was assassinated. Ali's martyrdom became a powerful symbol for all who objected to the reigning caliph's government.

The political division that occurred with Ali's death led to a permanent religious split in the Muslim community. The **Sunnis,** the "people of custom and the community," held that the leader of the Islamic community could be chosen by consensus and that the only legitimate claim to descent was through the male line. In Muhammad's case, his uncles could succeed him, since he left no sons. Although Sunnis accept Ali as one of the four rightly guided caliphs that succeeded Muhammad, they do not believe that Ali and Fatima's children, or their descendants, can become caliph because their claim to descent was through the female line of Fatima.

Opposed to the Sunnis were the "shia" or "party of Ali," usually referred to as **Shi'ites** in English. Shi'ites not only support Ali's claim to succeed Muhammad but also believe that the grandchildren born to Ali and Fatima should lead the community. They denied the legitimacy of the three caliphs before Ali, who were related to Muhammad only by marriage, not by blood.

The breach between Sunnis and Shi'ites became the major fault line within Islam down to the present. (Today, Iran, Iraq, and Bahrain are predominantly Shi'ite, and the rest of the Islamic world is mainly Sunni.) The two groups have frequently come into conflict, not only over the issue of succession but also over other issues, like property rights. For example, Shi'ite Muslims grant direct female kin, such as daughters, preference in inheritance law over more distant male relatives, such as uncles, a direct consequence of their view that descent from Muhammad could be traced through his daughter Fatima.

Early Conquests, 632–661

The early Muslims forged a powerful army that attacked non-Muslim lands, including the now-weak Byzantine and Sasanian Empires, with great success. When the army attacked a

---

● **Quran** The book that Muslims believe is the direct word of God as revealed to Muhammad. Written sometime around 650.

🅒🅛 **Primary Source:**
The Quran
These selections contain a number of the tenets of Islam and shed light on the connections among Islam, Judaism, and Christianity.

● **hadith** Testimony recorded from Muhammad's friends and associates about his speech and actions. Formed an integral part of the Islamic textual tradition, second in importance only to the Quran.

● **Five Pillars of Islam** (1) To bear witness to Allah as the sole god and accept Muhammad as his messenger: (2) to pray five times a day in the direction of Mecca; (3) to pay a fixed share of one's income to the state in support of the poor and needy; (4) to refrain from eating, drinking, and sexual activity during day-time hours in the month of Ramadan; and (5) if feasible, to do the hajj pilgrimage to Mecca.

● **Sunnis** The larger of the two main Islamic groups that formed after Ali's death. Sunnis, meaning the "people of custom and the community," hold that the leader of Islam should be chosen by consensus and that legitimate claims to descent are only through the male line. Sunnis do not believe Ali and Fatima's descendants can become caliph.

The Five Pillars of Islam

One of the most important Islamic texts, the Hadith of Gabriel, is associated with the second caliph, Umar, who described an encounter he had witnessed between the prophet Muhammad and the angel Gabriel. The Hadith of Gabriel summarizes the core beliefs of Islam as they were understood in Muhammad's lifetime. The Five Pillars proved crucial to the expansion of Islam because these concise teachings encapsulated its most important practices. One did not have to learn Arabic or memorize the entire Quran to be a Muslim; nor did one require access to a mosque or to educated teachers. The second passage, from the Islamic geographer al-Bakri writing in 1068, describes how a Muslim teacher persuaded a king in Mali, in West Africa, to convert to Islam. Al-Bakri lived in Spain his entire life and did not himself witness the Mali king's conversion or the rain that followed it. Thus his account may not be entirely factual, but it shows how an educated Muslim scholar believed one ruler's conversion occurred at the edge of the Islamic world. Observe how, according to al-Bakri, the teacher condensed the Five Pillars even further.

Sources: Hadith of Gabriel as translated in Vincent J. Cornell, "Fruit of the Tree of Knowledge: The Relationship Between Faith and Practice in Islam," in *The Oxford History of Islam,* ed. John L. Esposito (New York: Oxford University Press, 1999), pp. 75–76 (brackets removed to enhance readability); al-Bakri's *The Book of Routes and Realms,* as translated in *Corpus of Early Arabic Sources for West African History,* ed. N. Levtzion and J. F. P. Hopkins (New York: Cambridge University Press, 1981), pp. 82–83.

From the Hadith of Gabriel

Umar ibn al-Khattab reported: One day, while we were sitting with the Messenger of God (may God bless and preserve him), there came upon us a man whose clothes were exceedingly white and whose hair was exceedingly black. No dust of travel could be seen upon him, and none of us knew him. He sat down in front of the Prophet (may God bless and preserve him), rested his knees against the Prophet's knees and placed his palms on the Prophet's thighs. "Oh Muhammad, tell me about Islam," he said. The Messenger of God (may God bless and preserve him) replied: "Islam means to bear witness that there is no god but Allah, that Muhammad is the Messenger of Allah, to maintain the required prayers, to pay the poor-tax, to fast in the month of Ramadan, and to perform the pilgrimage to the House of God at Mecca if you are able to do so."

"You are correct," the man said. We were amazed at his questioning of the Prophet and then saying that the Prophet had answered correctly. Then he said, "Tell me about faith." The Prophet said: "It is to believe in Allah, His angels, His books, His messengers, and the Last Day, and to believe in Allah's determination of affairs, whether good comes of it or bad."

"You are correct," he said. "Now tell me about virtue [*ihsan*]." The Prophet said: "It is to worship Allah as if you see Him; for if you do not see Him, surely He sees you." . . . Then the man left. I remained for a while, and the Prophet said to me: "Oh, Umar, do you know who the questioner was?" "Allah and His Messenger know best," I replied. He said: "It was the angel Gabriel, who came to you to teach you your religion."

From al-Bakri's *The Book of Routes and Realms*, about the Malal region (modern-day Mali)

Beyond this country lies another called Malal, the king of which is known as al-musulmani [the Muslim]. He is thus called because his country became afflicted with drought one year following another; the inhabitants prayed for rain, sacrificing cattle till they had exterminated almost all of them, but the drought and the misery only increased. The king had as his guest a Muslim who used to read the Quran and was acquainted with the Sunna [the model of behavior that all Muslims were expected to follow]. To this man the king complained of the calamities that assailed him and his people.

The man said: "O King, if you believed in God (who is exalted) and testified that He is One, and testified as to the prophetic mission of Muhammad (God bless him and give him peace), and if you accepted all the religious laws of Islam, I would pray for your deliverance from your plight and that God's mercy would envelop all the people of your country, and that your enemies and adversaries might envy you on that account."

Thus he continued to press the king until the latter accepted Islam and became a sincere Muslim. The man made him recite from the Quran some easy passages and taught him religious obligations and practices which no man be excused from knowing. Then the Muslim made him wait till the eve of the following Friday, when he ordered him to purify himself by a complete ablution, and clothed him in a cotton garment which he had. The two of them came out towards a mound of earth, and there the Muslim stood praying while the king, standing at this right side, imitated him. Thus they prayed for a part of the night, the Muslim reciting invocations and the king saying "Amen." The dawn had just started to break when God caused abundant rain to descend upon them. So the king ordered the idols to be broken and expelled the sorcerers from his country. He and his descendants after him as well as his nobles were sincerely attached to Islam, while the common people of his kingdom remained polytheists. Since then their rulers have been given the title of al-musulmani [the Muslim].

QUESTIONS FOR ANALYSIS

▶ Which of the Five Pillars marked one's conversion to Islam?

▶ Which, according to the Hadith of Gabriel, was optional?

▶ Which Pillar do you think would have been the most difficult for the king of Mali to observe?

new region, the front ranks of infantry advanced using bows and arrows and crossbows. Their task was to break into the enemy's frontlines so that the mounted cavalry, the backbone of the army, could attack.

In the first stage of conquest, the troops seized all the movable property of the conquered people and reserved a fixed share, called *zakat* (literally "purification," officially set at one-fifth), for the commander. The remaining four-fifths were distributed among the troops and provided a powerful incentive to keep on fighting. The caliph headed the army, which was divided into units of one hundred men and subunits of ten.

Once the Islamic armies pacified a new region, a process that sometimes took generations, the regional governor had to implement a more regular system of taxation. The Muslims levied the same tax rates on conquering and conquered peoples alike, provided that the conquered peoples converted to Islam.

Islam stressed the equality of all believers before God, and all Muslims, whether born to Muslim parents or converts, paid two types of taxes: one on the land, usually fixed at one-tenth of the annual harvest, and the zakat tax, originally set by Muhammad at one-fifth of all plunder. The zakat tax evolved into a property tax with different rates for different possessions. Because the revenue was to be used to help the needy or to serve God, it is often called an "alms-tax" or "poor tax." Exempt from the zakat tax, non-Muslims paid the *jizya* tax, usually set at a higher rate than the taxes paid by Muslims.

Islamic forces conquered city after city and ruled the entire Arabian peninsula by 634. Then they crossed overland to Egypt from the Sinai Peninsula. Although Egypt had a majority Christian population, Egyptians chose to ally with the invading Islamic armies to throw off Byzantine rule. By 642 the Islamic armies controlled Egypt, and by 650 they controlled an enormous swath of territory from Libya to Central Asia. In 650, they vanquished the once-powerful Sasanian empire.

The new Islamic state in Iran aspired to build an empire as large and long-lasting as the Sasanian empire, which had governed modern-day Iran and Iraq for more than four centuries. The caliphate's armies divided conquered peoples into three groups. Those who converted became Muslims. Those who continued to adhere to Judaism or Christianity were given the status of "protected subjects" (*dhimmi* in Arabic), because they too were "peoples of the book" who honored the same prophets from the Hebrew Bible and the New Testament that Muhammad had. Non-Muslims and nonprotected subjects formed the lowest group. Dhimmi status was later extended to Zoroastrians as well.

The Umayyad Caliphate, 661–750

Although the Islamic community had not resolved the issue of succession, by 661 Muslims had created their own expanding empire whose religious and political leader was the caliph. After Ali was assassinated in 661, Muawiya, a member of the Umayyad clan like the caliph Uthman, unified the Muslim community. In 680, when he died, Ali's son Husain tried to become caliph, but Muawiya's son defeated him and became caliph instead. Since only members of this family became caliphs until 750, this period is called the Umayyad dynasty.

The Umayyads built their capital at Damascus, the home of their many Syrian supporters, not in the Arabian peninsula, the original homeland of Islam. Initially they used local languages for administration, but after 685 they chose Arabic as the language of the empire.

🔳 **Portraying Paradise on Earth: The Umayyad Mosque of Damascus**   The most beautiful building in the Umayyad capital of Damascus was the mosque, where some 12,000 Byzantine craftsmen incorporated mosaics, made from thousands of glass tiles, into the building's structure. Notice how the trees grow naturally from the columns at the bottom of the photograph and how the twin windows allow viewers to glimpse the beautiful flowers on the ceiling above. These compositions portray the paradise that Muhammad promised his followers would enter after their deaths. (© Bernard O'Kane/Alamy)

In Damascus, the Umayyads erected the Great Mosque on the site of a church housing the relics of John the Baptist (see Chapter 7). Architects modified the building's Christian layout to create a large space where devotees could pray toward Mecca. This was the first Islamic building to have a place to wash one's hands and feet, a large courtyard, and a tall tower, or minaret, from which Muslims issued the call for prayer. Since Muslims honored the Ten Commandments, including the Second Commandment, "You shall not make for yourself a graven image," the Byzantine workmen depicted no human figures or living animals. Instead their mosaics showed landscapes in an imaginary paradise.

The Conquest of North Africa, 661–750

Under the leadership of the Umayyads, Islamic armies conquered the part of North Africa known as the Maghrib—modern-day Morocco, Algeria, and Tunisia. Strong economic and cultural ties dating back to the Roman Empire bound the Maghrib to western Asia. Its fertile fields provided the entire Mediterranean with grain, olive oil, and fruits like figs and bananas. In addition, the region exported handicrafts such as textiles, ceramics, and glass. Slaves and gold moved from the interior of Africa to the coastal ports, where they, too, were loaded into ships crossing the Mediterranean.

While Egypt had fallen in only a few years, the conquest of the rest of the Maghrib took many years. Islamic armies took Tunis (formerly Carthage, Tunisia) in 670 and Fez (Morocco) in 711, and then crossed the Strait of Gibraltar to enter Spain.

Arab culture and the religion of Islam eventually took root in North Africa, expanding from urban centers into the countryside. By the tenth century, Christians had become a minority in Egypt, outnumbered by Muslims, and by the twelfth century, Arabic had replaced both Egyptian and the Berber languages of the Maghrib as the dominant language. Annual performance of the hajj pilgrimage strengthened the ties between the people of North Africa and the Arabian peninsula. Starting from different places along the Mediterranean coast and along the Nile, pilgrim caravans converged in Cairo, from where large groups then proceeded to Mecca.

Islamic rule reoriented North Africa. Before it, the Mediterranean coast of Africa formed the southern edge of the Roman Empire, where Christianity was the dominant religion and Latin the language of learning (see Chapter 7). Under Muslim rule, North Africa lay at the western edge of the Islamic realm, and Arabic was spoken everywhere.

● The Abbasid Caliphate United, 750–945

In 744, a group of Syrian soldiers assassinated the Umayyad caliph, prompting an all-out civil war among all those hoping to control the caliphate. In 750, a section of the army based in western Iran, in the Khurasan region, triumphed and then shifted the capital some 500 miles (800 km) east from Damascus to Baghdad, closer to their base of support. Because the new caliph claimed descent from Muhammad's uncle Abbas, the new dynasty was called the Abbasid dynasty and their empire the **Abbasid caliphate.** Under Abbasid rule, the Islamic empire continued to expand east into Central Asia. At its greatest extent, it included present-day Morocco, Tunisia, Egypt, Saudi Arabia, Iraq, Iran, southern Pakistan, and Uzbekistan. In Spain, however, the leaders of the vanquished Umayyad clan established a separate Islamic state.

● **Abbasid caliphate** Dynasty of rulers (750–1258) who ruled a united empire from their capital at Baghdad until the empire fragmented in 945. They continued as religious leaders until 1258, when the last Abbasid caliph was killed by the Mongols.

Baghdad, City of Learning

The new Abbasid capital was built by the second Abbasid caliph Mansur (r. 754–775). Baghdad was on the Tigris River in the heart of Mesopotamia, near the point where the Tigris and Euphrates Rivers come closest together (see Chapter 2). Several canals linked the two rivers. Mansur explained his choice:

Indeed, this island between the Tigris in the East and the Euphrates in the West is the harbor of the world. All the ships that sail up the Tigris . . . and the adjacent areas will anchor here. . . . It will indeed be the most flourishing city in the world.[3]

Baghdad more than fulfilled his hopes. Located at the crossroads of Africa, Europe, and Asia, it was home to a half a million residents who included the majority Muslim community and smaller communities of Christians, Jews, and Zoroastrians. The city's residents lived side by side, celebrated each other's festivals, and spoke Arabic, Persian, Greek, and Hebrew.

Mansur, we learn from the historian Masudi,

> was the first caliph to have foreign works of literature translated into Arabic . . . various of Aristotle's treatises on logic and other subjects; Ptolemy's *Almagest;* the *Book of Euclid;* the treatise on arithmetic and all the other ancient works. . . . Once in possession of these books, the public read and studied them avidly.[4]

Local scholars benefited from the support of both the caliph and the city's residents, who paid for the manuscripts to be copied and studied them in their schools. The city's cosmopolitan environment encouraged scholars to study the scientific and mathematical discoveries of Greece, India, and Mesopotamia. Historians call their collective efforts, which lasted several centuries, the **translation movement.** In translating astronomy, medical, mathematical, and geography books from ancient Greek, Sanskrit, and Persian into Arabic, they created a body of scientific knowledge unsurpassed in the world. Certain works by ancient Greek scholars, such as the medical scholar Galen, survive only in their Arabic translations. When, beginning in the eleventh and twelfth centuries, Europeans once again became interested in the learning of the Greeks, they gladly used the Arabic translations, which preserved the legacy of the past while adding many distinguished advances (see the "Movement of Ideas" feature in Chapter 13).

• **translation movement** The collective effort of Islamic scholars, many living in Baghdad, between 750 and 1000 to translate astronomy, medical, mathematical, and geography books from ancient Greek, Sanskrit, and Persian into Arabic.

Islamic scholars also made many scientific and mathematical discoveries of their own. The great mathematician al-Khwarizmi (al-HWAR-ez-mee) (d. 830) combined the Indian and Babylonian number systems to create the world's first workable decimal system. Al-Khwarizmi invented algebra (from the Arabic word *al-jabr,* meaning "transposition") to solve math problems more easily through the use of equations. He also developed a system of computation that divided complex problems into shorter steps, or algorithms (the word *algorithm* is derived from al-Khwarizmi's name).

One of the Five Pillars of Islam (see page 245) is to pray five times a day facing toward Mecca. Islamic scholars developed increasingly sophisticated instruments to determine this position for prayer. The **astrolabe** allowed observers to calculate their location on earth once they had set the appropriate dials for the date, the time of day, and the angle of the sun's course through the sky; they could then determine the direction of Mecca for their prayers. The astrolabe also functioned as a slide rule, one of the world's first hand-held mathematical calculators. It became the most significant computational tool of its time.

• **astrolabe** Computational instrument that allowed observers to calculate their location on earth to determine the direction of Mecca for their prayers. Also functioned as a slide rule, one of the world's first hand-held mathematical calculators.

In a significant technological advance, a paper-making factory was opened in Baghdad in 794–795 that used Chinese techniques (see Chapter 4) to produce the first paper in the Islamic world. Muslim scholars had previously written on either papyrus, a dried plant grown in Egypt, or dried, scraped leather, called parchment. Both were much more costly than paper, and the new writing material spread quickly throughout the empire. By 850, Baghdad housed one hundred paper-making workshops.

The low cost of paper greatly increased the availability of books. Manuals on agriculture, botany, and pharmacology contributed to the spread of agricultural

■ **Determining the Direction of Mecca: The Astrolabe** This astrolabe, made in 1216, is a sophisticated mathematical device. After holding the astrolabe up to the sun to determine the angle of the sun's rays and thus fix the viewer's latitude on earth, one inserted the appropriate metal plate (this example has three) into the mechanism, which allowed one to chart the movement of the stars. (Musée Paul Dupuy, Toulous, France/Eric Lessing, Art Resource, NY)

techniques and crops from one end of the empire to the other. Cookbooks show the extent to which the empire's residents embraced Asian foodstuffs like rice, egg-plant, and processed sugar. Cotton for clothing, grown by Persians at the time of the founding of the Abbasid dynasty, gradually spread to Egypt, and, by the twelfth century, West Africans began to cultivate the crop as well.

Abbasid Governance

Baghdad, the city of learning, was the capital of an enor-mous empire headed by the caliph, who presided over the military, the bureaucracy, and the judiciary. His chief minister, or vizier, stood at the head of a bureaucracy based in the capital. In the provinces, the caliph del-egated power to regional governors, who were charged with maintaining local armies and transmitting revenues to the center; however, they often tried to keep revenues for themselves.

In the early centuries of Islamic rule, local populations often continued their pre-Islamic religious practices. For example, in 750 fewer than 8 percent of the people living in the Abbasid heartland of Iran were Muslims. By the ninth cen-tury, the Muslim proportion of the population had increased to 40 percent, but only in the tenth century did converts become a majority—70 or 80 percent—of the population.[5]

The caliphate offered all of its subjects access to a developed judicial system that implemented Islamic law. He appointed a chief judge, or qadi, for the city of Baghdad and a qadi for each of the empire's provinces. These judges were drawn from the learned men of Islam, or **ulama** (also spelled *ulema*), who gained their positions after years of study. The ulama took no special vows and could marry and have families. Some specialized in the Quran, others scrutinized records of Muhammad's sayings in the hadith to establish their veracity, and still others concentrated on legal texts. Scholars taught at schools, sometimes in mosques and sometimes in separate buildings. On Fridays, at the weekly services, the ulama preached to the congregation (women and men sat separately, with the men in front), and afterward they heard legal disputes in the mosques.

The judiciary enjoyed an unusually high position, for even members of the caliph's immediate family were subject to their decisions. In one example, an employee who brought goods for Zubaydah, the wife of the caliph Harun al-Rashid, refused to pay a merchant. When the merchant consulted a judge, the judge advised the merchant to file suit and then ordered the queen's agent to pay the debt. The angry queen ordered the judge transferred and Harun complied with his wife's request, but only after he himself paid the money owed to the merchant.

At first glance, it might seem that the queen had prevailed; after all, she managed to have the judge transferred. But she had not ordered him killed, and the judge continued to hear cases in his new post. A comparison with other contemporary empires demonstrates the power of the judiciary in the Abbasid empire: no Chinese subject of the Tang dynasty would have dared to sue the emperor, and no one in Europe had access to a comparable judicial system.

● **ulama** Learned Islamic scholars who studied the Quran, the hadith, and legal texts. They taught classes, preached, and heard legal disputes; they took no special vows and could marry and have families.

Abbasid Society

When compared with its Asian and European contemporaries, Islamic society appears surprisingly egalitarian. It had divisions, of course: rural/urban, Muslim/non-Muslim, free person/slave. Apart from gender differences, however, none of these divisions were insurmountable. Rural people could move to the city, non-Muslims could convert to Islam, and slaves could be, and often were, freed.

In the royal ranks, however, much had changed since the time of Muhammad, whose supporters treated him as an equal. The Abbasid rulers rejected the egalitarianism of early Islam to embrace the lavish court ceremonies of the Sasanians. To the horror of the ulama, the caliph received visitors from behind a curtained throne, and visitors had to kiss the ground in front of his throne even though only God, the learned felt, should receive such a form of submission. Equally reprehensible in the eyes of the ulama, his subjects addressed the caliph as "the shadow of God on earth," a title modeled on the Sasanian "king of kings." At the right of the caliph stood an executioner, ready to kill any visitor who might offend the caliph.

The one group in Islamic society to inherit privileges on the basis of birth were those who could claim descent from Muhammad's family. All the Abbasid caliphs belonged to this group, and their many relatives occupied a privileged position at the top of Baghdad society. Descent from Muhammad did not bring any financial advantage; it simply commanded more respect.

Under the royal family, two large groups enjoyed considerable prestige and respect: the ulama, on the one hand, and the cultured elite, who included courtiers surrounding the caliph, bureaucrats staffing his government, and educated land-owners throughout the empire. These groups often patronized poets, painters, and musicians, themselves also members of the cultured elite. Generally speaking the cultured elite were not as observant as the ulama.

Like the caliph's more educated subjects, ordinary people varied in the extent of their compliance with the religious teachings of Islam. In the cities they worked carrying goods, and in the countryside they farmed. Most farmers prayed five times a day and attended Friday prayers at their local mosques, but they could not always afford to go on the hajj.

Farmers aspired to send their sons, but not their daughters, to study at the local mosque for a few years. Here they acquired the rudiments of Arabic so that they could recite the Quran before starting work full-time as cultivators. Families that educated their daughters did so at home. Boys who demonstrated scholarly ability hoped to become members of the ulama, while those gifted in mathematics might become merchants.

Muhammad and two of his immediate successors had been merchants, and trade continued to enjoy a privileged position in the Abbasid caliphate. Merchants were supposed to adhere to a high standard of conduct: to be true to their word and to sell merchandise free from defects. Many merchants contributed money for the upkeep of mosques or to help the less fortunate. Because Islamic law forbade usury (charging interest on loans), Muslim merchants used credit mechanisms like checks, letters of credit, and bills of exchange.

While the most successful merchants became bankers and traders who special-ized in large-scale transactions that spanned the empire, other merchants ran single shops or peddled their goods, some of which they made themselves, from town to town. The state regulated the quality of goods such as textiles, which had to be stamped by the government before being placed on sale.

The shift of the capital to Baghdad in the eighth century brought a dramatic increase in trade within the empire and beyond. Long-distance merchants sent ships to India and China that were loaded with locally produced goods—such as Arabian horses, textiles, and carpets—and nonlocal goods, such as African ivory and Southeast Asian pearls. The ships returned with spices, medicines, and textiles. Islamic merchants were at home in a world stretching from China to Africa; Aladdin, the famous fictional hero of a tale from *The Thousand and One Nights,* was born in China and adopted by an African merchant. As early as the ninth century, ships trav-eled routinely between the Arabian Sea and south Chinese ports, and the China-Mecca route was the longest regularly traveled sea route in the world before 1500.

Slavery   Much long-distance trade involved the import of slaves from three ma-jor areas: Central Africa, Central Asia, and central and eastern Europe, by far the largest source (see Map 9.1). The Arabs referred to the region of modern Poland and Bohemia as the "slave country." (The English word *slave* is derived from the Latin word for *slav,* because so many slaves were originally Slavic.)

An extraordinary sailor's tale from the mid-tenth century tells of the abduc-tion of an East African slave.[6] Although the tale is clearly a literary creation, the narrator, a Muslim slave trader, describes real-world trading routes. In 922, an Arab ship set out from the port of Oman in the Persian Gulf, was caught in a storm, and landed on the coast of East Africa, in modern Somalia or Kenya, regions that had become Islamicized under the Abbasids. "The canoes of the negroes

MAP 9.1

The Abbasid Caliphate Between 750 and 950, the Abbasid caliphate lost huge chunks of territory in North Africa, the Arabian peninsula, Iran, and Central Asia, yet a shared Islamic identity held the former empire together, as Ibn Jubayr learned in his 1183–1185 journey (see page 262). The people living in the empire's core around Baghdad imported slaves, many of whom converted to Islam, from Africa, northern Europe, and Central Asia.

Interactive Map

surrounded us and brought us into the harbour," the narrator explains, and the local king gave him permission to trade.

At the conclusion of their trip, the African king and seven companions boarded the ship to bid the Arab merchants good-bye. The narrator explains the ship's captain's thoughts:

> When I saw them there, I said to myself: In the Oman market this young king would certainly fetch thirty dinars [a *dinar* coin contained 4.25 grams of gold], and his seven companions sixty dinars. Their clothes are not worth less than twenty dinars. One way and another this would give us a profit of at least 3,000 dirhams [a silver coin] and without any trouble. Reflecting thus, I gave the crew their orders. They raised the sails and weighed anchor.

The captain's split-second calculation of the king's value chills the blood. Unable to escape, the captive king joined two hundred other slaves in the ship's hold and was sold when the ship reached Oman.

Several years later, the same captain and the same ship were caught in a storm, and, to their horror, they landed in the same harbor. They were brought to the king, and to their amazement, it was the same king they had sold at the Oman slave market. The king explained that he had been purchased by a Muslim in the Persian Gulf port of Basra, who had first taught him the Quran and then had sold him to a man living in Baghdad. After converting to Islam, the king joined a group of hajj pilgrims on their way to Mecca, and in Mecca he joined a group going to Cairo. On the way home from Cairo, slave traders captured him twice, he escaped both times, and finally he reached his former kingdom where his countrymen welcomed him back.

The king then explained why he had forgiven the narrator and his fellow slave traders: "And here I am, happy and satisfied with the grace God has given me and mine, of knowing the precepts of Islam, the true faith, prayers, fasting, the pilgrimage, and what is permitted and what is forbidden." In short, the chain of events that began with his capture led to his conversion and finally his freedom.

Although fictional, this tale sheds light on a poorly documented process: under the Abbasids, the coastal cities of East Africa, particularly those north of Madagascar, became Muslim, not because they were conquered by invading armies but because traveling merchants introduced Islam to them. The merchants came to the coast to buy slaves and other products, including gold and ivory. In many cases, the rulers converted first, and the population later followed.

Like this fictional enslaved king, most Islamic slaves worked as servants or concubines, not as field hands like the slaves of the American South before the Civil War. The caliph's household purchased thousands of slaves each year. The women entered the secluded women's quarters in the palace, or harem, where they were guarded by eunuchs, or castrated men. Many slave buyers particularly valued eunuchs because they could trust them with their female kin.

Since Islamic law held that no Muslim could be sold as a slave, any slave who converted to Islam had to be freed. Former slaves often continued to work for their original owners for wages. All levels of society, from the caliph with his hundreds of female slaves down to the petty trader who could afford only one, respected the teaching that children born to a slave woman and a Muslim father should be raised as free Muslims. As a result, these children were granted identical rights as their siblings born to Muslim mothers.

Harun al-Rashid was himself the child of a slave mother, Khaizuran. Like many young slave children, she learned to read and write because educated slaves could command a higher price on the slave market. When the caliph Mansur gave her to his son Mahdi sometime in the late 750s, Mahdi took an immediate liking to the young girl, who was "slender and graceful as a reed," the root meaning of her name *khaizuran*.

Politics of the Harem   Like most ordinary people living within the Abbasid Empire, Khaizuran had grown up in a nuclear family headed by her father and his one wife, her mother. Islamic law permitted Muslim men to marry as many as four wives, but most men could afford to support only one. The caliphs took the four wives Islamic law entitled them to, and their enormous revenues also permitted them to support unlimited numbers of concubines.

When Khaizuran joined the royal household, she left behind her life in the streets of Mecca, where women had some freedom of movement, and entered a world whose customs were completely unfamiliar. The higher a woman's class, the greater the degree of seclusion, and the caliph's wives were the most secluded of all. An army of eunuchs guarded the secluded women's quarters and prevented illicit contact with any men. Khaizuran was free to leave the palace only on rare occasions, and then only under escort.

When Khaizuran entered the harem, she told everyone she had no living kin. Only after giving birth to two sons, and only after she was certain of her status as one of the future caliph's favorites, did she reveal that her mother, two sisters, and a brother were still alive in Yemen. The caliph Mansur immediately summoned them to live in the palace and arranged for Khaizuran's sister to marry another of his sons. The sister subsequently gave birth to a daughter, whose nickname was "little butter ball," or Zubaydah.

Khaizuran's relations with her son Hadi soured soon after he, and not Harun, became caliph in 785. Hadi was particularly upset to discover that his mother was meeting with his generals and courtiers on her own. He chastised her, saying: "Do not overstep the essential limits of womanly modesty. . . . It is not dignified for women to enter upon affairs of state. Take to your prayer and worship and devote yourself to the service of Allah. Hereafter, submit to the womanly role that is required of your sex."[7]

But Khaizuran did not back down. Hadi then asked his generals how they would feel if their mothers interfered in politics, and they all agreed, "Not any one of us would like that."[8] This description by the historian al-Tabari (at-TAH-bah-ree) (d. 923) seems to suggest that all the commanders felt the same: that no woman, and certainly not Khaizuran, should intervene in matters of state. Contrary to the expectation of these men, Khaizuran did, however, intervene in court politics. Hadi died suddenly, in mysterious circumstances, and Khaizuran made sure that Harun succeeded him as caliph. (No one knows exactly how.)

Unlike her mother and her famous aunt Khaizuran, who had come to the harem as adults, Zubaydah grew up entirely within the women's quarter of the palace. After her marriage she devoted herself to public works. While in Mecca, she contributed an additional 1,700,000 dinars, or nearly eight tons of gold, from her own funds to construct a giant reservoir. She also ordered wells dug to provide hajj pilgrims with fresh water. The resulting stone water tunnels, running above and below ground for 12 miles (20 km), constituted a genuine feat of engineering. Finally, she made extensive repairs to the road linking Kufa, a city outside Baghdad, with Mecca and Medina. (See the feature "Visual Evidence: Zubaydah's Road.")

The Breakup of the Abbasid Empire, 809–936

Like her mother-in-law Khaizuran, Zubaydah tried to manipulate the succession after Harun's death in 809, but she sided with the losing son, who was defeated by his brother Mamun in 813. The empire Mamun won, however, was not as prosperous as it appeared. The costs of governing the Abbasid Empire often exceeded its revenues. Even during Harun's reign the caliphs were often forced to seek emergency loans. The central government frequently ran short of money because regional governors did not forward the taxes they collected to the caliph. The frequent civil wars between rivals for the caliphate destroyed the irrigation works that underpinned the agrarian economy, and, because no one rebuilt them, tax revenues continuously declined.

As a temporary expedient, the caliph occasionally appointed someone, usually called a tax farmer, to collect a fixed amount in a region where the caliph's bureaucrats had trouble raising revenue. In these cases the caliph still retained direct political control. If tax farmers failed to raise the necessary revenues, the caliph

ZUBAYDAH'S ROAD

Zubaydah devoted considerable resources to the project that brought her lasting fame: the road linking Kufa, a city outside Baghdad, with Mecca and Medina. Although the road existed before her reign, she made so many improvements to it that it came to be called Darb Zubaydah, or Zubaydah's Road.

When Saudi archaeologists surveyed the desert in the 1970s, they found identifiable traces of a roadway 18 yards (17 m) yards wide. The road's builders had faced the challenge of designing a road for pedestrians even though it ran through long stretches of sand, some muddy ground, and rough lava fields. They cleared the road of stones, paved the sections of the road that went through the mud, and smoothed rough lava fields before covering them with soft sand on which pilgrims could easily walk. One archaeologist has called the project "the finest and most remarkable and extensive road system in the earlier period of Islamic history."[*]

————

[*]Saad A. al-Rashid, *Darb Zubaydah: The Pilgrim Road from Kufa to Mecca* (Riyad: Riyad University, 1980), p. 330.

• The stones of the lava field were so sharp that they hurt the feet of the pilgrims and their camels.

• After clearing the road, engineers covered it with a smooth layer of sand for the convenience of the pilgrims and their camels, who traveled over 700 miles (1,100 km).

(John Herbert)

QUESTION FOR ANALYSIS

What preparations did hajj travelers going overland have to make, and how would these differ for those traveling by boat?

Because Zubaydah was particularly concerned about poorer pilgrims who traveled the difficult route on foot, she added nine new rest stations at convenient intervals between existing stations, for a total of fifty-four rest stops. All the new stations had a pool, and they often included some kind of shelter and sometimes even a small mosque. This painting, from an illustrated thirteenth-century manuscript of collected anecdotes, shows what a resting place on the Darb Zubaydah might have looked like.

The nimbus, or cloud, behind the head was originally an Iranian artistic convention used to show royalty. In this picture, however, the nimbus seems purely decorative, since all the human figures have one.

(Institute of Oriental Studies, St. Petersburg, Russia/The Bridgeman Library)

This figure uses bellows to light a fire below a cooking pot.

This is a shrine, most likely to a prominent Islamic teacher whose grave lies inside it, where Muslims came to pray.

Two camels bray with their mouths open. Although often ill-tempered, camels were the one draft animal that could withstand the hot, dry climate of the desert.

Inside a tent made from beautiful textiles, these two men lean on portable wooden furniture as they converse with each other.

Three camels feed from saddlebags placed on the ground. Able to survive for up to nine days without water, camels can carry loads over 300 pounds (140 kg).

259

● iqta grant A grant given by the caliph to someone who promised to collect taxes from a certain region and pay the caliph a certain amount of money. Grant holders became military governors and rulers of their regions, over which the caliph had only nominal control.

might go a step further and make an **iqta grant,** ceding all political control to the man who promised to pay a certain amount. The iqta (ICK-tah) grant-holder became the military governor and ruler of the area, and the caliph retained only nominal control. In 789 and 800, Harun granted independence to two Islamic states in North Africa in exchange for annual tax payments; his successors made similar arrangements with other regions.

Until the middle of the tenth century, none of the iqta holders directly challenged the authority of the caliph. Then, in 936, the caliph took the final step and ceded all his power to an Iraqi grant holder, giving him the title *commander of commanders*. The grant holder disbanded the entire Abbasid army and replaced it with an army loyal to himself. He eliminated the Abbasid bureaucracy as well, sentencing the last vizier to life imprisonment in a dungeon.

This new arrangement did not last long. In 945, the Buyids, a group of Shi'ite Iranian mercenaries based in the mountains south of the Caspian Sea, conquered Baghdad and took over the government. Rather than depose the caliphs and risk alienating their Muslim subjects, the Buyids retained them as figureheads who led the Islamic caliphate but had no political power. The caliph received a small allowance so that he could reside in his crumbling palace in Baghdad, and Islamic preachers continued to cite his name in their Friday prayers. The extensive territory of the Abbasid Empire proved ungovernable as a single political unit, and it broke up into different regions, all still part of the Islamic cultural and religious world.

● The Rise of Regional Centers After the Abbasids, 945–1258

Although no one knew how the caliph's loss of political authority would affect the caliphate, Muslims found it surprisingly easy to accept the new division of political and religious authority. The caliphs continued as the titular heads of the Islamic religious community, but they were entirely dependent on temporal rulers for financial support. No longer politically united, the Islamic world was still bound by religious ties and the obligation to perform the hajj. Under the leadership of committed Muslim rulers, Islam continued to spread throughout South Asia and the interior of Africa. Rulers all over the Islamic world continued to patronize Islamic scholars, and Islamic learning, particularly in the field of geography, continued to thrive.

Regional Islamic States, 945–1258

Many different states formed in the centuries after the caliph's loss of political authority. In 1055, Baghdad fell to yet a different group of soldiers, the Turkish-speaking Seljuqs (also spelled Seljuk) from Central Asia. With the accession of the Seljuqs (sell-JOOKs), other sections of the empire broke off and, like Baghdad, experienced rule by different dynasties. In most periods, the former Abbasid Empire was divided into four regions: the former heartland of the Euphrates and Tigris River basins, Egypt and Syria, North Africa and Spain, and the Amu Darya and Syr Daria River Valleys in Central Asia.

Two centuries of Abbasid rule had transformed these four regions into Islamic realms whose residents, whether Sunni or Shi'ite, observed the tenets of Islam. Their societies retained the basic patterns of Abbasid society. When Muslims traveled anywhere in the former Abbasid territories, they could be confident of finding mosques, being received as honored guests, and having access to the same basic legal system (even if some legal schools differed in their interpretations). As in the Roman Empire, where Greek and Latin prevailed, just two languages could take a traveler through the entire realm: Arabic, the language of the Quran and high Islamic learning, and Persian, the Iranian language of much poetry, literature, and history.

Map of Eurasia, 1182 This map, like all Islamic maps, is oriented with the south on top and the north below. It is a copy of a silver map made by the geographer al-Idrisi, which no longer survives. With greater precision than any other contemporary map, it shows the blue Mediterranean Sea in the middle with Africa above (notice the three sources of the Nile on the right) and Eurasia below. (National Library [Dar-al-Katub], Cairo, Egypt/Erich Lessing/Art Resource, NY)

Sometime around 1000, the city of Córdoba in Islamic Spain replaced Baghdad as the leading center of Islamic learning. The Umayyad capital from around 750 to 1031, Córdoba served as the capital for the Almoravid (1031–1147) and Almohad (1130–1269) dynasties who succeeded the Umayyads and ruled North Africa and Spain in the eleventh through thirteenth centuries. All visitors to Córdoba admired its gardens, fountains, paved streets, and most of all, its running water (the first in Europe since the fall of Rome).

Córdoba played a crucial role in the transmission of learning from the Islamic world to Christian Europe. Craftsmen learned how to make paper in the eleventh century and transmitted the technique to the rest of Europe. Córdoba's residents, both male and female, specialized in copying manuscripts and translated treatises from Arabic into Latin for European audiences.

The study of geography also flourished in the eleventh and twelfth centuries as Muslims learned about the most distant places within the Islamic community. Al-Bakri, a geographer based in Córdoba, provided a rare, detailed description of Central Africa. He reported that the two kingdoms of Ghana and Gao had capital cities with separate districts for Muslims and for local religious practitioners who prayed to images. He explained that although rulers often converted to Islam after contact with Muslim traders, their subjects, as in the case of Mali, did not always follow suit.

This religious division between rulers who converted to Islam and subjects who did not held true in the other major area that was brought into the Islamic world in the eleventh and twelfth centuries: Afghanistan, Pakistan, and north India. Muslim conquerors moved into north India from their base in Afghanistan. During the actual conquest they tore down Hindu temples, but once they gained power they allowed Hindu temples to remain, even as they endowed mosques. Ordinary Indians continued to worship Hindu deities (see Chapter 8), while the ruling family, who were based in Delhi and who are thus known as the Delhi sultanate, observed the tenets of Islam.

During this long period of division, Muslim cartographers made some of the most advanced maps of their day. Working in Sicily, the geographer al-Idrisi (1100–1166) drew a map of the world engraved on a silver tablet 3 yards by 1.5 yards (3 m by 1.5 m). Although the map was destroyed during his lifetime, the book al-Idrisi wrote to accompany his map is so detailed that scholars have been able to reconstruct the seven climatic zones, each with ten sections, that appeared on his original map. Like all Islamic maps, his looks upside down to modern viewers because he oriented the map to the south. His map showed the outlines of the Mediterranean, Africa, and Central Asia with far greater accuracy than contemporary maps made elsewhere in the world.

Ibn Jubayr's Hajj in 1183   By the twelfth century, different Islamic governments ruled the different sections of the former Abbasid Empire. Since the realm of Islam was no longer unified, devout Muslims had to cross from one Islamic polity to the next as they performed the hajj. Local Islamic rulers might take advantage of the pilgrims by charging them extra taxes or exacting customs duties, but sometimes they also facilitated the pilgrims' journey. Pilgrims were often unsure of the correct rituals to perform in Mecca, and as the number of pilgrims increased over the centuries, a new genre of book, called "travels" (*rihla* in Arabic), appeared that described the trip to Mecca and the most

The Hajj Today

The world's fastest-growing religion, Islam is second only to Christianity in the number of adherents, with a total of 1.2 billion Muslims in the world today. The four countries with the greatest number of Muslims lie far from the heartland of Islam in Saudi Arabia: Indonesia (170 million), Pakistan (136 million), Bangladesh (106 million), and India (103 million). The world region with the greatest number of recent converts is Africa.

Each Muslim hopes to go on the hajj at least once in his or her lifetime, and more than two million people travel to Saudi Arabia each year on this pilgrimage. The number would be even greater except that the government of Saudi Arabia limits the number of visas issued annually to one thousand pilgrims for each one million citizens in each country.

Because the visitors all want to visit the different sites in the prescribed order on the same days, crowding poses a major problem. As in Ibn Jubayr's day, the stoning of the Devil at Mina is one of the most dangerous rites. After staying up most of the night, pilgrims throw rocks, yell insults, or hurl their shoes at one of three stone pillars. The highest number of casualties occurred in 1990, when 1,426 pilgrims died in a stampede in a tunnel. Stampedes have also occurred in 1998, 2001, 2004, and 2006. Still, because it is such an important part of the hajj experience, authorities are reluctant to limit the number of people visiting Mina.

Sources: adherents.com; various newspaper reports accessed via Lexis Nexus.

important rituals performed there. Although Muslims came from different regional states and spoke different languages, their participation in the same rituals of the hajj bound them together. (See "World History in Today's World: The Hajj Today.")

The most famous travel book is *The Travels* of **Ibn Jubayr** (1145–1217), a courtier from Granada, Spain, who went on the hajj in 1183–1185. Ibn Jubayr (IH-buhn joo-BAH-eer) decided to go to Mecca to repent for drinking seven cups of wine, a drink forbidden to Muslims. He financed his trip with a gift of seven cups of gold coins received from the governor of Granada, his superior, who felt contrite about having forced Ibn Jubayr to drink so much. Ibn Jubayr's book serves as a guide to the sequence of hajj observances that had been fixed by Muhammad; Muslims today continue to perform the same rituals (see Table 9.1, "The Nine Steps of the Hajj").

 After thirty days' sail across the Mediterranean, Ibn Jubayr arrived in the port of Alexandria, Egypt, then under the rule of Saladin (1137/38–1193), the founder of the Ayyubid dynasty (1171–1250) in Egypt. When Saladin, whose father had served in the Seljuq army, defeated the Fatimid dynasty, the caliph in Baghdad granted him an iqta for all of Egypt and Syria.

Because their boat was from another country, all the travelers with Ibn Jubayr had to go through customs. Ibn Jubayr praised Saladin's generosity as a host but criticized the port officials for requiring the pilgrims to pay the zakat tax on the goods they carried. From Egypt, Ibn Jubayr traveled south and crossed the Red Sea; on his arrival, he once again had to pay a tax. Before 945, all territory was under Abbasid rule, and there were no border crossings; after 945, Muslim travelers, even those going in the hajj, had to pay the costs of leaving one country and entering another.

• **Ibn Jubayr** (1145–1217) Spanish courtier from Granada, Spain, who went on the hajj pilgrimage in 1183–1185. Wrote *The Travels,* the most famous example of a travel book, called a *rihla* in Arabic, that described the author's trip to Mecca.

263

Table 9.1   The Nine Steps of the Hajj
1. To put on pilgrim's robes
2. To walk around the Kaaba seven times counterclockwise
3. To stand at Arafat on the ninth day of the twelfth month
4. To stay overnight near Arafat
5. To throw stones at three different locations where, Muslims believe, Satan tempted the prophet Ishmael
6. To sacrifice an animal at Mina
7. To repeat the circumambulation of the Kaaba (see step 2)
8. To drink water from the Zamzam well
9. To recite two sets of prayers at the Station of Abraham, where Abraham and Ishmael, Muslims believe, prayed together after the Kaaba was built

Source: Vincent J. Cornell, "Fruit of the Tree of Knowledge: The Relationship Between Faith and Practice in Islam," in *The Oxford History of Islam,* ed. John Esposito (New York: Oxford University Press, 1999), pp. 84–87.

When Ibn Jubayr arrived at the outskirts of Mecca, he put on the two pieces of unsewn cloth permitted to the male pilgrim. (Because women pilgrims were obliged to cover all but their face, hands, and feet, they required more cloth.) While Sunni and Shi'ite rules differed slightly, all concurred that pilgrims should refrain from having sex, eating meat, and cutting their hair or nails during the hajj. Muslims could fulfill their obligation to go on the hajj only once a year: on the eighth, ninth, and tenth days of the twelfth month in the Islamic lunar calendar. After Ibn Jubayr had been in Mecca for some eight months, the month of the hajj arrived.

The number of Muslims going on the hajj had increased dramatically over time. By 1184, Ibn Jubayr writes that the total number of pilgrims from Iraq alone "formed a multitude whose number only God Most High could count."[9] The more unruly pilgrims (especially from Yemen, in Ibn Jubayr's opinion) forced the Meccan authorities to replace the Kaaba's wooden covering with a strong iron dome.

Once pilgrims arrived in Mecca, they walked around the Kaaba seven times in a counterclockwise direction. On the eighth day of the month Ibn Jubayr and all the other pilgrims departed for Mina, which lay halfway to Mount Arafat. The hajj celebrated Abraham's release of his son Ishmael. The most important rite, the Standing, commemorated the last sermon given by the prophet Muhammad.

Fear of bandits prevented the pilgrims from spending the night at Arafat as was customary. When they arrived at Mount Arafat early in the morning of the ninth day, they first climbed the mountain and then descended to the plain, where they remained on their feet throughout the Standing:

> When, on Friday, the midday and afternoon prayers were said together, the people stood contrite and in tears, humbly beseeching the mercy of Great and Glorious God. The cries of "God is Great" rose high, and loud were the voices of men in prayer. Never has there been seen a day of such weeping, such penitence of heart, and such bending of the neck in reverential submission and humility before God.

As soon as the sun had set, the pilgrims proceeded quickly in the dark toward a mosque some three hours away for final prayers. They spent the rest of the night there.

When the pilgrims arrived at Mina the next day, their religious observance shifted suddenly from solemn piety to raucous celebration. They first threw stones at the wall where Muslims believe Satan tempted Ishmael, and they then slaughtered sheep to celebrate Abraham's substitution of a sacrificial ram for his son Ishmael. The change of pace was abrupt, and disturbances often broke out at Mina. Ibn Jubayr saw "dissension and riot between the negro inhabitants of Mecca and the Turks of Iraq in which there were some hurts. Swords were drawn, arrow notches were put to the bow-string, and spears were thrown, while some of the goods of the merchants were plundered."

After the religious observances were completed, giant bazaars sprang up in which Ibn Jubayr saw "wares ranging from precious jewels to the cheapest strings of beads, together with other articles and various merchandises of the world." The hajj may have been a religious duty, but it also had a distinctly commercial side: merchants from all over the Islamic world found a ready market among the pilgrims.

Finally, Ibn Jubayr, like almost all pilgrims, went to see Muhammad's tomb and mosque at Medina, even though this was not an obligatory part of the hajj. From Medina to Baghdad, Ibn Jubayr traveled along Zubaydah's Road, which he covered at a rapid 30 miles (50 km) per day:

> These tanks, pools, wells, and stations on the road from Baghdad to Mecca are monuments to Zubaydah. . . . But for her generous acts in this direction this road could not have been traversed.

In Baghdad, he visited the palace where the family members of the figurehead caliph "live in sumptuous confinement in those palaces, neither going forth nor being seen."

For the return trip, Ibn Jubayr chose a different route: after going to Damascus, he traveled to the kingdom of Jerusalem, which was under the rule of the Crusader states (see Chapter 13). In 1185, Saladin had already begun his campaign to win Jerusalem back (he did so in 1187), and on his way to Jerusalem, Ibn Jubayr saw hundreds of Christian prisoners taken captive by Saladin. The incongruity of the situation struck him: "One of the strangest things in the world is that Muslim caravans go forth to Frankish [meaning the Christians from modern-day France and Germany] lands, while Frankish captives enter Muslim lands." Ibn Jubayr's caravan entered the Crusader-ruled territory without paying any taxes, and he caught a ship to Europe from Acre [Akka], in modern Israel. Because of several months' delay caused by a shipwreck, he arrived back in Spain more than two years after his departure in 1185.

Ibn Jubayr's rihla offers a precious eyewitness account of the Islamic world in the late twelfth century, when the Abbasid caliphs continued as figureheads in Baghdad but all real power lay with different regional rulers. This arrangement came to an abrupt end in 1258, when the Mongols (see Chapter 14) invaded Baghdad and ended even that minimal symbolic role for the caliph.

Chapter Review

KEY TERMS

Khaizuran (238)

Muhammad (240)

jihad (244)

hajj (244)

caliph (244)

Quran (245)

hadith (245)

Five Pillars of Islam (245)

Sunnis (245)

Shi'ites (245)

Abbasid caliphate (250)

translation movement (251)

astrolabe (251)

ulama (253)

iqta grant (260)

Ibn Jubayr (263)

Download the MP3 audio file of the Chapter Review and listen to it on the go.

When Muhammad instructed his followers to perform the annual hajj pilgrimage, the Islamic world was limited to the west coast of the Arabian peninsula. In the eighth century, Khaizuran was able to fulfill her obligation with a journey only a few weeks long, and Ibn Jubayr traveled all the way from Spain to Mecca in a few months. However, Muslims who lived at the edges of the Islamic world in Central Africa, Central Asia, or Afghanistan measured their journeys in years. Although living in widely dispersed areas, they were bound together by many ties, including loyalty to the caliph.

 Who was the prophet Muhammad, and what were his main teachings?

Muhammad was a merchant who, in the early 600s, had a series of visions in which, according to Muslim belief, he received revelations from God as transmitted by the angel Gabriel. The Five Pillars of Islam specified the obligations of each Muslim: (1) to bear witness to Allah as the sole god and to accept Muhammad as his messenger, (2) to pray five times daily in the direction of Mecca, (3) to pay a fixed share of one's income to the state in support of the poor and needy, (4) to refrain from eating, drinking, and sexual activity during the daytime hours of the month of Ramadan, and (5) provided one has the necessary resources, to do the hajj pilgrimage to Mecca.

Between Muhammad's death in 632 and the founding of the Abbasid caliphate in 750, what were the different ways that the Islamic community chose the new caliph?

At first, the Islamic community chose the caliph by consensus, but the murder of the third caliph threw the umma into turmoil. Sunnis believed that only those chosen by consensus, even if not related to Muhammad, could serve as caliphs. Shi'ites believed that only those like Muhammad's cousin and son-in-law Ali were qualified. During the first century after Muhammad's death, Muslims struggled with the question of choosing his successor, until they eventually accepted the idea of dynastic succession in 680, when the son of the first Umayyad caliph succeeded him.

Which economic, political, and social forces held the many peoples and territories of the Abbasid caliphate together?

Between its founding in 750 and its disintegration in 945, the Abbasid rulers used a common political structure—of provinces paying taxes to the center at Baghdad—to tie the empire together. Muslims throughout the empire honored the caliph as their political and religious leader and revered the learned religious teachers of the ulama; they also went on the hajj. Those who knew Arabic (the language of the Quran) and Persian (the language of learning) could make themselves understood anywhere in the Abbasid Empire.

 After the fragmentation of the Abbasid Empire in 945, which cultural practices, technologies, and customs held Islamic believers in different regions together?

After the breakup of the Abbasid Empire in 945, Muslims in different regions accepted the deposed caliph as their religious leader even as they served the different regional rulers based in Spain and North Africa, sub-Saharan Africa, Egypt and Syria, Iraq, and Central and South Asia.

Although originally a religious obligation, by 1200 the hajj had a profound effect on trade, navigation, and technology. The hajj, and the resulting trade, pushed Muslims to adopt or to discover the fastest and most efficient means of transport from different places to Mecca and to equip those vessels with the best astronomical instruments, maps, and navigational devices. Despite the hardships, all Muslims viewed a trip to Mecca, no matter how distant, as an obligation to be fulfilled if at all possible. The result was clear: ordinary Muslims were far better traveled and more knowledgeable than their contemporaries in other parts of the world.

In the years after 945, multiple political and cultural centers arose that challenged Baghdad's position in the previously united Islamic world. As the next chapter will show, something similar happened in Europe as political and cultural centers first appeared and then overtook the Byzantine capital at Constantinople.

 WEB RESOURCES

Pronunciation Guide

Interactive Maps

MAP 9.1 Abbasid Caliphate

Primary Sources

Chapter Objectives

ACE Multiple-Choice Quiz

Flashcards

For Further Reference

Abbott, Nadia. *Two Queens of Baghdad: Mother and Wife of Harun al-Rashid.* London: Al Saqi Books, 1986, reprint of 1946 original.

Allen, Roger. *An Introduction to Arabic Literature.* New York: Cambridge University Press, 2000.

Broadhurst, R. J. C., trans. *The Travels of Ibn Jubayr.* London: Jonathan Cape, 1952.

Esposito, John L., ed. *The Oxford History of Islam.* New York: Oxford University Press, 1999.

Freeman-Grenville, G. S. P. *The East African Coast: Select Documents from the First to the Earlier Nineteenth Century.* Oxford: Clarendon Press, 1962.

Gutas, Dmitri. *Greek Thought, Arabic Culture: The Graeco-Arabic Translation Movement in Baghdad and Early 'Abbāsid Society (2nd–4th/8th–10th centuries).* New York: Routledge, 1998.

Hodgson, Marshall. *Venture of Islam.* Vols. 1–3. Chicago: University of Chicago Press, 1974.

Hourani, George F. *Arab Seafaring.* Exp. ed. Princeton: Princeton University Press, 1995.

Kennedy, Hugh. *The Prophet and the Age of the Caliphates.* 2d ed. London: Pearson Education Limited, 2004.

Levtzion, N., and J. F. P. Hopkins, eds. *Corpus of Early Arabic Sources for West African History.* New York: Cambridge University Press, 1981.

Lunde, Paul, and Caroline Stone, trans. *The Meadows of Gold: The Abbasids by Mas'udi.* New York: Kegan Paul International, 1989.

Turner, Howard R. *Science in Medieval Islam: An Illustrated Introduction.* Austin: University of Texas Press, 1995.

Websites

Adherents.com
(www.adherents.com).   Takes an informed Religious Studies approach to the world's many religions, including Islam.

Discover Islam
(http://www.Islamicity.com).   An introduction to Islam on an educational website that also sells products related to Islam.

Internet Medieval Sourcebook
(http://www.fordham.edu/halsall/sbook.html).   Many primary sources listed under the link "Islam."

The Multiple Centers of Europe, 500–1000

Sometime around the year 1000, Leif Eriksson (LEAF ERIC-son) sailed with some forty companions from Greenland across the North Atlantic to New-foundland in today's Canada. His former sister-in-law **Gudrid** and her second husband **Thorfinn Karlsefni** followed in a subsequent voyage. The travelers were originally from Norway in the Scandinavian region of Europe, which also includes Sweden, Finland, and Denmark. The Europe of 1000 differed dramati-cally from the Europe of 500. In 500, it contained only one major empire, By-zantium, with its capital at Constantinople (modern Istanbul, Turkey). Over the next five hundred years, migrating peoples completely reshaped Europe. By 1000, it was home to multiple centers—modern-day France and Germany, Scandinavia, and Russia—that today are still the most important European powers.

Competition among these multiple centers provided a powerful stimulus to develop, as the Scandinavian voyages to the Americas amply demonstrate. An account recorded several hundred years later, but based on oral history, reports that, after the Scandinavians arrived in the Americas, Karlsefni set off to explore with a man named Snorri:

GUDRID AND
THORFINN KARLSEFNI

(Arni Magnusson Institute, Reykjavik, Iceland/
The Bridgeman Art Library)

Karlsefni sailed south along the coast. . . . Karlsefni and his men sailed into the estuary and named the place Hope (Tidal Lake). Here they found wild wheat growing in fields on all the low ground and grape vines on all the higher ground. Every stream was teaming with fish. They dug trenches at the high-tide mark, and when the tide went out there were halibut trapped in all the trenches. In the woods there was a great number of animals of all kinds.

They stayed there for a fortnight [two weeks], enjoying themselves and noticing nothing untoward. They had their livestock with them. But early one morning as they looked

Ⓒ This icon will direct you to interactive activities and study materials on the *Voyages* website:
www.cengage.com/history/hansen/voyages1e

268

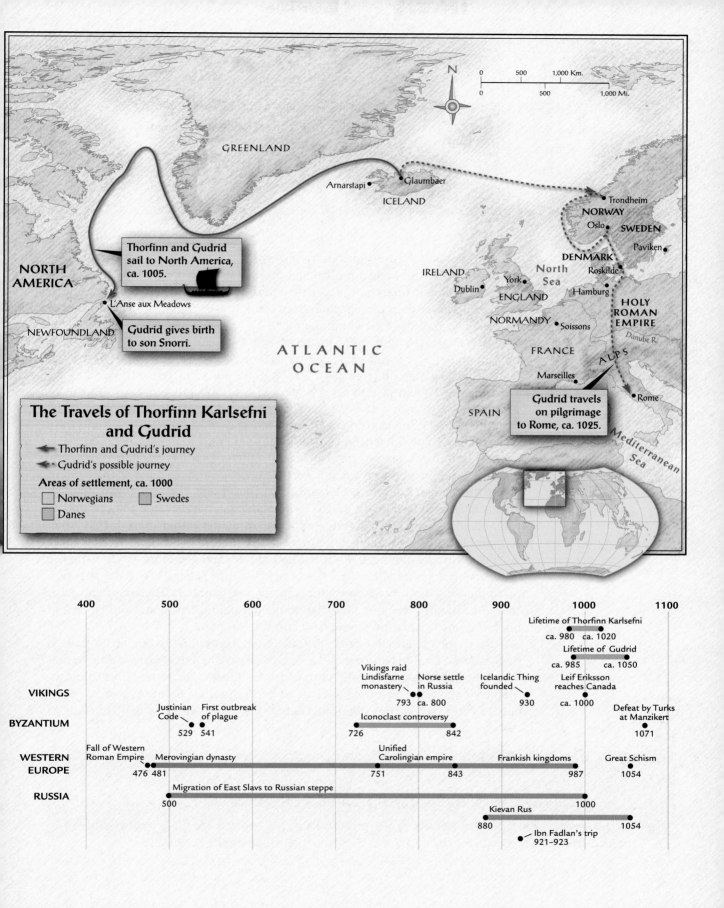

The Travels of Thorfinn Karlsefni and Gudrid

← Thorfinn and Gudrid's journey
←•• Gudrid's possible journey

Areas of settlement, ca. 1000
☐ Norwegians ☐ Swedes
☐ Danes

Thorfinn and Gudrid sail to North America, ca. 1005.

Gudrid gives birth to son Snorri.

Gudrid travels on pilgrimage to Rome, ca. 1025.

GREENLAND

Arnarstapi   Glaumbaer
ICELAND

Trondheim
NORWAY
Oslo
SWEDEN
Paviken

DENMARK
Roskilde

IRELAND   North Sea
York   Hamburg
Dublin
ENGLAND   HOLY
ROMAN
NORMANDY   EMPIRE
Soissons   Danube R.

FRANCE   ALPS

Marseilles   Rome

SPAIN   Mediterranean Sea

NORTH
AMERICA

L'Anse aux Meadows

NEWFOUNDLAND

ATLANTIC
OCEAN

	400	**500**	**600**	**700**	**800**	**900**	**1000**	**1100**

Lifetime of Thorfinn Karlsefni
ca. 980   ca. 1020

Lifetime of Gudrid
ca. 985   ca. 1050

VIKINGS

Vikings raid Lindisfarne monastery — 793
Norse settle in Russia — ca. 800
Icelandic Thing founded — 930
Leif Eriksson reaches Canada — ca. 1000

BYZANTIUM

Justinian Code — 529
First outbreak of plague — 541
Iconoclast controversy — 726 842
Defeat by Turks at Manzikert — 1071

WESTERN EUROPE

Fall of Western Roman Empire — 476
Merovingian dynasty — 481
Unified Carolingian empire — 751 ... 843
Frankish kingdoms — 987
Great Schism — 1054

RUSSIA

Migration of East Slavs to Russian steppe — 500 1000
Kievan Rus — 880 1054
Ibn Fadlan's trip 921–923

around they caught sight of nine skin-boats; the men in them were waving sticks which made a noise like flails [tools used to thresh grain], and the motion was sunwise [clockwise].

Karlsefni said, "What can this signify!"

"It could well be a token of peace," said Snorri. "Let us take a white shield and go to meet them with it."[1]

> **● Gudrid and Thorfinn Karlsefni**
> A couple originally from Iceland who settled in about 1000 in Greenland and then Canada, which the Scandinavians called Vinland. Eventually left the Americas and returned to Iceland.

Karlsefni and Snorri went out to meet the men in boats, who stared at them and then left without incident. Although this incident is recorded in a later source, archaeological evidence shows that these Scandinavians built at least one settlement; evidence of their presence has been found in the Canadian town of L'Anse aux Meadows in today's Newfoundland.

Possessing faster and more maneuverable wooden boats than any of their contemporaries, the Scandinavians went as far as Russia, Greenland, Iceland, and Canada (see the map on page 269). Although we are accustomed to think of the distance between Europe and the Americas as enormous, the voyage from Greenland to the northeastern coast of Canada was only 1,350 miles (2,200 km). If the Scandinavians had hugged the coast of Greenland and Canada, they could have traveled farther but still within constant sight of land.

The Scandinavians were one of several different groups speaking Germanic languages that lived in western and northern Europe after the loss of the western half of the Roman Empire (see Chapter 7). Around 500, the residents of the late Roman Empire looked down on these Germanic peoples because they could not read and write, worshiped a variety of different deities rather than the Christian God, and lived in simple villages much smaller than Rome or the eastern capital of Constantinople. But by 1000, the situation had changed dramatically. The rise of Germanic states paralleled the rise of the Buddhist states of East Asia that borrowed the Tang dynasty blueprint for empire (see Chapter 8). These new European states, like Byzantium, were Christian, but their political structures differed from those of Rome because they were based on the war-band.

This chapter begins in Constantinople, the successor to the Roman Empire. As the Byzantine Empire contracted, new centers arose: first in Germany and France, then in Scandinavia, and finally in modern-day Russia. The residents of Constantinople viewed these regions as uncivilized backwaters, good only as sources of raw materials and slaves. They did not recognize the vitality of these new centers.

Focus Questions

 What events caused the urban society of the Byzantines to decline and resulted in the loss of so much territory to the Sasanian and Abbasid Empires?

⛵ **What was the war-band of traditional Germanic society? How did the political structures of the Merovingians and the Carolingians reflect their origins in the war-band?**

⛵ **When, where, how, and why did the Scandinavians go on their voyages, and what was the significance of those voyages?**

⛵ **What were the earliest states to form in the area that is now Russia, and what role did religion play in their establishment and development?**

⛵ **What did all the new states have in common?**

Byzantium, the Eastern Roman Empire, 476–1071

To distinguish it from the western empire based in Rome, historians call the Eastern Roman Empire, with its capital at Constantinople, the **Byzantine Empire,** or simply Byzantium (see Map 10.1). The Byzantine Empire lasted for over a thousand years after the western empire ended, in spite of continuous attacks by surrounding peoples. Far worse than any attack by a foreign power, the bubonic plague struck the empire in 541 and then at regular intervals for two more centuries. The massive decline in population, coupled with the cutting off of shipping lines across the Mediterranean, resulted in a sharp economic downturn. Through all these events the empire's scholars continued to preserve Greek learning, systematize Roman law, and write new Christian texts. Over the centuries, however, the amount of territory under Byzantine rule shrank, providing an opportunity for other European centers to develop.

● **Byzantine Empire** (476–1453) Eastern half of the Roman Empire after the loss of the western half in 476. Sometimes simply called Byzantium. Headed by an emperor in its capital of Constantinople (modern-day Istanbul).

● **patriarch** In the 400s and 500s, the highest-ranking bishop of the four major Christian church centers at Constantinople, Alexandria, Jerusalem, and Antioch. By 1000, the patriarch of Constantinople had become head of the Orthodox church of Byzantium.

● **pope** In the 400s and 500s the pope was the highest-ranking bishop in Rome, equal in rank to the patriarchs of Constantinople, Alexandria, Jerusalem, and Antioch. By 1000, the pope was recognized as leader of the Catholic Church in Rome.

Justinian and the Legacy of Rome, 476–565

Constantinople, the city named for the emperor Constantine, had been a capital of the Eastern Roman Empire since 330. Between 395 and 476 different rulers governed the eastern and western sections of the empire, but after 476 the eastern emperor often had no counterpart in Rome. The Christian church at this time had five major centers: in Constantinople, Alexandria, Jerusalem, Antioch, and Rome. The top church bishops in the first four cities were called **patriarchs,** but by 1000 the highest-ranking bishop in Rome had the title of **pope.**

Culturally the residents of the eastern and western halves of the empire had much in common: educated people often spoke both Greek and Latin, almost everyone was Christian, and citizens accepted Roman law. Sometimes people in the west referred to those living in the eastern half as "Greeks" since nearly everyone there, including Armenians, Syrians, and Egyptians, spoke Greek, not Latin, although not always as their mother tongue. In the year 500, few observers realized that the urbanized life of the Roman Empire was soon to decline, but decline did begin with the first outbreak of plague in 541, which occurred during the long reign of the emperor Justinian I and had lasting repercussions.

MAP 10.1

The Byzantine Empire

The Byzantine empire grew dramatically during the reign of Justinian (r. 527–565), expanding its territory in North Africa, the Balkans, and Italy. Yet the plague struck for the first of at least fifteen times in 541–544, killing seven million of his twenty-six million subjects.

CL Interactive Map

Justinian I was a native of Thrace, the region north of Greece, and grew up speaking the local language and Latin. Like many Byzantine emperors, he was chosen by his predecessor, an illiterate soldier also from Thrace, who adopted him and raised him in Byzantium. In 520, Justinian met his future wife: an actress and circus performer named Theodora (497–548), who had given birth to at least one child before she met Justinian. She did not fulfill Byzantine ideals of modesty, yet Justinian succeeded in changing the law so that he could marry her, and the two ruled together for more than twenty years.

In 532, early in their reign, a commission of legal scholars completed one of the most important legal works ever written: the Justinian Corpus of Civil Law. The corpus consists of three works: the Code (completed in 529), the Digest (533), and the Institutes (also 533). Working for three years, the commission gathered together all the valid laws of the Roman Empire and reduced some three million laws, many no longer in effect, to a manageable body 1,500 pages long in its modern edition. The texts of the laws and the extensive legal commentary were written in Latin, still the official language of the central government, but the laws issued by Justinian himself were in Greek, which was rapidly becoming the administrative language of the empire. The Justinian Corpus preserved the core of Roman law not just for sixth-century jurists but also for all time.

Justinian and Theodora managed the empire's relations with its neighbors with considerable success. Unlike his predecessors, Justinian challenged the Vandals, one of the Germanic peoples who had conquered North Africa in the fifth century (see Chapter 7). His successful military campaigns in Northwest Africa, coastal Spain, and Italy added territory to the empire. Yet, on the eastern front, the armies of the Sasanian empire in Iran (see Chapter 6) captured Antioch, the third-largest city in the Byzantine Empire. This Persian display of military might revealed how vulnerable the eastern empire was.

The Impact of the Plague and the Arab Conquests, 541–767

The fighting on both the eastern and western frontiers subsided immediately after the first recorded outbreak of the bubonic plague in Europe in 541. Many people, including Justinian himself, became terribly ill. In modern usage, the term **plague** refers to two distinct illnesses, bubonic plague and pneumonic plague, which form two phases of an outbreak. First, fleas that have drunk the blood of infected rodents transmit the bubonic plague to people. Lymph glands on the neck, under the arm, and on the groin swell up and turn black. Once part of the human population is infected with bubonic plague, the pneumonic plague spreads as one victim sneezes or coughs onto another. Pneumonic plague is almost always fatal.

One contemporary observer, the historian Procopius (pro-COE-pee-uhs), observed that the disease first appeared in towns along the coast and then moved inland, but he did not know why. Only in the late nineteenth century did scientists realize that black rats living on ships were the main agents responsible for spreading the disease.

The first outbreak hit the Egyptian port of Pelusium (pell-OOZE-ee-uhm) on the mouth of the Nile in 541 and spread across the Mediterranean to Constantinople in the following year. Ports such as Carthage, Rome, and Marseilles were affected in 543. Further outbreaks followed; historians have counted at least fifteen different outbreaks between 541 and 767, when the plague finally came to an end.

In the absence of accurate population statistics, historians have to estimate the deaths resulting from the plague. The deaths in the large cities were massive: some 230,000 out of 375,000 died in Constantinople alone.[2] High estimates put the death toll from the plague at one-quarter of the empire's population during Justinian's reign: of 26 million subjects, only 19 million survived.

Before the plague the Roman Empire had been an urban society where powerful people met at the marketplace each day to discuss their affairs, enjoying theater and circus performances alongside their poorer neighbors. By 600 such an urban type of life had become a memory. Constantinople may have begun as the emperor's glorious second capital, but the deaths resulting from the Justinian plague severely damaged the empire's economy.

Starting in 541 and continuing to sometime in the ninth century, the population declined, cities shrank, the economy contracted, and tax revenues plummeted. In these centuries of declining tax revenues, the government minted far fewer coins than earlier, and a barter economy replaced the partially monetized economy. Craftsmen and merchants gave up their occupations to become farmers.

Another consequence of these catastrophes was that the government could no longer afford to pay its soldiers. Instead, militias were formed by part-time soldiers who farmed the land during peacetime. When Islamic forces began to expand around 640 (see Chapter 9), the Sasani and Byzantine Empires had just finished an exhausting war, and the Byzantine Empire ceded to the victorious Islamic forces large chunks of territory in Armenia and Africa.

In contrast to the multiple officials of Roman times, the basic administrative unit of the Byzantine Empire during the seventh and eighth centuries was the *theme* (Greek plural form: *themata*) headed by a single governor rather than the multiple officials of Roman times. This governor heard legal disputes, collected taxes, and commanded the local militia. Society had also changed from Roman times. The high and low in rank led almost identical lives, and people no longer used a clan name and a personal name; a simple Christian name (first name) sufficed. Fewer

plague Refers to two distinct illnesses, bubonic plague and the almost always fatal pneumonic plague, forming two phases of an outbreak. The plague struck Byzantium more than fifteen times between 541 and 767.

people knew Latin. Some people possessed more land than others, but they now worked the land alongside their poorer dependents. Slavery declined as well because no one could afford to feed slaves. Most of the people in the countryside were legally independent peasants who farmed the land intensively, often with two oxen and a plow, and grew only enough food to feed their own families.

The final outbreak of plague hit Constantinople in 747 and ended in 767. In the following years a slow revival began. The government minted more small coins, and trade and commerce increased slightly. The writing of manuscripts resumed, especially in monasteries, where scribes devised a new, smaller minuscule script that allowed them to write more words on a piece of parchment, the most common writing material. (Parchment was made by scraping the hair from the skin of sheep, goats, or calves and then stretching and cleaning it.) Literacy was mainly concentrated among monks and nuns. Although monasteries had little land and not much wealth, like the monasteries of Egypt (see Chapter 7), they offered an appealing alternative to family life.

◼ **The Striking Dome of Hagia Sophia**   Built in a mere five years, the dome of the Hagia Sophia cathedral in Constantinople (modern Istanbul, Turkey) is more than 100 feet (30 m) in diameter and over 180 feet (55 m) tall. Forty windows at the bottom of the dome give the impression that it floated in the air, and later observers believed that such a beautiful dome could only have been made with divine help.   (Color lithograph from the original drawing by Chevalier Caspar Fussati/© Historical Picture Archive/Corbis)

Religion and State, 767–1071

The Byzantine emperor ruled the empire, while the patriarch of Constantinople presided over the church, which held property throughout the empire. While the Christian emperors sometimes tried to impose their own views on the church, they also served as patrons. For example, the emperor Justinian financed the rebuilding of the most beautiful cathedral in Constantinople, the Hagia Sophia (hah-GHEE-ah so-FEE-ah), whose literal meaning "Divine Wisdom" refers to an attribute of Jesus.

Byzantine opinion during the eighth century was sharply divided over the use of images in Christian worship. The iconoclasts, literally "image-breakers," advocated the removal of all images of Jesus, Mary, and any saints yet permitted prayers directed to crosses. Like the Umayyads, who also banned images (see Chapter 9), the iconoclasts justified their position by citing the Second Commandment of the Hebrew Bible forbidding the worship of graven images. The iconoclast movement appalled many Christians in western Europe, however, who frequently prayed to the statues of saints. When one emperor ordered the removal of a statue of Jesus from the main entrance to his palace, an angry crowd of women killed the man who took the image down.

In 780, the widow of the emperor Leo IV came to power when in her mid-20s and served as regent for her 9-year-old son. Few expected Irene to rule for long, but she surprised her opponents by tackling some of the major issues facing the empire. Whenever Byzantine rulers wanted to resolve a controversy within the church, they summoned a church council that included the patriarch (the top-ranking cleric in Constantinople) and bishops from all over the Christian world. Irene summoned such a council in the hope of working out a compromise to end the iconoclast controversy. In 787, the Second Council of Nicaea met and condemned iconoclasm. Those at the meeting cited passages from the Bible approving the veneration of images, and they permitted all previous iconoclasts to repudiate their earlier positions against icons. Images that had been removed from different churches were returned.

During her reign, Irene tried, not always successfully, to negotiate foreign relations with the Abbasid caliphate and the Franks, the powerful Germanic group that controlled most of modern France (see next page). By agreeing to make various large payments of both books and money, she managed to keep the Abbasid armies under the leadership of Harun al-Rashid from taking the city of Constantinople (see Chapter 9), but she could not prevent the powerful Islamic army from making incursions into the empire's shrunken territory.

Irene and her son did not share power easily. First he tried to seize power from her, then they ruled together, and then, in 797, she tried to overthrow him. Her allies blinded her son, possibly without her knowledge, and he died soon after. Irene then became the first woman to rule the Byzantine Empire in her own right and called herself emperor (not empress).

■ **The Sin of Iconoclasm**   The ninth-century Byzantine artist who painted this miniature equated the application of whitewash to a round icon of Jesus (*lower center*) with the Roman centurions giving vinegar to the dying Jesus on the cross at Jerusalem (*upper right*). The text in the upper left hand is written in minuscule script, first developed in the eighth century, that allowed scribes to squeeze more words onto each page of costly parchment.   (State Historical Museum, Moscow. Photo courtesy the Weitzmann Collection, Department of Art and Archaeology, Princeton University)

A great blow to the Byzantines came from Rome in 800 when the pope crowned the ruler of the Franks, Charlemagne, emperor of Rome (see page 281). The pope used the pretext that Irene could not be emperor because she was female. The Byzantines were horrified. They thought of Charlemagne as the unlettered leader of primitive peoples, not as a monarch comparable to their own. The pope's crowning of Charlemagne was significant because it marked the rise of a new state outside the Byzantine Empire that claimed to be the legitimate heir to the Roman Empire.

In 802, the empress's courtiers deposed the elderly Irene and installed a general as her successor. The empire that Irene relinquished was less than a third the size it had been in the mid-sixth century. Justinian had ruled over an empire that controlled the eastern half of the Mediterranean, but Islamic forces had conquered large blocks of territory throughout the seventh century. By 800, the Byzantine Empire, consisting largely of the region of Anatolia, could easily fit inside the modern borders of Turkey, and its population was only seven million.

In the centuries after 800 Byzantium, though small, continued to be an important intellectual center where scholars studied, copied, and preserved Greek texts from the past, analyzed Roman law, and studied Christian doctrine. Between 800 and 1000, Byzantine rulers sometimes won military victories to the east in modern-day Bulgaria or farther west in Anatolia, but in 1071 they suffered a massive defeat at the battle of Manzikert (modern-day Malazgirt, Turkey) at the hands of the Seljuq Turks, who captured the emperor himself. A new emperor took power in Constantinople. After 1071, the Byzantine emperors continued to rule from their capital at Constantinople, but with a much-weakened army over much less territory.

The Germanic Peoples of Western Europe, 481–1000

After the fall of the Western Roman Empire, the Byzantines often referred to the peoples living in the north of Europe as *barbarians*, a Greek word meaning "uncivilized." The largest group were the Franks in modern-day France and Germany. Although uncivilized in Byzantine eyes, they commanded powerful armies who defeated the Byzantine armies in battle. The Franks were ruled first by the kings of the Merovingian dynasty (481–751) and then by the Carolingians (751–ca. 1000). And in 800, as we have seen above, the pope crowned the king of the Franks, Charlemagne, the emperor of Rome. Unlike the Byzantine emperors, who governed an empire divided into regular administrative districts called *themata*, the Merovingian and Carolingian monarchs ruled as the leaders of war-bands, the most important unit of Germanic society.

Germanic Society Before 500

Many different peoples lived in the regions of northern and central Europe and crowded the borders of the Western Roman Empire before it fell in 476. They spoke a group of related languages now classed as Germanic, about which little is known because none was written down. Even so, analysts have been able to sketch some broad similarities among Germanic peoples, usually on the basis of archaeological evidence.

The basic unit of Germanic society was the extended family, which was headed by the father, who might have more than one wife, as well as children and slaves. Since cattle herding was the basis of the economy, the more cattle an individual had, the higher his rank. Freemen looked down on slaves, who were usually war captives.

Beyond the immediate family were larger kinship groups consisting of several households bound by family ties on both the male and female sides. These groups feuded often and developed a complex set of rules for determining the correct handling of disputes. The best source for understanding the practices of the Germanic peoples is the Salic Law, a list of punishments for different crimes recorded early in the sixth century. Although written in Latin, the Salic Law shows little Roman influence.

One of the most important Germanic legal concepts was that of **wergeld** (literally "man-payment"), which set the monetary value of a human life. Wergeld (WEAR-geld) payments served to prevent an endless cycle of killing and counterkilling among feuding families. Different wergeld penalties were specified for men and women, both free and unfree. For example, the section of the Salic Law "On Killing Pregnant Women" says the following:

> **wergeld** Literally "man-payment," an important Germanic legal concept that set the monetary value of a human life. The function of wergeld payments was to prevent an endless cycle of killing and counterkilling among feuding families.

1. He who kills a pregnant woman shall be liable to pay twenty-four thousand denarii [six hundred solidi, or 6 pounds, or 2.73 kg, of gold]. And if it is proved that the fetus was a boy, he shall also be liable to pay six hundred solidi for the child.

2. He who kills a girl less than twelve years old or up to the end of her twelfth year shall be liable to pay two hundred solidi [2 pounds, or .9 kg, of gold].

3. He who kills a woman of mature age up to her sixtieth year, as long as she is able to bear children, shall be liable to pay twenty-four thousand denarii [six hundred solidi, or 6 pounds, or 2.73 kg, of gold].

4. But if she is killed afterwards when she is no longer able to bear children he shall be liable to pay two hundred solidi [2 pounds, or .9 kg, of gold].[3]

Penalties were levied in either silver denarius coins or gold solidus coins and varied depending on whether a woman had reached or passed child-bearing age, and if pregnant, whether she was carrying a male or female child. These payments were the sole form of punishment: no one was imprisoned or banished.

In times of war, groups of warriors called **war-bands** gathered behind a leader, whose main claim to their allegiance was the distribution of plunder. A successful leader took his men into battle and rewarded them liberally with the spoils of victory. He not only fed and clothed them but also provided them with horses, armor, and a place to live. His supporters, in turn, fought next to him in battles and banqueted with him when at peace.

> **war-band** The most important social unit of Germanic society. In times of war, warriors formed bands behind a leader, who provided them with horses, armor, and a place to live. Successful leaders rewarded their men with the spoils of victory to claim their allegiance.

Germanic society was extremely fluid, because war-bands could form rapidly and collapse equally quickly. Members of a war-band distinguished themselves from others by wearing a certain kind of clothing, having similar hairstyles, or carrying similar weapons. They often believed that they and the other members of the war-band had a common ancestor, sometimes a god, from whom they all claimed descent. According to Germanic custom, freemen were obliged to fight in wars while slaves were not. The freemen in these bands often gathered in assemblies, called Thing (TING), to settle internal disputes or to plan military campaigns.

The Merovingians, 481–751

The most important leader to emerge from the constantly evolving alliances of Frankish society was Clovis (r. 481–511), who established the **Merovingian dynasty** that ruled modern-day France and Germany from 481 to 751. He combined great military successes, such as defeating the Visigoths of Spain, with skillful marriage alliances to build a dynasty that lasted two centuries, far longer than any earlier Germanic dynasty. The Merovingian army consisted of different war-bands linked by their loyalty to Clovis.

● **Merovingian dynasty** A Germanic dynasty (481–751) in modern-day France and Germany whose founder Clovis (r. 481–511) converted to Christianity and ruled as a war-band leader.

One incident, recounted by the chronicler Gregory of Tours (538/39–594?), vividly illustrates the ties between Clovis and his followers. In 486, Clovis and his men removed many items from the treasuries of several churches, including a "vase of marvelous size and beauty" from Soissons. The bishop of the robbed church requested the vase's return. After Clovis and his followers had divided the goods they had stolen, Clovis addressed his men: "I ask you, O most valiant warriors, not to refuse to me the vase in addition to my rightful part." Most of his men agreed to do so, but one man crushed the vase with his battle-ax because he felt that Clovis, although their leader, was not entitled to more than his fair share. The humiliated Clovis returned the pieces of the broken vase to the bishop.

One year later, Clovis summoned his troops for a review so that he could inspect their spears, swords, and axes, the iron weapons that helped to make his armies invincible. When he reached the man who had destroyed the vase, he threw the soldier's ax to the ground. As the soldier bent down to pick it up, Clovis grabbed his head and smashed it down on the weapon. "Thus," he said, "didst thou to the vase at Soissons."[4]

This incident shows that, though called a king, Clovis was a war-band leader who ruled his men only as long as he commanded their respect, and he had to use brute strength coupled with rewards to do so. One sign of the Merovingian king's power was his hair, which only he was allowed to grow long. If someone challenged the ruler's hold on power and defeated the leader, he was forced to shave off his hair — a visible reminder that he was no longer fit to rule — and the challenger took over.

The Franks, a tiny minority of perhaps 200,000 people, lived among 7 million Gallo-Romans in modern-day France and Germany.[5] Like many of his subjects, Clovis worshiped both Roman and Germanic deities. However, as Gregory of Tours reports, Clovis converted to Christianity a few years before his death in 511, thus eliminating the largest cultural barrier between the Germanic peoples and the Gallo-Romans they governed. Like the Roman emperor Constantine (see Chapter 7), Clovis promised to convert if Jesus Christ brought him victory in battle; when his enemy surrendered, he was baptized, along with three thousand of his men. This battle may have occurred in 496, 498, or 506. So few records about the early Merovingians survive that even the basic chronology of Clovis's reign is unknown. When Clovis died in 511, he divided his realm among his four sons, according to Germanic custom, and they and their descendents continued to rule until the mid-eighth century.

Under the Romans, large landowners had lived with their slaves in widely dispersed estates. Under the Merovingians, the basic farming unit changed to the Germanic village. The many wars with Rome during the fourth and fifth centuries forced Roman villa owners to leave their homes and move near streams or forests, where they lived with others in small settlements and reclaimed small plots from Roman agricultural land that had been allowed to go wild. They engaged in slash-and-burn agriculture and changed plots whenever a field's productivity gave out.

Ordinary people consumed a diet composed largely of hunted animals, fish caught in rivers, or plants foraged from the forest.

At the beginning of the Merovingian dynasty, many urban residents had embraced Christianity, while most of those living in the countryside continued to pray to shrines housing Germanic or Roman gods. In the fourth and fifth centuries, early Christians had experimented with extreme forms of asceticism and different types of religious communities. Monasteries—small communities under the supervision of the local bishop—gradually spread to western Europe from the eastern Mediterranean. Many were modeled on a monastery founded in 529 near Rome by Benedict of Nursia (ca. 480–545), who composed a concise set of practical rules for running a monastery. Benedictine monks devoted themselves full-time to manual labor and the worship of God, usually through public prayer conducted eight times each day. Unlike monks in more extreme monasteries, they ate an adequate diet and received enough sleep. The adult members of the community selected their leader, or abbot, who was to obey the local bishop.

Around 590 an Irish monk named Saint Columbanus (543–615) arrived in the Merovingian kingdom and founded many monasteries that encouraged monks to be even more devout and disciplined. Columbanus (COH-luhm-bahn-us) taught that laypeople could contribute land and money to monasteries, read religious texts (or have them read aloud), and recite Psalms from the Hebrew Bible. Irish monks copied, and so preserved, many manuscripts that would have otherwise been lost.

Bishops were among the few educated men in Merovingian society. Bishops tended to have varied backgrounds. While some had served as priests, others had worked for the king; still others had been monks or abbots in monasteries, and some had no ties to the church except that they belonged to an important lay family, often one that controlled a fair amount of land. Many learned to read and write by studying with other bishops or in monasteries.

Most Merovingian bishops had married before assuming office. After they became bishops, their wives continued to assist them with their duties, but the popes in Rome frequently urged them to treat their wives as their sisters and stop sleeping with them. In some cases bishops slept surrounded by their male assistants so that everyone could see that they maintained their vows of celibacy.[6]

The head cleric of the Western church, the pope, was elected by the clergy in Rome. Before the rise of Islam, Rome and the Christian church had been securely under the control of the Byzantines, who controlled Italy. As Byzantine power declined, and after 568, when the Byzantines lost control of northern and central Italy to a Germanic people

CL **Primary Source:**
The Rule of Saint Benedict: Work and Pray
In this selection from his rules for monastic life, Benedict urged monks to avoid idleness by devoting themselves to physical labor, prayer— and reading!

Lindisfarne Gospel   In 793, the Vikings raided the island of Lindisfarne, an important center of Christian learning famed for its illuminated manuscripts. Here, the artist monk portrays Matthew using a stylus to write the first page of the gospel named for books. The artist first made a sketch on the reverse side of an individual sheet of parchment, turned it over, and shone a candle through the animal skin so that they could see the outline, which they then filled in with paint.   (British Library, London/HIP/Art Resource, NY)

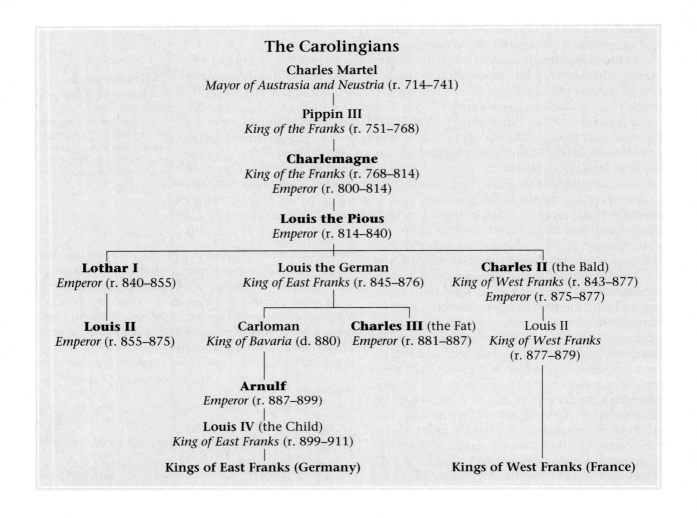

The Carolingians

Charles Martel
Mayor of Austrasia and Neustria (r. 714–741)

Pippin III
King of the Franks (r. 751–768)

Charlemagne
King of the Franks (r. 768–814)
Emperor (r. 800–814)

Louis the Pious
Emperor (r. 814–840)

Lothar I
Emperor (r. 840–855)

Louis the German
King of East Franks (r. 845–876)

Charles II (the Bald)
King of West Franks (r. 843–877)
Emperor (r. 875–877)

Louis II
Emperor (r. 855–875)

Carloman
King of Bavaria (d. 880)

Charles III (the Fat)
Emperor (r. 881–887)

Louis II
King of West Franks
(r. 877–879)

Arnulf
Emperor (r. 887–899)

Louis IV (the Child)
King of East Franks (r. 899–911)

Kings of East Franks (Germany)

Kings of West Franks (France)

called the Lombards, the popes needed military protection because they had no armies of their own. Moreover, the Lombards were Arians, and the popes did not accept Arius's teachings that God the Father was superior to Jesus and the Holy Ghost (see Chapter 7). The pope eventually turned to the Carolingians, an important family living in the Merovingian realm, for help.

Charlemagne and the Carolingians, 751–ca. 1000

In 751, the **Carolingian dynasty**, an important aristocratic family living in the eastern part of the Merovingian realm, overthrew the Merovingian rulers. (See the chart "The Carolingians.") The most powerful Carolingian ruler was Charles "the Great" ("le Magne" in old French), or Charlemagne (SHAHR-leh-maine). The events of his reign (768–814) demonstrated that the Carolingian realm (the region of modern-day France and Germany) exceeded Byzantium in importance. By 800, Europe had two powerful centers: Byzantium, which had inherited the legacy of Rome, and the new kingdom of the Franks.

Since the pope needed protection against the Lombards, he looked north to the Franks, and in 753 he formed an alliance with the Carolingians against the

• **Carolingian dynasty**
(751–ca. 1000) An important aristocratic family who overthrew the Merovingian rulers in 751. Their most powerful ruler was Charlemagne. After his death, the empire split into three sections, each under a different Carolingian ruler.

⊕ MAP 10.2
The Carolingian Realms

After coming to power in 768, Charlemagne continuously expanded the area under Carolingian rule. The unified empire did not last long. In 843, his grandsons divided his realm into three separate regions. The West Frankish kingdom eventually became modern-day France, while the East Frankish kingdom developed into modern Germany. The two states regularly vied for control of the territory between them.

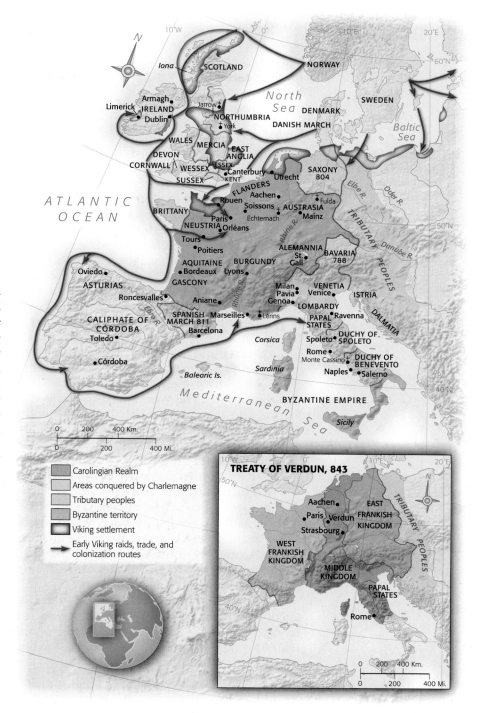

Lombards. The geographical origins of the popes changed almost immediately. Of the seventeen popes in office between 654 and 752, five came from Byzantium and five from Rome. After 753, there was never again another Greek-speaking pope. Most were Roman, and a few came from Frankish lands.[7]

Charlemagne became king of the Franks in 768 and then launched a series of wars against the neighboring Germanic peoples. The pope in Rome supported him against the Lombards, who controlled much of Italy, and Charlemagne rapidly conquered northern and central Italy, some parts of Spain, and much of Germany (see Map 10.2). In 800, during Irene's reign as Byzantine emperor (see page 275), the pope crowned Charlemagne emperor. By accepting this title, Charlemagne claimed that he, and not Irene, was the rightful successor of the emperors of Rome.

Diverging from its roots in the war-band, Carolingian society was divided into two groups: the powerful (potentes) and the powerless (paupers), literally the poor. The powerful owned their own land and could command others to obey them. Although some paupers owned land, they had no one to command. Among the powerless were slaves, a minority of the laborers in the countryside.

Interactive Map

During Charlemagne's many conquests, his armies took vast numbers of prisoners from enemy forces; they sold these slaves to buyers, sometimes in distant lands. Writers in the eighth and ninth centuries used the word *captive*, not *slave*, for these prisoners of war. Charlemagne's Christian advisers urged him to stop the sale of Christian slaves to non-Christians, but he continued to do so. One of Europe's main exports to the Abbasids under Charlemagne and his successors was slaves (see Chapter 9).

Despite his title of emperor, Charlemagne was still very much a Germanic warband leader. Although he had conquered more territory than any Germanic leader, he was much less educated than the Byzantine or Abbasid rulers of his day. His biographer, Einhard, reports that "he also attempted to learn how to write, and, for this reason, used to place wax-tablets and notebooks under the pillows on his bed, so that, if he had any free time, he might accustom his hand to forming letters. But his effort came too late in life and achieved little success."[8] Unable to write his name, Charlemagne liked having books read aloud to him.

Nevertheless, Charlemagne founded an academy where the sons of the powerful could be educated. He and his successors also established schools, one at the imperial court, others in monasteries. As in the Byzantine Empire, a new minuscule script came into use that permitted more words to be written on a single page of parchment. (Carolingian minuscule is the basis of today's lowercase Roman fonts.) During this revival of learning, monastic authors wrote Latin grammars, medical texts, and liturgies with detailed instruction for church ceremonies.

When Charlemagne died in 814, he left his empire intact to his son Louis the Pious (r. 814–840), but when Louis died in 840, his feuding sons divided the kingdom into thirds. The West Frankish kingdom would eventually become modern France, and the East Frankish kingdom, modern Germany. The East and West kingdoms continuously fought over the territory of the former Middle kingdom, which today contains portions of France, Germany, Italy, the Netherlands, and Switzerland. The Carolingians ruled until 911 in Germany and until 987 in the region of modern France, when they were succeeded by new dynasties.

Historians often describe the Carolingians as more centralized than the Merovingians, but in fact the two Frankish dynasties were more alike than different. Both dynasties were led by rulers who rewarded their followers with gifts and whose main source of revenue was plunder. Throughout this period, literacy remained extremely restricted, with only a tiny number of officials able to read and write. The rulers of both dynasties were Christian, but many of their subjects did not observe basic Christian teachings.

By the tenth century, when Carolingian rule came to an end, the region of the Franks, sometimes called the Latin West, was no longer united. Its major sections—modern-day France and Germany—were beginning to become powerful centers in their own right. By 1000, Byzantium was no longer the only empire in Europe.

The Age of the Vikings, 793–1050

In 793, a group of **Viking** raiders came by boat and seized the valuables held in an island monastery off the English coast. The term *Viking* refers to those Scandinavians who left home to loot coastal towns. For the next three centuries the

Vikings were the most successful plunderers in Europe, and no one could withstand their attacks. The peoples living in Scandinavia had many of the same Germanic customs as the Franks: their leaders commanded the loyalty of war-bands, plunder was their main source of income, and they gradually adopted Christianity and gave up their traditional Germanic gods. Some Scandinavian boatmen lived by stealing from coastal peoples, while others eventually settled in Iceland, Greenland, England, Scotland, Ireland, and Russia; ultimately, however, they decided not to stay on the Atlantic coast of Canada. Between 800 and 1000, several new states formed in Greenland, Iceland, Denmark, Norway, and Sweden, creating even more centers in Europe (see Map 10.3).

> **• Viking** Term used for those Scandinavians who left home to loot coastal towns and who were most active between 793 and 1066.

🌐 **MAP 10.3   The Viking Raids, 793–1066**   From their homeland in Scandinavia, the Vikings launched their first raid on Lindisfarne on the North Sea in 793 and moved on to attack Iceland, Greenland, France, Spain, and Russia for more than two hundred years. They often settled in the lands they raided. In around 1000, they even reached North America.

Ⓒ Interactive Map

Viking Raids on Great Britain, 793–1066

The Viking homeland was north of Charlemagne's realm in Scandinavia, a region consisting of modern-day Norway, Sweden, and Denmark (see the map on page 269), where the languages spoken were Germanic. The region had a cold climate with a short growing season, and many of its residents hunted walrus and whale for their meat or maintained herds on farms.

Since the Scandinavians conducted their raids by sea, the greatest difference between the Viking and the Frankish war-bands was the **longboat,** a large wooden boat held together by iron rivets and washers. The combination of oars and sails made these boats the fastest mode of transport in the world before 1000. Like the ancient Polynesians (see Chapter 5), the Scandinavian navigators recognized the shapes of different landmasses, sometimes sighting them from mountaintops. No evidence of Scandinavian navigational instruments survives. Their first targets were the monasteries of the British Isles in England, Ireland, and Scotland, which lay closest to the southwestern coast of Norway.

Before 500, Britain was home to a group of indigenous peoples whom the Romans had encountered, but after 500 these groups were absorbed by the Anglo-Saxons, a general term for the many Germanic groups who migrated to Britain from present-day Denmark and northern Germany. Anglo-Saxon society retained the basic characteristics of Germanic society on the continent: a sharp distinction between free and unfree, with a legal system emphasizing the concept of wergeld. (See the feature "World History in Today's World: The Days of the Week.")

The Anglo-Saxons converted to Christianity during the sixth and seventh centuries. Bede (ca. 672–735) became their most famous Christian thinker. He also

● **longboat** Boat used by the Vikings to make raids, made of wood held together by iron rivets and washers. Equipped with both oars and sails, they were the fastest mode of transport before 1000.

■ **The Longboats of the Scandinavians**   Sewn between 1066 and 1082, the Bayeux tapestry (held in northern France) is an embroidered piece of linen that stretches 231 feet (70 m). This detail shows the longboats in full sail. The boats are moving so quickly that the men seated in the first and third boats do not need to row. Notice that the middle and last boats are large enough to transport horses.   (© Michael Holford)

The Days of the Week

Where do Tuesday, Wednesday, Thursday, and Friday come from? Each of these names combines the name of a Scandinavian god with the suffix -day. Thursday, or Thor's day, is named for the vigorous god who ruled the sky and controlled thunder, wind, rain, and the harvest. Germanic peoples prayed to him to prevent famine and disease. Friday is named for Frey, the powerful god of fertility, who was honored at weddings. Odin, the powerful god of war, was thought to have created the first man and the first woman. His name is also spelled Wodin, the root of the modern Wednesday. Odin's son Tiu gave his name to Tuesday.

What about Sunday, Monday, and Saturday? They date back to 321 C.E., when the Romans adopted the seven-day week; Emperor Constantine named the days for different astronomical bodies: the sun, the moon, and the planet Saturn. The English names for the days of the week, which combine both the Scandinavian and Roman names, date to the fifth and sixth centuries C.E., when the Anglo-Saxons migrated to England from Germany.

Source: www.indepthinfo.com/weekdays/index.shtml.

wrote a history of the Anglo-Saxons that dated events before and after Christ's birth, the same system used in most of the world today.

Monasteries made an appealing target for Viking raiders because they contained much detailed metalwork, whether reliquaries that held fragments of saints' bones or bejeweled gold and silver covers for illustrated manuscripts. The raiders also captured many slaves, keeping some for use in Scandinavia and selling others to the Byzantine and Abbasid Empires. In 866, a large Viking army arrived in England, just north of London, and established a long-term base camp. This was the first Scandinavian settlement in England.

Between 866 and 954, the Scandinavians retained tenuous control of much of northern and eastern England, a region called the **Danelaw.** The residents paid an annual indemnity to their conquerors, and the Scandinavians settled throughout the Danelaw, Ireland, and Scotland. Alfred I (r. 871–899), who called himself "king of the Anglo-Saxons," managed to survive in the face of Viking attacks. After his death, various English, Anglo-Saxon, and Scandinavian leaders vied with each other for control of England, but no one succeeded for very long. In the tenth century, some Scandinavians settled in Normandy ("Northman's land") in northern France. From this base William the Conqueror launched an invasion of England in 1066, and his descendants ruled England for more than a hundred years.

● **Danelaw** Region including much of northern and eastern England, over which the Scandinavians maintained tenuous control between 866 and 954. The conquered residents paid an annual indemnity to the Scandinavians.

Scandinavian Society

Since the Scandinavians left only brief written texts on runestones, historians must draw on archaeological evidence and orally transmitted epics. Composed in Old Norse, a Germanic language, these epics were written down between 1200 and 1400. Two fascinating works, entitled *Erik the Red's Saga* and *The Greenlanders' Saga*, recount events around the year 1000. Together they are called **The Vinland Sagas,** since the Scandinavians called the Americas Vinland, meaning either grape land or fertile land. Like all oral sources, they must be used cautiously; both epics glorify certain ancestors while denigrating others, and both exaggerate the extent of Christian belief while minimizing the extent of non-Christian practices.

● *The Vinland Sagas* Term for *Erik the Red's Saga* and *The Greenlanders' Saga,* two sagas composed in Old Norse that recount events around the year 1000. Both were written between 1200 and 1400.

The peoples of Scandinavia lived in communities of small farms in large, extended families of parents, children, grandchildren, unmarried siblings, and their servants. Women had considerable authority in Scandinavian society. They had property rights equal to those of their husbands and could institute divorce proceedings.

Leif Eriksson's sister-in-law Gudrid plays such a major role in *Erik the Red's Saga* that some have suggested that it should have been named for her, and not for Leif's father Erik. She married three times, once to Leif Eriksson's brother, was widowed twice, and possibly went to Rome on a pilgrimage at the end of her life. In the saga, whereas Gudrid is virtuous, Leif's illegitimate sister Freydis (FRY-duhs) is a murderer who will stop at nothing to get her way. Both women, however one-dimensional, are intelligent, strong leaders.

Like the Germanic peoples living on the European continent, the Scandinavians formed war-bands around leaders. Leaders recruited their retinues with gifts, and their followers accompanied them into battle and fought vigorously for shares of the plunder they took from the defeated. In the years before 1000, new trade routes appeared linking Scandinavia with the Abbasid Empire. Muslims bought slaves and furs from Scandinavians with silver dirham coins, over 130,000 of which have been found around the Baltic Sea.

At this time Scandinavian society produced a leader who played a comparable role to King Clovis of the Merovingians: Harald Bluetooth, who ruled the region of modern Denmark between approximately 940 and 985. After unifying Denmark, he conquered southern Norway. In 965 he became the first Scandinavian ruler to convert to Christianity, and the rulers of Norway and Sweden did so around 1030.

Scandinavian Religion

Women played an especially active role in pre-Christian religion because some served as seers who could predict the future. Once when famine hit a Greenland community, *Erik the Red's Saga* relates, a wealthy landowner hosted a feast to which he invited a prophetess. The next day she asked the women of the community who among them knew "the spells needed for performing the witchcraft, known as Warlock songs." Gudrid reluctantly volunteered and "sang the songs so well and beautifully that those present were sure they had never heard lovelier singing." When she finished, the seer explained that the famine would end soon, since "many spirits are now present which were charmed to hear the singing."[9]

The Scandinavians worshiped many gods. One traveler described a pre-Christian temple in Sweden that held three images. In the center was Thor, the most powerful deity who controlled the harvest. On either side of him stood the war-god Odin and the fertility goddess, Frey. Scandinavian burials often contain small metal items associated with Thor, such as hammers.

Burial customs varied. In some areas burials contained many grave goods, including full-size boats filled with clothing and tools, while in other areas the living cremated the dead and burned all their grave goods. (See the feature "Movement of Ideas: Ibn Fadlan's Description of a Rus Burial" on page 294.) When people converted to Christianity, they were not supposed to bury grave goods because Christians believed that the dead could not bring these goods to the afterlife, but many who still believed in the gods were reluctant to follow this prohibition for fear that the dead might starve or freeze as a result. In one gruesome anecdote from *The Vinland Sagas,* the ghost of a dead man comes to Gudrid and instructs her to give the dead a Christian burial in consecrated ground near a church but to burn the body of a bad man, presumably to stop him from haunting the living. The tale captures the dilemma of those deciding between Christian and pre-Christian burial.

The Scandinavian Migrations to Iceland and Greenland, 870–980

As in Merovingian and Carolingian society, slaves and former slaves ranked at the bottom of society. When a former slave proposes to Gudrid, her father is furious: "I never expected to hear such a suggestion from you— that I should marry my daughter to the son of a slave! My lack of money must be very obvious to you!" The proposal prompts him to give up his farm and leave for Greenland, where he hopes to find more fertile land. This was the impetus for migration: everyone hoped to get more fertile land than was available in Scandinavia, which was becoming increasingly crowded.

In the first wave, between 870 and 930, Scandinavians went to Iceland. In 930 they established an assembly, called the Thing, that resembled the assemblies of other Germanic peoples to their south. The Thing had the power to pass laws and to hear disputes. Some have called Iceland's Thing the world's first legislature, but wealthy landowners had a greater say than the poor.

The Vinland Sagas describe events occurring in Iceland sometime around 980, when Erik the Red and his father had already left Norway "because of some killings." They were forced to give up their home, where Leif was born, after Erik killed two neighbors. When they became involved in a second dispute, the Thing assembly exiled Erik for being a thief.

Erik then told a group of followers that he was going to look for an island that he had heard about. He sailed west 200 miles (320 km) to Greenland, which he so named because he hoped to entice more people to settle there. After his term of exile ended, he returned to Iceland, which was becoming increasingly crowded with a population of thirty thousand, and recruited Scandinavians to go with him. In 985 or 986, Erik led a fleet of twenty-five boats on a migration to Greenland; fourteen reached Greenland, and the others either turned back to Iceland or perished.

These stories roughly describe how migrations occurred. Scandinavian explorations generally began with a ship being blown off course. Those navigators who successfully steered their way home described what they had seen. Then someone, such as Erik the Red, sailed in search of the new place. Finally, a small expedition of ships led a group of settlers to the new lands.

The Scandinavians established two settlements on Greenland, the Eastern and Western Settlements. At that time Greenland was slightly warmer than it is now. The settlers lived much as they had on Iceland, grazing animals on the narrow coast between the ocean and the interior ice, fishing for walrus, whales, and seals, and hunting polar bears and reindeer. They had to trade furs and walrus tusks to obtain the grain, wood, and iron they needed to survive. The Greenlanders established their own Thing assembly, which voted to adopt Christianity soon after the Icelandic Thing voted to do so in 1000.

The Scandinavians in Vinland, ca. 1000

Around 1000, Leif Eriksson, the son of Erik the Red, decided to lead an exploratory voyage because he had heard from a man named Bjarni Herjolfsson (bee-YARN-ee hair-YOLF-son) of lands lying to the west of Greenland. It is possible that others had preceded Bjarni to the Americas, but *The Vinland Sagas* do not give their

THE SCANDINAVIAN SETTLEMENT AT L'ANSE AUX MEADOWS

In 1960, a Norwegian diplomat-turned-explorer, Helge Ingstad, and his archaeologist wife, Anne Stine Ingstad, explored the Canadian coastline hoping to find a place where, as *The Vinland Sagas* said, "the country was flat and wooded, with white sandy beaches wherever they went; and the land sloped gently down to the sea."* This description fit an inlet near the town of L'Anse aux Meadows on the northern tip of Newfoundland, and here Helge and Anne Ingstad found a small settlement.

Pollen analysis revealed that the climate in about 1000 was similar to today's and could have easily supported a settlement. Lumber, whether live trees or driftwood, was abundant. It was so cold that in most years the ice did not melt until June or July, an impossible climate for wild grapes. Still, the growing season was long enough for cloudberries, raspberries, blueberries, and red and black currants to thrive. Caribou, wolves, and foxes lived on the land, while walruses, whales, and seals flourished in the bay.

Originally, the Ingstads were not certain whether local Amerindians or Scandinavians had lived at the site. The small settlement contained eight houses that dated to between 980 and 1020, precisely at the time of the Scandinavian exploration of Vinland. Many finds indicated that it was a Scandinavian settlement.

---

*Magnus Magnusson, ed., *The Vinland Sagas* (New York: Penguin Books, 1965), p. 55.

Identical in structure to Icelandic buildings of the same period, the houses had walls and roofs made of sod that rested on wooden supports. Three were quite large halls for perhaps fifty people measuring 65 feet (20 m) long, with five smaller structures nearby. They formed three clusters of houses, each with a main dwelling for the group's leader and smaller, outlying houses for his dependents and slaves. Archaeologists found no large objects, an indication that the residents of the site systematically packed their possessions and left for home. The most revealing artifact was a small ringed pin, identical in design to thirteen others found on Iceland.

Many small artifacts indicate the kinds of tasks done on site. Needles and spindle whorls point to textile manufacture and mending, which, according to the sagas, were traditional women's work. The residents also collected iron ore, which forms naturally in bogs containing iron and manganese, and melted it in a furnace to obtain metal, which they hammered into nails for their boats. The place where the Scandinavians worked iron (the smith) contained an anvil and a big stone for hammering iron, iron fragments, and lumps of iron found in local bogs. The presence of a single locally produced iron nail makes this the earliest site of ironworking in the Americas (since none of the indigenous peoples living in the Americas could work iron).

Butternuts, a kind of a walnut, were found at the site but do not grow that far north. Archaeologists reason that the Scandinavians probably traveled

QUESTIONS FOR ANALYSIS

What finds from the site of L'Anse aux Meadows indicated that it was a Scandinavian settlement and not an Amerindian site?

What activities did men and women do separately in the different rooms of Hall F, and which together?

How did archaeologists use information from *The Vinland Sagas* to analyze the site?

south to collect them and possibly the grapes mentioned so often in the sagas. The site may have been a base camp for launching different expeditions to southern regions.

Some analysts believe that l'Anse aux Meadows was the main settlement of the Scandinavians where Leif Eriksson landed. The site was not occupied for long because little garbage was found, and no one was buried there. Even if it was not actually Leif's settlement, it is undeniable that the Scandinavians lived at l'Anse aux Meadows, however briefly, before deciding to return home.

Archaeologists injected a chemical preservative to harden the original walls, which were 5 feet (1.5 m) thick.

The bay, which opens onto the Atlantic Ocean, remains icy until June and freezes again in November or December.

This picture shows Hall F, the great hall, 65 feet (20 m) long and 16 feet (5 m) wide, that occupied the center of the structure.

(Parks Canada National Photo Collection)

Here, archaeologists found a sandstone whetstone for sharpening needles and scissors as well as the flywheel of a hand-held spindle, both signs of a women's sewing area.

Archaeologists found iron rivets in this iron-smelting workshop.

This hearth produced a small soapstone lamp of Icelandic design.

289

- **Bjarni Herjolfsson**
The first European,
according to *The Vinland
Sagas*, to sail to the
Americas, most likely
sometime in the 990s.

names, so we should probably credit **Bjarni Herjolfsson**—and not Christopher Columbus—with being the first European to sail to the Americas. First Leif and then Thorfinn Karlsefni made several voyages to the Americas, landing in modern-day L'Anse aux Meadows, Newfoundland, Canada, and possibly farther south in Maine. The Scandinavians landed in North America after the end of the Maya classic era and before the great Mississippian cities of the Midwest were built (see Chapter 5). (See the feature "Visual Evidence: The Scandinavian Settlement at L'Anse aux Meadows.")

Leif's brother-in-law, Thorfinn Karlsefni (see the beginning of the chapter), decided to lead a group of sixty men and five women to settle in Vinland, the Scandinavian name for their settlements in North America. Their first year went well because they found much wild game. Then "they had their first encounter with **Skraelings**" (literally "wretches"), the term that the Scandinavians used for indigenous peoples. At first the Skraelings traded furs for cow's milk or scraps of red cloth, because Karlsefni would not allow his men to trade their iron weapons. But relations soon deteriorated, and the Scandinavians and the Skraelings fought each other in several battles involving hand-to-hand combat. *Erik the Red's Saga* reports that the Skraelings "were using catapults. Karlsefni and Snorri saw them hoist a large sphere on a pole; it was dark blue in color. It came flying in over the heads of Karlsefni's men and made an ugly din when it struck the ground."

- **Skraelings**   Term in
The Vinland Sagas for
the Amerindians living
on the coast of Canada
and possibly northern
Maine, where the Scan-
dinavians established
temporary settlements.

The settlers in this story probably belonged to Karlsefni's war-band. Many had kin ties to him, whether direct or through marriage, and they probably gave him a share of the lumber they shipped to Greenland, much as they would have given him a share of any loot they collected in battle. Whenever the Scandinavians went to a new place, they captured slaves, and North America was no exception. Karlsefni enslaved two Skraeling boys, who lived with the Scandinavians and later learned their language. The boys told them about their homeland: "there were no houses there and that people lived in caves or holes in the ground. They said that there was a country across from their own land where the people went about in white clothing and uttered loud cries and carried poles with pieces of cloth attached." This intriguing report is one of the earliest we have about Amerindians.

The Scandinavians had a technological advantage over the Amerindians because they could fight using metal knives and daggers, which the indigenous peoples lacked because they did not know how to work iron. But while iron weapons gave the Scandinavians a slight advantage over a band of Amerindians equal in size to their own small population, they could never have prevailed against a much larger force. The sagas succinctly explain why the Scandinavians decided to leave the Americas: "Karlsefni and his men had realized by now that although the land was excellent they could never live there in safety or freedom from fear, because of the native inhabitants."

After a few years on the Canadian coast, the Scandinavians returned to Greenland, and in later centuries they sometimes returned to Canada to gather wood but never to settle. Sometime in the fifteenth century they also abandoned their settlements on Greenland because a drop in global temperature made life there much more difficult. The Scandinavian voyages are significant because they were the first Europeans to settle in the Americas. Their decision to leave resulted in no long-term consequences, a result utterly different from that of Columbus's voyages in the 1490s (see Chapter 15).

Russia, Land of the Rus, to 1054

Long before they set foot in Iceland, Greenland, or the Americas, around 800, early Scandinavians, mostly from Sweden, found that they could sail their longboats along the several major river courses, including the Volga and Dnieper Rivers, through the huge expanse of land lying to their east (see Map 10.4). The peoples living in this region called themselves and their polity **Rus,** the root of the word *Russia.* This region offered many riches, primarily furs and slaves, to the raiders. Local rulers sometimes allied with a neighboring empire, such as Byzantium or the Abbasids, to enhance their power. When forming such an alliance the rulers

> • **Rus**   Name given to themselves by people who lived in the region stretching from the Arctic to the north shore of the Black Sea and from the Baltic Sea to the Caspian Sea.

🌐 **MAP 10.4   Kievan Rus**   Before 970, the leaders of different war-bands controlled the region between the Baltic, Black, and Caspian Seas. In the 970s Prince Vladimir gained control of the trading post at Kiev and gradually expanded the territory under his rule to form the state of Kievan Rus.

Ⓒ Ⓛ **Interactive Map**

had to choose among Judaism, Islam, or the Christianity of Rome or Constantinople, and the decisions they made had a lasting effect. The region of modern-day Russia also saw the rise of important centers before 1000, contributing to even more centers in Europe.

The Peoples Living in Modern-Day Russia

Stretching from the Arctic to the north shore of the Black Sea and from the Baltic Sea to the Caspian, the region of Russia (which was much larger than today's modern nation) housed different ecosystems and different peoples deriving their living from the land. To the north, peoples exploited the treeless tundra and the taiga (sub-Arctic coniferous forest) to fish and to hunt reindeer, bear, and walrus. On the steppe grasslands extending far to the west, nomadic peoples migrated with their herds in search of fertile pasture. In the forests, where most people lived, they raised herds and grew crops on small family farms. Too poor to dedicate much land to raising hay, they had no draft animals and could clear the land only with fire and hand-tools. The lack of natural fertilizer from draft animals forced them to clear new lands every few years, with the result that their agriculture resembled slash-and-burn cultivation. These cultivators and foragers never could have survived had they depended entirely on agriculture.

The various peoples living in Russia spoke many different languages, none of which were written down. In 500, the **Slavs** occupied much of the territory in the lower Danube River Valley near the Black Sea. As they moved north and east for the next five hundred years, they enlarged the area in which their language, an ancestor of Russian, Ukrainian, Polish, and Czech, was spoken.

All these peoples, whatever their ecological niche, lived on the edge of subsistence and were vulnerable to Scandinavian slave raiders. After 700, the Scandinavians established trade outposts on the southeast coast of the Baltic and on the Dnieper and Volga Rivers. By 800, they had learned how to navigate these rivers to reach the Black and Caspian Seas.

The lack of written sources, whether by outsiders or Slavs, makes it difficult to reconstruct the early history of the Rus. Scholars have intensely debated their identity, some arguing that they were entirely Scandinavian, and others, entirely Slav. Modern scholars tentatively agree that the Rus were a multiethnic group including Balts, Finns, and Slavs, with Scandinavians the most prominent among them. Of these groups, the Balts and the Finns stayed in the region of the Baltic and Finland, while the Slavs and the Scandinavians traveled throughout the region.

Much of what we know about Russia before 900 comes from Byzantine accounts. The Byzantine Empire had the most sustained contact with the peoples who lived on the north shore of the Black Sea, particularly the Crimean peninsula. The Khazars, a formerly nomadic Turkic people, gained control of the southern part of Kievan Russia. In 900 their rulers converted to Judaism, a religion of the book that was neither the Christianity of their Byzantine enemies nor the Islam of their Abbasid rivals. The Khazar state continued to rule the Crimea for much of the tenth century.

During the tenth century, the Bulgars, a Turkic nomadic people previously subject to the Khazars, formed their own state along the Volga River. The Bulgars of modern Bulgaria are descended from these people. The Bulgars paid the Khazars one sable pelt each year for every household they ruled, but they converted to Islam partially in the hope of breaking away from the Khazars and avoiding this

● **Slavs** The people who, around 500, occupied much of the lower Danube River Valley near the Black Sea. They moved north and east for the next five hundred years and enlarged the area where their language, an ancestor of Russian, Ukrainian, Polish, and Czech, was spoken.

payment. After they received a visit by an envoy from the Abbasid caliph in 921–923, the ruler of the Bulgars assumed the title *emir,* and this state is therefore known as the Volga Bulgar Emirate.

Ibn Fadlan, an envoy from the Abbasid court, says that one merchant prayed, saying, "Lord, I have come from a distant land, bringing so and so many slave-girls priced at such and such per head and so many sables priced at such and such per pelt."[10] He then asked the deity to find him a merchant who would accept his asking price without haggling. (See "Movement of Ideas: Ibn Fadlan's Description of a Rus Burial.")

Rus traders used the currency of the Abbasid Empire: gold dinars and silver dirhams. The Rus gave their wives a gold or silver neckband for each ten thousand dirhams they accumulated. Archaeologists have found many such neckbands, frequently decorated with small Thor's hammers like those found in Scandinavian graves.

In addition to amber, swords, and wax, the main goods the Rus sold to the Islamic world were furs and slaves. Scandinavian merchants sold so many Slavs into slavery that, in the tenth century, the Europeans coined a new word for slaves: the Latin *sclavus* (SCLAV-uhs), derived from the Latin word for the Slavic peoples. This is the source of the English word *slave.*

Kievan Rus, 880–1054

Before 930, the Rus consisted of war-bands who paid tribute to rulers like the Khazars and the Volga Bulgar Emirate so that they could sell slaves and furs in their territories. After 930, the Rus war-bands evolved into early states called principalities, political units led by princes who exercised control over their own trading posts. The history of Kiev, a trading outpost on the Dnieper River, illustrates this development. Before 900, Kiev had a population of only one or two hundred residents who lived in villages. After 900, as trade grew, its population increased to several thousand, including specialized craftsmen who made goods for the wealthy. In 911, and again in 945, the Rus **Principality of Kiev** signed a treaty with Byzantium that specified the terms under which the Rus were to do business in Constantinople. Throughout the tenth century, the princes of Kiev eliminated their political rivals, including the Khazars and the Bulgars.

Since the middle of the ninth century, Byzantine missionaries had been active among the Rus and had modified the Greek alphabet to make the Cyrillic alphabet, named for a Byzantine missionary, Saint Cyril (827–869), who had been active a century earlier in modern-day Moravia. Using this alphabet, they devised a written language, called Old Church Slavonic, into which they translated Christian scriptures.

In the 970s Prince Vladimir emerged as leader of the Kievan Rus. Like the Khazar and Bulgar rulers, he had to decide which religion would best unify his realm, so he summoned the leaders of his kingdom and asked their advice. Our main source for this period, *The Primary Chronicle,* written down around 1100, gives a year-by-year chronology after 850 for the Rus (leaving many years blank). Its detailed entry for 987 explains that Vladimir decided to send ten "good and wise men" to compare the religions of the Volga Emirate, the Germans (the successors of the Carolingians), and the Byzantines. When the men returned, they criticized both the Islamic practices of the Volga Emirate and the Christianity of the Germans.

▨ **Tangible Evidence of the European Slave Trade** European slave traders used this set of shackles, found in modern Bulgaria, to restrain a slave. They wrapped the long chain of iron links around his arms and legs and then connected it to the large ring, which they fastened around the captive's neck. Iron was expensive, though, so wooden and rope restraints would have been more common. (Krivina Museum, Ruse, Bulgaria)

● **Principality of Kiev** A new state that began as a trading post on the Dnieper River and evolved into a principality, led by a prince, around 900.

Ibn Fadlan's Description of a Rus Burial

Although Ibn Fadlan, an envoy from the Abbasid court, looked down on the Rus as coarse and uncivilized, his account of a king's funeral is the most detailed description of pre-Christian Rus religious beliefs and practices surviving today. It is particularly moving because he was able to observe a young girl who died so that she could be buried with her lord. The Angel of Death who kills the girl may have been a priestess of either Frey or Odin, whose devotees some-times engaged in sex as part of their fertility rites. While Ibn Fadlan clearly finds the Rus funerary practices strange, the Scandinavian he quotes at the end of this selection finds the Islamic practice of burial equally alien.

Source: James E. Montgomery, "Ibn Fadlan and the Rusiyyah," *Journal of Arabic and Islamic Studies* 3 (2000): 12–20. Online at www.uib.no/jais/content3.htm.

I was told that when their chieftains die, the least they do is cremate them. I was very keen to verify this, when I learned of the death of one of their great men. They placed him in his grave and erected a canopy over it for ten days, until they had finished making and sewing his funeral garments.

In the case of a poor man they build a small boat, place him inside and burn it. In the case of a rich man, they gather together his possessions and divide them into three, one third for his family, one third to use for his funeral garments, and one third with which they purchase alcohol which they drink on the day when his slave-girl kills herself and is cremated together with her master. (They are addicted to alcohol, which they drink night and day. Sometimes one of them dies with the cup still in his hand.)

When their chieftain dies, his family ask his slave-girls and slave-boys, "Who among you will die with him?" and some of them reply, "I shall." Having said this, it becomes incumbent on the person and it is impossible ever to turn back. Should that person try to, he is not permitted to do so. It is usually slave-girls who make this offer.

When that man whom I mentioned earlier died, they said to his slave-girls, "Who will die with him?" and one of them said, "I shall." So they placed two slave-girls in charge of her to take care of her and accompany her wherever she went, even to the point of occasionally washing her feet with their own hands. They set about attending to the dead man, preparing his clothes for him and setting right all that he needed. Every day the slave-girl would drink alcohol and would sing merrily and cheerfully.

On the day when he and the slave-girl were to be burned I arrived at the river where his ship was. To my surprise I discovered that it had been beached and that four planks of birch and other types of wood had been placed in such a way as to resemble scaffolding. Then the ship was hauled and placed on top of this wood. They advanced, going to and fro around the boat uttering words which I did not understand, while he was still in his grave and had not been exhumed.

Then they produced a couch and placed it on the ship, covering it with quilts made of Byzantine silk brocade and cushions made of Byzantine silk brocade. Then a crone arrived whom they called the "Angel of Death" and she spread on the couch the coverings we have mentioned. She is responsible for having his garments sewn up and putting him in order and it is she who kills the slave-girls. I myself saw her: a gloomy, corpulent woman, neither young nor old.

When they came to his grave, they removed the soil from the wood and then removed the wood, exhuming him still dressed in the *izar* [clothing] in which he had died. . . . They carried him inside the pavilion on the ship and laid him to rest on the quilt, propping him with cushions. . . . Next they brought bread, meat, and onions, which they cast in front of him, a dog, which they cut in two and which they threw onto the ship, and all of his weaponry, which they placed beside him. . . .

At the time of the evening prayer on Friday, they brought the slave-girl to a thing they had constructed, like a door-frame. She placed her feet on the hands of the men and was raised above the door-frame. She said something and they brought her down. [This happened two more times.] They next handed her a hen. She cut off its head and threw it away. They took the hen and threw it on board the ship.

I quizzed the interpreter about her actions and he said, "The first time they lifted her, she said, 'Behold, I see my father and my mother.' The second time she said, 'Behold, I see all of my dead kindred, seated.' The third time she said, 'Behold I see my master, seated in Paradise. Paradise is beautiful and verdant. He is accompanied by his men and his male-slaves. He summons me, so bring me to him.'" . . .

The men came with their shields and sticks and handed her a cup of alcohol over which she chanted and then drank.

Six men entered the pavilion and all had intercourse with the slave girl. They laid her down beside her master and two of them took hold of her feet, two her hands. The crone called the "Angel of Death" placed a rope around her neck in such a way that the ends crossed one another and handed it to two of the men to pull on it. She advanced with a broad-bladed dagger and began to thrust it in and out between her ribs, now here, now there, while the two men throttled her with the rope until she died.

Then the deceased's next of kin approached and took hold of a piece of wood and set fire to it. . . . A dreadful wind arose and the flames leapt higher and blazed fiercely.

One of the Rus stood beside me and I heard him speaking to my interpreter. I quizzed him about what he had said, and he replied, "He said, 'You Arabs are a foolish lot!'" So I said, "Why is that?" and he replied, "Because you purposely take those who are dearest to you and whom you hold in highest esteem and throw them under the earth, where they are eaten by the earth, by vermin and by worms, whereas we burn them in the fire there and then, so that they enter Paradise immediately." Then he laughed loud and long.

QUESTIONS FOR ANALYSIS

As you read the above passage carefully, note the events that Ibn Fadlan did not witness himself.

▶ Which of these events do you think could have occurred?

▶ Which events seem less likely?

▶ How did Muslim and Scandinavian burial customs differ?

▶ What is Ibn Fadlan's attitude toward peoples whose practices differ from those in the Islamic world?

But when they went to the Hagia Sophia church in Byzantium (see photo on page 274), they reported the following:

> We knew not whether we were in heaven or on earth. For on earth there is no such splendor or such beauty, and we are at a loss how to describe it. We know only that God dwells there among men, and their service is fairer than the ceremonies of other nations. For we cannot forget that beauty.[11]

Vladimir did not immediately accept their recommendation, but instead asked the reigning Byzantine emperor Basil II (r. 963–1025) to send his sister Anna to him as his bride. Although the Byzantine emperors rarely allowed imperial princesses to marry foreign rulers, Basil agreed because he desperately needed the assistance of Vladimir's troops to suppress a rebellion. He agreed, the *Primary Chronicle* reports, to the engagement on the condition that Vladimir be baptized before the marriage. Vladimir made a counteroffer: he would receive baptism only from the priests accompanying Anna to the wedding. Basil acceded. Once baptized, Vladimir then ordered, on penalty of death, all the inhabitants of Kiev to come to the riverbank and surprised them all by performing a mass baptism. Kiev and all its inhabitants converted to Christianity.

The Growing Divide Between the Eastern and Western Churches

Prince Vladimir and his ten advisers conceived of the Christianity of the Germans and of the Byzantines as two separate religions, which we now call Roman Catholicism and Eastern Orthodoxy. The two churches used different languages, Latin in Rome and Greek in Constantinople, and after 500 they became increasingly separate. Since 751, the pope had been allied with the rulers of the Franks, not the Byzantine emperors.

By 1000, the practices of the Eastern and Western clergy diverged in important ways. Members of the Western church accepted the pope as head, while members of the Eastern church recognized the patriarch of Constantinople as leader. Western priests were supposed to be celibate, even if not all were; their Eastern counterparts could marry. Eastern priests were required to have beards, while Western priests did not. Orthodox Christians put yeast in the communion bread, while Roman Catholics ate unleavened bread.

Although the cultural differences were greater, the teachings of the two churches also diverged on certain doctrinal points. Sometime in the sixth century, probably in Spain, Western Christians had added a new phrase to the basic statement of Christian belief, the Nicene Creed, saying that the Holy Spirit proceeded from both the Father (God) and the Son (Jesus). Charlemagne adopted this phrasing. In contrast, Eastern theologians held that the Holy Spirit proceeded from God alone and did not approve of the phrasing introduced by the Western church. The dispute was not just about a doctrinal point: the Eastern church objected to the Roman church making such a fundamental change on its own.

In 1054, a bishop in Bulgaria wrote to an Italian bishop criticizing certain practices of the Western church, such as the use of unleavened bread in communion and the failure to fast on Saturdays. The pope responded by sending an envoy who carried two letters (one was 17,000 words long) to the patriarch in Constantinople defending these practices and asserting his right as the pope to lead the Western church. As the level of rhetoric escalated, the pope's envoy excommunicated the patriarch of Constantinople, and the patriarch did the same to the pope's envoy. Historians call this the Great Schism of 1054.

Although similar disputes had been resolved in the past, 1054 marked the final break between the two churches. (The dispute was resolved only in 1965, but the two churches stayed separate.) After 1054, the pope in Rome, whose wealth and influence made him the equal of European monarchs, led the Roman Catholic Church. In Constantinople, the patriarch led the Eastern Orthodox Church, the church of both the Byzantine Empire and its close ally, the Kievan princes.

The new Christian states of Europe that formed between 500 and 1000 provided slaves and different raw materials, like fur, to the Abbasids, their powerful neighbors to the southeast. So many of the enslaved captives came from the homeland of the Slavs that Europeans coined the Latin word *sclavus* (meaning "slave") from Slav. As we have seen in Chapter 9, slaves entered the Islamic world from three major sources: Scandinavia, Russia, and Africa, but the expanding trade with Europe and the Islamic world had different results in Africa, as we will see in the next chapter.

Chapter Review

Download the MP3 audio file of the Chapter Review and listen to it on the go.

Between 500 and 1000, Europe became multicentered. In 500 the Byzantine Empire was the sole power throughout Europe, but by 1000 many other centers had formed: in Germany, Scandinavia, and Russia. Gudrid, *Erik the Red's Saga* reports, personally visited Greenland and the Scandinavian settlement in Canada before returning to live in Iceland; at the end of her life, she may have traveled to the center of the Christian church in Rome. Thorfinn, who came originally from Iceland, also visited Greenland, Canada, and Norway.

What events caused the urban society of the Byzantines to decline and resulted in the loss of so much territory to the Sasanian and Abbasid Empires?

After the fall of Rome in 476, only one empire existed in Europe: the Eastern Roman Empire of Byzantium. In 500, the urban life of Constantinople varied little from ancient Rome's: urban residents continued to gather at marketplaces, watch the circus, and attend the theater. But when plague struck in 541 and continued for more than two centuries, the cities of the empire contracted, trade fell off, and people took up subsistence farming. Their urban way of life all but disappeared. The weakened army lost extensive lands in Anatolia to the Sasanians and in Armenia and Africa to the powerful Abbasid Empire. After its disastrous defeat by the Seljuq armies at Manzikert in 1071, Byzantium retained control only of Constantinople and parts of Anatolia, a fraction of its original empire.

KEY TERMS

Gudrid and Thorfinn Karlsefni (268)
Byzantine Empire (271)
patriarch (271)
pope (271)
plague (273)
wergeld (277)
war-band (277)
Merovingian dynasty (278)
Carolingian dynasty (280)
Viking (282)
longboat (284)
Danelaw (285)
The Vinland Sagas (285)
Bjarni Herjolfsson (290)
Skraelings (290)
Rus (291)
Slavs (292)
Principality of Kiev (293)

What was the war-band of traditional Germanic society? How did the political structures of the Merovingians and the Carolingians reflect their origins in the war-band?

To the west in Germany and France lived various Germanic peoples whose primary social unit was the war-band. Each war-band had a leader who provided his followers with food, clothing, housing, and plunder from the places they raided; the followers in turn remained loyal to him in peace and fought with him in war. The Merovingians and the Carolingians called their leaders king, but their greatest leaders, including Clovis and Charlemagne, commanded the respect of their war-bands only as long as they could provide them with the spoils of battle.

 When, where, how, and why did the Scandinavians go on their voyages, and what was the significance of those voyages?

To the north, in Scandinavia, lived a different group of Germanic peoples, the Scandinavians. Unlike the Franks, who moved overland, they traveled by longboat, first to England and Ireland in the 790s, then to Iceland in 870, to Greenland in 980, and finally to the Atlantic coast of Canada around the year 1000, some fifteen years after Bjarni Herjolfsson first spotted land there. All the Scandinavian settlers shared the same goal: they wanted more farmland than was available to them in Scandinavia.

Their voyages were significant because they were the first Europeans to settle in the Americas. Their short-lived settlement in Canada preceded Columbus's by nearly five hundred years; unlike his, theirs had no long-term consequences.

 What were the earliest states to form in the area that is now Russia, and what role did religion play in their establishment and development?

In the centuries that some Scandinavians traveled west, others went east. The Rus took their longboats down the rivers of Russia, where they captured slaves, collected furs from subject peoples, and traded with the Islamic world. Before 970, these Rus traders paid taxes to the Khazars, who had adopted Judaism, and to the Volga Bulgars, who had converted to Islam. After 970, the Rus formed their own state, the Kievan Rus principality, whose ruler Prince Vladimir converted to Eastern Orthodoxy, the state church of Byzantium.

 What did all the new states have in common?

The new states that formed in France and Germany, Scandinavia, and Russia had much in common. The Germanic peoples who settled these regions all grouped into war-bands, and the first kings convened assemblies with their subjects as warband leaders. The early kings gave up their multiple deities for Christianity, although they often continued to worship their gods for a few generations. Unlike the complex legal system of the Romans, the legal systems of these societies were wergeld-based systems with clearly defined offenses and fines.

For Further Reference

Biraben, J. N., and Jacques Le Goff. "The Plague in the Early Middle Ages." In *Biology of Man in History: Selections from Annales Economies, Sociétés, Civilisations,* ed. Robert Forster et al. Baltimore: Johns Hopkins University Press, 1975, pp. 48–80.

Fitzhugh, William W., and Elisabeth I. Ward. *Vikings: The North Atlantic Saga.* Washington, D.C.: Smithsonian Institution Press, 2000.

Fletcher, Richard. *The Barbarian Conversion: From Paganism to Christianity.* Berkeley: University of California Press, 1999.

Geary, Patrick. *Before France and Germany: The Creation and Transformation of the Merovingian World.* New York: Oxford University Press, 1988.

Kazhdan, A. P., and Ann Wharton Epstein. *Change in Byzantine Culture in the Eleventh and Twelfth Centuries.* Berkeley: University of California Press, 1985.

Lynch, Joseph H. *The Medieval Church: A Brief History.* New York: Longman, 1992.

Magnusson, Magnus, and Hermann Palsson, trans. *The Vinland Sagas: The Norse Discovery of America.* New York: Penguin Books, 1965.

Martin, Janet. *Medieval Russia 980–1584.* New York: Cambridge University Press, 1995.

McCormick, Michael. *Origins of the European Economy: Communications and Commerce AD 300–900.* New York: Cambridge University Press, 2001.

McKitterick, Rosamond, ed. *The New Cambridge Medieval History,* vol. 2, c. 700–c. 900. New York: Cambridge University Press, 1995. Particularly the essays by Michael McCormick.

Reuter, Timothy. "Plunder and Tribute in the Carolingian Empire." *Transactions of the Royal Historical Society,* 5th ser., 35 (1985): 75–94.

Reuter, Timothy, ed. *The New Cambridge Medieval History,* vol. 3, c. 900–1024. New York: Cambridge University Press, 1999. Particularly the essay by Thomas S. Noonan.

Rosenwein, Barbara H. *A Short History of the Middle Ages.* Orchard Park, N.Y.: Broadview Press, 2002.

Southern, R. W. *Western Society and the Church in the Middle Ages.* New York: Penguin Books, 1970.

Treadgold, Warren. *A History of the Byzantine State and Society.* Stanford: Stanford University Press, 1997.

Wallace, Birgitta L. *Westward Vikings: The Saga of L'Anse aux Meadows.* St. John's, Newfoundland, Canada: Historic Sites Association of Newfoundland and Labrador, 2006.

 WEB RESOURCES

Pronunciation Guide

Interactive Maps

MAP 10.1 The Byzantine Empire

MAP 10.2 The Carolingian Realms

MAP 10.3 The Viking Raids, 793–1066

MAP 10.4 Kievan Rus

Primary Sources

Chapter Objectives

ACE Multiple-Choice Quiz

Flashcards

Websites

L'Anse aux Meadows
(http://www.pc.gc.ca/progs/spm-whs/itm2-/site1–E.asp). Canada Parks Service website about the Viking colony at L'Anse aux Meadows.

Internet Medieval Sourcebook
(http://www.fordham.edu/halsall/sbook.html). Excellent collection of primary sources under the following headings: Carolingians, The Early Germans, France, and England.

Vikings
(http://www.mnh.si.edu/vikings/). Information about the Vikings from the Smithsonian National Museum of Natural History.

Expanding Trade Networks in Africa and India, 1000–1500

In 1325, a 20-year-old legal scholar named **Ibn Battuta** (1304–1368/69[1]) set off on a hajj pilgrimage from his home in Tangier (tan-jeer), a Mediterranean port on the westernmost edge of the Islamic world (see Chapter 9). In Mecca Ibn Battuta (ibin bah-TOO-tuh) made a decision that changed his life: instead of returning home, he decided to keep going. A world traveler with no fixed destination and no set time of return, he followed trade routes that knitted the entire Islamic world together. These routes connected places like Mecca, which had been at the center of the Islamic world since Muhammad's first revelations (see Chapter 9), to others that had more recently joined that world, such as the sub-Saharan kingdom of Mali and the Delhi sultanate of north India. After his travels were over, Ibn Battuta dictated his adventures to a ghost writer. His account began:

MUSLIM TRAVELER, CA. 1300

(Bibliothèque nationale de France/Superstock, Inc.)

My departure from Tangier, my birthplace, took place . . . in the year seven hundred and twenty-five [1325] with the object of making the Pilgrimage to the Holy House at Mecca and of visiting the tomb of the Prophet . . . at Medina. I set out alone, having neither fellow-traveller in whose companionship I might find cheer, nor caravan whose party I might join, but swayed by an over-mastering impulse within me, and a desire long-cherished in my bosom to visit these illustrious sanctuaries.[2]

CL This icon will direct you to interactive activities and study materials on the *Voyages* website: www.cengage.com/history/hansen/voyages1e

The Travels of Ibn Battuta

← Selected journeys of Ibn Battuta

Ibn Battuta leaves Tangier on hajj pilgrimage to Mecca, 1325.

Ibn Battuta travels to and from Mali via camel caravan, 1349–1354.

Ibn Battuta sails to the trading centers of the Swahili coast, 1330–1332.

LEÓN · ARAGON · Genoa · Venice · Black Sea · CASTILE · Corsica · Rome · Constantinople · Lisbon · GRANADA · Granada · Sardinia · Caligari · BYZANTINE EMPIRE · IL-KHANATE · Tangier · Tunis · Sicily · Latakia · Baghdad · Salé · Fez · Mediterranean Sea · Damascus · Hormuz · Madeira Islands · Marrakech · MARINIDS · Sijilmasa · ZAYYANIDS · Tripoli · Jerusalem · Basra · Persian Gulf · Muscat · HAFSIDS · Alexandria · MAMLUK SULTANATE · Cairo · ARABIA · OMAN · Sur · Canary Islands · S A H A R A · Medina · Nile R. · Red Sea · Jiddah · Mecca · Aydhab · Taghaza · Suakin · Sanaa · RASULIDS · Oulata · Timbuktu · Meroë · Aden · MALI · GOLD · Gao · Agades · ALWA · Adulis · Gulf of Aden · Koumbi-Saleh · Jenne · Niger R. · SONGHAI · KANEM · Lake Chad · Aksum · Kano · BORNU · ETHIOPIA · IFAT · GOLD · Niani · S U D A N · INDIAN OCEAN · OYO · BENIN · ATLANTIC OCEAN · Mogadishu · Malindi · Mombasa · SWAHILI COAST · Zanzibar · Kilwa · Zambezi R. · GREAT ZIMBABWE · Great Zimbabwe · Sofala · Madagascar · N

THE TRAVELS OF IBN BATTUTA

ATLANTIC OCEAN · QIPCHAQ KHANATE · 1330–1333 · CHAGHATAI KHANATE · YUAN DYNASTY · 1325–1327 · IL-KHANATE · DELHI SULTANATE · SAHARA · MAMLUK SULTANATE · 1333–1341 · 1341–1349 · MALI SULTANATE · 1349–1354 · INDIAN OCEAN · 1327–1330

— Ibn Battuta's journeys
▨ Islamic world, ca. 1350

0 600 1200 Km.
0 600 1200 Mi.

0 400 800 Km.
0 400 800 Mi.

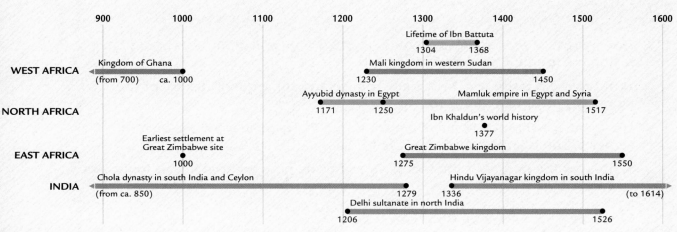

	900	1000	1100	1200	1300	1400	1500	1600

Lifetime of Ibn Battuta
1304   1368

WEST AFRICA
Kingdom of Ghana
(from 700)   ca. 1000
Mali kingdom in western Sudan
1230   1450

NORTH AFRICA
Ayyubid dynasty in Egypt
1171   1250
Mamluk empire in Egypt and Syria
1517
Ibn Khaldun's world history
1377

EAST AFRICA
Earliest settlement at Great Zimbabwe site
1000
Great Zimbabwe kingdom
1275   1550

INDIA
Chola dynasty in south India and Ceylon
(from ca. 850)   1279
Hindu Vijayanagar kingdom in south India
1336   (to 1614)
Delhi sultanate in north India
1206   1526

● **Ibn Battuta** (1304–1368/69) Legal scholar from Tangier, Morocco, who traveled throughout the Islamic world between 1325 and 1354 and wrote *The Travels* recounting his experiences in Africa, India, Central Asia, Spain, and China.

So begins the account of the longest known journey taken by any single individual before 1500. Proceeding on foot, riding camels and donkeys, and sailing by boat, Ibn Battuta covered an estimated 75,000 miles (120,000 km)—an extraordinary distance in the preindustrial world. Because the Five Pillars of Islam (see Chapter 9) obligated all Muslims to give alms, not just to the poor and the sick but also to travelers, Ibn Battuta was able to continue his travels even when his own funds were exhausted.

After setting out alone, Ibn Battuta soon fell in with a caravan of traders on their way to Cairo. Because he always traveled with Islamic merchants on established caravan routes, his itinerary provides ample evidence of the extensive trade networks connecting northern Africa, much of East and West Africa, and northern India. Many of the people he met accepted the teachings of the Quran, and he was able to communicate in Arabic everywhere he went. In each place he visited, he named the rulers, identified the highest-ranking judges, and then listed the important holy men of the town and their most important miracles. This narrow focus means that he rarely reported on some important topics, such as the local economy or the lives of women and non-Muslims.

Ibn Battuta was the first traveler to leave an eyewitness description of Africa south of the Sahara Desert, where he stayed in the kingdom of Mali. He visited Cairo, the capital city of the Mamluks (MAM-lukes) of Egypt, a powerful dynasty founded by military slaves, as well as several East African ports south of the equator. He remained for seven years in north India, then under Muslim rule, and visited many Indian Ocean ports. He did not, however, go to the interior of southern Africa or see the majestic site of Great Zimbabwe.

Many legs of Ibn Battuta's journey would not have been possible three hundred years earlier. In 1000 many parts of Africa were not connected to the broader Islamic world, including the rainforest of the West African coastlands and Central Africa, the densely populated Great Lakes region around Lake Victoria, and the southern African savannah. By 1450, however, expanding networks of trade had brought West and East Africa into increasing contact with the Islamic world of northern Africa and western Asia.

Focus Questions

⛵ **How was sub-Saharan Africa settled before 1000 C.E.? What techniques have historians used to reconstruct the past?**

⛵ **What role did trade play in the emergence and subsequent history of the kingdoms of Ghana and Mali?**

⛵ **How and why did the Mamluk empire based in Egypt become the leading center of the Islamic world after 1258?**

⛵ **What was the nature of the Indian Ocean trade network that linked India, Arabia, and East Africa?**

Reconstructing the History of Sub-Saharan Africa Before 1000 C.E.

The Sahara Desert divides the enormous continent of Africa into two halves: sub-Saharan Africa in contrast to North and East Africa. As we have seen in Chapter 9, Islamic armies conquered North Africa in the seventh century, and East Africans had much contact with Muslim traders throughout the Abbasid period (750–1258). We know much less about sub-Saharan Africa before 1000 because few Muslims, the source of so much of our information, traveled there. Apart from Arabic accounts, historians of Africa must draw on archaeological excavation, oral traditions, and analysis of vocabulary from different languages to piece together sub-Saharan Africa's history before 1000.

The Geography and Languages of Sub-Saharan Africa

Africa is a large continent, with an area greater than that of the United States (including Alaska), Europe, and China combined. As we saw in Chapter 1, the first anatomically modern humans crossed the Sinai Peninsula from Africa into western Asia at least 150,000 years ago, possibly earlier. The Nile River Valley was the site of Africa's earliest complex societies, first in Egypt and then in Nubia (see Chapter 2). Rome's greatest rival, Carthage, operated from a base in North Africa, and after its defeat in 202 B.C.E., Romans bought much of their grain from Egypt. In the 300s, Christianity spread throughout the Mediterranean to Egypt, northern Africa, and Ethiopia (see Chapter 7). After 650, Islam replaced Christianity in much of northern Africa, but not Ethiopia.

A glance at Map 11.1 shows why only North and East Africa had such close contacts with the larger world: 3,000 miles (4,800 km) across and around 1,000 miles (1,600 km) from north to south, the Sahara Desert posed a formidable barrier between the coast and the sub-Saharan regions. The first traders to cross the Sahara did so riding camels. The single-humped camel they used originated in Arabia and reached North Africa sometime in the first century B.C.E. Domesticated in the third or fourth centuries C.E., camels were much cheaper than human porters because they were hardier—capable of going for long periods without water and carrying much heavier loads. Camels did not need roads and crossed the desert on sandy tracks.

Immediately to the south of the Sahara is a semidesert region called the Sahel (meaning "shore" in Arabic). South of the Sahel (SAH-hel), enough rainfall fell to support the tall grasses of the dry savanna, and then farther south, a band of wooded savanna where many trees grew. Rainfall was heaviest in Central Africa, and rainforest stretched from the Atlantic coast all the way to the Great Lakes region. The pattern repeated itself south of the rainforest: first a band of woodland savanna, then dry savanna, and then the Kalahari Desert near the tip of southern Africa.

Africans today speak nearly two thousand different languages, one-third of the total number of languages spoken in the world (see Map 11.1). Several languages spoken in North Africa, including Egyptian, Nubian, Ethiopian, and Arabic, have had written forms for a thousand years or longer (see Chapters 2, 7, and 9). But none of those spoken south of the Sahara were written down before 1800. Today about five hundred of Africa's two thousand languages have written forms.

Major climatic zones of Africa

- Wet equatorial
- Woodland savannah
- Dry savannah with long dry season (6–9 months)
- Sahel or subdesert
- Desert
- Mediterranean
- Highland (climate moderated by altitude)
- → Trans-Saharan trade routes
- → Traditional Arab spice routes
- ➡ Spread of Bantu-speakers, by ca. 1000

TEDA Major language

CL Interactive Map

⊕ MAP 11.1

African Trade Routes, 1200–1500 The Sahara Desert forms a natural boundary between Saharan Africa and sub-Saharan Africa. Overland camel routes across the Sahara Desert linked Mali with the Mediterranean coast, while Indian Ocean sea routes connected the important center of Great Zimbabwe in East Africa to the Islamic world and Asia.

The Spread of Bantu Languages

Africa's languages cluster in several major groups. Arabic is spoken throughout the Islamic regions, while the **Bantu** languages of the Niger-Congo language family are widely distributed throughout sub-Saharan Africa. Since many of these languages show surprising uniformity over a wide area, earlier analysts posited that the migration of a single people, all speaking an earlier form of the Bantu language, accounted for this modern language distribution.

Accordingly, many analysts assumed that the Bantu speakers set out from their homeland in Nigeria and Cameroon, in the western bend of Africa, and migrated all over central, eastern, and southern Africa. When they came to a new place, they conquered the indigenous peoples with their iron weapons and then used iron tools to till the land. This view, like earlier understandings of the Indo-European migrations discussed in Chapter 3, presumes that a single people were responsible for the spread of a single language family. It also credits them with technological superiority over the original residents of the regions who hunted, fished, and gathered wild plants.

But this model of a single wave of Bantu migration presents many problems, the most basic of which is timing. Agriculture and ironworking did spread throughout sub-Saharan Africa sometime before 1000 C.E., but not necessarily at the same time as the Bantu languages did.

African historians have pioneered the use of a linguistic method called *glottochronology* to analyze the history of languages. By comparing vocabulary lists, linguists can count how many words in two languages are the same and how many have changed. The greater the number of shared words, the closer two languages are; the fewer the number, the more distant. Those who practice glottochronology believe that linguistic change holds constant over time: some, for example, estimate that sixteen words out of one hundred will change over a five-hundred-year period.[3] Most analysts find glottochronology useful for determining which languages broke off from others and in what order; not everyone, however, is convinced of claims about the timing of those changes. The linguistic variation among modern Bantu languages suggests multiple waves of change. Accordingly, scholars today have discarded the theory of a single wave of Bantu migration.

A more persuasive model for the spread of Bantu languages sees three different, and often overlapping, processes taking place over an extended period of time: the planting of the first crops, the development of metallurgy, and the spread of the Bantu languages. First, archaeological evidence shows that, sometime between 1000 and 500 B.C.E., different peoples began to cultivate crops. Those in the drier regions grew sorghum, millet, and rice, while those in the rainforest raised tubers such as yams. Like the Maya (see Chapter 5), many of these peoples engaged in slash-and-burn agriculture, meaning they farmed the same place for only one or two seasons. Once the fertility of a plot gave out, cultivators moved to a new site, where they cleared fields by setting fire to the brush. As in other parts of the world, it took hundreds, possibly thousands, of years before people shifted to full-time agriculture.

During this transition to agriculture, different peoples learned how to work iron. Iron tools were much more effective than stone and wood tools in turning the earth and preparing it for seed, and Africans developed sophisticated technologies for making them. Archaeologists have traced the spread of ironworking techniques throughout sub-Saharan Africa. The first evidence of ironworking in Africa dates to about 600 B.C.E. Interestingly, people living north of the Sahara, along the Nile River in modern Sudan, and south of the Sahara in central Nigeria learned how to work iron at about the same time. The metallurgical techniques used north of the Sahara differ markedly from those used in the south, an indication that the peoples of the two regions discovered how to work iron independently of each other.

The African experience differs from that of other societies because most sub-Saharan African peoples started to work iron without any previous experience in

● **Bantu** Name for the languages of the Niger-Congo language family, which are widely distributed throughout sub-Saharan Africa. By extension, the word also refers to the speakers of those languages.

working copper. In Eurasia the usual pattern was first to combine copper and tin into bronze and then, as the Hittites did in 2000 B.C.E., build on that expertise to smelt iron (see Chapter 2); the peoples of the Americas, in contrast, never worked iron (see Chapter 5).

Africans built a greater variety of furnaces for smelting iron than people anywhere else in the world. Some furnaces had tall shafts; others used preheated air. These smelting techniques allowed Africans to make iron from much leaner ores than those used elsewhere. The technology for smelting iron spread throughout southern Africa by 300 C.E.

Although iron is an extremely useful metal that can be made into agricultural implements and military weapons, it is relatively soft and rusts. Steel is much stronger and more resistant to rusting. The difference between iron and steel is the amount of carbon in the metal: iron that has been worked by a blacksmith, or wrought iron, usually contains less than .2 percent carbon, while steel may contain up to 1.5 percent. African smelting furnaces often made iron with enough dissolved carbon to have the properties of steel.

In the same centuries that the sub-Saharan Africans were developing agriculture and refining their production of iron, the Bantu languages spread in a southward direction to the regions where rainfall was heavier. It is possible that different groups moved out from the heartland of the Bantu languages in modern-day Nigeria and Cameroon and that their ability to farm and to make iron tools enabled them to displace the indigenous populations, who hunted and gathered. Yet it is equally likely that indigenous peoples adopted the new farming and iron-smelting technologies and the Bantu languages in different phases in different regions.

By 1000, agricultural peoples who used iron tools had settled throughout sub-Saharan Africa, many of them speaking Bantu languages. Their iron tools allowed them to move into and settle heavily forested areas such as the Great Lakes regions.

Society and Family Life

The final centuries of these changes overlap with the first written records. As early as the eighth century, Arab geographers began to record some preliminary notes, often on the basis of hearsay, about sub-Saharan Africa (see the "Movement of Ideas" feature in Chapter 9), and Arabic sources dominate the historical record through the sixteenth century, particularly for North and East Africa. The lack of indigenous historical records means that, like their colleagues elsewhere, historians of sub-Saharan Africa must rely on **oral histories,** recited accounts passed from one generation to the next. Exciting breakthroughs in African history have come when historians have determined the exact date and location of a given event by linking events from oral histories with Arabic-language sources. Ibn Battuta's account occupies pride of place among these Arabic sources because he went to so many places and wrote at such great length. (The English translation of his account fills nearly a thousand pages in four volumes.)

Historians have been able to reconstruct the past through careful examination of historic accounts and judicious consideration of which aspects of social and economic life remained unchanged over the centuries. Jan Vansina, a prominent historian of Africa, coined the term *up-streaming* for their task because it resembles standing on a riverbank, observing what is in front of them, and making an intelligent guess about what happened upstream.[4]

●**oral histories**
Historical accounts passed from one generation to the next. In Africa, griots often recited the events of the past to the monarchs they advised. Particularly important in societies where no written accounts survive.

Up-streaming has led historians to concur that certain generalizations probably hold true for most of sub-Saharan Africa before 1000. While no estimates for Africa's overall population at this time exist, it is clear that people lived in villages of several hundred to several thousand residents and that fertile areas were more heavily populated than barren regions like the Sahara Desert. Often the people of one village claimed descent from the same ancestor, whether legendary or historical, and historians use the term **lineage** or *clan* for such family units. (Historians today avoid the word *tribe* because of its negative associations and condescending use in the past.)

Lineages and clans organized into villages were the bedrock of Africa's diverse societies. Men often dominated the tasks with the greatest prestige, like hunting or metallurgy, as well as anything requiring long-distance travel, such as military conquest, long-distance trade, and diplomatic negotiations. Women usually tilled the soil, gathered wild fruits and vegetables, made pottery, and prepared meals. Marriage patterns varied from village to village: a man might take a single wife or multiple wives, sometimes from within his own lineage, sometimes from other groups.

Men formed tight bonds with other men of the same age while undergoing initiations into adulthood. Men in the junior age grades respected the men of the more senior age grades, and when they grew old, they in turn expected younger men to obey them. A man who fathered many children and attained great wealth was called a "great man." Great men earned their position at the top of village society, often by military prowess.

Great men led villages, and, if continuously successful in battle, they might form larger political units such as a chieftaincy; if more successful, a kingdom. Historians usually describe villages as evolving into chieftaincies, and then chieftaincies into kingdoms or states, but the different stages were not sharply defined. The same political unit might seem to be a kingdom to an observer in the capital but more like a chieftaincy to someone in an outlying area. During the lifetimes of the great men who led them, the villages they had conquered would submit gifts to them; after their deaths, however, the fragile political units they formed could easily break apart. In the course of his travels, Ibn Battuta met several great men who headed their own kingdoms, one of whom was the ruler of Mali.

> • **lineage** Group of people claiming descent from the same ancestor, whether legendary or historical, who are not necessarily biologically related but see themselves as a family unit.

The Kingdom of Mali in Sub-Saharan Africa

The kingdom of **Mali,** centered on the Niger River basin, occupied much of West Africa south of the Sahara Desert. It straddled the Sahel (see above) and the vast savannah grasslands to the south. Because this territory included some of the world's biggest gold mines, merchants crossed the Sahara to this region perhaps as early as 500 C.E. Urbanization began in the West African Sahel with the development of the trans-Saharan trade. Ghana (ca. 700–1000) was the first kingdom to take advantage of its location at an important node of trade, and the kingdom of Mali built on these earlier achievements in using trans-Saharan trade as a pathway to power. Ibn Battuta offers a verbal snapshot of Mali's trade with the north in the 1350s: caravans brought slaves and gold from the south and exchanged them for cloth, pottery, and glass trinkets from the north.

> • **Mali** Kingdom founded ca. 1230 by Sundiata in West Africa south of the Sahara Desert and in the Niger River basin. Generated revenue by taxing the caravans of the trans-Saharan trade. Declined around 1450 after losing trading cities to the Songhai Empire.

The Kingdom of Ghana, ca. 700–1000

The Muslim geographer al-Bakri (d. 1094) provided the earliest and most detailed description of the kingdom of Ghana in his *Book of Routes and Realms* (see "Movement of Ideas," Chapter 9). Since al-Bakri never left his native Spain, he drew all of his information from earlier geographic accounts and from named informants who had been to the Sahara and the sub-Saharan trading kingdoms.

These kingdoms originated as small settlements located at points where different routes crossed each other. Sijilmasa (sih-jil-MAHS-suh), located on the northern edge of the Sahara in modern Morocco, began, al-Bakri reports, as a periodic market on a "bare plain" where local people came to buy and sell goods, like iron tools, only at certain times of year. He says, "That [the periodic market] was the beginning of its being populated, then it became a town." Sijilmasa grew into an important trade depot ruled by a royal lineage whose founder claimed descent from a family who sold iron tools at the earliest periodic market. Towns like Sijilmasa became city-states whose main source of revenue was the taxes their rulers collected from traders.[5]

The kingdom of Ghana arose through a similar process. In the mid-1000s, al-Bakri reported that the kingdom contained two cities: preachers and scholars lived in the Islamic one, which had twelve mosques where Friday prayers were said; and "six miles" away, the king and his "sorcerers" lived in the other. Al-Bakri's informants drew a sharp line between Muslims and "polytheists," whose "religion is paganism and the worship of idols." The king did not convert to Islam, but he welcomed Muslim visitors.

Archaeologists have not found any sites that match al-Bakri's description and have concluded that the kingdom did not have a fixed capital. Instead, the king and his retinue regularly moved among different cities. Excavations at Jenne (JENN-eh) and Koumbi Saleh (KOOM-bi sah-LEH) (200 miles north of Bamako, Mali) have found evidence of large cities: the population of Jenne in the 700s was around 20,000, with smaller surrounding towns of 500 to 1,500 people.[6]

The king taxed the goods going in and out of the cities he ruled. Merchants paid a tax in gold on each donkey load of goods they brought into the city. The tax was higher for more valuable goods, like copper, and lower for cheaper commodities, like salt. These revenues financed the king's military campaigns. The king, al-Bakri reported, could raise an army of 200,000 men, of whom 40,000 were archers.

Some states in pre-1500 Africa, like Ghana, controlled large amounts of territory, but usually they exercised direct political control over only a small core area. Even where such states existed, however, kings normally had little independent political power, usually serving as mediators and consensus-builders of councils of elders. The lineage and clan elders made the most important decisions at the local level.

Unlike Mesopotamia, Egypt, India, China, or the Americas, where the first complex societies tapped agricultural surplus, most African states arose through control of strategic natural resources like water or gold. The loss of several key trading depots to the Almoravid dynasty of Spain (see Chapter 9) drastically reduced the tax revenues paid to the kings of Ghana, and they lost their kingdom to a local lineage named the Sosso (SUE-sue) around 1150.

Sundiata and the Founding of the Mali Kingdom, ca. 1230

The best source about the rise of Mali is an oral epic, written down only in the twentieth century, that recounts the life and exploits of the founder of the Mali kingdom, Sundiata (soon-JAH-tuh) (r. ca. 1230).[7] The peoples of

West Africa spoke a group of related languages called Mande (MAHN-day), which included the Malinke (muh-LING-kay) language spoken in Mali. The Malinke version of the tale *Sundiata* tells how the son of a local ruler overthrew the Sosso king Soumaoro (sue-MAO-row) and united the different peoples of the region.

Each king of Mali had his own storyteller, or **griot** (GREE-oh; a French word), who had been taught the story of his dynastic predecessors and whose task was to compose new sections about the reigning king. The griots' extensive knowledge of the ancestral teachings granted them a prominent position in Mali society, and they often advised rulers on matters of state and accompanied them on diplomatic missions. Since Ibn Battuta did not speak Malinke, an interpreter must have told him about the griots; his description is one of the earliest we have of the griots and their close relationship to the **sultan.** Ibn Battuta used the word *sultan,* meaning "ruler" in Arabic, for the Mali king because his predecessors had converted to Islam sometime around 1000.

Ibn Battuta saw the sultan's griots when he visited Mali: "Each of them is inside a costume made of feathers resembling the green woodpecker on which is a wooden head with a red beak. . . . They stand before the Sultan in this laughable get-up and recite their poems. I have been told that their poetry is a sort of admonition. They say to the Sultan: 'This platform, formerly such and such a king sat on it and performed noble actions, and so and so did such and such; do you do noble acts which will be recounted after you.'" Once they were done reciting, the griots climbed up the platform on which the sultan was sitting and placed their head on his right shoulder, his left, and then his lap to show their respect. (See the feature "World History in Today's World: Griottes in Mali.")

The story of Sundiata remains our most detailed source about the early years of Mali. Mali's founder, Sundiata, was born to a king and his hump-backed wife,

• **griot/griotte** Royal storytellers who served as advisers to the rulers of Mali and other West African states. (A griotte is a female storyteller.)

• **sultan** "Ruler" in Arabic. Any head of an Islamic state. The states they governed were often called *sultanates*.

🖼 **A Modern Headdress from Mali** When Ibn Battuta visited the sultan of Mali, he described griots who wore a feathered costume topped by a bird's head with a beak. Perhaps he saw something like this bird mask, made in the twentieth century out of feathers, porcupine quills, antelope horns, and mud, from the same region of Mali that he visited. (Gift of Mr. William W. Brill. Photograph courtesy of the Herbert F. Johnson Museum of Art, Cornell University)

Griottes in Mali

When the historian D. T. Niane studied the epic of *Sundiata* in 1960, he transcribed the tale from a male griot named Mamadou Kouyaté (mah-mah-DEW koh-yah-TAY), who had learned the tale from his father and grandfather. Although the narrative presents a few vivid female characters, the story is focused on one man's exploits. One can easily imagine a largely male audience listening to a male griot tell the story of Sundiata.

Before 1960, it was difficult for women to leave home for extended periods so that they could learn new epics from experienced griots. Women storytellers therefore specialized in singing shorter narratives with little historical content, which did not attract large audiences. Now that epics are often performed on radio or television, women can learn to recite them from cassette recordings. As a result, the number of women griottes (GREE-ohts) has increased so much that they now dominate the storytelling profession in Mali, and the genre of the oral epic seems much less male-centered. Scholars are uncovering new tales, some with female heroines, told by griottes. Often women tell the stories while men accompany them on musical instruments.

Sources: Thomas A. Hale, *Griots and Griottes: Masters of Words and Music* (Bloomington: Indiana University Press, 1998). Video resource: *Griottes of the Sahel: Female Keepers of the Songhay Oral Tradition in Niger* (made by Thomas A. Hale; 11-minute video distributed by Audio-Visual Services, the Pennsylvania State University).

---

and he walked only at the age of 7. These traits indicated to the audience that both mother and son possessed unusual spiritual powers. In the hope that Sundiata would someday succeed to the throne, his father assigned him his own griot. One day, when his exasperated mother yelled at Sundiata because he was still entirely dependent on others for food, his griot sent word to the village blacksmith to send an iron bar so heavy that six men were needed to carry it. Sundiata easily picked up the bar with one hand and then stood up and walked. He grew into a strong and powerful warrior, eventually forced into exile by one of his father's envious wives. After nearly ten years away, Sundiata returned to his kingdom to find it under the oppressive rule of Soumaoro, the leader of the Sosso lineage that Sundiata resolved to overthrow.

The *Sundiata* narrative sketches the process of state formation as a series of conquests, some within Mali, others beyond; some of human enemies, others of supernatural forces. By the end of the epic, Sundiata rules the kingdom of Mali. (See the feature "Movement of Ideas: Mali Religion in the Epic of *Sundiata*.")

How many of the events described in *Sundiata* can be confirmed by other sources? Arab chronicles confirm that the kingdom of Mali existed in the thirteenth century, and the great Arab historian Ibn Khaldun (1332–1406), a native of Tunis in North Africa, recorded the names of the Mali kings and the major events of their reigns. Ibn Khaldun (IH-buhn hal-DOON), perhaps the most important Muslim historian of all times, formulated an entirely original definition of history as the study of human society and its transformations. His work makes it possible to date Sundiata's reign to around 1230.

The process of state formation that the *Sundiata* narrative describes is plausible: armies several thousand strong did fight with iron-tipped bows and other metal weapons. At its largest, reached some one hundred years after Sundiata's reign, the kingdom of Mali extended more than 1,000 miles (1,600 km) east to west and included the basins of both the Senegal and Niger Rivers.

As the *Sundiata* narrative shows, the Mali army consisted of different independent armies, each led by a local leader, who decided in each instance which leader he would support. When Soumaoro lost, a number of kings changed sides and supported Sundiata.

Although these kings may have exchanged gifts with Sundiata, the government's primary source of revenue was taxes on trade. One of Sundiata's most wealthy successors was Mansa Musa (r. 1307–1332), who visited Cairo on his way to Mecca in 1324. (*Mansa* is a word in the Malinke language meaning "supreme ruler," and *Musa* is Arabic for Moses; *Mansa Musa* means King Moses.) Five hundred servants, each carrying a staff of gold weighing 6 pounds (2.7 kg), walked in front of him. One hundred camels were required to carry his travel money, which was some 700 pounds (315 kg) of gold, making Mansa Musa one of the most talked-about and most welcome travelers of his day. A map of Afro-Eurasia made one hundred years after his death pictured Mansa Musa as a symbol of great wealth.[8]

| **Trans-Saharan Trade Networks** | In 1352, twenty years after Mansa Musa's death, Ibn Battuta went to Mali, then ruled by his grandson. The only eyewitness description we have of the fabulously wealthy kingdom, his |

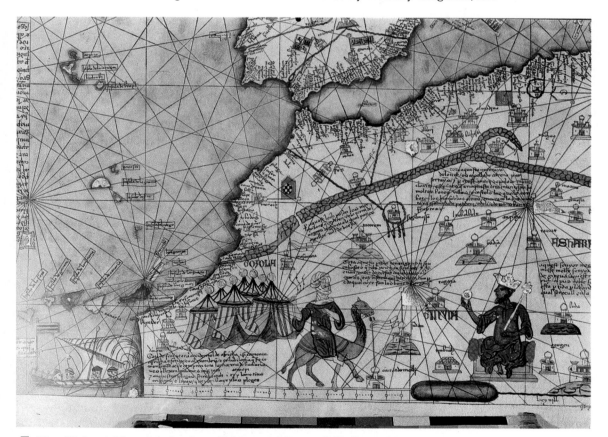

🔲 ***The Richest King in the Land? Mansa Musa of Mali*** In 1375, a European cartographer mapped Afro-Eurasia with unprecedented accuracy. This detail of the Catalan Atlas shows the green Mediterranean Ocean, southern Spain, and North Africa. The mapmaker has also included written labels that identify the seated figure on the lower right as Mansa Musa, the richest king in the land because of the abundant gold in his country. (Bibliothèque nationale de France/Bridgeman Art Library)

Mali Religion in the Epic of *Sundiata*

The *Sundiata* epic reveals much about African religions. Sundiata's enemy Soumaoro is a sorcerer who knows how to make small figurines, or fetishes, and recite spells to wound his enemies. Still, Soumaoro is not invincible. He tells his wife that he must observe a taboo against touching a cock's spur, the sharp talon a rooster uses to attack his enemies. If he does not, he will lose the power granted to him by his ancestors. Both Sundiata and his half-sister use the same word for the sorcerer's power: *jinn*, the Arabic word for a spirit or ghost (also the root of the English word *genie*), which they are able to overcome by attaching a cock's spur to the arrow that kills Soumaoro. The epic illustrates how local African religion absorbed religious conceptions from Islam. Notice that Sundiata never mentions God or the power of Islam, even though Mali's ruler converted to Islam around 1000, two centuries before the events described in the epic occurred. The selections below are taken from different parts of the epic.

Source: D. T. Niane, *Sundiata: An Epic of Old Mali,* trans. G. D. Pickett (London: Longman, 1965), pp. 52–53, 57–58, 65.

Sundiata's Description of Soumaoro's Powers

Soumaoro was now within spear range and Sundiata reared up his horse and hurled his weapon. It whistled away and bounced off Soumaoro's chest as off a rock and fell to the ground. Sogolon's son [Sundiata] bent his bow but with a motion of the hand Soumaoro caught the arrow in flight and showed it to Sundiata as if to say "Look, I am invulnerable."

Furious, Sundiata snatched up his spear and with his head bent charged at Soumaoro, but as he raised his arm to strike his enemy he noticed that Soumaoro had disappeared. Manding Bory [man-DING BORE-ee] riding at his side pointed to the hill and said, "Look, brother."

Sundiata saw Soumaoro on the hill, sitting on his black-coated horse. How could he have done it, he who was only two paces from Sundiata? By what power had he spirited himself away on to the hill? . . . The sun was already very low and Soumaoro's smiths gave way but Sundiata did not give the order to pursue the enemy. Suddenly Soumaoro disappeared!

How can I vanquish a man capable of disappearing and re-appearing where and when he likes? How can I affect a man invulnerable to iron? Such were the questions which Sogolon's son asked himself. He had been told many things about Sosso-Soumaoro but he had given little credence to so much gossip. Didn't people say that Soumaoro could assume sixty-nine different shapes to escape his enemies? According to some, he could transform himself into a fly in the middle of the battle and come and torment his opponent; he could melt into the wind when his enemies encircled him too closely—and many other things.

The battle of Neguéboria [neh-GAY-BOH-ria] showed Djata [Sundiata], if he needed to be shown, that to beat the king of Sosso [Soumaoro] other weapons were necessary.

The evening of Neguéboria, Sundiata was master of the field, but he was in a gloomy mood. He went away from the field of battle with its agonized cries of the wounded, and Manding Bory and Tabon Wana [TAY-ban WAH-nah] watched him go. He headed for the hill where he had seen Soumaoro after his miraculous disappearance from the midst of his troops. From the top of the hill he watched the compact mass of Soumaoro's smiths withdrawing in a cloud of dust.

"How was he able to escape me? Why did neither my spear nor my arrow wound him?" he wondered. "What is the jinn that protects Soumaoro? What is the mystery of his power?"

He dismounted from his horse and picked up a piece of the earth which Soumaoro's horse had trampled on. Complete darkness had already fallen, the village of Neguéboria was not far away and the Djallonkés came out in a crowd to greet Sundiata and his men. The fires were already lit in the camp and the soldiers were beginning to prepare a meal, but what was their joy when they saw a long procession of girls from Neguéboria carrying on their heads enormous gourds of rice. All the sofas [warriors] took up the girls' song in chorus. The chief of the village and its notables followed behind. Djata came down from the hill and received the Djallonké chief of Neguéboria, who was a vassal of Tabon Wana. For the sofas the day had been a victory because Soumaoro had fled, so the drums of war became drums of joy and Djata let his men celebrate what they called a victory. He stayed in his tent. In the life of every man there comes a moment when doubt settles in and the man questions himself on his own destiny, but on this evening it was not yet doubt which assailed Djata, for he was thinking rather of what powers he could employ to injure Sosso-Soumaoro.

Sundiata's Half-Sister Questions Her Husband Soumaoro Directly About the Source of His Powers

"Tell me, oh you whom kings mention with trembling, tell me Soumaoro, are you a man like others or are you the same as the jinn who protects humans? No one can bear the glare of your eyes, your arm has the strength of ten arms. Tell me, king of kings, tell me what jinn protects you so that I can worship him also." These words filled him with pride and he himself boasted to me of the might of his Tana•. That very night he took me into his magic chamber and told me all.

• **Tana**   the taboo he observed to keep his powers

The Loss of Soumaoro's Powers

Sogolon's son looked for Soumaoro and caught sight of him in the middle of the fray. Sundiata struck out right and left and the Sossos scrambled out of his way. The king of Sosso, who did not want Sundiata to get near him, retreated far behind his men, but Sundiata followed him with his eyes. He stopped and bent his bow. The arrow flew and grazed Soumaoro on the shoulder. The cock's spur no more than scratched him, but the effect was immediate and Soumaoro felt his powers leave him. His eyes met Sundiata's. Now trembling like a man in the grip of a fever, the vanquished Soumaoro looked up towards the sun. A great black bird flew over above the fray and he understood. It was a bird of misfortune.

QUESTIONS FOR ANALYSIS

▶ Where does Sundiata's power come from?

▶ What about Soumaoro's?

▶ Does this epic provide evidence about the religious beliefs of the storyteller? Of the audience?

▶ What evidence does the epic contain of Islamic beliefs?

• **trans-Saharan caravan trade network**   A network of overland trade linking sub-Saharan Africa with the Mediterranean. Starting around 500 C.E., camel caravans brought slaves and gold from the south and traded them for cloth, pottery, and glass trinkets from the north.

account provides our best source about the **trans-Saharan caravan trade network** connecting Mali with northern Africa. Traveling in caravans on well-established trade routes, Ibn Battuta witnessed the highly developed commercial network that traversed the sharply different geographic zones of the Sahara Desert, the Sahel, the grasslands, and the more heavily populated forests of Central Africa.

Those like Ibn Battuta who crossed the desert usually bought camels and provisions at towns like Sijilmasa, whose rise al-Bakri described (see above). After twenty-five days in the desert, Ibn Battuta's exhausted caravan arrived in Taghaza, one of the major salt-producing centers on the southern edge of the Sahara. "It is a village with no attractions," remarks Ibn Battuta, who describes only dwellings and a mosque with walls of salt blocks and roofs of camel skins. Salt structures were long-lasting because there was less than 8 inches (200 mm) of rain each year. The slaves who mined the salt lived on a monotonous diet of camel meat, dates from North Africa, and millet from Mali, so even they were enmeshed in a trading economy.

Salt is an essential nutrient for all human beings, and it is even more important in hot areas because it allows the body to replenish nutrients lost by sweating. Pure salt was so valuable that it was used as a currency. "The Blacks," Ibn Battuta remarks, "trade with salt as others trade with gold and silver; they cut it in pieces and buy and sell with these." As Ibn Battuta made his way south of the Sahara, he learned that travelers did not have to carry either food or silver coins because they could trade small amounts of salt, small glass trinkets, or spices for whatever food and lodging they required.

At the end of his stay, Ibn Battuta visited Timbuktu (tim-buk-TOO), a great trading city on the Niger River, whose ruler gave him a young male slave, a typical gift for an honored guest. The slave traders of Mali did not enslave their own countrymen; they captured slaves in the forest belt to the south. When Ibn Battuta returned to Morocco, he traveled with a caravan carrying six hundred female slaves. This figure is one of the few reliable statistics available to historians trying to measure the volume of the slave trade across the Sahara. Ibn Battuta's observation, combined with a handful of other sources, has led one historian to estimate that 5,500 slaves crossed the desert each year between 1100 and 1400.[9]

Ibn Battuta's caravan was indeed typical: more women than men crossed the Sahara because more buyers wanted female slaves than male slaves. Once sold in the markets of Morocco, women slaves would work as servants and concubines for urban dwellers, or perhaps for the royal court. Since slave owners feared that male slaves might impregnate the female members of the household, they preferred castrated males.

At the time of Ibn Battuta's visit, Mali had two major exports: slaves and gold. One historian has estimated that, in the thirteenth and fourteenth centuries, two-thirds of all the gold entering Europe passed through the North African cities of Tunis, Fez, and Cairo.[10] The gold originated in the mines of Bambuk (bam-BOOK) and Bure (boo-RAY) in Mali. Working conditions in the gold mines were grim: shafts could be over 60 feet (20 m) deep and frequently collapsed. Men dug out the ore while women extracted the gold. Since individual veins were not that rich, both tasks were laborious, but the mining allowed subsistence farmers to augment their incomes.

Society in Mali

Ibn Battuta visited Mali because it was on an established caravan route and he was confident that he would be received there as he was throughout the Islamic world. The first ruler of Mali to convert to Islam did so around 1000, but his subjects, according to the geographer al-Bakri, did not (see the "Movement of Ideas" feature in Chapter 9). By the time of Ibn Battuta's visit, Mali had become a Muslim kingdom, but people in Mali did not behave as Ibn Battuta felt observant Muslims should. Although he wrote as though there was a single standard of behavior that prevailed throughout the Islamic world, there was not. Within the structure of Islam, no supreme authority existed that could establish such a standard, which explains why Islamic religious and cultural practices were (and are) so diverse.

On his arrival in Mali, Ibn Battuta commented how unusual the kingdom was:

> No one takes his name from his father, but from his maternal uncle. Sons do not inherit, only sister's sons! This is something I have seen nowhere in the world except among the infidel Indians of al-Mulaibar [Malabar, on the east coast of India].

In short, Mali society was matrilineal, with descent determined by the mother, not the father. Royal women had much more power than their North African counterparts, but the rulers were male.

Ibn Battuta did not mince words when what he saw in Mali fell short of his expectations. He disdainfully described the social practices of the provincial town of Walata, where women were not secluded. On one occasion he visited his caravan leader and his wife, who were hosting a male friend of the wife. Indignantly, Ibn Battuta inquired: "Are you happy about this, you who have lived in our country and know the content of the religious law?" His host defended himself, explaining that the local women "are not like the women of your country," but Ibn Battuta refused to return to his host's house.

Ibn Battuta concluded his discussion of Mali with an "account of what I found good," namely, its secure roads, its high attendance at Friday services, and, most of all, the "great attention to memorizing the Holy Quran." He was deeply impressed by the example of several different children who had been placed in shackles because they had failed to memorize assigned passages from the Quran.

The kings of Mali continued to govern after Ibn Battuta's departure in 1353, but they faced rival armies as cavalry warfare became more common around 1400. To fight these battles, they had to import large horses from the north because horses bred locally often died from sleeping sickness and other parasitic diseases. They also bought saddles, iron stirrups, and bits to control their mounts. By 1400, they had added helmets and chain mail armor to their equipment. The kings lost control of several major cities, such as Timbuktu in 1433, and around 1450 Songhai (SONG-high), a neighboring kingdom that similarly profited by controlling the trans-Saharan trade, conquered Mali and brought Sundiata's dynasty to an end.

◼ **Mali Horseman** This terracotta figurine of a mounted warrior dates to around 1200 C.E., the time of Sundiata's reign. Local rulers began to import horses from North Africa around 1000 C.E., but initially only the most important leaders, like the imposing man shown here, rode on horses. By 1400, the kings of the Mali regularly led armies of mounted warriors into battle. (Photo © Heini Schneebeli/Bridgeman Art Library)

Islamic North Africa and the Mamluk Empire

By the time of Ibn Battuta's travels, North Africa had split into three separate sultanates, each ruled by a sultan. Each year these kingdoms sent thousands of pilgrims, like Ibn Battuta, to Cairo, where they joined pilgrims coming from North and West Africa to form even larger caravans for the final trip to Mecca. Cairo had become the cultural capital of the Islamic world in 1261, when the rulers of the **Mamluk empire** announced the re-establishment of the caliphate after the fall of Baghdad in 1258 to the Mongols (see Chapter 9). Ibn Battuta traveled through Mamluk territory in Egypt, Syria, and Arabia and personally experienced the ravages of the plague, which struck Eurasia for the first time since the eighth-century outbreaks in Constantinople (see Chapter 10).

> ● **Mamluk empire**
> (1250–1517). Dynasty founded by mamluk military slaves in Cairo that ruled Egypt, Syria, and the Arabian peninsula. In 1261, following the Mongol destruction of the caliphate of Baghdad, the Mamluk empire re-established the caliphate in Cairo.

The Sultanates of North Africa

Three months after his departure from Tangier in 1325, Ibn Battuta arrived at the trading port of Tunis, the capital of one of the three sultanates in North Africa, with a population near 100,000. Located on a point sticking out into the Mediterranean, it was ideally situated as a port for trade across the Strait of Gibraltar to southern Europe. European merchants traded fine textiles, weapons, and wine for animal hides and cloth from North Africa as well as gold and slaves transshipped from the interior.

In almost all the North African states, a sultan headed the government. In exchange for taxes paid by the inhabitants (Muslims paid a lower rate than non-Muslims), the government provided military and police protection. In addition, the sultan appointed a *qadi*, or chief jurist, who was assisted by subordinate jurists in settling disputes in court. Anyone who had studied law at Islamic schools was eligible to be appointed a qadi. These courts implemented Islamic law, called **sharia** (sha-REE-ah), which consisted of all the rules that Muslims were supposed to follow; legal authorities compiled these rules on the basis of the Quran, the hadith, and earlier legal decisions. Interpretation of certain points varied among the jurists belonging to different legal schools. Ibn Battuta had studied the legal interpretations of the Maliki school, one of the four major Sunni schools that interpreted the sharia.

> ● **sharia** Islamic law: all the rules that Muslims were supposed to follow, compiled on the basis of the Quran, the hadith, and earlier legal decisions.

The chief jurist in Tunis, Ibn Battuta informs us, heard disputes every Friday after prayers in the mosque: "people came to ask him to give a decision on various questions. When he had stated his opinion on forty questions he ended that session." The qadi's decision, called a *fatwa,* had the force of law and was enforced by the sultan's government.

Although Ibn Battuta had come to Tunis as an individual pilgrim, he left the city as the qadi for a caravan of Berber pilgrims going on the hajj. The caravan functioned like a small, mobile sultanate, with the caravan leader making all the important decisions about the route and Ibn Battuta serving as the traveling qadi. His new salary made it possible for him to marry the daughter of a fellow pilgrim, but the marriage did not last. "I became involved in a dispute with my father-in-law which made it necessary for me to separate from his daughter," Ibn Battuta comments without explaining further.

According to Islamic law, when a man and a woman married, they drew up a contract specifying the terms of the marriage and the property arrangements should they divorce. While a man could divorce his wife simply by saying "I divorce thee" three times, a woman had to demonstrate genuine maltreatment. Both husband and wife could remarry after divorce.

The Mamluk Empire, 1250–1517

Sometime in the spring of 1326, not quite a year after his departure from Tangier, Ibn Battuta arrived in the port city of Alexandria and went immediately to see the city's most famous tourist attraction: the lighthouse overlooking the Mediterranean. Alexandria marked the westernmost point of the Mamluk empire, which ruled all the way to Damascus.

The word **mamluk** originally referred to a type of non-Muslim slave used by Islamic states as warriors. In the ninth and tenth centuries, Islamic rulers in Afghanistan, North Africa, Spain, and Egypt, unable to recruit and train an efficient army from among their own populace, purchased large numbers of Turks from Central Asia to staff their armies. The number of slaves swelled in succeeding centuries.

Bought as children, the young mamluks studied Islam in preparation for their mandatory conversion. Living in isolation from the rest of the population, they continued to speak their own Turkic dialects and often could not read Arabic. They did no manual labor and could rise to high military rank. Once a mamluk soldier converted to Islam, he was freed, and his children would be born Muslim. This made his children ineligible for service as mamluks, a powerful check on the ability of any commander to develop his own power base.

Many of these mamluk slaves rose to high positions in the Ayyubid dynasty (1171–1250) founded by Saladin (which Ibn Jubayr visited in 1183–1185; see Chapter 9). Taking advantage of their growing power, the mamluk slave soldiers staged a coup in 1250 and founded the Mamluk dynasty. Only ten years later, Mamluk generals masterminded one of the greatest military victories in premodern times; in 1260, 120,000 Mamluk troops defeated 10,000 Mongol archers in 1260 at the battle of Ayn Jalut, north of Jerusalem in modern Israel (see Chapter 14). Hailing from the Central Asian grasslands and intimately familiar with horses, many Mamluk soldiers were skilled in the same fighting techniques used by the Mongols. The Mamluk forces were one of the few armies in the world to defeat the Mongols in direct combat.

mamluk
Non-Muslim slaves purchased by Islamic states in Afghanistan, North Africa, Spain, and Egypt as warriors to staff their armies. Mamluks were forced to convert to Islam.

Cairo, Baghad's Successor as the Cultural Capital of the Islamic World

Although the Mamluks were neither originally Muslim nor native speakers of Arabic, they positioned themselves as the protectors of the Islamic world. In 1261, they announced the re-establishment of the caliphate in Cairo, three years after its destruction by the Mongols in 1258 (see Chapter 9). Thousands of refugees, particularly Islamic teachers, poured into Cairo, where they taught in the city's many colleges, called *madrasas* in Arabic. The high number of Islamic schools, many located in mosques, impressed Ibn Battuta.

The thirteenth and fourteenth centuries saw the rise throughout the Islamic world of a new type of Islamic mystic, or **Sufi,** who taught that the individual could experience God directly without the intercession of others. Followers of individual Sufis also believed that their teachers had *baraka,* or divine grace, and could help others gain direct access to God. When alive, these Sufi teachers usually formed their own lodges where they taught groups of disciples and hosted visitors. When they died, their tombs became pilgrimage sites because their devotees believed that they retained their occupant's *baraka.*

Sufi Islamic mystic who taught that the individual could experience God directly without the intercession of others. Followers of individual Sufis believed their teachers had *baraka,* or divine grace, and could help others gain direct access to God.

Ibn Battuta stayed three days with a Sufi teacher named Burhan al-Din the Lame, whom he described as "learned, self-denying, pious and humble." Burhan al-Din urged Ibn Battuta to visit three teachers in India, Pakistan, and China. His advice is certain evidence of a Sufi network stretching all the way from Egypt to China, and Ibn Battuta eventually met all three men.

With a population between 500,000 and 600,000, Cairo was larger than most contemporary cities; only a few Chinese cities outranked it.[11] The city's population fell into distinct social groups. At the top were the Mamluk rulers, military commanders, and officials who kept records and supervised the tax system. Independent of the military were the Islamic notables, or *ulema*, who included religious teachers, scholars, preachers, and judges in the Islamic court system. Merchants, traders, and brokers formed a third influential group, who were often as wealthy and as respected as members of the Mamluk ruling class.

Below the military, religious, and mercantile elites were those who worked at respectable occupations: tradesmen, shopkeepers, and craftsmen. Farmers worked agricultural plots located in the center of Cairo and the outlying suburbs. At the bottom of society were the people whose occupations violated Islamic teachings, such as usurers (who lent money for interest) and slave dealers. Cairo residents looked down on their neighbors who sold wine or performed sex for a fee, and they shunned those whose occupations brought them into contact with human corpses or dead animals.

Eyewitness to the 1348 Outbreak of Plague in Damascus

The sultan of the Mamluk empire provided camels, food, and water for the poorer hajj travelers and guaranteed the safety of the pilgrims who gathered in Cairo before they journeyed together to Mecca. The number of pilgrims to Mecca in any given year varied enormously, depending on weather conditions and political uncertainty, but Ibn Battuta was probably traveling in the company of some ten thousand pilgrims. On his first pilgrimage (he arrived in Cairo in 1326), he hoped to journey to Mecca by boat, which was the most direct route from Cairo, but the closing of the sea route forced him to retrace his steps to Cairo, where he joined a group of pilgrims going overland to Damascus, a detour hundreds of miles out of his way. Damascus was the second-largest city in the Mamluk empire and a great cultural center in its own right, having been the capital of the Umayyads in the seventh century.

In Damascus, Ibn Battuta's route converged with Ibn Jubayr's, and his account borrowed, often without acknowledgment, as much as one-seventh of Ibn Jubayr's twelfth-century narrative.[12] From Damascus, Ibn Battuta proceeded to Mecca. After some time there (scholars are not certain how long), he decided to continue east on his journey.

Some twenty years later, Ibn Battuta again passed through Damascus on his journey home. This time he was unwittingly traveling with the rats that transmitted one of the most destructive diseases to strike humankind: the plague. Historians reserve the term *Black Death* for the outbreak in the mid-1300s. Because Europe, the Middle East, and North Africa had experienced no major outbreaks of plague since the eighth century (see Chapter 10), the effects of the Black Death were immediate and devastating.

The first new outbreak in western Europe occurred in 1346 in the Black Sea port of Kaffa. From there the dread disease traveled to Italy and Egypt (see Map 13.2). In May or June 1348, Ibn Battuta first heard of the plague in Ghazza, Syria, where "the number of dead there exceeded a thousand a day." He returned to Damascus, where the city's residents stayed up all night praying at the Great Mosque, and then joined a barefoot march in hopes of lowering the death toll: "The entire population of the city joined in the exodus, male and female, small and large; the Jews went out with their book of the Law and the Christians with their Gospel, their women and children with them; the whole concourse of them in tears and humble supplications, imploring the favour of God through His Books and His Prophets." Damascus lost two thousand people "in a single day," yet Ibn Battuta managed to stay well.

Modern historians estimate that the plague wiped out 33 to 40 percent of the population in Egypt and Syria alone.[13] By the beginning of 1349, daily losses began to diminish, but it would take two to three hundred years for the populations of Egypt and Syria to return to their pre-plague levels.

◍East Africa, India, and the Trade Networks of the Indian Ocean

The Indian Ocean touched three different regions, each with its own languages and political units: the East African coast, the southern edge of the Arabian peninsula, and the west coast of India. Much as the rulers of the trading posts on the Sahara survived by taxing overland trade, the sultans of the **Indian Ocean trade network**—the city-states and larger political units encircling the Indian Ocean—taxed the maritime trade. Some sultanates consisted of only a single port city like Kilwa in modern Tanzania, while others, like the Delhi sultanate, controlled as much Indian territory as the Mauryan and Gupta dynasties of the past (see Chapters 3 and 8). Although politically decentralized, the Indian Ocean was bound together by frequent boat crossings to its different ports. Merchants who had grown up along the African coast had operations in Arabia or India, and much intermarriage among the residents of different coasts took place, contributing to a genuine mixing of cultures along the coastlines of the Indian Ocean. Interior regions supplied goods to the coastal cities, but because so few outsiders visited them, we know much less about them.

> •**Indian Ocean trade network** Network that connected the ports around the Indian Ocean in East Africa, Arabia, and western India. Dhows traveled from port to port along the coast carrying goods.

The East African Coast

In January 1329, after leaving Mecca, Ibn Battuta traveled south to the port of Aden, on the Arabian peninsula, and sailed to East Africa, most likely in a **dhow** (DOW). Among the earliest and most seaworthy vessels ever made, dhows served as the camels of the Indian Ocean trade. Boatmakers made dhows by sewing teak or coconut planks together with a cord and constructing a single triangular sail. Because dhows had no deck, passengers sat and slept next to the ship's cargo. Traders frequently piloted their dhows along the coastline of East Africa, the Arabian peninsula, and India's west coast. Their expenses were low: dhows required no fuel and traders and their family members could staff their own boats.

Everywhere Ibn Battuta traveled, he saw Indian, Persian, and Arabian ships and merchants. After leaving Aden, he sailed for fifteen days before he reached the port city of Mogadishu, Somalia, which exported woven cotton textiles to Egypt

> •**dhow** Among the earliest and most seaworthy vessels and the main vessel used by Indian Ocean traders. Was made from teak or coconut planks sewn together with a cord; had a single triangular sail and no deck.

and other destinations. Mogadishu's political structure resembled that of other East African ports: headed by a sultan, the government maintained an army and administered justice through a network of qadi justices.

The sultan spoke his native Somali in addition to a little Arabic. The farther Ibn Battuta traveled from the Islamic heartland, the fewer people he would find who knew Arabic. Still, he could always be confident of finding an Arabic speaker, and the Mogadishu sultan's chief legal adviser turned out to be an Egyptian.

Because Ibn Battuta's stay in Mogadishu was brief, he did not go inland, where he would have seen villages growing the strange, colorful foodstuffs he ate, fewer people of Arabian descent, and more non-Islamic religious practices. After a short stop in Mombasa, Ibn Battuta proceeded to Kilwa, a small island off the coast of modern Tanzania (modern Kilwa Kivinye, 140 miles south of Dar es Salaam); there he saw "a large city on the seacoast, most of whose inhabitants are Zinj, jet-black in colour. They have tattoo marks on their faces." Ibn Battuta used the word *zinj,* meaning black, to refer to the indigenous peoples of East Africa. The people he encountered may have already begun to speak the creole mixture that later came to be called Swahili (swah-HEE-lee), a Bantu language that incorporated many vocabulary words from Arabic. (*Swahili* means "of the coast" in Arabic.)

Ibn Battuta arrived at Kilwa during a period of prosperity: a newly established dynasty had taken control of Sofala, a small port near the Zambezi River, which was a major entrepôt (trading center) for gold coming from the interior. Archaeological excavations have revealed that the city had a mosque and a palace built of stone, and its inhabitants lived in stone houses with indoor toilets, ate in kitchens equipped with Chinese porcelains, and wore imported silks and gold and silver ornaments.

We know more about the history of Kilwa than about many other East African ports because of the survival of *The Chronicle of the Kings of Kilwa* in both Portuguese and Arabic versions. This work gives the name of individual rulers but not their dates. By matching the names of rulers in *The Chronicle* with Ibn Battuta's detailed account, historians have concluded that the Kilwa dynasty began in the

■ **The Dhows of the Indian Ocean**
Unlike most other boats, the dhows of the Indian Ocean were sewn and not nailed together. Boatmakers sewed planks of teak or coconut trees together with a cord and added a single sail. This boat design was so practical that it is still in use today. (Hauke Dressler/LOOK Die Bildagentur der Fotografen GmbH/Alamy Images)

1200s. The kings of Kilwa were descended from Arabic-speaking settlers who came to the region from Yemen, further evidence of the ties linking the different societies on the Indian Ocean.

The sultan of Kilwa was a generous man, Ibn Battuta reports, who regularly gave gifts of slaves and ivory from elephant tusks, which he obtained in the interior: "He used to engage frequently in expeditions to the land of the Zinj people, raiding them and taking booty." Slaves and ivory, and less often gold, were Kilwa's main exports. Like the other East African ports, Kilwa imported high-fired ceramics from China, glass from Persia, and textiles from China and India.

Great Zimbabwe and Its Satellites, ca. 1275–1550

Although the interior of southern Africa supplied the Kilwa sultan with slaves and ivory, we know much less about it because Ibn Battuta and other travelers never described the region. There, on the high plateau between the Zambezi and Limpopo Rivers, stood a state that reached its greatest extent in the early 1300s. Its center was the imposing archaeological site of **Great Zimbabwe** (see Map 11.1).

Like other speakers of Bantu languages in sub-Saharan Africa, the people living on the Zimbabwe plateau cultivated sorghum with iron tools. Before 1000 C.E., most lived in small villages in houses made from wood beams held together by plaster. Even at this early date they traded ivory, animal skins, and gold.

Sometime around 1000 C.E., some villagers became wealthy enough to build stone enclosures for themselves. By the thirteenth and fourteenth centuries, the population had reached 10,000[14] and they built three hundred smaller stone enclosures over a large area on the plateau. The word for these enclosures in the local Shona language is *zimbabwe*, which means "venerated houses." Archaeologists use this name for the people who built the enclosures, and it is also the name of the modern nation of Zimbabwe where they are located.

The Elliptical Building is the largest single stone structure in sub-Saharan Africa built before 1500. One estimate holds that four hundred laborers could have built the wall of this building during the slack period of the agricultural season over the course of four years.[15] Because the walls of Great Zimbabwe do not resemble any Islamic buildings along the coast, including those at nearby Kilwa, all analysts concur that Great Zimbabwe was built by the local people, not by the Arabic-speaking peoples of the coast.

Since the people who lived there did not keep written records, archaeological finds provide our only information about local religion. Nothing indicates Islamic beliefs. On the northern edge of the site, the Eastern Enclosure held six stylized birds carved from soapstone, which may depict ancestors or deities. The Zimbabwe people also made and probably worshiped phalluses and female torsos with breasts in the hope of increasing the number of children. (See the feature "Visual Evidence: The Ruins of Great Zimbabwe.")

When excavated, the site contained a single hoard that one archaeologist has called "a cache of the most extraordinary variegated and abundant indigenous and imported objects ever discovered at Great Zimbabwe or, indeed, anywhere else in the interior of south-central Africa." Pieces of broken, imported, Chinese green high-fired celadon ceramic pots and colorful Persian earthenware plates with script on them make it possible to date the site's occupation to the thirteenth and fourteenth centuries. The presence of a single coin at the site, embossed with the name of the king Ibn Battuta met at Kilwa, reveals that the site's residents traded with the coastal towns and were part of existing trade networks.

• **Great Zimbabwe** Large city in Zimbabwe surrounded by smaller outlying settlements, all distinguished by stone enclosures called "zimbabwe" in the local Shona language. The location of the largest stone structure built in sub-Saharan Africa before 1500.

THE RUINS OF GREAT ZIMBABWE

Located near Masvingo, Zimbabwe, the Great Zimbabwe site contains several large ruins and many smaller stone structures whose original purpose is undocumented and therefore still not well understood. The ruins, covering almost 1,800 acres (7.2 sq km), fall into three groups: the Hill Complex, the Valley Complex, and the Great Enclosure. The site was first settled before 1000, when the first stone structures were built, and continued to grow through the 1300s. Little evidence of cereal agriculture survives, indicating that the city's population depended largely on cattle for their food supply.

Like other Bantu peoples, the Zimbabwe people living at the site knew how to work iron. Archaeolo-

The Hill Complex, a group of stone buildings forming a ritual space, stood above a granite cliff 330 feet (100 m) long and 100 feet (30 m) high on the northern edge of the site.

Area of detail

(© Georg Gerster/Photo Researchers, Inc.)

QUESTIONS FOR ANALYSIS

What methods have archaeologists used to analyze the function of the stone buildings at Great Zimbabwe? Whose analysis do you find more convincing?

gists have found nodules of iron ore from mines and alluvial gold collected from riverbeds. The site also contained a workshop where metal-smiths heated copper ingots in crucibles to make wire.

The Great Enclosure holds two large structures: the Elliptical Building and the solid Conical Tower inside it. The outer wall of the Elliptical Building is made of evenly cut granite blocks, fitted together without mortar, that are elegantly trimmed with an intricate (V-shaped) design on the top. What was the purpose of these two buildings? Two analysts, Peter S. Garlake and Thomas N. Huffman, have taken radically different approaches to the problem.

Garlake bases his analysis on close examination of the construction techniques used to make the different types of walls and the location of different artifacts. The sheer size of the Elliptical Building suggests to him that it was the palace of the ruler. Its walls, he contends, stood too high to be mere guard walls:

they made a statement about the ruler's power to all his subjects.

Huffman, in contrast, examines the settlements of the Shona-speaking peoples who live near the site today. Since many of their houses are divided into areas for men to work and women to work, he wonders whether this might not be true of Great Zimbabwe as well. The one hundred smaller soapstone carvings of phalluses and female torsos with breasts found in the Elliptical Building resemble some figurines used in modern schools to teach adolescent girls about family life. The high walls of the Elliptical Building, Huffman believes, kept outsiders from observing the activities at a girls' initiation school.

Sources: P. S. Garlake, *Great Zimbabwe* (New York: Stein and Day, 1973); Thomas N. Huffman, "Where You Are the Girls Gather to Play: The Great Enclosure at Great Zimbabwe," in *Frontiers: Southern African Archaeology Today,* ed. M. Hall et al., *Cambridge Monographs in African Archaeology* 10 (Oxford: B. A. R., 1984), pp. 252–265.

The Eastern Enclosure contained six stone bird statues, suggesting that it was a ritual center.

Detail

In the Valley Complex, Enclosure 12 contained the largest hoard found on the site: over 220 pounds (100 kg) of iron hoes, 44 pounds (20 kg) of iron for wire, warthog and elephant tusks, thousands of Indian beads, and broken ceramic vessels from China and Iran.

With three entrances, the Great Enclosure contains the Elliptical Building, the Conical Tower, and mud and thatch huts where individual families lived.

The Conical Tower—possibly a symbolic granary—is a completely solid stone structure with an outer wall over 30 feet (9 m) high.

The Elliptical Building has an outer wall that runs 800 feet (250 m) long and contains 182,000 cubic feet (5,150 cubic m) of stone.

Kilwa was most prosperous at exactly the same time that Great Zimbabwe was—in the thirteenth and fourteenth centuries when Ibn Battuta visited the city. When the Portuguese arrived on the East African coast after 1500, both Kilwa and the Great Zimbabwe site had already declined dramatically from their earlier, glorious days, but we do not know why.

The Delhi Sultanate and the Hindu Kingdoms of Southern India

When Ibn Battuta sailed away from Kilwa, he embarked on a fifteen-year-long journey along the trade routes linking Africa with India and China. He traveled first to Constantinople and to Central Asia, where he learned that the Muslim ruler of India, Muhammad Tughluq (r. 1324–1351), had defeated his rivals to become the ruler of the **Delhi sultanate** (1206–1526), a powerful sultanate that ruled from their capital at Delhi.

The Delhi sultanate, like the Mamluk empire of Egypt and Syria, was founded by former mamluk slaves. It was not the first Islamic dynasty in South Asia. In the eighth century, conquering caliphate armies had established Islamic states in the Sind region of modern Pakistan. In the 1200s, when a group of mamluks based in today's Afghanistan conquered large sections of northern India, they considerably expanded the extent of territory under Muslim control. These Afghans established their capital in Delhi, which remained the capital of many later northern Indian dynasties and is India's capital today.

Ibn Battuta's patron Muhammad Tughluq, the son of a Turkish slave and an Indian woman, was a powerful leader. His armies, fueled by a desire for plunder, succeeding in conquering almost all of India, including south India. To be closer to the lands he had conquered, in 1326, he ordered his officials to move the capital 400 miles (650 km) south. This measure had disastrous consequences, including the loss of much territory by his enraged subordinates.

● **Delhi sultanate** (1206–1526). Islamic state led by former mamluk slaves originally from Afghanistan, who governed north India from their capital at Delhi. At their height, in the early 1300s, they controlled nearly all of the Indian subcontinent.

■ **The Earliest Islamic Building in Delhi, India**   In 1311, the ruler of the Delhi sultanate planned to build an enormous mosque with four gates, but construction stopped after only the southern gate, the Alai Darwaza shown here, was completed. The Indian architects who built the gate had little familiarity with the classic Islamic elements of arches and domed roofs, so they used extremely thick walls (10.5 feet, or 3.2 m, deep) to support a very shallow dome. (Alai Darwaza/DK Images)

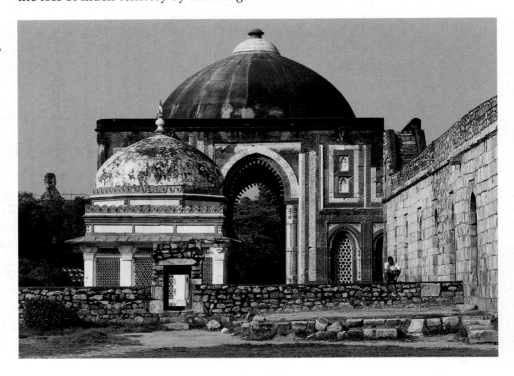

In yet another departure from the practices of earlier rulers, Muhammad Tughluq decided to hire only foreigners to administer his empire. He named Ibn Battuta to be the highest qadi jurist in Delhi, a very high-ranking position, even though Ibn Battuta did not speak Persian, the language of the government, and had studied the writings of a different legal school from that of the Delhi sultanate. In fact, Ibn Battuta kept so busy attending court ceremonials and hunting expeditions that he heard no legal cases.

Throughout this reign, south India remained largely Hindu. After Muhammad Tughluq's government withdrew from the failed new capital, Hindu rulers gained control of urban centers in the south and established temple-centered kingdoms like that of the earlier Cholas (see Chapter 8). The most important Hindu empire was based at **Vijayanagar** (vihj-eye-NUH-gah), which means "city of victory" in Sanskrit, in the modern Indian state of Karnataka. The Vijayanagar rulers (ca. 1336–1614) patronized Sanskrit learning and Hindu temples while creating a powerful army that enabled them to rule for more than two centuries.

Ibn Battuta remained in Delhi for seven years before the sultan named him his emissary to China. When he departed in August 1341, he was traveling with fifteen Chinese envoys, over two hundred slaves, one hundred horses, and various lavish gifts of textiles, dishes, and weapons—all intended for the Mongol rulers of China. His party traveled overland until they reached the Indian Ocean port of Cambay, where they boarded ships.

As Ibn Battuta made his way down the west coast of India, he visited towns that resembled the ports on the African side of the Indian Ocean. A sultan governed each port, where qadis administered justice, and each town had a bazaar and a mosque. Ibn Battuta arrived in Calicut at the head of a large embassy carrying Muhammad Tughluq's gifts for the ruler of China and accompanied by several concubines, one pregnant with his child. At the time of his visit, thirteen Chinese-built vessels were in the port waiting for the winds to shift so they could return to China. "On the sea of China," Ibn Battuta comments, "traveling is done in Chinese ships only."

The Chinese ships docked at Calicut differed markedly from dhows. Unlike dhows, the Chinese-built ships had wooden decks and multiple levels with compartments with doors. Some had up to twelve sails, made of "bamboo rods plaited like mats." These enormous ships, over 100 feet (30 m) long, carried six hundred sailors and four hundred armed men; Ibn Battuta took their massive size as an indication of China's prosperity: "There is no people in the world wealthier than the Chinese."

Ibn Battuta much preferred the Chinese-built ships with their private cabins to dhows, which had no deck and no cabins. On the day he sailed, he discovered that the best staterooms, those with lavatories, were taken by Chinese merchants. He indignantly changed to a smaller vessel, where he could have a room big enough for him to stay with his female companions, "for it is my habit," he said, "never to travel without them." Since it was a Friday, Ibn Battuta went to the mosque for prayers and arranged for his luggage to be transferred to the smaller boat, leaving his traveling companions on the larger vessel.

A violent storm broke that night, and the captains of the two ships removed their vessels from the shallow harbor to the safety of the sea. The smaller boat survived, but the big ship was totally destroyed. Ibn Battuta stood horror-struck on the beach, watching corpses whose faces he recognized float to the top of the water. Having utterly failed to protect the envoys he accompanied, Ibn Battuta fled. Eight years more in India, the Maldive Islands, and China passed before he returned home to Morocco.

● **Vijayanagar** (ca. 1336–1614) "City of victory" in Sanskrit. Important Hindu empire based in the modern Indian state of Karnataka. Vijayanagar rulers created a powerful army that enabled them to rule in central India for more than two centuries.

Chapter Review

 Download the MP3 audio file of the Chapter Review and listen to it on the go.

As Ibn Battuta discovered, many roads led to Mecca. His travels along existing trade routes brought him to much of the Islamic world of the 1300s: overland across the Sahara to Mali, to the ports of northern and eastern Africa, around the Indian Ocean, and to China. He encountered Islamic practices everywhere he went: rulers and the well-off received him generously; students learned to recite the Quran in Arabic; Friday prayers were conducted in mosques; and he could always find companions, often hajj pilgrims or merchants, to accompany him on another leg of his journey. Yet some places, like southern Africa, remained beyond his reach even though they, too, were embedded in the expanding trade networks of Africa and India. The arrival of the Europeans after 1500 did not mark a break with the past but simply extended further the well-developed trade routes already linking the interior of Africa with its coastal ports on the Mediterranean and the Indian Ocean.

How was sub-Saharan Africa settled before 1000 C.E.? What techniques have historians used to reconstruct the past?

Historians have combined oral histories, glottochronology, and archaeological analysis to reconstruct the different phases of the Bantu migrations before 1000 C.E. Most people in sub-Saharan Africa lived in villages, which varied in size and were usually ruled by great men who had demonstrated military prowess and had large families. Sometime around 500 B.C.E., some sub-Saharan peoples planted their first crops. Over the centuries, as they refined their techniques of cultivation, they learned how to make tools and weapons from smelted iron. Iron technology spread throughout sub-Saharan Africa by 300 C.E. The Bantu languages spread in multiple waves until 1000 C.E., when they blanketed much, but not all, of sub-Saharan Africa.

What role did trade play in the emergence and subsequent history of the kingdoms of Ghana and Mali?

The kingdoms of Ghana and Mali both arose at important nodes on trade networks linking the Mediterranean with the Sahel. The Islamic historian al-Bakri described how Sijilmasa began as a periodic market and then became a year-round trading center, then a town, and finally a city. Ghana and Mali followed this same pattern. Their rulers taxed trade, charging merchants for each donkey cart loaded with goods that they brought in and led out of major cities. They used these tax revenues to finance their armies; when they lost important trading cities to rival armies, tax revenues dwindled, and their kingdoms contracted.

How and why did the Mamluk empire based in Egypt become the leading center of the Islamic world after 1258?

The rulers of Cairo, the Mamluks, started as military slaves brought to Egypt from Central Asia and the Caucasus Mountains. After a coup in 1250 in which they seized power from their predecessors, they became great patrons of Islam. In 1261 they announced the establishment in Cairo of the caliphate, which had been destroyed in 1258 when the Mongols took Baghdad. The Mamluks gave large donations to many mosques, hostels, and Islamic schools.

 What was the nature of the Indian Ocean trade network that linked India, Arabia, and East Africa?

Dhows crisscrossed the Indian Ocean, carrying African slaves, gold, textiles, and ivory; Iranian glass; Chinese porcelains; and Indian textiles and beads from one port to the other. All along the coast, different sultanates, some big, some small, survived by taxing the trade. The ports on the Indian Ocean were Islamic city-states governed by sultans and administered by qadi jurists. The merchants who spoke the different languages in this area—Swahili, Arabic, various Indian languages—intermarried with local people and created a new composite Indian Ocean culture.

For Further Reference

Childs, S. Terry, and David Killick. "Indigenous African Metallurgy: Nature and Culture." *Annual Reviews Anthropology* 1993 (22): 317–337.

Dunn, Ross. *The Adventures of Ibn Battuta: A Muslim Traveler of the 14th Century.* Berkeley: University of California Press, 2005.

Garlake, P. S. *Great Zimbabwe.* New York: Stein and Day, 1973.

Hale, Thomas A. *Griots and Griottes: Masters of Words and Music.* Bloomington: Indiana University Press, 1998.

Hall, Martin. *Farmers, Kings, and Traders: The People of Southern Africa 200–1860.* Chicago: University of Chicago Press, 1990.

Hopkins, J. F. P. *Corpus of Early Arabic Sources for West African History.* New York: Cambridge University Press, 1981.

Huffman, Thomas N. "Where You Are the Girls Gather to Play: The Great Enclosure at Great Zimbabwe." In *Frontiers: Southern African Archaeology Today,* ed. M. Hall et al. *Cambridge Monographs in African Archaeology* 10. Oxford: B. A. R., 1984, pp. 252–265.

Irwin, Robert. *The Middle East in the Middle Ages: The Early Mamluk Sultanate 1250–1382.* London: Croom Helm, 1986.

Isichei, Elizabeth. *A History of African Societies to 1870.* Cambridge: Cambridge University Press, 1997.

Lapidus, Ira M. *Muslim Cities in the Later Middle Ages.* Cambridge: Harvard University Press, 1967.

Letzvion, Nehemia, and Randall L. Pouwels, eds. *The History of Islam in Africa.* Athens: Ohio University Press, 2000.

Schoenbrun, David Lee. *A Green Place, a Good Place: Agrarian Change, Gender, and Social Identity in the Great Lakes Region to the 15th Century.* Portsmouth, N.H.: Heineman, 1998.

Vansina, J. "New Linguistic Evidence and 'The Bantu Expansion.'" *Journal of African History* 36 (1995): 173–195.

Vansina, J. *Paths in the Rainforest: Towards a History of Political Tradition in Equatorial Africa.* Madison: University of Wisconsin Press, 1990.

Websites

National Geographic: Xpeditions (http://www.nationalgeographic.com/xpeditions/lessons/10/g35/tgbattuta.html). This website is a lesson plan on Ibn Battuta and his travels.

PBS: Africa (http://www.pbs.org/wnet/africa/. Various resources about Africa. Teacher Tools are particularly helpful.

African Studies Center Outreach Program at Boston University (www.bu.edu/africa/outreach). Offers some online materials, as well as a list of materials for borrowing.

China's Commercial Revolution, ca. 900–1276

(The Collected Works of Li Qingzhao [Beijing: Zhonghua shuju, 1962], plate 3)

In 1127, **Li Qingzhao** (LEE CHING-jow) (ca. 1084–ca. 1151) and her husband Zhao Mingcheng (JOW MING-chung) (1081–1129), a low-ranking Chinese official, abandoned their home in Shandong (SHAN-dong) province and joined half a million refugees fleeing to the south. After Zhao's death only two years later, Li recorded her memoir, which depicts the long-term economic changes of the Song (soong) dynasty (960–1276), when China's prosperity made it the world's most advanced economy, and the short-term consequences of military defeat, when the Song emperors were forced to surrender all of north China to a non-Chinese dynasty named the Jin (GIN) (1115–1234).

As she explains, Li and Zhao fled from their home in north China and traveled 500 miles (800 km) to the Yangzi River:

In 1126, the first year of the Jingkang [JEENG-kong] Reign, my husband was governing Zichuan [DZE-chwan; in Shandong province] when we heard that the Jin Tartars were moving against the capital. He was in a daze, realizing that all those full trunks and overflowing chests, which he regarded so lovingly and mournfully, would surely soon be his possessions no longer. . . . Since we could not take the overabundance of our possessions with us, we first gave up the bulky printed volumes, the albums of paintings, and the most cumbersome of the vessels. Thus we reduced the size of the collection several times, and still we had fifteen cartloads of books. When we reached Donghai [DONG-high; Jiangsu], it took a string of boats to ferry them all across the Huai, and again across the Yangzi River to Jiankang [JI-AHN-kong; modern Nanjing, Jiangsu].[1]

LI QINGZHAO

CL This icon will direct you to interactive activities and study materials on the *Voyages* website: www.cengage.com/history/hansen/voyages1e

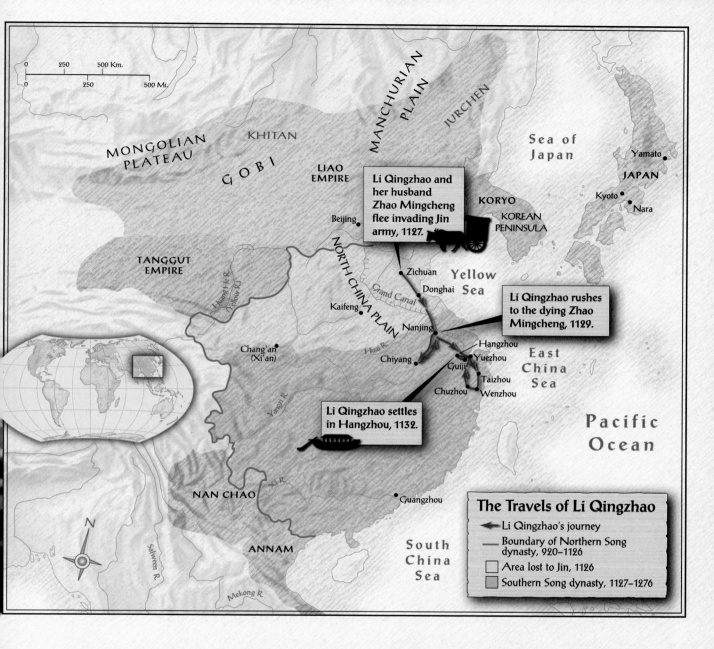

Li Qingzhao and her husband Zhao Mingcheng flee invading Jin army, 1127.

Li Qingzhao rushes to the dying Zhao Mingcheng, 1129.

Li Qingzhao settles in Hangzhou, 1132.

MONGOLIAN PLATEAU

KHITAN

GOBI

MANCHURIAN PLAIN

JURCHEN

Sea of Japan

LIAO EMPIRE

KORYO

KOREAN PENINSULA

JAPAN

Yamato

Kyoto

Nara

Beijing

TANGGUT EMPIRE

Huang He R. (Yellow R.)

NORTH CHINA PLAIN

Zichuan

Donghai

Yellow Sea

Grand Canal

Kaifeng

Nanjing

Hangzhou

Yuezhou

East China Sea

Chang'an (Xi'an)

Huai R.

Chiyang

Guiji

Taizhou

Chuzhou

Wenzhou

Yangzi R.

Pacific Ocean

NAN CHAO

Xi R.

Guangzhou

N

Salween R.

ANNAM

South China Sea

Mekong R.

The Travels of Li Qingzhao

Li Qingzhao's journey

Boundary of Northern Song dynasty, 920–1126

Area lost to Jin, 1126

Southern Song dynasty, 1127–1276

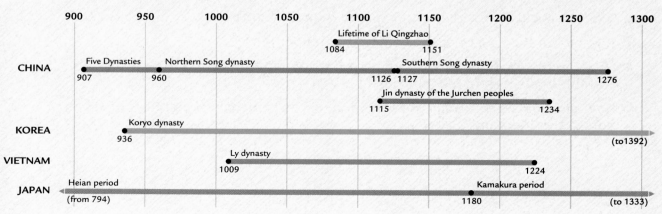

	900	950	1000	1050	1100	1150	1200	1250	1300

Lifetime of Li Qingzhao
1084 — 1151

CHINA
Five Dynasties
907
Northern Song dynasty
960
Southern Song dynasty
1126 1127
1276

Jin dynasty of the Jurchen peoples
1115 — 1234

KOREA
Koryo dynasty
936
(to 1392)

VIETNAM
Ly dynasty
1009 — 1224

JAPAN
Heian period
(from 794)
Kamakura period
1180
(to 1333)

● **Li Qingzhao** (ca. 1084–ca. 1151) Famous woman poet of the Song dynasty who fled south with her husband Zhao Mingcheng when the Jurchen armies conquered north China. Wrote a first-person memoir about their marriage.

After they reached Nanjing (NAHN-jeeng), Li explains, they were forced to abandon their last fifteen carts of books. Li was in her early 40s at the time of her flight. She and her husband Zhao had been born into the top level of Song society, and their fathers had both served as high officials. The couple went by boat to south China, where they hoped they would be safe from the invading armies.

Li Qingzhao's memoir permits a glimpse of Chinese life at a time of wrenching political chaos. Seldom has the world seen such a mass panic as when the Jin armies defeated the Northern Song dynasty. While half a million other people made the same trip south as Li Qingzhao, her account stands out. For one, a woman wrote it. Highly educated in an age when the vast majority of women could not read, Li Qingzhao was the only woman of her time to achieve lasting fame as a poet. Even though only fifty of her poems survive today, many people consider her China's greatest woman poet, and she remains some people's favorite poet, male or female.

The fall of the Northern Song intensified a long-term migration from north to south China that had started centuries before Li Qingzhao's lifetime and continued centuries after it. Starting around 750, farmers realized they could grow more food in south China than in north China. In addition, during the years following the An Lushan rebellion of 755–763 (see Chapter 8), north China suffered continuous political instability that pushed people to migrate to the south.

These long-term migrations resulted in economic growth so dramatic that this period is called China's "commercial revolution." Before the revolution, most of China's farmers grew the food they ate. Largely self-sufficient, they bought little at markets. After the revolution, farmers and craftsmen produced full-time for the market, and China's economic growth affected her neighbors in Korea, Japan, and Vietnam as well.

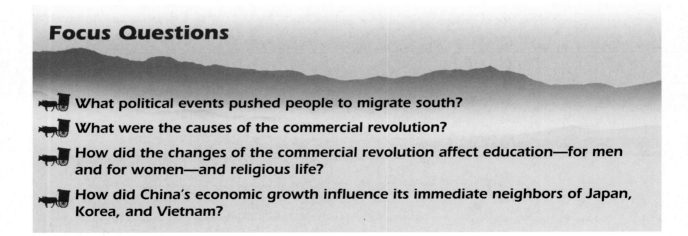

Focus Questions

🐂 **What political events pushed people to migrate south?**

🐂 **What were the causes of the commercial revolution?**

🐂 **How did the changes of the commercial revolution affect education—for men and for women—and religious life?**

🐂 **How did China's economic growth influence its immediate neighbors of Japan, Korea, and Vietnam?**

The Five Dynasties Period and the Song Dynasty, 907–1276

The Tang dynasty (618–907), permanently weakened by the An Lushan rebellion of 755, came to an end in 907 (see Chapter 8). China then broke apart until 960, when the founder of the Song dynasty (960–1276) reunited the empire. The dramatic rise and fall of Chinese dynasties sometimes left the political structure basically unchanged, and this happened during the transition from the Tang dynasty to the Song. The new Song emperor presided over the central government. Almost all government officials were recruited by means of the civil service examinations, making the Song the world's first genuine bureaucracy. Despite the loss of north China to the Jin, Song officials successfully managed the transfer of the central government to a new capital in the south, where they presided over two centuries of unprecedented economic growth.

The Rise of the Northern Song Dynasty, 960–1126

The fifty-three years between the Tang and Song dynasties is known as the Five Dynasties period (907–960) because during this time China was ruled by different regional governments, of which five were most important. The Five Dynasties, in turn, came to an end when a powerful general overthrew a boy ruler of one of the regions and founded the **Song dynasty** in 960. By 976, he had united both north and south China and made his capital in Kaifeng (kie-fuhng). Since the reign of the First Emperor (see Chapter 4), China's capital had always been in the heartland of China, in the valley of the Yellow River. When the founder of the Song dynasty established his capital in Kaifeng (in Henan province) in 976, he was also continuing this tradition.

The Song founder kept in place the old political structure, with the emperor at the top of a central bureaucracy that oversaw local government. But there was one major difference. After unifying the empire in 976, the emperor summoned his most important generals and explained that the Tang dynasty had fallen apart because the regional governors, many of them also generals, exercised too much power. His generals agreed to retire, setting an important precedent. The Song initiated a period of greater civilian rule, as opposed to military rule, with genuine power remaining in the hands of bureaucrats, not generals.

Those officials stationed in the capital held the highest positions in the Song bureaucracy. The Song government referred all matters of state to six ministries: Revenue, Civil Appointments, Rites, Works, Punishments, and War. The heads of these six ministries all reported to the grand councilor, the highest official in the government, who was named to office by the emperor. If the emperor chose, he could, like the Song founder, be active in government matters. However, some emperors preferred to delegate their authority to the grand councilor and devote themselves to leisurely pursuits like the study of calligraphy and art.

The largest administrative districts during the Tang had been the prefectures. There were 220 such prefectures during the Song dynasty. Officials grouped these into over twenty larger units called circuits. Each prefecture in a circuit was further divided into subprefectures headed by a magistrate, who was in charge of collecting

● **Song dynasty** (960–1276) Dynasty that ruled a united China from the northern capital of Kaifeng from 960 to 1126 and only the southern half of the empire from 1127 to 1276.

taxes and implementing justice. Aided by two or three subordinate officials and a clerical staff, the magistrate depended on powerful local families to help him govern. When he encountered problems that he could not solve, he could petition his superiors in the prefecture and in the larger circuit. At every level of the bureaucracy, officials were required to carry out the directives of the central government.

The Collapse of the Northern Song, 1126–1127

Since its founding, the Song dynasty faced a problem common to earlier dynasties: keeping peace with the nomads to the north, in this case the Khitan (KEE-tan), a nomadic people living in modern-day Mongolia. To counter this threat, the Song formed an alliance with the Jurchen (JIR-chen), a forest-dwelling, fishing people based in Manchuria who proved to be skilled horsemen and who raised a powerful army of their own. They spoke Jurchen, an Altaic language similar in structure to Japanese. Originally a subject people of the Khitan, the Jurchen declared their independence by founding their own dynasty, the **Jin dynasty** ("gold" in Chinese), in 1115. The Song-Jurchen forces defeated the Khitan in 1125, yet their alliance proved to be short-lived. As soon as victory was certain, the Jurchen leader ordered his troops to attack the Song. The Jurchen army, with its superior horses, defeated the Song handily and conquered Kaifeng.

The superiority of the Jurchen cavalry proved decisive in battles with the Song army, but a powerful cavalry alone could not conquer the huge walled cities of north China like Kaifeng. For that, the Jurchen had to use weapons fueled by gunpowder, a Chinese invention. Gunpowder is an explosive material made with different ratios of potassium nitrate (also called saltpeter), sulfur, and charcoal. Before 900, the Chinese used different combinations of these materials, primarily for fireworks. But sometime around 900 they realized that they could use gunpowder as a weapon.

Chinese soldiers employed gunpowder in both simple and complex ways. In the most basic use, archers tied small bags of gunpowder onto their arrows, which then detonated on impact. One of the most complex and powerful weapons used in the siege of Kaifeng was the flame-thrower, which emitted a continuous stream of fire. Military engineers used gunpowder to keep the fuse lit and designed a cart of high-quality brass that did not melt when the lit fuel touched it.

When the Jurchen armies first attacked Kaifeng in early 1126, forty-eight thousand Song defenders fended them off with stone-throwers and flame-throwers. The Jurchen troops retreated and then returned a second time in the winter of 1126 and built siege towers, taller than the city's walls, from which they could shoot incendiary bombs made of bamboo shells containing gunpowder and fragments of porcelain that shot in all directions. Unable to devise an effective defense to this horrific new weapon, the residents of Kaifeng surrendered in January 1127.

The loss of the capital marked the end of the Northern Song dynasty (960–1126) and the beginning of the Southern Song dynasty (1127–1276). When the Jurchen captured Kaifeng, they took two emperors prisoner. One, Huizong (HWAY-dzong), had reigned from 1101 to 1125 and then abdicated in favor of his eldest son. The most artistically talented of China's emperors, Huizong did many paintings of birds and flowers and also perfected his own distinctive calligraphic style. His Jurchen captors forced him and his son to wear the plain clothes of commoners. They gave Huizong the humiliating title *Marquis of Muddled Virtue,* and his son, *Doubly Muddled Marquis.*

• **Jin dynasty** (1115–1234) Dynasty of the Jurchen people of Manchuria that ruled north China from 1127 to 1234, when the Mongols defeated their armies. They modeled their government on that of the Song dynasty.

■ The Emperor as Painter   Emperor Huizong (r. 1101—1125) is famous for his bird-and-flower paintings and his distinctive calligraphy, but recently art historians have carefully analyzed the brushstrokes in several paintings labeled "imperially brushed" and have discovered that they were made by different artists, probably those in the imperial workshop. They argue that Huizong's idiosyncratic calligraphy, in fact, lent itself to replication by others. (Palace Museum, Beijing, China/Cultural Relics Press)

Despite their success, Jurchen armies could not conquer the region south of the Huai River. One of Huizong's ten living sons managed to escape from Kaifeng and was named emperor in May of 1127. He did not realize it at the time, but both his father and his brother would die in captivity, making him the first emperor of the Southern Song dynasty. He named Hangzhou (HAHNG-jo), in Zhejiang province, his temporary capital. This placed China's capital south of the Yangzi River for the first time in Chinese history and marked the new importance of southern China. He and his supporters hoped that they would eventually reconquer north China, but they never did, and Hangzhou became the capital of the Southern Song. Historians refer to the period when the capital was in Kaifeng as the Northern Song (960–1126) and the period when the capital was in Hangzhou as the Southern Song (1127–1276). The period of the Song dynasty covers its founding in 960 to its collapse in 1276.

The military defeat of the Northern Song triggered one of the greatest migrations in human history. Most of the people who left Kaifeng worked for the Song government; they included 20,000 officials, 100,000 clerks, and 400,000 army soldiers and their families. In sum, nearly 500,000 people, out of a population in north and south China of an estimated 100 million, crossed the Yangzi River in 1126 and 1127. Like Li Qingzhao, most never returned to north China.

China Divided: The Jin and the Southern Song, 1127–1234

Life in the south was extremely difficult for many northerners, who viewed the north and south as two distinct cultural regions. Northerners ate wheat and millet, often in the form of noodles or bread, while southerners ate rice. Worse, their spoken dialects were mutually incomprehensible. Many of the refugees moved to Hangzhou, which had been a small, regional city, and its population was hard-pressed to accept 500,000 new residents. Within a few years the migrants built housing, and the population of Hangzhou soon reached one million, making it a worthy successor to the Northern Song capital of Kaifeng.

Li Qingzhao's memoir provides a rare eyewitness account of the migration south. She and her husband Zhao Mingcheng fled their home in 1127 to avoid the invading troops. They left behind belongings and artwork that filled ten rooms in their home, which was burnt to the ground by the Jurchen invaders a few months later. In the south, crisscrossed by many rivers and lakes, the couple moved more rapidly by boat.

In the summer of 1129, when the Southern Song emperor summoned Zhao Mingcheng to Nanjing for a personal audience, the couple were forced to separate, with Li Qingzhao remaining behind. Six weeks later, Li Qingzhao received a letter from her husband saying that he had contracted malaria. She frantically traveled the 100 miles (160 km) to Nanjing in twenty-four hours by boat, reaching his side just in time to watch him succumb to dysentery and die at the age of 49.

Li Qingzhao closes her memoir with this sentence: "From the time I was eighteen until now at the age of fifty-two—a span of thirty years—how much calamity, how much gain and loss I have witnessed!" Alone and widowed, Li Qingzhao wrote some of her most moving poems:

> The wind subsides—the dust carries a fragrance of fallen petals;
> It's late in the day—I'm too tired to comb my hair.
> Things remain but he is gone, and with him everything.
> On the verge of words, tears flow.

> I hear at Twin Creek spring's still lovely;
> How I long to float there on a small boat—
> But I fear that at Twin Creek my frail grasshopper boat
> Could not carry this load of grief.[2]

Li Qingzhao gave voice to the losses suffered by the many people displaced by the Jurchen conquest. In the south, the Southern Song dynasty governed some sixty million people from the capital at Hangzhou, where Li Qingzhao settled. For more than a century and a half after 1127, China was divided. With a government structure modeled after the Song dynasty, one million Jurchen ruled a population of some forty million Chinese in the north until 1234.

After fourteen years of more fighting, the Southern Song and the Jurchen signed a peace treaty in 1142, but it came at a high price for the Southern Song. According to the humiliating terms of the treaty, the Southern Song, an "insignificant state," agreed to pay the Jurchen, a "superior state," tribute of 250,000 ounces of silver and 250,000 bolts of silk each year. This tribute was an enormous burden on the Song state and its people, who were well aware that earlier dynasties had received tribute from weaker neighbors, not paid it. The payments, however, stimulated trade and economic growth because the Jurchen used the money to buy Chinese goods. After the peace treaty of 1142 was signed, the people of south China turned to the task of rebuilding the economy, and theirs became one of the richest societies in the world.

The Commercial Revolution in China, 900–1300

The expansion of markets throughout China between 900 and 1300 brought such rapid economic growth that scholars refer to these changes as a commercial revolution. We do not usually think of a change that takes place over more than four hundred years as revolutionary, and the commercial revolution affected different regions at different times. But for the people who personally experienced the expansion of markets, the changes were indeed dramatic.

Before the commercial revolution, farmers grew their own food in a largely self-sufficient barter economy and bought salt, if that, at the market. Officials strictly monitored all trade, and markets opened only at noon and closed promptly at dusk. As markets sprang up in different towns and more people went to them, these restrictions became increasingly difficult to enforce, and, by Li Qingzhao's day, they had long been forgotten. At the height of the commercial revolution in the Song dynasty, China's farmers sold cash crops such as tangerines and handicrafts such as pottery, baskets, and textiles at markets. They used their earnings to buy a variety of products, including food. Dependent on the marketplace for their incomes, they led totally different lives from those who had lived before the commercial revolution.

Changes in Agriculture and the Rise of the South

The origins of the commercial revolution go back centuries before Li Qingzhao's lifetime. In north China, where rainfall was lower (see Chapter 4), farmers planted wheat and millet; in south China, where rainfall was greater, farmers grew rice, which produced a larger surplus. This surplus freed others to grow cash crops or to produce handicrafts.

Before the commercial revolution, south China was universally viewed as a remote backwater whose many swamps provided a breeding ground for malaria and other diseases. When northerners moved south in search of more land, they settled in the highlands and drained the swamps. They used pumps to regulate the flow of water into walled fields. After planting rice seeds in small gardens, they transplanted the rice plants into a field drained of water. Once the plants had taken root, they flooded the fields with water until the crop ripened.

Southern farmers experimented with different rice strains, and in the late tenth century they realized that a type of rice imported from Vietnam had a higher yield than indigenous rice. The Vietnamese rice had a shorter growing season, making it possible to harvest two crops a year rather than just one. Initially this double-cropped rice tasted and smelled bad, but farmers mixed different strains of rice and eventually developed high-yielding hybrids that tasted better.

The shift from wheat and millet to rice had a dramatic impact on China's population. In 742, 60 percent of the population of sixty million lived in north China, where wheat and millet were grown. By 980, 62 percent were living in south China, where they cultivated the higher-yielding rice. With more food available, the overall population increased to one hundred million in the year 1000. Thus one of the most important changes in China's history was this shift south. During the Song dynasty, for the first time, the majority of China's population lived in the south, a trend that continues today.

The Currency of the Song Dynasty

- **paper money**
Money issued around 1000 by the Song dynasty that could be used instead of bronze coins. The Song dynasty was the first government in world history to issue paper money.

- **New Policies**
Reforms introduced by Wang Anshi, a grand councilor of the Song dynasty, implemented between 1069 and 1086. These included paying all government salaries in money and extending interest-free loans to poor peasants.

As more and more people began to produce for markets, they needed a way to pay for their purchases. In response, Song authorities greatly increased the money supply, which consisted of round bronze coins with square holes; a string consisted of a thousand coins strung together. By the eleventh century, the Song government was minting twenty times more coins than had the Tang dynasty at its height.[3]

Li Qingzhao's description of her husband's many shopping trips offers a rare glimpse into the new market economy under the Northern Song: "On the first and fifteenth day of every month, my husband would get a short vacation from the Academy: he would 'pawn some clothes' for five hundred cash and go to the market at Xiangguo [SHE-AHNG-gwaw] Temple, where he would buy fruit and rubbings of inscriptions." Many people in the Song enjoyed tangerines and oranges, which were grown in south China but were available at reasonable cost at markets all over the empire. Zhao used bronze coins to purchase rubbings of inscriptions, art objects that only the richest people could afford. Sometime near the year 1000, the government introduced **paper money**, which was printed on paper and could be used instead of bronze coins. Paper money was much lighter than bronze coins; a string of one thousand coins could weigh as much as 2 pounds (1 kg). The new currency appeared at a time when China's paper-making technology was just reaching the Islamic world (see Chapter 9) and had not yet spread to Europe. While people continued to use coins, paper money expanded the money supply, further contributing to the economic growth of the commercial revolution.

Right from its start, the question of how much paper money to print was intensely controversial. Some wanted to print vast quantities of paper money; other officials urged caution. The debate came to a head in 1069, when the reigning emperor appointed a new grand councilor, named Wang Anshi (WAHNG AHN-shih), who held more radical views. He instituted the **New Policies,** which included paying all government salaries in money and extending interest-free loans to poor peasants. But peasants could not earn enough money to pay back their loans, and by 1086 the reforms had failed.

The World's First Paper Money   This early example of paper money, which the Song dynasty first issued around the year 1000, has three frames. The top section shows ten round bronze coins with square centers, the distinctive currency of the Chinese that paper money supplemented. The middle band of text explains that this sheet of money is worth 770 coins and valid everywhere in the empire except for Sichuan (which had its own iron currency), while the bottom shows men carrying grain into a storehouse.   (Neimenggu jinrong yanjiusuo [The Research Center for Finance in Inner Mongolia], *Zhongguo guchao tuji*, 1987, plate 1.1)

Iron and Steel   The commercial revolution led to the increased production of all goods, not just of rice and fruit. Iron production boomed as entrepreneurs built large-scale workshops to make iron products in factory-like spaces with hundreds of workers. Song metallurgists made two kinds of iron: cast and wrought. Cast iron was poured into a mold and was so hard that it could not be worked with a hammer; wrought iron was malleable enough that blacksmiths could work it. The capital's demand for both types of iron was considerable. For centuries Chinese metallurgists had used blast furnaces to make cast iron, and by the Song their technology was so advanced that they cast an entire pagoda 78 feet (24 m) high, section by section.

Soldiers needed iron armor and weapons, while government workshops produced iron tools and iron fittings, like nails and locks, for buildings and bridges. These goods were not mass-produced in the modern sense, with assembly lines and factories. But they were made in large quantities and at low prices and so were available to rural and urban residents.

The metal-smiths of the Song even learned to how to produce steel, one of the strongest metals known. They heated sheets of wrought and cast iron together in a superheated furnace and then worked them by hand to make steel swords. After the forests around Kaifeng had been depleted for fuel and housing, Chinese metal-smiths fired their smelters with coke, a fuel made from preheated coal that produced high temperatures.

The area around Kaifeng became the world's leading producer of iron. By 1078, China was producing 125,000 tons of iron or 3.1 pounds per person in the entire country, a ratio matched in Europe only in 1700, on the eve of the Industrial Revolution. China's iron and steel production has prompted historians to ask why, if the Song reached such an advanced stage of metal production, China did not experience a sustained industrial revolution. The answer most often given is that Britain's Industrial Revolution occurred under a unique set of circumstances. For example, the British invented machines to make up for a labor shortage, while the Song had no corresponding shortage of labor and therefore no need to develop labor-saving machinery.

Urban Life   As newlyweds, Li Qingzhao and her husband had lived in Kaifeng, one of the world's most prosperous cities and possibly the largest city in the world, rivaled only by Cairo, with a population of 500,000. (At that time London and Paris each had fewer than 100,000 residents.) After one of her husband's shopping expeditions, Li and her husband played a drinking game that shows how close they were:

> I happen to have an excellent memory, and every evening after we finished eating, we would sit in the hall called "Return Home" and make tea. Pointing to the heaps of books and histories, we would guess on which line of what page in which chapter of which book a certain passage could be found. Success in guessing determined who got to drink his or her tea first. Whenever I got it right, I would raise the teacup, laughing so hard that the tea would spill in my lap, and I would get up, not having been able to drink anything at all. I would have been glad to grow old in such a world.

Li Qingzhao and her husband clearly enjoyed each other's company, and he treated her as his intellectual equal. As wealthy urbanites living in Kaifeng before 1127, they were able to enjoy all the fruits of the commercial revolution.

THE COMMERCIAL VITALITY OF A CHINESE CITY

L i Qingzhao's memoir makes the reader wonder what the markets and cities of the Northern Song looked like. One of the masterpieces of Song painting, an extraordinary hand scroll sometimes called the *Mona Lisa* of China, depicts a city with many markets during the Northern Song. We are told in a brief biographical notice at the end of the painting that the scroll's painter, Zhang Zeduan (JAHNG zeh-dwon) (flourished 1150), specialized in technical drawing: "He showed talent for fine-lined architectural drawing, and especially liked boats and carts, markets and bridges, moats and paths." The artist

(National Palace Museum, Beijing/Cultural Relics Press)

This vendor has laid out his tools on a cloth for customers to see.

Three lightly clothed carriers put down their loaded baskets outside a stand serving drinks under two large umbrellas.

QUESTIONS FOR ANALYSIS

What are people buying and selling in the Qingming scroll? What do these transactions reveal about the commercial revolution of the Song dynasty?

intended that viewers look at the hand scroll slowly, rolling it out inch by inch, from right to left, and savoring the extraordinary detail that extends a full 17.25 feet (5.25 m) long. The painting, often referred to as the Qingming scroll, was completed sometime before 1186. Entitled *Peace Reigns over the River,* the scroll celebrates commercial life.

The dramatic high point of the painting comes right in the middle of the scroll. At first one views a boat with sailors hurriedly pulling the mast down. Then, as the scroll unfurls, the viewer understands why: the boat is going under the rainbow bridge, yet its towline has snapped. In his efforts to keep the boat from crashing, one sailor grabs a rope thrown by a passerby standing on the bridge, just as the men at the ship's bow gesture frantically to the oncoming boat to stay out of the way.

The bridge scene vividly illustrates the major change of the commercial revolution: commerce had exploded out of restricted market districts to blanket the cities of the twelfth century. Restaurants and food stands line the side of the river, and they have even crept up the bridge where passersby can eat a snack purchased from a seated baker or can buy

ropes or scissors from vendors who have laid out their goods on the ground. As the scroll ends, when one goes through a large gate and finally enters the city proper, it dawns on the viewer that all the commercial activity seen so far has taken place outside the city walls—a location where all markets were banned during the Tang dynasty.

The detail of the scroll is so mesmerizing that one can easily forget that one is looking at a painting by an artist and not at a photograph. Zhang Zeduan has fit the city into an artfully constructed composition, complete with the rainbow bridge at the exact midpoint of the scroll, and has depicted a city without dirt, illness, or crowding. Curiously, Zhang has nearly omitted women from his cityscape. Of the over five hundred people in the scroll, only twenty or so are female. Surely a real city would have had more women outside, even if women from prestigious families, like Li Qingzhao, often remained indoors.

A collision is about to occur on top of the bridge: an official riding a horse confronts someone (a woman?) in a sedan chair. Several feisty servants gesture emphatically to the horseman to get out of the way.

A bystander on top of the bridge tosses a rope to the boat's frantic crew, who hope to avert a crash with a boat coming toward them from under the bridge.

The details of the bridge's construction—a round arch made from straight wooden beams wrapped together with iron—are clear from this angle. A wooden walkway at the water's edge allows pedestrians to pass underneath the bridge.

339

Kaifeng was a city with many sensual pleasures for those who could afford them, and the prosperity of the commercial revolution meant that many people could. Restaurants were the most prominent establishments catering to consumers. Kaifeng alone had seventy-two major restaurants, each standing three floors high and licensed by the government. Many smaller establishments had menus listing over one hundred kinds of different dishes. Even working people could afford to eat noodles or a snack at the many stands dotting the city.

Although Li Qingzhao does not write about crowding, Kaifeng's one million residents were packed into a small space just over 23 square miles (60 sq km), resulting in a density of 32,000 people per square mile (2,000 per sq km). With people so crowded, sanitation posed a genuine problem, and disease must have spread quickly. (See the feature "Visual Evidence: The Commercial Vitality of a Chinese City.")

Footbinding

The southward migration eventually brought greater wealth to most people and eroded the distinctions among social groups. Although merchants continued to be at the bottom of the ideal social hierarchy—below scholars, peasants, artisans, and merchants—others envied their wealth. The continued expansion of the market turned many peasants into part-time and full-time artisans. Many of those making money selling goods at the market aspired to the high social position of the officials they saw above them.

Both in cities and the countryside, wealthy men sought second and third wives, called concubines, whom they hoped would give them more children. Being able to support a large family with concubines and many children was a mark of prestige. Many observers complained about unscrupulous merchants who kidnapped women and sold them as concubines to newly wealthy men.

Brokers in women found that those with bound feet attracted a higher price than those with natural feet. Li Qingzhao's mother did not bind her daughter's feet, but by 1300 the wives and daughters of officials throughout south China did. The practice appeared first in the tenth century, when dancers at the imperial court, who were probably in their late teens, had begun to wrap their own feet to make them smaller. By the Southern Song, women from good families began to wrap their daughters' feet in the hopes of enhancing their chances of making a good match. The mothers started when the girls were young, around 10, so that their feet would never grow to their natural size.

In the Song period, feet were shortened only slightly, to around 7 or 8 inches (18 or 20 cm), but by the nineteenth century a foot only 3 inches

A Bound Foot Superimposed on a Normal Foot When girls turned 10, their mothers started to bind their feet by wrapping long strips of cloth around them and gradually tightening them until the foot shrank. During the Song dynasty, bound feet were only slightly smaller than normal feet, but in the nineteenth century the ideal bound foot measured only 3 inches (8 cm) long.

(Illustration from John K. Fairbank, Edwin O. Reischauer, and Albert M. Craig, *East Asia: Tradition and Transformation*, rev. ed. [Boston: Houghton Mifflin, 1989], p. 142.)

(8 cm) long was the ideal. To bind her daughter's feet, a mother took a long cloth, some 10 feet (3 m) long, and wrapped it around her daughter's foot so that the small toes were bent inward toward the sole while the big toe was left unbound. Over the years, the mother would tighten the bindings to make the foot smaller. The initial binding was very painful, but eventually girls could resume walking, though always with difficulty. Footbinding transformed a woman's foot into a sexual object that only her husband was supposed to see, wash, or fondle.

Book Publishing and the Education Boom

The commercial revolution brought an information revolution parallel to today's Internet boom, brought on by a deceptively simple innovation, woodblock printing. Before 700, creating a book was a slow, laborious process, since all manuscript copies were done by hand (see Chapter 8). The introduction of woodblock printing sped up book publishing dramatically and significantly lowered the cost of books.

The effect on everyday life was profound, as many more men and women could afford books and learned to read. Because people had more disposable income, they could finance the education of their children. The rise in wealth and educational opportunity also prompted more people to take the government's civil service examination, the door to a job in the bureaucracy (see Chapters 4 and 8).

Woodblock Printing and the Invention of Movable Type

For centuries Chinese scholars had made ink rubbings from stone carvings of Buddhist, Daoist, and Confucian texts. Woodblock printing applied this technique to woodblocks. First, a literate but low-level craftsman with good, clear handwriting wrote the desired text on a piece of paper, which was glued face down on the wood. When the paper was scraped off, the ink from the text remained on the surface of the wood. Then a carver removed the wood around the characters. When the block was completed, the text remained in relief. He then inked the woodblock, placed a sheet of paper over it, and rubbed with a brush. Printers could make hundreds of copies from the same block of wood. Folding each page in half, they sewed the pages into bound chapters of thirty or so pages. Often people calculated the size of libraries in sewn chapters, which were stored in boxes.

Shortly after 1040, a Chinese bookmaker invented **movable type,** in which each character is made separately and arranged on a frame to form a page. An eleventh-century description explains:

> Bi Sheng [bee shung], a man of unofficial position, made moveable type. His method was as follows: he took sticky clay and cut in it characters as thin as the edge of a coin. . . . When he wished to print, he took an iron frame. . . . In this he placed the types, set close together. . . . If one were to print only two or three copies, this method would be neither simple nor easy. But for printing hundreds or thousands of copies, it was marvelously quick.[4]

● **movable type**
First developed in China after 1040. Printers made individual characters from clay, fired them in a kiln, set them in an iron frame, and printed pages by pressing paper against the inked type.

◼ The World's First Movable Type

This model reconstructs the movable type Bi Sheng invented for printing in the 1040s. Because the printer had to cut out an individual type for each character out of clay, the cost of movable type was much higher than the traditional Chinese method of woodblock printing. For large print runs of over one hundred thousand, however, movable print made sense. The world's earliest surviving books printed with movable type were made in Korea around 1400, some fifty years before the German printer Gutenberg used movable type to print the Bible. (Ontario Science Centre, Toronto, Canada)

Since Chinese has thousands of different characters, making a different piece of type for each character was a slow and expensive process. For this reason, it was cheaper to carve woodblocks for smaller runs, such as a thousand books. Movable type made sense only for few large-scale printing projects.

The low cost of books combined with sustained economic growth produced an education boom that intensified the competition for government jobs. More and more families hired scholars who had failed the civil service examinations as tutors for their sons and daughters, buying books and study aids in large numbers. Though only a few passed the exams, many boys gained basic literacy.

The Education of Women

Some women began to enjoy increased educational opportunities in the twelfth and thirteenth centuries, exactly the time when footbinding began to spread. Although they were not allowed to take the civil service exams, many women learned to read and write and take care of their families' finances. We know a good deal about wealthy women in the Song dynasty from biographies, called **epitaphs,** that were buried in their tombs.

The epitaphs reveal what kind of woman was most admired in the twelfth and thirteenth centuries. Whereas Tang dynasty epitaphs emphasized women's physical appearance and ancestry, Song epitaphs frequently praised women for successfully managing their household finances, a skill requiring knowledge of math. In 1250, one official wrote an epitaph for Lady Fang, the wife of his younger brother:

● **epitaph** A biography of someone who has died that was placed in their tomb. An important source for Chinese ideals about model women in the twelfth and thirteenth centuries.

My brother was untalented at making a living but loved antiques and would spend every cent to collect famous paintings and calligraphies. Lady Fang calmly made secret economies and never complained of lacking anything. . . .

Lady Fang was a widow for over ten years. During this time she arranged for her husband's tomb, completed marriage arrangements for her children, repaired the old house, and brought new fields into cultivation in order to continue the thread of our family and preserve the orphans. . . .[5]

Note that the author commends her ability to manage her family's income after her husband's death. Widows frequently figure in epitaphs from the twelfth and thirteenth centuries, and they are often praised for tutoring their young children at home and for making economies that allow their offspring to attend school when older.

The Growth of Civil Service Examinations

The Song dynasty was the only government in the twelfth- and thirteenth-century world to recruit its bureaucrats via merit, as measured by a grueling series of examinations. At the time of the dynasty's founding in 960, civil service examinations had been in use for over a thousand years (see Chapters 4 and 8). But the system had expanded slowly. It was only in the Song era that the proportion of the bureaucracy who had passed the civil service examinations exceeded 90 percent. The tests were not always fair, but they were more equitable than the system of appointments by heredity or social position used elsewhere in the world.

During the Song dynasty, exam candidates took two rounds of exams: the first in their home prefecture and the second in the capital. Originally examiners often met the candidates and knew whose paper they were grading; after 1000, the candidates' names were covered up and the exam papers recopied so that examiners could not recognize their acquaintances' handwriting. The emperor himself conducted the final stage, the palace examinations, in which those placing highest in the written exams were examined orally, with one lucky man named number one in the empire. Those placing highest in the exams were given prestigious entry-level jobs, often drafting decrees for the emperor, because even they had to work their way up the bureaucracy.

The government examiners devised different types of exams over the centuries. Successful candidates had to demonstrate mastery of a classic text, often within the Confucian tradition, by explaining from which text an unidentified passage had been taken. They were asked to compose poetry or essays with a fixed number of lines and a set number of words per line (like a sonnet in English). The candidates also wrote essays about problems the central government had faced in the past or might face in the future, such as inflation or defeating border peoples. Many of these literary skills did not relate directly to what officials would do once in office. Still, those who wrote the questions were seeking to test a broad range of learning with the expectation that they could select the most educated, and so, they believed, the most virtuous, men to become officials.

By 1046, more than 89 percent of the estimated 10,000 to 20,000 officials[6] in China's bureaucracy had received examination degrees, compared to 5 percent under the Tang. As a result, the Song era saw a decisive shift from government by aristocracy to government by merit-based bureaucracy.

Exams in Today's China

In 2007, 10.1 million people competed for 5.67 million spots in China's colleges; only 2.6 million slots are in four-year universities. For the two days in early June when the exams are held, officials implore—not always successfully—construction workers to stop the pounding of jackhammers and partygoers to turn off their outdoor karaoke machines. Urban couples often accompany their only child (one-child families are the norm among China's urban middle class) to the examination site and wait outside for them with meals and snacks; in 2007, one 46-year-old father in the northeastern city of Harbin even attended high school so that he could take the examinations alongside his 18-year-old son.

Cheating is a problem. In 2005, the authorities caught 1,300 people cheating; in 2006, they apprehended 3,000. A new system allows officials to monitor each of the 346 test sites (each with an average of just under 3,000 people) throughout the country. Some officials require that exam-takers sign written pledges, while others equip examination halls with mobile phone detectors (so that exam-takers cannot call people outside for the answers).

In 2007, police captured three men in Anhui province who had hired current university students to sit the exams using the false names of current high school students. If the cheaters did well on the exams, they could make over $1,000. Students and their ambitious parents are not the only ones cheating. Some school principals have leaked the contents of the exams ahead of time so that students from their schools can do better than students from rival schools.

Nowadays, many college graduates have trouble finding jobs, especially in the cities where most want to live. Increasing numbers are turning to the civil service examinations, which were introduced in 1995. (Before that year, the universities placed their graduates in various positions.) In 2007, 530,000 college graduates took the first round of the civil service examinations, which consisted of a general multiple-choice test, an essay question, and a specialized test in law or various types of management. Those who do well on the examination are then interviewed in person. Twelve thousand people—one out of forty-two—will receive positions in different ministries, such as Commerce, Information, Construction, and Justice.

In recent years, as competition to enter universities has eased, many people see the civil service examinations as the true heir to the examinations of the Song dynasty.

The examinations were not open to everyone. Local officials permitted only young men from well-established families to register for the first round of exams. Unlike farmers' sons, who were lucky to attend village school for a year or two, the sons of privileged families had the time and money to study for the exams, often at home with a tutor. Preparation required long years of study. A few brilliant men passed the exams after fifteen years of study, but most continued to study part-time in their 20s and 30s, and some did not pass the examinations until later. (See the feature "World History in Today's World: Exams in Today's China.")

In the eleventh century, successful exam candidates tended to come from a small group of one hundred families living in the capital, Kaifeng. This was the elite into which Li Qingzhao and Zhao Mingcheng were born, and both her father and her father-in-law had received the highest possible degree of advanced scholar.

As the population grew and printed books became more widely available, examinations became more competitive. In 1100, some 80,000 men participated in the civil service exams; in 1270, the number had increased to 400,000, or about 1 out of every 250 people. By that time, in some prefectures in southeast China (particularly in modern Fujian), as many as 700 men competed for a single place in the first round of the examinations. The high number of candidates must have increased the literacy rate: some historians believe that one in ten men, but many fewer women, could read.[7]

The examinations maintained the anonymity of candidates and were outwardly fair. But in fact, the examinations favored the sons of powerful families. Sons and relatives of high officials were eligible to take a less competitive series of examinations, often with a pass-rate of 50 percent, an advantage called the **shadow privilege.** Since Zhao Mingcheng's father was grand councilor, the highest official in the bureaucracy, his shadow privilege extended to his sons, grandsons, sons-in-law, brothers, cousins, and nephews. In the twelfth and thirteenth centuries, as more men became eligible for the shadow privilege, fewer candidates took the open examinations.

● **shadow privilege** Privilege extended to sons and relatives of Song dynasty officials who were allowed to take a less competitive series of examinations, often with a pass-rate of 50 percent.

As competition increased, so did the pressure to cheat. Some candidates paid others to take the exams in their place, or they copied others' answers. In one scandal in Sichuan province, officials grading the exams took bribes, changed the names on the exams, and secretly marked the booklets to which they were supposed to give passing grades. Crafty students also bought commercial aids, like miniature books with tiny characters the size of a fly, that they could smuggle into the examination halls.

Cheating and heightened competition prompted many men to turn away from the examinations and government service altogether. In 1101, when Li Qingzhao married, she assumed that her husband would become an official, and he did. One hundred years later, many families of equally prominent rank chose instead to educate their sons at private academies and to keep them at home to run their family estates once their education was completed. As a book critical of the examination system explained:

> If the sons of a gentleman have no hereditary stipend to maintain and no permanent holdings to depend on, and they wish to be filial to their parents and to support children, then nothing is as good as being a scholar. . . . For those who cannot be scholars, then medicine, Buddhism and Daoism, agriculture, trade, or crafts are all possible.[8]

This author uses the word *scholar* for everyone who earned a living by reading, writing, teaching, or editing. Many young men followed the book's advice. After studying at private academies, they returned to their family estates and pursued the alternate careers the author suggested.

● Religious Life During the Song

The prosperity created by the commercial revolution allowed the Chinese to give money to practitioners of many different religions. Most Chinese did not adhere to a specific religion: they worshiped the deities and consulted the religious specialists they thought most powerful. Lay Chinese made offerings to their ancestors, to Buddhist and Daoist deities, and to gods not associated with any organized religion. Many educated families, particularly those whose sons did not do well on the civil service examinations, were drawn to the teachings of Neo-Confucianism.

Neo-Confucian Teachings

The most influential private academy, the White Deer Academy, was founded in 1181 by the thinker **Zhu Xi** (1130–1200). Zhu Xi's curriculum emphasized moral cultivation. He wanted his students to become true Confucian gentlemen, not civil service officials, and he thought the best guidelines were the Confucian classics. Four texts: *The Analects* (which contained the conversations of Confucius with his students), *Mencius* (written by a follower of Confucius), and two chapters from a ritual manual. These writings are known collectively as *The Four Books*.

Zhu Xi (JOO She) criticized Buddhism as a non-Chinese religion and urged his followers to give up all Buddhist practices, yet Buddhist teachings about meditating and reaching enlightenment clearly influenced Zhu Xi's understanding of the transmission of the Way. He also claimed that studying and thinking on his own had allowed him to understand the Way as it had passed from Confucius to Mencius, from Mencius to a Tang dynasty thinker named Han Yu (768–824), and then to himself. Moreover, he was not the first thinker to focus on the two chapters from the ritual manual included in *The Four Books:* Buddhist teachers in the early 1000s had noticed that these books contained ideas that overlapped with Buddhism, and the two chapters had already circulated as independent texts studied in Buddhist monasteries.

Because Zhu Xi's teachings were based on Confucianism but introduced major revisions, they are called **Neo-Confucianism.** Rather than focusing on ritual and inner humanity as Confucius had (see Chapter 4), Zhu Xi urged students to apprehend the principle in things. If students examined the world around them and studied *The Four Books* carefully, Neo-Confucians believed that they could discern a coherent pattern underlying all human affairs. Armed with that knowledge, an individual could attain sagehood, the goal of all Neo-Confucian education. (See the feature "Movement of Ideas: The Teachings of Neo-Confucianism.")

Zhu Xi did not attract a great following during his lifetime, and the government banned his teachings during the last years of his life. But after the ban was rescinded in 1202, his teachings gained in popularity, and, in the fourteenth century, his edition of *The Four Books* became the basis of the civil service examinations—an outcome Zhu Xi could never have anticipated. Zhu Xi's teachings continued to be influential in China long after his death, and by the seventeenth century they had gained a wide following in Japan, Korea, and Vietnam.

Day-to-Day Religious Life

At the time that Zhu Xi and his followers were formulating their teachings, Neo-Confucian shrines spread throughout south China. At the beginning of the Song dynasty, a few community leaders and teachers had erected shrines to classical thinkers in their schools, but, by the end of the dynasty, shrines to worthies had proliferated throughout the empire. A "worthy" was someone who had lived a virtuous life and embodied the Neo-Confucian virtues of being educated, honest, and concerned about his community's welfare. All worthies were male.

These shrines provided a physical reminder of Neo-Confucian teachers and teachings to ordinary people who might not otherwise have encountered them. They often housed a portrait of the person to be worshiped. Members of the local community or the school that housed the shrine gathered on certain holidays to make offerings to the worthy: bolts of cloth, food, and drinks like wine or tea. A member of the community led a prayer asking the worthy to descend, listen to the prayer, and receive offerings. [9]

Many other types of religion coexisted with the shrines to worthies. Li Qing-zhao's account mentions ancestor worship in particular. When she and her husband parted, Zhao instructed her to "carry the sacrificial vessels for the ancestral temple yourself; live or die with them; don't give *them* up." Each household had an altar for ancestor worship. The wealthy put bronze vessels on their altars; ordinary people used pottery or wooden bowls and cups.

Much religious activity took place outside the home. Some religious practitioners going from market-town to market-town were associated with organized religions, like Daoism and Buddhism, while others, like the spirit mediums, tended to work on their own. Believing that evil spirits caused illness, many people consulted religious specialists, such as exorcists, in the hope of curing sick family members. Daoist practitioners claimed to intervene with the spirits of the underworld and dead ancestors on behalf of the ill, while spirit mediums professed the ability to communicate directly with the spirit world.

Buddhist monasteries offered many women a place where they could go unaccompanied by men and listen to Buddhist texts recited aloud (see Chapter 8). At home the educated few could read Buddhist texts themselves, while the wealthy could afford to hire monks to come to their homes to read to them. Thousands forswore marriage and became monks and nuns living in monasteries and nunneries. Male clerics outnumbered women six to one during the Song dynasty.

●Vietnam, Korea, Japan, and the World Beyond

At the beginning of the Song dynasty, few knew much about the regions beyond China's frontiers, with the exception of places like Central Asia that could be reached overland. As the commercial revolution led to technological breakthroughs, particularly in ocean exploration, the vastness of the larger world became apparent to educated Chinese. Chinese navigators continued to modify their designs for ships, whose large wooden construction profoundly impressed Ibn Battuta (see Chapter 11), and techniques for surveying extensive stretches of territory—so crucial to mapmaking—also improved.

After the Song ruler signed the peace treaty of 1142 with the Jurchen, his dynasty entered a multistate world. The Southern Song was only one of several regional powers in East Asia at the time, of whom the Jurchen were the most powerful. Foreign trade with these powers played an important role in China's commercial revolution. Anyone traveling to Vietnam, Korea, or Japan in the thirteenth century would have seen signs of Chinese influence everywhere: people using chopsticks, Buddhist monasteries and Confucian schools, books printed in Chinese, and Chinese characters on all signposts and government documents. Chinese bronze coins, or local copies, circulated throughout the region, forming a Song dynasty currency sphere. But Vietnam, Korea, and Japan also had their own distinctive political structures and their own ways of modifying the collection of institutions, laws, education systems, and religions they had adopted from the Tang (see Chapter 8).

The Teachings of Neo-Confucianism

The first selection is from a Chinese primer. During the Song dynasty, children learned to read by using primers that taught a core vocabulary. One of the most popular, *The Three-Character Classic*, written circa 1200, consisted of rhyming lines of three Chinese characters each, which students had to learn by heart. Because almost everyone studied *The Three-Character Classic* while only more advanced students studied Zhu Xi's teachings, this version of Confucianism had great influence, not only in China but also all over East Asia, where many students learned to read Chinese characters (even if they pronounced them in Japanese or Korean) using this primer.

The second selection is a memorial to the emperor in which Zhu Xi provides a succinct description of Neo-Confucianism. Zhu Xi formulated his curriculum of the Four Books for advanced students who could read difficult texts. Again and again, he returns to the importance of education. One could apprehend the "principle in things" only through education, by which Zhu Xi meant careful study of the Confucian classics. Here he cites both Confucius (see "Movement of Ideas," Chapter 4) and his later follower Mencius in support of his views.

In the fourteenth century, when Zhu Xi's teachings were chosen as the basis of the civil service examinations, one of his followers included this essay in a widely read anthology. Zhu Xi's teachings spread to Korea around 1400 and to Japan around 1600. One Japanese proponent summarized them in this way: "Study widely. Question thoroughly. Deliberate carefully. Analyze clearly. Act conscientiously."* Although neither the Japanese nor Korean governments recruited bureaucrats via exams as the Song had, both valued Zhu Xi's emphasis on education.

Sources: (*The Three-Character Classic*) Pei-yi Wu, "Education of Children in the Sung," in *Neo-Confucian Education: The Formative Stage*, ed. Wm. Theodore de Bary and John W. Chaffee (Berkeley: University of California Press, 1989), pp. 322–323; (Zhu Xi's memorial) Patricia Buckley Ebrey, *Chinese Civilization and Society: A Sourcebook* (New York: The Free Press, 1981), pp. 116–117.

Selections from *The Three-Character Classic*

Men, one and all, in infancy are virtuous at
    heart.
Their moral tendencies the same, the practice
    wide apart.
Without Instruction's friendly aid, our instinct
    grew less pure;
But application only can proficiency ensure. . . .

To feed the body, not the mind—fathers, on you
    the blame!
Instruction without discipline, the idle teacher's
    shame.
Study alone directs the course of youthful minds
    aright;
How, with a youth of idleness, can age escape
    the blight?
Each shapeless mass of jade must by the artisan
    be wrought,
And man by constant study moral rectitude be
    taught.

Be wise in time, nor idly spend youth's fleeting
    days and nights;
Love tutor, friend, and practice oft Decorum's
    sacred rights. . . .

Father and son should live in love, in peace the
    married pair:
Kindness the elder brother's and respect the
    younger's care.
Let deference due to age be paid, comrades feel
    friendship's glow,
Princes treat well their minister—*they* loyalty
    should show.
These moral duties binding are on all men here
    below. . . .

Men's hearts rejoice to leave their children
    wealth and golden store!
I give my sons this little book and give them
    nothing more.

*Totman, *Japan Before Perry* (Berkeley: University of California Press, 1981), p. 152.

Zhu Xi on Learning

Of all the methods of learning, the first is to explore the basic principle of things. To get at the basic principle of things, one must study. The best way to study is to proceed slowly and in sequence, so as to learn everything well. In order to learn everything well, one must be serious-minded and able to concentrate. These are the unchanging principles of study.

There is a principle for everything under the sun: there is a principle behind the relationship between an Emperor and his subjects, between a father and his son, between brothers, between friends, and between a man and wife. Even in such trivial matters as entering and leaving a house, rising in the morning and going to bed at night, dealing with people and conducting daily affairs, there are set principles. Once we have explored the basic principles of things, we will understand all phenomena as well as the reasons behind them. There no longer will be doubts in our minds. We will naturally follow good and reject evil. Such are the reasons why learning should begin with the exploration of the true principles of things.

There are many theories about the principles of things in our world, some simple, others subtle, some clear, others obscure. Yet only the ancient sages were able to formulate a constant, eternal theory of the world, and their words and deeds have become the model for the ages. If we follow the teachings of these ancient sages, we can become superior men; if not, we will become ignorant fellows. We are inspired by the superior men who govern the realm within the four seas; we are frightened by the ignorant ones who lose their lives. All these deeds and results are recorded in the classics, historical writings, and memorials to the throne. A student who wishes to comprehend the basic truth of things yet fails to study these materials might as well place himself in front of a wall—he will not get anywhere. This is why I say that study is the only key to the comprehension of the principles of the world. . . .

The comprehension of essential knowledge depends on the mind. The mind is the most abstract, most mysterious, most delicate, and most unpredictable of all things. It is always the master of a person, for everything depends on it, and it cannot be absent for even a second. Once a person's mind wanders beyond his body, he will no longer have control over himself. Even in movements and perception he will not be the master of himself, let alone in the comprehension of the teachings of the ancient sages or in the investigation of the true nature of the myriad of things. Therefore Confucius said, "If a gentleman is not serious-minded, he will not inspire awe and his learning will not be solid." And Mencius said, "There is no principle in learning other than the freeing of the mind." . . . This is why concentration is the basis of learning. I, your humble subject, have tried these principles in the course of my own studies and found them most effective. I believe that even if the ancient sages should return to life, they would have no better methods for educating people. I believe these principles are fit even for the education of Kings and Emperors.

QUESTIONS FOR ANALYSIS

▶ Compare and contrast the two different texts: how do their authors view education?

▶ Which of Zhu Xi's ideas do not appear in *The Three-Character Classic* or in *The Analects* (see "Movement of Ideas," Chapter 4)?

▶ Which ideas do you think students in Japan and Korea would have found most understandable?

Technological Breakthroughs Although Chinese ships traveled to Southeast Asia and India as early as the fifth century, they stayed close to the coastline because their ships did not have compasses. Already in the fourth century B.C.E. the Chinese had known that naturally magnetic lodestones would point north when placed on a board. The lodestones, however, eventually lost their magnetism and so were not suited to long sea voyages.

Sometime between 850 and 1050, Chinese metallurgists realized that, if they heated steel needles to a high temperature that we now call the Curie point (which varies depending on the metal in question) and then cooled them rapidly, they could magnetize the needles. Placed in water on a float of some kind, the buoyant needles pointed north. The use of a steel-needle compass floating in water made deep-water navigation possible in the twelfth and thirteenth centuries and facilitated travel to distant places like Vietnam and Cambodia in Southeast Asia, farther than Chinese navigators had gone before.

Two maps (shown below), carved back to back on a stone tablet in 1136, illustrate the limits of Song dynasty knowledge of the outside world. Drawn sometime

◼ What Song Dynasty Cartographers Knew About the World Beyond China These two maps were carved back to back on a single stone tablet in 1136. The map on the front of the tablet (*left*), "The Map of the Tracks of Yu," uses a grid to map the territory under Northern Song rule. This map shows nothing beyond China's borders. The cartographer of the map on the back of the stone tablet (*right*), "The Map of China and Foreign Countries," depicts China's major rivers and provinces spatially and provides short verbal descriptions of foreign peoples. (left: Zhengjiang Museum; right: Shaanxi Provincial Museum; both from Cao, Wan-Ru, with Zheng Xihuang, *An Atlas of Ancient Maps in China* [Beijing: Cultural Relics Publishing House, 1990], maps 56 and 62)

🌐 **MAP 12.1**

China's Trade Relations with the External World, 1225 In 1225, most of Song dynasty China's foreign trade was with Japan, Korea, and Vietnam. China exported silk and high-quality ceramics, while these different societies traded different minerals, raw materials, and foodstuffs in return. Chinese bronze coins circulated throughout the region, creating a currency sphere.

between 1081 and 1084, the map on the front, "The Map of the Tracks of Yu," maps the rivers and coastline of north and south China onto a grid. The map is named for Yu, a legendary ruler of ancient China who controlled floods. Each square covers the same amount of territory. Drawn to a scale of 1:3,500,000, the map is so accurate that it has been called "the most remarkable cartographic work of its age in any culture."[10] Depicting the territory under Northern Song rule, this map shows nothing beyond China's borders, so it omits Vietnam, Korea, and Japan.

As the title reveals, the second map, "The Map of China and Foreign Countries," includes non-Chinese areas. Composed in 1117, it covers much of the same territory as "The Map of the Tracks of Yu" but without a grid and so with much less precision. The map's anonymous cartographer had a good reason for leaving outlying areas blank: he simply did not know the locations of many foreign peoples. Accordingly, he devised a different way to show what he knew about them: he used words, not graphics. In tiny black characters surrounding the map, he provided capsule descriptions of certain foreign peoples. These written descriptions provide the names of Vietnam, Korea, and Japan yet give no further information, an indication that even mapmakers knew little about China's immediate neighbors in the early twelfth century.

The tradition of writing about foreign peoples continued with the publication in 1225 of *The Description of Foreign Peoples*[11] by **Zhao Rugua** (see Map 12.1). Zhao Rugua (JAO RUE-gwah) served as the director of the Department of Overseas Trade in Quanzhou, China's largest international trade port, in Fujian province on the southeast coast. Not a traveler himself, he combined information from encyclopedias with what he learned from speaking with foreign and Chinese traders, which enabled him to go beyond the 1117 map and describe the three states of East Asia most influenced by the Tang: Vietnam, Korea, and Japan.

CL **Interactive Map**

• **Zhao Rugua** (fl. 1225) Author of *The Description of Foreign Peoples* (published in 1225), a compendium of information about China's closest trading partners—Korea, Vietnam, and Japan—and distant places such as the east coast of Africa and Spain.

• **Ly dynasty** (1009–1224) The independent rulers of Vietnam who claimed to have the Mandate of Heaven to rule the southern empire. Adopted the *Tang Code* in 1042 and accepted tributary status, acknowledging the superiority of the Chinese emperor.

Vietnam Since Vietnam directly bordered China on the south, it received the most extensive Chinese influence. Zhao did not consider it a separate country. Under direct Chinese rule during the Han and Tang dynasties, Vietnam, under the **Ly dynasty** (1009–1224), remained nominally independent during the

Song. Because it was a tributary of China, its king acknowledged the superiority of the Chinese emperor and periodically sent delegations to the Chinese capital to present him with gifts. The Chinese emperor bestowed gifts on the emissaries in return.

The Chinese-educated scholars of the Ly (LEE) dynasty argued that their king, the southern emperor, ruled the southern kingdom of Vietnam because he, like the Chinese emperor, had the Mandate of Heaven (see Chapter 4). The Vietnamese kings credited local spirits with protecting the royal house and supported Buddhism. Since at least the fourth century, Buddhist monks had traveled back and forth between China and Vietnam, and Buddhist texts had circulated in both directions (see Chapter 8).

The Vietnamese king and his courtiers had received a Chinese-style education and could read and write Chinese. In 1042, the Ly emperor adopted a modified form of the *Tang Code* (see Chapter 8) so that his subjects would understand the laws of the kingdom. In fact, though, the dynasty's control beyond the major administrative centers was weak. In much of the kingdom's territory, largely independent chieftains ruled groups who lived in bands in the highlands and submitted valued items like rhinoceros horns and elephant tusks to the king. At the time of Zhao's writing, the Vietnamese exported to China the same unprocessed goods, including rhinoceros horns, elephant tusks, camphor, musk, and sandalwood, that they had for the previous thousand years.

Korea

Koryo dynasty
(936–1392) Dynasty that gave its name to the modern country of Korea. Its founder modeled the structure of the central government on the Tang dnasty and divided the region into administrative districts like those in China.

Like Vietnam, Korea did not strike Zhao Rugua as foreign: "Their houses, utensils and implements, their mode of dressing and their methods of administration are," Zhao remarked, "more or less copies of what we have in China." In 936, the founder of the **Koryo dynasty** (936–1392) defeated his last rival and founded the dynasty that gave its name to the modern country of Korea. He modeled the structure of the central government on the Tang dynasty and divided the region into administrative districts like those in China.

The king used a Chinese-style exam to recruit officials and thereby reduce the influence of his main rivals, powerful families who formed a hereditary local aristocracy who controlled their own troops. This policy succeeded for over two hundred years until 1170, when aristocrats and their military supporters overthrew the Chinese-style administration. Military officers took over all government positions, and men of letters retreated to the countryside, where they continued their studies. Kings continued to rule as figureheads, but the top generals could and did replace them at will.

Trade with China persisted even during these politically unstable times. Korea exported precious metals like gold, silver, and copper and edible goods like ginseng and pine nuts in exchange for Chinese silks, books, and high-quality ceramics. Korean potters built high-firing kilns in which they made pale green celadon pots even more beautiful than Chinese export ware.

Koreans also embraced woodblock printing. In 1251, Korean printers created a library of Buddhist texts several thousand sewn chapters long that is universally acknowledged to be the highest-quality set made anywhere in East Asia. Much more so than their Chinese counterparts, Korean printers adopted the technology of movable type. The world's first surviving book printed with movable type was made in Korea and dates to around 1400, some three centuries after the Chinese first invented movable type and half a century before Johannes Gutenberg printed the first Bible in Germany using movable type (see Chapter 15).

Japan

Zhao Rugua called Japan the "Land of the Rising Sun," because "this country is situated near the place where the sun rises." The Japanese, Zhao reported, exported cedar trees, some as tall as 15 yards (15 m). "The natives split them into planks, which they transport in large junks to our port of Quanzhou for sale."

Although the Japanese emperors had earlier looked to China as a model (see Chapter 8), after 900 certain warrior clans gradually gained power and forced the emperor to retire to Kyoto, abandon Chinese-style government, and remain as a figurehead. In 1185, the Minamoto (ME-nah-MOE-toe) clan defeated its rivals and established a new capital at Kamakura, a city just outside modern Tokyo.

During the **Kamakura period** (1185–1333), political power rested in the hands of the shogun, or general, who claimed to govern on behalf of the emperor. The shogun did not conduct Chinese-style civil service examinations but appointed members of powerful clans to office. Still, scholars continued to study both Buddhist and Confucian texts, many of them imported from China and written in Chinese characters; they also used the kana alphabet to represent the sounds of spoken Japanese.

The shogun patronized Buddhism, and the teachings of Zen Buddhism attracted many followers. Zen masters posed puzzling questions with no clear answer: for example, what is the sound of one hand clapping? As disciples meditated on these questions, their masters hoped that they would suddenly understand the teachings of the master and attain enlightenment.

> • **Kamakura period** (1185–1333) Era in Japanese history when political power rested in the hands of the shogun, or general, who governed on the emperor's behalf. The shogun appointed members of powerful clans to office without civil service examinations.

The World Beyond East Asia

Going beyond East Asia, Zhao Rugua's book covers the Islamic heartland of Arabia and Mecca and the Islamic periphery; the southern coast of Europe; and the northern and eastern coasts of Africa. Clearly dependent on Arab geographers for his knowledge of these places, Zhao's entries mix accurate information with sheer fantasy. For example, he begins his description of Madagascar in vague terms— "The country is in the sea to the south-west"—and then reports that a giant bird lives there who swallows camels whole.

But Zhao's information is not all myth. He is particularly knowledgeable about foreign products, such as dark-skinned African slaves, that he has seen with his own eyes in Quanzhou. "In the West there is an island in the sea on which there are many savages, with bodies as black as lacquer and with frizzed hair. They are enticed by offers of food and then caught and carried off for slaves to the Arabian countries, where they fetch a high price."

Zhao's knowledge of the non-Chinese was the product of the trading environment of Quanzhou. Almost every place on his list is located on a seacoast, and the goods he describes came to China on seagoing vessels. Knowing nothing of the nomadic peoples of the north, Zhao was completely unaware that as he was writing a powerful confederation of Mongols was taking shape on the grasslands of Eurasia (see Chapter 14).

> ⒸⓁ **Primary Source:**
> A Description of Foreign Peoples
> *Discover the rich commodities and unusual customs of Arabia and southern Spain, as seen by Zhao Rugua, a thirteenth-century Chinese trade official.*

Chapter Review

 Download the MP3 audio file of the Chapter Review and listen to it on the go.

When later Chinese looked back on the Song dynasty, they had much reason to be proud. To be sure, the dynasty's military forces had suffered the massive loss in 1126 of all north China to the Jurchen, as Li Qingzhao so movingly recorded. Her memoir captures the civilized, cosmopolitan life of the Song dynasty. The expansion of markets during the commercial revolution had changed people's lives dramatically for the better. The sustained prosperity made it possible for couples like Li Qingzhao and Zhao Mingcheng to attain a high level of education. In the next chapter, we will meet a similarly talented couple who lived through a period of comparable economic growth in Europe.

What political events pushed people to migrate south?

The turmoil of the An Lushan rebellion of 755–763 prompted many living in north China to move south, and the migrations continued in the closing years of the Tang dynasty and the Five Dynasties period. The fall of north China in 1126–1127 to the invading armies of the Jin dynasty accelerated the migrations south. Some 20,000 officials, including Li Qingzhao's husband Zhao Mingcheng, 100,000 clerks, and 400,000 soldiers and their families moved to the new capital at Hangzhou.

What were the causes of the commercial revolution?

The more productive rice agriculture of south China produced a surplus that freed some family members to grow cash crops, like tangerines, or to make handicrafts, like baskets and textiles, to sell at market. The Song dynasty government increased the money supply, both by minting more bronze coins and, after 1100, by printing the world's first paper money.

How did the changes of the commercial revolution affect education—for men and for women—and religious life?

The era's prosperity, coupled with the development of woodblock printing, sustained an educational boom. While sons of official families might have bemoaned the increased competition in the open civil service examinations, hundreds of thousands of boys and even girls learned to read and write in schools or at home with tutors. The economic growth also meant that more people had money to give to religious practitioners who claimed to be able to cure the ill and to pray on behalf of the dead. Devotees gave money to Buddhist and Daoist monasteries, temples to deities, and Confucian shrines to worthies. The teachings of Zhu Xi attracted a wide following, particularly among elite families whose sons did not attain positions in the bureaucracy.

How did China's economic growth influence its immediate neighbors of Japan, Korea, and Vietnam?

Consumers in Vietnam, Korea, and Japan purchased Chinese ceramics, textiles, and books even as they exported metals, food, and lumber to the Song Empire. They did not accept Chinese culture passively but modified it to suit their own societies. Korean potters and printers surpassed Chinese accomplishments in high-fired porcelain and movable type printing.

For Further Reference

Bol, Peter K. "The Sung Examination System and the Shih." *Asia Major,* 3rd ser., 3.2 (1990): 149–171.

Chaffee, John. *The Thorny Gates of Learning in Sung China: A Social History of Examinations.* New York: Cambridge University Press, 1985.

Ebrey, Patricia. *The Inner Quarters: Marriage and the Lives of Chinese Women in the Sung Period.* Berkeley: University of California Press, 1993.

Ebrey, Patricia Buckley, Anne Walthall, and James B. Palais. *East Asia: A Cultural, Social, and Political History.* 2d ed. Boston: Wadsworth/Cengage Learning, 2009.

Franke, Herbert. "The Chin Dynasty." In Denis C. Twitchett and Herbert Franke, eds., *Alien Regimes and Border States, 907–1368,* vol. 6 of *The Cambridge History of China.* New York: Cambridge University Press, 1994.

Hansen, Valerie. *The Open Empire: A History of China to 1600.* New York: W. W. Norton, 2000.

Heng Chye Kiang. *Cities of Aristocrats and Bureaucrats: The Development of Medieval Chinese Cityscapes.* Singapore: University of Singapore Press, 1999.

Owen, Stephen. "The Snares of Memory." In *Remembrances: The Experience of the Past in Classical Chinese Literature.* Cambridge: Harvard University Press, 1986, pp. 80–98.

Tarling, Nicholas, ed. *The Cambridge History of Southeast Asia.* Cambridge: Cambridge University Press, 1999.

Temple, Robert. *The Genius of China; 3,000 Years of Science, Discovery, and Invention.* New York: Simon and Schuster, 1986.

Totman, Conrad. *A History of Japan.* Malden, Mass: Blackwell Publishers, 2000.

 ## WEB RESOURCES

Pronunciation Guide

Interactive Maps

MAP 12.1 China's Trade Relations with the External World, 1225

Primary Sources

Chapter Objectives

ACE Multiple-Choice Quiz

Flashcards

Websites

The Beijing Qingming Scroll and Its Significance for the Study of Chinese History, by Valerie Hansen (http://www.yale.edu/history/faculty/materials/hansen-qingming-scroll.html).   Introduction to the Qingming Scroll, with captions and detailed images of the painting.

Li Qingzhao (http://home.infionline.net/~ddisse/liquinzh.html).   A short biography and translations of poems by Li Qingzhao.

Nova Online: Secrets of Lost Empires: China Bridge (http://www.pbs.org/wgbh/nova/lostempires/china/). A website to accompany the show "China Bridge," including resources and teacher's guide.

Europe's Commercial Revolution, 1000–1400

Sometime around 1132, when he was in his early 40s, **Peter Abelard** (1079–1142/44) wrote an account of his own life entitled *The Story of His Misfortunes*. The title was apt. Abelard wrote about his love affair with **Heloise** (ca. 1090–1163/64), a woman at least ten years younger than he was; when her guardian discovered that Heloise was pregnant, he ordered several of his men to castrate Abelard. After the assault, Abelard and Heloise separated and lived in religious institutions for the rest of their lives, he as a learned teacher, she as the abbess of a nunnery. Over the course of their event-filled lives, Heloise and Abelard personally experienced the changes occurring in Europe between 1000 and 1400. Like China of the Song dynasty (see Chapter 12), Europe underwent a dramatic commercial revolution, especially in agriculture. Most of the land in Europe was brought under cultivation in a process called *cerealization*. The economic surplus financed the first universities of Europe, new religious institutions, the Crusades, and trade with East Asia, all of which made the Europeans in 1400 richer and more knowledgeable about distant places than they had been in 1000.

We can learn about the dramatic changes of this period from Abelard's memoir, which begins with the story of his childhood:

ABELARD AND HELOISE

(Musée Condé, Chantilly, France/Giraudon/Art Resource, NY)

> I was born on the borders of Brittany, about eight miles I think to the east of Nantes (NAHNT), in a town called Le Pallet (luh PAH-lay). I owe my volatile temperament to my native soil and ancestry and also my natural ability for learning. My father had acquired some knowledge of letters before he was a knight, and later on his passion for learning was such that he intended all his sons to have instruction in letters before they were trained to arms. His purpose was fulfilled. I was his first-born, and being specially dear to him had the greatest care taken over my education. For my part, the more rapid and easy my progress in my

 This icon will direct you to interactive activities and study materials on the *Voyages* website: www.cengage.com/history/hansen/voyages1e

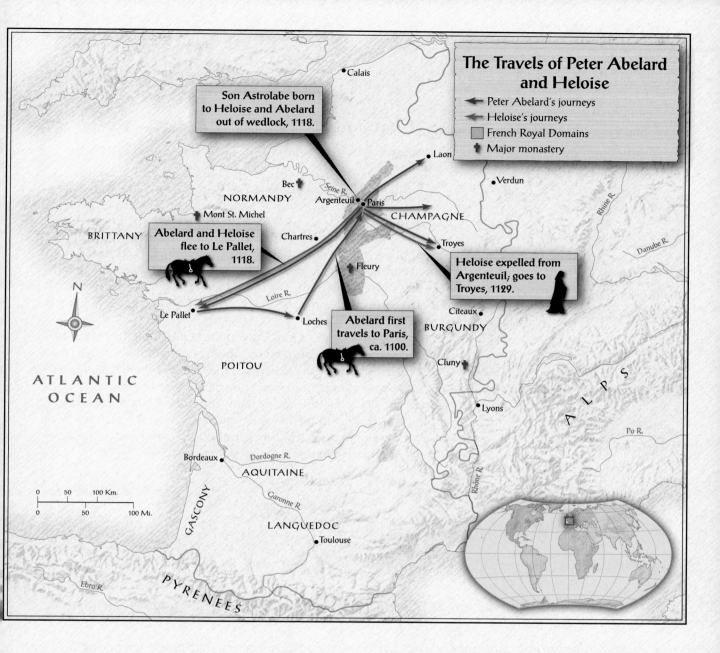

The Travels of Peter Abelard and Heloise

→ Peter Abelard's journeys
→ Heloise's journeys
◻ French Royal Domains
✝ Major monastery

Son Astrolabe born to Heloise and Abelard out of wedlock, 1118.

Abelard and Heloise flee to Le Pallet, 1118.

Heloise expelled from Argenteuil; goes to Troyes, 1129.

Abelard first travels to Paris, ca. 1100.

Calais

Bec

Seine R.

NORMANDY

Argenteuil • Paris

Mont St. Michel

Laon

Verdun

Rhine R.

BRITTANY

Chartres

CHAMPAGNE

Danube R.

Fleury

Troyes

Le Pallet

Loches

Loire R.

Citeaux

BURGUNDY

POITOU

Cluny

ATLANTIC OCEAN

Lyons

ALPS

Po R.

Bordeaux

Dordogne R.

AQUITAINE

N

0   50   100 Km.
0   50   100 Mi.

GASCONY

Garonne R.

Rhône R.

LANGUEDOC

• Toulouse

PYRENEES

Ebro R.

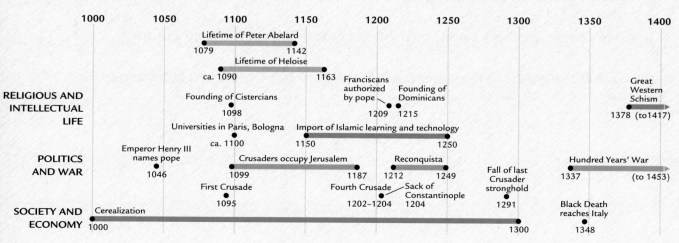

	1000	1050	1100	1150	1200	1250	1300	1350	1400

Lifetime of Peter Abelard
1079 — 1142

Lifetime of Heloise
ca. 1090 — 1163

RELIGIOUS AND INTELLECTUAL LIFE

Franciscans authorized by pope 1209

Founding of Dominicans 1215

Great Western Schism 1378 (to 1417)

Founding of Cistercians 1098

Universities in Paris, Bologna ca. 1100

Import of Islamic learning and technology 1150 — 1250

POLITICS AND WAR

Emperor Henry III names pope 1046

Crusaders occupy Jerusalem 1099 — 1187

Reconquista 1212 — 1249

Fall of last Crusader stronghold 1291

Hundred Years' War 1337 (to 1453)

First Crusade 1095

Fourth Crusade 1202–1204

Sack of Constantinople 1204

SOCIETY AND ECONOMY

Cerealization 1000 — 1300

Black Death reaches Italy 1348

studies, the more eagerly I applied myself, until I was so carried away by my love of learning that I renounced the glory of a military life. . . . I began to travel about in several provinces disputing, like a true peripatetic philosopher, wherever I had heard there was a keen interest in the art of dialectic.[1]

● **Peter Abelard** (1079–1142/44) Prominent scholastic thinker who wrote about his affair with Heloise in his autobiography, *The Story of His Misfortunes.*

● **Heloise** (ca. 1090–1163/64) French nun who wrote many letters to Peter Abelard, her former lover and the father of her child Astrolabe, which survive in the *Letters of Abelard and Heloise.*

Abelard's speaking abilities and ferocious intelligence made him one of the best-known philosophers and most famous teachers in Europe. He traveled from one French town to another until he arrived in the great intellectual center of Paris, where one of the first universities in the world was taking shape. Students from all over Europe flocked to hear his lectures before returning home to serve their kings as officials or their churches as clergy.

During this time, new methods of farming produced much higher yields, and Europe's population increased as a result. Many landowning families initiated new inheritance practices that gave only the eldest sons the right to inherit their father's estates, forcing the other sons to go into education, as Abelard chose to do voluntarily, or the church, which, after undergoing many different reforms, became one of the most vibrant institutions in medieval European society. The century from 1300 to 1400 saw a temporary halt in growth caused by a massive outbreak of plague but also changes that strengthened European monarchies.

Focus Questions

♦ **What caused the cerealization of Europe, and what were its results?**

♦ **What led to the foundation of Europe's universities? How did they gain the right to govern themselves?**

♦ **How did economic prosperity affect the Christian church and different monastic orders?**

♦ **What did the Crusaders hope to achieve outside Europe? Within Europe?**

♦ **How did the major developments of the century from 1300 to 1400 strengthen European monarchies?**

The Cerealization and Urbanization of Europe

Europe experienced sustained economic prosperity between 1000 and 1300. The growth resulted not from migration to rice-growing regions as in China (see Chapter 12) but from the intensification of agriculture. Quite simply, Europeans grew the same staple crops of wheat and barley, but they reclaimed more land and farmed it more intensively than they had before. The main innovations—crop rotation, horse-drawn plows, use of iron tools, and water mills and windmills—were known in earlier times but became widespread after 1000. Europe's population grew dramatically as a result. As in China, the creation of a large agricultural surplus freed some people from having to work the land and allowed them to pursue a variety of careers.

Agricultural Innovation

The agricultural innovations from 1000 to 1300 can be summed up in a single word: *cerealization*. Like the term *industrialization,* the word **cerealization** indicates a broad transformation that profoundly affected everyone who experienced it. Before cerealization, much of the land in Europe was not cultivated regularly; after it, much of it was. In Carolingian France at the time of Charlemagne in 800 (see Chapter 10), many farmers had engaged in slash-and-burn, or swidden, agriculture. Since they worked different plots at different times, as much as half of the land remained uncultivated at any moment. Farmers had to fish and hunt to supplement their diets. But the advanced agricultural techniques that came into use after 1000 allowed them to keep more land under cultivation.

Not all these changes occurred at the same time throughout Europe. Northern France and England were the most advanced regions. Farmers before 1000 realized that land became less fertile if they planted the same crop year after year, so each year they allowed a third to half of their land to lie fallow. After 1000, a few farmers began to rotate their crops so that they could keep their land under continuous cultivation. One popular rotation of turnips, clover, and grain took advantage of different nutrients in the soil each year. This practice, so crucial to increasing agricultural yield, spread only slowly.

European farmers also began to exploit more sheep, horses, and cows in their farming. They raised sheep for their wool, while they could use both horses and oxen for transport. In the centuries after 1100, horses, which worked harder and faster, gradually replaced oxen on European farms. By 1200, very few farmers in northern France used oxen any longer.

Before 1000, most of the plows used in Europe to prepare the earth for planting had wooden blades, which broke easily and could not penetrate far into the soil. Gradually farmers, particularly in northern France, added pieces of iron to their blades, which allowed them to dig deeper and increase productivity. In addition, iron horseshoes protected the hooves of the horses that pulled the plows. Farmers also experimented with better harnesses for draft horses that allowed them to pull plows more efficiently. By 1200, many villages had their own blacksmiths who repaired horseshoes and plow blades.

The final innovation left the deepest imprint on the landscape. As early as 500, but particularly after 1000, farmers began to harness the water in flowing rivers to

cerealization Term comprising many agricultural practices that allowed Europeans between 1000 and 1300 to cultivate most of the land in Europe: crop rotation, use of draft animals, the addition of iron blades to plows, and the spread of water mills and windmills.

operate mills. Water mills were first used to grind grain and then were adapted to other uses, such as beating wool to make it thicker ("fulling" cloth), sawing wood, and sharpening or polishing iron. By 1100, records show that at least 5,600 water mills existed throughout England, or one mill for every thirty-five families.

Even more powerful than water mills were those powered by wind. The world's first windmills were built in Iran around 700; positioned on a vertical axis, the blades drove pumps that moved water from one irrigation channel to another. They came into use in Europe just before 1200. Since windmills required a steady wind, they could only be used in certain regions, often by the sea.

Each farming family performed a wide variety of tasks. Women tended to do the jobs closer to the home, like raising children, cooking food, tending the garden, milking cows, and caring for the other livestock. Men did the plowing and sowed seed, but both sexes helped to bring in the harvest. Many households hired temporary help, both male and female, at busy times of year to assist with shearing sheep, picking hops for beer, and mowing hay.

Population Growth and Urbanization

The clear result of Europe's cerealization was the marked population growth that occurred between 1000 and 1340. In 1000, Europe had a population of less than 40 million; by 1340 the population had nearly doubled to around 75 million. Even more significant was the geographic pattern of population growth. The number of people living in southern and eastern Europe—in Italy, Spain, and the Balkans—increased 50 percent, from 17 to 25 million. But the population of northern Europe shot up by a factor of three, with the result that half of Europe's people lived in northern Europe by 1340.[2]

■ **Cutting-Edge Farming Techniques in Europe, 1300–1340** At first glance, the two men working the land may seem to be using traditional farming techniques. In fact, though, this detail from a manuscript illustrates two of the most important innovations in the cerealization of Europe: horse-drawn plowing equipment and the use of iron tools. The horse is pulling a harrow, a large rakelike tool with many teeth that broke up lumps of earth after the soil had already been plowed. (British Library, London/HIP/ Art Resource, NY)

The process of cerealization freed large numbers of people from working the land full-time. Individual households began to produce food products such as butter, cheese, and eggs or handicrafts like textiles and soap to sell at local markets. At first, people went to periodic markets to trade for the goods they needed. This began to change around 1000, when rulers minted the first coins since the fall of the Western Roman Empire. With the new currency, many periodic markets gradually evolved into permanent markets that opened daily. Markets were usually located near castles or large monasteries; inside the walls of most European market towns were the marketplace, the lord's castle, and several churches.

These market towns arose first on the coasts of the Mediterranean, the English Channel, and the Baltic or along inland rivers like the Rhine. During the 1000s and 1100s, more and more people traveled from one market to another, sometimes going overland on new roads, to attend the fairs that occurred with increasing frequency.

Before 1000, only a handful of cities, all the sites of castles or church centers, existed north of the Alps. After 1000, the number of cities there increased sharply. European cities between 1000 and 1348 were not large. One of the largest, Paris, had a population of 80,000 in 1200, much less than the 450,000 people living in Islamic Córdoba and a mere fraction of Song dynasty Hangzhou's one million.

Yet the people who lived in Europe's cities had crossed an important divide: because they had stopped working the land, they were dependent on the city's markets for their food supply. Many urban artisans worked either in food preparation, like butchers and bakers, or in the field of apparel, like tailors and shoemakers. Because one-third to one-half of these artisans worked with no assistants, they depended on their wives and children to sell their goods. Some merchants specialized in transporting goods from one place to another; for example, a German woman in 1420 bought and sold "crossbows, saddle bags, bridles, harnesses, halters, spurs, and stirrups, as well as sulphur, copperas [a chemical used in tanning], verdigris [a green pigment], arrow quivers, soap, parchment, wax, paper, and spices."[3]

The people who lived in cities were intensely aware that they differed from those who worked the estates and those who owned them. Tradesmen in the same occupations formed **guilds** that regulated prices and working hours; they also covered their members' burial costs. Most important, they decided who could enter the guild and who could not; only those who belonged to the guild could engage in the business the guild regulated. One visible sign of the guilds' influence was the cathedrals they financed throughout Europe, sometimes with contributions from others. (See the feature "Visual Evidence: The Gothic Cathedral at Chartres.")

After 1000, urban residents frequently petitioned their rulers for the right to pass regulations concerning trade and to mint coins. Local rulers often granted these rights in the hope that the guilds would support them against their rivals.

> • **guilds** Associations formed by members of the same trade that regulated prices and working hours and covered members' burial costs. Only those who belonged to the guild could engage in the business the guild regulated.

Land Use and Social Change, 1000–1350

The sharp increases in productivity brought dramatic changes throughout society. These changes did not occur everywhere at the same time, and in some areas they did not occur at all, but they definitely took place in northern France between 1000 and 1200.

One change was that slavery all but disappeared, while serfs did most of the work for those who owned land. Some of the most informative sources are the lists of customs that detail the obligations of serfs to their landlords. Although their

THE GOTHIC CATHEDRAL AT CHARTRES

Starting around 1150, people throughout Europe built cathedrals in the Gothic style, of which the Cathedral of Notre Dame at Chartres, France, is one of the best examples. The cathedral has an unusual front because the south tower (on the left) was built in 1160, while the much more opulent north tower was added in 1513 after a fire destroyed the original.

High arched ceilings inspired awe in those who entered cathedrals, but medieval builders faced a major engineering challenge. Arches built in the traditional manner required thick walls to support them; otherwise the walls would buckle from the outward pressure. Two innovations allowed stoneworkers to deflect the pressure away from the walls and build taller structures: vaults with ribs inside the church and flying buttresses outside the walls. With the help of these supports, the ceiling of Chartres rises a glorious 121 feet (37 m) above the ground.

Since the walls did not bear the weight of the ceiling, they could be cut away to hold glass windows. Unlike many other cathedrals, Chartres preserves much of its original stained glass. Of 186 original stained-glass windows, 152 have survived. Many

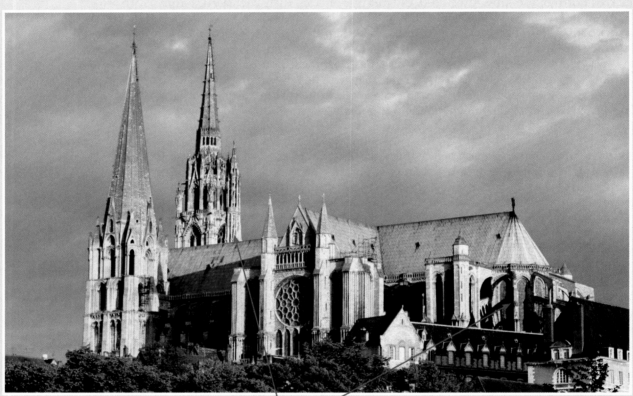

(Sandro Vannini/Corbis)

The north tower, completed in 1507, is so heavily decorated that architectural historians call its style "flamboyant style." It contrasts sharply with the original Gothic style of the south tower.

Half arches connect these flying buttresses outside to the cathedral wall, which they support, making it possible to build a high interior roof.

QUESTION FOR ANALYSIS

What does the Cathedral at Chartres reveal about the local economy in the 1100s, and how did it contribute to the local economy?

windows were dedicated by guild members and portray biblical scenes above and scenes of that guild's work below.

The window shown here was dedicated to Saint Lubin (Saint Leobinus), the bishop of Chartres in 558, whose devotees believed that he performed miracles, including curing people afflicted with edema, an illness that caused excess swelling. Wine merchants and local innkeepers paid for the window, which was completed in 1210.

Chartres was both a religious and an economic center. Pilgrims flocked to the cathedral to worship Mary, the Virgin Mother of Jesus, and her robe, which they believed survived, inside the cathedral. The pilgrims hoped that Mary would heal their illnesses and grant their prayers. Wealthy worshipers could afford to buy copies of her robe made for tourists, while others could purchase cheaper, lead figurines that they could pray to at home.

The young Lubin studies his alphabet while behind him his companion quaffs a glass of wine. All the round windows portray scenes from the life of Saint Lubin.

His hand holding a whip, a wine merchant transports a cask of wine tied onto a donkey cart.

In each of the side panels, people wearing different-colored robes hold cups of wine.

A wine seller gives a goblet of wine to a seated traveler, while the young boy behind him announces that a new barrel of wine has been opened. Above his head is a barrel hoop, the sign of a tavern.

(Erich Lessing/Art Resource, NY)

landlords did not own them, and they were not slaves, a series of obligations tied serfs to the land. Each year, their most important duty was to give their lord a fixed share of the crop and of their herds. Serfs were also obliged to build roads, give lodging to guests, and perform many other tasks for their lords. After 1000, a majority of those working the land became serfs.

Many serfs lived in settlements built around either the castles of lords or churches. The prevailing mental image of a medieval castle town is one in which a lord lives protected by his knights and surrounded by his serfs, who go outside the walls each day to work in the fields. Some use the term **feudal** for such a society. Yet historians today often avoid the word *feudal* because no one alive between 1000 and 1350 used such a word, and the term came into use only after 1600 as a legal concept.

The prominent French historian Georges Duby has described the social revolution of the eleventh and twelfth centuries in the following way. In Carolingian society, around 800, the powerful used loot and plunder to support themselves, usually by engaging in military conquest. Society consisted of two major groups: the powerful and the powerless. In the new society after 1000, the powerful comprised several clearly defined social orders—lords, knights, clergy—who held specific rights over the serfs below them. Many lords also commanded the service of a group of warriors, or knights, who offered them military service in exchange for military protection from others.

Knights began their training as children, when they learned how to ride and to handle a dagger. At the age of 14, knights-in-training accompanied a mature knight into battle. They usually wore tunics made of metal loops, or chain mail, as well as headgear that could repel arrows. This type of clothing was heavy and hot. Their main weapons were iron-and-steel swords and crossbows that shot metal bolts.

One characteristic of the age was weak centralized rule. Although many countries, like England and France, continued to have monarchs, these kings' power was severely limited because their armies were no stronger than those of the nobles who ranked below them. They controlled the lands immediately under them but not much else. The king of France, for example, ruled the region in the immediate vicinity of Paris, but other nobles had authority over the rest of France. In other countries as well, kings vied with rival nobles to gain control of a given region, and they often lost.

In the eleventh and twelfth centuries, landowners frequently gave large tracts of land to various monasteries (see page 372). The monasteries did not pay any taxes on this land, and no one dared to encroach on church-owned land for fear of the consequences from God. By the end of the twelfth century, the church owned one-third of the land in northern France and one-sixth of all the land in France and Italy combined.

One of the most perplexing changes was the rise of primogeniture in northern France, England, Belgium, and the Netherlands. Before 1000, when the head of the family died, aristocratic families divided their property among their sons, and sometimes even granted their daughters a share of the estate. After 1000, they kept their estates intact by passing the property on to only one son. As we have seen, Peter Abelard explained that he, the first-born son, was entitled to his father's lands but chose to give up his inheritance to pursue his studies.

He was an exception. Much more often first-born sons kept their family estates, and their brothers pursued other careers, whether as bureaucrats, churchmen, or

feudal The legal and social system in Europe from 1000 to 1400 in which serfs worked the land and subordinates performed military service for their lords in return for protection. The term came into use after 1600 as a legal concept.

knights in someone else's service. In many cases these second sons attended schools and universities before embarking on their chosen careers.

●The Rise of the European Universities, 1100–1400

Although schools had existed in Europe at least since the time of the Roman Empire, rates of literacy remained low throughout the continent. Starting around 1100, groups of teachers gathered in two major centers—Paris, France, and Bologna, Italy—and began to attract large numbers of male students, many of them from well-off families who used their surplus wealth, the product of cerealization, to finance their sons' education. In this early period, the universities were unregulated and free, as Peter Abelard experienced himself. Soon, however, the curriculum became more standardized. In a crucial development, cities, kings, and popes granted the universities a certain amount of self-rule and the right to grant degrees, rights that allowed universities to develop into independent centers of learning.

Education in Europe Before the Universities, ca. 1100

Latin remained the language of all educated people, the church, and administrative documents, and students had to learn to read and write Latin before they could advance to other subjects. The most basic schools also taught the simple mathematics needed by peddlers. Before 1100, most people who learned to read and write did so in local schools or at home with tutors or their parents. Some of these schools admitted girls, whether in separate classrooms or together with boys. Many schools were headed by a couple so that the father could teach the boys and the mother the girls. Often they were located close to the cathedrals that administered them. Heloise studied at a convent outside Paris.

Peter Abelard has little to say about his early education except that he loved learning and that his favorite subject was "dialectic," by which he meant the study of logic. Dialectic was one of three subjects, along with grammar and rhetoric, that formed the trivium. The roots of the trivium curriculum lay in ancient Greece and Rome: one studied the structure of language in grammar, expression in rhetoric, and meaning in dialectic, the most advanced subject of the three. Then one advanced to the quadrivium, which included arithmetic, astronomy, geometry, and music theory. The trivium and quadrivium formed the basic core of the curriculum and together were known as the **liberal arts.** The highest-level subjects, beyond the trivium and the quadrivium, were theology, church law, and medicine.

Abelard wrote a treatise called *Sic et Non* (Yes and No) whose prologue explained his method of instruction:

> It is my purpose, according to my original intention, to gather together the various sayings of the holy Fathers which have occurred to me as being surrounded by some degree of uncertainty because of their seeming incompatibility. These may encourage inexperienced readers to engage in that most

● **liberal arts** Basic core of the curriculum in Europe between 500 and 1500 that consisted of the trivium (logic, grammar, and rhetoric) and the quadrivium (arithmetic, astronomy, geometry, and music theory).

important exercise, enquiry into truth. . . . For by doubting we come to inquiry, and by inquiry we perceive the truth.[4]

Sic et Non poses a series of questions and then provides citations from classical sources and the Bible without directly providing any solutions. If one posed the question correctly and considered the proper authorities, one could draw on the powers of reasoning to arrive at the correct answer, Abelard and his contemporaries believed. This optimism about the ability of human reason to resolve the long-standing debates of the past characterizes **scholasticism,** the prevailing method of instruction in Europe between 1100 and 1500.

In 1114, Abelard was named to his first teaching position in Paris as master of the cathedral school at Notre-Dame. He became a canon, that is, a member of the small group of salaried clerics living close to the cathedral who served its religious needs. When Peter Abelard began teaching, he focused on explicating the single book Ezekiel of the Hebrew Bible. Teachers at universities explicated ideas and concepts slowly. The goal of most instructors was to cover an entire book in a year or two of instruction.

Books remained expensive. The main writing material was parchment, made by scraping the hair from the skin of a sheep or goat and drying it. One copy of the Bible made in Winchester, England, was made from the skins of 250 calves selected from 2,500 imperfect ones.[5] Booksellers formed copying workshops in which literate craftsmen copied texts at maximum speed. They no longer used the minuscule handwriting popular in Charlemagne's day: instead they adopted the even faster Gothic script, with short, upright strokes.

When the news of Abelard's affair with Heloise broke in 1118, he left Paris and returned only in the 1130s, when he again took up a teaching post. In 1136, when John of Salisbury arrived from England to study with Abelard, he reported that Paris had become the most important center of learning in Europe because more people taught there than anywhere else.

During the early 1100s, the university at Bologna in Italy became a center for the study of law. Legal study flourished as people realized that law could be used to resolve the disputes that occurred constantly between kings and subjects, churches and nobles, and merchants and customers. All kinds of groups, whether in monasteries, guilds, or universities, began to write down previously unwritten laws. The Magna Carta, which formalized the relationships between the English king and his barons in 1215, is a good example.

> **• scholasticism**
> Prevailing method of instruction in Europe between 1100 and 1500. Held that students could arrive at a correct answer if they used their powers of reasoning to derive the answer from multiple citations of classical sources and the Bible.

> **CL Primary Source:**
> Magna Carta: The Great Charter of Liberties
> *Learn what rights and liberties the English nobility, on behalf of all free Englishmen, forced King John to grant them in 1215.*

The Import of Learning and Technology from the Islamic World, 1150–1250

From about 1150 to 1250, scholars recovered hundreds of Greek texts that had disappeared from Europe after the loss of the Western Roman Empire in 476 (see Chapter 10). Arabic versions of these texts had been preserved in the Islamic world, and their recovery fueled a period of great intellectual growth. Between 1160 and 1200, all of Aristotle's works were first translated from Arabic into Latin and then checked against the original Greek. Like many of his contemporaries, Abelard did not know more than a few words of Greek (Heloise seems to have known more), so the translation of Greek texts into Latin had a direct impact on Europe's intellectual life. (See the feature "Movement of Ideas: Adelard of Bath.")

As Islamic learning entered Europe, Europeans encountered paper, which the Chinese had first invented and which was transmitted to the Islamic world in the eighth century. Paper appeared first in Spain in the tenth century and then in Sicily in the eleventh, but it won wide use only between 1250 and 1350 as Italian-made paper spread throughout Europe. Following the same route as paper, the ship's compass and the adjustable rudder originated in China and came to Europe via the Islamic world.

Other technologies from the Islamic world, such as magnifying glasses, entered Europe around 1200. Eyeglasses were first made from transparent, naturally occurring quartz, and only later from glass. Europeans also profited from Islamic knowledge of medicine, which was much more advanced than European; students at European universities studied the works of the Greek doctor Galen (129–ca. 216) that had been updated by Islamic commentators. Muslim observers were shocked to see European surgeons cut off the legs of wounded soldiers with axes instead of with the precise metal instruments used throughout the Islamic world.

Some European scholars clearly admired Islamic learning. Among them were Peter Abelard and Heloise, who named their son Astrolabe (born in 1118, year of death unknown) for the Islamic navigation instrument. Others, however, remained suspicious of the Islamic world because it was not Christian, and the interest in Arab learning waned after 1250 once the important Greek thinkers had been translated into Latin.

The Universities Come of Age, 1150–1250

As contact with the Islamic world began to invigorate learning, the universities at Paris and Bologna gained significant independence in the century after Abelard's death in the 1140s. Although the two universities had arisen at the same time, they were quite different. In Paris, most of the masters had independent incomes provided by the church, so they were not dependent on the tuition paid by students. Their counterparts in Italy were more often laypeople without independent incomes who earned their living with the money the students paid. Accordingly, Bologna's students had far more power than those in Paris, and they hired the masters for the following year.

In 1200, Paris had a population of some eighty thousand, while Bologna, with forty thousand residents, was half its size. In both cities, the student population fluctuated around 10 percent. As trade guilds regulated their own membership, so too did students and instructors decide who could join the university.

Modern degrees have their origins in the different steps to full membership in the guild of university teachers. Starting students, like apprentices, paid fees, while more advanced bachelors, like journeymen, helped to instruct the starting students. Those who attained the level of masters were the equivalent of full members of the guild. In the 1170s, the masters of Paris gained the right to determine the composition of the assigned reading, the content of examinations, and the recipients for each degree. This structure was much more formalized than anything during Peter Abelard's lifetime.

Most students came from well-off families and had ample spending money; therefore, they formed a large body of consumers whose business was crucial to local shopkeepers. Whenever students had a dispute with local authorities, whether with the city government or the church, they could boycott all local merchants.

Adelard of Bath

Adelard of Bath (ca. 1080–ca. 1152) is best known for his translation of Euclid's geometry into Latin from an Arabic translation of the original Greek text, which was written around 300 B.C.E. He also translated other works, including al-Khwarizmi's astronomical tables (see Chapter 9), and he is credited with introducing the use of the abacus to the treasury officials of the English king Henry I. Born most likely in Bath, he studied first in France in Laôn and then went to Salerno, Italy, and Syracuse, Sicily, both centers of Islamic learning.

Although Adelard consistently praises Islamic learning, scholars have not found any quotations from Arabic books in his writing. Although he studied in Italy, his transcriptions of Arabic words reflect Spanish pronunciation, not Italian as one would expect. It seems likely, therefore, that he spoke Arabic to an informant, probably from Spain, who explained Islamic books to him, and he then wrote down what he had been told. This kind of translation using native informants is exactly how the early Buddhist translators in China handled difficult Sanskrit texts (see Chapter 8).

The selections below are drawn from Adelard's Questions on Natural Science, a series of dialogues with his "nephew," who may have been a fictitious conversational partner. Their conversation illustrates how the great teachers of the twelfth century, including Adelard, taught by using the Socratic method (see Chapter 6), in which they guided their students with pointed questions. The nephew's suspicion of Islamic learning was the typical European view. Few learned Arabic as Adelard had, and most saw Islam as the source of teachings that were contrary to Christianity. The uncle and nephew agree to accept reason as their guide, a conclusion that both the ancient Greeks and Adelard would have applauded.

Source: Charles Burnett et al., eds., *Adelard of Bath: Conversations with His Nephew: On the Same and the Different, Questions About Natural Science, and on Birds* (New York: Cambridge University Press, 1998), pp. 91, 103–105.

ADELARD: You remember, dear nephew, that, seven years ago, when I dismissed you (still almost a boy) with my other students in French studies at Laôn, we agreed amongst ourselves that I would investigate the studies of Arabs according to my ability, but you would become no less proficient in the insecurity of French opinions.

NEPHEW: I remember, and all the more so because when you left me you bound me with a promise on my word that I would apply myself to philosophy. I was always anxious to know why I should be more attentive to this subject. This is an excellent opportunity to test whether I have been successful by putting my study into practice, because since, as a listener only, I took note of you when often you explained the opinions of the Saracens [Muslims], and quite a few of them appeared to me to be quite useless. I shall for a brief while refuse to be patient and shall take you up as you expound these opinions, wherever it seems right to do so. For you both extol the Arabs shamelessly and invidiously accuse our people of ignorance in a disparaging way. It will therefore be worthwhile for you to reap the fruit of your labor, if you acquit yourself well, and likewise for me not to have been cheated in my promise, if I oppose you with probable arguments.

ADELARD: Perhaps you are being more bold in your presumption than you are capable. But because this disputation will be useful both to you and to many others, I shall put up with your impudence, as long as this inconvenience is avoided: that no one should think that when I am putting forward unknown ideas, I am doing this out of my own head, but that I am giving the views of the studies of the Arabs. For I do not want it to happen that, even though what I say may displease those who are less advanced, I myself should also displease them. For I know what those who profess the truth suffer at the hands of the vulgar crowd. Therefore, I shall defend the cause of the Arabs, not my own.

NEPHEW: Agreed, so that you may have no occasion for silence.

ADELARD: Well then, I think we should begin from the easier subjects. For if I speak sensibly about these, you may have the same hope concerning greater things. So let us start from the lowest objects and end with the highest.

(The two then discuss the sources of nourishment for plants, and then the nephew asks about animals.)

ADELARD: About animals my conversation with you is difficult. For I have learnt one thing from my Arab masters, with reason as guide, but you another: you follow a halter, being enthralled by the picture of authority. For what else can authority be called other than a halter? As brute animals are led wherever one pleases by a halter, but do not know where or why they are led, and only follow the rope by which they are held, so the authority of written words leads not a few of you into danger, since you are enthralled and bound by brutish credulity. Hence too, certain people, usurping the name of "an authority" for themselves, have used too great a license to write, to such an extent that they have not hesitated to trick brutish men with false words instead of true. For why should you not fill pages, why not write on the back too, when these days you generally have the kind of listeners that demand no argument based on judgment, but trust only in the name of an ancient authority? For they do not understand that reason has been given to each single individual in order to discern between true and false with reason as the prime judge. For unless it were the duty of reason to be everybody's judge, she would have been given to each person in vain. . . .

Rather I assert that first, reason should be sought, and when it is found, an authority, if one is at hand, should be added later. But authority alone cannot win credibility for a philosopher, nor should it be adduced for this purpose. Hence the logicians have agreed than an argument from authority is probable, not necessary. Therefore, if you wish to hear anything more from me, give and receive reason. . . .

NEPHEW: By all means let us do as you demand, since it is easy for me to oppose with reasonable arguments, nor is it safe to follow the authorities of your Arabs. Therefore, let us keep to this rule: between you and me reason alone should be the judge.

QUESTIONS FOR ANALYSIS

▶ **What does Islamic learning represent to Adelard? To his nephew?**

▶ **How do the two view European learning?**

▶ **On what basis will they decide if a given explanation is true or false?**

The most dramatic conflicts occurred in Paris. In 1229, during the Mardi Gras season, a disturbance broke out, and the authorities killed several students in the confusion. The masters of the university demanded that the city officials be punished, but the monarch sided with the officials. The masters left the city and returned only two years later when the ruler gave in. The pope then issued an order recognizing the masters as a guild with the right to boycott. Thereafter, the papacy always supported university masters in disputes with French rulers.

By 1200, Paris and Bologna were firmly established as Europe's first universities, and other universities formed in England, France, and Italy and later in Germany and eastern Europe. Universities offered their home cities many advantages, all linked to the buying power of a large group of wealthy consumer-students.

As in both the Islamic world and Song China, young men came to large cities to study with teachers to prepare for careers in government, law, religious institutions, or education. The largest schools provided facilities for a wide variety of instructors to teach many different topics. Unlike either Islamic schools or Song dynasty schools, however, only European universities had the power to grant degrees independently of the state or the church.

Most students did not study long enough to get their first degree, which was the equivalent of a modern master's degree. Instead, many concentrated on improving their command of Latin, which remained the language of educated people and the church throughout Europe before 1500. Learning to take notes in Latin during a lecture greatly enhanced a young man's ability to draft a Latin document quickly. Some knowledge of mathematics was also useful. University studies prepared young men for careers in government administration or the church. Many received employment as literate bureaucrats working for a noble or for members of the clergy, often near their hometown. Over time, as more and more families sent their sons to university, it became the norm for officials and clergy to be literate, and the proportion of students finishing their degrees consistently increased over time.

The Movement for Church Reform, 1000–1300

Although historians often speak of the church when talking about medieval Europe, Peter Abelard and Heloise's experiences make it clear that no single, unified entity called the church existed. The pope in Rome presided over many different local churches and monasteries, but he was not consistently able to enforce decisions. Below him, but not necessarily obedient to him, were many churches and monasteries throughout Europe that possessed their own lands and directly benefited from the greater yields of cerealization; in addition, their devotees often gave a share of their increasing personal wealth to religious institutions. As a result, monastic leaders had sufficient income to act independently, whether or not they had higher approval.

Starting in 1000, different reformers tried to streamline the church and reform the clergy. Yet reform from within did not always succeed. The new orders founded in the thirteenth century, like the Franciscans and the Dominicans, explicitly rejected what they saw as lavish spending in favor of new begging orders in which monks and nuns demonstrated their faith by renouncing wealth.

The Structure of the Church

By 1000, the European countryside was completely blanketed with churches, each one the center of a parish in which the clergy lived together with laypeople. Some churches were small shrines that had little land of their own, while others were magnificent cathedrals with extensive monasteries, and sometimes nunneries, attached to them. The laity were expected to pay a tithe of 10 percent of their income to their local parish priest, and he, in turn, performed the sacraments for each individual as he or she passed through the major stages of life: baptism at birth, confirmation and marriage at young adulthood, and funeral at death. The parish priest also gave communion to his congregation.

By the year 1000, this system had become so well established in western Europe that no one questioned it. Much as we agree to the obligation of all citizens to pay taxes, medieval Europeans accepted, for example, that all those born in a parish had to undergo baptism. Baptism guaranteed passage to heaven; failure to be baptized ensured permanent suffering in hell. The other sacraments and the tithe were similarly accepted.

The clergy fell into two categories: the secular clergy and the regular clergy. The secular clergy worked with the laity as local priests or schoolmasters. Those who lived in monasteries and had no contact with laypeople were called regular clergy because they lived by the rule, or *regula* in Latin, of the church or by monastic rules, such as those of Saint Benedict (see Chapter 10).

Reform from Above

In 1046, a crisis occurred in the papacy when three different Italian candidates vied for the position of pope; one had bought his position from an earlier pope who decided that he wanted to marry. A church office was considered sacred, and its sale, or **simony,** was universally considered a sin.

The ruler of Germany, Henry III (1039–1056), then intervened in the dispute and named Leo IX (in office between 1048 and 1056) pope. For the first time in over two hundred years, the pope traveled north of the Alps to modern-day Germany and France, where he conducted public ceremonies in which priests vowed, sometimes in the presence of saints' relics, that they had not bought their offices. This was the first reform campaign led by a pope. Leo's main goals were to end simony and to enforce celibacy.

Although many people recognized the dangers of simony in corrupting church officials, fewer agreed that marriage of the clergy should be forbidden. Many priests' wives came from locally prominent families who felt strongly that their female kin had done nothing wrong in marrying a member of the clergy. In 1072, when one French archbishop tried to punish priests who had married, the laity threw stones at him, and he barely escaped serious injury. Those who supported celibacy believed that childless clergy would have no incentive to divert church property toward their own family, and their view eventually prevailed.

Pope Gregory VII (1073–1085) also sought to reform the papacy by drafting twenty-seven papal declarations asserting the supremacy of the pope. Only the pope could decide issues facing the church, Gregory VII averred, and only the pope had

• simony   The sale of church office in Europe. Since church office was considered sacred, its sale was a sin.

Pope Innocent III Approves the Franciscan Rule One of the most famous painters of the fourteenth century, Giotto (1266–1336), painted the most important events in the life of Saint Francis (ca. 1181–1226) directly on fresh plaster, which preserved the intense reds and blues for all time. Here Pope Innocent III (*right*) grants Francis and his followers (*left*) the right to preach among the poor. Note the sharp contrast between the elegant robes of the pope and the cardinals and the coarse brown robes of the Franciscan friars. (Upper Church, S. Francesco, Assisi, Italy/Alinari/Art Resource, NY)

the right to appoint bishops. In his efforts to strengthen the papacy, he even claimed "that the Roman Church has never erred, nor will it ever err, as the scripture testifies."[6] Many of the twenty-seven points had been realized by 1200 as more Europeans came to accept the pope's claim to be head of the Christian church.

In 1215, Pope Innocent III (1198–1216) presided over the fourth Lateran Council. Over twelve hundred bishops, abbots, and representatives of different European monarchs met in the Lateran Palace in the Vatican to pass decrees regulating Christian practice, some of which are in effect today. For example, they agreed that all Christians should receive Communion at least once a year and should also confess their sins annually. The fourth Lateran Council marked the high point of the pope's political power; subsequent popes never commanded such power over secular leaders.

Reform Within the Established Monastic Orders

● **heresy** The offense of believing in teachings that the Roman Catholic Church condemned as incorrect.

Abelard was condemned twice, once after his affair with Heloise, and again near the end of his life for heresy. **Heresy,** the offense of believing in teachings that the church condemned as incorrect, was a grave charge. The details of the charges against Abelard are complex, and historians may never understand them fully because many of the original documents are lost. Though found guilty, Abelard was able to continue teaching and writing because powerful patrons protected him. In 1140, Peter the Venerable (abbot from 1122 to 1156) invited him to Cluny (CLUE-nee), the largest monastery in Europe, and refused to give him up to those who had condemned him. Peter's invitation quite possibly saved Abelard's life.

Cluny's holdings in land and money were greater than those of the church in Rome, and the abbot of Cluny, Peter the Venerable, was more powerful than anyone in the church, except for the pope. Founded in 910, the monastery at Cluny followed the rules of Saint Benedict. Three hundred monks, many from the most prominent families in France, lived at Cluny itself, and one thousand monasteries, home to twenty thousand monks, were associated with Cluny.

Since the abbot did not visit most of these monasteries, monastic discipline at Cluny suffered. In 1098, several monks broke away from Cluny because they wanted reform. This was the beginning of the Cistercian Order, which called for a return to the original rules of Saint Benedict. Unlike the Cluniac monasteries, each Cistercian monastery had its own abbot, and no one was admitted until he was over 15 and had served a full year as a novice. The Cistercian monasteries established a fixed procedure for the creation of new monasteries: a new abbot went with twelve monks to each new site. The resulting daughter monasteries retained close ties with their mother monasteries, whose abbots visited each year. All Cistercian abbots convened at regular intervals to ensure that everyone followed the same regulations. The Cistercians lived more austerely than the monks at Cluny, wearing simple clothes of undyed wool, eating only vegetarian food, and building undecorated churches. The Cistercian monasteries proved enormously popular, as did other movements for monastic reform. From 5 monasteries in 1119, the order mushroomed to 350 in 1150 and to 647 by 1250.

About half of the Cistercian monasteries were nunneries for women. After 1000, as Europe's population surged, many more women joined nunneries. But because their contemporaries did not think it appropriate for them to do the work monks did, a nunnery needed male staff to run its estates, farm the land, and perform religious services. The chronic lack of revenue created by this problem made the nunneries vulnerable to outside intervention.

The day after Abelard's castration, he ordered Heloise to become a nun at the convent in Argenteuil, France, where she had been educated as a child. She reluctantly agreed and left her son Astrolabe to be raised by Abelard's sister. Heloise rose to the rank of prioress, the second in command at the convent. When the king abruptly ordered the nuns to move elsewhere because he wanted their land, Heloise received a letter from Abelard for the first time since they had parted. He offered his own church, which had its own lands given by supporters, to Heloise. She accepted Abelard's invitation and served as abbess until her death in the 1160s.

Reform Outside the Established Orders

Although the Cistercians certainly thought of themselves as reformers, they still accepted the need for groups of men or women to live on landed monasteries or nunneries. But as the drive to reform continued, some asked members of religious orders to live exactly as Jesus and his followers had, not in monasteries with their own incomes but as beggars dependent on ordinary people for contributions. Between 1100 and 1200, reformers established at least nine different begging orders, the most important of which was the Franciscans founded by Saint Francis of Assisi (ca. 1181–1226). Members of these orders were called **friars.**

Francis was born to the well-off Italian family of a textile merchant, but while in his 20s he abandoned his family and began to live as a beggar. After attracting a small group of followers, he requested formal permission from Pope Innocent III

● **friars** Members of the begging orders established in Europe between 1100 and 1200, of which the Franciscans were the best known.

(CL) **Primary Source:**
Summa Theologica:
On Free Will
This selection from Thomas Aquinas, on the question of free will, shows a synthesis of Aristotelian logic and Christian theology.

• **Thomas Aquinas** (1224/25–1274) One of the most famous scholastic thinkers and a member of the Dominican order. He wrote a book, *Summa Theologica* (Summary of Theology), juxtaposing the teachings of various church authorities on various difficult questions.

to be allowed to preach. In 1209, the pope granted the Franciscans the right to speak on simple topics like the correct conduct of a Christian but not on complex theological issues.

The Franciscan movement grew rapidly even though Francis allowed none of his followers to keep any money, to own books or extra clothes, or to live in a permanent dwelling. In 1217, Francis had 5,000 followers; by 1326, some 28,000 Franciscans were active. Francis also created the order of Saint Clare for women, who lived in austere nunneries where they were not allowed to accumulate any property of their own.

In 1215, Saint Dominic (1170?–1221) founded the order of Friars Preachers in Spain. Unlike Francis, he stressed education and sent some of his brightest followers to the new universities. Since he hoped to eliminate heresy everywhere, he created a structure in which all his followers, and not just bishops, could convert non-Christian peoples. **Thomas Aquinas** (1224/25–1274), one of the most famous scholastic thinkers, belonged to the Dominican order. Aquinas wrote *Summa Theologica* (Summary of Theology), a book juxtaposing the teachings of various church authorities on various difficult questions, just as Abelard had; but where Abelard had trusted each reader to determine the correct interpretation, Aquinas wrote detailed explanations that remained definitive for centuries.

● The Crusades, 1095–1291

The founding of the Franciscans and the Dominicans was only one aspect of a broader movement to spread Christianity through Crusades. Some Crusades within Europe targeted Jews, Muslims, and members of other non-Christian groups. In addition, the economic surplus resulting from cerealization and urban growth financed a series of expeditions to the Holy Land. During the twelfth and thirteenth centuries, thousands of Crusaders left Europe in the hope that they could conquer Jerusalem, the symbolic center of the Christian world because Jesus had preached and died there, and make it Christian again (see Map 13.1). They succeeded in conquering Jerusalem but held it for only eighty-eight years.

• **Crusader** Term, meaning "one who is signed by the cross," that indicated anyone who attached a cross to his or her clothes as a sign of belonging to a large, volunteer force against Muslims. Between 1095 and 1291, eight different groups of Crusaders traveled to the Holy Land in the hope of capturing Jerusalem.

The Crusades to the Holy Land

Historians use the term *Crusades* to refer to the period between 1095, when the pope first called for Europeans to take back Jerusalem, and 1291, when the last European possession in Syria was lost. The word **Crusader,** literally "one who is signed by the cross," indicates anyone who attached a cross to his or her clothes as a sign of belonging to a large, volunteer force against Muslims. In 1095, Pope Urban II (1088–1099) told a large meeting of church leaders that the Byzantine emperor requested help against the Seljuq Turks (see Chapters 9 and 10). He urged those assembled to recover the territory lost to "the wicked race" (meaning Muslims) so that they could govern it: his audience cried, "It is the will of God" in response.[7] If they died en route, the pope promised, they could be certain that God would forgive their sins because God forgave all pilgrims' sins. This marked the beginning of the First Crusade.

From the outset, the Crusader forces consisted of self-financed individuals who, unlike soldiers in an army, did not receive pay and had no line of command. The

Interactive Map

problems of disorganization extended to the top ranks, which included some of France and England's most prominent nobles. Rarely agreeing with each other about military strategy, they often could not even decide on their main commander.

An estimated 50,000 combatants responded to the pope's plea in 1095; of these, only 10,000 reached Jerusalem. Of those 10,000, some 1,500 were knights, the only fighters properly equipped for siege warfare. Nevertheless, the Crusaders succeeded in taking Jerusalem in 1099 from the rulers of Egypt, who controlled it at the time. After the city fell, the out-of-control troops massacred everyone still in the city.

The Crusaders ruled Jerusalem for eighty-eight years, long enough that the first generation of Europeans died and were succeeded by generations who saw themselves first as residents of Outremer (OU-truh-mare), the term the Crusaders used for the eastern edge of the Mediterranean. The Crusaders' fervent belief that they had the right to remove the non-Christian government of Jerusalem led to the creation of the Crusader kingdom in the city. Despite the fact that Jerusalem was also a holy site for both Jews and Muslims, the Crusaders were convinced that the city belonged to them.

In 1169, Saladin overthrew the reigning Egyptian dynasty and in 1171 founded the Ayyubid dynasty (see Chapter 9). He then married the widow of the Seljuq ruler of Central Asia, effectively allying the two great powers of the Islamic world.

**MAP 13.1
The Crusades** In response to the pope's request, thousands of Europeans walked over 2,000 miles (3,200 km) overland through the Byzantine Empire to reach Jerusalem, which the Europeans governed from 1099 to 1187. Others traveled to the Holy Land by sea. The Europeans who lived in Jerusalem for nearly a century developed their own hybrid culture that combined French, German, and Italian elements with the indigenous practices of the eastern Mediterranean.

With this combined power, he was poised to fight the Crusaders. His biographer explained the extent of Saladin's commitment to jihad, or holy war:

> The Holy War and the suffering involved in it weighed heavily on his heart and his whole being in every limb: he spoke of nothing else, thought only about equipment for the fight, was interested only in those who had taken up arms.[8]

Saladin devoted himself to raising an army strong enough to repulse the Crusaders. By 1187 he had gathered an army of thirty thousand men on horseback carrying lances and swords like knights but without chain-mail armor. Half of his army consisted of light cavalry who could maneuver much more quickly than the twenty thousand Crusaders they faced. Saladin laid a trap for the Crusaders in an extinct Syrian volcano called the Horns of Hattin. While the Crusader forces had no way to replenish their water supply, the Muslim armies made sure that each camp had water storage tanks supplied by camels carrying goat skins filled with water. On the day of the battle, Saladin's well-rested forces baited the parched and exhausted Crusaders by pouring fresh water out on the ground instead of giving it to them to drink. They easily defeated the Crusaders.

When Saladin's victorious troops took Jerusalem back, they restored the mosques as houses of worship and removed the crosses from all Christian churches, although they did allow Christians to visit the city. The English king Richard the Lion-Hearted (1189–1199) led armies provided by different European rulers in an effort to recapture Jerusalem from Saladin. Traveling by sea, Richard conquered the Mediterranean island of Cyprus from its ruler in 1191. After several years of fighting, however, he realized that the Crusaders could not recapture Jerusalem unless they conquered Egypt first, and they returned to Europe without having taken Jerusalem.

In 1201, the Europeans decided to make one further attempt, in the Fourth Crusade, to retake Jerusalem. Because they did not have enough ships, they promised to pay the Venetian navy to transport them to the Holy Land. In June 1203, the Crusaders reached Constantinople and were astounded by its size: the ten biggest cities in Europe could easily fit within its imposing walls, and its population surpassed one million. One awe-struck soldier wrote home:

> If anyone should recount to you the hundredth part of the richness and the beauty and the nobility that was found in the abbeys and in the churches and the palaces and in the city, it would seem like a lie and you would not believe it.[9]

When one of the claimants to the Byzantine throne refused to pay the crusaders, the commanders gave the fateful command to their troops to attack the city in the hope that they could plunder what they needed to pay the Venetians to transport them to Jerusalem.

One of the worst atrocities in world history resulted: the Crusaders rampaged throughout the beautiful city, killing all who opposed them and raping thousands of women. They treated the Eastern Orthodox Christians of Constantinople precisely as if they were the Muslim enemy. (See the feature "World History in Today's World: The Memory of the Crusades in Istanbul.") The Crusaders' conduct in Constantinople turned the diplomatic dispute between the two churches, which had begun in 1054, into a genuine and lasting schism between Roman Catholics and Eastern Orthodox adherents (see page 296).

(CL) **Primary Source: Annals**
Read a harrowing, firsthand account of the pillage of Constantinople by Western Crusaders on April 13, 1204.

The Memory of the Crusades in Istanbul

"After eight centuries, how can we not share the disgust and pain?" Pope John Paul asked Bartholomew I, the patriarch of Constantinople (modern Istanbul), who visited the Vatican on June 29, 2004. "In particular, in these circumstances we cannot forget what happened in the month of April in the year 1204. An army, which left to recover the Holy Land for Christianity, headed toward Constantinople to take and sack it, spilling the blood of brothers in faith."

Since 1964, the pope and the patriarch have exchanged annual visits in an attempt to maintain dialogue between the two churches. In April 2004, Bartholomew granted a formal pardon to the Catholics who had sacked Constantinople.

John Paul II's successor, Pope Benedict XVI, visited Istanbul in November 2006 and met with Bartholomew. The two church leaders issued a joint declaration that stated their shared desire to move toward "full unity" at some point in the future.

Pope Benedict's visit triggered protests by Turkish Muslims, who greatly outnumber Orthodox Christians. As one protestor explained: "The popes—were they not the ones who tried to destroy Turks and Islam? Who organized the crusades? They should not give lessons of peace here."

Sources: Religion News Service, June 29, 2004 (Tuesday 3:16 PM Eastern Time); *The Australian,* July 1, 2004; BBC Monitoring Europe—Political, November 30, 2006; *Los Angeles Times,* December 1, 2006, all accessed via Lexis/Nexis.

After 1204, individual European monarchs sent armies to attack Egypt or Jerusalem, but they never again sent a multinational force. Europeans did not regain control of Jerusalem, and by 1291 they had lost control of the little territory around it, like the port city of Acre in modern-day Israel, that they retained after the Battle of Hattin. Cyprus, however, remained in European hands until 1570 and provided an important precedent that gave subsequent generations of Europeans the belief that the conquest of foreign territory for Christianity was acceptable. When Europeans went to new lands in Africa and the Americas, they founded colonies similar to those of the Crusaders in the Mediterranean (see Chapter 15).

The Crusades Within Europe   Muslims in West Asia were not the Crusaders' only target. European Christians, convinced that they were right about the superiority of Christianity, also attacked enemies within Europe, sometimes on their own, sometimes in direct response to the pope's command.

Many European Christians looked down on Jews, who were banned from many occupations, could not marry Christians, and often lived in separate parts of cities, called *ghettos*. But before 1095, Christians had largely respected the right of Jews to practice their own religion; they neither forced them to convert nor attacked their temples. This fragile coexistence fell apart in 1096, as the out-of-control crowds traveling through on the First Crusade attacked the Jews living in the three German towns of Mainz, Worms, and Speyer and killed all who did not convert to Christianity. Thousands died in the violence. Anti-Jewish prejudice worsened over the next two centuries; England expelled the Jews in 1290 and France in 1306.

These spontaneous attacks on Jews differed from two campaigns launched by the pope against enemies of the church. The first was against the Cathars, a group of Christian heretics who lived in the Languedoc region of southern France. Like the Zoroastrians of Iran (see Chapter 6), the Cathars believed that the forces of good in the spiritual world and of evil in the material world were engaged in a perpetual fight for dominance. Jesus, they thought, never assumed material form but remained a spirit the entire time he was visible on earth.

In 1208, Pope Innocent III launched a crusade to Languedoc in which he promised that God would forgive the sins of those who fought the Cathars for forty days in France just as he would forgive those who went on the Crusades for a much longer time. The campaign attracted numerous supporters, and gradually the pope's forces killed many of the lords and bishops who supported Catharism.

Because mass campaigns against heretics often spun out of control, in the early thirteenth century the pope established a special court, called the **inquisition,** to hear charges against accused heretics. Unlike other church courts, which operated according to established legal norms, the inquisition used anonymous informants, forced interrogations, and torture to identify heretics. Those found guilty were usually burned at the stake. One inquisitor in south France, active between 1308 and 1323, sentenced 633 offenders, many to life imprisonment.[10] The inquisition remained active in the region of the Cathars until 1330, and later popes established inquisition courts whenever they felt it necessary.

The leader of the crusade against the Cathars begged to be allowed to continue his fight against non-Christians in Spain, and the pope granted his request in 1212. Historians use the Spanish word *Reconquista* ("Reconquest") to refer to these military campaigns by Christians against the Muslims of Spain and Portugal. Before 1200, various Christian rulers had recovered isolated cities, such as Toledo, Spain, and Lisbon, Portugal, and the Crusader army won a decisive victory in 1212 and captured Córdoba and Seville in the following decades. After 1249, only the kingdom of Granada, on the southern tip of Spain, remained Muslim.

● **inquisition** Special court established by the pope to hear charges against those accused of heresy. The inquisition used anonymous informants, forced interrogations, and torture to identify heretics. Those found guilty were usually burned at the stake.

● Disaster and Recovery, 1300–1400

The three centuries of prosperity and growth caused by cerealization and urbanization came to a sudden halt in the early 1300s, when first a series of food shortages rocked the north European countryside and then the Black Death, which Ibn Battuta had seen in Damascus (see Chapter 11), traveled along established trade routes to reach Europe's major cities first in 1348 and several times thereafter. The fighting of the Hundred Years' War (1337–1453) between England and France caused more deaths. In the long run, however, the economy recovered, and by 1500 the population had returned to pre–Black Death levels. The structure of European society also changed, and European kings, especially in France and England, emerged from this difficult century with more extensive powers than their predecessors.

Continuing Expansion of Trade Outside Europe

The Crusaders who returned from the Holy Land were one source of information for those seeking to learn about the world beyond Europe. Europeans gained access to other sources of information as trade networks linking Europe with Asia expanded. During the 1300s, merchants, usually from the Italian city-states of Venice or Genoa, traveled to West Asia, and sometimes to East Asia, to pursue trading opportunities (see Map 13.2).

In the twelfth and thirteenth centuries, Europeans consumed huge quantities of the new spices—such as pepper, cinnamon, ginger, cloves, and nutmeg—that entered Europe from Southeast Asia. Europeans used spices to enhance dishes' flavor and as medicines, not to preserve rotten meat, as is often said. (Rotten meat could not be salvaged once it spoiled; the wealthy ate freshly killed meat.) Surprisingly large quantities of spices went into a single meal: in 1319, the pope presided at a dinner for six guests in which he served lamb, pork, chicken, and partridges seasoned with one pound each of ginger and cloves.[11] To obtain spices, European merchants often traveled to Constantinople, the Black Sea, or Iran, where they

⊕ MAP 13.2
Movement of the Plague and Trade Routes   The complex network of trade routes linking Europe with Asia and Africa facilitated the movement of goods, like Asian spices, but also disease, like the Black Death. Europeans learned about Asia from travelers like Marco Polo, who went to Mongolia and China, and John of Mandeville, who did not. Small communities of Europeans lived in the nodes of the network: in Constantinople, Kaffa, Khara Khorum, and the Chinese capital of Beijing.

CL Interactive Map

Tombstone for an Italian Girl Who Died in China In 1342, the daughter of a Venetian merchant died in Yangzhou, near the mouth of the Yangzi River, and her family commissioned a tombstone for her. The tombstone shows scenes from the life of a haloed figure, most likely Saint Catherine of Alexandria, for whom the deceased was named. To the left of the Latin text, four Chinese characters appear in a small rectangle; the artist's signature in stone is the equivalent of the red-colored seals Chinese painters stamped on their paintings. (Harvard Yenching Library)

Primary Source:
Description of the World
Follow Marco Polo, and hear him relate the natural—and sometimes supernatural— wonders he encountered on his journey to Khubilai Khan.

established small commercial colonies with warehouses and homes. During the 1330s and 1340s, a small group of merchants even lived in the Mongols' capital at Beijing, China, where a bishop served the Christian congregation.

During these years, readers avidly devoured books about distant foreign places, especially those that purported to describe the actual travels of their authors. Marco Polo (1254–1324), a Venetian merchant who traveled to Asia, portrayed the wonders of the known world and painted China as especially wealthy. Even more popular was *The Travels of Sir John Mandeville*, published in the 1350s, which described a legendary Christian king named Prester John who ruled over a realm distant from Europe. Polo combined some firsthand knowledge with hearsay; Mandeville's writing was based on pure hearsay. Even so, both books created an optimistic impression of Asian wealth that inspired later explorers like Columbus to found overseas colonies (covered in Chapter 15).

The Losses from Rural Famines and the Black Death

Europeans living in the 1300s could see signs of expansion but also troubling indications that the prosperity might end. The first signs that three centuries of growth had come to an end were internal. The Great Famine of 1315–1322 affected all of northern Europe, and it was the first of repeated food shortages. Many starved to death, and thousands fled the barren countryside to beg in the cities.

These difficult times caused financial strains that, in turn, led to changes in rural society as rulers and feudal lords struggled to increase their tax revenues. Rulers found that they needed more money than they could obtain from the traditional obligations tying peasants to their lords. In 1315, therefore, the French king freed all the serfs on royal land so that he could charge them new and higher taxes. Landlords in other places, like England and Germany, adopted short-term leases that replaced the lists of customary obligations and fixed rents at higher rates.

During these difficult decades, the Black Death came first to Europe's ports from somewhere in Asia, possibly North China (see Map 13.2). In 1346, the rats

Portraying the Black Death

This painting, made more than a century after the Black Death struck Europe between 1346 and 1348, shows Saint Sebastian praying for those who had fallen ill with the plague. The artist shows the plague victim wrapped in a white shroud, presumably because the black swellings on the bodies were too grisly to include in a painting displayed in a church. (Walters Art Museum, Baltimore/Bridgeman Art Library)

infected with the Black Death traveled by ship to the Genoese colony of Kaffa on the Black Sea. In 1348, the year in which Ibn Battuta observed the plague's toll in Damascus, the plague struck Italy, and then France and Germany one year later. Like the plague in sixth-century Byzantium (see Chapter 10), it had two phases: bubonic plague and pneumonic plague, which was almost always fatal. Historians reserve the term *Black Death* for the outbreak in the 1300s.

Since nearly six hundred years had passed since the most recent outbreak of 767, Europeans had lost whatever immunity they had developed, and the plague's initial toll was devastating. The Black Death reduced Europe's population from about seventy-five to about fifty-five million, and it only returned to pre-plague levels after 1500.

The losses of the first outbreak were greatest. One doctor in Avignon, France, reported that, in 1349, two-thirds of the city's population fell ill, and almost all died. In the second occurrence, in 1361, half the city's population was affected, and, again, almost all died. But in a third outbreak in 1371, only one-tenth of the people caught the illness, and some of them survived. By the fourth outbreak, in 1382, only one-twentieth of the population was afflicted, and almost everyone survived.[12]

The Hundred Years' War Between England and France, 1337–1453

During this difficult century, the rulers of England and France engaged in a long series of battles now known as the **Hundred Years' War** (1337–1453). In 1328, the French king died without leaving an heir. Edward III of England (1327–1377), who owned extensive lands, was next in line to the throne, but in 1337 the French nobles selected his cousin as king instead.

• Hundred Years' War War between the English and French fought entirely on French soil. At the end of the war (1337–1453), the kings of England and France had gained the power to tax and to maintain a standing army.

Edward III sent an army to France and launched a conflict that took more than a century to resolve.

France, with a population of some fifteen million, was far richer than England, which had only around four million. The war was conducted entirely on French soil, and the opportunity to obtain plunder provided a strong incentive for the English troops.

The long conflict saw the end of battles fought by mounted knights. Early in the war, the English won significant victories because they used a new type of long-bow 6 feet (1.8 m) tall that shot metal-tipped arrows farther and more accurately than the crossbows then in use. Knights donned even heavier armor to protect themselves, but they could not protect their horses. Moreover, the armor was so heavy that a knight who had fallen off his horse could not get up to fight an as-sailant armed with a staff. By the final years of the war, both sides were using gunpowder to shoot stones or cannonballs. Although difficult to aim accurately, these new weapons could destroy the walls surrounding a castle or town under siege and make it possible to take the city.

Not restricting their contest to the battlefield, the English and French kings both tried to enlist the support of the pope. In 1309, a pope moved to the French town of Avignon to avoid the factional disputes in Rome, and his seven successors, all French, acknowledged the supremacy of the French monarch. In 1378, a crisis oc-curred when two popes, one based in Rome, the other in Avignon, simultaneously claimed to be the rightful pope; each excommunicated the other. The French mon-arch backed the Avignon pope, while the English king supported the pope in Rome. Between 1409 and 1417, a third man claimed to be the legitimate pope as well. This **Great Western Schism** only ended in 1417, when a church council deposed all three claimants and appointed a new pope, who accepted the council's authority.

The Hundred Years' War continued through the time of the Great Western Schism, and in 1429 a young illiterate peasant woman named Joan of Arc (1412–1431), who claimed divine guidance, succeeded in rallying the French forces and won a surprise victory. After capturing her in 1430, the English burned her as a heretic in 1431. In the years after her death, the French forces won more victories, recovering all the territory that had been under English rule—with the sole excep-tion of the port of Calais—until they defeated the English in 1453, when the French and the English signed a treaty marking the end of the war.

• **Great Western Schism** Dispute that divided the Roman Catholic Church (1378–1417), in which two, sometimes three, men claimed to be the legiti-mate pope. The French kings backed the popes living in Avignon; the English king supported the pope in Rome.

The Consolidation of Monarchy in France and England

When they assess the significance of the Hundred Years' War, historians note how the political structure of France and England changed: at the beginning of the war, the two kingdoms consisted of patchworks of territory ruled by a king who shared power with his nobles. By the end of the war, the two coun-tries had become centralized monarchies governed by kings with considerably more power.

This result had much to do with the changing nature of warfare. In conflicts during the early 1300s, the French and English kings summoned their nobles, who provided knights and soldiers. But the men best able to use first the longbow and then cannon were specialists who had to be paid. At first, when the kings needed money, they asked for it on an emergency basis, often allowing their subordinates to substitute financial payment for military aid. Over time, kings demanded money each year and so gained the right to tax the lords of their country.

In England, the king had summoned groups of advisers since the 1200s; contemporaries called these meetings "Parliament," which literally means "to talk." **Parliament** consisted of different groups, some nobles and some well-off city dwellers. It met whenever the English king convened his most powerful subordinates to inform them of new taxes. Though they always paid what he asked for, they were entitled to an explanation for why he needed the money. Most European rulers convened bodies similar to Parliament; the French equivalent, weaker than Parliament, was called the Estates General and included the nobles, clergy, and townsfolk.

The monarchy as it evolved in France and England differed from earlier political structures. France and England were smaller than the earlier Roman and Byzantine Empires, and their rulers consulted with their subordinates more often. The new monarchies, though, proved to be extremely effective, partially because they could command the allegiance of their subjects.

> • **Parliament** (literally "to talk"). Name for the different councils that advised the English kings and approved their requests for taxation.

Chapter Review

[CL] Download the MP3 audio file of the Chapter Review and listen to it on the go.

Peter Abelard and Heloise experienced the changes of Europe's commercial revolution, particularly the changes in education, organization of the church, and city life. The losses of the 1300s caused by food shortages, the Black Death, and prolonged warfare brought a halt to Europe's developing economy, but only a temporary one.

What caused the cerealization of Europe, and what were its results?

Between 1000 and 1300, Europe experienced enormous growth, much of it fueled by cerealization, the reclamation and planting of land with grain. The European countryside in 1300 looked very different than it had in 1000: livestock, iron tools, and wind mills or watermills were in use everywhere, and crop rotation was systematically practiced. The increasing crop yields caused Europe's population to grow from some forty million in 1000 to around seventy-five million in 1340. In addition, society became more complex as lords, knights, and clergy acquired specific rights over serfs.

What led to the foundation of Europe's universities? How did they gain the right to govern themselves?

The universities had their roots in privately run schools or church-run schools like those at which Peter Abelard taught. Structured like commercial guilds, the universities gradually implemented rules about the curriculum, examinations, and the

KEY TERMS

Peter Abelard (356)

Heloise (356)

cerealization (359)

guilds (361)

feudal (364)

liberal arts (365)

scholasticism (366)

simony (371)

heresy (372)

friars (373)

Thomas Aquinas (374)

Crusader (374)

inquisition (378)

Hundred Years' War (381)

Great Western Schism (382)

Parliament (383)

granting of degrees. Because students and masters threatened to, and sometimes did, leave the towns that hosted them, the townspeople supported them in their quest for autonomy, which universities achieved by the mid-thirteenth century.

How did economic prosperity affect the Christian church and different monastic orders?

Since individual churches had their own lands and benefited from cerealization, their leaders often had their own incomes and considerable independence. Many people outside the church called for an end to the sale of church office, or simony, and for members of the clergy to be celibate. Reformers founded different monastic orders, each demanding greater sacrifices from its members. During the twelfth century, the pope granted permission for the founding of at least nine different begging orders, including the Franciscans and the Dominicans. The church, after undergoing many different reforms, became one of the most vibrant institutions in medieval European society.

What did the Crusaders hope to achieve outside Europe? Within Europe?

The Crusaders' main purpose was to recapture Jerusalem, the symbolic center of the Christian world where Jesus had lived and died. They held Jerusalem for eighty-eight years, and after it fell in 1187, they tried to recover it. In the same years that they fought Muslims for control of the Holy Land, they also tried to make Europe more Christian: out-of-control crowds attacked Jews, the pope authorized a Crusade against the Cathars of France, and Christian armies fought to reconquer the Muslim cities of Spain and Portugal. In later centuries, the Crusades provided an important precedent for those who believed that Europeans were entitled to colonize non-Christian lands outside Europe.

How did the major developments of the century from 1300 to 1400 strengthen European monarchies?

The tremendous growth of the twelfth and thirteenth centuries began to slow around the year 1300, when the first food shortages occurred, and then stopped almost entirely when the Black Death of 1348 struck. The fourteenth century was also a time of military conflict between France and England, which fought the Hundred Years' War between 1337 and 1453, and of conflict in the church, which had two, sometimes even three, candidates for pope during the Great Schism (1378–1417). The long years of fighting gave the monarchs new powers, most notably the power to tax their subordinates (who no longer provided them with armies of knights) and to keep standing armies. Once the difficult fourteenth century ended, a renewed Europe emerged.

For Further Reference

Baldwin, John W. *The Scholastic Culture of the Middle Ages, 1000–1300.* Prospect Heights, Ill.: Waveland Press, 1971, 1997.

Cipolla, Carlo M. *Before the Industrial Revolution: European Society and Economy, 1000–1700.* New York: W. W. Norton, 1994.

Clanchy, M. T. *Abelard: A Medieval Life.* Malden, Mass.: Blackwell, 1997.

Lynch, Joseph H. *The Medieval Church: A Brief History.* New York: Longman, 1992.

Madden, Thomas F. *The New Concise History of the Crusades.* Updated ed. New York: Rowman and Littlefield, 2005.

Moore, R. I. *The First European Revolution, c. 970–1215.* Malden, Mass.: Blackwell, 2000.

Opitz, Claudia. "Life in the Late Middle Ages." In *Silence of the Middle Ages,* ed. Chistiane Klapisch-Zuber, vol. 2 of *A History of Women in the West.* Cambridge, Mass.: Belknap Press of Harvard University Press, 1992, pp. 259–317.

Radice, Betty, trans. *The Letters of Abelard and Heloise.* Revised by M. T. Clanchy. New York: Penguin Books, 2003.

Rosenwein, Barbara. *A Short History of the Middle Ages.* Orchard Park, N.Y.: Broadview Press, 2002.

Spufford, Peter. *Power and Profit: The Merchant in Medieval Europe.* New York: Thames and Hudson, 2002.

 WEB RESOURCES

Pronunciation Guide

Interactive Maps

MAP 13.1 The Crusades

MAP 13.2 Movement of the Plague and Trade Routes

Primary Sources

Chapter Objectives

ACE Multiple-Choice Quiz

Flashcards

Websites

Chartres Cathedral
(http://gallery.sjsu.edu/chartres/tour.html).   Photographs and information on Chartres.

The Cloisters
(http://www.metmuseum.org/cloisters).   Introduction to America's most prominent museum of medieval art.

Internet Medieval Sourcebook
(http://www.fordham.edu/halsall/sbook.html).   Many valuable primary sources under the entries for Crusades, Iberia, Empire and Papacy, France, and England.

The Mongols and Their Successors, 1200–1500

In 1255, after his return from Mongolia, **William of Rubruck** (ca. 1215–ca. 1295) wrote a confidential report about his attempt to convert the Mongols to Christianity. He addressed it to his sponsor, the pious French king Louis IX (1214–1270). William's letter runs nearly three hundred pages long in translation and contains the most detailed, accurate, and penetrating description of the Mongols and their empire that exists today. In 1206, the Mongols exploded out of their homeland just north of China and conquered most of Eurasia by 1242. For the first time in world history, it became possible for individual travelers, like William, to move easily across a united Eurasia. Such movement prompted an unprecedented exchange of ideas, goods, and technologies. William's report is just one example of the different cultural exchanges that resulted and whose effects persisted long after different successor states replaced the Mongol Empire. His description of his trip to the Mongol empire begins as follows:

WILLIAM OF RUBRUCK

(The Masters and Fellows of Corpus Christi College, Cambridge)

We began our journey, then, around June 1, with our four covered wagons and two others which the Mongols had provided for us, in which was carried the bedding for sleeping on at night. They gave us five horses to ride, since we numbered five persons: I and my colleague, Friar Bartholomew of Cremona; Gosset, the bearer of this letter; the interpreter Homo Dei, and a boy, Nichols, whom I had bought at Constantinople with the alms you gave me. They supplied us in addition with two men who drove the wagons and tended the oxen and horses. . . .

Now on the third day after we left Soldaia, we encountered the Tartars [the Mongols]; and when I came among them, I really felt as if I were entering some other world. Their life and character I shall describe for you as best I can.[1]

CL This icon will direct you to interactive activities and study materials on the *Voyages* website: www.cengage.com/history/hansen/voyages1e

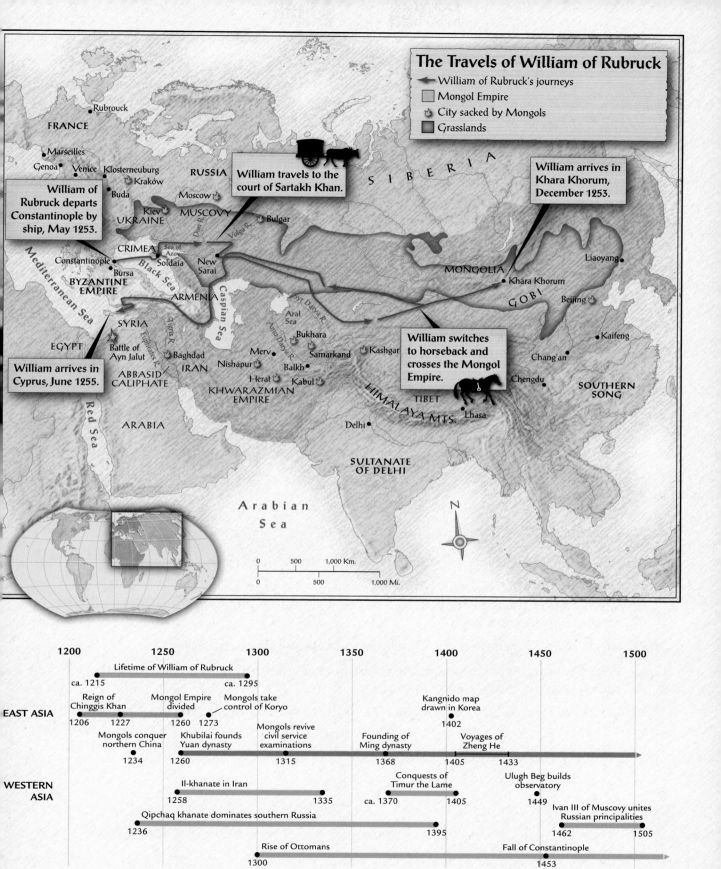

The Travels of William of Rubruck

- ← William of Rubruck's journeys
- Mongol Empire
- ☽ City sacked by Mongols
- Grasslands

William of Rubruck departs Constantinople by ship, May 1253.

William travels to the court of Sartakh Khan.

William arrives in Khara Khorum, December 1253.

William arrives in Cyprus, June 1255.

William switches to horseback and crosses the Mongol Empire.

FRANCE
Rubrouck
Marseilles
Genoa
Venice
Klosterneuburg
Kraków
Buda
Moscow
RUSSIA
SIBERIA
Kiev
UKRAINE
MUSCOVY
Bulgar
CRIMEA
Sea of Azov
Soldaia
New Sarai
Don R.
Volga R.
MONGOLIA
Liaoyang
Constantinople
Bursa
Black Sea
Khara Khorum
BYZANTINE EMPIRE
Caspian Sea
ARMENIA
GOBI
Beijing
Mediterranean Sea
SYRIA
Syr Darya R.
Aral Sea
Kaifeng
EGYPT
Battle of Ayn Jalut
Baghdad
Tigris R.
Euphrates R.
Merv
Nishapur
Bukhara
Anu Darya R.
Samarkand
Kashgar
Chang'an
Chengdu
SOUTHERN SONG
ABBASID CALIPHATE
IRAN
Balkh
Herat
Kabul
KHWARAZMIAN EMPIRE
HIMALAYA MTS.
TIBET
Lhasa
Red Sea
ARABIA
Delhi
SULTANATE OF DELHI
Arabian Sea
N

0   500   1,000 Km.
0   500   1,000 Mi.

	1200	1250	1300	1350	1400	1450	1500

Lifetime of William of Rubruck
ca. 1215 — ca. 1295

EAST ASIA

Reign of Chinggis Khan
1206 — 1227

Mongol Empire divided
1260

Mongols take control of Koryo
1273

Kangnido map drawn in Korea
1402

Mongols conquer northern China
1234

Khubilai founds Yuan dynasty
1260

Mongols revive civil service examinations
1315

Founding of Ming dynasty
1368

Voyages of Zheng He
1405 — 1433

WESTERN ASIA

Il-khanate in Iran
1258 — 1335

Conquests of Timur the Lame
ca. 1370 — 1405

Ulugh Beg builds observatory
1449

Qipchaq khanate dominates southern Russia
1236 — 1395

Ivan III of Muscovy unites Russian principalities
1462 — 1505

Rise of Ottomans
1300

Fall of Constantinople
1453

In December 1253, after nine months of traveling—first by cart, then on horseback—through modern-day Turkey, Russia, the Ukraine, Siberia, and Mongolia, William arrived at the court of the Mongol leader Möngke (MUNG-keh) (d. 1259), the grandson of Chinggis Khan (the Mongolian spelling; Genghis Khan in Persian).

Called William of Rubruck because he was born sometime around 1215 in the village of Rubrouck, France, William was educated at Paris. A follower of Saint Francis, he went to Syria, then under the control of the Crusaders (see Chapter 13) in 1248, from where he departed for Mongolia.

As an outsider, William writes about the appearance of Mongol men and women, the process for making fermented horse's milk, and their worship of household spirits. No comparably detailed account by a Mongol survives. William visited the Mongols at the height of their power, during the years after Chinggis Khan had united the empire and before it broke apart.

William's gripping description of the Mongols allows us to understand how the Mongols created the largest contiguous land empire in world history, stretching from Hungary to the Pacific. Once they conquered a region or the local rulers surrendered, the Mongols placed a governor in charge and granted him considerable autonomy. Their loosely structured empire allowed many people, including William, to cross Eurasia and resulted in the interaction of societies and cultures that had been previously isolated. This chapter will also examine the states that succeeded the Mongols: the principality of Muscovy (Moscow) in Russia, the Ottomans in Turkey, the Yuan and Ming dynasties in China, and the successor states of Korea, Japan, and Vietnam.

Focus Questions

How did the Mongols' nomadic way of life contribute to their success as conquerors?

What bound the different sectors of the Mongol Empire together? What caused its breakup in the 1260s?

What states succeeded the Qipchaq and Chaghatai khanates?

What military innovations marked Ottoman expansion, and what cultural developments typified Ottoman rule?

What was the legacy of Mongol rule in East and Southeast Asia?

From Nomads to World Conquerors, 1200–1227

Founded by **Chinggis Khan** (ca. 1167–1227), the Mongol Empire formed between 1200 and 1250. At the time of Chinggis's birth around 1167, the Mongols lived in modern-day Mongolia with their herds of sheep, cattle, and horses and pursued a nomadic existence, trading with their sedentary neighbors primarily for grain, tea, textiles, and metal goods. After conquering the different peoples in Mongolia, Chinggis forged them into a fearsome fighting force that conquered gigantic sections of Europe, Central Asia, and China. The Mongols' skill with horses and systematic use of terror brought them unprecedented military success.

> • **Chinggis Khan** (ca. 1167–1227) Founder of the Mongol Empire who united the different peoples living in modern-day Mongolia in 1206, when he took the title Chinggis Khan.

The Mongols' Nomadic Way of Life Before 1200

Nomadic peoples lived in the Mongolian grasslands even before the Mongols moved into Central Asia around 1000. The Mongols spoke Mongolian and different Turkic languages that are the basis of modern Turkish. The only source in Mongolian about the Mongols' early history is *The Origin of Chinggis Khan,* an anonymous oral epic that took shape in 1228 and was committed to writing a century or more later. (Many English translations are entitled *The Secret History of the Mongols.*) In 1206, Chinggis Khan ordered a Central Asian prisoner of war to record something he said in Mongolian. The prisoner wrote in his native Uighur, a Central Asian language spoken in Central Asia and in modern-day Xinjiang in west China. After this incident, the Mongols used the Uighur script to write the Mongolian language.

The Origin of Chinggis Khan gives a vivid sense of how the Mongols lived before they were unified. The Mongols' traditional homeland occupies much of the modern-day Mongolian People's Republic as well as the Inner Mongolian autonomous region just northwest of Beijing. This steppe region consists largely of grasslands, watered by a few rivers. Few trees grow there. While the soil and limited rainfall could not support a sedentary, farming population, the extensive grasslands perfectly suited pastoral nomads grazing their herds. (See the feature "World History in Today's World: Modern Nomads.")

After exhausting the available grass in a location, the Mongols moved to new pastures. Ranging from ten to several hundred people, an individual band might travel 100 miles (160 km) in its annual migration, usually on a fixed route. When the Mongols began their conquests, the fighters covered much larger distances and left their parents, wives, and children behind to tend their herds.

Religious Practices of the Mongols

The Mongols worshiped a variety of nature spirits. Each of the Mongols' tents, William noticed, contained several figurines made of felt, a textile made by pressing layers of wool together. All these figurines represented protective spirits who watched over the tent's residents as they performed their daily tasks.

The supreme deities of the Mongols were the sky-god Tengri and his counterpart, the earth-goddess Itügen. Certain people, called **shamans,** specialized in interceding with these gods. Sometimes they traveled to high mountains thought

> • **shamans** Mongol religious specialists who interceded with the gods. Traveled to high mountains, thought to be the residence of high gods, to prostrate themselves. Also contacted deities by burning bones and interpreting the cracks to interpret the gods' will.

Modern Nomads

The population of Mongolia today is 2.65 million; about one-third are nomadic and keep herds totaling twenty-five million sheep, goats, horses, cattle, camels, and yaks. (The other two-thirds live in cities.) Many are struggling to maintain their traditional nomadic way of life. From the 1920s to 1990, Mongolia, sometimes called Outer Mongolia, was a satellite state dependent on the Soviet Union. During those years many nomads stopped herding and lived instead on large state farms with collectively owned herds. In 1990, after the fall of the Berlin Wall, Mongolia became independent. The withdrawal of massive Soviet subsidies caused its economy to collapse, forcing many to return to private herding. The state farms were disbanded, and each person received thirty animals.

Many of these nomads live in the traditional felt tents with a wooden frame, called *ger* (GAIR), but have added some modern conveniences. Some use solar-energy generators to fuel small refrigerators, while others receive television signals from sat-ellite dishes. The most prosperous have bought dirt bikes, motorcycles, or pickup trucks, which they use if they move their ger to a new location. A few have tried tending their herds with motor vehicles, but the high cost of gasoline means that most rely on horses for herding.

Few modern nomads have retained traditional herding skills. In 2000 and 2001, two harsh winters in a row covered much of Mongolia's extensive grasslands with ice and snow, preventing millions of animals from grazing. A few knowledgeable families prepared by taking their animals on a traditional monthlong trek covering some 100 miles (160 km) in the fall, and their fattened animals survived the difficult winter. Others fared less well: 3.5 million livestock died in 2000, and 4.8 million in 2001. Many of those who lost their flocks have given up herding and moved to the capital, Ulan Bator, to seek their livelihood, where fully one-third of the population consists of migrants from the countryside.

to be the residence of the sky-god and the other high gods, where they prostrated themselves. On other occasions, shamans burned bones and interpreted the cracks as indicators of the gods' will, much like Shang dynasty diviners in ancient China (see Chapter 4).

The Mongols in central and western Mongolia had some contact with Christian missionaries from the Church of the East, which was based in Syria and used Syriac as its primary liturgical language. These missionaries, the Christians most active in Central Asia, spoke the Turkic language Uighur when they preached among the Mongols. Williams called them Nestorians after Nestorius, a Syrian patriarch in Constantinople in 428, but in fact the Church of the East did not accept the teachings of Nestorius, whom successive church councils had declared a heretic.

Throughout his travels William encountered Eastern Christians and acknowledged them as fellow Christians while profoundly disagreeing with them about their beliefs. Like other Roman Catholics, William believed that Jesus had a single nature, not two distinct ones, and that Mary was Jesus' mother. William gradually realized that the Mongols saw no contradiction between worshiping their traditional deities and praying to the Christian God. They also saw no significant differences between Western and Eastern teachings about Jesus.

Mongol Society Mongol society had two basic levels: ordinary Mongols and the families of the chiefs. The chief's sons and grandsons formed a privileged group from which all future rulers were chosen. Differences in wealth certainly existed, with some men having larger herds or better clothes than others, but no rigid social divisions or inherited ranks separated ordinary Mongols. Below them in rank, however, were slaves who had often been captured in battle.

The chiefs periodically collected a 1 percent tax simply by taking one of every hundred animals. They could use this tax as they liked or to meet the group's needs. Unlike sedentary peoples, who collected taxes once a year, usually in the fall after the harvest was in, Mongol chiefs imposed the tax whenever they chose.

The Mongols lived in felt tents that could be put up and dismantled rapidly. While the men led their herds to new grazing areas, the women packed up their households and organized the pitching of tents at the new campsite. William described the Mongols' traditional division of labor:

> It is the women's task to drive the wagons, to load the dwellings on them and to unload again, to milk the cows, to make butter and curd cheese, and to dress the skins and stitch them together, which they do with a thread made from sinew. . . . They never wash clothes, for they claim that this makes God angry and that if they were hung out to dry it would thunder. . . .
>
> The men make bows and arrows, manufacture stirrups and bits, fashion saddles, construct the dwellings and the wagons, tend the horses and milk the mares, churn the khumis (that is, the fermented mare's milk), produce the skins in which it is stored and tend and load the camels. Both sexes tend the sheep and goats, and they are milked on some occasions by the men, on others by the women.

Because Mongol women ran their households when their menfolk were away and often sat at their husbands' side during meetings, they had much more decision-making power than women in sedentary societies, William realized. Living in close proximity to their animals, the Mongols used the products of their own herds whenever possible: they made their tents from felt, wore clothes of skins and wool, ate meat and cheese, and drank fermented horse's milk, or khumis. William describes his first reaction to this drink with unusual frankness: "on swallowing it I broke out in a sweat all over from alarm and surprise, since I had never drunk it before. But for all that I found it very palatable, as indeed it is."

The Mongols, however, could not obtain everything they needed from their herds and depended on their agricultural neighbors to provide grain, which they valued as a supplement to their monotonous diet. The Mongols also relied on settled peoples to obtain the silks and cottons that were so much softer and lighter than the Mongols' rough wool and felt. Although they could make do, if necessary, without grain, tea, or textiles, they required metal objects like the knives, daggers, and spears used in hunting and war.

Before 1200, an uneasy peace prevailed among the Mongols and their neighbors. Individual Mongol groups might occasionally plunder a farming community, but they never expanded outside their traditional homelands. Under the powerful leadership of Chinggis Khan, all that changed.

The Rise of Chinggis Khan

Sometime around 1167, *The Origin of Chinggis Khan* reports, a chieftain of a small Mongol band and his wife gave birth to a son they named Temüjin, the future Chinggis Khan. He enjoyed a normal family life for a mere nine years before a rival poisoned his father. His widowed mother and her children were able to eke out a living only by grazing a small herd of nine horses and eating wild plants.

• **tanistry** Process the Mongols used to choose a new leader. Under tanistry, the most qualified member of the chief's family led the band. All contenders for power had to prove their ability to lead by defeating their rivals in battle.

• **khuriltai** Name of the Mongols' assembly that gathered to acclaim the new leader after he had defeated his rivals. Not an electoral body.

Difficult as it was for his mother, his father's untimely death brought Temüjin some advantages. Though only a teenager, he could forge alliances with other leaders who declared their loyalty to him. He allied himself with one band to fight a third band, and when that band had been defeated and joined his forces, he would then attack another. In this way, Temüjin eventually formed a confederation of all the peoples in the grasslands of modern Mongolia. In 1206, in recognition of his leadership, the Mongols awarded the 39-year-old Temüjin the title of universal ruler: Chinggis (literally "oceanic") Khan ("ruler").

The Mongols used a political process called **tanistry** to choose a new leader. Its basic rule was that the most qualified member of the chief's family led the band.[2] In practice, this meant that each time a chief died or was killed by a challenger, all contenders for power had to prove their ability to lead by defeating their rivals in battle. Then the warriors gathered at an assembly, or **khuriltai,** to acclaim the new leader. When this leader died, the destabilizing and bloody selection process began again. Each time a Mongol leader died, his followers disbanded; only a powerful successor could reunite them.

Chinggis's Army Once he had united the Mongols, Chinggis weakened their group loyalties by dividing all his soldiers into units that crossed group lines. Each soldier belonged to four units: a unit of ten was part of a unit of one hundred, within a larger unit of one thousand, which finally belonged to one of ten thousand men. All able-bodied men between the ages of 15 and 70 fought in the army, and women did so if necessary. Scholars estimate the total population of the Mongols at one million, far less than the populations of the lands they conquered and governed. With such a small population, the Mongols did not have enough warriors to staff an enormous army. Numbering only one hundred thousand in 1206, the Mongol forces reached several hundred thousand at the height of Chinggis's power in the 1220s.

A Mongol Archer in Italian Eyes
This Mongol warrior's skull-like face stares menacingly at the viewer. He clasps a compound bow in his left hand, an arrow in his right. Ordinary bows were too big for a mounted warrior to shoot, but the compound bow was short enough for use on horseback. When the Mongols laid siege to cities, row after row of mounted archers shot showers of arrows with devastating effect. (Louvre, Paris, France/Réunion des Musées Nationaux/Art Resource, NY)

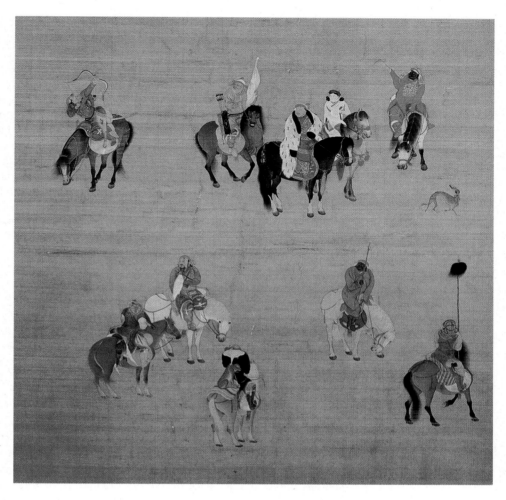

A Mongol Hunting Party as Seen by a Chinese Artist In painting the hunting party of Khubilai Khan (see page 410), the Chinese artist Liu Guandao rendered the horses' different stances and the varied facial features of the retainers in exquisite detail. Note the different animals the Mongols, but not the Chinese, used for hunting: a greyhound dog to the right of the khan and a cheetah, prized for its speed, on the saddle of the lowermost horse. The archer (*far left*) leans backward to shoot a bird flying high above in the sky; the skills the Mongols developed while hunting were directly transferable to warfare. (National Palace Museum, Taipei, Taiwan/The Bridgeman Art Library)

The Mongols started with only one significant advantage over the European and Asian powers they conquered: horses. Their grassy homeland provided them with an unending supply of horses, and, because Mongol children were raised on horseback, they matured into highly skilled riders who could shoot from horseback with their compound bows of wood, horn, and sinew. The Mongols had so many horses that they could change their mounts three times a day, and they frequently put dummies on riderless horses to make their army look larger.

The overriding goal of the Mongol armies was to conquer as much territory as quickly as possible. It was much cheaper and faster, the Mongols realized, to take a city whose occupants surrendered without a fight than to lay siege to a walled, medieval settlement that could take months to fall. The Mongols placed captives on their front lines to be killed by their own countrymen, in the hope that the rulers of the cities on their path could surrender. In exchange, the Mongols promised not to destroy their homes.

Mongol traditions held that Chinggis Khan could command the total obedience of his warriors in wartime but not in peacetime. Accordingly, he had good reason to keep conquering new territory. In war, the Mongols viewed all plunder as their due, but they limited their requisition to one-tenth of all the enemy's movable property if the enemy submitted voluntarily. Because the ruler shared the spoils with his men whenever he conquered a city, his followers had a strong incentive to follow him, and the ruler had no reason to stop fighting. Under Chinggis's leadership, the Mongols built one of the most effective fighting forces the world had ever seen.

At first Chinggis led his troops into north China, which was under the rule of the Jin dynasty (see Chapter 12), and conquered the important city of Beijing in 1215, forcing the Jin dynasty to occupy a small sliver of land between the Southern Song and the Mongol realms. In 1219, Chinggis turned his attention to Transoxiana, the region between the Amu Darya and Syr Darya Rivers, then under the rule of the Islamic Khoresmian empire. In rapid succession the Mongols conquered the glorious cities of Bukhara (in modern Uzbekistan), Balkh (Afghanistan), Nishapur (Iran), Merv (Turkmenistan), and Herat (Afghanistan). The Persian historian Juvaini (1226–1283) quotes an eyewitness: "They came, they sapped, they burnt, they slew, they plundered, and they departed."[3]

Mongol Governance

● **darughachi**
Regional governor appointed by the leaders of the Mongols after they had conquered a new territory. The darughachi's main tasks were to administer the region and to collect taxes.

Before departing from Bukhara, Chinggis summoned all the local notables to explain how the new regime would work. He appointed one man, usually a Mongol, to be governor, or **darughachi** (dah-roo-GAH-chee), of the conquered region. The darughachi's main responsibility was to collect the required taxes.

The darughachi were free to try different types of taxes in the various parts of the empire as long as they produced sufficient revenue. The Mongols continued to levy irregular taxes, like their traditional 1 percent tax on herds, in addition to taxes on agriculture, and in many locations they also instituted a 5 percent tax on commercial transactions. Since the Mongols allowed the local governments to rule as they had before the conquest, the darughachi resembled the satraps of the Achaemenid Empire of Persia (see Chapter 6).

The Mongols reserved the highest positions in the occupying government, such as the darughachi, for Mongols. Above the darughachi were the Mongol khan and his kin, who did not hold official titles but made all the major decisions affecting the empire. Below the darughachi were the conquered peoples, who staffed the lower branches of government and were permitted to continue their own religious practices. Religious institutions did not have to pay taxes. The Mongols' willingness to leave much of the local government and customs intact meant that they could conquer enormous swaths of territory quickly without having to leave behind a large occupying force to rule the conquered lands.

● The United Mongol Empire After Chinggis, 1229–1260

When Chinggis Khan died in 1227, no one knew whether his empire would survive him. From 1229 to 1260, the Mongols remained united but were led by different rulers (see the chart "Mongol Rulers, 1206–1260"). They continued their conquests and took eastern Europe and northern China. During this time, they also introduced important innovations, such as the postal relay system, and began

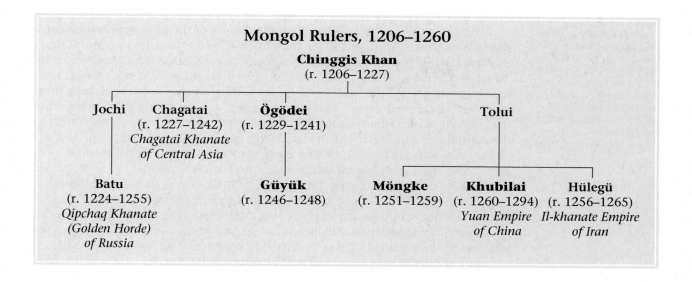

Mongol Rulers, 1206–1260

- **Chinggis Khan** (r. 1206–1227)
  - **Jochi**
    - **Batu** (r. 1224–1255)
      Qipchaq Khanate (Golden Horde) of Russia
  - **Chagatai** (r. 1227–1242)
    Chagatai Khanate of Central Asia
  - **Ögödei** (r. 1229–1241)
    - **Güyük** (r. 1246–1248)
  - **Tolui**
    - **Möngke** (r. 1251–1259)
    - **Khubilai** (r. 1260–1294)
      Yuan Empire of China
    - **Hülegü** (r. 1256–1265)
      Il-khanate Empire of Iran

work on the Mongol capital at Khara Khorum. The postal relay system, the requirements for receiving envoys, and the court-financed merchant networks were the only institutions holding the different parts of the far-flung Mongol Empire together, as William of Rubruck discovered when he traveled to Khara Khorum in the 1250s. His trip exemplifies the ease of movement across Eurasia and the resulting cultural exchanges that came with the Mongol conquest.

The Reign of Ögödei, 1229–1241

Chinggis Khan died in Mongolia in 1227 at the age of 60. Before he died, Chinggis had divided his entire realm into four sections, each for one of his sons. If the Mongols had followed the traditional election process, the succession dispute could have been protracted. Instead, at a khuriltai held two years after Chinggis's death, they acquiesced to Chinggis's request that his third son, Ögödei (r. 1229–1241), govern all four sections of the Mongols' realm.

In the 1230s, the Mongols attacked Russia repeatedly and subdued the Russian principalities. With nothing now standing between the Mongols and Europe, western European rulers, including the king of France and the pope, belatedly realized how vulnerable they were to Mongol attack. Until then, they had been preoccupied with taking back Jerusalem (see Chapter 13). Ignorantly assuming that any enemy of Islam had to be Christian and so a natural ally of theirs, the Europeans hoped to enlist the Mongols in the Crusades. Each European envoy returned with the same report: the Mongols demanded that the Europeans submit to them and give up one-tenth of all their wealth. The Europeans refused. In 1241–1242, the Mongols attacked Poland, crossed the Danube, and reached Klosterneuburg, only a few miles from Vienna, Austria.

There, on the brink of overrunning western Europe, the Mongols suddenly halted. News of Ögödei's death reached the troops, and, according to custom, all the warriors returned home to attend the khuriltai. They were unable to choose a new leader quickly from among the brothers, sons, and nephews of Chinggis Khan, and the troops never returned to eastern Europe. The western European powers were spared invasion by the Mongols.

●**postal relay system**
Mongol institution of fixed routes with regular stops where messengers could eat and get fresh mounts, which took shape during Ögödei's reign. Functioned as the central nervous system of the sprawling empire.

The Postal Relay System   The warriors in Europe learned of Ögödei's death fairly quickly because of the **postal relay system,** which took shape during his reign and which allowed the ruler to communicate with officials in the furthest regions of the Mongol Empire. The Mongols established fixed routes, with regular stops every 30 or so miles (50 km) at which messengers could eat and get fresh mounts. As official messengers, they carried a silver or bronze tablet of authority that entitled them to food and horses. Because the riders could cover some 60 miles (100 km) a day, the relay system functioned as the central nervous system of the sprawling empire. The Mongols also used the postal relay stations to host visiting envoys, to provide them with escorts, food, and shelter, and, most important, to guarantee their safe return.

William of Rubruck began his journey in 1253, two years after the Mongols had finally settled on Möngke, one of Chinggis Khan's grandsons, as Ögödei's successor. William wore a brown robe and went barefoot because he was a Franciscan missionary, not a diplomat. Just before he entered Mongol territory, however, he learned that if he denied he was an envoy, he might lose his safe-conduct guarantee and the right to provisions and travel assistance. He decided to accept the privileges granted to envoys.

The system for receiving envoys functioned well but not flawlessly, as William discovered. When he crossed the Don River, local people refused to help. To his dismay William found that the money he brought from Europe was useless: in one village, no one would sell him food or animals. After three difficult days, William's party once again received the mounts to which they were entitled. For two months, William reported, he and his compatriots "never slept in a house or a tent, but always in the open air or underneath our wagons."

On July 31, 1253, they arrived at the court of Sartakh, a great-grandson of Chinggis. Earlier envoys had reported that Sartakh was an observant Christian, and William hoped that Sartakh would permit him to stay. In his quest to obtain permission to preach, William personally experienced the decision-making structure of the Mongol government. Although the Mongols respected envoys, they feared spies. Sartakh said that, to preach, William needed the approval of Sartakh's father, Batu, a grandson of Chinggis Khan who ruled the western section of the empire. Batu in turn decided that William needed the approval of the highest ruler of all, Möngke, before he could preach among the Mongols. Each ruler chose to send William in person to see his superior.

William and his companion Bartholomew departed for Khara Khorum with a Mongol escort who told them: "I am to take you to Möngke Khan. It is a four month journey, and the cold there is so intense that rocks and trees split apart with the frost: see whether you can bear it." He provided them each with a sheepskin coat, trousers, felt boots, and fur hoods. At last, taking advantage of the postal relay system, William began to travel at the pace of a Mongol warrior, covering some 60 miles (100 km) each day:

> On occasions we changed horses two or three times in one day; on others we would travel for two or three days without coming across habitation, in which case we were obliged to move at a gentler pace. Out of the twenty or thirty horses we, as foreigners, were invariably given the most inferior, for everyone would take their pick of the horses before us; though I was always provided a strong mount in view of my very great weight.

William's reference to his bulk provides a rare personal detail. The Mongols ate solid food only in the evening and breakfasted on either broth or millet soup. They had no lunch. Although William and Bartholomew found the conditions extremely trying, the speed at which they traveled illustrates the postal relay system's crucial role in sending messages to officials and orders to the armies throughout the Mongol Empire.

At Möngke's Court   On December 27, 1253, William arrived at the winter court of Möngke on the River Ongin in modern Mongolia, where he and his retinue pitched their tents and where their herds stayed with them. On January 4, 1254, the two Franciscans entered the ruler's tent, whose interior was covered with gold cloth. Möngke "was sitting on a couch, dressed in a fur which was spotted and very glossy like a sealskin. He is snub-nosed, a man of medium build, and aged about forty-five." William asked Möngke for permission to preach in his territory. When his interpreter began to explain the khan's reply, William "was unable to grasp a single complete sentence." To his dismay, he realized that Möngke and the interpreter were both drunk.

His interpreter later informed him that he had been granted permission to stay two months, and William ended up staying three months at Möngke's court and another three at the capital of Khara Khorum, where he arrived in the spring of 1254. Khara Khorum was home to a small but genuinely international group of foreigners, who introduced important innovations from their home societies to the Mongols. Although they had originally come as captives and were not free to go home, these Europeans possessed valuable skills and enjoyed a much higher standard of living than the typical Mongol warrior. Whenever the Mongols conquered a new city, they first identified all the skilled craftsmen and divided them into two groups: siege-warfare engineers and skilled craftsmen. These engineers made catapults to propel large stones that cracked holes in city walls, and Chinese and Jurchen experts taught the Mongols how to use gunpowder (see Chapter 12). Mongol commanders sent all the other skilled craftsmen to help build Khara Khorum. The Mongols' willingness to learn from their captives prompted extensive cultural exchange.

The Mongol rulers designated a group of Central Asian merchants as their commercial agents who would convert the Mongols' plunder into money and then buy goods the rulers desired. As a nomadic people, the Mongols particularly liked textiles because they could be transported easily. Instead of a fixed salary, rulers gave their followers suits of clothes at regular intervals. The Mongols had two types of tents: their traditional felt tents held up with poles on the interior and new-style tents with guy ropes on the outside. Both could be very large, holding as many as a thousand people, and could be lined with thousands of yards of lavishly patterned silks. Most of the merchants traveling along caravan routes and supplying the Mongol rulers were Central Asian Muslims, whom William does not mention in his account.

Understandably, William writes much about the Europeans resident in Khara Khorum, including a French goldsmith named William. Captured in Hungary and technically a slave, the goldsmith worked for Möngke, who paid him a large amount for each project he completed. The goldsmith made an elaborate drinking fountain that dispensed khumis, honey wine, grape wine, and rice ale. This fountain illustrates the many cultural exchanges of the time: the technology was French, while the drinks were both European and Mongol. The goldsmith generously offered his bilingual son as a replacement for William's incompetent interpreter, and the son interpreted for William when Möngke invited him to debate with Nestorian, Muslim, and Buddhist representatives at court. (See the feature "Movement of Ideas: A Debate Among Christians, Buddhists, and Muslims at the Mongol Court.")

A Debate Among Christians, Buddhists, and Muslims at the Mongol Court

In May 1254, Möngke sent word to William that, before departing, the Christians, Muslims, and Buddhists should meet and debate religious teachings, since Möngke hoped to "learn the truth." William agreed to participate, and he and the Nestorians had a practice session in which he even took the part of an imaginary Buddhist opponent. On the appointed day, Möngke sent three of his secretaries—a Christian, a Muslim, and a Buddhist—to be the judges.

Since William's report is the only record that survives, historians cannot compare it with other descriptions of what happened. It is possible, for example, that he exaggerated his own role in the debate or misunderstood the arguments of his opponents.

The debate began with William arguing points with a Chinese Buddhist, whom William identifies by the Mongolian word *tuin* (TWUN). Like the Crusaders, William refers to the Muslims as Saracens and reports that they said little.

Source: Peter Jackson, trans., *The Mission of Friar William of Rubruck: His Journey to the Court of the Great Khan Möngke 1253–1255* (London: The Hakluyt Society, 1990), pp. 231–235.

The Christians then placed me in the middle and told the tuins to address me; and the latter, who were there in considerable numbers, began to murmur against Möngke Khan, since no Khan had ever attempted to probe their secrets. They confronted me with someone who had come from Cataia [China]: he had his own interpreter, while I had Master William's son.

He began by saying to me, "Friend, if you are brought to a halt, you may look for a wiser man than yourself."

I did not reply.

Next he enquired what I wanted to debate first: either how the world had been made, or what becomes of souls after death.

"Friend," I answered, "that ought not to be the starting-point of our discussion. All things are from God, and He is the fountain-head of all. Therefore we should begin by speaking about God, for you hold a different view of Him from us and Möngke wishes to learn whose belief is superior." The umpires ruled that this was fair.

They wanted to begin with the issues I have mentioned because they regard them as more important. All of them belong to the Manichaean heresy, to the effect that one half of things is evil and the other half good, or at least that there are two principles; and as regards souls, they all believe that they pass from one body to another.

Even one of the wiser of the Nestorian priests asked me whether it was possible for the souls of animals to escape after death to any place where they would not be compelled to suffer. In support of this fallacy, moreover, so Master William told me, a boy was brought from Cataia [China], who to judge by his physical size was not three years old, yet was fully capable of rational thought: he said of himself that he was in his third incarnation, and he knew how to read and write.

I said, then, to the *tuin*: "We firmly believe in our hearts and acknowledge with our lips that God exists, that there is only one God, and that He is one in perfect unity. What do you believe?"

"It is fools," he said, "who claim there is only one God. Wise men say that there are several. Are there not great rulers in your country, and is not Möngke Khan the chief lord here? It is the same with gods, inasmuch as there are different gods in different regions."

"You choose a bad example," I told him, "in drawing a parallel between men and God: that way any powerful figure could be called a god in his own dominions."

But as I was seeking to demolish the analogy, he distracted me by asking, "What is your God like, of Whom you claim that there is no other?"

"Our God," I replied, "beside Whom there is no other, is all-powerful and therefore needs assistance from no one; in fact we all stand in need of His. With men it is not so: no man is capable of all things, and for this reason there have to be a number of rulers on earth, since no one has the power to undertake the whole. Again, He is all-knowing and therefore needs no one as counsellor: in fact all wisdom is from Him. And again He is the supreme Good and has no need of our goods: rather, 'in Him we live and move and are.' This is the nature of our God, and it is unnecessary, therefore, to postulate any other."

"That is not so," he declared. "On the contrary, there is one supreme god in Heaven, of whose origin we are still ignorant, with ten others under him and one of the lowest rank beneath them; while on earth they are without number."

As he was about to spin yet more yarns, I asked about this supreme god: did he believe he was all-powerful, or was some other god?

He was afraid to answer, and asked: "If your God is as you say, why has He made half of things evil?"

"That is an error," I said. "It is not God who created evil. Everything that exists is good." All the *tuins* were amazed at this statement and recorded it in writing as something erroneous and impossible. . . .

He sat for a long while reluctant to answer, with the result that the secretaries who were listening on the Khan's behalf had to order him to reply. Finally he gave the answer that no god was all-powerful, at which all the Saracens burst into loud laughter. When silence was restored I said: "So, then, not one of your gods is capable of rescuing you in every danger, inasmuch as a predicament may be met with where he does not have the power. Further, 'no man can serve two masters': so how is it that you can serve so many gods in Heaven and on earth?" The audience told him to reply; yet he remained speechless. But when I was seeking to put forward arguments for the unity of the Divine essence and for the Trinity while everyone was listening, the local Nestorians told me it was enough, as they wanted to speak themselves.

At this point I made way for them [the Nestorians]. But when they sought to argue with the Saracens, the latter replied: "We concede that your religion is true and that everything in the Gospel is true; and therefore we have no wish to debate any issue with you." And they admitted that in all their prayers they beg God that they may die a Christian death. . . .

Everybody listened without challenging a single word. But for all that no one said, "I believe, and wish to become a Christian." When it was all over, the Nestorians and Saracens alike sang in loud voices, while the *tuins* remained silent; and after that everyone drank heavily.

QUESTIONS FOR ANALYSIS

▶ **What is William's main point?**

▶ **How does William present the main teachings of Buddhism? Of Islam?**

▶ **In William's account of the debate, does anyone say anything that you think they probably did not? Support your position with specific examples.**

Möngke's invitation to debate illustrates the Mongols' tolerance for and interest in other religious beliefs. Yet, on the one occasion he had a competent interpreter, even William realized that he had made no converts. William returned to Acre, the city in the Holy Land from which he departed, and then proceeded to France, where, in 1257, he met Roger Bacon (ca. 1214–1294), who preserved William's letter. After 1257, William disappears from the historical record, leaving the date of his death uncertain.

William's lack of success as a missionary is confirmed by one contemporary: in 1259, the king of Armenia, Hetum I (1226–1269), reported what the Mongols had told him about William. When William "appeared before the great king of the Tartars [Batu], he began to press on him the Christian faith, saying that the Tartar— and every infidel—would perish eternally and be condemned to everlasting fire." William might have been more successful as a missionary, the Mongol ruler Batu wryly commented, if he had tried to persuade the Mongols of the benefits of being a Christian, rather than threatening them with "everlasting punishment." The Armenian king's report seems all too believable: we can easily imagine William haranguing the unconvinced Mongol ruler.

The Empire Comes Apart, 1259–1263

William's letter to his monarch reveals that only the postal relay stations bound the different parts of the Mongol Empire together. The Mongols granted the darughachi governors wide latitude in governing, and they never developed an empire-wide bureaucracy. Officials from one part of the empire were not transferred to other regions, and they did not implement uniform standards and policies.

Because the Mongols allowed the darughachi governors to use the local language for administration and the recruitment of local officials, Chinese, Persian, and Turkish continued to be spoken throughout the empire. The Mongols did not impose Mongolian as the language of administration. During William's trip, the different sections of the empire continued to forward some taxes to the center, but the empire broke apart after Möngke's death in 1259.

A year earlier, Möngke's brother Hülegü had led the Mongols on one of the bloodiest campaigns in their history, the conquest of Baghdad, in which some 800,000 people died. Hülegü also ordered the execution of the caliph and so, in 1258, put a final end to the Abbasid caliphate, founded in 750 (see Chapter 9). In 1260, the Mamluk dynasty of Egypt (see Chapter 11) defeated the remnants of Hülegü's army in Syria at the battle of Ayn Jalut.

This defeat was the first time the Mongols had lost a battle and also marked the end of a united Mongol Empire. One of Möngke's surviving brothers, Khubilai (KOO-bih-leye) (d. 1294), engineered a khuriltai that named him the rightful successor, while a rival khuriltai named his brother Arigh Boke (d. 1264) the new khan. After 1260 it was impossible to maintain any pretense of imperial unity.

Another setback occurred in 1263, when the ruler of the Qipchaq (KIP-chack) khanate in Russia actively sought an alliance with the Mamluks against his cousin Hülegü in Iran. Never before had a Mongol allied with a non-Mongol force against another Mongol leader, and the alliance provides a clear date for the end of the unified Mongol Empire.

● Successor States in Western Asia, 1263–1500

After this breakup the Mongol Empire divided into four sections, each ruled by a different Mongol prince, generally the son or grandson of a former ruler (see Map 14.1). The eastern sector consisted of the Mongolian heartland and China (discussed later in this chapter). In the western sectors, each time a ruler died his living sons divided his territory, and succession disputes were common, fragmenting authority even further. Three important realms dominated the western sector. The Il-khanate in Iran governed the Tigris and Euphrates River basins, the Iranian Plateau, and Anatolia in Turkey. Their northern neighbor, the Qipchaq khanate or the Golden Horde, ruled the region north of the Black, Caspian, and Aral Seas (modern Ukraine, Russia, and Kazakhstan). Both the Il-khanate and the Qipchaq khanate shared a border with the third region, the Chaghatai khanate, which controlled the Syr Darya and Amu Darya Rivers of Central Asia around Samarkand. Each of these khanates inherited the legacy of the larger Mongol Empire but could not build territories as large. Border disputes often prompted war among these three realms. The Mongol tradition of learning from other peoples continued as each of the three ruling families converted to Islam, the religion of their most educated subjects (see Chapter 9).

The Il-khanate in Iran, 1256–1335

Since the Mongols had conquered Iran in 1258, only two years before the empire broke apart in 1260, they were not well established there. Hülegü took the title *il-khan* ("subordinate khan" in Persian) to indicate that he was lower in rank than his brother Möngke; he ruled the **Il-khanate.** As elsewhere, the Mongols faced the immediate problem of establishing order and ensuring the continued flow of taxes from the Muslim peoples of Iran.

● **Il-khanate** Mongol government of the region of Iran (1256–1335), founded by Hülegü, who took the title *il-khan* ("subordinate khan" in Persian) to indicate that he was lower in rank than his brother Möngke.

Hülegü, like his brother Möngke, was primarily a believer in shamanism. Five of Hülegü's sons and grandsons ruled Iran between 1265 and 1295. They, like other Mongol rulers, allowed Muslims, Buddhists, and Nestorian Christians to continue to worship their own belief systems. When Hülegü's great-grandson Ghazan (r. 1295–1304) took the throne in 1295, he announced his conversion to Islam, the religion of most of his subjects, and his fellow Mongols followed suit.

The Il-khanate never succeeded in establishing an efficient way to tax Iran. Infamous for collecting taxes twenty or more times a year, officials frequently resorted to force before they could get Iran's cultivators to pay. The end result was severe impoverishment of the countryside, which had already been devastated in the 1250s during the Mongol invasions. The Il-khanate had regular contact with the Yuan dynasty in China (covered later in this chapter), and in the 1290s the government introduced paper money (using the Chinese word for it) in the hopes that people would turn in all their gold and silver to the government. The paper money failed completely, bringing commerce to a standstill, but the experiment testifies to the Il-khanate's willingness to borrow from neighboring peoples.

After 1295, several Il-khanate rulers, in an attempt to bring reform, stipulated how much taxation should occur and when, encouraged farmers to reclaim abandoned land, and closely supervised Islamic judges, or qadi. Revenues seem to have

MAP 14.1

The Four Quadrants of the Mongol Empire After 1263 The first three Mongol rulers had governed the largest contiguous land empire in world history. But the Mongols were unable to choose a single successor to Möngke, the grandson of Chinggis Khan who died in 1259. The empire broke into four quadrants, each governed by a different member of the founder's family.

Interactive Map

Mongol domains, ca. 1300

- Qipchaq Khanate
- Vassal state of Qipchaq Khanate
- Il-Khanate
- Vassal state of Il-Khanate
- Chaghatai Khanate
- Vassal state of Chaghatai Khanate
- Yuan dynasty
- Vassal state of Yuan dynasty
- Mongol campaigns

increased, but the Il-khanate ended in 1335 when the last of Hülegü's descendants died, and Iran broke up into many small regions.

The Qipchaq Khanate and the Rise of Moscow

Although individual rulers of the Qipchaq khanate converted to Islam as early as the 1250s, Islam became the official religion only during the reign of Muhammad Özbeg (r. 1313–1341). The Qipchaq ruled the lower and middle Volga River valley, the home of the Bulgars, who had converted to Islam in the tenth century (see Chapter 10). Many Qipchaq subjects in Russian cities to the north and west continued to belong to the Eastern Orthodox Church.

Before the Mongols conquered the region in the 1230s, the descendants of Prince Vladimir of Kiev had governed the various Rus principalities (see Chapter 10). Unable to mount a successful defense against the Mongols, the different Russian princes surrendered. At the beginning of the Mongol era, Kiev had been the most important city in Russia, but the conquests devastated the city, prompting many to move to other places. Like all conquered peoples, the Russian princes of various cities paid the Mongols tribute, and the Qipchaq khanate, in turn, gave certain princes written permission to govern a given territory.

The **principality of Muscovy** (Moscow) eventually emerged as Kiev's successor, partially because the rulers of Moscow were frequently better able to pay their share of tribute and so were favored by the Qipchaq khanate. Ivan III (r. 1462–1505) defeated other Russian families to become the undisputed leader of the region; in 1480 he stopped submitting tribute to the Qipchaq khanate, and in 1502 he brought the khanate to an end. Ivan III controlled large chunks of modern-day Russia: from the Black Sea in the south to Novgorod in the north and much of modern-day Poland.

The Chaghatai Khanate and Timur the Lame

Straddling the Amu Darya and Syr Darya River valleys, the Chaghatai khanate included the eastern grasslands in what is now modern Mongolia and a western half that included the great Silk Road cities of Bukhara and Samarkand. In the grasslands to the east, the Mongols could follow their traditional nomadic way of life, and different chieftains continued to rule this region after the breakup of the empire.

Starting around 1350, a Turkish-speaking leader of Mongol descent took power first in the city of Samarkand and then in the surrounding western section of the Chaghatai khanate. This leader, known to his Persian enemies as **Timur the Lame** (1336?–1405), contracted to *Tamerlane* in English, succeeded in forming a powerful confederation.

Timur the Lame united the different peoples of the steppe much as Chinggis Khan had done around 1200: fighting one band until he defeated them, and then allying with them against another. In this way, he conquered much of modern Iran, Uzbekistan, Afghanistan, and the Anatolian region of Turkey. He married a descendant of Chinggis so that he could claim to be his successor, and he, too, used terror to reduce resistance. Timur was famous for setting his enemies on fire or throwing them off cliffs.

Like the Mongols, Timur the Lame forcibly resettled artisans and architects from among the conquered townspeople of India, Iran, and Syria. In his capital of

CL **Primary Source:** Russia's Conquest by the Mongols: A Song to Lost Lands *This song mournfully describes Russia before its conquest by the Mongols.*

• **principality of Muscovy** Successor to the Qipchaq khanate in modern-day Russia. Its most important leader, Ivan III, defeated other Russian families to become the region's undisputed leader; overthrew the Qipchaq khanate in 1502.

• **Timur the Lame** Also known in English as Tamerlane. Successor to the Chaghatai khanate, he conquered much of modern Iran, Uzbekistan, Afghanistan, and the Anatolian region of Turkey.

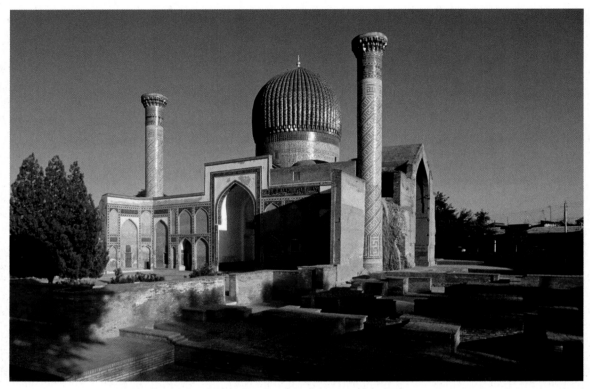

■ **The Tomb of Timur the Lame in Samarkand**   Completed in 1401, this building was originally intended as a madrasa, or school, but, when Timur died suddenly in 1405, his son buried his father there. The dome has a diameter of 49 feet (15 m) and is 41 feet (12.5 m) tall, but its design, with sixty-four distinctive ribs, gives an impression of lightness. The brilliant mosaic of light and dark blue tiles, the culmination of several centuries of experimenting, makes this one of the most striking buildings in modern Samarkand.   (© Tom Ang/drr.net)

Samarkand, these craftspeople built foreign-influenced buildings with elaborate mosaic tilework that is still visible today. As a result of this work, Samarkand became one of the most beautiful of all Central Asian cities.

Timur died in 1405 as he was preparing to lead his troops into China. Continuing the Mongol legacy of patronizing learning, his grandson Ulugh Beg (1394–1449, r. 1447–1449) built an enormous astronomical observatory and compiled a star chart based on ancient Greek and Islamic learning. Ulugh Beg ruled for only two years before his son ordered him killed and took over as ruler, in keeping with the Mongol tradition of tanistry. Timur's empire soon fragmented because the different members of the royal house, unable to decide on a successor, simply divided it among themselves.

By 1500, almost all the Mongol successor states had ceased to exist in western Asia. The region of Iran had broken into smaller states, as had the territory of the former Chaghatai khanate. Muscovy emerged as the major power in the Volga region, leaving only a small Mongol successor state in the Crimea.

●The Ottomans, 1300–1500

In the centuries that saw the fragmentation of the khanates in the west, a new power arose that initially replicated many elements of Mongol rule but then made crucial innovations that allowed it to build an empire that outlasted all the Mongol successor states. The **Ottomans,** a group of Turkic Muslim nomads, first gained control of Anatolia, in modern Turkey, which lay between the eastern edge of the Byzantine Empire and the western edge of the Il-khanate. Like the Mongols, the Ottomans were a nomadic people who conquered their sedentary neighbors and paid their soldiers with plunder. They put local rulers in place and granted them considerable autonomy in exchange for the regular payment of tribute and provision of troops when needed. Over time, however, they shifted from a Mongol-type army to an army who received a fixed salary—and not a share of plunder. Their conquest of Constantinople in 1453 marked the end of the Byzantine Empire and the establishment of a major Islamic power in western Asia.

● **Ottomans** Group of Turkic Muslim nomads who gained control of the Anatolia region in modern Turkey around 1300. Their conquest of Constantinople in 1453 marked the end of the Byzantine Empire and the establishment of a major Islamic power in western Asia.

The Rise of the Ottomans, 1300–1400

Even at the height of their power during the thirteenth century, the Mongols sent few troops to Anatolia, which lay on the western edge of their empire. After sacking Constantinople in 1204 (see Chapter 13), the Crusader forces occupied the city, while different Byzantine contenders tried to organize the opposition; as a result they, too, neglected the region of Anatolia. Around 1300 a man named Osman (the origin of the name *Ottoman*) emerged as the leader of a group of nomads who successfully conquered different sections of the Anatolian peninsula.

In 1326, the Ottomans conquered the port city of Bursa, which lay across the Sea of Marmora from Constantinople, and made it their first fixed capital. Because their armies were powerful, different claimants to the throne of the Byzantine Empire formed alliances with them. In 1354, Ottoman forces bypassed Constantinople and crossed the narrow straits of Dardanelles into modern-day Bulgaria. From this base, they conquered much of Greece and the Balkans by 1400, when they became the most powerful group professing loyalty to the Byzantine ruler, who controlled only the city of Constantinople and its immediate environs.

As the Ottomans swallowed up large chunks of the Byzantine territory, they became less hostile to the Christian residents of Anatolia and the Balkans, who were, after all, peoples of the book. The Ottomans could not stand up to the armies of Timur the Lame, but they resumed their conquests after his death in 1405.

As the Ottoman realm expanded, Ottoman rulers began to see themselves as protectors of local society, with Islamic law as their main tool. They paid mosque officials salaries and included them as part of their government bureaucracy. Agriculture thrived under their rule, and they were able to collect high revenues from their agricultural taxes, which they used to build roads for foot soldiers.

The Ottoman Military

The Ottomans enjoyed unusual military success because of their innovative policies. Unlike their enemies, they paid market prices for food and did not simply steal supplies from the local people. As a result, farmers willingly brought their produce to market to sell to the Ottomans.

As the Ottomans moved through the countryside, they frequently captured soldiers from among the conquered Christians. These enslaved prisoners of war were forced to join the army. Many eventually converted to Islam. They were called **Janissaries,** a Turkish word that means "new soldier." To prevent the Janissaries from building up large private estates, the Ottomans required them to be celibate so that they would not have descendants. Even so, many local people volunteered their sons for Janissary units because the boys could rise to a much higher position than if they remained on family farms.

The Ottomans also took advantage of new weapons using gunpowder. Although the Mongols had used some gunpowder, their most effective troops were mounted cavalry with bows and arrows. Nomadic peoples had the advantage over sedentary peoples because people living in cities could not defend themselves against the mobile, mounted nomad warriors armed with crossbows.

Around 1400, however, gunpowder weapons improved noticeably. Siege engineers realized that they could use wrought-iron launches powered by gunpowder to propel stone cannonballs weighing 440 pounds (200 kg) against city walls. While settled peoples could store gunpowder in safe stone storehouses, called *magazines,* nomadic peoples could not transport large quantities of gunpowder because they exploded too easily. Sedentary peoples then gained the advantage over nomadic peoples.

The Ottoman Conquest of Constantinople, 1453

The Ottomans demonstrated their command of the new gunpowder technology in 1453. When the Byzantine emperor requested the doubling of an annual subsidy from the Turks, the young Ottoman emperor Mehmet II (r. 1451–1481) decided to end the fiction of Byzantine rule. Mehmet, who is known as **Mehmet the Conqueror,** began construction of a large fort on the western shore of the Bosphorus, just across from Constantinople, and positioned three cannon on the fort's walls where they could hit all ships that entered the harbor to provision the Byzantine troops. (See the feature "Visual Evidence: The Siege of Constantinople, 1453.")

Eight thousand men on the Byzantine side faced an Ottoman force of some eighty thousand, assisted by a navy of over one hundred ships and armed with powerful cannon that could shoot a ball weighing 1,340 pounds (607 kg). Even so, the walls of Constantinople were so strong that it took two long months before the Ottomans defeated the Byzantine Empire.

When the city fell, Mehmet promised his troops the customary three days of looting a fallen non-Islamic city, but he called an end to the sacking after a single day. At the end of that day he led a small group of guards and advisers to the Hagia Sophia, the largest and most striking church in the city, which he planned to convert into a mosque. The Ottomans transformed Constantinople from a Christian into a Muslim city by turning many churches into mosques, often by adding four minarets around the original church building and clearing a prayer hall inside. The official name of the city was Qustantiniyya, "city of Constantine," but its residents referred to it as Istanbul, meaning simply "the city" in Greek.

Once the city came under Ottoman rule, the Greek, Slavic, and Turkic peoples living in the region moved to the city, bringing great prosperity. Priding himself

---

●**Janissaries** (Turkish word meaning "new soldier"). Soldiers of the Ottomans, recruited from conquered Christians. The Ottomans required them to be celibate so that they would not have descendants.

●**Mehmet the Conqueror** (r. 1451–1481) Leader of the Ottomans who conquered Constantinople in 1453 and commissioned scholars to copy ancient Greek classics, write epic poetry in Italian, and produce scholarly works in other languages.

(CL) **Primary Source:** The Fall of Constantinople to the Ottomans: A Lamentation *This account offers a mournful reflection on Constantinople before its fall to the Ottomans.*

Converting a Church into a Mosque   In 1453, on the day Mehmet's troops took Constantinople, he summoned his advisers to the most beautiful church in the city, the Hagia Sophia, to discuss their postconquest plans. The Ottomans transformed the Hagia Sophia into a mosque by adding four minarets outside the original church building and by clearing a giant hall for prayer inside. They also constructed a traditional Islamic garden, complete with fountain, behind the mosque.   (Steve McCurry/ Magnum Photos)

on his patronage of scholars and artists, Mehmet commissioned scholars to copy the ancient Greek classics, to write epic poetry in Italian, and to produce scholarly works in other languages, like Arabic and Persian. Realizing that the state needed educated officials, he established Islamic schools (madrasas) in the different cities of the realm.

Fresh from their 1453 victory, the Ottomans consolidated their control of the former Byzantine lands. Although they had started in 1300 as nomadic warriors who, like the Mongols, attacked sedentary peoples to take their agricultural surplus, by 1500 they had become the undisputed rulers of western Asia, and the salaried Janissary army was much more stable than the Mongol army, which had been propelled by the desire for plunder. Like the Mongols, the Ottomans adopted new technologies from the peoples they conquered.

THE SIEGE OF CONSTANTINOPLE, 1453

Although the fall of Constantinople was one of the major turning points in world history, surprisingly few portrayals of the event survive. One of the most detailed illustrations is from a manuscript describing the travels of Bertrandon de la Broquière (BEAR-trahn-dohn duh lah BROKE-ee-air) (d. 1459) from Dijon, France, to the Ottoman Empire in 1432–1433. Traveling on a mission for a French nobleman, Bertrandon hoped to find out whether it was feasible to launch a new crusade to free the Holy Land from Muslim rule. Although he visited Constantinople twenty years before 1453, his book included a picture of the fall, which he must have learned about after his return to France and before his death in 1459.

Bertrandon's *Voyage d'Outremer*, or *Voyage to Outremer,* offered European readers an eyewitness description of the Ottomans' power during the reign of Murad II (r. 1421–1451). The sultan's army impressed Bertrandon because his men ate only small amounts when traveling and rode strong horses. The soldiers' armor, made of chain mail, was lighter than the plated armor of the French, and their level of discipline seemed high to Bertrandon.

Bertrandon visited Adrianople (modern-day Edirne, Turkey), where the ambassador of Milan hosted him and took him to court. Here he saw the Ottoman sultan, who, he reported, had four major advisers who had to approve anyone's request to speak in person to the ruler. The painting (see inset 3 on the facing page) shows two of these advisers standing in an ornate tent in the foreground.

(Bibliothèque nationale de France/The Bridgeman Art Library)

This label, in medieval French, reads, "The headquarters of the Grand Turk with two of his principal advisers; The headquarters of the captain-general of the Turks."

QUESTION FOR ANALYSIS

Which different weapons and fighting techniques does the painting portray?

The artist painted a view of Constantinople, the peninsula of the Golden Horn, from the western shore of the Bosphorus. To protect the city, the Byzantines connected a giant chain (not shown in the painting) across the entrance to the Golden Horn to block the Ottoman warships, but the Ottomans simply transported their ships overland in wooden cradles along metal tracks to just outside the city, where they could fire on the walls. They carried a total of seventy ships, of which the artist shows only a handful, over the 200-foot-tall (60-m-tall) hill on the left of the painting. Outside the city the Ottomans arrayed a force of eighty thousand to lay siege; inside the city, a combined force of eight thousand Byzantines and their non-Byzantine allies succeeded in defending the city for two months before it fell.

This painting, though based on secondhand information, is surprisingly accurate. The artist captures the city's vulnerability: on all sides the Ottoman forces gather, while the Byzantines are concentrated in the central walled triangle extending into the Bosphorus. The painting does not convey the noise and confusion of cannon warfare; the scene is sunny and the setting idyllic. But it is not hard to imagine that all the forces arrayed outside the walls will soon be able to conquer the city.

These men are pulling the Ottoman boats on wooden carriages along a metal track to get around the chain blocking water access.

The Byzantines had triremes, or boats with three tiers of rowers, which could row faster than the one- or two-tiered Ottoman boats, but the Ottomans commanded many more ships than the Byzantines.

Ottoman engineers constructed this pontoon bridge so that their armies could get closer to the city walls, where their artillery was more effective.

A fishmonger offers fish for sale, a reminder that daily life continued in the city during the two-month-long siege.

The headquarters of the Ottomans. An elderly prisoner kneels before an officer.

⬤ East Asia During and After Mongol Rule, 1263–1500

At the time the empire broke apart in 1260, Chinggis's grandson Khubilai Khan (r. 1260–1294) controlled the traditional homeland of Mongolia as well as north China. Conquering south China, where the wet terrain proved extremely difficult for the Mongol horsemen to traverse, posed a genuine challenge. Only after building a Chinese-style navy did the Mongols succeed in taking south China, but they never conquered Japan or Southeast Asia. The Mongols ruled China for nearly one hundred years, until, in 1368, a peasant uprising overthrew them. The cultural exchanges of the Mongols continued to influence Ming dynasty (1368–1644) China, most clearly in the sea voyages of the 1400s.

⬤ **Khubilai Khan**
(1215–1294) Grandson of Chinggis Khan who became ruler of Mongolia and north China in 1260 and who succeeded in 1276 in conquering south China, but not Japan or Vietnam.

The Conquests of Khubilai Khan and Their Limits

Of the Mongol rulers who took over after 1260, **Khubilai Khan** (1215–1294) lived the longest and is the most famous. Suspicious of classical Chinese learning, Khubilai learned to speak some Chinese but not to read Chinese characters. During his administration in China, the Mongols suspended the civil service examinations (see Chapter 12); preferring to appoint officials, they tried to pair a non-Chinese official, either a Mongol or a Central Asian, with each Chinese appointee, though the small number of Mongol officials available made it difficult to do so. Even so, the Mongol administration in China absorbed many local customs. For example, in 1271, Khubilai adopted a Chinese name for his dynasty, the Yuan, meaning "origin."

Khubilai Khan's most significant accomplishment was the conquest of south China, resulting in the unification of north and south China for the first time since the tenth century. Demonstrating a genuine willingness to learn from other peoples, Khubilai Khan commissioned a giant navy that conquered all of south China by 1276. The Mongols became the first non-Chinese people in history to conquer and unify north and south China. As elsewhere in the Mongol Empire, they left much of the machinery of local government intact.

Like all Mongol armies, Khubilai's generals and soldiers wanted to keep conquering to obtain even more plunder. The Mongols made forays into Korea, Japan, and Vietnam even before 1260, and they continued their attacks under Khubilai's rule.

Of these three places, Korea, under the rule of the Koryo dynasty (936–1392), was the only one to come under direct Mongol rule. In 1231, a Mongol force active in north China invaded, prompting the Korean ruler to surrender. He agreed to disband his army, made heavy payments to the Mongols, and sent five hundred young men and five hundred young women as hostages to the Mongol court. Sporadic fighting continued, and the Mongols gained firm control only in 1273. Acknowledging the Mongols as their overlords, the Koryo rulers continued on the throne, but the Mongols forced them to intermarry with Mongol princesses, and the Koreans adopted many Mongol customs.

Once they had subdued Korea and gained control of north and south China, the Mongols tried to invade Japan, then under the rule of the Kamakura (see Chapter 12), in 1274 and 1281. To this end the Mongols forced the Koreans to provide nine hundred ships as well as many soldiers and supplies. Later sources report that a powerful wind destroyed the Mongol ships, an event described to this day by Japanese as *kamikaze* or "divine wind." (In World War II, Japanese fliers who went on suicide missions were called kamikaze pilots.) Contemporary sources do not mention the weather but describe a Mongol force of no more than ten thousand on either occasion being turned back by the fortifications the Japanese had built on their coastline. The costs of repelling the invasion weakened the Kamakura government, which fell in 1333, and Japan began three centuries of divided political rule that would end only in 1600 when the country was reunified.

The Mongols also proved unable to invade Vietnam, then under the rule of the Tran dynasty (1225–1400). Mongol armies sacked the capital city at Hanoi three times (in 1257, 1284, and 1287), but on each occasion an army staffed by local peoples regained the city and promised to pay tribute to the Mongols, who then retreated.

When Khubilai Khan died in 1294, a new generation of leaders took over who had grown up in China, spoke and wrote Chinese, and knew little of life on the steppes. The fourth emperor in the Yuan dynasty, Renzong (r. 1312–1321), received the classical Chinese education of a Chinese scholar and reinstated the civil service exams in 1315. Under his direction, the Mongols introduced a new Neo-Confucian examination curriculum testing the candidates' knowledge of Zhu Xi's commentary on *The Four Books* (see Chapter 12). Adopted by subsequent dynasties, this curriculum remained in use until 1905.

After Emperor Renzong's death, the Yuan government entered several decades of decline. The 1330s and 1340s saw outbreaks of disease that caused mass deaths; a single epidemic in 1331 killed one-tenth of the people living in one province. Scholars suspect that these deaths may have been linked to the Black Death that hit Europe in 1348, but they cannot be certain because the Chinese sources do not describe the symptoms of those who died.

Faced with a sharp drop in population and a corresponding decline in revenue, the Yuan dynasty raised taxes, causing a series of peasant rebellions. In 1368, a peasant who had been briefly educated in a monastery led a peasant revolt that succeeded in overthrowing the Yuan dynasty and driving the Mongols back to their homeland, from which they continued to launch attacks on the Chinese. He named his dynasty the Ming, meaning "light" or "bright" (1368–1644).

The Reign of the First Ming Emperor, 1368–1398

The founder of the **Ming dynasty,** Ming Taizu, prided himself on founding a native Chinese dynasty but in fact continued many Mongol practices. In addition to the core areas ruled earlier by the Northern Song dynasty, the Ming realm included Manchuria, Inner Mongolia, Xinjiang in the northwest, and Tibet, which had all been conquered by the Mongols. The Ming also took over the provincial administrative districts established by the Mongols, which still define modern China.

When the Ming founder assumed office, he appointed all new officials and suspended the civil service examinations because he was suspicious of Confucian learning. Later, though, he came to believe that bureaucrats were best able to govern China and in 1381 reinstated the civil service examinations with a Confucian curriculum identical to that of the Mongols. Competition for the exams intensified in succeeding centuries, and the ruling elite remained Confucian because of this decision.

• **Ming dynasty** (1368–1644) Ruling dynasty in China founded by the leader of a peasant rebellion against the Yuan. Its founder prided himself on founding a native Chinese dynasty but in fact continued many of the practices of his Mongol predecessors.

Oddly, the Ming founder, the one emperor in Chinese history who was born a peasant, had a conservative vision of China's society and believed that no one could change his or her social position. Ming officials assigned each household a category of labor such as agriculture, military service, or salt mining and required that each household contribute a fixed number of days of that type of labor annually. In fact, many people paid others to fulfill their labor obligations.

When the Ming founder died in 1398, he hoped that his grandson would succeed him, but one of the emperor's brothers led an army to the capital and set the imperial palace on fire. The unfortunate new emperor, only 21 at the time, probably died in the fire, making it possible for his uncle to name himself the third emperor of the Ming dynasty, or the Yongle emperor (r. 1403–1424).

The Chinese Voyages to South and Southeast Asia and Africa, 1405–1433

Viewed as a usurper his entire life, the Yongle emperor pursued several policies to show that he was the equal of the Ming founder. He ordered all written materials to be copied into a single, enormous set of books called *The Yongle Encyclopedia*. He moved the capital from Nanjing, where many remained sympathetic to the deposed emperor, to Beijing, the former capital of the Mongols. He sent five military expeditions to Mongolia in the hope of vanquishing the Mongols, but none succeeded. The Yongle emperor also launched a series of imperially sponsored voyages to demonstrate the strength of his dynasty to all of China's trading partners.

Chinese geographical knowledge of the world had grown considerably since the maps of the mid-twelfth century (see the maps on page 350). No maps made under the Mongols survive today, but a Korean map copied around 1470, the Kangnido map, was based on earlier maps and includes both the Islamic world and Europe, a vivid illustration of how the Mongol unification of Eurasia led to a dramatic increase in geographic knowledge.

This increase in geographical knowledge prompted the most ambitious voyages in Chinese history, which were led by the admiral named Zheng He (JUHNG huh) (1371–1433). Zheng He's ancestors had moved from Bukhara (Uzbekistan) to southwest China to serve as officials under the Yuan dynasty. Both his father and grandfather went on the hajj pilgrimage to Mecca, and the family was well informed about the geography of the larger Islamic world.

Zheng He was captured at the age of 10, castrated, and forced into the Chinese military, where he rose quickly and eventually put in charge of maritime expeditions to display the power of the Yongle emperor. The Chinese junks of the **Zheng He expeditions** visited Sumatra (SOO-mah-trah), Sri Lanka, and the western Indian ports of Calicut, Cochin, and Quilon (KEE-lahn), and they also crossed the Persian Gulf. The farthest they went was the coast of East Africa, which they visited in 1418, 1421–1422, and 1431–1433. In leading China's navy to India and Africa, Admiral Zheng He was following well-established hajj routes taken by both pilgrims and Muslim merchants. His route to East Africa from China was simply the mirror image of Ibn Battuta's from East Africa to China (see Chapter 11). Although they covered enormous distances, Zheng He's ships never ventured into unknown waters. They were not exploring: their goal was to display the might of the Yongle emperor.

Admiral Zheng He's fleet must have impressed everyone who saw it. Twenty-eight thousand men staffed the full fleet of over three hundred massive wooden

• **Zheng He expeditions** From 1405 to 1433, a fleet of Chinese junks under the leadership of the eunuch admiral Zheng He (1371–1433) traveled on well-established hajj routes from China to Southeast Asia, India, the Islamic world, and East Africa to display the might of the Yongle emperor.

State-of-the-Art Cartography in 1470: The Kangnido Map In 1470, Korean cartographers made this map of Afro-Eurasia. Although the proportions are wrong (Korea is disproportionately large) and India is missing, the map testifies to the wide circulation of information under the Mongols. The three sources of the Nile are exactly the same as those on the map shown in Chapter 9 (see page 261), the Islamic map of al-Idrisi completed in 1182, because the Korean mapmakers copied Africa from an Islamic original. (Ryukoku University Library, Kyoto, Japan)

ships. The biggest Chinese ships—200-foot-long (61-m-long) "treasure ships"— were the largest ships in the world at that time.[4] In 1341, at Calicut, Ibn Battuta had praised Chinese ships for their wooden compartments that offered individual travelers privacy; Zheng He's sailors filled similar compartments with fresh water and stocked them with fish for their dining pleasure.

Although none of the sailors has left an eyewitness account of the East African coast, one of Zheng He's men, Fei Xin (1385–1436?), did record what he had been able "to collect as true facts from the explanations" of others about Africa. Much more detailed than Zhao Rugua's 1225 descriptions of Africa (see Chapter 12) are Fei Xin's descriptions of Mogadishu in modern-day Somalia: "This place lies on the sea-shore. Piles of stones constitute the city-wall. . . . The houses are of layers of stone and four or five storeys high, the places for dwelling, cooking, easing oneself [going to the bathroom], and entertaining guests all being on the upper floors."[5] Fei Xin's informant describes what he saw from onboard ship; the Chinese did not venture inland.

Because Zheng He's ships also engaged in trade, usually giving suits of clothing in exchange for horses, animal skins, gold, and silver, his men were well informed about local trading conditions. The commodities traded at Mogadishu included such things as "gold and silver, colored satins, sandalwood, rice and cereals, porcelain articles, and colored thin silk." Fei Xin's description of the known world ends with a description of Mecca, an indication that his account, although written in Chinese, was modeled on the Islamic genre of rihla travel accounts used by Ibn Jubayr, Ibn Fadlan, and Ibn Battuta to record their journeys (see Chapters 9, 10, and 11), further evidence that the Chinese of the Ming dynasty inherited the shared intellectual traditions of the Mongols.

The Chinese voyagers who participated in the trade did so as members of the imperial navy, not as independent entrepreneurs. When the Ming government suspended the voyages in 1433, the year Admiral Zheng He died, the trips to Africa came to an abrupt halt. Placed in storage, the treasure ships subsequently rotted away. The Ming dynasty shifted its resources from the sea to the north and rebuilt the Great Wall (see Chapter 4) in the hope of keeping the Mongols from invading. (The Great Wall visitors see today is the Ming wall.) The Ming stayed in power until 1644, with its attention fixed firmly on its main foreign enemy, the Mongols to the north.

Chapter Review

KEY TERMS

William of Rubruck (386)

Chinggis Khan (389)

shamans (389)

tanistry (392)

khuriltai (392)

darughachi (394)

postal relay system (396)

Il-khanate (401)

principality of Muscovy (403)

Timur the Lame (403)

Ottomans (405)

Janissaries (406)

Mehmet the Conqueror (406)

Khubilai Khan (410)

Ming dynasty (411)

Zheng He expeditions (412)

CL Download the MP3 audio file of the Chapter Review and listen to it on the go.

In 1253–1254, William of Rubruck traveled through a unified Mongol territory; in 1263, the empire split apart. The rulers of the different successor dynasties, like Chinggis and his descendants, led powerful armies fueled by the desire for plunder; once they conquered a given region, they proved unusually willing to learn from conquered peoples and adopt their technologies. Although their empire was short-lived, the Mongols unified much of Eurasia for the first time. They were able to conquer so much territory because their cavalry was more powerful than that of the various sedentary peoples they defeated. After 1400, the development of new weapons powered by gunpowder, particularly cannon and small firearms, shifted the military advantage away from nomadic peoples decisively in favor of sedentary societies. As we will see in the next chapter, the Europeans who landed in the Americas in the 1490s used the same gunpowder weapons with far-reaching consequences.

 How did the Mongols' nomadic way of life contribute to their success as conquerors?

Before 1200, the Mongols moved within the region of modern Mongolia with their flocks in search of fresh grass. After Chinggis unified them in 1206, their mobility allowed them to conquer much of Eurasia. The Mongols' skillful use of terror prompted many people to surrender rather than fight, enabling the Mongols to conquer vast amounts of territory rapidly.

What bound the different sectors of the Mongol Empire together? What caused its breakup in the 1260s?

Even when the Mongol Empire was at its strongest, during the first fifty years of its existence, only the postal relay system and the system of hosting envoys held it together. After the third Mongol ruler Möngke died in 1259, the traditional method for selecting a new ruler, tanistry, did not work because two rival candidates each held their own khuriltai and the empire broke into western and eastern halves. In 1263, the alliance between the Qipchaq khanate in Russia and the Mamluks of Egypt against the Il-khanate of Iran provides a clear date for the end of the unified Mongol Empire.

What states succeeded the Qipchaq and Chaghatai khanates?

In the western half, all the Mongol rulers eventually converted to Islam. Ivan III's principality of Moscow emerged as the strongest power in Russia after the breakup of the Qipchaq khanate, and Timur the Lame succeeded the Chaghatai khanate.

What military innovations marked Ottoman expansion, and what cultural developments typified Ottoman rule?

Although the Ottomans were a nomadic people whose army initially resembled that of the Mongols, they shifted to a more stable army of Janissaries. The Ottomans took advantage of the new gunpowder weapons, particularly cannon, when they attacked and conquered Constantinople in 1453. After taking the city, the Ottoman rulers commissioned scholars to copy the ancient Greek classics, to write epic poetry in Italian, and to produce scholarly works in other languages.

What was the legacy of Mongol rule in East and Southeast Asia?

The legacy of the Mongols was most visible in Ming dynasty China, whose borders overlapped with those of the Yuan dynasty. The Ming founder implemented the Neo-Confucian examination curriculum of the Mongols. Although the Mongols ruled Korea only briefly and never conquered either Japan or Vietnam, all peoples in East Asia knew more about Eurasia than they had before the Mongol conquests. The Kangnido map of the world and the Zheng He voyages vividly illustrate this increase in knowledge.

For Further Reference

Allsen, Thomas T. *Mongol Imperialism: The Politics of the Grand Qan Möngke in China, Russia, and the Islamic Lands, 1251–1259.* Berkeley: University of California Press, 1987.

Dawson, Christopher, ed. *The Mongol Mission: Narratives and Letters of the Franciscan Missionaries in Mongolia and China in the Thirteenth and Fourteenth Centuries.* New York: Sheed and Ward, 1955.

De Rachewiltz, Igor. *Papal Envoys to the Great Khans.* London: Faber and Faber, 1971.

Finlay, Robert. "How Not to (Re)Write World History: Gavin Menzies and the Chinese Discovery of America." *Journal of World History* 15, no. 2 (2004): 225–241.

Fletcher, Joseph. "The Mongols: Ecological and Social Perspectives." *Harvard Journal of Asiatic Studies* 46, no. 1 (1986): 1–56.

Hodgson, Marshall G. S. *The Venture of Islam: Conscience and History in a World Civilization,* vol. 2, *The Expansion of Islam in the Middle Periods.* Chicago: University of Chicago Press, 1974.

Inalcik, Halil. *The Ottoman Empire: The Classical Age, 1300–1600.* Translated by Norman Itzkowitz and Colin Imber. London: Weidenfeld and Nicolson, 1973.

Jackson, Peter, trans. *The Mission of Friar William of Rubruck: His Journey to the Court of the Great Khan Möngke 1253–1255.* London: The Hakluyt Society, 1990.

Kennedy, Hugh. *Mongols, Huns and Vikings.* London: Cassell, 2002.

Latham, Ronald, trans. *The Travels of Marco Polo.* New York: Penguin Books, 1958.

Morgan, David. *The Mongols.* 2d ed. New York: Blackwell, 2007.

Wood, Frances. *Did Marco Polo Go to China?* London: Secker and Warburg, 1995.

 WEB RESOURCES

Pronunciation Guide

Interactive Maps

MAP 14.1 The Four Quadrants of the Mongol Empire After 1263

Primary Sources

Chapter Objectives

ACE Multiple-Choice Quiz

Flashcards

Websites

The Mongols in World History (http://afe.easia.columbia.edu/mongols/).   This website provides general information on the Mongols.

Popular History and Bunkum (http://maritimeasia.ws/topic/1421bunkum.html). A detailed critique of the evidence that allegedly shows that Zheng He visited the Americas.

Silk Road Narratives: A Collection of Historical Texts (http://depts.washington.edu/silkroad/texts/texts. html).   A valuable collection of primary sources, including Rubruck's, with helpful introductions.

Film

Mongol, a commercial movie epic released in 2008 about Chinggis Khan's rise to power, departs from *The Origin of Chinggis Khan* in many places but still gives a vivid sense of Mongol society in the early 1200s.

Maritime Expansion in the Atlantic World, 1400–1600

With two of his ships separated from the third in a storm and uncertain that he would make it back to Spain, **Christopher Columbus** (1451–1506) summarized his journey and then wrapped the parchment document in cloth, sealed it with wax, and dropped it overboard in a wine casket. He survived the storm and returned to Spain, where he presented a long letter describing his first voyage to his backers Queen Isabella (1451–1504) and King Ferdinand (1452–1516) of Spain. Columbus's voyage connected Europe with the Americas in a way that no previous contact had; the resulting exchange of plants, animals, people, and disease shaped the modern world. In his letter describing the people he encountered in the Caribbean, he voices the twin motivations of the Spanish and the Portuguese: in search of gold, they also hoped to convert the indigenous peoples to Christianity.

CHRISTOPHER COLUMBUS

(The Metropolitan Museum of Art, New York. Image copyright © The Metropolitan Museum of Art/Art Resource, NY)

Hispaniola is a wonder. The mountains and hills, the plains and the meadow lands are both fertile and beautiful. They are most suitable for planting crops and for raising cattle of all kinds, and there are good sites for building towns and villages. The harbors are incredibly fine and there are many great rivers with broad channels and the majority contain gold. . . .

The inhabitants of this island, and all the rest that I discovered or heard of, go naked, as their mothers bore them, men and women alike. A few of the women, however, cover a single place with a leaf of a plant or piece of cotton which they weave for the purpose. They have no iron or steel or arms and are not capable of

CL This icon will direct you to interactive activities and study materials on the *Voyages* website: **www.cengage.com/history/hansen/voyages1e**

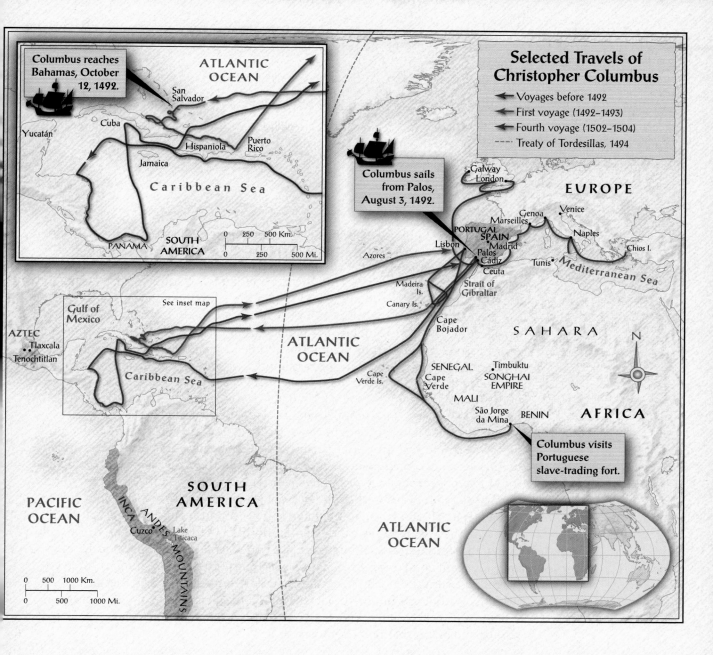

Selected Travels of Christopher Columbus

← Voyages before 1492
← First voyage (1492–1493)
← Fourth voyage (1502–1504)
--- Treaty of Tordesillas, 1494

Columbus reaches Bahamas, October 12, 1492.

Columbus sails from Palos, August 3, 1492.

Columbus visits Portuguese slave-trading fort.

ATLANTIC OCEAN

San Salvador

Yucatán

Cuba

Hispaniola

Puerto Rico

Jamaica

Caribbean Sea

PANAMA

SOUTH AMERICA

| 0 | 250 | 500 Km. |
| 0 | 250 | 500 Mi. |

Galway
London
EUROPE

Genoa
Venice
Marseilles
Naples
PORTUGAL
SPAIN
Lisbon
Madrid
Palos
Cádiz
Ceuta
Chios I.
Tunis
Mediterranean Sea

Azores

Madeira Is.

Canary Is.

Strait of Gibraltar

Cape Bojador

SAHARA

SENEGAL
Cape Verde
Timbuktu
SONGHAI EMPIRE

Cape Verde Is.

MALI

São Jorge da Mina
BENIN
AFRICA

N

Gulf of Mexico

See inset map

AZTEC
Tlaxcala
Tenochtitlan

Caribbean Sea

ATLANTIC OCEAN

PACIFIC OCEAN

SOUTH AMERICA

Inca
Cuzco
Lake Titicaca
ANDES MOUNTAINS

ATLANTIC OCEAN

| 0 | 500 | 1000 Km. |
| 0 | 500 | 1000 Mi. |

	1300	1350	1400	1450	1500	1550	1600
				Lifetime of Christopher Columbus 1451 1506			
MEXICO AND CARIBBEAN		Aztec settle Tenochtitlan 1325	Triple Alliance Aztec Empire 1428		Viceroyalty of New Spain 1521		
SOUTH AMERICA			Inca settle Cuzco 1400	Inca Empire 1438	1532 Viceroyalty of Peru 1543		
				Cabral reaches Brazil 1500	Portuguese organize settlement of Brazil 1533		
CONQUEST AND EXCHANGE		Portugal settles Azores 1350	Portugal begins Atlantic slave trade 1444	Columbus reaches Hispaniola 1492	Conquest of Aztec 1519–1521	Conquest of Inca 1532 1550	
				Gutenberg Bible printed 1454	Columbus brings European plants and animals to America 1493	First smallpox in America 1518	

using them, not because they are not strong and well built but because they are amazingly timid. . . .

I gave them a thousand pretty things that I had brought, in order to gain their love and incline them to become Christians.[1]

● **Christopher Columbus** (1451–1506) Visited European colonies in the Mediterranean, the Atlantic Ocean, and the west coast of Africa before voyaging to the island of Hispaniola in 1492. Made three subsequent voyages before being removed as viceroy in 1499.

At the time of his first voyage to the Americas, Columbus was in his early 40s. Born in Genoa, Italy, as a teenager he had sailed on wooden boats to the different settlements of Genoese and Venetian merchants in the Mediterranean. Later, in his 30s, he lived for three years in the Madeira Islands, a Portuguese possession off the African coast in the Atlantic, and visited the Portuguese slave-trading fort at Sao Jorge da Mina on the west coast of Africa. Madeira, the world's largest sugar producer in 1492, hired indigenous peoples from the nearby Canary Islands and African slaves to work on its plantations. While in the Canary Islands, Columbus heard that one could sail west, and, assuming he could reach Asia by doing so, he persuaded the rulers of Spain to finance a trial voyage across the Atlantic in search of the Indies, the source of so many valuable spices. After the first voyage in 1492, he made three more trips to the Americas before his death in 1506.

Unlike the Viking voyages to Newfoundland (see Chapter 10) and unlike the Ming voyages to East Africa (see Chapter 14), the Spanish and Portuguese voyages had far-reaching consequences. After 1300, while the Aztec in Mexico and the Inca in Peru were creating powerful expansionist empires, on the opposite side of the Atlantic Europeans were learning about geography as part of their humanistic studies. Spanish and Portuguese explorers traveled farther and farther, first to the islands of the Mediterranean and the Atlantic, then to the west coast of Africa, and finally to the Americas, claiming each place they landed as colonies for the monarchs of Spain and Portugal. The Europeans transported plants, animals, and people (often against their will) to entirely new environments on the other side of the Atlantic. Within one hundred years of Columbus's first voyage, millions of Amerindians (the death toll reached 95 percent in some areas) had perished, victims of European diseases that no one understood.

Focus Questions

 How did the Aztec form their empire? How did the Inca form theirs? How did each hold their empire together, and what was each empire's major weakness?

 How did humanist scholarship encourage oceanic exploration? What motivated the Portuguese, particularly Prince Henry the Navigator, to explore West Africa?

How did the Spanish and the Portuguese establish their empires in the Americas so quickly?

 What was the Columbian exchange? Which elements of the exchange had the greatest impact on the Americas? On Afro-Eurasia?

●The Aztec Empire of Mexico, 1325–1519

Starting sometime around 1325, the Aztec, a people based in western Mexico, moved into central Mexico to Tenochtitlan (some 30 miles, or 50 km, northeast of modern-day Mexico City), a site near the ancient city of Teotihuacan (see Chapter 5). The Aztec were one of many Nahua (NAH-wah) peoples who spoke the Nahuatl (NAH-waht) language. Like the Maya, the Nahua peoples had a complex calendrical system combining both lunar and solar calculations, built large stone monuments, and played a ritual ball game. The Aztec believed in a pantheon of gods headed by the sun that demanded blood sacrifices from their devotees. To sustain these gods, they continually went to war, gradually conquering many of the city-states in central Mexico to form the **Aztec Empire.**

The Aztec Settlement of Tenochtitlan

The Toltec, the most powerful successors to the Maya, collapsed in the 1200s (see Chapter 5). Though each people tells the story of its past differently, disparate accounts agree that around this time various groups migrated to central Mexico. The heart of this area is the Valley of Mexico, 10,000 feet (3,000 m) above sea level and surrounded by volcanoes. The Valley of Mexico contains many shallow lakes and much fertile land.

The first Nahua groups to arrive obtained the best land in the Valley of Mexico. Those who came twenty years later settled nearby, and the final group, who claimed their homeland was in a place called Aztlan, literally "heron-land," arrived last. It is not clear whether Aztlan was a genuine or a legendary place, but linguistic analysis of the Nahuatl language indicates that its speakers originated somewhere in the southwest United States or northern Mexico. *Aztlan* is the origin of the modern word *Aztec,* a term that no one at the time used but that this text will use despite its imperfections. The Aztlan migrants referred to themselves as "Mexica" (meh-SHE-kah), the origin of the word *Mexico.*

By the 1300s, some fifty city-states, called **altepetl,** occupied central Mexico, each with its own leader, or "speaker," and its own government. Each altepetl had a palace for its ruler, a pyramid-shaped temple, and a market. The Aztec migrated to the region around the historic urban center of Teotihuacan, a large city with many lakes. Since this region was already home to several rival altepetl, the Aztec were forced to settle in a swampland called **Tenochtitlan** (teh-noch-TIT-lan).

Traditional accounts say the Aztec people arrived at Tenochtitlan in 1325, a date confirmed by archaeological excavation. The Aztec gradually reclaimed large areas of the swamps and on the drier, more stable areas erected stone buildings

● **Aztec Empire** An empire based in Tenochtitlan (modern-day Mexico City). Founded in 1325, the dynasty formed the Triple Alliance and began to expand its territory in 1428. At its peak it included 450 separate altepetl city-states in modern-day Mexico and Guatemala and ruled over a population of four to six million.

● **altepetl** The 450 city-states of the Aztec Empire. Each altepetl had its own leader, or "speaker," its own government, a palace for its ruler, a pyramid-shaped temple, and a market.

● **Tenochtitlan** Capital city of the Aztec, which they reclaimed from swampland. Housed a population of some 200,000 people.

MAP 15.1
The Aztec Empire
Starting from their capital at Tenochtitlan (modern Mexico City), the Aztec conquered different neighboring peoples living between the Gulf of Mexico and the Pacific Ocean. Aztec rulers required the conquered peoples to pay taxes and submit tribute but gave few benefits in return. When Cortés landed on the coast of Mexico, he quickly found allies among the conquered peoples, particularly the Tlaxcalans.

(CL) Interactive Map

held together with mortar. They planted flowers everywhere and walked on planks or traveled by canoe from one reclaimed area to another.

At its height, Tenochtitlan contained 60,000 dwellings, home to perhaps 200,000 people in an area of 5 square miles (13 sq km). The central marketplace offered cooked and uncooked food, slaves, tobacco products, and luxury goods made from gold, silver, and feathers. Consumers used cotton cloaks, cacao beans, and feather quills filled with gold dust as media of exchange, since the Aztec had no coins.

Nahua Religion and Writing System

The most important Nahua deity, the sun, controlled agriculture, and crops—primarily corn, beans, and peppers—were the main source of food. Engaged in a constant struggle with the forces of dark, the sun needed regular offerings of "precious water," the Nahuatl term for human blood. Ranking just under the sun-god were the gods of rain and agriculture. In addition, each altepetl had several deities associated with its native place. The Aztec believed that their patron god was Huitzilopochtli (wheat-zeel-oh-POSHT-lee), the hummingbird of the south, whom they worshiped along with the god of rain, Tlaloc. A third important god was Quetzalcoatl (kate-zahl-CO-ah-tal), a creator god who was credited with devising the Nahuatl writing system.

The Nahua wrote on bark paper or deerskin covered with a thin white layer of limestone plaster. Their writing system functioned quite differently from Mayan. Nahuatl texts combine pictures with rebus writing, which uses images to represent something with the same sound; in English, for example, a picture of an eye functions as a rebus for the word *I*.

The Nahua writing system served as a trigger to memory; people who had been trained to tell a certain story could look at a Nahua manuscript and be reminded of the details. But if one did not know the original story beforehand, it was impossible to make it out.

Nahua Society

The Nahua peoples treated certain human beings like gods. The leader of the Aztec, their Great Speaker, was carried in a feathered chair. His advisers never looked at the Great Speaker or addressed him directly: a screen always separated them from him. The Great Speaker was in charge of all external matters, including war, the receipt of gifts, and relations with other altepetl. A group of nobles, priests, and successful warriors chose the new Great Speaker, and although they treated him as their ritual superior, they could depose him if they did not approve of his rule.

The second-highest leader, a man called the Female Snake, took charge of all internal affairs. Usually a close relative of the Great Speaker, he consulted with him frequently. All the top officials came from the royal family and had large private estates.

Most of the Nahuas were commoners, each of whom belonged to a "big house," a group who believed they were descended from a common ancestor. The Aztec capital contained some twenty big-house groups, and more lived in other regions. They had their own lands, and some had schools for warriors. The lowest-ranking people in Nahua society were slaves, often the original residents of the Valley of Mexico.

Ordinary people and slaves farmed the land and generated the surplus that underpinned the expansion of the Aztec altepetl. The Nahua prepared the soil and planted seeds by hand, often planting bean and pepper seeds in the same hole as corn seeds. Because they had no draft animals, metal tools, or wheels, everything had to be carried and cultivated by hand.

Corn ripened in only fifty days, providing sufficient food for a family as well as a surplus. Grinding corn was exclusively women's work; for fear that they might antagonize the gods, men were forbidden to help. Ordinary people were required to pay tribute to their Aztec overlords by contributing a share of the crop, performing labor service for a certain time, paying other goods, and most onerous of all, providing victims for human sacrifice.

The Military and the Conquests of the Aztec

If successful in battle, warriors could rise in Aztec society to a high position. They then received lands of their own and were not required to pay taxes on them. Conversely, the best human sacrifice one could offer to the gods, the Nahua believed, was a warrior taken captive in battle. In their system of thirteen heavens and eight underworlds, the highest heaven, the Paradise of the Sun God, was for men who had killed the enemy in battle and for women who had died in childbirth, a type of battle in its own right.

The Aztec troops fitted their clubs, spears, and darts with blades made from obsidian, a volcanic glass that was sharp and easy to work but dulled easily. They protected themselves with thick cotton armor. The Aztec also hired as mercenaries mountain peoples who used bows and arrows. Hand-to-hand combat was considered the most honorable form of warfare.

In 1428, the Aztec formed the Triple Alliance with two other peoples and launched a series of conquests that led to the creation of an empire. By 1500, they had conquered 450 altepetl in modern Mexico, extending all the way to Guatemala, and ruled over a subject population estimated between four and six million who lived in an area of 8,000 square miles (20,810 sq km).[2]

The Aztec conquered other peoples not simply to gain the wealth of subject peoples but also to feed their own deities. Conducting mass sacrifices at their temples, the Aztec killed tens of thousands of victims at a time and displayed their skulls on racks for all to see.

The Aztec empire, though large and with a beautiful capital, had one major weakness. Once the Aztec conquered a given people, they demanded tribute and took sacrificial victims from them, yet they did nothing to incorporate them further into their empire.

⬤The Inca Empire, 1400–1532

• Inca Empire
Founded in 1438 by Pachakuti (d. 1471), who launched a series of conquests outward from the capital at Cuzco. At its peak, the empire ruled over a population of ten to twelve million.

The **Inca Empire,** 2,500 miles (4,000 km) to the south in the highlands of the Andes, was structured differently. Each time the Inca conquered a new group, they integrated them into the empire, requiring them to perform labor and military service and resettling some groups to minimize the chances of revolt. Like the Aztec, the Inca worshiped deities that demanded human sacrifices, but never as many as in Mexico. Although the Inca successfully integrated subject peoples into their empire, they did not have an orderly system of succession. Each time their ruler died, everyone who hoped to succeed him plunged into full-time conflict until a new leader emerged victorious.

Inca Religion and Andean Society

The ordinary people of the Andes lived in kin groups called **ayllu** (aye-YOU) that worked the land in several adjacent ecological zones so they could maximize their yield should the crops in one zone fail. (See the feature "World History in Today's World: Miss Bolivia Speaks Out.") Most ayllu were divided into smaller subgroups, and men tended to marry women from another subgroup. All the people in a given ayllu recognized one person as a common ancestor. Ordinary people believed that, in addition to their ancestors, hundreds of spirits (*wak'a*) inhabited places in the landscape such as streams, caves, rocks, and hills.

> **ayllu** Andean kin groups of the Inca Empire that worked the land in several adjacent ecological zones so they could maximize their yield should the crops in one zone fail.

The Inca believed that some deities ranked far above these local spirits. The most important deities were the Creator (Wiraqocha), the Creator's child the Sun (Inti), and the Thunder (Inti-Illapa) gods.

By 1500, the sun-god had become the most important deity, probably because the Inca ruler, the Sapa Inca, or "Unique Inca," claimed descent from him. The priest of the sun-god was the highest-ranking priest in Inca society and the second most powerful person in the Inca Empire.

Both the Sapa Inca and the sun-god priest belonged to the aristocracy, which was divided into three tiers: the close relatives of the ruler and previous rulers, more distant relatives, and then the leaders of the groups who had been conquered by the Inca. Although most Inca traced their ancestry through their father's line, the ruler's mother's family played a central role in court politics because the ruler took his wives from his mother's family.

The Inca had no orderly system of succession. Each time the Inca ruler died, all contestants for the position from among his male kin launched an all-out war until a single man emerged victorious, much like the system of tanistry prevalent among the Mongols (see Chapter 14). The new ruler was then installed in an elaborate coronation honoring the sun-god. During his reign the Sapa Inca lived as a deity among his subjects, eating special foods and wearing unusual clothing. Even so, he had to keep the support of the aristocracy, who could easily overthrow him at any time.

Like the ayllu ancestors, the ruler was believed to continue to live even after death. The Inca mummified the bodies of deceased rulers and other high-ranking family members and then placed the mummies in houses around the main square of Cuzco, their capital city high in the Andes at an elevation of 11,300 feet (3,450 m). One Spanish observer described their interaction with these mummies:

> Most of the people of Cuzco served the dead, I have heard it said, who they daily brought out to the main square, setting them down in a ring, each one according to his age, and there the male and female attendants ate and drank. . . . The mummies toasted each other and the living, and the living toasted the dead.[3]

He did not explain how the living communicated with the dead, but it seems likely that priests intervened.

The Inca organized the worship of all the local spirits, ancestors of the rulers, and deities into a complex ritual calendar specifying which one was to be worshiped on a given day. Of 332 shrines in Cuzco, 31 received human sacrifices. These usually occurred in times of hardship, like an epidemic, or during unusual astronomical events like eclipses. In many cases, believers sacrificed a young boy and a young girl, a symbolic married couple, in the hope of pleasing the god involved and ending the suffering. Occasionally larger sacrifices occurred, such as when a ruler died, but the largest number of sacrificial victims killed at a single time was four thousand (as opposed to eighty thousand for the Aztec).

Miss Bolivia Speaks Out

Not all Bolivians are "poor people and very short people and Indian people," Miss Bolivia in the 2004 Miss Universe contest explained. "I'm from the other side of the country, from the east, where it's not cold. It's very hot, and we're tall, and we are white and can speak English."

Controversy immediately erupted because Gabriela Oviedo had dared to say out loud what many people only think. The divisions between the indigenous peoples and the descendents of Europeans run deep throughout Latin America, and nowhere deeper than in Bolivia, where fully 62 percent of the population of 8.8 million is Amerindian, members of thirty-six different groups.

Many of the indigenous peoples of Bolivia live on less than two dollars a day and have no electricity or gas in their homes. Bolivia's average national income is the lowest in Latin America, even though the country has both natural gas and oil reserves. Miss Bolivia lives in the city of Santa Cruz, whose prosperity is fueled by the export of large natural gas reserves, and many of her fellow citizens support further economic globalization, while most Amerindian groups remain vehemently opposed.

In December 2005, Evo Morales became the first Amerindian to be elected president of a Latin American nation since the mid-1800s. Before being elected, Morales raised the coca plant (from which cocaine is processed), played the trumpet, laid bricks, and worked as a union organizer. He staunchly defends the right of Bolivia's farmers to raise coca, which he maintains is a "sacred leaf" to the indigenous peoples of Bolivia.

Some indigenous leaders advocate nationalization of the natural gas industry and urge the government to buy out the foreign exporters. Threatening to secede, they propose forming a new Inca nation composed of the indigenous peoples who live in western Bolivia and the indigenous Aymara-speaking peoples of Peru and Chile. In this new Inca state, they suggest, all decisions would be made by councils called ayllus, a term drawn from the Inca Empire. Though illegal, discrimination against Amerindians persists; Bolivia's indigenous peoples gained the right to vote and to attend school only in 1952.

The Inca Expansion   As the Aztec believed their history began with their occupation of Tenochtitlan, the Incas traced their beginnings to their settlement in Cuzco. Archaeological evidence suggests that the Inca moved to Cuzco sometime around 1400. Although oral accounts conflict, most accept the date of 1438 as the year Pachakuti (patch-ah-KOO-tee) (d. 1471), the first great Inca ruler, seized the throne from his brother in a coup and launched the military campaigns outward from Cuzco. The Inca conquered neighboring lands because they desired the goods produced in each ecological zone: the herds of llamas and alpaca, crops like grain and potatoes, and the gold, feathers, shells, and minerals from the jungle lowlands and the shore.

Much of Inca warfare consisted of storming enemy forts with a large infantry, often after cutting off access to food and water. For several days enemy forces traded insults and sang hostile songs such as this: "We will drink from the skull of the traitor, we will adorn ourselves with a necklace of his teeth, we play the melody of the pinkullu [a musical instrument resembling a flute] with flutes made from his bones, we will beat the drum made from his skin, and thus we will dance." Attackers in quilted cotton launched arrows, stones from slingshots, and stone spears,

🌐 MAP 15.2

The Inca Empire   In 1438, the Inca ruler Pachakuti took power in the capital at Cuzco and led his armies to conquer large chunks of territory along the Andes Mountains. Two north-south trunk routes, with subsidiary east-west routes, formed a system of over 25,000 miles (40,000 km) of roads. By 1532, the Inca ruled ten to twelve million people in an empire of 1,500 square miles (4,000 sq km).

and in hand-to-hand combat used spears and clubs, some topped with stone or with bronze stars.

Like other Andean peoples (see Chapter 5), the Inca knew how to extract metallic ore from rocks and how to heat different metals to form alloys. They made bronze by combining copper with tin, as did most other Bronze Age peoples, and by combining copper with arsenic. But the Inca did not develop their metallurgical expertise beyond making club heads, decorative masks, and ear spools for the nobility.

At its height, the Inca army could field as many as 100,000 men in a single battle, most of the rank-and-file drawn from subject peoples who were required to serve in the army. Although soldiers fought only seasonally and returned home at harvesttime, the rate of Inca expansion was breathtaking. Starting from a single location, Cuzco, the Inca conquered large chunks of southern, central, and coastal Peru, Equador, the eastern lowlands of Peru and Bolivia, and the mountains of Argentina and Chile (see Map 15.2). By 1532, they ruled over an area of 1,500 square miles (4,000 sq km) with a population estimated at ten to twelve million inhabitants.

CL Interactive Map

| **Inca Rule of Subject Populations** | Unique among the Andean peoples, the Inca incorporated each conquered land and its occupants into their kingdom. They resettled thousands of people, forcing them to move to regions far from their original homes. The Inca also brought many images of subjects' ancestral deities to Cuzco, holding the images hostage so that their devotees would not rise up against their Inca overlords. |

The Inca, like the Mongols, encouraged different peoples to submit to them by treating those who surrendered gently. They allowed local leaders to continue to serve but required everyone to swear loyalty to the Inca ruler, to grant him all rights to their lands, and to perform labor service as the Inca state required.

Inca officials also delegated power to indigenous leaders. Those of high birth could serve in the Inca government as long as they learned Quechua (keh-chew-ah), the language of the Inca. Each official was in charge of a certain number of households: top officials supervised ten thousand households, while the lowest functionaries watched over ten. Inca officials registered the population in a census and

THE TEN STAGES OF INCA LIFE ACCORDING TO GUAMÁN POMA

In 1613, Felipe Guamán Poma de Ayala (FAY-leep gua-MAHN POH-mah duh AIE-ah-lah) wrote an illustrated letter of over one thousand pages to the king of Spain. The Spaniards, he charged, had violated Christian teachings (he himself was a convert), and he asked the Spanish king to return the former Inca Empire to local leaders. The child of a Spanish father and an Inca mother, he used the two languages of Spanish and Quechua. One part of his letter, which was discovered and published only in the 1900s, describes the Inca labor system. Since Inca officials were most concerned with an individual's ability to perform labor service, they placed those best able to work, the middle-aged, in the highest

This woman is too old to work. The writing above her head says "blind people," "lame," "dumb," and "always sick."

The fifth girl represents the category of "very beautiful girls of marriageable age" and is standing up, bigger than any of the other women or girls.

(Royal Library Copenhagen)

This infant girl represents the tenth road. The Inca did not name their children before they reached the age of 2, since too many died before that age.

428

categories. Those less able to work, the elderly, came next, with young children and infants ranking last. Guamán Poma diagrammed the ten stages, or "roads," of life for both men and women; each drawing has a title at the top, and some have additional captions as well.

The ten "roads" for women begin with a middle-aged woman at the peak of her productivity who is weaving, and this is followed by three frames showing successively older women. Then the order shifts to a young girl, with the final five frames showing younger and younger girls. The men's roads follow roughly the same order, starting in middle age, followed by old age, and then progressing from adolescence to newborns.

Guamán Poma's drawings allot equal space for men and women and depict them as the same size, suggesting that the labor they contributed was equally important to the Inca state.

In the first stage for men, a proud warrior stands up straight, his weapon in his left hand and the head of his captive in the right.

The boy of 18 or 20 in the fifth box is poised to carry a message, possibly a quipu set of tied ropes.

(Royal Library Copenhagen)

QUESTIONS FOR ANALYSIS

What do Guamán Poma's illustrations indicate about Inca conceptions of gender?

How did men and women contribute to the labor service system?

• **quipu** Inca system of record keeping that used knots on strings to record the population in a census and divide people into groups of 10, 50, 100, 500, 1,000, 5,000, and 10,000.

(CL) **Primary Source:**
Chronicles
Learn how the Incas used the mysterious knotted ropes called quipu as record-keeping devices that helped them govern a vast and prosperous empire.

assigned each person to groups of 10, 50, 100, 500, 1,000, 5,000, and 10,000. Each year they recorded the number of people in each group not with a written script but by using a system of knotted strings, called **quipu** (key-POOH). Each town had a knot keeper who maintained and interpreted the knot records, which were updated annually to record changes in the population.

To fulfill the Inca's main service tax, male household heads between 25 and 50 had to perform two to three months' labor each year. Once assigned a task, a man could get as much help as he liked from his children or wife, a practice that favored families with many children (See the feature "Visual Evidence: The Ten Stages of Inca Life According to Guamán Poma.")

The Inca did not treat all subject peoples alike. From some resettled peoples they exacted months of labor, and many subject groups who possessed a specific artistic skill, such as carving stones or making spears, performed that skill for the state. Others did far less. For example, many Inca looked down on a people they called Uru, literally meaning "worm," who lived on the southern edge of Lake Titicaca. The Uru were supposed to catch fish, gather grasses, and weave textiles, but they performed no other labor service. An even more despised group was required each year to submit a single basket filled with lice, not because the Inca wanted the lice, but because they hoped to teach this group the nature of their tax obligations.

Each household also contributed certain goods, such as blankets, textiles, and tools, that were kept in thousands of storehouses throughout the empire. One Spaniard described a storehouse in Cuzco that particularly impressed him: "There is a house in which are kept more than 100,000 dried birds, for from their feathers articles of clothing are made." This system functioned so well that the corn and potatoes in the storehouses could support an army for months.

One lasting product of the Inca labor system was their magnificent highways, which included over 25,000 miles (40,000 km) of roads (see Map 15.2). While some of these routes predated the Inca conquest, the Inca linked them together into an overall system with two main trunk roads running north-south that were linked by twenty different

■ **Keeping Records with Knots** The Inca kept all their records by using knotted strings, called quipu, attaching subsidiary cords, sometimes in several tiers, to a main cord. Different types of knots represented different numeric units; skipped knots indicated a zero; the color of the string indicated the item being counted. (The Granger Collection) east-west routes. Since the Inca did not have the wheel, most of the traffic was by foot, and llamas could carry small loads only short distances each day. With no surveying instruments, the Inca constructed these roads across deserts, yawning chasms, and mountains over 16,000 feet (5,000 m) high. Individual messengers working in shifts could move at an estimated rate of 150 miles (240 km) per day, but troops moved much more slowly, covering perhaps 7 to 9 miles (12–15 km) per day.

Despite its extent, the Inca Empire appeared stronger than it was. Many of the subject peoples resented their heavy labor obligations, and each time an Inca ruler died, the ensuing succession disputes threatened to tear the empire apart.

◉ Intellectual and Geographic Exploration in Europe, 1300–1500

Between 1300 and 1500, as the Aztec and Inca were expanding their empires overland in the Americas, Portuguese and Spanish ships colonized lands farther and farther away, ultimately reaching the Americas. In the years after the Black Death (see Chapter 13), European scholars extended their fields of study to include many new topics. They found that the traditional Greek and Latin sources they revered often contradicted each other, and they struggled to make sense of these differences. Meanwhile, new printing technology made books more available and affordable, enabling people like Christopher Columbus to read and compare many different books.

During the same period, European navigators between 1350 and 1492 began to venture into previously unexplored waters and sailed past the Strait of Gibraltar into the Atlantic. Portuguese and Spanish voyagers founded colonies on the Canary Islands, which were inhabited by an indigenous Stone Age people, and on the uninhabited Madeira Islands. Columbus's own trips to the Americas extended the expeditions of earlier explorers.

The Rise of Humanism

Since the founding of universities in Europe around 1200 (see Chapter 13), students had read Greek and Latin texts and the Bible. Instructors like Peter Abelard used scholastic approaches to study the authors of the past. The main goal of instruction was to reconcile the many differences among ancient authorities to form a logical system of thought.

Around 1350, a group of Italian scholars opposed to scholasticism pioneered a new intellectual movement called **humanism.** Humanists claimed expertise in the humanities, a broad field of study including the traditional liberal arts (see Chapter 13) as well as newer subjects like language, history, literature, and philosophy. The humanists studied many of the same texts that the scholastics had, but they tried to impart a more general understanding of them to their students in the hope that students would improve morally and be able to help others do the same.

One of the earliest humanist writers was the Italian poet Petrarch (1304–1374). Scholasticism was misguided, Petrarch felt, because it was too abstract. It did not

> ● **humanism** Intellectual movement begun around 1350 in Italy by scholars who opposed scholasticism. Humanists claimed expertise in the humanities, which included traditional liberal arts as well as fields of study like language, history, literature, and philosophy.

teach people how to live and how to obtain salvation. Petrarch searched for previously unknown Latin texts that could serve as literary models and also as moral treatises. Although he composed much poetry in Latin, he is remembered for the poetry he composed in Italian, one of several European vernacular languages that came into written use in the fourteenth and fifteenth centuries.

The ideals of humanism do not lend themselves to easy summary. In 1487, a Venetian woman named Cassandra Fedele (fay-DAY-lay) (1465–1558) addressed the students and faculty of the University of Padua in a public oration that set out her own understanding of humanism. Having studied Greek and Latin with a tutor, Fedele urged her audience to devote themselves to studying Cicero, Plato, and Aristotle because, she maintained, while wealth and physical strength cannot last, "those things which are produced by virtue and intelligence are useful to those who follow." She continued: "And how much more humane, praiseworthy and noble do those states and princes become who support and cultivate these studies! Certainly for this reason this part of philosophy has laid claim for itself to the name of 'humanity,' since those who are rough by nature become by these studies more civil and mild-mannered." She eloquently expressed the major tenet of humanism: studying the humanities made students, whether from noble or low-born families, more refined and better people.[4]

■ **The Art of Humanism** In 1487, the scientist, artist, and engineer Leonardo da Vinci portrayed man, not God, as the center of the universe. Above and below the ink drawing, the left-handed Da Vinci wrote notes in mirror writing to explain that his drawing illustrated a text about proportions by the Roman architect Vitruvius (ca. 75–ca. 15 B.C.E.). Unlike earlier artists, da Vinci personally dissected corpses so that he could portray the structure of human muscles as accurately as possible. (Accademia, Venice, Italy/Cameraphoto/Art Resource, NY)

Rather than treat Latin translations as flawless, the humanists checked them against texts in the original languages, including the Greek of the Bible. When they did, they found that many of the most difficult-to-understand passages were corrupted by translation errors. One product of humanist scholarship was multilingual editions of the Bible that printed the Latin, Greek, Hebrew, and Aramaic texts on the same page so that scholars could compare them.

Historians call this period of humanist revival the Renaissance, which means "rebirth," to contrast it with the earlier centuries, but many continuities linked the intellectual advances of the twelfth and thirteenth centuries with those of the humanist era.

Europe's First Books Printed with Movable Type

The introduction of printing in Europe contributed greatly to the humanist movement because movable type made books cheaper, enabling scholars to more easily compare different versions of the same text. Johannes Gutenberg (ca. 1400–1468) printed the first European book, a Bible, using movable type sometime before 1454. This was not the first book in the world made using movable type; we have seen that the Chinese knew about movable type as early as the eleventh century and that the world's earliest surviving book using movable type was made in Korea in 1403 (see Chapter 12). We should remember, too, that Gutenberg could not have printed the Bible if paper, a Chinese invention, had not come into widespread use in Europe between 1250 and 1350 (see Chapter 13).

Movable type, however unsuited to Chinese with its thousands of characters, functioned beautifully for alphabetic languages like Latin. Gutenberg made several crucial innovations: a mold with rows in which different letters could be placed, an oil-based ink, and the type itself. Close analysis of Gutenberg's earliest books shows variation among individual letters, suggesting that he may have made hundreds of the same letter by hand, maybe even from wood, and did not cast them from a metal mold as is often supposed.

Within fifty years of its introduction, printing had transformed the European book. Although European readers had once prized illuminated manuscripts prepared by hand, with beautiful illustrations and exquisite lettering, now typesetters streamlined texts so that they could be printed more easily. Some of the most popular books described the marvels from around the world and included the first Latin translation in 1409 of the Greek geographer Ptolemy (see Chapter 7) and the travel account of Marco Polo (see Chapter 13). Columbus's personal library included copies of both books, and he carefully wrote long notes in the margins of the passages that interested him.

Early European Exploration in the Mediterranean and the Atlantic, 1350–1440

Widely read travel accounts whetted the appetite for trade and exploration. European merchants, primarily from the Italian city-states of Venice and Genoa, maintained settlements in certain locations far from Europe, such as Constantinople, the island of Cyprus, and other smaller islands in the Mediterranean (see Map 15.3). These communities, which existed primarily for the convenience of the merchants, had walled enclosures called *factories* that held warehouses, a place for ships to refit, and houses for short- and long-term stays.

The government of Venice appointed an official, the rector, to serve every two years in each of the city's various settlements. In deciding disputes, he could choose whether to apply local or Venetian law. The primary support the Venetians offered to their colonies was naval protection for the merchant fleet.

Starting around 1350, European navigators began to sail past the Strait of Gibraltar into the Atlantic Ocean. In 1350, two Italian explorers wrote the first book about the Canary Islands and their non-Christian inhabitants. The Europeans captured some of these Canary Islanders and sold them in the slave markets of Europe, where they were much in demand. Also around 1350, the Portuguese reached the Azores, which lie one-third of the distance from Europe to the Americas. After 1350, cartographers began to show the various Atlantic islands off the coast of Africa on their maps.

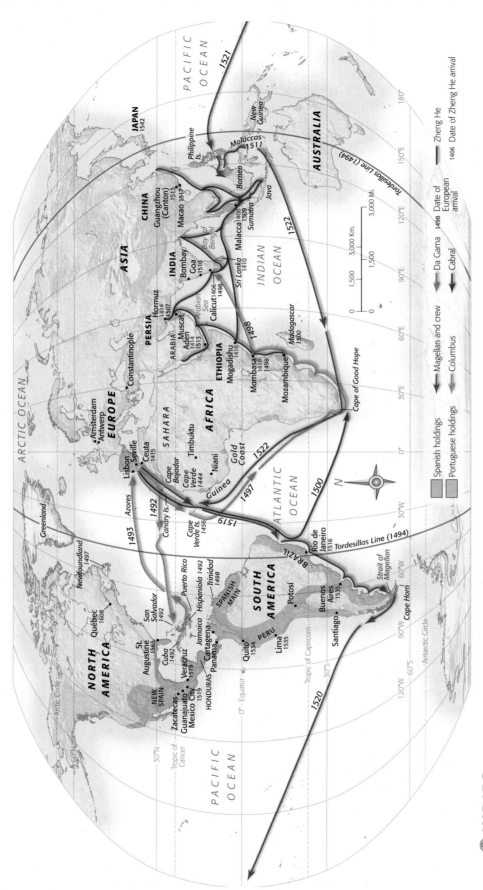

MAP 15.3

The Age of Maritime Expansion, 1400–1600 Between 1400 and 1600, maritime explorers pioneered three major new routes: (1) across the Atlantic Ocean from Europe to the Americas, (2) across the Pacific from the Americas to Asia, and (3) south along the west coast of Africa to the Cape of Good Hope. Once the Portuguese Vasco da Gama rounded the Cape in 1498, he connected with the well-traveled hajj route linking East Africa with China that Zheng He's ships had taken in the early 1400s.

CL Interactive Map

One motivation for exploring these unknown islands was religious. As the Catholic rulers of Spain and Portugal regained different Islamic cities in Iberia during the Reconquista of the thirteenth and fourteenth centuries, they hoped to expand Christian territory into North Africa. At the time, Portugal was separate from Spain, which itself contained several distinct kingdoms. In 1415, a Portuguese prince named Henry, now known as **Henry the Navigator** (1394–1460), led a force of several thousand men that captured the Moroccan fortress of Ceuta (say-OO-tuh). Using the rhetoric of the Crusades and armed with an order from the pope, his goal was to convert the inhabitants to Christianity.

Henry tried to take the Canary Islands for Christianity in 1424, but the inhabitants, armed only with stone tools, repelled the invaders; nevertheless, the Portuguese continued to capture and enslave Canary islanders on a regular basis. The Portuguese occupied the island of Madeira, and in 1454 they established plantations there, which soon exported large amounts of sugar.

Many navigators were afraid to venture past the Madeira Islands because of the dreaded torrid zone. Greek and Roman geographers had posited that all the peoples of the known world lived in the northern temperate zone, which was bordered by an uninhabitable frigid zone to the north and a torrid zone to the south, whose scorching heat made it impossible to cross. Following the revival of interest in Greek and Roman geography in the twelfth century, all informed people realized, as the ancients had, that the globe was round. (The American writer Washington Irving invented the myth that everyone before Columbus thought the world was flat.)

Portuguese exploration along the west coast of Africa forced people to reconsider the existence of a torrid zone. Many Europeans had assumed that Cape Bojador (see Map 15.3), just south of the Canary Islands in modern Morocco, marked the beginning of the impenetrable torrid zone. But in 1434 the Portuguese successfully sailed past the Cape. An Arabic-speaking courtier sent by Henry to learn about the region's geography returned to his monarch after seven months to report that no torrid zone existed.

● **Henry the Navigator** (1394–1460) Portuguese prince who supported Portuguese explorations across the Mediterranean to the Moroccan city of Ceuta, across the Atlantic to the Canary and Madeira Islands, and along the West African coast past Cape Bojador (in modern Mauritania).

Portuguese Exploration of Africa and the Slave Trade After 1444

If there were no torrid zone, Henry realized, the Portuguese could transport slaves from the west coast of Africa and sell them in Europe. Portuguese vessels had already brought back thirty-eight African slaves from West Africa. In 1444, Henry dispatched six caravels to bring back slaves from the Arguin bank, south of Cape Bojador in modern-day Mauritania. The caravel was a small sailing ship, usually about 75 feet (23 m) long, that had two or three masts with square sails. Its main advantage was that it could sail close to the wind.

In 1444, Henry staged a huge public reception of the slaves for his subjects. The ships' captains presented one slave each to a church and to a Franciscan convent to demonstrate their intention to convert the slaves to Christianity. An eyewitness description captures the scene:

> These people, assembled together on that open space, were an astonishing sight to behold. Among them were some who were quite white-skinned, handsome and of good appearance; others were less white, seeming more like brown men; others still were as black as Ethiopians, so deformed of face and body that, to those who stared at them, it almost seemed that they were looking at spirits from the lowest hemisphere. But what heart, however hardened it might be, could not be pierced by a feeling of pity at the sight of that company?[5]

One could easily assume that this description is an early critique of slavery, but, in fact, the author, like many of his contemporaries, accepted the need for slavery. These Europeans saw the trade in slaves as a Christian act: the Africans, as non-Christians, were doomed to suffer in the afterlife, but, if they converted, they could attain salvation. From its very beginnings, the European slave trade combined the profit motive with a missionary impulse.

Within ten years the Portuguese slave traders had reached agreements with two rulers in northern Senegal to trade horses for slaves each year. The price of a horse varied from nine to fourteen slaves. Horses did not live long in Africa's tropical climate, but because rulers liked them as a symbol of power and a war tool, the demand never flagged. By the time of Henry's death in 1460, Portuguese ships had transported about 1,000 slaves a year, fewer than the 4,300 slaves who crossed the Sahara overland each year at the time. After 1460, the oceanic trade continued to grow because the Portuguese deliberately hoped to bypass the Sahara caravans, which they did not control.

Many of the African slaves worked on sugar plantations, either in the Canary Islands or on Madeira. Portugal and the Spanish kingdom of Castile, which ruled central Spain, signed the Treaty of Alcaçovas in 1479 in which they agreed that the Atlantic islands belonged to Castile while the Azores, Madeira, the Cape Verde islands, and any still-to-be-discovered islands beyond the Canaries belonged to Portugal. This treaty recognized the Portuguese right to continue their explorations along the African coast, and, in 1487, a Portuguese ship commanded by Bartholomew Dias rounded the Cape of Good Hope at Africa's southern tip. The Portuguese became convinced that the quickest way to Asia and the riches of the spice trade was around Africa, as Chapter 16 will show.

● The Iberian Conquest of Mexico, Peru, and Brazil, 1492–1580

Columbus's landfall in the Caribbean had immediate and long-lasting consequences. Representatives of the Spanish and Portuguese crowns conquered most of Mexico and Latin America with breathtaking speed. In 1517, the Spanish landed for the first time on the Aztec mainland; by 1540, they controlled all of Mexico, Central America, and the northern sections of South America. Portugal controlled Brazil by 1550. By 1580, Spain had subdued the peoples of the southern regions of South America. Given that the residents of the Canary Islands, armed only with stone tools, managed to repel all attempts to conquer them for 150 years, how did the Spanish and Portuguese move into the Americas and conquer two sophisticated empires so quickly?

The subject peoples of the Aztec, who had not been incorporated into the empire, welcomed the Spanish as an ally who might help them overthrow their overlords. Moreover, the Spanish arrived in Peru just after the installation of a new Sapa Inca, whose opponents still hoped to wrest power from him. The Europeans had other advantages, like guns and horses, which the Amerindians lacked. Finally, the Europeans were completely unaware of their most powerful weapon: the disease pools of Europe.

Columbus's First Voyage to the Americas, 1492

In 1479, Isabella (1451–1504) ascended to the throne of Castile and married Ferdinand of Aragon, unifying the two major kingdoms of Spain. Throughout the 1480s, Columbus approached both the Spanish and the Portuguese monarchs to request funds for a voyage to the Indies by sailing west from the Canary Islands.

In keeping with the scholastic and humanist traditions, Columbus cited several authorities in support of the new route he proposed. One passage in the Bible (II Esdras 6:42) stated that the world was six parts land, one part water. Columbus interpreted this to mean that the distance from the Iberian Peninsula to the western edge of Asia in Japan was only 2,700 miles (4,445 km). In actuality, the distance is over 6,000 miles (10,000 km), and the world is about 70 percent water and 30 percent land, but no one at the time knew this.

In rejecting his proposal, the scholars advising the Portuguese and Spanish monarchs agreed on its main flaws: the world, they thought, was bigger than Columbus realized. Moreover, no ship carrying its own provisions could sail all the way to Japan because the men on board would die of starvation before reaching Asia. These scholars were correct about the distance from Iberia to Japan, but they did not realize that any ship crossing the Atlantic would be able to stop in the Americas and obtain food.

Several developments occurred in 1492 that prompted Isabella and Ferdinand to overturn their earlier decision. Granada, the last Muslim outpost, fell in 1492, and all of Spain came under Catholic rule. In that same year the rulers of Aragon and Castile expelled all Jews from Spain, a measure that had been enacted by France and England centuries earlier. Delighted with these developments, Ferdinand and Isabella decided to fund Columbus, primarily because they did not want the Portuguese to do so, and also because he was asking for only a small amount of money, enough to host a foreign prince for a week.

Isabella and Ferdinand gave Columbus two titles: *admiral of the ocean sea* and *viceroy*. An admiral commanded a fleet, but *viceroy* was a new title indicating a representative of the monarch who would govern any lands to which he sailed. Columbus was entitled to one-tenth of any precious metals or spices he found, with the remaining nine-tenths going to Isabella and Ferdinand. No provision was made for his men.

Columbus departed with three ships from Granada on August 3, 1492, and on October 12 of the same year arrived in Hispaniola, a Caribbean island occupied by the modern nations of Haiti and the Dominican Republic. Although Europeans knew about Islamic astrolabes and sextants, Columbus did not use them. He sailed primarily by dead reckoning: he used a compass to stay on a westerly course and, with the help of a clock, estimated his speed and so the approximate distance he traveled in a day. Columbus was not certain where he had arrived, but he suspected that he was in Japan.

His first encounter with the people on the island was peaceful: "In order to win their friendship," Columbus wrote in his logbook, "I gave some of them red caps and glass beads which they hung round their necks, and also other trifles. These things pleased them greatly and they became marvelously friendly to us." The two sides exchanged gifts and tried to make sense of each other's languages. The island's residents spoke **Arawak,** a language used over a large region spanning modern Venezuela to Florida. "They are the color of Canary Islanders (neither black nor white)," Columbus noted, an indication that he thought of the Arawak as potential slaves.

CL **Primary Source: The Agreement with Columbus of April 17 and April 30, 1492** *Read the contract signed by Columbus and his royal patrons, and see what riches he hoped to gain from his expedition.*

• Arawak General name for a language of families spoken in the 1500s over a large region spanning modern Venezuela to Florida. The term also includes all the Arawak-speaking peoples, including those Columbus met on Hispaniola in 1492.

A Comparison of Columbus's and Zheng He's Voyages

Many people have wondered why the Spanish and the Portuguese, and not the Chinese of the Ming dynasty, established the first overseas empires. The Chinese, who first set off in 1405, had almost a century's head start on the Europeans (see Chapter 14). Their biggest ships extended a full 200 feet (61 m) in length, while Columbus's ships were two-fifths of that length. The full fleet of 317 Chinese treasure ships carried 28,000 men; the doctors on board outnumbered Columbus's entire crew.

Yet the size of the treasure ships did not give the Chinese an advantage, because they were too big to take into unknown waters. One of Columbus's original

■ **The Santa Maria Versus Chinese Treasure Ships: Is Bigger Always Better?** Columbus and Zheng He made journeys of about the same length—5,000 miles (8,000 km)—but in very different vessels. The *Santa Maria* (*left*) measured 80 feet (24 m) long, while the treasure ships of Zheng He (*below*) were over twice that length. Chinese ships, with watertight compartments and movable rudders, were technologically much more sophisticated than European boats of the same period. Still, Columbus complained that his ships were too large to venture into unknown shallow waters, a reminder that smaller boats were better suited for exploration. (From *The Ship, an Illustrated History*, by Bjorn Landstrom. Copyright © 1961 by Bokforlaget Forum AB. Used by permission of the Royal Library Copenhagen)

three ships ran aground during the first voyage, and he complained that his ships—only 80 feet (24 m) long—were too large for successful exploration.

China was richer than either Spain or Portugal. It was arguably the richest country in the world in the early fifteenth century, while Spain and Portugal were far smaller. Yet their small size gave both the Portuguese and the Spanish powerful motivation to seek new lands.

Columbus's voyages differed from the Chinese voyages led by Admiral Zheng He in another critical sense. The navigators on the Chinese treasure ships knew each destination because they followed the best-traveled oceanic route in the world before 1500. Muslim pilgrims from East Africa traveled up the East African coast to reach Mecca, and Chinese pilgrims sailed around Southeast Asia and India to reach the Arabian peninsula. The Zheng He voyages simply linked the two hajj routes together. In contrast, when Columbus and other later explorers set off, they were consciously exploring, looking for new places to colonize. Columbus's voyages were genuine voyages of exploration because he was going where no one else (or at least no one else that anyone remembered) had gone before him.

The Ming dynasty governed a huge empire, and there is no indication that the Yongle emperor (r. 1403–1424) wanted to make it bigger by using the voyages. He simply hoped that the various nations of the world would acknowledge him as the rightful ruler of the Chinese. The Chinese had no concept of a "colony"—no colonies comparable to the Madeira or Canary Islands or even to the factories built by European merchants on different Mediterranean islands. Rulers of earlier Chinese dynasties had sometimes conquered other peoples, but always in contiguous neighboring lands, never overseas.

The Ming government ordered an end to the voyages in 1433 because they brought no financial benefit to the Chinese. In contrast, the Spanish and Portuguese voyages brought their countries immediate returns in gold and slaves and the promise of long-term profits if settlers could establish enterprises such as sugar plantations.

Spanish Exploration After Columbus's First Voyage, 1493–1517

From the beginning Columbus did not exercise tight control over his ships. When he first reached the Americas, the ship *Niña* set off on its own to search for gold, and Columbus had no choice but to welcome it back. The *Santa Maria* had already run aground and been dismantled to make a fort, and Columbus needed both remaining ships to return home. With only two ships, he was forced to leave thirty-nine men behind in the fort, but when he returned on his second voyage in 1493, he found that all had been killed, presumably in disputes with the Arawak over women. Relations between the Arawak and the Spanish were never again as harmonious as they had been during the first voyage.

Once the Spanish realized that Columbus had discovered a new landmass, they negotiated the **Treaty of Tordesillas** (tor-duh-SEE-yuhs) with the Portuguese in 1494, while Columbus was away on his second voyage. The treaty established a dividing line: all territory 1,185 miles (1,910 km) west of the line belonged to Castile, while all the islands to the east were reserved for Portugal. Lands already ruled by a Christian monarch were unaffected by the agreement. Although the pope, himself a Spaniard, supported the treaty, no other European power accepted its terms. Portugal gained Africa, the route to India, and, although no one knew it at the time, Brazil, which both the Spanish Vicente Pinzon and the Portuguese Pedro Álvares Cabral (1467/68–1520) reached six years later in 1500.

• Treaty of Tordesillas Treaty signed by the Portuguese and the Spanish in 1494 that established a dividing line: all territory 1,185 miles (1,910 km) west of the line belonged to Castile, while all the islands to the east were reserved for Portugal.

This treaty made the peoples of the Americas subjects of Ferdinand and Isabella. When Columbus returned from the second voyage with five hundred slaves on board, Isabella freed all of them on the grounds that her subjects could not be enslaved. Only non-Spanish subjects, like those of African rulers, could.

Columbus never solved the problem of how to compensate his men. When recruiting sailors in Spain he spoke of great riches, but the agreement he had signed with Ferdinand and Isabella left no share of wealth for his men. On his first voyage, his men expected to sail with him to Asia and return, but on subsequent voyages many joined him expressly so that they could settle in the Americas, where they hoped to make fortunes. In 1497, the settlers revolted against Columbus, and he agreed to allow them to use Indians as agricultural laborers. Because Columbus was unpopular with the settlers, in 1499 the Crown removed him from office and replaced him with a new viceroy.

In 1503 the Spanish established the **encomienda system** in the hope of clarifying arrangements with the colonists and of ending the abuse of American indigenous peoples. Under this system, the Spanish monarchs "entrusted" (the literal meaning of *encomienda*) a specified number of Amerindians to a Spanish settler, who gained the right to extract labor, gold, or other goods from them in exchange for teaching them about Christianity. The monarchs took as their model the governmental structure used to administer lands newly recovered from Muslim kingdoms in the Reconquista. Although designed to protect the indigenous peoples, the encomienda system often resulted in further exploitation.

Spanish and Portuguese navigators continued to land in new places after 1503. The Spanish crossed 120 miles (193 km) from Cuba to the Yucatán Peninsula in 1508–1509 and reached Florida in 1510. In 1513, Vasco Núñez de Balboa (bal-BOH-uh) crossed through Panama to see the Pacific, and by 1522 the Portuguese navigator Magellan had circumnavigated the globe, although he died before his ship returned home.

The Conquest of Mexico, 1517–1540

Hernán Cortés (kor-TEZ), the Spaniard who led the conquest of Mexico, came first to Hispaniola in 1506 and moved to Cuba in 1509. Like many of the other Spanish **conquistadors** ("conquerors"), he came from a family of middling social influence and made his fortune in the Americas. After rumors reached Cuba from the Maya peoples of the Yucatán about a larger, richer empire to the north, Cortés sought to launch an expedition. Within two weeks he had recruited 530 men to travel with him.

When Cortés landed in the Yucatán in early 1519, he immediately met a woman who helped him penetrate the language barrier separating the Spanish- and the Nahua-speakers: a Nahua noblewoman named **Malinché** (mah-lin-HAY) who had grown up among the Maya and could speak both the Nahuatl and Mayan languages. Given to Cortés as a gift, Malinché learned Spanish quickly. The Spaniards called her Dona Marina. As adviser to Cortés, she played a crucial role in the Spanish conquest of Mexico, partially because she commanded the respect of the Nahua peoples.

Cortés landed on the coast of Mexico on April 20, 1519, and slightly over two years later the Aztec had surrendered their capital and their empire to him. Yet this outcome had been far from certain. The Spanish had only 1,500 men.

The encounter between the Nahua and the Spaniards is unusual because we have surviving sources from both sides—the European colonizers and the

---

• encomienda system (Literally "entrusted.") System established in 1503 by the Spanish in the hope of clarifying arrangements with the colonists and of ending the abuse of indigenous peoples of the Americas.

• conquistadors Literally "conquerors," the term for the Spaniards who conquered Mexico, Peru, and Central America in the 1500s. Many came from families of middling social influence and made their fortunes in the Americas.

• Malinché Nahua noblewoman who served as translator for and adviser to Cortés. Trilingual in Spanish, Nahuatl, and Mayan, she played a crucial role in the Spanish conquest of Mexico because she commanded the respect of the Nahua peoples.

■ **Cortés's Interpreter, Malinché** This image dates to the 1500s and shows what Cortés's army looked like when it first landed in Mexico. The Spaniards, with their heavy armor and horse, contrast sharply with the local peoples, who use bands tied around their foreheads to bear the weight of food in containers as well as to carry a small child (*far left*). The army was a mixed force: Malinché, who was Cortés's mistress and interpreter, stands at the far right, with the bearded Cortés on her left. (Bibliothèque nationale de France/Snark/Art Resource, NY)

indigenous peoples. One of Cortés's foot soldiers, Bernal Díaz del Castillo, wrote the most detailed account from the Spanish point of view. On the Nahua side, a Franciscan missionary named Fray Bernardino de Sahagún (FRAY burr-NARD-ee-noh duh sah-hah-GWUN) compiled the **Florentine Codex** in the 1550s on the basis of interviews he and his research assistants conducted and recorded in an alphabet for Nahuatl developed by Spanish missionaries. This account is not the same as a first-person contemporary account, yet, since Sahagún and his team systematically crosschecked what their informants reported, it is the best Nahuatl-language account we have.

The *Florentine Codex* records the response of the reigning Great Speaker Moctezuma (also spelled Montezuma) to the first envoy from the Spanish:

> It especially made him faint when he heard how the guns went off at the Spaniards' command, sounding like thunder. . . . And when it went off, something

● *Florentine Codex*
The main source in Nahuatl about the events of the Spanish conquest. Compiled by a Franciscan missionary named Fray Bernardino de Sahagún in the 1550s on the basis of interviews he and his research assistants conducted and recorded.

like a ball came out from inside, and fire went showering and spitting out. . . .
And if they shot at a hill, it seemed to crumble and come apart. . . . Their war
gear was all iron. They clothed their bodies in iron, they put iron on their
heads, their swords were iron. . . .

And their deer that carried them were as tall as the roof.[6]

The Spaniards' "deer" were horses, an animal not native to the Americas, whose
size greatly impressed the Aztec.

On their way to Tenochtitlan, the Spaniards fought a major battle lasting
nearly three weeks with the people of Tlaxcala (tlash-CAH-lah). After their defeat
the Tlaxcalans became the Spaniards' most important allies against their own hated
Aztec overlords. When, in November 1519, the Spaniards first arrived at the capital
city of Tenochtitlan, the Great Speaker Moctezuma allowed them to come in un-
harmed. The Spaniards could not believe how beautiful the city was. Bernal Díaz
described this event:

> Gazing on such wonderful sights, we did not know what to say, or whether
> what appeared before us was real, for on one side, on the land, there were great
> cities, and in the lake ever so many more, and the lake itself was crowded with
> canoes, and in the Causeway were many bridges at intervals, and in front of
> us stood the great City of Mexico.

For one week the Spaniards and the Aztec coexisted uneasily, until the Spanish
placed Moctezuma under house arrest. Then, in the spring of 1520, while Cortés
was away, one of his subordinates ordered his men to massacre the city's inhabitants, and prolonged battles resulted. The Spaniards killed Moctezuma and, after
suffering hundreds of casualties, retreated to Tlaxcala, the city of their allies. At
this point, it seemed that the Aztec would win.

But by then smallpox had reached the Americas. The native peoples of America
had little or no resistance to European smallpox, measles, malaria, sexually transmitted diseases, or even the common cold. In December 1518, one-third of Hispaniola's population died; in 1519, disease ravaged Puerto Rico, Jamaica, and Cuba;
and in the spring of 1520, smallpox crossed into the Yucatán, arriving in Tenochtitlan by October. Moctezuma's successor died of smallpox in early December, and
the mass deaths threw the entire city into disarray.

Even so the Spaniards had great difficulty conquering the Aztec. They laid siege
to Tenochtitlan for eighty days of sustained fighting before the city surrendered in
August of 1521. Spanish guns and cannon were not decisive. Some 100,000 troops
and a portable fleet of boats supplied by the Tlaxcalans enabled the Spaniards to win.

In 1524, twelve Franciscan friars arrived in Mexico, where they were welcomed
by Cortés. The Franciscans became the most important missionary order among the
Nahuatl speakers. They searched for parallels between native beliefs and Christian
teachings at the same time that they suppressed practices, like human sacrifice
and polygamy, that they saw as un-Christian. (See the feature "Movement of Ideas:
The Sacrifice of Isaac: A Sixteenth-Century Nahuatl Play.") The Spanish gradually imposed a more regular administration over Mexico under the governance of a viceroy.

**The Spanish Conquest
of Peru, 1532–1550**

The order of events in the Spanish conquest of Peru differed from that in Mexico, where Cortés had arrived
before smallpox. The smallpox virus traveled overland

from Mexico and, in 1528, caused an epidemic in which many Inca, including the Inca Sapa, died, four years before the first Spaniards arrived in Peru. War among the contenders to the throne broke out. In November 1532, when the Spanish forces, led by Francisco Pizarro (pih-ZAHR-oh) (1475–1541), arrived, they happened upon the moment of greatest instability in the Inca kingdom: when the newly enthroned Sapa Inca had not yet completely subdued his main rival. Atahualpa (ah-tuh-WAHL-puh; also spelled Atawallpa) had become ruler only after defeating his older half-brother, whom he still held in captivity. Atahualpa had taken severe counter-measures against his brother's supporters, many of whom sided immediately with the Spaniards.

When Pizarro and his 168 men arrived at Cajamarca, an important city in the Peruvian highlands where Atahualpa was living, Atahualpa initially received the Spanish peacefully. Then, on their second day in Cajamarca, the Spanish staged a crisis: a Dominican missionary gave a prayer book to Atahualpa, and an interpreter explained that the Spanish wanted to spread the teachings of God. Atahualpa threw the book down on the ground, and the Spanish charged out from behind the stone buildings where they had been hiding. Their guns, armor, and horses gave them an initial advantage. An estimated seven thousand Inca, yet not a single Spaniard, died in the ensuing carnage.

Pizarro himself captured Atahualpa, who offered to pay an enormous ransom for his release: he promised to fill a room 2,600 cubic feet (74 cubic m) half with gold and half with silver. By April, the Inca had amassed the metal for the ransom, which the Spaniards melted down and divided among Pizarro's troops. Those with horses received 90 pounds (41 kg), equivalent today to perhaps $500,000, and those on foot half that amount. Then the Spanish reneged on their agreement and killed Atahualpa.

It took twenty years for the Spanish to gain control of Peru. With the support of those who opposed Atahualpa, they installed a puppet Sapa Inca and played off different Inca groups against each other. Since the Inca maintained no standing army, their warriors had to return home for the harvest while their Spanish opponents did not.

As the Spanish conquered different sections of Inca territory, they imposed the encomienda system. In 1551, they named the first viceroy for Peru and gradually established a more stable administration. The first census, taken in the 1570s, showed that half the population had died from European disease, with the toll in some places reaching as high as 95 percent of the population. The Amerindians who lived at high altitudes suffered much fewer losses than those living on the coast.

The Portuguese Settlement of Brazil, 1500–1580

In 1500, Pedro Álvares Cabral (kah-BRAHL) (1467/68–1520) landed in Brazil. Although the Portuguese claimed Brazil following Cabral's voyage, few of them came to this resource-poor country. Most Portuguese sought their wealth in Asia, as discussed in the next chapter. In 1533 the Portuguese monarch John III (r. 1521–1557) made a systematic effort to encourage the settlement of Brazil by dividing it into fifteen slices, each occupying 160 miles (260 km) of the coastline and extending inland indefinitely. He granted these territories to Portuguese nobles, many of them his courtiers.

John III also authorized the Jesuits, a new order of Catholic priests founded in 1540, to preach in Brazil. Many Jesuits traveled to the interior, converted the

The Sacrifice of Isaac: A Sixteenth-Century Nahuatl Play

The members of the Catholic orders who lived in Mexico used different approaches to teach the Nahua peoples about Christianity. In addition to printing bilingual catechisms in Spanish and Nahuatl, they sponsored the composition of plays in Nahuatl on religious themes. Since these plays were not published but only circulated in handwritten manuscripts, very few survive. The short play *The Sacrifice of Isaac* recounts the story from the Hebrew Bible of Abraham and Isaac (see pages 52 and 244), which addresses a topic of great interest to the Nahua peoples: human sacrifice.

God the Father appears in the play to ask Abraham to sacrifice his son Isaac, but he later sends an angel to instruct Abraham to offer a lamb instead. Abraham, his first wife, and Isaac all embody obedience, a virtue prized both by the ancient Hebrews and the Nahua peoples. Abraham's slave Hagar and her son Ishmael urge Isaac to disobey his father; both still worship the sun (not God), a sure clue to the audience that they are evil.

Corresponding faithfully to the version in the Hebrew Bible, the play shows an obedient Isaac offering himself for sacrifice until the moment the angel instructs Abraham to free him and sacrifice a lamb instead. The lively quality of the Nahuatl language suggests that it was written sometime after the Spanish conquest, probably by a native speaker who converted to Christianity.

Source: Marilyn Ekdahl Ravicz, *Early Colonial Religious Drama in Mexico: From Tzompantli to Golgotha* (Washington, D.C.: The Catholic University of America Press, 1970), pp. 83–97. The first selection is from pp. 87–90; the second, pp. 95–96.

The Devil, Ishmael, and Hagar Trick Isaac

(A demon enters, dressed either as an angel or as an old man.)

DEMON: What are you doing, young man? For I see your affliction is very great.

ISHMAEL: Most certainly my affliction is great! But how is it that you know if I have pain? Who told you this?

DEMON: Do you not see that I am a messenger from heaven? I was sent here from there in order to tell you what you are to do here on earth.

ISHMAEL: Then I wait to hear your command.

DEMON: Hear then why it is that you are troubled. Do I astound you? Truly it is because of the beloved child, Isaac! Because he is a person of a good life, and because he always has confidence in the commands of his father. So you contrive and wish with all your energy that he not be obedient to his father and mother. Most assuredly I can tell you what you must do to accomplish this.

ISHMAEL: Oh how you comfort me when I hear your advice. Nor do I merit your aid. You are most truly a dweller in heaven and my protector!

DEMON: Open your heart wide to my command! Look now—his father and mother have invited many others to a banquet; they are relaxing and greatly enjoying themselves. Now is the time to give Isaac bad advice so that he might forget his father and his mother and go with you to amuse himself in some other place. And if he should obey you, they will certainly punish their son for this, however well they love him.

ISHMAEL: I shall do just as you command.

DEMON: Then, indeed, I am going to return to heaven. For I came only to console you and tell you what you must do. . . .

(Hagar the slave and her son Ishmael enter.)

HAGAR: Now while the great lord Abraham once again entertains many for the sake of his son whom he so greatly loves, we are only servants. He values us but little. And you, my son, merit nothing, are worthy of nothing. Oh that I might placate myself through you, and that you might calm all my torment upon earth! But so it is; your birth and its reward are eternal tears.

(Here they both weep—also the son.)

ISHMAEL: Oh you sun! You who are so high! Warm us even here with your great splendor as well as in every part of the world, and—in the way which you are able—prosper all the peoples of the earth! And to us, yes, even to us two poor ones—who merit nothing and who are worthy of nothing! Know now, oh my mother, what I shall do: later, when they are all feasting, perhaps I shall be able to lead Isaac away with some deceit, so that we might go to divert ourselves in some other quarter. With this action he will violate the precept of his father, who will not then love him with all of his heart.

Hagar: What you are thinking is very good. Do it in that way.

Abraham and Isaac on the Mountain

ABRAHAM: Now hear me, my beloved son! Truly this is what the almighty God has commanded me in order that His loving and divine precept might be fulfilled; and so that He might see whether we—the inhabitants of the earth— love Him and execute His Divine Will. For He is the Lord of the living and of the dead. Now with great humility, accept death! For assuredly He says this: "Truly I shall be able to raise the dead back to life, I who am the Life Eternal." Then let His will be done in every part of the earth.

(Here Abraham weeps. The Music of the "Misericordia" is heard.)

ISAAC: Do not weep, my beloved and honored father! For truly I accept death with great happiness. May the precious will of God be done as He has commanded you. . . .

ANGEL: Abraham! Abraham!

(Here an angel appears and seizes Abraham's hand so that he is unable to kill his son.)

ABRAHAM: Who are you, you who speak to me?

ANGEL: Now know the following by the authority and word of God. For He has seen how much you love Him; that you fulfill His divine precept; that you do not infringe it; that you brought your cherished son—he whom you love so much—here to the peak of the mountain; and that you have come to offer him here as a burnt sacrifice to God the almighty Father. Now truly for all this, by His loving Will, I have come to tell you to desist, for your cherished son Isaac does not have to die.

Abraham: May His adored will be done as He wishes it. Come here, oh my beloved son! Truly you have now been saved by death by His hand.

(Here he [Abraham or Isaac] unties the cloth with which he was blindfolded, and loosens the ropes with which his hands were bound.)

ANGEL: Then understand this: as a substitute for your beloved son, you shall prepare a lamb as God wishes it. Go, for I shall accompany you and leave you at your house.

QUESTIONS FOR ANALYSIS

▸ What information does the author include to make the audience think Ishmael is bad and Isaac good?

▸ What does the text propose as an appropriate substitute for human sacrifice?

indigenous peoples, and then resettled them in villages. The settlers searched for gold throughout the sixteenth century but never found significant amounts.

Instead the Portuguese began to build sugar plantations with the guidance of technicians brought from the Canary Islands. Since so many of the indigenous Amerindians had died, the plantation owners imported slaves from Africa, who had learned how to cultivate sugar in the Canary Islands and the Madeiras.

In 1580 Philip II succeeded to the throne of both Spain and Portugal, and the two countries remained under a single king until 1640. The Portuguese and Spanish empires had evolved parallel structures independently. The highest colonial official, the viceroy, presided over a royal colony and governed in concert with an advisory council who could appeal any decisions to the king.

The social structure in the colonies was basically the same throughout Latin America. At the top of society were those born in Europe, who served as military leaders, royal officials, or high church figures. Below them were creoles, those with two European parents but born in the Americas. Those of mixed descent (mestizos in Spanish-speaking regions, memlucos in Brazil) ranked even lower, with only Amerindians and African slaves below them. By 1600, 100,000 Africans lived in Brazil, many working in the hundreds of sugar mills all over the colony.

● The Columbian Exchange

● Columbian exchange All the plants, animals, goods, and diseases that crossed the Atlantic, and sometimes the Pacific, after 1492.

The term **Columbian exchange** refers to all the plants, animals, goods, and diseases that crossed the Atlantic, and sometimes the Pacific, after 1492. At the same time that European diseases like smallpox devastated the peoples living in America, European animals like the horse, cow, and sheep came to the Americas and flourished. In the other direction came plant foods indigenous to the Americas like tomatoes, potatoes, peanuts, and chili peppers.

Of all the European imports, smallpox had the most devastating effect on the Americas. It did not strike until 1518, probably because no Spaniard who came to the Americas before suffered from an active outbreak. Only someone suffering an outbreak can transmit smallpox, which is contagious for about a month: after two weeks of incubation, fever and vomiting strike; the ill person's skin then breaks out with the pox, small pustules that dry up after about ten days. Either the victim dies during those ten days or survives, typically with a pock-marked face and body.

One Nahuatl description captures the extent of the suffering:

> Sores erupted on our faces, our breasts, our bellies. . . . The sick were so utterly helpless that they could only lie on their beds like corpses, unable to move their limbs or even their heads. . . . If they did move their bodies, they screamed with pain.[7]

Although no plants or animals had an effect as immediate as smallpox, the long-term effects of the Columbian exchange in plants and animals indelibly altered the landscape, diets, and population histories of both the Americas and Europe. When Columbus landed on Hispaniola, he immediately realized how different the plants were: "All the trees were as different from ours as day from night, and so the fruits, the herbage, the rocks, and all things." He also remarked on the absence of livestock: "I saw neither sheep nor goats nor any other beast."[8]

On his second voyage in 1493, Columbus carried cuttings of European plants, including wheat, melons, sugar cane, and other fruits and vegetables. He also brought pigs, horses, chickens, sheep, goats, and cattle. More like wild boars than modern hogs, pigs were the first to adapt to the Americas, eating wild grasses, reproducing in large numbers, and moving into many areas emptied of humans by the depredations of smallpox.

While smallpox traveled from Europe to the Americas, there is evidence that syphilis traveled in the other direction. The first well-documented outbreaks of syphilis in Europe occurred around 1495, and one physician claimed that Columbus's men brought it to Madrid soon after 1492 but that he did not recognize it until many years later. It is also possible that diseases resembling syphilis, often labeled "leprosy," existed in Europe before this time but that the modern form of syphilis only arose after 1492. No European skeletons with signs of syphilis before 1500 have been found, but an Amerindian skeleton with syphilis has, suggesting that the disease did indeed move from the Americas to Europe. Causing genuine pain, syphilis could be passed to the next generation and was fatal for about one-quarter of those who contracted it, but it did not cause mass deaths.

Assessing the loss of Amerindian life due to smallpox and the other European diseases has caused much debate among historians because no population statistics exist for the Americas before 1492. Different historians have come up with estimates for the regions with the heaviest populations—Mexico, between four and six million, and Peru, between ten and twelve million—but even these numbers are controversial. Figures for the population of the entire Americas can be little more than guesswork. The first reliable figures for Amerindian populations came with Spanish colonization. In 1568, Spanish authorities counted 970,000 non-Spanish living in Mexico and 1.2 million living in Peru.[9] For the entire period of European colonization in all parts of the Americas, guesses at the total death toll from European diseases, based on controversial estimates of precontact populations, range from a low of 10 million to a high of over 100 million.

By 1600, two extremely successful agricultural enterprises had spread through the Americas. One was sugar, and the other was cattle raising. The Spaniards who landed in the Americas had long experience with cattle. They knew how to lasso, to lead cattle to grass, and to round up cattle and bring them in for slaughter. The Americas contained huge expanses of grasslands in Venezuela and Colombia, from Mexico north to Canada, and in Argentina and Uruguay. In each case the Spaniards began on the coastal edge of a grassland and followed their rapidly multiplying herds of cattle to the interior.

As European food crops transformed the diet of those living in the Americas, so too did American food crops transform the eating habits of people in Afro-Eurasia. The climate of Latin America closely resembled that of Africa, and American food crops moved into West Africa, particularly modern Nigeria, where even today people eat corn, peanuts, squash, manioc (cassava), and sweet potatoes.

Two crops in particular played an important role throughout Afro-Eurasia: corn and potatoes (including sweet potatoes). Both produced higher yields than wheat and grew in less desirable fields, such as on the slopes of hills. Although few people anywhere in the world preferred corn or potatoes to their original wheat-based or rice-based diet, if the main crop failed, hungry people gratefully ate the American transplants. By the eighteenth century corn and potatoes had reached as far as India and China, and the population in both places increased markedly.

Chapter Review

Download the MP3 audio file of the Chapter Review and listen to it on the go.

Unlike the Viking voyages to Newfoundland and the Chinese expeditions to East Africa, Columbus's landfall in 1492 had lasting consequences. The major difference was that the arrival of the Spaniards and the Portuguese initiated the Columbian exchange, an unprecedented transfer of diseases, plants, and animals from one continent to another. The mass deaths of the Amerindians preceded the large-scale movement of Europeans and Africans to the Americas. The migrations in the first hundred years after Columbus's arrival in Hispaniola produced the mixed composition of the population of the Americas today. As we will see in the next chapter, the arrival of the Europeans had a very different impact on Asia.

How did the Aztec form their empire? How did the Inca form theirs? How did each hold their empire together, and what was each empire's major weakness?

The Aztec, based in modern Mexico, demanded much from their subject peoples, including payments of grain and other goods, a certain number of days of work each year, and sacrificial victims to provide the gods with precious "water," but they gave little in return. Living in their own communities, the subject peoples had little reason to be loyal to the Aztec and every reason to ally with any power against them.

The Inca Empire of the Andes was organized differently. Once the Inca conquered a locality, they incorporated its residents in their empire, sometimes even relocating them. Their weakness was that whenever the Sapa Inca died or became weak, all those desiring to succeed him engaged in a free-for-all struggle, which created great instability in the empire. When one leader emerged victorious, he took severe measures against all his rivals, who would readily ally with any enemy of the new Sapa Inca if doing so gave them a chance to reassert themselves.

How did humanist scholarship encourage oceanic exploration? What motivated the Portuguese, particularly Prince Henry the Navigator, to explore West Africa?

Benefiting from the lowered cost of printed books, the humanists emphasized the rigorous re-examination of the classics, preferably in the original Latin and Greek, including geographical works. Christopher Columbus owned copies of Ptolemy's geography and Marco Polo's travel account. Although ancient geographers posited the existence of a torrid zone that could not be crossed because it was scorchingly hot, Portuguese navigators, many sponsored by Prince Henry the Navigator, made their way down the coast of West Africa and realized that the zone did not exist. Hoping to make Portugal a wealthy slave-trading state, the Portuguese rulers professed a desire to convert the Africans they captured and brought to Europe as slaves.

How did the Spanish and the Portuguese establish their empires in the Americas so quickly?

The Spanish tapped the resentment of the subject peoples, including both the Tlaxcalans in Mexico and the Inca supporters of the unsuccessful brother of Atahualpa, against their rulers. European horses and guns frightened the Amerindians, but the most powerful European weapon was invisible: European smallpox and other diseases to which Amerindians had no resistance. The mass deaths made it possible for the Spanish and Portuguese to gain control over modern-day Mexico, Central America, and South America within one hundred years after Columbus's 1492 arrival in Hispaniola.

What was the Columbian exchange? Which elements of the exchange had the greatest impact on the Americas? On Afro-Eurasia?

Of all the plants, animals, and microbes going between the Americas and Afro-Eurasia after 1492, disease had the greatest impact. The death toll from smallpox ranged between 50 and 90 percent, and estimates suggest that at least ten million Amerindians died in the years after the first outbreak of smallpox in 1518. American food crops traveling in the other direction, particularly corn and potatoes, spread throughout Afro-Eurasia and enabled many to survive famines.

WEB RESOURCES

Pronunciation Guide

Interactive Maps

MAP 15.1 The Aztec Empire

MAP 15.2 The Inca Empire

MAP 15.3 The Age of Maritime Expansion, 1400–1600

Primary Sources

Chapter Objectives

ACE Multiple-Choice Quiz

Flashcards

For Further Reference

Coe, Michael. *Mexico*. London: Thames and Hudson, 1984.

Cohen, J. M., trans. *The Four Voyages of Christopher Columbus*. New York: Penguin, 1969.

D'Altroy, Terence. *The Incas*. Malden, Mass.: Blackwell Publishing, 2002.

Flint, Valerie I. J. *The Imaginative Landscape of Christopher Columbus*. Princeton: Princeton University Press, 1992.

Grafton, Anthony, et al. *New Worlds, Ancient Texts: The Power of Tradition and the Shock of Discovery*. Cambridge: The Belknap Press of Harvard University Press, 1992.

Lockhart, James. *The Nahuas After the Conquest: A Social and Cultural History of the Indians of Central Mexico, Sixteenth Through Eighteenth Centuries*. Stanford: Stanford University Press, 1992.

Lockhart, James, and Stuart Schwartz. *Early Latin America: A History of Colonial Spanish America and Brazil*. New York: Cambridge University Press, 1983.

Russell, Peter. *Prince Henry "the Navigator": A Life*. New Haven: Yale University Press, 2000.

Schwartz, Stuart B. *The Iberian Mediterranean and Atlantic Traditions in the Formation of Columbus as a Colonizer*. Minneapolis: The Associates of the James Ford Bell Library, University of Minnesota, 1986.

Schwartz, Stuart B. *Victors and Vanquished: Spanish and Nahua Views of the Conquest of Mexico*. New York: Bedford/St. Martin's, 2000.

Smith, Michael E. *The Aztecs*. Malden, Mass.: Blackwell Publishing, 1996.

Websites

Foundation for the Advancement of Mesoamerican Studies, Inc. (http://www.famsi.org/research/pohl/pohl-aztec6.html). Detailed description of the daily life of the Aztecs.

National Humanities Center: American Beginnings (http://nationalhumanitiescenter.org/pds/amerbegin/). Extensive collection of primary documents on European exploration and the first encounters between the Europeans and the Amerindians.

The Roots of the City (http://www.mexicocity.com.mx/history1.html). Excellent information about Tenochtitlan.

Maritime Expansion in Afro-Eurasia, 1500–1700

The Italian priest **Matteo Ricci** (1552–1610) knew more about China than any other European of his time. Though frustrated by the small number of converts he made to Christianity during his two decades as a missionary, Ricci (REE-chee) described Chinese political and social life in positive terms. Though Ricci was sometimes less complimentary, in the following passage his idealized view of China was meant as a criticism of his own society. Ricci was correct in his assessment that China was more populous, more prosperous, and more stable than Europe in the first decade of the seventeenth century:

MATTEO RICCI (LEFT) AND ANOTHER MISSIONARY

(Private Collection/The Bridgeman Art Library)

It seems to be quite remarkable . . . that in a kingdom of almost limitless expanse and innumerable population, and abounding in copious supplies of every description, though they have a well-equipped army and navy that could easily conquer the neighboring nations, neither the King nor his people ever think of waging a war of aggression. . . . In this respect they are much different from the people of Europe, who are frequently discontent with their own governments and covetous of what others enjoy. . . .

Another remarkable fact and . . . marking a difference from the West, is that the entire kingdom is administered by . . . Philosophers. The responsibility for orderly management of the entire realm is wholly and completely committed to their charge and care. . . . Fighting and violence among the people are practically unheard of. . . . On the contrary, one who will not fight and restrains himself from returning a blow is praised for his prudence and bravery.[1]

This icon will direct you to interactive activities and study materials on the *Voyages* website: **www.cengage.com/history/hansen/voyages1e**

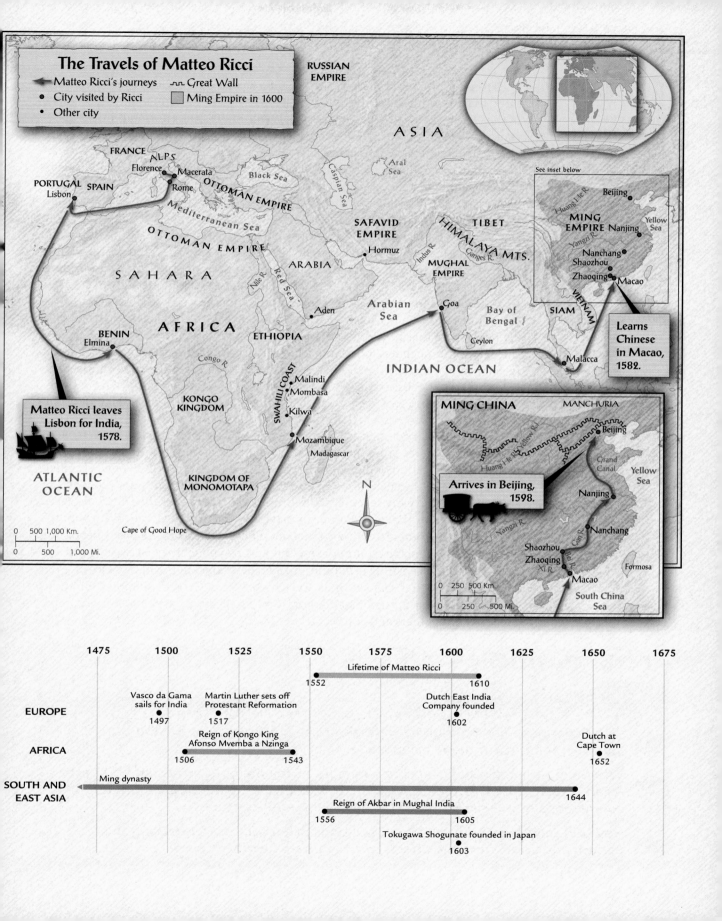

The Travels of Matteo Ricci

- → Matteo Ricci's journeys   ⌐ Great Wall
- • City visited by Ricci   ▨ Ming Empire in 1600
- • Other city

RUSSIAN EMPIRE

ASIA

See inset below

FRANCE
ALPS
Florence
Macerata
Rome
OTTOMAN EMPIRE
Black Sea
Caspian Sea
Aral Sea

PORTUGAL SPAIN
Lisbon

Mediterranean Sea
OTTOMAN EMPIRE

SAFAVID EMPIRE
Hormuz

TIBET
HIMALAYA MTS.

MING EMPIRE
Beijing
Huang He R.
Nanjing
Yellow Sea
Nanchang
Shaozhou
Zhaoqing
Macao

Learns Chinese in Macao, 1582.

SAHARA

ARABIA
Nile R.
Red Sea

MUGHAL EMPIRE
Indus R.
Ganges R.

AFRICA

ETHIOPIA

Aden

Arabian Sea
Goa

Bay of Bengal
Ceylon

SIAM
VIETNAM

Malacca

BENIN
Elmina

Congo R.

KONGO KINGDOM

SWAHILI COAST
Malindi
Mombasa
Kilwa

INDIAN OCEAN

Matteo Ricci leaves Lisbon for India, 1578.

Mozambique
Madagascar

ATLANTIC OCEAN

KINGDOM OF MONOMOTAPA

N

Cape of Good Hope

0   500 1,000 Km.
0   500   1,000 Mi.

MING CHINA

MANCHURIA

Beijing
Huang He (Yellow R.)
Grand Canal
Yellow Sea

Arrives in Beijing, 1598.

Nanjing

Nanchang
Gan R.
Shaozhou
Zhaoqing
Xi R.
Macao

Formosa

South China Sea

0   250   500 Km.
0   250   500 Mi.

	1475	1500	1525	1550	1575	1600	1625	1650	1675

Lifetime of Matteo Ricci
1552 — 1610

EUROPE

Vasco da Gama sails for India
1497

Martin Luther sets off Protestant Reformation
1517

Dutch East India Company founded
1602

AFRICA

Reign of Kongo King Afonso Mvemba a Nzinga
1506 — 1543

Dutch at Cape Town
1652

SOUTH AND EAST ASIA

Ming dynasty ————————————————— 1644

Reign of Akbar in Mughal India
1556 — 1605

Tokugawa Shogunate founded in Japan
1603

● **Matteo Ricci** (1552–1610) Italian Jesuit missionary who traveled to China in the sixteenth century. Tried unsuccessfully to reconcile Christianity with Confucianism and convert Ming scholar-officials.

Ⓒ **Primary Source:**
Journals: Matteo Ricci
This story about Jesuit missionaries in China provides an interesting look at the link between religion and politics in the early seventeenth century.

From Ricci's point of view, all that China lacked was religious truth. He understood that to communicate his Christian ideas he had to conform to the expectations of the "Philosophers," the scholar-officials who staffed the enormous imperial bureaucracy of Ming China. To this end, he learned Mandarin Chinese, studied Confucian texts, and dressed in silk garments to show a social status "equal of a Magistrate."

Italian by birth, Ricci joined the Jesuits, a Catholic religious order dedicated to "conversion of the Infidels." Because it was the Portuguese who pioneered the direct oceanic route from Europe to Asia, Ricci traveled from Rome to Lisbon to learn Portuguese and prepare for his mission. He then spent four years in India before traveling to China, where he lived from 1582 until his death in 1610. Meanwhile, other Jesuits were traveling to Japan, Brazil, Quebec, West Africa, and the Mississippi River Valley. The Jesuits were taking advantage of the new maritime connections established in the sixteenth century by the navigators who pioneered direct routes from Europe to the Americas, West Africa, the Indian Ocean, and East Asia.

While European mariners were a new presence in the Indian Ocean, they traveled on routes that had long been used by Asian and African merchants. In fact, the new maritime routes from Europe to Africa, the Indian Ocean, and East Asia first developed by Portuguese sailors were far less revolutionary than the connections between Europe, Africa, and the Americas that followed from the voyages of Christopher Columbus (see Chapter 15). The dominant powers in Asia remained land-based empires, such as Mughal (MOO-gahl) India and Ming China, rather than European overseas colonies. As Matteo Ricci's story shows, Europeans who traveled the maritime routes often operated on the margins of powerful Asian empires.

Still, the creation of more direct and sustained networks accelerated commercial and cultural interaction between Europe, Africa, and South and East Asia in the sixteenth and early seventeenth centuries, especially after the Dutch displaced the Portuguese as the main European players in the Indian Ocean. Following the maritime trade routes to China, Matteo Ricci became a key figure in the beginning of an ongoing "great encounter" between Europe and China.[2] Between 1400 and 1600, new and deepening economic linkages developed in the Indian Ocean, even as the Asian empires, such as India and China, became larger and more ambitious. In both Europe and Asia, major cultural and intellectual developments accompanied new encounters and connections.

Focus Questions

 What changes and continuities were associated with Portuguese and Dutch involvement in the Indian Ocean trade?

 What were the main political characteristics of the major South Asian and East Asian states? How was their development influenced by the new maritime connections of the sixteenth and early seventeenth centuries?

 How did religious and intellectual traditions of Eurasia change during this period, and what were the effects of encounters between them?

Maritime Trade Connections: Europe, the Indian Ocean, and Africa, 1500–1660

Unlike the Atlantic, the Indian Ocean had long served to connect rather than divide, facilitating trade between East Africa, the Persian Gulf, India, Southeast Asia, and China. The Portuguese added a new element to this network when their ships appeared in Indian Ocean waters in the early 1500s. Though their intention was to create an empire like that being constructed by Spain in the Americas, their political and military ambitions went largely unmet. The Dutch followed the Portuguese, bringing with them innovations in naval technology and business organization that stimulated the older oceanic trade networks while also building new ones.

Africa was connected to both the Atlantic and Indian Ocean systems. In East Africa the Portuguese merely inserted themselves into an existing commercial network along the East African coast. In West Africa, however, an entirely new oceanic trade began: the Atlantic slave trade.

Portugal's Entry into the Indian Ocean, 1498–1600

Henry the Navigator's exploration of the coasts and currents of the Atlantic Ocean culminated in 1488 when Bartholomew Dias and his crew rounded the southern tip of Africa at the Cape of Good Hope (see Chapter 15). These journeys had both economic and religious motives: in seeking an oceanic trade link with Asia, the Portuguese were trying to outflank Muslim intermediaries who controlled the land routes through western Asia and North Africa.

In 1497 the Portuguese explorer **Vasco da Gama** (1460–1524) sailed for India. The trip was not an easy one. After reaching the Cape of Good Hope, most of the crew wanted to return home and nearly mutinied. Sailing up the East African coast, da Gama hired a local pilot who used Arabic-language charts and navigational guides to guide the Portuguese from Africa to western India. One of these books boasted of the superiority of Arab knowledge: "We possess scientific books that give stellar altitudes. . . . [Europeans] have no science and no books, only the compass. . . . They admit we have a better knowledge of the sea and navigation and the wisdom of the stars." The Portuguese were sailing into well-charted waters, the same ones visited by Zheng He one hundred years earlier (see Chapter 15).

When they reached India, the Portuguese anchored their ships in well-established, cosmopolitan ports. India was at the center of the world's most extensive maritime trading system. In the western Indian Ocean, merchants transported East African gold, ivory, slaves, and timber to markets in southern Arabia, the Persian Gulf, and western India. Among the many goods exported from India along the same routes was highly valuable cotton cloth, often dyed by Indian craftsman specifically to appeal to customers in distant markets across the ocean.

On the east coast of India another set of maritime networks connected the Bay of Bengal and the markets of island and mainland Southeast Asia with Ming China. Muslim-ruled Malacca (mah-LAK-eh), which controlled trade through the straits between Sumatra and the Malaya Peninsula, had a population of over fifteen thousand traders from all over the Indian Ocean world. Here silk and sugar joined the long list of traded commodities. Cinnamon from the fabled "spice islands" was particularly precious. Whoever controlled the narrow straits at Malacca would profit handsomely from all this commercial activity.

• Vasco da Gama (1460–1524) Portuguese explorer who in 1497–1498 led the first European naval expedition to reach India by sailing around the Cape of Good Hope, laying the foundation for the Portuguese presence in the Indian Ocean in the century.

Economically, the Portuguese had almost nothing to offer: the first Indian king with whom they negotiated was insulted by the poor quality of their gifts. But what the Portuguese lacked in trade resources they made up for with military technology. Their ship-mounted cannon allowed them not only to blow their competitors out of the water but also to destroy the coastal defenses of political authorities at strategic points around the Indian Ocean. Seizing important trading centers from East Africa to Malacca, the Portuguese controlled a huge area after 1582. Their aggressive behavior earned them a widespread reputation as rough, greedy, and uncivilized.

In some cases the Portuguese redirected trade to profit themselves at the expense of previous merchant groups. For example, one of the main sources of gold for the Indian Ocean was the kingdom of Monomotapa in the interior of south-central Africa. For centuries the gold trade had been dominated by Swahili (swah-HEE-lee) merchants, African Muslims who lived on the coast. The Swahili town of Kilwa was ideally suited for this trade, since it was the furthest point south that mariners from India, Persia, and Arabia could safely reach and return in the same year using the monsoon winds. The Portuguese used their cannon to destroy the sea walls of Kilwa and tried to divert the gold southward through their settlement at Mozambique. The fact that they did so while flying militant crusader crosses on their sails did not endear them to local Muslim merchants and rulers.

But the degree of disruption the Portuguese caused at Kilwa was exceptional. More often they simply inserted themselves into existing commercial networks and used military force to extort payments from Asian and African rulers and traders. "What they set up was not an empire," argues one historian, "but a vast protection racket." Portuguese officials required that all ships trading in the ocean purchase a license, and if an Indian Ocean captain was found trading without one he risked Portuguese cannon fire; according to this historian, "the Portuguese were selling protection from violence which they themselves had created."[3]

Thailand (or Siam as it was then known) is a good barometer of both the extent and limitations of Portuguese power. Siam was a rising kingdom in the 1500s, struggling to establish its independence from Burma. The Portuguese were welcomed as trading partners and military allies. Access to European cannon and local adaptation of Portuguese styles of military fortification helped Siamese leaders centralize power and establish their independence. Siam later remained open to the Dutch and French and benefited greatly from the expansion of Indian Ocean trade. There were limits on European influence, however. Popular culture remained rooted in Thai adaptations of Hinduism and Buddhism. Asian traders, including Japanese, Chinese, and Malays, far outnumbered European ones. And trade with China, not with Europe, was central to Thailand's commercial life.

The biggest gap between Portuguese ambition and achievement was in religion. They made few converts to Christianity, while Islam continued to spread. The Portuguese did form an alliance with the Christian king of Ethiopia to help secure access to the Red Sea. In fact, in 1542 Cristovão da Gama, son of the navigator, died while leading Portuguese forces against a Muslim enemy of the Ethiopian king. But the Portuguese/Ethiopian alliance did not last. Members of the Orthodox branch of Christianity, the Ethiopians rejected Catholic teachings of the missionaries from Portugal. In the sixteenth century these African Christians were surrounded by expanding Muslim states. Here in the Red Sea region, as in South and Southeast Asia and all across the Indian Ocean world, it was Islam rather than Christianity that proved most attractive to new converts.

Fort Jesus, Mombasa Still standing on the Kenyan coast today, Fort Jesus was built by the Portuguese in 1593. The fort was built not only to protect Portuguese trade interests in the Indian Ocean, but also to assert the Christian conquest of the Swahili-speaking Muslims of Mombasa. The Swahili word for a jail, *gereza*, derives from the Portuguese word for a church, *igreja*, indicating how the residents of Mombasa themselves saw Fort Jesus. (© Adriane Van Zandbergen/ Alamy)

By the early seventeenth century the Portuguese position in the Indian Ocean was growing tenuous. Other powers, both European and Asian, were now using ship-based cannon and challenging Portuguese fortifications. In 1622, for example, the British allied themselves with Safavid Iran (see Chapter 17) to take the strategic port of Hormuz, at the mouth of the Persian Gulf, from the Portuguese, and in 1631 a local uprising drove the Portuguese from their strategic East African fortification of Fort Jesus. But the most potent challenge to Portuguese commercial profit came from Dutch merchants, who were, by the early seventeenth century, developing both more efficient business systems and more advanced shipping technologies.

The Dutch East India Company, 1600–1660

Early Dutch trading ventures in Europe and the Atlantic were often very profitable, but merchants could be financially ruined if violent storms sank their ships or if pirates stole their cargo. To spread the risk they developed joint-stock companies, a new form of business enterprise based on the sale of shares to multiple owners. In addition to helping investors avoid bankruptcy if a single venture failed, the joint-stock system allowed men and women of small means to buy a few shares and reap a modest profit with little risk.

The development of joint-stock companies put the Dutch at the forefront of early modern commercial capitalism. The development of financial institutions

■ **A Portrait of a Dutch Merchant**
Although Dutch merchants were among the most successful traders in the seventeenth-century world, the austerity of their clothing reflected their Calvinist religious beliefs. Here a ship-owner and his family are shown with the trading vessels that provided them with great wealth.
(Musée des Beaux-Arts, Valenciennes, France/Erich Lessing/Art Resource, NY)

such as banks, stock exchanges, and insurance companies increased the efficiency with which capital could be accumulated and invested. Rather than simply look for a single big windfall that would allow them to retire in comfort, investors now looked for more modest but regular gain through shrewd reinvestment of their profits. This dynamic of using profit for reinvestment and further profit was at the core of the new capitalist ethos associated with the bourgeoisie, the rising social group in Amsterdam and other urban areas of western Europe in the seventeenth century. The bourgeoisie based their social and economic power, and their political ambitions, on ownership of property rather than inherited titles.

Dutch culture reflected the rise of this commercially dynamic bourgeoisie. In many cultures trade was a low-status activity, it being assumed that a merchant could only be rich if he had made someone else poor. Seeking higher social status for their families, successful merchants in cultures as diverse as Spain and China would often use their assets to educate their sons to be "gentlemen" (in Spain) or members of the "literati" (in China). In Holland, by contrast, the leading citizens were all involved in trade, and commerce was seen as a noble calling.

The greatest of the joint-stock companies, and the largest commercial enterprise of the seventeenth century, was the **Dutch East India Company,** founded by a group of Amsterdam merchants in 1602. The government of the Netherlands granted a charter to the company giving it a monopoly on Dutch trade with Asia. As a "chartered company," the Dutch East India Company was also granted administrative and military responsibilities overseen from their headquarters in Batavia in what became the Dutch East Indies (today's Indonesia). In the coming centuries other European powers would copy the Dutch model and use chartered companies of their own to extend their national interests.

Dutch capitalism was not based on free-market principles. The Dutch East India Company was a heavily armed corporate entity that maintained its monopoly through force. "Trade cannot be maintained without war," said one governor of the East India Company, "nor war without trade."[4] The Dutch thus repeated

• **Dutch East India Company** Founded in 1602 in Amsterdam, a merchant company chartered to exercise a monopoly on all Dutch trade in Asia. The company was the effective ruler of Dutch colonial possessions in the East Indies.

the Portuguese pattern of using military force in the Indian Ocean to secure commercial profit, while at the same time introducing modern business and administrative techniques that made them more efficient and effective.

The Portuguese were no match for Dutch competition. In addition to their commercial innovations, the Dutch had made major advances in ship design and construction. In 1641 they took Malacca, the strategic choke point for Southeast Asian trade, from the Portuguese. They became a power in South Asia after they took the island of Sri Lanka (south of India) in 1658. The Dutch presence in Africa was focused on the settlement of Cape Town, established at the far southern tip of the continent in 1652. The fort at Cape Town was built to supply passing Dutch ships with water, meat, brandy, and fruit. At the other end of this vast oceanic expanse, ships of the Dutch East India Company made annual calls at the Japanese port of Nagasaki.

The Dutch East India Company made huge profits, especially from the spice trade. Sometimes they violently intervened in local affairs to increase production, as on the Bandas Islands, where they removed most of the local population and replaced them with slaves drawn from East Africa, Japan, and India to grow nutmeg. The estimated rate of profit ranged from several hundred to several thousand percent. Investors back in Holland were delighted.

The Dutch were lucky that at this time the entire Indian Ocean economy was being stimulated by the introduction of large quantities of American silver being mined by the Spanish in South America and shipped across the Pacific. In fact, the increased supply of silver into China and the Indian Ocean trade networks in the late sixteenth and early seventeenth centuries probably had a greater effect on those economies than the activities of European merchants. Still, the Dutch, with their efficient business organization and shipping infrastructure, were in an ideal position to profit from this development.

Origins of the Atlantic Slave Trade, 1483–1660

When their ships first ventured south in the fifteenth century, the Portuguese had regarded Africa primarily as a source of gold to finance their Asian trade. Almost immediately, however, slaves became part of European-African commerce (see Chapter 15). During the sixteenth century the foundation was laid for what became the largest movement of people to that point in human history: the forced migration of Africans across the Atlantic Ocean.

The lucrative and expanding market for sugar played a central role in the process. The Portuguese brought knowledge of slave-produced sugar from the Mediterranean to the Atlantic and first used African slaves to grow sugar on islands off the West African coast. By the early seventeenth century sugar plantations in Brazil and the Caribbean were generating huge profits (see Chapter 19). Looking to supply labor for expanding sugar plantations, Portuguese merchants found that they could purchase slaves in the markets of West Africa.

The **Kongo kingdom** was one of many African societies that were destabilized by the Atlantic slave trade. When the Portuguese arrived at the capital city of Mbanza Kongo in 1483, they found a prosperous, well-organized kingdom with extensive markets in cloth and iron goods. The Kongo king and aristocracy were quite interested in Portuguese technology. Firearms, though of limited military use in a forest environment, made a large impact when used for ceremonial purposes. The stone buildings that the Europeans constructed amid the mud-brick and thatch structures of the capital city aroused curiosity as well. (See the feature "Visual Evidence: An Ivory Mask from Benin, West Africa.")

● **Kongo kingdom** West-central African kingdom whose king converted to Christianity in the early sixteenth century and established diplomatic relations with the Portuguese. Became an early source of slaves for the new Atlantic slave trade.

AN IVORY MASK FROM BENIN, WEST AFRICA

The kingdom of Benin already had a long history of political and cultural achievement before the arrival of the first Europeans in the sixteenth century. Descendents of Oduduwa (oh-doo-doo-wah), ancestor of all Yoruba kings, Benin's rulers, the *obas*, were associated with great spiritual powers. Starting in the fourteenth century Beninese artists, organized into a guild by the king, began producing magnificent brass sculptures of royalty. Using a sophisticated "lost wax" technique, they made a beeswax model, covered it with bronze, molded it with clay, and then fired the sculpture, melting the wax and allowing the metal to flow into the open cavity. Their achievement was not only technical but also artistic. The Benin bronzes are known for their naturalism, a quality that made them highly attractive to European collectors. In fact, in 1897 the British colonial government looted over a thousand of these invaluable pieces, and the fight to return them to West Africa continues.

The bronze used in these sculptures was imported from the Mediterranean and was therefore extremely expensive. More often than lost-wax casting, Beninese artists carved masks and wall decorations directly from wood and ivory, sometimes incorporating cowrie shells imported from the Indian Ocean. This ivory mask, made around 1520, depicts Idia (ee-DEE-ah), the Queen Mother of Oba Esigie (eh-see-GEE-ay). Like the Benin bronzes, this ivory mask conveys a powerful sense of the individuality of its subject. The Portuguese were present in West Africa by this time and had allied with King Esigie and helped him fight off an enemy invasion. Their role in West African politics was still quite marginal, however, as indicated by the minor representation of European figures at the top.

A century and a half after this mask was made, a Dutch visitor was impressed with the capital city:

> The houses in this town stand in good order, one close and evenly placed with its neighbor, just as the houses in Holland stand. . . . The king's court is very great. It is built around many square-shaped yards. These yards have surrounding galleries where guards are always placed. I myself went into the court far enough to pass through four great yards like this, and yet wherever I looked I could still see gate after gate which opened into other yards.*

Earlier, in the sixteenth century, the pepper trade was so profitable that Benin's *obas* (kings) had closed the slave market. By the time the Dutch visitor came to Benin in 1688, however, slavery had become a major item of commerce, as elsewhere in West Africa. Nevertheless, Benin's artistic tradition continues until today.

---

*Olfert Dapper, *Description of Benin* (Madison: University of Wisconsin Press, 1998), p. 40.

QUESTION FOR ANALYSIS

 From the way they are represented on this mask, what might we infer about the extent of Portuguese influence on the artists of Benin?

In Benin, as in many African societies, the Queen Mother was a pivotal figure in the king's council, and he often relied on her to gain a consensus of opinion among clan leaders.

The Queen Mother had a special role in representing the interests and opinions of women.

The oba of Benin, King Esigie, is said to have worn this mask on his hip at a commemoration ceremony for Queen Idia.

The figures on top represent the Portuguese who allied with King Esigie and helped him thwart an enemy invasion. These Portuguese figures resemble the mudfish often found in Beninese sculptures. Like mudfish, the Portuguese could travel both in the water and on land.

(© Trustees of the British Museum)

459

Portuguese missionaries in Kongo found a royal family and aristocracy open to the message of Christianity. A baptized Christian, King Afonso Mvemba a Nzinga (uh-fahn-so mm-VEM-bah ah nn-ZING-ah) (r. 1506–1543), renamed his capital San Salvador, sent his son Enrique to study in Lisbon, and exchanged diplomatic envoys with both Portugal and the Vatican. It seemed that this would be an alliance of equals. Afonso, aided by the Portuguese, undertook wars of conquest that added additional territory to the Kongo kingdom.

Afonso's wars also had the side effect of stimulating the slave trade. In West Africa, as in many parts of the world, captives taken during war were in a precarious position. War captives might simply be killed, but more often they were exchanged, redeemed for a ransom, or kept as dependent workers. Into this traditional system came the new labor demands of the Atlantic plantation system. As demand for slaves increased, so did the supply.

King Afonso complained to his "brother king" in Portugal that some of the European Christians had lost interest in spreading the faith and were enslaving and exporting Afonso's own subjects:

> In our Kingdoms there is another great inconvenience which is of little service to God, and this is that many of our people, keenly desirous as they are of the wares and things of your Kingdoms, which are brought here by your people, and in order to satisfy their voracious appetite, seize many of our people, freed and exempt men . . . and so great, Sir, is the corruption and licentiousness that our country is being completely depopulated. . . . That is why we beg of your Highness to help and assist us in this matter . . . because it is our will that in these Kingdoms there should not be any trade of slaves nor outlet for them.[5]

Foreign goods and foreign traders had distorted the traditional market in slaves, which had previously been a byproduct of warfare, into an economic activity in its own right. Afonso's complaints fell on deaf ears.

As sugar production surged, the demand for slaves increased decade by decade. Not all parts of Africa were affected. On the east coast, Swahili merchants continued to participate in the Indian Ocean trade without engaging in the rising slave trade of the Atlantic. Most Central Africans had as yet little or no connection to the commercial and cultural influences of either the Atlantic or Indian Ocean networks. Yet over time the rise of the Atlantic slave trade would fundamentally alter the terms of Africans' interactions with the wider world (see Chapter 19).

The Politics of Empire in Southern and Eastern Asia, 1500–1660

In the course of Matteo Ricci's long journey he came in contact with a great variety of cultural and political systems. The largest and most powerful were Mughal India and Ming China.

Mughal India was a young and rising state in sixteenth-century South Asia with an economy stimulated by internal trade and expanding Indian Ocean commerce. Great political skill was needed to keep the vast Mughal realms at peace, however. The prosperity of South Asia depended on the extent to which India's Muslim rulers could maintain a stable political structure in the midst of great religious and ethnic diversity.

In the sixteenth century Ming China was the most populous and most productive society in the world. As we saw in the introduction to this chapter, Matteo Ricci was impressed with the order and good governance maintained by the Chinese emperors and their extensive official networks. But even while the Ming Dynasty earned Ricci's admiration in the early seventeenth century, it was about to begin a downward spiral that would end in 1644 in loss of power and a change of dynasty.

Since political leaders in the neighboring East Asian states of Vietnam and Korea had long emulated Chinese systems and philosophies of statecraft, Ming officials recognized these states as "civilized." Japan, while also influenced by China in many ways, was by Ming standards disordered and militaristic in this period, though it did achieve a more stable political system in the seventeenth century.

The Rise of Mughal India, 1526–1627

During Matteo Ricci's four-year stay in western India, the **Mughal dynasty,** the dominant power in South Asia, was at the height of its glory under its greatest leader, **Emperor Akbar** (r. 1556–1605). Building on the military achievements of his grandfather, who had swept into northern India from Afghanistan in the early sixteenth century, Akbar's armies controlled most of the Indian subcontinent. Ruling 100 million subjects from his northern capital of Delhi, the "Great Mughal" was one of the most powerful men in the world.

The Mughal state was well positioned to take advantage of expanding Indian Ocean trade. It licensed imperial mints that struck hundreds of millions of gold, silver, and copper coins of uniform value and trusted purity. The influx of silver from the Americas starting in the sixteenth century stimulated market exchanges. Dyed cotton textiles were a major export, along with sugar, pepper, diamonds, and other luxury goods.

Agriculture was the ultimate basis of Mughal wealth and power, providing 90 percent of the tax income that paid for Mughal armies and the ceremonial pomp of the court at Delhi. By insisting that taxes be paid in currency, Mughal officials forced villagers into the money economy, selling surplus produce for the coins needed to pay their taxes. State investment in roads helped traders move goods to market. The Mughals also supported movement of populations into previously underutilized lands by granting tax-exempt status to new settlements. The eastern half of Bengal (today's Bangladesh) was transformed from a lightly populated land of tropical forests into a densely populated rice-producing region.

The tax collection system also had political implications. In many parts of India a pre-Mughal aristocracy was used to collecting and retaining revenue from local production. The Mughals intruded on their prerogatives by sending tax clerks out to the provinces, surveying the lands, and diverting much of the revenue to Delhi. But they also confirmed the old aristocracy's rights to 10 percent of the local revenue and thus assured their loyalty.

Finding ways to bring such existing Indian authorities into Mughal structures of governance was the principal political challenge faced by Akbar and his successors. People may be conquered by the sword, but more stable forms of administration are usually necessary if conquest is to turn into long-term rule. In this case, the challenge was that the Islamic faith of the Mughal rulers differed from the Hindu beliefs of most of their subjects.

Mughal dynasty (1526–1857) During the height of their power in the sixteenth and seventeenth centuries, Mughal emperors controlled most of the Indian subcontinent from their capital at Delhi.

Emperor Akbar (r. 1556–1605) The most powerful of the Mughal emperors, Akbar pursued a policy of toleration toward the Hindu majority and presided over a cosmopolitan court.

Conflict at Ayodhya

Peace and harmony have not always characterized relations between Muslims and Hindus in India. While the nation has a secular constitution, some Hindu nationalists feel that it is and should be a Hindu nation. The large Muslim minority has felt threatened by the growth of this Hindu nationalism in recent years.

A flashpoint of conflict is the town of Ayodhya in northern India. According to legend, it was the birthplace of the Hindu god Rama and the site of a great Hindu temple. Hindu nationalists claim that the temple was torn down by an early Mughal ruler and replaced with a mosque. After Indian independence in 1947, Muslims were offended after some Hindu statues were smuggled in; to avoid conflict, the government fenced off the site and strictly limited access to the mosque. Then in 1992 a group of militant Hindu nationalists tore down the fence and destroyed the mosque. Thousands were killed in the rioting that followed.

One of the groups involved in the destruction of the mosque, the Bharatiya Janata Party (BJP),

was the leader of a coalition of parties that won the 1998 national elections. Though the BJP had promised to rebuild the Temple of Rama, it took no action and kept the site closed off. In 2002 the conflict escalated once again when a train carrying Hindu activists returning to western India from Ayodhya was set on fire, allegedly by Muslims, resulting in fifty deaths. In the retaliatory violence that followed over one thousand people, mainly Muslim, were killed.

Although nationalists continue to agitate and raise funds for a rebuilt temple, archaeologists have turned up no firm evidence that a temple to Rama ever stood on the site. Partially for that reason, a stone-cutting project begun in anticipation of building a new temple was halted in 2007 because of lack of donations. Still, the Ayodhya controversy continues to strain the tradition of peaceful religious coexistence established by Akbar, as well as the tradition of secular government enshrined in India's constitution.

(CL) **Primary Source:**
Akbarnama
These selections from the history of the house of Akbar offer a glimpse inside the policies and religious outlook of the Mughal emperor.

• **Nur Jahan** (1577–1645) Mughal empress who dominated politics during the reign of her husband Jahangir. By patronizing the arts and architecture and by favoring Persian styles, she had a lasting cultural influence on north India.

Akbar's policy was one of toleration and inclusion. He canceled the special tax that Islamic law allows Muslim rulers to collect from nonbelievers and granted Hindu communities the right to follow their own social and legal customs. Hindu *maharajahs* were incorporated into the Mughal administrative system at the imperial and regional levels just as rural aristocrats were at the local level. For their part, the Hindu population was accustomed to a social system in which people paid little attention to matters outside their own caste groups. Thus the ruling Muslims were simply another caste with their own rituals and beliefs. (See the feature "World History in Today's World: Conflict at Ayodhya.")

Akbar's policy of religious tolerance was continued by his successor Jahangir (r. 1605–1627) and his remarkable wife **Nur Jahan** (1577–1645). When Jahangir was faced with regional rebellions, Nur Jahan (noor ja-HAN), an intelligent and skilled politician, took charge and kept Mughal power intact. Since women were secluded in the *zezana,* or women's quarters, she could not appear at court in person. Instead she issued government decrees through trusted family members. She took a special interest in women's affairs, such as by donating land and dowries for orphan girls. Originally from Iran, Nur Jahan had a great cultural influence through her patronage of Persian-influenced art and architecture. She built many of the most beautiful mosques and gardens in north India.

Nur Jahan was also interested in commerce and owned a fleet of ships that took religious pilgrims and trade goods to Mecca. Even more than Akbar, her policies facilitated both domestic and foreign trade. Though she dictated policy from behind the closed doors of the zezana, Nur Jahan's favorable attitude toward trade and entrepreneurship had a strong influence on the wider world. Indian merchants, sailors, bankers, and shipbuilders were important participants in Indian Ocean markets, and the cosmopolitan ports of Mughal India teemed with visitors from Europe, Africa, Arabia, and Southeast Asia (see Map 16.1). But there was little Chinese presence in the Indian Ocean, and no followthrough to the fifteenth-century voyages of Zheng He (see Chapter 15). Unlike the Mughal rulers of India, the leaders of Ming China saw maritime trade more as a threat than as an opportunity.

The Apogee and Decline of Ming China, 1500–1644

By 1500 the **Ming dynasty** in China was at the height of its power and prestige. In 1368 the Ming had replaced the Mongol Yuan dynasty, and the early Ming rulers were highly conscious of the need to restore Confucian virtue after years of what they saw as "barbarian" rule. Like earlier Chinese dynasties, the Ming defined their country as the "Middle Kingdom" and called the emperor the "Son of Heaven." China was at the center of the world, and the emperor ruled with the "Mandate of Heaven."

The emperor's residence in the Forbidden City in Beijing (bay-JING), constructed during the early Ming period and still standing today, was at the center of a Confucian social order based on strict hierarchical relationships. The emperor stood at the top of the social hierarchy, and everyone owed him unquestioning obedience. For his part, the emperor was expected to emulate the benevolent behavior of the greatest Confucian sages, seeking the best interests of those dependent on him. The junior official owed obeisance to the senior one, the younger brother to the older one, the wife to the husband, and so on throughout society.

Hierarchy governed foreign relations as well. Ming officials respected those societies that had most successfully emulated Chinese political, intellectual, and cultural models, such as Korea and Vietnam. Japan and the societies of Inner Asia were usually thought of as "inner barbarians," peoples touched by Chinese civilization but still uncouth. All the rest of the world's peoples were regarded as "outer barbarians." From a Ming standpoint, the only conceivable relationship between any of these other kingdoms and China was a tributary one. Foreign kings were expected to send annual missions bearing tribute in acknowledgement of China's pre-eminent position.

Confucians believed that if such stable hierarchies of obeisance and benevolence were maintained, then the people would prosper. And in the early sixteenth century peace and prosperity were the norm in Ming China. The network of canals and irrigation works on which so much of the empire's trade and agriculture depended were refurbished and extended. Most important for trade and governance was the Grand Canal connecting the political and military capital Beijing with the productive Yangzi River Valley and fertile rice-producing regions further south. Public granaries were maintained as a hedge against famine. New food crops, including high-yield strains of rice from Southeast Asia and crops like maize, peanuts, and potatoes from the Americas, improved the health of the population, which had reached about 120 million people by the time of Matteo Ricci's arrival in 1582.

The **examination system,** based on the Confucian classics, helped ensure that the extensive Ming bureaucracy was staffed by competent officials at the local, county, and imperial levels. Years of study and tremendous powers of recall were

• **Ming dynasty** (1368–1644) Chinese imperial dynasty in power during the travels of Matteo Ricci. At its height during the fifteenth century, by 1610 the Ming dynasty was showing signs of the troubles that would lead to its overthrow.

• **examination system** Chinese system for choosing officials for positions in the Ming imperial bureaucracy. Candidates needed to pass one or more examinations that increased in difficulty for higher positions.

🖱 **Interactive Map**

🌐 **MAP 16.1**

Maritime Trade in the Eastern Indian Ocean and East Asia

By 1630 the Dutch had overtaken the Portuguese in Indian Ocean trade, the French and English were becoming more active, and Spanish silver from American mines was stimulating trade across South, Southeast, and East Asia. Dutch ships passed through Cape Town in South Africa bearing Asian and African cargo, such as valuable spices, for European markets. Still, the dominant powers in Asia remained land-based empires such as the Mughal Empire in India and the Ming Empire in China. Traditional trade routes controlled by local sailors and merchants—between Japan and China, between the South China Sea and the Bay of Bengal, and between western India, the Persian Gulf, and East Africa—were also growing in volume in the seventeenth century.

necessary to succeed on the highest and most difficult levels of the civil service examination. With a hierarchy of well-educated officials supervised by dynamic emperors, the early Ming efficiently carried out such basic tasks of government as the collection of taxes and maintenance of public order.

The elaborate and expensive Ming bureaucracy required an efficient system of tax collections. In 1571 Ming officials decided that only payments in silver would be acceptable, generating a surge in global demand for silver. While Japan was the traditional source of silver for China, its mines could not keep up with demand. But at that time massive new silver discoveries in the Americas, combined with technological advances that increased the yield of silver from ore, made huge quantities of silver available to China (see Chapter 17). The Spanish city of Manila in the Philippines became the destination for the Manila Galleons, an annual shipment of silver from Mexico. Thus, silver was central to an emerging trans-Pacific trade, which was from the beginning connected to the Indian Ocean network. In the late sixteenth century this flow of silver between the Americas and Asia was helping to lay the foundation of a global economy.

Ming officials saw the development of these more intensive commercial networks as a mixed blessing. On the one hand, the flow of silver was essential to the functioning of the Chinese economy and the taxation it made possible. On the other hand, Ming officials regarded the sea with suspicion. It was unpredictable and difficult to control, the realm of "pirates" like the Japanese and Portuguese. Unlike the Mughal rulers of India, therefore, Ming officials tried to limit and control seaborne commerce. Their efforts met only limited success because the momentum of foreign trade driven by the demand for silver had become too powerful.

In this emerging world economy, reliance on foreign silver supplies made the Ming economy vulnerable to distant economic shocks. While the influx of silver stimulated Chinese economic growth, it also caused inflation. Rising prices caused distress to people less well poised to benefit from commercial expansion. Even more

The Destitute of Ming China While acknowledging the power of the Ming dynasty and other great kingdoms and empires of the past, we might also remember that even amidst wealth and luxury, poverty was the fate of many. These scenes of the poor of Suzhou were painted in 1516 by the artist Zhou Chen as "a warning and admonition to the world." (The Cleveland Museum of Art [1964.94])

severe was the effect of declining silver supplies on the world market after 1620. By that date economic contraction was contributing to an accelerating crisis in Ming governance.

The decline of the Ming is associated with the **Wanli Emperor** (r. 1573–1620), whose apathetic attitude toward his duties did much to undermine the achievements of his predecessors. Within the walls of the Forbidden City personalities and petty jealousies became more important as the influence of uneducated court eunuchs rose at the expense of scholar-officials. Without imperial oversight, corruption increased: gifts could determine the outcome of court cases, grain intended for famine relief was sold on the market, and irrigation works went untended. Bandits vexed merchants on the roads, and local peasant uprisings became more common. When Matteo Ricci was finally granted permission to enter the Forbidden City and performed the ritual *kowtow,* prostrating himself with his forehead on the ground, he did so before a vacant Dragon Throne. The Wanli Emperor was inaccessible, remaining deep in the recesses of the Forbidden City.

Matteo Ricci, in his tribute to Ming governance cited in the chapter opening, appears to have failed to notice the decay that was setting in below the impressive façade of the Wanli Emperor's court. In 1644 northern invaders from Manchuria breached the walls of Beijing and drove the Ming from power (see Chapter 20).

Tradition and Innovation: Korea, Vietnam, and Japan, 1500–1650

The societies most strongly connected to Chinese civilization in the early modern period were Korea, Vietnam, and, more loosely, Japan. The Chosŏn (choh-SAN) dynasty of Korea, who closely followed the Ming imperial model, established one of the world's most stable political systems, ruling the Korean peninsula from 1392 until the early twentieth century. The capital at Seoul (sole) was home to a Confucian academy that trained young men for examinations that led to social prominence and political power.

While early modern Korea was not as commercially dynamic as Ming China, it did benefit from a remarkable series of innovations undertaken by the **Emperor Sejong** (r. 1418–1450). Before his time, learning to read and write required years of training in the complexities of Chinese script. Then in 1446, Sejong (SAY-jung) brought together a group of scholars to devise a new phonetic script based on the Korean language. This distinctive *han'gul* (HAHN-goor) writing system, still in use today, enabled many more Koreans to read and write. Emperor Sejong supported projects to write the history of the country in the new Korean script and also to translate key Buddhist texts. He also patronized printers who were developing a more efficient technology to produce large books more cheaply. Korea became one of the world's most literate societies.

The Vietnamese were also strongly influenced by China, but their leaders, having repulsed fifteenth-century Ming armies, were protective of their political independence. In 1428 the general who took power in Vietnam after defeating a Ming army gave his name to the new **Lê dynasty.** One story relates that General Lê (lee) sent a gift of cattle to his retreating Ming counterpart, as if to say that the invasion would not stop Vietnam from pursuing positive relations with China. Indeed, Lê monarchs closely copied Chinese imperial models. Confucianism rose in importance in traditionally Buddhist Vietnam as scholar-officials gained influence at court. Military expeditions expanded the size and strength of the Vietnamese state, and

Himeji Castle
Incessant warfare during the Ashikaga period led the Japanese *daimyo* barons to build well-fortified stone castles. The introduction of cannon in the sixteenth century made the need for such fortifications even greater. Himeji Castle was begun in 1346; Toyotomi Hideyoshi greatly expanded and beautified it in the late sixteenth century. Now a UNESCO World Cultural and Heritage Site, Himeji is the best-preserved castle in all of Japan.   (© Jon Arnold Images Ltd/Alamy)

agrarian reforms led to greater equality in landholding and greater productivity in agriculture.

Japan lay further outside the orbit of Chinese civilization than either Korea or Vietnam. Unlike in Ming China, political power was decentralized during Japan's Ashikaga (ah-shee-KAH-gah) Shogunate (1336–1568), and the Japanese emperor, unlike his Chinese, Korean and Vietnamese counterparts, was a ritual figure with no real authority. The greatest political power was the *shogun,* a supreme military ruler who acted independently of the imperial court. But the Ashikaga shoguns themselves had little control over the *daimyo* (DIE-mee-oh), barons who ruled their own rural domains. As each daimyo had an army of *samurai* (SAH-moo-rye) military retainers, incessant warfare spread chaos through the islands.

Ashikaga Japan was a land of contrasts. While the daimyo lords engaged in violent competition for land and power, they also acted as benefactors of Buddhist monasteries, which promoted spiritual reflection. The samurai warriors, with their strict *bushido* code of honor and loyalty, were also practitioners of the Zen school of Buddhism, with its emphasis on mental discipline and acute awareness. Flower arranging and the intricate refinement of the tea ceremony were also highly developed, peaceful counterpoints to the ceaseless military competition of the daimyo.

In the late sixteenth century several Japanese lords aspired to replace the Ashikaga family; the most ambitious was **Toyotomi Hideyoshi** (r. 1585–1598), whose plans included not only the consolidation of power on the Japanese islands but also conquest of the mainland. In 1592, as Matteo Ricci was journeying in southern China, Hideyoshi's forces attacked Korea with an army of 200,000 soldiers. A statue of Admiral Yi in central Seoul still commemorates his use of heavily fortified "turtle ships," armed with multiple cannon and wooden planks shielding their decks, to defend Korea against the Japanese attack.

● **Toyotomi Hideyoshi** (r. 1585–1598) A *daimyo* (baron) who aspired to unify Japan under his own rule. His attempts to conquer Korea and China failed, and members of the competing Tokugawa family became shoguns and unified the islands.

In a power struggle following Hideyoshi's death, the Tokugawa (TOH-koo-GAH-wah) clan emerged victorious. After 1603, the **Tokugawa Shogunate** centralized power by restraining independence of the daimyo, forcing them to spend half the year in the shogun's new capital of Edo (today's Tokyo). Compared with the highly centralized imperial model of Korea, which persisted even after the fall of the Ming, political power in Japan was still diffuse, with many regional barons controlling their own domains. But the Tokugawa system brought a long-term stability that made possible economic and demographic growth. In the seventeenth century, as market exchanges became central to the Japanese economy (see Chapter 20), Japanese cities such as Osaka and Nagasaki emerged as vibrant commercial centers.

Despite this increased unity, some daimyo formed diplomatic and trade alliances with Christian missionaries, undercutting the centralizing ambitions of the Tokugawa court at Edo. As a result, Jesuit missionaries attracted many converts, and the shoguns became deeply suspicious of both European and Japanese Christians. After 1614 they outlawed the foreign faith; hundreds of Japanese Christians were killed, some by crucifixion, when they refused to recant their faith. Apart from an annual Dutch trade mission confined to an island in the port of Nagasaki, no Christians were allowed to enter the country. Japanese trade with China and Korea, however, continued to flourish.

●Eurasian Intellectual and Religious Encounters, 1500–1620

In the early modern Afro-Eurasian world, increased maritime trade networks also led to increased cultural interactions. Intellectual ferment in this period was often associated with new religious ideas. In western Europe the Protestant Reformation divided Christians over basic matters of faith. Matteo Ricci himself was a representative of the Catholic Reformation, which sought to re-energize Roman Catholicism. In Mughal India, many people converted to Islam and the new faith of Sikhism was founded, while the emperor himself promoted his own "Divine Faith" to reconcile diverse religious traditions. In China, Matteo Ricci attempted to convince Ming scholar-officials that Christianity was compatible with the oldest and purest versions of Confucianism.

Challenges to Catholicism, 1517–1620

While Renaissance humanism had led to significant artistic and intellectual achievement in western Europe (see Chapter 15), it coincided with increasing corruption in the Catholic Church. For example, popes and bishops raised money for prestigious building projects, such as Saint Peter's Basilica in Rome, by selling "indulgences," certificates that, according to church authorities, had the power to liberate souls from purgatory and allow them to enter into heaven. Thus the cultural richness of the Roman Church was underwritten by practices that some European Christians viewed as mere corruption and worldliness.

One of these, a cleric named **Martin Luther** (1483–1546), was infuriated. Surely, he argued, salvation could not be purchased; only God could determine the spiritual condition of a human soul. Luther made his challenge public in 1517 and refused to stand down when brought before church and civil authorities. Excommunicated by the church, he began to lead his own religious services, and the Protestant Reformation was under way. The Christian church, already divided since the eleventh century between its Eastern Orthodox and Roman Catholic branches, was now divided within western Europe itself (see Map 16.2).

As a significant minority of sixteenth-century western Europeans left Catholicism, they developed a variety of alternative church structures, rituals, and beliefs. Lutherans, as the followers of Martin Luther were called, downgraded the importance of intermediaries between the individual and God and therefore challenged the whole edifice of the Catholic priestly hierarchy. Taking advantage of increased literacy and the wider availability of printed Bibles after the fifteenth-century development of movable-type printing, Luther argued that individuals should read their own Bibles and not rely on priests to interpret God's word for them. He translated the Bible into the German language, making the scriptures available for the first time to the many who could read German but not Latin. In the seventeenth century the Protestant Reformation led to significant political violence as some leaders of western European states defended the reformers while others took up arms to defend Roman Catholicism (see Chapter 17).

There were no Protestants in Matteo Ricci's hometown in central Italy, where the pope held both civil and religious authority. In secure Catholic areas like this the inquisition, a church bureaucracy devoted to the suppression of heresy, was always on guard to squelch "heretical" ideas such as those of Martin Luther. But even here the impact of the Reformation was profound, for the Catholic Church was shaken out of its complacency and launched a response known as the **Catholic Reformation,** or Counter-Reformation.

A major focus of the Catholic Reformation was more rigorous training of priests to avoid the abuses that had left the church open to Protestant criticism. As a member of the Jesuit order, or Society of Jesus, Ricci was especially trained in the debating skills needed to fend off Protestant theological challenges. The Jesuits were one of several new Catholic orders developed to confront the Protestant challenge and, especially in the Jesuit case, to take advantage of the new maritime routes to spread their faith around the world.

Another challenge to Catholic belief that developed during Ricci's lifetime was the "new science" associated with his fellow Italian the great scientist **Galileo Galilei** (1564–1642). Catholic theologians had reconciled faith and reason by incorporating classical Greek thinkers, especially Aristotle, into church teachings. The work of Galileo (gal-uh-LAY-oh) struck at the heart of that intellectual system by challenging the authority of Aristotle. Carefully measuring the acceleration of balls rolled down inclined planes, he overturned Aristotle's law of inertia by arguing that a body in motion would stay in motion unless acted upon by some external force, an insight that would later prove essential to new understandings of planetary motion. Pointing his telescope toward the heavens, Galileo discovered things the church could not explain: spots on the sun, craters on the moon, and other indications that the heavens were not a place of absolute, unchanging perfection.

Galileo became convinced of the validity of the heliocentric theory first proposed in 1543 by the Polish astronomer Nicolaus Copernicus, which placed the sun rather than the earth at the center of the solar system. Further support for the Copernican system was offered by the German mathematician Johannes Kepler, who argued that elliptical rather than circular orbits best explained planetary motion,

CL **Primary Source: Table Talk** *Read Martin Luther in his own words, speaking out forcefully and candidly—and sometimes with humor— against Catholic institutions.*

● **Catholic Reformation** Reform movement in the Catholic Church, also called the Counter-Reformation, that developed in response to the Protestant Reformation. The church clarified church doctrines and instituted a program for better training of priests.

CL **Primary Source: Letter to the Grand Duchess Christina** *Read Galileo's passionate defense of his scientific research against those who would condemn it as un-Christian.*

● **Galileo Galilei** (1564–1642) Italian scientist who provided evidence to support the heliocentric theory, challenging church doctrine and the authority of Aristotle. He was forced to recant his position by the inquisition, but his theories were vindicated during the Scientific Revolution.

MAP 16.2

The Protestant Reformation By the middle of the sixteenth century Protestant churches were dominant in England, Scotland, the Netherlands, Switzerland, and Scandinavia. German principalities were
divided between Protestants and Catholics. Catholicism remained dominant across most of southern
Europe, though Protestants formed a significant minority in France. The religious landscape was especially complex in southeastern Europe, where, under Ottoman authority, there were substantial communities of Catholics, Protestants, Orthodox Christians, and Muslims.

CL Interactive Map

a theory contrary to both classical tradition and church teachings. Church authorities saw the "new science" as a direct challenge to Christianity; the heliocentric theory, they argued, contradicted the book of Genesis by displacing the earth from its central place in God's creation. The church put Galileo on trial and forced him to recant his support for the heliocentric theory.

The ferment of the new ideas arising from the Protestant Reformation and the "new science" helped sharpen Matteo Ricci's intellectual training and prepare him for his travels. In India he took part in lively religious and philosophical debates that were valuable preparation for his missionary work in China.

Islam, Sikhism, and Akbar's "Divine Faith," 1500–1605

The Mughal capital of Delhi was a cosmopolitan place. In addition to bringing Hindus and Muslims together, Akbar attracted to his court scholars, artists, and officials from Iran, Afghanistan, and Central Asia. Mughal India proved a fertile environment for artistic growth as Persian, Turkish, and Indian influences flowed together. The Taj Mahal, a "love poem in marble" built by Akbar's grandson as a memorial to his wife, is the best-known example of the Persian-influenced architecture inspired by Nur Jahan and other Mughal leaders.

Akbar was keenly interested in religion, and he routinely invited leaders from various religious traditions to debate at his court. In 1579, the year after Ricci arrived at Goa, a diplomatic embassy arrived from the Great Mughal requesting that Catholic missionaries come to Delhi. "We hope for nothing less than the conversion of all India," wrote Ricci. Two missionaries went to Delhi, bringing a richly produced, lavishly illustrated, and very costly Bible as a gift for the emperor. Although the emperor did not convert, his interest in the Jesuit mission was characteristic of his open-minded exploration of diverse faiths.

During this time Sufism was also attracting new converts. In addition to obeying the Muslim laws of submission, Sufis were often loyal to personal religious leaders who claimed to have special means of approaching God. The mystical Sufis often used rhythmic motion and special chants to create a meditative state in which they could feel God's presence. Some Muslim scholars, especially those who stressed the more legalistic aspects of

Akbar with Representatives of Various Religions at His Court   For years, the Mughal Emperor Akbar hosted weekly conversations among scholars and priests of numerous religions, including the Jesuits seen here on the left. Akbar sponsored the translation of varied religious texts, including the Christian Bible, into Persian, even though he himself was illiterate. When criticized by some Muslim scholars for his patronage of Hindu arts and his openness to other religious traditions, Akbar is said to have replied, "God loves beauty." (The Chester Beatty Library, Dublin)

Islam, looked with suspicion on the more emotional Sufi forms of religious devotion. Akbar brought both the legal scholars and the Sufi mystics to his court and listened intently to their debates.

Akbar also brought Jews, Hindus, and representatives of other faiths to Delhi. Having encountered so many different spiritual traditions, he announced his own adherence to a "Divine Faith" that he said both included and transcended them all:

> O God, in every temple I see people that seek Thee; in every language I hear spoken, people praise Thee; if it be a mosque, people murmur in prayer; if it be a Christian church they ring the bell for love of Thee . . . it is Thou whom I seek from temple to temple.[6]

Akbar extended to the new faith of Sikhism the same tolerance he had granted more established religions. While Akbar's "Divine Faith" never spread beyond the Mughal court and disappeared after his own death, Sikhism grew into a successful new faith community. The first Sikh (sick) spiritual leader (*guru*) was Nanak (1469–1539). Through conversations with a wide range of religious thinkers, Nanak became convinced that Hinduism, despite its outward appearance of polytheism, had at its core a belief in a single God, and that this made Hinduism and Islam compatible. His reconciliation of the two faiths emphasized the equality of all believers, and he rejected the Hindu caste system.

Although Nanak emphasized peace and harmony, the Sikh community developed a formidable military tradition when a later Mughal emperor canceled Akbar's policy of tolerance and had their guru beheaded (see Chapter 20). The dead leader's son reorganized the Sikhs into an "army of the pure" with distinctive dress and appearance: unshaved beards, uncut hair beneath a turban, and a military style of dress with a sword prominently displayed. Ironically, Nanak's attempt to reconcile Hinduism and Islam led to the formation of a separatist religious community.

Hinduism was also undergoing important changes and reforms in the early modern period. The epic story of the *Ramayana*, formerly read only by priests trained in the ancient Sanskrit language, was retold in 1575 by a prominent poet using the commonly spoken Hindi language, making this story of the ancient king, a manifestation of the god Vishnu, more accessible. This development was part of a broader development of new forms of Hindu devotion that de-emphasized the role of Brahmin priests. The new version of the *Ramayana* was an achievement parallel to the translation of the Bible into languages like English and German and to the new availability of Buddhist texts in the Korean *han'gul* script. In all of these cases religious inquiry was not limited to kings and philosophers but could be found at all levels of society.

Ricci in China: Catholicism Meets Neo-Confucianism, 1582–1610

Ming China was less religiously diverse than Mughal India, with Buddhism as the empire's majority faith. In fact, when Ricci first arrived in Ming China, he adopted the dress of a Buddhist priest, with a shaved head, a beard, and flowing robes. Soon he came to understand, however, that affiliating himself with Buddhism would not carry much weight with the most prominent people in Chinese society, the scholar-officials who manifested the power of the emperor. Many of these *literati* looked down on the poorly educated Buddhist clergy. Ricci subsequently changed his appearance and habits to appeal to this prestigious class of individuals. His plan was to convert China through its leading Confucian scholars, from the top down.

Confucian scholars emphasized education as the main route to self-cultivation. While most of the emperor's subjects remained nonliterate peasant cultivators, young children from more privileged households were taught to read from a young age, often by memorizing a list of one thousand different characters that taught Confucian virtues like hard work and respect for elders and teachers. After they had mastered such basics, boys had to memorize the classic texts of Confucianism, collections of poems, and histories of past times that usually focused on the virtues of ancient sages.

In theory, any young man could take the annual examinations and, if successful, become an imperial official. In reality, the cost of private tutors meant that children of the elite held an advantage. Still, the Ming system was based on merit: wealth and status could not purchase high office, and even the privileged had to undergo years of intensive study.

Though women were barred from taking the examinations, the Ming emphasis on education did contribute to the spread of female literacy. Foreign observers noted how many girls were able to read and write. However, education for girls reinforced Confucian views of gender. Rather than reading histories of sages and virtuous officials, girls usually read stories about women who submitted to their parents when they were young, obeyed their husbands once they were married, and listened to their sons when they became widowed. Singled out for special praise were widows who demonstrated eternal loyalty to their husbands by declining to be remarried. Chinese girls were thereby indoctrinated into the Confucian ideal of strict gender hierarchy.

Matteo Ricci paid careful attention to debates between advocates of various schools of Confucianism as he built up an argument for the compatibility of Confucianism and Christianity. At this time the Neo-Confucian philosophy of Wang Yangming (1472–1529) was especially influential. While other Confucians had emphasized close observation of the external world as the path of the sage, Wang stressed self-reflection, arguing that "everybody, from the infant in swaddling clothes to the old, is in full possession of . . . innate knowledge." Ricci accused Wang's Neo-Confucian followers of distorting Confucianism. By returning to the original works of the ancient sages, Ricci said, the Chinese literati would discover that one could convert to Christianity while retaining the ethical and philosophical traditions of Confucius.

Once his language skills were sufficiently developed, Ricci took advantage of a favorite Ming pastime to share his views. Scholar-officials would often invite interesting speakers to a banquet and, after dinner, hold philosophical debates. For many in the audience Ricci's well-known ability to instantly memorize and repeat long lists of information, and even repeat them backwards, would have been of greater interest than his views on Confucian philosophy and Christian theology. It was a highly relevant skill in a society where difficult exams were the main path to power and status. But while his hosts might have been entertained by his arguments, few were persuaded by them.

Ricci also impressed his hosts with examples of European art and technology, especially printed books, paintings, clocks, and maps. Lavishly illustrated and beautifully bound books contrasted with the austerity of Chinese woodblock prints. Chinese artists adapted European techniques of landscape painting, and Ming astronomers were impressed by European telescopes and the precision with

Christianity in China

Are Christianity and Confucianism compatible? Matteo Ricci thought so, though other Jesuits disagreed. How did Chinese officials and intellectuals address this question?

At first, Ming toleration of Christianity continued during the Qing dynasty (see Chapter 20), as an edict of the Emperor Kangxi in 1692 proclaimed: "The Europeans . . . commit no crimes, and their doctrine has nothing in common with that of the false sects in the empire, nor has it any tendency to excite sedition." The emperor ordered that Christian churches be protected and open to worshipers. In 1715, however, the church reversed Ricci's policy by declaring that

Confucian rites were incompatible with Christianity. Emperor Kangxi was furious: "To judge from this proclamation, their religion is no different from other small, bigoted sects of Buddhism." In 1721 he banned Christians from preaching in his empire.

Earlier, in the seventeenth century, Confucian intellectuals had given assessments of the Catholic faith, examples of which are given below.

Source: Jacques Gernet, *China and the Christian Impact: A Conflict of Cultures,* (New York: Cambridge University Press, 1986), pp. 39–40, 53, 82, 107, 108, 120, 159, 161.

Chinese Commentaries on Christianity

1) [The Jesuits] are extremely intelligent. Their studies concern astronomy, the calendar, medicine and mathematics; their customs are compounded of loyalty, good faith, constancy and integrity; their skill is wonderful. Truly they have the means to win minds. . . . The only trouble is that it is a pity that they speak of a Master of Heaven, an incorrect and distasteful term which leads them into nonsense. . . . Our Confucianism has never held that Heaven had a mother or a bodily form, and it has never spoken of events that are supposed to have occurred before and after his birth. Is it not true that herein lies the difference between our Confucianism and their doctrine?

2) Compared with the contents of the Buddhist books, what [the Christians] say is straightforward and full of substance. The principal idea comes down to respecting the Master of Heaven, leading a life that conforms with morality, controlling one's desires and studying with zeal. . . . Nevertheless . . . what they say about paradise and hell appears to differ barely at all from what the Buddhists maintain and they go even further than the latter when it comes to extravagance and nonsense.

3) [The Jesuits] openly take issue with the false ideas of Buddhism. . . . Meanwhile, where they do take issue with Confucianism, they do not

dare to open their mouths wide for they wish to use the cap and gown of the literate elite to introduce their doctrine even into Court, so as to spread their poison more effectively.

4) The superiority of Western teaching lies in their calculations; their inferiority lies in their veneration of a Master of Heaven of a kind to upset men's minds. . . . When they require people to consider the Master of Heaven as their closest relative and to abandon their fathers and mothers and place their sovereign [king] in second place, giving the direction of the state to those who spread the doctrine of the Master of Heaven, this entails an unprecedented infringement on the most constant rules. How could their doctrine possibly be admissible in China?

5) [The Ming emperor] sacrifices to Heaven and to Earth; the princes sacrifice to the mountains and rivers within the domains; holders of high office sacrifice to the ancestral temple of the founder of their lineage; gentlemen and ordinary individuals sacrifice to the tables of their own [immediate] ancestors. . . . In this way . . . there is an order in the sacrifices that cannot be upset. To suggest that each person should revere a single Master of Heaven and represent Heaven by means of statues before which one prays each day . . . is it not to profane Heaven by making unseemly requests?

6) In their kingdom they recognize two sovereigns. One is the political sovereign [the king] the other is the doctrinal sovereign [the pope]. . . . The former reigns by right of succession and passes on his responsibilities to his descendents. He nevertheless depends upon the doctrinal sovereign, to whom he must offer gifts and tokens of tribute. . . . It comes down to having two suns in the sky, two masters in a single kingdom. . . . What audacity it is on the part of these calamitous Barbarians who would like to upset the [political and moral] unity of China by introducing the Barbarian concept of the two sovereigns!

7) We Confucians follow a level and unified path. Confucius used to say . . . "To study realities of the most humble kind in order to raise oneself to the comprehension of the highest matters, what is that if not 'serving heaven?'" . . . To abandon all this in order to rally to this Jesus who died nailed to a cross . . . to prostrate oneself before him and pray with zeal, imploring his supernatural aid, that would be madness. And to go so far as to enter darkened halls, wash oneself with holy water and wear amulets about one's person, all that resembles the vicious practices of witchcraft.

8) In the case of Jesus there is not a single [miracle] that is comparable [to those of the ancient sages]. Healing the sick and raising the dead are things that can be done by great magicians, not actions worthy of one who is supposed to have created Heaven, Earth and the Ten Thousand Beings. If one considers those to be exploits, how is it that he did not arrange for people never to be sick again and never to die? That *would* have increased his merit.

9) Our father is the one who engendered us, our mother the one who raised us. Filial piety consists solely in loving our parents. . . . Even when one of our parents behaves in a tyrannical fashion, we must try to reason with him or her. Even if a sovereign behaves in an unjust way, we must try to get him to return to human sentiments. How could one justify criticizing one's parents or resisting one's sovereign on the grounds of filial piety toward the Master of Heaven?

QUESTIONS FOR ANALYSIS

▶ In which documents is Christianity judged to be incompatible with China's social and political traditions? How is that incompatibility described?

▶ Matteo Ricci was critical toward Buddhism. In these documents, where and how do Chinese authors equate Christianity with Buddhism?

▶ Do these critiques seem to be based on a deep or superficial understanding of seventeenth-century Christianity?

which the Jesuits could predict such events as eclipses. Late-sixteenth-century European clocks, while not very reliable by later standards, were much more accurate than the water clocks used by the Chinese. And Ricci's world map, locating the "western barbarians" for the first time in relation to the "Middle Kingdom," was such a success that Chinese artisans were employed to print reproductions.

For Ricci, however, mnemonic tricks, maps, and clocks were only a means to convert his audience to Christianity. Criticizing both Buddhism and Neo-Confucianism, Ricci emphasized those aspects of the Western tradition that appealed most to Confucian intellectuals: its moral and ethical dimensions rather than its character as a revealed religion. For example, after learning that Chinese scholars were usually upset to hear about the suffering and death of Jesus, he largely avoided that central aspect of Christianity. (See the feature "Movement of Ideas: Christianity in China.")

Ricci's most influential work published in Chinese was *The True Meaning of the Lord of Heaven*. Composed with the aid of the small number of Chinese Christian converts, it is a dialogue between a "Chinese Scholar" and a "Western Scholar." In the following passage Ricci criticizes Buddhism and argues for the compatibility of Confucianism and Christianity:

> *Chinese Scholar:* The Buddha taught that the visible world emerges from "voidness" and made "voidness" the end of all effort. The Confucians say: "In the processes of *Yi* there exists the Supreme Ultimate" and therefore make "existence" the basic principle [of all things] and "sincerity" the subject of the study of self-cultivation. I wonder who, in your revered view, is correct?

> *Western Scholar:* The "voidness" taught by the Buddha [is] totally at variance with the doctrine concerning the Lord of Heaven [i.e., Christianity], and it is therefore abundantly clear that [it does] not merit esteem. When it comes to the "existence" and "sincerity" of the Confucians, however . . . they would seem to be close to the truth.[7]

Such arguments did not convince many, but at least the Jesuits in China, unlike their brethren in Japan, were accepted as representatives of a legitimate school of philosophy.

Some Jesuits and Vatican officials felt that *The True Meaning of the Lord of Heaven* and other attempts by Ricci to reconcile Christianity and Confucianism went too far. For example, Ricci argued that veneration of ancestors was compatible with Christianity and the biblical command to "honor your father and your mother." Less flexible church authorities felt that Chinese ancestor rites were pagan and should be rejected. Ricci knew that such a rigid interpretation of cultural practice would limit the appeal of Christianity among potential converts, who would be ostracized by family and friends if they abandoned their household shrines. Although Matteo Ricci made no more than a handful of converts, he played an important role in world history as the first major figure in the ongoing "great encounter" between Europe and China.

Chapter Review

The new maritime route from Europe to Asia that took Matteo Ricci from Europe through the Indian Ocean to Ming China, while not as revolutionary as the one that connected Europe with the Americas, stimulated important new economic, political, and cultural connections across early modern Afro-Eurasia. Among the important outcomes were the beginnings of the Atlantic slave trade, increased interaction between the great land-based Asian empires and European states, and competition among European states for dominance in Asian trade.

 ## What changes and continuities were associated with Portuguese and Dutch involvement in the Indian Ocean trade?

Even as the Portuguese and Dutch intruded on the Indian Ocean, there was significant continuity with earlier patterns of trade. While the Portuguese did manage to control strategic coastal locations, they did not create an overarching imperial structure for the Indian Ocean. In West Africa they had a significant effect on the Kongo kingdom and helped lay the foundations of the Atlantic slave trade, and they displaced some Swahili rulers along the Indian Ocean coast and became involved in the Christian kingdom of Ethiopia. But most Africans remained unaffected by such Portuguese initiatives. During the seventeenth century, the Dutch East India Company brought deeper changes, especially in commerce. Significant quantities of goods, such as Indian textiles, Chinese porcelain, and Southeast Asian spices, were now carried to Europe, often purchased with American silver. In fact, the huge inflow of silver was a greater stimulus to the Asian economies ringing the Indian Ocean than European merchant activity itself.

While the Dutch were a formidable new military presence, their direct influence, like that of the Portuguese, was limited to the few islands and coastal fortifications under their control. African and Asian rulers were still the key to politics in places like the Swahili city-states of East Africa, the Persian Gulf and Bay of Bengal, and mainland Southeast Asia.

KEY TERMS

Matteo Ricci (450)
Vasco da Gama (453)
Dutch East India Company (456)
Kongo kingdom (457)
Mughal dynasty (461)
Emperor Akbar (461)
Nur Jahan (462)
Ming dynasty (463)
examination system (463)
Wanli Emperor (466)
Emperor Sejong (466)
Lê dynasty (466)
Toyotomi Hideyoshi (467)
Tokugawa Shogunate (468)
Martin Luther (468)
Catholic Reformation (469)
Galileo Galilei (469)

What were the main political characteristics of the major South Asian and East Asian states? How was their development influenced by the new maritime connections of the sixteenth and early seventeenth centuries?

The dominant political players in East and South Asia were land-based empires with leaders who paid little attention to maritime affairs. Ming China, the most populous and most powerful, had ended its state-sponsored oceanic voyages even while benefiting from the increased tempo of maritime trade. Agriculture was the principal foundation on which the complex Ming imperial bureaucracy rested. By the time of Matteo Ricci's arrival in Beijing late in the sixteenth century, however, political and economic crises were about to undermine the Ming dynasty, and in 1644 the Forbidden City fell to northern invaders.

Korea, Vietnam, and Japan derived at least part of their political culture from China. The Korean state modeled its imperial system most closely on Ming China, and Vietnam, even after fending off a Ming military incursion, emulated the Chinese imperial system and sent tribute to the Forbidden City. Sixteenth-century Japan, by contrast, was a disordered land with little central authority. In the seventeenth century, the Tokugawa Shogunate consolidated power and brought greater stability that produced a surge in commercial activity and artistic innovation.

Like Ming China, Mughal India benefited from increased Indian Ocean commerce even as its wealth and power were primarily derived from taxation on agriculture. Under Akbar, India possessed military might, economic productivity, and cultural creativity. With a Muslim ruling class, a Hindu majority, and a royal court that looked to Persia, Turkey, and Central Asia for artistic stimulation, the artistic and administrative achievements of the Mughal Empire reflected the culture of tolerance promoted by Akbar.

 How did religious and intellectual traditions of Eurasia change during this period, and what were the effects of encounters between them?

Akbar's exploration of various religious traditions was characteristic of a Eurasian intellectual climate in which cultural encounters were becoming more frequent. His open-minded attitude was not universal, however. In western Europe differences between Protestants and Catholics increasingly led to violence and warfare (see Chapter 17), and in India Akbar's policy of tolerance would be reversed by his successors. Most Chinese literati were ethnocentric in their belief that Chinese traditions such as Confucianism gave them all the guidance they needed, and Ricci gained few converts. European clocks, paintings, telescopes, and maps impressed them, but mostly as novelties. Nevertheless, Ricci was usually received in a respectful manner and helped lay the foundations for ongoing encounters between China and Europe.

For Further Reference

Brook, Timothy. *The Confusions of Pleasure: Commerce and Culture in Ming China.* Berkeley: University of California Press, 1998.

Chaudhuri, K. N. *Asia Before Europe: Economy and Civilization of the Indian Ocean from the Rise of Islam to 1750.* Cambridge: Cambridge University Press, 1990.

Dale, Stephen Frederick. *Indian Merchants and Eurasian Trade, 1600–1750.* Cambridge: Cambridge University Press, 1994.

Hilton, Anne. *The Kingdom of Kongo.* Oxford: Clarendon Press, 1985.

Pearson, Michael. *The Indian Ocean.* New York: Routledge, 2007.

Richards, John. *The Mughal Empire.* New York: Cambridge University Press, 1996.

Spence, Jonathan. *The Memory Palace of Matteo Ricci.* New York: Viking Penguin, 1984.

Subrahmanyam, Sanjay. *The Portuguese Empire in Asia, 1500–1700.* New York: Longman, 1993.

Websites

Jesuit History (http://www.sjweb.info/jesuits/jeshistory.cfm). A website of historical material on the Society of Jesus, maintained by the Catholic religious order.

WEB RESOURCES

Pronunciation Guide

Interactive Maps

MAP 16.1 Maritime Trade in the Eastern Indian Ocean and East Asia

MAP 16.2 The Protestant Reformation

Primary Sources

Chapter Objectives

ACE Multiple-Choice Quiz

Flashcards

Portuguese and Dutch Colonial History (http://www.colonialvoyage.com/). Links to historical materials and contemporary legacies of Portuguese and Dutch colonialism.

World History Matters (http://worldhistorymatters.org/). A useful portal to primary sources on world history, including Asian empires, organized chronologically and geographically, with a dedicated section on women in world history.

Religion, Politics, and the Balance of Power in Western Eurasia, 1500–1750

In 1673 the Frenchman **Jean de Chardin** (1643–1713) started on the second of his long journeys to Iran. On his first visit the shah had made a deal with Chardin to come back with European jewelry for the royal collection. But when Chardin returned he found that the shah had died, and he had to renegotiate the sale. Those negotiations led to frustration on both sides.

Cultural differences lay at the heart of this disagreement. Jean de Chardin (JAHN duh shar-DAN) expected his original contract to be honored, while his Iranian hosts saw haggling over price as an essential part of commercial life that helped to establish a personal relationship between buyer and seller. Even though Chardin had spent years in Persia (as Europeans called Iran) and spoke the language well, he still had difficulty adjusting to its business culture:

JEAN DE CHARDIN

(Private Collection/The Bridgeman Art Library)

I shall not say anything of the deceits, tricks, wiles, disputes, threats and promises with which I was plagued for ten days . . . to make me lower the price. I was so weary of all the indirect means the nazir [minister] made use of that . . . I begged he would rather give back my jewels. . . . What provoked him the most, as he said, was that I kept firm to my first agreement without the least abatement. He had put himself in so violent a passion . . . that one would have thought he was going to devour me, and indeed I should have dreaded some bad consequences from so vehement an indignation if I had not been well acquainted with the Persians' manner

This icon will direct you to interactive activities and study materials on the *Voyages* website:
www.cengage.com/history/hansen/voyages1e

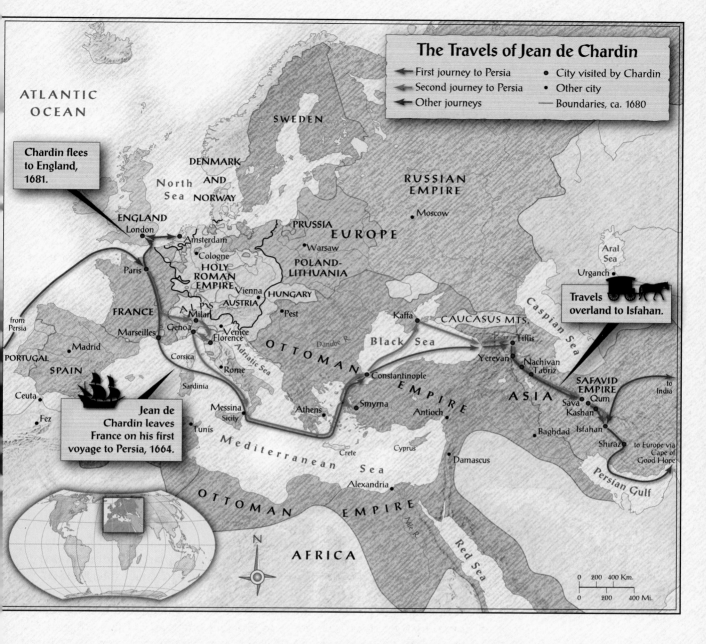

The Travels of Jean de Chardin

→ First journey to Persia
→ Second journey to Persia
→ Other journeys
• City visited by Chardin
• Other city
— Boundaries, ca. 1680

ATLANTIC OCEAN

Chardin flees to England, 1681.

North Sea

SWEDEN

DENMARK AND NORWAY

RUSSIAN EMPIRE

Moscow

ENGLAND
London

Amsterdam

Cologne

PRUSSIA

EUROPE

Warsaw

POLAND-LITHUANIA

HOLY ROMAN EMPIRE

Paris

Vienna

AUSTRIA

HUNGARY

Pest

Aral Sea

Urganch

Travels overland to Isfahan.

FRANCE

ALPS

Milan

Genoa

Venice
Florence

Danube R.

OTTOMAN

Kaffa

Black Sea

CAUCASUS MTS.

Caspian Sea

Tiflis

from Persia

Marseilles

Corsica

Adriatic Sea

EMPIRE

Constantinople

Yerevan

Nachivan
Tabriz

SAFAVID EMPIRE

to India

PORTUGAL

Madrid

SPAIN

Rome

Sardinia

Athens

Smyrna

Antioch

ASIA

Sava
Kashan

Qum

Ceuta

Jean de Chardin leaves France on his first voyage to Persia, 1664.

Messina
Sicily

Tunis

Mediterranean Sea

Crete

Cyprus

Damascus

Baghdad

Isfahan

Shiraz

to Europe via Cape of Good Hope

Fez

Alexandria

OTTOMAN EMPIRE

Persian Gulf

AFRICA

Nile R.

Red Sea

N

0 200 400 Km.
0 200 400 Mi.

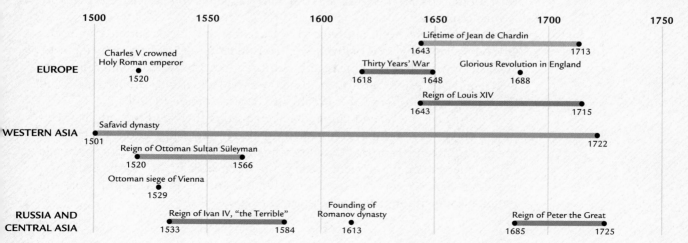

	1500	1550	1600	1650	1700	1750
EUROPE				Lifetime of Jean de Chardin 1643 — 1713		
	Charles V crowned Holy Roman emperor 1520			Thirty Years' War 1618 — 1648	Glorious Revolution in England 1688	
				Reign of Louis XIV 1643 — 1715		
WESTERN ASIA	Safavid dynasty 1501					1722
		Reign of Ottoman Sultan Süleyman 1520 — 1566				
		Ottoman siege of Vienna 1529				
RUSSIA AND CENTRAL ASIA		Reign of Ivan IV, "the Terrible" 1533 — 1584	Founding of Romanov dynasty 1613		Reign of Peter the Great 1685 — 1725	

of acting on like occasions. What I found most difficult to bear was the reproaches of the courtiers who . . . found it very strange that I should stick so stiffly to my first word; some of them ascribed it to my obstinacy and others to an over-greediness of excessive gain.[1]

Jean de Chardin (1643–1713) French traveler and business-man who voyaged to Iran in 1665; learned the language and made a contract with the shah to return with jewelry. On a second trip in 1673, he reached Iran after passing through the Ottoman Empire.

On a positive note, Chardin complimented Persians for their warm generosity: "The most commendable property of the manners of the Persians is their kindness to strangers; the reception and protection they afford them and their universal hospitality." He also praised the Iranians' general "toleration in regard to religion," with the exception of the "the clergy of the country who, as in all other places, hate to a furious degree all those who differ from their own opinion."

Coming from a country where Protestants faced persecution from a Catholic king, Chardin had deep personal experience with religious intolerance. Himself a Protestant, he would eventually have to abandon his native France to settle in Protestant-governed Britain. As in Shi'ite-governed Iran, where Sunni Muslims were a persecuted minority, religion and politics were closely connected in early modern Europe. In both Christian and Islamic lands, religious fervor fueled competition for wealth and power at a time when the refinement of gunpowder technologies was making warfare more lethal.

Chardin's experiences were also characteristic of this period's global interconnections. The previous two chapters traced increasing political, economic, biological, and cultural interactions in the Atlantic and Indian Ocean worlds. This chapter focuses on the complex interplay between religion and politics within and between Christian and Muslim societies and on the shifting balance of power between major states in western Eurasia and the Mediterranean.

In addition to Mughal India (see Chapter 16), two other Muslim-ruled states were on the rise in sixteenth-century Eurasia. One was the Safavid (SAH-fah-vihd) Empire in Iran visited by Chardin. To reach its capital of Isfahan, Chardin traveled across the even more powerful Ottoman Empire. Already well established by 1500, the Ottomans continued to expand their power westward across North Africa and northward into Europe. The antagonism between the Ottomans and the Safavids was reinforced by their rulers' adherence to different branches of Islam. Together with Mughal India, the Ottomans and Safavids represented a sixteenth-century Islamic resurgence.

Powerful states were also emerging in sixteenth-century Europe. While the Orthodox Christian rulers of Russia were consolidating and extending their power, Spanish kings were attempting to unite Christendom against Protestant resistance. By the mid-eighteenth century, Spanish power was fading, and Catholic France and the Protestant nations of Great Britain and Prussia were on the rise.

Meanwhile, the Safavid Empire had collapsed entirely and the Ottoman Empire, while still powerful, had lost the initiative to the rising European states. By the mid-eighteenth century the ability to maintain and extend military power had come to depend on the efficient use of gunpowder weapons. The balance of power in western Eurasia now favored France, Britain, Austria, Prussia, and Russia, and national competition had largely replaced religious rivalry.

Focus Questions

When, where, and how were religion and politics most closely intertwined in western Eurasian societies? When and why did religion come to play a less prominent political role?

How did the balance of power between the dominant states of western Eurasia shift during this period?

What do Jean de Chardin's travel writings tell us, both about Safavid Iran and about his own culture and values?

Land Empires of Western Eurasia and North Africa, 1500–1685

Unlike the maritime empires described in the last two chapters, the Ottoman, Safavid, and Russian Empires were land-based, created by the expansion of political and military power into neighboring territories. Since their core areas had earlier been conquered and administered by the Mongols, their origins lay in the relationship between steppe nomads and settled agricultural peoples.

The rulers of the Ottoman Empire, already well established in the fifteenth century when their power was magnified by their seizure of Constantinople in 1453, were the most successful of the Turkic-speaking peoples who had migrated westward from the steppes to conquer sedentary agricultural societies. The Safavids were also Turkic-speaking and nomadic in origin. Both societies inherited Islamic law and tradition, even while the Sunni (SOO-nee) Ottomans and the Shi'ite (shee-ite) Safavids had different interpretations of Islam.

The rulers of Russia, by contrast, were products of a settled agrarian society, though their southern frontier had long-term contact with steppe nomads. Starting in the mid-fifteenth century, the Russians turned the tables on the Mongols and conquered parts of the steppe that had once been ruled by the Golden Horde. By the mid-seventeenth century, under the Romanov dynasty, the Russian Empire was moving westward toward Poland, eastward into Siberia, and southward toward the edges of Ottoman and Safavid power. The influence of the Russian Orthodox Church spread along with the empire.

The Ottoman Empire, 1500–1650

The legendary splendor of the Sublime Porte, center of Ottoman power in Constantinople, reflected the success of the Ottoman military elite in governing and taxing the peasants, craftsmen, and merchants in their sprawling and productive domains. In the sixteenth century those lands expanded to include Palestine, Syria, Arabia,

Iraq, much of Hungary, and most of the Black Sea. From southeastern Europe Ottoman armies marched into the German-speaking lands of central Europe. The Ottomans also ruled Greece and conquered the Mediterranean coast of North Africa up to Morocco, which remained the only significant Arab-ruled kingdom. In Egypt, Arabia, and Syria, Arabs were ruled by Turkish-speaking Ottoman administrators.

The Ottomans' military strength derived from their cavalry, infantry, artillery, and naval power. Ottoman fleets came to dominate the Black Sea and the eastern and southern shores of the Mediterranean, and the Ottoman navy challenged Christian fleets in the Red Sea, Persian Gulf, and Indian Ocean.

Early Ottoman expansion was driven by soldiers known as *ghazis* (GAH-zeez), horsemen of nomadic origin driven by their zeal to conquer the Christian infidels of Byzantium for Islam. But the increasing scale of Ottoman military operations and the organization necessary to use gunpowder weapons such as muskets and cannon led to greater military professionalism. As ghazis were given land grants in conquered territories with responsibilities for maintaining order and collecting taxes, they became administrators rather than fighters. At the same time, slaves became more important in the Ottoman military and in the central administration of the empire.

An old saying has it that a state "conquered on horseback" cannot be "governed on horseback." While old-style cavalry were still necessary to defend the empire's frontiers, the Ottomans needed better-trained employees for stable administration. They began to rely on **Janissaries,** slave soldiers who were recruited from conquered Christian lands and trained as professional soldiers. Janissaries trained year-round and became skilled at using gunpowder weapons. As the need for such soldiers increased, the Ottomans regularly enslaved Christian youth in the Balkan and Caucasus Mountains to meet the demand.

The concept of "elite slaves" strikes the modern ear as strange. But relying on slaves as soldiers and administrators was an old tradition. A sultan might not trust his own brothers or sons because they were vying for power of their own, but the loyalty of a slave general was absolute. If he disobeyed he could simply be killed: he had no local family to protect him. By the sixteenth century the Janissaries were playing a central role in administration as well as in the military. Even the sultan's chief minister was a slave.

After conquering Arabia and Palestine, the Ottomans controlled Mecca, Medina, and Jerusalem, the three holiest cities for Muslims. Since these were the pilgrimage sites to which all Muslims hoped one day to travel, the Ottomans came to emphasize their role as guardians of Islam. The question was how to reconcile protection of Islam with the extraordinary diversity of the sultan's subjects. While Akbar in Mughal India had to devise a strategy to stabilize Islamic rule over a Hindu majority (see Chapter 16), Ottoman rulers had to incorporate dozens of different communities with many different religious and legal traditions.

The master strategist who reconciled central authority with local autonomy was Sultan **Süleyman** (r. 1520–1566). A strong military leader who greatly expanded the empire, Süleyman (soo-lay-MAHN) also devised an administrative system that regularized relations between the government and its population. His court reflected the ethnic and linguistic diversity of the empire. Turkish was the language of administration and military command, Arabic the language of theology and philosophy, and Persian the language of poetry and the arts. Europeans called him "Süleyman the Magnificent" for the dazzling opulence and splendor of his court. But within the empire he became known as "Süleyman the Lawgiver" for bringing peace and stability to the realm. An Austrian ambassador made special mention of the quality of the sultan's officials, who gained power through merit rather than family lineage:

●**Janissaries** An elite corps in the Ottoman military. Janissary soldiers were Christian youths from the Balkans who were pressed into service and forced to convert to Islam.

●**Süleyman** (r. 1520–1566) Also known as "Süleyman the Magnificent" and "Süleyman the Lawgiver," he extended the Ottoman Empire while maintaining economic and political stability. Credited with the development of literature, art, architecture, and law and for inclusive policies toward religious minorities.

"Those who are dishonest, lazy and slothful never attain to distinction, but remain in obscurity and contempt. That is why they succeed in all they attempt . . . and daily extend the bounds of their rule."[2]

Süleyman centralized religious authority and sponsored the building of mosques and religious schools, partly to combat the intermixture of residual pagan practices with Islam. While most peasants in rural Anatolia were Muslim, many of their practices reflected older beliefs, deities, and rituals. Süleyman sent religious scholars and legal experts to these areas to create a greater degree of Islamic orthodoxy. Nevertheless, the Ottomans did not impose a single legal system on existing cultural and religious traditions. Instead, they developed a flexible system that allowed local Christian and Jewish populations to govern their own affairs and maintain their own courts as long as they remained loyal to the sultan and paid their taxes promptly.

This relative tolerance is demonstrated by the safe haven found in North Africa, Egypt, and other Ottoman lands by many of the Iberian Jews who were driven from Catholic Spain in 1492. Many of these Jews came to live in Ottoman North Africa and the Arab-ruled kingdom of Morocco. After 1492, Ladino-speaking Jews, with a language derived from medieval Spanish, made significant contributions to the intellectual and commercial life of Ottoman North Africa. Jean de Chardin himself experienced the empire's tolerance, passing unmolested through Ottoman lands even though the empire was at war with various European states. His journey was a testament to the safety, security, and stability that had been bequeathed by Süleyman the Lawgiver.

In Süleyman's day the Ottomans were a substantial threat to central Europe, as the letter written to Vienna from Constantinople by the Austrian ambassador emphasized:

> On their side are the resources of a mighty empire, strength unimpaired, experience and practice in fighting . . . endurance of toil, unity, discipline, frugality and watchfulness. On our side is public poverty, private luxury, impaired strength, broken spirit. . . . [W]orst of all, the enemy is accustomed to victory, and we to defeat. Can we doubt what the result will be?

In fact, the Austrian ambassador overestimated Ottoman strength. The Ottoman siege of Vienna in was turned back by the city's defenders, and in the Mediterranean a combined European fleet under Spanish command defeated the Ottoman navy in the Battle of Lepanto in 1571. But the navy was rebuilt and the Ottomans stayed on the offensive in southeastern Europe into the later seventeenth century. (See the feature "Movement of Ideas: The Travels of Evliya Çelebi.")

The European diplomats that Jean de Chardin found attending the shah's court at Isfahan were seeking an ally against the persistent threat of the Ottoman

Süleyman the Magnificent This portrait of Süleyman the Magnificent, also known as "the Lawgiver," shows the influence of Persian miniature painting on the arts of the Ottoman Empire. Though most Muslim scholars rejected the practice of representing the human form in paintings and illuminated book manuscripts, fearing the sin of idol worship, the Ottomans borrowed these old artistic practices from their Iranian rivals. (British Library, London/Art Resource, NY)

The Travels of Evliya Çelebi

In the Turkish language, you say of someone who feels a constant urge for travel, "Evliya Çelebi gibi": "He is like Evliya Çelebi." Evliya Çelebi (1610–1683) was one of the great travelers of the seventeenth century. Son of an Ottoman official, he was raised in the sultan's palace in Constantinople. Guided, he wrote, by a dream that assured him the Prophet's blessing on his voyages, his journeys encompassed all of the Ottoman lands, including Greece, Syria, Egypt, Baghdad, Bosnia, Jerusalem, and Armenia. He also traveled beyond the sultan's domain to Vienna, Poland, and Russia.

The passages below are from Çelebi's descriptions of Europe and Europeans. In the first, he shares with his Ottoman readers his impressions of Austrian Catholics, Hungarian Protestants, and Jews. In the second he records his impressions of a surgical procedure he witnessed in Vienna.

Sources: Robert Dankoff and Robert Elsie, eds., *Evliya Çelebi in Albania and Adjacent Regions* (Boston: Brill, 2000), pp. 65–66, 68; J. W. Livingstone, "Evliya Çelebi on Surgical Operations in Vienna," *Al-Abath* (1970), vol. 23, pp. 230–232; translation modified.

Descriptions of Hungarian Protestants, Austrian Catholics, and Jews

The Hungarians are Lutherans while the Germans [or Austrians] are Catholics. Therefore these two infidel groups are opposed to one another, despite their both being Christians. . . . They communicate at the point of a spear. . . . The Hungarian state is quite puny ever since the time of Sultan Süleyman when . . . 300 walled towns were lost to the Ottomans. After that happened the Austrians prevailed over the Hungarians and made them into their subjects.

Still, compared to the Hungarians the Austrians are like the Jews: they have no stomach for a fight and are not swordsmen and horsemen. Their infantry musketeers, to be sure, are real fire-shooters; but . . . they can't shoot from the shoulder as Ottoman soldiers do. Also, they shut their eyes and shoot at random. . . .

The Hungarians, on the other hand, though they have lost their power, still have fine tables, are hospitable to guests, and are capable cultivators of their fertile land. And they are true warriors. . . . Indeed, they look just like our frontier soldiers, wearing the same dress as they and riding the same thoroughbred horses. They are clean in their ways and in their eating, and honor their guests. They do not torture their prisoners as the Austrians do. They practice sword play like the Ottomans. In short, though both of them are unbelievers without faith, the Hungarians are the more honorable and cleaner infidels.

The Jews never accept food and drink from other people. Indeed, they do not mingle with others—if they join your company it is an artificial companionship. All their deeds are calculated to treachery and the killing of Muslims, especially anyone named Muhammad. Even wine they refuse to buy from other people.

Observation of a Surgical Procedure in Vienna

Since there are many doctors in the hospital [of St. Stephan] the likes of Plato [and] Hippocrates . . . the king himself comes to it when ill. These doctors wear pure white [gowns] and on their heads a type of linen skull cap of Russian leather. . . . Upon taking the patient's pulse, they immediately know the disease and accordingly know the [proper] treatment for it. So when a close relative of the king's was wounded . . . by a bullet that penetrated deeply and was lodged in the side of his skull near his ear [he was brought to this hospital].

. . . I came to the Chief Surgeon and introduced myself [asking to be allowed to witness the operation]. Thereupon he had the wounded infidel brought in. . . . [He was] given a cup of liquid resembling saffron to drink, and passed out. The chief surgeon . . . cut the skin of his forehead from ear to ear and flayed the skin effortlessly from the side of his right ear. The skull-bone appeared pure white. Not a drop of blood flowed. Then the surgeon lightly pierced the wounded fellow's skull from his ear to the temple. After this he inserted an iron clamp. When the handle of the clamp was turned, the skull began to rise up from where the fellow's scalp had been cut. The wounded man made a light movement at that moment.

When the clamp was turned again . . . the top of the fellow's head was opened. . . . Inside his head the brains were visible. . . . Then he quickly took the bullet from the man's brain with a pair of forceps. With a sponge he wiped away the hard, dry blood from the spot where the bullet had been lodged all this time. . . .

[A] giant ant was taken from [a] box with iron tongs. It was placed on the fellow's head where the skin had been cut. When the hungry ant bit the two edges of the skin, the surgeon cut the ant at the waist with scissors, leaving the head still biting the edges of the skin. . . . Eighty ants were made to bite the skin of the wounded fellow's head from ear to ear. . . . Gauze was inserted into the bullet hole in his skull and this was smeared with salve and bandaged.

Foul smelling incense was burned inside the room. Wine of a forty or fifty year-old vintage was poured in the wounded man's nose, and clay was smeared over [his entire body]. . . . I remained there seven complete days observing the [convalescence]. On the eighth day the pleasant fellow had recovered, and began to move around the hospital with ease. . . .

In the city of Vienna there are perfect masters of surgery . . . and scholars of such wisdom and skill the equal of Ibn Sinā and Pythagoras together.

QUESTIONS FOR ANALYSIS

▶ What does Çelebi criticize and what does he admire about various Europeans?

▶ Are there passages where he expresses prejudices and stereotypes about them?

military. The Austrian ambassador noted the strategic importance of Safavid Iran: "Persia alone interposes in our favor; for the enemy, as he hastens to attack, must keep an eye on this menace in his rear." For all their religious and cultural divergences, the Europeans and the Safavids found that mutual antipathy to the Ottomans gave them a starting point for cooperation.

Foundations of Safavid Iran, 1500–1629

Iran is a rich and productive land with a long tradition of political and cultural influence in western and southern Asia. With Mesopotamia and the Mediterranean to the west and the Indus Valley and India to the south and east, Persian civilization had benefited from cultural and commercial contacts with other civilizations. Its agricultural wealth and position as a commercial crossroads have also long attracted invaders. In the early sixteenth century some of these invaders founded the **Safavid dynasty** (1501–1722) and challenged the power of the Ottoman Empire.

Like the early Ottoman ghazis, the Safavid invaders had a religious motivation. Known as *kizilbash* ("redheads") because of the color of their turbans, they swept down from Azerbaijan in the name of the Shi'ite interpretation of Islam. Behind their leader **Ismail** (r. 1501–1524) the "redheads" conquered the Persian-speaking lands and drove west, capturing the important cities of Baghdad and Basra.

Shi'ites believed that when Muhammad died religious and political authority should have passed to his son-in-law Ali. Sunni Muslims, by contrast, argued that the Prophet's successors could be chosen freely from among Muhammad's close companions. In the seventh century the two sides came to blows. First Ali was killed, and then his son Hussein fell to the Sunni caliph. Shi'ites curse the names of the Sunni caliphs, and every year an elaborate festival of mourning is held to commemorate the death of Hussein.

Before the Safavids most people in Iran had been Sunni Muslims living alongside many small Sufi brotherhoods. Under Ismail, the Shi'ite version of Islam became the state religion, and Sunnis who would not agree to curse the early caliphs were driven into exile. It was the first time that Shi'ites, long a repressed minority, controlled a major Islamic state. Later the Ottoman army retook the Tigris-Euphrates River Valley, including Baghdad and Basra, where the cultural boundary between Arabic- and Persian-speaking populations and the religious boundary between Sunni and Shi'ite majorities were located.

Although the shift toward Shi'ism in Iran was permanent, over time the religious passions that drove initial Safavid policies died down. The greatest Safavid ruler, Shah **Abbas I** (r. 1587–1629), built a new capital at Isfahan (is-fah-HAHN), a city of half a million residents by the time Jean de Chardin commented on "the great number of magnificent palaces, the agreeable and pleasant houses . . . the really fine bazaars, the water channels and the streets of which the sides were covered with tall plane trees."[3] The gardens of Isfahan were legendary, and under Abbas Persian culture continued to spread both east and west. Persian verse was widely admired, influencing Swahili poets in East Africa and Urdu poets in India. Isfahan, a showcase for Persian architecture and engineering, influenced the graceful silhouette of the Taj Mahal in India. In addition to creating beautiful abstract patterns on rich carpets, Persian artists were famous for miniature paintings depicting scenes from everyday life.

The economy also blossomed under the security afforded by Abbas's long and stable rule, with new irrigation works supporting agricultural productivity, new

●**Safavid dynasty** (1501–1722) Dynasty that established Shi'ite Islam as the state religion in Iran and challenged the powerful Ottoman Empire. The Safavids fell to invaders from Central Asia in the early eighteenth century.

●**Ismail** (r. 1501–1524) Founder of the Safavid dynasty in Iran who forced his subjects to adopt Shi'ite Islam. Came into military and religious conflict with the Ottoman Empire, which was Sunni.

●**Abbas I** (r. 1587–1629) Safavid ruler who created a long and stable reign, beautified the capital city of Isfahan, promoted foreign trade, and repelled Ottoman invaders.

markets for Iranian handicrafts, and a pilgrim trade bringing visitors to the holy sites of Shi'ite Islam. Iranian silks, carpets, and ceramics were traded on overland markets to the east and west and also into Indian Ocean circuits. As Chardin noted, Armenian merchants played a crucial role in Iranian trade. Minorities in the lands where they traded, from the Mediterranean to Southeast Asia, Armenian traders relied on their shared linguistic and religious heritage for security while at the same time adjusting to the legal and cultural environment in which they worked. The Armenians in Isfahan certainly had a better appreciation of Iranian bargaining strategies than did Jean de Chardin!

In addition to protecting and patronizing the Armenian community, Shah Abbas invited other European merchants and diplomatic representatives to Isfahan, mainly to support the Europeans' rear-guard action against the Ottomans. Abbas was also anxious to acquire guns and cannon and to train professional soldiers who could use them efficiently.

The safety and security with which Chardin traveled through Persia in the later seventeenth century was part of Shah Abbas's legacy. While in Iran, he also benefited from the hostility between the Ottomans and Safavids. The antagonism of the Shah's chief minister to all things European was offset by the Safavid need to cultivate European alliances in their struggle with the Ottomans. Iranians, Chardin reported, "know no more of what passes in Europe than in the world of the moon" and looked upon it as "some little island in the North Sea." But the Safavid rulers used the old philosophy "the enemy of my enemy is my friend" to seek European alliances against Constantinople.

When Chardin observed the jockeying for position among the Europeans at the Safavid court, he noted that the Russian ambassador was given precedence and was told by the grand vizier: "The Muscovite [Russian] is our neighbor and our friend, and the commerce has been a long time settled between us, and without interruption. We send ambassadors to each other reciprocally almost every year, but we hardly know the other [Europeans]." As the Russian Empire expanded to the south, commercial and diplomatic relations between the two powers intensified.

Origins of the Russian Empire, 1500–1685

Before the sixteenth century the Slavic-speaking Russian people had been deeply influenced by Greek-speaking Byzantium. Medieval Russian princes and merchants cultivated relations with Constantinople, and after the conversion of its ruler the city of Kiev became a central point for the diffusion of literacy and Orthodox Christianity. The monastic tradition of Orthodox Christianity took deep root.

The first phase in the consolidation of a Russian state is largely the story of two Ivans, Ivan III (r. 1440–1505) and Ivan IV (r. 1533–1584). Ivan III ruled Muscovy from his capital at Moscow. After the Ottoman seizure of Constantinople in 1453, the increased political importance of the Russian Orthodox Church worked in Ivan's favor. Driving out the weakened Mongols and asserting his authority over the other Russian states, Ivan III made an explicit connection between his own power and the Byzantine legacy, calling himself "tsar" ("caesar") and declaring that Russia would defend the Orthodox Christian heritage. Ivan's concern to build a large territorial buffer around the core Russian lands to protect them from invasion would become a persistent aspect of Russian imperial policy.

His successor Tsar Ivan IV centralized royal authority even further and extended Russian power to the west, east, and south, earning the nickname "Ivan the Terrible" for the random cruelty that characterized his later years. To the west, the tsar's armies engaged Catholic Poland and Protestant Sweden. To the south they conquered Muslim populations in rich steppe grasslands and began to drive into the Caucasus Mountains between the Black and Caspian Seas. To the east, across the Ural Mountains, lay the forbidding lands of Siberia. The quest for animal furs lured the first Russian frontiersmen to these lands, and state power followed later (see Chapter 20). Defense and expansion of the Orthodox faith inspired Ivan's conquests.

Following the death of Ivan the Terrible came a "time of troubles" with no clear successor to the title of tsar. That period of uncertainty ended in 1613 when the Russian nobles offered royal power to Mikhail Romanov. The Romanov dynasty (1613–1917) continued imperial expansion and proved to be one of the most enduring dynasties in world history (see Chapters 20 and 27). Like the sultans of the Ottoman Empire, the Romanov tsars remained in power into the early twentieth century.

While trade and commerce brought wealth to Moscow, the main source of revenue for the tsars and the nobility was agricultural surpluses. Village-based farming was the foundation of all of the land-based empires, not only Russia but also the Ottoman and Safavid Empires, Mughal India, and Ming China (see Chapter 16). What was unique about Russia was the persistence of serfdom. By the mid-seventeenth century peasants were tightly bound to their villages, and the tsars and the Russian aristocracy increasingly saw these "souls," as they called the peasants, as property that could be bought and sold. The oppressive conditions of serfdom in Russia contrasted with developments in western Europe, where serfdom had either disappeared altogether or where peasant obligations were becoming less burdensome.

CL Primary Source:
A Russian Serf Explains the Facts of Life to an Enlightened Russian Nobleman
Read a firsthand account on the conditions of Russian serfdom, from a serf's perspective.

● The Struggle for Stability in Western Europe, 1500–1653

The sixteenth century and the first half of the seventeenth century were a time of turmoil in western Europe. Warfare became common as the religious divisions arising from the Protestant Reformation (see Chapter 16) became entangled with the ambitions of emperors, kings, and princes. Attempts at political centralization were often met with resistance, and social and economic changes associated with urbanization and commercialization also led to tensions.

The Habsburgs were the most powerful family in Europe at the beginning of this period. Originally from central Europe, through marriages and diplomatic maneuvers the **Habsburg dynasty** came to rule Spain, the Netherlands, parts of Italy, and much of German-speaking Europe. Also commanding the vast resources of Spain's American empire, the Habsburgs aspired to control a pan-European Catholic empire. Their failure meant the permanent political and religious division of western Europe.

Conflict with the Ottoman Empire, including the need to protect Vienna from Ottoman attack, was one check on Habsburg power. Another was the rising power of England and France. Beginning with the reign of Queen Elizabeth I (r. 1558–1603), England's Tudor monarchs were solidly Protestant and stridently anti-Spanish, while the Catholic monarchs of France competed with the Spanish

● **Habsburg dynasty** Powerful ruling house that expanded from Austria to Spain, the Netherlands, and the Spanish Empire, as well as throughout the German-speaking world when Charles V (r. 1516–1555) was elected Holy Roman Emperor.

Habsburgs for power and influence. The rebellious provinces of the Netherlands were another major distraction and expense.

By the mid-seventeenth century Habsburg power had started to fade, while religious and dynastic conflict brought civil war to England and France. Violence was greatest in central Europe, where thirty years of religiously driven warfare devastated much of the countryside.

The Rise and Decline of Habsburg Power, 1519–1648

The greatest of the Habsburg monarchs was Charles I, who ruled Spain from 1516 to 1556. Educated in the Netherlands, he inherited both the Spanish crown at Madrid and the Habsburg domains in central Europe. His Dutch experience tied him to one of the most dynamic commercial economies in the world, the central European territories dominated from Vienna were crucial in the European military balance, and his Spanish possessions included all the riches of the Americas. His family connections also made him king of Naples, controlling the southern part of Italy.

In 1520 Charles was crowned Holy Roman Emperor under the title Charles V, having defeated the French king to win that title. The Holy Roman Empire was a vestige of a much earlier attempt to recreate Roman unity in Europe in collaboration with the Catholic Church. By the sixteenth century the "emperor," elected by the many princes who ruled over German-speaking lands, had little real power. However, it was a prestigious position, and, having been crowned emperor by the pope, Charles became the principal defender of the Catholic faith.

With such extensive territorial possessions in Europe and all the wealth of the Americas at their disposal, it seemed that the Habsburgs might be able to create a political unity in western Europe. But for all of the military campaigns undertaken by Charles V during his long reign, it was not to be. The French were too powerful a rival in the west, while the Ottoman Turks challenged Habsburg supremacy in eastern Europe and the Mediterranean. Equally significant were the violent political repercussions from the Protestant Reformation that began to appear in the mid-sixteenth century.

Charles V became Holy Roman Emperor just as Martin Luther was publicly challenging church authority (see Chapter 16). In 1521 Charles V presided over a meeting intended to bring Luther back under papal authority. Luther refused to back down

Martin Luther Preaching Martin Luther was known as a powerful preacher, as seen in this contemporary depiction. The rapid spread of his Protestant ideas, however, resulted from the printing press as well. In 1455 the first metal movable type outside of Asia was invented by a German goldsmith; a hundred years later that invention allowed Martin Luther's ideas to spread far and wide. (British Library, London/HIP/Art Resource, NY)

and was declared an outlaw. The German princes chose sides, some declaring themselves "Lutherans," others remaining loyal to the pope and Holy Roman Emperor. Decades of inconclusive warfare followed, and religious division became a permanent part of the western European scene. Exhausted, in 1555 Charles agreed to a peace that recognized the principle that princes could impose either Catholicism or Lutheranism within their own territories. He then abdicated his throne and split his inheritance between his brother Ferdinand, who took control of the Habsburg's central European domains, and his son Philip, who became king of Spain.

● **Philip II** (r. 1556–1598)   Son of Charles V and king of Spain. Considering himself a defender of Catholicism, Philip launched attacks on Protestants in England and the Netherlands.

While **Philip II** (r. 1556–1598) ruled over a magnificent court at Madrid, the Viceroyalties of New Spain were firmly established, the Ottomans were defeated at a great naval battle at Lepanto (1571), and the Philippines (named for Philip himself) were brought under Spanish control. All was not well, however. Even with the vast riches of New Spain, his father's wars had severely strained the treasury, and increased taxes led to unrest. Since Philip was also more militant than his father in attempting to impose Catholic orthodoxy on his subjects, religious divisions became even more acute.

One example is the rebellion of the Spanish *Moriscos* (mohr-EES-kos) in 1568, Arabic-speaking Iberians who stayed in Spain after the completion of the Reconquista (reh-con-KEES-tah) in 1492. Though forced to convert to Christianity, many Morisco families continued to practice Islam in private. When the church, with Philip's support, tried to impose Catholic orthodoxy on them, the resulting rebellion took two years to suppress; Philip later ordered the expulsion of all remaining Iberian Muslims.

Religious conflict was also an important component of Philip's ongoing struggles with the Calvinists in his Dutch provinces. John Calvin was a Protestant theologian whose Reformed Church emphasized the absolute power of God over weak and sinful humanity. The possibility of salvation for human souls lay entirely with God, Calvin argued: "eternal life is foreordained for some, eternal damnation for others."

Philip regarded these Calvinists as heretics, and when he tried to seize their property they armed themselves in self-defense. The nobleman sent to put down the rebellion unleashed terrible violence that only stiffened Dutch resistance. This constant warfare was a drain on the Spanish treasury. The struggle was never resolved in Philip's lifetime, but in 1609 a treaty was signed that led to the effective independence of the Dutch United Provinces. It was in this political context that the Dutch East India Company emerged as a powerful trading company (see Chapter 16).

England was another constant source of concern to Philip. Its Protestant rulers harassed the Spanish at every turn, such as by supporting the privateers who plundered Spanish treasure ships in the Caribbean. In 1588, Philip's attempt to assert his dominance over England failed when poor weather combined with clever English naval strategy to defeat Spain's great naval Armada.

By the early seventeenth century the powerful empire constructed by the Habsburg family a century earlier was falling apart from religious divisions and the expensive necessity of fighting wars on so many fronts. At this same time silver imports began to decline. Like the rulers of Ming China, another great empire for which expanding supplies of silver was a necessity, the Spanish Habsburgs found themselves in a difficult position. By the mid-seventeenth century their Italian possessions, though Catholic, were also in revolt.

Things were no better in the eastern Habsburg domains. The peace of 1555 had broken down, and warfare continued to rock central Europe. The constant state of political unrest between Catholic and Lutheran rulers finally led to a catastrophic showdown, the **Thirty Years' War** (1618–1648), that was a disaster for the people of central Europe. As the armies rampaged through the countryside, as much as 30 percent of the rural population was killed from famine and disease in some areas, a loss of population almost as great as that brought by the Black Death three hundred years earlier. Finally the Peace of Westphalia (1648) recognized a permanent division between Catholic and Protestant Germany. The ideal of a single overarching imperial structure was gone, replaced by the concept of separate national states that, though often in conflict, would recognize one another's sovereignty. By 1648 the nominal unity that the Holy Roman Empire had once given German-speaking lands was shattered, and the era of Habsburg dominance in western European history was over.

Religious and Political Conflict in France and England, 1500–1653

France and England had the most to gain from the decline of Habsburg power. But in this same period these two societies also had to deal with their own religious divisions and political conflicts.

While Protestants, like the family of Jean de Chardin, were always a minority in French society, they had an influence on French life and politics beyond their numbers. Many French Calvinists, knows as Huguenots (HEW-guh-noh), followed John Calvin into exile in Switzerland; those who remained faced increasing persecution. In 1572, after ten years of constant conflict, religious violence reached a new level with the St. Bartholomew's Day Massacre, when the French king ordered the assassination of Protestant leaders. When news of the killing hit the streets of Paris, a mass slaughter of Huguenots began and soon spread to other French cities.

The situation was made even more dangerous by the fact that the heir to the throne, Henry of Navarre, was a member of the Protestant Bourbon family. When he became king as Henry IV in 1589, he had to face Catholic armies and a largely hostile Parisian population. But Henry proved the right man for the times. He publicly converted to Catholicism and then, in 1598, issued the Edict of Nantes granting limited toleration of Protestant worship. Still, Catholic/Protestant tensions persisted.

The dominant French political figure of the time was **Cardinal Richelieu** (1585–1642). Although Richelieu (RISH-el-yeuh) was a church official, his policies were guided by the interests of the French monarchy rather than by religious affiliation. He was willing, for example, to ally France with German Protestants against the Spanish Habsburgs, whom he saw as the main rivals to French power. Increased taxes to pay for military campaigns led to social unrest. Though the French nobility were exempt from taxes, they resented the fact that he challenged their monopoly on local affairs by sending royal officials known as *intendants* out to the provinces. These officials, granted their posts through royal patronage, were part of Richelieu's attempt to amass greater power for the king and his ministers.

The situation was volatile when the king and Cardinal Richelieu both died within a few months of each other and a child-king, **Louis XIV** (r. 1643–1715), came to the throne. Revolts broke out almost right away, and from 1648 to 1653 France was racked once again by civil war. This time the country was divided not along religious lines but between the monarchy and the many elements of French society that were fed up with high taxes and the centralization of authority at court. But the French monarchy survived these challenges, and, as we will see below, the long reign of Louis would mark a high point in French prestige and power.

● **Thirty Years' War** (1618–1648) Series of wars fought by various European powers on German-speaking lands. Began as a competition between Catholic and Lutheran rulers and was complicated by the dynastic and strategic interests of Europe's major powers.

● **Cardinal Richelieu** (1585–1642) Influential adviser to French kings who centralized the administrative system of the French state and positioned the Bourbon rulers of France to replace the Habsburgs as the dominant Catholic force in Europe.

● **Louis XIV** (r. 1643–1715) Known as the "Sun King," Louis epitomized royal absolutism and established firm control over the French state. Aggressively pursued military domination of Europe while patronizing French arts from his court at Versailles.

■ **Louis XIV at Court**   King Louis XIV was an active patron of the new science. It was his finance minister, Jean-Baptiste Colbert, who suggested that the king form the Royal Academy of Sciences in 1666. Here Colbert is shown presenting members of the Academy to the king; two globes and a large map indicate that the French monarch saw the development of science as a means of expanding his empire.   (Musée de Versailles/ Art Resource, NY)

English society entered the seventeenth century in relative tranquility under its powerful Queen Elizabeth. The "Elizabethan Age" was a time of increasing confidence of England's role in the world, as reflected in the verses of its greatest writer, William Shakespeare (1564–1616):

> This royal throne of kings, this sceptred isle . . .
> This happy breed of men, this little world,
> This precious stone set in the silver sea . . .
> This blessed plot, this earth, this realm, this England.[4]

But the peace did not last, and, like the French, the English would experience the first half of the seventeenth century as a time of turbulence.

In religious matters, Elizabeth had followed the Anglican Church tradition established by her father, King Henry VIII. Although Catholicism was made illegal and suppressed, Henry had actually retained many Catholic rites and traditions, including a hierarchical structure with powerful bishops. Many English Protestants wanted a more thorough reform that would purge it of Catholic influences like the emphasis on saints, statues, and elaborate rituals.

Protestant reformers known as **Puritans** grew increasingly discontent with the Stuart kings who came to power after Elizabeth. They looked with scorn on the increasingly lavish court life and complained of the culture of luxury of Anglican

● **Puritans**
Seventeenth-century reformers of the Church of England who attempted to purge the church of all Catholic influences. They were Calvinists who emphasized Bible reading, simplicity and modesty, and the rejection of priestly authority and elaborate rituals.

Church bishops. For the less religiously inclined, increased taxes and the assertion of centralized royal power were, as in France, potent causes of public complaint.

Under King **Charles I** (r. 1625–1649) these tensions exploded into civil war. The fiscal situation grew ever worse as Charles pursued war with Spain and supported Huguenot rebels in France. The problem was that Charles could not raise taxes to finance his wars without the approval of Parliament. In 1628, when Parliament presented a petition of protest against the king's policy, he disbanded it and did not call another for eleven years. By then Charles was so desperate for money that he had no choice but to reconvene another Parliament. Reformers in Parliament used their power over the purse to try to compel Charles into dramatic reform, such as the abolition of the Anglican bishop hierarchy in favor of a more decentralized church organization. The reformers were backed by the populace of London, which reacted with violence when Charles arrested several parliamentary leaders on charges of treason. The king fled from London, and the English Civil War (1642–1649) began.

Opposition to the king's forces was organized by the Puritan leader Oliver Cromwell (1599–1658). Although his New Model Army was generally more disciplined than the king's forces, Puritan soldiers showed their disdain by stabling their horses inside Anglican churches, smashing statues, and knocking out stained-glass windows. After seven years of fighting Cromwell prevailed, and the king was captured. Though the majority in Parliament favored negotiations, radicals insisted on summary justice. In 1649, King Charles was executed.

Oliver Cromwell became Lord Protectorate of the English Commonwealth and instituted a series of radical reforms. But the Commonwealth was held together by little other than his own will and his control of the army, and some of his policies were highly unpopular. Puritan suppression of the theaters, for example, while in keeping with strict Calvinist ideals, was resented by many. When Cromwell died in 1658, the Commonwealth went with him, and in 1660 Parliament invited Charles's son home from exile to re-establish the monarchy. The English had not yet found a way to balance monarchical and parliamentary power.

> ● **Charles I** (r. 1625–1649)   King of England whose attempts to centralize royal power led to conflict with Parliament, where some members also resented the influence of his Catholic wife. His execution marked the end of the English Civil War.

●The Shifting Balance of Power in Western Eurasia and the Mediterranean, 1650–1750

Religious divisions had further inflamed European political and military competition in the sixteenth and early seventeenth centuries. By the middle of the eighteenth century, however, the situation had stabilized as Catholic and Protestant dynasties increasingly pursued warfare and diplomacy on the basis of dynastic and national interests rather than religious ones.

New powers were emerging to challenge and displace the old empires. In the later seventeenth century, Russia, England, and France all arose as great powers and were joined by Austria, still ruled by the Habsburg family, and Prussia, a rising German-speaking power. As these five great powers jockeyed for military and diplomatic advantage, others saw their power decline. Formerly powerful Poland was divided; Safavid Iran was invaded and conquered. The Ottomans remained powerful, but by the eighteenth century their days of expansion were over.

The general direction of the power shift in western Eurasia between 1650 and 1750 was toward the north and west. Even the rulers of imperial Russia, with an empire that continued to expand to the south and east, looked to western Europe as a source of power and innovation.

Safavid Collapse and Ottoman Stasis, 1650–1750

In 1722 Afghan invaders descended on Isfahan and left Shah Abbas's city in ruins. A new Iranian leader then tried to reassemble the central power that had subsequently collapsed, but by 1747 he had been assassinated and the cultural and political legacy of the Safavid Empire was gone.

Jean de Chardin's account suggests that corruption and poor leadership were weakening the Safavids in the late seventeenth century. Shah Abbas, jealous of his own power, had neglected to groom a competent successor. The new king, Chardin reported, had been secluded in the royal harem his whole life, receiving little education, having no experience of government or administration, and being spoiled by his father's wives and concubines.

Chardin's portrait of the Safavid court in the 1670s is not complimentary. With the exception of the stern, religious, and honest grand vizier, almost everyone seemed to follow the young shah's example of drunkenness, debauchery, and petty corruption. Chardin says that several times the pious grand vizier, abiding by Islamic law in not drinking wine, was attacked by the king, who "caused full glasses of wine to be thrown in his face, poured down upon his head, and all over his clothes."[5] Shi'ite clerics, who had been principal supporters of the Safavid dynasty in its earliest days, were appalled by such behavior.

The last Safavid shah made a desperate attempt to reverse these trends and regain the support of the clergy by imposing harsh conditions of public morality. Like the unbending Puritans in England, he banned music, coffee, and public entertainments, restricted women to the home, and even destroyed the imperial wine cellar. (See the feature "World History in Today's World: The Coffeehouse in World History.") Though perhaps popular with some more radical Shi'ites, such actions were insufficient to revive Safavid claims to legitimacy.

Weakness at the top of Iranian society was a recipe for disaster. Lacking strong central direction, the Safavid bureaucracy became little more than a drain on Iranian productivity. Bribery became constant, damaging trade and the legal system. Provincial governors raised taxes on their own account, depriving the shah of revenue and the rural population of food. The Safavid Empire was therefore easy pickings for the Afghan invaders of 1722.

The Ottoman story in this same period is less dramatic, a story of relative stasis rather than collapse. In 1750 the Ottoman Empire was still impressive in its extent. In 1683 Ottoman armies had once again laid siege to Vienna, threatening to expand even further into central Europe, and as late as 1739 Ottoman forces defeated the Austrians; the Habsburgs were forced to cede Balkan territory to Constantinople. Such victories were, however, increasingly exceptional. In general, eighteenth-century Ottoman leaders found themselves defending their borders against rising powers like Russia.

As the "gunpowder revolution" continued to make warfare more deadly, it also made it more expensive to sustain an adequate military establishment to defend an empire with expansive and diverse frontiers. The difficulty that Ottoman leaders had in matching the rising power of European challengers in the eighteenth century had economic and demographic origins. Sustained population growth was not matched by an equivalent rise in economic output. Agricultural and

The Coffeehouse in World History

One of the most enduring institutions arising from the early modern Islamic world is that of the coffeehouse. Coffee is of African origin and spread to southern Arabia, where it was used by Sufi mystics to fuel their nighttime rituals. By the mid-sixteenth century the habit of coffee drinking had spread to the major cities of Islam, where coffeehouses were popular with men from all social positions as places for leisure, discussion, and games such as chess and backgammon. Women, barred from coffeehouses, drank coffee at public baths, which served a similar social function. By 1650 there were over six hundred coffeehouses in Constantinople alone.

From here coffee and coffeehouses spread to both Europe and India. Legend has it that European coffee drinking began after the Turks left bags of coffee behind when they lifted their siege of Vienna in 1683. In reality, Armenian merchants had already brought coffee to Italy and France, and it was the university town of Oxford in England that was probably the site of the first European coffeehouse. The spread of printing meant that cheap newspapers became available to fuel argumentation and debate. Men from the emerging English middle class found the coffeehouse a respectable, convivial, and inexpensive way to spend an evening.

Because of this connection with political and intellectual debate, authorities in Europe, as well as in the Islamic world, associated coffeehouses with radical and subversive ideas. In 1656 the Ottoman sultan tried to shut down Constantinople's coffeehouses, but all such attempts to limit their appeal proved futile.

In the nineteenth and twentieth centuries many European coffeehouses became more genteel, attracting a bourgeois clientele and serving chocolates and cakes. But the grittier, smoke-filled tradition of the coffeehouse as a place of independent thought and discussion endured. In the 1950s, American coffeehouses were associated with artistic forms such as free jazz and countercultural poetry. In the 1960s this association with youth culture continued, as coffeehouses became centers of protest music in the folk tradition.

More recently, coffeehouses in the United States have become the domain of large corporations. In many places, corporate homogenization now threatens the individuality and eccentricity of older coffeehouses. However, there are still many coffeehouses in Europe, in the Middle East, and in American university towns that carry on the old traditions of free thinking, argumentation, and debate.

---

commercial production was indeed on the increase at the time of Süleyman, but by the early seventeenth century economic expansion was no longer keeping up with population growth. When hunger and hardship resulted, the Ottoman government attempted to control prices and prevent exports of grain. Their success was limited, however, because global economic changes were limiting their control over their own economy.

These changes included the vast influx of American resources into western Europe, especially silver, which created steep inflation. While high prices in Europe facilitated the export of Ottoman commodities to the west, silver flowed out of the Ottoman economy at an even greater rate, used to pay for luxury goods, furs from Russia, and porcelain and silk from Iran and China for the imperial elite. Attempts at government control of imports and exports only encouraged smuggling. Meanwhile, the continuing development of all-water routes to the markets of the Indian Ocean meant that goods that had previously been transported through the Ottoman realm, and taxed in transit, were now carried directly to Europe. To finance their large army and navy and to sustain the vast imperial bureaucracy, Ottoman rulers raised taxes. But the debilitating effects of inflation and increased corruption combined with ever more strained relations between the Ottomans and their subject peoples.

As with the Safavids, problems for the Ottoman Empire represented opportunities for both subject peoples chafing under Ottoman rule and for aspiring empires like Russia, which envied the warm water ports of the Black Sea. But unlike the Safavids, the Ottomans persisted, and in the eighteenth century their realm remained one of the world's great land-based empires.

Political Consolidation and the Changing Balance of Power in Europe, 1650–1750

In the latter part of the seventeenth century, stability returned to European political life. With the failure of the Habsburg ambition to create a united Catholic empire, the permanent division of western Europe, both politically and religiously, was now taken for granted. In France, the Bourbon king Louis XIV triumphed over mid-seventeenth-century rebels to create a court of legendary power, with his Versailles Palace rivaling the Sublime Porte in Constantinople in its reputation for splendor and luxury. Louis, the "Sun King," was a model for all European kings who aspired to absolute power.

Of course, royal authority could not be made effective unless other challengers were contained. Louis completed the total identification of the French state with Catholicism in 1685 when he formally revoked the Edict of Nantes. Jean de Chardin was already living in London at this time; soon hundreds of thousands of French Protestants had fled to England, Switzerland, and the Netherlands. Some also went to join the Dutch East India Company settlement at Cape Town in South Africa (see Chapter 16). Ironically, Louis's motto, "One King, One Law, One Faith," did not lead to a policy of cooperation with other Catholic kingdoms: the French monarchy was determined to weaken Spain and Austria and so position itself as the world's dominant Catholic power.

Another obstacle to the centralization of the state was the French nobility, which was jealous of its power and prerogatives. Although serfdom had disappeared, the nobles still dominated the countryside, and many basic aspects of governance were still highly local. As a carryover from the medieval period, peasants still owed traditional labor obligations on the lords' estates and were subject to justice dispensed in manorial courts. Both lords and peasants lived in a world where local customs and traditions were much more important than national ones. The dialects they spoke were specific to their localities and regions, and the world of Paris and the royal court seemed distant indeed. Trade was hampered by local tolls, by poorly integrated transportation networks, and even by the various weights and measures used in different parts of the country.

With the uprisings of the early 1650s suppressed, Louis XIV went even further than Cardinal Richelieu to assert greater central control. The use of intendants, often men from the middle class or the lower ranks of the nobility, increased. Lacking their own estates, they relied on royal patronage and were therefore loyal to the king. They were dispatched across the country to enforce royal edicts, many of which, such as those having to do with courts and taxes, cut into the power of the landed nobility. Most nobles, having lost some of their local power and realizing they could benefit from cooperation with the king, sought royal patronage and enjoyed lavish banquets, plays, operas, and ballets provided for their entertainment at Versailles.

While the nobles were exempt from taxation, French commoners shouldered an increasing financial burden to support Louis's costly wars. After years of conflict with Spain, the Netherlands, and the Austrian Habsburgs, a settlement was finally reached in 1713 that brought some order to the dynastic politics of Europe. Faced with the possibility that the Habsburgs might reunify Madrid and Vienna under a single ruler, the European powers supported a plan to put a Bourbon relation of Louis XIV on the Spanish throne, with the stipulation that the French and Spanish crowns could never be united. Now Louis and his successors could put even more energy into challenging England in what would soon become a global competition for power (see Map 17.1).

The struggle between France and England had economic and military components. In the seventeenth century both countries had adopted **mercantilism,** which put national economic interests at the forefront of foreign policy. Under mercantilism, restrictive tariffs were placed on imports to raise their prices, maximize the country's exports, and build up its supplies of gold and silver bullion. Through the use of monopolistic chartered companies on the model of the Dutch East India Company (see Chapter 16), Louis XIV's government attempted to closely control foreign trade, directing colonial resources to the benefit of the motherland and restricting the access of the English and other rivals to French colonial markets.

Louis XIV's form of government has been termed "royal absolutism." "I am the state," he said, implying that all of public life should be directed by his own will. When Charles II returned to England in 1660 to re-establish the Stuart monarchy after civil war and Puritan rule, he was perhaps envious of Louis's power. But Charles was in a difficult position. He preferred relatively tolerant policies, and although the extremes of Puritan rule under Cromwell had given Calvinists something of a bad reputation, Charles welcomed Huguenot refugees from France, appointing Jean de Chardin as his royal jeweler. But Parliament imposed stringent restrictions on both Catholics and Protestant "dissenters," that is, those who rejected the Anglican Church in favor of a more thoroughly reformed Protestantism. Only Anglicans were allowed to hold public office.

With the death of Charles, religious tension rose to the point of crisis when his Catholic brother came to the throne as King James II (r. 1685–1689). While James II did not try to impose Catholicism on the largely Protestant kingdom, he did seek greater tolerance for his own faith. The question of succession was the main problem for many members of Parliament, since James's son and heir was also a Catholic. To prevent a Catholic succession, they invited Charles's reliably Protestant daughter Mary, together with her Dutch husband William of Orange, to take the throne. James II went into exile and assembled an army to restore himself to power, but in 1690 he was defeated by Protestant forces led by William at the the Battle of the Boyne in Ireland. William's victory made permanent the Protestant character of the British monarchy and established a long-standing Protestant ascendency over the Catholic population of Northern Ireland.

The so-called Glorious Revolution of 1689 was neither very glorious nor very revolutionary, but it did come with a constitutional innovation that would eventually have global repercussions. Since they had been invited to rule by Parliament, William and Mary were required to accept the principle of annual parliamentary meetings. They also approved a **Bill of Rights** that defended freedom of speech and protected all Englishmen against arbitrary seizure of their person or property. While restrictions on individual liberty remained, most people had no real voice in their own governance, and discrimination against Catholics and dissenting

● **mercantilism**
Dominant economic theory in seventeenth- and eighteenth-century Europe that emphasized the role of international economics in interstate competition. Restrictive tariffs limited imports and protected bullion supplies, and chartered companies maximized revenue from overseas colonies.

● **Bill of Rights**
In 1689, King William and Queen Mary of England recognized a Bill of Rights that protected their subjects against arbitrary seizure of person or property and that required annual meetings of Parliament.

MAP 17.1

Western Eurasia in 1715 By the early eighteenth century the Habsburg attempt to unify western Europe had failed, and the continent was permanently divided between Catholic and Protestant powers. In 1715 the dominant powers in the west were France, Great Britain, Austria, and Prussia. The Russian and Ottoman Empires to the east were formidable military powers, but the golden age of Spain had ended.

CL Interactive Map

Key:
- French Bourbon lands
- Spanish Bourbon lands
- Austrian Habsburg lands
- Prussian lands
- Great Britain
- Boundary of the Holy Roman Empire
- Russian Empire
- Russian gains, by 1725
- Ottoman Empire, 1722

Protestants continued, the English Bill of Rights was a check on royal power that created important precedents for the future.

The English solution to the crisis of the seventeenth century was therefore very different from the French one of royal absolutism. The balance between king and Parliament worked well and gave English society a stable foundation. English commerce thrived, both domestically and across the world, and the British navy, already envied by Louis XIV in the late seventeenth century, became the dominant world power in the eighteenth century. Rising from religious strife and civil war, England had become a great power, and the French and the British would soon be engaged in a global contest for power and influence that brought war to both the Americas and Asia.

Austria, Prussia, and Russia, the remaining great powers of eighteenth-century Europe, all followed the French model of royal absolutism. The Ottomans remained formidable rivals in southeastern Europe, while the Habsburgs still controlled an expansive empire from their capital at Vienna and were secure in their core territories after the second Ottoman siege of Vienna was lifted. The Austrian Habsburgs ruled over an ethnically and religiously heterogeneous population. Facing the same challenge as the Ottomans—how to assert a single royal authority over a diverse population—the Habsburgs generally pursued a similar policy: as long as the authority of the king was acknowledged and taxes were paid, local autonomy would be accepted. Thus after a Hungarian rebellion was suppressed, the privileges of the Hungarian nobility and many traditional Hungarian legal customs were retained. In the mid-eighteenth century Habsburg Austria was a formidable power.

In Protestant-dominated northern Germany, Prussia was the rising power in the aftermath of the Thirty Years' War. Although the German-speaking lands were still divided into numerous small territories, Prussia, from its capital at Berlin, was emerging as the largest, strongest, and most centralized German state. Under Frederick William I (r. 1713–1740) military affairs took precedence. If Prussia had not been a pioneer in military technology and organization, using the latest cannon and muskets and developing a professional standing army of well-trained and disciplined troops, it would not have been able to push itself into the ranks of the great powers. Many features of modern military life, such as precision marching, were pioneered under Frederick William. In comparison with France and especially with England, the Prussian middle class had little political influence. Instead, it was the Junkers (YUNG-kurz), the traditional rural aristocracy, who were the social bedrock of royal absolutism. Their cooperation in taxing and controlling the peasants gave Frederick William and his successors resources to expand the military and make Prussia a force to be reckoned with.

We have seen that, when Jean de Chardin visited Iran, the Russians already had a special diplomatic relationship with their Safavid rulers. From Chardin's perspective, the Russians at Isfahan were almost as exotic as the Iranians:

> The [Russian] Ambassador was clad in a robe of yellow satin, over which he had a large vest of red velvet lined with marten furs. . . . His cap was also of the same fur, covered with crimson velvet, embroidered with small pearls in the front and with two tresses of pearls that hung down his back to his waist.

This description reminds us that Russian culture and the Russian state had developed in interaction not with western Europe but with steppe nomads and Byzantine Christianity. A major shift in the balance between European and Asian elements came with Tsar **Peter the Great** (r. 1685–1725). After visiting the Netherlands as

• **Peter the Great** (r. 1685–1725) Powerful Romanov tsar who built a new Russian capital at St. Petersburg, emulated Western advances in military technology, and extended the Russian Empire further into Asia.

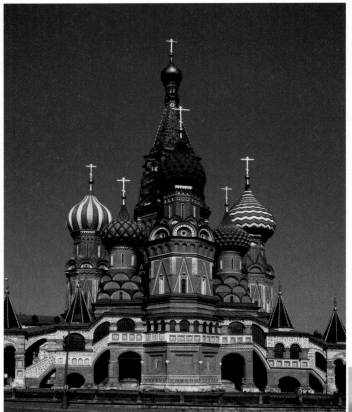

St. Basil's Church and the Winter Palace Architecture demonstrates Russia's diverse cultural influences. St. Basil's Cathedral (*left*) in Moscow highlights the impact of Byzantine and Persian traditions on Orthodox church architecture, while Peter the Great's Winter Palace (*below*), today part of the Hermitage Museum complex, testifies to the tsar's emulation of Western models in the construction of his new capital at St. Petersburg. (left: © Steve Vidler/Superstock; below: Peter Christopher/Masterfile)

a young man, Peter came back strongly aware of Russian backwardness and undertook reforms designed to put Russian power on a par with that of the rising Western states. He built the new city of St. Petersburg on the Baltic Sea as Russia's "window on the west." Its elegant baroque buildings, emulating those of Rome and Vienna, stood in contrast to the churches and palaces of Moscow, which were more influenced by Central Asian architecture. Peter also tightened the dependence of the nobility on the Russian state. In a move that symbolized his desire to bring the country in line with Western models, he ordered Russian nobles to shave off their luxurious beards. From now on they would dress not like the ambassador described by Chardin but according to the latest European fashions.

Peter's ultimate goal, however, was power, and that meant focusing on the military. He established a regular standing army that was larger than any in Europe and bought the latest military technology from the West while working toward Russian self-sufficiency in the production of modern guns, cannon, and ships for his Baltic fleet. He also sponsored a new educational system that focused on technical skills appropriate to the emergence of more efficient civilian and military bureaucracies. But the middle class remained small, weak, and dependent on state patronage. The situation of the serfs was worse than ever. It was their heavy taxes that paid for the grandeur of St. Petersburg and the power of the Russian military, and it was their sons who fought Peter's wars.

Peter won victories against Poland, Sweden, and the Ottoman Empire, pushing the imperial frontiers from the Baltic Sea in the north to the Black Sea in the south. The Siberian and Central Asian frontiers of the Russian Empire also continued to expand, in the latter case bringing more Muslims under Russian rule. Pragmatism dictated that there would be no systematic attempt to convert subject peoples to Orthodox Christianity.

By 1750 the great power roster was in place that would dominate western Eurasian political and military competition for centuries. Prussia, Russia, and Austria would control central and eastern Europe. France, the major land power in the West, would also build its navy to challenge England for control of the sea-lanes and the overseas empire on which commercial success increasingly depended.

CL Primary Source: Edicts and Decrees
Read a selection of Peter the Great's decrees and find out how he wished to modernize, and Westernize, Russia.

● Bourgeois Values and Chardin's View of the "Orient"

When reading travel writings, we often learn as much about the traveler as about the places that he or she has visited. That is certainly true of Chardin's *Travels in Persia,* which reveals his own values by contrasting them with Iranian norms. As we saw at the beginning of the chapter, Chardin's model of commercial negotiation differed from the one practiced by his Iranian counterparts: he thought they were duplicitous, and they thought he was rude. Throughout the book Chardin contrasts the values of his own society with those of the "oriental" societies through which he moves. (See the feature "Visual Evidence: Portrait of the Safavid Court.")

Chardin was not close-minded. He noted strong Iranian traditions in medicine and astronomy, saying that "the Persian genius lies in the direction of the sciences

PORTRAIT OF THE SAFAVID COURT

The artistic contributions of Iranian artists to world culture have been numerous and significant, especially across the Islamic world. In the Safavid period, Persian carpets, ceramics, glazed tiles, and jewelry brought a refined aesthetic to useful objects. Safavid Iranians brought Persian traditions of poetry, literature, and architecture to many lands, including Renaissance Italy and Mughal India (see Chapter 16).

Like other Muslim artists, Iranians emphasized abstract and floral designs. Most Muslim artists avoided realistic representations of the human form, fearing the temptation of idol worship. At the Safavid court,

This is a portrait of royal leisure rather than royal power. The shah is clearly identified by his central place in the portrait, but he is not elevated above his courtiers. Musicians entertain him, while attendants stand ready with bows and arrows for an evening hunt.

The influence of European artistic traditions is seen in Jabbadar's use of vanishing perspective to create a pastoral background, conventional in European but not in Iranian painting. The highly individualized facial characteristics of the courtiers, as well as close attention to their diversity of dress and therefore ethnic background, may also derive from European influence.

(Institute of Oriental Studies, St. Petersburg, Russia/The Bridgeman Art Library)

however, the shahs lavishly patronized painting that portrayed people. *Shah Sulayman and His Courtiers*, seen here, was painted in watercolor, gold, and ink in about 1670 by 'Ali Quli Jabbadar. This work is in the tradition of Persian miniature painting. While incorporating intricate details, it measures only 11 by 16 inches.

Shah Sulayman II (soo-lay-mahn) (r. 1666–1694) was in power when Jean de Chardin returned to Isfahan. The elder son of Shah Abbas II, Sulayman was born to a slave girl and raised in the highly protected harem, with no experience of the world. Chardin commented on Sulayman's erratic behavior and his frequent drunkenness. One pious official who refused to join the Shah in drinking wine provoked the drunken king's anger so that "he one time went even so far as to strike him upon that account, [the king] has caused full glasses of wine to be thrown in his face." Shiite clerics were appalled by such behavior at court. Their disaffection was an important indicator that by the late seventeenth century the Safavids were losing popular support.

Indeed, while Isfahan remained a magnificent capital under Shah Sulayman II, the beginning of Safavid decline had begun. Raiders from the east took advantage of the weak court and lack of discipline in the military to invade from the east, while to the west Sulayman's forces were unable to take advantage of the Ottoman defeat at Vienna in 1683. In this portrait the young Shah does not seem aware of the trouble to come.

Area of detail

• The European figure in the upper left, shown bowing to the shah or perhaps lighting his pipe, looks somewhat like Jean de Chardin. It was with Sulayman's officials that the Frenchman had his dispute over the price of jewelry.

• Sulayman was criticized by Muslim clerics for his moral laxity. They frowned on the use of hashish, opium, or tobacco, all of which were smoked through waterpipes like this one, and were especially disgusted by the shah's fondness for wine.

QUESTION FOR ANALYSIS

How do Sulayman's pose and facial expression, and the poses and facial expressions of the others, relate to the general mood of the portrait?

more than toward any other profession." He recognized the linguistic skills of educated Safavid subjects, women as well as men, and complimented their poetry: "The number of figures of speech of which Persian poetry makes full use is almost limitless. Nevertheless all of them are sublime." He praised Iranian architecture, describing the shah's residence as "one of the most imposing palaces that can be seen in any capital city."

Even regarding gender relations, Chardin kept an open mind. He understood that the tradition of veiling women was older than Islam, "the most ancient of anything their histories speak of," and correctly identified the practice as more of a social custom than a religious mandate. He even wondered if the Iranian custom of gender segregation might be preferable. "When [the men] do not see another man's wife," he wrote, they will not lose "the affection which they have, or ought to have, for their own." Of course, Chardin himself was unable to enter the women's quarters of the shah's palace, so he had no direct knowledge of the degree to which elite Safavid women, on the model of Nur Jahan in Mughal India (see Chapter 16), might wield significant influence even while remaining secluded.

More frequently, however, Chardin reveals his own value system by criticizing the Iranians. It is a common human characteristic to define your own positive attributes by pointing out their supposed absence in another group of people. Each of the following critiques of Iranian behavior might, by negative example, define Chardin's own sense of correct behavior:

- "They love to enjoy the present, and deny themselves nothing that they are able to procure, taking no thoughts for the morrow and relying wholly on providence, and their own fate they firmly believe to be sure and unalterable."

- "They cannot conceive that there should be such a country where people will do their duty from a motive of virtue only, without any other recompense."

- "They are not desirous of new inventions and discoveries [but] rest contented, choosing rather to buy goods from strangers than to learn the art of making them."

None of these statements should be taken as an accurate record of Iranian values. They can, however, reveal those that Chardin himself most appreciated: thrift, foresight, plainspeaking, hard work, and detached curiosity.

Such values were characteristic of Chardin's own social group, the urban middle class of northwestern Europe. Like Chardin, middle-class members of the bourgeoisie did not have the advantages of the nobility, such as aristocratic titles, landed estates, and exemption from taxes. But they did possess property, education, and ambition, and they often asserted the superiority of their own codes of conduct over both foreigners and other social groups in their own countries.

The counting and measuring of time is an example. Whereas peasants marked time by the changing of the seasons and religious authorities by a ritual calendar, the bourgeoisie increasingly saw time not as slow cycles but as something akin to money, to be saved and invested. The development of ever smaller and more accurate timepieces reinforced that attitude. When middle-class civic authorities in Europe built town clocks with bells to strike every quarter hour, trying to promote a stricter and more quantified sense of timekeeping, they were sometimes resisted by artisans who preferred the slower pace of the past. Some town clocks were smashed as a result.

To Safavid officials, Chardin's close observance of minutes and hours must have seemed an irrational obsession. But such perspectives were rarely, if ever, represented in Western texts. Instead, stereotypes of "Asiatic" societies began to multiply. As more members of Europe's growing middle class traveled abroad in the eighteenth and nineteenth centuries, a market developed for travel books from "exotic" Asian locations. Deeply engrained prejudices and misunderstandings resulted, such as an assumption that "oriental" societies were static and unchanging. Though Chardin himself, with his knowledge of Iranian language and culture, was less guilty than many of inflating the virtues of his own society by denigrating others, his *Travels in Persia* provides a preview of what was to come.

After leaving France to avoid religious persecution from Catholic authorities, Chardin achieved even greater wealth and prestige after he was appointed court jeweler to the British king. He then took employment with the British East India Company and moved to Holland. In Amsterdam his Calvinist beliefs and bourgeois values fit right in. As the eighteenth century progressed, Europe's urban middle class also began to contrast their own emphasis on thrift, foresight, plainspeaking, and hard work with the luxury and privilege enjoyed by their social superiors. By the end of the eighteenth century such bourgeois critiques of the European aristocracy would have revolutionary implications (see Chapter 22).

Chapter Review

CL Download the MP3 audio file of the Chapter Review and listen to it on the go.

The early modern period was a time of heightened competition between the empires and states of western Eurasia and, as the travels of Jean de Chardin show, also of increased commercial and cultural interaction. Religious divisions heightened political and military competition both in western Europe, divided between Catholics and Protestants, and in western Asia, where the Sunni-dominated Ottoman Empire struggled to assert its domination over the Shi'ite rulers of Safavid Iran.

When, where, and how were religion and politics most closely intertwined in western Eurasian societies? When and why did religion come to play a less prominent political role?

In the seventeenth and early eighteenth centuries, religion and politics became closely intertwined across western Eurasia. Ruling dynasties usually saw themselves as defenders of the faith, whether it was Orthodox Christianity for the Russian tsars, Roman Catholicism for the Habsburg emperors, Protestantism for the kings and queens of England, Sunni Islam for the Ottoman sultans, or Shi'ism for the Safavid shahs. Conflicting religious ideologies often added fuel to the fire of political and military competition, as in the Ottoman/Safavid competition for territory and influence, or in the Thirty Years' War that ravaged central Europe. Rulers differed, however, in how they responded to religious diversity *within* their domains. The Spanish, French, and British dynasties were the least tolerant of religious diversity.

KEY TERMS

Jean de Chardin (480)

Janissaries (484)

Süleyman (484)

Safavid dynasty (488)

Ismail (488)

Abbas I (488)

Habsburg dynasty (490)

Philip II (492)

Thirty Years' War (493)

Cardinal Richelieu (493)

Louis XIV (493)

Puritans (494)

Charles I (495)

mercantilism (499)

Bill of Rights (499)

Peter the Great (501)

The Safavids also imposed a single faith from the top down, but they tolerated Christian and Jewish minorities who played important commercial roles. The Ottomans, following the tradition established by Süleyman the Lawgiver, were more tolerant of religious diversity, recognizing that their vast empire could not be effectively ruled without the acquiescence of subject peoples.

By the eighteenth century religion had become less central to politics. With the fall of the Safavid dynasty, Shi'ite Islam no longer had a powerful imperial patron. In Europe, the ambitious rulers and dynasties were no longer as interested in religious affiliations as in power and profit.

How did the balance of power between the dominant states of western Eurasia shift during this period?

In the early eighteenth century the balance of power between states and empires in western Eurasia began to shift. At the beginning of the sixteenth century the Ottoman, Safavid, and Spanish Habsburg empires were each in an expansive phase. Two hundred years later the situation was quite different. The Safavid dynasty was gone. Madrid and Constantinople were still important capitals, but they had lost the initiative to other powers. Instead it was France, England, Austria, Prussia, and the quickly growing Russian Empire that dominated political and military competition in early eighteenth-century western Eurasia.

What do Jean de Chardin's travel writings tell us, both about Safavid Iran and about his own culture and values?

Jean de Chardin viewed Safavid culture through the lens of his own experiences. Like all good travel writers, he provides us with key insights into seventeenth-century Iranian life, but we must be careful not to take his assessments at face value. His criticisms of his Iranian hosts often came from differences in cultural orientation. As a French Protestant from an urban background, Chardin embodied the ideas and ideals of the rising middle class of northern Europe. Literate, commercially oriented, and increasingly impatient with political and cultural customs that did not suit their interests, bourgeois men like Chardin would play an increasingly prominent role in world history.

For Further Reference

Beik, William. *Louis XIV and Absolutism: A Brief Study with Documents*. New York: Bedford/St. Martin's, 2000.

Bergin, Joseph. *The Seventeenth Century: Europe 1598–1715*. New York: Oxford University Press, 2001.

Braudel, Fernand. *The Mediterranean and the Mediterranean World in the Age of Philp II*. Sian Reynolds, trans. New York: Harper and Row, 1972.

Chardin, Jean de. *A Journey to Persia: Jean Chardin's Portrait of a Seventeenth Century Empire*. Ronald W. Ferrier, trans. and ed. London: I. B. Tauris, 1996.

Clot, Andre. *Suleiman the Magnificent*. London: Saqi Books, 2004.

Coward, Barry. *The Stuart Age: England, 1603–1714*. 3d ed. New York: Longman, 2003.

Fichtner, Paula Sutter. *Terror and Toleration: The Habsburg Empire Confronts Islam, 1526–1850*. New York: Reaktion Books, 2008.

Faroghi, Suraiya. *The Ottoman Empire and the World Around It*. London: I. B. Tauris, 2006.

Hughes, Lindsay. *Russia in the Age of Peter the Great*. New Haven: Yale University Press, 2000.

Savory, Roger. *Iran Under the Safavids*. New York: Cambridge University Press, 2007.

Websites

Islamic History Sourcebook (http://vlib.iue.it/hist-russia/Index.html).   Links to materials on Ottoman and Safavid history and a wealth of other topics related to the Islamic world.

Modern History Sourcebook (http://www.fordham.edu/halsall/mod/modsbook.html).   An extensive collection of primary sources on the Reformation and other topics.

Russian History Index (http://vlib.iue.it/hist-russia/Index.html).   Materials and links on Russian history, presented both chronologically and topically.

WEB RESOURCES

Pronunciation Guide

Interactive Maps

MAP 17.1 Western Eurasia in 1715

Primary Sources

Chapter Objectives

ACE Multiple-Choice Quiz

Flashcards

Empires, Colonies, and Peoples of the Americas, 1600–1750

By the early 1600s the Spanish had conquered the once-mighty Aztec and Inca and were secure in their American empire. But some areas had not been effectively occupied, and some Amerindian peoples held on to their independence. A battle-hardened young soldier, **Catalina de Erauso** (1585–1650), described an encounter with one such group in South America:

CATALINA DE ERAUSO

(*Lieutenant Nun: Memoir of a Basque Transvestite in the New World*, by Catalina de Erauso [Boston: Beacon Press, 1996])

On the third day we came to an Indian village whose inhabitants immediately laid hold of their weapons, and as we drew nearer scattered at the sound of our guns, leaving behind some dead. . . . [A soldier] took off his helmet to mop his brow, and a devil of a boy about twelve years old fired an arrow at him from where he was perched in a tree beside the road. . . . The arrow lodged in the [soldier's] eye. . . . We carved the boy into a thousand pieces. Meanwhile, the Indians had returned to the village more than ten thousand strong. We fell at them again with such spirit, and butchered so many of them, that blood ran like a river across the plaza. . . . The men had found more than sixty thousand pesos' worth of gold dust in the huts of the village, and an infinity more of it along the banks of the river, and they filled their helmets with it.[1]

This icon will direct you to interactive activities and study materials on the *Voyages* website: www.cengage.com/history/hansen/voyages1e

510

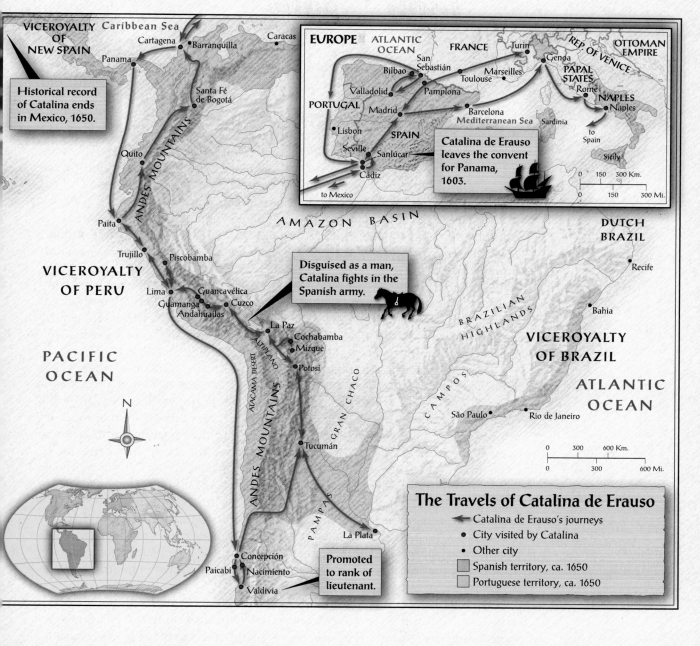

VICEROYALTY OF NEW SPAIN

Caribbean Sea

Cartagena • Barranquilla • Caracas

Panama

Historical record of Catalina ends in Mexico, 1650.

Santa Fé de Bogotá

Quito

ANDES MOUNTAINS

Paita

Trujillo • Piscobamba

VICEROYALTY OF PERU

Lima • Guancavélica
Guamanga • Cuzco
Andahuailas

PACIFIC OCEAN

AMAZON BASIN

La Paz
Cochabamba
Mizque
Potosí

ALTIPLANO

ATACAMA DESERT

ANDES MOUNTAINS

GRAN CHACO

Tucumán

PAMPAS

La Plata

Concepción
Paicabí • Nacimiento
Valdivia

Disguised as a man, Catalina fights in the Spanish army.

BRAZILIAN HIGHLANDS

CAMPOS

São Paulo • Rio de Janeiro

DUTCH BRAZIL

Recife

Bahia

VICEROYALTY OF BRAZIL

ATLANTIC OCEAN

Promoted to rank of lieutenant.

N

EUROPE ATLANTIC OCEAN **FRANCE** Turin REP. OF VENICE **OTTOMAN EMPIRE**

San Sebastián
Bilbao
Marseilles
Genoa
Toulouse
PAPAL STATES
Valladolid
Pamplona
Rome
NAPLES
PORTUGAL
Madrid
Barcelona
Naples
Mediterranean Sea
Sardinia
Lisbon
SPAIN
to Spain
Seville • Sanlúcar
Sicily
Cádiz

Catalina de Erauso leaves the convent for Panama, 1603.

to Mexico

0   150   300 Km.
0   150   300 Mi.

0   300   600 Km.
0   300   600 Mi.

The Travels of Catalina de Erauso
— Catalina de Erauso's journeys
• City visited by Catalina
• Other city
▢ Spanish territory, ca. 1650
▢ Portuguese territory, ca. 1650

	1500	1550	1600	1650	1700	1750
			Lifetime of Catalina de Erauso 1585 — 1650			
NORTH AMERICA			Samuel de Champlain founds New France 1608	Huron population is decimated by disease 1640s		
			First African slaves in Virginia 1619			
MEXICO AND THE CARIBBEAN		Viceroyalty of New Spain founded 1535		Lifetime of Sor Juana Ines de la Cruz 1648 — 1695		
CENTRAL AND SOUTH AMERICA		Discovery of silver at Potosí 1545		Kingdom of Palmares 1630 — 1694	Discovery of gold in Brazil 1695	

It was a woman, Catalina de Erauso (kat-ah-LEE-nah day eh-rah-OO-so), one of the most remarkable figures of seventeenth-century America, who painted this matter-of-fact picture of slaughter.

Erauso, born in northeastern Spain, was put into a convent by her family at the age of 4. At the age of 15, when she was being prepared to take the permanent vows that would confine her for a lifetime, she stole the keys and escaped: "I shook off my veil and went out into a street I had never seen. . . . I holed up for three days, planning and re-planning and cutting myself out a suit of clothes. . . . I cut my hair and set off without knowing where I was going."

Disguised as a boy, Erauso found employment as a personal assistant for a local nobleman, but she left when he "finally went so far as to lay hands on me." She stole some money, boarded a ship for Panama in 1603, and joined the Spanish army. For twenty years Erauso traveled, disguised as a man, around Peru, Chile, Bolivia, and Argentina. A member of Spain's ethnically distinct Basque (bask) community, Erauso often teamed up with fellow Basques as she soldiered her way across the Spanish Americas. According to her own story, her violent streak kept getting her into trouble. Card games often ended with insults and drawn swords, and more than once she had to run from the law after killing a man.

Erauso's exploits have become part of Latin American folklore, where she is known as *la monja alférez* (la mon-ha al-FAIR-ez), "the lieutenant nun." Her story is compelling because it is exceptional. But her deception was made easier by the unsettled conditions of the early colonial frontier. New arrivals from Europe and Africa increased decade by decade, interacting with the remaining inhabitants to forever alter the cultural landscape of the Americas. For Erauso and many others, it was literally a "new world"—new for European officials, settlers, and adventurers, and new for African slaves who did much of the work building the new American societies. It was also new for America's indigenous inhabitants, who saw their old ways of life undermined, sometimes quickly and sometimes more slowly, as they came under the political control and economic influence of European powers like Spain, Portugal, France, and England. Interactions between peoples from Europe, Africa, and the Americas were the foundation on which new American societies were built.

This chapter examines the political, economic, social, and cultural life of colonial America in the seventeenth and early eighteenth centuries, focusing especially on gender and race relations, the role of the Americas in the global economy, and the differences between the various European colonial ventures.

Focus Questions

What were the principal forms of political and economic organization in the Americas in this period?

What were the key demographic and cultural outcomes of the interaction of European, African, and Amerindian peoples in various regions of the Americas?

 What connections and comparisons can we draw between the different European colonial ventures in the Americas?

The Spanish Empire in the Americas, 1600–1700

In a remarkably short time the Spanish conquistadors had laid waste to the Aztec and Inca Empires (see Chapter 15) and established a firm foothold in much of the region we now call Latin America. To rule these vast territories, the Spanish set up a highly centralized government that relied on close cooperation between crown and church. It was a strictly hierarchical power structure, with officials from Spain and locally born Spaniards at the top, the increasing number of people of mixed descent in the middle, and conquered Indians, and sometimes African slaves, at the bottom. As Erauso's story shows, however, the farther one went from such centers of Spanish authority the more fluid relations of gender and race became, giving at least some people with modest backgrounds new possibilities in life.

From Conquest to Control

When Erauso arrived in Panama in 1603, the Spanish Empire was the most powerful of the European colonial ventures. True, a Spanish Armada had been defeated by England in 1588, and the Dutch, still under Spanish rule, were laying the foundations for their own global enterprise. But Philip II of Spain could count on American resources as a foundation of his power (see Chapter 17). The Spanish continued to subjugate Amerindian peoples even while in some remote regions indigenous societies remained independent into the eighteenth century.

During the sixteenth century the Spanish Habsburgs were asserting greater royal authority. Having created a more centralized bureaucracy headed by the Council of the Indies, in 1535 they sent the first viceroy to Mexico City, and in 1542 a second was dispatched to Lima. From that time forward, the emperor in Madrid sent officials to America as representatives of Spanish power. Eventually four **viceroyalties** were created: New Spain (with a capital at Mexico City), New Granada (Bogotá), Peru (Lima), and La Plata (Buenos Aires; see Map 18.1). Below the viceroys were presidencies, captaincy-generals, governors, and municipal authorities.

The other great institution of Spanish rule was the Catholic Church. The pope granted the Spanish crown the right to exercise power over the church in the Americas in all but purely spiritual affairs. The boundaries between church and state therefore became blurred. Civil authorities appointed and dismissed bishops, while church leaders often served as top government officials. In some cases the church helped extend the frontier of Spanish rule and make it effective, such as on the northern frontiers of New Spain, where missionaries brought Catholicism and

> **• viceroyalties** Seats of power of the Spanish officials representing the king. Originally there were two viceroyalties, in New Spain (Mexico City) and Peru (Lima). Later, New Granada (Bogotá) and La Plata (Buenos Aires) were added.

NEW FRANCE
(Conquered by England, 1760)

ENGLISH COLONIES
(Independence declared, 1776)

ATLANTIC OCEAN

40°N

40°W

Effective frontier of Spanish settlement

Silver
Silver
COAHUILA

Colorado R.
Rio Grande

Gulf of Mexico

FLORIDA
(Ceded to England, 1763–1783)

VICEROYALTY OF NEW SPAIN
BAJÍO LEÓN (1535)
Guadalajara ✕ Zacatecas
✕ Guanajuato
Mexico City   Veracruz
Silver
Cacao
Sugar cane
Cochineal
Cochineal
Cacao
Indigo
BRITISH HONDURAS
Guatemala
Silver

Sugar cane

Sugar cane
Indigo

Havana

Sugar cane
Beef
Tobacco

HAITI [SAINT-DOMINGUE]
(Ceded to France, 1697)

Beef

Sugar cane
JAMAICA
(Conquered by England, 1655)

SANTO DOMINGO

PUERTO RICO

Sugar cane

Caribbean Sea

20°N

N

Caracas
Pearls
Cacao
Gold

Bogotá

Orinoco R.

GUIANA

Magdalena R.

VICEROYALTY OF NEW GRANADA
(Separated from Viceroyalty of Peru, 1717, 1739)

Quito

Equator   0°

Amazon R.

Forest products

PACIFIC OCEAN

VICEROYALTY OF PERU
(1590s)
Lima

Sugar cane

Cuzco

Sugar cane
La Paz
Chuquisaca
(La Plata; Sucre)
Potosí

ANDES

VICEROYALTY OF BRAZIL
(1720)

Sugar cane   Pernambuco

Sugar cane   Salvador

Cacao

Paraná R.

Diamonds
Gold
Rio de Janeiro
(Capital, 1763)

São Paulo

20°S

Yerba
Tobacco

VICEROYALTY OF LA PLATA
(Separated from Viceroyalty of Peru, 1776)

Wheat

Beef and hides

0   500   1,000 Km.
0   500   1,000 Mi.

AUDIENCIA OF CHILE
(Retained by Viceroyalty of Peru, 1776)

Santiago

Buenos Aires

Montevideo

Beef and hides

Claimed but not settled by Spain

Islas Malvinas
(Falkland Islands)

Cape Horn
80°W   60°W

Territories claimed by Spain
Viceroyalty of New Spain
Viceroyalty of New Granada
Viceroyalty of Peru and Audiencia of Chile
Viceroyalty of Rio de la Plata

Territories claimed by Portugal
Viceroyalty of Brazil

✕ Silver mine

CL Interactive Map

🌐 **MAP 18.1   The Spanish Empire in the Americas**
This map of the early-eighteenth-century Americas shows the territorial dominance of the Spanish Empire and its four viceroyalties. Though Portuguese Brazil was also large and rich, British and French colonial possessions were small and poor in resources by comparison. We should remember that this map shows European *claims* to territory. Some Amerindian societies remained autonomous and unconquered, especially in more remote regions of mountains, forests, and deserts.

Spanish rule to the Amerindian peoples of California. In the early colonial period, bishops sent directly from Spain occupied the higher church positions.

As more Iberians crossed the ocean, American-born Spaniards known as *criollos* (kree-OY-os) began to grow in number, and by the seventeenth century they were participating in government, even though the top positions continued to be held by officials sent directly from Spain. Criollos became a social and economic elite, pursuing wealth and power often by seizing Amerindian land and exploiting Amerindian labor.

Although lust for gold had been a principal motive of the early conquistadors, it was silver that filled the Spanish treasury and transformed the world economy. In 1545, shortly after silver deposits were found in Mexico, the greatest discovery of silver in world history was made high in the Andes at **Potosí** (poh-toh-SEE). The

> ● **Potosí**   Location high in the Andes in modern Bolivia where the Spanish found huge quantities of silver. Silver exports from Potosí and other American mines helped finance development of the early modern world economy.

▗ **The Silver Mine at Potosí**   The silver mines of Spanish America, of which Potosí was the greatest, enriched the Spanish treasury and facilitated the expansion of global trade. As this engraving from 1590 shows, however, it was the heavy toil of Amerindian workers on Potosí's mountain of silver that made it all possible. Spanish mine operators used the mercury amalgamation process to increase the yield of silver from ore, resulting in the frequently lethal mercury poisoning of workers such as those seen here.   (The Granger Collection)

Spanish had found a whole mountain of silver, and Potosí soon became crucial to the development of the early modern world economy: Andean silver made possible European trade with China and other Asian economies, and much of the silver extracted from Potosí ended up in China (see Chapter 16).

Silver mining and the trade it made possible generated huge profits, but not for the workers who dug open the mountain. Mining has always been difficult and dangerous work. With the technology available in the sixteenth century, conditions were so brutal that force was needed to get workers for the mines. Though the Crown had placed restrictions on *encomienda* (in-coh-mee-EN-dah) holders (see Chapter 15), a new legal system called the *repartimiento* (reh-par-TEE-me-en-toh) gave Spaniards the right to coerce Amerindian labor for specific tasks. Although the original intent in reforming the encomienda system had been to limit abuses, most Spaniards still casually assumed they had a right to enslave Amerindians. Erauso, for example, commented that during one of her trading ventures a civic leader "gave me ten thousand head of llama to drive and a hundred-some-odd Indians." It does not seem that these Amerindians had any say in the matter.

The Spanish called their Andean labor system *mita* (mee-tah), the same name that was used by the Inca for their system of labor tribute. In spite of the name, the Spanish system differed greatly from the earlier Inca one. Under the Inca, mita required every household to contribute labor for tasks such as military service, road construction, and the maintenance of irrigation works. Exemptions were given for people whose families were in difficult circumstances, and the workers were fed, clothed, and well treated. By contrast, the voracious Spanish appetite for silver meant that little attention was paid to the well-being of local communities or individual laborers. Every adult male had to spend one full year out of every seven working in the mines at wages that were not sufficient for his own support, let alone for his family. The use of poisonous mercury to separate silver from ore led to sickness and death for many Amerindian workers. In addition, women, children, and the elderly back in their villages had to work harder to compensate for the drain of adult male labor from their communities.

By 1600 Potosí, with a population over 100,000, was a major market for foodstuffs and other supplies. When Erauso set off with her llamas and one hundred Indians, she intended to exploit this market: "[The official] also gave me a great deal of money to buy wheat in the Cochabamba plains. My job was to grind it and get it to Potosí, where the scarcity of wheat made for high prices. I went and bought eight thousand bushels . . . hauled them by llama to the mills . . . and took them to Potosí. I then sold them all . . . and brought the cash back to my master." The llamas she used as transport were indigenous, but the wheat they hauled grew from seeds brought from Europe, an example of the ongoing Columbian exchange (see Chapter 15).

Expanding market opportunities also came with the growth of administrative centers such as Mexico City, Lima, and Buenos Aires, which stimulated local and regional trade in foodstuffs. In colonial Latin America market-based agriculture was based on large estates known as **haciendas** (ha-cee-EN-das). While many Amerindian communities remained largely self-sufficient, farming small village plots, the Spanish hacienda owners focused on meeting rising demand for agricultural produce. In addition to growing crops for sale, many grazed vast herds of cattle.

The hacienda owners were closely integrated into the larger networks of church, state, and market. But within the boundaries of their own large estates they often had almost total control, governing their lands and the people who lived on them

---

CL Primary Source:
Complaint of the Indians of Tecama Against Their Encomendero, Juan Ponce de León
Read the testimony of several Indians on the conditions of Indian labor in New Spain, as reported by a notary.

• **haciendas** Large agrarian estates characteristic of colonial agriculture in Latin America.

without reference to outside authority. Spanish landowners used debt peonage as a way to control labor. They would make loans to "their" Indians that were to be repaid in labor, but the wages were never enough to repay the debt. In fact, the sons of the original borrowers often inherited these debts, and many families became permanently bound to a single estate. Since Amerindians were legally prevented from leaving the hacienda to escape their debts, they had difficulty seeking higher wages or better working conditions, and their families often remained desperately poor and ill educated across the generations. Debt peonage, like much of the hacienda system, would long persist in Latin America.

Spain's main economic goal was to extract minerals and other raw materials from America. Although it imported such goods as dyes, cotton, and hides from livestock for the manufacture of leather, no product came close in value to the silver bullion sent in two annual armadas to Spain. Taking much from its American empire and investing little, Spain's economy did not lay the foundations for long-term growth and stability; while other Europeans were developing new military and commercial technologies and organizations (see Chapter 17), the Spanish crown and nobility were becoming overly reliant on mineral wealth. As a result, the Dutch, English, and French effectively challenged Spain in the seventeenth and eighteenth centuries.

By 1750 the basic patterns of political and economic life in the Spanish-speaking Americas had been established. The process of subjugating and incorporating indigenous societies into the Spanish Empire was well advanced. Large-scale haciendas and mining operations were the foundation of commercial economies. Officials sent from Spain dominated the upper ranks of both church and state, while locally born criollos became colonial and municipal officials, hacienda landowners, and merchants.

Colonial Society: Gender and Race on the Margins of Empire

Between the small Spanish elite at the top of the social hierarchy and the Amerindians who continued to speak indigenous languages and practice ancient cultural traditions, there emerged a complex mix of peoples and cultures in this society. European immigration, the forced migration of African slaves, and the continued loss of American populations because of disease and economic deprivation were the ingredients of this mix.

The Spanish elite imported their cultural models into the new context of the Americas and were concerned with enforcing strict hierarchies of caste, gender, and religious or ethnic identity. Men were guided by a code of family honor, responsible for the virginity of their daughters and the fidelity of their wives. At the same time, they did not hold themselves to the same standards, often boasting of their own multiple sexual conquests.

A fixation among the Spanish elite with "purity of blood" went back to the Reconquista (see Chapter 15), when reserving public office for men of pure Spanish descent was a means of keeping converted Jews and Muslims out of positions of power. This Iberian tradition was transferred to the Americas: the king's subjects of non-Spanish or non-Catholic origin were expected to defer to their superiors.

It was easy for the Spanish elite to maintain such hierarchies in the courts, schools, and urban spaces of Mexico City, Lima, and other bastions of Spanish power. Outside the cities, however, the social environment was much more fluid and Spanish men far outnumbered Spanish women, making "purity of blood" a

CL **Primary Source: The Problem of the Indian and the Problem of the Land**
Read a Marxist's analysis of the oppression of Peru's Indians and his prescription for political change.

difficult ideal to maintain. By the seventeenth century a distinct *mestizo* (mes-TEE-zoh), or mixed Spanish/Amerindian, category had emerged that led to the biological and cultural blending that would come to characterize Mexican society.

Also difficult to maintain under frontier conditions was the power of the Catholic bishops to impose traditional Iberian religious ideas. In Spain itself, the inquisition monitored the beliefs and behavior of the population to keep them in line with strict Catholic orthodoxy. Families of *conversos* and *moriscos* (mohr-EES-koz), who had been forcibly converted from Judaism and Islam, were subjected to special scrutiny. Sometimes, however, such groups were able to retain elements of their old faith on the colonial frontier. Even today some Mexican families discover Jewish elements in their family traditions.

By the seventeenth century, converted Amerindians were the largest group of Catholics deviating from the church's theology and ritual. In the sixteenth century missionaries had baptized many indigenous people in Mexico and Peru, while in China Matteo Ricci had adapted Christianity to the Confucian traditions of his intended converts (see Chapter 16). In Spanish America, it was not the missionaries but the Amerindians themselves who blended their cosmologies and rituals into Catholicism. While some church leaders campaigned against the continuation of "idol worship" among baptized Amerindians, more often Spanish missionaries tolerated such practices. Amerindian populations had stabilized after the great losses of the sixteenth century, and where they formed a majority, as in the Andes, missionaries had little choice but to work through Amerindian cultures.

This process of **syncretism,** the blending of existing and imported religious ideas, is a theme in world history also seen, for example, when Islam spread to Africa and Buddhism to China. A thousand years before the conquest of the Americas, European converts to Christianity had adapted some of their pagan ideas to the new faith. For both ancient Europeans and colonized Amerindians, former gods reappeared as Christian saints. And while the Christian God was male, worship of Mary as the Virgin Mother allowed a spiritual space in the new religion for Aztecs who previously worshiped the fertility goddess Tonantzin.

In Mexico, the cult of the **Virgin of Guadalupe** epitomized the process of religious syncretism. In 1531 a peasant named Juan Diego reported to a Spanish bishop that the Virgin Mary had appeared to him. The bishop was initially doubtful, but the cult of the Virgin of Guadalupe proved remarkably popular. Though apparitions of the Virgin Mary were relatively common in Spain, the Virgin of Guadalupe had a special appeal in Mesoamerica. Represented as dark in complexion, like most of her devotees, she remains a symbol of Mexican identity.

In Catalina de Erauso's story, however, the Catholic Church plays a much more practical role. Once after she had stabbed a man in a fight she sought refuge in a church, where the civil authorities could not pursue her without the bishop's permission. In tough spots such as these she also relied on fellow members of the Basque-speaking minority for protection. Facing discrimination in Iberia, many Basques joined the Spanish army in the Americas. Erauso was exceptionally proud of her Basque heritage, but when dealing with Italians or Portuguese she was always quick to identify herself with Spain and assert Spanish superiority. Erauso's multiple identities are another example of the fluidity of frontier life.

Erauso's autobiography also gives us fascinating insights into race and gender relations in Spanish America. Once in Peru she deserted the army and wandered into the mountains, where, she tells us, she nearly died from exposure but was rescued by two men who took her to their mistress's ranch:

syncretism The fusion of cultural elements from more than one tradition. In colonial Latin America religious syncretism was common, with both Amerindians and Africans blending their existing beliefs and rituals with Catholicism.

Virgin of Guadalupe An apparition of the Virgin Mary said to have appeared to a Mexican farmer in 1531. She exerted a powerful attraction to Mesoamerica's surviving Amerindians and became an icon of Mexican identity.

The lady was a half-breed, the daughter of a Spaniard and an Indian woman, a widow and a good woman. . . . The next morning she fed me well, and seeing that I was so entirely destitute she gave me a decent cloth suit. . . . The lady was well-off, with a good deal of livestock and cattle, and it seems that, since Spaniards were scarce in those parts, she began to fancy me as a husband for her daughter . . . a girl as black and ugly as the devil himself, quite the opposite of my taste, which has always run to pretty faces.

Erauso went along with this plan, not intending to marry the girl but merely to receive the widow's gifts. She then writes, "In the two months I was putting off the Indian woman, I struck up a friendship with the Bishop's secretary," who introduced Erauso to his niece with the indication that they might get married. Again, Erauso accepted gifts from this potential in-law, but then "saddled up and vanished."

We cannot know how much of this story is true and how much was embellished to appeal to Erauso's audience. But, apart from the twist of a woman pretending to woo other young women in the guise of a man, this passage indicates that Iberian men (as Erauso presented herself to be) were highly desirable marriage partners for families wishing to sustain or improve their social status. Marriage to a Spaniard would "improve" the family bloodline. On the frontier, Spanish men were in such short supply that Erauso was able, at least by her own account, to contract multiple engagements with ease. Of course, Spanish women were even less available as marriage partners. Most Spanish men could not afford to "import" wives from Iberia, so they made the best unions they could, usually fathering mixed-race children.

Erauso's narrative also shows the complex racial mixture in the Spanish Empire. Erauso describes the widow as a "half-breed" who is "good" and "well-off." The daughter, on the other hand, is described as "black" and "ugly," though that was not enough to stop Erauso from wooing the young woman. Here we see the two fundamental racial realities of the Spanish Americas. On the one hand, racial mixing was taken for granted as a normal part of life. On the other hand, whiteness was always linked with higher status, wealth, and beauty. So even in the many places where **mestizos** (of mixed Spanish/Amerindian descent) or mulattos (of mixed Spanish/African descent) formed the majority of the population, the ideal was Spanish "pure blood." Perhaps the widow thought marriage to a white soldier like Erauso could improve the color and status of her "ugly" daughter's children. (See the feature "Visual Evidence: Representing the Casta System.")

Gender relations and the social roles of women varied by social class. As in many societies, including the North African ones that had so strongly influenced Spanish culture, elite Spanish men demonstrated their wealth and status by keeping women out of the public realm. Elite parents, preoccupied with protecting the family honor, arranged unions for adolescent daughters who would, upon marriage, lead restricted lives. Those for whom no acceptable marriage could be found were sent to convents. Poorer families in which women played vital economic roles as farmers and artisans could not imitate such behavior.

At the same time, elite women sometimes had access to education, and those in convents also might enjoy some power and authority within their all-female community. **Sor Juana Inés de la Cruz** (1648–1695) was the most famous of such women. Born into a modest family, she was a child prodigy who learned to read Latin before the age of 10. She became a lady-in-waiting for the viceroy's wife in Mexico City and a popular figure at court. But after her application to the

mestizo Offspring of an Amerindian and Spanish union. Cultural and biological blending became characteristic of Mexican society, marked by a complex racial hierarchy, the *casta* system, in which people were carefully categorized into dozens of categories of racial descent.

Sor Juana Inés de la Cruz One of the great literary figures of colonial New Spain. Wrote poetry, prose, and philosophy despite having been denied a university education. Best known for her defense of the intellectual equality of men and women.

REPRESENTING THE CASTA SYSTEM

In New Spain, a complex racial hierarchy, known as the *casta* system involved the use of dozens of terms to describe various racial mixtures and skin tones. Brothers and sisters of mixed ancestry might themselves vary in skin tones, facial structure, hair quality, eye color, and other markers of descent. Still, the way an individual was classified and observed would affect his or her chances in life: marriage and inheritance, education, access to the royal bureaucracy, or leadership roles in the church. Judgments of character, honor, and morality were linked to one's rank on the ladder of the castas. This meant that individuals of mixed background would usually do their best to emphasize their Spanish heritage in appearance, culture, and language.

In eighteenth-century Mexico *casta* paintings were a well-developed tradition. These paintings represented racial and ethnic mixture by portraying a father and mother of different backgrounds and at least one of their children. These two works by Miguel Carbrera are part of a larger series of casta portraits of remarkable sensitivity and beauty.

De Español y d'India, Mestisa .

- These people seem to be well-to-do cloth merchants. This cloth looks like imported silk, perhaps from China. It was, however, locally woven: note the Amerindian motifs.

- The pineapple was unknown to Europeans before Columbus and was associated with the exoticism of the Americas.

(Private Collection. Photographer: Camilo Garza/Fotocam, Monterrey, Mexico)

In the first example Carbrera shows a Spanish man, an Indian woman, and their mestiza daughter. The second illustrates a mestizo husband, his Indian wife, and their sons, labeled coyotes. Cabrera's other portraits are labeled as follows:

- From a Spaniard and a *Mestiza*, *Castiza*
- From a Black and an Indian, *China Cambuja*
- From a *China Cambujo* and a Indian, *Loba*
- From a *Lobo* and an Indian, *Albarazado*
- From an *Albrazado* and a *Mestiza*, *Barcino*
- From a Spaniard and a Negro, *Mulata*
- From a Spaniard and a *Mulata*, *Morisca*

This complex list is only a small sample of the names and combinations of racial and ethnic mixture found in Mexican casta paintings.

De MeſtizoydIndia;Coyote

(Collection of Elisabeth Waddo-Dentzel, Multicultural Music and Art Foundation of Northridge, Calif.)

Note how the figures touch and/or look at each other. What impression do we get of the relationship between husbands and wives and between parents and children?

The child's cap stands out against the group's otherwise drab apparel. How might we determine its significance?

The couple seem poor, but the burro indicates that the man has work and the vegetables indicate that they have enough to eat.

QUESTION FOR ANALYSIS

What do these paintings tell us about the relationship between social status, clothing, and physical appearance in eighteenth-century New Spain?

University of Mexico was denied, she entered the convent. In contrast to Catalina de Erauso, who saw convent life as a prison, Sor Juana recognized that only by restricting herself to an all-women's community would she be able to develop her remarkable literary and intellectual skills.

Sor Juana's writings cover many topics, and her poetry is still taught to Mexican children. She is best known for her passionate defense of the spiritual and intellectual equality of women with men: "There is no obstacle to love / in gender or in absence, / for souls, as you are well aware, / transcend both sex and distance."[2] Conservatives wrote strong denunciations of her work. After years of correspondence and debate with church leaders, she saw the futility of trying to change their minds and stopped publishing altogether. In 1694 church officials forced her to sell her library of four thousand books, and the next year she died in an outbreak of plague. One of the finest minds in the Spanish-speaking world was silenced.

Sor Juana's story indicates the degree to which New Spain recreated the Spanish social order. But Erauso's narrative reminds us that the "New World" could also mean new possibilities. Would she have been able to carry on her deception for so long had she remained in Spain? In frontier conditions the watchfulness of church and state was not as strong as it was in Europe or in Mexico City, giving Erauso a chance to carve out a life appropriate for her personality and ambition.

⬤ Brazil, the Dutch, New France, and England's Mainland Colonies

Throughout the sixteenth century and into the seventeenth century, Spain remained the dominant imperial force in the Americas. But it was not the only European kingdom using American resources to advance its place in the world. Portugal, though it placed a greater emphasis on its Asian empire, controlled Brazil, with its vast economic potential. Likewise the Dutch, while focusing on Asia, during the height of their world power in the seventeenth century harassed the Spanish and Portuguese in the Western Hemisphere. The French and English were latecomers to the American colonial game, starting their settlements in North America only after the Spanish had created their great empire to the south. As in the Spanish colonies, diverse demographic and cultural patterns arose from the interactions of Europeans and Africans with indigenous Amerindian populations; the further one moved from European-dominated centers to the frontier, the more fluid were the interactions among European, African, and Amerindian peoples.

The Portuguese and Brazil

In the sixteenth century Portugal's overseas efforts focused on the Indian Ocean (see Chapter 16). Brazil was an afterthought. Having been discovered accidentally and secured through treaty with Spain, Brazil turned out to have no large cities or empires to conquer and no easily accessible treasuries of gold or silver to pillage. Portuguese settlement was initially limited to small coastal enclaves, and apart from a lucrative trade in precious types of wood, the Portuguese initially had little economic interest in Brazil.

This situation changed dramatically in the later sixteenth century with the expansion of sugar plantations in northeastern Brazil. By the end of the seventeenth century there were about 150,000 African slaves in Brazil, about half of the colony's total population. Meanwhile Portuguese adventurers were moving into the interior looking for slaves, gold, and exotic goods such as brightly colored feathers from the Amazon. In 1695, major gold deposits were discovered in the southern interior in a region that thereby gained its name: Minas Gerais, "General Mines." European prospectors brought African slaves to exploit the mineral discoveries, displacing Amerindian peoples in the process. By the early eighteenth century profits from sugar and gold had turned Brazil into Portugal's most important overseas colony, and for the next three hundred years, until today, the settlement of the interior of Brazil by a predominantly Euro-African population continued.

In Brazil, missionaries were powerful players. The Jesuits (see Chapter 16) used their large cattle ranches and sugar mills to raise funds for church construction and missionary endeavors among the Amerindians of the interior. While many missionaries tried to stop the worst abuses of colonization and often defended Indian interests, they unwittingly spread epidemic diseases and undercut indigenous life by helping extend imperial borders.

Both Catholicism and African religions were practiced in colonial Brazil. As soon as the sugar plantation economy was established in the northeast, slaves began to run away into the interior. Some of the runaways, called maroons, assimilated into Amerindian groups. Others formed their own runaway communities known as *quilombos*. Since the members of a quilombos had usually been born and raised in different African societies, their political and religious practices were usually mixtures of various African traditions and gods. The largest and most powerful of the quilombos was **Palmares** (pal-MAHR-es), founded in the early seventeenth century.

Since slavery had erased the original affiliations and identifications of the people at Palmares, they adapted the Central African institution of *kilombo,* a merit-based league of warriors that cut across family ties. Religious life seems to have been based on the traditions of the Kongo kingdom (see Chapter 16), mixed with other African traditions and Catholicism. With tens of thousands of residents ruled by their elected *Ganga Zumba* (Great Lord), Palmares defended itself against decades of Portuguese military assaults until it was finally defeated in 1694. However, the adaptation of African religion and culture to the American environment continued in Brazil, and other parts of the Americas, long after the fall of Palmares (see Chapter 19).

By 1750, Brazil had an exceptionally diverse culture. The Brazilian elite remained entirely white, dominating laborers who were, in this case, primarily African rather than Amerindian. As in Spanish America, a large mixed-race group emerged along with a similarly complex hierarchy that paralleled the Spanish castas, though with more Africans than Amerindians. Brazilian Catholicism, which became infused with African deities and beliefs, underwent a process of religious syncretism parallel to the one taking place in New Spain.

In Brazil, "black" and "African" were associated with slavery, the lowest condition of all. But like the Spanish casta system, the social and racial hierarchy in Brazil was flexible enough so that individuals or families might try to improve their standing. Dress, speech, education, marital status, and, above all, economic success were means by which colonial Brazilians of mixed descent might try to

● **Palmares** The largest and most powerful maroon community (1630–1694) established by escaped slaves in the colonial Americas. Using military and diplomatic means, their leaders retained autonomy from Portuguese Brazil for over half a century.

negotiate higher status. Still, the basic polarities remained clear: white at the top, black at the bottom.

The Dutch in the Americas Like the Portuguese, the Dutch were initially focused on Indian Ocean trade (see Chapter 16). However, from 1630 to 1654 the Protestant Dutch seized control of the northeastern coast of Brazil as part of their larger global offensive against the Catholic empires of Spain and Portugal.

In 1619 the Protestant Dutch, after an extremely violent conflict, had won their independence from Catholic Spain, which at that time also ruled over Portugal, and therefore Brazil. Following the model of the successful Dutch East India Company, a group of merchants formed the Dutch West India Company in 1621 to penetrate markets and challenge Spanish supremacy in the Americas. Their main advantage was an aggressive form of capitalism in which they constantly reinvested their profits in faster ships and larger financial ventures. In Brazil the most important of these were the sugar plantations, to which the Dutch brought more capital investment and a larger supply of slaves.

Ousted by the Portuguese in 1654, some of the Dutch planters went to the Caribbean, where they transferred their business techniques and more advanced sugar-processing technology. Spanish-ruled islands like Cuba and Puerto Rico, as well as English ones like Jamaica and Barbados, were transformed by the seventeenth-century explosion of sugar production in the Caribbean, with dramatic consequences for Africa and the world economy (see Chapter 19).

Farther north, in 1624 the Dutch West India Company founded the colony of New Netherland. They traded up the Hudson River Valley, allying with the powerful Iroquois Confederacy to tap into the lucrative fur trade of the northern interior. In addition, a small number of Dutch immigrants came as settlers to farm these rich and well-watered lands. But these American settlements remained marginal to overall Dutch commercial goals, which were still focused on Southeast Asia. In 1664, with the English pressing in on all sides, the Dutch surrendered New Netherland to them. Their largest settlement, New Amsterdam, was then renamed New York. Henceforth, the French and English would compete for dominance in North America.

New France, 1608–1754 Like other European powers since before the days of Columbus, the French were focused on finding a direct maritime route to Asia. In the second half of the sixteenth century French mariners sailed up the St. Lawrence River looking for a "northwest passage" to Chinese markets. What they found instead was the world's largest concentration of fresh water lakes and a land teeming with wildlife. In 1608, Samuel de Champlain founded the colony of New France with its capital at Québec (kwa-BEC).

Even prior to the establishment of Québec, French fur traders had made their way up the St. Lawrence and into the Great Lakes. Like the Russians, who were expanding fur markets into Siberia at the same time, these French fur traders went beyond the frontiers of formal colonial control, driven by lucrative European, Ottoman, and Safavid markets. They developed cooperative relations with their indigenous trading partners, who did the actual work of trapping beaver and bringing the pelts to accessible trade depots. The efficiency of the Amerindian hunters

French Fur Trader French traders ventured far beyond the borders of European colonial society in their quest for valuable furs such as beaver pelts. They frequently adopted the technologies, languages, and customs of Amerindian peoples, and they sometimes married into Amerindian societies. At the same time, on the other side of the world, the global fur market was also driving Russian traders deep into the forests of Siberia. (Museum of Fine Arts, Boston/Laurie Platt Winfrey/The Art Archive)

increased as they became more proficient in using iron-tipped spears and axes imported from Europe, driving the fur frontier ever deeper into the interior.

Living far from other Europeans, French fur traders had to adjust to the cultural norms of the First Nations peoples (as they are called in Canada). For example, tobacco smoking was an important ritual that cemented trade and diplomatic alliances. Sometimes French traders became fully assimilated into First Nations communities and bore children who were Amerindian in language and culture. More often French trappers and traders visited only seasonally; their mixed-race children, known in French as **métis** (may-TEE), were usually fluent in both French and indigenous languages such as Cree and served as commercial and cultural intermediaries between First Nations and European societies.

The fur trade had significant environmental and political effects. Once their traditional hunting grounds were exhausted, Amerindians had to venture farther afield to lay their traps. The competition for beaver pelts put them increasingly in conflict with other indigenous peoples, while the availability of guns, one of the main commodities for which furs were traded, made such warfare more lethal. New technologies and the desire for new commodities (iron tools and alcohol, as well as firearms) affected indigenous life well beyond the frontiers of European colonial control. For example, on the Great Plains the introduction of firearms from New France and of horses from New Spain led to both more efficient buffalo hunting and more effective mobile warfare among groups like the Sioux.

In the St. Lawrence region the French were strongly allied with the indigenous **Huron** people, who were receptive to the Jesuit missionaries who came up the river. French traders established residence in Huron country and negotiated with local chiefs to supply them with furs. Division of labor by gender facilitated the process. Since Huron men worked in agriculture only when clearing fields in early

métis In colonial New France, the off-spring of a European and Amerindian union.

Huron A matriarchal, Iroquoian-speaking Amerindian group in the St. Lawrence region that was devastated by the smallpox brought by French fur traders and missionaries in the mid-seventeenth century.

spring, they were available for hunting and trading parties during the rest of the year, while the women stayed behind to tend the fields. The political power and economic resources that came from the fur trade therefore went mainly to men, and the traditional power of Huron women was undercut: male chiefs became more powerful at the expense of the matriarchs chosen by their clans to represent them on the Huron confederacy council.

While some Huron chiefs and hunters became powerful as a result of fur trading, the overall effects of contact with the French were disastrous. By 1641, half of the Huron population had been killed by disease. Many Huron sought baptism, praying that the priests' holy water would save them from the smallpox that the missionaries themselves had unknowingly introduced.

• **Québec** (est. 1608) Founded by Samuel de Champlain in 1608 as the capital of New France (in modern Canada), Québec became a hub for the French fur trade and the center from which French settlement in the Americas first began to expand.

Meanwhile, French settlers were attracted to the farmlands surrounding the city of **Québec,** where some fifty thousand French men and women lived by 1750. These farmers, and the small urban population they supported with food and supplies, represented the beginnings of quite a different European presence in what would later become Canada. While the fur traders and missionaries sought to integrate themselves into indigenous societies in their search for pelts to sell or souls to save, the settlers were driven by the search for cheap land and lumber. In later years, as their numbers swelled and the frontier advanced, settlers would increasingly displace First Nations peoples (see Chapter 25).

In the first half of the eighteenth century, however, the most valuable French possessions in the Americas were not vast North American territories but relatively small Caribbean islands. French plantations in the West Indies were generating huge profits using African slave labor to produce sugar for European markets. The same was true for England.

Mainland English Colonies in North America

For the English, as for the French, the Caribbean was the economic focal point of their American venture, especially after they began their own sugar plantations there in the later seventeenth century (see Chapter 19). On the mainland the English, again like the French, were relative newcomers to American settlement in the first half of the seventeenth century, with initial settlements in what Europeans considered less desirable northern areas such as Virginia and Massachusetts.

• **Virginia** (est. 1607) English colony in North America with an export economy based on tobacco production. The use of European indentured servants gave way to dependence on slave labor.

Though the first English settlement of **Virginia,** in 1607, was nearly wiped out, by the 1630s the colony was thriving. The soil was rich, and the Virginia colonists discovered a lucrative Atlantic market for tobacco. Long used by Amerindian peoples for social and ritual purposes, tobacco laid the foundation for Virginia's prosperity and generated a strong demand for labor. The option of using Amerindian labor was never seriously pursued, partly because in woodland societies men were not usually engaged in agriculture and were therefore resistant to such work. Another reason was that by the second decade of the seventeenth century diseases such as smallpox had already begun to decimate local populations.

English policy was another factor in excluding Amerindians from participation, even as laborers, in the evolving economy of Virginia. Unlike the French, who cooperated with Amerindian societies, the English, acting as they had in Ireland, drove indigenous peoples beyond the frontier and replaced them with "civilized" English farmers. Sir Walter Raleigh, a major investor in Virginia settlement, had taken this approach when sent to put down a late-sixteenth-century Irish rebellion. In Virginia, the "savages" to be brought under control were Amerindian rather than Irish, but Raleigh pursued the same strategy in both places.

But plantations required more work than free settlers could provide. One solution was indentured labor. In this system, employers paid for the transportation costs of poor English and Irish peasants in return for four to seven years of work, after which time they received either a return passage or a small plot of land. Cheap as this labor was, tobacco planters, who had to compete in Atlantic markets by producing a good-quality crop at a low price, were driven to seek a labor force that was more easily controlled. In 1619 the first shipment of slaves arrived, and by the late seventeenth century traders were marketing African slaves in Virginia markets in increasing numbers.

Virginia's population developed, therefore, through exclusion of Amerindian peoples, free immigration of English settlers, and forced immigration of African slaves. Colonial authorities were worried about the social contacts and sexual unions between white settlers and African slaves; as early as 1630 one Hugh Davis was whipped "for abusing himself to the dishonor of God and the shame of Christians, by defiling his body in lying with a Negro."[3] In the later seventeenth century, Virginia developed stringent laws that prohibited interracial unions. These liaisons nevertheless continued, such as between African men and female indentured servants from Ireland. The offspring of such unions were discriminated against both legally and socially. Though terms such as *mulatto* were commonly used for a person of mixed race, by the eighteenth century the English generally viewed anyone with any sign of African parentage as "black," a status closely associated with that of "slave."

Even as the importance of slave bondage increased, Virginia's institutions evolved toward a system in which free, propertied white men had a voice in their own governance. Virginia had become a royal colony in 1624, with a governor-general appointed by the king. By the 1660s Virginia's assembly, the House of Burgesses, was increasingly acting as an independent deliberative body. Political unrest in England, most notably the Civil War that raged from 1642 to 1649, made it more difficult to impose centralized administration from above. By the eighteenth century Virginia's ruling class of planters were accustomed to running their own affairs and would resist renewed attempts by the English monarchy to impose central control (see Chapter 22).

Farther south, in the colony of **Carolina,** English settlers established a demographic and economic pattern more like that of the West Indies, especially on the coast and the coastal islands. Carolina's plantations were generally much larger than Virginia's. Rice and indigo (used to produce a rich blue dye) were the main crops. Because Africans greatly outnumbered the few English settlers, they were able to retain much of their culture. West African words, language patterns, stories, and crafts persisted among African Americans along Carolina's coast and on offshore islands into the twentieth century.

Slavery was also present though less prominent in the middle colonies, where New York and Philadelphia emerged as vibrant political and economic centers. The twenty thousand German settlers who had arrived in Pennsylvania by 1700 added an ethnic variable, but the European immigrant population was still primarily English and Scottish.

The settlement of **New England** began with the arrival in the 1620s and 1630s of Calvinist dissenters from the established Church of England (see Chapter 17). Soon more English settlers were attracted for economic reasons: land was relatively cheap, and wages were relatively high. Entire families migrated to New England intending to recreate the best features of the rural life they knew in England and combine them with American economic opportunity.

Carolina (est. 1663) English colony that modeled West Indian social and economic patterns, with large plantations growing rice and indigo with slave labor. Unlike in Virginia, Africans were a majority of the seventeenth-century population.

New England Beginning with the arrival of English Calvinists in 1620s, colonial New England was characterized by homogeneous, self-sufficient farming communities.

Thanksgiving and the Mashpee Wampanoag

Though not many could identify a group of Native Americans in Massachusetts called the Mashpee Wampanoag, many people around the world are familiar with the role their ancestors played in colonial American history as guests at the first Thanksgiving feast. In 1621 they taught a group of English immigrants how to survive and joined them for an autumn feast of corn and turkey.

The Mashpee received little benefit from their hospitality. Smallpox killed many, and relations with the English soured as competition over land increased. In 1675 the Mashpee leader Metacom, "King Phillip" to the English, launched a war to defend his people and their way of life. But the Mashpee were not completely united behind Metacom; those who had converted to Christianity mostly stayed neutral in the conflict. Defeat in "King Phillip's War" was a disaster for the Mashpee. Hundreds of men were sold into slavery, and Mashpee women and children were forced to become servants to English colonists. Over time their ancestral lands on and around Cape Cod were purchased by outsiders, lost, it seemed, forever.

Finally, however, on March 31, 2007, the Mashpee Wampanoag had cause for celebration. After decades of petitions, the United States Bureau of Indian Affairs officially declared that "the Mashpee exists as an Indian tribe." The tribal chairman of the Mashpee Wampanoag declared that "this is truly a day of Thanksgiving."*

Federal recognition comes with a number of benefits, among them the possibility of building a casino for the financial benefit of tribal members, though as of early 2008 the federal Department of the Interior had yet to approve that proposal. Only with the resources that come from tourism and gaming, says Chief Vernon "Silent Drum" Lopez, can the two thousand Mashpee Wampanoag who remain in Massachusetts have a chance to preserve what is left of their heritage and to thrive in contemporary Massachusetts.

*Sean Gonsalves, "Mashpee Wampanoag Win Tribal Status," *Cape Cod Times*, February 15, 2007, http://www.capecodonline.com/cgi-bin/print/printstory.cgi.

These new farming communities were self-sufficient both economically and demographically. Whereas elsewhere European men outnumbered European immigrant women, in New England men and women were equally balanced, making cultural and racial mixture much less common. Since families did their own farmwork, there was little need to import African labor. Regarding the indigenous peoples as competitors for land and water resources, the settlers drove those Amerindians who were not destroyed by disease beyond the colonial boundaries. New England developed as an exceptionally homogeneous place. (See the feature "World History in Today's World: Thanksgiving and the Mashpee Wampanoag.")

The city of Boston was the commercial center of New England, its merchants oriented not to the farming settlements of the interior but to the maritime trade of the Atlantic. The cod fisheries of the North Atlantic provided the original foundation of Boston's wealth. Dried and salted cod from the seemingly limitless bounty of the ocean were an important source of protein and improved health throughout the Atlantic region and beyond. The highest-quality fish was consumed locally or exported to Europe. Lower-quality fish was sent to the Caribbean as cheap food for plantation slaves.

The colonial population of New England was troublesome for English authorities almost from the start. Because most of the early settlers were dissenting Protestants, the Church of England did not have the same authority as the church in the

Spanish colonies. And, as in Virginia, the Civil War in England meant that there was little oversight of colonial affairs in the crucial middle decades of the seventeenth century. When British monarchs in the eighteenth century tried to impose a more centralized administrative system, they found that New Englanders had become accustomed to having a voice in public affairs and would not give it up willingly (see Chapter 22).

In the seventeenth and early eighteenth centuries, Britain's mainland colonies were of limited economic and strategic importance. The silver of New Spain and the sugar of the West Indies generated profits on a much greater scale than Carolina's rice, Virginia's tobacco, or New England's grain. Faced with a hostile alliance of French and Indian societies to the north and west, the potential for expansion beyond the Atlantic seaboard seemed uncertain. These tensions were not confined to North America. By 1750, England and France were poised to battle for control of such diverse colonial territories as the Ohio River Valley, plantation colonies in the Caribbean, and trade settlements in South Asia (see Chapters 19 and 20). By that time the significance of Britain's mainland American colonies had grown substantially.

Connections and Comparisons Across the Colonial Americas

By 1750, the European impact on the Americas was profound yet full of variety. While different geographic environments led to diverse economic and demographic outcomes, the various political, religious, and cultural traditions of the European colonial powers also left their mark on the evolving colonial societies.

One common feature was the continuing effects of the Columbian exchange (see Chapter 15). The spread of horses and cattle on the wide-open South American plains (and, somewhat later, on the North American plains) allowed European colonists to convert grass into protein in a way never before possible and also promoted an export industry in hides and skins. In other regions, such as Virginia, hogs thrived. European food crops like wheat and barley combined with American crops like maize, potatoes, squash, and tomatoes to increase agricultural productivity.

Few Amerindians shared in this bounty. Disease and death accompanied the expansion of European colonial frontiers, and by the middle of the eighteenth century Amerindian peoples were unaffected only in remote areas, such as the Arctic north or the furthest Amazonian interior. More commonly, high mortality among Amerindians transformed the landscape. In Mexico, former Amerindian farmlands were converted into grazing grounds for European livestock; in the Chesapeake, tobacco plantations replaced the more varied Amerindian agricultural and hunting landscapes.

All of the European powers applied mercantilist economic theories (see Chapter 17) to their colonial enterprises, harnessing American profits to augment the wealth and power of their monarchs. The Spanish and Portuguese in particular benefited from the supplies of gold and silver flowing from American mines, lubricating their own trade with the dynamic economies of Asia. Actual government control of commerce was never as great in practice as it was in theory, however. In the seventeenth century smuggling and piracy were common, and Spanish, Portuguese, French, and English colonists were frequently able to evade laws that required them to trade only with their mother countries. In the middle and late eighteenth century, when European states attempted to apply mercantilist regulations in the Americas more strictly, tensions with colonial settlers in both Spanish and British colonies resulted (see Chapter 22).

Within the colonies quite different economic regimes took hold. Some enterprises were merely extractive: mines in Spanish America, furs in New France. Here indigenous people formed the workforce (often by compulsion in New Spain, usually voluntarily in Canada). Sustaining the great silver mines such as Potosí in the Andes and feeding the expanding urban centers created opportunities in agriculture and meat production for hacienda owners, exceptionally powerful men who commanded the labor and obedience of their dependents, usually Indians or mixed-race mestizos.

Lacking minerals, the economies of the English colonies all relied on agriculture (and, in New England, fishing), though their agricultural regimes and settlement patterns differed. In temperate New England, independent farmers worked small but productive plots, largely with family labor, and provided most of their own sustenance. In contrast, large plantations were the characteristic form of landholding in colonial Carolina. In the coastal lowlands and offshore islands, Carolina resembled the West Indian pattern of settlement, with a majority of African slaves focusing their labor on high-value crops for export. In Virginia a mixed pattern emerged. Slave-worked plantations were central to the Virginian economy, but the scale of production was much smaller than in Carolina. Often European owners worked relatively small Virginia farms using a few slaves to supplement family labor.

Religious traditions were important in the development of all the colonial American cultures. Not surprisingly, the religious competition of the Reformation period (see Chapter 17) was imported to the Americas. The Catholic kings of France, Portugal, and Spain, seeing themselves as defenders of a single universal church, collaborated with church officials in the administration of their territories. The politics of the Reformation period magnified territorial and commercial competition between the Catholic Spanish and Protestant English, as well as between Catholic Portugal and the Protestant Dutch. These politics also affected French settlement. After 1627 the French monarchy, doubtful of Huguenot loyalty, banned Protestant emigration to New France.

In some English colonies, specific Protestant groups were dominant. The Church of England was the established church of Virginia and Carolina, while the Congregationalist Church was dominant in Massachusetts and Connecticut. Rhode Island and Pennsylvania were the only colonies that guaranteed freedom of religious worship, accommodating the few Catholic settlers who were not welcome in New England or Virginia.

As part of the religious divide of the early modern period, the English developed a strongly negative view of the Spanish and their empire. Associating Spain with religious intolerance and violent treatment of native peoples, the "black legend" of Spanish barbarism and cruelty infused English literature and philosophy. In the twentieth century the Mexican poet Octavio Paz turned the "black legend" on its head, arguing that the English were exceptionally harsh in their exclusion of Amerindians from colonial life, while the Spanish church at least allowed them "to form a part of one social order and one religion." The chance to be an accepted part of

🔲 **Catholic and Protestant Churches in the Americas**   There is a sharp contrast between the interior of the Spanish colonial church of Santa Maria Tonantzintla (*left*) in Puebla, Mexico, and that of the Old Whaler's Church (*right*) in Martha's Vineyard, Massachusetts. The Spanish church embodies the Catholic preference for richly embellished church interiors associated with elaborate rituals, and incorporates indigenous Amerindian themes. The New England church reflects the asceticism and simplicity of the Calvinist tradition, and bears no trace of Amerindian influence. (left: © Robert Frerck/Odyssey Productions, Inc.; right: © David Lyons/Alamy)

colonial society, "even if it was at the bottom of the social pyramid," Paz wrote, "was cruelly denied to the Indians by the Protestants of New England."[4] (See the feature "Movement of Ideas: Prospero and Caliban.")

Paz underestimated the missionary impulse among Protestant settlers in North America, some of whom made a strong effort toward conversion. He was correct, however, in pointing out the difference between the casta hierarchy of the Spanish Empire and the very different racial and ethnic system that developed in British North America. The Spanish system, though based on hierarchy and inequality, was flexible, allowing for gradations of identification and classification between people of mixed European, African, and Amerindian backgrounds. The English system of racial classification was more sharply segregated. Though there was substantial

Prospero and Caliban

When Catalina de Erauso arrived in New Spain, William Shakespeare was the leading playwright in the English-speaking world. Shakespeare's imagination, like that of many Europeans in the early seventeenth century, was stimulated by tales of exotic adventure in what one of Shakespeare's characters referred to as "this brave new world." That line comes from *The Tempest* (1611), a drama that reflects European fascination with new discoveries in the Americas. Shakespeare used reports from Virginia settlers who had survived a shipwreck to weave a fantastic tale of magic, revenge, and the triumph of justice.

Stranded on an island is the great magician named Prospero and his daughter, Miranda. In the scene below, Prospero speaks with a misshapen monster named Caliban, the only native inhabitant of the island. From Prospero's perspective, Caliban deserves harsh treatment. In spite of the kindness shown by the magician, the monster attempted to rape Miranda. Things look very different from Caliban's viewpoint. The powers he inherited from his mother, Sycorax, cannot counter Prospero's magic, and he has no choice but to serve as the magician's slave while plotting his vengeance. Their unequal positions are even reflected in their names, which might be translated as "Prosperity" and "Cannibal." Though Shakespeare presents Prospero as having justice on his side, he also allows Caliban to voice his complaints as an abused native imprisoned by a colonial master.

The text is adapted from the following website: http://the-tech.mit.edu/Shakespeare/tempest/index.html. The glossary is original.

The Tempest, Act I, Scene 2

PROSPERO:
>Thou poisonous slave, got• by the devil himself
>Upon thy wicked dam•, come forth!

CALIBAN:
>As wicked dew as e'er my mother brush'd
>With raven's feather from unwholesome fen
>Drop on you! a south-west blow on ye
>And blister you all o'er!

PROSPERO:
>For this, be sure, to-night thou shalt have cramps,
>Side-stitches that shall pen thy breath up; urchins•
>Shall, for that vast of night that they may work,
>All exercise on thee•; thou shalt be pinch'd
>As thick as honeycomb, each pinch more stinging
>Than bees that made 'em.

CALIBAN:
>This island's mine, by Sycorax my mother,
>Which thou takest from me. When thou camest first,
>Thou strokedst me and madest much of me, wouldst give me
>Water with berries in't, and teach me how
>To name the bigger light, and how the less,
>That burn by day and night•: and then I loved thee
>And show'd thee all the qualities o' the isle,
>The fresh springs, brine-pits, barren place and fertile:
>Cursed be I that did so! All the charms
>Of Sycorax, toads, beetles, bats, light on you!
>For I am all the subjects that you have,
>Which first was mine own king: and here you sty• me
>In this hard rock, whiles you do keep from me
>The rest o' the island.

PROSPERO:
>Thou most lying slave,
>Whom stripes• may move, not kindness! I have used• thee,
>Filth as thou art, with human care, and lodged thee

* **got** begotten.　• **dam** mother.　• **urchins** goblins.
* **exercise on thee** torment you.
* **day and night** the sun and moon.
* **sty** imprison.　• **stripes** whippings.　• **used** treated.

In mine own cell, till thou didst seek to
    violate
The honour of my child.

CALIBAN:
O ho, O ho! would't had been done!
Thou didst prevent me; I had peopled else●
This isle with Calibans.

PROSPERO:
Abhorred slave,
Which any print of goodness wilt not take,
Being capable of all ill! I pitied thee,
Took pains to make thee speak, taught
    thee each hour
One thing or other: when thou didst not,
    savage,
Know thine own meaning, but wouldst
    gabble like
A thing most brutish, I endow'd thy
    purposes
With words that made them known. But
    thy vile race,
Though thou didst learn, had that in't
    which good natures
Could not abide to be with; therefore wast
    thou

Deservedly confined into this rock,
Who hadst deserved more than a prison.

CALIBAN:
You taught me language; and my profit on't
Is, I know how to curse. The red plague rid you
For learning me your language!

PROSPERO:
Hag-seed●, hence!
Fetch us in fuel; and be quick, thou'rt best,
To answer other business. Shrug'st thou,
    malice?
If thou neglect'st or dost unwillingly
What I command, I'll rack thee with old
    cramps,
Fill all thy bones with aches, make thee roar
That beasts shall tremble at thy din.

CALIBAN:
No, pray thee.
Aside
I must obey: his art is of such power,
It would control my dam's god, Setebos,
and make a vassal of him.

PROSPERO:
So, slave; hence!

● **else** otherwise.

● **Hag-seed** child of a witch.

QUESTIONS FOR ANALYSIS

▶ To what extent does Shakespeare encourage us to empathize with Caliban?

▶ Is Caliban's situation in any way analogous to that of conquered Amerindian peoples?

intermixing between the three main population groups in the early colonial period, English authorities made little accommodation for mixed-race identities.

Gender identities were strongly fixed in every colonial society. As in Europe at that time, even modes of dress were regulated by law: no one was allowed to dress above his or her station, and mixing of clothing by gender was not permitted. However, as we have seen, social realities could be more fluid on the frontier, as when French fur traders interacted with matrilineal First Nations peoples.

Catalina de Erauso was, of course, exceptional. Badly wounded in a fight, and thinking she had better confess her sins before she died, Erauso told a priest about her deception. He did not believe her, but the nuns sent to confirm her true gender identity confirmed the fact. After she recovered, Erauso went to Spain to seek a pension from the king for her service as a soldier, and to Rome to meet the pope. News of her strange story spread across Europe, and as Erauso journeyed by horseback across France on her way to Italy, people came out to the road to see the famous woman warrior in a man's uniform. During her papal audience at the Vatican, she was told to restrain herself from violent behavior, but then the pope gave her formal permission to dress as a man for the rest of her life.

While in Rome, Erauso narrated her story to an unknown scribe, ending with the following anecdote:

> And one day in Naples, as I was strolling about the wharves, I was struck by the tittering laughter of two ladies, who leaned against a wall making conversation with two young men. They looked at me, and I looked at them, and one said, "Señora Catalina, where are you going all by your lonesome?" "My dear harlots," I replied, "I have come to deliver one hundred strokes to your pretty little necks, and a hundred gashes with this blade to the fool who would defend your honor." The women fell dead silent, and they hurried off.

How did Erauso see herself? Did she resent having to act as a man in order to live her own life as she pleased? Or was her cross-dressing more than a masquerade? History provides no additional evidence.

It seems that Erauso preferred the life of the colonial frontier. According to legend, she returned to Mexico, disappeared into the mountains with a pack of burros, and was never heard from again. She was one of many European immigrants for whom the Americas represented new possibilities.

Chapter Review

The Spanish were the dominant power in the colonial Americas, controlling the largest territories and populations while extracting considerable wealth, especially in silver, from New World mines. The Portuguese colony of Brazil, with large sugar plantations and profitable gold mines, was also significant. By the eighteenth century the French and English were also profiting substantially from sugar production in the West Indies, while their frontiers of settlement in North America expanded at the expense of Amerindian peoples.

What were the principal forms of political and economic organization in the Americas in this period?

In the sixteenth and early seventeenth centuries the Spanish were the dominant colonial power in the Americas. The flow of gold and silver from American mines, supplemented by other commodities extracted from the American environment through the mobilization of Amerindian labor, financed the splendor of the royal court and provided the wherewithal for increased European trade with Asia. At first it was Spaniards sent from Iberia who dominated colonial society, but by the seventeenth century American-born criollos were becoming more prominent, for example, through their control of large haciendas.

In Portuguese Brazil large landholdings were also characteristic of colonial society. Main exports included sugar from coastal plantations and gold from mines in the south. Like all the European colonial powers, Portugal pursued mercantilist policies that emphasized extraction of colonial resources for the benefit of the court at Lisbon, with slaves providing much of the labor. The Dutch ruled Brazil (and New Netherland to the north) only briefly, but they had a significant impact on the sugar industry, improving methods of production and helping to transfer sugar production from Brazil to the Caribbean.

The economy of New France was driven by the highly lucrative fur trade. Since the French relied on Amerindian hunters and political leaders for their supply of pelts, diplomacy and alliances were central to their colonial policy, even as a colony of European settlement grew up around Québec.

The mainland colonies of England were diverse in political structure and economic orientation. Virginia and the Chesapeake specialized in the export of tobacco and imported slaves as a workforce. However, they also attracted many settlers. Further south in Carolina, plantations were larger and Africans were in the majority. The immigrant farmers of New England pursued a different strategy of agricultural self-sufficiency, though cod fisheries represented another means by which the bounty of the Americas was exported to Europe and beyond. The settlers of

KEY TERMS

Catalina de Erauso (510)

viceroyalties (513)

Potosí (515)

haciendas (516)

syncretism (518)

Virgin of Guadalupe (518)

mestizo (519)

Sor Juana Inés de la Cruz (519)

Palmares (523)

métis (525)

Huron (525)

Québec (526)

Virginia (526)

Carolina (527)

New England (527)

Virginia and New England developed a relatively strong expectation of being involved in government.

What were the key demographic and cultural outcomes of the interaction of European, African, and Amerindian peoples in various regions of the Americas?

Cultural developments in the Americas were related to demographic ones, especially the changing balance of population between European settlers, Amerindian survivors, and African slaves. In some regions Amerindian peoples remained a majority. In Mesoamerica and the higher Andes, for example, Amerindian populations stabilized after the huge losses of the sixteenth century. Indigenous languages and cultures remained strong, even while labor systems such as the mita in the Andes and the appearance of large Spanish-owned haciendas subordinated Amerindian peoples to European power.

In other, more remote parts of the Americas, Amerindian peoples who were far from the frontiers of European power retained not only their own languages and cultures but also political autonomy. The other extreme was found in areas such as New England, where European settlers almost completely displaced the original inhabitants. This pattern was exceptional, however; across much of the colonial Americas the more common pattern was demographic and cultural mixture. Both the mestizo population of New Spain and the métis of New France are examples of important mixed European/Amerindian groups in the colonial period. In Brazil, Africans were a larger part of the population, and European/African mixture became a defining feature of Brazilian life.

What connections and comparisons can we draw between the different European colonial ventures in the Americas?

Religion is one important area where comparisons can be drawn. In Iberia, the Catholic Reformation had led to a firm church policy of monitoring and enforcing religious orthodoxy. In the frontier conditions of the Americas, however, the failure to stamp out alternative beliefs and practices is shown by the infusion of Amerindian beliefs into Christianity in New Spain and New France, and of African ones in Brazil. While Protestants in North America also tried to convert Amerindians to Christianity, their congregational and theological traditions made it much more difficult for religious syncretism to take place. In religion as in social life more generally, English colonists were less tolerant of syncretism than Spanish colonists.

Whatever political, economic, or religious rules and regulations colonial governments put in place, the fact remained that, outside the major centers of European control, life on the American frontiers remained fluid as European, Amerindian, and African peoples created new societies with new cultural traditions. The story of Catalina de Erauso and of millions of other people in the colonial Americas could not otherwise have taken place.

For Further Reference

Benton, Lauren A. *Law and Colonial Cultures: Legal Regimes in World History, 1400–1900.* New York: Cambridge University Press, 2002.

Burkholder, Mark, and Lyman Johnson. *Colonial Latin America.* 6th ed. New York: Oxford University Press, 2007.

Eccles, William J. *The French in North America, 1500–1783.* Rev. ed. Lansing: Michigan State University Press, 1998.

Erauso, Catalina de. *Lieutenant Nun: Memoir of a Basque Transvestite in the New World.* Translated by Michele Stepto and Gabriel Stepto. Boston: Beacon Press, 1996.

Fernandez-Armesto, Felipe. *The Americas: The History of a Hemisphere.* London: George Weidenfeld and Nicholson, 2003.

Kamen, Henry. *Empire: How Spain Became a World Power, 1492–1763.* New York: HarperCollins, 2003.

Lavrin, Asunción. *Sexuality and Marriage in Colonial Latin America.* Lincoln: University of Nebraska, 1992.

Nash, Gary. *Red, White and Black: The Peoples of Early North America.* 5th ed. New York: Prentice Hall, 2005.

Paz, Octavio. *Sor Juana.* Translated by Margaret Sayers Peden. Cambridge: Harvard University Press, 1988.

Sweet, James H. *Recreating Africa: Culture, Kinship, and Religion in the African-Portuguese World, 1441–1770.* Durham: University of North Carolina Press, 2006.

Taylor, William. *Magistrates of the Sacred: Priests and Parishioners in Eighteenth Century Mexico.* Stanford, Calif.: Stanford University Press, 1996.

 WEB RESOURCES

Pronunciation Guide

Interactive Maps

MAP 18.1 The Spanish Empire in the Americas

Primary Sources

Chapter Objectives

ACE Multiple-Choice Quiz

Flashcards

Websites

Canadian History
(http://bubl.ac.uk/link/c/canadianhistory.htm).
A helpfully annotated guide with links to sources on
Canadian history.

Colonial North America
(http://www.earlyamerica.com/).   Offer extensive access
to documents on Britain's North American colonies.

Internet Resources for Latin America
(http://lib.nmsu.edu/subject/bord/laguia/).   A wide-
ranging site with quality links to both historical and
contemporary materials.

The Atlantic System: Africa, the Americas, and Europe, 1550–1807

In 1789, members of England's growing abolitionist movement, campaigning against the slave trade, provided an eager audience for a new publication, *The Interesting Narrative of the Life of Olaudah Equiano, or Gustavus Vassa, the African.* For many, it was the first time they heard an African voice narrate the horrors of slavery. **Olaudah Equiano** (ca. 1745–1797) purchased his own freedom, pursued a career as a sailor, and became a leader of the black community in Britain and an important contributor to the abolitionist movement. His story shows how he suffered as a slave but also how he beat the odds. Equiano's readers learned of the horrors of the infamous Middle Passage across the Atlantic:

(British Library, London/The Bridgeman Art Library)

OLAUDAH EQUIANO

The first object which saluted my eyes when I arrived on the coast was the sea, and a slave-ship. . . . These filled me with astonishment, which was soon converted into terror. . . . I was now persuaded that I had gotten into a world of bad spirits, and that they were going to kill me. . . . [T]hey made ready with many fearful noises, and we were all put under deck . . . now that the whole ship's cargo was confined together [the stench of the hold] was absolutely pestilential. The closeness of the place, and the heat of the climate, added to the number in the ship, which was so crowded that each had scarcely room to turn himself, almost suffocated us. . . . This wretched situation was again aggravated by the galling of the chains, now become insupportable; and the filth of the [latrines], into which the children often fell, and were almost suffocated. The shrieks of the women, and the groans of the dying, rendered the whole a scene of horror almost inconceivable.[1]

CL This icon will direct you to interactive activities and study materials on the *Voyages* website:
www.cengage.com/history/hansen/voyages1e

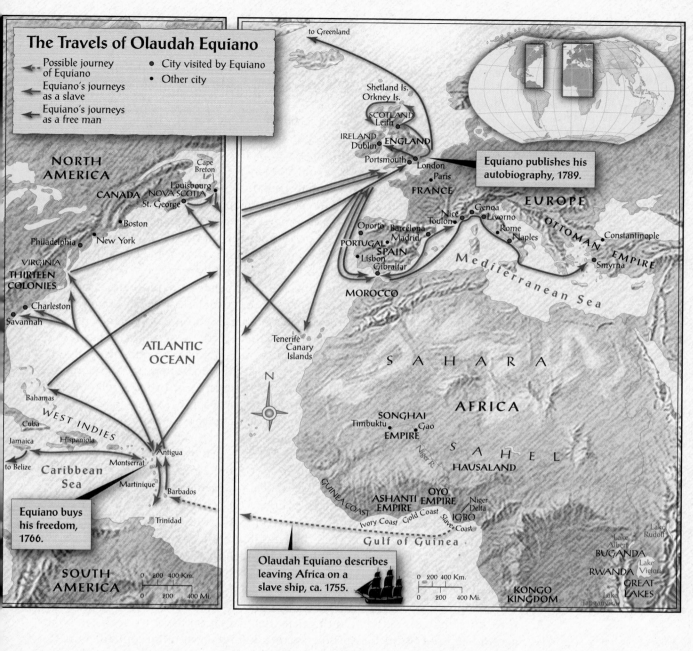

The Travels of Olaudah Equiano

Legend:
- Possible journey of Equiano
- Equiano's journeys as a slave
- Equiano's journeys as a free man
- ● City visited by Equiano
- ● Other city

Equiano publishes his autobiography, 1789.

Equiano buys his freedom, 1766.

Olaudah Equiano describes leaving Africa on a slave ship, ca. 1755.

Map labels:

NORTH AMERICA

Cape Breton
Louisbourg
NOVA SCOTIA
St. George
CANADA

Boston
Philadelphia
New York

VIRGINIA
THIRTEEN COLONIES

Charleston
Savannah

ATLANTIC OCEAN

Bahamas
Cuba
Jamaica
Hispaniola
WEST INDIES
Antigua
Montserrat
Martinique
Barbados
Trinidad
to Belize
Caribbean Sea

SOUTH AMERICA

0   200 400 Km.
0   200 400 Mi.

to Greenland

Shetland Is.
Orkney Is.
SCOTLAND
Leith
IRELAND
Dublin
ENGLAND
Portsmouth
London
Paris
FRANCE
Oporto
Barcelona
Madrid
PORTUGAL
SPAIN
Lisbon
Gibraltar
MOROCCO
Nice
Toulon
Genoa
Livorno
Rome
Naples
EUROPE
OTTOMAN EMPIRE
Constantinople
Smyrna
Mediterranean Sea

Tenerife
Canary Islands

SAHARA
AFRICA
SAHEL

SONGHAI EMPIRE
Timbuktu
Gao
Niger R.
HAUSALAND

GUINEA COAST
ASHANTI EMPIRE
OYO EMPIRE
Niger Delta
IGBO
Ivory Coast   Gold Coast   Slave Coast
Gulf of Guinea

Lake Rudolf
Lake Albert
BUGANDA
Lake Victoria
RWANDA
GREAT LAKES
KONGO KINGDOM
Lake Tanganyika

0   200 400 Km.
0   200 400 Mi.

N

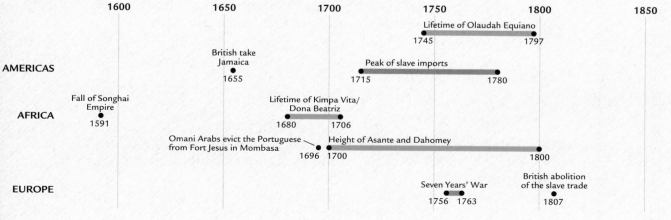

Timeline:

	1600	1650	1700	1750	1800	1850

Lifetime of Olaudah Equiano — 1745–1797

AMERICAS
- British take Jamaica — 1655
- Peak of slave imports — 1715–1780

AFRICA
- Fall of Songhai Empire — 1591
- Lifetime of Kimpa Vita/Dona Beatriz — 1680–1706
- Omani Arabs evict the Portuguese from Fort Jesus in Mombasa — 1696
- Height of Asante and Dahomey — 1700–1800

EUROPE
- Seven Years' War — 1756–1763
- British abolition of the slave trade — 1807

●**Olaudah Equiano**
(1745–1797) Afro-British author and abolitionist who told of his enslavement as a child in Africa, his purchase of his own freedom in the West Indies, his move to England, and his wide travels as a sailor.

(CL) **Primary Source:**
The Interesting Narrative of Olaudah Equiano and Written by Himself
Read selections from an ex-slave's autobiography, one of the most influential abolitionist books published in England.

At least twelve million African had similar experiences between the sixteenth and nineteenth centuries, and an unknown number perished in Africa even before they reached the slave ports on the coast.

The historical importance of Equiano's *Interesting Narrative* has been established, even though some scholars have begun to question the authenticity of its earliest passages. Some disputed evidence suggests that the author was born in the Americas and created his account of Africa and the voyage across the Atlantic by retelling other slaves' stories. Whether Olaudah Equiano (oh-lah-OO-dah ek-wee-AHN-oh) actually experienced the terror he reports in the passage above or based the story on other accounts, few other sources bring us closer to the reality faced by millions of Africans in this period or offer a more eloquent critique of slavery.

By 1745, when Equiano's life began, the Atlantic slave trade was at its height. Hundreds of thousands of Africans crossed the Atlantic every year. They lived in diverse environments—the Brazilian tropics, the temperate lands of Virginia, the rocky shores of Nova Scotia—and performed a great variety of tasks. The fate of most of the twelve million Africans sent to the Americas in the seventeenth and eighteenth centuries, however, was tied to the sugar plantations of the West Indies. Sugar was the foundation of the Atlantic economy, a source of great profit and immense suffering.

A complex set of interconnections between African, American, and European societies characterized the Atlantic system. The most basic of these relationships was economic. The so-called triangular trade sent Africans to the Americas as slaves; sugar, tobacco, and natural resources from the Americas to Europe; and manufactured goods from Europe to both Africa and the Americas. Africans provided the labor for American plantations financed and managed by Europeans. The planters sent their profits back to Europe, stimulating economic growth, while in those parts of Africa afflicted by the Atlantic slave trade, life became much less secure.

The Atlantic system also fostered political competition. Warfare in West Africa increased, and European powers competed for Atlantic supremacy; Equiano was involved in naval clashes between the English and the French. The Atlantic slave trade also had demographic and cultural consequences. Africans arrived in the Americas not simply as slaves but also as carriers of traditions that had a profound influence on the cultural development of American societies (see also Chapter 18).

Finally, the abolition of slavery was itself a complex process involving actors from different parts of the Atlantic, including plantation slaves who resisted bondage and European Christians who grew uncomfortable with the contradictions between their beliefs and the practice of slavery. It was to his fellow Christians that Olaudah Equiano especially appealed with his *Interesting Narrative*.

Focus Questions

 How were existing African economic and political systems integrated into the Atlantic plantation system? What were the effects of this interaction on Africans and African societies?

What were the major social and economic features of the plantation complex in the West Indies and on the American mainland? What cultural patterns were associated with forced African migration to the Americas?

How did the plantation complex affect political and economic developments in Europe in the eighteenth century?

African History and Afro-Eurasian Connections, 1550–1700

The impact of the Atlantic slave trade on African societies, and its overall importance in African history, cannot be judged without a larger cultural and geographic context. Contrary to common assumptions, Africa was not an isolated continent; it had been part of world history since the most ancient of times, with long-standing connections to Europe and Asia across the Mediterranean, the Red Sea, and the Indian Ocean (see Chapter 16). It was therefore fitting for Equiano's tale to begin in Africa.

Africa's diverse environments, such as deserts, grassland savannas, and rainforests, produced a great variety of political systems. In the mid-sixteenth century some Africans lived in small bands of hunter-gatherers, while others were subjects of powerful monarchs. Basing his story either on childhood memories or the stories told by other slaves, Equiano described the Igbo-speaking villages in the Niger Delta region of West Africa as productive communities where yam-based agriculture supported a dense population. Other nearby societies had more centralized and hierarchical political structures, but the Igbo (ee-BWOH) seem to have preferred their merit-based system, in which men and women accumulated titles and authority on the basis of their achievements rather than birth. As in other African societies, clan elders played a crucial role in negotiating the consensus needed for group decisions. Such institutions were nearly universal in Africa. Even when a more distant chief or king required tribute and obeisance, African villages had their own mechanisms for keeping peace and administering justice.

Much of the cultural and economic energy of the continent came from interaction among African peoples. In the well-populated **Great Lakes region** of east-central Africa, for example, migration had led to encounters between Africans from different linguistic and cultural backgrounds. Bantu-speaking migrants from the west brought knowledge of grain agriculture. Their sophisticated iron technology is now thought by scholars to have been independently invented rather than borrowed from the Nile Valley. From pastoralist neighbors these farmers also gained access to cattle. In the Great Lakes, agriculture provided the bulk of calories and was the focus of work, but people associated cattle with wealth and prestige. No proper marriage contract could be negotiated unless the young man's family gave a gift of cattle to the family of his intended bride. The prosperity of African agriculture in the Great Lakes was also stimulated by the incorporation of plantains (bananas) into the farm cycle, a Southeast Asian plant that had been brought across the Indian Ocean. Supported by agricultural surpluses and dominated by powerful

• Great Lakes region
A temperate highland region in and around the Great Rift Valley in east-central Africa. Characterized by agriculture and cattle pastoralism, a substantial iron industry, and dense populations.

clans with great wealth in cattle, a number of powerful kingdoms, such as Rwanda and Buganda, were emerging in the seventeenth-century Great Lakes region.

Some societies, like those in the Great Lakes region, developed without direct contact beyond the continent. But for other African societies, contacts with external political systems, commercial markets, and religious traditions were very important. For example, Ethiopia, Kongo, and South Africa had connections to the wider Christian world. The Ethiopian Church was the oldest, already over a thousand years old when the Portuguese vainly attempted a military alliance in the sixteenth century (see Chapter 16).

In the Kongo kingdom, civil war and invasion by outside forces led to the disintegration of the monarchy and the abandonment of the Kongo capital of San Salvador in the seventeenth century. Into this political vacuum stepped **Kimpa Vita,** a remarkable religious figure also known as Dona Beatriz (ca. 1680–1706). In a powerful example of religious syncretism (see Chapter 18), Kimpa Vita declared that she had been visited by St. Anthony and is reported to have said that she died each Friday, only to arise each Sunday after having conversed with God, who told her that the people of Kongo must unite under a new king. She taught that Christ and the apostles were black men who had lived and died in the Kongo, and she was hostile to the Portuguese missionaries who regarded her beliefs as heresy. Nevertheless, her doctrine was popular, and her followers repopulated the old capital city. She was captured by one of the contestants for the Kongo throne, tried for witchcraft and heresy, and burned at the stake. But the tradition of depicting Jesus Christ as an African endured in this part of Africa after Kimpa Vita's death.

Another religious tradition was the ascetic Calvinist version of Christianity brought to South Africa by Dutch and French Huguenot immigrants in the late seventeenth century. Calvinism was worlds apart from the mystical Ethiopian faith and the religious syncretism of Kimpa Vita in Kongo. Dutch and Huguenot settlers, sponsored by the Dutch East India Company, arrived in the only part of Africa where the disease environment favored European settlement. In the very southeastern tip of Africa, where Cape Town was founded in 1652, the indigenous Khoisan (KOI-sahn)-speaking peoples were few in number, had no metal weapons, and, most important, no resistance to diseases such as smallpox. Within a hundred years white settlers had enslaved them or driven them beyond the expanding colonial border.

The world of Islam continued to provide another gateway for Africa's global interconnections. On the East African coast, African Muslims participated in long-established maritime trade routes even while political circumstances changed. After initial conquest, the Portuguese had a difficult time maintaining their power on the Swahili coast (see Chapter 16). In the seventeenth century the ambitious sultan of Oman (oh-maan), at the entrance to the Persian Gulf, challenged the Portuguese for control and evicted them from Fort Jesus in Mombasa in 1696. In the eighteenth century Swahili princes and aristocrats ruled over their own local affairs, while generally acknowledging the Omani sultan as their overlord.

The other major focal point of African Islam was the **Sahel,** the arid region south of the Sahara Desert. Here urban civilization developed from trade between grain farmers and cattle pastoralists and between the products of the grassland savanna and those of the rainforest further south. Fishermen drew in the resources of the great Niger River. Rising in the mountains of the west, flowing through the savanna to the edge of the desert and on through the rainforests of the Niger Delta where Equiano placed his childhood home, the river was a highway of trade; West Africa's most important cities were located on its banks. This urban, commercial

---

• **Kimpa Vita** (ca. 1680–1706) Christian reformer in the Kongo kingdom, also known as Dona Beatriz. She preached that Jesus Christ was an African. Was executed as a heretic by forces loyal to the Kongo king.

• **Sahel** Arid region south of the Sahara Desert that played an important historic role as a West African center of trade and urbanization. Islam traveled with the caravans across the Sahara, making the Sahel a diffusion point for Islam in West Africa.

dynamic was further stimulated by the trans-Saharan trade. Cities like Timbuktu were the southern destinations for camel caravans from North Africa.

The **Songhai Empire,** with its capital at Gao along the Niger River, was built on a thousand-year-old tradition of large-scale states in this region (see Map 19.1). In addition to leading armies of conquest, the *askias* (emperors) of Songhai (song-GAH-ee) were great patrons of the Islamic arts and sciences. The Sankore Mosque in Timbuktu became a center of intellectual debate, and scholars were drawn from far and wide by its impressive library. Timbuktu was famous for its gold trade and its book market, where finely bound Moroccan volumes were eagerly sought after by Muslim scholars, both Arab and African. When rulers, traders, and intellectuals from Songhai went on the *hajj* (pilgrimage) to Arabia, they amplified the empire's connections with the broader Islamic world.

Even within the mighty Songhai Empire, however, most Africans lived in small agricultural villages far from the urban, Islamic world of kings, cavalry, and long-distance trade. In the rural societies of the Sahel that paid tribute to Songhai overlords, Islam spread slowly. Here older gods and ritual practices endured, though sometimes villagers incorporated elements of Islamic practice. Even in cities like Timbuktu and at the court of powerful Songhai kings, syncretism was characteristic of West African Islam.

The success of the askias (AH-skee-as) of Songhai in enlarging their territory and expanding their trade ultimately proved their undoing because it attracted the

● **Songhai Empire** (1464–1591)   Important Islamic empire with a prosperity based on both interregional and trans-Saharan trade. Stretched from the Atlantic into present-day Nigeria, reaching its height in the sixteenth century before being invaded from Morocco.

The Great Mosque at Jenne   The city of Jenne (Djenné) is an ancient West African trade site on the upper Niger River. Jenne's merchants benefited from trans-Saharan trade, and in the thirteenth century, when the original mosque on this site was built, the city's people embraced the Islamic faith. This mosque, a World Heritage Site, is the largest mud brick structure in the world and shows how Islamic architecture was influenced by the use of local materials and by West African aesthetic principles. The current structure is over one hundred years old.   (Wolfgang Kaehler/Getty Images)

MAP 19.1

West African States and Trade, ca. 1500

In 1500 Africa's primary global connections were across the Sahara desert, up the Nile, across the Red Sea, and into the Indian Ocean. Large kingdoms and empires such as those of Songhai in the west and Ethiopia in the northeast benefited from participation in world trade, as did the Swahili city-states in the east. The arrival of Europeans added a new set of interconnections along the West African coast, but only in South Africa did Europeans come as settlers. Large states were the exception in Africa; societies smaller in scale populated vast regions of the continent.

attention of their powerful Moroccan neighbors to the north. Morocco's leaders had remained independent of the expanding Ottoman Empire and had successfully driven off the Portuguese from their Atlantic and Mediterranean shores. The Moroccan sultan, envious of Songhai's gold and salt mines, decided on conquest, and in 1591 the army he sent out from Marrakesh conquered Songhai. But the Moroccans were unable to sustain direct rule over such a long distance, and the once mighty Songhai Empire splintered into numerous smaller kingdoms, chiefdoms, and sultanates. Never again would a large-scale African state rise to such dominance in the Sahel.

While Songhai was at its height in the sixteenth century, Europeans were constructing fortifications on the West African coast. Though the major centers of population and prosperity in the savanna interior were connected to the wider world across the Sahara, the Portuguese, French, English, and others were finding a way to redirect West African trade to the coast, focusing on the commodity in which they were soon most interested: slaves. The economic geography of West Africa began a long, slow shift away from the interior and toward the coast. By the eighteenth century, Africans from the Sahel who may once have crossed the Sahara to Morocco might be enslaved and sent to Jamaica. While connections across the Sahara Desert and the Indian Ocean continued, Africa's international connection was now more linked to the Atlantic Ocean and, beyond, to the Americas.

⬤ Africa and the Americas: The Plantation Complex

The lives of at least twelve million Africans were utterly transformed when they experienced the horrors of the voyage from Africa to the Americas, called the Middle Passage. This forced emigration was the basis of the **Atlantic plantation system,** in which the use of slaves to grow crops like sugar led to a new set of interchanges between Europe, Africa, and the Americas. Huge profits came to European planters and governments through the sugar trade, sharpening competition between European states. In the Americas, plantation regions were completely remade ecologically, demographically, and economically. Imported plants and animals replaced indigenous ones, Africans became the majority population of the Caribbean islands, and sugar planters implemented a proto-industrial system of production to supply expanding global markets for sugar and related products like molasses and rum.

● **Atlantic plantation system** The focal point in the new set of interchanges between Africa, Europe, and the Americas that peaked in the eighteenth century. Utilized African slave labor to produce large quantities of agricultural products, particularly sugar, for international markets.

As Equiano's story shows, Africans were more than passive victims of the Atlantic slave trade and plantation system. Many resisted slavery. And though mortality rates were high and survivors usually could not retain their own languages, Africans kept much of their culture and contributed it to the new American societies (see Chapter 18). Meanwhile, on the continent of Africa, the social and political systems of some African societies were distorted after their integration into Atlantic markets.

The Ecology and Economics of Plantation Production

European conquest of the Americas and the continuing outcomes of the Columbia exchange, along with the Portuguese opening of new trade links with West Africa, set the stage for the rise of the Atlantic plantation system (see Chapters 16 and 18). A newly interconnected Atlantic world was created that combined the financial, political, and military power of Europe, American land and natural resources, and African labor.

When the Spanish first conquered the Caribbean islands, they could not exploit the labor of the Amerindians, who could stand neither the strain of European rule nor the deadly effects of the new diseases. While European indentured servants were imported, for example, to work on tobacco plantations on Barbados in the 1620s, they were vulnerable to the tropical diseases such as yellow fever and malaria that had been brought across the ocean from Africa. Starting in the mid-seventeenth century, when sugar became the sole focus of West Indian agriculture, neither Europeans nor Amerindians could provide sufficient labor.

Enslaved Africans filled the void. They were expensive, and became more so over time. But from a sugar planter's perspective they were worth the investment because they could survive in the Caribbean environment. Through migration and trade contacts, West Africans had long been connected with the wider Afro-Eurasian disease environment and had developed resistance to the same diseases as had Europeans. Through genetic adaptation and childhood exposure, Africans were also more likely to survive malaria and yellow fever. Ironically, what should have been a great advantage in life, the ability to survive in difficult disease environments, proved to be a tragic disadvantage to the Africans hauled across the ocean to toil on sugar plantations.

Slavery was by no means uncommon in previous human history, but the scale and commercial orientation of the sugar industry were something new. When comparing institutions of slavery in different times and places, one must distinguish between "societies with slaves" and "slave societies." Many societies have had social institutions that allow for slavery, but such "societies with slaves" are different from more extreme "slave societies," where the master/slave relationship is at the heart of social and economic life. "Societies with slaves" were common in the Islamic world and in Africa itself. Equiano described a mild form of servitude in the Niger Delta region, where the "slaves" had a lower place in society but retained legal rights. "Societies with slaves" developed in the Americas as well. In seventeenth-century Pennsylvania and Mexico, for example, African slaves were part of the population, but slavery was by no means the main engine of economic life. In fact, only 5 percent of the Africans who crossed the Atlantic during the era of the Atlantic slave trade came to British North America. Most became part of genuine "slave societies" in Brazil and the Caribbean, which together accounted for 80 percent of slave imports. In the West Indies slavery was at the heart of social and economic life.

Purchasing and provisioning a sugar plantation, and buying the slaves needed to work it, took substantial capital. Sugar planters were usually men of property, either nobles with estates and aristocratic titles or middle-class entrepreneurs. For the latter, profits from sugar could improve not only their finances but also their social standing. Some of the great estates and chateaux of eighteenth-century France and Britain were built on the financial foundation of slave labor.

On a typical Caribbean plantation, the owner and his family occupied a "great house." Over time, absentee ownership became more common, especially on British islands such as Jamaica, so that the master's house might stand empty for long periods waiting for his occasional arrival from Europe. The work of overseeing slave labor was often performed by lower-status European immigrants, legendary for their harshness. In other cases the overseers were men of mixed race, though

Caribbean Sugar Mill Sugar production was an industrial as well as agricultural enterprise. Here wind power is used to crush the sugarcane; the rising smoke indicates the intense heat of the furnaces used to boil down the juice. The slaves' work was hard, dangerous, and unceasing: such machinery was usually operated six days a week year-round. (From William Clark, *Ten Views in the Islands of Antigua*, 1823, British Library)

mulattos did not automatically have higher status on the plantation. Equiano told of a French sugar planter on Martinique with "many mulattoes working in the fields [who] *were all the produce of his own loins!*"

Slaves performed the backbreaking work of planting, weeding, and harvesting, and they were also involved in the complicated task of turning the raw cane into a semiprocessed product for export. Because sugar is bulky in its raw state, the juice had to be squeezed out of the cane and boiled down for profitable shipment to distant markets. Sugar production was, in fact, an agro-industrial enterprise, organized like a modern factory where profitable operation requires that the assembly line is always rolling and raw materials are always at hand. Sugarcane was planted year round so that it could be harvested and processed year round, with full-time use of the complex machinery that crushed the juice from the cane and the large copper kettles that were used to boil down the juice. The industrial process was physically strenuous, and the copper kettles sometimes exploded, taking African lives in the process.

Under such harsh conditions many Africans were worked to death. Statistics from the island of Barbados are representative. In 1680 there were 50,000 African slaves on the island. Over the next forty years another 50,000 slaves were imported, but the total black population actually *dropped* to 45,000 slaves in 1713. Even with massive imports, slave populations were not self-sustaining. The mortality rate was high, and the fertility of slave women was adversely affected by harsh working conditions and poor diet. As Equiano noted, the overseers, "human butchers" left in charge by their absentee masters, "pay no regard to the situation of pregnant women. . . . The neglect certainly conspires with many others to cause a decrease in the births, as well as in the lives of the grown negroes." In the late eighteenth century Equiano calculated that Barbados, not the worst island in terms of African mortality, required a thousand fresh imports annually just to maintain a level population.

Equiano himself escaped the harsh fate of working on a Caribbean sugar plantation. While still a boy he was sold to a British naval officer; he spent much of his early life aboard ships and developed a lifelong fondness for London, where, as a teenager, he was baptized as a Christian in 1759. He was then sold to a Philadelphia merchant with business interests in the West Indies. By this time Equiano was very familiar with the types of ships that had once caused him such alarm. Literate in English, he had developed a good head for numbers. His new owner treated him well, and Equiano had significant freedom in tending to his master's business, which sometimes included trading in slaves. He witnessed many cruelties:

> It was very common in several of the islands, particularly in St. Kitt's, for the slaves to be branded with the initial letters of their master's name, and a load of heavy iron hooks hung around their necks. . . . I have seen a negro beaten till some of his bones were broken, for only letting a pot boil over. It is not uncommon, after a flogging, to make slaves go on their knees and thank their owners and . . . say "God Bless You."

While distressed by his own bondage, Equiano was keenly aware of the much worse fate he could have faced as a field slave.

Of course, sugar was not the only slave-produced plantation crop in the Americas. Slaves were also used on the tobacco plantations of Virginia and the indigo plantations of Carolina (see Chapter 18). But while Carolina plantations were organized much like those of the West Indies, the British colonies of the Chesapeake were actually at the margins of the plantation complex. Here there was a more equal balance between male and female slaves. Better diet and higher fertility made the slave population self-reproducing in British North America by 1720, a sharp contrast to conditions in the Caribbean.

African Culture and Resistance to Slavery

Previously some historians argued that the psychological effects of the Middle Passage and of slavery itself were overwhelming for Africans. Deprived of any connection with previous cultural values, the slaves became like children completely dependent on their master's authority and lost their will to resist. More recent historical research has shown the complete inadequacy of this passive image of enslaved Africans. Resistance to slavery was widespread.

Slave traders, owners, and overseers had to be always vigilant. Slaves were constantly looking for ways to escape their bondage and, failing that, to resist their captivity in large or small ways. Planters, however, paid great attention to security, and the penalties for open insubordination or revolt were gruesome. Slaves often found safer, more subtle ways to assert their humanity and critique their condition. Songs and stories derived from African cultural traditions might be used to ridicule an evil master using coded language that he could not understand. Religious rites—African, Christian, or a synthesis of multiple belief systems and rituals—could be assertions of dignity and spiritual force. External appearances of deference to the slave master could be deceiving.

Resistance to slavery sometimes began even before the slave ships arrived in America. Equiano describes the nets that were used to keep Africans from jumping overboard and relates that "one day . . . two of my wearied countrymen, who were chained together . . . preferring death to such a life of misery, somehow made through the nettings and jumped into the sea." Insurrections aboard slave ships were also common, as this dramatic description from 1673 attests:

> A master of a ship . . . did not, as the manner is, shackle [the slaves] one to another . . . and they being double the number of those in the ship found their advantages, got weapons in their hands, and fell upon the sailors, knocking them on the heads, and cutting their throats so fast as the master found they were all lost . . . and so went down into the hold and blew up all with himself.[2]

Equiano tells of a slave trader who had once cut off the leg of a slave for running away. When Equiano asked how such an action could be squared with the man's Christian conscience, he was simply told "that his scheme had the desired effect— it cured that man and some others of running away."

Some Africans were freed by their masters (see below), but many others simply escaped. But if an individual or a small group escaped from a slave plantation, where would they go, and how would they live? Options for escaped slaves included joining pirate communities in the Caribbean, which in spite of their reputation for brutality were relatively egalitarian, forming autonomous communities of runaway slaves, or settling among Amerindian populations.

Already in the sixteenth century Africans were banding together to form **maroon communities,** societies formed by escaped slaves. Perhaps the best known was Palmares in northeastern Brazil (see Chapter 18). Palmares was unique in scale, but smaller maroon communities, where escaped slaves guarded their independence and made their own rules, were common in the eighteenth-century Caribbean. Some of the islands were too small for maroons to successfully avoid recapture, but the interior mountains of Jamaica were perfect for that purpose.

When the Spanish fled Jamaica in 1655 during a British attack, they left behind hundreds of African slaves who fled to the hills. The livelihood of the Jamaican maroons came from farming, fishing, and occasionally raiding the British sugar plantations on the coasts. The threat to the British came not so much from those raids but from the sanctuary that the maroons could provide to other escaped slaves. After several slave uprisings in the early eighteenth century, the British increased their attacks on the maroons. The British and maroons fought to a stalemate, leading to a treaty that allowed the maroons control of their own communities under a British supervisor in exchange for a promise that they would hunt, capture, and return future runaways.

In some places runaway slaves formed alliances with Amerindians, sometimes assimilating into their societies. A small group of Africans might seek sanctuary in an Amerindian village and become a part of that society; sometimes larger-scale cooperation between maroons and Amerindians occurred. In Florida, Africans who escaped from slavery in Carolina and Georgia formed an alliance with Creek Indians, and the cultural interaction between the two groups led the "Black Seminoles" to adopt many elements of Creek culture.

●maroon communities
Self-governing communities of escaped slaves common in the early modern Caribbean and in coastal areas of Central and South America.

A Coromantyn Free Negro, or Ranger, armed

🔲 **A Jamaican Maroon** In Jamaica and elsewhere in the Caribbean escaped slaves banded together to form maroon communities. This man's gun and sword show that the maroons organized themselves to protect their independence from European colonialists. While some joined maroon communities, other escaped slaves joined Amerindian socities or the crews of pirate ships. (Private Collection/ The Bridgeman Art Library)

Of course, slaves who escaped were taking a risk: they could be recaptured and face terrible punishments, or they could find survival in an unknown environment to be extremely difficult. Even if Africans had to resign themselves to their fate as plantation slaves, however, covert resistance was common. Slowing down and subverting the work process was one method of self-assertion, even if the risk of the whip was ever present.

Slave religion is perhaps the area where Africans could best resist the psychological and spiritual torments of slavery without risking flight or outright rebellion. Where Africans formed a strong majority, such as the Caribbean and northwestern Brazil, their religious practices showed the greatest continuity. In both Brazil and Cuba, for example, Africans brought their beliefs and rituals into Roman Catholicism. In both colonies the *orisas* (or-EE-shahs), gods of the Yoruba people (of present-day western Nigeria), were transformed into Catholic saints. Xangó, the Yoruba deity of thunder and lightning, is still venerated today in the Cuban and Brazilian syntheses of Catholicism and African religion called *Santeria* (san-ta-REE-ah) and *Candomblé* (candome-blay). Like Amerindians in Mexico, Africans in Brazil and Cuba transformed their old gods into Catholic saints and thereby merged their existing beliefs with Christianity (see Chapter 18). (See the feature "Movement of Ideas: Afro-Brazilian Religion.")

In areas where Africans were a smaller percentage of the population, as in most of British North America, European cultural influences were more dominant. But religion allowed for cultural expression and spiritual self-assertion here as well. While white Christian preachers delivered sermons to the slaves that emphasized obedience now and rewards in the afterlife, the slave hymns and choral traditions tended to focus on biblical motifs of liberation, such as the story of Moses leading his enslaved people to freedom.

Equiano's story shows us another, though unusual, strategy of escape from slavery: working within the system. His freedom came about through a combination of good fortune and business acumen. He was fortunate that his final owner, a Philadelphia merchant, was a member of the Society of Friends, a Christian group that had strong doubts about whether Christians should own slaves. This master agreed that if Equiano could repay the money he had spent on him, Equiano would have his freedom, and he allowed Equiano to trade on his own account in his spare time. In this way the young man saved enough money to buy his own freedom. He returned to England, which he regarded as his home, but frequently went back to sea, working as a sailor in the Atlantic and the Mediterranean and even joining an unsuccessful voyage to the North Pole. He worked as a hairdresser for the London elite and learned to play the French horn.

Equiano's story reminds us of the situation of free Africans in the Atlantic world and of the many roles that Africans played in the Americas beyond that of field slave. In many parts of the Americas, Africans were essential to the economy as skilled artisans. The long familiarity of most African societies with iron production and ironworking often gave them the skills needed to perform this function. Africans, whether as slaves or free men, also served as frontier soldiers for expansionist European states.

In some places, like Brazil, **manumission,** the voluntary freeing of slaves, was encouraged as an act of Christian religious charity. Of course, those most likely to be freed were women, children, and the elderly, and adult male Africans had little chance of attaining freedom through a simple act of charity. However, because the legal system in colonial Latin America operated on the principle that all persons are free *unless* proven otherwise, it was possible for black men who escaped their masters to move far enough away that they might "pass" as free men.

In British North America, however, manumission was uncommon and legal codes made little or no distinction between free blacks and slaves. Here the equation between skin color and slave status was so strong that free blacks were in a very uncomfortable situation, as this story from Equiano's stay in Georgia attests:

> After our arrival we went up to the town of Savannah; and the same evening I went to a friend's house . . . a black man. We were very happy at meeting each other . . . after supper . . . the watch or patrol came by, and, discerning a light in the house . . . came in and sat down, and drank some punch with us. . . . A little after this they told me I must go to the watch-house with them; this surprised me a good deal after our kindness to them, and I asked them "Why so?" They said, that all Negroes who had a light in their houses after nine o'clock were to be taken into custody, and either pay some dollars or be flogged.

This was not an isolated incident: on other occasions Equiano's trade goods were confiscated for no reason other than his vulnerability as a black man, and several times he was nearly re-enslaved in spite of the document he always carried with him attesting to his freedom. Thereafter he avoided Georgia and Carolina altogether. In such places, legal freedom did not mean true liberty for Equiano or other free blacks.

Effects of the Atlantic Slave Trade on West Africa

Beginning in the sixteenth century, the Atlantic slave trade had profound reverberations in West African societies such as the Kongo kingdom (see Chapter 16). Here Portuguese traders found that they could buy slaves in African markets and sell them for a considerable profit. The slaves available for purchase were often war captives. As the demand for labor from American plantations increased, traditional African sources of supply proved insufficient, and in some regions new motives for African participation in the slave trade began to transform existing social, economic, and military systems.

The **Asante kingdom** was an expanding power in the forest region of eighteenth-century West Africa. As the ruling kings, the *Asantehenes,* pursued their ambitions for greater power through military expansion, many prisoners were taken captive. These war captives might be exchanged for Asante (uh-SHAN-tee) soldiers also taken prisoner, redeemed to their homes in exchange for payment, or kept and integrated into Asante households as servants. Before the rise of the Atlantic slave trade, in fact, one of those three options would most certainly have

•manumission
The voluntary freeing of slaves by their masters.

•Asante kingdom
(ca. 1700–1896) A rising state in eighteenth-century West Africa, with its capital at Kumasi in the rainforest region of what is now Ghana. Asante's wars of expansion produced prisoners who were often sold into the Atlantic slave circuit.

Afro-Brazilian Religion

The strong African element in the religious life of Brazil is not surprising given that more people of African descent live in Brazil than in any other country outside of Africa. Africans infused their beliefs into Roman Catholicism during the age of colonialism and slavery. Although Catholics were supposed to receive the sacraments and religious instruction from ordained priests, many slaves did not have access to regular church services. Instead they elevated their own spiritual leaders and devised their own rituals, infusing their faith with African elements.

In Roman Catholicism only men could be priests, but in many African societies from which Brazilian slaves originated women played important roles as seers, prophets, and healers. Such women prophets would sometimes enter a trance as if possessed by spirits and deities; a Christian might say they were possessed by the Holy Spirit or by a saint, and her utterances might be described as "speaking in tongues." This tradition, in which women were intermediaries between humans and powerful deities and spirits, was carried to the Americas and continues in Brazil today in the heavily African form of spirituality called Candomblé.

In the eighteenth century, leaders of the Catholic Church worried that this process of religious syncretism was leading to heretical ideas. Sometimes they would use ecclesiastical courts (church courts) to try to suppress what they saw as unacceptable beliefs and rituals. For example, they sometimes saw drums and dancing as satanic. The two eighteenth-century documents below, which describe African elements in Brazilian Catholicism, are both taken from court documents at which African priestesses were on trial for heresy.

Source: Paulo Simões, *Tupã, olorum, Jesus and the Holy Spirit: An Analysis of the Cultural and Ideological Implications of Religious Change in Brazil*, M.A. thesis, California State University Long Beach, 1999, pp. 55–56.

Document 1

Most conspicuous in the . . . diabolic dance was one Negress Caetana . . . and in the occasion of the dance she would preach to the others and say that she was God who made the sky and earth, the waters and the stones. To join in this dance they would first build a doll which they made with the appearance in imitation of the devil, and place him on an iron lance and with a cape of white cloth. . . . They would put him in the middle of the house, on a small rug, on top of some crosses, and around them they would place pots, some with cooked herbs. . . . After having arranged this effigy, all would begin dancing and saying their sayings, that that was the saint of their homeland, and in this way worshipped the dummy. In the same dance the priestess would feign death and fall to the ground, and others would lift her and take her into a room, and after this dance one named Quitéria would emerge from the room and would climb to the top of the house, and would begin preaching in her tongue saying that she was God and daughter of Our Lady of the Rosary and of Saint Anthony [also a Catholic patron saint of slaves]. . . . And after this practice, she would leave the [temple] and a Negress would bring in a dead chicken and another a small cauldron [from which] with a bundle of leaves she would sprinkle holy water.

Document 2

[Luzia was] dressed as the angel . . . with a saber in her hand, with a wide ribbon tied to her head. . . . [She was attended by] two Negresses, also Angolan, and one black man playing . . . a little drum . . . and playing and signing for the space of one or two hours, [Luzia] would become as if out of her own judgment, saying things that no one understood, and the people would lie on the ground that she would cure, and she would reach over them various times, and on these occasions say that she had the winds of prophecy.

QUESTIONS FOR ANALYSIS

▶ How do the African slaves described in these documents seem to be combining African rituals and Catholic beliefs?

▶ What similarities and differences are there between the rituals ascribed to Caetana and those of Luzia? What was the principal spiritual role of each of these women?

(CL) **Primary Source:**
A Voyage to New Calabar River in the Year 1699
Learn about the slave trade in West Africa, from a Frenchman on an English slave-trading expedition.

● **Dahomey** (ca. 1650–1894)   African kingdom in present-day southern Benin, reaching its height of influence in the eighteenth century. Its leaders sought regional power by raiding for slaves in other kingdoms and selling them for firearms and European goods.

been the fate of a war captive. But now a powerful fourth option, sale to Europeans and transport across the ocean, had developed. Where war captives had once been a mere byproduct of wars fought for other purposes, now Asante generals had an additional motive for military expansion: profit from the slave trade. British slave traders sailed to Cape Coast Castle, one of many coastal fortifications built by Europeans to facilitate the slave trade, to pay with currency, rum, cloth, and guns for these unfortunate victims.

The rising kingdom of **Dahomey** (dah-HOH-mee) was even more proactive than Asante in using the slave trade to advance state interests. Its kings traded slaves for guns to build a military advantage over their neighbors. More and more guns were imported into West Africa in the eighteenth century as rising prices for slaves put African participants in a better bargaining position. Faced with aggressive neighbors like Dahomey, other African rulers sometimes found they needed to be involved in the slaves-for-guns trade out of self-defense. Keeping your own people from being enslaved sometimes meant selling Africans from other societies to protect your own. It was a vicious cycle.

🔹 **A Slave Sacrifice at Dahomey**   The Atlantic slave trade cheapened life in Africa as well as in the Americas. The kings of Dahomey based their power on slave raiding and trade with the Europeans. Here members of the the Dahomean royal family, and two European observers, await the sacrifice of slaves about to be thrown from the heights in honor of the king. The umbrella is a symbol of monarchy in parts of West Africa.   (Mary Evans Picture Library)

African systems of slavery were transformed by the impact of the Atlantic trade. Before the Atlantic system developed, if children became enslaved it was usually because their parents had suffered some catastrophe that made it difficult or impossible for them to care for their own offspring. In that case, a parent might "pawn" a child to someone with sufficient resources to keep him or her alive. It was a desperate move, but sometimes a necessary one. A child who was enslaved in this way was not viewed as mere "chattel," the simple property of his or her master. Rather, the chances were good that he would be incorporated into the social network of his new village.

In Africa, where land was usually plentiful and people were the scarce (and therefore valuable) resource, this process of incorporation sometimes took the form of what anthropologists have called "fictive kinship." Descendants of captive outsiders (such as pawned children or war captives) would come to be identified with local lineages. Though the stigma of slave origins might never be completely forgotten, their descendants would gradually become recognized as members of the community.

Female slaves, who were preferred for both their productive and reproductive capabilities, helped further this process of assimilation. In patrilineal societies, where descent is traced through the father's line, children of a free man and a slave women had rights in their father's lineage. Here African practice stood in contrast to the situation in the Americas, where European masters seldom acknowledged responsibility for their own slave-borne offspring. African slave raiders profited from the complementary preference of African masters for female slaves and European plantation owners for male ones. Male slaves could be exported, while female captives were more likely to be sold within West Africa's own slave markets. The fates of their children were likely to be quite different, however. In Africa the women's offspring would often be assimilated into the host community; in the Americas assimilation into European society was rarely an option.

As an abolitionist, Equiano perhaps had an interest in downplaying the negative aspects of indigenous slavery. But he addresses the issue of slavery in Africa in a forthright way, whether the account is based on his own childhood memories or on accounts he had heard from other slaves:

> Each master of a family has a large square of ground. . . . Within this are his houses to accommodate his family and slaves; which, if numerous, frequently cause these tenements to present the appearance of a village. In the middle stands the principal building, appropriated to the sole use of the master. . . . On each side are the apartments of his wives. . . . The habituations of the slaves and the rest of his family are distributed throughout the rest of the enclosure.

In such a village, where there was so little physical distance between master and slave, where conditions of housing and diet were relatively equal, and where the ability to exploit the labor of slaves carried with it a responsibility to protect them, there was little chance that the type of chattel slavery characteristic of the American plantation could ever develop.

But the transformation of West African systems of slavery under the impact of the Atlantic trade is shown in another passage from the *Interesting Narrative* where Equiano, being taken to the coast, is purchased by an African master:

> A wealthy widow . . . saw me; and having taken a fancy to me, I was bought off the merchant, and went home with them. Her house and premises . . . were the finest I ever saw in Africa: they were very extensive, and she had a number

of slaves to attend her. The next day I was washed and perfumed, and when mealtime came, I was led into the presence of my mistress, and ate and drank before her with her son. That filled me with astonishment; and I could scarcely avoid expressing my surprise that the young gentleman should suffer me, who was bound, to eat with him who was free. . . . Indeed everything here, and their treatment of me, made me forget that I was a slave. The language of these people resembled ours so nearly, that we understood each other perfectly. They had also the very same customs as we. . . . In this resemblance to my former happy state, I passed about two months; and now I began to think I was to be adopted into the family. . . .

In Equiano's account we see an example of the traditional practice of incorporating outsiders. As in times past, his new mistress could have kept the young man and by marriage he and his descendants would likely have become integrated into that society. However, by Equiano's time traditional systems had been transformed under the influence of the Atlantic trade. Now she had the option of selling him for ready cash; in Equiano's account she sold him back into the slave export channel that led to the coast.

In such ways, on scales large and small, traditional institutions were transformed by the Atlantic market. Warfare increased, and the climate of insecurity often led to more centralized political structures. African merchants and political leaders who traded slaves for valuable imported commodities gained in power and status. By the later eighteenth century, as more African states came to rely on slaves not just as commodities for export but also to play essential domestic roles as soldiers and laborers, some African "societies with slaves" started to become "slave societies." This transformation of slavery under the influence of the Atlantic trade meant that there were now kingdoms in Africa itself where conditions of servitude had become essential to the functioning of state and society. The power of some Africans was thereby greatly strengthened, but by far the biggest political and economic advantages went to European slave traders and plantation owners.

Some historians have warned that we should not exaggerate the impact of the Atlantic slave trade on continental Africa. It is true that many African societies had no connection with external slave markets in this period, while others were part of Muslim commercial networks that included long-standing slave markets. Farming and herding remained the principal economic activities in Africa. But it is hard not to conclude that the Atlantic slave trade had sharply negative effects, not only for those taken captive and shipped to the Americas but also for the continent they were forced to leave behind.

Most of the world was experiencing a population surge in the eighteenth century. One factor was increasing agricultural productivity associated with the diffusion to Eurasia of new food crops from the Americas. Many African farmers benefited as well, planting maize (from Mesoamerica), which produces more calories per acre than some traditional crops, and cassava (from Brazil), which is very drought-resistant. In spite of such innovations, however, the total population of the African continent remained stagnant. It is hard to avoid concluding that the large-scale export of slaves had a deeply damaging effect on Africa's overall economic productivity.

●Europe and the Atlantic World, 1650–1807

By the eighteenth century the Atlantic Ocean had become a dense network of interchange: people, goods, plants, animals, diseases, religious and political ideas, and cultural forms such as music and storytelling traditions circulated freely back and forth between Europe, Africa, and the Americas.

The high point of the Atlantic slave trade in the eighteenth century coincided with other important developments in world history. Britain and France, now surpassing the Spanish, Portuguese, and Dutch as the world's dominant naval powers, were locked in nearly constant conflict. In spite of great profits from sugar plantations and other commercial enterprises, increased military costs strained the fiscal and political systems of both countries. Mercantilist policies, intended to generate the funds necessary to fight these wars, created incentives for smuggling for both respectable New England merchants and the ever-present pirates of the Caribbean. As a result, the Atlantic world emerged as a transcultural zone where ambitious youths, sometimes even former slaves like Olaudah Equiano, could seek their fortune.

Economic and Military Competition in the Atlantic Ocean, 1650–1763

The economic exchange between Europe, Africa, and the Americas is often called the **triangular trade,** which refers to the movement of manufactured goods from Europe to Africa, of African humanity to the Americas, and of colonial products, such as sugar, tobacco, and timber, back to Europe.

While the triangular notion is a useful one, it simplifies the realities of world trade in this period. For example, Indian Ocean trade networks connected to Atlantic ones whenever West African consumers showed a preference for cotton textiles from India (see Map 19.2). American silver was used to purchase Indian textiles, which were then exported to Africa, Europe, and the Americas. Cowrie shells, harvested from the Indian Ocean and used as currency in West Africa, were imported in huge quantities by European traders during this era. Thus early modern Africa's global trade links were not simply triangular but interoceanic; the Atlantic system was itself part of an emerging global economy (see Chapter 16).

With the major European powers using mercantilist policies in both the Indian and Atlantic Oceans to limit competitors' access to their own colonial markets (see Chapter 17), economic competition resulted in political and military conflict. While the Portuguese, Spanish, and Dutch still profited from their American and Asian possessions in the eighteenth century, none of them could compete with the growing military strength of France and England. The War of Jenkin's Ear (1739–1742) was symptomatic of Spain's slow decline. The Spanish crown, after asserting that only its own ships could trade with its own American colonies, apprehended an Englishman, Captain Robert Jenkins, when they found him smuggling goods to and from their territory. When he got back to England, Jenkins claimed the Spaniards had tortured him and cut off his ear, and he held it up in Parliament demanding revenge.

The outbreak of the War of Jenkin's Ear between the British and the Spanish in the Caribbean was paralleled by political competition and military conflict back in Europe. The great powers—Britain, France, Prussia, Russia, and Austria—were still

● **triangular trade**
The network of interchange between Europe, Africa, and the colonial Americas. Consisted of raw materials and agricultural produce sent from the Americas to Europe; manufactures sent to Africa and used for the purchase of slaves; and slaves exported from Africa to the Americas.

From 1518 to 1850 approximately 11,000,000 slaves were shipped from Africa to the Western Hemisphere; of these about 500,000, or 5 percent, were imported into areas now part of the United States.

Main sources of African slaves

Main slave-trade routes from Africa

Main areas of slave importation in the Western Hemisphere

CL Interactive Map

🌐 **MAP 19.2**
The Atlantic Slave Trade
The Middle Passage from Africa to the Americas was the greatest forced migration in human history. The vast majority of the Africans who lived through it were put to work on Caribbean islands or coastal plantations. The Arab trade in African slaves, across the Sahara desert and the Indian Ocean, was much older, but at no time matched the scale of the Atlantic trade.

jockeying for position (see Chapter 18). When the Prussian army invaded Austrian territory, the resulting War of the Austrian Succession (1740–1748) soon involved all the major European powers. France allied with Prussia, and Britain with Austria. While the British dominated the French in naval battles, the French were dominant on the continent, producing a stalemate, and the war was settled with little effect on the existing European balance of power and no effect on the distribution of colonies in the Americas.

These conflicts focused the attention of British and French leaders on the economic and strategic importance of their American possessions. In 1745 the English Parliament considered raising the tax on sugar imports to finance the war. A lobbyist for the sugar planters argued against the bill, claiming that a tax increase would harm the very industry on which Britain relied for so much of its economic strength. If increased taxation meant that "our sugar colonies should decline, those of our neighbors, our enemies and rivals in trade and navigation, would advance."[3] The lobbyist was probably thinking of Saint-Domingue (san doh-MANGH), the western half of the island of Hispaniola that the French had taken from Spain in 1697, which produced more sugar than any other West Indian colony. (See the feature "World History in Today's World: The World's Sweet Tooth.")

The World's Sweet Tooth

A driving force of the Atlantic slave trade was demand for sugar, which previously had been scarce and expensive. By the eighteenth century England was leading the world in the consumption of cane sugar, and it became cheap enough for middle-class consumers to add to the tea they were now importing in large quantities from Asia.

From England the taste for sweet beverages spread to the rest of Europe and then the world. Today, large quantities of soft drinks are consumed in every corner of the globe as the development of high-fructose corn syrup as a cheap substitute for cane sugar has made soft drinks and other sweetened drinks and foods more widespread than ever.

Though associated with health risks such as tooth decay and obesity, modern soft drinks first emerged from the pharmacy, and well into the twentieth century people in the United States would drink them at "soda fountains" in drug stores. First pharmacists discovered how to add artificial "fizz" to plain water, imitating naturally carbonated mineral water. Then they began to add various natural ingredients, inventing tastes such as root beer and ginger ale. Even

Coca-Cola, first sold in Atlanta, Georgia, in 1886 and named for two main ingredients, the coca leaf and the kola nut, was marketed in drug stores as a "brain and nerve tonic." Today the health risks of excessive consumption of soft drinks are well understood. In the United States, 81 percent of teenage girls are lacking enough calcium in their diet, partly from consuming soft drinks rather than milk.

While the United States leads the world at 56 gallons of soft drinks consumed per capita each year, the fastest-growing markets are in Latin America (especially Mexico and Brazil), eastern Europe (led by Poland), and Asia (where both China and India represent enormous market potential for soft drink manufacturers). While the soft drink market now spans the world, control over these markets has become increasingly consolidated, with Coca-Cola and PepsiCo now responsible for 68 percent of sales. These corporate giants have increased their advertising efforts in emerging markets, doing their best to get young Asians, Africans, and Latin Americans to associate their soft drink brands with the "good life" of Western consumer societies.

With such economic competition fueling political and military tensions, the French and British were soon back at war. Skirmishes that began in the Ohio River Valley in North America led to the outbreak of the **Seven Years' War** (1756–1763). Fought simultaneously in Europe, the West Indies, North America (in the British colonies it was known as the "French and Indian War"), and India, this tricontinental conflict may be thought of as the first "world war." In 1758, while still the property of a Royal Navy officer, Olaudah Equiano saw action as a combatant at the important British siege of Louisbourg:

> The engagement now commenced with great fury on both sides: [the French ship] immediately returned our fire and we continued engaged with each other for some time; during which I was frequently stunned with the thundering of the great guns, whose dreadful contents burned many of my companions into eternity.

The British victory in this engagement at the gateway to the St. Lawrence River soon led to the conquest of Québec and New France. At the same time, the British were scoring victories over the French in India (see Chapter 20).

Like the Spanish and French, the British pursued mercantilist policies in North America and the Caribbean, but they could never limit trade to officially sanctioned traders and trade routes. For example, the sugar and molasses produced on

● **Seven Years' War** (1756–1763) Fought simultaneously in Europe, the West Indies, North America, and South Asia, this war shifted the balance of power between Britain and France in favor of the British, making their influence paramount in India and Canada.

islands like Jamaica and Barbados in the British West Indies were supposed to be sent directly to England. However, New England merchants, seeing an opportunity, traded directly with the Caribbean, exchanging North American products such as timber, cattle, horses, and foodstuffs for sugar. They then refined the sugar into molasses or rum and used it to trade directly for slaves on the West African coast, contrary to mercantilist regulations.

Although American merchants found ways to evade mercantilist restrictions on trade, many deeply resented them. The anger of colonial traders was strongest in commercially oriented cities such as Boston, Philadelphia, and New York. The Seven Years' War added to this increasing set of tensions between the British crown and American commercial interests. Having spent a huge sum to defend the American colonies from France, the British reasoned that it was only logical to have the Americans help pay for their own protection. But new taxes and further mercantilist restrictions on trade soon prompted the Americans to rally to the slogan "no taxation without representation." The Boston Tea Party (1773), during which merchants dressed as Amerindians threw bricks of tea into Boston Harbor, arose from resentment at the monopoly on tea imports that had been given to the British East India Company (see Chapters 20 and 22).

The eighteenth-century Atlantic was therefore the scene of increasing tensions between European powers and colonial societies, and frustrated merchants were not the only source of trouble. Rimming the Atlantic, and manning the ships that transported goods and people around it, was a multitude of uprooted people whose story should also be told.

Life on the Eighteenth-Century Atlantic Ocean

Olaudah Equiano, who spent almost half his life aboard ships, was familiar with the turbulent mass of humanity that made its living from the sea: slave traders, cod fishermen, pirates, and officers and crew fighting for king and country.

Violence was common. Press gangs haunted the banks of the Thames River and other English ports looking for a chance to seize sailors and force them onto ships, a situation that Equiano and many others saw as akin to slavery. English peasants, driven from the countryside by land enclosures that favored the landed gentry, often ended up as sailors, as did Irishmen forced off their lands by English settlement. The sea was often a refuge for the desperate.

Life aboard ship was rough, nearly as much like a prison for the sailors above as for the slaves who might be in the hold below. Their actions were closely controlled; there was no privacy. Captains had to be alert to any signs of indiscipline or they might lose command of the men. Sometimes the sailors, like the slaves below, felt they had nothing to lose and risked their lives in mutiny. The great lexicographer Samuel Johnson commented: "A ship is worse than a jail. There is, in a jail, better air, better company, better convenience of every kind; and a ship has the additional disadvantage of being in danger."[4]

Johnson went on to say that once men had become accustomed to the life of the sea they could not adjust to any other. That seemed to fit Equiano, who "being still of a roving disposition" after he gained his liberty, never went more than a few years without going once again to sea. Contrary to Johnson's grim view, however, life at sea could also mean opportunity for an ambitious person from a poor background. Military success, commercial profit, the safety of those on board—all required the competence of those in charge. Thus life at sea rewarded ability, in contrast to almost every other arena of British life, where inherited social status trumped knowledge and competence.

Even as a slave and a black youth, Equiano was able to earn a promotion to the rank of "able seaman" for his service during the Seven Years' War. He equated that promotion with status as a freeman, and it made him eligible for a payment from the Crown at war's end. He was bitterly disappointed when his master, who was also his commanding officer, not only kept his pension but also sold him to a new slave master. Still, it was life at sea that gave Equiano his greatest opportunities. It was also at this time that Captain James Cook (1728–1770) was rising to prominence in the British Navy. The son of a farmer, Cook rose through the ranks on the basis of his leadership abilities and navigational expertise to become one of the most famous men in the British Empire (see Chapter 21).

The Atlantic Ocean also represented opportunities for fishermen. Enormous quantities of cod were pulled from the **Grand Banks,** off the coast of Newfoundland. Basque fisherman had first discovered this area in medieval times, and salted cod became a staple of the Mediterranean diet. By the eighteenth century ships from places as diverse as England, Spain, France, Iceland, Portugal, and Massachusetts could be found exploiting this rich source of protein, which once cured was easily stored and transported.

In New England, the codfish became a symbol of prosperity. In the early eighteenth century the Boston Town Hall had a gilded cod hanging from its ceiling. The fishing communities of the North Atlantic provided an alternative to the slave-based plantation model that was dominant to the south:

> New Englanders were becoming a commercial people, independent and prosperous and resentful of monopolies. While the West Indies sugar planters were thriving on their protected markets, New Englanders were growing rich on free-trade capitalism. . . . Even the fishermen were independent entrepreneurs, working not on salary but, as they still do in much of the world, for a share of the catch.[5]

Here was another constituency brought forth by the Atlantic economy that would cause political trouble (see Chapter 22). Some of the participants in the Boston Tea Party were involved in trading salt cod to the West Indies in exchange for molasses, which would then be refined and sold on the west coast of Africa for slaves.

Ironically, while cod fishing brought a sense of freedom to New England, it also reinforced slavery in the West Indies by giving plantation owners a cheap source of both protein and salt with which to feed captive Africans. In the Atlantic world, slavery and freedom were two sides of the same coin.

● **Grand Banks**
Fishing area located south and southeast of present-day Newfoundland, Canada. Noted for its immense quantities of cod, a source of protein for the residents in and around the Atlantic and of large profits for British colonial traders.

●Abolition of the British Slave Trade, 1772–1807

In 1775 Olaudah Equiano accepted an opportunity to work as a plantation supervisor on the Central American coast. Equiano did not seem to mind, and even congratulated himself on a job well done: "All my poor countrymen, the slaves, when they heard of my leaving them were very sorry, as I had always treated them with care and affection, and did everything I could to comfort the poor creatures."

In this passage from the *Interesting Narrative* Equiano seems to imply that slavery could be made humane.

Equiano's opinions about slavery changed over the next decade, however, when he came to believe that slavery was inherently evil and needed to be abolished rather than merely reformed. His change in thinking was partly an outcome of deepening religious conviction. After surviving a shipwreck, Equiano became involved in the Methodist movement, whose founder had argued that slavery was incompatible with Christian morality. In that vein, Equiano wrote, "O, ye nominal Christians! Might not an African ask you, 'learned you this from your God, who says unto you, Do unto all men as you would men should do unto you?'" In his increasing consciousness of the incompatibility of Christianity and slavery, Equiano was a man of his times. Throughout the 1780s more and more British Christians raised their voices in opposition. Though the slave owners and slave traders formed a powerful lobby in the British Parliament, public opinion was turning against them.

Apart from Christian conscience, other factors aided the antislavery **abolitionist** cause. In 1772 a judge had ruled that no slave, once he or she reached England, could be compelled to return to a colony where slavery was practiced. Essentially, this meant that the condition of slavery had no legal basis in British law. National pride was a stimulus to abolitionism. Britons were proud of their tradition of "liberty," constitutionally guaranteed by the Bill of Rights of 1689. But the British constitution was also based on the protection of rights of property. Which rights were paramount: those of slaves to their own liberty, or those of slave owners to the use and disposition of their property?

One strategy of the British abolitionists was to show the link between British sugar consumption, by far the highest in the world, and the evils of slavery. In his poem "Poor Africans," William Cowper wrote:

> I pity them greatly, but I must be mum,
> For how could we do without sugar and rum?
> Especially sugar, so needful we see,
> What, give up our desserts, our coffee and tea?

As a result of this campaign more Britons saw slavery not as something distant and abstract, but as an evil in which they personally participated by consuming the products of slave labor. Abolitionist boycotts of West Indian sugar brought the debate home to the breakfast table.

Equiano intended his *Interesting Narrative* to be part of the accelerating abolitionist campaign. Like many authors at this time, he advertised for subscribers who would pay in advance and receive their copies once the book was written and printed. Subscriptions were a way for propertied men and women to support causes they believed in; the subscribers for Equiano's book included major antislavery campaigners: Thomas Clarkson, who wrote a university essay on the theme "Is enslaving others against their will ever justified?" decided the answer was "no" and became the movement's leading national organizer; Josiah Wedgwood, the highly successful ceramics entrepreneur whose plate featuring the image of an African in chains saying: "Am I Not a Man and a Brother?" was sold across the country; and William Wilberforce, the member of Parliament who took the abolitionist cause to the House of Commons. (See the feature "Visual Evidence: The Horrors of the Middle Passage.")

• abolitionist
A man or woman who advocated an end to the practice of slavery. In the late eighteenth century a powerful abolitionist movement was created in England.

After the publication of the *Interesting Narrative* in 1789, Equiano spent three years touring England, Scotland, and Ireland speaking at antislavery meetings. He was hugely successful in advancing the cause of abolitionism while doing well for himself financially. Book royalties made him the wealthiest black man in England; his property was moderately increased by the family income of the English wife he married in 1792.

As he began an English family, Equiano remained politically active. Wilberforce had decided to press only for the abolition of the slave trade, not of the condition of slavery itself. This more limited agenda had a better chance in Parliament. Many members thought it was permissible to stop slaves from being seized and transported but did not think it proper for the state to interfere in existing property relations, even when the property in question consisted of human beings.

Even with this more limited agenda, the abolition of the slave trade took much longer than its proponents had hoped. In fact, when Equiano passed away prematurely in 1797, he was still waiting. The radicalism of the French Revolution led the government to look on political reform with deep suspicion. Equiano even removed the names of some of his more radical subscribers from the *Interesting Narrative* to avoid guilt by association (see Chapter 22).

It was not until 1807 that Parliament finally passed the **Act for the Abolition of the Slave Trade,** ending the trade in slaves among British subjects. Another whole generation of Africans had to wait before slavery itself was abolished in the British Empire, an advance that did not help slaves in non-British territories such as Cuba, Brazil, and the southern United States. Meanwhile, the British government, with the full backing of public opinion, pursued a global campaign to eliminate slave markets. That was a significant turnabout, considering that Britain had perhaps benefited more than any other nation from four centuries of the Atlantic slave trade.

● **Act for the Abolition of the Slave Trade** Law passed in 1807 by English Parliament ending the trade in slaves among British subjects. The British government then used the Royal Navy to suppress the slave trade internationally.

THE HORRORS OF THE MIDDLE PASSAGE

Britstrisht abolitionists were well aware of the power of visual images to advance their cause, anticipating that a shocked public would pressure Parliament to end the trade in slaves. Political cartoons were one way to both express and influence public opinion. The cartoon below refers to the case of a slave trader, Captain John Kimber, who was accused in 1792 of torturing a 15-year-old African girl to death when she refused to "dance" for him. ("Dancing" was a required physical activity for slaves when they were

The ABOLITION of the SLAVE TRADE.
Or the Inhumanity of Dealers in human flesh exemplified in Capt.ⁿ Kimber's treatment of a Young Negro Girl of 15 for her Virgin Modesty

(Library of Congress)

Captain Kimber is clearly depicted as being responsible for the abuse of the African girl. He seems to be enjoying himself.

For his portrayal of the victim the artist chose to use dark ink, obscuring her features. What effect does this technique have on the viewer?

The sailor pulling the rope says: "Damn me if I like it I have a good mind to let go." The other two sailors say: "My Eyes Jack our Girls at Wapping are never flogged for their modesty," and "By G-d that's too bad if he had taken her to bed to him it would be well enough. Split me, I'm almost sick of this Black Business."

QUESTION FOR ANALYSIS

Of these two images, which gave the more powerful indictment of the slave trade?

brought up to the ship's deck for exercise; slave captains routinely enforced that rule with the lash.) Kimber was acquitted, and the sailors who gave evidence against him were convicted of perjury. Abolitionists were outraged and their opponents encouraged by this legal ruling. The title of the illustration reads: "The Abolition of the Slave Trade, or the inhumanity of the dealers in human flesh exemplified in Captn Kimbers treatment of a Young Negro Girl of 15 for her virgin modesty."

The image below, the slave ship *Brooks,* was widely circulated by abolitionists to show (in the words of a modern historian) "that the slaver itself was a place of barbarity, indeed a huge, complex technologically sophisticated instrument of torture."* First circu-

_____
*Marcus Rediker, *The Slave Ship: A Human History* (New York: Viking, 2007), p. 309.

lated by the Society for Effecting the Abolition of the Slave Trade in 1788, this engraving was widely known across Britain and the United States. Its depiction of a "close packed" slave ship made "an instantaneous impression of horror upon all who saw it" according to Thomas Clarkson, a prominent abolitionist who wrote the text that accompanied this image. Clarkson interviewed British sailors in slave ports like Bristol and Liverpool who told him bloodcurdling stories of inhumanity on ships like the *Brooks* where, another abolitionist wrote, "human creatures [were] reduced nearly to the state of being buried alive." The *Brooks* made ten voyages to Africa between 1781 and 1804, its captains purchasing 5,163 slaves, of whom 4,559 survived the Atlantic crossing. This image of the *Brooks* undoubtedly contributed to the abolition of the British slave trade in 1807.

Each adult African man aboard the *Brooks* was allocated a plank six feet by sixteen inches with no more than two feet six inches of vertical space, too little to allow him to sit up. Not shown are the tubs of excrement which fouled the air in the slave hold.

(Thomas Clarkson, *The History of the Rise, Progress, and Accomplishment of the Slave-Trade by the British Parliament*, 1808)

The artist who produced this engraving carefully drew every individual African on board, showing each wearing only a loincloth, and the men with their ankles chained.

Shown here are 482 slaves. On an earlier voyage, before a 1788 law that regulated the slave trade, one *Brooks* captain had crammed 609 Africans in this same space: 351 men, 127 women, 90 boys, and 41 girls.

Chapter Review

CL Download the MP3 audio file of the Chapter Review and listen to it on the go.

The Atlantic system as it developed in the seventeenth and eighteenth century encompassed a broad range of economic, environmental, cultural, and political interactions. Olaudah Equiano experienced many different facets of Atlantic life, but his story points most clearly to the centrality of slavery. By remaking himself as a free man and an abolitionist, Equiano played a pioneering role in purging slavery from the human story. The *Interesting Narrative of the Life of Olaudah Equiano, or Gustavus Vassa, the African* was a substantial contribution to that cause, guaranteeing the author's place in history.

 How were existing African economic and political systems integrated into the Atlantic plantation system? What were the effects of this interaction on Africans and African societies?

On the eve of the Atlantic slave trade, African history was unfolding in diverse ways. Most Africans lived in small societies where they farmed, tended their livestock, raised their children, and managed their own affairs through discussion and consensus. Large African states also arose from the cultural and economic interchange between African groups, as in the Great Lakes, or from trade across ecological frontiers, as in the Sahel. When African states were in direct contact with Asia and Europe, as were the Songhai Empire and the Swahili city-states, it was most often through Muslim routes of trade and pilgrimage. The rise of the Atlantic slave system transformed those African societies, especially in West Africa, into suppliers or sources of slaves for American plantations. While wealth and power went to those Africans who seized the opportunity to benefit from slavery and the slave trade, participation in the Atlantic system left much of Africa more violent, insecure, and less productive than before.

What were the major social and economic features of the plantation complex in the West Indies and on the American mainland? What cultural patterns were associated with forced African migration to the Americas?

The plantation complex of the Atlantic world, especially the sugar plantations of the West Indies, represented something new in world history: an agro-industrial enterprise geared specifically for commercial export markets. Sugar planters imported most of their labor, food, and equipment and focused on producing a single crop for distant markets. As a result, sugar became an essential part of the European diet. The cultural outcomes of the plantation system were complex. As in the mainland colonies, new societies emerged from the mixture of African, Amerindian, and European cultural and biological elements (see Chapter 18). Maroon communities were one form of resistance; persistence of African cultural traditions was another means by which slaves could assert their dignity and humanity. Meanwhile, out on the ocean, sailors, fishermen, pirates, and even a slave like Olaudah Equiano sometimes found greater opportunities than were available on land.

 ## How did the plantation complex affect political and economic developments in Europe in the eighteenth century?

Events in the Atlantic reinforced the shifting balance of power in Europe. Buoyed by the profits of sugar plantations, the French and British became the key players in the European power struggle by the late seventeenth century. Economic competition in the age of mercantilism set them into a conflict that culminated in the Seven Years' War (1756–1763), fought not only in the Atlantic but also in North America, continental Europe, and South Asia. British victory led to a British mastery of the seas of which Olaudah Equiano, having fought in the war, was quite proud.

 WEB RESOURCES

Pronunciation Guide

Interactive Maps

MAP 19.1 West African States and Trade, ca. 1500

MAP 19.2 The Atlantic Slave Trade

Primary Sources

Chapter Objectives

ACE Multiple-Choice Quiz

Flashcards

For Further Reference

Anstey, Roger. *The Atlantic Slave Trade and British Abolition, 1760–1810*. New York: Macmillan, 1975.

Carretta, Vincent. *Equiano, the African: Biography of a Self-Made Man*. New York: Penguin Books, 2007.

Curtin, Philip. *Africa Remembered: Narratives by West Africans from the Era of the Slave Trade*. 2d ed. Long Grove, Ill.: Waveland Press, 1997.

Curtin, Philip. *The Rise and Fall of the Plantation Complex: Essays in Atlantic History*. 2d ed. New York: Cambridge University Press, 1998.

Eltis, David. *Economic Growth and the Ending of the Trans-Atlantic Slave Trade*. New York: Oxford University Press, 1987.

Equiano, Olaudah. *The Interesting Narrative of the Life of Olaudah Equiano, or Gustavus Vassa, the African*. Edited by Vincent Carretta. 2d ed. New York: Penguin Putnam, 2003.

Lovejoy, Paul. *Transformations in Slavery: A History of Slavery in Africa*. 2d ed. New York: Cambridge University Press, 2000.

Mintz, Sidney. *Sweetness and Power: The Place of Sugar in Modern History*. New York: Penguin Books, 1985.

Northrup, David. *Africa's Discovery of Europe, 1450–1850*. New York: Oxford University Press, 2002.

Patterson, Orlando. *Slavery and Social Death: A Comparative Study*. Cambridge: Harvard University Press, 1985.

Rediker, Marcus. *The Slave Ship: A Human History*. New York: Viking, 2007.

Thornton, John. *Africa and Africans in the Making of the Atlantic World, 1400–1800*. 2d ed. New York: Cambridge University Press, 1998.

Websites

African Studies Library
(http://www.bu.edu/library/asl/index.shtml).   Boston University offers a searchable database of information about Africa.

Slavery, Abolition, and Emancipation
(http://www.brycchancarey.com/slavery/links.htm).
An extensive set of links hosted by a noted scholar of abolitionism.

The Transatlantic Slave Trade
(http://www.inmotionaame.org/migrations).   Portal to a wide variety of resources, including African experiences of slavery and the slave trade.

CHAPTER
20

Empires in Early Modern Asia, 1650–1818

The British were just consolidating their power in northeastern India in the late 1780s when a young Chinese sailor named **Xie Qinggao** (1765?–1821) visited Calcutta, India. Xie had been born in the Guangdong province of south China, a region with a long history of commercial interaction with foreign ships. His life was transformed when, at the age of 18, he was involved in a shipwreck and rescued by a Portuguese vessel. His subsequent travels extended beyond coastal China, the Japanese islands, the Korean peninsula, and Southeast Asia to include the entire Indian Ocean commercial world and Europe itself. Years later, he recalled his impressions of British rule in India:

(© North Wind Picture Archives)

SOUTHERN CHINESE SAILOR IN LOCAL ATTIRE, 1800s

Bengal is governed by the British. The military governor, who is named "La" ["Lord"] rules from Calcutta. There is a small walled city inside of which live officials and the military while merchants reside outside the wall in the surrounding district. . . . The buildings and towers form cloud-like clusters, the gardens and pavilions are strange and beautiful. . . . More than 10,000 English live there with fifty to sixty thousand soldiers from the local people. . . . When the top officials go out on parade it is particularly impressive. In the front are six men on horseback . . . all wearing big red robes. The two men on the left and the right are dressed just like the "La," but his chest is covered with strange embroidery that looks like a fortunetelling sign. . . . The local people are of several types. The Bengalis are relatively numerous, and the Brahmin caste is particularly well off. . . . The rich among them have clothing, food and dwellings like those of the English that are beautiful and impressive. The poor are almost naked . . . taking cloth several inches wide to wrap around their waists to cover their lower halves.[1]

This icon will direct you to interactive activities and study materials on the *Voyages* website: **www.cengage.com/history/hansen/voyages1e**

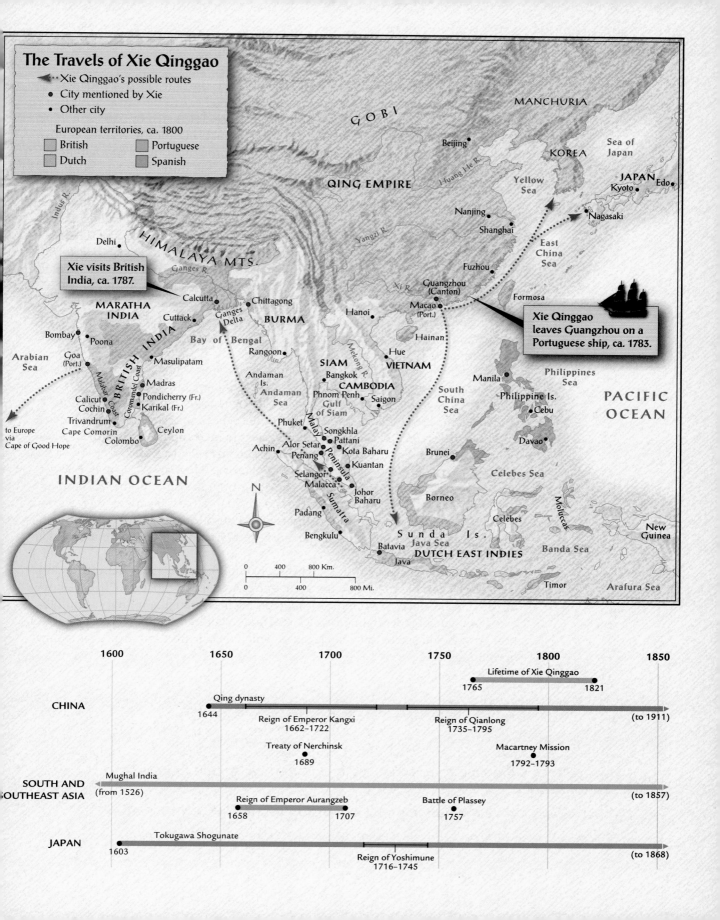

The Travels of Xie Qinggao

- Xie Qinggao's possible routes
- City mentioned by Xie
- Other city

European territories, ca. 1800
- British
- Dutch
- Portuguese
- Spanish

Xie visits British India, ca. 1787.

Xie Qinggao leaves Guangzhou on a Portuguese ship, ca. 1783.

GOBI

MANCHURIA

Beijing

QING EMPIRE

KOREA

Sea of Japan

JAPAN

Kyoto

Edo

Nagasaki

Huang He R.

Yellow Sea

Nanjing

Shanghai

East China Sea

Yangzi R.

Fuzhou

Xi R.

Guangzhou (Canton)

Macao (Port.)

Formosa

Delhi

HIMALAYA MTS.

Ganges R.

Calcutta

Chittagong

MARATHA INDIA

Cuttack

Ganges Delta

BURMA

Hanoi

Hainan

Bombay

Poona

Bay of Bengal

Rangoon

Hue

VIETNAM

Manila

Philippine Sea

Indus R.

Arabian Sea

Goa (Port.)

BRITISH INDIA

Masulipatam

SIAM

Bangkok

South China Sea

Philippine Is.

PACIFIC OCEAN

Cebu

Calicut

Cochin

Madras

Pondicherry (Fr.)

Karikal (Fr.)

Andaman Is.

Andaman Sea

Phnom Penh

CAMBODIA

Saigon

Malabar Coast

Coromandel Coast

Trivandrum

Cape Comorin

Ceylon

Colombo

Gulf of Siam

Phuket

Songkhla

Pattani

Kota Baharu

Kuantan

Brunei

Davao

to Europe via Cape of Good Hope

INDIAN OCEAN

Achin

Alor Setar

Penang

Malay Peninsula

Selangor

Malacca

Johor Baharu

Celebes Sea

Borneo

Celebes

Moluccas

New Guinea

N

Padang

Sumatra

Bengkulu

Batavia

Java

Sunda Is.

Java Sea

DUTCH EAST INDIES

Banda Sea

Timor

Arafura Sea

0   400   800 Km.

0   400   800 Mi.

	1600	1650	1700	1750	1800	1850

Lifetime of Xie Qinggao
1765 — 1821

CHINA

Qing dynasty
1644

Reign of Emperor Kangxi
1662–1722

Reign of Qianlong
1735–1795

(to 1911)

Treaty of Nerchinsk
1689

Macartney Mission
1792–1793

SOUTH AND SOUTHEAST ASIA

Mughal India
(from 1526)

(to 1857)

Reign of Emperor Aurangzeb
1658 — 1707

Battle of Plassey
1757

JAPAN

Tokugawa Shogunate
1603

(to 1868)

Reign of Yoshimune
1716–1745

● **Xie Qinggao** (1765?–1821) Sailor from southern China who traveled across the Indian Ocean and throughout Europe. After becoming blind, Xie retired from sailing and dictated his story, published as *Hai-Lu,* or *Record of Sea Journeys.*

Xie Qinggao (shee-ay ching-GOW) was living in the Portuguese settlement of Macao, working as a translator because blindness had ended his career as a sailor, when a visitor from a neighboring Chinese province, fascinated by Xie's stories of his adventurous sailor's life, decided to record them. If not for the visitor's curiosity, Xie's story, like that of most ordinary people throughout history, would never have been recorded. By 1820, when Xie recorded this story in his *Record of Sea Journeys* the British had conquered all of South Asia.

Xie's presence in Calcutta was part of an age-old trading network that connected the South China Sea with ports in Southeast Asia, India, the Persian Gulf, and East Africa. That network existed before the arrival of Portuguese ships in the sixteenth century and continued to exist even as the Dutch, British, and French developed more aggressive and heavily armed commercial organizations (see Chapter 16). But the officials of the British East India Company described by Xie Qinggao (called "Company men") were representative of an important new phase of this history. In their conquest of Bengal the British were striking at the authority of the Mughal Empire and so, for the first time, directly challenging one of the major Asian land-based empires.

Indeed, the creation and maintenance of empire were a consistent political theme in early modern South and East Asia. The Manchu emperors of the Qing (ching) dynasty, ruling not just China but also extensive Central Asian territories, controlled the greatest land-based empire of the age. As Qing armies and diplomats extended their influence to the east, they came into increasing contact with emissaries of the Russian Empire, which was expanding into Central Asia from the west. Meanwhile, the British were moving to supplant the Mughals as the major power of South Asia. Taken together, the expansion of the British and Russian Empires showed the increasing influence of Europe in Asian affairs. Japanese rulers, however, resisted these eighteenth-century trends, consolidating power on their own islands rather than seeking further territory, and rejecting European influence as a matter of state policy.

This chapter focuses on the expansion of empires in the late seventeenth and eighteenth centuries in East, South, and Central Asia. In the process we will see how imperial leaders had to contend with factors such as changing military technologies, commercial growth, increasing social and religious interactions, and population growth and ecological change, all of which might affect the success or failure of their policies.

Focus Questions

 How did the Qing emperors build and maintain their empire in East and Central Asia?

 What factors drove Russian imperial expansion in the eighteenth century?

What were the principal causes of the decline of Mughal power, and how were the British able to replace the Mughals as the dominant power in South Asia?

 In comparison with the Qing, Russian, and British Empires, what were some unique features of early modern Japanese history?

●The Power of the Qing Dynasty, 1644–1796

By the early seventeenth century underlying weaknesses made the Ming dynasty in China vulnerable to invasion and conquest (see Chapter 16). In 1644 Manchu armies from Manchuria to the northeast took Beijing and established the Qing dynasty. Qing emperors ruled China from 1644 to 1911.

From 1683 to 1796, just three long-ruling emperors ruled Qing China, bringing remarkable political stability to the empire. It was a time of explosive population growth, economic expansion, and intellectual and artistic dynamism. It was also at this time that imperial China expanded to its greatest extent, encompassing parts of Central Asia and Tibet and bringing the island of Taiwan under Qing control.

Establishment of Qing Rule, 1636–1661

The ancestors of the Manchu were steppe nomads who lived to the northeast of China beyond the Great Wall (see Map 20.1). By the sixteenth century some Chinese farmers had moved onto this frontier, and some Manchu had taken up agriculture. By the late Ming period Chinese literacy and Confucian philosophy were spreading among the Manchu.

Earlier Ming officials, using a time-honored strategy for maintaining peace along the borders, had bestowed favors on some Manchu leaders, such as the right to wear elaborate dragon-patterned robes made of silk. The Manchu in turn emulated Chinese-style imperial governance even while maintaining their own language and culture, including nomadic traditions such as cavalry warfare and a love of hunting. In the 1590s Ming generals called on the Manchu armies to help resist an attempted Japanese invasion (see Chapter 16). Unfortunately for the Ming, the previously divided Manchu armies united under a single ruler, who declared himself leader of the **Qing dynasty** and organized his fighters into eight "banners," named for the color of the flags that the different regiments carried in battle. As the Manchu army grew in strength and the Ming declined, some Mongol and Chinese generals allied themselves with the Qing (meaning "Brilliant"), keeping their own identities under their unique regimental banners.

The Manchu path to Beijing became clear in 1644 when one of China's own rebel armies stormed the capital and the last Ming emperor committed suicide. The Manchu soon established their power over Beijing and the north, but it took them close to four decades to establish themselves as masters of China. Ming holdouts waged fierce battles against Qing forces, especially in the south. But the Qing used diplomacy as well as force in dealing with the resistance. Chinese generals who

● **Qing dynasty** (1644–1911) Sometimes called the Manchu dynasty after the Manchurian origins of its rulers. Qing rule extended from Beijing as far as Mongolia and Tibet.

surrendered were well treated, and the banner system allowed Chinese forces to be incorporated into the Qing military system.

Qing rulers acted quickly to establish Confucianism as the official state ideology and to bring Chinese scholar-officials into the imperial bureaucracy, knowing that stable administration would require their support and collaboration. They retained the examination system and the Chinese system of ministries, assigning one Chinese and one Manchu official to each. The Chinese scholar-officials had the requisite knowledge and experience, but the Manchu officials, thought to be more loyal, were there to supervise their work.

Even while Qing rulers made political adjustments as part of their new role as the ruling elite, they carefully guarded core elements of Manchu culture and identity. Intermarriage between Manchu and Han Chinese was forbidden. Though fluent in Chinese, the Manchu elite continued to speak their own language and to practice their own form of Buddhism, of Central Asian origin. Qing emperors spent their

🌐 MAP 20.1
The Qing Empire, 1644–1783

Beginning from their homeland in the north, the Manchu rulers of the Qing dynasty not only conquered China but also built an empire stretching far into Central Asia, matching the contemporary expansion of the Russian Empire. The Qing Empire grew to more than twice the size of its Ming predecessor. Tibetans, Mongols, and other subject peoples were ruled indirectly through local authorities loyal to the Qing emperors.

 Interactive Map

The Qing Empire
- Qing homeland
- Dominant by 1644
- Dominant by 1659
- Acquired from Russia, 1689
- Dominant by 1783
- Principal tributary states
- ⌐⌐⌐⌐ Great Wall

summers at the great palace of Chengde (chungh-deh), beyond the Great Wall, where horsemanship, hunting, and camping were reminders of nomadic life.

While the Manchu made few efforts to impose their own culture on their Chinese subjects, the Qing did decree that all Chinese men had to cut their hair in the distinctive Manchu style, called a *queue* (kyoo), with a shaved forehead and a single long braid in back. Chinese men reluctantly complied, saying it was either "lose your hair or lose your head."

The Age of Three Emperors, 1661–1799

The success of the Qing emperors in retaining their own culture while earning the cooperation and loyalty of Han Chinese subjects was illustrated by the social, economic, and intellectual achievements of the late seventeenth and eighteenth centuries. When **Emperor Kangxi** (r. 1662–1722) ascended the Dragon Throne in 1662, the fate of the Qing was still in doubt. After six decades of Kangxi's rule, however, the Qing had established themselves as worthy successors of earlier Chinese dynasties and as masters of one of the greatest empires the world had ever known. His successors Yongzheng (r. 1723–1735) and Qianlong (r. 1736–1795) consolidated that achievement. Together, these three emperors ruled the world's largest and richest state for more than 130 years.

Kangxi's first order of business was to suppress Ming resistance in the south, a task that was successfully concluded by 1683. Since some Ming rebels had fled to the island of Taiwan, Qing forces followed them there and brought Taiwan under the control of Beijing for the first time. At the same time, Kangxi (kang-shee), aspiring to be a "sage ruler," studied the Confucian classics closely, and official portraits often show him in scholarly poses. Because the Manchu were of "barbarian" origin, it was important for Kangxi to convince his Chinese subjects, especially the scholar-officials, that his rule was soundly based on Confucian principles.

Kangxi adhered to the Confucian belief that land and agriculture are the ultimate source of all wealth and that a large population is the most important sign of prosperity. In a demographic sense, Qing China was prosperous indeed. In the early modern period China's population boomed, growing from about 100 million in 1500 to about 250 million by 1750. One result was the growth of cities, with Beijing, Nanjing (nahn-JING), and Guangzhou (gwahng-jo) all with over a million residents. Population growth was made possible by increasing agriculture productivity. Farmers brought new areas into production, and the planting of American crops like peanuts, sweet potatoes, and maize allowed their fields to expand into previously marginal areas. Population growth in China was therefore another important outcome of the Columbian exchange (see Chapter 15).

The emperor Yongzheng promoted an empirical form of Confucianism, encouraging scholars to gather data in minute detail from across the empire and sponsoring the compilation of an 800,000-page encyclopedia to guide officials in formulating policies and applying them across so vast and complex an empire. By ordering a thorough census of landholding and basing rural taxation on accurate land registers, Yongzheng both increased state revenue through more efficient tax collection and spread the burden of taxation more equitably between commoners and gentry.

It was during the reign of Qianlong (chee-YEN-loong) that the power of Qing China reached its height. Coming to the throne as a young man in 1736, **Qianlong** ruled for sixty years before abdicating in 1795: true to Confucian ideals of filial piety, he did not want his reign to exceed the length of that of his grandfather,

● **Emperor Kangxi** (r. 1662–1722) One of the most powerful and long-ruling emperors in Chinese imperial history, Kangxi extended the Qing Empire, expanded the economy, and cultivated an image as a Confucian scholar and sage.

● **Qianlong** (r. 1736–1795) Qing emperor who ruled during the empire's greatest territorial expansion and prosperity. Late in his reign, corruption began to infect the state bureaucracy. Rejected an English attempt to establish diplomatic relations.

Kangxi. During these six decades the commercial economy became even more dynamic. A mainstay of Chinese production was luxury goods for export, especially silk and porcelain. Vast quantities of silver from Japan and Spanish America continued to flow into Qing China, providing capital for public works and private investment. Some Chinese farmers found that tobacco, another American crop, was a profitable addition to their fields. Artisans and small-scale entrepreneurs expanded the glass-making, brewing, and coal-mining industries. Thus eighteenth-century China retained its long-established position as the leading industrial economy in the world.

The area of greatest commercialization in the eighteenth century was the lower **Yangzi River Valley,** around the important city of Nanjing, where the production of cotton textiles was emerging as a major industry. Unlike silk, which remained a luxury product, cotton cloth became sufficiently inexpensive that it found a market among all but the poorest Chinese consumers, bringing with it the advantages of being comfortable, durable, and easy to clean.

● **Yangzi River Valley** Agriculturally productive region with the important urban center of Nanjing. The Yangzi River delta was the site of strong industrial and commercial growth in the eighteenth century.

The expansion of the cotton industry reinforced traditional gender relations. All Chinese women were expected to work with their hands. Elite women, who were not expected to make a financial contribution to the household, often produced beautiful embroideries. For rural women, the tending of silkworms and the spinning of silk thread was considered both a virtuous activity and one that helped the family with additional income. This division of labor was summed up in the expression "Men plow, women weave."[2] The transition to the spinning and weaving of cotton within the household meshed neatly with earlier practices and ideals. In more commercialized regions of China such as the Yangzi (yang-zuh) delta, spinning and weaving cotton cloth helped drive economic growth.

Chinese women did not receive much benefit from this work. Upon marriage young women left their own families to join their husband's household, where they were often at the mercy of demanding mothers-in-law. As the economy became more commercialized, young women could spend more time spinning and weaving cloth than working in the fields. But while contributing to the income of their husband's family, they did not necessarily gain any additional wealth or status for themselves.

In one way, in fact, these activities might have made women's situation worse, since increased production within the household may have increased the severity of footbinding. The practice of binding young girls' feet tightly in cloth to reshape them into small points was an old one. Originally it had been an elite practice; by the time of the Ming dynasty footbinding had spread throughout the Han Chinese population. Young girls' feet were broken and compressed into 3-inch balls by binding the four smaller toes under the sole of the foot and forcing the big toe and heel together. Women suffered from constant pain, limited mobility, and frequent infections.

Qing officials were disgusted by the practice, and Manchu women never bound their own daughters' feet. The cultural traditions of the steppe required that women be able to ride horses and perform other strenuous physical tasks. But the practice was so well established among the Chinese that Qing officials did not try to abolish it.

On a more positive note, there seems to have been a decline in female infanticide during this period. The greater financial contribution made by women in textile production may have softened the attitude that boys are a blessing while girls are a burden. Elite women had opportunities for education and artistic expression. Unlike the sons of elite households, who were prepared by tutors for the state examinations, girls were educated to be refined in language and behavior and to bring honor to their husbands and their household. Many of the finest poems from Qing times were written by women.

The Weaving of Flower'd Silks, two Women at Work.

■ **Silk Weaving**
Silk weaving was a highly profitable enterprise in eighteenth-century China. Women played a central role in all stages of silk production, operating large and complex looms such as the one pictured here. The spinning of cotton thread and weaving of cotton cloth were also increasingly important at this time, and women dominated production in the cotton industry as well. (Stapleton Collection/ The Bridgeman Art Library)

Historians have wondered why the dynamic commercial economy in eighteenth-century China did not lead to a full-fledged industrial revolution. Older explanations pointed to the Confucian value system, which emphasized order over innovation and regarded commerce as a low-status occupation. More recently, scholars have focused on demographic factors. China had such a large pool of cheap labor that entrepreneurs had little incentive to invest in laborsaving methods of production. Women who spun and wove at home, and artisans in the cities who produced finished and dyed cloth, worked efficiently for little pay. Human labor therefore remained the dominant form of energy used for textile production. Meanwhile, by the end of Qianlong's reign in 1799, the small island of Britain on the other side of Eurasia was witnessing increasingly effective experiments with new sources of energy and more efficient methods of production (see Chapter 23).

The Qing Empire and Its Borderlands

Territorial expansion was one of the greatest Qing achievements. The emperors used both force and diplomacy to extend their power. The more effective use of guns and cannon, part of the "gunpowder revolution" of early modern Eurasia (see Chapter 17), was complemented by the use of the banner system to incorporate frontier peoples into the empire.

In the century following 1683, when the Manchu had secured control of southern China and Taiwan, the Qing Empire doubled in size. Manchu officials and generals then had to deal with the age-old Chinese problem of bringing stability to the unsettled western and northern fringes of their empire. That meant asserting their control over Mongolian nomads and Turkish-speaking Muslim peoples to their west, stationing soldiers as far away as Tibet, and contending with the challenge of the Russian Empire as it expanded into Central Asia.

The main threat came from the Zunghars, Central Asian Mongols who were devoted to the Tibetan branch of Buddhism. The spiritual leader of the Tibetans and of the Zunghar Mongols was the Dalai Lama (DAH-lie LAH-mah). The Manchu used both force and subterfuge against the Zunghars, sending an army to Tibet but also supporting one of the rival contenders for the title of Dalai Lama, correctly assuming that their support would win his loyalty. With Tibet in a tributary relationship to Beijing, the Zunghars were weakened and finally destroyed in 1757. Qianlong issued a genocide order: most of the men were slaughtered (a few survived by crossing into Russian-controlled territory), the women and children were enslaved, and the lands were repopulated with sedentary peoples, such as the Muslim farmers still found in China's western Xinjiang (shin-jyahng) province today. Qing authority now extended far beyond the Great Wall; after 1757 a Chinese dynasty was never again threatened by steppe nomads.

In other situations Qing officials relied on diplomacy. Like the Ming, they used the tributary system to organize their relations with states and societies outside their direct control. Annual tribute missions to Beijing continued to symbolize the subordination even of powerful leaders like the emperors of Korea and Vietnam, who maintained their own political autonomy through ritual recognition of the Qing as overlords (see Chapter 16). Tribute missions were also sent by non-Han groups living on the geographic margins of Chinese society, such as in the hills, jungles, and steppes.

The Train to Tibet

The $4.2 billion railway to Tibet made its inaugural run in July 2006. The route from Beijing to Lhasa, the Tibetan capital, takes passengers to a height of over 16,000 feet, skirting magnificent Himalayan peaks. Passengers are given supplementary oxygen for altitude sickness, while a complex engineering system keeps the tracks level as they cross long stretches of permafrost, where the ground alternately melts and freezes.

Always anxious to demonstrate their nation's technical competence, Chinese government leaders celebrated the achievement. The train to Tibet is just one part of a broader agenda for economic development that is spurring Han Chinese emigration to areas that were once remote borderlands of the Qing Empire. There are critics of the project, however. Human rights observers worry that Han Chinese immigrants seeking economic opportunity in Tibet are a threat to traditional Tibetan language, culture, and religion. Critics of the new railway also fear that economic development and resource extraction will upset the delicate environmental balance of the Tibetan plateau.

The controversy exploded into violence early in 2008. With the upcoming summer Olympic Games in Beijing focusing world attention on the People's Republic of China, Tibetan protestors took to the streets, replacing Chinese flags with Tibetan ones and, in some cases, attacking Han Chinese residents. Supporters of Tibetan autonomy dispute the Chinese claim on Tibet, arguing that there was never any direct imperial control of Tibetan affairs and that Chinese rule dates only from the invasion of the People's Liberation Army in 1950 and the suppression of a 1959 rebellion that forced the Dalai Lama, Tibet's spiritual leader, into exile in India.

The historical reality was more complex than either side would acknowledge. While Qing emperors did station soldiers on the Tibetan plateau, they ruled indirectly through Tibetan authorities, and regarded the Tibetan lamas as spiritual mentors. In fact, the model of Tibetan autonomy within the context of the Chinese state, a position advocated by the Dalai Lama, is consistent with previous imperial practice, though the Chinese government continues to insist on its unqualified sovereignty over the region.

Whatever political compromises might be made between the guardians of China's territorial integrity and the forces of Tibetan nationalism, the train to Tibet remains a symbol of the demographic changes that seem all but unstoppable as more Han Chinese move west looking for economic opportunity.

Though Tibet and the western region of Xinjiang had been conquered and brought under Qing rule, these areas were not, like the Chinese provinces, administered by scholar-officials. Rather, existing systems of political authority were allowed to continue under Manchu supervision as long as taxes were paid, order was kept, and loyalty to the Qing was maintained. For example, the Qing appointed a Tibetan official to communicate with the emperor on Tibetan affairs but otherwise did nothing to supplant the power and influence of powerful Buddhist monks. (See the feature "World History in Today's World: The Train to Tibet.") Tibetan and Mongol emissaries were often received at Chengde, the Manchu summer palace, rather than in the Forbidden City in Beijing.

Unlike the Ming, however, the Qing emperors were not interested in asserting their cultural superiority over these tributary societies. Ruling over a diverse empire, the Ming had actively assimilated linguistically and culturally foreign peoples into Han Chinese language and culture. But the Qing viewed China as just one distinct part of a wider Manchu empire. Eighteenth-century Qing maps had Chinese labels for Chinese provinces and Manchu labels for non-Chinese areas, illustrating that Qianlong saw himself not as a Chinese emperor but as a Manchu emperor whose authority included Chinese subjects, among others.

Trade and Foreign Relations

Not all of the Qing Empire's external relations could be encompassed within the tributary system. A growing European presence challenged traditional forms of diplomacy. Though the Qing quickly recognized that the Russians needed to be treated on more or less equal terms, they proved reluctant to grant diplomatic equality to the English and other European powers arriving by sea.

One challenge was from the Russian Empire, which was expanding into this region, its eastward thrust paralleling that of the Qing and its soldiers using similar gunpowder technologies. Kangxi was concerned that the Russians might ally with the steppe nomads against him. After some skirmishes along the border, the Russians and the Chinese agreed to the **Treaty of Nerchinsk** in 1689, according to which the Qing recognized Russian claims to the west of Mongolia, while the Russians agreed to disband some settlements to the east. Yongzheng and Qianlong continued this policy of avoiding conflict with the Russians through treaties that fixed the boundary between the two empires. The few Jesuit priests remaining in Beijing were now joined by a handful of Russian Orthodox ones; converts to Christianity remained very few (see Chapter 16).

Unlike the Russians, other European visitors came by sea. Like their late Ming predecessors, the three great Qing emperors looked on oceanic trade with suspicion. European trade was focused on south China, especially Guangzhou (called Canton by the Europeans), which had remained loyal to the Ming after the fall of Beijing. Qing emperors associated Guangzhou with "greedy" traders rather than sober scholar-officials and with adventurous sailors and emigrants like Xie Qinggao (who was born and raised in this area) rather than stable and dependable village-bound farmers.

As a result, officials reorganized the trade at Guangzhou around a system of official monopolies. European trade was restricted to this single port, and European traders were required to deal only with state-approved firms known as *cohongs*. Since the cohong merchants had a monopoly on trade with Europeans, they found it easy to fix prices and amass huge profits.

The British in particular were frustrated with the structure of the China trade. Having little to trade for Chinese goods but silver, they saw the continued outflow of money toward Asia as a major fiscal problem. Conflicts between British merchants and sailors and Chinese officials and residents of Guangzhou became more common, and tensions increased.

Finally the British government, responding to complaints from some of the major trading companies, decided to try to regularize Qing/British relations through diplomacy. In 1792 King George III sent the **Macartney Mission,** led by Lord George Macartney, to negotiate the exchange of ambassadors. Macartney was allowed to proceed from Guangzhou to Beijing. In his meeting with Qianlong, Macartney refused to perform the ritual *kowtow* of full prostration before the emperor, agreeing only to drop to one knee before him, as he would before his own king. He asked that more ports be opened to foreign trade and that restrictions on trade be removed.

• Treaty of Nerchinsk 1689 treaty between Romanov Russia and Qing China that fixed their Central Asian frontier.

• Macartney Mission The 1792–1793 mission in which Lord Macartney was sent by King George III of England to establish permanent diplomatic relations with the Qing Empire. Because he could not accept the British king as his equal, the Qianlong emperor politely refused.

Qianlong's response to King George III made it clear that diplomatic equality between them was impossible: "We have never valued ingenious articles, nor do we have the slightest need of your country's manufactures. Therefore, O King, as regards your request to send someone to remain at the capital, while it is not in harmony with the regulations of the Celestial Empire we also feel very much that it is of no advantage to your country."[3] Qianlong's letter made it clear that he still saw China as the Middle Kingdom, the center of the civilized world, and he insisted that the British should appear before him only if bearing tribute in recognition of his superior position.

Qianlong's attitude was understandable. The Qing controlled the largest and wealthiest empire on earth and had no need to look beyond their borders for resources. True, there were signs that all was not well. Inefficiency and corruption were creeping back into the system, and the power of the eunuchs was once again increasing at court as Qianlong grew old and more apt to delegate his immense authority to others. Since there were no real improvements in agricultural technology, the food supply could be increased only by bringing more marginal lands under cultivation. Ecological problems resulted. Deforestation led to increased silting up of rivers and devastating floods. As peasant rebellions became more common, some rebels saw the non-Chinese Manchu as illegitimate and dreamed of restoring the Ming dynasty.

When Qianlong abdicated the Dragon Throne in 1796, however, the gravity of these internal challenges was not yet clear, nor could he have anticipated how powerful the British would become when fifty years later they returned to impose their demands by force (see Chapter 26). As the nineteenth century began, Qing officials still believed that old solutions were sufficient to meet current challenges. But the threat to imperial China no longer came from steppe nomads, and in the nineteenth century no Great Wall could keep out the new invaders from the sea.

CL **Primary Source:**
Edict on Trade with Great Britain
Emperor Qianlong declines Britain's request for increased trade in China.

The Russian Empire, 1725–1800

Like the Chinese, the Russian people had long experience with steppe nomads. The Russian state had been founded as part of the dissolution of the Mongol Empire, and Russian leaders were conscious that control of the steppe was necessary for the security of their cultural heartland. Peter the Great had added momentum to that tradition by extending Russia's borders west, east, and south to make Russia a great power on two continents (see Chapter 17). For all the power and splendor of the Romanov court, however, conditions for the majority of Russians, serfs living in rural villages, remained grim.

Russian Imperial Expansion, 1725–1800

In the west, Russia had become the dominant power in the Baltic Sea region after Peter's army decisively defeated the Swedes in 1721. As the Polish kingdom weakened and then collapsed after the 1770s, Russia was one of the competing states, along with Prussia and Austria, sharing in its partition. The southward thrust of Russian power continued as well, largely at the expense of the Ottoman Empire. A great prize was the Crimean peninsula on the northern shore of the Black Sea, annexed by Russia in 1783 (see Map 20.2). A major trade emporium since ancient

The Russian Empire

- Russia in 1533
- Added by 1598
- Added by 1721
- Added by 1796
- ✴ Fort

PACIFIC OCEAN

Novo Arkhangelsk (Sitka)
TLINGIT

BRITISH NORTH AMERICA (CANADA)

Border set in 1826

RUSSIAN AMERICA (ALASKA)

ALEUTS

INUIT

INUIT

Bering Strait

Bering

INUIT

CHUKCHI

KORYAKS

Petropavlovsk
ALEUTS

Kamchatka Peninsula

50°N

60°N

70°N

Kolyma R.

Bering Sea

GREENLAND

ARCTIC OCEAN

Iceland

Zashiversk

Okhotsk

Sea of Okhotsk

Sakhalin I.

Arctic Circle

100°W 120°W 140°W 160°W 180° 160°E 140°E 120°E 100°E 80°E 60°E 40°E 20°E 0° 20°W 40°W 60°W 80°W

80°N

70°N

80°N

Kara Sea

Barents Sea

S I B E R I A

Yana R.

Zhigansk

Yakutsk

Lena R.

Olenek R.

Khatanga R.

EVENKI

Viluy R.

YAKUTS

LAMUTS

Amur R.

MANCHURIA

SWEDEN

NORWAY

GREAT BRITAIN

FINLAND

Arkhangelsk

Obdorsk

SAMOYEDS

OSTYAKS

Lower Tunguska R.

TUNGUSY

Nerchinsk

Yenisey R.

Ob R.

Toz R.

OSTYAKS

Bratsk

St. Petersburg

Baltic Sea

Novgorod

Riga

HOLY ROMAN EMPIRE

PRUSSIA

POLAND

AUSTRIA

HUNGARY

Moscow

Smolensk

Kiev

UKRAINIANS

Saratov

COSSACKS

COSSACKS

Dnieper R.

Dniester R.

OTTOMAN EMPIRE

Black Sea

GEORGIA

Verkhoturye

URAL MOUNTAINS

TARTARS

Tula R.

Nizhni Novgorod

Samara

Kama R.

Ural R.

Volga R.

Surgut

Kem R.

Krasnoyarsk

Irkutsk

Omsk

Biysk

Tobol R.

Ishim R.

Irtysh R.

KAZAKS

MONGOLIA

QING EMPIRE

Aral Sea

Caspian Sea

TIBET

BHUTAN

NEPAL

BURMA

AFGHANISTAN

IRAN

INDIA

⬡ Interactive Map

🌐 **MAP 20.2**
The Expansion of Russia, 1500–1800
By the end of the eighteenth century the Russian Empire extended westward into Europe, southward toward the Black Sea and Caspian Sea, and, most dramatically, eastward into Central Asia, Siberia, and the Americas.

times, the Crimea brought both strategic and economic benefits to the Russian Empire. In the late eighteenth century, the first Russian inroads were also made into the difficult mountainous terrain of the Caucasus Mountains.

In this same century the Russian Empire also continued its dramatic eastward expansion across Siberia, extending the fur-trapping frontier on which Russians had been active since the fifteenth century. The initial exploitation was not carried out by imperial forces but by wealthy Russian trading families who hired mercenary soldiers called **Cossacks** (from the Turkish word *kazakh,* meaning "free man") to extend their control. The Cossacks originated as fiercely independent horsemen, Slavic-speakers who had moved to the frontier and assimilated much of the technology and culture of their nomadic Mongol and Turkish neighbors on the steppes. The Cossack code of honor was based on strong group loyalty, tremendous skill in horsemanship, and skill with firearms. While Russian tsars used Cossack forces to conquer territories in the south, Russian fur traders relied on them in Siberia. Russian soldiers and administrators, including treasury officials sent to make sure the tsar got his share, followed the Cossacks and fur traders to the Siberian frontier, where they established more formal control.

As in North America, the fur trade required that European merchants and frontiersmen find ways to tap into indigenous expertise and labor. Indigenous Siberians, whom the Russians called the "small people of the north," were vulnerable to the military technology and diseases brought from the west. The Cossacks sometimes used compulsion to guarantee fur deliveries: if a community did not deliver their quota, they might be attacked, the women and children carried off into slavery. Though individual trappers and traders might profit by alliance with Russians, it was Russian merchants and the Russian treasury that reaped the lion's share.

As in North America, once the fur-bearing animals of a given area had been slaughtered to clothe the fashionable in Moscow, Paris, or Constantinople, the frontier moved on to virgin terrain. Thus the eastern frontier of the Russian Empire was extended to the Americas when, in 1741, the Bering Expedition crossed over into Alaska and claimed it for the tsar (see Map 20.2).

South of the Siberian frontier the Russian Empire was also establishing its influence over parts of Central Asia. Peter the Great had shown great interest in this region and thought that Russia might benefit from establishing direct trade links with India. While his armies maintained direct control over the steppes on Russia's immediate borderlands, Peter pursued a largely diplomatic strategy on the further Central Asian frontier. He ordered that young men be taught various Mongolian, Turkish, and Persian languages and sent them to the many small principalities of Central Asia as diplomatic representatives. This approach, relying on negotiation rather than force, was maintained until later Russian leaders adopted a more militarized policy in the nineteenth century. Meanwhile, as we have seen, Russia's eastward expansion brought it into contact with the Qing frontier. Skirmishes between Russian and Manchu soldiers led the emperors to approve of the negotiations that led to the Treaty of Nerchinsk.

Reform and Repression, 1750–1796

Much of the new imperial territory was acquired during the reign of **Catherine the Great** (r. 1762–1796). A German princess who married into the Romanov family and converted to the Orthodox faith, she was one of the dominating figures of eighteenth-century Eurasian politics.

• **Cossacks** Horsemen of the steppe who helped Russian rulers protect and extend their frontier into Central Asia and Siberia.

• **Catherine the Great** (r. 1762–1796) German princess who married into the Romanov family and became empress of Russia. Brought western European cultural and intellectual influences to the Russian elite. Her troops crushed a major peasant uprising.

■ **Catherine the Great** Equestrian portraits of monarchs on white horses were common in eighteenth-century Europe, though rarely were women represented this way. Catherine, a German princess who married into the Russian royal family, removed her husband from the throne in 1762 in a bloodless coup. Tough and brilliant, she ruled under her own authority for over three decades. (Musée des Beaux-Arts, Chartres, France/Erich Lessing/Art Resource, NY)

Primary Source:
Catherine the Great's Grand Instruction to the Legislative Commission *Catherine the Great gives instructions to the commissioners charged with developing a new code of laws for the Russian Empire.*

While ruling over an expanding Asian empire, Catherine brought new cultural and intellectual influences from western Europe to the tsarist court at St. Petersburg. Exciting new ideas were spreading from Europe's capitals, most notably Paris, energizing movements of reform and revolution in the West (see Chapter 22). Catherine brought the latest European trends in art, architecture, and fashion to Russia, but she adamantly ruled out political reform. Instead, she consolidated even greater power than her predecessors.

The Russian nobility benefited from her authoritarian policies. In return for their loyalty and their service in the bureaucracy and the military, Catherine gave the nobles more power over their serfs than ever before. At the same time, growing markets for grain in the cities of western Europe gave the nobles an incentive to increase production through increasingly harsh labor conditions. In their elegant townhouses and country estates, the Russian aristocracy saw imported Western commodities as an essential part of their lifestyle, paid for by those who toiled for them like slaves.

As the situation of the serfs deteriorated in the second half of the eighteenth century, social unrest led to open rebellion. In the 1770s a Cossack chieftain named Yemelyan Pugachev gained a huge following after claiming that he was the legitimate tsar. Pugachev promised the abolition of serfdom and an end to taxation and military conscription. It took several years for the tsarist army to suppress the rebels, but Pugachev was eventually captured, brought back to Moscow, and sliced to pieces in a public square. Catherine became even less tolerant of talk of reform after Pugachev's rebellion.

Catherine's imperial policies were pragmatic. Herself a convert to the Orthodox faith, she frequently restrained the church from attempting to convert non-Russian peoples. In some cases, as in Siberia, the reasons were financial. Converts to Orthodoxy had legal protections that other indigenous people lacked and could not be forced into supplementary tax payments. In other cases, especially on the steppe and the Central Asian frontier, Catherine was anxious to maintain stability and realized that working with local Muslim political and religious leaders was the most efficient way to do so. Even as the Crimea was added to the Russian Empire, for example, she protected the rights of the local Muslim nobility: "It is Our desire that without regard to his nationality or faith, each [nobleman] shall have the personal right to these lands and any advantages that will accrue from their use." (See the feature "Movement of Ideas: Petitioning Catherine the Great.")

Thus while the mobility and living conditions of Russian serfs deteriorated in the eighteenth century, and violence and disease spread on the Siberian frontier, Russian interactions with Asian societies were flexible. Like the Qing emperors in relation to Central Asia, Catherine the Great found that working with local rulers and institutions was often the most effective way to extend her influence and stabilize Russia's imperial frontiers.

India: From Mughal Empire to British Rule, 1650–1800

In the later seventeenth century the Mughal Empire was at the height of its wealth and power when the emperor **Aurangzeb** (ow-rang-ZEB) completed a series of conquests that extended his power throughout south India. Proud of his accomplishment, Aurangzeb took the title Alamgir, "World Seizer." A hundred years later, however, Mughal power was in retreat as the British East India Company established itself as the dominant political and military power in the region.

Even during Aurangzeb's long rule (1658–1707), ambitious regional leaders were starting to resist the central power of Delhi. Although Aurangzeb successfully reasserted and even extended imperial power, after his death the Mughal Empire began to fragment, leading to invasions from Iran and Afghanistan and the emergence of autonomous regional states. As in the past history of India and other land-based empires in Eurasia, great concentrations of wealth and power attracted invaders from the mountains and steppes who were strong enough to destabilize the existing political order without replacing it. In this case, however, the European seaborne empires represented something entirely new. Starting from their base in Bengal in the northeast, the British seized the initiative to fill the power vacuum left by the Mughal decline.

> • **Aurangzeb** (r. 1658–1707) Mughal emperor who used military force to extend his power but whose constant campaigns drained the treasury and whose policy of favoring Islam at the expense of India's other religions generated social and political tensions.

Aurangzeb and the Decline of Mughal Authority, 1658–1757

Aurangzeb was an energetic, capable, and determined ruler who presided over a stable and prosperous realm. The wealth he controlled was staggering. Some of this came from his territorial conquests, each of which brought treasure flowing back to Delhi. But agriculture, trade, and industry were the true foundations of India's wealth in the seventeenth century.

Mughal officials encouraged the planting of more commercial crops, such as sugarcane, indigo, and cotton, to enhance the tax base of the countryside, and many peasants benefited from a stronger focus on marketable crops. Another stimulus to growth was the planting of American crops like maize and tobacco. Population did not grow as rapidly as in China in the same period: epidemic diseases and periodic famines following from the failure of monsoon rains kept mortality rates high. Still, the population of India rose from about 150 million in 1600 to about 200 million in 1800. As in other land-based empires, taxes on peasant agriculture were the principal source of government revenue.

The stability of the Mughal heartland in north India was good for trade and industry. Participation in the expanding Indian Ocean economy brought an inflow of gold and silver that financed not only Aurangzeb's military adventures but also

Petitioning Catherine the Great

It was common in tsarist Russia for communities to petition the tsar or tsarina for redress of grievances. Often people felt that oppression resulted from the misuse of power by local and provincial officials: if only the tsarina herself knew of these abuses, surely she would correct them. Catherine the Great encouraged this attitude and invited her subjects (other than the serfs, who had no right to address her) to submit their petitions to her.

The first of the two petitions below was submitted by a group of Tartar nobles, that is, by the Muslim, Turkish-speaking elite of an area incorporated into the Russian Empire. The Kazan Tartars had ruled the Volga River region in the fourteenth century, but in the fifteenth century this region was conquered by the Russian tsar Ivan the Terrible. Ivan slaughtered much of the Muslim population and forcibly converted many of the survivors to Orthodox Christianity. Not until the reign of Catherine did the tsars allow new mosques to be built again in Kazan.

The second petition to Catherine was submitted by a group of Jewish leaders in Belarus. The majority of the population of Belarus (meaning "white Russia") consisted of Slavic speakers closely related to Russians in language and culture. Belarus was ruled from Poland/Lithuania until the eighteenth century, after which it was incorporated into the Russian Empire. The Jews of this region were known as *Ashkenazim*. Their liturgical language was a form of Hebrew, but their everyday language was Yiddish, a dialect of German infused with Hebrew vocabulary that was unintelligible to Russian speakers. To the greatest extent possible, the Ashkenazim took care of their own community affairs.

Source: Gregory L. Freeze, *From Supplication to Revolution: A Documentary Social History of Imperial Russia* (New York: Oxford University Press, 1988).

Petition from Tatar Nobles in Kazan Province, 1767

12. We the under-signed believe that nothing is more offensive to a person, regardless of his faith and rank, than to suffer disrespect and insults toward his religion. This makes one extremely agitated and provokes unnecessary words of abuse. But it often happens that people of various ranks say extremely contemptuous things about our religion and our Prophet . . . and this is a great affront for us. Therefore we request a law that anyone who curses our religion be held legally accountable. . . . [We further ask that] we Tatars and nobles not be forced to convert to Orthodoxy, but that only those who so wish . . . be baptized. . . .

15. If any of our people are voluntarily baptized into the faith of the Greek confession [i.e., into the Orthodox Church] they should be ordered to move to settlements with Russians the very same year in which the conversion takes place. . . . We ask that, under no circumstances, are converts to be permitted to sell their houses, garden plots, and pastures to Russians or people of other ranks, but are to sell only to us Tatars; they must sell either to unconverted kinsmen or other Tatars. . . . Also, without a special personal order from Her Imperial Majesty, no churches should be built in our localities and thereby put pressure upon us. . . .

Petition from Belarussian Jews, 1784

1. Some [Belarussian Jews] who live in towns engage in trade and, especially, in the distillation of spirits, beer and mead [honey beer], which they sell wholesale and retail. This privilege was extended to them when Belarus joined the Russian Empire. Hence everyone active in this business used all their resources to construct buildings suitable for distillation. . . . After the Belarussian region joined the Russian Empire, the Jews in some towns constructed more of these in the same fashion and at great expense. The imperial monarchical decree [on Jews] emboldens them to request tearfully some monarchical mercy.

2. According to an ancient custom, when the squires built a new village, they summoned the Jews to reside there and gave them certain privileges for several years and the permanent liberty to distill spirits, brew beer and mead, and sell these drinks. On this basis the Jews built houses and distillation plants at considerable expense. The squires, at their own volition, farmed out the inns to the Jews, with the freedom to distill and sell liquor. . . . But a decree of the governor-general of Belarus has now forbidden the squires to farm our distillation in their villages to Jews, even if the squires want to do this. As a result [these] poor Jews [have been left] completely impoverished. . . . They therefore request an imperial decree authorizing the squire, if he wishes, to farm out distillation to Jews in rural areas.

3. . . . Jews have no one to defend them in courts and find themselves in a desperate situation—given their fear, and ignorance of Russian—in case of misfortune, even if innocent. . . . To consummate all the good already bestowed, Jews dare to petition that . . . in matters involving Jews and non-Jews . . . a representative from the Jewish community . . . be present to accompany Jews in court and attend the interrogation of Jews. But cases involving only Jews . . . should be handled solely in Jewish courts, because Jews assume obligations among themselves, make agreements and conclude all kinds of deals in the Jewish language and in accordance with Jewish rites and law (which are not known to others.) Moreover, those who transgress their laws and order should be judged in Jewish courts. Similarly, preserve intact all their customs and holidays in the spirit of their faith, as is mercifully assured in the imperial manifesto. . . .

QUESTIONS FOR ANALYSIS

▶ What attitude did the writers of these petitions express toward Catherine's imperial authority?

▶ What do these documents tell us about the relationship of religion to empire in eighteenth-century Russia?

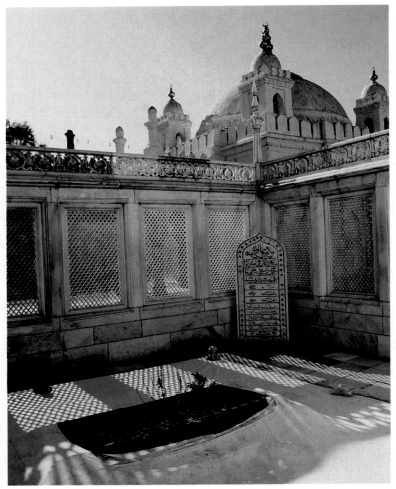

🔲 **The Tomb of Aurangzeb** The Mughal emperor Aurangzeb was a deeply spiritual man, but his advocacy of Islam in multireligious India weakened the empire. His simple grave contrasts with the ornate magnificence of most Mughal architecture. (© Art and Architecture/Danita Delimont Stock Photography)

entrepreneurial activity. Silk and opium were produced in greater quantities for Southeast Asian markets, but the principal mark of prosperity was the expansion of the textile sector. The European market for cotton cloth was a new and profitable one, as consumers in the Netherlands, France, and England found that Indian cottons were cheaper, more comfortable, and more easily washed than domestic woolens or linens. South Asian merchants and moneylenders were among the most powerful commercial agents in the world, using the silver that flowed in through Indian Ocean trade to pay cash advances to weavers, who then contracted with lower-caste women to spin cotton yarn for them.

Commercial wealth was not, however, an unmixed blessing for Mughal rulers. Increased prosperity gave some regional leaders resources to build up their own military forces as well as an incentive to try to keep their own wealth rather than pass it along to Delhi. The constant military campaigns undertaken by Aurangzeb were largely driven by the need to assert central control over such restive provinces.

In the process Aurangzeb reversed Akbar's earlier policy of religious tolerance (see Chapter 16). While many Muslims lived in major cities and in the northeast and northwest of the empire, most Mughal subjects were Hindus. Whereas Akbar had actively courted allies among Hindus, Sikhs, and other communities, Aurangzeb stressed the Islamic nature of his state, imposing on nonbelievers the special tax that the Quran allows but that Akbar had suspended. The tax caused great resentment among India's non-Muslim majority.

Hindu leaders trying to free themselves from central control, such as those in the **Maratha kingdoms** in western and central India, were now motivated by religious resentments as well as by political and economic ambition. Aurangzeb had fairly easily subdued other regions, but Maratha leaders successfully used guerilla tactics, well suited to the region's tough terrain, to keep the Mughal armies at bay. From 1695 to 1700, Aurangzeb left Delhi to live in military encampments. Vast sums were spent on his campaigns, and as the emperor became less attentive to other state affairs, corruption and incompetence crept into the government.

By the time of his death in 1707, Aurangzeb was full of despair. From his deathbed he wrote his son: "I have not done well to the country or to the people, and of

●**Maratha kingdoms** Loosely bound, west-central Indian confederacy that established its autonomy from Mughal rule in the eighteenth century and challenged the invading British in the nineteenth.

the future there is no hope." His passing brought a prolonged succession struggle that weakened the empire; regional leaders ignored Delhi, and tax collectors kept hold of revenue rather than forwarding it to the imperial treasury. The Mughals were now vulnerable to foreign invasion.

The main threat came from Iran. After the fall of the Safavid dynasty, a new leader named **Nader Shah** (1688–1747) had rallied Iranian forces to defend the country from Afghan invaders. In 1739 Nader Shah's forces seized key political and commercial centers in Afghanistan and entered northern India, defeated the Mughal army, and captured the emperor. Begging for mercy, the emperor handed over the keys to his treasury, and even the fabled Peacock Throne, before Nader Shah agreed to withdraw.

Nader Shah's invasion marked the death knell of Mughal authority. The Marathas tried to take advantage of Mughal weakness by themselves marching on Delhi, but they were decisively defeated by Afghani invaders in 1761. With Maratha expansion checked, it was now likely that India would become once again decentralized. Instead, the British took the mantle of Mughal imperial power.

• **Nader Shah** (1688–1747) Iranian ruler who invaded India from the north in 1739, defeating the Mughal army and capturing the Mughal emperor. He then retreated, but Mughal power went into permanent decline.

Foundations of British Rule, 1739–1818

The seaborne European empires in Asia were originally geared toward commercial profit rather than territorial control. Mughal rulers did not pay much attention to the Dutch, English, and French East India Companies operating on the fringes of their empire. In Amsterdam, Paris, and London, specialized bureaucracies handled shipping schedules, insurance, and warehousing. In Asia, Company agents identified profitable markets and negotiated with local political and commercial elites. The usual pattern was for Europeans to directly control only their own "factories," fortified outposts where they lived and kept their trade goods, and perhaps a bit of the immediately adjacent territory (see Chapter 17).

Cotton cloth has already been mentioned as a major trade item, but there was also opium (at first destined for Indonesian markets, and later for China), raw silk (exported to both Europe and Japan), and great quantities of pepper. Saltpeter, a key ingredient in gunpowder, was another important European import from Asia. European rulers, following the theory of mercantilism, believed that their own economies were damaged by the high silver exports needed to finance this trade. But commerce with India (and with China) was so profitable that silver exports continued.

With the decline of Mughal power, especially after Nader Shah's invasion of 1739, some Company employees were tempted to join in the general scramble to gain greater freedom from imperial authority. It was such "men on the spot," rather than policymakers in distant European capitals, who laid the foundations for European empires in Asia.

One of the first and most brilliant of these was **Joseph Francois Dupleix** (1697–1764), the governor-general in charge of all French establishments in India. During the 1740s he seized the British factory at Madras in south India. The French in turn were attacked by a local Indian ruler who wanted the wealth of Madras for himself. Dupleix (doo-PLAY) commanded just 230 French troops supported by some 700 *sepoys* (SEE-poyz), Indian soldiers employed and trained by the Europeans. Yet French superiority in both weaponry and organization allowed them to defeat a force of nearly 10,000 men. Dupleix then became an Indian ruler himself by seizing the position of his defeated Indian enemy. As part of the diplomatic maneuvers of the War of the Austrian Succession (see Chapter 19), however, Paris ordered

• **Joseph Francois Dupleix** (1697–1764) Governor-general in charge of all French establishments in India. Dupleix used diplomacy to forge alliances with local rulers and with their help defeated a much larger British force in the 1740s.

Dupleix to return Madras to the British. But Dupleix's example was followed with more lasting effect by Robert Clive, a British soldier of fortune.

The British East India Company factory at Calcutta tapped into the rich trade of the populous Mughal province of Bengal. The nawab (ruler) of Bengal, Siraj ud-Daulah (suh-raj uhd–duh-oo-lah), saw the British as a threat, and in 1756 his soldiers seized Calcutta. But Robert Clive cleverly outmaneuvered him. First, Clive secured the backing of some of Bengal's most powerful Hindu commercial and banking interests, who preferred to deal with the commercially minded British. Second, Clive made an alliance with the nawab's own uncle, who hoped to use this alliance to become nawab himself. In 1757, at the **Battle of Plassey,** the nawab's 50,000 troops faced only 800 Englishmen, plus about 2,000 sepoys. But some of Siraj ud-Daulah's troops had been secretly paid by Clive's moneylender friends not to fight, while the forces controlled by his uncle switched to the British side.

Siraj's uncle was duly installed as nawab, but he paid a high price when the Englishmen plundered his treasury. In the late eighteenth century Company officials drained fortunes from North India and returned to England to build stately London residences and palatial country homes. The chests full of silver they sent back home reversed the flow of bullion back toward Europe and away from the Indian Ocean economies.

From their base in Bengal the British could perhaps have marched on Delhi and ended the Mughal era once and for all. But Clive decided on a more subtle policy of recognizing the weakened Mughal emperor's status and inserting the Company into existing Mughal institutions. The East India Company became the official revenue collector of the rich northeastern provinces of Bengal, Bihar (bee-HAHR) and Oudh (OW-ad). Clive used the threat of military force to divide and conquer, making alliances with various nawabs, maharajahs, and sultans by offering them "protection" at a price.

Clive's success drew the attention of the English Parliament, and some members doubted whether he and the Company were serving the nation's interests. Some Englishmen were also horrified by the loss of life that followed the failure of the monsoon rains in 1769, resulting in a famine that killed as many as one-third of the population of Bengal. While the Company was able to feed its own employees and soldiers, it did nothing for the general population while continuing to extract its revenue. One member of Parliament complained: "We have outdone the Spaniards in Peru. They were at least butchers on a religious principle, however diabolical their zeal. We have murdered, deposed, plundered, usurped—nay, what think you of the famine in Bengal being caused by a monopoly of the servants of the East India Company?"[4]

The India Act in 1784 was Parliament's attempt to reform such abuses. **Lord Charles Cornwallis** was dispatched as governor-general and commander of British forces in India. Unlike Clive, whose public disgrace led to his suicide, Cornwallis was an aristocrat and a member of the British establishment. His assignment was to draw a strict line between administration and trade by implementing a system whereby Company employees could serve as either officials or traders, but not as both. Cornwallis believed that British rule could be fair and just; as his successor declared: "No greater benefit can be bestowed on the inhabitants of India than the extension of British authority."[5] That idea would long endure as a justification for British colonial rule.

British influence spread through negotiation as well as force. Some provincial Indian rulers looked to the British as patrons and protectors in the anarchy that accompanied Mughal decline. Negotiations also took place at institutional and

● **Battle of Plassey** 1757 battle that gave the British East India Company control of the rich eastern Mughal province of Bengal. Sir Robert Clive used alliances with Indian rulers to defeat the larger forces of Siraj ud-Daulah, the nawab of Bengal.

● **Lord Charles Cornwallis** (1738–1795) British general who surrendered to American forces at Yorktown and later served as governor-general of India and Ireland.

cultural levels as the British adjusted to Indian realities, learning Indian languages and adopting Mughal styles of dress and behavior. Because there were no English women in India, Company employees frequently associated with local consorts and even wives, who provided a cultural and linguistic bridge to local society.

In the field of law we see one example of the complex intercultural processes that developed. Xie Qinggao had witnessed a British court proceeding at Calcutta:

> The head judge sits, and ten guest judges [the jury] sit on his side. The head guest judge is the elder of the guest merchants. . . . On the day they consider the suit and then decide the outcome, if one of the guest judges does not agree they must hear the case again. Even if this happens two or three times, no one views this as inconvenient.[6]

But while the Company used British-style jury trials for disputes among themselves, they had neither the will nor the desire to replace South Asian legal traditions with their own. Instead, a situation of legal pluralism developed. Indian litigants might pursue their cases in local courts or in British ones. They might choose British courts because of corruption in the Mughal ones; however, they would still

A British East India Company Official Eighteenth-century Englishmen adopted many features of Mughal court life: dressing in Mughal fashion, smoking from a hookah, enjoying the entertainment of Indian musicians and dancers, and taking up the Mughal sport of polo. Many of these Mughal cultural practices, including the game of polo, had themselves been imported from Persia; this portrait bears comparison with that of the Safavid Shah Sulayman II (see page 504). (British Library, London/Werner Forman/Art Resource, NY)

expect their own customs to be respected. The British East India Company therefore hired Muslim and Hindu legal experts to help them in this complex, multi-layered legal system.

Another adaptation of a Mughal institution to British purposes was the revenue system that Cornwallis designed. The main tax collectors for the Mughal Empire had been *zamindars,* men with appointed positions that involved no land ownership. In the British tradition, however, landed property was an essential foundation of political order. Under the British, therefore, zamindars became landlords as well as tax collectors, merging Mughal and British roles.

In the 1770s the top Company official had declared: "The dominion of all India is what I never wish to see." But in the unsettled conditions of the late eighteenth century it was difficult to avoid greater involvement in the subcontinent's political and military affairs. In the west, when Maratha armies threatened the British East India Company's factory at Bombay, the British engaged in a series of alliances and interventions in that region. Finally, in 1818 they defeated the Marathas in battle and established their control over South Asia.

●Tokugawa Japan, 1630–1790

After the adventurism of Hideyoshi and his attempt to invade China at the end of the sixteenth century (see Chapter 16), early modern Japan remained largely aloof from empires and empire building. Unlike Korea and Vietnam, Japan was not part of the tributary system tying the local elite to the Chinese emperor. Unlike other offshore islands like the Spanish Philippines, the Dutch East Indies, or Qing-controlled Taiwan, it was subject to no foreign power. Instead, Japan developed its own distinctive and dynamic political, economic, and cultural systems. Yet this was a period of tremendous vitality in Japanese history. The Tokugawa (toe-koo-GAH-wah) shoguns and *daimyo* lords ruled over a rapidly growing society with a flourishing economy. Tokugawa Japan had a rich cultural and intellectual life, with major accomplishments in fields such as poetry, theater, and architecture.

The story of early modern Japan divides roughly into two periods. From 1630 to 1710 the Tokugawa system was at its height of affluence and creativity. But from 1710 to 1800 a series of financial and environmental problems left the Tokugawa, in the words of one historian, "struggling to stand still."[7] In this later period, population growth stalled, and a widening gap between the rich and the poor led to increasing social tensions.

Tokugawa Japan, 1630–1710

The Japanese emperor remained a shadowy figure. Real political power rested with the Tokugawa shoguns, the military leaders with their capital at Edo (Tokyo), who had partially reined in the independent power of Japan's lords, the daimyo (see Chapter 16). With stable leadership, seventeenth-century Japan harvested the fruits of peace.

Farmers brought back into production valuable lands they had abandoned in the sixteenth century because of violence and insecurity. They also devoted much time and labor to improving irrigation; yields were increased as rice paddies replaced dry field agriculture. After the most easily accessible lands were brought into production, Japanese farmers began to clear forests and terrace hillsides, while Japanese fishermen took greater advantage of the bounty of the surrounding seas.

The shoguns and daimyo tapped into this wealth through an efficient tax system based on precise surveys of land and population. Farmers, no longer subject to arbitrary taxes, had an incentive to boost production knowing that they would retain any additional surplus they produced. Mining was stimulated by heavy Chinese demand for silver and copper. Some of the new wealth was consumed by the administrative elite, who preferred finer Chinese silk to their own domestic product. But some of it also went toward the improvement of roads and irrigation works, further stimulating economic growth.

The expansion of Japanese cities was one of the most notable features of the period. Many of the castle towns, built as defensive fortifications during early centuries of civil war, developed into cultural and commercial centers. The most spectacular example was the capital of Edo (ED-doe), which grew from a small village to a city of more than a million people by 1720. An increase in coinage made possible a shift from local and regional self-sufficiency to a truly national economy.

One of the most pressing social questions of the early Tokugawa period was to find a role for the *samurai* warriors during times of peace. At this time the philosophy of *bushido,* "the way of the warrior," became codified. According to bushido, the samurai were to cultivate both the military and the civil arts, and in times of peace to emphasize the latter: "Within his heart [the samurai] keeps to the ways of peace, but . . . keeps his weapons ready for use. The . . . common people make him their teacher and respect him. . . . Herein lies the Way of the *samurai,* the means by which he earns his clothing, food and shelter."[8] The samurai therefore positioned themselves as the intellectual and cultural leaders of Tokugawa Japan. They established schools, wrote Confucian treatises, and patronized the arts. But they remained absolutely loyal to their daimyo masters and were willing to die for them if necessary.

Regulations stating that each rural family should be self-sufficient were also widely ignored as farming families increasingly geared their production toward urban markets. In gender relations as well, the Tokugawa theory of strict Confucian hierarchy was contradicted by the social dynamism of the period. As in China, elite women made prominent literary contributions. But in Japan women of other social classes also had some mobility. While women in most samurai families were subject to tight patriarchal control, urban merchant and artisan families were less restrictive. Thus women participated as performers as well as audience members in some of the new forms of dance and theater. (See the feature "Visual Evidence: The 'Floating World' of Tokugawa Japan.")

Tokugawa Japan and the Outside World

The conservative instincts of the Tokugawa shoguns were evident in foreign policy as well, and here their regulations were somewhat more effective. A series of **Seclusion Edicts** strictly limited Japanese contact with Europeans. After the 1630s only a single annual Dutch trading mission was allowed, with the stipulation that no Bibles or other Christian texts were to enter the country. Japanese were forbidden to practice Christianity or even to risk exposure to that religion through travel overseas.

But even in foreign relations these policies of exclusion and isolation were contradicted by a more dynamic reality of economic and intellectual interchange.

● **Seclusion Edicts** Series of edicts issued by the Tokugawa shoguns that, beginning in the 1630s, outlawed Christianity and strictly limited Japanese contact with Europeans.

THE "FLOATING WORLD" OF TOKUGAWA JAPAN

Three important cities played different roles in seventeenth-century Japan. Kyoto was the imperial capital, a city of temples and palaces. Here the emperor, his courtiers, and Buddhist monks and nuns kept alive ancient Japanese arts, such as the tea ceremony and the traditions of Zen Buddhism, including meditative gardens. Edo was the dynamic administrative center. Here daimyo kept palaces to remain close to the heart of political power, and many samurai turned themselves from warriors into scholars. Osaka was the country's commercial capital, the focal point of enlarged and intensified trade networks. New artistic forms accompanied social change in these cities. Poets experimented with a simple new form called *haiku*. Urban audiences patronized the new *kabuki* (ka-BOO-ki) theater, more realistic and emotive than previous forms of Japanese drama.

The shoguns favored a strictly hierarchical society along Confucian lines and preferred that everyone keep in his or her place. Their constant edicts ordering

(Hikone Castle Museum/DNPArchives.com)

This screen was owned by a noble daimyo family, but Tokugawa merchants were also important patrons of ukiyoe artists.

QUESTION FOR ANALYSIS

▶ The word *ukiyoe* had earlier been written with characters meaning "sorrowful world," with a Buddhist emphasis on impermanence. Do the figures on this screen seem to live in a "sorrowful world," or in a "floating world" as described by Ryōi?

people to dress in clothes and live in houses appropriate to their social status indicate that many people were *not* doing so. As in early modern western Europe, where the urban merchant class was also increasing its wealth and cultural influence, Japanese merchants ignored the laws that restricted the clothes they could wear: when they could afford it, they wore the fine silk robes presumably reserved for the daimyo.

The arts of the Tokugawa period demonstrate the cultural fluidity of seventeenth century Japanese culture. The image here is a detail from the *Hikone Screen,* produced in the 1640s and used by a Japanese lord as both a functional and decorative part of his home. The *Hikone Screen* is part of a new artistic genre that developed in the Tokugawa period depicting the *ukiyoe,* or "floating world," as described by Asai Ryōi: "Living only for the moment, turning our full attention to the pleasures of the moon, the snow, the cherry blossoms, and the maple leaves; singing songs, drinking wine, diverting ourselves in just floating, floating; caring not a whit for the pauperism staring us in the face, refusing to be disheartened, like a gourd floating along with the river current; this is what we call the *floating world.*"* Artists represented new art forms like *kabuki* theater and, as on this screen, bordellos that were as much about refined pastimes such as music and literature as about sexual gratification.

_____

*Quoted in Richard Lane, *Images from the Floating World* (New York: Putnam, 1978), p. 11.

Area of detail

● Earlier Japanese decorative artists emphasized calm landscapes and nature subjects. This screen-within-a-screen shows that older style in juxtaposition with the new Tokugawa ukiyoe theme.

One art critic writes: "A strong visual contrast is established between the ethereal realm of the monochrome landscape in a meticulously brushed Chinese style and the worldly ambiance of the bordello pursuits in the foreground."[†]

This is a scene from a brothel, but do the characters exhibit sexual tension?

● Urban Tokugawa culture is known for its emphasis on refinements in recreation and leisure activities such as music, backgammon, calligraphy, and painting.

_____

† John T. Carpenter, "The Human Figure in the Playground of Edo Artistic Imagination," in *Edo: Art in Japan, 1615–1868,* ed. Robert T. Singer et al. (Washington, D.C.: National Gallery of Art, 1998), p. 378.

For one thing, Japanese seclusion applied only to Europeans. Trade with Chinese and Korean merchants grew even as that with the Europeans declined, and as a result Japanese foreign trade increased throughout this period. Xie Qinggao, who visited Nagasaki as a sailor, noted the high volume of Japanese exports in silver, porcelain, paper and brushes, flower vases, and dying stamps, much of it destined for Chinese markets.

And while contact with Europeans was limited, the scientific and philosophical books that reached the islands through the annual Dutch trade missions found an eager audience, especially among samurai aspiring to a more scholarly peacetime role. In fact, for centuries Western knowledge in Japan was known by the term **Dutch learning,** and the ability to read Dutch was a sign of worldliness and sophistication (see Chapter 24).

While Dutch learning was new and exotic, the Chinese influence on Japanese intellectual life was deep and well established. Xie noted that "the king wears Chinese clothes" and that "the country uses Chinese writing." He overstated the degree of Chinese cultural influence on Japan, where both clothing styles and the writing system were unique Japanese adaptations of Chinese models rather than mere copies. Still, some Tokugawa thinkers, many of them samurai, were anxious to downplay Chinese influence. For one thing, they emphasized Japan's indigenous *Shinto* religious tradition, with its emphasis on the spiritual forces of the natural and ancestral worlds, while attacking Buddhism. Buddhism, some argued, led people to focus on empty and abstract thoughts, while Shinto connected believers to tangible forces in the world of experience. Other Japanese intellectuals argued that Japan, not China, should be regarded as the "Middle Kingdom" because of the greater purity of its Confucian traditions.

This sense of intellectual competition was not connected to empire building. The only territorial expansion of the Tokugawa Shogunate was to the lightly populated northern islands, especially Hokkaido (ho-KIE-do), whose indigenous Ainu people lived by hunting, gathering, and fishing and were no match for Japanese weapons. After losing several battles, the Ainu population became increasingly dependent on Japanese immigrants, primarily fishermen who exploited Ainu labor.

Eventually tensions would result when the Russians also extended their imperial frontier to the islands north of Japan. But in the eighteenth century Hokkaido was still very remote, and the increased Japanese presence was not an exception to the usual Tokugawa practice of seclusion and isolation. For several hundred years, Japanese rulers, in stark contrast to Qing, Russian, and British activities in Asia, simply opted out of the empire-building game.

• **Dutch learning** Traditional Japanese title for Western knowledge. Knowledge of Dutch in Tokugawa Japan was a sign of worldliness and sophistication.

Challenges, Reform, and Decline, 1710–1800

By 1710 Japan was a rich, populous, and united country. But the eighteenth century brought new challenges. The main problem was ecological. In the seventeenth century the population of Japan had doubled to over thirty million people. Farms became smaller and smaller, and with no significant improvements in technology or sources of energy, Japan had nearly reached its limit in food production. As in China, the spread of irrigation works had led to silting up of rivers and increased danger of floods. In addition, the growth of population, and especially the building of larger cities, had taken a toll on Japan's timber resources. Wood became more expensive, and excessive exploitation of forests led to soil erosion and a further decline in productivity.

In the 1720s and 1730s **Yoshimune** (r. 1716–1745), one of the greatest Tokugawa shoguns, launched a program of reform. Through constant edicts he urged people to be frugal and curtail unnecessary consumption and told the samurai to give up the ease of urban life and return to the countryside. True to the Confucian tradition, Yoshimune interpreted the economic and social problems of his time as resulting from moral failures. But his edicts were no more successful in changing people's behavior than those of previous shoguns.

Nevertheless, Yoshimune did sponsor some more practical and successful reforms. Most importantly, he tried to make life easier for the increasingly hard-pressed farmers. He reformed tax collections to eliminate the corruption that local officials had allowed to creep into the system, and he set strict limits on interest rates to help indebted farmers. His government also sponsored the cultivation of sugar and ginseng to replace imports from Korea and Southeast Asia, as well as promoted the planting of sweet potatoes on marginal land to increase the food supply. Support for increased exploitation of marine resources resulted in greater supplies of seafood as well as the production of fertilizer to refresh the exhausted soil.

Yoshimune, thinking that merchants were responsible for many of Japan's problems, tried to bring them under government control. Greater government involvement in commerce actually suited the interests of some merchants, especially larger trading houses that were anxious to secure government-backed monopolies. But Yoshimune's policies tended to undermine entrepreneurialism. His successors pursued similar policies, making Japanese business more regulated and monopolistic and less dynamic and inventive.

For all his effort and energy, however, Yoshimune reforms were mainly a matter of struggling to stand still. After 1750 the social problems arising from the ecological and economic crisis increased: incidents of rural unrest nearly doubled. Peasants particularly resented a system of unpaid labor that required them to toil on public works projects, such as road building. Tensions also grew within rural communities as families competed for access to scarce water and timber.

It is a testament to the solidity and effectiveness of Tokugawa institutions that the crises of the late eighteenth century did not lead to a general breakdown of the political order, such as was occurring in Mughal India. Instead the political, economic, and cultural legacies of the Tokugawa endured far into the nineteenth century. Not until then were the shoguns' policies of seclusion effectively challenged by outside powers, reigniting Japan's own imperial ambitions (see Chapter 24).

• **Yoshimune** (1738–1795) Eighth Tokugawa ruler to hold the title of shogun. A conservative but capable leader under whose rule Japan saw advances in agricultural productivity.

Chapter Review

CL Download the MP3 audio file of the Chapter Review and listen to it on the go.

Xie Qinggao's travels took him along the margins of great Asian empires. The Qing dynasty and the Russian Empire were extending their power further into Central Asia during Xie's lifetime, while the British East India Company was expanding its power in South Asia at the expense of the declining Mughal Empire.

Japan alone retained a largely nonexpansionist policy, its dynamic, urbanizing society protected from direct contact with Europeans by its conservative rulers.

In spite of Qing, Russian, and British imperial expansion in eighteenth-century Asia, many people still lived outside the control of large states and empires, and many boundaries between states were unclear. That would change in the later nineteenth century when even more powerful and aggressive imperial forces—western European, Russian, and Japanese—would encompass the globe with empires. The stage was set for more dramatic confrontations between the powers in Asia.

 How did the Qing emperors build and maintain their empire in East and Central Asia?

The Kangxi emperor and his successors were careful to emulate Chinese models of good governance to bolster their legitimacy with Han Chinese officials. Manchu rulers cultivated their image as Confucian sages while using the well-established examination system to staff the imperial bureaucracy. At the same time, the Manchu identity of the Qing emperors helped them control an immense domain and accommodate many diverse peoples besides their Han Chinese subjects. Tibetans, Mongols, and the Turkic-speaking Muslims of Xinjiang paid tribute to the Qing emperors.

 What factors drove Russian imperial expansion in the eighteenth century?

In the later eighteenth century Russian leaders continued the momentum they inherited from Peter the Great. Participation in the great power politics of Europe brought Baltic regions and Poland into the empire. Continuing aggression against the Ottoman Empire resulted in new territories being added to Russian control in the Caucasus Mountains and around the Black Sea. Most dramatically, the empire grew across Siberia to the Pacific, acquiring rich resources and vast economic potential. Like the Chinese, the Russians had often been invaded by Central Asian peoples, and their expansion in that direction was at least partially a pre-emptive strike. But at least two further motivations came into play: the profitability of the Siberian fur trade and ambitions to establish the Russian state as a great power in both Europe and Asia.

What were the principal causes of the decline of Mughal power, and how were the British able to replace the Mughals as the dominant power in South Asia?

Like the Qing, the rulers of the Mughal Empire governed a diverse population, but their Islamic religion set them apart from the majority of their subjects. Aurangzeb, the last powerful Mughal emperor, deviated from the policies of his predecessors by forcefully advocating Islam, thus provoking regional resistance to Mughal authority. At the same time, ambitious local rulers, benefiting from the economic expansion that came with increased regional and global trade, were asserting their autonomy. Aurangzeb was largely successful in keeping such forces in check, but his successors, distracted by succession struggles and foreign invasions, saw power slip from their hands.

The British East Indian Company was the main beneficiary of Mughal decline. Robert Clive manipulated local Indian politics to score a seemingly implausible victory at the Battle of Plassey. Then, taking advantage of Mughal weakness, Company officials redirected part of the vast wealth of north India to their own accounts. Amid accusations of corruption, the British Parliament intervened to regularize the administration of British India by separating it from the commercial activities of the British East India Company. Thus the British government, responding to events rather than implementing a proactive program of imperial expansion, had become deeply embroiled in the political and military affairs of India. The land-based empire of the Mughals was becoming part of the sea-based empire of the British.

WEB RESOURCES

Pronunciation Guide

Interactive Maps

MAP 20.1 The Qing Empire, 1644–1783

MAP 20.2 The Expansion of Russia, 1500–1800

Primary Sources

Chapter Objectives

ACE Multiple-Choice Quiz

Flashcards

 In comparison with the Qing, Russian, and British Empires, what were some unique features of early modern Japanese history?

The isolationism of the shoguns of Tokugawa Japan was a major exception to the rule of expanding empires in eighteenth-century Asia. Their Seclusion Edicts ran parallel to their domestic policies: in each case they intended to reinforce order, stability, and hierarchy. Still, Tokugawa society was exceptionally dynamic, characterized by economic and demographic growth, urbanization, and cultural creativity.

For Further Reference

Bayly, C. A. *Indian Society and the Making of the British Empire.* New York: Cambridge University Press, 1990.

Brower, Daniel R., and Edward J. Lazzarini. *Russia's Orient: Imperial Borderlands and Peoples, 1700–1917.* Bloomington: Indiana University Press, 1997.

Crossley, Pamela. *The Manchus.* Oxford: Blackwell Publishers, 2002.

Kappeler, Andreas. *The Russian Empire: A Multiethnic History.* Harlow, U.K.: Longman, 2001.

Keay, John. *The Honourable Company: A History of the English East India Company.* London: HarperCollins, 1991.

Matsunosuke, Nishiyama. *Edo Culture: Daily Life and Diversions in Urban Japan, 1600–1868.* Honolulu: University of Hawaii Press, 1997.

Perdue, Peter C. *China Marches West: The Qing Conquest of Central Eurasia.* Cambridge: Harvard University Press, 2005.

Richards, John. *The Mughal Empire.* New York: Cambridge University Press, 1996.

Spence, Jonathan. *Emperor of China: Self Portrait of K'ang Hsi.* New York: Knopf, 1974.

Totman, Conrad. *Early Modern Japan.* Berkeley: University of California Press, 1993.

Websites

British India (http://www.sscnet.ucla.edu/southasia/History/British/BrIndia.html).   Useful documents; hosted by the University of California Los Angeles.

A Journey to the Heart of Japan (http://www.nakasendoway.com/).   A virtual journey on the Nakasendo Highway, the road connecting the Tokugawa capital of Edo with the imperial residence at Kyoto.

The Virtual Library for Russian and East European Studies (http://www.ucis.pitt.edu/reesweb/).   A searchable database with numerous links.

A Visual Sourcebook of Chinese Civilization (http://depts.washington.edu/chinaciv/).   Created under the auspices of the National Endowment of the Humanities, with visual resources on such topics as calligraphy, military technology, painting, and architecture.

European Science and the Foundations of Modern Imperialism, 1600–1820

When the young British botanist **Joseph Banks** (1743–1820) sailed on the first European expedition to cross the Pacific Ocean in 1769–1771, his interest went beyond flora and fauna to include the people he encountered on the voyage. From the Amerindians of Tierra del Fuego (the southern tip of South America), to the Polynesians of the Pacific, to the Aboriginal peoples of Australia, Banks kept careful notes of his interactions with peoples of whom Europeans had little previous knowledge. His concern with these cultures went beyond mere curiosity. He was interested in understanding the relationships *between* societies. For example, when Banks learned that Tahitians understood the speech of the Maori (MAO-ree) of New Zealand, he recognized that there was a family connection between the two peoples. Banks was a pioneer of *ethnography*, the study of the linguistic and cultural relationships between peoples. Banks was also mystified by the behavior of the Polynesian people he and his shipmates met when they stepped ashore on the island of Tahiti:

(Private Collection/The Bridgeman Art Library)

Though at first they hardly dared approach us, after a little time they became very familiar. The first who approached us came crawling almost on his hands and knees and gave us a green bough. . . . This we received and immediately each of us gathered a green bough and carried it in our hands. They marched with us about ½ a mile and then made a general stop and, scraping the ground clean . . . every one of them threw his bough down upon

JOSEPH BANKS

 This icon will direct you to interactive activities and study materials on the *Voyages* website: www.cengage.com/history/hansen/voyages1e

598

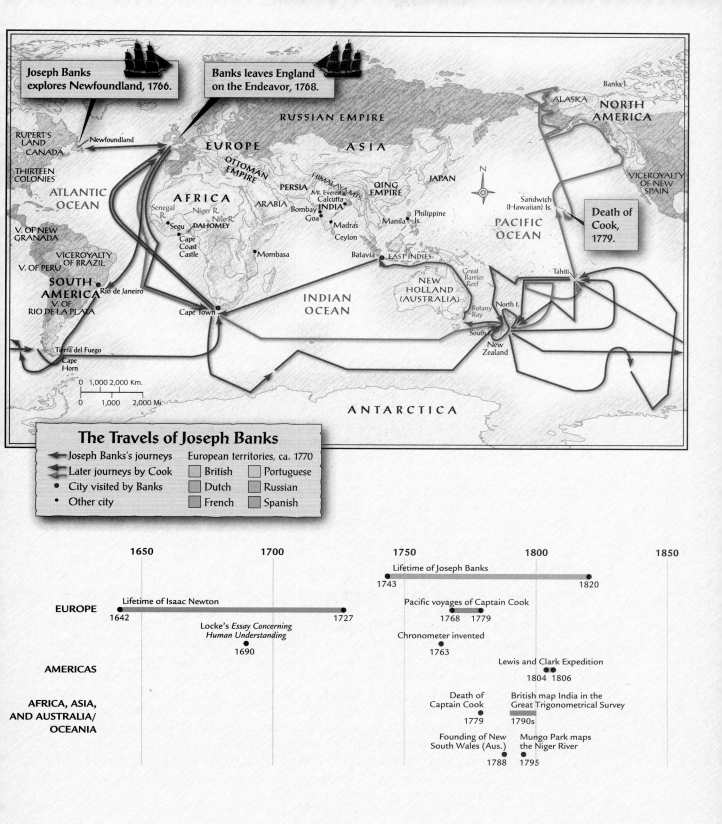

Joseph Banks explores Newfoundland, 1766.

Banks leaves England on the Endeavor, 1768.

Banks I.

ALASKA   NORTH AMERICA

RUSSIAN EMPIRE

RUPERT'S LAND
CANADA   Newfoundland

EUROPE   ASIA   JAPAN

THIRTEEN COLONIES

ATLANTIC OCEAN

OTTOMAN EMPIRE

PERSIA   HIMALAYA MTS.   QING EMPIRE

AFRICA   Mt. Everest   Calcutta

ARABIA   Bombay   INDIA

Senegal R.   Niger R.   Goa

Nile R.   Madras   Manila   Philippine Is.

Segu   DAHOMEY   Ceylon

Cape Coast Castle   Mombasa

AFRICA

Batavia   EAST INDIES

PACIFIC OCEAN

VICEROYALTY OF NEW SPAIN

Sandwich (Hawaiian) Is.

Death of Cook, 1779.

V. OF NEW GRANADA

V. OF PERU

SOUTH AMERICA   Rio de Janeiro

V. OF RIO DE LA PLATA

VICEROYALTY OF BRAZIL

Cape Town

INDIAN OCEAN

NEW HOLLAND (AUSTRALIA)

Great Barrier Reef

Botany Bay   North I.

Tahiti

Tierra del Fuego   South I.

Cape Horn   New Zealand

0   1,000 2,000 Km.

0   1,000   2,000 Mi.

ANTARCTICA

The Travels of Joseph Banks

- Joseph Banks's journeys
- Later journeys by Cook
- • City visited by Banks
- • Other city

European territories, ca. 1770

British	Portuguese
Dutch	Russian
French	Spanish

Timeline:

1650   1700   1750   1800   1850

Lifetime of Joseph Banks
1743 — 1820

EUROPE

Lifetime of Isaac Newton
1642 — 1727

Pacific voyages of Captain Cook
1768 — 1779

Locke's *Essay Concerning Human Understanding*
1690

Chronometer invented
1763

AMERICAS

Lewis and Clark Expedition
1804 1806

AFRICA, ASIA, AND AUSTRALIA/ OCEANIA

Death of Captain Cook
1779

British map India in the Great Trigonometrical Survey
1790s

Founding of New South Wales (Aus.)
1788

Mungo Park maps the Niger River
1795

the bare place and made signs that we should do the same. . . . Each of us dropped a bough upon those that the Indians had laid down, we all followed their example and thus peace was concluded.[1]

● **Joseph Banks** (1743–1820) English botanist on Captain James Cook's first voyage in the Pacific who categorized different species of plants and brought them back to England. Also established the Royal Botanic Gardens at Kew.

Such ceremonies became a bit less mysterious to Banks after he began to learn the Tahitian language and made friends with a high priest who helped him understand Polynesian customs. Still, even after years of contact, the cultural gulf between the Tahitians and the Englishmen remained immense.

Banks returned to England in 1771 after a three-year journey. The crewmen who had survived the *Endeavour*'s three years at sea were among the few at that time who had sailed around the entire world. Captain Cook became an instant celebrity. He had accomplished his mission of charting the Pacific Ocean, thus facilitating future European voyages to such places as Hawai'i, New Zealand, and Australia. He had also carried out important astronomical observations.

In fact, scientific inquiry was central to the *Endeavour*'s mission. The drawings and specimens of plant and animal life Banks brought back greatly expanded European knowledge of the natural world. He was interested not merely in collecting exotic flora and fauna but also in systematically classifying and cataloging his findings. While Cook was using his mathematical and navigational skills to chart the oceans, Banks was developing a system for naming and describing natural phenomena in order to clarify familial relationships in nature.

Why was Banks taken on board the *Endeavour* in the first place? There was no immediate, tangible benefit from his work. But science now enjoyed considerable social and political support. Especially in Britain and France, leaders understood the connection between science and empire. Banks's reconnaissance of the natural world, like that of the physical world undertaken by Cook, was a prelude to the more assertive European imperialism of the nineteenth century. While Polynesians were struggling to understand what they saw as the strange behavior of their British visitors, Cook was claiming their islands "for the use of his Brittanick majesty." Banks came home dreaming of "future dominions," an influential advocate of British settlement in Australia.[2] Science and empire would remain companions throughout the nineteenth century.

After the return of the *Endeavour*'s Banks never again traveled outside Europe. But from 1778 to 1820, as president of the Royal Society, the most prestigious scientific establishment in Europe, he focused on fields such as "economic botany," which linked science to technological and economic development. At the same time, men and women more philosophically inclined than Banks were extending the scientific model of inquiry, with its emphasis on reason, to human society, creating what is called the European Enlightenment.

Focus Questions

 When and how did Europe's Scientific Revolution begin to have practical applications?

 How did Enlightenment thought derive from the Scientific Revolution, and how did it differ from previous European thought systems?

 How did systematic classification and measurement support European imperialism in the late eighteenth and early nineteenth centuries?

 How did the societies of Oceania and Australia experience encounters with Europeans in this period?

● From Scientific Revolution to Practical Science, 1600–1800

Joseph Banks was heir to a scientific tradition that stretched back to the sixteenth century, when Nicolaus Copernicus first published his theory of a heliocentric solar system and Galileo Galilei upset church authorities by providing strong evidence that the earth rotates around the sun (see Chapter 16).

The Christian faith, in both its Catholic and various Protestant forms, continued to provide most western Europeans with answers to basic questions about relationships between God, humanity, and the natural world. By the eighteenth century, however, especially among the elite of northern Europe, an increasingly prominent group of men and women had embraced the "new science," with its emphasis on rational inquiry. Aided by the patronage of European monarchs, some members of the aristocracy and of the rising middle class began to pursue science as a vocation.

The development of science in eighteenth-century Europe was important from a purely intellectual standpoint. But Western science became "revolutionary" only when practical applications of science increased the political and military power of Europeans on the world stage. Joseph Banks contributed immensely to this development, both on his own English estate and more broadly in the British Empire. During his lifetime scientific inquiry became progressively more linked to real-world applications and economic purposes.

The Development of the Scientific Method

In seventeenth-century western Europe a sharp intellectual debate divided thinkers into two basic camps: the "ancients" and the "moderns." The "ancients" continued to emphasize the authority of Aristotle and other classical authors as the foundation on which knowledge in fields such as medicine, mathematics, and astronomy should be built. The "moderns" had a bolder idea. Rejecting the notion that one should always respect classical authorities (or Christian theology), they argued that the unfettered application of human reason provided the key to knowledge.

It was an optimistic viewpoint that contradicted the traditional Christian idea of humanity as "fallen" from God's grace, tainted by original sin, and capable of salvation only through God's mercy. The "moderns" believed instead that humankind was endowed by God with reason and through that reason could apprehend and accurately describe God's creation. "All our knowledge begins with the senses, proceeds then to understanding, and ends with reason. There is nothing higher than reason," wrote the eighteenth-century German philosopher Immanuel Kant.[3]

One seventeenth-century thinker who used a *deductive* approach to truth was the Frenchman **René Descartes** (1596–1650). Descartes (DAY-cart) argued that the axioms from which true philosophy should proceed had to be rigorously grounded in the human capacity to reason. He associated rationality with mathematics and thought the rigorous application of logic could result in a unified system of truth. He therefore emphasized systematic doubt as a key to knowledge, questioning even his own existence. His solution to that question, "I think, therefore I am," demonstrated that his ability to perceive the rational order of creation was at the core of his own existence. Descartes also had to doubt the existence of God before he could prove to his own satisfaction that God did, in fact, exist. Once again that proof came from rational thought rather than inherited wisdom or sacred texts.

Descartes is considered a philosopher and not a scientist because his works were based on logical reasoning rather than observation of the natural world. At the same time, others were laying the foundations for modern science based on experimentation and careful observation. The Englishman **Sir Francis Bacon** (1561–1626) was one of the main proponents of an *inductive* approach to science: working from modest, carefully controlled observations toward larger truths. Like Descartes, Bacon believed that doubt produced knowledge. "If a man will begin with certainties," he wrote, "he shall end in doubts; but if he will be content to begin with doubts he shall end in certainties."[4] (See the feature "Movement of Ideas: A Japanese View of European Science.")

Both Descartes, who used reason to deduce truths about existence, and Bacon, who used an inductive approach that emphasized close observation and careful record keeping, were part of an intellectual trend in western Europe that increasingly emphasized human possibilities. In spite of humanity's sinful nature, they argued, the ability to reason gave man an opportunity to comprehend the brilliance of God's creation, to strive toward truth on the basis of science. Such beliefs, controversial in Protestant England and Catholic France, were, as we have seen, actively repressed in seventeenth-century Italy at the time of Galileo (see Chapter 16).

Isaac Newton (1642–1727), born the same year that Galileo died, did more than anyone to create a systematic new architecture for science: his universal law of gravitation. Newton was a skilled experimental scientist in Bacon's inductive tradition. His work in optics, for example, led to the development of much more powerful telescopes. But he was pre-eminently a theorist who followed Descartes' lead in using reasoned, deductive thinking to establish general principles that tied together his own and others' findings. To achieve the mathematical rigor necessary to describe the acceleration and deceleration of bodies in motion, Newton became one of the inventors of differential calculus. He described a predictable

• René Descartes (1596–1650) French scientist, mathematician, and philosopher who developed the deductive method of reasoning, moving from general principles to particular facts.

• Sir Francis Bacon (1561–1626) English politician, essayist, and philosopher. Known for his *Novum Organum* (1620), in which he argues for inductive reasoning and the rejection of *a priori* hypotheses. His science was based on close observation of natural phenomena.

• Isaac Newton (1642–1727) Skilled theoretical and experimental scientist who created a systematic new architecture for science: the universal law of gravitation. Also one of the inventors of differential calculus and undertook extensive experiments with optics.

Advances in Astronomy

Apart from Galileo and Newton, many other European scientists were involved in the quest for astronomical knowledge. Here the Danish astronomer Tycho Brahe is depicted in the observatory from which he made the most detailed stellar observations since ancient Greek times. The German mathematician Johannes Kepler used Brahe's data to support the Copernican view of a sun-centered universe. (Bildarchiv Preussischer Kulturbesitz/ Art Resource, NY)

natural world in which all matter exerted gravitational attraction to all other matter, in inverse proportion to mass and distance.

Western Europe's educated elite were ready for such a solution. Whereas the new science had earlier caused anxiety by calling into question comfortable old ways of thinking, by the early eighteenth century an English poet could write: "Nature and Nature's laws lay hid in night; God said Let Newton Be! and all was light."[5] The association between God and Newton in this poem shows that the tension between science and faith was beginning to ease. Newton himself was a devout Christian. While many Christians continued to believe that God actively intervened in nature, those who adopted Newton's outlook tended to see the universe as a self-functioning outcome of God's perfect act of creation. He had embedded perfect proportionality and balance in nature, which was comprehensible to humanity through its ability to reason. God was like a master clock maker who, having set his elegant machine in motion, did not need to interfere further with its functioning.

With bold confidence Isaac Newton declared that he could use mathematics to "demonstrate the frame of the system of the world." Joseph Banks inherited not only Newton's optimism but also his position as president of the Royal Society, an assembly of leading thinkers. Starting with Newton and continuing with Banks, the Royal Society served as a nerve center for European science.

CL Primary Source: Sir Isaac Newton Lays Down the Ground Rules for the Scientific Method *Newton provides four detailed rules that define the principles of the Scientific Method.*

Practical Science: Economic Botany, Agriculture, and Empire

Close study of plant life has always been characteristic of human societies. Relying on the natural world for medicine as well as for food, people have always developed an intimate knowledge of their own local

A Japanese View of European Science

In the history of modern science, a common pattern has been repeated around the world. Those who generated new ideas, such as Galileo, were often attacked for their assault on tradition, but later their innovations were absorbed into the European status quo. When Europeans then took the new science to other continents, once again these ideas and approaches challenged established tradition. Here we have an example from anatomy, with a Japanese observation of the dissection of a human corpse.

For medieval Europeans the main authority in anatomy was the ancient Greek physician Galen, who, though he dissected many birds and animals, had theories about the inner workings of the human body that were based largely on speculation. Then, in 1543, a Belgian physician published a new scheme of human anatomy based on actual dissection of human cadav-

ers. Adherents of Galen's view were upset, as were those many Christians who saw the violation of dead bodies as sacrilegious. Over the next two hundred years, however, dissection became a routine process.

In the eighteenth century, the Tokugawa shoguns had severely limited Japanese contacts with Europeans. But through the annual Dutch trade mission to Nagasaki a few books entered the country, and some curious Japanese scholars learned Dutch so they could read them (see Chapter 20). Below, a physician named Sugita Gempaku (1733–1817) describes how, having looked at a Dutch anatomy text, he was astonished to see how accurate it was when he witnessed the dissection of a human body.

Source: David John Lu, ed., *Sources of Japanese History* (New York: McGraw-Hill, 1974), vol. 1, pp. 253–255.

A Dutch Lesson in Anatomy

Somehow, miraculously I obtained a [Dutch] book on anatomy. [Then] I received a letter from . . . the Town Commissioner: "A post-mortem examination of the body of a condemned criminal by a resident physician will be held tomorrow. . . . You are welcome to witness it if you so desire."

The next day, when we arrived at the location . . . Ryotaku reached under his kimono to produce a Dutch book and showed it to us. "This is a Dutch book of anatomy called *Tabulae Anatomicae*. I bought this a few years ago when I went to Nagasaki, and kept it." As I examined it, it was the same book I had and was of the same edition. We held each other's hands and exclaimed: "What a coincidence!" Ryotaku continued by saying, "When I went to Nagasaki, I learned and heard," and opened this book. "These are called *long* in Dutch, they are the lungs," he taught us. "This is *hart*, or the heart." . . . However, they did not look like the heart given in the Chinese medical books, and none of us were sure until we could actually see the dissection.

Thereafter we went together to the place that was especially set aside us to observe the dissection. . . . That day, the butcher pointed to this and that organ. After the heart, liver, gall bladder and stomach were identified, he pointed to other parts for which there were no names. "I don't know their names. But I have dissected quite a few bodies from my youthful days. . . . Every time I had a dissection, I pointed out to those physicians many of these parts, but not a single one of them questioned 'What was this,' or 'What was that?'" We compared the body as dissected against the charts both Ryotaku and I had, and could not find a single variance from the charts. The Chinese *Book of Medicine* says that the lungs are like the eight petals of the lotus flower, with three petals hanging in front, three in back, and two petals forming like two ears. . . . There were no such divisions, and the position and shapes of intestines and gastric organs were all different from those taught by the old theories. The official physicians . . . had witnessed dissection seven or eight times. Whenever they witnessed the dissection, they found that the old theories contradicted reality. Each time they were perplexed and could not resolve their doubts. Every time they wrote down what they thought was strange. They wrote in their books, "The more we think of it, there must be fundamental differences in the bodies of Chinese and of the eastern barbarians." I could see why they wrote this way. . . .

We decided that we should also examine the shape of the skeletons left exposed on the execution ground. We collected the bones, and examined a number of them. Again, we were struck by the fact that they all differed from the old theories while conforming to the Dutch charts. . . .

On the way home we spoke to each other and felt the same way. "How marvelous was our actual experience today. It is a shame that we were ignorant of these things until now. As physicians . . . we performed our duties in complete ignorance of the true form of the human body." . . . Then I spoke to my companion, "Somehow if we can translate anew this book called *Tabulae Anatomicae,* we can get a clear notion of the human body inside out. It will have great benefit in the treatment of our patients. Let us do our best to read it and understand it without the help of translators." . . .

The next day, we assembled at the house of Ryotaku and recalled the happenings of the previous day. When we faced the *Tabulae Anatomicae* we felt as if we were setting sail on a great ocean in a ship without oars or a rudder. With the magnitude of the work before us, we were dumbfounded by our own ignorance. . . . At that time I did not know the twenty-five letters of the Dutch alphabet. I decided to study the language with firm determination, but I had to acquaint myself with letters and words gradually.

QUESTIONS FOR ANALYSIS

▶ What was the basis of earlier Japanese views of anatomy, and how were they contradicted by the Dutch textbook?

▶ How does Gempaku's experience compare with that of "The Travels of Evliya Çelebi" (see Chapter 17)?

environment. But it was only with the rise of modern botany that scientists began to systematically collect and organize a global catalogue of the world's flora.

Carl Linnaeus (1707–1778) was the pioneering figure in this area. As a medical student, Linnaeus was initially trained to recognize plants for their curative properties, but as his enthusiasm for plant collecting grew, his focus switched to natural science. He traveled across Sweden gathering plant specimens, lavished attention on the botanical gardens at the university where he taught, and eventually sent nineteen of his students on voyages of trade and exploration around the world to increase the range of specimens available for scientific study. Two of Linnaeus's students were aboard the *Endeavour* serving as assistants to Joseph Banks.

As with Newton, the greatest scientists were those who combined experimentation and observation with theoretical system building. In 1735 Linnaeus published his *Systema Naturae,* laying out a scheme of classification that still influences the naming and categorization of plant life. Species were grouped into hierarchies of increasingly more general categories: genus/order/class/kingdom. Any new plant that was encountered anywhere in the world could therefore be classified in a well-ordered system that, to Linnaeus, demonstrated the beauty and orderliness of God's creation.

Linnaeus also developed a "binomial" ("two name") system for giving plants Latin names, the first name indicating the genus and the second the species. The world's plants were, of course, already named by the local people who were familiar with them. Now, as Linnaeus's students brought more and more specimens back to Europe, they received new names that made them, for the first time, part of a single knowledge system.

Linnaeus knew of Banks, and after the return of the *Endeavour* sent him a letter of congratulations. Though by far a more brilliant theoretician and more original thinker than Banks, Linnaeus had failed in his attempts to derive practical, economic lessons from his botany. But economic botany was precisely the area in which Banks excelled.

Banks was a leading figure in the late-eighteenth-century drive for "improvement," which in agriculture meant increasing the productivity of existing land and bringing new land under cultivation. Both Banks and King George III (r. 1760–1820), sometimes called "the farmer king," were eager supporters of the effort to bring to agriculture the insights gained from natural science. Progress had been made in the seventeenth century, when English farmers had made more efficient use of their land by planting soil-friendly crops like clover and turnips in fields that had previously been left fallow, and through the selective breeding of sheep and cattle had boosted their output of wool, meat, and milk.

Another innovation that was increasing production in this period was the draining of marshlands for farming. In low-lying Holland, Dutch engineers led the way by developing more and more sophisticated, wind-driven pumping systems to reclaim land from the sea. Later large amounts of marshy land in England were also drained and brought into agricultural production. Joseph Banks was just one of the wealthy landowners who, being able to afford the investment, borrowed this Dutch technology to extend their holdings and increase their profits. Banks's estate exemplified all the measures that were promoting agricultural productivity in eighteenth-century England: the draining of marshes, experiments with crop rotations, and crossbreeding of farm animals. The net effect has been called an "agricultural revolution."

● **Carl Linnaeus** (1707–1778) Swedish founder of the modern systems of botany and zoology. The basic parameters of his classification systems are still in use.

In Holland, the expense of the windmills, pumps, and dikes and the small size of the country made farmland a scarce resource. Nevertheless, land distribution remained fairly egalitarian. In England, by contrast, the agricultural revolution was characterized by rising inequality. The rural gentry were consolidating possession over larger and more efficient farms, while some poorer rural families were driven off the land.

Like traditional peasant societies in many parts of the world, English village society was oriented toward stability and security. For example, English farm families shared access to vital common resources such as pastures and woodlands. But in the seventeenth and eighteenth centuries ambitious members of the English gentry, like the Banks family, responded to growing urban markets for food by accumulating larger landholdings. They were aided by new laws that allowed them to "enclose" the common lands as their own private property, in what is called the enclosure movement. On these larger estates, "gentlemen farmers" like Banks were able to make investments and pursue innovations that dramatically increased English farm output.

Having lost access to the commons, many rural families had to either work for the gentry or drift to cities or coal mines looking for employment. One person's "improvement," therefore, could be another's ticket to unemployment. Banks himself received numerous letters from his farm manager complaining of protests from displaced farmers, and his London house was once attacked by people protesting a trade law that benefited landholders like Banks but made the price of bread much higher for the urban poor. The interests of "gentlemen" like Banks were well represented in Parliament, while those of the rural and urban poor were not.

Joseph Banks played a pivotal role in globalizing the practical application of science through his advocacy of "economic botany." To this end he developed a pioneering experimental facility at Kew Gardens, "a great botanical exchange house for the empire."[6] As other scientists followed his example from the *Endeavour*, collecting and describing new plant species from around the world, they would bring specimens to Kew to be further examined and cultivated. The benefits of this "economic botany" could then be disseminated both within Britain and in the wider colonial world.

Throughout the expanding British Empire, in such places as the West Indies, South Africa, and India, botanical gardens were created by British governors and commercial concerns as part of this wider effort to achieve agricultural "improvement" on a global scale. Rather than the haphazard circulation of species in the age of the Columbian exchange, this was biological diffusion aided by science. For example, when the British navy needed secure supplies of timber from tall trees for ship construction,

Botany and Art
Most scientific expeditions, starting with Banks's own journey to the Pacific and Australia, employed artists to catalog in fine detail the new flora they encountered. This exquisite rendering of a *Corypha Elata* plant, native to northern Australia, was produced by an anonymous Indian artist employed by the British. (By kind permission of the Trustees of the Royal Botanic Gardens, Kew)

English botanists identified South Asian mahogany as a possible supplement to British and North American oak and shipped seeds from India to botanical gardens in the British West Indies for study. Another example is the story of merino sheep, which Banks imported from Spain for crossbreeding purposes to improve British wool. While this experiment was not successful in England, merino sheep formed the basis of the early colonial economy of British Australia.

In addition to practical solutions to Britain's domestic and international economic concerns, the emphasis on science and "improvement" provided a set of ideas that justified the dominance of the English elite at home and abroad. The enclosure movement removed impediments to efficiency and productivity. Advocates argued that even those who were thrust aside in the short term would ultimately benefit from scientifically rational agriculture. The same idea could also be applied to the empire. Aboriginal Australians might neither understand nor accept the necessity of fencing off vast tracts of land for sheep herding, thus keeping them from their traditional hunting-and-gathering terrain. But no individual or group, the "improvers" said, should stand in the way of progress.

Francis Bacon, the great proponent of experimental science, had first applied the idea of bringing improvement to colonized peoples to Ireland:

> [We shall] reclaim them from their barbarous manners . . . populate, plant and make civil all the provinces of that kingdom . . . as we are persuaded that it is one of the chief causes for which God hath brought us to the imperial crown of these Kingdoms.[7]

By Banks's day the emphasis on God's will had lessened; the stress was now on the fulfillment of the earth's potential in line with a beneficent natural order. But the basic message was the same: we must "reclaim" land from "barbarous" people to make it more productive. Banks wrote, after the foundation of a botanical garden in Calcutta, that economic botany "would help to banish famine in India and win the love of the Asiatics for their British conquerors."[8] The connection between science and empire was deep and lasting.

The European Enlightenment, 1700–1800

• Enlightenment
Late-seventeenth-century European philosophical movement that stressed the use of reason rather than the authority of ancient philosophers or religious leaders in descriptions of society and the natural world.

The optimism characteristic of the new science influenced European views on human society as well. During the eighteenth century prominent **Enlightenment** thinkers argued that the same capacity for reason that allows scientists to unlock the secrets of the natural world should also be applied to social, political, and economic questions. Just as scientists like Newton believed that the inner workings of nature could be understood by human reason and described with mathematical precision, so Enlightenment philosophers saw rational, critical thinking as the best means of understanding and improving human society. By the late eighteenth century, some thought that progress in human affairs was not only possible but inevitable.

For these lofty ideas to find practical application, they needed to influence those in power, and Enlightenment philosophy did have an impact on Europe's kings, queens, and aristocracies. But there were limits to how far these "enlightened" rulers would follow through on the philosophers' call for reform. Since their own status was based on tradition, few eighteenth-century European rulers were willing to apply reason and critical thought in a way that undermined traditional power structures.

"Enlightened" Ideas: Politics, Economics, and Society

The contrast between two English political philosophers, Thomas Hobbes (1588–1679) and John Locke (1632–1704), demonstrates the growing optimism of the Enlightenment. Hobbes was a friend of René Descartes and applied the Frenchman's method of deductive reasoning to the question of how best to sustain political order in human society. His answer was deeply pessimistic. In the state of nature, he argued, there is no government, anarchy prevails, and life is "nasty, brutish, and short."[9] Social and political order, Hobbes argued, becomes possible only when individuals give up their autonomy and accept the need for a despotic ruler. Hobbes rejected the concept of the "divine right of kings," basing his support for absolute monarchy as the best form of government instead on reasoned arguments.

While Hobbes had used Descartes' method of deductive reasoning starting from axiomatic principles, **John Locke** (1632–1704) was a medical doctor who preferred Bacon's inductive approach, starting with experience and observation. His optimistic conclusions could not have been more different than those of Hobbes. In his *Essay Concerning Human Understanding* (1690), Locke argued that a stable, balanced political order is based on a contract in which individuals receive protection of their basic rights, "life, liberty and property," while they voluntarily give up some of their autonomy to the state, which was itself balanced between executive and legislative authorities. What Locke described was not a democracy: in his view only propertied males were capable of participating in government. But the rights of all would be protected regardless of gender or social class.

Hobbes's pessimism derived in part from his experience with the anarchy of the English Civil War, while Locke's optimism was connected to the role he played as an adviser to King William and Queen Mary during the Glorious Revolution (see Chapter 17). The balance between the powers of king and Parliament, and the protection of individual liberties through a Bill of Rights, were real-world applications of Locke's theories.

A French thinker who was influenced by English constitutional thought was the Baron de Montesquieu (1689–1755), who traveled to England to observe its very different constitutional system. This experience greatly influenced his book *The Spirit of the Laws* (1748), in which he argued for limitations on the power of government and a rational distribution of power between different social classes. Montesquieu (maw-tuh-SKYOO) believed that, as societies became more advanced, their political systems would become more liberal and their people more free. Following Locke, who argued that executive and legislative powers should be separate and balanced, Montesquieu maintained that judicial functions should also be protected from executive interference.

The most original economic thinker of the Enlightenment was Adam Smith, whose *Wealth of Nations* (1776) emphasized the self-regulating power of markets. Smith argued for the encouragement of free markets and unfettered economic interchange within and between nations. The French term **laissez faire** ("leave to do") (lay-say fair) has often been applied to Smith's vision of free-market capitalism. He argued that economic productivity was based on a division of labor. An

●**John Locke** (1632–1704)   Philosopher who applied Bacon's inductive reasoning to the study of politics and argued that a stable social order is based on a contract between rulers and ruled and requires the safeguarding of "life, liberty and property."

●*laissez faire* (French, "leave to do.") Economic philosophy attributed to Scottish Enlightenment thinker Adam Smith, who argued that businesses and nations benefit from a free market where each party seeks to maximize its comparative economic advantage.

individual who performed all the processes necessary to make a pin would be hard pressed to produce one a day. But if the process were subdivided among ten workers, each specializing in one aspect of production, Smith argued, thousands could be produced each day. He applied the same principle to international trade. If each nation specialized in the production of what it was best fit to produce, and trade with other nations specializing in products best fitted to their economic potential, everyone would gain through mutual exchange. Smith was also opposed to slavery because he thought that free labor contracts negotiated in the market would lead to more efficient production. He believed that the "invisible hand" of the market functioned like Isaac Newton's laws of gravitational attraction, maintaining balance and harmony in economic affairs. Like Locke, he also believed that protection of private property was a core function of government.

Smith's advocacy of the free market contradicted existing European economic policies based on monopoly and mercantilism. Like other Enlightenment thinkers, Smith was using reason to challenge existing traditions and assumptions. And whereas mercantilism had been based on a zero-sum view of economics, in which one nation could advance only at another's expense, Smith held the more optimistic view that freer international trade would lead to the generation of more wealth for all.

While philosophers across Europe aspired to the title "enlightened," it was through Paris that the main intellectual currents of the Western world flowed in the mid-eighteenth century. Indeed, we still use the French word for philosophers, ***philosophes*** (fill-uh-SOHF), to describe these intellectuals today. The most important of them was François-Marie Arouet, better known as Voltaire (1694–1778). Voltaire (vawl-TARE) was most famous as a satirist who used his reason like a searchlight to illuminate all the superstitions, prejudices, and follies of eighteenth-century European society. In his great novel *Candide* (1759), he mocked the corruption and injustice of the world around him. He believed that reason makes all phenomena and situations intelligible to the human intellect and thought that relativism, the ability to see yourself and your own social circumstances in a wider context, is a necessary component of enlightened thinking, since tolerance toward and understanding of others is a precondition for self-knowledge. Voltaire incurred the displeasure of religious authorities by arguing that organized religion is always and everywhere a hindrance to free and rational inquiry.

One place where Enlightenment ideas were discussed was in the *salons* (drawing rooms) of Paris. Often organized and hosted by women of means and education, these salons brought philosophical and artistic discussions into the homes of the elite; Voltaire and other notable philosophers were highly sought after as guests. But though women often were hostesses for these gatherings and participated in the lively discussions, few Enlightenment thinkers were willing to consider that traditional restrictions on the role of women were a matter of prejudice and tradition rather than reason.

Some women, however, protested their exclusion from full participation in intellectual life. At the same time as Sor Juana was meeting resistance from Catholic Church authorities in New Spain because of her writings (see Chapter 18), a seventeenth-century English scientist named Margaret Cavendish argued that restrictions on women's role resulted from nothing more than "the over-weening conceit men have of themselves."[10] Another Englishwoman, Mary Astell, challenged John Locke's idea that absolute authority, while unacceptable in the state, was appropriate within the family. Late in the eighteenth century Mary Wollenstonecraft

• ***philosophes*** French intellectuals who promoted Enlightenment principles.

Ⓒ**Primary Source:** Treatise on Toleration *Voltaire makes a powerful argument for cultural and religious tolerance.*

went even further in her *Vindication of the Rights of Women* (1792). Only through equal access to education, full citizenship, and financial autonomy, Wollenstone-craft argued, could women's full potential as individuals and as wives and mothers be achieved.

For many of the elite who attended the salons, arguing about such daring ideas as equality for women was more a matter of fashion than of passion. At the other extreme of the French social order, the Enlightenment had little immediate im-pact on the thinking of artisans and farmers, people whom Voltaire and most other philosophes considered irrational and tradition-bound. Of all the classes in French society, Enlightenment thought may have had the greatest impact on the *bourgeoisie,* or middle class.

The French bourgeoisie were economically successful but lacked the social sta-tus, and even the political rights, of the aristocrats. A more skeptical attitude toward religious and civil authority therefore came naturally to many of these educated, middle-class men and women. Expanding literacy meant that even those who did not travel in the refined circles of royal and aristocratic patronage, and who might never be invited to attend a salon, had access to these ideas. The most important publishing project of the age was the **Encyclopedia,** or *Rational Dictionary of the Arts, Sciences and Crafts,* a collection of all the great Enlightenment works that was compiled in Paris between 1751 and 1776, initially under the direction of Denis

• *Encyclopedia*
A collection of the works of all the great Enlightenment thinkers. Compiled in Paris be-tween 1751 and 1776, it promoted a new form of universal knowledge based on reason and the critical use of human intellect.

The *Encyclopedia*   Denis Diderot, the leading figure behind the *Encyclopedia,* aspired to collect all scientific and philosophical information in one publication. Essays numbering 70,000 were accompanied by 3000 illustrations, including "The Print Shop" shown here. The original essays were widely translated, spreading Enlightenment ideas across Europe.   (Division of Rare Books & Manuscripts Collection, Cornell University)

Diderot. More powerfully than any other work, this encyclopedia made the case for a new form of universal knowledge based on reason and the critical use of human intellect. The growth of the printing and publishing industries facilitated the widespread dissemination of the *Encyclopedia,* and translation into English, Spanish, and German meant it had an international impact.

The German philosopher Immanuel Kant (1724–1804) emphasized that cowardice stood in the way of enlightenment. Unquestioned tradition and blind faith, "man's inability to make use of his understanding without direction from another," hinders our progress. "Have courage to use your own reason," Kant concluded; "that is the motto of enlightenment."[11] But translating that motto into political reality meant confronting powerful vested interests, with radical, and potentially revolutionary, implications.

"Enlightened Despots" in Eighteenth-Century Europe

Voltaire and most other philosophes thought that if society were to become enlightened, the change would have to come from above. That provided some European monarchs, so-called **enlightened despots,** a new rationale for absolute power. Rather than simply claiming "divine right," they portrayed themselves as bringing order, harmony, and reason to their domains. In the late seventeenth century, Louis XIV is supposed to have said, "I am the state." Now in the eighteenth century, Frederick the Great of Prussia defined himself as "first servant of the state." It was a crucial difference, implying that the kingdom was greater than the king, who needed to demonstrate his competence in action.

• **enlightened despots** Eighteenth-century European rulers who sought to systematically apply Enlightenment ideals to the administration of government.

The Prussian leader Frederick the Great (r. 1740–1786) was perhaps the most "enlightened" of the great monarchs of the eighteenth century. As a young man, Frederick was engaged in the serious study of music and literature. He became a first-rate flute player, and his patronage made Prussia, previously considered only a military power, a center for the arts. Frederick was deeply interested in French literature and the ideas of the philosophes. After visiting with Voltaire in 1750, he kept up a long correspondence with the French thinker, trading philosophical ideas. He reformed the Prussian legal system to emphasize reason and justice over tradition, advocated freedom of conscience, and allowed some freedom of the press. However, the Prussian military tradition continued, and Frederick's Prussia was still a tightly regimented society. Under his rule Prussian territory doubled in size while the army became one of the largest and strongest in Europe.

The Enlightenment was also influential in two land-based European empires, Austria and Russia. In Austria, Empress Maria Theresa (r. 1740–1780) undertook significant reforms in the empire's linguistically and religiously complex domains. She put strict limits on landlords' power and was also the first European monarch to support compulsory education for all her subjects; though she failed to achieve that goal, it was an important precedent for the future. Maria Theresa's reforms were carried even further by her son and heir, Joseph II (r. 1780–1790), who abolished serfdom and liberalized laws restricting freedom of the press and religion. But some of Joseph's subjects, including the small but growing middle class, did not approve of his autocratic methods. Public participation in reform was not part of Joseph's plan, or of the plans of any other "enlightened despot."

In Russia, Catherine the Great took an active interest in Enlightenment philosophy and corresponded with Voltaire. She found the Enlightenment ideals enticing in theory, but not applicable to Russia. While her Austrian counterparts were reforming and then abolishing serfdom, under Catherine's rule the power of the Russian aristocracy over their serfs became greater than ever (see Chapter 20). Although Catherine consolidated Romanov power and expanded the Russian Empire, Russia remained the least open and least liberal of the European great powers.

In France, King Louis XV (r. 1715–1774) had inherited great power from his great-grandfather Louis XIV, but also a difficult set of political and financial challenges. Louis XV was only 5 years old when he came to the throne, and not until the 1740s did he take command. While his mistress patronized the philosophes, Louis contended with such difficult matters of state as the loss of the Seven Years' War to England (see Chapter 19). Unlike Frederick the Great in Prussia, who reformed his country's financial system to support his military efforts, Louis was blocked by vested interests when he tried to strengthen his financial position: the French nobility refused to pay any taxes at all.

In Britain, the constitutional balance of power established in 1689 prevented any kind of despotism, enlightened or otherwise. In 1714 a reliably Protestant German prince was crowned King George I. Speaking little English, George I accepted the powers of Parliament and hence the limitations on his own power. The British system of government evolved to meet new challenges as the eighteenth century progressed. The Scottish and English thrones were peacefully united to form Great Britain in 1707, and parliamentary factions developed into organized political parties.

There were unmet challenges in Great Britain as well. Restrictions on the civil rights of British Catholics remained, and attempts to reform the House of Commons to increase the representation of merchants and propertied professionals such as doctors and lawyers failed. These and other issues would be addressed in the course of the nineteenth century through parliamentary action and constitutional evolution. In many other parts of Europe, however, the failure of "enlightened despots" to substantially reform their societies led to conflict and revolution (see Chapters 22 and 23).

Measuring and Mapping: Exploration and Imperialism in Africa, India, and the Americas, 1763–1820

Enlightenment thinkers applied to human society science's emphasis on mathematical description of the natural world. In an age of expanding European empires, this quest for quantification had global implications. In the late eighteenth and early nineteenth centuries, the link between science and empire was firmly established through increasingly sophisticated measurement of time and mapping of space. Imperial officials in Qing China compiled maps and ethnographic information about subject peoples as part of their imperial project. However, the European efforts were more systematic, more widely spread, and ultimately more influential in shaping the modern world.

Europe's global control required much more detailed knowledge of world geography, and new procedures and technologies were developed to meet that need. For navigators the main challenge was the "problem of longitude," the need to find a way to accurately establish their position on an east/west axis. Across Africa, India, and the Americas, geographic expeditions gathered geographical information and communicated that knowledge through the many scientific societies of the Enlightenment, thereby expanding European power to new corners of the globe. The "future dominions" of which Joseph Banks dreamed at the time of the *Endeavour*'s journey were, by the early 1800s, becoming a reality in places like Canada, Australia, South Africa, and India.

Practical Science, the Royal Society, and the Quest for Longitude

As a natural scientist, Banks was most competent in the field of living organisms and their interconnections. Within the Royal Society over which he presided from 1778 to 1820, many saw mathematics and astronomy as the superior sciences. Whether dealing with flora and fauna or with calculus and planetary orbits, however, all scientists of his time were interested in practical applications of their theories. For a nation that was ascending to the top of the global power structure on the basis of its maritime prowess, the most important practical applications of mathematics and astronomy had to do with navigation. The **problem of longitude**—how to determine a ship's position on an east/west axis—occupied some of the best minds of the time.

The basic problem had puzzled mariners for much of human history. The best way to describe the location of any given point is with a set of imaginary intersecting lines that we know as latitude and longitude. Lines of latitude, determining position along a north/south axis, are easy to fix by observing natural phenomena, such as the height of the sun or familiar stars above the horizon. In the Middle Ages these techniques were advanced by Arab sailors, who introduced devices such as the quadrant and astrolabe (AS-truh-labe) to Europeans. Later refined, these navigational tools gave captains from Columbus to Cook an accurate way to chart latitude.

Much more difficult was the attempt to determine longitude, the relative position of a point on an east/west axis. Distance traveled in this direction could be determined only if the time at any two points could be accurately recorded. Until the late eighteenth century, ships' captains had no better solution than setting a log adrift and charting its motion to roughly calculate the speed and distance traveled. The inaccuracy of this system was demonstrated time and time again: captains often miscalculated their position by hundreds of miles, vainly looking for land when they expected to find it and crashing into rocky shores that suddenly appeared from nowhere. The toll in shipwrecks, and of lost lives and cargo, was great. Equally tragic was the suffering, including loss of life from dehydration and scurvy, that resulted when ships wandered endlessly looking for land, unsure how far away it was or whether it lay to the east or to the west.

The regular, clocklike cosmos described by scientists from Galileo to Newton offered hope. Longitude could be accurately fixed if a captain knew exactly what time it was on board relative to any other fixed location on earth. With the belief that the heavens moved in a regular, predictable way that could be mathematically described, European scientists set out to find a way to translate celestial time into local time on board a ship. To do so, they would have to strictly predict the positions of two known heavenly points—the sun, the moon, or a star—for one location on earth and then compared those with their actual position on a ship.

• **problem of longitude** The lack of an accurate means of determining a ship's position on an east/west axis. The problem was solved with the invention of an accurate shipboard chronometer by English cabinetmaker John Harrison.

The problem was that very few celestial events could be predicted with any certainty. Lunar and solar eclipses could be used this way, but they occurred too rarely to be useful. Galileo had shown that the moons of Jupiter eclipsed on a regular and predictable basis. If the timing of these eclipses could be charted, a ship's captain could compare the known time of the eclipse at a fixed location (such as his port of departure) and the actual observation of the eclipse at sea to determine his longitude. The system worked well on land, but on sea the method was impractical. The movement of the ship made it nearly impossible to keep the moons of Jupiter in telescopic vision while the calculations were made.

To an ambitious maritime power like England in the early eighteenth century, the "problem of longitude" became a matter of public policy. So valuable was a solution to this problem that in 1714 the British Parliament promised a large cash payment to anyone who could solve it. A Board of Longitude was established to consider applications, but for decades none were worthy of serious consideration. In popular speech, "discovering the longitude" came to mean "attempting the impossible."

But the astronomers in the Royal Society were persistent. The key to the problem, Isaac Newton believed, was to determine the "lunar distance" by finding a way to accurately measure the position of the moon relative to the sun by day, and to the stars by night. All that were needed were sky charts by which the future locations of these heavenly bodies could be accurately predicted. Astronomers spent hundreds of thousands of hours working on these charts. The problem was made even more complicated because, to be useful worldwide, separate star charts would have to be created for the entirely different night sky of the Southern Hemisphere.

By the 1760s the astronomers and mathematicians in the Royal Society were confident that they were close to a solution. The role of the *Endeavour,* which set out in 1769, was to observe the movement of Venus across the face of the sun, an event that occurred every eight years. By making identical observations in a wide variety of geographic locations, of which Cook's was by far the farthest from the Royal Observatory at Greenwich, astronomers would be able to predict much more accurately the future path of Venus. The solar, lunar, and stellar charts available to Cook on this journey were already much better than any other captain had ever used in the Pacific.

Meanwhile, there was another, potentially simpler solution: using a clock that accurately showed the current time at the point of departure, or any known location. A captain could easily calculate the time at his present location, compare it with the time kept by the clock, and calculate longitude. The problem was that eighteenth-century clocks were not accurate enough. Relying on a shipboard clock that was gaining or losing fifteen seconds a day could send a ship hundreds of miles off course.

John Harrison was an intrepid English cabinetmaker who took on the challenge of perfecting a timepiece that would be reliable enough to be carried to sea and would maintain its accuracy in spite of the constant motion from the waves, excessive humidity, and large changes in temperature. Harrison began work on his first "chronometer," as these timepieces came to be known, in 1727. It became his life's work: the last of his four versions was not finished until 1763, when he completed a compact chronometer that was accurate in oceanic conditions within one second per day.

The challenges Harrison faced were not only technical. Many of the astronomers in the Royal Society were highly status conscious and looked down on the

■ **Harrison's Chronometer**
John Harrison solved the "problem of longitude," greatly increasing the safety and efficiency of oceanic navigation, when he perfected his chronometer in 1763. An elegant piece of craftsmanship, Harrison's chronometer was a sophisticated and durable timepiece that kept accurate time even on rough seas and in high humidity, exemplifying the British tradition of "practical science." (Courtesy National Maritime Museum, London)

efforts of a mere "cabinetmaker" like Harrison, who was often frustrated by the board's unwillingness to give his prototypes the kind of trials that might lead him to the prize. They believed that only mathematics could provide a solution.

As it turned out, both Harrison and the astronomers were on the right track. On Cook's first voyage, he used the latest astronomical charts with great success. On Cook's second voyage he also took a chronometer and was very impressed, reporting that "it exceeded the expectations of its most zealous advocate and . . . has been our faithful guide through all vicissitudes of climate."[12] By the early nineteenth century Harrison's chronometer had become standard equipment on British naval vessels.

Scientists needed to set a fixed point from which the 360 degrees of longitude could be established. Not surprisingly given the dominant role that the British had played in the quest for longitude, that "prime meridian" was set at Greenwich, the site of the Royal Observatory. Even the French, who for a time used Paris as the zero point, eventually accepted the British standard. As a legacy of those days of British maritime dominance, longitude is still measured from Greenwich to this day.

Both John Harrison and Joseph Banks contributed to the "practical science" of the late eighteenth century. John Harrison's work, along with that of British astronomers, helped establish Greenwich as the "center of the world." Nearby, Banks developed Kew Gardens as the world center of botany. In both cases the ability to translate the scientific outlook into real-world applications supported the increasing power of Britain in particular, and Europe in general, across the globe.

Mapping Central Asia, Africa, India, and the Americas

The maritime empires of western Europe were not the only ones expanding in the eighteenth century (see Chapter 20). The Qing Empire was also expanding, including in its realm not only China but also parts of Central Asia. Matteo Ricci had earlier introduced modern maps to China (see Chapter 16), and in the eighteenth century Qing officials refined their mapmaking skills and applied them to their empire: "the Qing court," notes one scholar, "like other early modern states, chose to adopt these cutting-edge technologies for state building."[13] Qing participation in such projects shows one global aspect of the Enlightenment. Another was the influence that classical Confucian thought had on some European philosophers, who were inspired by the fact that Confucian morality is based on appeals to reason rather than religious faith. Still, the Enlightenment remained a primarily European phenomenon. Whereas Qing maps dealt only with a single empire, European maps encompassed the entire globe. European explorers from various nations contributed to a single, expanding network of knowledge.

Joseph Banks and the Royal Society promoted geographic expeditions, for example, by founding and helping to finance the **African Association.** Like many British efforts in this period, this association was a response to French competition. At this time, Europeans were still restricted to small coastal settlements that had arisen in connection with the Atlantic slave trade (see Chapter 19). But the French seemed to be in the best position to expand into the interior because of their long-established position at the mouth of the Senegal River, a potential gateway to the rich and populous lands of the predominantly Muslim lands of the Sahel.

The founders of the African Association knew that even more than the Senegal River, the key geographic feature of West Africa was the great Niger River, but they knew little of its origins and path. Discovering the course of the Niger would be a great addition to geographic, botanical, and ethnographic knowledge and might also promote British imperial expansion. Recruiting a young Scottish doctor named Mungo Park, whom Banks had earlier recommended as surgeon on a ship bound for Southeast Asia, the African Association sponsored a voyage of exploration to West Africa in 1795.

Park's voyage was a difficult one. The West African interior had been destabilized by the Atlantic slave trade, and the success or failure of his mission depended largely on the hospitality or animosity of the Africans he met en route. He made it safely to Segu, the most important city on the upper reaches of the Niger. Segu had been an important political and economic center ever since the empire of Songhai (see Chapter 19). Park was able to confirm that the Niger flowed from west to east, and his African hosts gave him a much clearer picture of how the river system moved people and goods through the region and into the wider Islamic world through North Africa and Egypt. But illness drove Park back to the coast before he could determine whether the river he had explored was the same one that flowed into the forested delta (in today's southern Nigeria) where British slave traders had long been active.

At the same time that Mungo Park was collecting basic information about the West African interior, the British were pursuing a more elaborate and systematic geographic project in India. The English East India Company ruled rich territories from its bases at Calcutta in the northeast and Madras in the south, and it was supplanting the Mughal Empire as the dominant military power on the subcontinent (see Chapter 20). British rule in India was established not only with guns and diplomacy but also with maps.

Beginning in the 1790s, the British undertook to capture the space of the Indian subcontinent in a mathematically precise grid. The **Great Trigonometrical Survey** established a baseline at an astronomically determined meridian of longitude in the south of India. From this point a precise triangular measurement was made between two other points and the first known location. Now three locations could be precisely defined in terms of longitude and latitude, and the survey could proceed with further triangular measurements.

Eventually the Great Trigonometrical Survey drove straight across India to the Himalayas. The highest mountain peak in the world, called Chomolungma, "Mother of the Universe," by the Tibetans, was renamed by the British "Mount Everest" after George Everest, the British surveyor-general. Such renaming occurred all over the world in this period.

● **African Association** (f. 1788) Society founded by Joseph Banks to sponsor geographical expeditions into Africa and chart the course of the Niger River, a feat achieved by Mungo Park.

● **Great Trigonometrical Survey** Beginning in the late 1790s, the British conducted this survey to plot the entire Indian subcontinent on a mathematically precise grid. The survey was a prelude to the expansion of Britain's Indian empire.

■ **The Great Trigonometrical Survey**   Beginning in southern India in the 1790s, British surveyors undertook a painstaking mapping project that by 1843 had reached the Himalayas. Accurate maps were a key source of British imperial power.   (From Matthew H. Edney, *Mapping an Empire* [Chicago: University of Chicago Press, 1997], p. 20)

Matthew Edney

The scientific purposes of the Great Trigonometrical Survey were entirely in keeping with the principles of the Enlightenment: rationality and order. Europeans had seen the Mughal Empire as an exotic and mystical land. The survey transformed the strange and unknowable "Hindustan" of earlier maps into a precisely ordered "India," a coherent world region. In a way, British surveyors were creating a new idea of India in the process of mapping it, and creating it in a way that implied British imperial control over regions that had not yet even been conquered. As one historian has written, "Imperialism and mapmaking intersect in the most basic manner. Both are fundamentally concerned with territory and knowledge."[14] The Great Trigonometric Survey created the skeletal structure onto which the bones, muscle, and skin of British India would be grafted.

In the Americas, Captain Cook's Pacific journeys had helped establish the dimensions of the North American continent; then in the 1790s Captain George Vancouver and his crew had charted its western coasts as far north as Alaska. (See the feature "World History in Today's World: A New Northwest Passage.") These maritime expeditions inspired transcontinental ones. After a first failed attempt to cross Canada on foot and canoe, the Scottish fur trader Alexander Mackenzie

A New Northwest Passage

The frozen north long presented an insurmountable barrier to commercial navigation. Though earlier centuries witnessed the futility of human ingenuity and effort in the quest to find a "northwest passage" to connect Europe and Asia by sea, now the effects of global climate change are making open Arctic seas a reality.

In 1794–1795 Captain George Vancouver repeated an earlier attempt by James Cook to find a Pacific outlet for a northwest passage, and though he charted much of what would become northernmost Canada, he failed to find one. It was not until 1906 that the Norwegian explorer Roald Amundsen managed to complete a three-year journey by water from the Atlantic to the Pacific.

Amundsen's route was neither commercially useful nor militarily significant, but that is changing as rapid temperature increases free parts of the Arctic Ocean of ice and open it up for competition. The fact that the climate change leading to the breakup of the ice is partly the result of human agency, and therefore a danger sign for the planet as a whole, is not the only cause for concern. National competition for control of the new northwest passage and other Arctic resources presents a potential new threat to global security.

Canada considers that much of the current northwest passage lies within its own territorial waters, but other nations, including the United States, contend that these are open waters where they have a free right of transit. As Canada considers building a deep-water port in the far north to assert its rights, the Russian government is also increasingly assertive in the Arctic. In 2007 the Russian president Vladimir Putin challenged international laws when he laid claim to vast underwater territories and to any energy and mineral resources that may be found there. The effects of global climate change in the Arctic are therefore not limited to the appearance of a new northwest passage, but include stepped-up geopolitical and economic competition across the entire region.

traveled from Montreal to London to equip himself with the latest technology: a sophisticated compass, sextant, chronometer, and telescope. Returning to Canada, and relying on the knowledge of indigenous First Nations people, Mackenzie and his party of nine became the first persons known to have crossed the entire American continent from east to west (see Map 21.1).

A parallel expedition also took place in the new United States of America (see Chapter 22), where separation from Britain in 1783 had opened the possibility of westward expansion. Americans considered the western lands to be wild, untamed, and savage. As in India, a principal means of bringing such "exotic" lands into "rationality" was to survey them and locate their spaces on a universal grid of longitude and latitude. The **Lewis and Clark Expedition** from the Mississippi River to the Pacific coast (1804–1806) was the pioneering effort.

One motivation for the government sponsors of Meriwether Lewis and William Clark, including President Thomas Jefferson, was to assess the potential for an American outlet to the Pacific Ocean to facilitate trade with Asia. Their reports, however, made clear the huge size and vast economic potential of the American interior itself. Like Banks and his protégés, Lewis and Clark carefully noted the flora and fauna on their journey, bringing the natural world of the American West into the orbit of European scientific knowledge. Also like Banks, they paid close attention to the customs of the indigenous peoples, speculating on their possible origins and the linguistic and cultural relationships between them. They carried

● **Lewis and Clark Expedition** (1804–1806) Government-sponsored team led by Meriwether Lewis and William Clark to open up a route through Native American territory to the Pacific. The expedition also collected new plant species and evaluated the potential for trade with Asia.

CL Interactive Map

🌐 MAP 21.1

The Exploration of Western North America   While Captain George Vancouver followed James Cook's Pacific expeditions and traced the Pacific coastline of North America, in the 1790s Alexander Mackenzie traced routes from the Pacific and Arctic Oceans into the frigid interior of British North America. A decade later Meriwether Lewis and William Clark investigated a transcontinental route from St. Louis to the Oregon coast. U.S. Army Captain Zebulon Pike led expeditions up the Mississippi River and explored the southern and western regions of the Louisiana Purchase, turning south from the Colorado Mountains into New Spain. Geographic exploration went hand-in-hand with expanding state frontiers across North America, as in the wider world.

surveying equipment with them and created maps that settlers would later use to help them occupy the land. In the American West we see another clear example of the relationship between science and empire.

All of the places visited by these Europeans were already well known to their local inhabitants. But the Europeans were adding this local knowledge to a central bank of data organized along hierarchical and mathematical lines. Whether it was a new plant species, the height of a mountain, or the location of a harbor, any new fact could be related to a centralized system of classification. Control of that knowledge system radically increased the global power of Europe in the nineteenth century.

Oceania and Australia, 1770–1820

The three journeys of Captain **James Cook** to the Pacific Ocean consolidated the role of science in advancing Britain's rise to global prominence and laid the foundations for the further expansion of the British Empire. As we have seen, his first expedition, accompanied by Joseph Banks aboard the *Endeavour,* returned to England in 1771 with significant astronomical, botanical, geographic, and cultural information. On his second and third journeys, Cook sailed near the coast of Antarctica and north to the Arctic Ocean; he also added the Hawaiian Islands to the European map of the Pacific.

Joseph Banks did not accompany Cook on the second two journeys. But from England he played a major role in the settlement of Australia. By 1820 the foundation had been laid for a British colony of settlement on a continent that had been virtually unknown to Europeans before Cook's voyage.

James Cook (1728–1779) British sea captain whose three voyages to the Pacific Ocean greatly expanded European knowledge of the region. Captain Cook, regarded as a great national hero by the British public, was killed in an altercation with Hawaiian islanders in 1779.

Captain Cook in Polynesia, 1769–1779

On the first voyage, Cook and Banks were greatly aided by the help of a Tahitian high priest named Tupaia (too-PUH-ee-uh). Tupaia understood several Polynesian languages and, coming from a family of navigators, was able to supplement Cook's instruments and charts with local knowledge of winds and currents. He also helped Banks understand Polynesian cultural practices, such as the meaning of the peace ritual that had so mystified the Englishman when he first set foot on the island.

In spite of Tupaia's help, misunderstandings between Europeans and Polynesians persisted. In his journals, Banks noted with frustration "how much these people are given to thieving." "All are of the opinion," he writes, "that if they can once get possession of anything it immediately becomes their own."[15] Usually it was small items that went missing, but when some of their important devices for astronomical observation disappeared, Cook was worried. Banks, with his developing knowledge of Tahitian society, was able to work with local people to get the equipment back.

Theft was also a problem among the English. Sailors kept stealing nails from the ship to trade with the islanders, for whom iron was a new and therefore valuable thing. However, one day a Tahitian woman refused to sell her stone axe for

VISUAL EVIDENCE

THE DEATH OF CAPTAIN COOK

James Cook had been sent off in royal fashion when his ships departed the Hawaiian islands in the summer of 1779. When they returned to mend a broken mast, however, the Hawaiians seemed disappointed and confused with their return. Tensions ran high, especially after a high chief was flogged for stealing a pair of iron tongs. Cook's crew noticed that some men were piling stones on the beach, as if getting ready for an attack. Cook invited one of the chiefs with whom he had been friends aboard his ship, but the *kahuna* (kah-HOO-nuh) was prevented by his own people from doing so. A warrior then

(© Dixson Galleries, State Library of New South Wales, Sydney, Australia. Pxd59, f.1/The Bridgeman Art Library)

The anger of the Hawaiians that led to this incident, Obeyesekere argues, came from Cook's unwillingness to help them in their war with Maui and his increasingly belligerent demands for food and supplies.

Obeyesekere notes that as soon as news of Cook's death reached England, his status as a Hawaiian god became a subject of music, art, and theater. Cook's godlike status, he argues, came about not from Hawaiian beliefs but from European myths of "conquest, imperialism, and civilization."*

---

*Gananath Obeyesekere, *The Apotheosis of Captain Cook: European Mythmaking in the Pacific* (Princeton: Princeton University Press, 1997), p. 3.

threatened Cook with an iron dagger. Cook shot at him, and a melee broke out. On that morning, July 14, 1779, on a beach at Kealakekua Bay, Captain James Cook was stabbed to death. That fact is certain. But the cause and context of Cook's death are controversial. The engraving reproduced here, made by John Webber, the officially appointed artist of the expedition, provides some evidence but does not resolve scholarly differences in the interpretation of Cook's death.

Anthropologist Marshall Sahlins argues that Cook had first arrived during the Makahiki (ma-kah-hee-kee) festival dedicated to the fertility god Lono. His appearance at that precise time, and his landing near the god's main temple, caused the Hawaiians to identify him with Lono. When Cook later returned to repair a broken mast, however, the Makahiki cycle had ended. Now it was time for Lono to be symbolically defeated, Sahlins explains, and replaced by the war god Ku. In conformity with the ritual cycle, Cook-Lono was killed.

Nonsense, says Gananath Obeyesekere, who maintains that Sahlins is guilty of typical European arrogance in saying that the Hawaiians saw Cook as a god. In fact, Obeyesekere argues, the Hawaiians were guided by "practical rationality," a universal common sense that would make it impossible for them to mistake a man for a god. Sahlins responds that he is the one interpreting events from within the logic of traditional Hawaiian beliefs, while it is actually Obeyesekere who is imposing foreign beliefs on the Hawaiians by ignoring their own cosmology and value structures. In Hawaiian belief, he notes, there was a strong equation between status as a powerful chief and affiliation with a god like Lono.

There is no clear conclusion to this debate, as Sahlins and Obeyesekere offer differing interpretations of this image.

Area of detail

Sahlins claims that he can identify the actual killer of Cook in this image: Nuha, a powerful warrior who was "an ideal champion for the aging king in the ritualistic murder of Lono-Cook."[†]

Accepting the overall accuracy of this image, Sahlins even claims to be able to identify the murder weapon: "an iron spike manufactured at [a] factory in Birmingham, requisitioned by Cook 'to be distributed to them as presents toward obtaining their friendship.' "[‡]

[†] Dan Lynch, "Gananath Obeyesekere v. Marshall Sahlins: Did Hawaiians Consider Captain Cook as a God?" Unpublished paper, California State University Long Beach, 2006.

[‡] Marshall Sahlins, *Islands of History* (Chicago: University of Chicago Press, 1985), p. 131.

QUESTION FOR ANALYSIS

Though John Webber was at the scene, he could not possibly have had the perspective on events that is shown in this drawing. Does the change in perspective from what he actually saw to how he represented the event diminish the reliability of the image as a historical source?

an iron nail. The sailor took it anyway, and Cook decided to make an example of him. He ordered the man to be flogged and invited some Tahitian chiefs to witness the punishment:

> [The chiefs] stood quietly and saw him stripped and fastened to the rigging, but as soon as the first blow was given they interfered with many tears, begging the punishment might cease, a request which the Captain would not comply with.[16]

It seems that the Tahitians had quite different views of property and punishment from those of the English. Cook's attitude toward such differences was utilitarian: he wanted to make his astronomical and navigational observations, get fresh supplies of food and water, and move on. Banks, however, considered his role as a scientist to include an attempt to try to understand the people of the island.

In 1779, cultural and political misunderstanding led to the death of Captain Cook on a Hawaiian beach. When they first arrived in Hawai'i, Cook and his men had received a joyous and generous reception. Nevertheless, there were tensions between the sailors and the islanders. His men were exhausted from a futile trip to the Arctic in search of a "northwest passage" linking Asia and Europe, and they resented Cook's attempts to stop them from their usual practice of trading iron nails for sex. Cook was trying to protect the Hawaiians from the venereal diseases that he knew were rampant on his ship. After he finally left Hawai'i, storm damage to his ship forced Cook to return. In great contrast to their earlier arrival, there was no one to greet them. An argument escalated into violence, and Cook was stabbed to death on the beach. (See the feature "Visual Evidence: The Death of Captain Cook.")

For all the power of predictability and prediction afforded by modern science, the death of Captain Cook shows that Enlightenment thinkers were perhaps overconfident in the degree to which they believed reason could govern human interactions. There were no chronometers, no astronomical sightings, no surveys or charts with which to safely navigate the waters of cross-cultural communication. The challenge for Polynesians came when they were drawn into a European-dominated global system that brought new economic relations, new technologies, and new belief systems that undermined the existing order of Oceanic societies.

Joseph Banks and the Settlement of Australia

The impact of Joseph Banks on the history of Australia is inscribed on one of its most famous geographic features, Botany Bay, where Banks undertook an intensive reconnaissance of eastern Australia's unique plant life. He is sometimes called "the Father of Australia" for the role he played in the foundation of the colony of New South Wales in 1788 with its capital at Sydney.

New South Wales began as a penal colony, its overwhelmingly male population consisting of prisoners, many of them Irish, who had little to lose from taking a chance on resettlement halfway around the world. The colony got off to a rocky start. Few of the convicts knew how to survive in this foreign terrain, nor could they rely on the local Koori population of Aboriginal Australians, which initially kept its distance and then launched a series of attacks.

A stronger economic foundation for the colonial economy of New South Wales came with the introduction of merino sheep in 1805, descendants of the same sheep that Joseph Banks had imported from Spain to Kew Gardens for the king's flock. The grasslands of New South Wales proved ideal grazing lands for these sheep, and wool exports financed the development of a more sophisticated colonial society. By the early nineteenth century most settlers were free immigrants rather than convicts, the cities of Sydney and Melbourne were on the path to prosperity, and new British colonies were founded across the continent. After 1817, the name *Australia* was used to refer to this collection of British colonies.

Joseph Banks regarded those developments as "improvement," another successful outcome of the application of practical science. But British settlement had a devastating impact on the original inhabitants of the continent. Indigenous Australians had rich and complex religious and artistic traditions, as well as keen knowledge of the local environment from which, as hunter-gatherers whose ancestors had lived on the continent for tens of thousands of years, they derived all the necessities of life. But they had no metal tools, no hierarchical political organization, and no resistance to Afro-Eurasian diseases like smallpox. As in the Americas in previous centuries, the Aborigines experienced the European territorial advance as a plague: more than half of them died in the nineteenth century. The survivors either fled to more and more remote deserts and mountains, worked for Europeans on their commercial ranches, or moved to the cities, where they formed a socially and economically disenfranchised subclass.

Chapter Review

(CL) Download the MP3 audio file of the Chapter Review and listen to it on the go.

Joseph Banks lived in an atmosphere of great optimism. As president of the Royal Society, he saw tremendous advances in scientific inquiry, not merely in the accumulation of data but also in the development of increasingly advanced systems of scientific classification. Banks was typical of many products of the Scientific Revolution and Enlightenment in his strong belief in progress, and he never seems to have worried that "progress" could have losers as well as winners. Yet the application of science to agriculture in England led to many farming families being dispossessed of their land. And, as we will see in future chapters, European imperial expansion, facilitated by the development of practical science, would lead to conflict all across the nineteenth-century world.

When and how did Europe's Scientific Revolution begin to have practical applications?

The calm confidence inspired by Sir Isaac Newton's description of an orderly, rational universe that could be described through the elegance of mathematics presented eighteenth-century European thinkers with a world that seemed full of promise. Science, it seemed, could not only accurately *describe* the natural world, but also through practical applications enhance nature for human purposes. In

KEY TERMS

the field of botany, for example, Linnaeus's system of classification was the foundation for the "practical science" of Joseph Banks's agricultural and botanical studies on his own estates and at Kew Gardens. Likewise, the development of a more refined system of measuring time and mapping both nautical and terrestrial space drew on scientific developments in astronomy and mathematics but also found real-world applications, most notably in the expansion of European empires.

 How did Enlightenment thought derive from the Scientific Revolution, and how did it differ from previous European thought systems?

The Scientific Revolution in Europe introduced the idea of a well-ordered universe that could be understood through close observation and the application of human reason. Enlightenment philosophers extended this belief in a rational, ordered universe to develop an optimistic view of human society in which political and economic affairs might also be governed by human reason. They rejected the pessimism of earlier Christian beliefs, which had focused on sin and human fallibility, and instead proposed that reason could show the way to reform and improve human societies. Most philosophes imagined that societal enlightenment would come from the actions of enlightened rulers applying reason to the problems of governance; however, "enlightened despots" were unable to fulfill the highest aspirations of the Enlightenment.

 How did systematic classification and measurement support European imperialism in the late eighteenth and early nineteenth centuries?

The link between "practical science" and the expansion of European empires gave the Scientific Revolution a global dimension. More than simple curiosity drove the mapping projects and surveying expeditions sent to Africa, India, and the Americas in this period. While the accumulation of scientific knowledge for its own sake was certainly one factor motivating explorers like Park, Mackenzie, and Cook, they all realized that British imperial ambitions were strengthened through the increase of geographic knowledge, the charting and mapping of space, and the accumulation of cultural information about indigenous societies.

 How did the societies of Oceania and Australia experience encounters with Europeans in this period?

The peoples of Oceania and Australia experienced their encounters with Europeans as a shock and a challenge. Tahitians, Hawaiians, and others were as baffled by the strange behavior of the Europeans as Joseph Banks was by his initial experiences with Polynesian culture. Soon at least some Europeans learned Polynesian languages and vice versa, and the cultural gap was narrowed. Still, as the death of Captain Cook demonstrates, there were severe limitations on cross-cultural communications. Soon the Europeans would be in a position to impose their own technologies and economic systems on Oceanic societies. The same was true to an even greater extent in Australia, where the indigenous Aborigines were even less able to resist European advances and Afro-Eurasian diseases.

For Further Reference

Crosby, Alfred. *The Measure of Reality: Quantification in Western Europe, 1250–1600*. Cambridge: Cambridge University Press, 1997.

Drayton, Richard. *Nature's Government: Science, Imperial Britain, and the "Improvement" of the World*. New Haven: Yale University Press, 2000.

Edney, Matthew H. *Mapping an Empire: The Geographical Construction of British India, 1765–1843*. Chicago: University of Chicago Press, 1990.

Fara, Patricia. *Sex, Botany and Empire: The Story of Carl Linnaeus and Joseph Banks*. New York: Columbia University Press, 2004.

Fernandez-Armesto, Felipe. *Pathfinders: A Global History of Exploration*. New York: W.W. Norton, 2007.

Gascoigne, John. *Joseph Banks and the English Enlightenment: Useful Knowledge and Polite Culture*. New York: Cambridge University Press, 2003.

Henry, John. *The Scientific Revolution and the Origins of Modern Science*. 3d ed. New York: Palgrave, 2008.

Israel, Jonathan. *Radical Enlightenment: Philosophy and the Making of Modernity, 1650–1750*. New York: Oxford University Press, 2002.

Jacob, Margaret. *The Cultural Meaning of the Scientific Revolution*. New York: McGraw-Hill, 1988.

Salmond, Anne. *The Trial of the Cannibal Dog: The Remarkable Story of Captain Cook's Encounter in the South Seas*. New Haven: Yale University Press, 2003.

Sorbel, Dava, and William J. H. Andrews. *The Illustrated Longitude: The True Story of a Lone Genius Who Solved the Greatest Scientific Problem of His Time*. New York: Walker & Co., 1998.

 WEB RESOURCES

Pronunciation Guide

Interactive Maps

MAP 21.1 The Exploration of Western North America

Primary Sources

Chapter Objectives

ACE Multiple-Choice Quiz

Flashcards

Websites

The Hakluyt Society:
(http://www.hakluyt.com/hak-soc-links.htm).
A reliable source of information and links to other sites on global exploration.

Internet Modern History Sourcebook: The Enlightenment
(http://www.fordham.edu/halsall/mod/modsbook10.html).   Access to a vast array of resources, including a searchable online version of the *Encyclopedia*.

The Papers of Sir Joseph Banks
(http://chnm.gmu.edu/worldhistorysources/r/58/whm.html).   This document collection provides access to much of the voluminous correspondence of Joseph Banks, including letters he both sent and received.

CHAPTER
22

Revolutions in the West, 1750–1830

In August of 1805 a young South American climbed one of the hills outside Rome to gain a panoramic view of the "eternal city." For **Simón Bolívar** (1783–1830) the history of Rome summed up all that was great and all that was tragic in history. Over the next two decades he became the most important military and political leader in the drive for the independence of Spain's South American colonies. In Latin America he is known simply as *El Libertador* (el lee-bir-TAH-door), "the Liberator."

Greatness was what he sought for Spain's American colonies as he dedicated himself to achieving their independence:

(Mirelle Vautier/The Art Archive)

SIMÓN BOLÍVAR

ere every manner of grandeur has had its type, all miseries their cradle. . . .

[Rome] has examples for everything, except the cause of humanity: . . . heroic warriors, rapacious consuls . . . golden virtues, and foul crimes; but for the emancipation of the spirit . . . the exaltation of man, and the final perfectibility of reason, little or nothing. . . . The resolution of the great problem of man set free seems to have been something . . . that would only be made clear in the New World. . . .

I swear before you, I swear by the God of my fathers, I swear on their graves, I swear by my Country that I will not rest body or soul until I have broken the chains binding us to the will of Spanish might![1]

 This icon will direct you to interactive activities and study materials on the *Voyages* website: **www.cengage.com/history/hansen/voyages1e**

628

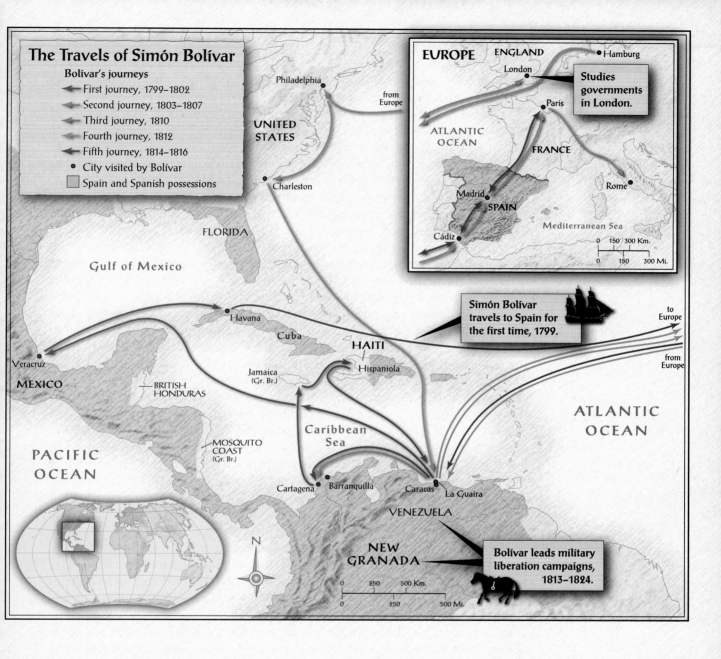

The Travels of Simón Bolívar

Bolívar's journeys
- First journey, 1799–1802
- Second journey, 1803–1807
- Third journey, 1810
- Fourth journey, 1812
- Fifth journey, 1814–1816
- • City visited by Bolívar
- ▨ Spain and Spanish possessions

EUROPE

ENGLAND
Hamburg
London
Studies governments in London.
ATLANTIC OCEAN
Paris
FRANCE
Rome
Madrid
SPAIN
Mediterranean Sea
Cádiz

0   150   300 Km.
0   150   300 Mi.

Philadelphia
from Europe
UNITED STATES
Charleston

FLORIDA
Gulf of Mexico

Havana
Cuba
HAITI
Hispaniola
Jamaica (Gr. Br.)

Veracruz
MEXICO
BRITISH HONDURAS
MOSQUITO COAST (Gr. Br.)

Caribbean Sea

PACIFIC OCEAN

Cartagena Barranquilla Caracas La Guaira
VENEZUELA

NEW GRANADA

Simón Bolívar travels to Spain for the first time, 1799.

to Europe
from Europe

ATLANTIC OCEAN

Bolívar leads military liberation campaigns, 1813–1824.

N

0   250   500 Km.
0   250   500 Mi.

	1725	1750	1775	1800	1825	1850

Lifetime of Simón Bolívar
1783   1830

SOUTH AMERICA AND THE CARIBBEAN

Lifetime of Tupac Amaru II
1741   1781

Haitian independence
1804

Congress of Angostura
1819

Lifetime of Toussaint L'Ouverture
1744   1803

"Grito de Dolores"
1810

Battle of Ayacucho
1824

NORTH AMERICA

Declaration of Independence
1776

U.S. Constitution adopted by Constitutional Convention
1787

EUROPE

Lifetime of Napoleon Bonaparte
1769   1821

National Assembly
1789

Reign of Terror
1793 1795

Congress of Vienna
1814–1815

Simón Bolívar's (see-MOAN bow-LEE-varh) oath changed not only his own life but also the course of Latin American history.

Growing up in one of the richest households in Venezuela, Bolivar had studied the great thinkers of the Enlightenment. He first went to Europe in 1799, when he was only 16, to visit an uncle in Madrid. There he spent his money freely while enjoying the life of the Spanish court. He fell in love and, in spite of his youth, married and returned with his bride to Caracas. Sadly, she died just eight months later. Now in his early 20s, inspired by the examples of revolution in North America and France, he returned to Europe to visit a former teacher, a revolutionary who had been driven into exile by the Spanish authorities in Venezuela.

Apart from visiting Rome, he spent most of this trip in Paris, the intellectual center of the Enlightenment and the political center of revolution. In the previous decade the French monarchy had been overthrown and replaced by a republic. Now the republic was being superseded by the dictatorship of Napoleon Bonaparte. Bolívar's worldview was greatly affected by his experience of postrevolutionary French politics. The French Revolution, like ancient Rome, had brought forth both "golden virtues" and "sordid crimes." Only in the Americas, thought Bolívar, could the full liberation of the human spirit be achieved.

Bolívar proved himself a brilliant military leader. Between 1813, when he entered his native Caracas at the head of a liberation army, and 1824, when he drove the Spanish army from Peru, he fulfilled the oath he had taken in Rome. Like other revolutionaries in the Americas and western Europe in the late eighteenth and early nineteenth centuries, Bolívar started out with high hopes founded in Enlightenment optimism. But turning independence from Spanish rule into true liberty for the people of South America proved difficult. By the time of Bolívar's death in 1830, many South Americans had become concerned about his dictatorial tendencies. His story, as one biographer has emphasized, is one of "liberation and disappointment."[2]

Elsewhere in Latin America and the Caribbean, and in North America and France, other revolutionaries also believed that prejudice and tradition would give way to rationality and enlightenment and that new political and social systems would both guarantee liberty and provide order and security. In 1776, Britain's North American colonists had broken free and founded a democratic republic that seemed to combine liberty with moderation. A more volatile historical precedent was the French Revolution, which swung violently from constitutional monarchy to radical republic to military dictatorship. In the Caribbean, the Republic of Haiti was created following one of the largest slave uprisings in world history.

The issue of slavery was very much on Bolívar's mind. Like his North American counterpart George Washington, Bolívar was a slave owner. Could the dream of liberty be compatible with the reality of slavery? Such discrepancies between dreams and harsher realities were, in fact, a central theme of the age. Reconciling the twin mandates of liberty and equality, and securing both within a stable and well-ordered state, was a tremendous challenge for revolutionaries across North and South America, the Caribbean, and France.

Focus Questions

 What political compromises were made in establishing the new United States of America?

 What were the major phases of the French Revolution?

 How were the revolutions in Latin America and the Caribbean influenced by the history of colonialism?

 How much did the outcomes of these revolutions in western Europe and the Americas represent a thorough transformation of existing political and social structures?

●The American War of Independence, 1763–1791

On April 19, 1775, a British force marched toward the Massachusetts town of Concord to destroy a stockpile of arms that had been accumulated by rebellious colonists. As they approached Concord Bridge, they were surprised by the size and discipline of the colonial forces they encountered. When the militiamen fired across the river, they focused on British officers, killing four of them. Surprised and confused, the British hastily retreated to Boston, facing further colonial fire along the way. The American Revolution had begun (see Map 22.1).

It is an overstatement to say that in the short run the shots at Concord, products of a skirmish in a small corner of the British Empire, were "heard 'round the world." Even the term *American Revolution* is misleading, since these events initially involved only a small part of the vast American landmass. Yet over time they would fundamentally change the world. The Declaration of Independence that justified the rebellion (1776) is one of the most influential political documents in world history, while the Constitution of the United States of America (1787) provided an example of limited yet effective government. Never before had the principles of the Enlightenment been so powerfully expressed in practical politics. But achievement of its highest aspirations, of universal liberty and equality, were undermined by the compromises that characterized the nation-building process, especially on the issue of slavery.

CL Primary Source:
The United States Declaration of Independence
Read a selection from Jefferson's famous text, which lays out the Enlightenment principles on which the United States was founded.

Revolution and War, 1763–1783

A key turning point in the relations between Britain and the colonists was the British victory in the French and Indian War. That North American conflict was only one

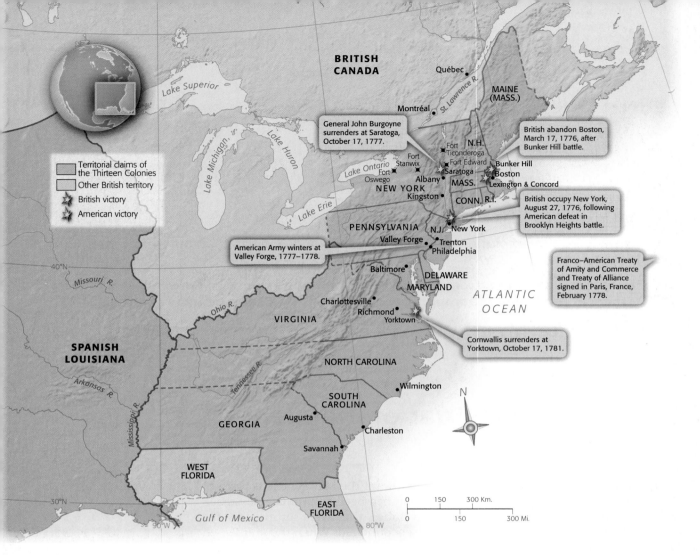

Interactive Map

🌐 **MAP 22.1**

The American Revolutionary War In terms of military firepower the British Empire far outmatched the American Continental Army. The British could deploy an almost unlimited number of well-armed professional soldiers and their navy was able to enforce a blockade of American ports. As would happen so often in modern world history, however, fighters who were highly motivated to throw off the imperial yoke managed to overcome the odds and win their independence.

theater of the Seven Years' War (1756–1763), which had pitted British against French imperial forces (see Chapter 19), and the British victory opened up new possibilities for expansion on the western frontier of Britain's North American colonies. Many colonists were excited about the economic opportunities that lay in the Ohio River Valley and other areas west of the Appalachian Mountains. But British leaders were cautious. As soon as they had defeated the French, they were faced with a large Native American uprising. It became clear that European settlement on the frontier would generate more such conflicts, which would inevitably require British troops and resources. The Proclamation of 1763, much to the disgust of colonists, established a fixed westward limit to colonial expansion.

■ **Protesting the Stamp Act**   Needing additional resources to control its expanded American frontier after victory in the Seven Years' War, the British Parliament imposed a Stamp Act on the North American colonies in 1765. In this engraving colonists angry at the new tax have strung up one of the king's officials on a "liberty pole," and they prepare to tar and feather another. Tarring and feathering, which often left the victim permanently disfigured, was an exceptionally violent form of vigilante justice. (The Granger Collection)

The TORY'S Day of JUDGMENT.

Not only had the British restrained colonial expansion, but they were also determined that the colonists would bear the cost of their own defense. New taxes, such as the Stamp Act of 1765, were bitterly resented. Attempts to restrict colonial trade with the West Indies threatened a profitable sector of the North American economy. Another grievance of New England merchants was the new monopoly granted by the British government to the East India Company (see Chapters 19 and 20) for the supply of tea to the colonies. Resistance to that law took the form of illegal smuggling, and more dramatically of the Boston Tea Party, where colonists dressed as Amerindians tossed a shipment of East India Company tea into Boston harbor. Lacking representation in Parliament, British subjects in the Americas had no direct way to influence British government policy. "No taxation without representation!" became one of the rallying cries of the rebellion.

Such grievances led many settlers to conclude that their rights as freeborn British subjects were being assailed. By forcibly repressing boycotts and urban demonstrations, British authorities increased the number of colonists whose self-identity was shifting from "British" to "American." The final straw was suspending the charter of the Massachusetts Bay Company in 1775, disbanding the colonial legislature, and imposing a British governor. By this time the colonists had formed militias for self-defense, and the scene was set for the confrontation at Concord.

In some areas, rebellious colonists had already taken over control of government and judicial affairs. Now larger-scale coordination was necessary. A Continental Congress was held in 1775 that brought together representatives from each of the thirteen colonies. **George Washington** (1732–1799) was appointed commander of its army. Washington, a Virginian, had served as an officer during British military campaigns in the Ohio River Valley.

On July 4, 1776, Congress approved Thomas Jefferson's **Declaration of Independence,** which contained not only a detailed list of colonists' grievances against the king but also a stirring announcement of universal political values:

> We hold these truths to be self-evident: That all men are created equal; that they are endowed by their creator with certain inalienable rights; that among these are life, liberty and the pursuit of happiness; that, to secure these rights,

● **George Washington** (1732–1799)   Commander of the Continental Army in the American War of Independence from Britain; also first president of the United States of America.

● **Declaration of Independence** (1776) Document written by Thomas Jefferson justifying the separation of Britain's North American colonies, declaring them free and independent states.

governments are instituted among men, deriving their just powers from the consent of the governed.

The phrase "consent of the governed" built on John Locke's theory of government as based on a contract in which individuals receive protection of their basic rights by voluntarily submitting to a legitimate government (see Chapter 21). Jefferson went further than Locke, however, by emphasizing the concept of popular sovereignty: government legitimacy derives directly from the "consent of the governed." When such legitimacy was lacking, rebellion was justified: "When a long train of abuses and usurpations . . . evinces a design to reduce them under absolute Despotism, it is their right, it is their duty, to throw off such Government and to provide new Guards for their future security."

The British had some advantages in the fight that began in 1776. The tens of thousands of "redcoat" soldiers in North America were well equipped and well trained. Moreover, many Loyalists in the colonies argued for compromise rather than confrontation. For Benjamin Franklin this was a family affair. Franklin found it difficult to exchange his British identity for an American one, and his son William, the royally appointed governor of New Jersey, refused to do so and remained loyal to the British throne. While a handful of African Americans participated in the rebellion, the Loyalist party included many free blacks who were aware that slavery had already been eliminated in England (see Chapter 19). Since prominent leaders of the rebellion included slave owners like Washington and Jefferson, it was logical for black Loyalists to associate Britain, rather than the Continental Congress, with "liberty."

Another key British ally was the Mohawk nation under their leader **Joseph Brant** (Mohawk name Thayendanegea) (1742–1807). Brant's sister had married an Irish fur trader who also served as a British frontier diplomat. Thereafter, the Brant family were important cultural and political mediators in the Iroquois/British alliance against the French. Brant had traveled to London to meet King George III (for later developments in Brant's family, see Chapter 25).

But in 1777 the rebellious colonists defeated a British force at Saratoga in New York. Not only did that surprise victory give the colonists a base from which to take the offensive against the Mohawk, but it also helped convince the French government that the American rebellion had a real chance of success. Early in 1778 a Franco-American treaty was signed, with France hoping to weaken its main global rival. The French supplied the rebel army with weapons and threatened the British fleet in the Atlantic and Caribbean.

Apart from the French alliance, the rebellious colonists had several advantages. One was the fact that the rural population generally supported the Continental Army and gave them supplies, information on British troop movements, and knowledge of the local terrain. Women played a notable role. They did extra work, including blacksmithing and other "male" jobs, in the absence of their soldier-husbands, and they also produced shoes, clothes, and munitions for the Continental Army. Finally, since British soldiers were reluctant to search them thoroughly, women made excellent spies and carriers of communication.

Another advantage for the rebels was the superior leadership abilities of General Washington, who managed to maintain the morale of his troops through the harsh winter spent at Valley Forge in 1777–1778 and to outmaneuver British forces at the culminating battle at Yorktown in 1781. French ships cut off the British route of retreat after they had been surrounded by Washington's army, and the war was over. The British commander who surrendered at Yorktown, Lord Cornwallis, would have more success in his next position as governor-general of British India (see Chapter 20).

Peace negotiations began almost immediately. With the Treaty of Paris (1783), the British government acknowledged the independence of the new United States of America. The rebel leaders had boldly declared their intentions in the Declaration of Independence; now they needed to create a constitutional order to make those dreams a reality.

Creating a Nation, 1783–1791

One of the mottos adopted by the founders of the new United States of America was *Novus Ordo Secolorum:* "A New Order of the Ages." They saw their enterprise of nation building not merely as a local effort but as a historical event that would usher in a new phase of human existence, "an epoch," as Washington put it, "when the rights of mankind were better understood and more clearly defined, than at any former period."

But separation from the British did not by itself bring about revolutionary changes in people's lives. Many conditions remained the same during these social, political, and economic changes; the same would be true in the French, Haitian, Latin American, and other revolutions to follow. For example, each of the thirteen colonies had developed a distinct political culture under British rule. In spite of another new motto of the United States, *E Pluribus Unum,* "one out of many," representatives of the individual states proved reluctant to sacrifice local sovereignty and local political traditions to create a more unified nation. The first constitution, the Articles of Confederation, required that the federal government request funds from the individual states. Lacking its own tax-raising power, however, the Confederation government had no army and therefore no effective power.

Shays's Rebellion (1786–1787) was the crisis that brought about negotiations for a more centralized federal constitution. In rural Massachusetts many revolutionary war veterans, led by veteran Daniel Shays, rose up over the old issues of taxation and representation. Under the Articles of Confederation, states were responsible for debts remaining from the war, and they used taxes to meet those obligations. Poorer farmers, who lived primarily through barter and had little cash to pay these taxes, often had to sell their land to meet their obligations. In addition to losing their land, these farmers also lost their right to vote, which at that time required property ownership. Shays was incensed that land speculators were benefiting at the expense of overtaxed veterans. The Massachusetts state militia suppressed the uprising, but those who argued for a stronger federal government with powers of taxation and the ability to assume war debts used Shays's Rebellion to make their point.

Mercy Otis Warren, one of the most prolific writers of her time, put it this way: "Our situation is truly delicate and critical. On the one hand we are in need of a strong federal government founded on principles that will support the prosperity and union of the colonies. On the other we have struggled for liberty . . . [and will not relinquish] the rights of man for the dignity of government." In addition to balancing the powers of government with the rights of individuals, the delegates from the thirteen states who met at the Constitutional Convention in 1787 faced the central issue of how to rebalance the relative power of the state and federal governments.

Compromise was the hallmark of the new **Constitution of the United States of America** (1787), which enhanced the powers of the federal government in such vital areas as taxation, judicial oversight, banking, and responsibility for diplomacy and warfare. At the same time specific powers, such as determining the voting franchise, were left to the states. A system of checks and balances, as earlier proposed by the French *philosophe* Montesquieu (see Chapter 21), ensured the separation of executive, legislative, and judicial authority. A balance was struck between the interests of large and small states by a two-house legislature with a House of Representatives in which each state was allocated a number of seats based on its population, and a Senate in which each state was equally represented by two senators.

• **Constitution of the United States of America** (1787) Agreement that created a more unified national structure for the United States, providing for a bicameral national legislature and independent executive and judicial authority, and incorporating a Bill of Rights.

One of the most important balances struck at the Constitutional Convention was between the power of majorities and the rights of minorities. Congress amended the Constitution in 1791 with a Bill of Rights to ensure that specific civil liberties would be guaranteed even in the face of majority opinion. For example, the Bill of Rights made the establishment of a state church impossible, protecting the rights of religious minorities. It also guaranteed freedom of the press, freedom of assembly, the right to bear arms as part of "well-regulated militias," and other fundamental freedoms.

The original document was not very democratic. Most states restricted the vote to property owners, women were not enfranchised, and the president and senators were elected indirectly rather than by popular vote. No political agency was given to Native Americans, slaves, or even most free blacks. Nevertheless, the Constitution of the United States of America has proved an enduring document, with both fixed principles and the flexibility to meet new challenges.

George Washington was the unanimous choice of the state electors as president in 1789. He served two terms and then retired. Washington, like Simón Bolívar on his European sojourn, looked to ancient Rome for political inspiration. One of his heroes was the general Cincinnatus, who, after leading Roman armies to victory, left the political stage to live as a simple citizen of the republic. In 1796, after two terms as president, Washington followed that example. He refused a third term and retired to his plantation. The important example he set was one of reluctant service rather than personal aggrandizement.

The Constitutional Convention, for all its achievements, proved unable to resolve the dichotomy between liberty and slavery. Southern delegates had no intention of applying the principle that "all men are created equal" to the 40 percent of southerners who were slaves. Though the abolitionist movement was gaining momentum at this time (*The Interesting Life of Olaudah Equiano* was published in 1789; see Chapter 19), the vested interests of the plantation owners prevailed. Adding insult to injury, the Constitution defined each slave as three-fifths of a person for calculating the size of congressional delegations but allowed the states to define slaves as nonpersons for all other legal purposes.

The issue of slavery shows that the new United States, like other postrevolutionary societies, did not start with a blank slate. The assertion that the people could seize their own liberty and command their own destiny inspired many future revolutionaries. Their enthusiasm might have been tempered if they had considered how difficult it might be to change deeply entrenched traditions, as the French experience would show.

●The French Revolution, 1789–1815

If the weight of the past made it difficult for the founders of the United States to fully implement Enlightenment ideals, French revolutionaries would have an even more difficult time reordering their established political system and society. Resistance to the French Revolution came not only from the monarchy and aristocracy but also from the Catholic Church and other European leaders who were fearful that the French revolt would be contagious. Compromise between France's various social and political interest groups would prove impossible.

The Revolution moved through three stages. The first was marked by the relatively moderate goal of constitutional monarchy. The second, most radical phase of the revolution was led by the Jacobins, extreme republicans who favored a complete transformation of French society. But the Jacobins are remembered less for their noble ideals than for the guillotine and the bloody Reign of Terror that marked their rule. After a period of confusion, an ambitious military genius named Napoleon Bonaparte not only restored order but also extended French power across Europe.

Louis XVI and the Early Revolution, 1789–1792

Louis XVI (r. 1774–1793) was one of the wealthiest and most powerful people in the world, ruling over twenty-four million subjects from his fabulous palace of Versailles. But the foundations on which the magnificence of the French Bourbon dynasty was built were growing rotten. When he took the throne in 1774, Louis found that the treasury was empty and public debt was out of control. The loss of the Seven Years' War (1756–1763) to the British had cost the French territory in both the Americas and Asia while leaving behind a pile of debt (see Chapter 19). The French government had received no economic benefit from backing the American rebels. The common people were crushed by taxes, while the nobility, who enjoyed the luxurious entertainments of Versailles as guests of the king, paid none at all.

The economic crisis led to a political one. In 1789, Louis and his ministers decided they had no choice but to convene an Estates-General in Paris to which each of the three Orders of French society would send representatives. The First Estate consisted of the Catholic Church, the Second Estate consisted of the nobility, and the Third Estate comprised everyone else, that is, the vast majority of French men and women. It was an extreme measure. Unlike Britain with its annual meetings of Parliament, no French king had called a meeting of the Estates-General since 1614.

In the provinces elections were held for delegates from the **Third Estate,** many of whose delegates were lawyers, merchants, and other members of the rising bourgeoisie, middle-class professional men who were frustrated with the social and economic predominance of the monarchy and the nobility. Revolution in the Americas inspired them to demand fundamental reforms, such as the creation of a representative legislative body. They collected notebooks of grievances in the French provinces to bring to Paris a catalogue of complaints and ideas for change.

But Louis was confident that he could control the Estates-General. Each Estate received only one collective vote. Many of the church representatives, the bishops and high officials, were also members of the nobility, and the Catholic Church, by far the biggest landowner in France, was, like the aristocratic members of the Second Estate, exempted from direct taxation. The king anticipated that the privileged

● **Louis XVI** (r. 1774–1793)   King of France whose inability to adequately reform the French fiscal system laid the foundation for the French Revolution. After showing reluctance to rule as a constitutional monarch, Louis was arrested and beheaded by republican revolutionaries.

● **Third Estate**   Before the Revolution, the order of French society that included most common people (the First Estate was aristocracy, the Second clergy, and the Third everyone else). Leaders of the Third Estate declared themselves a National Assembly in 1789, launching the French Revolution.

members of the First and Second Estates would vote together, canceling out any more radical proposals that came from the Third Estate.

Rather than accept this situation, delegates from the Third Estate took matters into their own hands. They declared themselves to be a **National Assembly** and took an oath that they would not disband until a constitutional monarchy had been established. Reacting with fear, Louis XVI summoned eighteen thousand troops to defend his palace at Versailles, 12 miles (19.3 km) outside of Paris. It was the summer of 1789, and the French Revolution had begun.

Thus far the contest was between the men of power, the king and his nobles, and the relatively wealthy and well-educated representatives of the Third Estate, men who *aspired* to power and influence. But events were pushed in a new direction by the actions of the common people. A group of Parisians stormed the Bastille (bass-TEEL), a building that served as both a jail and an armory. They freed prisoners, armed themselves from the arsenal's stockpile of weapons, and killed the mayor of Paris. The people of Paris were earning their reputation as a radical force of revolution.

Louis decided he had better compromise with some of the more moderate leaders of the Third Estate after all. He recognized the National Assembly, which promptly declared the principle of equality before the law, eliminated the special prerogatives of the nobility, and abolished serfdom and all the remaining feudal obligations of the peasantry. In the "Declaration of the Rights of Man and the Citizen," the National Assembly declared that "men are born and remain free and equal in rights," that "the natural and inalienable rights of man" are "liberty, property, security, and resistance to oppression," that all citizens are eligible for government positions "without other distinctions than that of virtues and talents," and that necessary taxation "must be assessed equally on all citizens in proportion to their means." Freedom of thought and religion were established, and mandatory payments to the Catholic Church were eliminated. The ideas of the philosophes were thus articulated as political principles.

In spite of this radical agenda, in other areas the National Assembly was quite conservative. For example, in spite of lobbying by middle-class Parisian women affiliated with groups like the *Cercle sociale* (Social Club), no rights were extended to women. In her *Declaration of the Rights of Women,* the author Olympe de Gouges (oh-limp duh GOOJ) protested: "The exercise of the natural rights of women has only been limited by the perpetual tyranny that man opposes to them; these limits should be reformed by the laws of nature and reason."[3] Though women were important to the Revolution, such appeals were ignored by the men who had seized power.

Within the National Assembly revolutionary zeal was secondary to cooperating with Louis XVI in establishing a new constitutional monarchy. But neither the king nor the assembly could control the pace of change. In the fall of 1789, in both urban and rural areas, the poor took direct action. Spurred on by hunger caused by the high price of bread and distrustful of the intentions of the king, twenty thousand Parisians marched to Versailles in what was called the "March of the Women" because of the preponderance of housewives and market women in its ranks. The marchers forced the king and his family to leave Versailles and return to his palace in the heart of Paris, where they could keep a closer eye on him.

Despite the political importance of Paris, the vast majority of French men and women were still village-based peasants who resented the political and economic rights the nobles still had over them. "Justice" came from courts presided over by their lord, they had to donate free labor to cultivating his estates, and they were

---

• **National Assembly** (1789) Revolutionary assembly formed by members of the Third Estate after the failure of the Estates-General. They agreed on the "Declaration of the Rights of Man and of the Citizen," forcing the king to sign the assembly's constitution.

CL **Primary Source:** The Declaration of the Rights of Man and of the Citizen *This document, drafted by the National Assembly of France, is an Enlightenment cousin of Jefferson's Declaration.*

often forced to grind their wheat into flour at the lord's mill, where lack of competition allowed him to charge whatever he liked. While the National Assembly debated the elimination of feudal practices, the peasants took matters into their own hands, sometimes burning only the manorial rolls that listed their feudal obligations, and sometimes burning the estates themselves to the ground.

In this tense atmosphere the National Assembly organized a Legislative Assembly to draft a new set of basic laws, following the United States example of a written constitution and the British example of sharing power between the king and representatives of the people. But the plan could not work without the king's cooperation; in the summer of 1791, he tried to escape from France, hoping to rally support from other European monarchs for his return as an absolute ruler. He was captured and held a virtual prisoner in his palace. Meanwhile, many members of the nobility had fled to other capitals, where they were trying to convince Europe's kings and aristocrats to help overthrow the revolution.

By the summer of 1792 French forces had fared badly in armed conflict with Habsburg regiments in the Netherlands, and there were fears of an Austrian invasion. A severe shortage of grain following the previous year's poor harvest increased tensions. The people of Paris staged demonstrations and then attacked the royal palace. Hundreds of citizens and soldiers died.

The time when compromise was possible was now at an end. Some members of the Legislative Assembly were disappointed that the king and his followers refused to play by the new rules of constitutional monarchy, but others were just as happy that the experiment did not work. They were republicans, who believed that any form of monarchy undermined liberty. The next phase of the French Revolution would belong to them.

Parisian Women March to Versailles Women played a distinctive role in the French Revolution. Elite women sponsored the gatherings that spread Enlightenment and revolutionary ideals in their *salons*, while the common women engaged in direct action, as here in 1789 where they are shown marching to Versailles to force the king to return to Paris. (The Granger Collection)

The Jacobins and the Reign of Terror, 1793–1795

The Legislative Assembly bowed to pressure from the people of Paris for the declaration of a republic and the institution of universal manhood suffrage. The National Assembly dissolved itself in favor of a National Convention, which immediately declared the end of the monarchy and began writing a republican constitution for France. They found Louis XVI guilty of treason, stripped him of his royal title, and beheaded him in January 1793.

The most radical faction in the National Convention were the **Jacobins** led by Maximilien Robespierre (ROBES-pee-air). Under the Jacobins the French Revolution passed through its most idealist and most violent phase. Robespierre had been deeply influenced by the philosophy of Jean-Jacques Rousseau, who had argued that the only legitimate state was one that expressed the "general will" of the people. Rousseau had envisioned a form of direct democracy practiced by enlightened citizens, but he rejected the checks on government power proposed by Montesquieu and implemented in the Constitution of the United States. Instead he talked of constructing a "Republic of Virtue" that would represent a radical new beginning.

The government confiscated lands belonging to the church and to the nobility, and slavery in the French Empire was abolished. The absolute equality of the French was demonstrated by their new salutation: everyone, rich and poor, expected to be addressed as "citizen." This new beginning of "liberty, equality, and fraternity" was symbolized by the creation of a new calendar. The year 1793 became Year One, marking the victory of reason over the old Christian faith. The months were divided into three weeks of ten days each, following the logic of the new metric system. The old names of the days of the week, irrationally based on pagan traditions, were replaced. Time itself would have a revolutionary new beginning.

But no fresh start was really possible; the past could not be so easily erased. Devout Catholics deeply resented Jacobin attacks on the church, and the bourgeoisie, though often republicans, were shocked by the Jacobins' seizure of property. Meanwhile, the kings of Prussia and Austria, alarmed by the execution of the king, had declared war on France, determined to end the revolution and restore the monarchy.

Robespierre felt justified in imposing a harsh dictatorship. Not for the last time in world history, a revolutionary leader declared that in order to save the revolution from its enemies its most cherished principle, liberty, would have to be sacrificed. A dictatorial Committee of Public Safety replaced democratic institutions. The committee quashed its enemies with a so-called Reign of Terror in which forty thousand people were killed. The symbol of the Revolution now became the guillotine (gee-yuh-TEEN), in which the condemned placed their head on a block before having it removed by the swift fall of a sharp, heavy blade. The fact that the guillotine became a symbol of revolutionary violence is ironic. The philosophes were horrified by grizzly public executions in which several swings of a heavy axe were often needed to fully decapitate the victim, or in which screaming victims were slowly burnt to death at the stake. Dr. Joseph Guillotin had intended his invention as an enlightened means of execution, clean and swift. Now his attempt at humane reform had been transformed into a means of terror.

The Jacobins were successful in one vital task: securing the republic against Austrian and Prussian invaders. They ordered a mass levy of conscripts and fielded an enormous army. The consequences of mass conscription were cultural and political as well as military. Most of the soldiers were peasants who had never before

• **Jacobins** Radical republican faction in the French Revolution. They organized a military force that saved the republic, but their leader Maximilien Robespierre, head of the Committee of Public Safety, ruled by decree and set in motion the Reign of Terror.

CL **Primary Source: Rousseau Espouses Popular Sovereignty and the General Will**
Modern political philosophy owes much to the ideas of this French philosopher.

traveled far from home. They had led very local lives, practicing local customs and speaking regional dialects. Once trained for defense of the Republic, many developed a stronger sense of French national identity.

Military success, however, emboldened the Jacobins' domestic enemies. People in the provinces were angry at the radicalism they associated with Paris, and many members of the middle class favored a more moderate republic. A further irony was added to the story of the guillotine: those who had used it to execute their enemies often ended with their own heads in a basket. Robespierre himself was executed before the end of 1794.

The Age of Napoleon, 1795–1815

The National Convention reasserted power and created a new constitution with a more limited electorate and a separation of powers. From 1795 to 1799, however, the country remained sharply divided. The Directory, which formed the executive of the new government, faced conspiracies both by the Jacobins trying to return to power and by monarchists trying to restore the Bourbon dynasty. Meanwhile, the French armies continued to gain victories as a young general named **Napoleon Bonaparte** (1769–1821) took northern Italy from the Austrians. In 1799 two members of the Directory, anxious to assert greater control over the country, plotted with Napoleon to launch a *coup d'état* and form a new government.

Like George Washington, Napoleon looked to Roman history for inspiration. But unlike the American general, who chose as a hero someone who had saved a republic from tyranny, Napoleon followed Rome's imperial example of transforming a republic into an empire. In 1804 he crowned himself Emperor Napoleon I. (See the feature "Visual Evidence: Portraits of Power: George Washington and Napoleon Bonaparte.") But first he secured the approval of the legislature and had the move ratified through a national referendum. In fact, Napoleon was quite popular. Tired of fractious republican politics, many French men and women were seeking an "enlightened dictatorship."

Indeed, by the orderliness and rationality of his administration, Napoleon seemed to fulfill many of the hopes of the eighteenth-century philosophes. In 1801 he had reached a compromise with the pope that allowed Catholic worship and restored government support for the clergy, thereby resolving one of the most contentious issues in French politics. The Bank of France was created to stabilize the government's financial situation, and a new legal system, the Napoleonic Code, recognized the legal equality of all French citizens. Napoleon also neutralized political opposition by bringing all but the most fervent monarchists into his administration and by tapping into the sense of French nationality that had been developed during the Revolution. The French were now citizens of a nation rather than subjects of a king, and Napoleon cultivated their sense of patriotism and national pride, promising them not liberty but glory. Napoleon's empire was a surprising outcome of the events of 1789.

French nationalism was greatly stimulated by Napoleon's remarkable military achievements. Though the emperor's planned invasion of England was stymied in 1805 by the victory of Lord Nelson's fleet at Trafalgar, a testament to Britain's continuing naval superiority, Napoleon's forces were unstoppable on the European continent. In some cases the French were greeted as liberators. The German composer Ludwig von Beethoven, for example, expected that the French were bringing liberty and enlightenment and initially dedicated his "Heroic" symphony to

Napoleon Bonaparte (1769–1821) Military commander who gained control of France after the French Revolution. Declared himself emperor in 1804 and attempted to expand French territory, but failed to defeat Great Britain and abdicated in 1814. Died in exile after a brief return to power in 1815.

PORTRAITS OF POWER: GEORGE WASHINGTON AND NAPOLEON BONAPARTE

During the eighteenth and nineteenth centuries in Europe and the Americas, political leaders commissioned paintings of themselves to project images of power. Portraits such as those reproduced here could inform people not merely of the *fact* of power but also of the particular *type* of power they were as-sociated with. President George Washington of the United States (r. 1789–1797) and Emperor Napoleon Bonaparte of France (r. 1799–1814), as well as their portraitists, were keenly aware of classical Greek and Roman models in projecting images of power. Washington identified himself with the democratic tradition

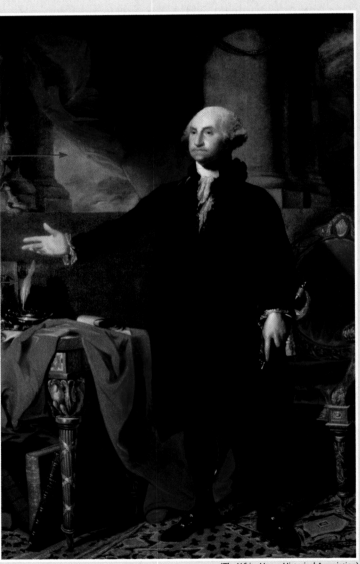

The stormy sky in the left background might illustrate the difficult times that Washington and his comrades passed through, while the rainbow in the upper right shows their ultimate victory.

The inkstand on the table and the books below, including a copy of the Constitution, show his importance in crafting the nation's foundational documents.

(The White House Historical Association)

Washington wears no signs of military rank, holds a sheathed sword with its point down, and offers his open hand. The impression is one of peace.

of Athens and the Republican period of Rome; Napoleon, by contrast, emphasized the imperial Roman tradition. Simón Bolívar, whose portrait at the beginning of the chapter can be compared with those here, was also keenly aware of both the republican and imperial traditions of ancient Rome.

Napoleon holds a scepter topped by a figure of Charlemagne, the early medieval king whose empire was one of his models.

At his coronation in 1804 Napoleon wore two different crowns, first a laurel crown like the one shown here and then a bejeweled reproduction of Charlemagne's crown. New rulers often seek legitimacy by associating themselves with older symbols of power.

(Musée de l'Armée, Paris, France/ Art Resource, NY)

What different reactions might Napoleon's supporters and detractors have had in viewing this portrait? Napoleon did not commission this painting, and we do not know what he himself thought of it.

QUESTIONS FOR ANALYSIS

In these portraits, what is similar or different about how Napoleon Bonaparte and George Washington are represented? Compare each with the portrait of Simón Bolívar at the beginning of the chapter with the same question in mind.

Napoleon. When he realized that personal ambition and the quest for French glory were the emperor's true motivations, he scratched that dedication from the title page. Simón Bolívar, living in Paris after his visit to Rome, was likewise disappointed by Napoleon's imperial pretensions. But like most observers, the young Bolívar admired Bonaparte's political and military skill.

French armies swept through Iberia and Italy and asserted control over the Netherlands, Poland, and the western half of Germany. The Austrians and Prussians suffered embarrassing losses to the French armies, who were commanded by the greatest general of the age and by a new breed of military officers chosen for their talent rather than their aristocratic connections.

But Napoleon's ambition caused him to overreach and bring about his own downfall. In 1812 he mounted a massive attack on Russia. The Russian army could in no way prevent this assault, but they used their vast spaces to military advantage. When Napoleon reached Moscow, he found that the city had been abandoned and largely burned to the ground by its own people. Napoleon had nothing to claim as a prize. The French army, retreating to the west in the harsh conditions of the Russian winter, was decimated. Of the 700,000 troops that had invaded Russia, fewer than 100,000 returned.

A broad coalition of anti-French forces then went on the offensive, invaded France, forced Napoleon to abdicate in 1814, and restored the Bourbon monarchy by placing Louis XVIII (r. 1814–1824) on the throne. Dramatically, Napoleon then escaped his exile, returned to Paris, and reformed his army before finally being defeated by British and Prussian forces at the Battle of Waterloo in 1815. He died in exile on a remote South Atlantic island.

By a roundabout route France had finally become a constitutional monarchy. Still, Napoleon's impact on world history was substantial. French conquests stimulated nationalism all across Europe and even, through Napoleon's invasion of Egypt, in North Africa (see Chapter 23). Napoleon's conquest of Spain created conditions favorable to the ambitions of Latin American revolutionaries like Simón Bolívar. And within France's overseas empire, the most dramatic developments took place on the Caribbean island of Saint-Domingue (san doe-MANG).

●The Haitian Revolution, 1791–1804

The colony of Saint-Domingue was by far France's richest overseas possession. Occupying the western half of the island of Hispaniola, Saint-Domingue generated incredible wealth for French merchants and sugar planters, accounting for as much as a third of the country's foreign trade. But the prosperity was based on misery. Half a million African slaves toiled on the plantations. Their conditions of work were so harsh, and the numbers who died of maltreatment and disease so great, that the planters constantly imported shipments of Africans to keep enough slaves working in the fields. Most of the blacks in Saint-Domingue had been born in Africa.

An elite of white planters stood over this vast African population. Their reaction to the revolutionary events starting in 1789 in Paris was complex. Many of them were inspired by the call to liberty and dreamed of forming their own independent republic. But the Revolution's other great goal, "equality," was more problematic. Abolishing slavery and establishing true equality had not been possible even in the United States, where slavery was relatively less important. In Saint-

Domingue, true equality, requiring the abolition of slavery, would have brought the entire plantation economy to a halt.

In fact, the white planters could not even conceive of offering the fruits of liberation to their slaves. The slaves themselves had little way of knowing what was happening in Paris or what the application of Enlightenment thought might mean for them. Initially, therefore, the central conflict was between the whites and the so-called *gens de couleur* (zhahn deh koo-LUHR), free men and women, mostly of mixed race, who were about equal in number to the whites. They were artisans and small farmers who supplied food and other commodities to the large plantations; some of them were prosperous enough to own a few slaves themselves. Many were literate, and having followed the events of the American and French Revolutions, they demanded liberty and equality for themselves. By 1791, civil war had broken out between the white planters and the gens de couleur.

While neither of these groups had any intention of ending slavery, the fight between them gave Africans an opening. Revolution from below came in the form of a vast slave uprising organized by a *Voudun* (voh-doon) priest popularly called Boukman (because he was literate). As in Brazil, where *Candomblé* showed the strong presence of African religious traditions (see Chapter 19), Voudun religious beliefs and rituals derived from West and Central Africa. Boukman's role as the leader of the African-based religion of Voudun gave him great authority, while his position as a field manager and coach driver for his master gave him wide-ranging connections in the slave community. He secretly organized thousands of slaves to rise up at his signal. When they did so, in the summer of 1791, they were spontaneously joined by tens of thousands of slaves from across Saint-Domingue, as well as by maroons, former slaves who had fled plantations to live in the mountains.

Just as French peasants had burned the manor houses of their aristocratic overlords in 1789, now Boukman's slave army attacked the planters' estates in the countryside. Then forty thousand of them marched on the city of Le Cap, where whites and gens de couleur had taken refuge. The slaughter lasted for weeks. When planter forces finally captured and killed the rebel leader, they fixed his head to a pole with a sign that read: "This is the head of Boukman, chief of the rebels."

In 1792 the French government sent an army to restore order, trusting that the slave rebels would falter from lack of leadership. But then a new commander emerged. François-Dominique Toussaint was born a slave but was educated by a priest and worked in his master's house rather than in the fields. The name by which he is remembered, **Toussaint L'Ouverture** (1744–1803), reflects his military skill: *l'ouverture* refers to the "opening" he would make in the enemy lines. But Toussaint's political, intellectual, and diplomatic strengths were equally important in turning the raw material of a slave uprising into an independent nation freed from the savage inequalities of slavery.

Like Olaudah Equiano, who was touring England in support of his abolitionist writing at this time (see Chapter 19), Toussaint L'Ouverture (too-SAN loo-ver-CHUR) could bridge the worlds of slave and master. He could organize the slaves to fight while forging alliances with whites, gens de couleur, and the foreign forces that intervened in the conflict. By 1801 his army controlled most of the island. Toussaint supported the creation of a new constitution that granted equality to all and that declared him governor-general for life.

Initially some radical French revolutionaries supported the rebels, but Napoleon had other ideas, and in 1802 he sent an expedition to crush Toussaint's new state. Although Toussaint was open to compromise as long as slavery would not be restored, he was arrested by the French commander and sent to France. Toussaint

● **Toussaint L'Ouverture** (1744–1803)   Leader of the Haitian revolution. Under his military and political leadership, Haiti gained independence and abolished slavery, becoming the first black-ruled republic in the Americas. He died in exile in France.

Toussaint L'Ouverture   In this contemporary engraving the Haitian revolutionary leader Toussaint L'Ouverture is shown in an equestrian pose associated with civil and military power. Toussaint brought Enlightenment ideals to the elemental struggle of Haiti's slaves for liberation. His leadership was sorely missed in Haiti after he was tricked into negotiations with France and died in a French prison.   (Bibliothèque nationale de France/Archives Charmet/The Bridgeman Art Library)

was harshly treated and died in a French prison in 1803.

Meanwhile, Haitian military leaders kept up the fight long enough for environmental factors to intervene on their side. Napoleon's soldiers, with no immunity to tropical diseases, succumbed to yellow fever. Just as the Russian winter would later spoil Napoleon's plan for eastward expansion, so in the West Indies he failed to adequately consider the effects of climate on his invading forces. His troops withdrew, and in 1804 the independent nation of Haiti was born.

The independence of Haiti had ramifications throughout the Atlantic world. Slave owners in the United States were terrified by the Haitian example. Some plantations owners stepped up security measures on their plantations, such as by placing even tighter limits on slaves' movements, while the U.S. government at first ostracized Haiti by refusing to grant it diplomatic recognition. Venezuela was even more directly influenced by the Haitian revolution. In 1795 a Venezuelan who returned from Haiti, a free *zombo* (of mixed African/Amerindian ancestry), led a local rebellion of slaves and free persons of color, sending the elite of Caracas into a panic. Simón Bolívar was just 12 at that time, but later he would seek the support of the Haitian government in his own fight for freedom and would argue for the abolition of slavery as a means of avoiding a Haitian-style revolution in the plantation zone of South America.

The Latin American Wars of Independence, 1800–1824

Simón Bolívar and other Latin American revolutionaries looked to the ideals of the Enlightenment and the examples of the United States, France, and Haiti in charting their own wars of independence in the early nineteenth century. At the same time, the experiences of Mexico and South America reflected their unique experiences with the social, cultural, demographic, and economic conditions of Spanish rule (see Chapter 18). Coalitions and conflicts between *criollos* (American-born Spaniards) and people of African, Amerindian, or mixed descent conditioned the course of revolution in many areas. Beyond widespread agreement on the need to expel the Spanish, the great diversity of Latin American voices and interests made it exceptionally difficult to establish common political ground.

In Mexico as in South America, a major question was whether the revolutionaries would be content fighting for independence from Spain or would also want more substantial social and economic reforms. Frightened by the radical Jacobin experience in France and the slave uprising in Haiti, Latin America's elites were cautious. But in Mexico, Bolivia, Venezuela, and elsewhere, Amerindians and slaves organized for a more complete transformation of their societies, aided by some establishment figures who took seriously such revolutionary mottos as "liberty," "equality," and "brotherhood."

Simón Bolívar and South American Independence

The conditions for Latin American independence were closely connected to events in Europe. In 1808 Napoleon had put his own brother on the Spanish throne, forcing the Spanish king to abdicate. (The king of Portugal, by contrast, fled to Brazil, which was ruled as a monarchy throughout this period.) In the Spanish-speaking Americas, loyalty to the king meant opposition to the French-imposed regime in Madrid, and local elites created *juntas* (ruling groups) to assert local rule. But were these juntas (HUN-tah) temporary organizations to be disbanded when the legitimate king returned to power or the precursors to a permanent transfer of power from Madrid to the Americas? Loyalists made the former argument, while Republicans like Bolívar and his Argentinean counterpart José de San Martín (1778–1850) saw the chance to win complete independence. This division of opinion meant that they would have to fight against powerful local loyalists as well as Spanish troops.

A focal point of grievance was the dominant position of the direct representatives of royal authority in Spanish America. These *peninsulares* dominated the affairs of church and state in a way that was frustrating to the ambitious members of the American-born elite, the criollos (see Chapter 18). Somewhat like the bourgeois leaders of the Third Estate in the French Revolution, many criollos felt that the existing system was an impediment to their rightful place as leading members of their communities. Criollo merchants were often frustrated by the restrictions on trade imposed by the peninsulares as representatives of Madrid.

But the struggle involved more than just imperial representatives and local elites. In most parts of the continent, building a popular base of support for independence required going beyond the white elite to appeal to Indians, Africans, *mestizos,* and other people of mixed descent. While the revolutionaries who built the new United States of America had largely avoided involving people of color in their revolution, there was little choice but to include them in Latin America, where they were usually the majority of the population.

For example, Bolívar's home city of Caracas, facing the sea, was culturally and economically connected to the Caribbean. Slave plantations were an important part of its economy, and Bolívar spent part of his childhood on a plantation worked by slaves. In addition, Caracas had a large community of *pardos,* free men and women of mixed African-Spanish-Native American ancestry. As in Haiti, with its bitter tensions between French planters, gens de coleur, and African slaves, in coastal Venezuela unity across lines of class and race was hard to achieve.

In the Venezuelan interior Bolívar would need to cooperate with a very different group: the *llaneros* (yah-neyr-ohs), tough frontier cowboys of mixed Spanish/Amerindian descent (like the *gauchos* of Argentina and the *vaqueros* of Mexico). Farther south, Bolívar's armies eventually entered the Viceroyalty of Peru, where the basic social divide was between the coastal areas dominated by Spanish-speaking colonists and the still considerable Amerindian population of the Andes. Bolívar's skills as a political leader were constantly tested by his need to forge alliances among such disparate groups.

As elsewhere in Spanish America, a junta composed of local elites had been formed in Caracas following Napoleon's removal of the Spanish king from power. These leaders saw themselves as holding power temporarily until the rightful monarchy was restored. The conservative junta chose the well-traveled Bolívar to represent them on diplomatic missions to London and Washington in 1810, but he betrayed them when he lobbied the British to support his plan for independence. Upon his return to Caracas, Bolívar attended the first Congress of Venezuela, which on July 3, 1811, became the first such body in Latin America to declare independence from Spain.

But just saying it did not make it so. Racial, ethnic, and regional division meant that there was no deep sense of "Venezuelan" identity upon which a new nation could be founded. The constitution restricted voting rights to a small minority of overwhelmingly white property owners and did nothing to abolish slavery. In addition, the llaneros of the interior felt threatened by a constitutional provision that extended private property ownership to the previously uncharted plains. Ironically, independence for Venezuela could mean their loss of liberty: if the lands where they rounded up wild cattle were fenced off by wealthy ranchers, the cowboys might lose their livelihood and their independence.

A huge earthquake in the spring of 1812 added to the instability of the new Venezuelan republic. Soon forces loyal to Spain were on the offensive. The young republic collapsed, and Bolívar set out on the military path he would pursue for the next twelve years, proclaiming a "war to the death" with the Spanish (see Map 22.2). Captured Spaniards would be executed, he declared, while American-born Spanish loyalists would be given a chance to mend their ways.

In the summer of 1813 Bolívar's army entered Caracas, but divisions within Venezuelan society worked against him. To broaden the revolutionary appeal, Bolívar had forged alliances with groups that had been excluded from the first congress and constitution. He sought out the cooperation of the leader of the llaneros and pledged himself to the abolition of slavery. But many criollos in the capital regarded the cowboys as bandits and, still haunted by memories of the violent Haitian Revolution, reacted with suspicion to Bolívar's coalition.

In addition to weaknesses arising from such internal dissension, the cause of independence suffered a setback in 1815 after Napoleon's defeat at Waterloo and the restoration of the Spanish monarchy. The Madrid government sent a fleet of fifty ships carrying over ten thousand soldiers to restore imperial authority in South America. Bolívar fled to the island of Jamaica, where he once again sought British help. (See the feature "Movement of Ideas: Simón Bolívar's Jamaica Letter.") He also traveled to Haiti, asking for support from its government and expanding his previous support of abolition with the pledge to seek "the absolute liberty of the slaves who have groaned beneath the Spanish yoke in the past three centuries."[4]

⊕ MAP 22.2
Independence in Latin America

Paraguay led the way toward Latin American independence in 1811, followed by rebels in Buenos Aires who declared the independence of the United Provinces of Rio de la Plata (the core of today's Argentina) in 1816. The next year forces led by José de San Martín crossed the Andes, linked with the rebel army of Bernardo O'Higgins, and secured Chilean independence. The Chilean rebels then traveled north by sea to attack Spanish positions at Lima, with inconclusive results. By that time, however, Simón Bolívar had secured the independence of Venezuela and Ecuador, uniting them into the independent state of Gran Colombia. Combined Chilean and Colombian forces defeated the Spanish at Ayachuco in 1824, finalizing the independence of Spanish Latin America.

CL Interactive Map

Most importantly from a military standpoint, he began to recruit battle-hardened British soldiers as mercenaries who would serve as his elite force.

Returning to Venezuela in 1817, Bolívar established himself in the interior of the country and was quickly recognized as the supreme commander of the various patriotic forces that were contesting Spain's effort to re-establish control. To slaves who joined his army he offered freedom, and he revived his alliance with the llaneros of the plains. Bolívar's toughness in battle and his willingness to share the privations of his men—once spending a whole night immersed in a lake to avoid Spanish forces—won him their absolute loyalty.

In 1819, even while the Spanish still held Caracas and other important cities, delegates to the **Congress of Angostura** planned for the resuscitation of

● **Congress of Angostura** (1819) Congress that declared Venezuelan independence after Simón Bolívar gave an opening address arguing for a strong central government with effective executive powers.

Simón Bolívar's Jamaica Letter

An important starting point for Simón Bolívar's political philosophy was the work of the great Enlightenment thinker the Baron de Montesquieu. In his *Spirit of the Laws* (1748), Montesquieu had argued that there was no universal template for human governance; rather, any given society is best governed by a political and legal system suited to its own culture and traditions. Bolívar argued that the institutions of independent Latin America must mesh with its own traditions rather than merely copy models imported from the outside. In this statement from 1815, written before the major experiments with republican independence had taken place in Latin America, Bolívar assesses the background to the postindependence constitutional order.

Source: *El Libertador: Writings of Simón Bolívar*, ed. David Bushnell, trans. Frederick H. Fornoff (New York: Oxford University Press, 2003), pp. 12–30.

Bolívar's Jamaica Letter

In my opinion, this is the image of our situation. We are a small segment of the human race; we possess a world apart, surrounded by vast seas, new in almost every art and science. . . . [We are] moreover neither Indians nor Europeans, but a race halfway between the legitimate owners of the land and the Spanish usurpers—in short, being Americans by birth and endowed with rights from Europe—find ourselves forced to defend these rights against the natives while maintaining our position in the land against the intrusion of the invaders. . . .

The posture of those who dwell in the American hemisphere has been over the centuries purely passive. We were at a level even lower than servitude, and by that very reason hindered from elevating ourselves to the enjoyment of freedom. . . . From the beginning we were plagued by a practice that in addition to depriving us of the rights to which we were entitled left us in a kind of permanent infancy with respect to public affairs. If we had been allowed to manage even the domestic aspects of our internal administration, we would understand the processes and mechanisms of public affairs. . . .

The Americans, within the Spanish system still in force, and perhaps now more than ever, occupy no other place in society other than that of servants suited for work, or, at best, that of simple consumers, and even this role is limited by appalling restrictions. . . . We were . . . lost, or worse, absent from the universe in all things relative to the science of government and the administration of the state. We were never viceroys, never governors . . . hardly ever bishops or archbishops; never diplomats; soldiers, only in lower ranks. . . . In short, we were never leaders, never financiers, hardly even merchants. . . .

The Americans have made their debut on the world stage suddenly and without prior knowledge . . . having to enact the eminent roles of legislators, magistrates, ministers of the treasury, diplomats, generals, and all the other supreme and subordinate authorities that make up the hierarchy of a well-organized state. . . .

Perfectly representative institutions are not appropriate to our character, our customs, and our current level of knowledge and experience. . . . Until our compatriots acquire the political skills and virtues that distinguish our brothers to the north, entirely popular systems, far from being favorable to us, will, I greatly fear, lead to our ruin. . . .

The people of South America have manifested the inclination to establish liberal and even perfect institutions, an effect, no doubt, of the instinct all men share of aspiring to the highest possible degree of happiness, which is invariably achieved in civil societies founded on the principles of justice, freedom and equality. . . . More than anyone, I would like to see America become the greatest nation on earth, regarded not so much for its size and wealth as for its freedom and glory. Although I aspire to a perfect government for my country, I can't persuade myself that the New World is ready at this time to be governed by a grand republic. . . . The American states need the stewardship of paternalistic governments to cure the wounds and ravages of despotism and war. . . .

The idea of merging the entire New World into a single nation with a single unifying principle to provide coherence to the parts and to the whole is both grandiose and impractical. Because it has a common origin, a common language, similar customs, and one religion, we might conclude that it should be possible for a single government to oversee a federation of the different states eventually to emerge. However, this is not possible, because America is divided by remote climates, diverse geographies, conflicting interests, and dissimilar characteristics. . . .

When success is uncertain, when the state is weak . . . all men vacillate; opinions are divided, inflamed by passion and by the enemy, which seeks to win easy victory in this way. When we are at last strong, under the auspices of a liberal nation that lends us its protection, then we will cultivate in harmony the virtues and talents that lead to glory; then we will follow the majestic path toward abundant prosperity marked out by destiny for South America; then the arts and sciences that were born in the Orient and that brought Enlightenment to Europe will fly to a free Colombia, which will nurture and shelter them.

QUESTIONS FOR ANALYSIS

▶ What forces does Bolívar think must be taken into account when planning Latin America's future?

▶ What limits does he feel those forces place on the continent's political aspirations?

▶ What comparisons does he draw between North and South America?

independent Venezuela. In his opening address Bolívar argued for a strong central government with effective executive powers, fearing that a federal system with a strong legislature would lead to division and instability. Rather than stay in his native country to see these plans carried out, however, Bolívar moved south and west to confront imperial forces in the Spanish stronghold of Bogotá. Seeking a broader foundation for Latin American liberty, he began his fight for *Gran Colombia*, a political union that he hoped would include the area covered by the contemporary nations of Venezuela, Colombia, Panama, Ecuador, and Peru.

Bolívar and his troops, natives of the tropical coast or the arid interior, suffered greatly on their campaign into the frigid Andean mountains. But they attracted local recruits to their cause, including many from the area's Indian population. The demoralized Spanish forces, led by generals who could not match the brilliance of Bolívar's strategies, quickly gave way, first in Bogotá and then in Ecuador. Meanwhile, further south, other liberators were scoring equivalent successes. José de San Martín (hoe-SAY deh san mar-TEEN) had taken the region of Rio de la Plata (today's Argentina), while Chile's successful republican forces were led by Bernardo O'Higgins (the Spanish-speaking son of an Irish immigrant). Together San Martín and O'Higgins had occupied the coastal regions of Peru, leaving only its Andean region in loyalist hands.

The situation in the Andes had been tense since an Amerindian uprising in 1780 led by a descendant of the last Inca ruler named **Tupac Amaru II** (1741–1781) (TOO-pack ah-MAR-oo). Tupac had been educated by Jesuit priests and for a time served the Spanish government. But the poverty, illiteracy, and oppression faced by his own people caused him first to petition for reform and then, when his pleas were ignored, to change his name, adopt indigenous dress, and organize a rebellion. It was the first uprising against Spanish rule in the highlands for over two hundred years.

Tupac Amaru's revolt was savagely suppressed. He was forced to witness the torture and death of his own wife and family members before his own execution. The Spanish government then tried to ban the wearing of indigenous cloth and the use of the indigenous Quechua (KEH-chwah) language. These Spanish attempts at cultural assimilation were not successful, however, as the local Amerindian population responded to the rebels' defeat by avoiding contact with the Spanish officials whenever they could. Though the Amerindians of the highlands were potential allies of Bolívar, most remained aloof from the fight, more concerned with the autonomy of their own communities than the independence of nations.

Nevertheless, Bolívar's troops engaged the Spanish in the Andes in 1824 at the Battle of Ayacucho. Their victory was complete, and South America was free from Spanish control. Still unanswered, however, was how independence from Spain would translate into liberty for the diverse peoples of South America.

● **Tupac Amaru II** (1741–1781) José Gabriel Condorcanqui Noguera, a descendant of the last Inca ruler; called himself Tupac Amaru II while leading a large-scale rebellion in the Andes against Spanish rule. He was defeated and executed.

● **Miguel de Hidalgo y Costilla** (1753–1811) Mexican priest who launched the first stage of the Mexican war for independence. Hidalgo appealed to Indians and mestizos and was thus viewed with suspicion by Mexican criollos. In 1811, he was captured and executed. The Spanish publicly displayed his severed and mutilated head in Guanajuato as a warning to other rebels.

Mexico and Brazil, 1810–1831

Mexico's path to independence ran parallel to the South American revolutions but had a different starting point. Whereas leadership in the first phase of the struggle in Venezuela was led by socially conservative criollos, in Mexico the deposition of the Spanish king quickly led to a popular uprising of mestizos and Indians. A parish priest named **Miguel de Hidalgo y Costilla** (1753–1811) rallied the poor not just for Mexican independence but also in the name of justice for the oppressed.

■ **Padre Hildalgo**   In 1810 Padre Hidalgo rallied the common people of Mexico, especially mestizos and Indians, under the banner of the Virgin of Guadalupe, for independence from Spain. Mexican elites opposed him, however, and cooperated with Spanish authorities to crush the uprising. Hidalgo was executed. When Mexican independence was achieved in 1821, the criollo elite was firmly in charge of the new nation. (Schaalwijk/Art Resource, NY)

From his pulpit in the town of Dolores, Father Hidalgo issued his famous *Grito* ("cry"): "Long live Our Lady of Guadalupe! Long live the Americas and death to the corrupt government!" His appeal to the Virgin of Guadalupe, a dark-skinned representation of the Virgin Mary as she had appeared to a lowly peasant (see Chapter 18), symbolized Hidalgo's appeal to downtrodden Indians and mestizos. Hidalgo called for the creation of a Mexican nation with the words "*¡Mexicanos, Viva México!*"

Shocking to Spanish officials, Hidalgo's actions had also alarmed Mexico's criollo elite, who flocked to the loyalist banner. His forces were scattered, and Hidalgo was excommunicated from the church and then executed. As late as 1820, Spanish authority seemed secure.

When independence did come in 1821, it resulted not from a renewal of popular insurgency but from a backlash by Mexican conservatives against changes in Madrid of which they did not approve. Afraid of liberal reform coming from Spain, these elite conservatives supported Mexican military officers who turned on their former Spanish allies. Contrary to Father Hildago's vision, Mexican independence brought no social or economic reform to the country. Nevertheless, Hidalgo still symbolizes Mexican independence, and the anniversary of the *Grito de Dolores*, September 16, is still celebrated as Mexico's national day.

Brazil followed an entirely different path in the early nineteenth century. In 1808 the Portuguese royal family reacted to Napoleon's invasion by seeking refuge in Brazil. In 1821 the king returned to Portugal, leaving his son Pedro behind as his representative. Pedro, however, recognizing that public opinion was turning strongly in favor of independence, declared himself sympathetic to this cause, and in 1824 Pedro I (r. 1824–1831) became the constitutional monarch of an independent Brazil. Although he was unpopular with some people, such as sugar planters who disapproved of his 1830 treaty with Britain to abolish the slave trade, the constitutional monarchy proved stable and lasted until it was finally overthrown by a republican movement in 1889 (see Chapter 25).

Interactive Map

🌐 **MAP 22.3**
Europe in 1815   After the disruptions to the political map of Europe caused by
the French Revolution and the expansion of Napoleon's empire, in 1815 European
diplomats restored earlier boundaries and established a conservative status quo at the
Congress of Vienna. One important change was the appearance of the Prussian-led
German Confederation, a tariff union that helped lay the foundation for the later unification of Germany (see Chapter 23).

Revolutionary Outcomes and Comparisons, to 1830

In the first half of the nineteenth century the new United States of America established itself as a vigorous republic. By 1830 there were twenty-four states in the Union; settlers moved to new territories as high wages and cheap land attracted swelling numbers of European immigrants, especially from Britain, Ireland, and Germany.

Liberated from British controls, American colonists pursued what they considered their "manifest destiny," a clear and divinely approved mission to settle the lands between the original thirteen colonies and the Pacific. The Lewis and Clark Expedition pointed the way west (see Chapter 21), and the vast Louisiana Purchase (purchased from Napoleon in 1803, who had lost Haiti and needed a quick source of funds) gave the new republic plenty of space to grow. The lands into which the citizens of the United States sought to expand were not, however, empty. As the military and transportation technologies available to settlers improved in the course of the nineteenth century, the western frontier of the United States would be marked by blood and violence. And since the issue of slavery remained unresolved, regional tensions in the young republic were bound to increase. As new states entered the Union, would they be free or would they be slave? It would take a violent civil war to solve that question (see Chapter 25).

In France and central Europe, conservative elites used the defeat of Napoleon to suppress reform. The Bourbon dynasty was restored to power, and Prince Metternich of Austria coordinated the diplomacy leading to the **Congress of Vienna** (1815), which restored the traditional balance of power among Britain, France, Austria, Prussia, and Russia (see Map 22.3). Aristocrats once again flouted their wealth and status in the capitals of Europe, no longer afraid of revolutionary violence.

Change was not so easily repressed, however. In particular, the spread of nationalism and the association of that idea with progressive reform proved a constant challenge, and sometimes a grave threat, to European rulers. It was Greek nationalists who showed the way, winning their independence from the Ottoman Empire in 1829. Backed by Britain, Greek nationalists did not threaten the European status quo. But it was not long before ethnic minorities in the Austrian and Russian Empires began organizing along national lines, while the idea of a single, powerful German nation began to spread as well. The embers of other radical ideals of the French Revolution also remained alight, such as the idea that equality could only be achieved through a more equitable distribution of wealth. Though basic liberal concepts such as the equality of all citizens before the law still had not been achieved by 1830, a rising generation of revolutionaries would soon try once again to overturn Europe's conservative status quo (see Chapter 23).

In Haiti, where most people had been slaves before the revolution, legal freedom was a clear outcome of revolution. But the transition from slave colony to free republic proved difficult. Independence saw a massive decline in plantation production as freed slaves established their own farms on small plots of land. Though individuals who were formerly slaves were certainly happy to become independent peasant farmers, the sharp decline in plantation exports robbed the new government of its tax base. The political transition to independence proved equally difficult. The personal ambitions of early Haitian rulers, fueled by deep historical tensions

• Congress of Vienna (1815)   Conference at which the balance of power of European states was restored after the defeat of Napoleon Bonaparte.

Bolivian Politics

The only country named for Simón Bolívar, Bolivia is the poorest country in South America. Liberation from Spanish rule meant little to the Aymara- and Quechua-speaking Amerindian peoples of the Andes. Through the nineteenth and twentieth centuries, most Amerindians had no rights except those they maintained within their own poverty-stricken communities. Military service in the lowest ranks was one option for employment. Often the only other was dangerous work in the tin mines, a modern parallel to the misery faced by their ancestors in the colonial silver mines.

Then in 2005 the first Amerindian president was elected. Evo Morales was not only the first Amerindian president of Bolivia; he was also the first anywhere in the Americas. Campaigning on a socialist platform, Morales promised to roll back five hundred years of racism and exploitation and to bring the benefits of the country's endowments in natural gas to the Bolivian people by nationalizing the energy sector. He began a program of land reform so that poor farmers could leave the mountains for better land in the plains. Morales also defended peasants' right to grow and consume coca, traditionally used as a local remedy for cold and hunger. In each case, Morales's emphasis on the rights of indigenous peoples won him many enthusiastic supporters.

But all of Morales's policies proved controversial. Faced with nationalization, the energy companies, including a powerful Brazilian conglomerate, threatened to withdraw much-needed investments. Farmers in the richer, more export-oriented eastern part of the country declared their opposition to a land reform they said would strip them of the fruits of their own hard work. To opposition leaders Morales was just another caudillo using populist rhetoric to amass authoritarian political power, and they boycotted the 2007 constituent assembly that strengthened the presidency. The United States reacted with hostility to Morales's friendship with left-wing leaders Hugo Chavez of Venezuela and Fidel Castro of Cuba, and it disapproved of his protection of the coca industry, vital to the Andean poor but a target of the U.S. "war on drugs."

In fall 2008 President Morales took a tough stand, expelling the U.S. ambassador as tensions with the rebellious eastern province of Santa Clara continued to escalate. The outcome of his attempt to rebalance the economic and political power structure of the country away from traditional elites and toward the Amerindians of the western mountains was still far from clear.

between the mixed-race gens de couleur and Haitians of African/slave descent, created a long-standing culture of corruption and dictatorship in Haitian politics.

The results of independence in Latin America were also disappointing, at least by the high standards set by Simón Bolívar. His vision of a state of *Gran Colombia* was not achieved. Military commanders preferred to take power as presidents of their own separate republics, and regionalism triumphed over federalism as South America became a patchwork of separate, often squabbling nations. Moreover, the new republics lacked strong traditions of local civic governance, a legacy of centralized Spanish rule. And after independence, as before, they were dominated by a small number of wealthy landowners. Concentrated land ownership proved a weak foundation on which to build democracy, and, as Bolívar predicted, the fragmentation of *Gran Colombia* into smaller nations left the people of South America vulnerable when faced with the power of Great Britain and the United States.

It was one of Bolívar's top commanders, José Antonio Páez, who declared Venezuela a separate republic in 1830, repudiating the connection with *Gran Colombia*.

Páez then established an authoritarian style of rule that would have ominous implications for his own country and for all of Latin America. He was one of the **caudillos,** dictatorial rulers who looked after their own interests and those of the military above all else. If Napoleon had been something of an "enlightened despot," the same could rarely be said of the men who seized power as caudillos in many of the new South American nations.

As we have seen, Africans, Amerindians, and people of mixed descent often played important roles in the Latin American wars of independence. But in the years immediately following independence, it was clear that their efforts were not to be rewarded with any systematic redistribution of power and privilege. (See the feature "World History in Today's World: Bolivian Politics.") It was a real step forward for equality where slavery was abolished, as in Venezuela. For the most part, however, the social group that benefited from independence was the criollos, who consolidated their political and economic dominance by stepping into the positions abandoned by the departing peninsulares. Although individual Catholic priests might still follow Father Hidalgo's tradition of siding with the poor and powerless, the Catholic Church hierarchy in Latin America continued to support the wealthy and powerful.

> • *caudillos* Latin American military men who gained power through violence during the early nineteenth and twentieth centuries.

Chapter Review

 Download the MP3 audio file of the Chapter Review and listen to it on the go.

Simón Bolívar had a forceful personality, and in his impatience with the feuding and squabbling that jeopardized his great project he sometimes resorted to dictatorial means. But in the end he resisted the allure of dictatorship and resigned as leader of *Gran Colombia*. He died in sad exile, experiencing neither the might of Napoleon Bonaparte in power nor the peace of George Washington in retirement. A recent biographer admits that Bolívar "never found the ideal balance between order and freedom" and that he was "better at analyzing the ills of Latin America than in devising remedies." But the fact remains that virtually all South Americans, whatever their differences of political ideology, social class, or ethnic or racial identity, take Simón Bolívar as their starting point for discussions of who they are and what they might be. That legacy makes him one of the great figures of nineteenth-century world history.

What political compromises were made in establishing the new United States of America?

The founders of the United States of America created an effective set of institutions by compromising on issues such as the influence of larger and smaller states on the federal government and on the balance between executive, judicial, and legislative power. One compromise that came out of the constitutional negotiations, however, both contradicted the noblest aspirations of the Enlightenment and laid the groundwork for future conflict. The persistence of slavery in the United States, and the expansion of slavery through the admission of new slave states to the Union, highlighted the contradiction between a status quo inherited from the colonial era and the United States' self-definition as the "land of the free." The War of Independence set the country on a new path, but it did not completely overcome such legacies of the past.

 ### What were the major phases of the French Revolution?

In the first phase, representatives of the Third Estate tried to create a constitutional monarchy. But the storming of the Bastille and attacks on the manor houses of the nobility created a more confrontational environment. Rather than compromise, Louis XVI and the nobility sought help from other European rulers to restore their power. In the next, most radical phase of the Revolution, the Jacobins under Maximilien Robespierre mobilized mass armies to fight off the invaders and instituted a harsh security regime: the Reign of Terror. It was not long before the Jacobins were swallowed up by the violence they had unleashed. The rise of Napoleon Bonaparte represented the final phase of the Revolution. Now it was national glory rather than individual liberty that inspired Napoleon's troops and the French nation. Though he instituted many social and political reforms in the tradition of Enlightenment rationality, Napoleon's imperial project contradicted the revolution's early emphasis on individual rights.

 ### How were the revolutions in Latin America and the Caribbean influenced by the history of colonialism?

In Latin America and the Caribbean, as in the United States and France, the possibilities of revolution were conditioned by continuities with the past. The French island colony of Saint-Domingue, one the world's largest producers of sugar, had a sharply divided social system with French planters at the top, mixed-race gens de couleur below, and, at the very bottom, a large population of African slaves. Toussaint L'Overture brought not just military leadership to the slave revolt but also an ability to connect the raw power of the slave rebellion with Enlightenment ideals. His attempt to reconcile those two realities was, however, frustrated by French treachery. Simón Bolívar did at least have an opportunity to put his dreams into reality, but here again history and tradition seemed to work against the fulfillment of his vision. The stark differences in wealth between the large landowners and the majority of the population, and the related cultural divide between the Spanish-descended elite and the mestizos (Indian and African majorities), meant that there was but a weak middle class of shopkeepers and small independent farmers as a foundation on which to build democratic republics. And, in spite of the example of Father Hidalgo in Mexico, the Catholic Church remained aligned with powerful Spanish elites.

How much did the outcomes of these revolutions in western Europe and the Americas represent a thorough transformation of existing political and social structures?

In each case, the persistence of the past blocked the full realization of the revolutionary intentions. In the United States, slavery persisted in spite of a rhetorical commitment to "liberty and equality." In France, revolutionary excesses led from a vision of democracy to the reality of Napoleonic dictatorship. In Latin America and the Caribbean, continuing social inequality undermined efforts to establish stable republican governments. And nowhere were women fully included in the agenda of equality. A French revolutionary argued in 1792 that "the perfectibility of man is unlimited," not just possible, but inevitable. Study of the political processes examined in this chapter leads to a more cautious conclusion. Even in the wake of revolution, societies are not blank slates ready for entirely fresh characters to be written. Reconciling the twin mandates of "liberty" and "equality" remained a challenge for every postrevolutionary society.

 WEB RESOURCES

Pronunciation Guide

Interactive Maps

MAP 22.1 The American Revolutionary War

MAP 22.2 Independence in Latin America

MAP 22.3 Napoleonic Europe in 1815

Primary Sources

Chapter Objectives

ACE Multiple-Choice Quiz

Flashcards

For Further Reference

Bailyn, Bernard. *The Ideological Origins of the American Revolution*. Cambridge, Mass.: Belknap, 1992.

Bell, Madison Smartt. *Toussaint Louverture: A Biography*. New York: Pantheon, 2007.

Bushnell, David. *Simón Bolívar: Liberation and Disappointment*. New York: Pearson Longman, 2004.

Bushnell, David, and Neill MacAuley. *The Emergence of Latin America in the Nineteenth Century*. New York: Oxford University Press, 1994.

Doyle, William. *Origins of the French Revolution*. New York: Oxford University Press, 1999.

Englund, Steven. *Napoleon: A Political Life*. New York: Scribner's, 2004.

Geggus, David P. *The Impact of the Haitian Revolution in the Atlantic World*. Columbia: University of South Carolina Press, 2002.

Rowe, Michael (ed.). *Collaboration and Resistance in Napoleonic Europe: State Formation in an Age of Upheaval*. New York: Palgrave Macmillian, 2003.

Van Young, Eric. *The Other Rebellion: Popular Violence, Ideology, and the Mexican Struggle for Independence, 1810–1821*. Stanford: Stanford University Press, 2001.

Wood, Gordon S. *The American Revolution*. New York: Modern Library, 2002.

Websites

The American Revolution (http://www.historyteacher.net/APUSH-Course/Weblinks/Weblinks4.htm). Extensive web links and primary source documents related to the American War of Independence.

The French Revolution (http://www9.georgetown.edu/faculty/schneidz/web.html). Extensive, high-quality links to information on French history, including the Revolution and Napoleonic empire.

Latin American Independence (http://www.pachami.com/English/latinoamericaE.html). Links to information on a great variety of Latin American independence leaders, including sources in both English and Spanish.

The Industrial Revolution and European Politics, 1780–1880

Driven into exile by the Russian government, the socialist thinker **Alexander Herzen** (1812–1870) took his family and fled west; their "covered sledge crunched through the snow" as they set off in the bitter Russian winter. Friends and servants accompanied them to the border: "There for the last time we clinked glasses and parted, sobbing."[1] In early 1848 they were enjoying the relative warmth of Italy when news came of revolution in Paris. "The name of the city," Herzen wrote, "is bound up with all the loftiest aspirations, with all the greatest hopes of contemporary man—I entered it with a trembling heart, with reverence, as men used to enter Jerusalem and Rome."[2]

Like Simón Bolívar four decades earlier, Herzen was seeking revolutionary inspiration in hopes of transforming his native land. In the spring of 1848 revolution spread from Paris across western Europe, but by summer conservative authorities were re-establishing control. Herzen was bitterly disappointed. After 1848 he saw the West as decadent and corrupt; he argued that the Russians, though suffering from political repression and economic backwardness, had the greatest potential for bringing socialism to the world:

(State History Museum/RIA Novosti, akg-images)

What a blessing it is for Russia that the rural commune has never been broken up, that private property has never replaced the property of the commune: how fortunate it is for the Russian people that they have remained . . . outside European civilization, which would undoubtedly have sapped the life of the commune. . . . The future of Russia lies with the peasant.[3]

ALEXANDER HERZEN

 This icon will direct you to interactive activities and study materials on the *Voyages* website:
www.cengage.com/history/hansen/voyages1e

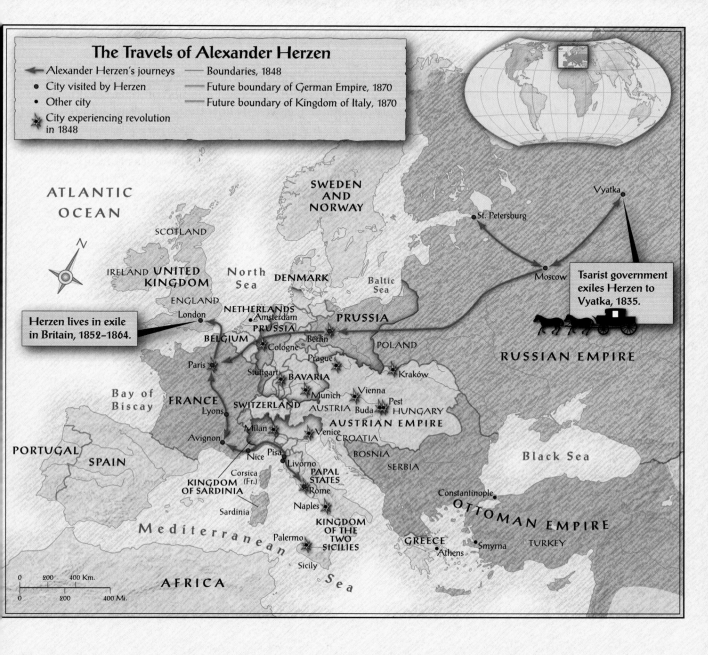

The Travels of Alexander Herzen

- → Alexander Herzen's journeys
- ● City visited by Herzen
- ● Other city
- ✳ City experiencing revolution in 1848
- —— Boundaries, 1848
- —— Future boundary of German Empire, 1870
- —— Future boundary of Kingdom of Italy, 1870

ATLANTIC OCEAN

SCOTLAND

IRELAND **UNITED KINGDOM**

North Sea

SWEDEN AND NORWAY

DENMARK

Baltic Sea

St. Petersburg

Vyatka

Moscow

Tsarist government exiles Herzen to Vyatka, 1835.

RUSSIAN EMPIRE

ENGLAND

London

NETHERLANDS

Amsterdam

PRUSSIA

Berlin

PRUSSIA

POLAND

Herzen lives in exile in Britain, 1852–1864.

BELGIUM

Cologne

Prague

Kraków

Paris

Stuttgart

BAVARIA

Munich

Vienna

FRANCE

SWITZERLAND

AUSTRIA

Buda

Pest

HUNGARY

Lyons

Milan

Venice

AUSTRIAN EMPIRE

CROATIA

Bay of Biscay

Avignon

Nice

Pisa

Livorno

CROATIA

BOSNIA

SERBIA

Black Sea

Corsica (Fr.)

KINGDOM OF SARDINIA

PAPAL STATES

Rome

Constantinople

OTTOMAN EMPIRE

PORTUGAL

SPAIN

Sardinia

Naples

KINGDOM OF THE TWO SICILIES

GREECE

Smyrna

TURKEY

Palermo

Athens

Sicily

Mediterranean Sea

AFRICA

0   200   400 Km.
0   200   400 Mi.

	1800	1820	1840	1860	1880

Lifetime of Alexander Herzen
1812 — 1870

EUROPE

British Reform Bill
1832

Second French Empire
1852 — 1870

European Revolutions
1848

Unification of Italy
1860

Unification of Germany
1871

RUSSIA

Crimean War
1853 — 1856

Emancipation Edict
1861

OTTOMAN EMPIRE

Reign of Muhammad Ali, Egypt
1808 — 1848

Tanzimat Reforms
1839 — 1876

● **Alexander Herzen** (1812–1870) Russian socialist and revolutionary thinker who published journals smuggled into Russia that influenced radical opinion toward reform and emancipation of the serfs. His philosophy combined socialism with fierce commitment to individual liberty.

In this passage Herzen combines two of the most powerful ideas of his age, socialism and nationalism, in his argument that the collectivist tradition of the Russian peasantry, modernized for the industrial age, would show the way toward a more equitable world.

Alexander Herzen lived through one of the most eventful periods of human history: the Industrial Revolution. Coal-driven steam engines unleashed the power of fossil fuels in the industrializing economies of western Europe and the United States, driving the machinery of new factories and propelling steamships and locomotives. More efficient transportation bound the entire world's people more tightly in networks of trade and communication. The sleigh that took Herzen's family to the West would soon be replaced by a railroad, and some of those peasants he celebrated would leave their rural communes to work in mines and factories.

The Industrial Revolution not only transformed methods of production and transportation but also stimulated new social conditions and political ideologies. More people moved to cities, where they often lived in squalid conditions. Rapid social change stimulated debates among reformers and revolutionaries. Alexander Herzen absorbed the sometimes conflicting ideals of liberals, who emphasized individual liberty; socialists, who stressed the collective good; and nationalists, who gave more thought to the advancement of their own group and less to the fate of humanity as a whole.

Debates in social theory were sparked by the writings of the German socialist Karl Marx and the English evolutionary biologist Charles Darwin, each of whom, in different ways, contributed to the widespread belief that the industrial age was a time of progress. But the Industrial Revolution posed particular challenges to the Russian and Ottoman Empires. Political elites in these old land-based empires, now on the fringe of industrializing Europe, were torn between policies of reform, including the adaptation to Western models of law and governance, and conservative policies that stressed continuity over change.

Focus Questions

🐎 **What were the most important outcomes of the Industrial Revolution?**

🐎 **What were the main features of European political development during and after the revolutions of 1848?**

🐎 **Why were the ideas of Karl Marx and Charles Darwin of such great significance for world history?**

🐎 **How did the leaders of the Russian and Ottoman Empires respond to the challenge of an industrializing western Europe?**

The Industrial Revolution: Origins and Global Consequences, 1780–1870

Innovations in three primary areas lay at the foundation of the **Industrial Revolution:** new means of harnessing energy, new inventions, and new ways of more productively organizing human labor. By unleashing the power of fossil fuels in the form of coal, harnessing that power to drive steam engines, applying those steam engines to mechanized systems of production, and organizing the process in more centralized and efficient factories with a more complex division of labor, industrial societies achieved unprecedented economic growth.

British industrialists took the lead, soon followed by their counterparts in continental Europe and the United States. By the middle of the nineteenth century these industrializing societies had significantly raised their economic productivity and technological development. These nations were then poised to translate economic power into military and political predominance on the world stage.

The Industrial Revolution was a global process. Improvements in transportation and communications—the steamship, railroad, and telegraph—helped develop a global market for industrial raw materials. At the same time, as more efficient production outstripped consumer demand in domestic markets, owners of industries looked to world markets and global resources as they competed to expand production even further.

> **• Industrial Revolution** Changes that began in late-eighteenth-century Britain and transformed the global economy by creating new markets for raw materials and finished goods. Accompanied by technological changes that revolutionized production processes, living and working conditions, and the environment.

Origins of the Industrial Revolution, 1780–1850

The agricultural revolution was a precondition for the industrial one. Joseph Banks and other "improving farmers" had greatly increased food production, while the enclosure movement had driven many rural people off the land (see Chapter 21). Driven by economic necessity, these people moved toward cities, mines, and emerging centers of factory production. Before the Industrial Revolution most people's lives were governed by the seasons, and their work was limited by the constraints of human and animal power. Now their lives became dominated by the relentless power of steam-driven machines and the screeching of clock-driven horns and whistles. People who had once known virtually everyone around them now found themselves living in the anonymity of cities, where even neighbors might treat each other as strangers.

Meanwhile the uncommon fluidity of the British elite was a spur to economic innovation. Whereas elsewhere in Europe the titled nobility remained aloof from commerce, in England lines were less firmly drawn between aristocrats, members of the gentry, and merchant families. Magnificent country houses were occupied not only by aristocrats of ancient lineage but also by families whose wealth came from Caribbean sugar plantations or the exploitation of Indian wealth. And while continental European philosophers usually concerned themselves with pure science over practical applications, "the English genius," Herzen remarked, "finds repellent an abstract generalization."[4] The "practical science" promoted by Joseph Banks during his long tenure as president of the Royal Society demonstrated Herzen's point.

Another stimulus to the British economy was the significant resource base provided by its empire. Timber and furs from Canada, sugar from the Caribbean, cotton textiles from India, and tea from China were part of a global trade network dominated by British shipping. Previously the boards of the banks, stock exchanges, and insurance houses that dominated the City of London were primarily directed toward trade. In the late eighteenth and nineteenth century, they expanded their investments to include industrial production as well. Industrial capitalism was born.

The Industrial Revolution was primarily an energy revolution: one of the major turning points in human history was the discovery of how to tap into the vast energy supplied by fossil fuels, first coal and later petroleum. Early British industrialists had relatively easy access to coal, but it was usually too impure for iron production. Iron producers (in Africa and China as well as Europe) had long burnt wood to make charcoal for iron smelting, but that led to deforestation, setting an environmental limit on production.

Then in the early eighteenth century an English inventor discovered a means of purifying coal to make a more concentrated product called coke. In the 1760s another innovator found a way to remove impurities from the coke-iron product. Now the fossil fuel energy of coal could be readily used to make low-cost, high-quality iron.

The full potential of the energy revolution was realized, however, only with the development of the steam engine. In 1764 James Watt, building on earlier crude designs, developed a much more efficient version, and for the first time it became possible to turn coal into cheap steam power.

Meanwhile, other entrepreneurs were focusing on the social organization of production. In his *Wealth of Nations,* Adam Smith (see Chapter 21) had argued that division of labor was a key to increased productivity. Smith used the example of pins. A single person making a pin from start to finish, Smith explained, would be much less productive than a group of artisans who each focused on a single step in the process. The division of labor was key to the development of the factory system of production.

In the 1760s an entrepreneur and abolitionist named Josiah Wedgwood began to experiment with a more complex division of labor in his ceramics factory, breaking the production process down into specialized tasks. As a result, his factory produced great quantities of less expensive, identical plates that were easily stacked and shipped. The days when a master potter and a few apprentices painstakingly produced pottery by hand were coming to an end. Wedgwood advanced the new factory system of production even further when, in 1782, he was the first to install a steam engine at his factory, combining Smith's division of labor and Watt's innovations with steam power. The age of mass production had begun (for Wedgwood's role in the abolitionist movement, see Chapter 19).

But it was in the textile industry that division of labor and steam power fully demonstrated the potential of this new system. Britain had long been a center for the production of woolen goods. But in the eighteenth century English consumers strongly preferred cotton clothing, which was lighter, more comfortable, and easier to wash. At that time, India was by far the world's largest producer of cotton textiles, and Indian calico cloth flooded the British market. British wool producers, unhappy with this competition, convinced Parliament to impose high tariffs on Indian calicoes, which became so expensive that few could afford them.

The tariffs did not apply to raw cotton, which British entrepreneurs began importing from India. They then used a decentralized "putting-out" system in which the merchant provided raw materials to a rural family, who would manufacture the cloth. The family used a traditional gender division of labor, the women spinning the raw cotton into thread and the men weaving it into cloth. Since spinning was much more time consuming than weaving, men were frequently underemployed while they waited for their wives, who had many other family and farm obligations, to catch up.

The problem was solved in the late eighteenth century when British inventors found ways to mechanize the spinning process, making it possible to produce much greater quantities of high-quality cotton thread. But with spinning now more efficient, it was the old methods of weaving that held back production. Extra weavers had to be hired, cutting into industrialists' profits and giving them a motive to mechanize the entire process. Experiments with steam-driven power looms took several decades, but by the 1830s the entire process of cloth production had been mechanized and consolidated into centralized factories.

Growth in textile production increased the demand for raw cotton. After 1793 supplies from India were augmented by new production in the United States. That was the year when the American inventor Eli Whitney invented the cotton gin, which efficiently separated seeds from cotton. Whitney's machine stimulated cotton production in the United States, which became the world's biggest supplier in the early nineteenth century.

Though textile manufacturing played a leading role, virtually every field of production had been transformed by the mid-nineteenth century. The social organization of the factory, combined with the energy revolution of coal and steam, created the most efficient industrial enterprises to that point in history. Britain's early lead in industrial production combined with its existing strength in international commerce to make the small island nation the dominant global power. But it was not long before the British model was copied by others. The small nation of Belgium, with large and accessible deposits of coal, was the first to develop a substantial network of steam-fired factories, soon followed by France and Germany. Industrial production was also increasing in the United States, particularly in northern states like Massachusetts (see Chapter 25).

Global Dimensions of the Industrial Revolution, 1820–1880

The Industrial Revolution was, from the beginning, a global process. Most nineteenth-century societies did not make the transition to fossil fuels and the factory system but were connected to the European and North American economies through the transportation and communications revolution that accompanied the industrial one. Railroads, steamships, and the telegraph dramatically increased the pace of global interactions. Many people around the world were also connected to factories as consumers of inexpensive factory-produced goods. By the later nineteenth century most of humankind was involved in the global commodity markets driven by industrial capitalism.

Early industrial Britain had benefited from its transportation network. The country's coastal shipping, combined with river transport helped by numerous canals, stimulated domestic markets. The general rule had always been that water transport was more efficient than transport by land. But then the price of iron dropped to the point where engineers began experimenting with railroads. At first railroad cars were drawn by horses. Then a British engineer began experimenting with steam locomotives. In 1829 the industrial cities of Manchester and Liverpool in northern England were connected by rail.

By midcentury a dense network of railroads covered western Europe (see Map 23.1). Railroads not only represented a radically more efficient and less expensive means of transporting heavy goods and bulk commodities by land, but they also made it possible for people to travel much more cheaply and comfortably than in the old days of the stagecoach. Geographic mobility and increased urbanization were two important outcomes. In North America, transcontinental railroads in the United States and Canada allowed European settlers to tap the vast productivity of the Great Plains (see Chapter 25). By 1880 railroad construction had also begun in Russia, British India, and Mexico.

Steamships were another product of what historians have called "the age of steam and iron." By 1850 steamships had improved domestic transportation in industrial nations, especially in the United States, where large waterways like the Mississippi River meant that people and goods needed to be moved over large distances. The international influence of steamships was in some ways even more revolutionary. The first steam-powered crossing of the Atlantic took place in 1838 and of the Pacific in 1853. Though sailing ships remained common, by the 1870s developments in steamship construction were dramatically reducing transportation

⊕ MAP 23.1

Continental Industrialization, ca. 1850   Ease of access to iron and coal spurred industrialization in parts of Europe, such as northeastern France, Belgium, and north-western regions of the German Confederation. By 1850 railroad connections supplemented rivers and canals as means of transport with an efficiency that lowered the cost of both raw materials and finished products. By the end of the century every nation in Europe was tightly integrated by rail, facilitating as well the movement of people and goods across the continent.

Interactive Map

times and shipping costs around the world and further enhanced the military superiority of Western nations in their dealings with African and Asian societies. The completion of the Suez Canal in 1869 (linking the Mediterranean and Red Seas), combined with the power of steamships, cut the transportation time from Europe to South Asia from months to weeks. Advances in communications and transportation were a prerequisite for the expansion of European imperialism in Africa and Southeast Asia (see Chapter 26) and for the tightening of administration over existing colonies, like British India.

Once experiments with electricity facilitated the invention of the telegraph, information could move even more quickly than people and trade goods. The first long-range telegraph message was sent in 1844. In 1869 a submarine cable was laid below the surface of the Atlantic Ocean, allowing for instantaneous transcontinental communication. Shipping companies took advantage of the telegraph to become more efficient, once more lowering the cost of shipping and increasing global trade. Military officers with telegraphic information had a powerful tactical advantage.

Industrialists expanded their search for raw materials, especially cotton. After the British secured political control of India (see Chapter 20), the export of finished cloth was replaced by the export of raw cotton. Partly because of the increased efficiency and hence lower cost of factory-produced textiles, and partly because the British government manipulated tariff structures to aid British industrialists, India actually suffered a process of deindustrialization in the early mid-nineteenth century. Unemployment drove many Indian spinners, weavers, and dyers from towns into the countryside, reversing the British pattern of urbanization.

Another supplier of cotton was Egypt. After Napoleon's invasion of Egypt in 1798 (see Chapter 22), an ambitious Ottoman military commander seized power. **Muhammad Ali** (r. 1808–1848) had witnessed firsthand the superiority of European weaponry and knew that his regime needed to keep up with the latest industrial and technological advances. Muhammad Ali (moo-HAH-muhd AH-lee) encouraged cotton production to generate the income that he used to pay for railroads, factories, and guns, while sending science and engineering students to study in France. Egyptian peasants, however, saw little or no benefit from heightened participation in global markets. That was even truer for the slaves who did the harsh work of planting, weeding, and picking cotton in the United States (see Chapter 25). For many people in India, Egypt, and North America, the Industrial Revolution and its appetite for raw cotton were a curse rather than a blessing.

The list of products drawn from around the world into the web of industry grew longer. Palm oil and peanuts from West Africa helped lubricate Europe's industrial machinery. Beef hides from the *pampas* (PAHM-pahs) grasslands of Argentina spurred a proliferation of leather goods. Sisal from Mexican plantations was exported for the manufacture of rope. In Africa and Latin America, people participated in the Industrial Revolution primarily as suppliers of raw materials in an integrated global market.

As we will see in the following three chapters, many people in the Americas, Africa, Asia, and the Pacific experienced the Industrial Revolution as a challenge to established political, social, economic, and cultural ways of life. In fact, similar challenges faced the peoples of Europe. In England, a group of skilled artisans known as Luddites broke into factories and smashed the machinery, believing that mechanization was a threat to their livelihoods. Kings, aristocrats, and religious leaders often saw growing cities as breeding grounds for moral decay and social disorder. But there were many in Europe, Alexander Herzen among them, who emphasized the new possibilities of the industrial age.

● **Muhammad Ali** (r. 1808–1848) Egyptian ruler who attempted to modernize his country's economy by promoting cotton cultivation and textile manufacturing and by sending young Egyptians to study in Europe.

⬤Reform and Revolution in Nineteenth-Century Europe, 1815–1880

In 1815 the great powers of Europe had banded together to put out the political fires of the French Revolution and its Napoleonic aftermath (see Chapter 22). Their success did not last long. The rising social classes of industrializing Europe, an invigorated and ambitious urban middle class and a new industrial working class, did not fit comfortably with old traditions of monarchical and aristocratic dominance.

Even when faced with repression, many Europeans retained dreams of liberty and freedom, adding some powerful new ideas to those they inherited from the Enlightenment and French Revolution. Liberals, most influential in Britain, emphasized the freedom of the individual and the sanctity of private property. Socialists, growing in numbers and influence throughout this period, stressed their belief in collective organization for the betterment of society. In the romantic movement, especially strong among Germans, artists increasingly emphasized drama and emotion over the cool rationality of the Enlightenment. The passion of romanticism became linked with nationalism, the most powerful of the ideologies swirling through industrial Europe.

The social tensions arising from industrial change led to a political crescendo in 1848, when revolutions spread across Europe. In Paris, Berlin, Vienna, Budapest, Rome, and other European cities, it seemed that the old order was being swept away. But the fire of revolution soon died down. Revolutionaries like Alexander Herzen were shocked and disappointed when conservative, authoritarian leaders re-established control.

Nineteenth-Century Ideologies: Liberalism, Socialism, Romanticism, and Nationalism

Alexander Herzen embodied the new ideas that would soon spread across the world. His writings show the deep influence of four different, sometimes contradictory, ideas: liberalism, socialism, romanticism, and nationalism.

Liberalism implied open-mindedness and acceptance of the need for social and political reform. In the nineteenth century, Britain was most strongly associated with liberal tendencies; most European monarchs and their conservative supporters resisted substantial reform. Liberals favored such policies as freedom of conscience, freedom of trade and protection of property rights, and limitations on the political power of religious authorities. While liberals approved of the extension of voting rights to men with property and education, only late in the century did liberalism become associated with universal male suffrage.

Socialism was better developed in France and Germany. Some nineteenth-century European socialists favored the revolutionary overthrow of the state as a precondition for the collectivization of property and the realization of social equality. Other socialists thought their cause could be advanced by working within existing institutions, while advocates of yet another strand of socialism created utopian communities outside the state. In liberal Britain, democracy and socialism developed together, while in Russia, with its more authoritarian government, the revolutionary strand of socialism predominated.

Romanticism, a cultural and intellectual movement that was strong among Germans, prioritized emotional intensity and authenticity over the rationalism and formality of the Enlightenment. "You can no more bridle passions with logic than you can justify them in the law courts," Herzen wrote, even as a series of love affairs tore his marriage apart.[5] Starting with Ludwig von Beethoven, German composers developed themes of musical romanticism culminating in the long, complex, and powerful operas of Richard Wagner (1813–1883).

Romanticism was strongly connected to *nationalism,* the most powerful political ideology of the industrial age. Nationalists, like Wagner, often hoped to develop cultural and historical pedigrees for national groups who entered the nineteenth century without states to represent them. Some nationalists worked to bring together members of language groups, such as Germans and Italians, who were divided by political boundaries. Others sought to separate their group from multinational empires: Poles from Russia, Greeks from the Ottoman Empire, and Hungarians from Austria. Unlike liberalism and socialism, which emphasized the betterment of humanity as a whole, nationalism focused on the particular interests of separate groups.

Victorian Britain, 1815–1867

In 1815 Britain, like other European countries, was dominated by conservatives who associated change with the excesses of the French Revolution. The landed classes who dominated Parliament imposed tariffs on imported grain, raising the price of bread. Unemployment was high among returning soldiers. The enclosure movement and the new factory system were driving many out of villages and into urban slums.

Conditions in the growing cities were appalling. Wages were low, and many employers preferred children, especially girls, as factory workers because they were nimble, could fit into tight spaces, and were easy to control. The growing industrial cities were unhealthy places. The lack of proper drainage and sanitation was

The Crystal Palace
The Crystal Palace, one of the great feats of Victorian engineering, was completed in 1851 as the centerpiece of Britain's Great Exhibition. The designers of this imposing structure, made entirely of iron and glass, intended it as a monument to industrial, technological, and commercial progress. (Victoria and Albert Museum, London/Art Resource, NY)

noted by Friedrich Engels, a German socialist leader, during his visit to Manchester in 1844:

> Right and left a multitude of covered passages lead from the main street into numerous courts, and he who turns in thither gets into a filth and disgusting grime, the equal of which is not to be found. . . . Inhabitants can pass into and out of the court only by passing through foul pools of stagnant urine and excrement. . . . At the bottom flows, or rather stagnates, the Irk, a narrow, coal-black, foul-smelling stream, full of debris and refuse, which it deposits on the shallower right bank. In dry weather, a long string of the most disgusting, blackish-green, slime pools are left standing on this bank, from the depths of which bubbles of miasmatic gas constantly arise and give forth a stench unendurable even on the bridge forty or fifty feet above the surface of the stream.[6]

Disease spread rapidly in such neighborhoods. Lack of proper sanitation became even more deadly after increased contact with India brought cholera to England for the first time. Thousands died from infected water supplies in nineteenth-century London.

The response of English families of property was to live in pleasant suburbs, isolated from filth, disease, and the pollution spewed by what poet Robert Blake had called England's "dark, satanic mills." The prevailing view of the upper class was that the poor were responsible for their own fate, an attitude satirized by the great Victorian novelist Charles Dickens in *A Christmas Carol* when Ebenezer Scrooge says that if people are so poor that they are likely to die, "they should do so and decrease the surplus population."

British subjects of the middle and lower classes did not have the right to vote and thus had no direct means of influencing government policy. Attempts by industrial workers to form unions to protect their interests were outlawed by Parliament as dangerous "combinations." Many factory workers found comfort and a sense of solidarity in churches. Methodism, with an egalitarian ethos, allowed workers to assert spiritual, if not social and political, equality. Others sought solace in gin and opium.

By the beginning of the stable and prosperous reign of Queen Victoria (r. 1837–1901), however, the reform impulse that had animated the abolitionist movement (see Chapter 19) was returning to British politics. Charitable organizations were growing in size and influence, their leaders arguing that the poor could improve their lot if only they would adopt middle-class values like thrift and sobriety. But it was clear to many that the government also had a role to play, especially in improving health and sanitation.

The result was a series of reforms in the Victorian era guided by a philosophy called utilitarianism. Jeremy Bentham, a strong proponent of *utilitarianism*, argued that all political and social policies needed to be rigorously judged by their utility in light of present-day circumstances. In 1840 the government built a model prison based on Bentham's designs in which each prisoner had a separate cell with more light and air than in the notoriously dark and dank prisons of an earlier age. Following utilitarian philosophy, the number of crimes for which the death penalty could be applied was radically reduced.

Animated by the British tradition of "practical science" (see Chapter 21), the government sponsored scientific studies of social conditions that improved urban planning, water supplies, and hygiene. Parliamentary investigations of child labor led to a public outcry and to legislation that regulated the abhorrent labor conditions of the early Industrial Revolution. Old restrictions on the political activities of Catholics were lifted. And by the 1850s wages were on the increase: even some less skilled workers were beginning to benefit from the productivity of British industry and from the nation's global dominance in trade.

The conservatism of the immediate post-Napoleonic period was giving way to a more liberal political environment. Middle-class liberals, believers in free trade and individual autonomy, were frustrated by their lack of representation in Parliament and by policies that favored landed interests over urban ones. Most did not, however, believe in democracy: education and possession of adequate property were still preconditions for political participation.

Liberals and utilitarians argued that British political institutions needed to be brought up to date. **The Reform Bill of 1832** made two changes in the British franchise that brought Parliament into closer accord with the social changes brought on by industrialization. First, seats in Parliament were redistributed to take account of the growth of cities. Second, the property requirements for voting were lowered so that better-off members of the middle class, such as male shopkeepers, could vote. This new Parliament better reflected the interests of industrialists and the urban middle class.

As a result of these political changes, economic policies also began to shift toward free trade. Powerful vested interests still favored tariffs to protect the interests of the rural gentry, but as improvements in transportation were making less expensive grain available from the Americas and eastern Europe, factory owners lobbied for the end of agricultural tariffs, arguing that cheaper bread would help keep wages down. In 1846 Parliament opened British markets to foreign grain, showing the new power of urban interests in British politics.

A powerful voice of British liberalism, praised by Alexander Herzen, was **John Stuart Mill** (1806–1873). In his book *On Liberty* (1859), Mill argued that liberty involved freedom not only from arbitrary government interference but also from "the tendency of society to impose, by other means than civil penalties, its own ideas and practices as rules of conduct on those who dissent from them."[7] His emphasis on freedom from both political oppression and social conformity led Mill to some conclusions that were radical for the time: he thought the vote should be extended not only to working men but also to women.

Though most would not go as far as Mill on the issue of gender, by the 1860s many British liberals did see that social change again necessitated political reform. The Reform Bill of 1867 lowered property qualifications and nearly doubled the number of voters. Once again working-class leaders were frustrated that property ownership remained a barrier to political participation. But the easing of restrictions on trade union organization gave them greater lobbying power, and by the end of the 1880s another reform bill had given most British men the vote. (See "Visual Evidence: The Beehive of Victorian Britain.")

> **The Reform Bill of 1832** Bill that significantly reformed the English House of Commons by lowering property qualifications for the vote. Still, only wealthier middle-class men were enfranchised.

> **John Stuart Mill** (1806–1873) English philosopher and economist who argued for the importance of individual liberty.

France: Revolution, Republic, and Empire

In 1815 the diplomats meeting at the Congress of Vienna decided to restore the Bourbon dynasty to power in France. After the revolutionary and Napoleonic years, however, it was impossible to return to the old status quo. The unpopular Bourbon monarch was overthrown by a popular uprising in 1830.

Some of those who organized street protests against the king clamored for the return of republican government. Many middle-class liberals, however, were afraid

THE BEEHIVE OF VICTORIAN BRITAIN

One Englishman proudly proclaimed in 1848, the year of revolutions elsewhere in Europe, "We have order in the midst of anarchy." Indeed, the slow evolution of British institutions under the influence of Victorian liberalism stood in contrast to more dramatic events on the continent of Europe. From the abolition of the slave trade in 1809 through the Reform Bill of 1832 and subsequent legislation to extend the franchise, the British Constitution gradually changed to accommodate liberal ideals and, eventually, democratic principles.

An important cause of this constitutional evolution was the concern of British elites, aristocrats as well as industrial and commercial leaders, to stave off more radical changes. To members of the British elite, the Chartist movement of 1848—during which millions of signatures were collected among common people in favor of universal manhood suffrage, a secret ballot, and salaries for members of Parliament so that common men could afford to serve—represented a real threat that change might be forced by popular organization. Constitutional reform, such as the

Order comes from the top down, represented by the figure of Queen Victoria, the "pillar of the state," and the "royal family by lineal descent" surmounting the British Constitution.

Three levels show a hierarchy of work starting with unskilled labor (e.g., chimney sweeps) followed by artisans (e.g., masons) and shopkeepers (e. g., bakers.)

Commercial and military institutions, along with the Bank of England, are shown as forming the foundation of "the richest country in the world."

(Hulton-Deutsch Collection/Corbis)

Cruikshank's biographer calls this "an unrelievedly static representation of an extraordinarily dynamic society."*

*Robert L. Patten, *George Cruikshank's Life, Times and Art*, vol. 2: *1835–1878* (New Brunswick, N.J.: Rutgers University Press, 1996), p. 445.

extension of the vote to a greater proportion of the middle class in 1867, was at least partially an attempt to anticipate and moderate such demands.

Many Victorians believed that the smooth ordering of society, and the greatest possible extension of individual liberty, come when people at all levels of society know their place and stay within in. That idea is beautifully illustrated in this lithograph by George Cruikshank, one of the most prolific and influential graphic artists of Victorian Britain. In addition to providing illustrations for the stories of Charles Dickens and the fairy tales of the Brothers Grimm, Cruikshank produced many caricatures that poked gentle fun at English men and women from all levels of society. The image from 1867 reproduced here is more serious in purpose. The beehive was a well-established symbol of cooperative activity, in which each individual bee has a particular role in sustaining the queen.

In an earlier sketch from 1848, Cruikshank had drawn a beehive with signs of disorder: the bottom level of society showed signs of drunkenness, disorder, and violence. The 1848 drawing was Cruikshank's negative response to the Chartist movement. Like most Victorian liberals, Cruikshank believed that property and education were prerequisites for responsible participation in politics.

By 1867, when this version of the beehive was produced, the tensions of the Chartist era were over. "The British Bee Hive" conveys a strong sense of hierarchy and stability.

Few shopkeepers could vote even after the Reform Bill of 1832, but most became enfranchised after the reforms of 1867, the year this drawing was made.

Few girls and women are shown, even though they formed a large part of the Victorian working population. Why might the artist have overlooked their importance?

QUESTION FOR ANALYSIS

How much potential does the artist show for movement up or down the British social hierarchy?

that a republic would be too susceptible to working-class opinion and not give enough respect to private property. Their leaders advocated a constitutional monarchy and invited Louis Philippe, a nobleman with moderate views, to take the throne. More interested in business than in royal protocol, King Louis Philippe was called the "bourgeois king." His regime was certainly more open than that of the Bourbons, though voting was restricted to a small minority of property-owning men. Republicans despised him, and it was they who took center stage early in 1848.

Herzen had rushed to Paris after hearing the news: police had fired on a crowd of demonstrators and 1,500 barricades had gone up around the city. Louis Philippe abdicated and fled the country, and for the first time in fifty years France became a republic in which the people themselves were sovereign. The change had come about so suddenly that the men who met in a newspaper office to plan the country's future were divided on how to proceed. One influential voice was that of a socialist named **Louis Blanc** (loo-EE blawnk) (1811–1882). Blanc argued that private ownership of industry was inefficient, leaving many unemployed, and unfair, giving workers no say in how the factories were run. He called instead for cooperative workshops to be set up by the government and run by the workers. Employment would be guaranteed for all.

Blanc was popular with the poor and unemployed, but his plan was strongly opposed by defenders of property rights. The republican government put into effect only a weakened version of Blanc's plan. Employment was provided on public works projects, such as the planting of trees, while those who still could not find work were guaranteed enough money to live on. Almost all this money was spent in Paris, a fact resented by the rural majority. Many of them backed the presidential candidacy of the conservative nephew of Napoleon Bonaparte, **Louis Napoleon** (1808–1873).

One Paris evening in the summer of 1848, Alexander Herzen heard a delegation marching past his window. They were, he said, "clumsy, rascally fellows, half peasants, half shopkeepers, somewhat drunk . . . they moved rapidly but in disorder, with shouts of '*Vive Louis-Napoleon!*'" Herzen wrote, "[I] shouted at the top of my voice: '*Vive la République!*' Those who were near the windows shook their fists at me and an officer muttered some abuse, threatening me with his sword."[8] As conservative forces gained strength, Herzen's revolutionary vision crumbled before him.

Louis Napoleon represented, in his own words, "order, authority, religion, popular welfare at home, national dignity abroad." His presidential candidacy was supported not only by liberals fearful of Blanc's radicalism but also by the many French peasants who resented the workers of Paris and still recalled the glorious days of Napoleon Bonaparte. After being elected president, Louis Napoleon followed his uncle's example by declaring himself Napoleon III, emperor of France. As in the 1790s, France had swiftly gone from constitutional monarchy, to republic, to empire (see Chapter 22).

Napoleon III presided over the Second Empire (1852–1870), a period of stability, prosperity, and expanding French power. As president Louis Napoleon had eliminated Blanc's socialist program, but he still recognized that the state should encourage trade and industry, such as by selling government bonds to finance the building of railroads and by backing semipublic financial institutions to provide capital for commerce and industry. Although Napoleon III was an authoritarian ruler, he respected the rule of law and basic civil liberties. Like Napoleon Bonaparte, he gained support by appealing to French nationalism and by expanding the French Empire.

● **Louis Blanc** (1811–1882) French socialist who advocated the use of the state to rectify problems of unemployment and exploitation in the workplace. His ideas were briefly put into practice during the revolution of 1848 in Paris.

● **Louis Napoleon** (1852–1870) Nephew of Napoleon I who was elected president of the Second Republic before declaring himself emperor in 1852. Was forced to abdicate in 1871 after losing the Franco-Prussian War.

Napoleon III was eventually brought down by his inability to cope with the rising power of Prussia. In 1870 German armies invaded France and drove him from power. He was replaced in 1871 by the Third Republic, the final nineteenth-century swing of the French constitutional pendulum. Leaders of the Third Republic would change many of Napoleon III's policies but would retain his emphasis on overseas imperial expansion (see Chapter 26).

The Habsburg Monarchy, 1848–1870

News of the 1848 uprising in France spread like wildfire across Europe. The dominant power in central Europe was the Austrian Empire, still ruled by the Habsburg family as in the days of the old Holy Roman Empire. Protestors took to the streets of Vienna in early 1848 demanding new rights. The befuddled emperor reportedly responded, "Are they allowed to do that?" Prince Metternich, the conservative architect of the Congress of Vienna, resigned his position as chancellor and fled to England. University students were prominent in the demonstrations that drove him from power.

Another challenge to the Habsburgs was the demand from their Italian and Hungarian subjects for national rights, a concept that threatened the existence of a multinational state like the Austrian Empire. In Budapest a Hungarian assembly created a new constitution that established religious freedom, equality before the law, and an end to the privileges of the old feudal nobility. Revolution also swept Austria's northern Italian possessions, its Czech-speaking provinces, and Balkan territories like Croatia.

The young Emperor Franz Joseph II (r. 1848–1916) tried to regain the upper hand by cultivating the support of the rural majority. As in France, many peasants were shocked by the radicalism of university students and urban workers, and their support helped Habsburg authorities re-establish control within the German-speaking territories of the empire. But Franz Joseph's success was far from complete. By 1859 Italian rebels had won independence from Austria (see below), and in 1866 Prussian forces had defeated the Habsburg army. The discontent of subject nationalities like the Hungarians and the Czechs continued. With crises looming, the emperor proclaimed the Dual Monarchy in 1867, creating a federal structure for the empire. He would be simultaneously emperor of Austria and king of Hungary, each state having its own separate representative institutions.

Through this compromise Austria retained its great power status and settled the long struggle between German rulers and Hungarian subjects. However, it did nothing to address the grievances of peoples such as the Czechs and the Croats. Failure to resolve the regional, ethnic, and class divisions in the empire created a hornet's nest of tensions that would help spark a world war early in the twentieth century (see Chapter 27).

The Unification of Italy, 1848–1870

In 1848 Italian liberals dreamt of a new political order based on ties of language, culture, and history. But they would have to overcome significant regional differences and the political division of the Italian peninsula into numerous states. The north was subject to the same forces of industrialization and urbanization as western Europe, while the south was still largely peasant and traditional in its Catholicism. Differences in dialect made it difficult for Italians from different parts of the peninsula even to communicate with one another. Such divisions played into the hands of conservatives, who soon stifled both liberal reforms and attempts at unification.

One of the men most responsible for the creation of a new Italian identity was the romantic revolutionary **Giuseppe Garibaldi** (jew-SEP-pay gar-uh-BOWL-dee) (1807–1882). Like other Italian idealists of the time, Garibaldi believed in the need for a *risorgimento,* a political and cultural renewal of Italy that would restore its historic greatness. Condemned to death for leading an uprising in Genoa, he fled to South America, where he took part in a Brazilian uprising. In 1848 he returned to Italy and fought in the northern wars against Austria.

Then in 1860 a rebellion broke out in southern Italy. With the kingdom of Naples tottering, Garibaldi landed on the island of Sicily with only a thousand poorly trained troops, overthrew its corrupt ruler, and crossed to the mainland. His army was joined by enthusiastic rebels as he marched north toward Naples. His forces brought Naples and Sicily into the new, united Italy.

Garibaldi had fought to establish an Italian republic, but he was outmaneuvered by royalists, who established the new Italy as a constitutional monarchy. By 1870 the Papal States had been incorporated into the kingdom, and the process of unification was complete. Italy was a new addition to the list of the great powers of Europe, and like the others its leaders set out to further develop its industrial base and military capacities and to view the wider world with an eye toward empire.

Germany: Nationalism and Unification, 1848–1871

Before 1848 German speakers were still ruled by over thirty different governments, from small kingdoms to powerful states like Austria and Prussia. Realizing that these political divisions could hamper economic growth, the Prussian government had begun organizing a customs union. But Prussian leadership was not welcomed by all Germans. German liberals viewed Prussian traditions of conservatism and militarism with suspicion.

When the revolutionary impulse hit Berlin, Friedrich Wilhelm IV of Prussia (r. 1840–1857) took a hard line against protestors, using military force to crush demonstrators who had stormed an arsenal and seized a royal palace. Although the king did grant Prussia a constitution in 1848, it was a very conservative one. While representatives to the new Prussian assembly were to be elected through universal manhood suffrage, the king and his ministers were free to ignore it and rule as they liked. Friedrich William made it clear that he saw the constitution as a personal gift to his subjects, not a matter of rights but of royal beneficence.

The Prussian government, like that of Austria, did not support German political unification in 1848, fearing that its power would be undermined. In other German states, however, there was significant support for the idea of a unified Germany under a liberal constitution. A committee of prominent liberals organized an election, and in 1848 the **Frankfurt Assembly** met to create a constitution for a united German confederation. The delegates drafted a Declaration of Fundamental Rights that embodied the best of liberal political principles, including freedom of assembly and freedom of speech. Seeking a symbol of unity, they offered the crown to Friedrich Wilhelm as constitutional monarch of a democratic German state. But the Prussian king refused to accept what he called "a crown from the gutter," rejecting the principle of popular sovereignty upon which the proposed constitution was based.

• Giuseppe Garibaldi (1807–1882) Italian nationalist revolutionary who unified Italy in 1860 by conquering Sicily and Naples.

• Frankfurt Assembly Assembly held in 1848 to create a constitution for a united German confederation. Elected Frederick William IV as constitutional monarch, but William refused the offer on the principle that people did not have the right to choose their own king.

■ **German Industrialization**   The Krupp family had been important innovators and manufacturers of armaments since the period of the Thirty Years' War (1630–1648). In the nineteenth century, with the foundations of the Krupp Steelworks, they became the most important of German industrialists, their field cannon playing an important role in securing victory in the Franco-Prussian War (1870–1871). Here the sprawling Krupp steel factory in the town of Essen shows that fields and factories could still be found close together in late-nineteenth-century Europe.   (Ullstein/The Granger Collection)

Friedrich Wilhelm's refusal killed any hope of unifying Germany under a liberal constitution. But the forces of industrialization, the building of railroads, and rapid urbanization were creating conditions in which a unified Germany seemed more desirable than ever. In the 1860s, under the initiative of its chancellor, **Otto von Bismarck** (1815–1898), Prussia started to create a new German nation.

Bismarck, Prussia's "iron chancellor," was of aristocratic background. A strict conservative, he told a committee of the German Confederation in 1862: "Not through speeches and majority decisions are the great questions of the day decided—that was the mistake of 1848—but by iron and blood."[9] Bismarck pursued a policy of militarization that led to victories over Denmark and Austria, sparking German national pride even outside of Prussia. In the wake of 1848 some Germans had grown cynical about representative government, associating it with the petty quarrels of politicians. Now they were inspired by a romantic vision of a grand German state fulfilling the people's destiny as a great world power.

Napoleon III's opposition to Prussian expansion led to the Franco-Prussian War of 1870–1871, during which the French emperor was captured by German forces. The unification of Germany in 1871, accomplished in the wake of Bismarck's victory over France, was to have profound implications for world history. The rise of a

● **Otto von Bismarck** (1815–1898)   Unified Germany in 1871 and became its first chancellor. Previously, as chancellor of Prussia, had led his state to victories against Austria and France.

unified Germany with the fastest-growing industrial economy in the world helped propel a new scramble for colonies in the late nineteenth century (see Chapter 26) and set the stage for two world wars in the twentieth.

New Paradigms of the Industrial Age: Marx and Darwin

Even more than during the Scientific Revolution, Europeans in this era believed that science could reveal the secrets of the natural world and that human society could be described and improved through the Enlightenment tradition of rational inquiry (see Chapter 21). Of the many scientists and social theorists of Europe's industrial age, Karl Marx and Charles Darwin stand out for the enduring global influence of their work. Marx, in his dissection of capitalism and explanation of the inevitability of socialist revolution, developed a systematic framework for the analysis of human history. Darwin, in describing how natural selection drives the process of evolution, developed a new framework for understanding natural history. Both developed new paradigms for understanding the world, new ways of ordering knowledge that substantially altered previous modes of thought.

Karl Marx, Socialism, and Communism

• **Karl Marx** (1818–1883) German author and philosopher who founded the Marxist branch of socialism; wrote *The Communist Manifesto* (1848) and *Das Kapital*.

Primary Source: "Working Men of All Countries, Unite!" *Read these excerpts from The Manifesto of the Communist Party and find out why "the proletarians have nothing to lose but their chains."*

The Manifesto of the Communist Party, published in 1848 by **Karl Marx** (1818–1883) and Friedrich Engels, directly challenged the status quo:

The Communists . . . openly declare that their ends can only be attained by the forceful overthrow of all existing social conditions. Let the ruling classes tremble at a Communistic revolution. The proletarians have nothing to lose but their chains. They have a world to win. WORKING MEN OF ALL COUNTRIES UNITE![10]

In spite of setbacks as conservatives retook control after 1849, Marx believed that the victory of socialist revolutionaries in Europe was not only possible but also inevitable.

Marx was a brilliant student who had earned a doctoral degree in philosophy. He absorbed from the works of Hegel a philosophy that the human mind progresses through stages toward absolute knowledge. While accepting this theory of progress, he rejected the idea that it takes place primarily at the level of consciousness. Marx instead developed a materialist view that saw history as propelled by changes in "modes of production." To greatly simplify Marx's complex view of history, his concept of scientific materialism held that it is economic forces, the way things are produced, that generate the social, political, and even ideological characteristics of a given society.

Hegel's dialectic described a process in which a dominant idea, called a thesis, generates a contending idea called an antithesis. These two ideas come into conflict until they generate a new, superior idea called a synthesis. Marx interpreted the dialectic in terms of material relations rather than abstract ideas. Changing modes of production produce antagonistic social classes. These social classes come into conflict in the political arena, generating ideas that match their class interests.

As Marx analyzed the original French Revolution, for example, he explained that the rise of capitalism challenged the old feudal system of production, leading to the rise of the bourgeoisie (the propertied middle class that stood between the aristocracy and mass of French society) and its overthrow of the monarchy and aristocracy. Whereas the aristocracy had promoted an ideology of power that emphasized family lineage, the bourgeoisie put forward ideas that focused on rights of property. The liberalism of Mill and Herzen, Marx argued, was simply the self-interested philosophy of the property-owning bourgeoisie.

Marx recognized that the bourgeoisie, "during its rule of scarce one hundred years, has created more massive and more colossal productive forces than have all preceding generations together."[11] But he felt that capitalism contains a fatal flaw that dooms it to destruction. The very efficiency of capitalism causes recurrent crises of overproduction when more goods are produced than the market can absorb. Wages are slashed and factories are closed. Then the economy recovers, but with each crash the division between the property owners and the workers increases: "Society as a whole," Marx wrote, "is more and more splitting up into two great hostile camps, into two classes directly facing each other: Bourgeoisie and Proletariat."[12] The struggle between these two classes, the propertied middle class and the industrial working class, was made inevitable by the capitalist mode of production, and the victory of the working class, Marx argued, would lead to the realization of socialism. The full establishment of socialism, though it might take a long time, would be the *final* stage in human progress, after which there would be no further class conflict.

From a global perspective, Marx explained the link between industrial capitalism and European imperialism:

> The need of constantly expanding market for its products chases the bourgeoisie over the whole surface of the globe. . . . It has drawn from under the feet of industry the national ground on which it stood. . . . In place of the old local and national seclusion and self-sufficiency, we have intercourse in every direction, universal inter-dependence of nations. . . . The bourgeoisie, by the rapid improvement of all instruments of production and by the immensely facilitated means of communication draws all . . . nations into civilization.[13]

Global expansion, however, can only delay the collapse of capitalism, not prevent it.

Marx's internationalist philosophy challenged the idea of nationalism. Nationalists argued that bonds of culture and history unified a people across lines of social class. To them, a German was a German, whether she was a princess or a chambermaid, whether she lived in Prussia or in Austria. To Marx such romanticized notions merely distracted proletarians from recognizing that their true interests lay not with the rich and powerful who spoke the same language, but with workers across the world. The Socialist International, which Marx helped to organize, was dedicated to fostering such working-class solidarity. But while Marx clearly explained why internationalism rather than nationalism was in the best interest of Europe's workers, nationalism increasingly exerted a powerful influence among all social classes.

After the failures of 1848, Marx spent the next thirty-five years of his life refining his theories. Though by the time of his death in 1883 there had been no socialist revolutions, his ideas were spreading widely and the number of his followers was increasing, especially in Germany. In the twentieth century the works of Karl Marx would be read and studied in many languages, and his image would be reproduced across the world.

Religious Leaders Comment on Science and Progress

While the nineteenth century saw the rise of secular ideologies such as liberalism, socialism, and nationalism, religion continued to shape the views of most people around the world. The excerpts below illustrate the implications of modern industrial ideologies for religious faith as interpreted by a Sunni Muslim scholar and a Roman Catholic pope.

The first selection comes from Sayyid Jamāl ad-dīn al-Afghani (1838–1897). He was educated in Islamic schools in Afghanistan and Iran and then spent twenty years in British-ruled India, also traveling to western Europe and the Ottoman Empire. Al-Afghani saw Pan-Islamic unity as necessary for effective resistance to European dominance and worked to heal divisions between the Sunni and Shi'ite Muslim communities.

The second passage is by Pope Pius IX (r. 1846–1878), who became a staunch conservative when Roman revolutionaries forced him to temporarily flee the Vatican in 1848. Pius IX greatly increased papal authority when he proclaimed the doctrine of papal infallibility, which stated that the pope's statements on central issues of faith were to be regarded as coming directly from God and could not be challenged.

Sources: Sayyid Jamāl ad-dīn al-Afghani, cited and translated in Nikki Keddie, *Sayyid Jamāl ad-dīn "al-Afghani": A Political Biography* (Berkeley: University of California Press, 1972), pp. 161, 186; *Quanta Cura* from Eternal Word Television Network, www.ewtn.com.

Sayyid Jamāl ad-dīn al-Afghani

1. "Lecture on Teaching and Learning" (1882)

If someone looks deeply into the question, he will see that science rules the world. There was, is, and will be no other ruler in the world but science. . . . In reality, sovereignty has never left the abode of science. However, this true ruler, which is science, is continually changing capitals. Sometimes it has moved from East to West, and other times from West to East. . . . The acquisitions of men for themselves and their governments are proportional to their science. Thus, every government for its own benefit must strive to lay the foundation of the sciences and to disseminate knowledge. . . .

The strangest thing of all is that our *ulama* [scholarly community] these days have divided science into two parts. One they call Muslim science, and one European science. Because of this they forbid others to teach some of the useful sciences. They have not understood that science is that noble thing that has no connection with any nation, and is not distinguished by anything but itself. Rather, everything that is known is known by science, and every nation that becomes renowned becomes renowned through science. . . .

How very strange it is that the Muslims study those sciences that are ascribed to Aristotle with the greatest delight, as if Aristotle were one of the pillars of the Muslims. However, if the discussion relates to Galileo, Newton and Kepler, they consider them infidels. The father and mother of science is proof, and proof is neither Aristotle nor Galileo. The truth is where there is proof, and those who forbid science and knowledge in the belief that they are safeguarding the Islamic religion are really enemies of that religion. The Islamic religion is the closest of religions to science and knowledge, and there is no incompatibility between science and knowledge and the foundation of the Islamic faith. . . .

2. "Answer of Jamal al-Din to Renan" (1883)

All religions are intolerant, each one in its way. The Christian religion, I mean the society that follows its inspirations and its teachings . . . seems to advance rapidly on the road of progress and science, whereas Muslim society has not yet freed itself from the tutelage of religion. . . .

I cannot keep from hoping that Muslim society will succeed someday in breaking its bonds and marching resolutely in the path of civilization after the manner of Western society. . . . No I cannot admit that this hope be denied to Islam.

Pope Pius IX

Quanta Cura (Condemning Current Errors), 1864

For well you know, my brothers, that at this time there are many men who applying to civil society the impious and absurd principle of "naturalism," dare to teach that "the best constitution of public society . . . requires that human society be conducted and governed without regard being had to religion any more than if it did not exist; or, at least, without any distinction between true religion and false one." From which false idea . . . they foster the erroneous opinion . . . that "liberty of conscience and worship is each man's personal right, which ought to be legally proclaimed and asserted in every rightly constituted society; and that a right resides in the citizens to an absolute liberty, which should be restrained by no authority whether ecclesiastical or civil, whereby they may be able openly and publicly to manifest and declare any of their ideas whatever, either by word of mouth, by the press, or in any other way." Whereas we know, from the very

teaching of our Lord Jesus Christ, how carefully Christian faith and wisdom should avoid this most injurious babbling.

And, since where religion has been removed from civil society, and the doctrine and authority of divine revelation repudiated, the genuine notion itself of justice and human right is darkened and lost, and the place of true justice and legitimate right is supplied by material force. . . . [Then] human society, when set loose from the bonds of religion and true justice, can have, in truth, no other end than the purpose of obtaining and amassing wealth, and . . . follows no other law . . . except . . . ministering to its own pleasure and interests.

Amidst, therefore, such great perversity of depraved opinions . . . and (solicitous also) for the welfare of human society itself, [we] have thought it right again to raise up our Apostolic voice.

QUESTIONS FOR ANALYSIS

▶ How do Pius IX and al-Afghani differ in their views of the relationship between religion and the ideas and ideals of industrial modernity?

▶ Are there any connections between these nineteenth-century debates and current controversies concerning science and faith in the Christian and Islamic worlds?

Charles Darwin, Evolution, and Social Darwinism

Prior to publishing his groundbreaking book *On the Origin of the Species by Means of Natural Selection* in 1859, the British scientist **Charles Darwin** (1809–1882) had spent many years gathering evidence. Geologists had already determined that the earth was millions of years old and that its surface features had greatly changed over time. Darwin was among those scientists who believed that long-term biological change, evolution, also characterized natural history. His search was for the mechanism of the evolutionary process.

In the Galapagos Islands off the coast of South America, Darwin observed that finches and turtles differed from those on the mainland and even in other areas of the islands. He theorized that the variations resulted not from separate acts of creation but from the adaptation of species to different environments. His principal contribution was the idea that natural selection drove this process.

Darwin explained the origins of all life on earth as resulting from competition for survival. Organisms with traits that gave them a better chance of survival passed those traits along to their offspring. Over time, the accumulation of diverse traits led to the appearance of new species, while failure in the struggle for existence led to the extinction of unsuccessful ones. Like Newton's theory of gravitation, Darwin's evolutionary theory was elegant, universally applicable, and a substantial advance in human understanding of the natural world.

In *The Descent of Man* (1871), Darwin made it clear that human beings had also undergone natural selection in their evolution as a species, an idea that generated considerably controversy. Just as Copernicus and Galileo had removed the earth from the center of the universe (see Chapter 16), Darwin seemed to be removing humankind from a central place in the natural world. Some religious leaders angrily denounced his work, seeing it as an extreme example of the amoral materialism of modern life and thought. (See the feature "Movement of Ideas: Religious Leaders Comment on Science and Progress.") Darwin's insights were, however, quickly accepted by virtually all natural scientists.

Beyond the domain of natural science, Darwin's ideas reflected and contributed to the broader intellectual trends of Europe's industrial age. The great increase in productivity and communications inspired the belief that human history is the story of progress. Karl Marx had absorbed this idea as a student and saw Darwin's theory of evolution as reinforcing his own argument that human history proceeds through stages (feudalism, capitalism, socialism). Marx was just one of many observers who thought that Darwin's work reinforced an optimistic view of human history.

But Darwin's concept of a "struggle for existence" in the natural world could also have less positive implications when applied to political, social, and economic competition. *Social Darwinism* was the idea that inequality of wealth and power could be explained by the superiority of some and the inferiority of others. In the open competition of the marketplace, Social Darwinists argued, the riches of some were proper reward for their exceptional talent. The poor were those with inferior traits. Analogies from nature were thus used to justify differences in wealth and power. Social Darwinism was also used to explain Europe's increasing global dominance: European imperialism was simply natural selection at work. "Inferior peoples" would be replaced by the superior Europeans as part of a natural and inevitable scientific process. As a scientist, Darwin did not draw such broad social and political corollaries from his work.

Reform and Reaction: Russia and the Ottoman Empire, 1825–1881

In 1798 Napoleon had invaded Egypt, one of the wealthiest Ottoman provinces. Then in 1812 his army marched on Moscow. Though the French retreated in both cases, both Russian and Ottoman leaders had been put on notice. Developments to their west and north, including the Industrial Revolution, were challenges to which they would have to respond. In both societies a deep divide separated conservatives and reformers. The question was whether it was better to emulate the legal, educational, social, and political trends of western Europe, as reformers argued, or to follow a conservative policy that emphasized continuity with the past.

Emancipation and Reaction in Russia

Alexander Herzen was from a generation of educated young Russians who were inspired by the revolutionary changes that had taken place to the west. He saw Russia as a backward place, "coarse and unpolished" compared with western European society.[14] But Russia could be reinvigorated if it joined the mainstream of European cultural and intellectual life. Westernizers like Herzen were inspired by the Decembrist Revolt of 1825, a failed uprising by a group of military officers striving to bring constitutional government to Russia. They were opposed by the conservative Slavophiles, who believed that Russia should stand by her Slavic traditions, especially Orthodox Christianity and the tsarist state.

After 1815, Russian tsars commanded the world's largest army and controlled an empire that spread from Poland in the west across Central Asia and Siberia to Alaska. But their imperial power had not been paralleled by similar advances elsewhere in society. Russia was overwhelmingly rural and agricultural. It had a powerful aristocracy and a weak middle class. The institutions of capitalism that facilitated British industrialization were weak, and Russia had almost no modern industry. Lacking a strong bourgeoisie or a growing proletariat, the main social divide was between the landowning nobility and the vast population of serfs. The serfs were poor, illiterate, and so lacking in rights that they could be won or lost in card games.

The nobility profited from this system, as did the government, which depended on serf conscripts for its huge army. Change was not likely to come from above. The Decembrist revolt put the new tsar, Nicholas I (r. 1825–1855), in an even more conservative mood. It was under Nicholas that the secret police force was established that would send Alexander Herzen and other dissenters into exile.

With the development of modern industry, the economic and technological gap between Russia and the other great powers widened. The price Russia paid for its lack of progress became clear during the **Crimean War** (1853–1856). Russia had secured control of the valuable Crimean peninsula, on the northern shore of the Black Sea, in the late eighteenth century (see Chapter 20), when it became part of the contested frontier with the Ottomans. In the 1850s the Russians attacked, claiming to be protecting Orthodox Christians from Ottoman mistreatment. In reality the tsar's military was planning to expand even further at Ottoman expense.

The British and the French came to the defense of the Ottoman Empire because they feared that Russian expansion to the south would upset the European

● **Crimean War** (1853–1856) War fought in the Crimean peninsula between the Russian and Ottoman Empires. France and Britain sent troops to aid the Ottomans and prevent Russian expansion.

balance of power. The Russian army was defeated, unable to make up in numbers what it lacked in modern military technology and organization. Poorly trained conscripts were given badly outdated rifles, while modern British and French naval vessels dominated the Black Sea. The lesson was clear: modern wars could not be won without an industrial foundation.

Tsar Alexander II (r. 1855–1881), who succeeded to the throne near the end of the Crimean conflict, recognized that Russia's social structure, based on serfdom, could not support a powerful modern state. In 1861 Alexander II freed the serfs with his **Emancipation Edict.** Increased labor mobility was one rationale for emancipation, since industrial development would require the movement of peasants into cities.

Neither the nobility nor their former serfs were satisfied. To avoid antagonizing the nobility, the edict required that emancipated serfs pay their former owners for their own freedom, and the amount of land they were allocated was often insufficient to meet that cost. Moreover, the communal organization of the peasant villages, where collective decisions were made about what and when to plant, made it difficult to increase agricultural efficiency through capital investment and scientific principles. Even after emancipation, the rural poor were the majority in Russia.

Alexander Herzen saw the Emancipation Edict as a wasted opportunity for more meaningful reform in the Russian countryside. But he did not give up hope. Since 1848 he had become disillusioned with the West, and he hoped that soon Russia's very lack of development would give it a fresh start. He thought that a liberal state could be created that guaranteed individual freedoms, while the communal organization of the Russian peasantry could be used to build a productive and humane social order. He explained these ideas in his journal *The Bell,* which he edited from London and which was smuggled into Russia. Though *The Bell* was banned by the tsar's censors, it was widely read, even by top government officials.

● **Tsar Alexander II** (r. 1855–1881) Also known as Alexander the Liberator, best known for his emancipation of the serfs.

● **Emancipation Edict** 1861 edict by Tsar Alexander II that freed the Russian serfs. However, serfs had to pay their former owners for their freedom, and the land they were allocated was often insufficient to produce the money needed to meet that cost for freedom.

Emancipated Serfs As with freed slaves in the U.S. South during the late nineteenth century, living conditions for most Russian serfs were not immediately transformed by emancipation in 1861. Most were illiterate and like the wheat threshers shown here had to rely on their own labor power. Even so, Alexander Herzen, admiring their collective village institutions, saw the peasants as the foundation of Russia's socialist future. (Adoc-Photos/Art Resource, NY)

Even so, political reforms under Alexander II were timid. Even after the Emancipation Edict, the agenda of the Slavophiles, those who wished for as little change as possible, predominated, while Westernizers hoping for more substantial reform feared the networks of spies and secret police whose job it was to identify "troublemakers" and exile them, often to harsh labor camps in Siberia.

At the same time, however, the tsar's government was now taking action in support of industrialization. During the 1870s government support led to a boom in railroad construction, also stimulating the local coal and iron industries. High tariffs were placed on foreign goods to encourage the development of Russian factories. Even as Russia continued to lag well behind the pace of western European growth, the beginnings of industrial production brought social problems. While by 1880 English, French, and German workers were beginning to enjoy some of the benefits of increased productivity, such as better clothing and housing, Russian workers were suffering from the kind of dangerous work environments and squalid living conditions that had marked the first phase of industrialization in the West.

Another challenge for Alexander's government was the question of nationalities. Bismarck had shown in Germany that nationalism could help overcome differences of region and social class and serve as the ideological foundation of a modern state. In Russia such a use of nationalism to bolster the power of conservative elites was impossible because over half the people in the empire were not Russian. Russia was more like multiethnic Austria, where nationalism was a divisive force. The tsars therefore responded harshly to nationalist uprisings, such as an 1863 rebellion in Poland. Observing from London, Herzen was distraught at the violent suppression of the Poles. He had hoped that Polish success would pave the way for liberal reforms in Russia.

By that time the generation of 1848 was losing influence to a younger group of Russian revolutionaries. This group had little patience for Herzen's philosophical debates. The secret police were everywhere, forcing Russian rebels to work in a secretive, conspiratorial environment. The anarchists among them thought that freedom could be achieved only through the complete abolition of the state and its instruments of power, the bureaucracy and the army. Some accepted the need for violence and even terrorism to achieve their ends: a bomb explosion killed Tsar Alexander II in 1881, causing the regime to crack down more on dissidence. Herzen died in exile, his dream that Russia could show the way to a better future unfulfilled.

Reform and Reaction in the Ottoman Empire

In the early nineteenth century the Ottoman Empire was a large and powerful state, but it was under increasing pressure. The Ottomans had lost effective control of the rich land of Egypt to the independent regime of Muhammad Ali, Greece to an independence movement in 1829, and Algeria to French invaders in 1830. Ottoman control was also slipping in the Balkans, the mountainous region of southeastern Europe they had controlled since the days of Süleyman the Magnificent.

After the loss of Greece, Sultan Mahmud II (r. 1808–1839) made an attempt at reform. His initiatives were expanded after his death during the mid-nineteenth-century era of the **Tanzimat reforms.** The reforming Ottoman bureaucrats who put these reforms into effect acted to break the power of the elite Janissary corps of the military (see Chapter 17) so that the army could be reorganized along modern lines. Like Muhammad Ali in Egypt, the Ottoman government established new types

• Tanzimat reforms (1839–1876) Restructuring of the Ottoman Empire. Control over civil law was taken away from religious authorities, while the military and government bureaucracies were reorganized to gain efficiency.

■ **Turkish Factory** Nineteenth-century industrialization was a global process, with many world regions tied to industrial processes solely as suppliers of raw materials and consumers of finished products. Here we see that in the western Ottoman Empire, factory production itself became a part of economic life. In this factory girls and women are weaving silk thread into cloth; the factory supervisor, however, is a man. In Japan as well (see Chapter 24) early textile production relied primarily on women's labor. (© Roger-Viollet/The Image Works)

CL **Primary Source:**
Imperial Rescript
In this proclamation, Abdul Mejid announces plans to reform and modernize the Ottoman Empire, while protecting the rights of non-Muslims.

of schools within the empire, such as colleges of military science and medicine, and sponsored students to travel and study in western Europe. A new system of primary and secondary schools following a European-style curriculum supplemented the existing *madrasas,* where the study of religious texts had long been emphasized. The urban elite began to travel more widely and to read French, Armenian, and Turkish newspapers, and European-style buildings were erected in Istanbul in an attempt to modernize the Ottoman capital. Partially in response to the restlessness of subject peoples, the legal system was revamped so that the same civil code applied to everyone, Muslim and non-Muslim alike, with full equality before the law. Finally, to facilitate trade with the West, the Tanzimat (TAHNZ-ee-MAT) reformers introduced a new commercial code modeled on European rather than Islamic principles.

The Tanzimat reforms went too far for Ottoman conservatives. Some Muslim religious leaders, like the Slavophiles in Russia, worried that by borrowing so many ideas from the West the government was undercutting the traditional religious and cultural foundations of their society. Some religious authorities resented their loss

Turkey and the European Union

The modern nation of Turkey, like the old Ottoman Empire, straddles the geographic boundary between Asia and Europe. Like the Tanzimat reformers of the nineteenth century, Turkish politicians have been remodeling their system along Western lines. In 1999 Turkey formally requested consideration for European Union (EU) membership. The first step, meeting a set of economic preconditions, had been accomplished by 2002.

Meeting the EU's human rights benchmarks, however, has proven more challenging. Freedom of speech is restricted by a law making it illegal to "insult Turkishness," a vague statute that has often been used to silence critics of the government. One journalist was recently assassinated by an extreme nationalist after he used the word *genocide* to describe Turkey's policy toward its Armenian minority in the First World War.

The human rights of Turkey's Kurdish minority are another issue of concern to members of the European Union. (Kurdish minorities are also located in neighboring Syria, Iran, and Iraq.) The Turkish government must distinguish, they say, between the legitimate cultural and political rights of Kurds and the terrorist methods that some organizations have used to try to achieve them. The military prefers to take a hard line, especially along the sensitive Kurdish-populated border with Iraq. The environment thawed a bit in 2007, however, when the government approved the opening of a Kurdish-language radio station.

Some EU members oppose Turkish membership for geographic and cultural reasons. French presidential candidate Nicolas Sarkozy stated during his 2007 campaign: "I won't be able to explain to French school kids that Europe's border neighbors are Iraq and Syria. . . . I don't believe that we can reinforce stability in the world by killing Europe."* Many European opponents of the plan focus on issues of immigration, fearing that Turkish membership would bring a flood of unassimilated Muslim immigrants. Other Europeans criticize such arguments as racist.

Within Turkey itself, entry into the European Union has the broad support of Western-oriented liberals. As in the nineteenth century, some conservative Muslims fear that reform along European lines will have damaging cultural effects. To date, however, the tensions between Turkey's secular liberals and its religious conservatives have not derailed momentum toward EU membership. The reform process has principally been overseen by the Justice and Development (AK) Party, which though it advocates a moderate form of Islamism is still distrusted by defenders of modern Turkey's secular tradition. A constitutional crisis was barely avoided in the summer of 2008 when a narrow majority of judges ruled against a motion to disband the AK altogether.

---

*As reported in the English-language *Turkish Daily News*, May 4, 2007.

of control over the educational and legal systems that, prior to the reforms, had been a principal source of their power and prestige. Others felt that the reforms did not go far enough. Some progressive Ottoman officials were dissatisfied with the centralized and bureaucratic nature of the Tanzimat program and argued for a constitutional monarchy guided by the principles of liberalism. (See the feature "World History in Today's World: Turkey and the European Union.")

When Sultan Abd al-Hamid (AHB-dahl-ha-med) III came to power in 1876, he at first agreed to create a representative government. With the backing of conservatives, however, he suspended the constitution a year after its creation and ruled as a dictator. Vacillating between reform and reaction, Ottoman authorities proved unable to strike a stable balance. As in Russia after 1881, reactionary policies largely replaced reformist ones in the late-nineteenth-century Ottoman Empire.

Chapter Review

CL Download the MP3 audio file of the Chapter Review and listen to it on the go.

Alexander Herzen's outlook was transformed by the disappointments of 1848, but he never gave up his belief that socialism and individual liberty would one day be achieved, with Russia showing the way. In 1870, the very year that Herzen died, Vladimir Ilyich Lenin was born. It was Lenin who would bring socialism to Russia in the form of Marxian communism (see Chapter 27); Herzen's dream of liberty for the Russian people would be long deferred.

What were the most important outcomes of the Industrial Revolution?

The Industrial Revolution transformed the world. More energy was available for human use than ever before once technological breakthroughs unleashed the power of coal. Steam engines drove the factories, ships, and railways of the industrial era. The more centralized organization of the factory system increased productivity, even as early industrial workers suffered from poor living conditions. On a global level, improved transportation and communication stimulated global commodity markets as industrialists sought out raw materials for their factories and markets for their finished goods.

What were the main features of European political development during and after the revolutions of 1848?

In 1815, European leaders thought they had finally contained the disruption to older patterns of authority represented by the French Revolution and the Napoleonic era. At that very time, however, the shift toward industrial factories was starting to undermine traditional social and economic relationships. Across Europe conservative leaders struggled to contain the new ideologies of liberalism, socialism, and nationalism. In early 1848 it seemed that the reformers and revolutionaries would be able to sweep away the old power structures in the name of freedom. But in the end their achievements were negligible. France and Austria were empires, the new Italy was a monarchy, and the kaiser who ruled a newly unified Germany after 1871 was a conservative Prussian. Britain was the exception to the European rule of revolutionary enthusiasm followed by conservative response. Victorian Britain was characterized instead by an evolutionary process of liberal reform that gradually enfranchised more of the queen's subjects.

Why were the ideas of Karl Marx and Charles Darwin of such great significance for world history?

Two European thinkers of the industrial era whose ideas would have a powerful global influence were Karl Marx and Charles Darwin. Marx analyzed the economic and historical foundations of industrial civilization, concluding that socialist revolution was the inevitable outcome of capitalist development. Marx's combination of idealism and scientific analysis was appealing to many who sought a blueprint for revolutionary change, not only in Europe but also around the world. The power of Charles Darwin's identification of natural selection as the mechanism of evolutionary change lay in its simplicity and universality. Darwin reinforced the growing faith of the industrial age in the explanatory power of science. At the same time, Social Darwinists applied his insights to political and economic conditions in ways that emphasized struggle and conflict.

WEB RESOURCES

Pronunciation Guide

Interactive Maps

MAP 23.1 Continental Industrialization, ca. 1850

Primary Sources

Chapter Objectives

ACE Multiple-Choice Quiz

Flashcards

 ## How did the leaders of the Russian and Ottoman Empires respond to the challenge of an industrializing western Europe?

Many within Europe were disturbed by the new social and political conditions of the Industrial Revolution and the ideas that came with them. The challenge of adapting to the industrial age was also faced by the Russians and the Ottomans, two empires located on the margins of European industrial development. In both cases conservatives and reformers vied for influence. In the Ottoman Empire, reformers instituted significant changes in educational, legal, and military structures during the Tanzimat period, before losing ground to conservatives later in the century. In spite of the emancipation of the serfs in 1861, the Russian tsars became even more conservative. While sponsoring railroad construction and industrial development, the Romanov tsars opposed all moves toward liberalism.

For Further Reference

Anderson, Benedict. *Imagined Communities: Reflections on the Origin and Spread of Nationalism.* London: Verso, 1991.

Auerbach, Jeffrey. *The Great Exhibition of 1851: A Nation on Display.* New Haven: Yale University Press, 1999.

Berlin, Isaiah. *Russian Thinkers.* New York: Viking, 1978.

Goodwin, Jason. *Lords of the Horizons: A History of the Ottoman Empire.* New York: Picador, 2003.

Herzen, Alexander. *My Past and Thoughts.* Translated by Constance Garnett. Berkeley: University of California Press, 1982.

Hobsbawm, Eric. *The Age of Capital, 1848–1875.* New York: Simon and Schuster, 1975.

Mayr, Ernst. *One Long Argument: Charles Darwin and the Genesis of Modern Evolutionary Thought.* Cambridge, Mass.: Harvard University Press, 1993.

Mokyr, Joel. *The Lever of Riches: Technological Creativity and Economic Progress.* New York: Oxford University Press, 1992.

Tilly, Louise. *Industrialization and Gender Inequality.* Washington, D.C.: American Historical Association, 1993.

Wheen, Francis. *Karl Marx: A Life.* New York: W.W. Norton, 2000.

Websites

The Industrial Revolution in Britain (http://www.historyteacher.net/APEuroCourse/WebLinks/WebLinks-IndustrialRevolution.htm). Extensive web links and access to primary sources.

Nationalism (http://www.socresonline.org.uk/2/1/natlinks.html). An exhaustive set of links to scholarship on the nature and history of nationalism.

Russian History (http://bubl.ac.uk/link/r/russianhistory.htm). A catalog of Russian history Internet sources.

China, Japan, and India Confront the Modern World, 1800–1910

I n 1859 the government of Japan sent its first delegation to visit the United States. On the crossing **Fukuzawa Yûkichi** (foo-koo-ZAH-wah yoo-KII-chi) (1835–1901), a 24-year-old samurai, studied *Webster's Dictionary*, but it did not prepare him very well for his experiences in San Francisco. "There were many confusing and embarrassing moments," he later wrote, "for we were quite ignorant of the customs of American life." At his hotel he was amazed when his hosts walked across expensive carpets with their shoes on. Fukuzawa attended a dance wearing the outfit of a samurai, with two swords and hemp sandals:

FUKUZAWA YÛKICHI

(Fukuzawa Memorial Center at Keio University/DNPArchives.com)

T o our dismay we could not make out what they were doing. The ladies and gentlemen seemed to be hopping around the room together. As funny as it was, we knew it would be rude to laugh, and we controlled our expressions with difficulty as the dancing went on. . . . Things social, political, and economic proved most inexplicable. . . . I asked a gentleman where the descendants of George Washington might be. . . . His answer was so very casual that it shocked me. Of course, I know that America is a republic with a new president every four years, but I could not help feeling that the family of Washington would be revered above all other families. My reasoning was based on the reverence in Japan for the founders of the great lines of rulers—like that for Ieyasu of the Tokugawa family of Shoguns.

CL This icon will direct you to interactive activities and study materials on the *Voyages* website: www.cengage.com/history/hansen/voyages1e

The Travels of Fukuzawa Yûkichi

Amsterdam
GREAT
BRITAIN
London
Paris   Berlin
Marseilles   Rome
Lisbon   OTTOMAN
          EMPIRE   PERSIA
Cairo
AFRICA

St. Petersburg
Moscow
RUSSIAN EMPIRE
Constantinople

QING CHINA
Beijing   Edo JAPAN
                 See inset
                 below
Hong Kong
(Gr. Br.)
Calcutta
INDIA

ALASKA

Fukuzawa Yûkichi
joins delegation to
San Francisco, 1860.

CANADA
San
Francisco   UNITED STATES   New York
                              Washington,
                              D.C.
Hawaiian
Is.   MEXICO
                                        PANAMA

ATLANTIC
OCEAN

INDIAN
OCEAN

Singapore (Gr. Br.)
DUTCH EAST INDIES
Batavia
(Neth.)

PACIFIC OCEAN

CAPE
COLONY

AUSTRALIA

N

NEW
ZEALAND

0   1500   3000 Km.
0   1500   3000 Mi.

The Travels of Fukuzawa Yûkichi

⟵ Fukuzawa Yûkichi's journeys
⟵⋯ Possible route of Fukuzawa
• City visited by Fukuzawa
• Other city
☐ British Empire, 1870

JAPAN, CA. 1860

QING
CHINA

RUSSIAN
EMPIRE

Hokkaido

0   150   300 Km.
0   150   300 Mi.

Vladivostok

Sea of Japan

KOREA
Seoul

JAPAN
Inland   Honshu
Sea   Kyoto   Edo (Tokyo)
Osaka   Nara   to
Fukuzawa walks   San Francisco
from Nagasaki   Shikoku
to Osaka.   Nakatsu
Nagasaki   Kyushu   PACIFIC
                               OCEAN
East China Sea   to
                        Hong Kong

1820	1840	1860	1880	1900	1920

Lifetime of Fukuzawa Yûkichi
1835   1901

EAST ASIA

Opening of   Meiji
Opium War   Japan by Perry   Restoration   Japanese colonization
1839 1842   1853   1867–1868   of Korea and Taiwan
                                                      1910
Treaty of Nanjing   Taiping Rebellion
1842   1850   1864   Boxer Rebellion
                                         1898

SOUTH ASIA

Indian Revolt   Indian National
1857   Congress established   Partition of Bengal
                 1885   1905

Lifetime of Gopal K. Gokhale
1866   1915

Though he was much more knowledgeable about the Western world than most Japanese, Fukuzawa said of himself and his American hosts, "neither of us really knew much about the other at all."[1]

Fukuzawa had grown up in a low-ranking samurai family who were expected to give unconditional support and service to their lord, but he was an ambitious nonconformist. As a young man he dedicated himself to "Dutch learning," and becoming convinced of the merits of Western science, he developed a philosophy that emphasized independence over subservience and science over tradition.

Fukuzawa's lifetime was one of remarkable change. All across the world societies struggled to adapt to the new industrial age with its advances in transportation and communications technologies, the spread of new religious and secular ideologies, and the dynamics of a changing global economy. In western Europe rulers, reformers, and rebels all struggled for control over the direction of change. Russian and Ottoman elites debated whether to emulate Western models (see Chapter 23). In East Asia, Japanese, Chinese, and Koreans were also divided when faced with increasingly aggressive Western powers. While Japanese reformers like Fukuzawa embraced change along Western lines as a means of empowerment, conservatives here and elsewhere in East Asia saw Europe and the United States as hostile threats to their established social, political, and economic systems.

Fukuzawa was a leader of the Westernizing faction that came to dominate Japan after the Tokugawa Shogunate was overthrown in 1868. The new Japanese government was able to resist the Western powers and, with military victories over China and Russia, expand its own empire. The leaders of Qing China, by contrast, proved incapable of reforming their society quickly or thoroughly enough to turn aside the Western challenge. By the late nineteenth century, China had been carved into spheres of influence by Britain, France, Germany, Japan, and the United States. Korean leaders were also slow to adapt to the industrial age, and the Korean peninsula was incorporated into the Japanese Empire.

South Asians also had to adapt to the industrial age, as well as balance their own traditions with powerful new economic forces and cultural influences. A major rebellion in 1857 signaled how deeply many Indians resented British rule. The failure of that revolt stimulated Indian intellectuals and political leaders to develop new ideas and organizations to achieve self-government. Indian nationalists, like those in Japan and China, struggled with the question of how to deal with the power of Western models in everything from clothing to house design to political philosophy.

This chapter focuses on the various strategies of resistance and accommodation used by the peoples of China, Japan, and British India in their attempts to come to terms with the industrial age. All these societies had to respond to the rising challenge from the West. Fukuzawa Yûkichi's proposal that Japan should emulate the West to become strengthened and modernized was just one of the solutions put forward in nineteenth-century East and South Asia.

Focus Questions

 What were the main forces that undermined the power of the Qing dynasty in the nineteenth century?

 What made it possible for Japan to be transformed from a relatively isolated society to a major world power in less than half a century?

 What were the principal ways that British-ruled Indians responded to imperialism?

China's World Inverted, 1800–1906

Four decades after the Qianlong Emperor dismissed an English diplomatic mission (see Chapter 20), the British returned with firepower to forcibly open Chinese markets. Qing officials, suddenly faced with Europe's industrial and technological progress, were forced to agree to a series of unequal treaties. Soon after, a major rebellion shook the Qing dynasty to its foundations. Some officials and scholars, humiliated by the decline in imperial prestige, were willing to consider change. However, as in the Russian and Ottoman Empires (see Chapter 23), reformers were outmaneuvered by conservatives who opposed the adoption of Western political, educational, and economic models. At the end of the century soldiers from Britain, France, the United States, and Japan occupied the Forbidden City. Imperial China had lost its ancient status as the "Middle Kingdom" to become a chessboard on which the great powers moved their pieces, dividing Chinese provinces into their own "spheres of influence."

The policies of the conservatives had proved disastrous. Fukuzawa Yûkichi, who had successfully helped implement in Japan precisely the type of reform that had been rejected by Chinese conservatives, observed in 1899: "I am sure that it is impossible to lead [the Chinese] people to civilization so long as the old government is left to stand as it is."[2] Seven years later the last Manchu emperor abdicated, and so ended the last of China's millennial-old imperial dynasties. China's dominant role in East Asia had been usurped by Japan.

Qing China Confronts the Industrial World, 1800–1850

In the late eighteenth century the British East India Company faced an old problem for Western traders in China: apart from silver, they had no goods that were of much value in Chinese markets. Their solution was to sponsor the development of large poppy plantations in newly conquered South Asia, refine the poppy seeds into opium, and smuggle the highly addictive narcotic into China. Commercially, it was a brilliant strategy, since narcotics create their own demand through the spiral of drug addiction. But profiting from the misery of those entrapped by drugs was ethically problematic and even hypocritical. Even as Victorian reformers worked to stamp out opium use in Britain, the East India Company continued to pursue its lucrative opium-for-tea strategy.

Qing officials were concerned for several reasons. Opium makes the user lethargic and often induces a sense of hopelessness. Addicts would neglect their own health and even the care of their own children and parents. The open flouting of government authority by opium traders was also intolerable to Qing officials. Finally, the opium trade undermined the Chinese economy when the traditional flow of silver bullion was reversed. For the first time silver was draining *out* of the Chinese economy, jeopardizing the silver-based Chinese fiscal system (see Chapter 16).

The opium crisis magnified the tensions between the British and Qing governments. Following their traditional tributary system of foreign relations, the Qing refused to allow any permanent European diplomatic presence in China. Tensions worsened after 1834, when the East India Company lost its monopoly on Anglo/Chinese trade. The new British commercial houses that entered the Chinese market were frustrated by Qing regulations that forced them to deal only with specified Chinese merchants backed by government monopolies. While the illegal opium trade fed the addiction of millions, these commercial interests lobbied the British government for more open access to Chinese markets.

By 1839 Sino-British relations were in crisis. The Qing government declared that drug traders would be beheaded and sent a scholar-official named Lin Zezu (lin say-shoe) to Guangzhou to see that the law was carried out and the opium trade suppressed. In a letter to Queen Victoria, Lin made his government's position clear:

> [By] introducing opium by stealth [the British] have seduced our Chinese people, and caused every province in the land to overflow with that poison. They know merely how to advantage themselves; they care not about injuring others! . . . Therefore those foreigners who now import opium into the Central Land are condemned to be beheaded and strangled.[3]

To the British government, however, the issue was not opium but free trade. According to liberal economic theory, free trade is always and everywhere best for everyone. If the Chinese could not understand this simple idea, then they would have to be *forced* to open their markets. The British responded to Lin's appeal with war.

The Opium War (1839–1842) was a severe shock to the Qing government. The British used their iron-clad gunboats to blockade the Chinese coast and bombard coastal cities such as Guangzhou and Shanghai. Unable to respond, many Qing commanders committed suicide at the disgrace of being so easily defeated by the "western barbarians." In 1842, as the British sailed up the Yangzi River and prepared to blast apart the walls of Nanjing, Qing officials realized that they would have to negotiate.

With no bargaining power, the Qing were forced to agree to the humiliating terms of the **Treaty of Nanjing,** the first of a series of unequal treaties that eroded Chinese sovereignty in the coming decades. The agreement opened five "treaty ports" to unrestricted foreign trade and gave possession of Hong Kong, upriver from the great port of Guangzhou, to the British. The treaty's provision of extraterritoriality, through which British subjects were governed by British rather than Chinese law at the treaty ports, was a grave blow to Chinese pride.

[CL] Primary Source:
Letter to Queen Victoria, 1839
On behalf of the emperor, Lin Zezu implores Queen Victoria to halt the British opium trade in China.

• **Treaty of Nanjing** (1842) One-sided treaty that concluded the Opium War. Britain was allowed to trade in additional Chinese ports and took control of Hong Kong. The provision for extraterritoriality meant that Britons were subject to British rather than Chinese law.

The Treaty of Nanjing left the British and other European nations eager for even greater power over China. Using supposed Qing violations of the Nanjing treaty as a pretext, in 1856 the British and French invaded and marched toward Beijing. They burned to the ground Qianlong's magnificent summer palace and briefly occupied the Forbidden City. In 1860, the Qing agreed to another, even more unequal treaty that opened more ports to Western trade and allowed "international settlements" in key Chinese cities such as Shanghai and Guangzhou. These settlements, where only Europeans were allowed to live, were foreign enclaves on Chinese soil. The British also mandated that imperial documents were no longer to use the Chinese character for "barbarian" to describe the British.

The Taiping Rebellion, 1850–1864

The Opium War and the unequal treaties that followed had exposed Qing weakness, leading some Chinese to conclude that the Manchu had lost the "Mandate of Heaven." China's peasant majority was suffering from neglect, misrule, and hunger. Behind the political chaos of nineteenth-century China was a startling fact: the population had grown by over 100 million between 1800 and 1850. Farmers brought marginal lands into production, and agricultural yields declined. Villages were devastated when the Huang He River repeatedly flooded. Although imperial governments had long been responsible for flood control and famine relief, the Qing bureaucracy, fighting foreign invaders, raised taxes for its military in the midst of the people's suffering.

In the mid-nineteenth century China was shaken by many revolts, including a major Muslim uprising in the northwest. The situation was especially desperate in the southeastern Guangdong province, where the **Taiping Rebellion** (1850–1864) began and then spread throughout southern China, sending the empire into chaos. The leader of the Taiping (tie-PING) was Hong Xiuquan (1813–1864). After traveling to Guangzhou and failing the imperial examinations several times, Hong Xiuquan (hoong shee-OH-chew-an) studied with some Western missionaries, adding his own interpretation to their message.

Hong claimed to be the younger brother of Jesus Christ come to earth to establish a "Heavenly Kingdom of Great Peace." Mixing a version of Christianity with an appeal to traditional peasant yearnings for fairness and justice, Hong gained hundreds of thousands of followers to his vision of a purified and reformed society. In their Heavenly Kingdom, the Taiping proclaimed, "inequality [will not] exist, and [everyone will] be well fed and clothed."[4]

At the core of the Taiping movement was a band of highly committed followers who practiced severe self-discipline. Many of these initiates were, like Hong, from the Hakka ethnic group. The Hakka were only brought under imperial control during Ming times and had never fully assimilated Confucian ideas of hierarchy. Women had relatively powerful and independent roles, and their feet were never bound. Hong's "long-haired rebels" refused to wear the long, braided ponytail, or queue, mandated by Manchu authorities as a sign of subservience. "Ever since the Manchus poisoned China," he said, "the influence of demons has distressed the empire while the Chinese with bowed heads and dejected spirits willingly became subjects and servants."[5]

The strength and confidence of Hong and his original converts soon attracted a mass following. In late 1850 some twenty thousand Taiping rebels defeated an imperial army sent to crush them; they then went on the offensive and began a

• **Taiping Rebellion** (1850–1864) Massive rebellion against the Qing led by Hong Xiuquan, who claimed to be the younger brother of Jesus Christ come to earth to create a "Heavenly Kingdom of Great Peace." The imperial system was greatly weakened as a result of the uprising.

■ **The Taiping Rebellion**   This contemporary print shows the defense of Shanghai by Qing forces in 1860. Though the Taiping controlled China's "southern capital" of Nanjing, the support given to the Qing military by Western powers, fearful of the anarchy that might accompany the loss of Manchu control, kept Shanghai under Manchu authority. Nanjing fell to the imperial army in 1864.   (School of Oriental and African Studies/The Art Archive)

long northward march that ended in 1853 with an invasion of Nanjing. Of the tens of thousands of Manchu living within the city walls, those who did not die in battle were systematically slaughtered. Hong moved into a former Ming imperial palace and declared Nanjing the capital of his Heavenly Kingdom of Great Peace.

After 1853, however, the Taiping rebels gained no more great victories. Their rhetoric of equality alienated the educated elite, and many influential members of the gentry organized militias to fight the Taiping when Qing defenses proved inadequate. As the Taiping movement grew in wealth and power, some leaders abandoned the plain living advocated by Hong and indulged in expensive clothing, fine food, and elaborate rituals. In addition, the Taiping were unable to recruit experienced administrators for the territory they controlled because their religious beliefs were at odds with the Confucian ideals of scholar-officials. Perhaps most important, the unsophisticated Taiping leaders did nothing to form the kind of foreign alliances that might have altered the balance of power in their favor.

In the early 1860s the British and French, who had done so much to undercut the Qing, now rallied to the dynasty's defense. From their base at Nanjing, the Taiping threatened Shanghai and the European interests that were rapidly developing there. In 1864, Qing forces, supported by European soldiers and armaments, stormed Nanjing. A Manchu official reported: "Not one of the 100,000 rebels in Nanjing surrendered themselves when the city was taken but in many cases gathered together and burned themselves and passed away without repentance."[6] By that time as many as thirty million people had been killed, and China's rulers were more beholden to European powers than ever before. The principal question facing China's government and intellectual elite became even more insistent: how to respond to the Western challenge?

"Self-Strengthening" and the Boxer Rebellion, 1842–1901

In the wake of the Opium War, some educated Chinese began calling for reform, arguing that only fundamental change would enable the empire to meet the rising Western challenge. Those calls became louder after the debacle of the Taiping Rebellion. The drug trade was no longer the issue. Now representatives of industrial capitalism arrived by steamship looking for markets and cheap labor, while an increasing number of missionaries sought the salvation of Chinese souls. The educated reform faction joined the **Self-Strengthening Movement** with the motto "Confucian ethics, Western science." China, these reformers said, could acquire modern technology, and the scientific knowledge underlying it, without sacrificing the ethical superiority of its Confucian tradition. As one of their leaders stated: "What we have to learn from the barbarians is only one thing, solid ships and effective guns."[7]

In the wake of the Taiping disaster the reformers established government institutions for the translation of Western scientific texts, the first since the days of Jesuit influence in the seventeenth century. Members of the gentry established new educational institutions that merged the study of classical Confucian texts with geographic and scientific ones. (See the feature "Visual Evidence: Family Photographs from Late Qing China.") And for the first time some young Manchu and Chinese men ventured to Europe and the United States to study Western achievements firsthand. Conservatives scoffed at their efforts. A prominent Neo-Confucian commented that since the most ancient times no one "could use mathematics to raise a nation from a state of decline or to strengthen it in times of weakness."[8]

As with Muslim scholars in the Ottoman Empire, Chinese scholar-officials based their power and prestige on special training in a long-standing and historically successful body of knowledge. To accept foreign principles in such fundamental areas as education would undercut the influence of the scholarly elite, and to emphasize military over scholarly pursuits would have gone against Confucianism. "One does not waste good sons by making them soldiers," went an old saying; it was a disparaging view of the military that Matteo Ricci had noted centuries earlier (see Chapter 16).

Conservative attitudes were reinforced at the top of the imperial hierarchy. During the reign of two child emperors, real power lay in the hands of a conservative regent, the **Empress Ci Xi** (1835–1908), an intelligent and ambitious concubine of the former emperor who came to dominate the highest reaches of the Qing bureaucracy. Conservatives rallied around Ci Xi (kee shee). She discouraged talk of reform and frequently diverted funds from modernization efforts, such as programs to build railways and warships, for spending on prestige projects, such as the rebuilding of the ruined summer palace.

Ci Xi's power was severely checked by the unequal treaties with Western nations, whose arrogant attitude toward the Celestial Empire severely irritated the "Dowager Empress." In spite of limited beginnings of industrialization and the acquisition of some modern armaments, the Qing military was no match for its rivals. In 1884, during a dispute over rights to Vietnam, French gunboats obliterated the Qing southern fleet within an hour. Southeast Asia, no longer tributary to the Qing, would now belong to France (see Chapter 26).

The European powers were not the only ones threatening the integrity of the Qing Empire; by this time Japan was also pursuing an aggressive policy of

● **Self-Strengthening Movement** Nineteenth century Chinese reform movement with the motto, "Confucian ethics, Western science." Advocates of self-strengthening helped to find a way to reconcile Western and Chinese systems of thought.

● **Empress Ci Xi** (1835–1908) The "Dowager Empress" who dominated Qing politics in the late nineteenth century, ruling as regent for the Emperor Guangxi. She blocked the Hundred Days' Reforms and other "self-strengthening" measures.

FAMILY PHOTOGRAPHS FROM LATE QING CHINA

The first photographic studio in China opened in British-controlled Hong Kong in 1846. Many more Western photographers followed, and as the Qing Empire declined they gained access to more parts of the empire. We therefore have a remarkable visual record of street scenes, buildings, ceremonies, soldiers, battlefields, ordinary people going about their work, and religious communities.

These two photographs of family groups were both taken by Englishmen. The photo below was taken by M. Miller in Guangzhou (then called Canton) between 1861 and 1864; it was labeled "A Mandarin and His Family." The photo opposite was taken by John Thomson in Beijing in 1871–1872; it was titled "House of the Official, Yang." Most of Miller's work was done for clients in his studio; Thomson, by contrast, traveled around the country collecting images for his *Illustrations of China and Its People,* a book that introduced many Western readers to the often harsh realities of late imperial China.

Guangzhou

This portrait was taken in the photographer's studio. During the early years of photography, slow shutter speeds meant that the family had to stay very still to achieve a clear image, too big a challenge for the infant on his grandfather's lap.

(Royal Asiatic Society, London)

The *queue* hairstyle of the men and boys, shaved in front with a long ponytail behind, was imposed on the Chinese by their Manchu rulers. In the later nineteenth century, Taiping rebels and Chinese nationalist saw the *queue* as a sign of servitude.

The bound feet of the mother and daughter indicates that this is a Han Chinese rather than a Manchu family.

QUESTION FOR ANALYSIS

How differently are the relationships among the members of these two families represented in these two photographs?

The Beijing photo shows an entire household, while the one from Guangzhou shows a nuclear family without servants. The former is a more traditional family assemblage, while the latter seems to have been affected by Western influences. Either the English photographer decided on the grouping, or perhaps the family itself, living in the treaty port of Guangzhou, was culturally influenced by Westerners.

Beijing

The house is called "Pavilion Among the Clouds." The fact that it is two stories high indicates that its owner was a man of great wealth.

(Wellcome Library, London)

This woman's headdress is typical of styles often found in Manchu families.

699

MAP 24.1

Asia in 1910 By 1910, empire was the status quo across Asia. In addition to the established British, French, and Dutch possessions, the United States (Philippines) and Japan (Korea and Taiwan) were new imperial players. The Russian Empire was also a powerful presence, expanding at the expense of Iran, though its defeat by Japan in 1905 showed the limits of its influence in East Asia. Qing China was still technically a sovereign state; however, the "concessions" controlled by Western powers after the imposition of unequal treaties meant that important coastal regions were under de facto European colonial control.

CL Interactive Map

Map labels

Sea of Okhotsk
Sakhalin
Karafuto (1905)
JAPANESE EMPIRE
PACIFIC OCEAN
Tropic of Cancer
New Guinea
(Portugal 1859)
Timor
Equator 0°
20°N
40°N

SIBERIA
AMUR DISTRICT (1858)
Khabarovsk (1858)
MANCHURIA
Vladivostok (1860)
Harbin
Sea of Japan
KOREA (1905, 1910)
JEHOL
Shenyang (Mukden)
Lüshun (Port Arthur) (Japan 1905)
Weihai (Gr. Br. 1898)
Jiaozhou (Ger. 1898)
Tianjin
Beijing
Ryuku Is. (Jap.)
East China Sea
Shanghai (Gr. Br. 1842)
Nanjing
Formosa (1895)
Wuhan
Fuzhou
Xiamen (Gr. Br. 1842)
Guangzhou (Gr. Br. 1842)
Macao (Port. 1557)
Hong Kong (France 1898)
Zhanjiang (France 1898)
Hainan
Philippine Is. (U.S. 1898)
Manila
South China Sea
BRITISH NORTH BORNEO (1888)
SARAWAK (1888)
Borneo
Celebes
DUTCH EAST INDIES

RUSSIAN EMPIRE
Lake Baikal
Chita
Irkutsk
OUTER MONGOLIA (Russian influence, 1912)
INNER MONGOLIA
Huang He R.
CHINA
Chongqing
Kunming
Yangzi R.
Hanoi
Haiphong
FRENCH INDOCHINA (1859, 1907)
Saigon
SIAM
Bangkok
MALAY STATES (1874, 1909)
Singapore (Gr. Br. 1819)
Sumatra
Java (1619)
Batavia (Neth.)
SOUTH China Sea

Trans-Siberian Railway
Omsk
Samara
SINKIANG
TIBET
HIMALAYA MTS.
BHUTAN
NEPAL
BURMA (1852, 1885)
Rangoon
Bay of Bengal
Andaman Is. (Gr. Br.)
Yanaon (Fr.)
Calcutta
Ganges R.

Helsinki
St. Petersburg
Riga
Moscow
Kiev
Dnieper R.
Orenburg
Kazalinsk
Aral Sea
Lake Balkash
Tashkent (1864)
Andizhan (1871)
Samarkand (1868)
Bukhara
Merv (1884)
Kushka
AFGHANISTAN
KASHMIR (1846)
PUNJAB
Delhi
INDIA
Madras
Pondicherry (Fr.)
Karikal (Fr.)
Ceylon
Goa (Port.)

Warsaw
Brest-Litovsk
Krasnovodsk
Ashkhabad (1881)
Caspian Sea
Baku
IRAN
RUSSIAN SPHERE (1907)
Tehran
BRITISH SPHERE (1907)
BALUCHISTAN (1883)
Karachi
Bombay
Diu (Port.)
Arabian Sea
INDIAN OCEAN

Black Sea
Batum (1878)
Kars (1878)
Angora
Constantinople
OTTOMAN EMPIRE
Damascus
Beirut
Baghdad
Mediterranean Sea
Medina
ARABIA
Medina
KUWAIT (1899)
Persian Gulf
OMAN (1891)
HADRAMAUT (1888)
WEST ADEN (1903)

AFRICA
Nile R.
Red Sea
Danube R.
Volga R.

Legend

Territories held by Western powers
- Great Britain
- France
- Netherlands
- United States
- Russian Empire

- Japan and its territories
- Independent Asian states
- Ottoman Empire
- Major railroads

0   500   1,000 Mi.
0   500   1,000 Km.

N

industrialization and militarization. Japan and Qing China came into conflict over Korea, where the Chosŏn dynasty still ruled what Westerners called "the hermit kingdom." An uprising against the emperor brought both Japanese and Chinese military forces to Korea, resulting in the Sino-Japanese War of 1894–1895 (see page 707). The Qing, who had earlier lost their southern fleet to France, now lost almost their entire northern fleet to Japan. The treaty that ended the war gave Japan possession not only of Korea but also of the island of Taiwan.

Once again the reformers stepped forward. This time they secured support from the young Guangxu (gwahng-shoo) emperor (r. 1875–1908), who tried to step out from Ci Xi's shadow in the summer of 1898 by issuing an unprecedented series of edicts that came to be called the Hundred Days' Reforms. Guangxu was inspired by a group of young scholars who had traveled to Beijing to present a petition urging the founding of a state bank, the raising of government bonds for large-scale building of railroads, and the creation of a modern postal system. The most fundamental of the Hundred Days' Reforms concerned education. Expertise in poetry and calligraphy would no longer be required. Instead, the examination essays would focus on practical issues of governance and administration. Beijing College was to add a medical school, and all the Confucian academies were to add Western learning to their curricula.

Ci Xi ended the Hundred Days' Reforms by proclaiming that Guangxu had asked her to rule in his name and confining him, along with his most progressive advisers, in the palace. Some advocates of self-strengthening were charged with conspiracy and executed; others left the country or lapsed into silence.

Meanwhile the aggression of external powers intensified. Germany seized the port city of Qingdao (ching-dow) and claimed mineral and railway rights on the Shandong peninsula; the British expanded their holdings from Hong Kong; and the Russians increased their presence in Manchuria (see Map 24.1). Public anger was growing, much of it directed at the Manchu for letting the power of the empire slip so dramatically.

During the difficult nineteenth century, many Chinese had sought security by joining secret societies. One of these, the "Society of Righteous and Harmonious Fists," also known as the Boxers because of their emphasis on martial arts, now rose to prominence. The Boxers were virulently antiforeign. In 1898 they attacked European missionaries and Chinese Christian converts, thus beginning the **Boxer Rebellion.** Empress Ci Xi, having resisted progressive reforms, decided to side with the rebels and declared the Boxers a patriotic group: "The foreigners have been aggressive towards us, infringed upon our territorial integrity, trampled our people under their feet. . . . They oppress our people and blaspheme our gods."[9]

Imperial support for the Boxers proved disastrous. In the summer of 1900, twenty thousand foreign troops from over a dozen different nations marched on Beijing and occupied the Forbidden City. Another humiliating treaty followed. The Qing were required to pay 450 million ounces of silver (twice the country's annual revenue) to the occupying forces. Like the Taiping, the Boxer Rebellion left China weaker and more beholden to foreign interests than ever before.

Finally, after the disaster of the Boxer Rebellion, Ci Xi's government implemented the Hundred Days' Reforms, abolishing the examination system and making plans for a constitutional order with some degree of popular representation. But it was too little, too late. In 1911 the first of two twentieth-century Chinese revolutions thrust the Qing dynasty into historical oblivion (see Chapter 27).

● **Boxer Rebellion** (1898)   Chinese uprising triggered by a secret society called the Society of Righteous and Harmonious Fists, a fiercely anti-Western group. Intended to drive out Westerners, it resulted instead in foreign occupation of Beijing.

The Rise of Modern Japan, 1830–1905

When Fukuzawa Yûkichi wrote that China could never move forward under Qing leadership, he was in a good position to judge. He was an important participant in Japan's own transformation from weakness and isolation to industrialism, centralized state power, and imperialism. After the Meiji (MAY-jee) Restoration of 1868 Japan had adapted to the new industrial age by looking to the West not just for its technology but also for its principles of education, economic organization, and state building. Yet socially, culturally, and spiritually, the Japanese maintained strong continuities with their ancient traditions. Japanese society actually achieved the "self-strengthening" that was advocated by late-nineteenth-century Chinese reformers, borrowing foreign ideas and adapting them to Japanese culture.

The turning point had come in 1853 with the arrival of a U.S. fleet. Isolation from the West was no longer possible. Having observed the devastating aftereffects of the Opium War in China, Fukuzawa and others advocated a radical reform program based on the rapid acquisition of Western knowledge and technology. As in China (as indeed in western Europe and the Russian, Ottoman, and Qing Empires), the reformers and revolutionaries were opposed by conservative defenders of the status quo. In Japan, Meiji reformers took charge of imperial policy. They laid the foundations of modern industry and began the technological and organizational transformation of the Japanese military. Military victories over China in 1895 and Russia in 1905 confirmed their success and fulfilled Fukuzawa's dream that his country would be recognized as a player equal to the Europeans and Americans in Asian affairs.

Late Tokugawa Society, 1830–1867

Growing up in the busy commercial center of Osaka, where his father had been sent to look after his *daimyo* lord's affairs, Fukuzawa was highly conscious of the gap between his family's samurai status and its low income. Samurai were not supposed to deal with mundane affairs such as shopping and handling money. But since they could not afford servants, lower samurai like the Fukuzawa family had no choice but to do so. Fukuzawa remembered how they would do their shopping at night, with towels over their faces to hide their shame. Even worse was the scornful treatment they met when they returned to their home village: "Children of lower samurai families like ours were obliged to use a respectful manner of address in speaking to the children of high samurai families, while these children invariably used an arrogant form of address to us. Then what fun was there in playing together?"[10] Although Fukuzawa's father was an educated man and well versed in the Chinese classics, no achievement on his part could raise his family's status.

Even at the bottom of the samurai hierarchy, the Fukuzawa family had higher status than most. Below them were first the farmers, then the artisans, then the merchants, and finally the outcasts who performed such unsavory tasks as working in leather and handling the bodies of executed criminals. As a young man Fukuzawa tested the attitude of the peasants by addressing them first in the haughty tones of the samurai and then speaking to them in the dialect of an Osaka merchant. The peasants abased themselves with humility when Fukuzawa spoke as a samurai, but they treated him with scorn when he imitated the speech of a merchant.

The young Fukuzawa regarded this castelike hierarchy as a prison from which he needed to escape. Education proved the key. Fukuzawa received no formal education until he was 14, and then it was the traditional curriculum of Confucian classics taught in Chinese. Frustrated at home, he sought his family's permission to travel to the port city of Nagasaki, the site of the annual Dutch trade mission. This was the only opening the Tokugawa government allowed to Europeans, and it was therefore also the center of "Dutch learning" (see Chapter 20). In 1843, Fukuzawa began to study the medical and scientific texts that would convince him of the superiority of Western over Chinese styles of education.

Just a few months earlier an American emissary, **Commodore Matthew Perry** (1794–1858), had sailed from the United States into Edo harbor, his steam-powered "black ships" sending shock waves through Japanese society. Perry's mission was to impress on the Tokugawa government the power of Western military technology and force it to establish diplomatic relations with the United States and open Japanese ports to foreign trade. Fearing that the Americans and Europeans might unleash

●**Commodore Matthew Perry** (1794–1858) American naval officer and diplomat whose 1853 visit to Japan opened that country's trade to the United States and other Western countries.

🖼 **Commodore Perry's Arrival in Japan** This Japanese print shows the arrival of Commodore Matthew Perry's steam-powered "black ships" near Edo (modern Tokyo) in 1853. After Perry's return to Japan in 1854, demanding that Japan be opened to Western trade, Japanese leaders debated how best to respond. The 1859 Tokugawa mission to San Francisco on which Fukuzawa Yûkichi served was an attempt to discover more about the U.S. government and its motives in East Asia. (Courtesy of the Trustees of the British Museum/The Art Archive)

a destructive barrage to open Japan to the outside word, the Tokugawa government submitted and, in 1858, signed an unequal treaty with the United States and five European powers granting access to treaty ports and rights of extraterritoriality.

Among those who accused the shogun of having humiliated the nation by signing this treaty were some daimyo who hoped to use the crisis to increase their independent power. Some even began to seek modern weapons for themselves and to fire at passing European ships. In the early 1860s it was not clear whether the Tokugawa government even retained enough authority to enforce its edicts. Seeking some breathing space, in 1862 the shogun sent a delegation to Europe hoping to delay further unequal treaties. Fukuzawa, who was part of this delegation, used the journey to make the close observations of European life later published in a widely read book called *Western Ways*.

By the time of his return in 1863, things were becoming more and more dangerous. Apart from the rebellious lords, another rising source of anti-Tokugawa pressure was coming from a group of *rônin* (ROH-neen), samurai without masters. The rônin were a floating population of proud men of limited means, many of whom were nostalgic for a glorious past when their military skills were highly prized. "The whole spirit," Fukuzawa said, "was one of war and worship of ancient warriors."[11] These rônin were stridently antiforeign. Fukuzawa, who had now learned English and was working as a government translator, was a potential target for their anger. For years he never left his home at night, fearful of being assaulted by anti-Western thugs.

The Meiji Restoration, 1867–1890

The challenge of the West required a coordinated national response, and neither the weakened Tokugawa government nor the rebellious daimyo could provide one. But there was another possible source of national unity, the imperial court at Kyoto. Some of the rebels against Tokugawa rule flocked to the banner of the child emperor under the slogan: "Revere the Emperor! Expel the Barbarians!"

In 1867 supporters of the emperor fought a brief but intense war with the shogun's forces. Fukuzawa was now a teacher, and when the fighting came to Edo he was lecturing on economics from an American textbook: "Once in a while . . . my pupils would amuse themselves by bringing out a ladder and climbing up on the roof to gaze at the smoke overhanging the attack."[12] He was doing his best to stay neutral, for his own safety and that of his students, fearing that the imperial forces would prove to be just as antiforeign as those of the shogun.

The armies affiliated with the imperial party were successful. In 1868 the **Meiji Restoration** brought a new government to power at Edo, now renamed Tokyo. Fukuzawa was delighted to discover that the administration of the Meiji ("enlightened") emperor, then only a child, was dominated by a powerful group of reformers who soon began to issue edicts that utterly transformed the closed, conservative society that Fukuzawa had known as a child. Most of these powerful behind-the-scenes oligarchs were, like Fukuzawa himself, men from middle and lower samurai families that placed a strong emphasis on scholarship.

The Meiji reforms eliminated the daimyo-ruled domains and replaced them with regional prefectures under the control of the central government. Tax collections were centralized to solidify the government's economic base. For the first time commoners were allowed to carry arms, as the Meiji government created a national conscript army armed with the latest rifles and led by officers trained in

● **Meiji Restoration** (1868)   A dramatic revolution in Japan that overthrew the Tokugawa and put the country on a path of political and economic reform under the slogans "Revere the Emperor" and "Expel the Barbarians." Meiji industrialization turned Japan into a major world power.

modern military organization. All the old distinctions between samurai and commoners were erased: "The samurai abandoned their swords," Fukuzawa noted, and "non-samurai were allowed to have surnames and ride horses."[13] The rice allowances on which samurai families had lived were replaced by modest cash stipends. Many former samurai had to face the indignity of looking for work.

Fukuzawa Yûkichi, a prominent supporter of the Meiji reformers, coined two of their most popular slogans: "Civilization and Enlightenment" and "Rich Nation, Strong Army." The government also agreed with Fukuzawa that education was the key to progress and set up a national system of compulsory schooling. Fukuzawa was pressured to join the new government and head the Education Ministry, but he preferred to keep his independence, founding both a university and a newspaper.

The goal that the Meiji oligarchs shared with Fukuzawa was to do anything possible to make Japan strong so it could resist Western intrusion and engage the world as an equal. Their policy was therefore one of adopting Western methods to challenge Western power. In 1873 another mission was sent to Europe. Its leaders were stunned by the West's industrial and technological development and were particularly impressed with the newly unified Germany and the politics of its chancellor, Otto von Bismarck. In Germany the delegation found a combination of nationalism and military-industrial power that they could use as a model.

Many Japanese in the 1870s and 1880s, however, were critical of this new direction. Some samurai took up arms against the Meiji regime, most notably the forty-two thousand who participated in the Satsuma Rebellion of 1877. Their leader, Saigō Takamori, ritually disemboweled himself when the battle turned against his men, and he later became a hero to the conservatives. But the Meiji reformers countered by creating their own cult of Saigō and helping turn him into a romantic hero. As they had used the phrase "Revere the Emperor" to modernize Japan, they again used appeals to tradition to support policies of change.

As during the early Industrial Revolution in Europe, the rewards of increased productivity were unequally distributed in Meiji Japan. Landlords benefited most from advances in agriculture such as the importation of new seeds and fertilizer and the government creation of agricultural colleges to improve methods of cultivation. Rice output increased 30 percent between 1870 and 1895, but high rents meant that peasants often paid half their crop to a landlord and now had to pay taxes to the government as well. To make ends meet, many rural families sent their daughters to work in the new factories the government was setting up around the country. Here the poorly paid girls and young women were housed in dormitories and strictly supervised, their dexterity and docility exploited for the benefit of others.

The Meiji went even further than the Germans in giving the state a direct role in industrial development. The government constructed railroads, harbors, and telegraph lines and made direct investments in industry. Meiji ministers and the oligarchs behind them did not leave economic development to market forces. In fact, Fukuzawa discovered how ignorant some were of the most basic principles of market economies when he showed one official his translation of an American economics textbook. Since there was no Japanese word for *competition*, he had substituted a word of his own invention, *kyōsō*, literally, "race-fight." When a treasury official objected to the use of the term, Fukuzawa explained that the concept was fundamental to the world of commerce. "I understand the idea," said the official, "but that word 'fight' is not conducive to peace. I could not take the paper with that word to the chancellor."[14]

The early industrial economy of Japan was based on a tight connection between state and industry, which continued even after the government began selling most of its industrial assets to private interests. After 1880, Japanese industry was largely controlled by *zaibatsu* (zye-BOT-soo), large industrial cartels that collaborated closely with the civil service. Some of the nineteenth-century zaibatsu, like Mitsubishi, still exist today. Liberal, free-trade economic notions were never as strong in Japan as in Britain and the United States.

Political liberalism was also part of late-nineteenth-century Japanese life. Fukuzawa had helped plant the liberal seed with an influential essay on John Stuart Mill's *On Liberty* (see Chapter 23). Like Mill, Fukuzawa addressed issues of gender, writing that "the position of women must be raised at once" and that education should be the first step toward greater gender equality.[15] A 20-year-old woman named Toshiko Kishida (toe-she-ko KEE-she-dah) went even further, speaking eloquently for women's rights in meetings across the country, even adding a little humor: "If it is true that men are better than women because they are stronger, why aren't our sumo wrestlers in the government?"[16]

One of Fukuzawa's greatest contributions in resolving the strains of the early Meiji period was in creating a space for "public opinion" in Japanese politics. Even if he disagreed with what Toshiko said, when she traveled the country arguing for women's rights she embodied Fukuzawa's principle of *enzetsu,* a word he created to describe something that had never existed in Japan before: "public speaking." In becoming a modern nation, Japan was also becoming a mass society where rulers had to take account of popular feelings and opinions. Here Fukuzawa played a prominent role. As a newspaper editor his views were widely discussed, and as a writer and publisher he was the principal source of the Japanese public's view of the Western world. In fact, *all* Western books in Japan came to be known as *Fukuzawa-bon.* (See the feature "World History in Today's World: Japanese Baseball.")

Fukuzawa was particularly proud of his part in using public opinion to pressure the Meiji oligarchs for a formal constitution that provided for a popularly elected legislature. After years of debate, in 1889 Japan became a constitutional empire, with a legislature elected by propertied male voters. But the new government was less liberal than many had hoped. The Japanese constitution was based on the German one, where the emperor himself rather than elected representatives controlled cabinet-level appointments and therefore the real levers of power. Like Germany under Bismarck, Meiji Japan had achieved unification and power through conservative nationalism rather than a broader liberalism based on individual rights. The slogan "for the sake of the country" encapsulated the idea that individuals were to sacrifice for the larger good. And like Germany, Japanese militarism combined with nationalism to make the country more aggressively imperialistic.

Japanese Imperialism, 1890–1910

The idea that Japanese national prestige required the acquisition of an empire was reinforced by global trends. The last two decades of the nineteenth century saw a spurt of imperial activity by the Europeans and the United States around the world. Doctrines of Social Darwinism became increasingly popular, portraying international relations as a "struggle for existence." Fukuzawa, who had earlier held more liberal and idealistic views, adopted this harder-edged attitude, saying: "There are only two ways in international relations: to destroy, or to be destroyed."[17] His opinion mattered, not only because of his books and his newspaper, but also because graduates of his own Keio Academy were now rising to power in the Meiji bureaucracy.

Japanese Baseball

The rules are the same: nine players to a side, nine innings to a game, three strikes and you're out. But when "America's national pastime" becomes Japanese *bēsubōru* many subtle changes result.

The Japanese attitude to the game can be summed up in two words: *wa,* "team harmony," and *doryoku,* "effort."* In Japan, the authority of the coaches and the decisions of the umpires are unquestioned, and players are expected to have a single-minded dedication reminiscent of the *bushido* code of the ancient samurai. Players prove themselves through endless repetitive drills that are meant to refine their skills and build team spirit. Wa and doryoku extend to the stands, where fans chant in unison under the guidance of cheerleaders, happily return foul balls to the ushers, and loyally purchase the products of the corporation that owns their favorite team.

Baseball came to Japan during the Meiji period and immediately became popular at elite high schools and universities, including Fukuzawa Yûkichi's Keio School. The transformation of an imported game into something truly Japanese was symbolic of Meiji Japan's drive to prove it could engage the modern world as an equal. The college game remains popular, but professional baseball, also called *yakyu* ("field-ball"), took off in the twentieth century, especially after a visit in 1934 by a group of American all-stars. A total of sixty-five thousand fans attended one game, and Babe Ruth told Japanese reporters, "There are no bad people among lovers of baseball."

American players who have gone to Japan have often had a hard time adjusting to the Japanese game. They are often seen as too individualistic, resisting the orders of their managers, arguing with umpires, and following their own training regimen rather than that of the team. Despite their talent, the Americans often upset their team's wa, the chemistry without which collective success is impossible, and show insufficient doryoku by refusing to participate in daylong practices and long team meetings. The Americans sometimes learn the hard way the old Japanese adage: "The nail that sticks up will be hammered down."

The greatest professional player in Japanese history was Sadaharu Oh, who hit 868 home runs between 1959 and 1980, surpassing the totals of Babe Ruth, Hank Aaron, and Barry Bonds. His batting coach was a martial arts instructor who emphasized the importance of Zen Buddhism in sharpening concentration. Oh stayed in the game as a manager, and in 2006 he led the Japanese national team to a stunning victory over Cuba to win the inaugural World Baseball Classic. Unlike the American "world series," it was a truly international event.

While in the past American players often went to Japan, often near the end of their careers, now it is more common for Japanese players to come to the United States. American fans are becoming accustomed to names like Matsui, Suzuki, Matsuzaka, and Fukudome, players who inspire large numbers of Japanese television viewers to watch American baseball.

---

*Robert Whiting, *You've Gotta Have Wa* (New York: Macmillan, 1987).

Japan flexed its imperial muscles first in Korea, the most tradition-bound kingdom in East Asia. As we have seen, both Japan and Qing China sent forces to the peninsula in response to an 1894 rebellion. Earlier tensions in Meiji society were swept away by the wave of national pride that followed from Japanese victory in the **Sino-Japanese War** (1894–1895). In addition to acquiring control over Korea and Taiwan, the Meiji government forced Qing China to grant it access to treaty ports and rights of extraterritoriality similar to those enjoyed by European powers. At the same time, Japan's own unequal treaties with Europe were renegotiated, this time on a basis of equality. Japan had become a player in the game of empire.

Japanese advisers forced Korea's imperial administration to promote a series of reforms that paralleled those of the early Meiji period. At first the Korean king

• Sino-Japanese War (1894–1895) A war caused by a rivalry over the Korean peninsula; ended with a one-sided treaty that favored Japan, which obtained treaty rights in China as well as control of Korea and Taiwan.

Peace Negotiations   This print by Kiyochika Kobayashi shows Japanese and Chinese negotiations at the end of the Sino-Japanese War. By terms of the Treaty of Shimonoseki (1895) the Qing Empire ceded the island of Taiwan to Japan, recognized Japanese rights over Korea, and agreed to make substantial reparations payments. The Qing and Meiji diplomats in this portrait are clearly differentiated by their clothing. (Musée des Asiatiques-Guimet, Paris, France/Réunion des Musées Nationaux/Art Resource, NY)

allied himself with the Japanese, sending his troops to aid in the suppression of a major peasant uprising. Then, in 1896, he sought protection from the Russians. For the next eight years Korean reformers allied themselves with Japan while the king and other conservatives promoted Russian interests on the peninsula. Meanwhile, Meiji rulers saw the presence of Russian troops in the Qing province of Manchuria as a direct threat to their own sphere of influence in northeastern Asia.

• **Russo-Japanese War** (1904–1905) War caused by territorial disputes in Manchuria and Korea. Japan's defeat of Russia was the first victory by an Asian military power over a European one in the industrial age.

The result of these tensions was the **Russo-Japanese War** of 1904–1905. Just as the Japanese navy had decimated the northern Qing fleet ten years earlier, now they scored a major naval victory over Russia. The Japanese navy, led by its impressive flagship the *Mikasa,* destroyed or disabled most of Russia's Pacific fleet. While the United States brokered peace negotiations, the Japanese government posted advisers to all the important Korean ministries. In 1910, after a Korean nationalist assassinated the Japanese prime minister, the Meiji government annexed Korea as a protectorate.

Japanese victory in the Russo-Japanese war had important consequences for world history. Russia was a traditional great power, and the tsar commanded the world's largest military. There was now no question that Japan must be counted among the great powers of the world. And there was also the question of race. The Russo-Japanese War was the first major defeat of a European power by an Asian one in the industrial era. Across East Asia, as well as in Africa, British India, and Southeast

Asia, nationalists looked to the Japanese victory for inspiration. European superiority was not inevitable after all.

As Japanese imperial ambitions grew in Asia and the Pacific in the last decade of the nineteenth century, the Germans, French, and English were also expanding their presence in the region, while the United States annexed Hawai'i and took over the Philippines. The world was becoming a smaller place, and the imperial aspirations of the great powers, now including Japan, would become a touchstone of conflict in the twentieth century.

● British India, 1818–1905

By the early nineteenth century the British had secured their position as the "new Mughals," the dominant political force on the Indian subcontinent. The effects were felt not only by South Asian political elites, who usually cooperated with the British or faced removal from power, but also by hundreds of millions of artisans and farmers whose livelihoods were deeply affected by the extension of industrial markets. Unlike the rulers of Qing China and Tokugawa Japan, who initially retained their authority as they struggled to adapt to industrial modernity, Indian elites were subject to more direct colonial control.

Even under foreign rule, however, South Asians carried on the same type of debate that could be heard in China and Japan, as well as in Russia and the Ottoman Empire: whether to adjust to the new circumstances by rejecting Western cultural models, by embracing them, or by finding a way to balance them with indigenous cultural traditions. A major rebellion in 1857 was inspired by the first of those choices, but after the British had suppressed the revolt and consolidated their rule even further, the option of holding on to the past was no longer viable. Indian nationalists then began developing new ideas and organizations in response to the problem of British rule and by the beginning of the twentieth century the foundations of modern Indian nationalism had been laid.

India Under Company Rule, 1800–1857

There was no exact date on which the British took control of India. The Battle of Plassey in 1757, which laid the riches of Bengal in the northeast open to the British East India Company, was certainly a turning point (see Chapter 20). The defeat of the Maratha confederacy in 1818 was important as well, adding to the empire the rich and populous territories in the hinterland of Bombay (today's Mumbai). The Sikhs of the Punjab in the northwest, with their strong allegiance to their religious leaders and deep military tradition, held out longer, succumbing to British military power only in 1849. By that time the British East India Company controlled virtually the entire subcontinent. By 1850 the British "Raj" in India was one of the great empires of world history.

Britain could not control so much territory and so many people without the active participation of powerful Indian allies. Much of the subcontinent was ruled through a "princely state" system whereby traditional rulers were kept in nominal charge with the guidance of British advisers. These princely rulers became part of the British East India Company's administrative machinery, helping them in such crucial areas as tax collection while maintaining an appearance of continuity with the past.

There was no mistaking the economic changes that came to India with British rule. Whereas early Mughal rulers had stimulated the South Asian commercial economy by promoting its connection with Indian Ocean markets, the British yoked the Indian economy to British interests. As a result, deindustrialization became a major problem (see Chapter 23). By 1830, unemployment among India's textile workers was reaching a critical level. India's initial experience of the Industrial Revolution under British rule was harsh, causing it "to fall backward in time . . . losing most of its artisan manufacturing abilities, forcing millions of unemployed craftsmen to return to the soil to scratch meager livelihoods directly from crowded land."[18] In India, the rural-to-urban migration of the European Industrial Revolution was reversed.

Technological and social changes were also responsible for important shifts in Anglo-Indian social and cultural interactions. In the eighteenth century, almost all the Europeans in India had been men. They often spoke Indian languages on a daily basis, wore Indian clothing, established relationships with Indian women, and played Mughal games like polo. But in the age of steamships and the telegraph, British officials were more likely to bring their families with them and to live in segregated communities. Speaking English and carefully following the rituals of Victorian social life, such as dressing formally for dinner no matter what the temperature, British rulers gradually grew more distant from the Indians among whom they lived.

Now it was more frequently Indians who tried to adjust to English language and culture. In the northeastern city of Calcutta, Britain's main commercial center, young Indians like **Rammohun Roy** (1772–1833) explored ways to assimilate European cultural influences into India's diversity. A native speaker of Bengali, Roy studied Sanskrit so he could read ancient Vedic texts in their original language, and he also wrote in Arabic, Persian, and English. A businessman as well as a scholar, Roy learned about liberal ideas from close contact with British traders and officials. He used those ideas to promote a reformed Hinduism that combined both

• **Rammohun Roy** (1772–1833) Bengali reformer and religious philosopher who opposed the caste system, polygamy, the prohibition of widow remarriage, the lack of education for common people, and discrimination against women.

Rammohun Roy Rammohun Roy was the leading thinker of the Bengal Renaissance, striving to reconcile liberal ideas from the West with Bengali, Persian, Mughal, and Hindu cultural and intellectual traditions. Himself a Hindu, Roy advocated reform of the caste system and restrictions on child marriage, while promoting the idea that Hinduism could be reformed from within by returning to the original principles of its ancient sacred texts.   (© Bristol City Museum and Art Gallery, U.K./The Bridgeman Art Library)

a return to the religion's most ancient philosophical principles and a series of reforms in the liberal spirit, such as an end to child marriage.

Roy became the leader of an intellectual movement called the Bengal Renaissance, an important influence on later Indians who absorbed Western culture and
thought into their own traditions. He was also politically active, lobbying the British government for changes to policies that favored English business interests at
the expense of Indian ones.

The efforts of men like Roy were encouraged by British liberals, who believed
that free trade and individual liberty were universally valid and could show India
the path to progress. In the 1830s one East India Company official declared that British education should create a "class of persons Indian in blood and color, but English in taste, in opinions, in morals, and in intellect." Though not limiting Indians
for their race, this highly ethnocentric attitude defined progress as the replacement
of Indian culture by British culture. Roy and most of his successors rejected that
approach, believing instead that they could use European ideas to reinvigorate
Indian traditions.

Although only a tiny number of Indians ever converted to Christianity, by the
mid-nineteenth century an increase in British missionaries traveling to India was
adding to a wider concern about the true intentions of the British. Many suspected
that the British had come not just to rule but also to overturn Indians' cultural traditions and convert them to a foreign religion. When combined with loss of support from some of India's traditional rulers and landed elites for the British presence
and the economic strains that were appearing in the vast countryside, the missionary presence created a volatile situation.

The Indian Revolt of 1857 and Its Aftermath

The **Indian Revolt of 1857** began with a mutiny
among the *sepoys* (SEE-poyz), the 200,000 Indian soldiers commanded by British officers. The sepoys were
essential to British rule, and their revolt sent shock waves across north India.

The immediate cause of the Indian Revolt was the introduction of a new type
of rifle that was far more accurate and faster-loading than previous guns. The British required soldiers to bite off the ends of the guns' ammunition cartridge casings,
which were greased. The rumor spread among Muslim troops that the cartridge had
been greased with pig fat; many Hindus believed that fat from cattle had been used.
Both groups suspected that the British were trying to pollute them, since contact
with pork was forbidden to Muslims and cattle were sacred to Hindus. The rebellious soldiers saw the new cartridges as part of a plot to convert them to Christianity. (See the feature "Movement of Ideas: Religion and Rebellion: India in 1858.")

Outraged that some sepoys had been imprisoned for refusing to use the greased
cartridges, a group of soldiers killed their British officers, marched to Delhi, and
rallied support for the restoration of the aging Mughal emperor. The revolt quickly
spread across northern and western India. The rani (queen) of Jhansi (jan-see), one
of the Maratha kingdoms, rallied her troops and rode into battle. Violence was terrible on both sides, the rebels sometimes killing English women and children, and
the British strapping rebels to cannon and blowing them to pieces. Even after order
was restored, the bitterness caused by such violence was an enduring tension underlying race relations in the British Raj.

Most British observers believed that the cause of the rebellion was simply the
backwardness of the Indian people. Prior to 1857, many had held the liberal belief

● **Indian Revolt of
1857** Revolt of Indian
soldiers against British
officers when they were
required to use greased
ammunition cartridges
they suspected were
being used to pollute
them and cause them to
convert to Christianity.
The revolt spread across
north India.

Religion and Rebellion: India in 1858

The following passage was written in the Urdu language in 1858 by an Indian Muslim, Maulvi Syed Kutb Shah Sahib. Maulvi Syed saw the rebellion as a chance to drive the British out of India. In this letter to Hindu leaders, he urged Hindu/Muslim cooperation to accomplish that goal, arguing that the British were consciously defiling both religions in an attempt to force conversions to Christianity.

One of the grievances Maulvi Syed mentions are British laws concerning widows. Islamic law encourages the remarriage of widows, following the example of Muhammad, whose wife Khadijah was a widow. Among Hindus, however, patriarchal beliefs dictated that a wife's life was essentially over once her husband died. The custom of *sati* encouraged widows to throw themselves on the fire when their husbands were cremated to demonstrate their devotion and to allow them to be reunited in the next life. In fact, relatively few Hindu women, usually from the highest castes,

actually did so. The Hindu reformer Rammohun Roy had argued that Hindus should give up the practice of sati, and in 1829 the British abolished it by law. They also issued another order that widows should be allowed to remarry.

Another controversy to which the author refers is the "doctrine of lapse," a colonial ruling that if an Indian prince died without a male heir, direct control over his territory would go to the British. In 1856 the city of Lucknow and the rich province of Oudh had been taken over by the British through this device. The author's references to food pollution may refer to the widespread suspicion that the British were forcing Indians under their control (such as sepoys and prisoners) into contact with forbidden animal fats.

Source: *Records of the Government of the Punjab and Its Dependencies,* New Series, No. VII (Lahore: Punjab Printing Company, 1870), pp. 173–175.

Maulvi Syed on British Christians

The English are people who overthrow all religions. You should understand well the object of destroying the religions of Hindustan [India]; they have for a long time been causing books to be written and circulated throughout the country by the hands of their priests, and, exercising their authority, have brought out numbers of preachers to spread their own tenets. . . .

Consider, then, what systematic contrivances they have adopted to destroy our religions. For instance, first, when a woman became a widow they ordered her to make a second marriage. Secondly, the self-immolation of wives [sati] on the funeral pyres of their deceased husbands was an ancient religious custom; the English . . . enacted their own regulations prohibiting it. Thirdly, they told people it was their wish that they . . . should adopt their faith, promising that if they did so they would be respected by Government; and further required them to attend churches, and hear the tenets preached there.

Moreover, they decided and told the rajahs that such only as were born of their wives would inherit the government and property, and that

adopted heirs would not be allowed to succeed, although, according to your [Hindu] Scriptures, ten different sorts of heirs are allowed to share in the inheritance. By this contrivance they will rob you of your governments and possessions, as they have already done with Nagpur and Lucknow.

Consider now another of their designing plans: they resolved on compelling prisoners, with the forcible exercise of their authority, to eat their bread. Numbers died of starvation, but did not eat it, others ate it, and sacrificed their faith. They now perceived that this expedient did not succeed well, and accordingly determined on having bones ground and mixed with flour and sugar, so that people might unsuspectingly eat them in this way. They had, moreover, bones and flesh broken small and mixed with rice, which they caused to be placed in the markets for sale, and tried, besides, every other possible plan to destroy our religions.

They accordingly now ordered the Brahmins and others of their army to bite cartridges, in the making of which fat had been used. The Muslim soldiers perceived that by this expedient the religion of the Brahmans and Hindus only was in danger, but nevertheless they also refused to bite them. On this the British resolved on ruining the faith of both, and [lashed to the cannons] all those soldiers who persisted in their refusal [and blew them to pieces]. Seeing this excessive tyranny, the soldiery now, in self-preservation, began killing the English, and slew them wherever they were found, and are now considering means for slaying the few still alive here and there. It is now my firm conviction that if these English continue in Hindustan they will kill everyone in the country, and will utterly overthrow our religions; but there are some of my countrymen who have joined the English, and are fighting on their side. . . .

Under these circumstances, I would ask, what course have you decided on to protect your lives and faith? Were your views and mine the same we might destroy them entirely with a very little trouble; and if we do so, we shall protect our religions and save the country. . . .

All you Hindus are hereby solemnly adjured, by your faith in Ganges; and all you Muslims, by your belief in God and the Koran, as these English are the common enemy of both, to unite in considering their slaughter extremely expedient, for by this alone will the lives and faith of both be saved. . . .

The slaughter of cows is regarded by the Hindus as a great insult to their religion. To prevent this a solemn compact and agreement has been entered into by all the Muslim chiefs of Hindustan, binding themselves, that if the Hindus will come forward to slay the English, the Muslims will from that very day put a stop to the slaughter of cows, and those of them who will not do so will be considered to have abjured the Koran, and such of them as will eat beef will be regarded as though they had eaten pork. . . .

The English are always deceitful. Once their ends are gained they will infringe their engagements, for deception has ever been habitual with them, and the treachery they have always practiced on the people of Hindustan is known to rich and poor. Do not therefore give heed to what they say. Be well assured you will never have such an opportunity again. We all know that writing a letter is an advance halfway towards fellowship. I trust you will all write letters approving of what has been proposed herein.

QUESTIONS FOR ANALYSIS

▶ **What reasons does Maulvi Syed give to justify the rebellion? Which of those reasons does he feel are most important?**

▶ **What actions does he think are necessary for the rebellion to succeed? Given what you know about Indian history, what might have prevented such actions from being taken?**

that Indians were perfectly capable of "becoming English" through education and assimilation. After 1857, racial stereotypes became much more powerful, with many in Britain believing that Indians (like Africans) were naturally and permanently inferior. Social Darwinism reinforced this emerging belief in race as the physical manifestation of not just cultural but also biological inferiority.

The Indian rebels knew what they were fighting against, but they were less clear about what they were fighting for. Loyalty to an aged and obscure Mughal emperor was not enough to build a broad sense of Indian unity. In South Asia the cultural, linguistic, and religious landscape was exceptionally diverse, making it all the more necessary to develop a sense of identity embracing all the peoples under British rule. Failure to do so, and the lack of coordination between different regional rebellions, made it easy for the British to retake control.

By 1858 the revolt was over, and the British government responded by disbanding the East India Company and abolishing the last vestiges of Mughal authority. In 1876, Queen Victoria added "Empress of India" to her titles. Direct control was extended over many of the princely states. Still, alliances were maintained with many traditional rulers, who were pampered financially even if they had no real political power. The British colonial administration was centralized and given enhanced fiscal responsibilities. At the top of that system stood the Indian Civil Service, elite government officials selected on the basis of a rigorous examination. In theory, anyone who passed the examination could join the Indian Civil Service. Since the exams were only administered in England, however, Indian candidates did not have a realistic chance.

While some British officials retained a liberal belief in equality before the law regardless of color, the general trend was toward a much harsher racial division in colonial society. When a British viceroy ruled that an Indian could testify against a British subject in court, he was widely attacked by the British community. The racial dynamics of postrebellion India made life difficult for Westernized Indians, who were frustrated that the British had turned to the remnants of the old aristocracy for allies and who found that many of the British mocked them for trying to assimilate into English culture. In 1885 they organized a new political movement called the Indian National Congress.

The Origins of Indian Nationalism, 1885–1906

Amidst all the political and social tensions of the British Raj, the Indian economy continued to grow. As in Europe, railroads played a major role (see Map 24.2). All the tracks and engines were imported from England, creating profits for English manufacturers and employment for English workers, while Indian taxpayers had to pay off the bonds that financed the building of the 50,000 miles (80,500 km) of rail constructed under British rule. But there were benefits as well. By the late nineteenth century the railroads, along with telegraphs and the post office (a letter could be sent anywhere across India for the cost of a single penny stamp), were also having strong social and political effects, creating a communications infrastructure that put India's diverse peoples and regions in closer contact with one another than ever before.

It was members of India's emerging middle class, often educated in India in the English language following a British school curriculum, who often had the clearest vision of "India" as a single political space that, under proper leadership, could come together and speak with one voice. In the beginning, however, the **Indian National Congress** was composed of relatively advantaged men who cared most

● **Indian National Congress** (1885) Formed by wealthy, Western-educated Indians to advance the cause of Indian involvement in their own governance. In the twentieth century, it would become the vehicle for India's independence under the leadership of Mohandas K. Gandhi.

🌐 **MAP 24.2**   CL Interactive Map

Indian Railroads, 1893   After provoking the Indian Revolt of 1857 by seizing the lands of an Indian ruler, the British learned to treat traditional rulers with greater respect. Some of the princely states were very extensive and their rulers, such as the Nizams of Hyderabad, quite wealthy. Even in the princely states, however, there was no question of British predominance. After 1857 the British built an extensive railroad and telegraph network to tighten their control, though improved transport and communications had the unintended consequence of helping bring Indians together from across the subcontinent, fueling the growth of Indian nationalism.

about the interests of their own social class. For example, it campaigned to have the examination for the elite Indian Civil Service (ICS) administered in India so that Indians would have a better opportunity to compete.

    Since they were in closer personal contact with whites than most Indians, the congress members were sensitive to the racism that permeated British India. Every British outpost in the empire had a "club" where British officials and merchants gathered to gossip, drink, play billiards and tennis, and talk of home. No matter how great the accomplishments of Indians, they were not allowed to set foot in this racially segregated center of power, except as servants.

Following in the tradition of Rammohun Roy, young congress members like **Gopal K. Gokhale** (1866–1915) took a moderate approach, trying to reconcile the British and Indian values they had absorbed through upbringing and education. They challenged their rulers to live up to the high ideal enunciated by Queen Victoria in 1858: "And it is our further will that, so far as may be, our subjects, of whatever race or creed, be freely and impartially admitted to offices in our service, the duties of which they may be qualified, by their education, ability and integrity." At the beginning, Gokhale (go-KAHL-ee) and the Indian National Congress were fighting not to change the system but to find a place within it. Like the mid-Victorians back in England, they believed that slow reform was better than revolutionary change. They did not seek independence, but self-rule for India within the British Empire. And self-rule could not be achieved, they acknowledged, until its people learned to respect one another more fully across lines of religion, caste, language, and gender.

Other Indian nationalists, such as **Bal Gangadhar Tilak** (1856–1920), took a more confrontational approach. They questioned why the British had any right to be in India at all. Tilak (tih-lak) declared: "*Swaraj* ("self-rule") is my birthright, and I must have it!"[19] Tilak's appeal was more emotional, and his plan much simpler than that of the congress: organize the masses to pressure the British, and they will leave. Tilak's radicalism was both a threat to the British and a challenge to the Indian National Congress. Because he used Hindu symbols to rally support, his movement also alarmed the country's large Muslim minority. While Indian nationalists accused the British of using "divide and rule" tactics, the British justified their rule by claiming that only they could be neutral among the subcontinent's diverse cultural and religious groups.

A major test of the British promise of "good government" came with the failure of the monsoon rains in 1896–1897. With its command of railroads and telegraphs, the British government could be expected to move food from regions with a surplus to those in need. Instead the government left matters up to the market. As grain prices climbed, merchants stockpiled food. Millions starved to death in the ensuing famine. One of the main arguments the British used to defend their right to rule, the supposed competency of their officials, was called into question.

The government meanwhile continued to use spectacular public rituals to display its power and legitimize its rule. The most impressive was the great pomp and circumstance of the "durbar" procession, a combination of circus, parade, and political theater held at Delhi in 1903. Organized to celebrate the coronation of the new English king, it featured *maharajahs* in ceremonial garb, hundreds of parading elephants, tens of thousands of marching soldiers, and elaborate salutes to India's new emperor.

But grand political theater was not enough to smooth over increasing tensions as British India entered the twentieth century. A flashpoint of conflict arose in 1905 when British bureaucrats, for no reason other than administrative expediency, decided to split the northeastern province of Bengal in two. No Indians were consulted about the **Partition of Bengal,** which created a predominantly Muslim province in the east. Nationalists again accused the British of using "divide and rule" tactics to reinforce their power by dividing Hindus from Muslims.

•Gopal K. Gokhale (1866–1915)   Indian political leader, social reformer, and advocate of Indian self-government to be achieved through negotiation.

•Bal Gangadhar Tilak (1856–1920) Indian nationalist who demanded immediate independence from Britain, mobilizing Hindu religious symbolism to develop a mass following and arguing that violence was an acceptable tactic for anticolonial partisans.

•Partition of Bengal (1905)   A British partition of the wealthy northeastern Indian province of Bengal for administrative expediency; became a touchpoint of anticolonial agitation. The Indian National Congress organized a boycott of British goods in protest.

Delhi Durbar of 1903   The British rulers of India used lavish political ceremonies to awe their subjects. Never was the pomp and circumstance greater than at the Durbar held in Delhi in 1903 to celebrate the coronation of King Edward VII as Emperor of India. Representing the absent king was his viceroy, Lord Curzon, who accepted the congratulations of the Indian princes seen here in procession before the Mughal-era Red Fort riding on magnificently outfitted elephants.   (© Christie's Images/Corbis)

In protest, the Indian National Congress organized a boycott of British goods. Bengali activists made huge bonfires of English cloth across the province, showing the connection between their economic and political grievances. Conditions were now ripe for the development of mass nationalism, bringing together the Western-educated elite of the congress and the millions of urban and rural Indians struggling toward a better future.

In 1906, the same year of the anti-Partition protests, the man who would be most responsible for forging that alliance between leaders and people returned to India. Mohandas K. Gandhi (1869–1948) was then a little-known lawyer coming home from South Africa, where he had led that country's Indian community in protests against racial discrimination. Gandhi (GAHN-dee) would come to symbolize a new India in the twentieth century.

Chapter Review

KEY TERMS

Fukuzawa Yûkichi (690)

Treaty of Nanjing (694)

Taiping Rebellion (695)

Self-Strengthening Movement (697)

Empress Ci Xi (697)

Boxer Rebellion (701)

Commodore Matthew Perry (703)

Meiji Restoration (704)

Sino-Japanese War (707)

Russo-Japanese War (708)

Rammohun Roy (710)

Indian Revolt of 1857 (711)

Indian National Congress (714)

Gopal K. Gokhale (716)

Bal Gangadhar Tilak (716)

Partition of Bengal (716)

Fukuzawa Yûkichi was just one voice in a global debate over appropriate responses to the disruptive influences of modern industrialism and Western imperialism. The decisiveness and success of the Meiji reformers stood in sharp contrast to the conservative response of the Manchu rulers of China, and while Japan became an imperial power China was carved up into spheres of influence. Nationalism, an ideology initially derived from Western historical experience, was now being used by Asians to critique the European-dominated global order of the industrial age. In Japan, national feeling was reinforced by military victory. In China, modern ideas of nationalism were central to the movement to overthrow imperial rule and create a modern state. In India nationalists struggled to create a unified nationalist movement in response to British rule. In the late-nineteenth-century world, it seemed that societies could be competitive only if they achieved a strong sense of national purpose.

What were the main forces that undermined the power of the Qing dynasty in the nineteenth century?

Corruption was one factor that undermined Qing power, but the real problem was the inability of Manchu and Chinese elites to find an adequate response to rising external pressure. The opium trade was the main focus of Chinese anger with the West, and in 1839 the industrial age burst in upon the Qing Empire with the British victory in the Opium War. Internal rebellions, especially the Taiping uprising, compounded the problem for Qing officials. Attempts at reform based on principles of "self-strengthening" were rejected by conservative opponents of change. The Qing Empire's lack of dynamic leadership culminated in imperial support for the Boxer rebels, with their virulent antiforeign ideology and lack of any vision on which a modern, industrial China could be built. China entered the twentieth century in an unprecedented position of weakness.

What made it possible for Japan to be transformed from a relatively isolated society to a major world power in less than half a century?

The challenges facing the Tokugawa shoguns were similar to those facing China, but the outcome was very different. Having witnessed the devastating effect of modern weapons in China, Tokugawa officials had no real choice but to open to the West after the arrival of Admiral Perry in 1853, even if doing so badly tarnished their domestic reputation. Japan entered a period of unrest as officials oscillated between the conservative desire to fend off the noxious foreigners and the reformist program embraced by Fukuzawa Yûkichi. Shortly after the shogun was removed and the emperor returned to power during the Meiji Restoration of 1868, it became clear that the new regime had embraced and even exceeded the reformers' agenda. The modernization of the Japanese economy and military was accomplished with astonishing rapidity. While at first there was some resistance, and even outright rebellion, from former samurai and peasants, military victories over China and Russia consolidated support for the Meiji regime. Japan entered the twentieth century as a major industrial power and a player in the game of imperialism in East Asia.

 WEB RESOURCES

Pronunciation Guide

Interactive Maps

MAP 24.1 Asia in 1910

MAP 24.2 Indian Railroads, 1893

Primary Sources

Chapter Objectives

ACE Multiple-Choice Quiz

Flashcards

 ## What were the principal ways that British-ruled Indians responded to imperialism?

Under Company rule, some Indian intellectuals, such as Rammohun Roy, sought to create an intellectual synthesis that would bridge British and Indian culture, much as Mughal culture had once been synthesized with north Indian elements. Anglo/Indian relations deteriorated, however, in the wake of the Indian Revolt of 1857. After suppressing the rebellion, the British began a more direct form of administration. South Asian resistance to British rule then moved in the direction of mass nationalism. Moderates like Gokhale argued that compromise and accommodation with the British was the best path for Indian self-rule, while radical nationalists like Tikal demanded immediate self-rule as a right. The protests that followed from the Partition of Bengal showed that popular discontent with British rule might be mobilized to support the nationalist agenda. In the early twentieth century the forces of mass nationalism were gathering as Mohandas K. Gandhi returned to lead the Indian National Congress in a four-decade struggle for independence.

For Further Reference

Cohn, Bernard S. *Colonialism and Its Forms of Knowledge: The British in India*. Princeton: Princeton University Press, 1996.

Fogel, Joshua A., ed. *Late Qing China and Meiji Japan: Political and Cultural Aspects*. Norwalk, Conn.: Eastbridge Press, 2004.

Fukazawa, Yûkichi. *The Autobiography of Yûkichi Fukazawa*. Translated by Eiichi Kiyooka. New York: Columbia University Press, 1960.

Hobsbawm, Eric. *The Age of Empire, 1875–1914*. New York: Vintage, 1989.

Hopper, Helen. *Fukazawa Yûkichi: From Samurai to Capitalist*. New York: Pearson Longman, 2005.

Jansen, Marius B. *The Making of Modern Japan*. Cambridge, Mass.: Harvard University Press, 2000.

Sievers, Sharon. *Flowers in Salt: The Beginnings of Feminist Consciousness in Modern Japan*. Stanford: Stanford University Press, 1987.

Spence, Jonathan. *God's Chinese Son: The Taiping Heavenly Kingdom of Hong Xiuquan*. New York: W.W. Norton, 1997.

Wiley, Peter Booth. *Yankees in the Land of the Gods: Commodore Perry and the Opening of Japan*. New York: Penguin, 1991.

Wolpert, Stanley. *A New History of India*. 7th ed. New York: Oxford University Press, 2003.

Websites

Japan Links: (http://web-japan.org/links/culture/museums/culture.html).   A comprehensive set of links to English-language information on museums and archives in Japan, including the Japanese Baseball Hall of Fame and Museum (http://english.baseball-museum.or.jp/index.html).

The Late Imperial Era in Chinese History (http://newton.uor.edu/Departments&Programs/AsianStudiesDept/china-late.html) and (http://newton.uor.edu/Departments&Programs/AsianStudiesDept/china-mod.html).   Links from the East and Southeast Asia Annotated Directory of Internet Resources.

SARAI: South Asian Resource Access on the Internet (http://www.columbia.edu/cu/lweb/indiv/southasia/cuvl/).   Maintained at Columbia University, with extensive links to contemporary and historical information on India and the South Asian region.

CHAPTER
25

State Building and Social Change in the Americas, 1830–1895

- **Political Consolidation in Canada and the United States** (p. 723)
- **Reform and Reaction in Latin America** (p. 733)
- **Connections and Comparisons in the Nineteenth-Century Americas** (p. 740)

Pauline Johnson-Tekahionwake (1861–1913) watched nervously as several older male poets recited their verse. It was the winter of 1892, and the hall in Toronto was packed for an "Evening with Canadian Authors." Her ambition was to be a well-known, financially independent poet, and here was her chance to make an impression. She chose to recite "A Cry from an Indian Wife," a poem that focused on her concern with Canada's First Nations, its indigenous inhabitants:

They but forget we Indians owned the land
From ocean unto ocean; that they stand
Upon a soil that centuries agone
Was our sole kingdom and our right alone.
They never think how they would feel today,
If some great nation came from far away,
Wresting their country from their hapless braves,
Giving what they gave us—but war and graves . . .
Go forth, nor bend to greed of white man's hands,
By right, by birth we Indians own these lands,
Though starved, crushed, plundered, lies our nation low . . .
Perhaps the white man's God has willed it so.[1]

PAULINE JOHNSON-
TEKAHIONWAKE

CL This icon will direct you to interactive activities and study materials on the *Voyages* website: www.cengage.com/history/hansen/voyages1e

The Travels of Pauline Johnson-Tekahionwake

← Pauline Johnson's journeys by ship
— Canadian transcontinental railroad
— Other Canadian railroad
— Cariboo Road

○ Johnson's permanent residences
● City visited by Johnson
KANSAS U.S. state visited by Johnson
▢ U.S. state visited by Johnson during 1907 Chautauqua tour

Performs in Cariboo Road, 1893.

Pauline Johnson-Tekahionwake performs in more than 75 cities in Canada and the U.S., 1891–1906.

Johnson's first trip to London, 1894

YUKON TERRITORY 1898

Great Slave Lake

BRITISH COLUMBIA 1871

NORTHWEST TERRITORIES
Hudson Bay

Labrador Sea

NEWFOUNDLAND (Gr. Br.)

to St. John's / London

Barkerville
Edmonton
ALBERTA 1905
SASKATCHEWAN 1905
Peace R.
Athabasca R.
Lake Athabasca
Churchill R.
Nelson R.
Saskatchewan R.
Lake Winnipeg

Ashcroft
Vancouver
Kamloops
Nakusp
Victoria
Chilliwack
ROCKY MOUNTAINS
Banff
Calgary
Medicine Hat
Lethbridge
Pincher Creek
Regina
Brandon
Boissevain
Saskatoon
Yorkton
MANITOBA 1870
Portage la Prairie
Winnipeg

QUÉBEC 1867

PRINCE EDWARD ISLAND 1873
Charlottetown

to London

St. Lawrence R.
Moncton
Québec
Fredericton
Saint John
Halifax
NOVA SCOTIA 1867
NEW BRUNSWICK

to Liverpool & London

WASHINGTON
OREGON
IDAHO
MONTANA
WYOMING
NORTH DAKOTA
SOUTH DAKOTA
NEBRASKA
NEVADA
UTAH
CALIFORNIA
COLORADO
KANSAS
MISSOURI
IOWA
WISC.
MINNESOTA
Port Arthur (Thunder Bay)
Albany R.
Lake Winnipeg

CANADA
ONTARIO 1867

Montréal

Sudbury
Sault Ste. Marie
Lake Superior
Lake Huron
MICH.
Toronto
Chiefswood/ Brantford
Hamilton
Detroit
Lake Michigan
Lake Ontario
Lake Erie
Ottawa
Orillia
VT.
N.H.
Boston
MASS.
R.I.
CONN.
NEW YORK
New York City
PENNSYLVANIA
NEW JERSEY
DEL.
MD.
W. VA.
VIRGINIA
OHIO
IND.
ILL.
KENTUCKY
TENNESSEE
NORTH CAROLINA

UNITED STATES

ATLANTIC OCEAN

N

0   200   400 Km.
0   200   400 Mi.

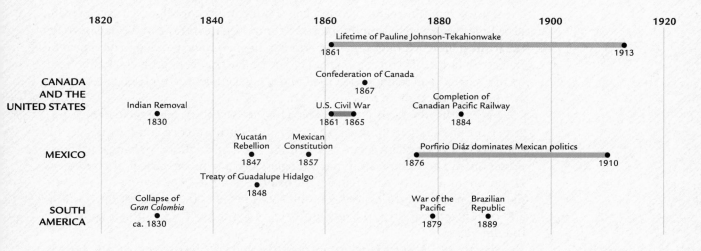

	1820	1840	1860	1880	1900	1920

Lifetime of Pauline Johnson-Tekahionwake
1861 — 1913

CANADA AND THE UNITED STATES

Indian Removal
1830

Confederation of Canada
1867

U.S. Civil War
1861 1865

Completion of Canadian Pacific Railway
1884

MEXICO

Yucatán Rebellion
1847

Mexican Constitution
1857

Treaty of Guadalupe Hidalgo
1848

Porfirio Díaz dominates Mexican politics
1876 — 1910

SOUTH AMERICA

Collapse of *Gran Colombia*
ca. 1830

War of the Pacific
1879

Brazilian Republic
1889

• **Pauline Johnson-Tekahionwake** (1861–1913) Canadian poet of mixed British and Mohawk ancestry.

Patriotic Canadians might have heard these as dissonant words; nevertheless; they gave Johnson's powerful performance loud applause.

"A Cry from an Indian Wife" reflected Johnson's own mixed ancestry. Her father's family was Mohawk, an Iroquois (ir-UH-kwoi) band that had established a close alliance with the British during the colonial period. As a child Pauline would listen to Mohawk legends and tales of a family history that included Joseph Brant, the Mohawk leader who had fought with the British in the American War of Independence (see Chapter 22). The British family connection was deepened when Pauline's father married an Englishwoman. Their wedding photograph shows optimism toward this cultural mixture: the groom wears both British medals and an Iroquois wampum belt, while the English bride's stiff Victorian attire is offset by the ceremonial tomahawk she holds in her lap.

Her father balanced two worlds, serving as both a Canadian government employee and a respected member of the Six Nations Band Council. Her mother instilled strict Victorian values in her children on the Six Nations Reserve in Ontario. Johnson-Tekahionwake (da-geh-eeon-wa-geh) would have a lifelong challenge trying to balance her Mohawk with her English ancestry. Though she grew up on the Iroquois reserve, she spoke only English, and though fascinated by Mohawk tales, she was most influenced by British literature. She was a loyal and patriotic Canadian, yet she spoke out against her country's policies toward indigenous First Nations societies.

As an adult, Pauline Johnson began to use her father's Mohawk family name Tekahionwake ("double life") in advertisements for a new career: traveling across Canada performing her poetry. Before radio and movies, there was a big audience for traveling artists, and Pauline Johnson-Tekahionwake became one of the nation's best-known entertainers. Her performances drew attention to her dual heritage. She appeared on stage in a dramatic buckskin outfit to perform poems such as "A Cry from an Indian Wife," after intermission reappearing in a Victorian evening gown to recite poems of nature and love. Having found a way to earn a living through her art—a challenge for a woman of her time—Johnson-Tekahionwake crossed Canada nineteen times, often performing in the United States as well, before retiring to Vancouver on the Pacific coast, where she collected native stories.

But the late nineteenth century was a difficult time for a mixed-race person. Racial divisions were becoming more and more sharply drawn in Canada, where the white majority thought that Amerindian peoples were doomed to disappear in the face of industrial and commercial progress. The engine of progress, symbolized by the very railroad that Johnson used to reach her audience, threatened to overrun anyone who stood in its way.

Indeed, the nineteenth century was a time of relentless change across the Western Hemisphere. In 1830, much of North and South America still lay outside the control of European-derived governments. By 1895, revolutionary changes in transportation and communication technologies, along with the arrival of many new European immigrants, had changed the balance of power. The frontiers of modern nations expanded at the expense of indigenous peoples. Industrialization, mining, and commercial forestry and agriculture became the keys to wealth and power in the Americas.

Perhaps the most striking feature of this period was the rise of the United States as both the dominant hemispheric power and a global force. Canada was also a growing economic power, where many shared in rising prosperity. In Latin America, by contrast, only the privileged elites enjoyed the benefits of state building.

Telegraphs, steamships and railroads, massive new cities, and enormous industrial fortunes posed challenges to many older ways of life. Social readjustments in the nineteenth-century Americas included the abolition of slavery, the arrival of new immigrants, changing gender relations, and, as Johnson-Tekahionwake's story indicates, difficult times for indigenous peoples.

Focus Questions

What challenges did Canada and the United States need to overcome in establishing themselves as transcontinental powers?

What factors help explain conditions of inequality in nineteenth-century Latin America?

Across the Americas, did nineteenth-century developments represent progress for indigenous peoples, ethnic and racial minorities, and women?

Political Consolidation in Canada and the United States

Consolidation of state power was a major feature of the nineteenth century in North America. Canada overcame deep regional divisions to become a nation, while the United States emerged from the Civil War with a more powerful and ambitious federal government than ever before. In both cases, governments extended their authority more deeply into society and more broadly across expanded territories as increased immigration from Europe brought the Great Plains and the Pacific coast under the control of Ottawa and Washington.

Confederation in Canada   Unlike other American nations, Canada was the product of slow evolution rather than revolutionary transformation. In 1830 British North America consisted of a scattering of separate colonies. Yet by 1892, when Pauline Johnson-Tekahionwake made her debut on a Toronto stage, many Canadians were developing a national identity even while affiliating themselves with the British Empire. Like many, Johnson-Tekahionwake was proud of being both Canadian and British: "And we, the men of Canada, can face the world and brag / That we were born in Canada beneath the British flag."

In 1830, British North America consisted of more than half a dozen disconnected colonies representing a great diversity of peoples and landscapes. Upper

Canada, with its capital at Toronto on the northern shore of Lake Ontario, was the fastest-growing region, where cheap land attracted English, Irish, and Scottish immigrants. Lower Canada, the lands along the St. Lawrence River now known as Québec, retained its French-speaking Catholic majority, the *Québecois* (kay-bek-kwah). The Atlantic colonies were primarily populated by seafaring people dependent on the bounty of the Atlantic Ocean. And at the opposite end of what would become Canada was British Columbia, its Pacific capital of Victoria more accessible to San Francisco than to Toronto. Far from the main population centers lay trading posts and settlements that had arisen during the fur-trading days (see Chapter 18). Stretching beyond formal British political control, these trade frontiers brought commercial opportunity but also guns, alcohol, and violence to indigenous communities.

Several First Nations, such as the Cree, Ojibwa (oh-jib-wuh), Sioux (soo), and Squamish (skwaw-mish), remained independent in the early nineteenth century. Mingled among them were communities of French-speaking *métis* (may-TEE), frontiersmen of mixed European/Amerindian descent. They could be found on the Great Plains, which were still lightly populated by buffalo hunters and fur trappers. Even farther from the main areas of European settlement and British control were the Inuit hunters of the far north.

Having learned a lesson from the American War of Independence, the British government no longer refused to offer Britons who emigrated to British North America (or to Australia, New Zealand, or South Africa) rights to political representation. Instead they were allowed limited participation in government while a governor appointed from London would watch out for British imperial interests. By 1830, however, this attempted compromise had not achieved stability. British North Americans increasingly called for **responsible government,** an elected government

> **•responsible government**
> Nineteenth-century constitutional arrangement in North America that allowed colonies to achieve dominion status within the British Empire and elect parliaments responsible for internal affairs. The British appointed governors as their sovereign's representative and retained control of foreign policy.

🔲 **A Métis Man and His Wives** The métis of the Canadian frontier were culturally and biologically mixed descendants of French traders and First Nations women. Protective of their independence, many métis resisted incorporation into the Canadian confederation, often in alliance with First Nations communities. These rebellions were defeated by Canadian forces in 1869 and 1885. (Library and Archive of Canada, acc. 1973-84-1)

in which the leader of the majority party would become prime minister, as in the Westminster Parliament in Britain. Lack of British action led to a series of uprisings in 1837, but they were easily suppressed for lack of mass support. No George Washington or Simón Bolívar emerged to lead Canada to independence, and most British North Americans, English as well as French speaking, seemed to think that progress could and should be achieved gradually through negotiations.

During the 1840s, as the climate for reform was increasing in Britain, an official report recommended responsible government for Canada. New British tariff policies lowered or eliminated duties on many North American goods reaching British markets, such as timber, fish, and grain. British North America had been in a protected imperial market, its economic security coming at the expense of economic growth. The removal of the old restrictions led to a boom in trade, especially with the United States, and undermined the mercantilist logic of direct imperial control.

In this atmosphere of reform, even most French Canadians looked favorably on continued association with the British Empire. As far back as 1763 the British Parliament had guaranteed equal rights for French-speaking Catholics. Though the influx of British settlers had alarmed the Québecois, most political leaders trusted that British constitutional models would protect their linguistic, religious, and cultural traditions. Likewise, many First Nations peoples in east and west Canada favored continuing association with the British Empire. For the Johnson family, whose ancestors had fought with the British against American rebels in the 1770s and against the United States in 1812, the beneficence of Britain and of Queen Victoria was unquestioned.

By the 1860s the British Parliament had granted responsible government to most British North American colonies. A bigger challenge was to bring them under a single constitution. Each colony wanted to retain control over its own internal affairs and saw little incentive to give up local power to a central government. Common anxiety about relations with the United States, however, soon moved the various colonial leaders toward compromise. Though abolitionist sentiment was strong in Canada, many felt sympathetic to the cause of the southern states during the American Civil War. As a result the U.S. government distrusted the British colonies to the north. Border tensions ran high after Confederate guerillas raided Vermont from Québec in 1864.

In 1867 the British Parliament passed the British North America Act, creating the **Confederation of Canada** with a federal capital at Ottawa. Though only four of the current Canadian provinces were included in the original confederation, the legal framework for its further evolution was in place. Canada was now a "dominion" within the British Empire. All local affairs, including economic and taxation policy, were in the hands of the Canadian and provincial governments. However, Queen Victoria appointed a governor-general to represent the Crown, and Britain continued to control Canada's foreign relations.

The dominant political figure in the confederation and its first prime minister was the Scottish-born leader of the Conservative Party, **Sir John A. MacDonald** (1815–1891). MacDonald led Canada for most of its first twenty-five years, ably compromising with both Britain and with the provinces while building an effective central government in Ottawa. He was fortunate to be able to do so during a time of rapid economic growth.

The building of the Canadian Pacific Railway (1869–1884), one of Prime Minister MacDonald's first priorities, was of central importance to both political consolidation and economic growth, facilitating the incorporation of Manitoba and the

•**Confederation of Canada** (1867) Confederation of former British colonies united under a single federal constitution. Recognized under the British North America Act, the confederation was a dominion within the British Empire.

•**Sir John A. MacDonald** (1815–1891) Dominant political figure of the Confederation of Canada whose Conservative Party dominated Canadian politics from 1867 until his death. A stable constitutional order and the Canadian Pacific Railway were two of his most important legacies.

Northwestern Territories into the Canadian confederation. British Columbia, which entered the confederation in 1871, was effectively tied to the rest of Canada only with the completion of this railway.

Canada's Great Plains were utterly transformed. Before the Industrial Revolution, only buffalo (later, horses and cattle) could convert the tough grasses of the plains into nutrients for human populations. Now, with the advent of cheap steel plows, grain production boomed. Canadian wheat exports rose from 10 million bushels in 1896 to 145 million bushels in 1914. Over a million farmers and their families took advantage of free land and the cheap agricultural implements churned out by the new industrial plants to move out onto the prairie. They were the audience for Pauline Johnson-Tekahionwake as she took her act to the town halls and opera houses springing up in the farming centers and mining camps of Canada. Two new western provinces, Alberta and Saskatchewan (sa-SKACH-uh-won), entered the confederation in 1905.

Economic growth was overseen and nurtured by a stable and effective federal government. The dominance of the Conservatives ended after MacDonald's death in 1891, but stability and continuity continued to mark Canadian politics when, starting in 1896, the Liberal Party won four consecutive elections based on a strong centrist base. The Liberals emphasized "race fusion," meaning the acceptance of Canada as a permanently and proudly bicultural land where English and French, Catholic and Protestant could live in peace and jointly forge a unique Canadian identity based on tolerance. Canadians did not always live up to that ideal; as we will later see, Amerindians and non-European immigrants were subject to brutal racism in these years. Still, at least for racially and economically dominant Canadians, a unique nationalism that acknowledged and celebrated Canada's continuing affiliation with the British Empire was taking shape.

Sectionalism and Civil War in the United States

Unlike Canada, the United States entered the nineteenth century with a strong constitution and a lively sense of national identity. (See the feature "Movement of Ideas: Alexis de Tocqueville's *Democracy in America*.") The Louisiana Purchase combined with the Lewis and Clark Expedition to the Pacific gave the young country a sense of unbounded opportunity (see Chapter 21). The way was open as never before for the westward expansion of the United States (see Map 25.1). But westward expansion also helped provoke a great crisis. As new states entered the Union, would they be slave or free? Could the balance between North and South be maintained in the scramble for new territory?

In 1820 Congress adopted the Missouri Compromise, which established the rules for admission of new western states. Tensions then resurfaced during the presidency of **Andrew Jackson** (r. 1829–1837). Unlike previous American presidents from elite New England or Virginia families, Jackson presented himself as representing the common man. He held a wild inaugural ball to which one and all were invited and at which a riot nearly broke out in the White House. As he campaigned for president, Jackson's supporters emphasized his humble southern origins and his military leadership in defeating a British invasion at New Orleans in 1814.

As president, Jackson supervised the enforcement of the forced migration of Amerindians stipulated by the **Indian Removal Act** passed by Congress in 1830. Ironically, before the act some Cherokee leaders, often of mixed European/ Amerindian background, tried to strengthen their society and preserve its sovereignty by giving it a constitution that melded traditional Cherokee ways with the

CL Primary Source: A New Model: Democracy in America *Read de Tocqueville's statement that in a democratic nation, although citizens can attain equality of conditions, they will never be content with their equality.*

● **Andrew Jackson** (r. 1829–1837) The seventh president of the United States after first serving in the military as general and in Congress as senator. An aggressive advocate of westward expansion, Jackson was responsible for implementing the Indian Removal Act.

● **Indian Removal Act** 1830 legislation leading to the dispossession of Amerindian peoples in the southeastern United States in order to promote gold mining and cotton growing. Thousands of Cherokee were killed when forcibly marched to Oklahoma along the "trail of tears."

American political model. But U.S. policies, driven by the discovery of gold in Georgia and the search for land on which to grow cotton, ended those experiments. A forced march to distant lands in Oklahoma killed over four thousand Cherokee on what their descendants call the *Nunna daul Tsuny,* the "Trail Where They Cried."

The Industrial Revolution provided both the means and the motive for the extension of the American national economy to the West. Steamships on rivers such as the Ohio and Mississippi lowered the cost of transport and connected the natural abundance of surrounding territories to national and global markets. The completion of the Transcontinental Railway in 1869 and the simultaneous extension

⊕ MAP 25.1

U.S. Expansion, 1783–1867   The United States expanded dramatically during the decades after independence. Vast territories were purchased from France (the Louisiana Purchase) and Russia (Alaska), acquired by treaty with Great Britain (the Pacific Northwest) and Spain (Florida), and annexed from Mexico after its defeat in the Mexican-American War. Contemporary observers regarded the growth of the United States into a transcontinental power as such an inevitability they called the process one of "manifest destiny."

[CL] Interactive Map

Alexis de Tocqueville's *Democracy in America*

The French historian Alexis de Tocqueville first traveled to the United States in 1831 at the age of 26, and at age 30 he published the original French version of *Democracy in America*. Later, as a deputy in the French National Assembly, he was a political moderate and opposed both the Socialists and Louis Napoleon (see Chapter 23). Based on extensive travels and personal observations, *Democracy in America* is still regarded as one of the most insightful analyses of the "American character" ever written.

Source: http://xroads.virginia.edu/~HYPER/DETOC/toc_indx.html.

Author's Introduction

Among the novel objects that attracted my attention during my stay in the United States, nothing struck me more forcibly than the general equality of condition among the people. . . . The more I advanced in the study of American society, the more I perceived that this equality of condition is the fundamental fact from which all others seem to be derived and the central point at which all my observations constantly terminated.

On Patriotism

As the American participates in all that is done in his country, he thinks himself obliged to defend whatever may be censured in it; for it is not only his country that is then attacked, it is himself. . . . Nothing is more embarrassing in the ordinary intercourse of life than this irritable patriotism of the Americans. A stranger may be well inclined to praise many of the institutions of their country, but he begs permission to blame some things in it, a permission that is inexorably refused.

Geography and Democracy

The chief circumstance which has favored the establishment and the maintenance of a democratic republic in the United States is the nature of the territory that the Americans inhabit. Their ancestors gave them the love of equality and of freedom; but God himself gave them the means of remaining equal and free, by placing them upon a boundless continent. General prosperity is favorable to the stability of all governments, but more particularly of a democratic one, which depends upon the will of the majority, and especially upon the will of that portion of the community which is most exposed to want. . . . In the United States not only is legislation democratic, but Nature herself favors the cause of the people.

In what part of human history can be found anything similar to what is passing before our eyes in North America? The celebrated communities of antiquity were all founded in the midst of hostile nations, which they were obliged to subjugate before they could flourish in their place. Even the moderns have found, in some parts of South America, vast regions inhabited by a people of inferior civilization, who nevertheless had already occupied and cultivated the soil. To found their new states it was necessary to extirpate or subdue a numerous population. . . . But North America was inhabited only by wandering tribes, who had no thought of profiting by the natural riches of the soil; that vast country was still, properly speaking, an empty continent, a desert land awaiting its inhabitants. . . .

Three or four thousand soldiers drive before them the wandering races of the aborigines; these are followed by the pioneers, who pierce the woods, scare off the beasts of prey, explore the courses of the inland streams, and make ready the triumphal march of civilization across the desert. . . . Millions of men are marching at once towards the same horizon; their language, their religion, their manners differ; their object is the same. Fortune has been promised to them somewhere in the West, and to the West they go to find it. . . .

Religion and Democracy

The Americans combine the notions of Christianity and of liberty so intimately in their minds that it is impossible to make them conceive the one without the other. . . .

In France I had almost always seen the spirit of religion and the spirit of freedom marching in opposite directions. . . . [American Catholics] attributed the peaceful dominion of religion in their country mainly to the separation of church and state. I do not hesitate to affirm that during my stay in America I did not meet a single individual, of the clergy or the laity, who was not of the same opinion on this point. . . .

Associations and Civil Society

In no country in the world has the principle of association been more successfully used or applied to a greater multitude of objects than in America. . . . The citizen of the United States is taught from infancy to rely upon his own exertions in order to resist the evils and the difficulties of life; he looks upon the social authority with an eye of mistrust and anxiety, and he claims its assistance only when he is unable to do without it. . . . If some public pleasure is concerned, an association is formed to give more splendor and regularity to the entertainment. Societies are formed to resist evils that are exclusively of a moral nature. . . . In the United States associations are established to promote the public safety, commerce, industry, morality, and religion. There is no end which the human will despairs of attaining through the combined power of individuals united into a society.

Tyranny of the Majority

I know of no country in which there is so little independence of mind and real freedom of discussion as in America. In any constitutional state in Europe every sort of religious and political theory may be freely preached and disseminated. . . . In America the majority raises formidable barriers around the liberty of opinion; within these barriers an author may write what he pleases, but woe to him if he goes beyond them.

QUESTIONS FOR ANALYSIS

▶ What does de Tocqueville see as the most essential features of American civilization, and what does he identify as its strengths and weaknesses?

▶ Are the Frenchman's observations still relevant to an understanding of the United States today?

of telegraph lines between merchants in distant cities further aided that process. Even ignoring the price paid by Amerindians for American political and economic growth (as did most American settlers), there was one big problem: western expansion increased conflicts between northern and southern states. Huge territories were added to the United States after 1848: Texas, California, the Great Plains, the desert Southwest, and the Rocky Mountains (see below). Would those vast spaces be settled by free white homesteaders or by plantation owners and black slaves?

The Democratic Party, which had become identified with southern planter interests, declared that the issue should be decided by "popular sovereignty," meaning by the voters within the new states. **Abraham Lincoln** (1809–1865), a leader of the new Republican Party founded by antislavery activists in 1854, disagreed. To put the issue in the hands of territorial voters, Lincoln declared, would be little more than "the liberty of making a slave of other people." More than most northern politicians, Lincoln stressed the moral dimension of the question. He was opposed to the westward spread of slavery "because of the monstrous injustice of slavery itself."[2] Other Republicans opposed the westward spread of slavery not because it was wrong but because they thought that slavery was incompatible with the spread of the free, independent farmers they saw as the bedrock of society.

Lincoln was a uniquely American figure who can also be understood in a global context, inspired as he was by the liberal nationalists who had led the revolutionary movements of 1848 in Europe. European development influenced Lincoln's idea that the United States needed a national consciousness to rise above local interests. Like his contemporary Alexander Herzen, Lincoln held a strong and romanticized vision of nationalism, but unlike Herzen and other European reformers, he defended free markets and rejected socialism (see Chapter 23). The Republicans believed firmly in the autonomous individual as the bedrock of social order, civil society, and economic growth.

For many white southerners, Lincoln and the Republican Party were a threat to essential freedoms long protected by the more intimate sovereignty of the states. To southern spokesmen, the Republicans represented a hard-edged industrialism that contrasted with a more gracious southern way of life based on older virtues like valor and honor rather than simple cold, commercial calculation. After all, some argued, a sick or elderly slave would be cared for by his or her master, while an industrial worker injured on the job would be thrown into the street to starve.

After Lincoln's election in 1860, there was virtually no chance that these divisions could be bridged: "A house divided against itself," he said, "cannot stand." Eleven southern states declared their independence as the Confederate States of America, plunging the country into a horrific civil war (1861–1865). Some people, thinking the war would soon be over, brought picnics to witness the first battles. They did not account for the technological changes that made modern warfare more deadly. More precise weapons and more powerful explosives, combined with tactics that threw masses of uniformed soldiers in waves upon each other, led to suffering on an unimagined scale. Over 600,000 people died, the most in any American armed conflict.

The fight between Union and Confederate forces was an unequal one in terms of resources. The North had a clear superiority in industrial infrastructure: railroads for moving men and materiel, iron foundries to produce guns and munitions, and textile factories to produce uniforms. The Confederates had several less tangible advantages: superior military leadership and soldiers who believed deeply in their cause and who were usually fighting to defend their home territories. However, the

• Abraham Lincoln (1809–1865) Sixteenth president of the United States and the country's first Republican president. His election on an antislavery platform led eleven states to secede from the Union, plunging the country into the Civil War.

South's export-oriented agricultural economy left it vulnerable to a Union naval blockade. Since the Confederate States were highly dependent on British markets for tobacco and cotton and British factories for arms and ammunition, it is remarkable that they stayed in the fight as long as they did. Still, unable to match the productivity of northern farms and factories, by 1865 southern resistance to Union forces had been overcome.

In 1863 Lincoln had issued the Emancipation Proclamation, making the abolition of slavery rather than the mere preservation of the Union a goal of the war. After the Union victory in 1865, the federal government was in a position to finally settle the question that had been left unresolved at the Constitutional Convention: how could the principle of liberty be reconciled with the reality of slavery? How should the northern victors treat their vanquished foes? The assassination of Abraham Lincoln in 1865 meant that the most able American politician would not be able to help resolve such issues.

The federal troops that occupied the South were mandated to ensure that federal law was observed as part of a process known as **Reconstruction.** Most white southerners strongly resented this military occupation and the pronouncements of radical Republican leaders that the old social and economic systems of the South would be crushed and its states remade in a northern image. In spite of new constitutional amendments intended to protect the civil and voting rights of freed slaves, southern politicians in the Democratic Party looked for an opportunity to end Reconstruction and restore a race-based system of governance.

The election of 1876 was a major turning point. The Democratic candidate narrowly won the majority of the popular vote, but the results in several states were disputed. An electoral commission was appointed that gave all the disputed votes to the Republican candidate, Rutherford B. Hayes. Southern Democrats were convinced to accept this outcome (of an election "without a free ballot and a fair count," as many said) when Hayes agreed to favor "states' rights," to withdraw federal troops from the former Confederacy, and to put an end to Reconstruction.

For some the end of Reconstruction was a positive development, since the Civil War had greatly magnified the power of the federal government, potentially violating the balance between state and federal authority intended by the Constitution. But for southern blacks, "states' rights" was a disaster. Violence against blacks increased dramatically with the rise of vigilante groups such as the Ku Klux Klan, and southern state legislatures enacted the harsh segregationist policies that came to be known as Jim Crow. Like Russian serfs, who were emancipated at about the same time (see Chapter 23), freed American slaves discovered that their freedom was far from complete.

CL **Primary Source:**
Four Score and Seven Years Ago . . .
Read an excerpt from Lincoln's Gettysburg Address.

• **Reconstruction**
(1865–1877)   Period immediately after the American Civil War during which the federal government took control of the former Confederate States and oversaw enforcement of constitutional provisions guaranteeing civil rights for freed slaves.

The Gilded Age

The Union victory prepared the United States for a great spurt of population growth and economic productivity. As in Canada, the opening of the Great Plains to European settlement and agriculture brought huge economic dividends. As the price of steel fell, even farmers of modest means could afford to cut the prairie soils as the spread of railroads and steamships lowered transport costs and made commercial agriculture possible in more regions. Increases in agricultural productivity led to falling grain prices in the cities, where industrial employment surged.

In the last two decades of the nineteenth century, the United States took a leadership position in the Second Industrial Revolution, when electricity and steel supplemented steam and iron and when huge steel firms and railroad corporations exceeded any level of economic organization the world had previously seen. This period of exhilarating growth is often called the **Gilded Age.** A gilded object is covered with gold on the outside, concealing base metal within. Looking beyond the fortunes of the most privileged in the Gilded Age revealed a host of continuing problems: grinding rural poverty for freed slaves as well as most whites across the South; an urban working class crammed into dirty and unsafe tenements in the industrial North; and political favors for sale to the highest bidder. Exuberant growth created deep inequalities: by 1890 less than 1 percent of the U.S. population controlled 90 percent of the nation's wealth.

In reaction to the excesses of the Gilded Age, small farmers in the Midwest and Plains states organized a movement to protest corporate interests, which they claimed used political influence to inflate their charges for storing and shipping grain. At the same time, industrial workers began to form unions to fight for better pay and working conditions. Some Americans even began to turn to ideas of socialism, thinking that capitalism needed to be tamed for the greater good. But they were a minority. When most Americans demanded equality, what they really meant was opportunity.

In 1893 the nation celebrated its achievements at the Great Columbian Exposition held in Chicago, designed to surpass the great world's fair held the previous year in Paris. Chicago was the most rapidly growing city in the Americas; the "city of broad shoulders," its wealth based on grain trading, stockyards, and industry, supported the construction of an amazing artificial city to hold the exhibits, which featured the world's first Ferris Wheel as a response to the Eiffel Tower of

• **Gilded Age** Period of economic prosperity in the last two decades of the nineteenth century. The opulence displayed by the wealthy masked the poverty, political corruption, and unsafe living and occupational conditions for the working class during this period.

■ **The Columbian Exposition** The Columbian Exposition, held in Chicago in 1893, was a self-congratulatory celebration of the "triumph of science and civilization" four hundred years after the voyage of Christopher Columbus. The illuminated exhibits were the first experience most of the awestruck visitors had ever had of electrical power. Walt Disney's father was a construction worker at the Exposition, and its architectural influence was obvious in Disney's theme parks in the United States, France, Japan, and Hong Kong. (Chicago Historical Society, ICHI-02554)

Paris. The Columbian Exposition was a monument to progress and to American self-confidence.

Attending the fair was Frederick Jackson Turner, a young historian from the University of Wisconsin and author of the paper "The Significance of the Frontier in American History." Turner noted that the cultural and political development of the United States had always been predicated on the availability of an open frontier. The exuberance and lack of class enmity of American life, compared with the harsher social conflicts of Europe, had everything to do with the frontier mentality. American democracy itself was a product of the frontier, Turner argued (ignoring the people who had lived there prior to white settlement). Now, however, the frontier was closing. How would Americans deal with these changed circumstances?

There were indeed signs that American society was in trouble. The economic boom turned to bust as overproduction led to a business slump. Thousands lost their jobs; farmers could not sell their grain or milk. The economic crisis proved to be temporary, but the historian's question still deserved an answer. At century's end the United States was clearly no longer a rough frontier society but a powerful modern industrial state. In the three decades following the Civil War it had become the world's leading industrial *and* agricultural producer. In the twentieth century the country would trade continental frontiers for global ones and make its influence felt among all the world's peoples.

Reform and Reaction in Latin America

The trend toward consolidation of power by ambitious national states was also characteristic of nineteenth-century Latin America. As in Canada and the United States, Latin American leaders would have to overcome regional and sectional differences in developing more effective national institutions. They also faced significant external challenges. In the middle of the nineteenth century Mexico lost vast northern territories to the United States and then suffered a decade of French occupation. All across Latin America, economic domination by Europe and the United States skewed economic production toward foreign markets, hindering the development of integrated national economies. Relying on exports of agricultural produce and natural resources while importing industrial goods and technologies, Latin Americans were highly susceptible to peaks and valleys in the global economy.

Conservatives, Liberals, and the Struggle for Stability in Mexico

After the failure of Padre Hidalgo's revolutionary movement by 1814, Mexico won its independence from Spain under conservative ideas and leaders (see Chapter 22). The government fell into the hands of ineffective military leaders, the *caudillos* (kouh-DEE-yohs), of which General Antonio Lopez de Santa Ana (1794–1876) was the most notorious. The postindependence authorities proved largely incapable of dealing with the challenges that lay before them.

One major problem arose when Mexico's territorial integrity was challenged in its northern state of Texas. Mexico's wealth in people, resources, settled agriculture, and culture was in its central and southern parts. The north, by contrast, was a relatively untamed frontier with only a few officials and missionaries mixed in with the *vaquero* (vah-KAIR-oh) cowboys, Amerindians such as Apache and Comanche, and the occasional American adventurer. None paid much attention to Mexican authorities.

In the 1820s Mexican authorities attempted to stabilize this distant frontier by inviting some English-speaking settlers into Texas. Most were Americans who planned to use slave labor to produce cotton. But since Mexico had already abolished slavery, the importation of slaves was illegal. President Santa Ana would either have to enforce that law or allow the Texans to flaunt his authority.

By 1836, when Santa Ana came north with his troops, there were thirty thousand American settlers in Texas. Unhappy with what they saw as the inefficiency and corruption of Mexican rule, they allied with discontented Spanish-speaking Texans to fight for independence. Despite his victory at the Alamo, Santa Ana lost Texas to the better-organized and well-armed rebels. Initially the rebels declared a republic, but a referendum in 1845 prepared the way for the annexation of Texas by the United States.

Mexico's loss of territory to the United States did not stop there. President James Polk, a southern Democrat, pursued an aggressive policy toward Mexico, provoking war in 1846. U.S. forces penetrated to Mexico City, and the Treaty of Guadalupe Hidalgo (1848) gave the United States the northern half of Mexico. Alta California entered the Union in 1850 as the state of California, adding its rich resources to the United States. The desert Southwest and mountain West were open for white settlement. Mexico's *"Norte"* had become the American Southwest.

Benito Juárez (beh-NEE-toh WAH-rez) (1806–1872) was the leader of a group of Mexican liberals who responded to this humiliating loss by calling for reform. Inspired by the European revolutions of 1848, Juárez and other middle-class Mexicans supported *La Reforma,* a movement to get rid of caudillo rule and create a more progressive Mexican nation. A Zapotec Amerindian, Juárez had to struggle to advance in a social structure in which opportunities were monopolized by the *criollo* elite (see Chapter 18). Nevertheless, he worked his way through law school and in 1848 was elected governor of the southern state of Oaxaca.

By 1855 even the conservatives had tired of Santa Ana and removed him from power in a coup d'état, but they were immediately challenged by an army led by Juárez and the liberals. The success of *La Reforma* was enshrined in the Mexican Constitution of 1857. The new constitution restricted the privileges of the Catholic clergy and the military, two groups the liberals saw as impediments to progress. It contained a Bill of Rights and established a strong unicameral legislature to offset executive power. The old caste system was eliminated: everyone was now equal before the law.

Most liberals saw the church as restricting individualism and progress while upholding the power of the large landowners. Conservatives, however, reacted angrily to such reforms, especially limitations on the church's power and the seizure of much of its land. While some in the church followed the example of Padre Hidalgo in supporting the rights of the majority (see Chapter 22), most priests allied with the conservative elites.

The struggle between liberals and conservatives gave an opening for the ambitions of the French emperor Napoleon III (see Chapter 23), who sent troops to Mexico in 1861. His stated intention was to force payments of Mexican debt, but his real motive was to resurrect a French empire in the Americas. The liberal government fought back. In 1862, on the fifth of May (*Cinco de Mayo*), a small army of Mexicans defeated a much larger French force at the Battle of Puebla. But Mexico lost the war with France after the conservatives cooperated with the French invaders and

● **Benito Juárez** (1806–1872) Mexican statesman and politician who was intermittently president of Mexico during the 1860s and 1870s and leader of *La Reforma*. His liberal principles were enshrined in the Constitution of 1857.

helped them take Mexico City. Pressure from Europe and the United States eventually forced the French to withdraw, but the struggle between liberals and conservatives for control of Mexico continued until the death of Juárez in 1872.

The coming to power of **Porfirio Diáz** (1830–1915) in 1876 altered the balance between conservatism and liberalism in Mexican politics, since he himself was a political conservative but an economic liberal. Like the old caudillos, he ruled as a dictator, and during his long tenure as president (1876–1880 and 1884–1911) he ignored the most important ideals of *La Reforma,* such as freedom of speech and assembly. He was, however, a firm believer in the economic platform of liberalism: free trade and foreign investment. The building of railroads, while central to his economic strategy, also had political implications: the power of the Mexican state expanded as improved transportation gave its officials and military forces greater access to the entire country. Mexican officials and businessmen actively sought investment from Britain and the United States to help stimulate the economy.

> **Porfirio Diáz** (1830–1915) President of Mexico during much of the last half of the nineteenth century and during the first decade of the twentieth century. While he ignored Mexican civil liberties, Diáz developed infrastructure and provided much needed stability.

Apart from railroads and mining, most of this new investment was in agriculture. Mexico had inherited from the colonial period a system of large landholdings known as *haciendas* (see Chapter 18). In the colonial era these large estates were only weakly connected to international markets; now, in response to the expansion of those markets, their owners were intensively planting export crops like cotton, sugar, and hemp. Commercial agriculture brought great wealth to Mexico's landowners, its urban commercial class, and foreign investors. Many formerly self-sufficient peasant communities, however, were driven by poverty to work on these commercial plantations for very low wages.

According to liberals, everyone should benefit from free markets. Indeed, nineteenth-century liberals believed that social, political, and economic freedoms all progressed as part of the same package. But the late-nineteenth-century Mexican economy showed the limitations of that theory, at least in the short run. The Diáz regime showed to Mexicans and the world that the open markets espoused by classical liberalism could be combined with authoritarian political rule.

Porfirio Diáz   During his long rule Porfirio Diáz improved Mexico's transportation infrastructure and invited foreign investment. He did nothing, however, to address the country's deep social and economic inequalities, or to respond to the demands of liberal Mexicans for democratic reforms. Like many dictators in world history, he was fond of bestowing medals and honors on himself.   (The Granger Collection)

Spanish-Speaking South America

By the time of his death in 1830, Simón Bolívar's vision of a great South American confederation, or at least a *Gran Columbia* in the north, was already defunct (see Chapter 22). Once the common enemy was defeated, regional diversities and the ambitions of politician-soldiers led to fragmentation. By the 1830s there were nine separate nations where the Spanish Empire in South America had once been, and, as in Mexico, their economies were largely geared toward exporting raw materials for industrial processes completed elsewhere and then importing the finished products. Plantation owners, commercial intermediaries, political elites, and foreign investors all prospered, but farmers and laborers were left behind.

The story of Bolívar's native Venezuela was fairly typical. The president, José Antonio Páez (1790–1873), was a self-made military leader for whom the liberation campaigns had been a personal opportunity as well as a political cause. After the collapse of *Gran Colombia* in 1830, Páez (PAH-ays) consolidated his power in typical caudillo fashion by forging an alliance with the old criollo aristocracy. While the president was a man of rough manners, fond of attending cockfights, the snobbish oligarchs were willing to overlook such behavior because Páez was able to control the common people.

Nevertheless, in the 1860s, after a brief civil war, Venezuelan reformers took charge and established a more liberal regime. Slavery was finally abolished, and the government borrowed money to build railroads and supervised an impressive expansion of primary school facilities. Still, the principal framework of Venezuelan society did not change: the export-oriented agricultural sector was controlled by an economic oligarchy with close ties to foreign investors.

■ **Buenos Aires**
The Argentine capital of Buenos Aires was an exceptionally prosperous city entering the twentieth century. As in Paris, New York, and Berlin, automobiles were beginning to compete with horse-drawn carriages along its spacious boulevards.
(Library of Congress)

Argentina was more economically successful. As in Texas, railroads made it much easier to get Argentine cattle to market, and the development of refrigerated steamship compartments in the 1860s gave European consumers access to Argentine beef. As the economy boomed, the capital, Buenos Aires, became one of the world's great cities. A cosmopolitan upper class of politicians, merchants, and lawyers enjoyed the city's broad boulevards, elegant plazas, and pleasant cafés. A growing working class, many of them recent immigrants from Italy, worked in meatpacking plants and other export-oriented industries. It was from their neighborhoods that the sensual café music known as the *tango* first developed, Argentina's enduring gift to global musical culture.

Apart from Argentina, the most successful South American republic was Chile. As elsewhere in Latin America, tensions between conservatives and liberals and between centralizers and believers in provincial autonomy squared off for influence in Chilean politics, but here a relatively conservative consensus emerged early on. The Catholic Church was especially powerful in Chile.

Political consensus may have been easier to achieve in Chile because of its success in competing with its neighbors, Peru and Bolivia. Starting in the 1840s, the three countries had greatly benefited from a valuable natural resource available along its Pacific coast: *guano* (GWA-noh), or bird droppings. Guano makes an excellent fertilizer, and the expansion of commercial agriculture created a worldwide demand; steamships provided low-cost transport. Of course, shoveling guano was not pleasant. When Chileans showed little interest, tens of thousands of Chinese laborers were transported to South America to do the job.

When Peruvian and Bolivian guano deposits declined, these countries began to develop nitrate mines in the same region, intensifying competition for national resources and leading to the **War of the Pacific** in 1879 among Peru, Bolivia, and Chile. The Chilean victory strongly enhanced its domestic and international reputation. The country's political institutions were strengthened, its economic situation was improved, and Chileans developed a stronger sense of national identity. The outcome of the war was disastrous for Bolivia, which became a landlocked country and one of the poorest societies in the Americas (see Map 25.2).

● **War of the Pacific** (1879)   War among Bolivia, Peru, and Chile over natural resources of the Pacific coast. Chile emerged victorious, gaining international prestige, while Bolivia's loss made it a poor, landlocked country.

From Empire to Republic in Brazil

The largest country in South America, Brazil followed a unique path, hardly surprising given its distinct ecology, demography, and relationship to Portugal. While the former Spanish colonies had fought their way to independence, Brazil became independent in 1822 as a constitutional monarchy (see Chapter 22). Pedro I, heir to the Portuguese throne, became the first emperor of Brazil. He was succeeded by his son, and Brazil remained a monarchy until 1889.

Despite this difference in constitutional form, the principal political tensions in Brazil were quite similar to those of its republican neighbors. Brazilian liberals, including its urban middle class, responded to progressive European trends, such as free trade and the protection of civil liberties, while the country's conservatives, large estate owners and military men, stressed traditional values such as the authority of the Catholic Church. The conservative nature of the Brazilian monarchy is shown by the fact that the abolition of slavery, a major liberal priority, was not achieved until 1888, later than anywhere else in the Americas.

In fact, slavery became even more widespread in nineteenth-century Brazil when coffee replaced sugar as the country's primary agricultural export. Coffee plantations expanded inland from initial bases of production in the south, and by 1880 Brazil was by far the world's largest coffee producer, with the crop making up well over half its exports. The expanding urban populations of the industrializing world, especially in the United States and western Europe, were the primary consumers of Brazilian coffee.

Another Brazilian export even more closely tied to industrialization was rubber. For the first time, improved transportation and communication technologies allowed Brazilian entrepreneurs, backed by foreign capital, to exploit the Amazon basin on a large scale. (See the feature "World History in Today's World: Pharmaceutical Riches of Amazonia.") The Brazilian government stimulated a rubber boom by granting gigantic land concessions, thus extending and deepening the reach of the Brazilian state.

As with guano, however, the rubber boom went bust. Brazil lost its monopoly when production spread to Central Africa and Southeast Asia, while overexploitation led to a decline in Amazonian yields (see Chapter 26). The bust in the rubber

⊕ MAP 25.2

Latin America, ca. 1895   By 1895 all of the nations of South America and Central America were independent except for British, French, and Dutch Guyana. Bolivia became landlocked after losing the War of the Pacific in 1879 and ceding coastal territory to Chile. Panama seceded from Colombia in 1903 with military backing from the United States, which was anxious to protect its canal zone interests. Many Caribbean islands remained British, French, and Dutch colonies. However, Cuba was freed from Spanish rule in 1898, the same year the United States took control over Puerto Rico. Dense railroad networks were a sign of foreign investment in exports like minerals and livestock products, as seen here in Mexico, Chile, Argentina, Uruguay, and southern Brazil.

Pharmaceutical Riches of Amazonia

South America has made many important contributions to the global pharmacopeia, the storehouse of drugs available to combat disease. In the nineteenth century, quinine from the bark of Peruvian trees offered protection against malaria. Today, scientists have high hopes for the slime of the giant monkey frog, which contains an opiate that produces a short bout of fever and dizziness soon replaced by a feeling of exceptional alertness. It is frequently used by Katukina men in the far west of the Brazilian Amazon to improve their hunting skills. They call it *kambô* and also use it to cure certain illnesses.

Connecting indigenous medical knowledge and modern science is central to Brazil's "Project Kambô," a program to protect and develop the country's "national genetic patrimony" by protecting the biodiversity of Amazonia.* That biodiversity is under attack as more and more species are threatened by the felling of the rainforest to make way for grazing and crop lands.

*Paula Prada, "Poisonous Tree Frog Could Bring Wealth to Tribe in Brazilian Amazon," *New York Times*, May 30, 2006.

Both the Katukina people and the Brazilian government are very sensitive about controlling research into any pharmaceuticals that might be developed from kambô. In the past it has usually been outsiders who have benefited from South America's genetic richness. In the nineteenth century, the cinchona used to make quinine was smuggled out of Peru, and the profits went to Dutch and English entrepreneurs. In the 1970s a major multinational drug company used the venom of an Amazonian snake to develop a drug to treat high blood pressure, making $1.6 billion from sales of that drug in 1991 alone.

Increasing competition for patents linked to biological resources has become a major issue in global diplomacy. The multinational pharmaceutical companies argue that years of investment in research and development are necessary to make the most of natural substances like kambô poison. Others call such appropriations of local resources "biopiracy." The Brazilian government says its own scientists can do the job, while Chief Fernando of the Katukina says: "The vaccine belongs to us. Science might help us develop it, but kambô knowledge is Katukina."

---

economy was matched by a sharp decline in coffee exports when a global economic slump in the 1890s led to falling demand and falling prices. Brazil found itself in the same dependency trap as other South American nations, too reliant on exports of agricultural products and raw materials and on imports of industrial goods and technologies from Europe, and thus increasingly exposed to downward trends in global markets.

At least the Brazilian economy finally became less reliant on slave labor. In the second half of the nineteenth century a surge of immigration provided a cheap and productive alternative. The northeastern plantation regions were becoming less important as coffee, cattle, and grain production surged in the south. As abolitionist sentiment grew, the monarchy, long associated with the conservative planter class, lost its credibility. In 1889 the emperor was deposed in a peaceful transition: Brazil became a republic, with the motto "Order and Progress" proudly displayed on its new green and gold flag. Slavery was finally purged from the Western Hemisphere.

● Connections and Comparisons in the Nineteenth-Century Americas

All across the Americas, deep changes in society resulted from economic integration into global markets and the expansion and consolidation of state power. One general result was the elimination of Amerindian sovereignty. In 1830 many indigenous societies still governed their own affairs using their own languages and cultural traditions; by 1895 such independence was found only in the most remote regions. Changing demographics were part of the story, as ever larger numbers of European immigrants crossed the Atlantic. In addition, with the end of the Atlantic slave trade and the abolition of slavery, racial categories began developing in diverse ways from changing balances between the descendants of Europeans, Amerindians, and Africans. Just as important were changes in gender roles. Pauline Johnson-Tekahionwake was not the only woman seeking greater autonomy in late-nineteenth-century society.

The Fates of Indigenous Societies

The nineteenth century was a decisive time for America's indigenous peoples. Before the Industrial Revolution, many Amerindian societies retained complete or substantial control over their own political, social, and cultural lives in regions as diverse as the Andes, the Arctic, Amazonia, and the Great Plains. Others, like the Johnson family and other Iroquois on the Six Nations Reserve, maintained connections with settler societies but decided for themselves how to balance old traditions and new influences. But as examples from Mexico, Canada, and the United States will show, by the end of the century almost all traces of Amerindian sovereignty had been wiped away.

The achievement of Mexican independence in 1821 had little immediate effect on the lives of the Mexican people. On the Yucatán (yoo-kah-THAN) peninsula, most Mayan-speaking villagers continued to live much as before, with little reference to Spanish-speaking government officials. They grew maize, beans, and other staple crops, supporting communities with deep roots in the pre-Columbian past. Although Christians, their Catholicism was a complex mix of local and imported beliefs and rituals. Though now part of a wider network with which they interacted as both producers and consumers, their basic self-sufficiency still allowed them to choose their own terms of economic contact with the outside world.

By the 1840s commercial agriculture in the Yucatán was booming. Although planters were looking for cheap Amerindian labor to grow sugar and henequen, they could not attract many workers at the wages they were willing to offer. Just at this time, however, Mexican tax collectors were becoming much more visible and aggressive because of the expensive wars with Texas. Forced, in many cases for the first time, to come up with cash to pay their taxes, some peasants resorted to debt peonage (see Chapter 18). Formerly independent peasants were becoming almost like slave laborers on large estates.

Meanwhile, the Spanish-speaking elite of the Yucatán revolted against the authority of Mexico City and declared the peninsula's independence. Maya communities used these divisions to advance their own case: in 1847, a small group of Maya militants began a guerilla campaign, known as the **Yucatán Rebellion,** attacking both Mexican government officials and local oligarchs. Since the Mexican army was fully engaged in war with the United States, the rebels soon controlled over half the Yucatán peninsula. Once the war in the north was over, however, Mexican officials redeployed their forces against the Maya rebels.

Even Mexican liberals, under the Zapotec leader Benito Juárez, supported repressing the rebellion, seeing the independent Maya communities as primitive folk standing in the way of "progress." Nation building and market economics were the engines of progress to the liberals, and the Yucatán rebels were attacking both. Although government authority had been reasserted in most places by the 1850s, scattered fighting in defense of Maya sovereignty continued until 1895. By then the economic autonomy of the Yucatán Maya had been broken: the need for cash to pay their taxes drove them to low-wage work on plantations producing agricultural commodities for export.

The life and customs of the indigenous communities of the Great Plains could hardly have been more different from those of the Maya. The Maya were farmers living in densely settled permanent villages, while most Plains Amerindians lived in mobile bands and depended on buffalo hunting for both food and a source of trade goods. But for both groups, the ways of life to which many were so deeply committed proved incompatible with industrial nation-states.

The ancient buffalo hunting culture of the Plains was given a new stimulus by the arrival of horses in the sixteenth and seventeenth centuries. Some formerly agricultural people like the Lakota (luh-KOH-tuh) Sioux and the Cheyenne moved to the Plains and used horses and rifles to develop an efficient hunting culture. Then the earlier trickle of Europeans passing through turned into a flood. After 1846, when Great Britain ceded Oregon to the United States, large numbers of settlers sought their fortune on the "Oregon Trail." By the time of the Civil War the U.S. government had built a series of forts in the Dakota Territory to protect settlers against Amerindians.

Still, for a time it seemed that negotiations between the Sioux and the U.S. government might provide a stable compromise. An 1868 treaty, for example, forbade white settlement for all time in the Black Hills, sacred to the Sioux and other Plains societies. Four years later gold was discovered, and waves of white prospectors descended on the new mining camp of Deadwood in the heart of sacred Sioux land. It seemed to Sioux leaders like **Sitting Bull** (ca. 1831–1890) that treaties with the U.S. government were worth less than the paper they were written on.

The Sioux prepared for war, and in the summer of 1876 Sitting Bull and his warriors defeated Lieutenant Colonel George Custer and the Seventh United States Cavalry at the Battle of Little Big Horn. In the American press, Custer's death was portrayed as a heroic "last stand" against savages. Emotions were intense, calls for vengeance swift. Some advocated not just the defeat of the Sioux but also the total annihilation of Amerindians.

The spread of railroads starting in the 1870s added fuel to the fire: European immigrants and American settlers were now arriving in the Dakota Territory as permanent homesteaders. Early in 1890 the U.S. government abolished key terms of its treaty with the Sioux to make land available for these settlers. The whole Lakota way of life, which depended on open grazing lands for buffalo, was now directly challenged.

Despairing of a political or military solution to their crisis, some Plains Amerindians were attracted to the teachings of a mystic named Wovoka (wuh-VOH-kuh),

• Yucatán Rebellion (1847) Maya uprising on Mexico's Yucatán peninsula, challenging the authority of the Mexican government and local landowners. Some Maya communities defended their sovereignty into the 1890s.

• Sitting Bull (ca. 1831–1890) Sioux chieftain who led Amerindian resistance to settlement of the Black Hills. After defeating the U.S. cavalry and General George Custer at the Battle of Little Bighorn in 1876, he was killed in 1890 for promoting the Ghost Dance Movement.

Sitting Bull and Buffalo Bill Cody　In the 1880s, before his death in 1890, the great Sioux war chieftain performed in Buffalo Bill Cody's Wild West Show, an indicator of how far his people had fallen in the decade since his defeat of George Custer at the Little Big Horn. As Native American resistance to white encroachment was overcome, patronizing notions of Amerindians as "noble savages" developed alongside the persistent Euro-American image of "blood-thirsty Indians." (Corbis)

leader of the Ghost Dance Movement, which combined indigenous beliefs and imported Christian ones. Most of Wovoka's followers believed that he was a messiah sent to liberate them and that by dancing the Ghost Dance they would hasten a millennium in which earthquakes would drive the invaders from the earth and leave the native peoples in permanent peace and prosperity.

The U.S. government regarded the Ghost Dance Movement as subversive and ordered the arrest of Sitting Bull in the mistaken belief that he was a leader of the movement. Early in 1890 Sitting Bull was killed in a skirmish; two weeks later, at Wounded Knee, units of the Seventh Cavalry fired into a captive group of Sioux, killing at least 150 people, nearly half of whom were unarmed women and children. An editorial writer at a South Dakota newspaper had this to say about the death of Sitting Bull and the massacre at Wounded Knee:

> The Whites, by law of conquest, by justice of civilization, are masters of the American continent, and the best safety of the frontier settlements will be secured by the total annihilation of the few remaining Indians. Why not annihilation? Their glory has fled, their spirit broken, their manhood effaced; better that they die than live the miserable wretches that they are.[3]

Such violent racism in support of a policy of genocide was not uncommon. (The author of this editorial was L. Frank Baum, who ten years later would write the beloved children's story *The Wonderful Wizard of Oz*.)

Rather than outright annihilation, however, the federal Bureau of Indian Affairs separated Amerindian children from their parents to prevent them from learning the language, culture, and rituals of their own people—a form of cultural genocide. The Ghost Dance and other ceremonies were forbidden and could be practiced only in secret. Amerindian military resistance was over. The frontier wars were now experienced only as entertainment, courtesy of Buffalo Bill Cody's tremendously popular Wild West shows.

When she began to travel across Canada in the 1890s, Pauline Johnson-Tekahionwake saw firsthand the tragedy of the Plains Amerindians. She witnessed the sad spectacle of "a sort of miniature Buffalo Bill's Wild West" in which Blackfoot warriors performed hokey versions of their old war maneuvers. Some of these men might have been veterans of the **Métis Rebellions,** the uprisings of mixed-race and First Nations peoples that had inspired Johnson to write "A Cry from an Indian Wife."

The Métis settlement (a particular settlement of métis frontier people; see page 724) in the Red River Valley of what is now the Canadian province of Manitoba represented an older form of European/First Nations interaction. During the heyday of the fur trade, when French trappers and traders relied on native communities for both profit and survival, mixed-race families were not uncommon. Sometimes Europeans were absorbed into indigenous communities, and sometimes, as with the Métis, the offspring of mixed unions established their own communities.

The first of two Métis Rebellions came immediately after Canadian Confederation in 1867. London had transferred authority over the vast territories of the Hudson's Bay Company to the Canadian government without consulting the people who lived there. The Métis leader Louis Riel organized his community to resist incorporation into Canada, which they feared would lead to loss of their lands and the erosion of their French language. Riel declared a provisional government and with minimal violence secured guarantees that Canada would protect the language and Catholic religion of the Métis. Negotiations led to the incorporation of Manitoba into Canada in 1870.

Meanwhile, the Canadian government began to implement a policy toward First Nations peoples based on the assumption that they were to disappear as a distinct population. The Plains dwellers were in an increasingly desperate situation. The buffalo were dwindling, and alcohol was becoming a scourge. The Canadian Pacific Railroad would bring settlers and markets to their lands, but their own hunting-based traditions and lack of access to capital made the transition to commercial farming almost impossible for them. In exchange for exclusive reserves and small annuities, band after band gave up claim to the lands of their forebears.

The Indian Act of 1876 asserted the authority of the Canadian state over First Nations communities. Children were separated from their families and sent to "industrial schools," given English names, and forbidden to speak their own languages. (See the feature "Visual Evidence: The Residential School System for First Nations Children.") The Indian Act also allowed Canadian officials to ban many traditional rituals, including the *potlatch* ceremony, in which men held enormous feasts to give away all the wealth they had accumulated in the previous years. This ceremony expressed the core cultural values of the peoples of the Pacific West. The idea of giving away all your wealth to solidify your social standing could not have stood in greater contrast to the ethos of industrial and commercial capitalism on which the new Canada was being built.

Meanwhile, government surveyors were dividing the prairie into 640-acre lots. The arrival of the expected flood of settlers would make the Métis a minority in their own land, and Louis Riel once again organized them to resist, this time forging an alliance with disaffected Cree, Assiniboine, and other First Nations peoples. In 1885, Riel again proclaimed himself to be the head of an independent provisional government. Métis partisans attacked a government outpost as Riel's indigenous allies burned down some white homesteads. But they were no match for Canadian government forces. Three thousand troops were sent west on the Canadian Pacific Railway, and Riel was arrested, convicted of high treason, and hanged.

●Métis Rebellions (1867 and 1885) Rebellions by the Métis of the Red River Settlement in Manitoba, a group with mixed French/Amerindian ancestry who resisted incorporation into the Canadian Confederation. In 1885 their leader Louis Riel again led them in rebellion against Canadian authority.

THE RESIDENTIAL SCHOOL SYSTEM FOR FIRST NATIONS CHILDREN

After the conquest of Amerindian communities, nineteenth-century governments in both the United States and Canada implemented residential school systems designed to separate children from their families and thus from the culture of their people. Amerindian children in these often church-run schools were given new names, converted to Christianity, forced to speak only English, and punished for speaking the language of their own people. Physical and sexual abuse was common, and rates of infectious disease, especially tuberculosis, were high. In Canada, attendance by First Nations children at residential schools was compulsory until 1948.

Finally, in 1998 the Canadian government formed the Aboriginal Healing Foundation to support community projects in reparation for the damage done by

In this photograph "Thomas" wears long braided hair and leans against a large fur robe. He holds what appears to be a toy gun, perhaps given to him as a prop by the photographer.

Assuming the photographer posed the boy, what impression does he seem to have wanted the photograph to have on its viewers?

One writer says that this image shows "the disorder and violence of warfare and of the cross-cultural partnerships of the fur trade . . . that had dominated life in Canada since the late sixteenth century."* How does the image show that?

(Saskatchewan Archives Board, Regina)

* John S. Milloy, *A National Crime: The Canadian Government and the Residential School System, 1879 to 1906* (Winnipeg: University of Manitoba Press, 1999), p. 4.

QUESTION FOR ANALYSIS

Taken together, what do these two photographs tell us about the ideology behind the residential school system in turn-of-the-century Canada?

this attempted cultural genocide of First Nations peoples. In 2008 the Canadian prime minister made a formal statement of apology, recognizing that "the consequences of the Indian residential schools policy were profoundly negative and that this policy has had a lasting and damaging impact on aboriginal culture, heritage, and language," and highlighting the "tragic accounts of the emotional, physical, and sexual abuse and neglect of helpless children, and their separation from powerless families and communities."

These two photographs were taken at the Regina Industrial School in the Canadian province of Saskatchewan and published in the *Annual Report* of the Canadian Department of Indian Affairs in 1904. They record the appearance of a First Nations child identified only as "Thomas Moore" (his true name was not recorded), supposedly upon first arrival and again a few years later.

(Saskatchewan Archives Board, Regina)

Apart from his hair and clothing, what is different and meaningful about Thomas's facial expression and posture in the second photograph?

The wall against which Thomas is leaning in this photograph seems much more solid and permanent that the fur robe in the earlier picture, perhaps symbolizing the superior strength of Christian Canadian society.

The goal of the Canadian government was to replace buffalo hunting with settled agriculture, a transformation perhaps symbolized by the potted plant included in this photograph.

When Pauline Johnson-Tekahionwake recited "A Cry from an Indian Wife" in 1892, these events were still fresh in the minds of her audience.

If we compare the Yucatán Rebellion, the struggles of the Lakota Sioux, and the Métis Rebellions, we might first be struck by their differences. Simple demography provides one contrast: whereas the Mexican government and economic oligarchy wanted to incorporate the Maya peasantry as laborers in the commercial plantation system, the United States and Canada had no use for Amerindians even as workers, instead driving them into reservations to make room for settlers.

But the three cases have this in common: in the Yucatán, the Black Hills, and Manitoba people rose up to defend long-established cultures against nation building and the spread of commercial agriculture. In all three places, indigenous and imported ideas had long been creatively merged: Maya beliefs and Catholicism, Sioux traditions with horse-based buffalo hunting, French and First Nations cultures in the days of the fur trade. Now all these peoples lost their ability to control their interactions with the national societies being constructed around them.

Abolition, Immigration, and Race

Race was a major issue across the Americas during Pauline Johnson-Tekahionwake's lifetime. During her childhood the lines were fairly simple: British (mostly Protestants), French and Irish (mostly Catholics), First Nations peoples (themselves quite diverse), and mixtures between them such as the Métis. By the time of her adult travels, that picture had become complicated by the arrival of new immigrants: Chinese, Italians, Russians, and others. Early in the twentieth century, half of the population on the prairies was born outside of Canada. The same was true across the Americas. The United States was the most favored destination, but Argentina and Brazil also attracted many European immigrants.

In some places, notably Brazil and the Caribbean, the abolition of slavery was connected to immigration patterns and policies. Slavery was abolished in the British West Indies in 1833 and on the French islands fifteen years later. Unable to keep the former slaves as poorly paid wage earners, landowners turned to indentured workers. In the English-speaking Caribbean, indentured laborers came largely from British India, part of a broader South Asian diaspora (scattering) that also took contract workers to South Africa, Malaya, and Fiji. In Cuba, where slavery was not abolished until 1878, the sugar plantations required so much additional labor that over a hundred thousand Chinese workers had come to the island as indentured workers to supplement slave labor.

Like Cuba, Brazil was bringing in new migrants even before slavery was abolished in 1888. Brazilian employers also took advantage of the global market in indentured workers, such as by bringing contract laborers from Japan to work on coffee farms. In fact, the largest group of Japanese-descended persons outside Japan is found in Brazil. Much larger, and more influential in Brazilian culture, however, was the Afro-Brazilian population with its origins in the old sugar plantation system. Brazilian art, music, dance, and religious worship all show a deep African influence.

Reflecting the racism so characteristic of the age, the rulers of republican Brazil were embarrassed by the country's African heritage. Their mottos were "order" and "progress," and in their minds black people represented neither. To "improve" the country racially, the government aggressively recruited immigrants from Europe. Germans, Italians, and others were given incentives to relocate and became an important presence in the economically dynamic southern part of the country. The northeast, site of the old plantation system, remained more African in population and culture.

Racism was also evident in immigration to the United States. The Anglo-Protestant majority portrayed Irish Catholics as drunk, violent, and lazy. Demeaning stereotypes also greeted new immigrants from southern and eastern Europe, such as Italian Catholics and Russian Jews. Prejudice against Chinese and Japanese immigrants on the west coast was even more intense, and Congress banned Chinese immigration altogether in 1882. Still, in 1890 fully 14.8 percent of the population had been born outside the United States, and some doubted whether these new arrivals, with their strange foods, languages, and customs, could ever be assimilated.

Racism drove restrictions on Asian immigration and continued to drive policy toward Americans of African descent. In 1896 the Supreme Court upheld the legality of racial segregation in the South. In northern cities recent immigrants, in spite of prejudices against them, often fared better than African Americans; many Irish Americans, for example, found good work as police officers and firemen, jobs that were closed to blacks. The cruel irony was that ancestors of most African Americans, whose ancestors had witnessed the birth of the republic, watched as new arrivals from Europe leaped past them to success.

The late nineteenth century was a time of harsh racial rhetoric and even harsher racial realities, not only in the United States but also across the Americas. The complex demographic and cultural interplay of Amerindians, Africans, Asians, and Europeans seemed to have been resolved decisively in favor of Europeans. For all the differences between the nations of North and South America, they had at least one thing in common: light-skinned men were in charge.

Gender and Women's Rights

In 1848, the same year as Marx's *Manifesto of the Communist Party* (see Chapter 23), the Seneca Falls Convention was held in upstate New York. The meeting is sometimes seen as the beginning of the modern women's movement. Inspired by the abolitionist movement and the revolutions of Europe, a group of talented women met to proclaim universal freedom and gender equality. The delegates to the Seneca Falls Convention declared: "Now, in view of this entire disfranchisement of one-half the people of this country, their social and religious degradation . . . and because women do feel themselves aggrieved, oppressed, and fraudulently deprived of their most sacred rights, we insist that they have immediate admission to all the rights and privileges which belong to them as citizens of these United States."

Such proclamations would, over time, have a broad effect on gender relations in the United States, Canada, and the world. In the short run, however, most women, like Pauline Johnson-Tekahionwake, had to explore their own possibilities without much external support. Just as she investigated her own complex identity through life and art, her public performances also explored her identity as a woman. The costume change she made halfway through her recitals—from buckskin to evening gown, from Tekahionwake to Pauline Johnson—transformed her from a passionate and even erotic persona to a distant and ethereal one.

For many middle-class women in the late-nineteenth-century United States and Canada, the bicycle was becoming a symbol of a new mobility and a new kind of freedom. For Pauline Johnson-Tekahionwake the canoe played this role. Her nature poems, such as "The Song My Paddle Sings," often involved canoe trips based on the many she took as a young woman on the Six Nations Reserve:

> . . . The river rolls in its rocky bed;
> My paddle is plying its way ahead . . .
> And up on the hills against the sky,
> A fir tree rocking its lullaby,
> Swings, swings,
> Its emerald wings,
> Swelling the song that my paddle sings.

In her canoe poems Johnson-Tekahionwake is always in control, even if, as is often the case, she has a male companion. The independence that she asserted in poetry was reflected in her personal life. She had several significant relationships but no marriage, and though money was a constant worry, she was financially independent. Perhaps Johnson-Tekahionwake's autonomy was itself a product of her mixed heritage, deriving from both the matriarchal tradition of the Mohawk and the new possibilities for women that had been proclaimed at Seneca Falls.

How exceptional were Pauline Johnson-Tekahionwake's attitudes and experiences for a woman of her time? The answer would depend on geographic location and class standing. Middle-class women in major commercial cities like Toronto, Chicago, or Buenos Aires had much in common. Some were politically active, seeking legal equality and the vote for women. Some organized campaigns for social improvement, working to limit abuses of child labor, to improve sanitary conditions, or to fight the evils of alcohol. Some took advantage of new educational opportunities. There were only a few women doctors, lawyers, and university professors in the Americas by the end of the nineteenth century, but there were many new openings for schoolteachers and nurses. Lower down the social order, the invention of the typewriter and the emergence of large corporations created a vast new job market for secretaries.

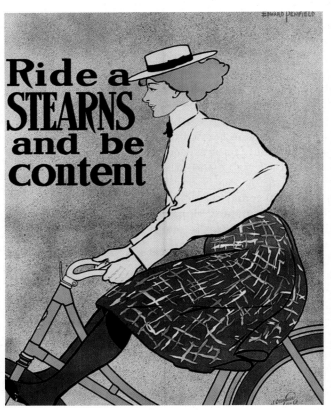

Often young women from the lower or middle classes took temporary positions as teachers, nurses, or secretaries to provide for themselves until they married. Such behavior was consistent with the "cult of true womanhood." Woman's role was in a "separate sphere": women were to maintain a refined home environment as sanctuary from the brutal and competitive "men's world" of business and industry. Even though many women like Johnson-Tekahionwake rejected the "cult of true womanhood," it was a powerful idea embraced by many urban middle-class women and by poorer women who aspired to middle-class status.

Women's progress toward equality and autonomy depended partly on where they lived. A middle-class homemaker in Buenos Aires would have had a much more comfortable life than a

Bicycle Advertisement This advertisement from 1896 associates the bicycle with the newfound mobility and independence of the "new woman." In the poems of Pauline Johnson-Tekahionwake, it was often a canoe that allowed women to "be content." (The Granger Collection)

Swedish pioneer getting her family through a first frigid winter on the Canadian prairie. Likewise, the circumstances of an Irish nun teaching immigrant children in a tough Chicago neighborhood would be difficult to compare with those of a Maya mother sending her sons off to work on a Yucatán plantation. The experiences of women varied tremendously according to their nation, culture, race, and social class. For her part, Pauline Johnson-Tekahionwake created a life of mobility and autonomy that would have been unimaginable to her foremothers.

Chapter Review

CL Download the MP3 audio file of the Chapter Review and listen to it on the go.

Earlier in the twentieth century, Pauline Johnson-Tekahionwake was routinely included in anthologies of Canadian poetry, and children learned "A Cry from an Indian Wife" and "The Song My Paddle Sings" by heart. Now her flowery, romantic poems have gone out of fashion. Still, she remains an important figure in Canadian literary history. In 1906, while on a voyage to London, she met and befriended the Squamish chief Joseph Capilano, who had journeyed to the imperial capital to protest violations of the treaty between his people and the Canadian government. When Pauline Johnson retired from the stage, she moved to the Pacific coast and spent the rest of her life collecting the Squamish tales, which were published as *The Legends of Vancouver*. In her quest to reconcile her own multiple identities, Johnson-Tekahionwake helped lay the literary foundations for what would later become a larger national dialogue about honoring the rich cultural heritage and protecting the rights of Canada's First Nations.

What challenges did Canada and the United States need to overcome in establishing themselves as transcontinental powers?

Unlike the thirteen British colonies that broke away to form the United States of America, Canadians built their confederation by gaining responsible government within the framework of the British Empire. The challenge was to find common constitutional ground on which to unite diverse regions and peoples. The Métis Rebellions showed how sharp the differences could be, but political compromise under strong but moderate leadership prevailed, while after 1867 the Canadian Pacific Railway and the extension of the telegraph provided the communications infrastructure for the new nation. The establishment of the United States as a transcontinental power was a substantially more violent process, as displayed in both the Mexican-American War, fought to wrench vast territories from Mexico, and in the American Civil War, when disputes over western expansion led to conflict between free and slave states. Once that war was over, the status of the United States as a continental power was ensured.

KEY TERMS

Pauline Johnson-Tekahionwake (720)

responsible government (724)

Confederation of Canada (725)

Sir John A. MacDonald (725)

Andrew Jackson (726)

Indian Removal Act (726)

Abraham Lincoln (730)

Reconstruction (731)

Gilded Age (732)

Benito Juárez (734)

Porfirio Diáz (735)

War of the Pacific (737)

Yucatán Rebellion (741)

Sitting Bull (741)

Métis Rebellions (743)

What factors help explain conditions of inequality in nineteenth-century Latin America?

The colonial inheritance in Latin America was one of sharp social and economic inequality. The criollo elites whose domination continued after independence gained even more power with the expansion of global markets, enriching themselves by allying with foreign investors and bringing more and more land into production for external markets. The vast majority of people saw little benefit from investments in land and transportation facilities. In fact, many people, such as Amerindian villagers, lost their autonomy as they became low-wage workers producing goods for distant markets.

Across the Americas, did nineteenth-century developments represent progress for indigenous peoples, ethnic and racial minorities, and women?

The powerful and the privileged in nineteenth-century America had a strong belief in progress, reinforced by rapid industrial growth and technological development. For indigenous peoples whose ancestors suffered and sometimes died at the hands of expanding national states, the word *progress* is a cruel misrepresentation of a bitter historical record. The experiences of ethnic and racial minorities were mixed. By 1888, slavery had finally been abolished across the Americas, a major step forward for peoples of African descent. As the histories of countries like Brazil, the United States, and Cuba demonstrate, however, even legal equality proved difficult or impossible to achieve, while the idea that blacks might achieve social and economic equality with dominant national groups was hardly even considered. Immigrants from Europe, while often facing initial prejudice, largely used the expansive opportunities offered in the Americas; Asian immigrants, by contrast, faced deeper, long-term restrictions on their mobility. The experience of women in the industrial age differed depending on nationality and social status. Amerindian women whose communities lost their lands to settlers and plantation owners lost both status and security. Urban middle-class women had more material comforts but were usually confined to the domestic sphere. By the 1890s, however, some educated women were organizing to fight for equal rights; in the twentieth century that struggle would become a global one.

For Further Reference

Bender, Thomas. *A Nation Among Nations: America's Place in World History.* New York: Hill and Wang, 2006.

Bushnell, David, and Neill Macauley. *The Emergence of Latin America in the Nineteenth Century.* 2d ed. New York: Oxford University Press, 1994.

Cronon, William. *Nature's Metropolis: Chicago and the Great West.* New York: W.W. Norton, 1992.

Dickason, Olive Patricia. *Canada's First Nations.* 3d ed. New York: Oxford University Press, 2001.

Fernández-Armesto, Felipe. *The Americas: A Hemispheric History.* New York: Modern Library, 2003.

Frazier, Donald S. *The United States and Mexico at War.* New York: Macmillan, 1998.

Gray, Charlotte. *Flint and Feather: The Life and Times of E. Pauline Johnson, Tekahionwake.* Toronto: HarperCollins, 2002.

Levine, Robert M. *The History of Brazil.* New York: Palgrave Macmillan, 2006.

Nelles, H. V. *A Little History of Canada.* New York: Oxford University Press, 2004.

Niven, John. *The Coming of the Civil War, 1837–1861.* Arlington Heights, Ill.: Harlan Davidson, 1990.

Wasserman, Mark. *Everyday Life and Politics in Nineteenth Century Mexico.* Albuquerque: University of New Mexico Press, 2000.

Websites

Canadian History
(http://www.canadainfolink.ca/history.htm). Links to a wealth of Canadian historical sources and perspectives.

 WEB RESOURCES

Pronunciation Guide

Interactive Maps

MAP 25.1 U.S. Expansion, 1783–1867

MAP 25.2 Latin America, ca. 1895

Primary Sources

Chapter Objectives

ACE Multiple-Choice Quiz

Flashcards

Mexican History
(http://historicaltextarchive.com/links.php?op=views link&sid=0&cid=1). Numerous links to information on Mexican history in the nineteenth century.

Pauline Johnson Archive
(http://www.humanities.mcmaster.ca/~pjohnson/home.html). Links to information on the life, family, career, and writings of the Canadian poet, including a selection of her letters.

U.S. History
(http://www.ipl.org/div/subject/browse/hum30.55.85.35.50/). The Internet Public Library provides extensive links related to the nineteenth-century history of the United States.

The New Imperialism in Africa and Southeast Asia, 1830–1914

In the short space of twenty years, between 1870 and 1890, European powers drew colonial boundaries on their maps of Africa, without the consent, and in most cases without even the knowledge, of those they planned to rule. In many places Africans mounted spirited resistance, but the Europeans' technological superiority proved impossible to overcome. As the British poet Hilaire Belloc observed: "Whatever else happens, we have got the Maxim gun, and they have not." During his lifetime, **King Khama III** (ca. 1837–1923) of the Bangwato (bahn-GWA-toe) people of southern Africa witnessed the great changes that came with the advance of the European empires. As a child, he was familiar with the occasional European hunter or missionary crossing the kingdom; as a king, he was forced to take drastic action to prevent the complete subjugation of his society:

At first we saw the white people pass, and we said, "They are going to hunt for elephant-tusks and ostrich-feathers, and then they will return where they came from." . . . But now when we see the white men we say "Jah! Jah!" ("Oh Dear!"). And now we think of the white people like rain, for they come down as a flood. When it rains too much, it puts a stop to us all. . . . It is not good for the black people that there should be a multitude of white men.[1]

KING KHAMA III

(Photo courtesy of Neil Parsons from The Botswana National Archives & Records Service)

CL This icon will direct you to interactive activities and study materials on the *Voyages* website: www.cengage.com/history/hansen/voyages1e

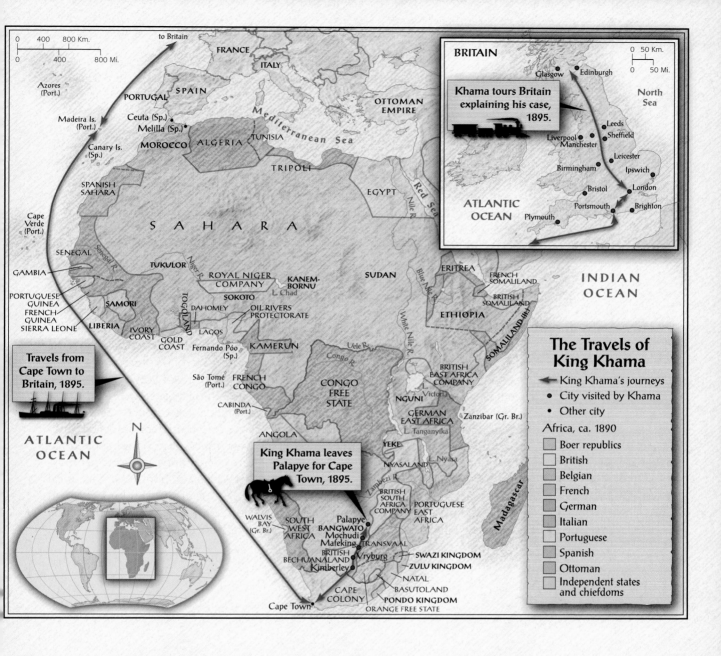

The Travels of King Khama

BRITAIN

Khama tours Britain explaining his case, 1895.

0   50 Km.
0   50 Mi.

Glasgow Edinburgh
North Sea
Leeds
Sheffield
Liverpool
Manchester
Birmingham
Leicester
Ipswich
Bristol
London
ATLANTIC OCEAN
Portsmouth Brighton
Plymouth

Travels from Cape Town to Britain, 1895.

King Khama leaves Palapye for Cape Town, 1895.

← King Khama's journeys
• City visited by Khama
• Other city

Africa, ca. 1890
- Boer republics
- British
- Belgian
- French
- German
- Italian
- Portuguese
- Spanish
- Ottoman
- Independent states and chiefdoms

to Britain

0   400   800 Km.
0   400   800 Mi.

Azores (Port.)

FRANCE
ITALY
SPAIN
PORTUGAL
Mediterranean Sea
OTTOMAN EMPIRE

Madeira Is. (Port.)
Ceuta (Sp.)
Melilla (Sp.)
Canary Is. (Sp.)
MOROCCO ALGERIA TUNISIA
TRIPOLI
EGYPT

Cape Verde (Port.)

SPANISH SAHARA

SAHARA

Red Sea
Nile R.

SENEGAL
GAMBIA
Senegal R.
TUKULOR
Niger R.
ROYAL NIGER COMPANY
KANEM-BORNU
L. Chad
SUDAN
Blue Nile R.
ERITREA
FRENCH SOMALILAND
BRITISH SOMALILAND

PORTUGUESE GUINEA
FRENCH GUINEA
SIERRA LEONE
LIBERIA
SAMORI
IVORY COAST
GOLD COAST
TOGOLAND
DAHOMEY
SOKOTO
OIL RIVERS PROTECTORATE
LAGOS
Fernando Póo (Sp.)
KAMERUN
Vele R.
Congo R.
White Nile R.
ETHIOPIA
SOMALILAND (It.)
BRITISH EAST AFRICA COMPANY

São Tomé (Port.)
FRENCH CONGO
CABINDA (Port.)
CONGO FREE STATE
NGUNI
L. Victoria
GERMAN EAST AFRICA
Zanzibar (Gr. Br.)
L. Tanganyika

ANGOLA
YEKE
L. Nyasa
NYASALAND
Zambezi R.
BRITISH SOUTH AFRICA COMPANY
PORTUGUESE EAST AFRICA
Madagascar

INDIAN OCEAN

ATLANTIC OCEAN

N

WALVIS BAY (Gr. Br.)
SOUTH WEST AFRICA
Palapye
BANGWATO
Mochudi
Mafeking
BRITISH BECHUANALAND
Kimberley
Vryburg
TRANSVAAL
SWAZI KINGDOM
ZULU KINGDOM
NATAL
BASUTOLAND
CAPE COLONY
PONDO KINGDOM
ORANGE FREE STATE
Cape Town

	1830	1850	1870	1890	1910	1930

Lifetime of King Khama of the Bangwato
1837 — 1923

AFRICA

Suez Canal
1869

Reign of Emperor Menelik II of Ethiopia
1889 — 1913

Xhosa Cattle Killing
1856–1857

Berlin Conference
1884

Battle of Omdurman
1898

Union of South Africa
1910

SOUTHEAST ASIA

Reign of King Chulalongkorn of Siam
1868 — 1910

Federation of Indochina
1897

U.S. possession of Philippines
1900

● **King Khama III**
(ca. 1837–1923) King of the Bangwato, a Tswana-speaking southern African group. His successful diplomacy helped establish the Bechuanaland Protectorate, putting the Bangwato and other kingdoms under British rather than South African rule.

In 1895, King Khama (KAH-ma) and two neighboring kings began a long diplomatic mission, journeying by ox-cart, railroad, and steamship from their homes in what is now the nation of Botswana, across South Africa, and all the way to London. They were in a difficult position. The frontier of white settlement already established in South Africa was moving northward, and the discovery of diamonds and gold had added further momentum to European expansion. The kings' goal was to have the British government declare a protectorate that would allow their people to retain their farming and grazing lands and at least some control over their own affairs. The British public responded positively to their appeals, the colonial secretary argued in their favor, and they even had an audience with Queen Victoria. Thanks in great part to their effort and skill, the people of Botswana were later spared the agonies of *apartheid* ("separateness") as practiced in twentieth-century South Africa (see Chapter 30).

Still, Khama's success was only partial. Individual African societies might make better or worse deals with the forces of imperialism, but none could escape them. The late nineteenth century was the time of the New Imperialism, when powerful industrial nations vied for control of colonial territories and resources all across the globe. In Southeast Asia as well, Europeans were competing for colonies, while American, French, German, and British flags went up over scattered Polynesian islands, Meiji Japan took control over Korea and Taiwan, and the last sovereign Amerindian societies were defeated in the United States and Canada (see Chapters 24 and 25).

Applied science and industrial productivity generated the technological, military, and economic advances that powered the New Imperialism. Those societies in possession of the tools of empire—modern firearms, telegraphs, and steamships—were able to assert their power as never before. In Africa and Southeast Asia, local leaders were able to resist only by manipulating European rivalries for their own ends. Even such independent states as Siam and Ethiopia were incorporated into the unequal global system based on empire. Indigenous leaders around the world could relate to King Khama's predicament.

Focus Questions

- What were the main causes of the New Imperialism?
- In what different ways did Africans respond to European imperialism?
- What were the main outcomes of the New Imperialism in Southeast Asia?
- What connections and comparisons can be made between Africa and Southeast Asia in the late nineteenth century?

The New Imperialism

Europeans and Africans had interacted long before the Industrial Revolution. After the sixteenth century, especially in western Africa, their relationship increasingly focused on the slave trade, though direct European involvement was limited to collecting and transporting slaves from their coastal fortifications (see Chapter 19). Before the late nineteenth century, Europeans in Africa's interior included only a small group of settlers moving out from Cape Town and a few intrepid explorers gathering geographic data (see Chapter 21).

The Industrial Revolution altered this pattern. The movement of African people across the Atlantic was replaced by the movement of African products to Western markets and increased imports of industrial manufactures into African markets. Still, for most of the nineteenth century, few Europeans penetrated the continent; rather, African merchants and African political authorities facilitated the new trade connections. Then something dramatic happened. As King Khama noted, suddenly after 1870 Africans confronted "a multitude of white men." The era of industrially backed European colonial expansion called the **New Imperialism** had begun. Heightened competition between European states for African raw materials and markets was one motive for the New Imperialism; personal ambition and religious inspiration were others. Modern technology made possible rapid partition and conquest during the "scramble for Africa" in the late nineteenth century.

●**New Imperialism** An increase in European imperial activity during the late nineteenth century, caused primarily by increased competition between industrial states for raw materials and markets and by the rise of a unified Germany as a threat to the British Empire.

Political and Economic Motives

The importance of the unification of Germany in 1871 (see Chapter 23) went beyond European politics. Germany, the fastest-growing industrial economy in the second half of the nineteenth century, was the newest member of the great power club and had something to prove. Having defeated the French, the Germans wanted to show that they were the equals of the British by acquiring an empire of their own. There was also a domestic logic to German imperialism. The German leader Otto von Bismarck recognized that rapid industrialization and urbanization were having destabilizing social effects and that the working class was becoming organized. From Bismarck's conservative standpoint, if the public's attention could be focused on military glory and imperial expansion, then nationalism would strengthen German unity and weaken the appeal of socialism.

For the French as well, international prestige, national glory, and domestic politics were all-important in stimulating imperial expansion after 1871. French politicians needed to restore their country's international standing after the humiliating defeat by the Germans. Imperial expansion in Africa and Southeast Asia accomplished that goal and gave legitimacy to the government of the Third Republic (see Chapter 23).

Britain already presided over a vast overseas empire that was largely a legacy of preindustrial commercial activities. In 1888 a British historian noted that they had accumulated their empire in a "fit of absentmindedness." Britain's centuries-old focus on maritime affairs, its early industrial lead, and its domination of global finance had brought control of resource-rich territories such as India and South Africa, even while Victorian liberals, with their belief in free trade, had tried to limit imperial expansion.

The rise of Germany caused Britain to more actively pursue imperial power. The Conservative Party (also called the Tories) had traditionally been the party of the rural gentry. But in the 1870s a new generation of Tory leaders, led by Benjamin Disraeli (1804–1881), saw an opportunity to broaden their base of support by becoming the party of empire. After the Reform Act of 1884 a majority of the country's male population could vote, and Disraeli found that appeals to patriotism and national glory could help him win elections. As in Germany and France, domestic politics helped drive imperial policy. The Liberal Party under W. E. Gladstone (1809–1898), always concerned that British taxpayers would have to bear the costs of colonial wars, tried unsuccessfully to resist this trend. The need to protect existing colonies meant that the British Empire continued to expand even during periods of Liberal rule.

Economic factors intensified the national competition that characterized the New Imperialism. The Second Industrial Revolution (see Chapter 25) brought dramatic innovations in technology and business organization. Large corporations that invested huge sums of money in the chemical and metals industries needed access to natural resources like tin, oil, and rubber from around the world to be competitive. As long as Britain was the dominant power and enforced global free trade, such resources were available to anyone with the ability to buy them. But as competition increased among the great powers, faith in the free market began to collapse.

The New Imperialism therefore brought a return to mercantilist policies. Countries attempted to have exclusive power over empires from which they could extract resources for the benefit of the home economy (see Chapter 16). With this zero-sum philosophy again on the rise, chartered companies such as those that had dominated Europe's eighteenth-century colonial enterprises came back. The imperial powers also had two other vital economic interests. First, they needed markets for the goods they were now producing with such efficiency. Second, they needed new investment opportunities. Empire was not the only way to achieve these economic ends, but by the 1890s imperial expansion was closely tied to the growth of industrial capitalism. As a result, the free-market preferences of economic liberals became less central to European policymakers.

Ideology and Personal Ambition

The New Imperialism was also associated with challenges to the social ideals of liberalism. Social Darwinism, the idea that races and nations were locked in a "struggle for existence" (see Chapter 23), had now become the dominant ideology in Europe and became even more potent when augmented by pseudo-scientific racial ideas. Most white people saw themselves as sitting atop an unchangeable hierarchy of races, a belief that justified colonial expansion as part of the natural order of things. Some predicted that the world's other peoples would gradually die out because of their biological and cultural weaknesses; others argued that it was the duty of "advanced" races to "civilize" the "inferior" ones for their own good (see Chapter 25).

Even as they preached a gospel of inclusion and love, Christian missionaries were influenced by racist attitudes. In the early nineteenth century, missionaries, inspired by the abolitionist movement (see Chapter 19), had dedicated themselves to the salvation of African souls and the redemption of the continent from spiritual practices that they regarded as primitive superstition. In the 1820s, the London Missionary Society established its first stations in South Africa (and Samoa). The career of **David Livingstone** (1813–1873), the great Scottish missionary and explorer, shows that in spite of cultural prejudices the early missionaries believed in the intellectual and spiritual capacities of African peoples.

● **David Livingstone** (1813–1873) Scottish missionary and explorer idolized in Britain for his commitment to the spiritual and moral salvation of Africans.

David Livingstone spent the better part of his life exploring the continent and preaching Christianity to its people. He spent most of his later years beyond the borders of European control, relying on African hospitality and protection. Livingstone saw Africans as fully capable in every way; his dream was eventually to have African Christians in positions of church leadership. In pursuit of this goal he spent time among the Bangwato, serving as a tutor to one of the kings who accompanied Khama to London.

Livingstone's goal was achieved by Samuel Ajayi Crowther, the first African bishop of the Church of England. Born in what is now western Nigeria, Crowther was sold into slavery in 1821. By then the British were committed to abolition, and the Royal Navy seized the Portuguese ship on which he was held captive along with his mother and brother. The British dropped the 12-year-old off at Freetown in Sierra Leone, earlier established as a home for such "re-captives." After education in Sierra Leone and England, and having served on a mission to the Niger River, Crowther was ordained as an Anglican priest. One of his enduring contributions to African Christianity was his translation of the Christian texts into his own native Yoruba and other African languages.

In 1864, Crowther became the Anglican bishop of West Africa. But he was disappointed to find that some white missionaries, influenced by Social Darwinism, resented the appointment of a black bishop and refused to follow his directives. Unlike Livingstone, they viewed blacks as permanent children, incapable of handling such a high office. Crowther was forced into retirement and replaced with an English bishop. (See the feature "Movement of Ideas: Bishop Turner's View of Africa.")

David Livingstone's story was well known in England (even if Samuel Ajayi Crowther's was not). When Khama and his friends visited England, they found that by using the name *Livingstone* they could always get a cheer from the crowd. Many in the audience remembered the dramatic story of how a young American journalist, Henry Morton Stanley (1841–1904), had located Livingstone in Central Africa when he was feared lost. Stanley exemplified the spirit of the New Imperialism, regarding Africans as savages and treating them as such.

Unlike Livingstone's expeditions, Stanley's explorations were made for his own benefit. Having traced the great Congo River from its source deep in Central Africa to its outlet on the Atlantic, Stanley formed an alliance with the ambitious **King Leopold II of Belgium** (r. 1865–1909) to profit from his discoveries.

Belgium was a small kingdom that had become independent from the Netherlands only in 1830. Leopold envied European monarchs like Queen Victoria who had claims to imperial territory, and he was convinced that great wealth could be gained in Africa. Declaring, "I must have my share of this magnificent African cake!"

■ **Samuel Ajayi Crowther**   A thoughtful theologian and talented linguist, Samuel Ajayi Crowther became the first Anglican bishop of West Africa in 1864. Increasing British racism undercut his authority, however. After Crowther, the Anglican church did not appoint another African bishop in West Africa for over fifty years.   (The Granger Collection)

● **King Leopold II of Belgium** (r. 1865–1909) Ignited a "scramble for Africa" when he claimed the large area of Central Africa he called the Congo Free State. The ruthless exploitation of Congolese rubber by Leopold's agents led to millions of deaths.

Bishop Turner's View of Africa

While the "scramble for Africa" was taking place, some people of African descent in the Americas began to develop a "Pan-African" perspective that stressed the common circumstances and aspirations of black people around the world. One strand of Pan-Africanism focused on the possible emigration of American blacks back to Africa. Here a major figure was Henry McNeal Turner (1834–1915). Born free but poor in South Carolina, Turner learned to read and write while working as a janitor at a law firm. After becoming a preacher, in 1857 he joined the African Methodist Episcopal Church (AME), an entirely black-run denomination, and during the Civil War served as the first black chaplain in the United States Army. After the war he was elected to the Georgia assembly but was prevented from taking his seat on racial grounds. The fact that he was of mixed race and fair skinned made no difference.

The failure of Reconstruction (see Chapter 25) to bring true liberty to black Americans left Turner bitter. As lynching and legalized segregation became the norm, he argued that it was foolish to suppose that blacks would ever be allowed to prosper in the United States, and he became a strong advocate for emigration to Africa. His first interest was Liberia, an independent nation founded by freed African Americans. He then became aware of South Africa, where black Christians were interested in affiliating themselves with the AME Church to escape the control of white missionaries. In the 1890s he traveled to both countries and ordained a number of South African bishops.

Source: Edwin S. Redkey, *Respect Black: The Writings and Speeches of Henry McNeal Turner* (New York: Arno Press, 1971), pp. 42–44, 52–55, 83, 143–144.

1883

There is no more doubt in my mind that we have ultimately to return to Africa than there is of the existence of a God; and the sooner we begin to recognize that fact and prepare for it, the better it will be for us as a people. We have there a country unsurpassed in productive and mineral resources, and we have some two hundred millions of our kindred there in moral and spiritual blindness. The four millions of us in this country are at school, learning the doctrines of Christianity and the elements of civil government. As soon as we are educated sufficiently to assume control of our vast ancestral domain, we will hear the voice of a mysterious Providence, saying, *"Return to the land of your fathers. . . ."*

Nothing less than nationality will bring large prosperity and acknowledged manhood to us as a people. How can we do this? Not by constantly complaining of bad treatment; by holding conventions and passing resolutions; by voting for white men for office; by serving as caterers and barbers, and by having our wives and daughters continue as washerwomen and servants to the whites. No—a government and nationality of our own can alone cure the evils under which we now labor, and are likely yet the more to suffer in this country.

It may be asked, where can we build up a respectable government? Certainly not in the United States. . . . I am sure there is no region so full of promise and where the probabilities of success are so great as the land of our ancestors. The continent appears to be kept by Providence in reserve for the Negro. There everything seems ready to raise him to deserved distinction, comfort and wealth. . . . And the time is near when the American people of color will . . . erect the UNITED STATES OF AFRICA.

The murders and outrages perpetrated upon our people . . . since 1867 [are] . . . an orgy of blood and death. . . . I know we are Americans to all intents and purposes. We were born here, raised here, fought, bled and died here, and have a thousand times more right here than hundreds of thousands of those who help to snub, proscribe and persecute us, and that is one of the reasons I almost despise the land of my birth. . . .

1891

You can ridicule it if you like, but Africa will be the thermometer that will determine the status of the Negro the world over. . . . The elevation of the Negro in this and all other countries is indissoluably connected with the enlightenment of Africa. . . .

1893

These black [Muslim] priests . . . walking around here with so much dignity, majesty and consciousness of their worth are driving me into respect for them. Some come from hundreds of miles from the country—out of the bush—better scholars than any in America. What fools we are to suppose these Africans are fools! . . . Since I reached here, I see native Africans running engines, manning oar and steamboats, and . . . two black ocean pilots and another black man measuring the depth of the ocean and guiding the ship amid the dangerous points. Poor black man, how the world tells lies about you! . . . .

I have found out another thing since I have come to Africa, gone scores of miles through the interior and noted the tact, taste, genius and manly bearing of the higher grade of the natives. . . . Those who think the receding forehead, the flat nose, the proboscidated mouth and the big flat-bottom foot are natural to the African are mistaken. There are heads here by the millions, as vertical or perpendicular as any white man's head God ever made. . . .

I have long ago learned that the rich Negro, the ignorant Negro . . . and the would-be white Negro care nothing for African redemption, or the honor and dignity of the race. . . . I have never advocated all the colored people going to Africa, for I am well aware that the bulk of them are lacking in common sense and are too fond of worshiping white gods. . . . [E]very man who has a drop of African blood in his veins should be interested in the civilization, if not the salvation, of her millions, and how any black man can speak in contemptuous language of that great continent and her millions, when they gave him existence . . . is a mystery to me.

QUESTIONS FOR ANALYSIS

▶ How did Turner think Africa could be useful to African Americans, and vice versa?

▶ How were his ideas about Africans in particular, and race issues in general, similar to or different from those of Social Darwinists?

he hired Stanley to organize a military expedition to stake a claim to the vast region surrounding the Congo River. The other European powers became alarmed. If Africa really were a vast source of wealth, they could not afford to miss out. In the 1880s all the other factors associated with the New Imperialism—political, strategic, economic, and ideological—came together in a rapid scramble for African territory.

Otto von Bismarck, concerned that Leopold's imperialism might destabilize the balance of power in Europe, brought together representatives of the European colonial powers at the **Berlin Conference** in 1884 to establish rules for the partition of the continent. No Africans were present. The European delegates declared that the boundaries of the French, British, Belgian, German, Portuguese, Italian, and Spanish possessions in Africa would be recognized only if those powers established "effective occupation" of the territories ceded to them in Berlin. For Africans, this meant that the next twenty years would be a time of constant warfare and instability as European governments launched a wave of invasions to secure the "effective occupation" of the territories they claimed. Millions of Africans would die.

● **Berlin Conference** (1884) Conference organized by the German chancellor Otto von Bismarck in which representatives of the major European states divided Africa among themselves, subject to "effective occupation."

● Africa and the New Imperialism

As late as 1878, the European colonial presence was almost entirely restricted to the African coast (see Map 26.1). The all-out scramble for control of African territory was therefore something new. In contrast to India, where British power had been expanding since the eighteenth century (see Chapter 24), most Africans confronted European power *after* the development of industrial technology: machine guns, field cannon, telegraphs, and steamships. The suddenness of the onslaught, aided by this technology, caught Africans off guard. Should they fight back? Seek diplomatic options? Ally themselves with the new intruders? African leaders tried all of these options, with little success.

Although European imperialists reduced Africa to a set of simple stereotypes in which "tribal Africa" represented the "heart of darkness," in reality Africa was immensely complex, a continent of great cultural and geographic variety. Africa's own historical dynamics, including the rise of new and powerful Muslim states in the West African savanna and the creation of the Zulu Empire in the far south, are an essential context for understanding the European partition of the continent.

(CL) **Primary Source: Parable of the Eagle, Limbo, Prayer for Peace, Vultures** *The literature of four African writers expresses the traumatic effects of colonialism.*

Western Africa   After abolition European merchants still visited the African coast to purchase raw materials for rapidly expanding industries. While Egypt under Muhammad Ali became a major source of raw cotton for British industry (see Chapter 23), the most important product coming from sub-Saharan Africa was palm oil. Responding to a growing demand for industrial lubricants starting in the 1820s, African farmers began to plant and process oil products for the export market, and many West African merchants became wealthy in this trade. Factory-produced cloth and iron goods were becoming cheaper at the same time as higher demand was increasing the price Europeans would pay for palm oil. At least in some regions, Africans found the terms of trade moving in their favor.

British — British
French — French
German — German
Italian — Italian
Portuguese — Portuguese
Belgian — Belgian
Spanish — Spanish
Independent African states — Independent African states
✴ Major battle
● Selected sites of African resistance to European occupation

Madeira Is. (Portugal)

Canary Is. (Spain)

SPANISH MOROCCO
Tangier
Casablanca
MOROCCO
IFNI
RIO DE ORO
Algiers
Mediterranean Sea
TUNISIA
Tripoli
Cyrene
ALGERIA
LIBYA
Sanusi 1912–1913
Arabi-Pasha 1881–1882
Cairo
EGYPT
Aswan
Tushki 1889
Mahdists
Tropic of Cancer
ARABIA
20°N

S A H A R A

FRENCH WEST AFRICA
Rabih 1892–1900
L. Chad
Omdurman 1898
Khartoum 1884
ANGLO-EGYPTIAN SUDAN
Fashoda
ERITREA
Adowa 1896
FRENCH SOMALILAND
BRITISH SOMALILAND
ETHIOPIA
Sayyid Muhammad 1891–1920

GAMBIA
Senegal R.
PORTUGUESE GUINEA
Bai Bureh 1898
SIERRA LEONE
1881–1892
1892–1898
Samori
Niger R.
Fon 1892
TOGOLAND
Asante 1900
Sokoto 1900
NORTHERN NIGERIA
LIBERIA
IVORY COAST
GOLD COAST
Ijebu 1892
S. NIGERIA
Fernando Po (Spain)
KAMERUN
SPANISH GUINEA
São Tomé (Portugal)
FRENCH EQUATORIAL AFRICA
Uele R.
Congo R.
Bunyoro 1890–1898
UGANDA
BRITISH EAST AFRICA
0° Equator

ATLANTIC OCEAN
CABINDA
BELGIAN CONGO
Tutsi and Hutu 1911–1917
L. Victoria
Mombasa
GERMAN EAST AFRICA
Abushiri 1888–1889
Zanzibar (Gr. Br.)
Hehe 1891–1898
Maji-Maji 1905–1907
L. Tanganyika
INDIAN OCEAN

ANGOLA
NORTHERN RHODESIA
Zambezi R.
Shona 1896–1903
NYASALAND
L. Nyasa
MOZAMBIQUE
MADAGASCAR
20°S
Tropic of Capricorn

GERMAN SOUTHWEST AFRICA
Herero 1904–1908
Nama 1905–1909
BECHUANALAND
SOUTHERN RHODESIA
Ndebele 1896
TRANSVAAL
SWAZILAND
ORANGE FREE STATE
Bambata 1906–1908
Isandhlwana 1879
BASUTOLAND
UNION OF SOUTH AFRICA
NATAL
Cape Town

0   400   800 Km.
0   400   800 Mi.

Inset map:
ALGERIA
EGYPT
S A H A R A
SENEGAL
Niger R.
Nile R.
20°N
Congo R.
0°
20°S
COLONIAL PRESENCE IN AFRICA, 1878
CAPE COLONY
0   800 Km.
0   800 Mi.
20°W   0°   20°E   40°E

🌐 **MAP 26.1**

Africa, 1878 and 1914 The dramatic expansion of European imperialism in Africa is seen in the comparison of maps from 1878 and 1914. Before the "scramble for Africa" the European colonial presence was largely limited to small coastal enclaves. At that time frontiers of European settlement were found only in Algeria and in the Cape Colony. By 1914 Europeans dominated the entire continent, with only Liberia and Ethiopia retaining their independence. The British were the main power in eastern and southern Africa, the French in west and north Africa, and the Belgians in central Africa.

CL Interactive Map

What the missionaries called a "legitimate trade" in agricultural products did not immediately bring an end to slavery or the slave trade in Africa. The long-standing Indian Ocean trade in slaves to Arabia and the Persian Gulf increased greatly even as the coastal slave trade in West Africa declined. And the use of slaves *within* West Africa actually increased after abolition: privileged Africans used slave labor on palm oil plantations in West Africa, and Arab plantation owners used slaves to grow cloves and other spices on the East African island of Zanzibar.

As West African economies became more integrated into world commodity markets, political power initially remained with African kingdoms and chiefdoms. A British-educated African surgeon named John Africanus Horton, in an influential essay in 1868, argued that existing African kingdoms should reform themselves by incorporating Western constitutional practice, much like the Meiji program in Japan (see Chapter 24). But Horton's call for a creative merging of African traditions with Western models was never successfully implemented. The European "scramble for Africa" came too suddenly for West Africans to carry out such reforms.

In 1874, with the pro-imperial Conservative Party of Benjamin Disraeli in power, Britain reversed its policy of noninvolvement in Africa's interior by attacking the powerful **Asante kingdom,** the dominant power in the West African forest in the eighteenth and nineteenth centuries. The Asante (uh-SHAN-tee) armies were badly outgunned. Besides being technologically inferior, even a relatively large and powerful state like Asante was too small compared to the British Empire to make the fight an equal one. Moreover, the Asante kingdom had incorporated smaller chiefdoms, some of which allied with the British to escape Asante control. As in Mesoamerica in the 1520s, old rivalries helped facilitate European conquest.

The French also had a limited but long-standing presence in West Africa that expanded dramatically in the last three decades of the nineteenth century. Most of the African societies the French encountered were Muslim. Although there were no successors to the once mighty empire of Songhai (see Chapter 19), by the early 1800s a string of powerful new states formed by Islamic reformers were spreading across the interior of West Africa.

The seeds of Islamic reform in West Africa were planted by charismatic leaders who established Sufi brotherhoods in which initiates practiced a mystical form of Islam, mastering complex prayers and rituals. Members of these brotherhoods were loyal to each other and devoted to their religious teachers. Striving for a return to the pure practices of early Islam, they moved to remote areas, hoping to escape the corruption and lack of piety in cities such as Timbuktu. The origins of the great *jihad* movements of nineteenth-century West Africa lay in their criticism of Muslim political leaders who tolerated the mixing of Islamic and traditional African practices and beliefs.

One of the most important West African jihad leaders was Usuman dan Fodio (1754–1817). In what is now northern Nigeria, dan Fodio launched constant calls for a local emir to put his government in line with Islamic law. When the emir tried to assassinate him, Usuman dan Fodio (OO-soo-mahn dahn FOH-dee-oh) and his followers went on the offensive. They built a large army and soon consolidated their power over the small emirates, combining them in the new Sokoto (SOH-kuh-toh) Caliphate. From here the jihadist impulse spread both east and west. Throughout the nineteenth century, existing West African Muslim populations became stricter in their practice, and Islam gained large numbers of new adherents.

In the mid-nineteenth century, the leaders of Sokoto and other jihadist movements focused on reforming their own Muslim societies and paid little attention

● **Asante kingdom**
Dominant power in the West African forest in the eighteenth and early nineteenth centuries. The Asante capital was sacked by British forces in 1874 and again in 1896. In 1900, Yaa Asantewa's War represented a final attempt to expel the British.

to Europeans. In the 1870s, however, when the French used their coastal bases to move up the Senegal River, they came into conflict. The West African Muslim who organized the most sustained resistance to French invasion was **Samori Toure** (ca. 1830–1900).

Samori Toure (sam-or-ee too-RAY), from a relatively humble merchant background, built a powerful new state on the upper Niger by training his soldiers in the use of imported rifles. At first his ambitions were merely political, but in 1884 he declared himself to be "commander of the faithful," leader of a jihad against lax Muslims and unbelievers. Even then, Samori avoided conflict with the French, focusing instead on control of lucrative trade routes in goods like slaves, salt, and gold. But once the French had conquered his weaker neighbors, they turned their attention on Samori.

Unable to prevail in conventional warfare, in 1891 Samori retreated with his army hundreds of miles to the east and launched a guerilla campaign. Cut off from access to the ammunition and gunpowder he had earlier imported from Sierra Leone, Samori's soldiers learned to manufacture their own from local materials. But even this most tenacious of African resistance leaders could not hold out for long. Because his soldiers oppressed the local people, he had no local base of support, and the French were relentless in their attacks. After Samori was captured and exiled in 1893, the French were masters of the region from the Senegal to the Niger Rivers.

The French march to the east threatened British control of Egypt and the Nile Valley. To head off the French advance, British forces moved to stake a claim of "effective occupation" over the savanna region still dominated by the Sokoto Caliphate. After the death of Usuman dan Fodio, the caliphate had become decentralized, with individual emirs controlling walled city-states and the surrounding countryside. Thus the British did not face the combined armies of a unified caliphate and could attack each city-state separately. The traditional tactics of savanna warfare, where peasants retreated into walled cities while mounted warriors mounted cavalry charges, were no match for rifles and machine guns; British field cannon easily blew breeches in the city walls. Some emirs fought, some fled, and some surrendered, as British forces took control of what is now northern Nigeria.

What might have happened if the Sokoto Caliphate had formed an alliance with the Asante kingdom in the forest to the south, or with Samori Toure? The lack of such alliances greatly accelerated the process of European imperialism, but there was no common identity to support them. Like King Khama of the Bangwato, African leaders dealt only with the local manifestations of the scramble for Africa, lacking organizational or ideological foundations for a broader unity. Even as they competed with one another, the Europeans had the advantage of having a broader overview of African developments, and they used their superior communications technology and geographic knowledge of the continent to great advantage.

Southern Africa

In southern Africa as well, a dynamic process of African historical development intersected with European imperialism. Long before the Dutch established their settlement at Cape Town (see Chapter 16), the ancestors of King Khama and his people, Bantu-speaking farmers, herders, and iron-makers, had populated the land. In the drier highland areas, they lived in centralized chiefdoms near permanent sources of water. In the moister region between the Drakensberg Mountains and the Indian Ocean, population density was historically

• Samori Toure (ca. 1830–1900) Founder of a major state in West Africa who adopted the pose of a jihadist leader in competition with neighboring kingdoms. After being forced into confrontation by the French, he launched a long but unsuccessful guerilla campaign against them.

lower, and the clan chiefs who presided over councils of elders had little autonomous power.

Centralization and warfare came to this region in the late eighteenth century, when drought led small chiefdoms to band together to secure permanent water sources. The most successful of the new states was the Zulu Empire of **Shaka** (r. 1820–1828), who created a great military machine that transformed much of southern Africa. He formed a standing army of soldiers from different clans, emphasizing their loyalty to him and to the Zulu state rather than to their own chiefdoms, and chose his generals on the basis of merit rather than chiefly status. Young women were organized into agricultural regiments, and no one was allowed to marry without Shaka's permission.

The conquests of Shaka's armies were known as the *mfecane* (mm-fuh-KAHN-ay), "the crushing." Many chiefdoms were violently absorbed into the Zulu Empire, though some neighboring chiefs voluntarily submitted. In either case, conquered peoples were taken into Zulu society and became Zulu. What had been one of many small, clan-based chiefdoms was becoming a powerful nation. The mfecane then set in motion a chain reaction as other leaders copied Zulu military tactics and carried the frontier of warfare a thousand miles north. The Bangwato and other societies in the interior fled to places of safety, abandoning much of their land to seek security.

Well aware of the Europeans who lived to his southwest, Shaka had several Englishmen as advisers. He was particularly interested in their guns, but he never gave up his reliance on well-forged iron spears to equip his army. The British were a new factor in southern Africa, having taken Cape Town from the Dutch during the Napoleonic Wars. Coveting the strategic control of the Cape, at first they had no interest in securing the interior, and in 1820 they tried to maintain a buffer between the settlement frontier and the African centers by moving English settlers into the boundary region. As Africans fled to the mountains to escape Zulu armies, these lands had become temporarily depopulated. But sending English settlers into these areas angered expansionistic Boer farmers, descendants of the original Dutch colonists who had established a fort at Cape Town in 1652 and who had moved into the African interior in the eighteenth century (see Chapter 19). On their Great Trek of 1834–1836, some Boer farmers moved north and staked their claim, involving the reluctant British more deeply in the affairs of the South African interior.

Boer settlement and British firepower overwhelmed many African societies, already weakened by the mfecane. The Xhosa (KOH-suh) chiefdoms, for example, were losing rich grazing lands to the colonists. Neither negotiation nor military resistance was successful at stemming the European tide. Moreover, contact with the colonial society had created deep divisions within Xhosa society. Some Xhosa had converted to Christianity and grew crops for colonial markets, and traditionalist Xhosa saw these converts and market-oriented farmers as having abandoned their own people.

Then another disaster struck, the **Xhosa Cattle Killing,** caused by a disease inadvertently introduced by the Europeans in the 1850s. The killing wiped out large numbers of Xhosa cattle. Facing starvation as well as invasion, some Xhosa turned to the prophecies of a young woman, Nongqawuse (ca. 1840–1898), who said the ancestors told her that evil would be driven from the land if the people slaughtered their remaining cattle. The ancestors would then return, defeat the whites and Xhosa traitors, and bring peace and prosperity.

Belief in the imminent power of ancestors was traditional to the Xhosa, and women often had the power to communicate with them. But the idea that the

Shaka (r. 1820–1828) Founder and ruler of the Zulu Empire. Zulu military tactics revolutionized warfare in southern Africa. Through the *mfecane,* or "crushing," Shaka violently absorbed many surrounding societies into his empire.

Xhosa Cattle Killing (1856–1857) A large cattle die-off in Africa caused by a European disease. Some Xhosa accepted the Nongqawuse prophecies that if the people cleansed themselves and killed their cattle their ancestors would return and bring peace and prosperity. The result was famine and Xhosa subjection to the British.

raising of the dead would accompany a new era of peace was borrowed by Nongqawuse's (nawng-ka-WOO-say) uncle from Methodist missionaries. Like Hong Xiuquan in China (see Chapter 24) and Wovoka on the Great Plains (see Chapter 25), the message of Nongqawuse was an example of syncretism, a combination of indigenous beliefs with the Christian concept of the "millennium," a period of perfect peace that awaits believers at the end of time. Seeing no other way out of their predicament, many Xhosa followed Nongqawuse's prophecy and killed their cattle. When the departed warriors failed to return and hunger spread throughout the land, British conquest of the Xhosa became inevitable. Over a hundred thousand lives were lost, and the remaining Xhosa were incorporated into Britain's Cape Colony. The British exiled Nongqawuse to Robben Island off the Cape coast (where, a century later, Nelson Mandela was also incarcerated; see Chapter 31).

Still, the Zulu and other African societies retained their sovereignty into the 1870s. Their colonial fate was not determined until mineral discoveries, diamonds in 1868 and gold in 1884, combined with New Imperialism to finally motivate the British to conquer the South African interior. The Boers, proud of their independence, sought a German alliance to protect themselves against British imperialism. Africans in the interior, like Khama's Bangwato, found themselves facing the full brunt of European military technology for the first time.

In 1879, British authorities issued an ultimatum demanding that the Zulu king Cetshwayo disband his regiments. Since military organization was at the heart of his power, Cetshwayo refused to comply. Zulu warriors did defeat the British at the major Battle of Isandhlwana, but like the Battle of Little Big Horn (see Chapter 25), this victory only made the invaders more determined. Zulu warriors had been trained to rush the enemy in dense regimental ranks, a suicide strategy when used against machine guns. In 1880 the British sacked the Zulu capital and sent Cetshwayo into exile.

The main figure of the New Imperialism in southern Africa was **Cecil Rhodes** (1853–1902), a mining magnate (and founder of the DeBeers diamond syndicate) who advocated a British empire "from Cape to Cairo." His British South Africa Company (BSAC) was a chartered company (see Chapter 16) with its own army and ambitions for conquest. It was to avoid annexation by the BSAC that Khama traveled to London, even as Rhodes was planning an invasion of the Boer republics, on whose land the great gold strikes were located.

THE RHODES COLOSSUS
STRIDING FROM CAPE TOWN TO CAIRO.

Cecil Rhodes The most important of Victorian imperialists, Cecil Rhodes dreamed of British imperial control of eastern and southern Africa "from Cape Town to Cairo." Combining political and economic clout, Rhodes was prime minister of the Cape Colony, founder of the DeBeers diamond syndicate, owner of some of the world's richest gold mines, and head of the British South African Company. He later endowed the Rhodes Scholarship program to bring elite Americans of British descent to Oxford University in England so that the United States might share Britain's imperial purpose. (The Granger Collection)

Cecil Rhodes (1853–1902) British entrepreneur, mining magnate, head of the British South Africa Company, and prime minister of the Cape Colony. Rhodes played a major role in the expansion of British territory in southern Africa.

After the failure of a BSAC invasion, the British government, with its strategic and economic interests threatened, went to war. The South African War (1899–1902) was a preview of the violence of twentieth-century warfare. The British had no trouble taking control of the towns and railway lines, but they were frustrated by the tactics of the Boer soldiers, who blended into the civilian population and launched guerilla attacks in the countryside. To separate civilians from soldiers, the British put Boer women and children into "concentration camps" (the first use of that term). Over twenty thousand Boer civilians, many of them women and children, died of illness. Though the South African War was between the British and the Boers, some twenty thousand Africans, enlisted to fight by both sides, were also killed.

The British won the war but then compromised with their defeated foes. The **Union of South Africa** (1910) was created by joining British colonies with former Boer republics under a single constitution. Like Canada (see Chapter 25), South Africa was now a self-governing dominion within the British Empire. The union has been called "an alliance of gold and maize," protecting both British capital in the mining sector and Boer agricultural interests. Both sides needed African labor. In 1913 the Native Land Act, passed by the new, all-white South African parliament, limited Africans to "native reserves" that represented a tiny proportion of their traditional landholdings. The goal was to create rural poverty and drive Africans to work in mines and on white farms at the lowest possible pay. The economic foundations for what would later be called apartheid had been laid (see Chapter 28).

Because of King Khama's successful negotiations with the British government, his people were not part of this new South Africa and were ruled by the British Colonial Office rather than by the South African parliament. (See the feature "World History in Today's World: Botswana: Diamonds and AIDS.") The Zulu and the Xhosa, meanwhile, like other Africans incorporated into the Union of South Africa, experienced the harshest form of colonial racism. As mineworkers and low-wage laborers on settler farms, they struggled at the lowest level of the global economy.

• **Union of South Africa** Self-governing dominion with the British Empire created in 1910 from a number of British colonies and Boer republics after the South African War. This compromise protected both British mining and Boer agriculture at the expense of African interests.

Conquest and Resistance

Between 1880 and 1900, European powers effectively occupied and partitioned Africa. France and Britain held the largest African empires; Portugal and Germany each had substantial territories in the east and south; Italy and Spain were relatively minor players; and King Leopold of Belgium claimed the vast Congo in the center of the continent.

The technological advantages enjoyed by the Europeans made their victory over Africans all but inevitable. The "tools of empire" included more than just rifles and machine guns. Steamships and telegraphs shrunk the distance between European centers of command and European officials on the ground, allowing for quicker coordination. Because African rivers drop sharply from highlands to the sea, sailing ships could not penetrate far inland. Now steam-powered ships allowed Europeans to more easily access the continent's interior regions. And beginning in the 1890s, railroads allowed the rapid movement of troops and colonial administrators.

Advances in medical technology also facilitated European conquest. One reason that Europeans had rarely ventured inland during the era of the slave trade was the danger of dying from malaria, against which they had no resistance. By the time of the "scramble for Africa" scientists had discovered that quinine, derived from the bark of a South American tree, allowed those with no immunity to malaria to survive multiple bouts of the disease.

Botswana: Diamonds and AIDS

Botswana became independent from Great Britain in 1966 under the leadership of Sir Seretse Khama, a direct descendant of King Khama III of the Bangwato. The constitutional order created in 1966 has endured to this day, with universal suffrage, separation of executive, legislative, and judicial powers, and a two-term limit on the presidency. In addition to the elected assembly, there is a House of Chiefs that must be consulted on matters pertaining to their chieftaincies. The current chief of the Bangwato is a member of this body.

Political stability has helped Botswana make the most of its economic resources. Half the country is desert, and the rest is subject to periodic droughts. Most people are farmers and herders with little disposable income. However, modern meat-processing facilities have allowed the villagers to benefit from the export of beef to neighboring South Africa, and careful development of the diamond industry has put the country's finances in good order. Botswana is the world's largest producer of gem-quality diamonds. Many of today's engagement rings come from beneath the same soil that King Khama worked to protect from Cecil Rhodes and the British South African Company in the nineteenth century.

Without a doubt the biggest challenge facing the people of Botswana is HIV/AIDS. The country has the highest known rate of HIV/AIDS infection in the world, and life expectancy is dropping. Astonishingly, 50 percent of women aged 25 test positive for HIV; one-third of all pregnant women in the country are infected. The costs of caring for AIDS orphans, often themselves HIV positive, is a huge drain on the country's resources that will only increase in the coming years.

Although the situation is grim, the progressive AIDS prevention program run by the government of Botswana, focusing on prevention of the disease among the young, could make a difference. The country has an impressive educational system, funded largely by income from diamonds. Virtually all of Botswana's children attend school, and the literacy rate of 81 percent is one of the highest in Africa. There is still hope that with education and good governance Botswana will surmount the HIV/AIDS challenge.

In spite of European technological superiority, Africans fought back. The Nile Valley was one arena of large-scale resistance to British imperialism. Its strategic value increased with the construction of the **Suez Canal** between the Mediterranean and the Red Sea in 1869. Built by a French engineer and financed by French and English capital, the canal became the main shipping route between Europe and Asia.

The Egyptian khedive, a descendant of Muhammad Ali (see Chapter 23), thought that revenue from the canal would allow Egypt to maintain its independence. But a fall in the price of cotton after 1865, when the end of the American Civil War brought U.S. cotton back onto the world market, reduced Egyptian government revenues. Unable to pay the country's debts, the khedive was forced to sell Egypt's shares in the Suez Canal to the British and to accept European oversight of government finances. European officers were imposed on the Egyptian military, which was reorganized as an Anglo-Egyptian force.

In 1882, nationalist officers in the Egyptian military led by Arabi Pasha rebelled against the khedive and his European backers. The British quickly suppressed the uprising and then forced the khedive to accept a governor-general who would "advise" the Egyptian government on all important affairs. The British thus came to dominate Egypt, much as they dominated the "princely states" in India (see Chapter 24), keeping real power in their own hands while allowing the indigenous rulers to retain their titles and their luxurious lifestyles.

Suez Canal (1869) French-designed canal built between the Mediterranean and the Red Sea that greatly shortened shipping times between Europe and Asia. The Suez Canal Company was dominated by European economic interests.

● **The Mahdi, Muhammad Ahmad** (1844–1885) *Mahdi* is the term some Muslims use for the "guided one" expected to appear before the end of days. Muhammad Ahmad took this title in the Sudan and called for a jihad against British-dominated Egypt.

Once they had taken control of Egypt, the British needed to secure the Upper Nile Valley as well. Here they faced fierce resistance from a jihadist state in Sudan, where a cleric named **Muhammad Ahmad** (1844–1885) proclaimed himself to be **The Mahdi** (MAH-dee), the "guided one" some Muslims believe will come to announce the end of days and the final judgment of mankind. In 1881, he declared a holy war against Egypt, which also brought him into conflict with Britain. The Mahdi's forces took the strategic city of Khartoum from the British in 1884, killing the British commander of a combined Anglo-Egyptian force. When Muhammad Ahmad died of typhus a few months later, however, his movement lost central direction.

The jihadist movement was reinvigorated in the 1890s under the leadership of the *khalifa* ("successor") to the Mahdi. Conflict with the Europeans could not be avoided: in response to French and German colonial claims, the British had become intent on establishing "effective occupation" over the entire Nile Valley. The Battle of Omdurman (1898) was the bloodiest battle between European and African forces in the entire period. Though outnumbered two-to-one, the Anglo-Egyptian forces used their Maxim guns to terrible effect, killing ten thousand Mahdist soldiers. British soldiers are reported to have killed Sudanese soldiers as they lay wounded, retribution for the siege of Khartoum.

Elsewhere African resistance to colonial occupation was on a smaller scale, as in the Asante kingdom. The British had sacked the Asante capital of Kumasi in 1874, but then withdrew. In the 1890s, however, with the Germans and French now active in the region, British forces once again moved toward Kumasi. The Asante reluctantly accepted a British protectorate and rebelled only after a new British governor arrived and demanded that the "golden stool" be brought before him. The golden stool was the sacred symbol of Asante kingship; according to legend, it had descended from the heavens to confirm the power of the first Asante king. Since it symbolized Asante sovereignty, the governor's request was an intolerable insult.

As the Asante prepared for war, some of the men expressed doubts about whether they could succeed. A queen mother from one of the confederated chiefdoms, Yaa Asantewa (YAH ah-san-TAY-wuh), stood forward and spoke: "[If] you the men of Asante will not go forward, then we will. We the women will. I shall call upon my fellow women. We will fight the white men. We will fight till the last of us falls in the battlefields." The Yaa Asantewa War of 1900 was a military defeat for the Asante, but it caused later British governors to treat the Asante royal family with greater respect and to acknowledge Asante legal traditions when codifying colonial laws.

Coordinating resistance was even more difficult in regions where traditional political organization was less centralized. The Maji Maji (MAH-jee MAH-jee) Revolt in German East Africa was led by a religious prophet, Kinjekitile, who attempted to forge an alliance between numerous small chiefdoms. German military conquest in the 1890s had been swift, meeting little opposition. By 1905, however, people in the region were angered when the Germans required them, under threat of force, to grow cotton. African farmers had little time to tend their own food crops while enduring the hard labor of planting, weeding, and harvesting cotton. The payment they received was barely enough to pay colonial taxes, and cotton robbed their fields of fertility. They rallied around Kinjekitile, a prophet who offered them hope.

Maji Maji meant "powerful water," a reference to a sacred pool that had for many years attracted pilgrims from across a wide area. Kinjekitile used this sacred shrine as a central point for communications, unifying scattered chiefdoms and coordinating their military intelligence. He promised his followers that bathing in the sacred stream would make them immune to German bullets. Of course, this did not happen, and the Germans ruthlessly suppressed the Maji Maji revolt. But they also learned not to press their African subjects too far, and no longer enforced mandatory cotton growing.

The aftermath of both the Asante and Maji Maji revolts shows that Africans' willingness to fight could force the Europeans to adjust their policies. Throughout the colonial period, Africans also used more subtle forms of resistance, such as songs and dances that criticized their European rulers, as a way to preserve their culture and express their humanity. (African slavers in the Americas had adopted similar strategies; see Chapter 19.)

Africans were, however, consistently demeaned by the imperial powers. A new fad at Western expositions was to display "natives" as a curiosity for the amusement of Western audiences. King Khama and his colleagues were taken to see a "Somali village" on display at London's Crystal Palace. One wonders what the southern African kings, dressed in formal Victorian attire, and the Somalis, presented to the public in their "primitive" state, thought of one another. The worst excess came in 1906, when a Central African named Ota Benga was displayed in a cage at the Bronx Zoo in New York. He later committed suicide. The disrespect and cruelty fostered by racist ideas such as Social Darwinism endured into the twentieth century.

●The New Imperialism in Southeast Asia

As in Africa, Europeans had long been competing for access to valuable trade goods and had established some imperial bases in Southeast Asia. But in the late nineteenth century the New Imperialism accelerated those trends and led to nearly complete domination by Western powers. In mainland Southeast Asia, the French used an alliance with Vietnamese emperors to extend their power over what became French Indochina. The British expanded from India into Burma and used the commercial city of Singapore to extend their empire into Malaya. On the thousands of islands that make up insular Southeast Asia, the Dutch were the dominant Western power; the United States joined the imperial club when it took the Philippines from Spain (see Map 26.2).

Mainland Southeast Asia

Vietnam's imperial structure was modeled on that of China (see Chapter 16), but central power was declining in the late eighteenth century. With the country wracked by rebellion, the Nguyen (NWIN) family, vying for control, allied with French missionaries and in 1802 established the new Nguyen dynasty, with Catholic missionaries representing French influence at the Vietnamese court.

The French moved from indirect influence to direct imperial control when Emperor Napoleon III, anxious to expand his country's global empire, sent an army of occupation to Vietnam in 1858 (and to Mexico a few years later; see Chapter 25). In 1862 the Nguyen ruler ceded control of the Mekong (MAY-kong) Delta and the commercial center of Saigon to France, opened three "treaty ports" to European

🌐 **MAP 26.2**

The New Imperialism in Southeast Asia, 1910 European nations had controlled parts of Southeast Asia, such as the Dutch East Indies and the Spanish Philippines, since the sixteenth and seventeenth centuries. The New Imperialism of the nineteenth century strengthened European control over those societies while bringing the entire region (with the exception of Siam, or Thailand) under Western colonial rule. In remote regions, such as the highlands of central Borneo, the process of conquest was not complete until the early twentieth century.

trade, and gave the French free passage up the Mekong River. Even that was not enough to satisfy the French government, which after 1871, here as in Africa, pursued an even bolder imperial strategy. By 1884 they were in nominal control of all of Vietnam but still had to suppress the tough resistance offered by guerillas. The French army of conquest killed thousands of rebels and civilians before establishing firm control. French authorities called the violence inflicted on the Vietnamese a campaign of "pacification."

By then French forces had conquered the neighboring kingdom of Cambodia and had taken Laos by agreement with the kingdom of Siam (see below). In 1897, they combined these territories into the **Federation of Indochina,** or simply French Indochina. French colonial authorities exploited Indochinese land and resources, taking over vast estates on which to grow rubber and turning rice into a major export crop. The profits went almost entirely to French traders and planters, though some Chinese and Vietnamese merchants in Saigon also benefited from the increase in commerce that came with the tighter integration of Southeast Asia into global markets.

Burma was also incorporated into the British Empire in stages, including several wars. By the 1870s, Britain controlled the south, while in the north a reformist Burmese king attempted to create the political and cultural infrastructure that he hoped would modernize the country under indigenous rule. British representatives had no patience for such experiments. They insulted the king by refusing to take off their shoes in his presence, a terrible affront to court protocol. Finally, in 1886 British forces invaded from India, took the capital of Mandalay, and over the next five years suppressed a number of regional rebellions. Having annexed Burma, the British brought in administrators from India and began building railroads to gain access to the rich timber resources of the Burmese jungles.

Since 1819, the trading city of Singapore had been Britain's most valuable possession in Southeast Asia. The British settlement attracted many Chinese immigrants and became the center of the Chinese merchant diaspora in the region. Before 1873 the British were content to control the main ports and grow rich on the trade between the Indian Ocean and the South China Sea, leaving politics to the dozens of Muslim rulers who dominated the sultanates of Malaya. But in the 1870s economic and strategic interests led to a more active imperialism. The completion of the Suez Canal in 1869 had shortened the shipping routes from Europe to the Indian

• Federation of Indochina (1897) Federation created in 1897 by the French after having conquered Vietnam, Cambodia, and Laos. Was an administrative convenience, as societies that made up the federation had little in common.

French Colonialism in Indochina   Like other European colonialists, the French argued that they were developing their imperial territories for the good of their subjects through both a "civilizing" cultural mission and economic development projects such as road building. As this photograph from southeast Asia indicates, however, it was the "natives" who did most of the work and their colonial overlords who grabbed the lion's share of profit.   (© Roger Viollet/The Image Works)

Ocean, and British merchants were particularly anxious to gain access to the rich tin resources of the Malay Peninsula, for which the Second Industrial Revolution had dramatically increased demand.

As in Africa, competition for power within and between indigenous states facilitated a policy of "divide and conquer." The British government appointed "residents" who would give the local rulers "advice" on the governance of their sultanates; if the sultan refused, they would simply recognize another ambitious man as ruler and work through him. As in Egypt and the princely states of India, the residency system left the indigenous rulers in place but put real power squarely in the hands of the Europeans. The British in Malaya, as in India and Burma, prided themselves on having brought solid, efficient administration to yet another corner of the globe. Meanwhile, as in Vietnam, plantation agriculture changed the agrarian landscape with expanding cultivation of commercial crops such as pepper, palm oil, and rubber.

Insular Southeast Asia

The Dutch had been the dominant European presence on the islands of Southeast Asia since the seventeenth century (see Chapter 16). After the Dutch East India Company was disbanded in 1799, colonial authorities imposed harsh economic conditions on their subjects in the Dutch East Indies. In 1830, for example, Dutch authorities forced rice farmers on the island of Java to convert to sugar production. One Dutch official declared that "they must be taught to work, and if they were unwilling out of ignorance, they must be ordered to work." Growing sugar, however, meant hard work for the benefit of others: the Dutch used political coercion to buy the sugar crop locally at low prices and then sold it for a great profit on world markets.

Fueled by such economic motives, Dutch authorities asserted more and more formal administrative control over the main islands of Java and Sumatra, where individual sultans had previously been left in charge of local affairs. At the same time, the increasing presence of other European powers motivated the Dutch to seek control of hundreds of other islands. Those who resisted, such as rebels on the Hindu-ruled island of Bali, were slaughtered. The New Imperialism significantly deepened Dutch power over the Indonesian archipelago.

While the Dutch were an old imperial power, the United States was a new presence in Asia and the Pacific. The arrival of Admiral Perry in Japan in 1853 (see Chapter 24) had significantly expanded American influence in Asia, and the United States claimed a direct territorial stake in the Pacific when it annexed the Hawaiian Islands in 1898. The extension of American imperialism to insular Southeast Asia came as a result of the Spanish-American War of 1898–1900. That conflict, initially centered on the Caribbean island of Cuba, spread to include the Philippines, where Spain had been in power since the foundation of Manila in 1571.

In the 1880s Filipino nationalists began organizing resistance to Spanish authority, and in 1896 they led a revolt to gain independence. In 1899, the Spanish, unable to suppress that revolt while at war with the United States, handed the islands over to the Americans by secret treaty. Some Americans protested that it was contrary to American principles to become a colonial power. The writer Mark Twain joined the Anti-Imperialist League, declaring that American motives in the Philippines were no more pure, and just as driven by economics, as those of European colonialists.

The Filipino revolutionaries continued to struggle for independence, now against an American army of occupation. Four years of tough fighting left five thousand U.S. soldiers and over sixteen thousand Filipino combatants dead. As in South Africa at the same time, thousands of civilians died from disease and mistreatment in the concentrated settlements used to separate them from the guerillas. While the Anti-Imperialist League continued its protests, President McKinley declared that "it is our duty to uplift and civilize and Christianize" the Filipinos, making Social Darwinism a driving idea behind United States foreign policy.

Observing the debate in American public opinion over colonial rule in the Philippines, the British poet of empire, Rudyard Kipling, urged the Americans to take on imperial responsibilities:

> Take up the White Man's burden—
> Send forth the best ye breed—
> Go bind your sons to exile
> To serve your captives' need;
> To wait in heavy harness,
> On fluttered folk and wild—
> Your new-caught, sullen peoples,
> Half-devil and half-child.

Kipling was afraid that the British Empire had begun to decline and that only an imperialistic United States could save the world for Anglo-Saxon civilization. Even if imperialism is a "burden," Kipling implied, Americans needed to take it up for the benefit of the Filipinos themselves, "to serve their captives' need."

One American observer had a much different view of events. The African American writer W. E. B. Du Bois (doo boyz), noting that the New Imperialism had led to white domination across the world, predicted in 1903 that "the problem of the twentieth century is the problem of the color-line."[2] His statement was as true for Southeast Asia as it was for Africa and the United States.

Imperial Connections and Comparisons

Whether in Africa or Southeast Asia, the New Imperialism was driven by the desire to control critical natural resources while building and retaining a strong military and strategic presence at the global level. The history of rubber shows how industrial and technological developments in Europe and the United States led to imperialism as a form of economic domination. Politically, a comparison of how the rulers of Siam (Thailand) in Southeast Asia and Ethiopia in East Africa managed to retain their independence in spite of the New Imperialism shows how these exceptions proved the rule of Western dominance. (See the feature "Visual Evidence: National Flags.")

A Case Study of the New Imperialism: Rubber

In the first half of the nineteenth century, inventors found new applications for rubber for such products as waterproof clothing and conveyor belts in factories. During the Second Industrial Revolution, the spread of telephones,

NATIONAL FLAGS

Banners and flags have a long history as markers of individual and group identity. Flags took on even more important symbolic power in the nineteenth century with the rise of European nation-states and the spread of their empires. In the West, where flags had earlier been closely associated with royal families, they now became the symbols of entire nations. The imposition of a nation's flag beyond the nation's frontier became a defining symbol of imperialism.

Here are nineteenth-century flags from societies that struggled to retain their independence: Liberia (West Africa), Ethiopia (East Africa), Siam (or Thailand, Southeast Asia), and Hawai'i. Creating these flags and preserving the right to fly them were important expressions of resistance to colonialism.

The West African Republic of **Liberia** was founded in 1847 by freed American slaves. An earlier version of the flag had a cross rather than a star in the upper left. When the flag was first presented, "many eyes were suffused with tears. . . . Who that looked back to America and remembered what he saw and felt there, could be otherwise than agitated?"

(All images courtesy Rick Wyatt, www.crwflags.com)

This flag, first used in 1897, features the "Lion of Judah" as a symbol for **Ethiopia**. Red stands for power and faith; yellow for peace, wealth, and love; and green for land and hope. These became the colors of global African nationalism, and they can now be found on the flags of nations such as Ghana, Zimbabwe, Guyana, and Grenada. The flag has deep religious symbolism for Jamaican Rastafarians.

This flag dates from 1891. One of several different flags from **Siam**, it was flown above the palace only when the king was present. At the center is the royal coat of arms, with a trident and golden crown above.

This flag was commissioned by Kamehameha the Great, the first Hawaiian to unify the islands, in 1816 (see Chapter 21) and it flew until 1893. The eight bars represent the major Hawaiian Islands, and the British Union Jack reflects the attempts of Hawaiian monarchs to use an alliance with Britain as protection against the United States and other imperialist powers. This is the current state flag of **Hawai'i**.

QUESTION FOR ANALYSIS

 How do these flags combine indigenous and imported design elements?

electrical lines, and bicycles generated a booming trade in rubber. At first the only source was the Brazilian Amazon (see Chapter 25), where "rubber barons" built palatial homes while indigenous Amerindian peoples suffered from the introduction of diseases to which they had no resistance.

The intensive exploitation of Brazil's natural rubber reserves was not enough to meet demand. To keep prices high and maintain its monopoly, Brazilians tried to prevent the export of rubber seeds. Nevertheless, a British agent smuggled enough out of the country to establish a nursery near London at Kew Gardens (see Chapter 21). Rubber seedlings were then sent from Kew to British colonies in Asia. Plantings in Singapore were successful, and from there rubber spread to Malaya, Thailand, Vietnam, and the Dutch East Indies. As in Brazil, great fortunes were made, usually at the expense of local farmers, and rainforests were felled to make room for large rubber plantations. British, French, and Dutch traders secured access to an essential commodity and reaped the lion's share of profits. Meanwhile, colonial taxation drove many Southeast Asian peasants to work for low wages and endure harsh conditions on rubber plantations.

The most notorious abuses took place in the Congo Free State, the personal domain of the Belgian king, Leopold II. Greedy for rubber revenue, Leopold ordered his agents to use whatever means necessary to maximize the harvest from Central African forests. The result was a reign of terror. Leopold's agents, who were paid bonuses based on the amount of rubber they delivered, would give villages unrealistic quotas to meet. Sometimes they kept African women in cages, promising to release them only after the men of the village had contributed enough rubber.

Like the farmers forced to grow cotton in East Africa, the families of rubber collectors went hungry when their own fields went untended.

If the quotas were still not met, the killing began. Free State soldiers, sometimes blacks under the command of Belgian officers and agents, were instructed to bring back the hands of those they killed to prove they had not wasted ammunition. To increase their own death quotas, these soldiers would sometimes chop off the hands of the living and bring them back to the Belgian trade stations for a cash reward. Eventually ten million people died, mostly from hunger.

⬛ Torture in King Leopold's Congo   Here two victims of Leopold's policies, Mola and Yoka, display their mutilated limbs. The hands of Mola were eaten by gangrene after his hands were tied too tightly by Leopold's agents. Yoka's right hand was cut off by soldiers who planned to receive a bounty at headquarters by using the hand as proof of a kill. Once the world learned about this extreme violence, humanitarian voices were raised against King Leopold.   (Anti-Slavery International)

Leopold hypocritically claimed to be a great humanitarian rescuing Africans from their "primitive" conditions and bringing them the light of Christianity. Although Europeans were initially inclined to believe him, by the late 1890s stories of violence from the Congo began to reach the outside world. A clerk in Brussels noticed that the ships that were arriving full of rubber and ivory were returning to the Congo with only guns and ammunition in their holds. His further investigation revealed the full horror of Leopold's crimes, and he helped form the Congo Reform Association to demand that they be ended. Finally, in 1908 King Leopold sold his African empire to the Belgian government, reaping a huge profit on the sale. A heritage of violence still affects the Congo today, while Brussels is filled with the many grand monuments that Leopold built with the fortune he made in the rubber trade.

Enduring Monarchies: Ethiopia and Siam

Given the strength of European empires in the age of the New Imperialism, it seems surprising that Ethiopia and Siam (present-day Thailand) managed to retain their independence. A comparison between them shows that while factors such as competent leadership were important, the continuing independence of these two states was not really an exception to overwhelming European domination in Africa and Southeast Asia.

The ancient Christian kingdom of Ethiopia was first introduced to modern European firepower in 1868 when a British relief column was sent to rescue an Englishman being held hostage by the Ethiopian king. The British easily crushed the poorly armed African army they encountered. When **Menelik II** (r. 1889–1913) became emperor, he was determined to strengthen the state against further assault. Ethiopia, like Tokugawa Japan, had long had a decentralized structure in which rural lords, commanding their own armies, were more powerful than the emperor himself. Menelik (men-uh-lik) consolidated power at the imperial court and created a standing army under his own command. Learning a lesson from 1868, he also equipped his soldiers with the latest repeating rifles. Finally, he used his credentials as a Christian to enhance his diplomatic influence in Europe, where his ambassadors did their best to play the European powers against one another to Ethiopia's advantage.

Menelik was also fortunate that when the European assault arrived it came from Italy, the weakest of the European imperial powers. At the Battle of Adowa (1896) the Ethiopians were victorious, though Italy did take the strategically important region of Eritrea on the Red Sea. Britain, the dominant power in northeastern Africa, was convinced that Menelik would be able to maintain security on the Egyptian frontier and allow European traders free access to his kingdom. Since it was a cheaper solution than occupying the country by force, the British sponsored the development of modern infrastructure, such as banks and railroads, during Menelik's reign. The benefits, however, went to the Ethiopian monarchy and aristocracy, and especially to European investors and merchants. The majority of Ethiopians scratched a meager living from the soil.

In the second half of the nineteenth century the kings of Siam also faced absorption into European empires, with the British expanding toward them from India to the west and the French posing a threat from Indochina to the east. The capable leadership of two long-ruling kings, Mongkut (r. 1851–1868) and Chulalongkorn (r. 1868–1910), transformed the ancient kingdom into a sovereign nation. Both

• Menelik II (r. 1889–1913)   Emperor who used diplomacy and military reorganization to retain Ethiopian independence, defeating an Italian army of invasion at Adowa in 1896.

kings used internal reform and diplomatic engagement with European powers to deal with the threat posed by the New Imperialism.

As a young man Mongkut (mang-koot) spent many years living in a Buddhist monastery. When he emerged to become king in 1851, he found that his monastic experience, where he had interacted with men from all social classes, prepared him to become a popular leader. He could interact not only with Siamese from diverse social backgrounds but also with Europeans; he also made contact with Western missionaries, learning English as well as mathematics and astronomy.

Having observed China's fate after the Opium Wars, Mongkut was determined to meet the Western challenge. As in China and Japan (see Chapter 24), some conservatives at the Siamese court opposed his reforms, arguing that they would undermine their own Buddhist traditions. Still, Mongkut invited Western emissaries to his capital, installed them as advisers, and exempted them from the usual court protocols, such as crawling on their knees before the king. Though Mongkut favored the British, he was careful to bring in French and Dutch advisers to balance their influence. He also opened Siam to foreign trade, giving European merchants from various countries a stake in his system.

● **Chulalongkorn** (r. 1868–1910) King of Siam (Thailand) who modernized his country through legal and constitutional reforms. Through successful diplomacy he ensured Siam's continued independence while neighboring societies were absorbed into European empires.

Most importantly, Mongkut chose an English tutor for his son and heir, **Chulalongkorn.** After Chulalongkorn (choo-luh-awhn-korn) came to power in 1868, he had an able set of Siamese advisers who understood that their traditions and sovereignty could be preserved only through reform. Chulalongkorn reformed the legal system to protect private property and abolish slavery and debt peonage, expanded access to education, and encouraged the introduction of telegraphs and railroads. Most important, he centralized government power through a streamlined bureaucracy that reached from the capital into the smallest villages.

Like his father, Chulalongkorn was an able diplomat who played the various European powers off one another. Lacking the strong army that Menelik had used to protect himself, the Siamese king even gave up claims to territories formerly part of his empire, such as Laos, to protect the core of his kingdom. Not only did this policy appease the French and the British, but it also gave his kingdom a more definable Thai character, much like the ethnically defined nation-states of Europe and Japan. While foreign advisers from various European countries were part of this reform process, the king oversaw government policy with the advice of a new Council of State.

Chulalongkorn was also fortunate that the British and the French were anxious to avoid military confrontation in Southeast Asia. Because their traders had access to Siamese markets and their missionaries were allowed to establish themselves in the kingdom, and because the Siamese leader was able to ensure peace and stability in his domain, the French and British agreed in 1896 to recognize the independence of the kingdom of Siam as a buffer between their empires (see Map 26.2).

As with Ethiopia, the independence of Siam was secured by internal reform, centralization of government power, and deft diplomatic maneuvering, all outcomes of effective political leadership. Nevertheless, had the British or French had a compelling reason to conquer Ethiopia or Siam, they would have done so. The achievement of Menelik and Chulalongkorn in the 1890s was to position their countries to take advantage of inter-European rivalries.

In the age of the New Imperialism, it was only under unusual circumstances that African and Southeast Asian societies could retain their sovereignty. King Khama's situation was much more common. He did his best with the diplomatic resources

King Chulalongkorn of Siam

This photograph from 1890 shows King Chulalongkorn of Siam with his son, the Crown Prince Vajiravudh Rama, who was studying in Britain. Chulalongkorn used deft diplomacy to maintain the independence of Siam (Thailand) during the height of the European scramble for colonial territory. Father and son are dressed in European style, but the warm embrace of their hands was a southeast Asian touch. British males rarely showed such affection in Victorian portraits. (Photo by W.&D. Downey/Getty Images)

at his disposal, but his kingdom was too small and too poorly armed to survive as an independent state. Unlike Menelik and Chulalongkorn, most African and Southeast Asian rulers did not command sufficient resources to protect themselves from the New Imperialism. Even in the exceptional cases of Ethiopia and Siam, the economic impact of Western industrial capitalism brought new and difficult challenges to rural peoples, who were now bound, like their counterparts in colonial empires, to a global economy to which they contributed much more than they received.

Chapter Review

KEY TERMS

Download the MP3 audio file of the Chapter Review and listen to it on the go.

During the course of a life that lasted 86 years, King Khama III of the Bangwato witnessed the transformation of his society. When he was a young man, his people were independent farmers and pastoralists under the leadership of their own kings and elders. During his adulthood they were connected, as subjects of a great empire, to global political and economic networks. The New Imperialism was the final stage of a process that had begun in the sixteenth century when Europeans first established overseas maritime empires. With the force of the Industrial Revolution behind them, nineteenth-century Western imperialists spread those empires more widely than ever before, planting their flags across Africa and Southeast Asia and bringing the entire world, directly or indirectly, under their control.

What were the main causes of the New Imperialism?

While European colonial outposts had been established in the previous centuries, the period of the New Imperialism saw a dramatic expansion of empire building, encompassing the entire planet. Political competition within and between European states, increased activity by Christian missionaries, and the private ambitions of men like Cecil Rhodes and King Leopold II of Belgium were all important causes of the New Imperialism, but the most important factor was the rising demand for global economic resources resulting from technological and industrial developments in Europe and the United States. Imperialism was fueled by global economic competition for gold and diamonds in southern Africa, rubber in Central Africa and Southeast Asia, and other commodities like palm oil, tin, and coffee.

In what different ways did Africans respond to European imperialism?

For most Africans, European encroachment in the late nineteenth century occurred suddenly and unexpectedly. They responded by forming alliances with the powerful new outsiders against traditional rivals, using diplomatic initiatives, and practicing military resistance. The Europeans had great technological advantages, and only in Ethiopia was the military option successful. Resistance often took the form of guerilla warfare, as in the Asante kingdom, or called upon spiritual forces and religiously inspired organization, as with the Xhosa and followers of the Maji Maji.

What were the main outcomes of the New Imperialism in Southeast Asia?

In the Dutch East Indies, the New Imperialism meant tighter administrative control and more systematic economic exploitation by the Dutch colonialists over their Asian subjects. Elsewhere, formerly independent states were divided among

European powers, with the French combining Vietnam, Cambodia, and Laos into French Indochina and the British taking control of Malaya and Burma. The former Spanish territory of the Philippines became a colony of the United States. The invaders established plantations and mines in their colonies to provide raw materials such as rubber and tin for their industries.

🚂 **What connections and comparisons can be made between Africa and Southeast Asia in the late nineteenth century?**

The history of rubber shows how the exploitation of colonial economies was connected to European industrial development. Production and consumption of rubber-based goods like boots and bicycle tires depended on the systematic extraction of raw materials and the coercive, and often violent, application of local labor in the forests of Central Africa and the plantations of Southeast Asia. In Ethiopia and Siam, able leaders were able to resist political incorporation, partially by playing on European rivalries. In both countries, however, political independence required that leaders like King Menelik II and King Chulalongkorn give European merchants and investors open access to their markets and raw materials.

For Further Reference

Headrick, Daniel. *The Tools of Empire: Technology and European Imperialism in the Nineteenth Century*. New York: Oxford University Press, 1981.

Hochschild, Adam. *King Leopold's Ghost: A Story of Greed, Terror and Heroism in Colonial Africa*. Boston: Houghton Mifflin, 1999.

Markus, Harold G. *The Life and Times of Menelik II: Ethiopia 1844–1913*. New York: Oxford University Press, 1975.

Martin, B. G., ed. *Muslim Brotherhoods in Nineteenth Century Africa*. New York: Cambridge University Press, 2003.

Owen, Norman G., ed. *The Emergence of Modern Southeast Asia*. Honolulu: University of Hawaii Press, 2004.

Packenham, Thomas. *The Scramble for Africa, 1976–1912*. 2d ed. London: Longman, 1999.

Parsons, Neil. *King Khama, Emperor Joe and the Great White Queen: Victorian Britain Through African Eyes*. Chicago: University of Chicago Press, 1998.

Peiers, J. B. *The Dead Will Arise: Nongqawuse and the Great Xhosa Cattle Killing Movement of 1856–1857*. London: James Currey, 1989.

Wyatt, David K. *A Short History of Thailand*. 2d ed. New Haven: Yale University Press, 2003.

Websites

African Colonial History (http://www-sul.stanford.edu/depts/ssrg/africa/history/hiscolonial.html). An exhaustive set of links to information on Africa's colonial history hosted by Stanford University.

Imperialism (http://www.fordham.edu/halsall/mod/modsbook34.html). The Internet Modern History Source Book provides numerous links on nineteenth-century imperialism, by both region and topic.

Southeast Asia Digital Library (http://sea.lib.niu.edu/). Organized both by country and type of resources, including links to historical image sets.

Film

Congo: White King, Red Rubber, Black Death.

CL WEB RESOURCES

Pronunciation Guide

Interactive Maps

MAP 26.1 Africa, 1878 and 1914

MAP 26.2 The New Imperialism in Southeast Asia

Primary Sources

Chapter Objectives

ACE Multiple-Choice Quiz

Flashcards

War, Revolution, and Global Uncertainty, 1905–1928

The violence and brutality of the First World War (1914–1918) made a mockery of the nineteenth-century idea of progress. Many people were left with doubt and pessimism about the future. Others, inspired by the revolutionary changes that accompanied the war, saw a brighter day dawning. Having witnessed the Russian Revolution of 1917 firsthand and interviewed many world leaders, the American journalist **Louise Bryant** (1885–1936) was in a good position to gauge the high stakes of the postwar world. She was entering the period of world history that one historian later called "the age of extremes." Bryant believed that the world was, for better or for worse, at a turning point:

(Hulton-Deutsch Collection/Corbis)

LOUISE BRYANT

On the grey horizon of human existence looms a great giant called Working Class Consciousness. He treads with thunderous step through all the countries of the world. There is no escape, we must go out and meet him. It all depends on us whether he will turn into a loathsome, ugly monster demanding human sacrifices or whether he shall be the savior of mankind.[1]

Bryant was an exceptional woman for her times. Impatient with restrictive conventions and an ardent feminist, she was described as someone who "refuses to be bound . . . an artist, a joyous, rampant individualist, a poet and a revolutionary." She was a child of the American West, born in San Francisco and then, after her father's premature death, raised on a remote ranch in Nevada with only her grandfather, a Chinese cook, and her imagination for company. After graduating from the University of Oregon, Bryant wanted to be a serious journalist, but the only job she could get was as a "society" writer for a Portland newspaper. It was 1909, and women were not expected to be involved with "hard"

This icon will direct you to interactive activities and study materials on the *Voyages* website: www.cengage.com/history/hansen/voyages1e

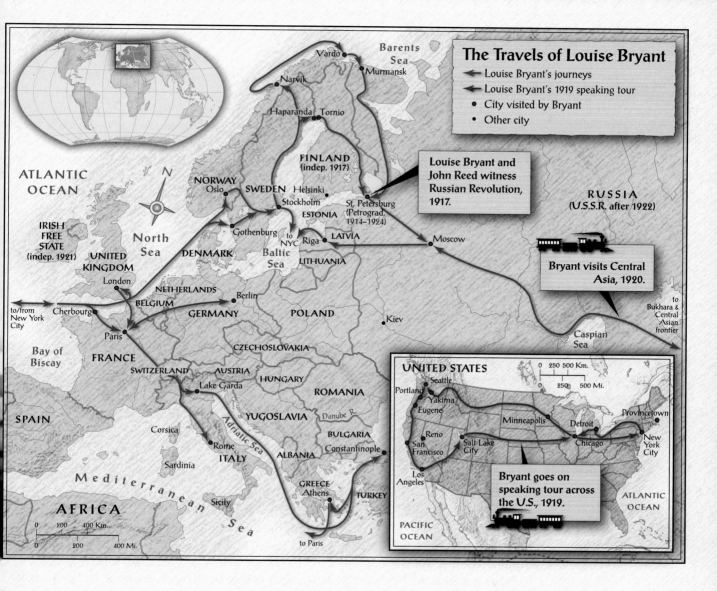

The Travels of Louise Bryant

← Louise Bryant's journeys
← Louise Bryant's 1919 speaking tour
● City visited by Bryant
● Other city

Louise Bryant and John Reed witness Russian Revolution, 1917.

Bryant visits Central Asia, 1920.

Bryant goes on speaking tour across the U.S., 1919.

ATLANTIC OCEAN

Barents Sea

Vardo
Murmansk
Narvik
Haparanda Tornio
FINLAND (indep. 1917)
NORWAY
Oslo
SWEDEN Helsinki
Stockholm
ESTONIA
St. Petersburg (Petrograd, 1914–1924)
RUSSIA (U.S.S.R. after 1922)
IRISH FREE STATE (indep. 1921)
UNITED KINGDOM
North Sea
Gothenburg
to NYC
Riga LATVIA
Moscow
DENMARK
Baltic Sea
LITHUANIA
London
NETHERLANDS
BELGIUM
Berlin
to/from New York City
Cherbourg
GERMANY
POLAND
Caspian Sea
to Bukhara & Central Asian frontier
Paris
Kiev
Bay of Biscay
FRANCE
CZECHOSLOVAKIA
SWITZERLAND
AUSTRIA
HUNGARY
Lake Garda
ROMANIA
SPAIN
Danube R.
YUGOSLAVIA
Adriatic Sea
BULGARIA
Corsica
Rome
ITALY
ALBANIA
Constantinople
Sardinia
Mediterranean Sea
GREECE
Athens
TURKEY
AFRICA
Sicily
0 200 400 Km.
0 200 400 Mi.
to Paris

UNITED STATES
Seattle
Portland
Yakima
Eugene
Minneapolis
Detroit
Provincetown
Reno
Salt Lake City
Chicago
New York City
San Francisco
Los Angeles
ATLANTIC OCEAN
PACIFIC OCEAN
0 250 500 Km.
0 250 500 Mi.

	1900	1910	1920	1930	1940

Lifetime of Louise Bryant
(b. 1885)   1936

EUROPE

World War I   Paris Peace Conference
1914   1918 1919

October Revolution in Russia   Union of Soviet Socialist Republics
1917   1922   (to 1991)

Weimar Republic
1919   1933

THE MIDDLE EAST AND ASIA

Chinese Revolution and fall of the Qing dynasty   End of the Ottoman Empire   British mandate in Palestine
1911   1919   1920

NORTH AMERICA

Mexican Revolution   United States enters World War I
1910   1917

● **Louise Bryant**
(1885–1936) American journalist, traveler, feminist, and author of several books on the Russian Revolution.

news. She married a dentist but felt increasingly hemmed in by her middle-class surroundings.

Then a young journalist named John Reed swept into her life. She left with him for New York, experiencing the cultural and intellectual dynamism of Greenwich Village. This was the life she craved, full of adventure and purpose. After a series of stormy love affairs that nearly tore their relationship apart, Bryant and Reed were married, and together they traveled to Russia in the summer of 1917. Both left important records of that experience, but Reed overshadowed Bryant in historical memory. Given the gender perceptions of the time, Bryant's journalism was never taken as seriously as that of her husband.

During her lifetime Bryant witnessed remarkable changes. In the industrialized world telephones and electricity became commonplace, and the automobile and airplane were invented: Bryant saw the great aviator Amelia Earhart, a symbol of female emancipation, as a role model. In some places, women fought for and won the right to vote. The creativity of African American musicians led to the creation of jazz music, the first significant influence of the United States on global culture. Scientific advances continued, as physicists such as Albert Einstein made huge strides toward understanding nature at both cosmic and atomic levels, while Sigmund Freud, whom Bryant once interviewed, plumbed the depths of the human psyche.

But a shadow of uncertainty hung over these accomplishments. The industrially driven devastation of the First World War in Europe caused immense suffering not only for soldiers but also for civilians. In mobilizing their empires for the war effort, the European powers made their local conflict a genuinely global one, severely disrupting the lives of many Africans, Asians, and peoples of the Pacific. While the president of the United States, Woodrow Wilson, confidently proclaimed that this was "the war to end all wars," one that would "make the world safe for democracy," competing national interests destabilized the postwar world.

Meanwhile, both before and during the war, major world societies—Mexico, China, and Russia—were rocked by revolution. Louise Bryant, a socialist, saw hope in uncertainty, applauding downtrodden people who rose up against local oppressors or imperial masters. But she recognized as well the dangers that war and revolution had unleashed.

Focus Questions

How can the First World War be regarded as a "total war," both for the domestic populations of the main combatants and for the entire world?

How did the postwar settlements fail to resolve global political tensions?

How did the outcomes of revolutions in Mexico, China, and Russia add to the uncertainty of the postwar world?

World War I as a "Total" War

Within Europe, World War I (1914–1918) represented a radical change from nineteenth-century warfare. Conditions of "total war" meant that the fight engaged masses of civilians and required the complete mobilization of economic and human resources. Governments assumed unprecedented powers to regulate social, political, and economic life. For each of the main combatants—Germany, Austria, Britain, France, Russia, and the United States—the war strained traditional social and political systems. The British called it simply the Great War.

The war can also be called "total" because it was a world war. While colonial peoples had been caught up in earlier European conflicts, the global involvement in World War I was unprecedented. Young men from the United States shipping out to Europe, Indian soldiers marching to Baghdad, and Southeast Asians working behind the lines on the western front all had life-changing experiences.

Causes of World War I, 1890–1914

On June 28, 1914, the Archduke Franz Ferdinand, heir to the Austrian throne, was assassinated in the Balkan city of Sarajevo (see Map 27.1). Archduke Ferdinand's killer was a Serbian nationalist. The politically unstable Balkan region had long been the boundary between the Austrian and Ottoman Empires. As the Ottomans declined in the nineteenth century, the Austrians asserted themselves in the region, provoking the anger of local nationalists who did not want to escape from one empire only to be dominated by another (see Chapter 23).

Balkan nationalists used religion to emphasize the differences between the Slavic people of the region, downplaying their cultural similarities and long history of coexistence. Serbian leaders, who were members of the Orthodox Christian faith, looked to their co-religionists in Russia for support, while Croatian nationalists allied themselves with Austria and Bosnian Muslims with the Ottoman Empire. These local tensions became globally important when the German government supported the Austrians against the Serbs.

German support for Austria in the Balkans angered the Russians and also alarmed the British and the French, who feared Germany's global ambitions. After Otto von Bismarck was dismissed in 1890, the ambitious **Kaiser Wilhelm II** (r. 1888–1918) abandoned careful diplomacy for a more aggressive foreign policy. The Kaiser's naval buildup caused Britain to reverse its practice of avoiding commitments on the continent. Likewise the French and Russian governments, alarmed by German ambitions, overcame their long-standing mutual distrust. Through a series of treaties a system of alliances was created that divided Europe into two opposing blocs: the Triple Entente (ahn-tahnt) of France, Britain, and Russia against the Triple Alliance of Germany, Austria, and Italy. The alliance system gave diplomats few options for the resolution of crises.

With Europe already sharply divided into two hostile and heavily armed camps, the assassination of the Archduke Franz Ferdinand detonated an explosive confrontation between the Triple Entente and the Triple Alliance. The Austrian government threatened Serbia with war if it did not comply with a set of humiliating demands. The Serbs appealed to Russia, while the Germans backed up the Austrians. Thus war between Austria and Serbia meant war between German and Russia. The Ottoman Empire, fearful of Russian and British designs on its territory, also allied itself with

Kaiser Wilhelm II (r. 1888–1918) German emperor whose aggressive foreign policy and military buildup changed the European balance of power and laid the foundation for the Triple Alliance and the Triple Entente.

MAP 27.1

World War I, 1914–1918 By the end of World War I horrific violence along the western front in Belgium, Luxembourg, and northeastern France, and on the eastern front in the Russian Empire and eastern Europe, had led to the deaths of over eight million soldiers, with twenty million wounded. On the southern front, defeat led to the dissolution of the Ottoman Empire. While these three theaters saw the fiercest fighting, the global effects of the conflict made this a truly world war.

Interactive Map

Germany. After a period of indecision, Italian leaders lived up to their treaty obligations and joined with Britain, France, and Russia.

Public opinion was also crucial in creating an atmosphere of war. In urban, industrial societies diplomacy was no longer the private concern of a small group of highly educated, cosmopolitan elites. Even in authoritarian countries like Germany, public opinion, as expressed and formulated through new media of communications such as inexpensive daily newspapers, was crucial to any significant government undertaking. Most people in western Europe were enthusiastically patriotic, and the declarations of war were met with excitement and prowar demonstrations. Only in Russia, where the tsar and his ministers were isolated from public opinion, did the government act without a clear mandate from the people. With a naiveté that seems remarkable in hindsight, most Europeans believed that the war would be quick and conclusive and that their side would win. (See the feature "Movement of Ideas: Emma Goldman's Critique of Militarism.")

Louise Bryant was cynical about the war, seeing it as nothing but a capitalist tactic to increase profits. It seemed clear to socialists like her that French and German workers had common interests against their bosses, and it was irrational for them to fight each other under the banner of patriotism. Nevertheless, even the Social Democratic Party in Germany, dominated by Marxists who had long urged "workers of the world unite!," now voted in favor of war.

Total War in Europe: The Western and Eastern Fronts

Unlike in 1870, when the Prussian army had moved rapidly to Paris (see Chapter 23), in 1914 the German advance was stopped 20 miles (32.2 km) from the French capital (see Map 27.1). The stalemate that developed on the **western front** in Belgium and northeastern France brought a new term to military vocabulary: *trench warfare.* On one side of the line French and British soldiers established well-fortified positions protected by razor wire; the Germans did the same on the other side. Miserable in the muddy trenches, soldiers were called on to go "over the top" into harrowing enemy fire in an attempt to dislodge the opposing forces from their position. With bombs exploding around them, sometimes choking on mustard gas (the first use of chemical weapons in history), they had little chance of survival, let alone of victory. Soldiers were immobilized in trenches, and the battle lines established in Belgium and northern France early in the war hardly shifted. Military planners then reinforced the trenches, connected them with tunnels, and built elaborate underground networks for supply and communications.

• **western front** During World War I, the line separating the elaborate trenches of German and Allied positions, which soon became almost immobile. Trench warfare was characteristic of the western front.

The casualties of trench warfare were horrific as the two sides fought year after year over the same small stretches of territory. At the Battle of Verdun in 1916, more than half a million young French and German troops lost their lives. The same year at the Battle of the Somme, nearly a million British and German soldiers were killed. The slaughter brought no military advantage to either side. In England, young men from the same neighborhood, school, or village often volunteered to join the same regiment, sometimes to be all wiped out in a single rush from the trenches. Many of those who survived lost not only their childhood companions but also their physical and mental health. Some survivors would suffer horrible trauma the rest of their lives from the "shell shock" that came from crouching in a trench with bombs exploding all around.

In an effort to undermine the economic and industrial foundation of the German military, the British established a naval blockade on German ports. The effects

CL **Primary Source: Mud and Khaki, Memoirs of an Incomplete Soldier** *Read from the memoirs of a British soldier, and imagine the horrors of trench warfare and poison gas in World War I.*

Emma Goldman's Critique of Militarism

Preparedness, the Road to Universal Slaughter" was written by the anarchist Emma Goldman and published in New York in 1915. Emma Goldman (1869–1940) was born into a Jewish family in Lithuania, then part of the Russian Empire. As a teenager she moved to St. Petersburg, where she was first exposed to radical politics, and at 16 she moved to New York. As a young woman she advocated violence and assassination, tactics that were deeply rooted in Russia's anarchist and revolutionary traditions. Later she became a pacifist, preferring mass organization as a means of countering the economic and political oppression of industrial capitalism. Louise Bryant, who attended a speech by Goldman in Portland in 1914, was just one of many young Americans stirred to radical political action by her oratory. The two became well acquainted, and Goldman attended the funeral of Bryant's husband John Reed in Moscow in 1921.

Goldman was arrested several times, once for heading an anticonscription campaign in the leadup to the First World War. After the Alien Act of 1918 allowed the deportation of "undesirable" immigrants without a trial, in 1919 the United States government deported her back to Russia. She left after two years, profoundly disappointed at the suppression of civil rights by Lenin and the Bolsheviks. Goldman then settled in Canada, traveling frequently to France and England, and continued to write and speak in defense of individual liberty.

Source: *Mother Earth* 10, no. 10 (December 1915).

Preparedness, the Road to Universal Slaughter

"Ammunition! Ammunition! O, Lord, thou who rulest heaven and earth, thou God of love, of mercy and of justice, provide us with enough ammunition to destroy our enemy." Such is the prayer which is ascending daily to the Christian heaven. . . . [All] of the European people have fallen over each other into the devouring flames of the furies of war, and America, pushed to the very brink by unscrupulous politicians, by ranting demagogues, and by military sharks, is preparing for the same terrible feat. In the face of this approaching disaster, it behooves men and women not yet overcome by the war madness to raise their voice of protest, to call the attention of the people to the crime and outrage which are about to be perpetrated upon them.

America is essentially the melting pot. No national unit composing it is in a position to boast of superior race purity, particular historic mission, or higher culture. Yet the jingoes and war speculators are filling the air with the sentimental slogan of hypocritical nationalism, "America for Americans," "America first, last, and all the time." This cry has caught the popular fancy from one end of the country to another. In order to maintain America, military preparedness must be engaged in at once. A billion dollars of the people's sweat and blood is to be expended for dreadnaughts and submarines for the army. The pathos of it all is that the America which is to be protected by a huge military force is not the America of the people, but that of the privileged class; the class which robs and exploits the masses, and controls their lives from the cradle to the grave. No less pathetic is it that so few people realize that preparedness never leads to peace, but that it is indeed the road to universal slaughter. . . .

Forty years ago Germany proclaimed the slogan: "Germany above everything. Germany for the Germans, first, last and always. We want peace; therefore we must prepare for war. Only a well armed and thoroughly prepared nation can maintain peace, can command respect, can be sure of its national integrity." And Germany continued to prepare, thereby forcing the other nations to do the same. The terrible European war is only the culminating fruition of the hydra-headed gospel, military preparedness. . . .

But though America grows fat on the manufacture of munitions and war loans to the Allies to help crush Prussians the same cry is now being raised in America which, if carried into national action, would build up an American militarism far more terrible than German or Prussian militarism could ever be, and that because nowhere in the world has capitalism become so brazen in its greed and nowhere is the state so ready to kneel at the feet of capital.

"Americanization" societies with well known liberals as members, they who but yesterday decried the patriotic clap-trap of today, are now lending themselves to befog the minds of the people and to help build up the same destructive institutions in America which they are directly and indirectly helping to pull down in Germany—militarism, the destroyer of youth, the raper of women, the annihilator of the best in the race, the very mower of life. . . .

The very proclaimers of "America first" have long before this betrayed the fundamental principles of real Americanism, of the kind of Americanism that Jefferson had in mind when he said that the best government is that which governs least; the kind of America that David Thoreau worked for when he proclaimed that the best government is the one that doesn't govern at all; or the other truly great Americans who aimed to make of this country a haven of refuge, who hoped that all the disinherited and oppressed people in coming to these shores would give character, quality and meaning to the country. That is not the America of the politician and munition speculators. . . .

Supposedly, America is to prepare for peace; but in reality it will be the cause of war. It always has been thus—all through bloodstained history, and it will continue until nation will refuse to fight against nation, and until the people of the world will stop preparing for slaughter. Preparedness is like the seed of a poisonous plant; placed in the soil, it will bear poisonous fruit. The European mass destruction is the fruit of that poisonous seed. It is imperative that the American workers realize this before they are driven by the jingoes into the madness that is forever haunted by the specter of danger and invasion; they must know that to prepare for peace means to invite war, means to unloose the furies of death.

QUESTIONS FOR ANALYSIS

▶ Based on these arguments, how would Goldman have responded to the criticism that as a Lithuanian Jew she had no right to question American patriotism?

▶ If we consider the actual experience of the United States during and after the war, were Goldman's warnings justified?

■ **The Western Front** Trench warfare on the western front was a harrowing experience. When officers called for the troops to "go over the top," the men had to navigate a gauntlet of razor wire while facing exploding shells, constant gunfire, and sometimes poison gas. There were more than 1.5 million casualties in the Battle of the Somme alone, including, undoubtedly, some of the British soldiers shown here. (Popperfoto/Getty Images)

were economically distressing not just to Germany but to Britain as well, since before the war the countries had been major trade partners. The British naval blockade also brought another relatively new military technology to the fore: the submarine, or "U-boat." Attacking without warning, German U-boats wrought havoc on British shipping early in the war.

Protracted total war had a deep and lasting impact on western European governments and societies. Because all of a nation's energies and capacities had to be tapped in the interests of survival, government power expanded. The transition to national economic planning was least revolutionary in Germany, where the state and large corporations were already in close cooperation before the war. In France, and especially in Britain, increased government intervention involved a major shift away from economic liberalism.

Government bureaucracies expanded dramatically, and unions lost the right to strike. Civilians could buy much less as access to imported goods declined and factories were converted from consumer to military production. The British Parliament even began to regulate the hours of the nation's "pubs," where working men and women sought relief from the drudgery of the wartime environment; less access to beer, it was thought, would improve industrial efficiency. Total war also meant restrictions on free speech and press censorship.

For European women, the war brought opportunities as well as costs. The profession of nursing expanded greatly, and, with so many men at the front, women became more important as factory workers. In wartime France, many women were running the family farms. This new situation undermined the idea that women should stay in the "private domain" of the home while men dominated the public sphere. Before the war, British suffragists, campaigners for women's voting rights, had used hunger strikes and public demonstrations to press their cause. The wartime contributions of British women helped swing public opinion in their favor, and in 1918 some British women—those over the age of 30, with property and education—were granted the right to vote.

In Russia, total war extracted a higher price than ever before for both soldiers and civilians. On the **eastern front** in Russia, the tsar's huge army could not match the military technology or organizational sophistication of the invading German army and fell rapidly before it. Hundreds of thousands of soldiers were taken prisoner, and the treatment they received from the Germans was noticeably harsher than that given to British or French soldiers. Morale among the conscripted peasants who made up the bulk of the Russian army was poor to begin with and deteriorated rapidly. Mutinies were common: the soldiers and sailors, mostly descendants of serfs, had little feeling of fellowship with their aristocratic officers. Sometimes they killed their own commanders rather than head into futile battles; frequently they simply abandoned their weapons and began a long walk home. Louise Bryant noticed them as she entered Russia, "great giants of men, mostly workers and peasants, in old, dirt-colored uniforms from which every emblem of Tsardom had been carefully removed."

Famine stalked the Russian countryside as war disrupted agricultural production. Factories closed when industrialists lost access to the Western capital on which Russian industrialization depended. In spite of growing discontent, Tsar Nicholas II refused to consider humiliating conditions of surrender to the Germans. By 1917, the Russian people were demoralized and exhausted.

Total War: Global Dimensions

Apart from the mobilization of civilian life in Europe, total war also required the mobilization of global resources. Battles were fought in Africa and the Middle East; the Japanese declared war on Germany with an eye toward taking over German concessions in China, and the British and French used their Asian and African empires as sources of men and materiel. By 1917, the Great War truly was a world war.

The decision by the Ottoman Empire to side with Germany opened a **southern front** that extended the war to the Middle East and North Africa. In the late nineteenth century German banks, commercial houses, and manufacturers had invested heavily in the Ottoman economy. The Ottomans saw the German alliance as a protection against the French, British, and Russians. The most important strategic Ottoman position was the Dardanelles, a narrow strait connecting the Black Sea with the Mediterranean. In 1915, British forces, including many Australians, attacked the heavily fortified Ottoman position at Gallipoli. In a scene reminiscent of the carnage on the western front, thousands of Australian soldiers who charged the Ottoman fortifications were mowed down. After a quarter of a million casualties, the British withdrew from Gallipoli.

In the wake of Gallipoli, the British could not spare men and materiel from their home islands to fight on the southern front, so they mobilized imperial forces from their African and Asian colonies. A force made up primarily of Egyptian soldiers under British command moved toward Ottoman-controlled Palestine, while Indian soldiers were brought up to engage Ottoman forces in Mesopotamia. Knowing that many of the Arab subjects of the Ottoman Empire were unhappy with Turkish rule, the British also forged an alliance with Arab leaders.

● **eastern front**
The front in Russia during World War I. The German army moved quickly across eastern Europe into Russia; low morale plagued the poorly equipped Russian army in the face of superior German technology.

● **southern front**
The front in World War I caused by the Ottoman Empire's decision to ally with the German army. Britain mobilized colonial forces from India, Egypt, and Australia to engage Ottoman forces at Gallipoli; British forces also occupied Mesopotamia and Palestine.

Indian Soldier   British imperial forces played a central role on the southern front fighting the Ottoman Empire. This Indian soldier combines a traditional turban with Western military clothing and gear as he prepares for battle in Mesopotamia (today's Iraq) in 1918. His division was successful; the Ottomans surrendered two days after this photograph was taken.   (Imperial War Museum, London)

Though the French did little fighting outside Europe, their military commanders were so desperate for men to hurl at the Germans that they also looked to their empire for support. The French had long recruited indigenous soldiers from their imperial possessions, but the number of volunteers was not enough to meet wartime demand. French colonial officials started putting strong pressure on local African leaders to produce more conscripts for the French army. One of the most famous regiments affected by this recruiting drive was the **Senegalese Sharpshooters,** young Muslims from French West Africa who developed a reputation as fearsome fighters. Many died or were maimed on the western front.

The geographic extent of total war is demonstrated by the role of East Africa, where battles were fought between German East Africa and British-controlled Kenya. On one side were African soldiers led by German officers, and on the other a largely Indian army commanded by the British. The German commander had little ambition other than tying down British imperial forces to keep them from being redeployed to the Middle East. He struck at British forces and then retreated into the countryside, requisitioning some of the Africans' food reserves for his army and burning what was left to deny supplies to the British army. Famine and disease stalked the land; total war reached even remote East African villages.

In Southeast Asia, the main consequence of the war was French recruitment of young Vietnamese men to serve in the Indochinese Labor Corps. The French needed laborers behind their lines on the western front and preferred to relieve French soldiers of hard work such as digging fortifications and maintaining roads. Vietnamese villagers in the Indo-Chinese Labor Corps were recruited to do such work, allowing the French to concentrate more of their regiments on the front line. At the same time the economic resources of Indochina, such as rice and rubber, were directed to support the French war effort.

● **Senegalese Sharpshooters**   Mostly Muslim soldiers from French West Africa who were conscripted by the French Empire in World War I and developed a reputation as fearsome fighters.

● **Woodrow Wilson** (r. 1913–1921) President of the United States during and after World War I. Wilson's idealistic view, enshrined in his Fourteen Points, was that the end of the war would lead to the spread of peace and democracy.

The Role of the United States

The entrance of the United States into the war was a major turning point in world history, again highlighting the global nature of total war. In 1914, the country had a small army, and most people were still inclined to follow George Washington's advice that the republic should not "entangle our peace and prosperity in the toils of European ambition." President **Woodrow Wilson** (r. 1913–1921) initially kept the United States

Wartime Propaganda   There is a strongly implied threat of sexual violence in this "liberty loan" poster, with a U.S. soldier protecting a mother and child who kneel helplessly before a German figure identified as a "Hun," or barbarian. Government attempts to arouse patriotism through such demonizing imagery were characteristic of twentieth-century "total war."   (© Corbis)

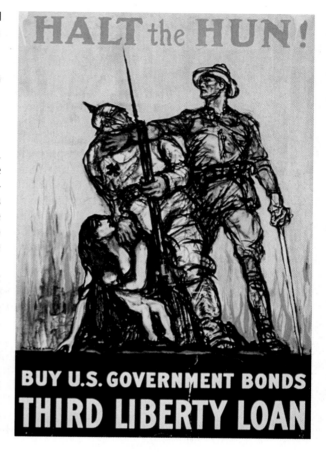

out of the war, but true neutrality proved impossible. The British naval blockade meant that almost all trade with Germany ceased, while American factories became major suppliers of industrial and military goods to France and Britain. Between 1914 and 1916 trade with these two countries grew from $824 million to $3.2 billion, bringing industrial expansion to the United States without any military cost.

The first step toward American entry into the war came with Germany's use of submarine warfare. In 1915, the Germans sank the *Lusitania,* a passenger ship that they correctly identified as secretly carrying armaments from the United States to England. President Wilson loudly protested, and the Germans promised to stop attacking ships without warning. Meanwhile, commercial and industrial interests in the United States lobbied for a rapid military buildup. While citing national security reasons, they were also aware, as critics like Louise Bryant pointed out, that government spending on armaments would expand their war profits even further.

Early in 1917 the Germans, anxious to stop American arms shipments to Britain, resumed submarine attacks. By that time Wilson had decided on war, but he still had to convince Congress and the American people. It was not enough to mention free trade, or even security. Americans, it seemed, could be persuaded to overcome their hesitation to fight only if they were offered some great moral purpose. Wilson filled that need when he told Congress: "The world must be made safe for democracy. Its peace must be planted upon the tested foundations of political liberty."

Wilson's idealism swung public opinion in favor of war, and a draft was instituted. Now the United States faced the same mandates of total war as the other combatants. The mobilization of a vast national army gave the government unprecedented power. Economic and political life became more centralized while restrictions were placed on free speech, the right of workers to strike, and freedom of the press.

The arrival of a million-strong American force helped turn the tide on the western front. On November 11, 1918, the war ended with the signing of an armistice. The United States was now in a strong position to influence the peace talks that followed, taking an unprecedented place along with the major European powers at the center of global diplomacy. But Asians and Africans, who were also deeply affected, gained no power in international affairs as a result of the war.

● The Postwar Settlements

As the war ended and diplomats headed to France to prepare the peace terms, the greatest outbreak of influenza in history raced around the world, killing tens of millions. The violence, dislocation, and population movements of the previous five years had paved the way for the disease, which deepened even further the world's distress. It also reinforced the idea that the world had changed in some fundamental way and that the future was uncertain.

In this atmosphere, representatives of the major Allied powers—Britain, France, Italy, and the United States—gathered at the **Paris Peace Conference** in 1919. In retrospect, the settlements negotiated in Paris were clearly inadequate to secure a stable and just global future. France insisted on punishing Germany for the war, undermining its new liberal constitution. The drawing of new national boundaries in eastern Europe and the Mediterranean generated violence, instability, and dictatorship. Britain and France absorbed former German colonies and Ottoman provinces into their own empires, stoking the flames of nationalism in Africa, the Middle East, and Asia. And the United States Senate voted against joining the new League of Nations, which Woodrow Wilson proposed precisely to avoid any recurrence of the catastrophe of global total war.

● **Paris Peace Conference** (1919) Conference that resulted in the Versailles treaty, which added to post–World War I tensions. A war guilt clause and reparations payments destabilized Germany, and efforts to create stable nations from former imperial provinces in eastern Europe were problematic.

The Paris Peace Conference

The principal leaders at the Paris Peace Conference—Woodrow Wilson of the United States, Georges Clemenceau of France, and David Lloyd George of Britain—faced an enormously complex task. Germany, which lay prostrate, had somehow to be reincorporated into the postwar international system. The Austrian and Ottoman Empires were in ruins, requiring the construction of entirely new political systems in central Europe and western Asia. Moreover, Germany had lost its global empire in Africa and the Pacific. Major sections of the world's map had to be redrawn (see Map 27.2).

Wilson brought to Paris the same high-minded attitude with which he earlier explained America's entry into the war. His Fourteen Points contained specific recommendations based on a few clear principles. Wilson stressed the importance of free trade, the right of peoples to national self-determination, and the creation of a permanent, international assembly to provide safeguards against future wars. The primary British goal, on the other hand, was to safeguard their global economic and colonial interests, and Clemenceau, wanting to punish the Germans for unleashing war on France, expected Germany to pay reparations in compensation for the cost of the war.

As the Allies tried to find compromises and solutions, others sought to influence the outcome as well. At a Pan-African Congress also held in Paris in 1919, black leaders from Africa, the West Indies, and the United States spoke up for the interests of Africans and peoples of African descent. A delegation of Egyptians also planned to attend the conference to represent Arab and Muslim interests, but the British government refused them permission to travel. The Chinese delegation, upset by concessions made to Japan, angrily returned home. Also in Paris was a young Vietnamese man named Ho Chi Minh (hoh chee min), who petitioned the Western powers to respect the rights of the Vietnamese and to apply the principle of national self-determination in French Indochina. Rebuffed by the great powers, Ho became a founding member of the French Communist Party and later the leader of

🌐 **MAP 27.2**

Territorial Changes in Europe After World War I The map of Europe was altered dramatically by the Versailles treaty through the application of Woodrow Wilson's policy of "national self-determination." New nations appeared in central and eastern Europe, carved from the former Russian, Austro-Hungarian, and Ottoman Empires, though the complex ethnic composition of the region often made it impossible to draw clear lines between "peoples" and "states." The handover of the key regions of Alsace and Lorraine from Germany to France caused much bitterness among German nationalists.

a Vietnamese insurgency against the French (see Chapter 29). Lacking any voice at the Paris Peace Conference, most of the world's people could only wait to see what fate was decided for them.

In the end, the Versailles treaty that resulted from the Paris Peace Conference fell far short of Wilson's goals. The Allies did agree to Wilson's plan for a **League of Nations** that would provide a permanent diplomatic forum in the hopes of avoiding future conflict. But tensions resulted from French insistence on the punishment

• **League of Nations**
Established in 1919, this international association was intended to promote international cooperation, peace, and security. However, it proved weak because of internal disputes and the United States's refusal of membership.

of Germany; from the difficulty in creating stable, democratic, and ethnically coherent states in eastern Europe; from the imperial ambitions of Britain and France, whose colonial policies contradicted the doctrine of national self-determination; and from the lack of participation in the League of Nations by both Russia, embroiled in revolution, and the United States, retreating into isolationism. The First World War was not a war to end all wars, and the world had not been made safe for democracy.

The Weimar Republic and Nation Building in Europe

After military surrender and the abdication of Kaiser Wilhelm II, liberals and moderate socialists cooperated in the creation of the new **Weimar Republic.** In 1919, many years after the revolutions of 1848, Germany finally had a liberal, democratic constitution. But postwar Germany was a difficult environment in which to cultivate a liberal political culture. A communist uprising in 1919 challenged the Weimar (vahy-mahr) leaders from the left, while on the right some angry veterans blamed liberal weakness for the nation's defeat. At war's end, many German people were hungry and cold.

The harsh peace terms insisted upon by the French made political and economic recovery many times more difficult than it had to be. First, the Weimar government was forced to sign a treaty that contained a "war guilt" clause. Germans did not believe that their country was solely responsible for the war, and signing a treaty that said so diminished the credibility of the new government. The French also insisted on huge reparation payments that crippled the German financial system. One British economist warned that the economic punishment of Germany was simply foolish in an era of interdependent industrial economies: everyone stood to lose. The treaty also called for the complete demilitarization of the Rhineland, the German province bordering France, and severe restrictions on German rearmament.

By 1923 the new Weimar Republic was rocking on its foundations. It was unable to meet its reparation obligations, and the French occupied the Ruhr Valley, Germany's industrial heartland, to take its resources in lieu of payment. When the government printed more money to make up for the shortfall in its treasury, inflation reached astronomical levels. People needed a wheelbarrow full of bank notes to buy a loaf of bread, and the savings of the middle class were wiped out. Although an attempt by right-wing military forces to take over from elected politicians was thwarted, the rebellious officers had a good deal of public support.

Signs of recovery appeared in 1925. International agreements eased Germany's reparation payments and ended the occupation of the Ruhr Valley. The German economy finally came back to prewar levels, and Berlin regained its status as a major cultural, intellectual, and artistic center. Soon, however, another set of crises would challenge the staying power of German liberalism (see Chapter 28).

In the meantime, postwar reconstruction resulted in a changing political geography in eastern, central, and southeastern Europe. While the collapse of the Austrian and Ottoman Empires seemed to create an opportunity to implement Wilson's ideal of national self-determination, the unleashing of competitive nationalism often led to conflict rather than consensus. The complex cultural geography of the region meant that ethnic, linguistic, and religious groups lived scattered among each other in many places. Delineating boundaries for states that neatly corresponded to such population groups was impossible.

● **Weimar Republic**
(1919–1933) After the abdication of Kaiser Wilhem II, the Weimar Republic created a new Germany based on a liberal constitution. However, the new republic was faced with huge war debts, political turmoil, and rising inflation.

Primary Source:
Comments of the German Delegation to the Paris Peace Conference on the Conditions of Peace, October 1919
Read Germany's response to the Treaty of Versailles, which deprived it of its colonies, 13 percent of its land, and 10 percent of its population.

Along the German/Polish cultural frontier, for example, people from the two linguistic groups often lived side by side in the same towns and villages, along with a substantial Jewish population. Poland, which had disappeared from the map of Europe in the eighteenth century (see Chapter 20), was now restored as a nation-state. But many Germans also lived in the new Poland. Polish nationalists felt that these Germans either had to be restricted or leave their homes and move to Germany, where they "belonged." The repression of Polish Jews was even more extreme.

Moreover, the new Poland, like the Weimar Republic, did not have strong historical foundations on which to build a liberal democracy. Tired of the endless squabbling of politicians, conservative army officers seized power in 1926 and imposed restrictions on free speech and political organization. The largely Serbian leaders of the new Balkan state of Yugoslavia also moved toward authoritarian control and repression of religious and ethnic minorities.

The slide toward dictatorship in much of eastern, central, and southern Europe arose from a contradiction that Wilson had not recognized: that nationalism is based on the rights of *groups,* while liberalism focuses on the rights of *individuals.* In many places nationalists with an "us versus them" mentality promoted restrictions on the rights of minority groups. The problem was particularly acute for peoples with no state to protect them, such as Europe's Jews and the Roma (or Gypsies). Nationalism as a basis for political reconstruction caused at least as many problems as it solved.

The Mandate System in Africa and the Middle East

In Africa and the Middle East, the French and British considered their colonial interests paramount and paid only token attention to the concept that peoples should have the right to govern themselves. Rather than apply Wilson's concept of national self-determination consistently, the Allies devised the **Mandate System,** which assumed that since not all the world's people were ready for self-governance, the great powers should rule over them under League of Nations auspices until they were "prepared" to govern themselves. It was an unspoken truth that race was used to determine which peoples would be judged capable of self-rule: the Mandate System was applied in Africa and Asia, but not in Europe.

In Africa, the Mandate System allowed the French, British, Belgian, and South African governments to take over former German colonies. With the addition of German East Africa (today's Tanzania) to her empire, Britain finally achieved Cecil Rhodes' dream of controlling a continuous stretch of territory "from Cape to Cairo" (see Chapter 26). The French expanded their West African holdings, and the Belgians enlarged their Central African empire. While they were required to submit reports to the League of Nations showing that they were looking out for "native rights," the European colonists ruled the mandated territories along the same lines as their existing colonies. Certainly they did little or nothing to prepare Africans for eventual self-determination, which most Europeans thought could be achieved only after centuries of European rule, if at all.

But the war had other effects on Africa as well. In South Africa, for example, the leaders of the African National Congress used the doctrine of national self-determination to argue for greater rights for Africans, including an extension of the right to vote to Western-educated African property owners. In West Africa

• **Mandate System** System by which former Ottoman provinces and German colonies were redistributed. Based on the idea that some societies were not ready for national self-determination, it expanded the empires of Britain, France, Belgium, and Japan while angering African, Arab, and Chinese nationalists.

also, the experience of war brought increasing consciousness of the continent's place in the wider world. More African students went to study in Europe and the United States and came back questioning the legitimacy of colonial rule. The seeds of African nationalism were being sown, but they would take time to germinate.

The most complex application of the Mandate System came in the Middle East, where the collapse of Ottoman authority had created a power vacuum. While the French and British wanted to control such rich and strategic areas as Turkey, Mesopotamia, Syria, and Palestine, they also contended with well-organized forces of Turkish, Arab, and Jewish nationalism.

As the Ottoman Empire collapsed, some of its subject peoples sought to liberate themselves. Hoping for an independent state, some Armenians had supported Russia during the war. Ottoman officials responded with a savage policy of dislocation, relocating millions of Armenians to the west of the empire. As many as 1.5 million Armenians died in what most historians consider to have been a genocide of the twentieth century. While the Armenians did gain a state of their own in the postwar settlements, the Kurdish-speaking people of the Ottoman Empire did not. Kurds were scattered across several new postwar states, their national aspirations unfulfilled.

In the Middle East the postwar situation was complicated by three contradictory promises made by the British during the war: the first to the Arabs, the second to the French, and the third to Jewish nationalists who hoped to establish a nation for themselves in the Middle East. The agreement reached by the British in 1915 with the Hashemites, a prominent Arab family, was part of the strategy of winning Arab support for the war against the Ottoman Empire. In return for that support, Britain promised to "recognize and support the independence of the Arabs." Contradicting that agreement, the British then signed a secret treaty with the French arranging to divide Ottoman provinces between themselves after the war.

A third agreement, difficult to reconcile with the previous two, came with the **Balfour Declaration** of 1917, which committed the British government to support the creation of a "national home" for the Jewish people in Palestine. The government was seeking additional support for the war effort from prominent British financiers and industrialists who advocated the creation of a Jewish national state to represent Jewish interests in the world and to offer Jews a refuge in times of crisis. These Zionists, as they called themselves, planned to build their new nation on the same site as the ancient Hebrew kingdoms. However, most Zionists had never been to the Middle East, and most of the people actually living in Palestine were Arab.

After the war, the British tried to use the Mandate System to reconcile these contradictory promises. True to their 1916 secret agreement, the British and the French divided the region between them. The French received a mandate over Syria and Lebanon, and the British stitched together three Ottoman provinces centered on the cities of Mosul, Baghdad, and Basra into a new entity they called Iraq. (See the feature "World History in Today's World: The Origins of Iraq.") Members of the Hashemite family were installed in Syria and Iraq as political leaders, though the French and British retained control over military, security, and economic issues. The British also drew a new line on the map at the Jordan River, separating Palestine, which they ruled directly, from the new kingdom of Jordan, where they installed yet another Hashemite ruler as king.

One problem with this compromise was that it took insufficient account of Arab nationalism. At the Congress of Damascus in 1919, Syrian nationalists protested their status of a mandate, saying that Arabs "are not naturally less than other more advanced races" and that they did "not stand in need of a mandatory power."

(CL) **Primary Source:**
Letter from Turkey, Summer 1915
Read an eyewitness account of the Armenian genocide by an American missionary from Massachusetts.

• **Balfour Declaration** (1917) Declaration that committed the British government to helping create "a national home for the Jewish people" in Palestine. Britain made this declaration to court support from Zionists during World War I.

(CL) **Primary Source:**
The Balfour Declaration, Stating the British Government's Support for a Jewish Homeland in Palestine, and Discussions Leading to Issuing It in 1917
Learn which questions were considered—and which were ignored—as Britain prepared to support the Zionist movement.

The Origins of Iraq

The world has become more familiar with Iraq's cultural geography since the U.S.-led invasion of 2003. Phrases like "the Sunni triangle," "the Kurdish north," and "the Shi'ite south" emphasize the country's ethnic and religious divisions (see Map 32.2 on page 955). This complex situation is due to agreements made at the end of World War I.

In 1916, by secret treaty, the French and British agreed to a division of Ottoman provinces after the war. Britain would control the Tigris/Euphrates region and the cities of Baghdad, at its center, and Basra, in the south. Mosul, the principal city to the north, was to be taken by the French. However, British forces had actually captured Mosul as part of their Mesopotamian campaign. Having taken possession of the city, the British did not want to give up this important center of oil production.

The French agreed that Britain could keep the Kurdish-populated area around Mosul in return for guarantees that French petroleum companies would be allowed to operate there. In 1921 the British added together the former Ottoman provinces administered from Baghdad and Basra to create Iraq; with the addition of Mosul in 1926, the boundaries of the country were finalized. In adding Mosul to Iraq, the British ignored the demand of Kurdish nationalists. Rather than living in a new state of Kurdistan, as their leaders demanded, the Kurds were scattered between Iran and the newly created states of Iraq, Turkey, and Syria.

Arabs rebelled against British authority in 1920, even before plans for the new country were finalized. Sunni and Shi'ite leaders cooperated in protesting that the Versailles treaty had given their homeland to Britain as part of the Mandate System. Having suppressed the three-month rebellion at great cost, the British then compromised. They created a provisional government with greater Arab participation and installed a Sunni Arab king from the Hashemite family as King Faisal, partially fulfilling promises they had made to secure Arab cooperation in the war against the Ottomans.

Shi'ite religious and political leaders were not part of this new political equation. From the country's creation in 1921 until the fall of Saddam Hussein in 2003, Sunni Arabs dominated Iraqi politics. The long ascendancy of the Sunni Arab minority stemmed from British policy. Gertrude Bell, the diplomat most responsible for the creation of modern Iraq, wrote in 1920: "I don't for a moment doubt that the final authority must be in the hands of the Sunnis, in spite of their numerical inferiority. . . . Otherwise you will have a . . . theocratic state, which is the very devil."

The lack of Arab unity still gave the Europeans the upper hand, however, and the French remained dominant in Syria, and the British in Iraq, even after they accelerated the timetable for transition from mandate status to fuller sovereignty.

The situation was even more complicated in Palestine, where the British needed to deal with both Arab and Zionist nationalism. Wartime anti-Semitism had increased the popularity of Zionism among American and European Jews, and even many who had no plans to move to Palestine began to contribute money to purchase land for those Jews who did decide to move. Arab leaders were alarmed. While they still formed the majority of the population of Palestine, they feared a future in which they would become a minority in the land where many of their families had lived for over a thousand years.

The British found it impossible to please both sides. Their declaration of support for a "national home" for Jews in Palestine fell short of support for a Jewish state, and Arab nationalists viewed any immigration of European Jews into Palestine with suspicion. When the British allowed such immigration in large numbers in the early 1920s, they faced massive Arab demonstrations. When they curtailed Jewish immigration in response, they were harshly criticized by Zionist leaders both in Palestine and abroad. The British were determined to keep Palestine because of its strategic location in the eastern Mediterranean, but they paid a high political price to do so.

The larger problem was that the British enlarged their global responsibilities at the end of the war at the same time that other factors, especially economic ones, made it unlikely that they would be able to manage such an extensive empire for very long. Having liquidated many of their foreign investments to fight the war, they slipped from being the world's largest creditor to facing significant debts, especially to the United States.

In the 1920 presidential election in the United States, the victorious Warren Harding coined the term *normalcy* to describe the plans to return the country to prewar peace and quiet and to avoid excessive involvement in international affairs. For the British and the French, "normalcy" meant empire. With the Russians distracted by their revolution, the Germans desperate and disarmed, and the Americans focused on their own internal affairs, the British and French could imagine that their imperial dominance was a lasting thing. That belief was an illusion. The forces of anticolonial nationalism were gathering throughout Africa and Asia, and eventually the United States and Russia would emerge as dominant global players.

It would be an exaggeration to say that total war in the second decade of the twentieth century had an immediate effect on all of the world's people. But the war and the postwar settlements had long-term global consequences. The same can be said of early-twentieth-century revolutions in Mexico, China, and Russia.

● Early-Twentieth-Century Revolutions

In the early twentieth century the revolutionary traditions first established in British North America and France became international. First in China, Mexico, and Russia and later in societies across Asia, Africa, and Latin America, masses of common people mobilized to topple existing elites and usher in entirely new political systems (see Chapter 29). As Louise Bryant indicated in the opening quotation, socialism would now play a much greater role. While nineteenth-century revolutionaries had often struggled to balance nationalism with liberalism, it was now the mixture of nationalism and socialism that proved most potent, much to the horror of conservatives everywhere.

The Mexican Revolution, 1910–1928

In 1915, when Louise Bryant first met her future husband and journalistic ally John Reed, he had just returned from Mexico, where he had accompanied the rebel leader Pancho Villa into battle. Reed's enthusiasm for the revolutionary cause was contagious, and Bryant was inspired by his exhilarating tales of downtrodden Mexican cowboys fighting for liberation from corrupt politicians, landowners, and priests.

Before 1910, Porfirio Diáz ruled Mexico as an elected dictator, winning rigged elections ever since 1880. Under Diáz's economic liberalism and political authoritarianism, foreign investment had led to the development of many large-scale commercial plantations producing crops for export (see Chapter 25). The benefits of growth were, however, monopolized by foreigners and the small group of oligarchs with connections to the Diáz regime. The new and increasingly important petroleum sector, for example, was almost entirely under foreign, largely American, control.

A younger generation was becoming dissatisfied with this status quo. Men like Francisco Madero, educated at the University of California in the United States, wanted liberal political rights that matched the free market policies of the Diáz regime. In 1910, Madero decided to run for the presidency in opposition to the old dictator. When Diáz was declared the victor, Madero refused to give up, rallying supporters under the slogan "Effective Suffrage and No Reelection." Madero's message resonated with Mexicans of all types; the aged Diáz gave up and fled to Europe.

But removing the dictator was only the beginning of the revolution. Madero was assassinated by an ambitious general in 1913, who was in turn defeated by a talented politician named Venustiano Carranza. Carranza held power in Mexico City and controlled the federal army, but two former partners in his revolutionary coalition, **Emiliano Zapata** (1879–1919) and Pancho Villa, now turned against him. As many as two million people were killed in the chaos of civil war that engulfed Mexico between 1913 and 1920.

Rallying support with the cry *¡Justicia, Tierra, y Liberdad!* ("Justice, Land, and Liberty!"), Zapata followed in the tradition of Father Hidalgo (see Chapter 22) in his passionate embrace of the rights of the poor. His rebel soldiers, mostly landless Indian peasants from the southern part of the country, strove to seize large plantations and redistribute them to the landless. Carranza, a middle-class moderate like Madero before him, saw that goal as an unacceptable intrusion on the rights of property owners. In 1919 Carranza's agents assassinated Zapata, and the southern rebel army fell apart.

In the north Pancho Villa, praised by John Reed for his "reckless and romantic bravery," led the fight against Carranza's government. His army was composed

● **Emiliano Zapata** (1879–1919) Leader of a popular uprising during the Mexican Revolution; mobilized the poor in southern and central Mexico to demand "justice, land, and liberty."

Villa and Zapata This photograph from 1915 shows Pancho Villa (sitting on the presidential throne in the National Palace) with Emiliano Zapata at his side, trademark hat on his knee. The two revolutionaries were soon chased from Mexico City, however, by forces loyal to Venustiano Carranza. Zapata was assassinated by Carranza's men in 1919, Villa by unknown assailants in 1923. (© Underwood & Underwood/Corbis)

mostly of small ranchers and cowboys (*vaqueros*) resentful that the elite controlled the best grazing lands and water sources. Villa was angered when the United States gave official recognition to the Carranza government in Mexico City. His downfall came after 1916, when his cross-border attack on a New Mexican town triggered a counterattack by the United States. From 1919 to 1923 he lived in hiding and was then assassinated. Villa's legendary exploits made him an enduring folk hero, and together he and Zapata represented the hopes and dreams of millions of the poorest Mexicans.

Carranza's government instituted a new constitution in 1917, trying to balance the different interests that had emerged during the revolution. While the Constitution of 1917 protected the rights of property owners, it also declared that "private property is a privilege created by the Nation," opening the path for land reform measures that would benefit the peasants. It also promised to protect working conditions, such as the eight-hour day. The mineral resources of the country, including oil, were declared to be the property of the nation as a whole, and not of any individual, local or foreign, a provision that would allow future Mexican governments to nationalize the energy sector of the economy (see Chapter 28).

These promises of land reform, workers' rights, and the use of oil resources for the good of the nation were not immediately implemented, however, and remained points of conflict and contention far into the future. Moreover, the revolution did not lay the foundation of a truly liberal political culture. Rather than a strong-armed dictator or a multiparty democracy, a single political party dominated Mexican politics. After 1929, leaders of the National Revolutionary Party used patronage, corruption, and backroom deals to try to reconcile the ongoing conflict between the interests of the rich and the poor, the needs of the nation and the influence of foreign investors, and rural and urban populations. Mostly, however, the party leaders acted to extend their own wealth and power. The revolution that had begun with such excitement ended with the stasis of the National Revolutionary Party's bureaucracy.

The Chinese Revolution

After the humiliations of the Boxer Rebellion (see Chapter 24), China entered the twentieth century in desperate need of a new government to unify its people and defend itself against foreign encroachment. In 1911 the last of Qing emperors, a boy at the time, abdicated when Yuan Shikai (yoo-ahn shee-KI), the most capable of the Qing generals, refused to come to the dynasty's defense. Nationalists led by Sun Zhongshan, better known as **Sun Yat-sen** (1866–1925), declared a new Republic of China. Lacking an army, Sun was dependent on Yuan's support. In 1912, after serving as president for only a few weeks, he stepped aside and delegates to the new national assembly elected Yuan as president.

Sun Yat-sen (soon yot-SEN) grew up near the treaty port of Guangzhou, the center of European influence in south China. He earned a medical degree in Hong Kong in 1892 and then moved to Hawai'i, where he started the political organizing that would put him at the head of the Guomindang (gwo-min-DAHNG), or Nationalist Party. Sun envisioned a stable, modernized China, with a liberal legal system and a just distribution of resources, taking its rightful place among the world's great powers.

The new Republic of China faced daunting challenges. Japanese imperialists were focused on China. Already in formal control of Taiwan and exercising great

● **Sun Yat-sen** (1866–1925) The founding father of the Republic of China after the revolution of 1911; established the Guomindang, or Nationalist Party.

power in Manchuria, in 1919 Japan was rewarded by Western diplomats, in acknowledgment of its wartime alliance with France and Britain. Japan was given control over northern Chinese territory on the Shandong peninsula formerly controlled by Germany. On May 4, 1919, Chinese university students staged an unprecedented public demonstration in Tiananmen Square in Beijing, appealing to the government to restore Chinese dignity in the face of Japanese aggression. Their May Fourth Movement led to strikes, demonstrations, and a boycott of Japanese goods. Mass nationalism was on the rise in China, but the republican government had little diplomatic or military ability to respond to the students' appeals.

The domestic military situation was another challenge for Sun and the Guomindang. In 1916 Yuan broke with the Nationalists and declared the foundation of a new imperial dynasty. When regional generals rejected Yuan's imperial pretensions, formed their own armies, and began to act as warlords, the country descended into a decade of chaos. The only stable and prosperous parts of China were the foreign enclaves. Sun fled south to Guangzhou, where the Guomindang was rebuilt by his brother-in-law and successor Jiang Jieshi, known in the west as Chiang Kai-shek (1887–1975). Chiang was a tough military man who in the mid-1920s defeated or co-opted the warlords into the Guomindang, finally establishing central authority over most of the country. Under Chiang's authoritarian command, however, Sun's idealism and emphasis on reform were replaced by a growing culture of corruption.

Meanwhile, in 1921, in the wake of May Fourth Movement, the Chinese Communist Party was formed in Shanghai. Seeking support from the new communist government in Russia, Sun and Chiang made a tactical alliance with the Communists. But in 1927, when Chiang felt more secure in power, he turned on his Communist allies. Guomindang soldiers and street thugs killed thousands of Communists

May Fourth Movement May 4, 1919, was an important day in the development of Chinese nationalism. Hundreds of thousands of protesters gathered in Tiananmen Square in Beijing angered by the Versailles treaty, which had given Chinese territory to Japan. Demonstrations were held across the country, with students playing a large role. In this photograph residents of Shanghai are waving signs that say, "Down with the traitors who buy Japanese goods!" (Eastfoto/Sovfoto)

in the coastal cities, and those remaining fled to the countryside. One Chinese Communist, Mao Zedong (1893–1976), argued that this development was necessary because the peasants would lead the way to socialism. Rejecting the traditional Marxist emphasis on the leading role of the industrial workers, Mao wrote: "In a very short time . . . several hundred million peasants will rise like a tornado . . . and rush forward along the road to liberation. They will send all imperialists, warlords, corrupt officials, local bullies, and bad gentry to their graves." By allying themselves with this elemental peasant force, Mao believed, the Communists could drive Chiang from power and bring about a true revolution.

In the late 1920s, when Chiang's Guomindang were in sole control of the Republic of China, they still had to reckon with Mao and the Communists, who were establishing bases in remote areas of the countryside (see Map 28.1 on page 835). It would be two decades before the contest of power between the Nationalists and the Communists would finally be resolved (see Chapter 30).

Russia's October Revolution	Even more than the Mexican and Chinese Revolutions, the Russian Revolution had a profound impact on world history.

Both those, like Louise Bryant, who were sympathetic to the revolution and those who saw the emergence of "godless communism" as a threat to freedom and decency agreed that a fundamental historical change had occurred. Indeed, the Bolsheviks and their leader V. I. Lenin saw themselves as fighting not just to control one country but also to change the destiny of all humanity.

Russia's first revolutionary crisis occurred in 1905, in the aftermath of defeat in the Russo-Japanese War (see Chapter 24). Protestors converged on the Winter Palace in St. Petersburg to petition the tsar for reform, carrying holy icons and petitions addressing the tsar respectfully as "our father." Mounted on horseback, the tsar's private guard rode the marchers down, killing many and shattering old bonds of trust.

Tsar Nicholas II (r. 1894–1917) responded to the ensuing crisis by authorizing a series of reforms, including, for the first time, a representative assembly called the Duma. The tsar also approved a crash program of industrialization that, though it achieved substantial progress by 1913, also created further social instability. The money for industrialization came largely from higher taxes on already miserable peasants, and the new industrial workers labored under much worse conditions and with much lower pay than their Western counterparts.

Although representatives of the Russian middle class could now express their desire for greater reform through the Duma, real power still lay with aristocrats, army officials, and the tsarist bureaucracy. While some reformers argued that the powers of the Duma could be expanded, others argued that a fresh start was needed to bring justice and progress to the country. One of the revolutionary groups was the Social Democratic Party, communist followers of the Marxist tradition.

After 1903, the Social Democrats split into two factions. One group, the Mensheviks, adhered to the traditional Marxist belief that socialism could only be built on the foundation of capitalism. Before Russia's workers could seize power for themselves, a modern industrial economy would have to be built. The Mensheviks therefore favored an alliance with the Russian middle class and supported a revolution that would lead to a liberal, multiparty constitutional republic.

V. I. Lenin (1870–1924), the leader of the opposing Bolshevik faction, had a different vision. Lenin's radicalism started in childhood, when his elder brother

●**V. I. Lenin** (1870–1924) Born Vladimir Ilyich Ulyanov, Lenin led the Bolsheviks to power during the Russian Revolution of 1917. Leader of the Communist Party until his death in 1924.

was hanged for plotting to assassinate the tsar. Lenin himself was exiled first to Siberia and then to western Europe. There he developed his theory of the "revolutionary vanguard," arguing that a small, dedicated group of professional revolutionists should represent the interests of the industrial proletariat. Rather than waiting for Russia's industrial workers to increase in numbers and in political consciousness, as the Mensheviks argued, the Bolshevik vanguard should seize state power and rule in the name of the working class.

Lenin's opportunity to implement his ideas came as a result of the war. With soldiers fleeing the eastern front, Tsar Nicholas was losing his ability to control events. Many blamed the ineptness of his government for the huge human and economic costs of war. Faced with mutinies in the army and near anarchy across the country, Tsar Nicholas abdicated in February 1917. When Louise Bryant arrived in the summer of 1917, the Provisional Government that had replaced him was also losing its popularity and legitimacy. In a country sick and tired of war, the leaders of the Provisional Government decided that Russia would continue to fight Germany and uphold its obligations to the Allies, hoping to maintain access to foreign loans and to share in the division of Ottoman lands if the Allies won.

Russians, however, were no longer willing to fight. Louise Bryant described the passionate appeal of one veteran for peace at a public meeting: "Comrades! I come from the place where men are digging their graves and calling them trenches! I tell you the army can't fight much longer!" A peasant delegate said that if they were not given sufficient land "they would go out and take it." "Over and over like the beat of the surf came the cry of all starving Russia," Bryant wrote, "'*Peace, land and bread!*'" The Provisional Government did not seem able to deliver on any of those demands.

After the tsarist bureaucracy collapsed, a new form of social and political organization emerged: the *soviets* (Russian for "committees"). As lines of authority broke down, they were spontaneously replaced by committees: of workers in factories, of residents in urban neighborhoods, of railway workers, and even of soldiers and sailors in the military. It was a radical form of democracy in which participants in a common enterprise had the right to speak and be represented, with decisions made through public discussion and consensus.

In this atmosphere, V. I. Lenin returned from exile. As Russian society slid from dictatorship to near anarchy, his clear vision and organizational abilities put the Bolsheviks in a position to make a play for power. In Bryant's words, "Lenin is a master propagandist. . . . He possesses all the qualities of a 'chief', including the absolute moral indifference which is so necessary to such a part." Though a sophisticated intellectual who wrote complex books on Marxist theory, in the summer of 1917 Lenin reduced the Bolshevik program to two simple slogans: "Peace, Land, and Bread!" and "All Power to the Soviets!" The fiery speeches and tireless organizing of another prominent Bolshevik, Leon Trotsky (1879–1940), did much to advance the Communist cause that summer.

By the fall of 1917, with the authority of the Provisional Government in decline, a vacuum appeared at the center of Russian politics. Lenin and the Bolsheviks planned and executed a coup d'état that later communists would celebrate as the October Revolution. Hardly a shot was fired in the Provisional Government's defense. Lenin shut the newly formed Constituent Assembly elected to write a new constitution. As Bryant wrote, "A big sailor marched into the elaborate red and gold assembly chamber and announced in a loud voice: 'Go along home!'" Russia's brief experiment with multiparty representative democracy had ended.

Civil War and the New Economic Policy, 1917–1924

The Communist Party, as the Bolsheviks were now called, regarded the Constituent Assembly as irrelevant. Defending the revolution, they thought, was the first order of the day. To fulfill their promise to bring peace, their delegates went to negotiate with the Germans and in 1918 signed a treaty ceding to Germany rich Ukrainian and Belarusian lands. The Communists saw this unequal treaty as only a temporary setback, being certain that soon the workers of Germany would rise up, overthrow their government, and establish a true and equitable peace with Russia. Their self-confidence in such dangerous circumstances was remarkable.

Lenin and his Communist government also dealt with powerful counter-revolutionary forces. Aristocratic generals turned their attention from the Germans to the Communists and threatened to undo the revolution. The Russian Civil War of 1919–1921 pitted the Communist Red Army, commanded by Leon Trotsky, against the "White Armies" organized by former tsarist generals and armed with the help of the United States and Great Britain. The Communists killed the tsar and his family to keep them from becoming a rallying point for the conservatives, and they developed a secret police organization just as terrifying as the old tsarist one.

The already weary Russian people suffered greatly during the civil war. By 1921, however, Lenin was securely in control and ruling with an iron hand. The anarchic democracy of freely elected soviets had been replaced by strict party discipline in the government, the army, the press, and the economy. Within the Communist Party the Central Committee, dominated by Lenin, allowed only limited debate even among themselves. All other political organizations were banned because, the Communists argued, they could only represent the interests of capitalists and counter-revolutionaries.

Bryant believed that circumstances pushed the Communists toward dictatorship. "In the beginning," she wrote of Lenin, "he imagined he could maintain a free press, free speech and be liberal toward his enemies. But he found himself faced by a situation where iron discipline was the only method capable of carrying the day." It is probably true that the Communists could not have held on to power without harsh measures; still, many would find Bryant's judgment of Lenin naive. Liberalism—the free play of ideas and organizations in civil society—was never part of his plan.

In a global context, one of the most important achievements of Lenin and the Communists in this period was to secure control over both Russia and the Russian Empire. Though they lost lands in the west (such as Poland, Finland, and Lithuania), they retained the rich lands of the Ukraine, the vastness of Siberia, the underdeveloped lands of Central Asia with their potential for agricultural development, and the strategic Caucasus Mountains in the south. These regions were brought together in 1922 in the Union of Soviet Socialist Republics (U.S.S.R.). Allegedly a federal republic, in reality the Soviet Union was a top-down dictatorship dominated by Moscow.

Once the crisis of civil war was over, Lenin created a positive plan for ruling his exhausted country. The New Economic Policy (1921–1924) ended the extreme economic regimentation of the civil war period. Peasants were allowed to keep the land they had recently won and to farm it as they saw fit. Restrictions on private business were lifted for all but the largest enterprises, such as transportation and heavy industry. Under the New Economic Policy the country experienced a brief respite of relative peace and the beginnings of economic recovery.

Stalin and "Socialism in One Country"

Louise Bryant never returned to Russia after Lenin's death in 1924, perhaps because she did not want to see how little her hopes for socialism were being realized after Joseph Stalin (r. 1926–1953) succeeded Lenin. Expelled from the seminary where he briefly studied, Stalin could not match Lenin's intellectual brilliance. While the exiled Lenin associated with European intellectuals, Stalin was robbing banks to raise funds for the party. Having spent time in jail, he knew the ways and means of the tsarist secret police from personal experience. *Stalin,* his chosen revolutionary name, means "man of steel."

From 1919 to 1924 Stalin demonstrated absolute personal loyalty to Lenin, who entrusted him with many secret and sensitive tasks. He stayed in the background while other Communists argued about policies and sought higher positions of authority, and he served on all the important committees but was part of no faction. When Lenin died, he used divisions in the Central Committee to position himself as a safe and neutral choice for leadership. But once Stalin held that power, he no longer acted as a mediator but as a dictator. By 1926 Stalin had consolidated his authority and established a personal dictatorship. He drove Leon Trotsky, his main competitor for the role of heir to Lenin, into exile. (See the feature "Visual Evidence: History, Photography, and Power.")

More than personal ambition was at stake. Stalin had a clear vision of how to move his country forward, a vision captured by the slogan **"Socialism in One Country."** Some Communists, like Trotsky, thought socialism could be built in Russia only with the help of revolutions in advanced industrial nations; others believed that the New Economic Policy was the correct course. Stalin rejected both ideas. Instead, socialism would be built through top-down government control of every aspect of economic, political, and social life.

In 1928 Stalin launched the first of his Five-Year Plans. The entire economy was nationalized in a crash policy of industrialization. Noting that Russia was far behind more advanced economies, Stalin said: "We must make good this lag in ten years . . . or we will be crushed." After the Soviet Union cut all ties with foreign economies, there was only one way Stalin could raise the capital needed for industrialization: by squeezing it out of the Soviet people. Low wages and harsh working conditions characterized new factories built to produce steel, electricity, chemicals, tractors, and other vital foundations of industrial growth. Especially productive workers received medals rather than higher wages, while poor performance could result in exile to a Siberian labor camp.

Faced with the brutality and deprivation resulting from Stalin's policies, people could no longer even turn to religion for solace. Portraying the Orthodox Church as a foundation of the old, tsarist regime, Stalin turned churches into municipal buildings and heavily regulated the few remaining monasteries. Communist theory, stripped of complexity and vitality, became the new orthodoxy in the world's first formally atheistic state.

Still, within ten years the successes of "Socialism in One Country" were notable. The Soviet Union had the fastest-growing industrial economy in the world, with production increasing as much as 14 percent a year. But the harshly repressive society Stalin created bore little resemblance to the hopeful scenario portrayed by Louise Bryant in the books she wrote during the early years of the revolution. Stalin's version of socialism was indeed a "loathsome, ugly monster demanding human sacrifices."

• **"Socialism in One Country"** Joseph Stalin's slogan declaring that Soviet socialism could be achieved without passing through a capitalist phase or revolutions in industrial societies. This policy led to an economy based on central planning for industrial growth and collectivization of agriculture.

HISTORY, PHOTOGRAPHY, AND POWER

As Joseph Stalin consolidated his power over the Soviet Union beginning in the late 1920s, he ordered that the history of the Russian Revolution be altered to magnify his own role. Stalin's propagandists portrayed him as having been exceptionally close to Vladimir Lenin, his close confidant and handpicked successor. In fact, while Lenin appreciated Stalin's discipline and loyalty, he regarded the younger man as of limited intelligence. In the 1930s, when Stalin began purging many of Lenin's closest allies from the Communist Party and executing many of the "Old Bolsheviks" who knew Lenin personally (see Chapter 28), the historical record was "adjusted" to remove many prominent revolutionists from the story.

> Though Lenin is shown here as a passionate orator, in fact he was not a good public speaker. To stir the masses with oratory the Bolsheviks relied on Leon Trotsky, who, as described by Louise Bryant, "swayed the assembly as a strong wind stirs the long grass."

(David King Collection)

During the revolution, Lev Kamenev served as editor of the Communist daily newspaper *Pravda* ("Truth"). He traveled to London to explain Communist policies to the British government but was deported after one week.

Although the Bolsheviks fought against Russia's deeply rooted anti-Semitism, it returned under Stalin's rule. Trotsky, born Lev Bronstein, was the most prominent of the Jewish Bolsheviks.

Stalin's propagandists altered the photographic as well as the historical record of the revolution. This picture of Lenin speaking in Moscow in 1920 (left) is an iconographic image that was reproduced around the world. From the later 1920s, when the retouched version (below) was first produced, until the 1990s, Soviet citizens saw only the altered image in which two prominent communists, Leon Trotsky and Lev Kamenev, had been erased and replaced with a set of wooden steps.

Stalin resented the leading role that Trotsky played as commander of the Red Army during the civil war of 1919–1921, and Trotsky was airbrushed out of all photographs from that period. In 1936 Kamenev was accused of plotting against Stalin and executed. Trotsky, exiled from Russia, died in Mexico in 1940 when one of Stalin's agents plunged an ice pick into his skull.

(David King Collection)

QUESTION FOR ANALYSIS

With today's widespread knowledge about digital editing, is it more or less likely that viewers would be fooled by such brazen alterations as seen in these photographs?

Chapter Review

KEY TERMS

Download the MP3 audio file of the Chapter Review and listen to it on the go.

Louise Bryant was part of a generation whose youthful idealism, inspired by the Mexican and Russian Revolutions, was crushed by the failure to create a more democratic and just postwar world. She spent the end of her life in Paris, where the earlier confidence of artists and intellectuals in human progress had been replaced by a much darker view of the human condition and a much grimmer set of expectations for the future. Their pessimism was justified: when Louise Bryant died in 1936, the drums of war were beating once again. Adolf Hitler had come to power in Germany.

How can the First World War be regarded as a "total war," both for the domestic populations of the main combatants and for the entire world?

Because industrial production was critical to the military balance of the First World War, it was essential for the combatant governments to mobilize their entire populations behind the war effort. Governments rationed consumer goods to prioritize the production of war materiel, placed limits on labor organization, and restricted free speech. Even in the most liberal societies, such as Great Britain, "total war" meant a much greater regimentation of daily life, bringing the war home to civilians. On a global scale, "total war" meant that colonial peoples were forced into the conflict by the imperial powers of Britain, France, and Germany. Africans and Southeast Asians fought in Europe, while Indian, Canadian, and Australian soldiers battled Ottoman armies in the Middle East. East Africa became a theater of war, and across the colonial world peasants and plantation workers stepped up production to feed the war machines of their colonial overlords.

How did the postwar settlements fail to resolve global political tensions?

Woodrow Wilson's vision that the war would "make the world safe for democracy" was not realized. At the Paris Peace Conference, the French delegation insisted on punishing Germany by inserting a "war guilt" clause and demanding financial reparations, thus undercutting the chances of success for the liberal Weimar Republic. At the same time, Wilson's ideal of "national self-determination" proved an ineffective roadmap to stability and democracy in eastern Europe, a region with an exceptionally complex ethnic tapestry and with societies long dominated by the Russian and Austrian Empires and therefore lacking in liberal and democratic traditions. Reordering the former Ottoman Empire was even more complicated; the British and French divided up former Ottoman provinces, and Turkish, Arab, and Jewish nationalists pursued their own interests. While the framers of the Versailles treaty created the Mandate System to restore order in former German colonies and Ottoman provinces, nationalist groups competed in the Middle East, and Asian and African nationalists became angry at their second-class status. The failures of the postwar settlements were global in scope.

How did the outcomes of revolutions in Mexico, China, and Russia add to the uncertainty of the postwar world?

While the romance of revolution appealed to many observers of the Mexican, Chinese, and Russian Revolutions, each of them failed to live up to the highest ideals of their supporters. The exploits of Pancho Villa and Emiliano Zapata in Mexico showed that common people could rise up to claim their rights, but their failure, and the subsequent dominance of the corrupt and bureaucratic National Revolutionary Party, undermined hopes for change from the bottom. Likewise Sun Yat-sen's aspirations for the new Chinese Republic remained unfulfilled after warlord resistance, communist opposition, and corruption led the Guomindang in an authoritarian direction. Most important, in Russia the transition from tsarist autocracy to communist dictatorship had a deep impact on global politics. Some of those who were dissatisfied with their own societies, including some labor leaders and anticolonial nationalists, idealized the new Soviet Union. Especially after the rise of Stalin, however, it became clear that the Russian Revolution had only added to the cloud of uncertainty and anxiety that lay over the postwar world.

WEB RESOURCES

Pronunciation Guide

Interactive Maps

MAP 27.1 World War I, 1914–1918

MAP 27.2 Territorial Changes in Europe After World War I

Primary Sources

Chapter Objectives

ACE Multiple-Choice Quiz

Flashcards

For Further Reference

Bryant, Louise. *Six Months in Red Russia*. Portland, Ore.: Powells, 2002.

Dearborn, Mary V. *Queen of Bohemia: The Life of Louise Bryant*. Bridgewater, N.J.: Replica, 1996.

Fromkin, David. *A Peace to End All Peace: The Fall of the Ottoman Empire and the Rise of the Modern Middle East*. New York: Holt, 2001.

Goldstone, Jack. *Revolutions: Theoretical, Comparative and Historical Studies*. Belmont, Calif.: Wadsworth, 2002.

Hart, John Mason. *Revolutionary Mexico*. Berkeley: University of California Press, 1997.

Keegan, John. *The First World War*. New York: Vintage, 2000.

Macmillan, Margaret. *Paris 1919: Six Months That Changed the World*. New York: Random House, 2003.

Neiberg, Michael S. *Fighting the Great War: A Global History*. New York: Cambridge University Press, 2005.

Service, Robert. *The Russian Revolution, 1900–1927*. 3d ed. New York: Palgrave Macmillan, 2007.

Strachan, Hew. *The First World War in Africa*. New York: Oxford University Press, 2004.

Websites

Mexican Revolution (http://historicaltextarchive.com/links.php?op=views link&sid=224). Historical texts with background on the Mexican Revolution.

Russian Revolution (http://www.fordham.edu/halsall/mod/modsbook39.html). The Internet Modern History Sourcebook has links to many primary source documents.

World War I (http://wwi.lib.byu.edu/index.php/Links-to-Other-WWI-Sites). A portal to information about World War I organized by country and by topic.

World War I in Documents (http://wwi.lib.byu.edu/index.php/Main-Page). Hundreds of primary source documents from the period.

Responses to Global Crisis, 1920–1939

After she had participated in the struggle for the creation of the new Turkey after the First World War, the novelist **Halide Edib** (1884–1964) was forced into exile in 1926 after falling out of favor with the country's president. For the next thirteen years she traveled to France, Britain, and the United States, writing books and lecturing at universities. In 1935 she went to India, a trip that resulted in the book *Inside India* and speculation about the future shape of the world. From her own experience in Turkey she understood the struggle of formerly powerful societies to overcome more recent Western domination and the difficulties in reconciling ancient cultures with modern influences. Edib's musings about the future importance of India and China were far-sighted:

HALIDE EDIB

(*Middle Eastern Muslim Women Speak*, ed. Elizabeth Warnock Fernea and Basima Qattan Bezirgan, University of Texas Press, 1977, p. 166)

[India] seemed to me like Allah's workshop: gods, men and nature abounded in their most beautiful and most hideous; ideas and all the arts in their ancient and most modern styles lay about pell-mell. Once I used to think that first-hand knowledge of Russia and America would enable one to sense the direction which the world was taking; but this India must certainly have its share in shaping the future. Not because of its immemorial age, but because of the new life throbbing in it! Perhaps the same is true of China. . . . How much must one see and understand before being able to have any idea of the working of history![1]

 This icon will direct you to interactive activities and study materials on the *Voyages* website:
www.cengage.com/history/hansen/voyages1e

812

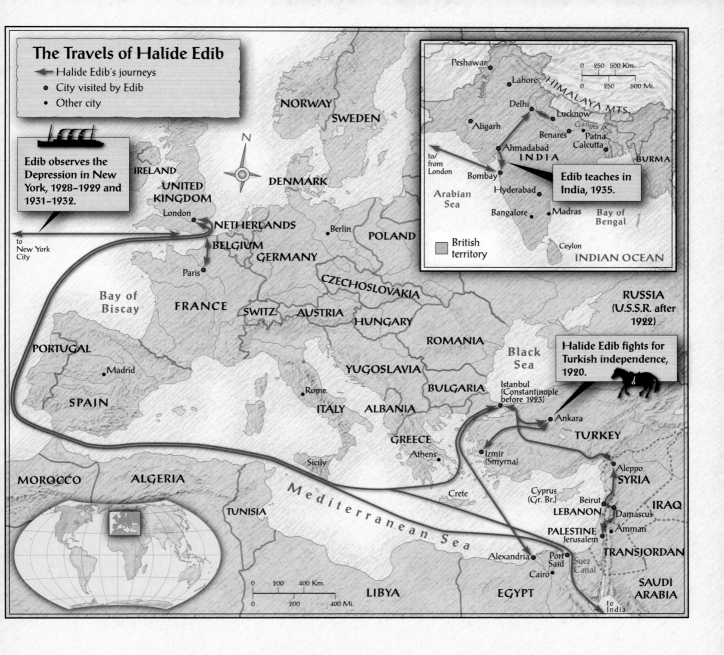

The Travels of Halide Edib

← Halide Edib's journeys
• City visited by Edib
• Other city

Edib observes the Depression in New York, 1928–1929 and 1931–1932.

to New York City

Edib teaches in India, 1935.

British territory

Halide Edib fights for Turkish independence, 1920.

NORWAY
SWEDEN
IRELAND
UNITED KINGDOM
London
DENMARK
NETHERLANDS
BELGIUM
GERMANY
Berlin
POLAND
Paris
CZECHOSLOVAKIA
Bay of Biscay
FRANCE
SWITZ.
AUSTRIA
HUNGARY
ROMANIA
PORTUGAL
Madrid
SPAIN
Rome
ITALY
YUGOSLAVIA
ALBANIA
BULGARIA
Black Sea
GREECE
Athens
RUSSIA (U.S.S.R. after 1922)
Istanbul (Constantinople before 1923)
Ankara
Izmir (Smyrna)
TURKEY
Aleppo
SYRIA
MOROCCO
ALGERIA
Sicily
Crete
Cyprus (Gr. Br.)
Beirut
LEBANON
Damascus
IRAQ
TUNISIA
Mediterranean Sea
Alexandria
Port Said
Suez Canal
PALESTINE
Jerusalem
Amman
TRANSJORDAN
LIBYA
EGYPT
Cairo
SAUDI ARABIA
to India

Peshawar
Lahore
HIMALAYA MTS.
Delhi
Lucknow
Aligarh
Benares
Patna
Ganges
Calcutta
Ahmadabad
INDIA
BURMA
to/from London
Bombay
Arabian Sea
Hyderabad
Bangalore
Madras
Bay of Bengal
Ceylon
INDIAN OCEAN

0 250 500 Km.
0 250 500 Mi.

0 200 400 Km.
0 200 400 Mi.

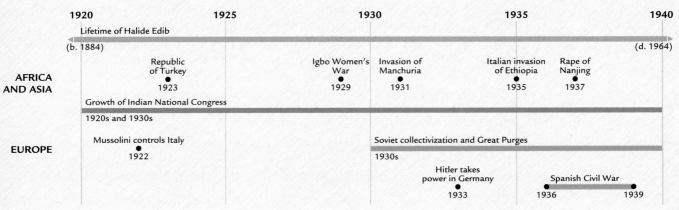

	1920	1925	1930	1935	1940
	Lifetime of Halide Edib				
	(b. 1884)				(d. 1964)
AFRICA AND ASIA	Republic of Turkey 1923		Igbo Women's War 1929	Invasion of Manchuria 1931	Italian invasion of Ethiopia 1935	Rape of Nanjing 1937
	Growth of Indian National Congress 1920s and 1930s				
EUROPE	Mussolini controls Italy 1922		Soviet collectivization and Great Purges 1930s		
			Hitler takes power in Germany 1933	Spanish Civil War 1936 1939	

Halide Edib (hall-ee-DEH eh-DEEP) was the daughter of a progressive Ottoman official who made sure she learned Arabic and studied the Quran but also had her tutored by an English governess and sent her to a Greek-run school. In 1901, fluent in Turkish, English, Greek, and Arabic, Edib was the first Muslim girl to graduate from the American College for Girls in Istanbul. As a child of privilege, she had the luxury of exploring many different ideas and forming her identity in a safe and secure environment. She remained a practicing Muslim.

After graduation Edib married and had two children: "My life was confined within the walls of my apartment. I led the life of an old-fashioned Turkish woman." But over the next two decades her life was thrown into turmoil. She grew beyond traditional gender roles, publishing her first novel in 1908 and helping to found the Society for the Elevation of Women. In 1910 she left her husband after he married a second wife, in conformity with Muslim law but against her wishes. After her divorce Edib became even more active in public affairs. In 1912 she was involved with the Turkish Hearth Club, where, for the first time, men and women attended public lectures together. It was the outbreak of war in 1914, however, that thoroughly transformed her life.

The Ottoman government sent Edib west to Damascus and Beirut to organize schools and orphanages for girls. Before long, however, the Ottoman armies were in retreat, and she returned to Istanbul with her second husband, a medical doctor. After British forces occupied Istanbul, she fled east in disguise, wearing a veil and carefully concealing her manicured fingernails as she and her husband rode on horseback to join the Turkish nationalist army headquartered at Ankara. She was given official rank and served the cause as a translator and press officer.

Though the nationalists were victorious—Turkey was recognized internationally in 1923—Edib's voyages were not over. During her years of exile, from 1926 to 1939, the uncertainties of the postwar world were turning into genuine global crises. When she came to New York as a visiting professor of literature at Columbia University in 1931–1932, the United States was suffering from the economic collapse that became known as the Great Depression. She witnessed the global effects of that economic downturn in Britain and France, from where she also viewed the emergence of fascism with the rise to power of Benito Mussolini in Italy and Adolf Hitler in Germany. Under these fascist regimes the liberal tradition was under assault, with state power growing at the expense of individual liberties. In the Soviet Union, Joseph Stalin was further consolidating his communist dictatorship.

With the global economy in crisis and political tensions on the rise, fewer people defended liberal ideals such as free trade and free political association. Ideologies that magnified the role of the state grew in popularity, while extreme nationalism allowed authoritarian rulers in many parts of the world to concentrate ever greater power. Even the liberal institutions of democratic states were sorely tested by the challenges of the 1930s. Authoritarian tendencies were reinforced wherever liberalism was weak or absent, such as in Russia, the European colonial empires, and the new nation of Turkey.

Nationalism could also be a positive force, however, providing a source of hope for many colonized Africans and Asians. The great Indian nationalist leader Mohandas K. Gandhi personified these hopes, while giving the entire world a model of peaceful political change. Like Halide Edib, Gandhi saw the fight for national independence as inseparable from the fight for justice, including equality for women, who had few rights under colonialism. Gandhi's peaceful philosophy, a source of inspiration to many, stood in sharp contrast to the renewed militarism that would soon lead to another world war.

Focus Questions

🏭 **How did governments in different parts of the world respond to the crisis of the Great Depression?**

🏭 **Why did liberal democracy decline in influence as fascism, communism, and other authoritarian regimes rose in power and popularity?**

🏭 **How successful were anticolonial nationalists in Asia and Africa during this period?**

🏭 **What major events led to the outbreak of the Second World War?**

◗The Great Depression, 1929–1939

In October 1929 prices on the New York Stock Exchange spiraled downward; within two months, stocks had lost half of their value. The next year a string of bank failures across Europe and the Americas spread economic turmoil around the world, bringing the **Great Depression** and years of misery. Massive unemployment struck industrialized countries, while plummeting agricultural prices brought difficult times to the world's farmers. In spite of various government policies intended to correct the problem, by 1939 global markets had still not recovered.

● **Great Depression**
Depression beginning in 1929 with the crash of stock prices in New York followed by a series of bank failures in Europe. Was marked by sustained deflation, unemployment in industrial nations, and depressed crop prices.

The Great Depression in the Industrialized World

The Great Depression revealed the central role now played by the United States in the global economy, as well as the degree to which finance and trade integrated nearly all the world's people into a single economic system. Historians continue to debate the causes of the Great Depression, but two factors clearly stand out: the speculative excesses of the American stock market, and the international debt structure that emerged after the First World War.

Financial markets reflected the frenetic pace of life in the United States during the "jazz age" of the 1920s, with its glamorous movie stars, mass-produced automobiles, and sensational gangsters. Speculators bought stock on borrowed money

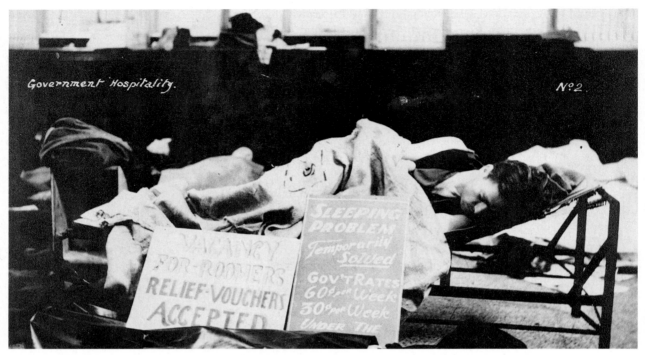

Government Hospitality.   No.2.

SLEEPING PROBLEM Temporarily Solved GOV'T RATIS 60 per Week 30 per Week

VACANCY FOR ROOMERS RELIEF VOUCHERS ACCEPTED

◾ The Great Depression   Those left unemployed by the Great Depression were often left homeless. Here a Canadian man takes shelter on a cot in an office, his plight seemingly left unsolved by his government's efforts to provide relief vouchers to "temporarily solve" the problem.   (Library and Archives Canada)

and, trusting that markets would endlessly increase in value, used paper profits to extend themselves even further. Then on October 24, 1929, the bubble burst. When the stock market collapsed, both investors and the bankers who had lent them money were ruined. As capital investment dried up, the stock market collapse turned into a general economic crisis.

The problem was magnified by a sharp division between rich and poor. By 1929, only 1 percent of the U.S. population controlled 20 percent of its wealth. Unable to purchase all the products being churned out of American factories, more and more workers found themselves staring at locked factory gates. By 1932, one-fourth of workers in the United States were unemployed.

During World War I the United States had replaced Great Britain as the world's leading source of investment capital, and European governments were in debt to American banks. The vulnerability of this system was revealed when the stock market crash led to a general run on banks. The banking crisis was particularly acute in Germany, where the Weimar government was forced to borrow heavily to make the huge payments to France required by the Versailles treaty (see Chapter 27). Financiers in the United States lent money to German banks, which paid it over to France in the form of reparation payments, and then the money came back to the United States as French payments on American loans. After the stock market collapse, American investors called in their loans to German banks, weakening them to the point of collapse. In the spring of 1931 the largest bank in Vienna declared bankruptcy as the Great Depression became global. By 1933 German factories produced only half the goods they had manufactured in 1929, and half the workforce was idle.

The policies of Western politicians, which sought domestic solutions to global problems, exacerbated the crisis. In 1930 the United States adopted high tariffs meant to protect American manufacturers from foreign competition. Great Britain followed suit in 1932, increasing interchange within its empire instead of participating in global free trade. Though designed to save jobs by protecting local manufacturers from international competition, such protectionist measures caused a steep decline in international trade and a further loss of jobs. By the early 1930s the world was locked in a vicious cycle of deflation, a downward spiral of both wages and prices.

In the United States, France, and Britain, governments responded with policies that gave the state a much larger economic role than before the war. In the United States President **Franklin Delano Roosevelt** (r. 1933–1945) implemented his New Deal programs, intended to stimulate the economy through government spending while taking care of those most in need. Social Security created a "safety net" for many of the nation's elderly, and the Works Progress Administration put the unemployed to work on public infrastructure. Price subsidies helped stabilize farm prices while legislation strengthened workers' rights to unionize and strike. Government protection of depositors' accounts restored faith in the banking system. Although conservatives complained that Roosevelt was taking the country down the path of socialism, the New Deal was quite popular. But it did not get at the root of the economic problem, and in 1939 unemployment in the United States still stood at 16 percent.

The same pattern of government economic activism unfolded in France and Britain, where socialist parties were actively involved in framing policy in the 1930s. The economic role of the state was most strongly developed in the Scandinavian countries of Sweden, Norway, and Denmark. Here Social Democrats were elected to office who pledged to construct a "welfare state" that would protect their citizens through comprehensive education, health care, housing subsidies, and unemployment insurance. But while such measures reduced suffering, they did not, any more than Roosevelt's policies, resolve underlying economic issues. No merely national solution could possibly solve the problem of depressed global markets caused by a shortage of credit.

> ● **Franklin Delano Roosevelt** (r. 1933–1945) President of the United States during the Great Depression and World War II. Created the New Deal, which intended to stimulate the economy through government spending, financial sector reform, and a safety net for those most in need.

The Great Depression in Global Perspective

Depressed agricultural prices hit hardest in those parts of the world most dependent on farming, except where peasant producers could withdraw from market production and simply grow crops for their own consumption. By 1930, however, few such producers were left. In Africa, for example, peasant production of commodities for export became the norm. Many small-scale African farming families grew crops like cocoa, cotton, and coffee not only to get the cash for imported commodities like cloth, kerosene lamps, and bicycles but also to pay the taxes demanded by European colonial governments. In the 1920s, African parents with extra money after paying their taxes often invested in school fees for their children. Thus in some areas, access to Western education was another stimulus for rural families to grow commercial crops.

When the world market price of coffee and cocoa fell by over half in early 1930, many African producers were unable to fully meet their tax obligations or pay the debts they had previously accumulated. Years of hardship followed during which school attendance dropped. Since Western manufactures had increasingly displaced indigenous industries, many African peasants had come to depend on imported goods like iron hoes and cotton clothing; now they could no longer afford them. A sensible strategy was to opt out of the market altogether and grow their own food. But colonial governments, unable to afford the loss of tax revenue that would follow, forced African villagers to plant cash crops for export even when they had little financial incentive to do so.

Conditions were equally bleak where export commodities were produced on plantations. Brazil, by far the world's largest producer of coffee, experienced a steep fall in prices when consumption of coffee in the United States and Europe declined. Exporters destroyed huge stockpiles of Brazilian coffee hoping that decreasing the supply would increase global prices, but stagnant global demand ensured that the deflationary cycle would continue. Agricultural workers left the plantations to scratch a living out of the soil or moved to cities like São Paulo to join the ranks of the destitute in the burgeoning *favelas,* or slums. The situation was similar in Southeast Asia, where a global decline in automobile and bicycle production caused the world market price of rubber to crash. In Vietnam, as in Brazil, unemployed plantation workers were left destitute.

In the villages of India, the drop in value of commercial crops further squeezed farmers who were already, in the words of Halide Edib, "at the mercy of rain, money-lender, and tax-gatherer." By 1932 peasant incomes had fallen by half, resulting in greater levels of debt for village families. To avoid losing their land, many families sold the gold jewelry they were saving for the dowry payment they needed before another family would consider their daughters for marriage. In the 1930s billions of rupees worth of such "distress gold" were sold, and many marriages were delayed or canceled. At the same time, declining incomes meant that many South Asian Muslims were forced to cancel plans to perform the *hajj,* the pilgrimage to Mecca and Medina that could take a lifetime of planning. As cotton prices plunged and textile factories in Europe and the United States cut production or closed, Egyptian farmers were struck equally hard. Whereas over 16,000 people a year traveled from Egypt to Arabia before 1929, only about 1,700 were able to make the pilgrimage in 1933.

These were also troubled times in Halide Edib's native Turkey. To build up its own industrial base and make the country less dependent on foreign imports, the government pursued a policy of "import substitution," using high tariffs to shield local producers from global competition. Also adopted in some of the larger Latin American countries, this approach was meant to stimulate local industry. But even if some new industrial jobs were created, the policy was, in global terms, economically dysfunctional. Like the protective tariffs imposed by the leading industrialized nations, the effect was to decrease international trade even further, hampering global economic recovery.

Fascism, Communism, and Authoritarianism

Even in countries where the liberal traditions of private enterprise and individual liberty had the deepest roots—such as the United States, Canada, Britain, France, Australia, and New Zealand—both total war in the 1910s and global depression in the 1930s brought greater government economic intervention. In Italy, Germany, and the Soviet Union, where liberalism had much shallower roots, the challenges of the early twentieth century created a climate in which explicitly antiliberal political ideologies—fascism and communism—flourished.

Fascists, most notably Benito Mussolini in Italy and Adolf Hitler in Germany, were contemptuous of representative government. Weak, vain, and vacillating politicians should be replaced by strong leaders who represented not self-interested factions but the people as a whole. Only then, they promised, could national greatness be achieved. Unity of purpose and the role of the state in organizing the collective will were more important in fascist thinking than individual rights. Fascists were extreme nationalists, and while racism was strongly present across the world—from the segregated cities and schools of the United States to the racially based empires of Britain and France—the German Nazis imposed racial policies of unprecedented severity. Germany's Jews were the principal target.

Communists also had no use for liberal democracy, following Karl Marx's idea that representative governments were merely committees for managing the affairs of the property-owning bourgeoisie (see Chapter 23). But in opposing the liberal emphasis on individual rights, communists traditionally underplayed national unity and emphasized class solidarity. The workers of each nation, after uniting to overthrow their oppressors, would unite to create global socialism. In reality, the Soviet Union was the only existing socialist society in the 1930s, and Stalin had already declared that his state would oversee the development of "Socialism in One Country." As Stalin collectivized agriculture, hastened the pace of industrialization, and purged the state and the army of his perceived enemies, the Soviet people lived in perpetual conditions of fear and deprivation.

Although fascists and communists were bitter enemies and hated each other passionately, they did share a common loathing for liberal democracy. Following the Great Depression, with the democratic nations struggling without much success to restore their economic vitality, many came to believe that the more radical prescriptions of fascism and communism were the cure.

Mussolini and the Rise of Fascism

For **Benito Mussolini** (1883–1945) the bond tying the people together was the Italian state: "Everything for the state, nothing against the state, no one outside the state." The term **fascism** derives from an ancient symbol of authority: the Roman *fascio*, wood branches tied tightly together around an axe. The idea was one of "strength through unity"; individual branches can be snapped, but when they are firmly bound they become unbreakable. Mussolini was bitterly disappointed by the lackluster performance of the Italian government and military during World War I, and he was also offended that Italy had been treated as a second-class citizen at the Paris Peace Conference. In the postwar period he organized quasi-military groups made up largely of former soldiers, the infamous Blackshirts, who used violence against Italian socialists and communists. Their belligerence also intimidated middle-class politicians, whose weakness, Mussolini thought, could allow Russian-style Bolshevism to spread to Italy. Mussolini's supporters called him *Il Duce* (ill DOO-chey), "the leader."

It was true that lack of unity made the country vulnerable to both outside powers and internal dissension. Social tension accompanied industrialization in the north, while the south was still mired in the poverty that drove many to emigrate to the United States and Argentina. Having no deep roots, the existing liberal constitution seemed unable to reconcile regional and class divisions. The Catholic Church, though dominating the lives of most Italians, was also powerless to bridge such divides.

Mussolini stepped in, with supreme confidence and determination, to fill the need that many Italians felt for order, discipline, and unity. The passion of his speeches contrasted sharply with the bland style of most politicians. Some landowners and industrialists gave the fascists financial backing as his Blackshirts harassed union leaders, broke strikes, and kept disaffected farm laborers and tenants

Benito Mussolini (1883–1945) Prime minister of Italy and the world's first fascist leader. Also known as Il Duce, he founded the Italian Fascist Party and formed an alliance with Hitler's Germany.

fascism Authoritarian political doctrine based on extreme nationalism, elevation of the state at the expense of the individual, and replacement of independent social organization in civil society with state organizations.

in line. In 1922 he maneuvered his way into the prime minister's position, and it seemed for a time that the fascists would be willing to work within the framework of Italy's representative, democratic constitution. As the violence of fascist thugs continued, however, many members of the Italian middle class who had been attracted by Mussolini's youth and vigor began to turn against him. Mussolini responded by taking active steps to consolidate his power, arresting opposition leaders and outlawing their political parties. Though the constitutional change was not immediate— the old Chamber of Deputies was retained until 1939—after 1926 Mussolini ruled as an authoritarian dictator.

The foundation of liberty in liberal societies was free associations: organizations formed voluntarily by people with similar regional, class, or political interests. Mussolini had no sympathy with this idea. Instead, he installed a system of "corporations" by which all citizens involved in a common undertaking would be organized by the state. His government replaced independent unions with state-sanctioned ones and took over the nation's youth organizations. In theory, the fascist government was thereby able to monitor and control the activities of everyone in the country, though the fascists never actually achieved that level of intrusion in the lives of individuals. (See the feature "Movement of Ideas: Fascism and Youth.")

For the dull compromises of parliamentary democracy Mussolini substituted a theatrical politics that involved singing, flag waving, marching, and stirring oratory. He often referred to Rome's imperial tradition and promised to make it once again the center of a mighty empire. In 1935, in defiance of the League of Nations, he invaded Ethiopia, successfully avenging his country's humiliating defeat at the Battle of Adowa by King Menelik's army in 1896 (see Chapter 26). Fervent patriotism in the cause of empire proved another effective way to bind the Italian people together.

Some Italians were active supporters of Mussolini's regime, willing to trade liberty for security and a renewed sense of national pride. Others paid for opposition to Mussolini with their lives, usually Italian communists. Most Italians probably did not care too much one way or the other. Rather than actively supporting the fascist cause or risking a fight against it, they simply went on with their daily lives.

Hitler and National Socialism in Germany

Germans also faced difficult conditions after World War I. The country was both humiliated and financially devastated by the war and the punitive Versailles treaty. Although the Weimar Republic had brought liberal democracy to Germany in the 1920s, progress toward stability and prosperity ended with the onset of the Great Depression. Germans were growing desperate for solutions to their seemingly intractable problems. By the early 1930s the center was falling out of German politics, as communists on the far left and fascists on the extreme right gained in popularity.

Into this environment stepped **Adolf Hitler** (1889–1945) and his followers in the National Socialist Party. Hitler had a very different idea than did liberals or socialists of what "the people" meant. Socialists believed that "the people" meant the masses of workers, and liberals believed that each individual was autonomous and that "the people" was simply the sum of those individuals. For Hitler, however, *das Volk* (dahs vohlk), "the people," was a single organism bound by history, tradition, and racial composition. Just as no cell is independent from the others in a living organism, so all Germans were connected by their racial destiny. Hitler defined Germans as an "Aryan" race superior to all others.

Adolf Hitler (1889–1945) Leader of the National Socialist Party who became chancellor of Germany and dismantled the Weimar constitution. His ultra-nationalist policies led to persecution of communists and Jews, and his aggressive foreign policies started World War II.

According to Nazism, any German who did not live up to the ideal of racial pride and racial purity was like a cancerous growth that needed to be excised. Nazi targets included communists, with their internationalist doctrine; homosexuals, with their supposed rejection of traditional family values; and the handicapped, considered physically inferior. Proponents of the racist pseudo-science of eugenics, also popular in the United States in the 1930s, argued that selective breeding could lead to superior human beings. If the smartest "Aryan" men and women married and had children, they could produce a "master race." Eugenic medical practices led to the sterilization of many girls from poor families to stop their "genetic defects" from being passed on to another generation.

But Hitler was even more concerned with the mixing of races. Looking for a scapegoat on which to blame the country's problems, he tapped into the centuries-old tradition of anti-Semitism. In spite of the fact that most German Jews were thoroughly assimilated into national life, he identified them as the main threat: "The personification of the devil as the symbol of all evil assumes the living shape of the Jew." For the Nazis, Jews were the people whose negative characteristics helped to define, by contrast, the virtues of the German *Volk*. Only by isolating the Jews could the goal of racial purity be achieved.

In the late 1920s such ideas were on the far fringe. But after the Great Depression revealed the weakness of the Weimar political system, voters increasingly abandoned the parties of the center-right and the center-left for the communists and the fascists. Between 1928 and 1932 the National Socialist share of the vote jumped from 2.6 to 37.3 percent of the national total, and Hitler's deputies controlled more than a third of the seats in the Reichstag. His main supporters came from lower-middle-class people who did not have savings or job security and were vulnerable during the depression, as well as from young people caught up in Hitler's emotional, patriotic appeals. Almost half the party members were under 30.

National Socialist Propaganda The Nazi Party often used images of healthy blond children to emphasize German vitality and racial superiority and organized young people into party-based boys' and girls' clubs. This poster for the "League of German Girls" solicits donations to a fund to "Build Youth Hostels and Homes." In spite of her smile, and the flowers on the swastika-labeled collection tin, all of the money collected actually went into weapons production. (Mary Evans Picture Library/The Image Works)

The German Communist Party also gained strong support in the elections of 1932. Alarmed by the threat of revolution, German business leaders increased their support for the ardently anticommunist National Socialists. Though many saw Hitler as wild and unrefined, they trusted him to rally the public against communism. Although President Hindenburg was reluctant to give Hitler a major political role, he needed Hitler's support to form a stable governing coalition. Hitler said he would join the conservative coalition only if he were made chancellor. The strategy worked: in 1933 President Hindenburg announced the formation of a new government with Hitler at its head.

Fascism and Youth

Fascists made a special appeal to youth, hoping to tap into the idealism of young people and their desire to be part of an exciting movement greater than themselves. Because fascism appealed to the emotions more than to reason, there were few philosophical statements of fascist principles. Perhaps the most coherent is the one extracted below, co-written by Benito Mussolini and the fascist political philosopher Giovanni Gentile in 1932.

The second document, published in a South African newspaper in 1938, shows how such fascist ideas spread to other parts of the world. It was an entry in a newspaper essay contest, written by a 16-year-old girl named Elsa Joubert. That year Afrikaner nationalists, descendants of the Boers who had claimed much of South Africa in the nineteenth century (see Chapter 26) staged an elaborate series of public ceremonies to mark the one-hundredth anniversary of the victory of "voortrekkers" ("pioneers") over a Zulu army. That miraculous victory, the nationalists claimed, had demonstrated God's covenant with the Afrikaner people to give them South Africa as their "promised land." Torches were carried by modern-day "voortrekkers" from across the country to the capital of Pretoria, where a bonfire was lit as part of the dedication of a nationalist museum, the Voortrekker Monument. In the 1930s Afrikaner nationalists used such rituals to unite their people against both South Africa's black majority and the English-speaking white immigrants who dominated the economy.

Sources: Mussolini from http://www.worldfuturefund.org/wffmaster/Reading/Germany/mussolini.htm, *Fascism Doctrine and Institutions*, 1935, pp. 7–42; Joubert quoted in T. Dunbar Moodie, *The Rise of Afrikanerdom: Power, Apartheid, and the Afrikaner Civil Religion* (Berkeley: University of California Press, 1975).

Benito Mussolini and Giovanni Gentile: "The Doctrine of Fascism"

Fascism sees in the world not only those superficial, material aspects in which man appears as an individual, standing by himself, self-centered, subject to natural law, which instinctively urges him toward a life of selfish and momentary pleasure; it sees not only the individual but the nation and the country; individuals and generations bound together by a moral law, with common traditions and a mission which suppressing the instinct for life closed in a brief circle of pleasure, builds up a higher life, founded on duty, a life free from the limitations of time and space, in which the individual, by self-sacrifice, the renunciation of self-interest, by death itself, can achieve that purely spiritual existence in which his value as a man consists. . . .

Therefore life, as conceived of by the Fascist, is serious, austere, and religious; all its manifestations are poised in a world sustained by moral forces and subject to spiritual responsibilities. The Fascist disdains an "easy" life. . . .

Anti-individualistic, the Fascist conception of life stresses the importance of the State and accepts the individual only in so far as his interests coincide with those of the State. . . . Liberalism denied the State in the name of the individual; Fascism reasserts the rights of the State as expressing the real essence of the individual. . . . Fascism stands for liberty, and for the only liberty worth having, the liberty of the State and of the individual within the State. The Fascist conception of the State is all embracing; outside of it no human or spiritual values can exist, much less have value. Thus understood, Fascism, is totalitarian, and the Fascist State . . . interprets [and] develops . . . the whole life of a people.

Elsa Joubert: "Young South Africa"

The hearts of three thousand Voortrekkers, each of whom in his own town had formed a link in the chain of the Torch Marathon, beat faster when they saw the light of the torch coming towards them over the hills in the dusk. . . .

The hill is on fire; on fire with Afrikaner fire; on fire with the enthusiasm of Young South Africa! You are nothing—your People is all. One light in the dusk is puny and small. But three thousand flames. Three thousand! And more! There's hope for your future, South Africa!

The mighty procession brings the torches to the festival ground where thousands await them. A matchless, unprecedented enthusiasm in the darkness of the night. Numerous prayers of thanks for the torches rise up, many a quiet tear is wiped away. The torches get their "Welcome home."

Behind them, like a blazing snake in the night, the belt of fire coils down the hillside. On the festival grounds the two torches set alight a huge joyous fire. Around it march the three thousand Voortrekkers and each throws his small puny torch upon it—to form one great might Afrikaner fire.

The logs crackle as they burn. As they crackle so they exult—"The torches set us alight. Now we again set you alight, O youth of our South Africa! Come along there's work to do."

QUESTIONS FOR ANALYSIS

▶ According to Mussolini and Gentile, how are fascist values different from liberal ones?

▶ To what extent does the essay by a teenage South African girl reflect the fascist values promoted in the first document?

A month after he took office, fire broke out in the Reichstag. The arson was the work of a single individual, but Hitler accused the Communist Party of treason and had all Communist members of the Reichstag arrested. The remaining representatives then passed a law that suspended constitutional protections of civil liberties for four years and allowed Hitler to rule as a dictator. The emergency powers granted to Hitler became permanent.

Hitler dismantled the Weimar institutions and became the *Führer* (leader) of an industrial state of huge potential power. Changes to German society were sudden and extreme. The Nazis abolished all political parties other than the National Socialists and replaced Germany's federal structure with a centralized dictatorship emanating from Berlin. As in Italy, they took over or replaced independent organizations in civil society such as labor unions. Protestant churches came under tight state control, and Hitler Youth replaced the Boy Scouts and church-sponsored youth groups as part of a plan, reinforced by a new school curriculum, to teach fascism to the next generation. Hitler promised a Third Reich ("Third Empire") that would last a thousand years.

Having sent the communists off to prison camps, the Führer (FY-ruh-r) turned to the "Jewish problem." In 1935 the Nazis imposed the Nuremburg Laws, which deprived Jews of all civil rights and strictly forbade intermarriage between Jews and other Germans. Some Jews began to flee the country, but others stayed, thinking that "good Germans" would prevent Hitler from turning his anti-Semitic rhetoric into action. Most German Jews were deeply assimilated into the country's cultural and social life and did not want to move. But in 1938 the threat to their safety became more extreme when the Nazis launched a series of coordinated attacks. After this "Crystal Night," named for the smashing of the windows of Jewish homes, synagogues, and stores, more Jews fled the country. Those who remained were forced into segregated ghettos.

Hitler's dictatorship, like Mussolini's, relied on either active support or passive consent from the majority of the population. Part of his appeal was negative: at a time of fear and insecurity, Hitler identified enemies, such as Communists and Jews, who could be blamed for the country's problems. But other economic, social, and psychological factors also help explain his popularity. While the Western democracies struggled to find solutions to the problems of unemployment and government finances, German unemployment dropped from over six million to under 200,000 between 1932 and 1938. Prices were fixed, and resources were allocated by a centralized bureaucracy working in close coordination with Germany's largest corporations. Massive public works projects, such as the world's first superhighways and a large military buildup, put millions of Germans back to work.

With communists and Jews out of the way, Hitler promised, traditional values of courage, order, and discipline would once again inspire and empower the German people. Women's highest calling was to stay in the home and nurture pure-bred Aryan children. The psychological appeal of fascism was apparent in the Nazis' massive rallies, with their precision marching, flag waving, and the spell-binding speeches by the Führer himself. Like the Italian fascists, the Nazis turned politics into theater and gave people a sense of being part of something much larger than themselves. By creating public rituals that helped meet the deep human need for experiences that transcend the individual, politics began to take on some of the functions of religion. Radio broadcasts and expertly made propaganda films spread the excitement throughout the land.

Of course, not everyone was taken in. But open opposition to Hitler would mean imprisonment or death. Many Germans were content to go about their daily

CL **Primary Source:**
The Centerpiece of Nazi Racial Legislation: The Nuremberg Laws
These laws defined who was a Jew, forbade marriage between Germans and Jews, and paved the way for the Holocaust.

CL **Primary Source:**
Speech to the National Socialist Women's Association, September 1935
Learn what the Nazis believed were the proper roles for women in society—from the woman appointed to disseminate their beliefs.

lives, perhaps regretting Hitler's excesses but appreciating his apparent restoration of relative order and prosperity.

Stalin: Collectivization and the Great Purges

For all the ambition of Mussolini and Hitler, neither could match the total control of society achieved by Joseph Stalin (1879–1953). While Stalin's totalitarian control predated the global depression and was independent of it (see Chapter 27), the Soviet Union also saw an escalation of state power in the 1930s.

Starting in 1928, Stalin launched the U.S.S.R. on a path of rapid industrialization based on centralized Five-Year Plans. Since most of the country was still agricultural, Stalin needed to find a way to apply his policy of "Socialism in One Country" to rural areas as well. Lenin had promised the peasants land in return for political support, and his New Economic Policy confirmed the move toward small-scale private ownership in the countryside (see Chapter 27). But for many communists this policy was an aberration, since private ownership would lead to agrarian capitalism. Stalin eliminated that option when he ordered the **collectivization** of the rural sector and suddenly moved millions of peasants into barracks on large, state-run collective farms.

There was substantial resistance to collectivization, which Stalin explained as the activity of *kulaks* (koo-LAHKS), rich peasants who were out to exploit their fellow villagers. When he sent the Red Army into the countryside, he said it was to help the masses defeat these kulaks. In reality, the Soviet state was waging war on its own people by using military power to enforce collectivization on a resistant population. In 1932–1933, Stalin's use of the army to impose collectivization created a famine that killed millions. Ukrainians suffered the most. The brutality in the Ukraine was Stalin's punishment for their attempt to establish an independent republic after the First World War.

But the industrial sector continued to expand rapidly. The Communist Party bureaucracy treated the non-Russian parts of the Soviet Union, especially in Central Asia, in colonial fashion, as sources of raw material for industrial growth in the Russian heartland. In sharp contrast with the economies of other industrial societies, there was no unemployment in the Soviet Union. But Soviet workers received almost no material benefit; wages were kept low to generate the capital that could be invested in further industrial expansion. Rapid industrialization also poisoned the air and water, leading to poor health for many. A network of *gulags* (GOO-lahgs), prison camps even harsher than those of tsarist times, became the destination for anyone who ran afoul of communist authority for even the smallest transgression.

In the later 1930s Stalin, always paranoid about plots against him, stepped up his repression of the Old Bolsheviks (see the "Visual Evidence" feature in Chapter 27). During the **Great Purges** of the later 1930s, Stalin ordered his secret police to arrest many former colleagues of Lenin—potential competitors for power—and forced them to confess to supposed crimes. Movie cameras recorded their statements before they were taken out and shot. In 1937 alone, half of the office corps of the army was imprisoned or executed.

The decimation of his own military leadership was an irrational move given that Hitler's rise to power was a direct threat. Even as he killed and imprisoned his generals, Stalin ordered a massive military buildup to protect the Soviet Union from the likely scenario of yet another German invasion.

● **collectivization**
Stalin's replacement of peasant villages with large, state-run collective farms, following the idea of "Socialism in One Country." Millions died.

● **Great Purges**
The execution by Stalin in the late 1930s of many "Old Bolsheviks" he regarded as competitors for power. Public trials and forced confessions marked the Great Purges.

Authoritarian Regimes in Asia

The challenge to liberalism was not limited to Europe and the Soviet Union. In many other parts of the world where liberal traditions were absent or only weakly developed, the uncertainty of the postwar period and the economic crisis of the Great Depression strengthened authoritarianism. In Japan and Turkey, charismatic rulers gained authority, the state intervened more in the economy and society, and single-party states developed.

Ultranationalism in Japan

Although the Versailles treaty had rewarded Japan with territorial concessions at China's expense (see Chapter 27), nationalists were still dissatisfied:

> We are like a great crowd of people packed into a small and narrow room, and there are only three doors through which we might escape, namely, emigration, advance into world markets, and expansion of territory. The first door has been barred to us by the anti-Japanese immigration policies of other countries. The second is being pushed shut by tariff barriers. . . . It is quite natural that Japan should rush upon the last remaining door . . . of territorial expansion.[2]

The Great Depression strengthened the arguments of nationalists and militarists for a more aggressive foreign and imperial policy.

In the 1920s there were some signs that the country was heading in a more democratic direction. Japan was a constitutional monarchy, with an emperor whose role was ceremonial rather than political. Though still quite limited, voting rights were extended to more Japanese men, and the cabinet was no longer chosen by imperial advisers but by the party that gained the most votes in elections.

But other factors limited liberal democracy in Japan. One was the power of the civil service bureaucrats, who controlled policy behind closed doors in coordination with the *zaibatsu*, Japan's large industrial conglomerates. In 1926, when the new emperor Hirohito came to the throne, ultranationalists saw an opportunity to move the nation further away from limited government and toward a more centralized state. A new requirement stipulated that the minister of defense be an active military officer with significant power in the cabinet, often equal to that of the prime minister. Even Fukuzawa Yûkichi, back at the turn of the century, had begun to emphasize national glory over individual liberty (see Chapter 24). That attitude was growing in the 1920s. After the market collapse of 1930 led to falling farm prices and tough times for the farm families whose sons made up most of the soldiers in the army, the military role in government became even greater.

● **Invasion of Manchuria** (1931) Invasion that occurred when Japanese military officers defied the civilian government and League of Nations by occupying this northeastern Chinese province, leading to the further militarization of the Japanese government.

Ultranationalists in Japan envisioned a new Asian economic system that would combine Japanese management and capital with the resources and cheap labor of East and Southeast Asia. The turning point came in 1931 with the **Invasion of Manchuria,** the seizure of northeastern China in the name of the Japanese emperor. As part of the postwar settlement, the Japanese had been allowed to keep soldiers in the Manchurian capital to safeguard their country's interests, but Manchuria was still formally a province of China. Then Japanese military commanders in Manchuria, in defiance of civilian politicians in Tokyo, ordered their soldiers to leave their barracks and occupy the main population centers and the transportation infrastructure. Brought to trial, the disobedient soldiers denounced the government and used the courtroom to whip up public support for the army's ambitions.

As imperial fever grew, civilian politicians lost what little control they had over the military.

As in Italy and Germany, the larger Japanese corporations were happy to play by the rules of the new game because militarization brought them lucrative government contracts. Japan was also like the fascist countries in the seeming success of its economic policies. Military spending, even if it required government borrowing, boosted the economy, as did the occupation of Manchuria. After 1932 expanding employment opportunities benefited the Japanese working class and helped solidify political support for the ultranationalists.

The Rise of Modern Turkey

The new nation of Turkey emerged from the violent collapse of the Ottoman Empire in an exceptionally hostile environment. Without the skillful military and political leadership of **Mustafa Kemal** (1881–1938), a former Ottoman officer, Turkey may well have been divided up by the victorious Allies. For his role in helping establish the new Turkish republic, Mustafa Kemal earned the name Atatürk, "Father Turk." With the success of Kemal's armies, by 1923 the great powers had agreed to recognize a sovereign Turkish republic that retained the core territories and population of the old empire.

Halide Edib played an important role. In 1919, as the Ottoman Empire crumbled before British and Greek invaders, she stood before a crowd of thousands and rallied them to the cause of Turkish nationalism. Her heart, she later wrote, "was beating in response to all Turkish hearts, warning of approaching disaster. . . . I was part of this sublime national madness. . . . Nothing else mattered for me in life at all." She and her husband then went to join Kemal's forces in Ankara, where she became one of the nationalist leader's closest confidantes. After independence was secured, however, they had a falling out. Whereas Edib and her husband were leaders of a political party that favored the expansion of liberal democracy, Kemal was planning to be the unchallenged leader of an absolutist state. "What I mean is this," he told her. "I want everyone to do as I wish. . . . I do not want any criticism or advice. I will have only my own way. All shall do as I command." According to her memoirs Edib responded, "I will obey you and do as you wish as long as I believe you are serving the cause." But Kemal ignored her conditional response and said only, "You shall obey me and do as I wish." Edib regarded his statement as a threat, and indeed shortly thereafter he banned her political party and she went into exile.

🔲 Turkey's New Alphabet
The Turkish leader Mustafa Kemal instituted a top-down program of modernization and westernization in the new nation of Turkey. In 1928, he declared that Turkish would no longer be written in Arabic script and that Latin characters would henceforth be used for all purposes, public and private. Here Kemal himself demonstrates the new alphabet. (© Photo12/The Image Works)

Kemal's authoritarian tendencies were not without precedent. Earlier Ottoman reformers had also taken a paternalistic view, regarding their subjects like children who needed guidance but also stern discipline. Such attitudes were also common during this era of postwar uncertainty and global economic crisis. Having forged a new country through war, Mustafa Kemal put his personal stamp on the ideas that would guide Turkey for decades to come. His goal was to put Turkey on an equal economic and military footing with the European powers, and he ordered rapid modernization to achieve that end. In the nineteenth century, the Ottoman Empire had vacillated about how much it should adopt Western models (see Chapter 23). Kemal had no second thoughts in imposing a secular constitution with a strict line between mosque and state.

Kemal's drive to separate religion from politics included laws to improve the status of women. Girls and young women were given increased access to education, a move Edib strongly supported. Not surprisingly, after the emotional pain she suffered when her first husband took a second wife, she also strongly favored the Turkish law abolishing polygamy. Edib applauded when, in 1930, Turkey became the first predominantly Muslim country in which women had the right to vote.

On the other hand, she critiqued the authoritarian means by which these reforms were attained. The issue of veiling was an important one. Edib argued that "wherever religion is interfered with by governments, it becomes a barrier, and an unremovable one, to peace and understanding."[3] But Kemal interfered with the religious practices of Turkish women by banning them from wearing the veil in all government buildings, schools, and public spaces. Liberal reformers like Edib argued that while the veil should never be imposed on women, neither should it be banned by governments. Education and freedom to choose were the keys to reform. Kemal had no patience for gradual reform; he simply imposed his own will on the nation.

Following the general trend of the times, Mustafa Kemal's modernization policies depended on the accumulation and application of centralized state power. After export prices fell in 1930, his government taxed the countryside heavily to finance a state-sponsored program of industrialization. This move was part of an import-substitution policy designed to replace imported goods with domestic manufactures; another part was protecting beginning industries with high tariffs on foreign products. By pursuing this policy, Turkey joined the many nations seeking a merely domestic solution to a global problem. High tariffs inhibited international trade, and as long as the global economy remained stagnant, the shadow of the Great Depression would remain. When Mustafa Kemal died in 1938 and Halide Edib returned home the next year to become Professor of English at the University of Istanbul, that problem still had not been solved.

Anticolonial Nationalism in Asia and Africa

Colonial governments are, by their nature, authoritarian. Such regimes were already well established in Africa, South Asia, and Southeast Asia by the 1920s. The economic crisis of the Great Depression, however, led powers such as the British and the French to exploit their colonies even more as they increasingly relied on imperial resources. Harsh policies, such as the use of forced labor, combined with the general decline in the global economy to spread distress through African and Asian societies in the 1930s. As a result, movements of anticolonial nationalism gathered in strength; the forces that would bring to an end the age of European global domination were gathering.

These forces were strongest in India, where **Mohandas K. Gandhi** (1869–1948) and the Indian National Congress organized mass resistance to British rule. In Africa and most of Southeast Asia, mass nationalism was in an earlier stage of development. Nevertheless, by the 1930s a new generation of Western-educated leaders in both Africa and Southeast Asia were working to forge the links between leaders and mass supporters that had made Gandhi's movement in India so effective.

Gandhi and the Indian National Congress

Halide Edib, in exile from Turkey, traveled to India in 1935. Speaking before an audience at the National Muslim University, her thoughts were more on someone in the audience than on her own speech. Looking out at the "fragile figure" before her, she wrote in her book *Inside India,* "I was thinking about the quality of Mahatma Gandhi's greatness." Gandhi had turned the Indian National Congress, before 1914 a small elite movement, into the voice of India.

The Great War was a major turning point. Before 1914, the Congress Party had been a reformist organization, seeking greater participation of Indians in their own governance but accepting the basic outlines of British rule. Given the huge contribution the country had made to the British war effort, Indians expected to be rewarded with substantial political reform. But the British developed only modest proposals for a gradual increase in Indian participation.

Then in 1919 the Amritsar Massacre shocked the nation. Although the British had banned public meetings, the peaceful, unarmed crowd that gathered for a religious ceremony was unaware of that order. In a horrible display of the violence on which colonial authority was based, a British officer ordered his Indian troops to fire directly into the crowd, which was trapped in a confined garden area. The soldiers fired 1,650 rounds of ammunition, leaving 400 dead and 1,200 wounded. Cooperation turned to confrontation, and in 1920 Gandhi and the Congress Party launched their first campaign of mass public protest to gain *Hind Swaraj,* Indian self-rule.

By then Gandhi, a Western-educated lawyer, had discarded European dress for the spare clothing of an ascetic Hindu holy man. His philosophy was in fact influenced by both traditions. Western ideals of equality informed his insistence that the so-called Untouchables, those considered outside and beneath the Hindu caste hierarchy, be given full rights and recognition as human beings. (See the feature "World History in Today's World: Caste and Affirmative Action in India.") But his two main principles were from the South Asian tradition. *Ahimsa* (uh-HIM-sah), or absolute nonviolence, was at the center of Gandhi's moral philosophy. *Satyagraha* (SUHT-yuh-gruh-huh), or "soul force," was the application of that philosophy to politics. Gandhi believed that it is self-defeating to use violence to counter violence, no matter how just the cause. The moral force of his arguments earned him the title *Mahatma,* "Great Soul."

But in 1920, after the British threw Gandhi and other Congress leaders in jail, depriving the movement of disciplined leadership, violence did accompany the first mass campaigns of civil disobedience. Deciding that the Indian people were not ready to achieve self-rule through satyagraha, Gandhi retreated to his *ashram* (AHSH-ruhm), a communal rural home, and spun cotton on a simple spinning wheel for hours at a time. The gentle clicking of the wheel stimulated meditation, and Gandhi stressed that Indians should produce their own simple cloth at home rather than

• **Mohandas K. Gandhi** (1869–1948) Indian political leader who organized mass support for the Indian National Congress against British rule. His political philosophy of nonviolent resistance had worldwide influence.

Caste and Affirmative Action in India

Is it appropriate to give social and political advantages to members of a group that has faced long-term historical discrimination? That is a question of great concern in India today.

Lying below and outside traditional Indian caste structures were the "Untouchables." Generation after generation they did the lowest and most degrading jobs. Their mere presence could "pollute" a caste individual. Mohandas K. Gandhi was outraged by the system of untouchability and made its abolition a central goal of his nationalist movement. He called them *Harijans,* "children of God," and declared, "I would far rather that Hinduism died than untouchability lived."

In 1950 the independent government of India "reserved" 22.5 percent of all university places and government jobs for what it called "scheduled castes." Today *dalit* is more often used, a term that also includes "tribal" peoples who, like the Untouchables, have historically been regarded as "unclean" by caste Hindus. Discrimination against *dalits* continues, and they (along with India's large and poorly educated Muslim minority) still make up much of the country's poor today.

Of course, many caste Hindus resent government affirmative action policies that indirectly require them to have higher credentials to gain admission to elite universities or to compete for coveted government jobs. Now the stakes are becoming even higher as the issue of affirmative action for *dalits* is entering the domain of private-sector employment as well.

Some employers have created special programs to help *dalits* compete for good jobs. At an Infosys facility, for example, a special training course helps *dalit* engineering graduates bring their skills up to the level necessary for employment in the global software sector. *Dalit* political leaders see such programs as insufficient and are calling for legislation that would "reserve" jobs for *dalits* in the private sector. Proponents of the legislation argue that positive action is still necessary to redress historical discrimination, while opponents say the proposal will hurt the Indian economy by preventing employers from simply hiring the best and brightest applicants.

import the British textiles that had, since the nineteenth century, represented imperial economic exploitation (see Chapter 23).

In 1932 Gandhi re-emerged to lead another campaign of mass civil disobedience. In his Salt March, he walked hundreds of miles to the sea to defy a British law that forbade Indians from using ocean water to make their own salt. While the Salt March galvanized his supporters and received international press coverage, the British responded with a combination of repression and concessions. After initially jailing Congress leaders, they then compromised with the Government of India Act of 1935, which called for elections of semirepresentative regional assemblies. The Congress Party won huge victories in the following elections, but the law fell far short of their goal of complete self-government.

While Gandhi remained the symbol of Indian nationalism, there were other strong political actors both within and outside the Congress Party. In 1928 the young Jawaharlal Nehru (1889–1964), a British-educated son of a wealthy Congress leader, was elected president of the party. Although a faithful follower of Gandhi, he differed in several ways. First, his politics were more pragmatic and realistic: he did not think the moral transformation of Indian society was a necessary prerequisite for self-rule. Second, he was a socialist who saw India's future as an industrial one. Whereas Gandhi idealized the simplicity of village life, Nehru saw the "backwardness" of village life as an obstacle to progress.

■ **Gandhi's Salt March**   In 1930 Mohandas K. Gandhi received significant international press coverage when he and his followers marched 240 miles from his ashram to the sea to make salt. It was a perfect example of nonviolent civil disobedience, since the manufacture of salt was a legal monopoly of the British Indian government. (© Dinodia Images/Alamy)

Though Gandhi used Hindu symbols to rally mass support, he and Nehru agreed that the Indian National Congress should be open to members of all faiths. That did not reassure leaders of the new Muslim League, who were concerned that if self-rule were achieved they would be vulnerable to oppression by future Hindu-majority governments.

Gandhi did his best to reassure the Muslim community, and Nehru's vision was of a secular state in which religion would play no part. Based on her visit to India, Halide Edib was confident that nationalist unity could transcend religious differences. Nevertheless, distrust between the two communities was increasing. During the 1930s, some members of the Muslim League developed the idea that a separate state should be established in Muslim-majority areas. But in 1939 state power still rested with the British. In spite of having played one group off the other as part of a "divide and rule" strategy, the British argued that their presence as a neutral arbiter between India's diverse peoples would be necessary far into the future.

Colonialism in Africa and Southeast Asia

Nationalist movements were also developing in Africa and Southeast Asia during this period. As in India somewhat earlier, in the 1930s Western-educated leaders were beginning to create political structures that could mobilize large numbers of people to challenge European authority. However, since such movements were not nearly as well developed as in India, European powers continued to rule Africa and most of Southeast Asia with great confidence.

One feature of colonialism is that the ruling powers must find indigenous allies to help them control and administer their territories. While the British, French, Dutch, Belgians, and Portuguese each developed particular modes of colonial rule, many of the same features were found throughout the colonial world. For example, it was too expensive to staff colonial administrations solely with European personnel. While the top positions were always reserved for Europeans, it made sense to educate some members of the colonized society to work as clerks, nurses, and primary school teachers. In so doing, however, Europeans were sowing the seeds of their own defeat. As part of a curriculum that focused on European history (rather than that of their own societies), young Africans and Southeast Asians learned about the French Revolution or the traditional liberties of British subjects. They could not help but compare their own situation with that of their colonial masters and aspire for greater freedom for themselves and for their people.

The gap between aspirations and realities for Western-educated members of colonized societies was particularly harsh in the French colonies. French colonialism developed the principle that if a "native" studied French history, spoke the French language perfectly, and was immersed in French culture, he would become an *évolué* ("evolved one"). However, since French colonial society remained deeply racist, the évolués (ay-vol-yoo-ay) were usually deeply frustrated because most French people still looked at them as *indigenes* (ihn-deh-JEN), "natives" who were automatically inferior.

The same dynamic was also found in the Dutch East Indies, where young adults of mixed race were educated in Dutch schools but found that legal equality was not matched by social equality in a racially informed colonial environment. The British also relied on Western-educated youth in places like Nigeria and Burma to carry out essential administrative tasks. In the British Empire, however, there was no concept of assimilation, no idea that Nigerians or Burmese could ever "become English." Still, Africans and Asian educated in the English language often emulated British cultural models, and they also might be shocked when racist colonizers rejected their attempts to be accepted as equals.

An additional resentment that often drove Western-educated Africans and Asians into the nationalist movement was the European policy of relying on indigenous authorities for much of the day-to-day administrative work. In Southeast Asia, for example, the Vietnamese emperors of the Nguyen dynasty continued in office. In Africa, the British brought the king of Asante back from exile and used him, and other "traditional" authorities, to maintain order and organize the collection of taxes (see Chapter 26). The British called their administrative structure "indirect rule," priding themselves on the respect they showed to "traditional" ruling elites.

In reality, European colonists forged alliances with conservative ruling elites to gain help in maintaining law and order and collecting taxes. Malaysian sultans, to take another example, were given privileged positions in return for helping to enforce existing laws. By the 1930s impatient nationalists increasingly saw such figures as hindrances to self-rule. "Indirect rule" focused attention on local issues, promoting local ethnic identities while forestalling the emergence of broader national ones.

The British in particular divided Africans into discrete "tribes" and played their leaders against one another to secure continued control. One of the nationalists who deplored this policy was the Nigerian Nnamdi Azikiwe (NAHM-dee ah-zee-KEE-way) (1904–1996). From the largely Christian southeast, Azikiwe argued that only if all Nigerians identified themselves with the nation as a whole, whatever their ethnic and religious backgrounds, would they be able to struggle effectively for self-rule. The young Azikiwe had a broader view of the African situation than most, having stowed away on a ship to the United States in 1925 and then graduated from the University of Pennsylvania. He returned to West Africa in 1937 and founded the Nigerian Youth Movement while editing the *West African Pilot,* a newspaper dedicated to inspiring Africans to challenge British colonial policies.

During the 1930s sporadic popular uprisings in Africa and Southeast Asia arose in response to colonial tax, trade, and land policies, but they had only limited and local effect because they were not connected to larger political organizations. In the **Igbo Women's War** of 1929, for example, women in southeastern Nigeria rebelled against what they felt to be an intrusion on their family privacy when the British insisted on counting every person in their households for tax purposes. These women targeted mainly the African chiefs who acted as tax collectors for the British. Using traditional Igbo (ee-BWOH) means of protesting male abuse of authority, the women dressed up in special costumes, gathered in large numbers, and sang songs of derision intended to shame the exploiter into better behavior. The British modified their tax system slightly in response, but there were no wider reforms. The women lacked a broader organization to connect their local efforts with a wider anticolonial struggle.

•**Igbo Women's War** (1929)   Rebellion led by women in colonial Nigeria who used traditional cultural practices to protest British taxation policies.

Colonial tensions were strongest in those few areas where the Europeans came not just as rulers but also as settlers, such as South Africa and Kenya. Here Africans had lost not only their sovereignty but also much of their best farming and herding land. The British colony of Kenya in East Africa saw the rise of a mass protest movement in the 1920s. Because the Kikuyu-speaking Kenyans were most affected by the land alienation policies of Britain, it was among this group that anticolonial feelings were strongest, and the first phase of resistance was organized ethnically rather than nationally. As in the Nigerian Women's War, however, merely local protest was not enough to gain substantial reform. Meanwhile, a young leader named Jomo Kenyatta (1895–1978) was earning a doctorate in anthropology from the London School of Economics. Only later, after the Second World War, would he return and provide the leadership necessary to create a nationalist and continental movement that connected Western-educated Africans with peasants and workers.

Across Africa and Southeast Asia, the Great Depression had made the already difficult conditions of colonialism even worse. In spite of a drop in world cotton prices that made their crop virtually worthless, farmers in equatorial Africa were forced to plant, weed, and harvest cotton because the French needed cheap supplies from the colonies to keep French textile factories open. Likewise, in East Africa a "grow more crops" campaign required African farmers to dedicate land and labor to export crops that were basically worthless. Hunger resulted when farmers' energy was diverted away from subsistence crops.

Unemployment rose in Malaya, Vietnam, and the Dutch East Indies when the drop in automobile manufacturing after 1929 depressed the world market for rubber, a major plantation crop in these British, French, and Dutch colonies. Small-scale farmers in Southeast Asia, as in Africa, sometimes stopped growing export crops and focused on food crops for their own consumption to lessen their exposure to world markets. However, colonial governments required cash payment of taxes and were willing to use force to compel those payments. The French penalized Vietnamese peasants who were not able to pay their taxes with forced labor on government projects and French-owned plantations, sparking occasional uprisings. As in Africa, however, the peoples of French Indochina still lacked the organizational and ideological means for effective resistance.

Africa and Southeast Asia have been called the "quiescent colonies" during this period. But in larger historical perspective, the 1930s were merely a pause following the resistance to colonial occupation that took place in the late nineteenth and early twentieth centuries. Nationalist leaders during this time were laying the foundations for the large-scale movements of mass nationalism that would emerge at the end of the new worldwide military conflict about to erupt. Ho Chi Minh, who had helped found the French Communist Party (see Chapter 27), spent the 1930s in China, Russia, and Thailand. He would return to Vietnam in 1941 to play a leading role in the decolonization of Southeast Asia.

The Road to War

World War II did not sneak up on anyone. In the 1930s numerous events in Asia, Africa, Asia, and Europe heralded the coming conflict. After the trauma of 1914–1918, the world's people barely had a chance to catch their breath before the coming of another, even more global and more violent total war.

Japanese militarists were not content with the occupation of Manchuria in 1931, seeing it as just one step toward a greater Asian empire. Having already left the League of Nations, the Japanese openly defied international law in 1937 when they launched a savage attack on coastal China. Fighting between the Guomindang government of Chiang Kai-shek and Communist revolutionaries led by Mao Zedong (see Chapter 27) left China particularly vulnerable to Japanese aggression. Attacked by their former Guomindang allies in 1927, the Communists had retreated to the interior. During the famous Long March of 1934–1936, they marched some 7,500 miles (12,000 km) to create a new base in the northeast. After the invasion of 1937, Chiang and Mao agreed to cease their mutual hostilities and fight the common Japanese enemy, but they never combined forces or coordinated their efforts (see Map 28.1).

Rape of Nanjing Slaughter in 1937 by the Japanese army of hundreds of thousands of Chinese civilians during their occupation of the city. The soldiers used tactics such as gang rape and child mutilation to spread terror among the Chinese population.

Convinced of their racial superiority, the Japanese invaders treated the Chinese, soldiers and civilians alike, with callous brutality. During the **Rape of Nanjing,** Japanese soldiers killed hundreds of thousands of Chinese civilians, using tactics such as gang rape and mutilation of children to spread terror among the population. Total war, with its disregard of the distinction between soldiers and civilians, was being taken to a new level.

The inability of international institutions to counter military aggression was also demonstrated by the Italian occupation of Ethiopia in 1935, an attack that featured airplanes dropping poison gas on both civilians and soldiers. The Ethiopian emperor Hailie Selassie (1892–1975) went to the League of Nations for help:

Legend:
- Areas under Communist control before Nov. 1934
- Areas under Communist control, 1929–1938
- Areas occupied by Japan by end of 1938
- → Route of the Long March, Oct. 1934–Oct. 1935: Main forces from Jiangxi Soviet
- → Other forces

SOVIET UNION

MANCHURIA
- Qiqihar
- Jiamusi
- Harbin

OUTER MONGOLIA
(Independent 1924)

Baotou

Zhangjiakou (Kalgan)
Jinzhou
Shenyang (Mukden)

Lanzhou

Yan'an
Taiyuan
Beijing
Tianjin
Lüshun (Port Arthur)

KOREA
(Japanese 1910–1945)

Sea of Japan

SHAANXI
Xi'an

Luoyang
Zhengzhou

SHANDONG
Jinan
Qingdao

Huang He R.

CHINA

Xuzhou

Yellow Sea

JAPAN

Chengdu
SICHUAN
Chongqing

Yangzi R.

Wuhan

Nanjing

Shanghai

Hangzhou

Zunyi

HUNAN
Changsha
Nanchang
Ji'an

Jiangxi Soviet under Mao Zedong and Chu Teh, 1929–1934

Guiyang

Kunming

Ruijin

Canton uprising, Dec. 1927

Xiamen (Amoy)

TAIWAN
(Japanese 1895–1945)

PACIFIC OCEAN

BURMA

Shantou

Guangzhou (Canton)

Hong Kong (Gr. Br.)

Hailufeng Soviet, 1927–1928

FRENCH INDOCHINA

SIAM

Hainan

🌐 **MAP 28.1**

The Japanese Invasion of China   Six years after the invasion of Manchuria (see Chapter 27) Japanese forces began conquest of coastal China in 1937, quickly taking Beijing, Shanghai, and other major cities. Chinese resistance was extensive, but limited by divisions between the Guomindang government of Chiang Kai-shek and the Communists led by Mao Zedong. Expelled from coastal cities by the Guomindang after 1927, the Communists relocated first to the southern interior and then, after their dramatic Long March, established a new base in the northeastern Shaanxi Province.

🖥 Interactive Map

■ **The Rape of Nanjing** One of the most brutal episodes during the Japanese invasion of China was the Rape of Nanjing. Here Japanese soldiers are seen using live captives for bayonet practice, with fellow soldiers and future victims looking on. Though the Chinese have long remembered such atrocities, until recently Japanese schoolchildren learned nothing about them. (Bettmann/Corbis)

I ask the fifty-two nations, who have given the Ethiopian people a promise to help them in their resistance to the aggressor, what are they willing to do for Ethiopia? And the great Powers who have promised the guarantee of collective security to small States on whom weighs the threat that they may one day suffer the fate of Ethiopia, I ask what measures do you intend to take? Representatives of the world, I have come to Geneva to discharge in your midst the most painful of the duties of the head of a State. What reply shall I have to take back to my people?

The emperor warned the international community that if it did not take effective action, no small nation would ever be safe. The League of Nations placed economic sanctions on Mussolini but took no further action. With access to colonial resources, such as Libyan oil, and with aid from the German government, the sanctions had little effect.

Meanwhile German and Italian fascists saw their movement gaining ground in Spain. In 1936, a democratically elected Spanish government was attempting to use socialist policies to deal with the crisis of the Great Depression. Spanish conservatives, rather than contesting such policies through the electoral process, took up arms under the leadership of General Francisco Franco (1892–1975) to overthrow the Republicans and the liberal constitution. During the **Spanish Civil War** (1936–1939) the Soviet Union supported the Republicans, while the Nazis supported Franco and his quasi-fascist movement. (See the feature "Visual Evidence: *Guernica*.") The liberal democracies of France, Britain, and the United States remained neutral. Mired in their own domestic concerns, they missed this chance to support democracy against fascism. But some young people in the Western democracies were so concerned that they formed volunteer brigades to fight with the Spanish Republicans. The Abraham Lincoln Brigade from the United States was one. Nevertheless, aided by the German air force, by 1939 Franco was victorious.

The Western democracies were also slow to respond to Hitler's challenge to the balance of power. Hitler was quite forthright about his imperial ambitions. He declared that the Germans needed *lebensraum* (LEY-buhns-rowm), "living space," in which to pursue their racial destiny. Jews had no role in this future, while the Slavic peoples of eastern Europe and Russia were looked upon as inferior peoples who would provide manual labor under German management. Hitler declared that the ethnic Germans scattered across eastern Europe needed to be reunited with the homeland. While Stalin took this threat seriously, most Western leaders thought that Hitler could be contained. In fact, there was sympathy in some Western circles for Hitler's anti-Semitism and anticommunism.

In 1936 Hitler moved military forces into the Rhineland region on the border of France, in direct violation of the Versailles treaty. In 1937 the British prime minister Neville Chamberlain (1869–1940) flew to Munich to deal directly with the German dictator. Chamberlain's policy of "active appeasement" was based on the premise that Hitler would be content with minor concessions and that by working with him Chamberlain could prevent a major European war. The British public, still scarred by the trauma of the Great War, largely supported Chamberlain's efforts to avoid another one.

Hitler then demanded that he be allowed to occupy the Sudetenland, a region of Czechoslovakia where, he claimed, ethnic Germans were being mistreated (see Map 28.2). Stalin was now thoroughly alarmed but lacked confidence that his army could withstand a German invasion, a problem partly of his own creation, since many Russian military officers had been killed during the Great Purges. Much as they hated and mistrusted each other, in the summer of 1939 Hitler and Stalin signed a nonaggression pact that secretly divided Poland between them. Hitler was merely delaying his planned attack on Russia, while Stalin was playing for time to ready his country for war.

When Hitler invaded Poland on September 1, 1939, Britain and France immediately declared war on Germany but took no active military steps to confront the German army. Meanwhile, in the United States public opinion was largely opposed to another intervention in European politics. Soon, however, peoples across Europe, Africa, Asia, and the Americas would be embroiled in a total war the likes of which humanity had never seen.

• **Spanish Civil War** (1936–1939) Conflict between conservative nationalist forces, led by General Francisco Franco and backed by Germany, and Republican forces, backed by the Soviet Union. The Spanish Civil War was seen by many as a prelude to renewed world war.

GUERNICA

The Spaniard Pablo Picasso (1881–1973) was one of the most influential visual artists of the twentieth century, his work reflecting the unsettled cultural climate of interwar Europe. Picasso's "cubist" paintings fractured images in surprising ways, often using African sculptures as models. Like other European artistic movements of the time—the strange, dream-like images of surrealism; the emotional violence of abstract expressionism—Picasso's cubist portraits characterized an "age of anxiety" during which modern artists undermined earlier ideals such as rationality, solidity, and conformity.

Though Picasso usually avoided political themes or direct reference to current events, he was so affected by the German bombing of the town of Guernica during the Spanish Civil War that he produced this painting, writing: "The Spanish struggle is the fight of reaction against the people, against freedom. My whole life as an artist has been nothing more than a continuous struggle against reaction and the death of art. . . . In the panel on which I am working, which I shall call *Guernica* . . . I clearly express my abhorrence of the military caste which has sunk Spain in an ocean of pain and death."

Before April 1937 Guernica was held by the elected Republican government, but it was under assault by insurgent Nationalist troops loyal to Francisco Franco. Anxious to aid the cause of Spanish fascism (and also to try out his new *Luftwaffe*, or air force), Adolf Hitler sent aerial squadrons to bombard Guernica. With no anti-aircraft defenses, the city was devastated by German bombs. Nearly two thousand civilians were killed or wounded. Picasso was so disturbed by the slaughter that he quickly produced this painting and displayed it in the Spanish Pavilion at the World's Fair in Paris. Many visitors to the exhibition saw it as a warning of terrible events about to unfold.

(Museo Nacional Centro de Arte Reina Sofia, Madrid, Spain/Art Resource, NY. © 2008 Estate of Pablo Picasso.
© Artists Rights Society [ARS], NY)

Francisco Franco remained in power in Spain until 1975, two years after Picasso's death. The artist refused to allow the painting to travel to his native country until democracy was restored. By 1981 that condition had been met, and *Guernica* was moved to the Prado Museum in Madrid.

The horse may represent the Spanish Republic, and the bull Franco.

The horse is illuminated by a sun containing an electric light (the only explicit symbol of modern technology) and by a lantern held by the arm of a woman entering the scene from above and beyond.

The bull stands over a weeping woman with a dead child in her arms; children were not spared from the bombing of Guernica.

Below the horse is a fallen warrior with a broken sword; just above the sword is a small flower, perhaps symbolizing renewed life and hope.

Picasso read about Guernica in the newspaper: the horse's body seems to be textured to look like newsprint, a feeling reinforced by the black, white, and grey color palette of the painting.

QUESTION FOR ANALYSIS

▶ Over seven decades after it was painted, does the symbolism and visual impact of Picasso's work still have the power to communicate the horrors of total war?

Key:
- International boundaries, 1936
- Germany in 1933
- Remilitarized in 1936
- Annexed in 1938
- Satellite states, March 1939
- Conquered by Germany in September 1939
- Annexed by Soviet Union in September 1939

Annexed by Germany, March 1939

Gained by plebiscite, 1935

To Hungary 1938–1939

Interactive Map

🌐 **MAP 28.2**
The Growth of Nazi Germany, 1933–1939   The major turning point in the expansion of Nazi Germany was the annexation of the Sudetenland from Czechoslovakia in 1938. Joseph Stalin interpreted British diplomatic efforts to avoid renewed world war as a sign of weakness, and he agreed to a secret treaty to divide Poland between Hitler's Germany and his own Soviet Union. The German invasion of Poland from the west in 1939 therefore triggered the annexation of eastern Poland by the Soviet Union.

Chapter Review

The decade of the 1930s was a harsh time, made harsher for Halide Edib by exile from Turkey, the country she loved and had helped to create. After her return in 1939, Edib continued to write novels, served one term as a member of parliament, and taught English literature at Istanbul University. It was a relatively peaceful life after her wartime adventures and later travels. The world context remained tense, however, as she lived to witness both the violence of the Second World War and, following that conflict, the bitter international divisions of the Cold War.

How did governments in different parts of the world respond to the crisis of the Great Depression?

Governments responded in a number of ways to the collapse of global markets. Liberal democracies like the United States, France, and Britain increased government involvement in the economy, trying to cushion their citizens from the effects of the depression while nudging their economies back to life. These attempts, which represented a compromise with the existing political, social, and economic order, were less effective than the more aggressive policies pursued in places like Germany and Japan, where more intensive state economic involvement and rapid military growth created millions of jobs. The governments of some recently industrializing economies, like Turkey and many Latin American nations, used import-substitution policies to stimulate modest increases in industrial activity. Meanwhile, the Soviet Union pursued a much more intensive policy of state industrial planning, resulting in rapid economic growth but no benefit for Soviet workers, while Stalin's policy of agricultural collectivization led to great hardship in the countryside.

Why did liberal democracy decline in influence as fascism, communism, and other authoritarian regimes rose in power and popularity?

In many countries, especially those that lacked strong liberal traditions, the economic crisis of the Great Depression weakened the political center as more people turned to ideologies of the extreme right and left in their search for solutions. Fascism in Italy and Germany, ultranationalism in Japan, and the authoritarianism of governments like that of Mustafa Kemal in Turkey are examples. China's conservative Nationalist government was challenged by communist forces, but in the 1930s the Soviet Union remained the world's only communist regime.

KEY TERMS

Halide Edib (812)

Great Depression (815)

Franklin Delano Roosevelt (817)

Benito Mussolini (819)

fascism (819)

Adolf Hitler (820)

collectivization (825)

Great Purges (825)

Invasion of Manchuria (826)

Mustafa Kemal (827)

Mohandas K. Gandhi (829)

Igbo Women's War (833)

Rape of Nanjing (834)

Spanish Civil War (837)

How successful were anticolonial nationalists in Asia and Africa during this period?

The authoritarian tradition of colonialism was reinforced when European powers used harsh measures such as forced labor to spur production among their imperial subjects in Africa and South and Southeast Asia, adding to the momentum of anti-colonial nationalism. The most successful resistance was led by the Indian National Congress, where Western-educated leaders like Gandhi and Nehru organized millions of Indians in their campaign for self-government. By 1935 they had extracted an agreement that allowed provincial elections, but the British remained in secure control at the top. In Africa and Southeast Asia, anticolonial protests were largely confined to the local level. Here urban-based, Western-educated nationalists were just beginning to build the political infrastructure that would later allow them to more effectively connect local resistance to national movements.

What major events led to the outbreak of the Second World War?

Throughout the 1930s militarism was on the rise. Japanese expansion, first into Manchuria and then into coastal China, the Italian invasion of Ethiopia, and Hitler's remilitarization of the Rhineland all demonstrated that the League of Nations was incapable of guaranteeing international security. The reluctance of the Western democracies to face up to the possibility of another total war was demonstrated by their neutrality in the Spanish Civil War and by Britain's policy of appeasement toward Hitler. The American novelist Ernest Hemingway wrote *For Whom the Bell Tolls* based on his experiences fighting with the Republicans in Spain. The title comes from a seventeenth-century poem by Englishman John Donne: "No man is an island, entire of itself; every man is a piece of the continent, a part of the main. . . . Any man's death diminishes me, because I am involved in mankind; and therefore never send to know for whom the bell tolls; it tolls for thee. . . ." The tolling bells of the 1930s, Hemingway warned, announced a looming catastrophe.

For Further Reference

Chang, Iris. *The Rape of Nanjing: The Forgotten Holocaust of World War II*. New York: Penguin, 1998.

Crozier, Andrew. *The Causes of the Second World War*. Malden, Mass.: Wiley-Blackwell, 1997.

Dalton, Dennis. *Mahatma Gandhi: Non-Violent Power in Action*. New York: Columbia University Press, 1993.

Edib, Halide. *House with Wisteria: Memoirs of Halide Edib*. Charlottesville, Va.: Leopolis Press, 2003.

Fitzpatrick, Sheila. *Stalin's Peasants: Resistance and Survival in the Russian Village after Collectivization*. New York: Oxford University Press, 1996.

Gellner, Ernest. *Nations and Nationalism*. Malden, Mass.: Wiley-Blackwell, 2006.

Hobsbawm, Eric. *The Age of Extremes: A History of the World, 1914–1991*. New York: Vintage, 1996.

Mango, Andrew. *Atatürk: The Biography of the Founder of Modern Turkey*. New York: Overlook, 2002.

Paxton, Robert. *The Anatomy of Fascism*. New York: Vintage, 2005.

Rothermund, Dietmar. *The Global Impact of the Great Depression, 1929–1939*. New York: Routledge, 1996.

Websites

An Age of Anxiety (http://www.fordham.edu/halsall/mod/modsbook40.html).   The Internet Modern History Sourcebook provides many primary source documents on the interwar years.

WEB RESOURCES

Pronunciation Guide

Interactive Maps

MAP 28.1 The Japanese Invasion of China

MAP 28.2 The Growth of Nazi Germany, 1933–1939

Primary Sources

Chapter Objectives

ACE Multiple-Choice Quiz

Flashcards

Armenian Genocide (http://news.bbc.co.uk/2/hi/europe/6045182.stm).   Debates over the 1915 Armenian genocide still generate controversy today. The BBC provides an overview and links to recent news stories on this topic.

Fascism (http://departments.kings.edu/history/20c/fascism.html).   A brief overview and solid bibliography, with links to specific figures and topics on the history of fascism.

Gandhi (http://www.gandhiserve.org/information/links/mk_gandhi/mk_gandhi.html).   Provides extensive links to information on Gandhi's historical role and on contemporary Gandhian movements.

The Second World War and the Origins of the Cold War, 1939–1949

By the spring of 1944, Nazi Germany had occupied France for nearly four years. In preparation for a British and American invasion at the Normandy coast, underground resistance fighters were being parachuted into the French countryside. **Nancy Wake** (b. 1912), a young Australian, was the only woman in her group. War can produce unlikely heroes, and Nancy Wake was one. While she had traveled to Paris in the 1930s looking for adventure, fun, and romance, now she was risking her life in the fight against Nazi Germany:

NANCY WAKE

(Australian War Memorial, Negative Number P00885.001)

As the Liberator bomber circled over the dropping zone in France I could see lights flashing and huge bonfires burning. I hoped the field was manned by the Resistance and not by German ambushers. Huddled in the belly of the bomber, airsick and vomiting, I was hardly Hollywood's idea of a glamorous spy. I probably looked grotesque. Over civilian clothes, silk-stockinged and high-heeled, I wore overalls, [and] carried revolvers in the pockets. . . . Even more incongruous was the matronly handbag, full of cash and secret instructions for D-Day. . . . But I'd spent years in France working as an escape courier . . . and I was desperate to return to France and continue working against Hitler. Neither airsickness nor looking like a clumsily wrapped parcel was going to deter me.[1]

CL This icon will direct you to interactive activities and study materials on the *Voyages* website: **www.cengage.com/history/hansen/voyages1e**

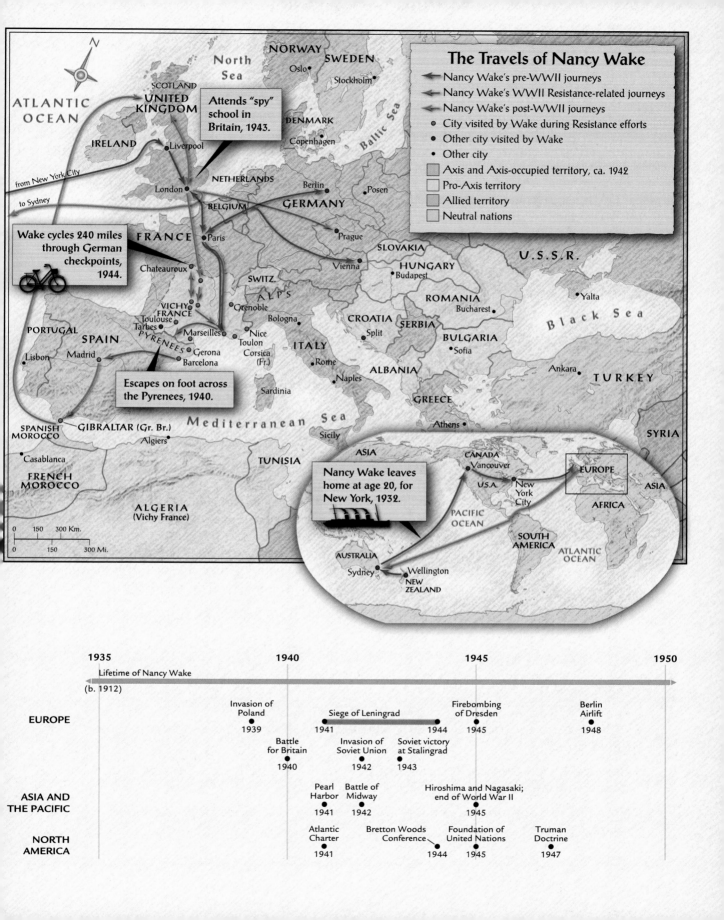

The Travels of Nancy Wake

→ Nancy Wake's pre-WWII journeys
→ Nancy Wake's WWII Resistance-related journeys
→ Nancy Wake's post-WWII journeys
• City visited by Wake during Resistance efforts
• Other city visited by Wake
• Other city
▢ Axis and Axis-occupied territory, ca. 1942
▢ Pro-Axis territory
▢ Allied territory
▢ Neutral nations

Attends "spy" school in Britain, 1943.

Wake cycles 240 miles through German checkpoints, 1944.

Escapes on foot across the Pyrenees, 1940.

Nancy Wake leaves home at age 20, for New York, 1932.

from New York City
to Sydney

0 150 300 Km.
0 150 300 Mi.

Timeline

	1935	**1940**	**1945**	**1950**
	Lifetime of Nancy Wake (b. 1912)			

EUROPE		Invasion of Poland 1939	Siege of Leningrad 1941 — 1944	Firebombing of Dresden 1945	Berlin Airlift 1948
		Battle for Britain 1940	Invasion of Soviet Union 1942	Soviet victory at Stalingrad 1943	
ASIA AND THE PACIFIC		Pearl Harbor 1941	Battle of Midway 1942	Hiroshima and Nagasaki; end of World War II 1945	
NORTH AMERICA		Atlantic Charter 1941	Bretton Woods Conference 1944	Foundation of United Nations 1945	Truman Doctrine 1947

• **Nancy Wake**
(b. 1912)   Highly decorated Australian veteran of the Second World War. After serving as courier for the French underground resistance early in the war, she traveled to England for training and parachuted into central France in 1944 during the Allied reoccupation.

The German secret police, the Gestapo, called her "the White Mouse" and put her at the top of their "most wanted" list. But Wake evaded capture and went on to become the most highly decorated female veteran of the war.

Born in a family that was originally from New Zealand, Wake had both English and Maori ancestors. Even as a child she "dreamt of seeing the world," and at the age of 20 she sailed from Australia to Canada and traveled by train to New York; in 1934 she settled in Paris. At that time Wake was more interested in parties than in politics, but she had an awakening when she traveled to Vienna. After witnessing German Jews being publicly humiliated by Nazi sympathizers, she wrote, "I resolved then and there that if I ever had the chance I would do anything, however big or small, stupid or dangerous, to try and make things more difficult for their rotten party."

Wake became engaged to a wealthy French industrialist and lived an exciting life, with a wide circle of Parisian friends and frequent vacations to the Alps. But there was an undercurrent of tension. "In common with many others I feared war was inevitable and then where would we all be? When would laughter end and the tears begin?" By 1937, civil war was raging in neighboring Spain and the threat of Hitler's Germany was growing.

After Hitler attacked Poland in 1939, there was an ominous pause before Germany opened a western front against France. After that invasion came in 1940, Wake served as a courier for the underground resistance, passing messages and helping the *maquis* (mah-KEE)—the antifascist fighters—escape from both the Gestapo and collaborating French authorities. Soon there was too much heat on the "White Mouse"; she hiked to Spain over difficult and dangerous mountain passes, and from there went to England. After training in Britain, she parachuted into central France and joined the maquis, the only woman in her group.

Wake's story puts a human face on the concept of total war. The military mobilization, civilian involvement, and global reach of this conflict were even greater than that of the First World War and had unprecedented global effects. The war deeply affected the world's peoples, and with its end came the rise of the United States and the Soviet Union as global superpowers and the beginning of their Cold War rivalry.

Focus Questions

 What factors contributed to early German and Japanese successes and later Allied ones?

How did civilians in various parts of the world experience the Second World War as a total war?

How did the outcome of the war affect the global balance of political and military power?

●The Second World War: Battlefields, 1939–1945

The Second World War (1939–1945) reached even more parts of the world than the First. The expansion of the Japanese Empire into China (see Chapter 26) made Asia and the Pacific a full-scale theater of war, and Mussolini's invasion of Ethiopia in 1935 and the desert war in North Africa brought African and Arab societies into the conflict. But control of Europe was still central to the struggle, with Britain and the Soviet Union allied against Germany (see Map 29.1). As during World War I, the United States made a delayed but decisive commitment to the war, this time fighting in both Asia and Europe.

After the German invasion of Poland in 1939, the Second World War proceeded in two phases. From 1940 to 1942, initiative and success lay with the **Axis powers:** Germany, Italy, and Japan. While the Germans and Italians advanced across continental Europe and the Mediterranean, Japanese armies were on the offensive in East and Southeast Asia. But after the Soviet Union was invaded by Germany in June 1941 and the United States was attacked by Japan in December of that same year, the momentum shifted as the Soviet Union and the United States mobilized their considerable resources. In 1943 the Soviet, British, and American Allies turned the tide, and by 1944, aided by resistance movements in France, Vietnam, the Philippines, and elsewhere, the Allies were on the offensive.

● **Axis powers**
Alliance of Germany, Italy, and Japan during the Second World War.

German *Blitzkrieg* and the Rising Sun of Japan, 1939–1942

When the German army invaded Poland, it unleashed a new form of warfare: the *blitzkrieg* (BLITS-kreeg) or "lightning war," which depended on the rapid mobility of tanks and mechanized infantry movements supported by massive air power. As western Poland was quickly overrun, Stalin made use of his secret agreement with Hitler to occupy the eastern part of the country. France and Britain declared war on Germany but took no steps to regain Poland. Instead, during the so-called Phony War of 1939–1940, they shored up their own defenses. Nancy Wake and her fiancé moved south from Paris to Marseilles (mahr-SEY), trying to put some distance between themselves and the anticipated German invasion.

In the spring of 1940, the Germans invaded Denmark and Norway and soon controlled Belgium, Holland, and northern France. In the 1930s the French had planned for a repetition of trench warfare by building an elaborate series of concrete bunkers, the Maginot Line, to protect the invasion route. But German military planners used their new blitzkrieg tactics and their control of Belgium to bypass the Maginot Line. In 1940, as in 1871, the Germans were in control of Paris. British forces sent to defend France had to evacuate their continental positions, while during the Battle for Britain the *Luftwaffe* (the German Air Force) pummeled Britain in preparation for a seaborne invasion.

The victory of the Royal Air Force in the Battle for Britain ensured that the planned invasion would never happen, but the Germans continued to bombard London to terrorize its citizens and sap their morale. During this "blitz," when Londoners crowded into subway stations to escape the bombing, Britain held together under the firm leadership of Prime Minister **Winston Churchill** (1874–1965): "Hitler knows that he will have to break us in this Island or lose the war. . . . Let

● **Winston Churchill** (1874–1965)   British prime minister during the Second World War who rallied his people to stand firm during the war's dark early days. A staunch anticommunist, he coined the term *iron curtain* to describe Stalin's domination of eastern Europe.

🌐 **MAP 29.1**

World War II in Europe and North Africa Through the summer of 1941 the Axis powers, led by Germany and Italy, held the momentum in the European theater of war, with Paris occupied, Britain isolated, the Soviet Union invaded, and eastern Europe and the Balkans under fascist domination. An important Allied triumph came with British victory Al Alamein in Egypt in 1942, but the real turning point was Soviet success in turning back the Germans at Stalingrad. After the United States entered the war, Allied invasions of Italy (1943) and of occupied France at Normandy (1944) turned the tide.

CL Interactive Map

🔲 **Blitzkrieg**   German *blitzkrieg* ("lightning war") tactics, based on rapid movement of mechanized forces, contrasted sharply with the immobility of trench warfare during World War I. The German forces seen here moved quickly across Belgium in 1940 and then overran French defenses en route to the occupation of Paris.   (Bettmann/Corbis)

us therefore brace ourselves to our duties, and so bear ourselves that, if the British Empire and its Commonwealth last for a thousand years, men will still say, 'This was their finest hour.'" Londoners took heart from the fact that the massive Cathedral of St. Paul's in the heart of their city, though surrounded by burning rubble, stood unscathed.

While the German army occupied and directly administered northern France, the south with its capital at Vichy (vee-shee) came under the authority of a regime that collaborated with the Nazis. Some officials in Vichy France hoped to build their own wealth and power by cooperating with the Germans, while others held anti-Semitic and anticommunist views and favored "order" over democracy. In other countries as well, some officials cooperated with Nazi rulers. In the Balkans, extreme Croatian nationalists in the Ustase Party forged an alliance with the Germans to get the upper hand on their Serbian competitors for regional power. In Asia, the kingdom of Thailand cooperated with the Japanese early in the war in exchange for Laos and half of Cambodia. The collaboration of Vichy France with Nazi Germany also had global implications: all but one of the French colonial governors in Africa and Southeast Asia acknowledged Vichy authority.

At the same time, men and women in various countries were organizing underground resistance cells. In France, Ethiopia, Italy, Yugoslavia, Vietnam, the Philippines, and elsewhere, partisans organized to defeat fascist invaders and their local allies. Polish leaders gathered in London and formed a government-in-exile. In 1940 Nancy Wake began to work as a courier for the French underground. Their hero was a maverick general, **Charles de Gaulle** (sharl du gawhl) (1890–1970), who formed a Free French government-in-exile in London and began to recruit an army of liberation. But in 1941 de Gaulle had few resources at his command and no way to link up with the maquis resistance within France.

War also came to North Africa and southeast Europe. Early in 1941, after the failed Italian offensive against British-dominated Egypt, German forces arrived to shore up the Italian position. Eighteen months of tough motorized warfare between German and British tank companies followed. Similarly, Mussolini's designs on the Balkans were undercut by the failure that same spring to conquer Greece. Again, the German high command had to divert troops to reinforce the Italian position. As a result, most of Hungary, Yugoslavia, Romania, and Greece were brought under Axis control.

Though the American president, Franklin Delano Roosevelt, privately agreed with Churchill about how much was at stake in the war, American public opinion was against the commitment of troops to Europe. Instead, Roosevelt declared that the United States would become the "arsenal of democracy" by negotiating a "lend lease" arrangement through which American arms would be supplied to Britain without the need for immediate payment.

In the summer of 1941 Churchill and Roosevelt met on a ship off the coast of Newfoundland and jointly issued the **Atlantic Charter,** a document that reaffirmed the Wilsonian principle of national self-determination: "[We] respect the right of all peoples to choose the form of government under which they will live; and . . . wish to see sovereign rights and self government restored to those who have been forcibly deprived of them." But moral and material support from the United States did no more than help the British to hold on. There seemed little hope that German advances could be rolled back.

Matters looked almost as bleak in East Asia. To justify attacks on the colonial possessions of the United States, the Netherlands, Britain, and France, Japanese propagandists spoke of a Greater East Asian Co-Prosperity Sphere that would free Asian peoples from Western imperialism under Japanese leadership. Having allied with Germany, in 1940 the Japanese demanded that the Vichy government give them access to ports and airfields in French Indochina. Vichy officials agreed and handed much of mainland Southeast Asia over to Japanese military administrators. Once Japanese naval assaults had given the empire control of southern Burma, the threat to British-held northern Burma, and to British India, was grave.

Tensions between Japan and the United States were growing in the summer of 1941. The United States beefed up its Pacific command in the Philippines, put a freeze on Japanese assets in the United States, and, most important, cut off petroleum and steel exports. Since the Japanese fleet was dependent on U.S. oil, the empire's military and industrial planners needed to find another source of supply and focused on the oil reserves of the Dutch East Indies. To get them, however, they would have to take the Philippines from the United States. Gauging that conflict was now inevitable, Japan decided to launch a pre-emptive surprise attack. On December 7, 1941—"a date," President Roosevelt said, "which would live in infamy"—Japanese fighters attacked the U.S. naval outpost at **Pearl Harbor,**

• Charles de Gaulle (1890–1970) French general and statesman who led the Free French Army in resistance to German occupation. Later elected president of France.

• Atlantic Charter (1941) Agreement between Winston Churchill and Franklin D. Roosevelt before the entry of the United States into the war; reaffirmed the Wilsonian principle of self-determination of nations.

• Pearl Harbor (1941) U.S. naval base in Hawai'i attacked by Japanese fighter planes on December 7, 1941, bringing the United States into the Second World War.

crippling much of the American battleship fleet. Simultaneously, Japan attacked American naval assets in the Philippines. The war for the Pacific had begun.

Once their own territory had been attacked, the American people rallied behind their president. A few days after Pearl Harbor, the German and Italian governments also declared war on the United States, and the country began an intensive mobilization to create armed forces that could match the Axis forces on both sides of Eurasia. While that mobilization was taking place, however, the Japanese occupied British Hong Kong, took the Philippines from the United States, and attacked the Dutch East Indies. Their brutality and exploitation in China was soon repeated in other occupied lands. In the spring of 1942, for example, thousands of Filipino and hundreds of American prisoners of war died when they were harshly treated in a forced march across the Bataan (buh-THAN) peninsula in the Japanese-occupied Philippines. Despite Japanese rhetoric, it was the quest for imperial wealth and power, not any vision of shared prosperity, that lay at the heart of the country's war plans.

The Allies on the Offensive, 1942–1945

Even before the Japanese attack on Pearl Harbor brought the United States into the war, Hitler reneged on his pact with Stalin (see Chapter 28) and invaded the Soviet Union. Hitler viewed Russia and the Ukraine as natural territory for the expansion of Germany (see Chapter 28), while his military planners projected that Soviet resources would be necessary to win the war. In one of the most consequential movements of the war, in June 1941 the German army moved from Poland into the Soviet Union. By early 1942 both the United States and the Soviet Union had joined with Britain to challenge the power of the Axis, and by 1943 these **Allied powers** were on the offensive. By then, Nancy Wake had escaped Vichy France by hiking across the Pyrenees; now she was in England, training to participate in a hoped-for Allied counter-offensive.

At first Hitler's eastward thrust was successful. His blitzkrieg tactics worked well on the Russian plains, and the Germans were soon nearing Moscow and Leningrad (as the historic capital of St. Petersburg was then called). In the **Siege of Leningrad,** the Germans blockaded the city from September 1941 until January 1944; the city's three million people were left without fuel in the freezing winter, and as food stocks dwindled many were reduced to hunting rats for food. Escape was possible only during winter, in convoys of trucks across a frozen lake north of the city. While some thereby fled to safety, others were drowned in the icy waters as German aircraft strafed and bombed these Soviet convoys. The German siege of Leningrad killed one million people.

Like Napoleon, Hitler had opened a second front in Russia while Britain remained unconquered. German supply lines were stretched thin, and Soviet generals were able to use the vastness of their country and the harshness of winter to their own advantage. German tanks became mired in the mud that came with spring rains, and Soviet resistance to the Nazis was unmatched in its toughness and resiliency. Stalin's propagandists emphasized heroic stands against earlier invaders and rallied the Soviet peoples behind the "Great Patriotic Homeland War."

If the Germans had treated the Soviet people well, they might have found allies, such as the Ukrainians, who had suffered under Stalin's harsh rule. Instead harsh treatment by the Nazi occupiers—who believed that Slavic peoples were only good for manual labor under German command—drove the various Soviet peoples

● **Allied powers** Alliance of Britain, the United States, and the Soviet Union during the Second World War.

● **Siege of Leningrad** (1941–1944) German siege of this Soviet city that left the city without food or fuel, resulting in over a million deaths.

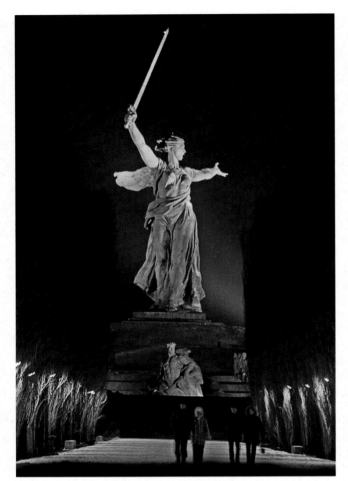

Stalingrad War Memorial   For Soviet citizens the Battle of Stalingrad symbolized their nation's toughness and resiliency in facing down the threat of fascism during the Great Patriotic Homeland War. The "Heroes of the Stalingrad Battle" complex, built on an epic scale, features this enormous "Mother of the Homeland" statue. It is still one of the most visited historical sites in Russia.   (© 2008 AP Images)

together under Stalin's leadership. If Stalin's secret police suspected people of having pro-German sympathies, as happened in the Baltic states of Latvia and Estonia, they were either killed outright or sent to Siberian labor camps.

As the United States and the Soviet Union mobilized for war, momentum shifted toward the Allies. Apart from the "Big Three," the antifascist alliance also included both the Guomindang government of Chiang Kai-shek and communist partisans led by Mao Zedong (see Chapter 28). After the Japanese invasion of China in 1937, Chiang moved his capital to the interior city of Chongqing and agreed to a cease-fire with Mao Zedong's Communists, even as tensions between them continued. Britain and the United States supplied arms to Chiang to keep up the fight against the Japanese in Burma and in China, while Mao's forces harassed the Japanese in the north. By 1942 it was becoming clear that holding on to China required a huge Japanese investment of men and material.

The first decisive military reversal for the Axis came in North Africa, where the British finally gained the upper hand. Victory at the Battle of El Alamein in Egypt (1942) not only protected Britain's control of the Suez Canal but also secured a base for a counter-attack against Italy across the Mediterranean. By 1943 British and American forces were driving northward up the Italian peninsula, aided by Italian partisans. Mussolini's forces collapsed. Though Germany propped him up until 1945, he was eventually captured and shot by the Italian resistance. In a sign of their contempt for Mussolini and what he stood for, his executioners hung his body by the heels from a public balcony.

In the Pacific, the Allies also gained momentum in 1942. The Japanese offensive continued over the first half of the year, until in early summer American aircraft inflicted severe damage on the Japanese fleet, sinking four of their six largest aircraft carriers

Battle of Stalingrad (1942–1944)   One of the major turning points of World War II, when the Soviet Army halted the German advance and annihilated the German Sixth Army. After victory at Stalingrad, the Soviets went on the offensive, driving the Germans out of Soviet territory.

at the Battle of Midway. Then the United States took the offensive at Guadalcanal, the beginning of a tough "island-hopping" campaign to drive the Japanese from well-entrenched positions. The fighting was tough, but with the huge U.S. economy now fully geared toward military production and with new ships and airplanes rolling off assembly lines at a staggering rate, American naval dominance in the Pacific was ensured.

Perhaps the single most important turning point of the war was the **Battle of Stalingrad.** Unable to take Moscow, in late 1942 the Germans swung south toward the Soviet Union's strategic oil fields. House-by-house fighting in Stalingrad gave the Red Army time to organize a counter-offensive, and in 1943 they surrounded and annihilated the German Sixth Army. Galvanized by their victory, the Soviets launched a series of punishing attacks on German positions. In January 1944 the siege of Leningrad ended as they forced the Germans from the city's outskirts, and in the spring of that year Stalin's forces drove Hitler's army out of Soviet territory altogether.

The Japanese were also on the defensive by 1943. The Allies retook the Burma Road, their main supply line to Chiang Kai-shek's Nationalist forces in China. Matching the Soviet thrust to drive the German army back toward Berlin, by 1944 American forces were pushing Japanese forces back toward their home islands. Local resistance in China, Vietnam, the Philippines, and the Dutch East Indies complemented British, Australian, Canadian, and American efforts.

When Churchill, Roosevelt, and Stalin met for the first time, in Teheran in 1943, they agreed to open a western front in addition to the front already opened in Italy. British and American commanders, led by General Dwight Eisenhower of the United States, began complex preparations for what would be a difficult landing on the beaches of Normandy in northwestern France. Meanwhile, Soviet forces drove the German army all the way to the Polish border.

In anticipation of the Normandy landing, Nancy Wake and her group parachuted into central France behind German lines. It was difficult and dangerous work. Once when her group of partisans lost their radio, and therefore contact with London, Wake bicycled more than a hundred miles over mountainous terrain to reestablish their communications link: "Every kilometer I pedaled was sheer agony. I knew if I ever got off the bike, I could never get on it again. . . . I couldn't stand up, I couldn't sit down, I couldn't walk and I couldn't sleep for days."

But Wake's efforts and those of the other maquis supported the Allied invasion of Normandy on D-Day, June 6, 1944, and helped defeat the Nazis. Moving north with her band of partisans, Wake reached Paris just as Allied forces drove the German army from the city she had once called home: "Paris was liberated on 25 August, 1944, and the whole country rejoiced. . . . After defeat and years of humiliation their beautiful capital was free. The aggressors were now the hunted. . . . The collaborators seemed to have vanished into thin air and the crowds in the street went wild with joy." But there was still hard fighting to do. A final German offensive in Belgium led to significant American casualties in the Battle of the Bulge in the winter of 1944 before British and United States forces regained the initiative. And Nancy Wake's happiness was tempered by personal loss: the Nazis had executed her husband and many of her friends.

By early 1945 Allied forces were poised to move into Germany from both east and west. The European war ended in a final fury of violence. As the Red Army moved into eastern Germany, some Soviet troops took their vengeance by raping, looting, and executing German civilians. British and American aircraft brought total war to a new level with the firebombing of Dresden. Tens of thousands of civilians who fled to underground shelters suffocated to death when the firebombs exploding above them sucked the oxygen from the air. As Soviet troops advanced into Berlin, Hitler killed himself in a bunker beneath the city. The nightmare of German fascism was over. On May 8, 1945—V-E Day—the possibility of peace returned.

It took the rest of the summer, however, for American forces to defeat Japan. Once the United States retook the Philippines late in 1944, the path toward invasion lay open (see Map 29.2). American submarines blockaded Japan, starving its military of supplies, while U.S. aircraft dropped incendiary bombs on Tokyo and other cities, reducing them to ashes. Still, some Americans thought that it would require a massive landing of troops to force a Japanese surrender, putting hundreds of thousands of American lives at risk.

CL Interactive Map

🌐 **MAP 29.2**
World War II in Asia and the Pacific   The Japanese Empire, like the Axis powers in Europe, dominated the early stages of the war in Asia, overrunning British, French, Dutch, and Chinese positions in Southeast and East Asia in 1940–1942, and threatening British India. By 1943, however, with the United States fully mobilized to fight the Pacific war, momentum shifted to the Allies. The war ended in the summer of 1945 when President Harry Truman, afraid of fierce Japanese resistance on their home islands and suspicious of Soviet intentions as Stalin's forces moved into the region, ordered the use of the atomic weapons dropped on Hiroshima and Nagasaki.

● Hiroshima and Nagasaki (1945) Two Japanese cities devastated by atomic bombs dropped by the United States in an attempt to end the Second World War. Hundreds of thousands were killed, many of slow radiation poisoning.

In 1945 a new American president, Harry S Truman, came to office after the death of Franklin Roosevelt and immediately had to make an important decision. Truman's choice to bring the war to a quick conclusion by dropping atomic bombs on Japan has been disputed ever since. The United States unleashed terrible devastation on **Hiroshima and Nagasaki.** Hundreds of thousands died, some instantly, others from the slow torture of radiation poisoning. Meanwhile, the Soviet Union occupied Manchuria and northern Korea, raising fears of Soviet occupation. Determining that immediate submission was Japan's best option, Emperor

Hirohito (hee-ro-HEE-to), whose voice his subjects had never before heard, went on the radio and announced Japan's unconditional surrender. On September 2, 1945—V-J Day—that surrender was made official. Finally, the Second World War was over.

⟨CL⟩ **Primary Source:**
The Decision to Use the Atomic Bomb
Learn why President Truman was advised to drop atomic bombs on Japan—from the chairman of the committee that gave him that advice.

● Total War and Civilian Life

Total war in the twentieth century intensely involved civilians in each conflict. Even more than during the First World War, tens of millions of ordinary people saw their routines and life plans disrupted; in that sense, Nancy Wake's experience was typical of the period.

In addition to being direct witnesses to the horrors of war, civilian populations were involved in myriad ways. The role of government in everyday life intensified. Media such as newspapers, radio, and film were censored and often incorporated government misinformation and propaganda. Once again colonized peoples were deeply involved in the global struggle. Many Africans, Indians, Arabs, and Southeast Asians participated directly in the war, were part of the mobilization for greater wartime production, or saw their destiny determined by the successes and failures of Allied and Axis armies.

Many different peoples suffered tragic population losses. Warfare and famine killed tens of millions of Chinese, and at least twenty-five million Soviet citizens lost their lives. Europe's Jewish community faced unparalleled tragedy. The genocide known as the Holocaust is the world's most painful and enduring memory of the ideological excess and savagery of fascism. Six million Jews were killed in concentration camps, death camps, and by other forms of abuse and execution. Of the entire European Jewish population, over 60 percent were murdered. The Nazis killed over 90 percent of Poland's Jews. Millions more people—homosexuals, disabled persons, Jehovah's Witnesses, and others deemed enemies of Aryan racial supremacy—were slaughtered as well. Eighty percent of Europe's Roma (Gypsies) were killed.

Civilians and Total War in Europe and the United States

Management of civilian economic production, especially in the industrial sector, was even more crucial to the war effort than during the First World War. Governments on all sides used centralized economic planning and coordinated the distribution of resources. Magnifying trends from the Great Depression, free trade became less of a factor in both domestic and international exchange.

The economic role of governments was part of a larger move toward greater state power. For example, radio and film allowed governments to engage in more effective campaigns of propaganda and misinformation. Nazi Germany's minister of information, Joseph Goebbels, was a master at using these new technologies, as well as mass public meetings, to inspire enthusiasm for Hitler and his ideas. Tokyo beamed radio broadcasts at American forces in the Pacific, using the seductive voice of "Tokyo Rose" to try to undercut the morale of U.S. forces. Even in liberal democracies like Britain and the United States, print and electronic media became tools of propaganda. (See the feature "Visual Evidence: Warfare and Racial Stereotypes.")

WARFARE AND RACIAL STEREOTYPES

Western democracies were not immune from the trend toward greater use of government propaganda to mobilize civilian populations during the total wars of the twentieth century. While authoritarian regimes like those in Nazi Germany and in communist societies like the Soviet Union had even greater control over what the public heard and saw, even in liberal societies wartime censors carefully checked the scripts for films and radio broadcasts and established government bureaus to feed information, and sometimes disinformation, to their citizens. They also restricted the political rights and liberties of individuals, outlawing strikes and sending workers where they were most needed.

The development and dissemination of racial stereotypes was part of government propaganda efforts during both global wars in the twentieth century. The most infamous case was Adolf Hitler's extreme anti-Semitism, as he stated clearly in *Mein Kampf* ("My Struggle"): "The personification of the devil as the symbol of all evil assumes the living shape of the Jew." In Asia the Japanese government also believed themselves a "master race" destined to rule over the "racially inferior" peoples of Korea, China, and Southeast Asia.

After the attack on Pearl Harbor, racial animosity toward people of Japanese descent increased in both Canada and the United States. Although most Japanese Americans and Japanese Canadians were citizens, governments stripped them of their property and forced them into detention camps on the assumption that their loyalty toward the Japanese emperor was stronger than that toward their adopted nations. As these illustrations show, wartime propaganda in the United States played on racial stereotypes.

These images are from the December 22, 1941, issue of *Life* magazine, one of the most widely circulated magazines of the period, its success stemming from its extensive use of photographs. This issue, which appeared two weeks after the assault on Pearl Harbor, featured an American flag on the cover. These images accompanied an article entitled "How to Tell Japs from the Chinese," about assaults that had just taken place on Asians in the United States. Many Americans used the single term *Orientals* to describe all Asians, and the editors of *Life* wanted to help their audience distinguish friends (the Chinese) from the Japanese foe.

(Time Inc. and Getty Images)

QUESTIONS FOR ANALYSIS

▶ In these images, how is physical appearance associated with behavior?

▶ How do these images seek to explain contemporary conflicts as related to fixed, unchanging racial characteristics?

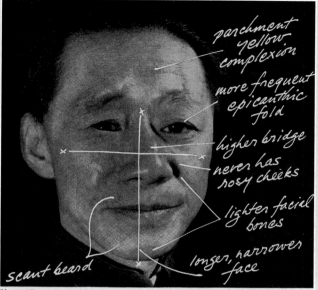

Handwritten annotations on photo:
- parchment yellow complexion
- more frequent epicanthic fold
- higher bridge
- never has rosy cheeks
- lighter facial bones
- longer, narrower face
- scant beard

Chinese public servant, Ong Wen-hao, is representative of North Chinese anthropological group with long, fine-boned face and scant beard. Epicanthic fold of skin above eyelid is found in 85% of Chinese. Southern Chinese have round, broad faces, not as massively boned as the Japanese. Except that their skin is darker, this description fits Filipinos who are often mistaken for Japs. Chinese sometimes pass for Europeans; but Japs more often approach Western types

The caption for this photo describes Ong Wen-Hao, a Chinese civil servant, as "representative of Northern Chinese anthropological group with long, fine-boned face and scant beard. Epicanthic fold of skin above eyelid is found in 85% of Chinese."

The editors make a further distinction: "Southern Chinese have round, broad faces, not as massively boned as the Japanese. Except that their skin is darker, this description fits Filipinos who are often mistaken for Japs. Chinese sometimes pass for Europeans; but Japs more often approach Western types."

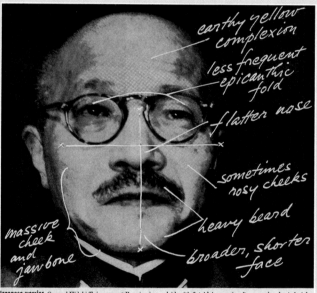

Handwritten annotations on photo:
- earthy yellow complexion
- less frequent epicanthic fold
- flatter nose
- sometimes rosy cheeks
- heavy beard
- broader, shorter face
- massive cheek and jaw bone

Japanese warrior, General Hideki Tojo, current Premier, is a Samurai, closer to type of humble Jap than highbred relatives of Imperial Household. Typical are his heavy beard, massive cheek and jaw bones. Peasant Jap is squat Mongoloid, with flat, blob nose. An often sounder clue is facial expression, shaped by cultural, not anthropological, factors. Chinese wear rational calm of tolerant realists. Japs, like General Tojo, show humorless intensity of ruthless mystics

In the caption General Hideki Tojo, the Japanese premier, is described as "a Samurai, closer to type of humble Jap than highbred relatives of Imperial Household. Typical are his heavy beard, massive cheek and jaw bones. Peasant Jap is squat Mongoloid, with flat, blob nose."

The editors of *Life* claimed that "an often sounder clue" in distinguishing Chinese from Japanese individuals "is facial expression, shaped by cultural, not anthropological, factors. Chinese wear rational calm of tolerant realists. Japs, like General Tojo, show humorless intensity of ruthless mystics."

During the Cold War, when the Japanese were allies of the United States and Communist China was an implacable enemy, these stereotypes were reversed, with the Chinese often depicted as ruthless fanatics and the Japanese as tolerant realists.

857

The American people sacrificed in the fight against fascism. Families were disrupted, sons and husbands were killed, and access to housing and basic consumer goods was restricted. With few exceptions, however, the war was not fought on American soil. Ironically, the war benefited American society in a number of ways. Massive state spending on munitions stimulated the economy, ending the Great Depression by putting the country back to work. The satisfaction of secure employment was a great psychological boost to those who had long been unemployed, even if there was relatively little to buy: many automobile plants, for example, were converted to military production.

For Americans who had long been at the bottom of the job ladder, especially women and African Americans, total war mobilization brought new opportunity. "Rosie the Riveter" became the symbol of women laboring on industrial production lines to produce the boots, bullets, and bombers needed by the military. Segregated African American military units, such as the famous "Tuskegee Airmen," distinguished themselves in the fighting, while other American blacks discovered that they had access to good industrial employment for the first time. More broadly, the camaraderie and discipline of both military and civilian life, dedicated to a successful fight against a great evil, gave an entire generation of Americans a powerful shared experience.

◾ British War Production Total war required the complete mobilization of civilian populations behind a nation's military. As in the United States and Soviet Union, traditional gender roles in Britain were transformed as women factory workers replaced departed servicemen. Here a British worker finalizes assembly of the nose cone of an Avro Lancaster bomber in 1943. (Hulton Archive/Getty Images)

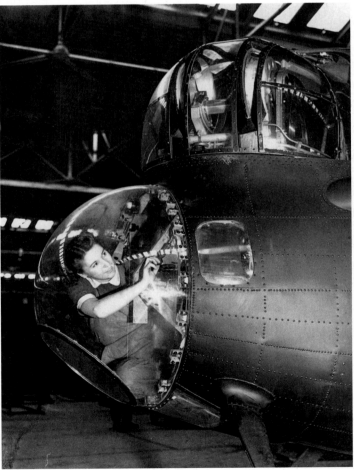

The people of the Soviet Union also experienced "the Great Patriotic Homeland War" as a powerful collective endeavor; however, their level of suffering and sacrifice, especially in the Siege of Leningrad, was much higher. Moreover, much of the Soviet Union's most productive agricultural and industrial regions lay directly in the path of the German advance, and even before the German invasion, factories were dismantled and moved to interior regions. Millions of people were likewise uprooted and put to work on farms in safer interior regions. Soviet women bore a special burden, caring for children and the elderly while often taking on dangerous jobs in mines and factories. Many Soviet women also served with distinction in the armed forces. Wartime suffering left Stalin and the Soviet people with a deep determination never to allow such an invasion from the West again.

The western European experience was more like the Soviet than the American one. Civilians in occupied western Europe—French, Belgians, Dutch, and others—saw the war come to their own cities and villages. British families were evacuated from cities under bombardment to safer rural areas, where farming families made sacrifices to take them in. In countries under occupation by the Nazis or local collaborators, such as France, Norway, and the Netherlands, the slightest sign of anti-German feeling, or any display of sympathy for the Jews, might result in imprisonment, torture, and death.

As the Second World War drew to a close, total war also came to the civilians of the original aggressor states: Germany, Italy, and Japan. During Hitler's final and futile attempt to save the "Fatherland" from invasion, old men and young boys were conscripted into the German army, facing the power and rage of better-armed and better-trained Allied forces. After 1945, German families that had been comfortable and secure saw the violence of fascism recoil on them, as during the firebombing of Dresden. Much of urban Germany lay in ruins, while hungry refugees wandered the roads.

The Japanese public experienced state intervention in all aspects of life, such as highly regulated economics, tightly controlled communications, and severe restrictions on freedom of speech and assembly. But other than the soldiers, few Japanese had any direct experience of the horrors of war or of the terrible violence that was inflicted on the empire's subjects early in the war. It was only in 1944–1945, with the aerial assault on Japan and the nuclear annihilation of Hiroshima and Nagasaki, that the Japanese people paid a severe—indeed, a terrible—price for their country's military adventure.

The civilian experience of total war had long-term effects on the political cultures of Europe, the Soviet Union, and the United States. In Europe, bitterness between those who resisted and those who collaborated would long be remembered. The Soviet Union was determined never to allow such a disaster to occur again and, as we will see in more detail, constructed a zone of buffer states to prevent future invasions from the West. And the people of the United States were, for the first time, fully willing to engage themselves as a great power in world affairs.

Civilians and Total War in Asia and the Colonial World

In the Asian theater of war, pre-existing issues of European colonialism became linked to the struggle between the Allied powers and Japan. Much of the territory gained by the Japanese early in the war was taken from the British, French, Dutch, and American colonial empires. To Winston Churchill, "liberating" such territories as Burma and Malaya meant returning them to British rule. But to local nationalists, who were aware of the doctrine of national self-determination as expressed in the Atlantic Charter, the fight against the Japanese could also be seen as a fight to throw off foreign rule altogether. Once the war against the Axis was complete, an intense conflict would arise between the European powers and local nationalists fighting to create new, independent nations.

As in Europe, civilians in Asia suffered a war fought on their own soil. Like the Germans, the Japanese thought of the people they conquered as useful for only hard labor, and they regarded exploitation of Southeast Asia's natural resources such as metal, oil, and rubber as essential to their imperial mission. Many Vietnamese, Malays, and Filipinos were forced to work in slavelike conditions, and women were forced into prostitution. (See the feature "World History in Today's World: Comfort Women.") American, British, Canadian, and Australian prisoners of war were also treated with great cruelty and often died in captivity.

Hunger and hardship were the lot of most Chinese civilians during the war. Those under Japanese occupation suffered from the harshness of imperial rule, but even those living in zones controlled by Chiang Kai-shek's Guomindang Army faced shortages of such necessities as food and medicine. With production and trade

Comfort Women

There is a long and sad connection between warfare and sexual abuse. During World War II that association became a matter of state policy as the Japanese military forced as many as 200,000 young Asian women into military brothels to provide "recreation" for their troops. The victims of this policy of forced prostitution were referred to as "comfort women." Most came from Korea, but women from the Philippines, Taiwan, and Indonesia were also victims.

For decades, most of the "comfort women" concealed their experiences to protect themselves and their families from shame. But starting in the 1980s, some of the now elderly survivors of the military brothels began to organize for both financial compensation and a formal apology from the Japanese government. Chung Yun-Hong, an 87-year-old Korean, said: "I decided to disclose my secret when I was 72 years old, after I was impressed by the brave decision by another comfort woman to speak out publicly. Only then could I have some peace of mind."*

Politicians in Tokyo initially refused to even discuss the matter, claiming that the brothels were organized by private companies and not the imperial government and that all claims to compensation had been precluded by postwar treaties. But the "comfort women" did not give up. Backed by their governments, as well as by international women's rights organizations, they continued their fight for justice.

Finally, in 1993 the Japanese government admitted that the imperial government had been directly involved in the system of forced military prostitution. In 1995, Tokyo set up a privately funded charity to pay compensation to some of its victims. The women and their advocates saw these steps as unsatisfactory, since by 2005 fewer than four hundred women had received any form of compensation. The Japanese government took a backward step in March 2007 when the prime minister denied that the comfort women had experienced sexual slavery, saying that "there is no evidence to prove there was coercion." Many of these elderly women passed away as the controversy continued to generate diplomatic tensions.

Some nationalist politicians in Japan are reluctant to acknowledge the brutality of that period, which involved harsh conditions of forced labor for millions of people, and they have tried to keep such information out of Japanese history books. But in other Asian nations, where the violence of empire is well remembered, there is strong public sentiment that the Japanese public needs to confront this difficult period of history more fully and truthfully.

*Cited in http://www.womensenews.org/article.cfm/dyn/aid/1851/context/archive.

thoroughly disrupted, malnutrition was common. Chinese resistance to the Japanese occupation was hampered by the lack of coordination or communication between Chiang's Guomindang and Mao's Red Army. The two armies achieved no more than a temporary cease-fire, made possible only by the common threat of Japan. Once the Japanese were expelled, the fight between them for China's future would be renewed.

Communist resistance was also important in neighboring Vietnam. Here a tough group of guerillas led by Ho Chi Minh used their bases in inaccessible northern regions to harass Japanese occupation forces, with American and British assistance. The principal Allied concern in Southeast Asia was the Burma Road, the primary supply line of weapons to Nationalist forces in China. Bitterly contested jungle warfare in Burma, involving African and Australian troops and supported by Allied

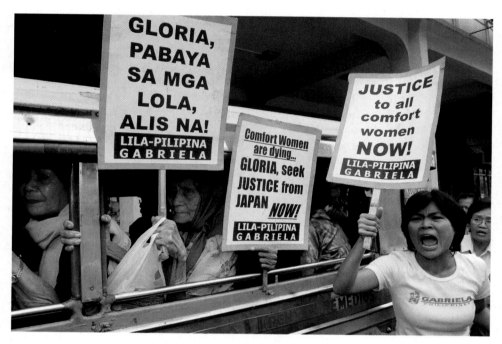

Filipina Women in Protest Memories of Japan's wartime atrocities run deep in East and Southeast Asia. These Filipina women are protesting the Japanese government's lack of restitution for the suffering of the "comfort women"—girls and women from the Philippines and other Asian countries who were forced to provide sexual services to Japanese soldiers during the war. (AFP/ Getty Images)

bombing missions, caught many peasant villagers in the crossfire. Late in the war, forced replacement of food crops with industrial ones, Japanese hoarding of food, and American bombing of rail and road lines contributed to the death by famine of two million Vietnamese.

Aware as they were of the conditions in the Japanese Empire, the British were astonished when Mohandas K. Gandhi and his Indian National Congress refused to back the British Empire in the war. During World War I Gandhi and the Congress Party had supported the British, hoping to be rewarded with concrete steps toward Indian self-government. But when the British-controlled Government of India declared war on Germany and Japan without consulting Indian public opinion, Congress leaders were frustrated by what they saw as British arrogance. Much to the disgust of British colonial officials, the Congress launched a **"Quit India"** campaign, insisting that the British leave immediately, even in the midst of war. Another Indian nationalist, Subhas Bose (Soob-ahs BOZ) (1897–1945), advocated an Indo-Japanese alliance against the British and traveled to Tokyo to organize captured Indian soldiers into an Indian National Army to fight alongside the Axis powers.

As Gandhi and other nationalist leaders were once again thrown into jail, and while Bose died in a plane crash before British officials could charge him with treason, the Indian army remained the bulwark of British defense in Asia. Under Britain's wartime economic management, Indian civilians also contributed their labor and economic resources to the Allied war effort. As in China and Vietnam, wartime economic policies led to great hardship for people in British India. In 1943, over two million people died in a famine in the northeastern province of Bengal.

British war strategies also provoked an anti-British backlash by some Arab nationalists. In Egypt they were outraged when the British mobilized their forces without seeking permission from the nominally independent government. As a result,

• **"Quit India"** Campaign by Mohandas K. Gandhi and the Indian National Congress during World War II to demand independence. They refused to support the British war effort and instead launched a campaign of civil disobedience demanding that the British "quit India" immediately.

Britain had to send police to Cairo to quell demonstrations even as they prepared for desert war with Italy and Germany. Arab nationalists were also upset at the increased Jewish immigration to Palestine, while in Iraq anti-British feelings were so strong that the government actually declared its sympathies with the Axis powers, prompting the British to invade and occupy Baghdad in the spring of 1941.

Britain's African subjects, perhaps surprisingly, showed greater loyalty to the empire. For example, the British recruited soldiers for the **King's African Rifles** from West African colonies such as Nigeria, and East African ones like Kenya, to buttress their forces in Asia, especially in the Burmese campaign. Many of these African soldiers had never traveled more than a few days' journey from their homes. Those lucky enough to return brought back an expanded view of the world and of Africa's place in it. In addition, the liberation of Ethiopia from Italian occupation in 1941, along with the return of Hailie Selassie to his throne, was of great symbolic importance, signifying the restoration of African dignity.

Africans learned that they were supporting the Allies in the name of such ideals as liberty, freedom, and national self-determination as enshrined in the Atlantic Charter. In South Africa, some younger members of the African National Congress specifically pointed to this charter in their calls for a mass-based movement against racial segregation and discrimination. In fact, some black South Africans found new opportunities during the war. As in the United States, the industrial economy boomed from the demand for war materiel. With many white working-class men conscripted into the army and with blacks forbidden from joining the military, some Africans found new and better job opportunities in the industrial sector, just as their counterparts did in the United States. On the other side of the racial divide, the war polarized South African whites. While mainstream white politicians, still loyal to the British Empire, brought South Africa into the war on the Allied side, some Afrikaner nationalists organized a pro-Axis underground movement.

Africans in the French Empire also helped in defeating fascism, providing soldiers for Charles de Gaulle's Free French Army. While most colonial officers allied with the Vichy government, the governor of French equatorial Africa, Félix Éboué (1884–1944), stood with de Gaulle. Éboué was from French Guiana in South America; a descendant of slaves, he had attained French citizenship through educational achievement. Under his leadership, the colonial city of Brazzaville became a staging ground for Free French recruitment of African soldiers.

• **King's African Rifles** African regiment recruited by Britain during the Second World War. These soldiers saw action in Burma, fighting against the Japanese to save India for Britain.

The Holocaust

Even among the many people who made great sacrifices in the war against fascism, few were aware of the magnitude of Hitler's assault on the Jews of Europe. Only when the death camps were liberated by Allied forces in 1945 did the scale of the horror known as the Holocaust become clear.

Some of the most calamitous events of the twentieth century occurred when political leaders tried to turn extremist ideologies into reality. The Nazi death camps of World War II are the most infamous example. The racial ideology that drove Hitler's National Socialism, described in the previous chapter, played to the fears of Germans disoriented by their disempowerment after World War I and by the catastrophe of the Great Depression. Now scapegoating turned to slaughter.

The Nazis regarded the peoples of eastern Europe, especially the Slavs, as an inferior "race" destined to work under the direction of their "Aryan" superiors, the German "master race." But Hitler identified two "races" that he claimed played no useful role at all. One was the Roma, or Gypsies, a traveling people whose ancestors had come from India. Clinging to their own language and traditions, the Roma of central Europe suffered prejudice and discrimination. Hitler's other outsider group was the much larger Jewish community. Thorough assimilation into German culture and society gave the country's Jews no protection from Hitler's racial obsession.

In the 1930s, the Nazis had segregated Jews into ghettos and then herded them into labor camps. Hitler, growing dissatisfied with that approach, contemplated a "final solution" to the "Jewish problem." Early in 1942, Nazi officials made plans for "death camps" where, instead of being worked to death, Europe's Jews would simply be liquidated. According to the minutes of the Wannsee Conference, a bureaucracy would be set up to "cleanse the German living space of Jews in a legal manner." Jews "capable of work" would be sent to camps in Poland, "whereby a large part will undoubtedly disappear through natural diminution." Those who were not worked to death "will have to be appropriately dealt with." The "appropriate" measure for those too young, too old, or too sick to work was simply to kill them outright. (See the feature "Movement of Ideas: Primo Levi's Memories of Auschwitz.")

Nazi officials used the latest technology to design a system whose outcome was the extermination of human beings. One death camp administrator observed that people died faster if they were already short of breath when they entered the "shower rooms" that were actually gas chambers. Determined to follow "the industrialist's logic," he forced Jewish captives to run to the showers in a panic, saving gas as well as time for further executions. Thousands of people could be killed in a single day. Scientific rationality and industrial progress were perverted to the most horrible of ends.

Not all Jews went meekly to their death. The **Warsaw Ghetto Uprising** was the most militant act of mass resistance to Nazi abuse. The Polish city of Warsaw had long been a Jewish cultural center, but shortly after their occupation the Nazis forced the city's Jews into a fenced-off ghetto where they found no work and very little food. In 1943, the Nazis began to remove residents for extermination at the Treblinka death camp. In response, sixty thousand Jewish residents of the ghetto rose up in revolt. Ten thousand paid with their lives, and the Nazis killed most of the rest at Treblinka. The heroism of Jewish resistance, and of the many people across Europe and the Middle East who risked their lives to aid Jewish neighbors, was not enough to prevent Hitler from carrying out his plans.

At the same time, the United States retained its racially discriminatory restrictions on Jewish immigration. In 1939, over nine hundred Jewish refugees seeking sanctuary were turned away by American immigration officers and returned to Europe. (Many of them later died in the Holocaust.) So where were Jewish refugees supposed to go? Britain also restricted Jewish immigration to both England and Palestine. Some Zionists, believers in the creation of a Jewish state to be called Israel, took matters in their own hands, forming guerilla groups in Palestine and developing an underground system to aid illegal Jewish immigration to the land of their ancient ancestors. After 1939, however, it was almost impossible for Jews under Nazi rule to escape. Those who did so were helped by people such as those in Denmark, who helped many Danish Jews flee to neutral Sweden, putting their own lives and livelihoods at risk.

The Nazi death machine continued even after it became clear that the Allies would win the war. The Allied soldiers who liberated the emaciated victims were sickened by the sight of mass graves. Many Holocaust survivors found that their entire families had been killed. Sometimes, however, after scattering to different parts

CL **Primary Source: Memoirs**
Read what the man responsible for administering and overseeing the Holocaust thought and felt about his "work."

● **Warsaw Ghetto Uprising** (1943) Unsuccessful revolt of Polish Jews confined to the Warsaw ghetto who rose up to resist being sent to the Treblinka death camp.

Primo Levi's Memories of Auschwitz

Primo Levi (1919–1987) was an Italian Jew who joined the underground resistance to fascism in his home country. Like millions of other European Jews, he was sent to a Nazi concentration camp, but he survived and became one of the world's most renowned writers. The extract below is taken from an interview that appeared on Italian television in 1983. The interview took place as Levi was returning for the first time to Auschwitz on a Polish train. Primo Levi took his own life in 1987.

Source: From the transcript of a 1983 Italian radio broadcast, http://www.inch.com/~ari/levi1.html. The English translation is by Mirto Stone, modified for clarity.

Return to Auschwitz

INTERVIEWER: Did you know where you were going [on the train to Auschwitz]?

PRIMO LEVI: We didn't know anything. We had seen on the cars at the station the writing "Auschwitz" but in those times, I don't think even the most informed people knew where Auschwitz was. . . .

INTERVIEWER: What was your first [experience of] Auschwitz?

LEVI: It was night time, after a disastrous journey during which some of the people in the car had died, and arriving in a place where we didn't understand the language, the purpose. . . . It was really an alienating experience. It seemed we had abandoned the ability to reason, we didn't reason.

INTERVIEWER: And how was the journey, those five days?

LEVI: There were forty-five of us in a very small car. We could barely sit, but there wasn't enough room to lie down. And there was a young mother breast-feeding a baby. They had told us to bring food. Foolishly we hadn't brought water. No one had told us, and we suffered from a terrifying thirst even though it was winter. This was our first, tormenting pain, for five days. The temperature was below zero and our breath would freeze on the bolts and we would compete, scraping off the frost, full of mist as it was, to have a few drops with which to wet our lips. And the baby cried from morning to night because his mother had no milk left.

INTERVIEWER: What happened to the children and their mothers when [you arrived at Auschwitz]?

LEVI: Ah well, they were killed right away: out of the 650 of us on the train, 400–500 died the same evening we arrived or the next. They were immediately sorted out into the gas chambers, in these grim night scenes, with people screaming and yelling. They were yelling like I never heard before. They were yelling orders we didn't understand. . . . There was an officer . . . who would ask each one of us, "Can you walk or not?" I consulted with the man next to me, a friend, from Padua. He was older than me and also in poor health. I told him I'll say I can work, and he answered, "You do as you please. For me, everything is the same." He had already abandoned any hope. In fact he said he couldn't work and didn't come into the camp. I never saw him again. . . .

INTERVIEWER: And the food, how was it there?

LEVI: They gave us a minimal ration equivalent to about 1600–1700 calories a day, but . . . there were thefts and we would always get less. . . . Now, as you know, a man who doesn't weigh much can live on 1600 calories without working, but just laying down. But we had to work, and in the cold, and at hard labor. Thus this ration of 1600 calories was a slow death by starvation. Later I read some research done by the Germans which said that a man could last, living off his own reserves and that diet, from two to three months.

INTERVIEWER: But in the concentration camps one would adapt to anything?

LEVI: Eh, the question is a curious one. The ones who adapted to everything are those who survived, but the majority did not adapt to everything, and died. They died because they were unable to adapt even to things which seem trivial to us. For example, they would throw a pair of mismatched shoes at you. . . . One was too tight, the other too big. . . . and those who were sensitive to infections would die. . . . The feet would swell, rub up against the shoes and one had to go to the hospital. But at the hospital swollen feet were not considered a disease. They were too common so those who had swollen feet would be sent to the gas chambers. . . .

INTERVIEWER: For the Italians, there was the language problem. . . .

LEVI: Understanding one another is very important. Between the man who makes himself understood and that one who doesn't there is an abysmal difference: the first saves himself. . . . The majority of Italians deported with me died in the first few days for being unable to understand. They didn't understand the orders, but there was no tolerance for those who didn't understand. An order was given once, yelled, and that was it. Afterwards there were beatings. . . .

INTERVIEWER: We are about to return to our hotel in Kracow. In your opinion, what did the holocaust represent for the Jewish people?

LEVI: It represented a turning point. . . . [It] was perhaps the first time in which anti-Semitism had been planned by the state, not only condoned or allowed as in the Russia of the Czars. And there was no escape: all of Europe had become a huge trap. It entailed a turning point, not only for European Jews, but also for American Jews, for the Jews of the entire world.

INTERVIEWER: In your opinion, another Auschwitz, another massacre like the one which took place forty years ago, could it happen again?

LEVI: Not in Europe, for reasons of immunity. Some kind of immunization must exist. It is [possible] that in a fifty or a hundred years Nazism may be reborn in Germany; or Fascism in Italy. . . . But the world is much bigger than Europe. I also think that there are countries in which there would be the desire, but not the means. The idea is not dead. Nothing ever dies. Everything arises renewed.

INTERVIEWER: Is it possible to abolish man's humanity?

LEVI: Unfortunately, yes. Unfortunately, yes. And that is really the characteristic of the Nazi camps. . . . It is to abolish man's personality, inside and outside: not only of the prisoner, but also of the jailer. He too lost his personality in the concentration camp. . . . Thus it happened to all, a profound modification in their personality. . . . The memory of family had fallen into second place in face of urgent needs, of hunger, of the necessity to protect oneself against cold, beatings, fatigue . . . all of this brought about some reactions which we could call animal-like. We were like work animals.

INTERVIEWER: Do you think that people today want to forget Auschwitz as soon as possible?

LEVI: Signs do exist that this is taking place: forgetting or even denying. This is meaningful. Those who deny Auschwitz would be ready to remake it.

QUESTIONS FOR ANALYSIS

▶ Apart from death itself, what were the effects of the physical and psychological torture endured by Levi and his fellow death camp inmates?

▶ Over two decades after this interview, how might we evaluate Levi's answer to the question of whether something like the horrors of Auschwitz might happen again?

of the world after the war, survivors were lucky enough to find relatives who were still alive.

How could the Holocaust have happened? It is not enough to blame the Nazis. Anti-Semitism was strong across Europe, and Nazi collaborators from France, Italy, Hungary, Poland, and elsewhere sent Jews to the camps. Moreover, the system could not have worked without the passive acquiescence, if not the active participation, of German civilians. There are still debates today about whether Europe's Christian churches could and should have done more to prevent the slaughter. The Catholic pope Pius XII, for example, sponsored a great deal of humanitarian work for refugees and prisoners of war, but some think he should have confronted the German government. For her part Nancy Wake, appalled by the treatment of Jews in Austria before the war, did everything in her power to prevent Nazi ideas from spreading. Too many others simply looked the other way.

● Origins of the Cold War, 1945–1949

Soviet and American troops met each other at the Elbe River in Germany in a spirit of friendship and joy at the end of the European war, celebrating their joint victory over fascism. Roosevelt envisioned that Allied cooperation would continue after the war in the new **United Nations,** which was founded in San Francisco in the spring of 1945. Instead, the world divided into two hostile camps.

● United Nations Organization established near the end of the Second World War to guarantee international peace and security through permanent diplomacy. A Security Council of five members with veto power was created to enhance its authority.

The New United Nations and Postwar Challenges, 1945–1947

The United Nations would include all sovereign nations in its General Assembly, but it also had a Security Council composed of the major war allies: Britain, France, China, the Soviet Union, and the United States. Since each member of the council had veto power, its decisions could only be reached through consensus. It was hoped that the Security Council's special powers would make the United Nations more effective than the League of Nations.

The spirit of Allied cooperation did not last. Soon the United States and the Soviet Union were bitter enemies, two potent "superpowers" that increasingly divided the postwar global system into a bipolar struggle between Washington and Moscow. But full-scale war between them never developed. This was a "cold" war, often fought by proxies (smaller nations on either side) but never by the main adversaries (see Chapter 30). The deployment of nuclear weapons, first by the United States in 1945 and then by the Soviet Union in 1949, meant that direct conflict between the two superpowers could lead to mutual annihilation. The stakes of total war were now beyond what any leader was willing to gamble.

By the time Roosevelt, Churchill, and Stalin met at the Yalta Conference in early 1945 to plan the end of the war and the subsequent peace, Europe was becoming divided into two regions. The British, Americans, and de Gaulle's Free French controlled western Europe while Stalin's Red Army controlled eastern Europe. Churchill was deeply suspicious of Stalin, a distrust rooted in both his hatred of communism and a traditional British fear of Russian imperial expansion. Roosevelt was more accommodating to Stalin's wishes, desperately hoping to lay the foundation for a safe and secure future.

One central issue was the fate of Poland. The British and Americans had promised the Polish government-in-exile that free elections would be held after the war to determine the country's future. Stalin, however, knew that any Polish government chosen through free elections would be highly suspicious of the Soviet Union, perhaps even actively hostile to it, and so insisted that it must have a "friendly government." At Yalta, while the fighting continued, the conference participants papered over the difference. But as soon as the war was over, it became clear that Stalin intended to retain a Red Army presence in eastern Europe and to install communist governments that would do his bidding.

Stalin saw no contradiction here, saying: "Everyone imposes his own system as far as his army can reach." In 1946, Churchill coined the term *iron curtain* to describe the imposition of communism in the Soviet sphere of influence:

> From Stettin in the Baltic to Trieste in the Adriatic an iron curtain has descended across the Continent. Behind that line lie all the capitals of the ancient states of Central and Eastern Europe. Warsaw, Berlin, Prague, Vienna, Budapest, Belgrade, Bucharest and Sofia; all these famous cities and the populations around them . . . are subject, in one form or another, not only to Soviet influence but to a very high and in some cases increasing measure of control from Moscow.

Ironically, in many of these countries local communists were actually a strong political force after the war, having played important roles in the antifascist resistance. But Stalin was not interested in working with communists who had their own legitimacy and bases of power. He wanted control from the top down through men of unquestioned loyalty to Moscow, whose rule would be enforced by the continued presence of the Soviet army.

When she traveled to Prague in 1947, Nancy Wake witnessed one of the most tragic examples of Soviet domination. Before Hitler's invasion, Czechoslovakia was a relatively liberal and prosperous society with a strong middle class and an emerging democratic tradition. But when Wake arrived to work at the British consulate, she found that the capital was tense: "Although the Russians were not visible, the majority of Czechs I met used to walk around looking over their shoulders in case someone was listening to their conversation."

Most Czechs saw themselves as a bridge between east and west. Local communists fared well in a free election held in 1946 and were part of a coalition government. But that was not good enough for Stalin, who wanted firmer control. In 1948, Czech communists loyal to Moscow seized power and ended their country's brief postwar experiment with democracy. "Yes, the Germans had gone," Wake commented, "but who would liberate the country from the liberators?"

The United States, the Soviet Union, and the Origins of a Bipolar World

The guiding Marxist-Leninist ideology of the Soviet Union proclaimed the desirability and inevitability of socialist revolution on a global scale. Stalin, however, was less focused on achieving worldwide communism than on gaining security for the Russian core of the Soviet Union. With large, exposed land frontiers, Soviet Russia needed a string of buffer states across its European and Asian borders to maintain its security and prevent the re-emergence of threats such as those posed by Napoleon and Hitler. Such "defensive expansion" had also been part of the earlier development of the Russian Empire (see Chapter 20).

CL **Primary Source:**
The Long Telegram
This critique of the Soviet Union's ideology, authored by an American diplomat in 1946, profoundly influenced the foreign policy of the United States.

CL Primary Source:
Telegram, September
27, 1946
*Read what the Soviet ambas-
sador wrote to his government regarding the foreign
policy goals of the United
States.*

• **Truman Doctrine**
(1947) Declaration, by
President Harry Truman,
that the United States
would aid all peoples
threatened by commu-
nism. In reality, his doctrine of "containment"
meant that the United
States did not try to
dislodge the Soviets from
their sphere of influence.

• **Marshall Plan**
U.S. effort to rebuild war-
ravaged Europe, named
after the American
secretary of state, George
C. Marshall.

American psychology in the postwar period was quite different. The American experience allowed most U.S. citizens to retain their characteristic optimism and idealism. Americans now stood ready to project their ideals—personal liberty, de-mocracy, technological progress, and market-driven economic efficiency—onto the world stage. But as Americans engaged the postwar world, they found impedi-ments to this global vision. Though Americans thought their ideals were universal, not everyone seemed to share them. Moreover, along with the communists, some cynical observers saw American idealism as a smokescreen for the expansion of American capitalism and American imperialism.

The **Truman Doctrine** boldly expressed the intention of the United States to stop the spread of communism. The context was civil war in Greece. Communist partisans who had fought the Germans for control of their homeland did not dis-arm at the war's end but continued fighting to bring about a communist revolution. The Greek government and army were unable to put down this rebellion on their own, and in 1947 Truman stood before a joint meeting of Congress and promised American aid to suppress the "terrorist activities" of the Greek communists, also promising aid to Greece's neighbor and traditional enemy Turkey and to any nation struggling for freedom: "I believe that it must be the policy of the United States to support free peoples who are resisting attempted subjugation by armed minorities or by outside pressures." Despite Truman's strong language, his policy was actually one of "containment" rather than frontal assault. The United States took no direct action in response to the Soviet takeover of Czechoslovakia, for example, but did install missiles in Turkey to deter the Soviets from advancing to the south. For his part, Stalin implicitly recognized an American sphere of influence in the Mediter-ranean by doing nothing to back the Greek communists.

The Cold War stalemate was most apparent in Germany, where the Soviets liberated the eastern part of the country and the British, Americans, and de Gaulle's Free French armies liberated the west. The capital city of Berlin, which lay within the zone of Soviet occupation, was divided into four sectors. With the breakdown of wartime collaboration between the Soviet Union and the Western powers, no agree-ment could be reached on Germany's future. While the British, French, and Ameri-cans combined their sectors, Stalin refused to cooperate. Border tensions escalated in 1948 when the Soviets cut off access to Berlin by land and the United States re-sponded by airlifting supplies to West Berlin in what is called the Berlin Airlift. In 1949, the rift resulted in the creation of two separate states, the German Federal Re-public (or West Germany) and the German Democratic Republic (or East Germany). Both sides blamed the other for preventing the reunification of Germany across the former Allied zones of occupation, but in reality neither France nor the Soviet Union were unhappy with the outcome, given that Germany had twice posed a grave threat to their peace and security. As long as the Cold War lasted, the division of Germany would symbolize the larger division of Europe between East and West.

Meanwhile, the United States took an active role in rebuilding war-ravaged western Europe, most famously through the **Marshall Plan,** named for the Amer-ican secretary of state. Some in the Truman administration wanted a return to the Versailles policy of forcing Germany to pay reparations; others advocated a more isolationist policy and wanted the United States to retreat from an active role in European affairs. Truman saw that the reconstruction of western European econo-mies was essential for two reasons. First, a revival of global trade, in which Europe would play a central role, was necessary for postwar American economic progress. Second, the communist parties of Italy and France were still quite strong, and continued economic difficulties might increase their popularity. In early 1948, the United States announced that $12 billion would be made available for European reconstruction.

In 1944, even before the war was over, the American-sponsored **Bretton Woods Conference** had formed a plan to prevent the economic catastrophe that had followed World War I. The World Bank was created to loan money to nations in need of a jumpstart for economic development, while the International Monetary Fund (IMF) would stabilize the international currency system and, later, provide emergency loans to prevent nations from going bankrupt. The Marshall Plan and the Bretton Woods institutions were designed to enhance the prosperity and stability of a free-market international economic order with a strong foundation in American

●**Bretton Woods Conference** (1944) Conference that led to creation of the World Bank and the International Monetary Fund (IMF), designed to secure international capitalism by preventing global economic catastrophes.

The Bretton Woods Conference   In 1944 delegates from forty-four countries met in New Hampshire to develop institutions to guide postwar economic reconstruction. The International Bank for Reconstruction and Development (part of today's World Bank) and the International Monetary Fund were designed to help the world avoid a repetition of the economic problems that followed from World War I. They were only partially successful, since the Soviet Union declined to join the IMF.   (AP Images)

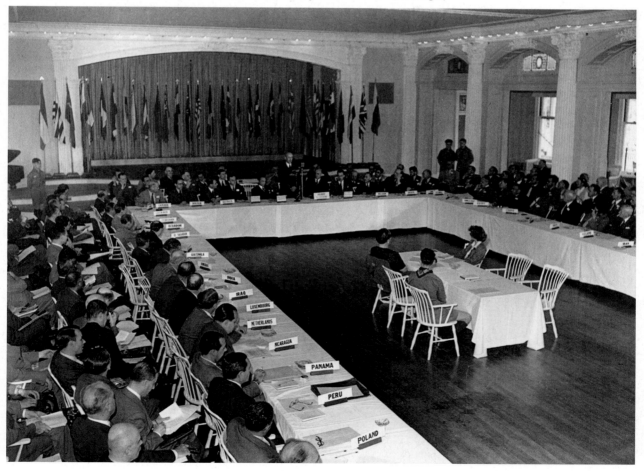

capitalism. Critics pointed out that the U.S. government was intent on creating international institutions that would favor its own brand of free-market economics.

The Soviet Union and its eastern European satellites were invited to join the Marshall Plan, but Stalin refused, not wanting to integrate communist economies into the market-based system of the West. It was therefore clear after 1948 that the Cold War political and military division in Europe would be an economic one as well. While the U.S. sphere of influence consisted of market-based, industrialized economies, the Soviet Union dominated another sphere in which command economies run by centralized planning shielded producers and consumers, at least initially, from direct contact with global market forces. To the weakest, least industrialized areas—Asian and African colonies, weak and dependent Latin American countries—the United States would promise development assistance, while the Soviet Union would advocate prosperity through socialist revolution.

The reality was that the United States, which experienced enormous industrial expansion during the war, was in a much better position to aid its allies. The Soviet Union, which had suffered widespread destruction, was itself in need of reconstruction. So while the United States offered the Marshall Plan, the Soviets exploited their eastern European satellites economically. Entire factories were dismantled and moved from eastern Germany to the Soviet Union. While the United States could use a combination of military strength, diplomacy, and economic aid to gain allies during the Cold War, the Soviet Union usually relied on more direct military control.

Both sides also expanded their intelligence operations, as international spy rings became a central Cold War feature. The Soviet spy agency, known by the initials KGB, worked through local proxies, like the East German *Stasi,* to maintain tight control over the domestic affairs of its satellites while trying to infiltrate Western political, military, and intelligence communities. In the United States, the Central Intelligence Agency (CIA) was formed out of the wartime intelligence service. This was the first time a U.S. government agency was dedicated to secretly collecting information and engaging in covert operations in other countries (see Chapter 30). One of the CIA's first operations involved paying Italian journalists to write negative stories about communist parliamentary candidates.

As we will see in the next two chapters, Cold War divisions became global ones as well. Outside Europe, communist regimes took power in the People's Republic of China, the Democratic People's Republic of Korea, the Democratic Republic of Vietnam, and the Republic of Cuba. As the British and French Empires declined in power, the new nations that emerged from colonialism in Asia and Africa were often pulled between East and West, between communist and liberal democratic alliances. Some of the larger former colonies, such as India after gaining independence in 1947, were able to steer a middle course between superpower rivalries. But other nations, like Vietnam, Angola, Afghanistan, and Nicaragua, would be torn by warfare as Cold War rivalries magnified local political tensions. Two generations of humanity lived in the shadow of the Cold War, with the terrible knowledge that it could one day lead to a nuclear doomsday.

Chapter Review

 Download the MP3 audio file of the Chapter Review and listen to it on the go.

Nancy Wake is one of the most decorated women veterans in history, having earned the George Medal from the United Kingdom and the Medal of Freedom from the United States. She was made a Companion of the Order of Australia, and from France she received the Resistance Medal, the *Croix de Guerre* (War Cross), and the title of Chevalier in the Legion of Honor. Wake made extraordinary sacrifices in the fight against fascism. Because of her resistance activities, the Gestapo tortured her first husband to death. She symbolizes the heroism of the many who resisted, while her story stands as a reprimand to those who aided the fascist cause, either directly or through passive acquiescence.

 What factors contributed to early German and Japanese successes and later Allied ones?

Having spent the 1930s building up their military capacities, Germany and Japan were in a strong position as the war began. Early Axis successes followed from the blitzkrieg tactics of the German army and from the ability of the imperial Japanese forces to overrun the European colonial positions in Southeast Asia after the surprise attack on Pearl Harbor. A key turning point was Adolf Hitler's decision to invade the Soviet Union in the summer of 1941. By early 1942, the huge productive potential of both the Soviet Union and the United States was fully mobilized. By 1943, victories by the British in the North African desert, the United States in the Pacific, and, most important, by the Soviets at Stalingrad paved the way for an American-led invasion of Italy. As the Soviets drove Hitler's army back toward Germany, the D-Day landing on the beaches of Normandy in 1944 created a pincer movement in which British and American troops moved east while the Soviets drove west. The enormous American naval effort in the Pacific stole the momentum from the Japanese, in concert with indigenous armies and resistance movements in China, the Philippines, the Dutch East Indies, and Vietnam. The Pacific war came to a swift and horrible conclusion soon after the United States dropped nuclear bombs on Hiroshima and Nagasaki.

KEY TERMS

Nancy Wake (844)
Axis powers (847)
Winston Churchill (847)
Charles de Gaulle (850)
Atlantic Charter (850)
Pearl Harbor (850)
Allied powers (851)
Siege of Leningrad (851)
Battle of Stalingrad (852)
Hiroshima and Nagasaki (854)
"Quit India" (861)
King's African Rifles (862)
Warsaw Ghetto Uprising (863)
United Nations (866)
Truman Doctrine (868)
Marshall Plan (868)
Bretton Woods Conference (869)

How did civilians in various parts of the world experience the Second World War as a total war?

The Second World War caused tremendous hardship not only for the soldiers who fought in its battles but also for civilian populations. Even in the most liberal societies, political leaders restricted individual liberties and subjected their citizens to wartime propaganda and misinformation. The totalitarian nature of the fascist states and Stalin's Soviet Union was grotesquely exaggerated when wartime crises justified government intrusion in every domain of life. Even in those societies where the economy expanded, most notably the United States, the cause was government spending on the military, not prosperity based on free markets.

In Asia and Africa, total war meant the involvement of colonial societies. The harsh experiences of the Chinese, Filipinos, and others under imperial occupation showed the hollowness of the Japanese claim that their empire was a Co-Prosperity Sphere meant to liberate Asian societies from the European colonial yoke. Still, the Indian National Congress refused to support the British war effort even as Japanese forces entered neighboring Burma, and many Arab peoples responded with hostility to the operation of Allied forces in the Middle East. On the other hand, Africans served loyally and with distinction in both the British and Free French armies, and across East and Southeast Asia local partisans joined the fight against Japan. In Africa and Asia, civilians suffered as well as soldiers and resistance fighters: food scarcity was the norm, and millions died in the Asian famines that followed from economic dislocation.

The Jews and Roma of Europe faced the greatest disaster: a genocidal attempt to eliminate them entirely. After the nightmare of the Holocaust and the nuclear annihilation of Hiroshima and Nagasaki, the age of limited wars seemed over.

How did the outcome of the war affect the global balance of political and military power?

The formation of the United Nations in 1945 brought the prospect that the international community could learn its lesson and build a future of hope and security. That sense of optimism proved short-lived as tensions developed between the two new superpowers, the United States and the Soviet Union. Western Europeans, who previously controlled much of the globe through colonial empires and industrial strength, were no longer able to dominate the international order. The Cold War rivalry of the United States and the Soviet Union split the world into two mutually antagonistic camps, with the threat of nuclear annihilation hanging over their heads.

For Further Reference

Burleigh, Michael. *Third Reich: A New History*. New York: Hill and Wang, 2001.

Dower, John. *War Without Mercy: Race and Power in the Pacific War*. New York: Pantheon, 1987.

Higgonet, Margaret, ed. *Behind the Lines: Gender and the Two World Wars*. New Haven: Yale University Press, 1989.

Iriye, Akira. *Power and Culture: The Japanese-American War, 1941–1945*. 2d ed. Cambridge, Mass.: Harvard University Press, 2004.

Keegan, John. *The Second World War*. New York: Penguin, 2005.

LeFeber, Walter. *The United States, Russia and the Cold War*. Updated ed. New York: McGraw Hill, 2002.

Leffler, Melvyn P., and David S. Painter. *Origins of the Cold War: An International History*. 2d edition. New York: Routledge, 2005.

Thurston, Robert W., and Bernd Bonwetsch, eds. *The People's War: Responses to World War II in the Soviet Union*. Champaign, Ill.: University of Illinois Press, 2000.

Wake, Nancy. *The White Mouse*. Melbourne: Macmillan, 1986.

Yahil, Leni. *The Holocaust: The Fate of European Jewry*. New York: Schocken, 1987.

Websites

Cold War Links on the Internet (http://history.sandiego.edu/gen/20th/coldwarlinks.html).   An exhaustive portal to primary and secondary source material on the Cold War.

WEB RESOURCES

Pronunciation Guide

Interactive Maps

MAP 29.1 World War II in Europe and North Africa

MAP 29.2 World War II in Asia and the Pacific

Primary Sources

Chapter Objectives

ACE Multiple-Choice Quiz

Flashcards

World War II Asia: Historical Text Archive (http://historicaltextarchive.com/links.php?op=views link&sid=293).   Links to a wealth of primary sources.

World War II Links on the Internet (http://history.sandiego.edu/GEN/ww2_links.html).   Hundreds of links on World War II, sorted by topic, date, and country, and including CD/DVD/MP3 resources.

The Cold War and Decolonization, 1949–1975

In 1952 Alberto Granado and **Ernesto Guevara** (1928–1967), two Argentine students with promising futures in medicine, decided to take an ambitious road trip across South America on an aging motorcycle. At first, their motive was fun and adventure, "not setting down roots in any land or staying long enough to see the substratum of things; the outer surface would suffice." Soon, however, their encounters with Indians, peasants, and miners changed the nature of Guevara's quest:

(Private Collection)

ERNESTO GUEVARA,
1951

We made friends with a [Chilean] couple. . . . In his simple, expressive language he recounted his three months in prison . . . his fruitless pilgrimage in search of work and his *compañeros,* mysteriously disappeared and said to be somewhere at the bottom of the sea. The couple, numb with cold, huddling against each other in the desert night, was a living representation of the proletariat in any part of the world. They had not one single miserable blanket to cover themselves with, so we gave them one of ours and Alberto and I wrapped the other around us as best we could. . . . The communism gnawing at [their] entrails was no more than a natural longing for something better, a protest against persistent hunger transformed into a love for this strange doctrine, whose essence they could never grasp but whose translation, "bread for the poor," was something which they understood and, more importantly, filled them with hope.[1]

CL This icon will direct you to interactive activities and study materials on the *Voyages* website: www.cengage.com/history/hansen/voyages1e

Che Guevara crosses South America on his first trip, 1951.

CANADA

NORTH AMERICA

UNITED STATES

New York City

MEXICO
Tuxpan
Miami
Havana
CUBA
Mexico City
GUATEMALA
Guatemala City
PANAMA
COLOMBIA
ECUADOR
Guayaquil
PERU
Lima
Cuzco
BOLIVIA
La Paz
Santa Cruz
PARAGUAY
ARGENTINA
Santiago
Buenos Aires
URUGUAY
Punta del Este
CHILE

Caracas
VENEZUELA
Bogotá

SOUTH AMERICA

BRAZIL

ATLANTIC OCEAN

PACIFIC OCEAN

0   750   1,500 Km.
0   750   1,500 Mi.

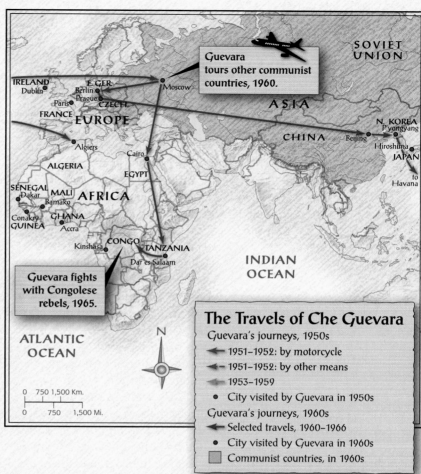

Guevara tours other communist countries, 1960.

SOVIET UNION

IRELAND
Dublin
E. GER.
Berlin
Paris
Prague
CZECH.
FRANCE
EUROPE
Moscow

ASIA

CHINA
Beijing
N. KOREA
Pyongyang
Hiroshima
JAPAN
to Havana

Algiers
ALGERIA
Cairo
EGYPT

SENEGAL
Dakar
MALI
Bamako
AFRICA
Conakry
GUINEA
GHANA
Accra

Kinshasa
CONGO
TANZANIA
Dar es Salaam

INDIAN OCEAN

Guevara fights with Congolese rebels, 1965.

ATLANTIC OCEAN

N

0   750   1,500 Km.
0   750   1,500 Mi.

The Travels of Che Guevara

Guevara's journeys, 1950s
- 1951–1952: by motorcycle
- 1951–1952: by other means
- 1953–1959
- • City visited by Guevara in 1950s

Guevara's journeys, 1960s
- Selected travels, 1960–1966
- • City visited by Guevara in 1960s
- ■ Communist countries, in 1960s

	1945	1950	1955	1960	1965	1970	1975
	Lifetime of Ernesto Guevara (b. 1928)				1967		
AMERICAS			Overthrow of Arbenz 1954	Cuban Revolution 1959	Cuban Missile Crisis 1962	Tlatelolco Massacre 1968	Overthrow of Allende 1973
ASIA		People's Republic of China 1949	Bandung Conference 1955	Great Leap Forward 1955	High point of Great Proletarian Cultural Revolution 1965 – 1970		
		Korean War 1950 – 1953			U.S. forces in Vietnam 1964 – 1975		
EUROPE			Hungarian Uprising 1956		Prague Spring 1968		
AFRICA AND THE MIDDLE EAST	Founding of Israel 1948		Algerian War 1954 – 1962		Six-Day War 1967		
			Suez Canal crisis 1956	Death of Patrice Lumumba 1961			

By the time Ernesto returned to Buenos Aires, he was a different man and on the path to becoming "Che," the most charismatic of twentieth-century revolutionaries.

It took one more trip to change Guevara's path from that of an Argentine doctor to that of a professional revolutionary. After completing his degree, he set out on another road trip, this time with heightened political consciousness. While in Guatemala in 1954, he witnessed the overthrow of its democratically elected government by a right-wing rebel army allied with the United States. Fearing arrest, Guevara fled to Mexico, where he met a group of Cuban exiles determined to overthrow their own dictator. Che joined them as a soldier and military commander, using guerilla tactics such as quick raids and surprise ambushes to defeat the Cuban army. After the success of the Cuban Revolution in 1959, Che's fame spread around the world.

Guevara identified completely with the downtrodden, especially those in the "Third World." In 1952 a French journalist had pointed out the tripartite division of the postwar world. The capitalist United States and its allies constituted the wealthy First World, and the socialist Soviet Union and its allies were the Second World. The Third World, lacking in industry and with little voice in world affairs, made up two-thirds of the world's population. Guevara chose to speak and act on behalf of this disempowered majority, the people Frantz Fanon, another advocate of Third World revolution, called "the wretched of the earth."

Rather than settling down in socialist Cuba, Guevara pursued his dream of revolution in Africa and South America. In 1965 he traveled to Congo and in 1967 to Bolivia, in both cases organizing guerilla armies in the name of socialist revolution. But there were to be no more glorious victories: in 1967, Che was captured and executed by Bolivian troops. Yet in death he became even more powerful and influential than in life. When his remains were discovered in 1998, they were sent to Cuba, where Che received a hero's burial. By then he had long been an icon of youth culture. The familiar image of "Che," reproduced on endless tee-shirts and posters, became emblematic of the social and political idealism of the 1960s. As a symbol Che was loved and admired, or hated and feared, by millions.

Guevara lived at the intersection of two great global struggles. One was the East/West division of the Cold War. The other was the North/South division between the global haves and have-nots. This was the age of decolonization, when many former colonies were moving toward national independence. Across Asia and Africa, mass political movements brought the

🔲 **El Che, 1958** The Cuban revolution succeeded exactly one year after this photograph, taken on January 1, 1958. By this time the transformation of Ernesto Guevara into "Che," the revolutionary icon, was complete. He addresses rebel soldiers wearing his trademark military fatigues, beret, and beard. (Corbis Sygma)

possibility of positive change. But there, as in Latin America, the Cold War environment increased the risk that violence and authoritarianism would triumph over democracy and liberation. In many societies, the conflict between the Soviet Union and the United States dampened hopes for democracy and reinforced trends toward dictatorship.

This chapter explores the turbulent quarter century between 1949 and 1974, when dozens of new nations were born from the dissolution of European empires; when communist revolutionaries took power in mainland China; when the United States and the Soviet Union, the new "superpowers" of the Cold War era, faced off across a deep nuclear chasm; when antidemocratic political forces in strategic parts of the world found sponsorship from the American and Soviet governments; and when young people dreamed of transforming the world. For many, Che Guevara symbolized their dreams, and their disappointments.

Focus Questions

- What were the implications of successful revolutions in China and Cuba for the Cold War rivalry of the United States and the Soviet Union?

- How were democratization and decolonization movements in the mid-twentieth century affected by the Cold War?

- What was the role of youth in the global upheavals of 1965–1974?

The Cold War and Revolution, 1949–1962

By the 1950s, the United States and Soviet Union were building huge arsenals of nuclear weapons, including hydrogen bombs many times more powerful than the devices dropped on Hiroshima and Nagasaki. Any direct conflict between the superpowers brought the possibility of mutual nuclear annihilation. Since conflict along the tense border between eastern and western Europe was likely to spark a high-stakes war, each side was cautious not to push the other too far. Official policy in the United States remained one of "containment," preventing the Soviet Union from expanding its sphere of influence but not intervening within it. Insults, propaganda, and espionage characterized United States/Soviet relations in Europe.

If the Cold War in Europe was a standoff, in two important cases elsewhere communist revolutions increased the potential sphere of Soviet influence. In 1949, after the victory of the People's Army, Mao Zedong stood in Tiananmen Square in Beijing and declared the foundation of the People's Republic of China. Ten years later a rebel army led by Fidel Castro and Che Guevara marched into Havana and founded a socialist government in Cuba. From the perspective of anticommunists

MAP 30.1

China and Taiwan   After World War II, the Communist forces of Mao Zedong took the offensive against the Guomindang, or Nationalist army, of Chiang Kai-shek. The Nationalists were driven off the mainland to the island of Taiwan. In Beijing, Mao declared the creation of the People's Republic of China on October 1, 1949. The Communists and Nationalists agreed that there was only "one China," and their continuing animosity became another zone of conflict in the global Cold War.

 Interactive Map

in the United States and elsewhere, the "Soviet menace" was greatly increased after communism spread first to China, the most populous country in the world, and then Cuba, an island located just 90 miles (145 km) from Florida.

The People's Republic of China, 1949–1962

Almost immediately after the defeat of Japan, the competition between Chiang Kai-shek's Guomindang and Mao Zedong's Chinese Communist Party for control of China resumed (see Chapter 28). At war's end in 1949, the Communists were in charge of the new People's Republic of China on the mainland, and Chiang Kai-shek and his Nationalist followers fled to the island of Taiwan, where they established the Republic of China (see Map 30.1).

The Communists succeeded even though the Nationalists started the fight with a larger army, a stockpile of weapons supplied by the Allies during World War II, and control of China's largest cities. Mao's army had built a strong base of support among the north Chinese peasantry while fighting Japanese invaders, and the People's Liberation Army had become a tough, disciplined organization. Mao used his popular base to great advantage, telling his soldiers to "swim like fishes in the sea" of rural China, camouflaging their activities behind the normal routines of village life. Since the People's Liberation Army treated rural Chinese with greater respect than did Chiang's Guomindang, they rode mass support to success.

Once in power, the Communists revolutionized China, using mass mobilization to reorganize it from the bottom up. Peasants were organized into agricultural cooperatives. Educational opportunities were greatly expanded, and young people were brought into youth organizations guided by the party. Workers became members of state-sponsored trade unions. Within the unions, the army, and other mass organizations, mandatory "thought reform" sessions focused on the study of "Mao Zedong Thought." Those who were said to have deviated from acceptable socialist ideas and practice were often shamed and publicly humiliated into confessing their "errors."

As under the Jacobins and Bolsheviks during earlier revolutions in France and Russia (see Chapters 22 and 27), external threats justified repressive policies. At the end of World War II, the Korean peninsula had been divided between a Soviet-backed Democratic Republic of Korea in the north and an American-allied Republic of Korea in the south. The Korean War (1950–1953) began with a North Korean attack on the south. When the United States, leading a United Nations coalition, rushed to defend its South Korean ally, the mainland Chinese government feared that the United States intended to attack them as well. The People's Liberation Army then threw massive forces into the battle in support of North Korea. In the end, American-led forces had protected the south from invasion, but there was still a stalemate along the tense demilitarized zone that separated the harsh communist regime in North Korea, which allowed no freedom at all, from the stern authoritarian regime in South Korea, which allowed very little.

Initially, the People's Republic of China was following a different set of economic policies based on the Soviet example of state-run heavy industry and collective farming. In 1953 a Five-Year Plan was drawn up following the Soviet model, and Chinese engineers and state planners were sent to Russia for training. For Mao, the results were disappointing. Not only was the growth of production slower than he expected, but the dull, bureaucratic socialism of the post-Stalinist Soviet Union did little to inspire him. Mao felt that the fire was going out of the revolution.

He decided to shake things up. In 1956, Mao launched a public call for new ideas, using the phrase "Let a hundred flowers bloom." China's intellectuals responded with open criticism of the Communist Party, and even of Mao himself. Either the critical response was greater than Mao had expected, or perhaps he had intended all along to use the "hundred flowers" campaign to trick his opponents out into the open, but during the savage repression of 1957, many intellectuals were arrested, imprisoned, or exiled to remote provinces. To Mao and his followers, all signs of independent, critical thought were seen as "rightist" deviations that needed to be purged from socialist society.

Mao saw that the Communist Party itself was divided into two factions, which he labeled "red" and "expert." The "experts" in charge of agricultural collectivization and industrial development were becoming an elite cut off from the masses. The "red" leadership, emphasizing socialist willpower rather than technical ability, would help China catch up with the world's dominant economic powers. If only the true revolutionary potential of China's peasants and workers could be unleashed, Mao thought, the people could move mountains.

● **Great Leap Forward** (1958) Mao Zedong's attempt to harness the revolutionary zeal of the Chinese masses for rapid industrialization. The result was a massive economic collapse and millions of deaths from famine.

In 1958 Mao launched the **Great Leap Forward,** decreeing that the agricultural collectives should be harnessed for industrial development. Rather than relying on large steel factories, the revolutionaries would set up small furnaces all across the country. The "masses" were directed to pour all their energy and enthusiasm into increasing communal production. Property rights were even more restricted than previously as peasants lost access to the small plots they had relied on to feed their families.

The results of the Great Leap Forward were disastrous. The steel produced in small communal furnaces was virtually useless, and food production suffered as the farm workers wasted their energies on Mao's inefficient scheme. It has been estimated that as many as thirty million people died in the famine that accompanied the Great Leap Forward. By 1961 the failures of these policies led the more pragmatic "experts" in the Communist Party to reduce Mao's authority behind the scenes (while still publicly acknowledging his leadership) and to reinstate a more rational, technocratic form of economic planning.

Still, Mao's emphasis on the power of revolutionary enthusiasm would prove appealing to some members of a younger generation, both in China and other parts of the world, who wanted to believe that their passion for justice would allow humanity to take a "great leap forward." Che Guevara was among those who found inspiration in the Chinese model as an alternative to both capitalism and the stodgy Soviet model of technocratic socialism.

The Cuban Revolution and the Cuban Missile Crisis

The island of Cuba presented great contrasts in the 1950s. The capital city of Havana was best known for its nightclubs and beaches. Its *mambo* musicians, fusing the nation's African and Latin cultural traditions, had a worldwide influence. But if the power and energy of Cuban culture was well known, there was a dark side to the island as well. Gangsters from the American Mafia controlled many of Havana's casinos and nightclubs, where prostitution flourished. Fulgencio Batista, the Cuban dictator, allowed no democratic freedoms, and most Cubans, the poorest of them descendants of slaves, worked for low wages with little access to health care or education. While Havana was a playground for wealthy tourists and elite Cubans, most of the island's inhabitants lived in desperate poverty.

Fidel Castro (b. 1926), like Ernesto Guevara, was an idealistic young man who gave up middle-class privileges in the name of revolution. In 1953 he had been arrested and imprisoned for leading an attack on an army barracks, and after his release in 1955 he went into exile in Mexico City. Here he formed a deep friendship with Che Guevara, newly arrived from Guatemala, who joined Castro's small rebel band for military training at a nearby secret base.

In 1956, Castro and Guevara left by boat for Cuba, reaching the relative safety of the Sierra Maestra Mountains. Gradually they replenished their ammunition supplies through daring attacks on police stations and military barracks and attracted recruits from a sympathetic peasant population. Like Mao in China, Castro and Guevara relied on peasants, with their intimate knowledge of the local terrain, for the intelligence that allowed them to outmaneuver government forces. During two years of hard fighting, Che's medical background came in handy as he tended to wounded colleagues. He played an even more important role, however, as a commander and military tactician. As conditions were tough and betrayal could mean death, Guevara had no second thoughts about executing soldiers or civilians he believed to be agents of the government. By 1958, the rebels were poised to launch an offensive on Havana, and on New Year's Day 1959 Batista fled the country as Castro's forces marched triumphantly into the capital.

Neither Castro nor Guevara had ever joined the Cuban Communist Party, and many Cubans expected that through a combination of socialist economics and liberal politics the new government could distribute wealth while protecting individual liberties. But "defense of the revolution" rather than protection of civil liberties quickly became the focal point of Castro's government. The new leaders found that they had to deal with the immediate danger of counter-revolution, as pro-Batista forces fled to the United States and lobbied for an American-backed invasion.

Initially, President Eisenhower hoped that Castro might be someone he could work with, as the Cuban leader toured Washington and New York seeking both public and official support. But relations deteriorated after Cuba's Agrarian Reform Law led to the nationalization of land previously owned by large American corporations. Both corporate lobbyists and Cold War hawks then portrayed Castro as a Soviet threat on America's doorstep. As tensions increased between the two countries, Castro sent Che Guevara to Moscow and Beijing to shore up socialist support for his regime and the Eisenhower administration imposed a trade embargo and drew up plans for an invasion of Cuba.

In the spring of 1961 a group of Cuban exiles stormed ashore at the Bay of Pigs in a U.S.-sponsored attempt to overthrow Castro. But the new American president, John F. Kennedy (1917–1963), having strong doubts about the prospects for success, gave the Cuban counter-revolutionaries only lukewarm support. Not only were Castro's forces easily victorious, but the invasion validated Castro's utter distrust of U.S. intentions and pushed him toward more repressive policies. In addition, the U.S. economic embargo placed on Cuba created a climate of hostility between the two nations that made diplomacy and compromise all but impossible. Castro then turned to the Soviet Union for support.

In the fall of 1962 came one of the most frightening events in modern history: the **Cuban Missile Crisis.** Convinced that the United States would never let his socialist experiment proceed in peace, Castro developed ever-closer ties with the Soviet Union. Soviet Premier Khrushchev took advantage of the situation to secretly ship nuclear missiles to Cuba. When American surveillance aircraft detected the missiles, Kennedy presented Khrushchev with an ultimatum: withdraw the missiles, or prepare for war. As the world stood on the brink of nuclear conflict, an agreement

● **Fidel Castro** (b. 1926) Cuban prime minister from 1959 to 1976 and president from 1976 to 2008. Led the successful revolution in 1959, after which his nationalization policies led to deteriorating relations with the United States and increasing dependence on Soviet support.

● **Cuban Missile Crisis** Tense 1962 confrontation between the United States and the Soviet Union over placement of nuclear missiles in Cuba. A compromise led to withdrawal of Soviet missiles from Cuba and American missiles from Turkey.

The Doomsday Clock

During the Cold War, citizens of both the United States and the Soviet Union saw the threat of nuclear warfare, and of nuclear annihilation, as very real. The governments of both countries organized elaborate civil defense procedures in the event of an attack, but in reality millions would have died had a full-scale nuclear war ever taken place.

In 1947 the Board of Directors of the *Bulletin of Atomic Scientists* devised the Doomsday Clock as a visual guide to the nuclear threat. The original setting was seven minutes to midnight. The clock, which has appeared on the cover of every *Bulletin* for over fifty years, has been reset periodically, either closer to midnight to reflect heightened tensions between nuclear powers, or farther away during periods of greater security.

In 1953 the Doomsday Clock was set at two minutes to midnight, closer than ever before or since, when within one month of each other the United States and the Soviet Union successfully tested thermonuclear devices. In 1972, conversely, the Board of Directors marked the signing of the Strategic Arms Limitation Treaty (SALT) between the United States and the Soviet Union by setting the clock back to twelve minutes to midnight.

With the end of the Cold War, public fears of nuclear annihilation have waned. But a look at the Doomsday Clock warns us not to be too complacent. In setting the clock forward from seven to five minutes to midnight in January 2007, the Board of the *Bulletin of Atomic Scientists* warned, "We stand at the brink of a second nuclear age. Not since the first atomic bombs were dropped on Hiroshima and Nagasaki has the world faced such perilous choices. North Korea's recent test of a nuclear weapon, Iran's nuclear ambitions, a renewed U.S. emphasis on the military utility of nuclear weapons, the failure to adequately secure nuclear materials, and the continued presence of some 26,000 nuclear weapons in the United States and Russia are symptomatic of a larger failure to solve the problems posed by the most destructive technology on Earth."

Though nuclear proliferation is proving difficult to stop, South Africa offers some hope. After the fall of apartheid in the early 1990s (see Chapter 31), it became the only country in the world to voluntarily give up its nuclear weapons.

Source: http://www.thebulletin.org/minutes-to-midnight/board-statements.html. Doomsday clock is reprinted by permission of the Bulletin of the Atomic Scientist, www.thebulletin.org.

was reached. Khrushchev agreed to remove Soviet missiles from Cuba, and the Kennedy administration quietly began to remove U.S. missiles from Turkey. The world's people breathed a sigh of relief. (See the feature "World History in Today's World: The Doomsday Clock.")

Feeling more vulnerable than ever, Castro threw himself into an even tighter alliance with Moscow. Most important for the Cuban economy, the Soviets helped Cuba withstand the American trade embargo by agreeing to buy the island's entire sugar output at above-market prices and to supply fuel and agricultural machinery to jumpstart the socialist transformation of the island. These Soviet subsidies helped Cuba regain its economic balance. By the mid-1960s, most of its people were better fed and better housed than they had been before the revolution; they also had free access to basic health care and were more likely to be able to read and write.

But underlying economic problems remained. As was common in Latin America, Cuba had long been a dependent economy, exporting agricultural produce (mostly sugar and tobacco) and importing higher-valued industrial goods (see Chapter 25). With the Soviet Union as an economic patron, Cuba's reliance on agricultural exports was as strong as ever. Economic development was also hampered by the Soviet-style command economy installed by Castro. Bureaucratic inefficiency and low worker morale characterized Cuba's large, mechanized state farms.

When Cuban workers agitated for higher wages, Che Guevara, as minister for industry, told them that they should be content to know that their hard work supported the glorious cause of socialism. Himself willing to work long hours for almost no material reward, Guevara thought that others should do the same. But not everyone was as idealistic as he was, and without material rewards for workers or free-market incentives to inspire creativity and entrepreneurship, the Cuban economy settled into a lethargic pattern.

Guevara was disappointed. A romantic revolutionary idealist, he could not abide the endless meetings and plodding pace that came with the routine business of government. The country's reliance on the Soviet Union bothered him; his distrust of Moscow had been heightened by the brutal suppression of popular uprisings in eastern Europe. In 1965 he left Cuba for Africa to pursue his revolutionary dreams on a global stage.

Spheres of Influence: Old Empires and New Superpowers

The Cuban Missile Crisis showed how dangerous it was for one superpower to intervene in the other's established sphere of influence. More often such interventions took place within the superpowers' own strategic domains, as when the United States helped overthrow the democratically elected government of Guatemala in 1953 or Soviet tanks crushed a prodemocracy uprising in Hungary in 1956.

But much of the world lay outside the Soviet and American spheres established immediately after World War II. In most of Asia and Africa, the weakening of the old European empires was accompanied by successful decolonization movements. How would these new nations fit into the international system? In some countries, especially in Africa, former European colonial powers managed to retain substantial economic and military influence even after national independence. Elsewhere, however, the power vacuum created by the decline of European empires meant that new African and Asian nations were caught up in the tensions stoked by the global bipolarity of the Cold War. Some, like Congo and Vietnam, were pulled apart in the process.

Recognizing the danger that the superpower rivalry posed to recently decolonized nations, in 1955 a group of African and Asian leaders met to discuss ways to maximize their sovereignty. Their goal in founding the Non-Aligned Movement was to avoid both neocolonial influence from Europe and, by refusing to associate themselves with either the Soviet Union or the United States, to avoid superpower intervention in their affairs. It was not a simple goal to achieve. The French withdrawal from Vietnam, followed by the intervention of the United States against Ho Chi Minh's communist forces, showed how the decline of European power could lead to superpower intervention.

MAP 30.2

Cold War Confrontations Two military alliances, the North Atlantic Treaty Organization (NATO) led by the United States, and the Warsaw Pact, dominated by the Soviet Union, were the principal antagonists in the Cold War. Fearful of mutual nuclear annihilation, however, they never engaged in direct combat. Instead, the Cold War turned hot in proxy struggles around the world—in Central America and the Caribbean, Africa, the Middle East, and southeast Asia.

 Interactive Map

Superpower Interventions, 1953–1956

During the Cold War, both the United States and the Soviet Union presented themselves as champions of freedom. Of course, they had very different interpretations of what that meant. The Soviets, identifying colonialism and imperialism as the main barriers to liberation, actively supported nationalists in the Third World who were fighting to throw off European colonialism, as well as socialists fighting against American political and economic domination in Latin America. But Moscow would not tolerate similar liberation movements within its own sphere. In the Soviet Union and its satellites (see Map 30.2), movements toward freedom of speech, association, or religion, as well as national self-determination, were brutally crushed.

In eastern Europe, extensive secret police networks were usually enough to keep the people from expressing any openly anticommunist or anti-Soviet opinions. In East Germany, for example, the feared *Stasi* maintained an icy atmosphere of paranoia by planting informers at all levels of society and encouraging neighbors to spy on neighbors. But after the death of Stalin in 1953, some eastern Europeans, and even some Russians, saw an opportunity for reform. The new Soviet leader, Nikita Khrushchev (1894–1971), denounced the excesses of Stalinism at a Communist Party congress. But while Khrushchev (KHROOS-chev) pursued limited reforms from above, he would not tolerate popular movements for change.

After 1953, when Soviet tanks crushed public demonstrations in East Berlin, it was clear that the communist government of the German Democratic Republic was based more on Soviet power than on popular legitimacy. Over the next eight years, thousands of East Berliners fled to the West. Finally, in 1961 the East German government ordered the construction of the Berlin Wall to ensure the captivity of its own people. Churchill's metaphoric "iron curtain" took physical shape in the bricks and mortar that disfigured one of Europe's great cities.

In Poland most people detested the pro-Moscow government that had been imposed by Stalin after the war. The Poles, being predominantly Catholic, resented the official atheism of the communist state. In 1956 a religious gathering attended by a million Poles turned into an antigovernment demonstration. Here the Soviet government compromised, allowing the Polish communists to introduce reforms, such as an end to collectivization of agriculture and some religious freedom. But it was clear that any Polish attempt to weaken their ties to the Soviet Union would not be tolerated.

The **Hungarian Uprising** of 1956 showed the seriousness of the situation. In that year Hungarian students, factory workers, and middle-class professionals all joined to protest the Soviet-imposed communist dictatorship. Faced with a mass uprising, the Hungarian government collapsed. Leaders of the new provisional government feared a Soviet invasion but expected support from the Western democracies. In spite of broadcasts on the Voice of America encouraging rebellion, however, the United States did not intervene; the risk of a Pan-European war escalating to the use of nuclear weaponry was too great. Khrushchev sent in the Soviet army, and the Hungarian revolt ended in mass arrests and executions.

The Americans were quick to point out the obvious contradiction between Soviet rhetoric, which equated socialism with democracy, and their practice of suppressing freedom. But U.S. practices were also at odds with American ideals. The covert actions of the **Central Intelligence Agency** (CIA) often thwarted democracy by supporting authoritarian leaders willing to back American economic and strategic interests. Since communism was defined as an absolute evil, many Americans assumed that anyone who opposed Marxism-Leninism was on the

Hungarian Uprising (1956) Popular revolt against the Soviet-controlled government of Hungary, leading to a Soviet invasion and reimposition of communist authority.

Central Intelligence Agency (CIA) U.S. federal agency created in 1947 whose responsibilities included coordinating intelligence activities abroad, including covert operations against the Soviet Union and its allies during the Cold War.

The Hungarian Uprising A rebellion against their Communist regime brought thousands of Hungarians onto the streets of Budapest in 1956, provoking a Soviet invasion. Great courage was shown by the Hungarians in confronting Soviet tanks and troops, but they were bitterly disappointed when the United States and NATO provided no military support for their freedom struggle. (Laszlo Almasi/Reuters/Landov)

side of freedom. In reality, many of the anticommunist regimes backed by the United States during this period were authoritarian dictatorships.

Iran was one example. Although a constitutional monarchy, Iran had difficulty maintaining a stable balance of power between king and parliament. In the early 1950s, Shah Muhammad Reza Pahlavi (pahl-ah-vee) aspired to greater power but was checked by an assertive parliament led by a popular prime minister, Muhammad Mossadegh (moh-sah-dehk). Pahlavi, an ardent anticommunist, cultivated a close alliance with the United States. The Eisenhower administration was concerned that the Soviet Union, which had occupied northern Iran during World War II, still had designs on these oil-rich lands.

For their part, Mossadegh and his parliamentary allies were upset that Britain's Anglo-Iranian Oil Company reaped the lion's share of profits from Iranian petroleum. Mossadegh tried to renegotiate Iran's contracts, and when negotiations failed he made plans to nationalize the oil industry. In 1953 the Iranian military, with the covert support of the CIA, arrested Mossadegh and greatly expanded the shah's authority. The chances for a more democratic Iranian future were fatally undermined, and many Iranians now saw their king as an American puppet.

The next year the United States similarly undermined democracy in Guatemala. Like other Central American countries, Guatemala had long been ruled by authoritarian dictators and had an economy dominated by foreign corporations, especially by the United Fruit Company, an American company that owned vast banana plantations, the only railroad, the only port, and the country's telephone system. The small Guatemalan elite benefited from this system, but the country was a study in inequality: 72 percent of the land was owned by 2 percent of the population.

During World War II reformist army officers seized control and organized elections. In 1946, the new democratic government promised land reform and labor reform, arguing that democracy could not flourish in a country where resources were concentrated in so few hands. In 1950 another election was held and the new president, **Jacobo Arbenz** (1913–1971), reaffirmed those policies. But the Eisenhower administration, thinking that the Arbenz government had been penetrated

Jacobo Arbenz (1913–1971) President of Guatemala from 1951 to 1954. A moderate socialist, Arbenz enacted comprehensive land reforms that angered Guatemalan elites and U.S. corporations. Was deposed by rebel forces backed by the United States.

by Soviet agents, invoked the "domino theory" and claimed that the "loss" of Guatemala would lead to communist victories elsewhere in the Americas. Most Americans, knowing nothing of Guatemala's economic and political realities, accepted this explanation. A rebel leader with U.S. backing overthrew Arbenz in 1954, and Guatemala reverted to a caudillo-style dictatorship.

Ernesto Guevara was deeply radicalized by his experiences in Guatemala City. His flight to Mexico and affiliation with Castro was the turning point when Ernesto Guevara became "Che," dedicating himself entirely to revolution. Though he distrusted the Soviet Union, especially after the violence with which it suppressed the Hungarian rebellion, his Guatemalan experience helped convince him that the United States represented the greater threat to freedom and justice.

Decolonization and Neocolonialism in Africa, 1945–1964

World War II had made many Africans aware of their place in the wider world and increasingly dissatisfied with the colonial status quo. The French, British, and Belgians initially underestimated the force of African nationalism; entering the decade of the 1950s, colonial officials thought they were in Africa to stay. Yet by 1960, nationalist movements had freed most of the continent from colonial rule and many new African nations had been established (see Map 30.3). The Swahili word *uhuru,* "freedom," was heard around the world, and Kwame Nkrumah (1909–1972), first president of independent Ghana after 1957, was an international symbol of rising African aspirations and the strength of global Pan-Africanism.

But reaping the fruits of independence proved difficult. For one thing, the economic structures of colonialism did not disappear simply by lowering a European flag and raising an African one. Economic development required capital and expertise, and both had to be imported. Economic dependency created ideal conditions for neocolonialism: the continuation of European influence even after independence had been attained. Some African leaders were more responsive to British, French, and American interests than to the needs of their own people.

The French government was a clever practitioner of neocolonialism. Even before independence,

Ghana's Independence In 1957 the British colony of the Gold Coast led the way toward continental decolonization when it became the independent state of Ghana, named after an ancient African kingdom. Here Prime Minister Kwame Nkrumah waves to a massive crowed during Ghana's independence ceremony. Nkrumah provided support for other anticolonial movements on the continent, and, through his emphasis on Pan-Africanism, became a spokesman for the ambitions of people of African descent around the world. (Bettmann/Corbis)

⊕ MAP 30.3

Decolonization In the three decades following Indian independence in 1947, the European colonial empires in Asia and Africa unraveled, adding many new "third world" representatives to the United Nations. Their aspirations of dignity and development were frequently thwarted, however, by Cold War politics, continued Western economic domination, poor leadership, and ethnic and religious rivalry.

 Interactive Map

the French had laid the foundations of neocolonial control in their former West and Central African colonies. Colonial policies of "assimilation" held out the promise of French citizenship for a few educated Africans, creating an elite African that identified strongly with French culture. Appealing to their sentiments and responding to the rise of nationalism in the French African empire, President Charles de Gaulle announced in 1958 that a referendum would be held across French Africa. A "yes" vote meant that the former French colonies would receive control over their own internal affairs but would remain part of a larger French "community" directed from Paris. The French government would retain control over economic policy, foreign affairs, and the military. A "no" vote meant complete and immediate independence, severing all ties to France.

All but one of the colonies voted to become members of the French community. The exception was Guinea, where a radical trade union leader named Sekou Toure (sey-koo too-rey) mounted a campaign for complete independence. The French government responded to Guinea's "no" vote by withdrawing their administrators overnight, stopping economic aid, and even ripping telephones from the walls as they abandoned their offices. The French message was clear: play by our rules, or suffer the consequences. There were actually more French soldiers in the Ivory Coast after independence than before; with their currencies pegged to the value of the French franc, leaders of new nations such as Senegal and Mali had little control over their own economic policies.

Meanwhile, some Africans were forced to take up arms to liberate themselves, especially in regions where Europeans had come not just as rulers but also as settlers. In North Africa, over a million French men and women lived in Algeria. After the Second World War, Algerian nationalists, some of whom had fought for De Gaulle's Free French Army, began to demand equal treatment with French citizens and a voice in their own governance. Harshly repressed, these nationalists formed the National Liberation Front and, in 1954, began their armed struggle. It was a brutal war, with the FLN (the French acronym) sometimes launching terrorist attacks on French civilians and the French military systematically using torture in its counter-insurgency campaign. Over time French public opinion soured on the violence, and in 1962 an agreement recognizing Algerian independence was finally negotiated. (See the feature "Movement of Ideas: *The Wretched of the Earth*.")

Like Algeria, Kenya in East Africa was a country with a large settler population. The main nationalist leader, Jomo Kenyatta (joh-moh ken-yah-tuh), hoped to develop a mass organization to force the British into negotiations. But a group of African rebels took a more militant stand, forming a secret society, stealing arms from police stations, assassinating a collaborationist chief, and naming themselves the Land and Freedom Army. The British called them the Mau Mau and depicted them as "savages" who had returned to a "primitive" state of irrationality. Hopelessly outgunned by colonial forces, the rebels used their knowledge of the forest and the support of the local population to carry on their fight. By the late 1950s the Kenyan rebellion was contained, after over twelve thousand Africans and one hundred Europeans had been killed. The British government was now determined to make the settlers compromise with moderate African nationalists. In 1964, Jomo Kenyatta became the first president of an independent Kenya.

In southern Africa, compromise between white settlers and African nationalists was impossible. The white settlers of Rhodesia declared their independence from Britain in 1965 rather than enter into negotiations over sharing power with African leaders, while in South Africa the apartheid regime was deeply entrenched. Because

CL **Primary Source: Comments on Algeria, April 11, 1961** *Read excerpts of a press conference held by Charles de Gaulle, in which he declares France's willingness to accept Algerian independence.*

The Wretched of the Earth

Frantz Fanon (1925–1961) was an advocate of Third World revolution, guerilla warfare, and socialism. Born on the Caribbean island of Martinique, in the French West Indies, Fanon volunteered for service in the Free French Army and was wounded during the liberation of France in 1944. After training in Paris as a psychiatrist, he was stationed in North Africa. During the Algerian war Fanon's medical practice included psychiatric treatment of both French practitioners and Arab and Berber victims of torture. From this experience he concluded that colonialism was in-trinsically violent and could only be removed by violence. He joined the Algerian National Liberation Front and became a prominent spokesman for their cause. Fanon was dying of leukemia in 1961 while writing his most bitter indictment of colonialism, *The Wretched of the Earth* (1961).

Sources: Frantz Fanon, *The Wretched of the Earth* (New York: Grove, 1963), pp. 36, 39–41, 43, 45, 59, 61, 312, 315–316; David Macy, *Frantz Fanon* (New York: Picador, 2000), p. 483.

Decolonization is the meeting of two forces, opposed to each other by their very nature. . . . Their first encounter was marked by violence and their existence together—that is to say the exploitation of the native by the settler—was carried on by dint of a great array of bayonets and cannons. . . .

The naked truth of decolonization evokes for us the searing bullets and bloodstained knives which emanate from it. For if the last shall be first, this will only come to pass after a murderous and decisive struggle between the two protagonists. . . .

The settlers' town is a strongly built town, all made of stone and steel. It is a brightly lit town; the streets are all covered with asphalt, and the garbage cans swallow all the leavings, unseen, unknown, and hardly thought about. . . . The settlers' town is a town of white people, of foreigners. . . .

The native town is a hungry town, starved for bread, of meat, of shoes, of coal, of light. The native town is a crouching village, a town on its knees, a town wallowing in the mire. . . . The look that the native turns on the settlers' town is a look of lust, a look of envy; it expresses his dreams of possession—all manner of possession: to sit at the settler's table, to sleep in the settler's bed, with his wife if possible. The colonized man is an envious man. . . .

The violence which has ruled over the ordering of the colonial world, which has ceaselessly drummed the rhythm for the destruction of native social forms and broken up without reserve the systems of reference of the economy . . . that same violence will be claimed and taken over by the native at the moment when, deciding to embody history in his own person, he surges into the forbidden quarters. . . .

As if to show the totalitarian character of colonial exploitation the settler paints the native as the quintessence of evil. Native society is not simply described as a society lacking in values. . . . The native is declared insensible to ethics; he represents not only the absence of values, but the negation of values . . . and in this sense he is the absolute evil. . . .

The violence with which the supremacy of white values is affirmed and the aggressiveness which has permeated the victory of these values over the ways of life and thought of the native mean that, in revenge, the native laughs in mockery when Western values are mentioned in front of him. . . . In the period of decolonization, the colonized masses mock at these very values, insult them, and vomit them up. . . .

[When the urban militants] get into the habit of talking to the peasants they discover that the rural masses have never ceased to pose the problem of their liberation in terms of violence, of taking back the land from the foreigners, in terms of a national struggle. Everything is simple. . . . They discover a generous people prepared to make sacrifices, willing to give of itself, impatient and with a stony pride. One can understand that the encounter between militants who are being hunted by the police and these impatient masses, who are instinctually rebellious, can produce an explosive mixture of unexpected power. . . .

Come, then, comrades, the European game has finally ended; we must find something different. We today can do everything so long as we do not imitate Europe, so long as we are not obsessed with desire to catch up with Europe. . . . European achievements, European techniques, and European style ought to no longer tempt us and to throw us off our balance.

When I search for Man in the technique and style of Europe, I see only a succession of negations of man, and an avalanche of murders. . . . It is a question of the Third World starting a new history of Man, a history which will have regard to the sometimes prodigious theses Europe has put forward, but which will also not forget Europe's crimes. . . . For Europe, for ourselves, for humanity, comrades, we must turn over a new leaf, we must work out new concepts, and try to set afoot a new man.

QUESTIONS FOR ANALYSIS

▶ What is similar and what is different between Fanon's ideas and those of Mohandas K. Gandhi (see Chapter 28)?

▶ What is Fanon's critique of European society, and how does he find hope in Third World revolution?

the Rhodesian and South African leaders were adamantly anticommunist, governments in London and Washington were willing to overlook their repressive policies. In 1964, when Nelson Mandela was sentenced to life in prison, hopes for transforming South Africa were at an all-time low (see Chapter 31).

The former Belgian Congo was the one place in postcolonial Africa where decolonization created a power vacuum so intense that it brought about direct superpower intervention. The Belgians had done even less than the British or the French to prepare Africans for independence. After the violence of King Leopold's reign (see Chapter 26), the Belgian government had created a tightly centralized, racially divided colonial administration. After eighty years of Belgian rule there were only sixteen Africans in the entire Congo with university degrees. Still, with Congo caught up in the nationalist excitement spreading across the continent, in 1960 the Belgians made hasty plans for independence, believing that the weakness of the new Congolese government would make it susceptible to neocolonial control.

The election was won by the Congolese National Movement, and a government was formed by Prime Minister **Patrice Lumumba** (loo-MOOM-buh) (1925–1961). The independence ceremony in 1960 was fraught with tension. After the Belgian king made a patronizing speech praising his country's "civilizing mission" in Africa, Lumumba responded with a catalogue of Belgian crimes against Africans. "Our wounds," he said, "are still too fresh and painful for us to be able to erase them from our memories." The speech made Lumumba a hero to African nationalists, but he was now regarded as a dangerous radical in Brussels and Washington.

Lumumba faced immediate challenges to his authority. African soldiers mutinied against their Belgian officers, and the mineral-rich southern province of Katanga seceded. When the United Nations sent in peacekeeping forces, Lumumba suspected their real purpose was to defend Western interests. Desperate to make his rule effective, he turned to the Soviet Union for military aid. Now branded in the West as a "communist," Lumumba was arrested, with the complicity of the CIA, and then beaten and murdered by rival Congolese forces. Rebel armies arose in several provinces as the Congo simmered in constant crisis. Finally Joseph Mobutu (mo-BOO-too), an army officer who had long been on the CIA payroll, took over dictatorial powers.

Che Guevara was among those who regarded Lumumba as a fallen hero and Mobutu as an American puppet. In 1965, Che and a small group of Cuban commandos headed for Central Africa to join the fight, linking up with Congolese rebels in the eastern part of the country. It was a disappointing experience, since the rebels were lacking in both discipline and ideological commitment: "I felt entirely alone," he later wrote, "in a way that I had never experienced before, neither in Cuba nor anywhere else, throughout my long pilgrimage across the world."[2] Sheer willpower, he learned, was not enough to change the world.

When Che returned to Cuba in 1966, the Congo was firmly under Joseph Mobutu's authoritarian control. The United States was the main power broker in Central Africa, using its alliance with Mobutu to secure access to the mineral riches of the Congo, some of which, such as cobalt, were vital to the aerospace industry.

The Bandung Generation, 1955–1965

Neocolonialism and superpower intervention were exactly what the leaders of former colonial states who met in Bandung (bahn-doong), Indonesia, for the first Asia-Africa conference in 1955 wished to avoid. The careers of the Indonesian, Indian, and Egyptian representatives at the Bandung Conference, leaders of large states

• Patrice Lumumba (1925–1961) The first prime minister of the Democratic Republic of Congo in 1960. Was deposed and assassinated by political rivals in 1961.

with significantly more regional influence than countries like Guatemala or the Congo, show how difficult it was to achieve their goal of nonalignment with either the United States or the Soviet Union.

Ahmed Sukarno (1901–1970) first emerged as a nationalist fighting against Dutch colonialism in the 1920s. In 1945 he and his party declared Indonesia free of both the Dutch and the Japanese, but it was not until 1950 and the defeat of Dutch reoccupation forces that this independence became a reality. The new country was scattered across hundreds of islands, with a great diversity of ethnic groups. Sukarno worked toward cultural and political unification by sponsoring the development of an Indonesian language with a simplified grammar to facilitate communication between citizens from various linguistic backgrounds.

Sukarno was widely popular at the time of independence, but like many leaders in recently decolonized countries, he had little experience in running a country. Sukarno saw himself as the key to Indonesia's development. After the Bandung Conference he became erratic and dictatorial, in 1963 declaring himself "president-for-life." As the popular base of his rule began to weaken, he was faced by a potent communist insurgency. Both the Indonesian military and their allies in Washington felt that Sukarno was either sympathetic to the communists or too weak to stave them off. The Indonesian military launched a brutal crackdown in 1964 to wipe out communist insurgents, killing hundreds of thousands. In 1967 General Suharto, a military commander backed by the United States, suspended the constitution and took power, and successive American administrations turned a blind eye to the dictatorial and corrupt aspects of Suharto's regime. As in Mobutu's Congo, they were glad to have a dependable ally in the struggle against communism.

Jawaharlal Nehru (juh-wah-her-lahl NAY-roo) (1889–1964) was much more successful than Sukarno in defending his country's sovereignty and non-alignment during the Cold War. Like other leaders of newly independent nations, Nehru faced tremendous problems. In the 1930s the Muslim League began to challenge the dominance of the Indian National Congress by arguing for a separate Muslim nation to be carved out of British India. In 1947, the British did indeed partition their colony into two separate independent states: India and Pakistan. It was not a simple solution, for there was a substantial Hindu minority in Pakistan and an even more substantial Muslim minority in the new state of India. In a climate of fear and uncertainty, millions of people tried desperately to find the borders of the country where they "belonged." In the intercommunal violence that followed, as many as ten million people were dislocated, perhaps seventy-five thousand women were raped or abducted, and more than one million people lost their lives.

In spite of India's difficult birth and of enduring challenges such as poverty and illiteracy, the country emerged in the 1950s as the world's largest democracy (see Chapter 32). Nehru and the Congress Party provided political stability, allowing the prime minister to make good on his promise to keep India nonaligned from superpower entanglements. Even when military tensions emerged on India's borders with Pakistan and China, Nehru kept his country nonaligned by purchasing military hardware from both the United States and the Soviet Union and by building up India's own defense industries. In Pakistan, by contrast, corruption and misrule led to a military seizure of power. In 1958, Pakistan's military government entered into a defense agreement with the United States, which was concerned about India's military ties with the Soviet Union and anxious to have a reliably anticommunist ally in this strategic region. These agreements meant that, in spite of India's nonalignment, the Cold War deeply affected South Asian politics.

• **Ahmed Sukarno** (1901–1970) Leader in the struggle for Indonesian independence from Holland, achieved in 1949. Indonesian military leaders, backed by the United States, thought Sukarno incapable of battling communism and removed him from power.

• **Jawaharlal Nehru** (1889–1964) Statesman who helped negotiate the end of British colonial rule and served as independent India's first prime minister from 1947 to 1964. Nehru was an influential advocate of the Non-Aligned Movement, refusing to choose sides in the Cold War.

Another prominent figure at Bandung was **Gamal Abdel Nasser** (1918–1970), the president of Egypt. In 1952 he had led a group of young military officers in over-throwing the ineffectual King Farouk, whom they saw as a pawn of foreign interests. Nasser was a nationalist who argued that Arabs should unite to fight against European neocolonialism and American imperialism. Like other Arab leaders at the time, he embraced secular Arab nationalism, rejecting religion as a basis for politics. He banned competing political parties such as the Egyptian Communist Party and the Muslim Brotherhood, which advocated an Egyptian constitution grounded in Islamic precepts.

In 1954 Nasser successfully negotiated the withdrawal of British troops from the Suez Canal Zone and began plans for building a giant dam on the Nile River to provide electricity for industrialization. He approached Britain and the United States but refused to accept their condition that he join an anti-Soviet alliance in return for help with the dam. In 1956 Nasser took a bold move, proclaiming the nationalization of the Suez Canal as a means of financing his dam project. The British government was outraged, feeling that its vital economic and security interests were threatened.

The Suez Crisis of 1956 resulted when the British, working with the French and Israelis, developed a secret plan: the British and the French would send "peace-keeping" troops to the Canal Zone in response to a prearranged Israeli incursion across the Egyptian border. Lacking support from the United States, which was not consulted in the plan, the British and Israelis withdrew when faced with Egyptian opposition and international criticism. For Nasser, it was a triumph. He became a hero across the Arab world for facing down British imperialism and Israeli aggression, and the Aswan Dam was later completed with Soviet aid.

Nasser's reputation in the Arab world was also grounded in his fierce support of the Palestinian cause and his belligerent attitude toward Israel. In 1947, the British withdrew their forces from Palestine, which they had occupied under a League of Nations Mandate after the First World War (see Chapter 27). Diplomats at the United Nations then finalized a plan to partition Palestine between Arab and Jewish states. In 1948, with Arab states refusing to accept the partition plan, Zionist leaders declared the independence of Israel. Egypt, Lebanon, Syria, Jordan, and Iraq immediately attacked Israel, in their eyes an illegitimate entity that had been carved from Arab lands. Nasser himself served in the Pan-Arab army that took up arms against Israel at the moment of its birth.

As Arab refugees fled the fighting, some driven from their homes by Israeli soldiers, the Israeli government expanded its borders beyond what the United Nations plan had envisioned, and the Israeli military routed the Arab armies. Shocked and humiliated by the events of 1948, many Arabs looked to Nasser as their best hope to destroy Israel and return Palestinian refugees to their native land.

Nasser's reputation, however, was severely damaged when he made a series of threatening moves toward Israel that prompted a pre-emptive Israeli attack. In the Six-Day War of 1967, virtually the entire Egyptian air force was destroyed as Israeli forces occupied Egypt's Sinai Desert, Syria's Golan Heights, and the West Bank of the Jordan River. Of great symbolic and strategic importance was the Israeli occupation of East Jerusalem, which was predominantly Arab. Military and economic support from the United States had helped make the Israeli victory possible, a fact that was resented across the Arab and Muslim worlds. While the Soviet Union gave rhetorical support to the Palestinians, its material and military support never came close to what the United States provided to its allies.

Sukarno, Nehru, and Nasser had all grown up in European-dominated colonial worlds and had dedicated themselves to the liberation of their peoples. While they were all aware that Cold War entanglements would compromise their ability to move their nations forward, they had different levels of success in achieving the nonalignment to which they had dedicated themselves at Bandung. Sukarno was the least successful; his fall brought to power an Indonesian military dictatorship allied with the United States. Nehru was by far the most successful, maintaining India's status as a genuinely nonaligned democracy throughout this period. Nasser chose to ally Egypt with the Soviet Union not out of any enthusiasm for communism, which he despised, but simply because the Soviets were enemies of the United States, and the United States was the main ally of his Israeli rivals.

Vietnam: The Cold War in Southeast Asia, 1956–1974

As in Indonesia, Vietnamese nationalists had to fight colonial reoccupation forces to win their independence. After helping drive the Japanese from Indochina during World War II, Ho Chi Minh had declared an independent Democratic Republic of Vietnam in 1945, explicitly referring to the American Declaration of Independence in asserting the right of the Vietnamese people to be free from foreign rule. That claim was disputed by France, which sent forces to re-establish colonial control.

Ho's Viet Minh fighters had developed tough fighting skills in the war against the Japanese. In spite of American subsidies for the French military, the Viet Minh won a battle at Dien Bien Phu (dyen byen foo) in 1954 that proved to be a turning point. French military officers told their government that they could not operate two counter-insurgency wars—in Algeria and Vietnam—simultaneously. Since Algeria was home to a million French citizens, its retention was a greater priority. The French therefore decided to negotiate an end to the war in Indochina.

But national elections planned for 1956 never took place. The United States, fearing that Ho Chi Minh would win the vote, supported the formation of a separate South Vietnamese regime. Conflict between the two Vietnams began as the United States supported the south with weapons and military training, while in 1960 North Vietnam sponsored the expansion of a southern-based rebel army, the National Front for the Liberation of South Vietnam, or Vietcong. The United States had a decision to make: risk allowing South Vietnam to fight its own war, or commit substantial American forces. In 1964, President Lyndon Johnson appealed to Congress and the American people for their support in launching a full-scale war against the communist regime in Hanoi, claiming that North Vietnamese ships had launched an unprovoked attack on American gunboats; in reality the American ships were within North Vietnamese waters on an intelligence-gathering mission. But members of Congress (and the American people) believed the version of events given by their commander-in-chief and gave Johnson authority to wage war. By 1965, there were 200,000 American military personnel in Vietnam.

In spite of this military commitment, which included massive bombing attacks on North Vietnam, the resistance of southern guerilla fighters supported by Hanoi held firm. American soldiers, drafted into the military, fighting in unfamiliar tropical terrain, and with little knowledge of the country and its culture, were often unable to distinguish friend from foe. Many American civilians did not want to believe the truth that their troops had brutally slaughtered innocent civilians in the village of My Lai (mee lie) in 1969 or that their military was spreading poisonous clouds

Primary Source: Letter to the French Chamber of Deputies *Read what the chairman of the Vietnamese Nationalist Party, 26 years old and awaiting execution, wrote to the parliament of France.*

■ **Vietnamese Protest** On June 11, 1963, Quang Duc, a Vietnamese Buddhist monk, burned himself to death on a Saigon street. His self-immolation was a protest of the policies of the U.S.-backed South Vietnamese government, which many Buddhists thought favored the Catholic minority. (Malcolm Browne/AP Images)

of defoliating chemicals across the Vietnamese countryside, leading to respiratory illnesses, especially among children and the elderly, while causing lasting environmental damage. Images of burning children fleeing napalm bomb blasts sickened global audiences. In this first "televised war," images of death and destruction were transmitted around the world.

In 1968, the Vietcong took the fight straight to the South Vietnamese capital of Saigon during the Tet Offensive. Antiwar protests were spreading across American college campuses, and anti-American feelings were also rising among students in much of Europe, Asia, Africa, and Latin America. With public opinion turning against the war, in 1969 the new administration of Richard Nixon promised a "secret plan" to win the war: even more intensive bombing of North Vietnam and the replacement of American ground forces with South Vietnamese ones. The South Vietnamese government and military, characterized by rampant corruption and low morale, were not up to the task. On April 30, 1975, after the United States withdrew its ground forces, communist forces entered Saigon, renamed it Ho Chi Minh City, and reunified the country under their dictatorship.

Entering the Vietnam War, Americans were inclined to think of the world in simple terms: democracy was good, communism was evil, and any fight against communism was necessarily a fight for democracy. In the course of the Vietnam

War many discovered that the world was, in fact, more complicated. While the Viet Minh were Marxists-Leninists dedicated to social revolution, especially in the redistribution of land, their movement also had roots in Vietnam's long history of resistance to foreign intrusion: China in former times and, more recently, Japan and France.

In Vietnam, as in Indonesia, the Congo, and many other parts of the world, the Cold War greatly complicated the transition from colonialism to national independence. While the outcomes in these three countries varied, they had one thing in common: in the mid-1970s not one of them was a democracy.

⬤A Time of Upheaval, 1966–1974

Americans who grew up during "the sixties" often remember this period vividly as a time of great political, social, and cultural ferment. The Civil Rights Movement under the leadership of figures like Dr. Martin Luther King paralleled the liberation movements taking place in other parts of the world. Young people took center stage, proclaiming that the world could, and should, be made a far better place. In 1963, the poet-musician Bob Dylan captured the spirit of the time:

> Come mothers and fathers throughout the land
> And don't criticize what you can't understand
> Your sons and your daughters are beyond your command
> Your old road is rapidly aging
> Please get out of the new one if you can't lend your hand
> For the times they are a-changing.

Students in many parts of the world became convinced that they could create a world of peace, love, and justice.

This global trend toward greater youth involvement in politics and society was led by students in Europe, Asia, Africa, and the Americas who had come of age after the Second World War. In dormitory rooms across the world, posters of Che Guevara represented the vitality, idealism, and revolutionary potential of youth. In most places, youth movements arose in opposition to traditional authority. In China, however, Mao Zedong harnessed the power of young people to drive his final experiment in radical revolutionary transformation.

In the end, global youth in the 1960s failed to change the world, at least as completely or quickly as many had hoped. In the United States, Europe, China, and Latin America, authorities reasserted control. The bipolarity of the Cold War, though somewhat softened by diplomatic initiatives in the 1970s, endured.

The Great Proletarian Cultural Revolution, 1965–1974

After the disaster of the Great Leap Forward, the People's Republic of China had returned to a more conventional planned economy. But Mao was still not content, feeling that the revolutionary enthusiasm of the masses was being squashed by elitists and technocrats. The Soviet model of top-down economic planning, which had never appealed to Mao, was even further discredited by a series of border clashes in 1960 that led to a deterioration of relations with Moscow. In 1965, Mao began a campaign to mobilize the revolutionary potential of the young, organizing them into units called the **Red Guards,** who were taught that Mao himself was the source of all wisdom. His thoughts were collected in a "little red book" that became the bible of the Red Guard movement, waved enthusiastically in the air by the millions of young people who came to Beijing to pay homage to the "Great Helmsman."

● **Red Guards** Young people who rallied to the cause of Maoism during the Great Proletarian Cultural Revolution. As their enthusiasm got out of control, the Red Guards spread anarchy across the People's Republic of China.

Mao used the Red Guards to attack his enemies within the Communist Party, the "rightists" and "experts" who had resisted him during the Great Leap Forward. Soon the Red Guards had created an atmosphere of anarchy, attacking party offices, publicly humiliating their teachers, destroying cultural artifacts that linked China to its past, and harassing anyone they thought needed "re-education." Educated Chinese were sent to farms and factories, where they were expected to humble themselves and absorb the authentic revolutionary spirit of the masses. Many died.

By 1968 the country was in a state of near anarchy and its economy was at a standstill. Pragmatic communist leaders realized that the Cultural Revolution had gone too far and convinced Mao to allow the People's Liberation Army to restore governmental authority. Many Red Guards themselves now faced "downward transfer" to remote villages and labor camps. But while the worst excesses of the Proletarian Revolution were curbed, a bitter power struggle was taking place behind the scenes. A radical faction called the "Gang of Four," led by Mao's wife, Jiang Qing (jyahng ching), schemed to restore the Cultural Revolution. Jiang was a former actress who used her power to purge Chinese art and intellectual life of Western influences and to take vengeance on her many enemies. On the other side were more pragmatic communists like Deng Xiaoping (dung shee-yao-ping), an "expert" who was struggling to regain his influence. With the Cultural Revolution reigned in, and an aging Mao no longer in complete command, Deng and the "expert" faction gradually reasserted themselves.

The pragmatists scored a victory in 1972 when the American president Richard Nixon came to Beijing. Relations between the two countries had long been tense, partly because the Americans supported the Nationalist government of Chiang Kai-shek on the island of Taiwan, which the communists regarded as a rebel province of China. But the Chinese were also worried about their long border with the Soviet Union, where armed confrontations had recently taken place. Although a die-hard anticommunist, Nixon judged that better relations with communist China would increase his own bargaining power with the U.S.S.R. and might help the United States extricate itself from Vietnam.

In spite of thawing relations with the United States, the restoration of party and army control, and the return of moderates to positions of influence, the shadow of the Cultural Revolution still hung over China at the time of Mao's death in 1976. The eventual victory of Deng Xiaoping's pragmatic faction over the Gang of Four sent the People's Republic of China in a direction that could scarcely have been imagined in the darkest days of the Cultural Revolution (see Chapter 31). The people of China had paid a terrible price for Mao's political adventures: the Great Leap Forward and the Great Proletarian Cultural Revolution had killed tens of million of people.

1968: A Year of Revolution

In 1968, just when the Chinese Communist Party was suppressing the Red Guard movement, the political power of youth was escalating elsewhere in the world. In the United States, the

■ **Nixon in China**   A lifelong anticommunist, President Richard Nixon nevertheless seized the chance for global realignment by visiting China in 1972, hoping that better relations with China would aid U.S. diplomacy with the Soviet Union. The agenda for the meeting was the work of Premier Chou En-lai (*far left*) and Nixon's national security adviser Henry Kissinger (*far right*) who were both practitioners of *realpolitik* ("realistic politics").   (Bettmann/Corbis)

"hippie" movement was in full flower. During the "summer of love" in 1967, long hair, psychedelic art and music, and slogans such as "make love, not war" emanated from college campuses. Some young people's interest in Eastern religions, and experimentation with consciousness-altering drugs, were part of their quest to remake themselves while remaking the world. (See the feature "Visual Evidence: *Sgt. Pepper's Lonely Hearts Club Band.*")

New thinking about gender roles was one of the most transformative of the assaults on what young people called "the establishment." Even though women had achieved legal equality in much of the world, social inequality persisted. In societies both rich and poor, a child's chances to develop his or her full potential through educational opportunities was shaped by gender. Professional opportunities for women were sharply limited; the universal expectation of men in charge was that young women could never advance in careers because they would quickly marry and devote themselves to motherhood. In the 1960s, the founders of the modern feminist movement demanded women's rights to full social and economic equality.

In the United States, as the Vietnam War polarized American society, the hopeful idealism that drove feminists, civil rights advocates, and student leaders in the early 1960s was soon tempered by harsher realities. Excessive drug use ruined lives. In 1967, a peace march on Washington turned violent as protestors confronted army troops defending the Pentagon, and mass arrests followed a series of "stop the draft" demonstrations in New York. The assassinations of civil rights leader Martin Luther King Jr. and Democratic presidential candidate Robert F. Kennedy in the spring and summer of 1968 removed two voices for peace and moderation from the scene. Violence spread through American cities.

During the 1968 Democratic National Convention, American television viewers watched in horror as Chicago police rained blows on the heads of youthful protestors; a few months later Republican Richard Nixon won the presidency. To those

SGT. PEPPER'S LONELY HEARTS CLUB BAND

Listen and compare two songs by the British group the Beatles, "I Want to Hold Your Hand" (1963) and "A Day in the Life" (1967), to get an idea of the depth and rapidity of cultural change in the mid-1960s. In a mere four years, John Lennon, Paul McCartney, George Harrison, and Ringo Starr went from pop stars adored by screaming adolescent girls to artists whose words, music, and rapidly evolving public images made them globally influential figures.

Millions anxiously anticipated the release of their new album, *Sgt. Pepper's Lonely Hearts Club Band,* on June 1, 1967. Their earlier albums had become more and more complex in musical structure and ambitious in lyrical content, influenced by the highly conceptual

Tribute is paid to the Rolling Stones, the Beatles' main rival on the rock music scene, and Bob Dylan, a strong influence on their musical development.

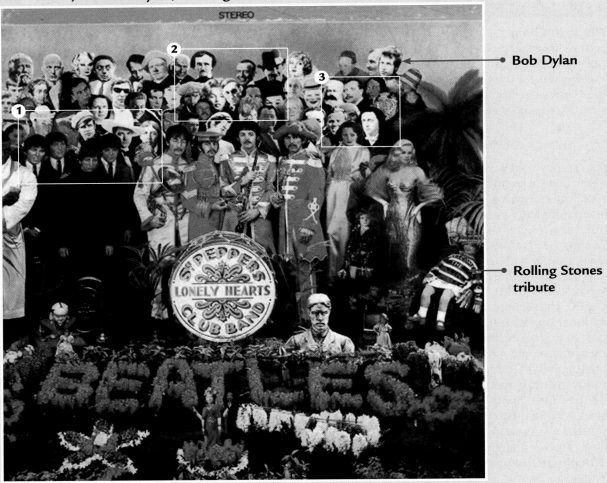

Bob Dylan

Rolling Stones tribute

(© Capitol Records/EMI/Michael Ochs Archives.com)

John Lennon's suggestion that Jesus, Gandhi, and Hitler all be included was vetoed. Lennon had been criticized the year earlier for declaring that the Beatles were "more popular than Jesus Christ," and the inclusion of Hitler would have been even more offensive. An image of Gandhi was included at the photo shoot, but was later removed at the request of the record company.

songwriting of Bob Dylan, an opening of the imagination commonly attributed to marijuana and psychedelic drugs, and the brilliance of their producer/engineer George Martin, with his strong background in classical music. While recording *Sgt. Pepper's,* the group traveled to India for training in transcendental meditation, a journey eagerly covered by the global media and one that provided further artistic stimulus.

The album lived up to expectations. No one had ever heard anything like it before. But the album was more than just a collection of songs. Eager fans sought symbolic meanings not only in the sometimes obscure lyrics but also in the visual images that adorned the large gatefold cover of the album. Peter Blake, the artist who designed the cover, recalls, "The concept of the album had already evolved: it would be as though the Beatles were another band, performing a concert. Paul and John said I should imagine that the band had just finished the concert, perhaps in a park. I then thought that we should have a crowd standing behind them, and this developed into the collage idea."* The resulting image was studied for meaning by millions of young people around the world.

_____

*Quoted in http://math.mercyhurst.edu/~griff/sgtpepper/sgt.html.

The inclusion of figurines of the Beatles (*a*) from Madame Tussaud's Wax Museum highlights the transformation of the group's visual self-representation between 1964 and 1967.

Scattered among the historical figures and film stars are three Indian spiritual leaders (*b*) included at the suggestion of George Harrison. The influence of both Indian instrumentation and Hindu philosophy on Harrison can be heard on the album track *Within You Without You.*

Famous historical figures include Karl Marx (*c*), T. E. Lawrence ("Lawrence of Arabia") (*d*), and writers such as Edgar Allan Poe (*e*), Lewis Carroll (*f*), and Oscar Wilde (*g*). Actors include Marlon Brando (*h*), Marilyn Monroe (*i*), and Stan Laurel (*j*).

QUESTION FOR ANALYSIS

 Given your knowledge of 1960s popular culture, what ideas and emotions would this image have evoked at the time of its first release?

Americans appalled by the tumult of the previous years, Nixon was an experienced, thoughtful anticommunist who would restore order. To those who imagined a societal leap into a new age of peace and justice, Nixon represented everything that was wrong with the existing power structure. The nation became even more bitterly divided after Ohio Army National Guardsmen shot four student protestors to death at Kent State University in the spring of 1970.

Meanwhile, Paris was one of the major centers of student activity in Europe. As in the United States, the number of university students had risen sharply in the post-1945 period. After three college students were arrested for occupying a dean's office, students all over France rose to their defense. By May the Sorbonne University in Paris was festooned with portraits of Che Guevara and other revolutionary heroes. Student marchers, assaulted by riot police, built barricades of overturned cars and garbage cans.

Whereas in the United States most working Americans, including most union members, tended to side with the forces of "law and order," in France the major trade unions joined the protests. Two million French workers went on strike, joining with the students to reject the principles of top-down management. Just as students took over universities, so workers took over factories, proclaiming that bosses were unnecessary. Art students expressed this philosophy in the hundreds of different posters they plastered on the walls of Paris, combining stark expressionist images with slogans such as "Be realistic, ask for the impossible," "The boss needs you, you don't need him," and "It is forbidden to forbid."

In response to this chaos, French president Charles De Gaulle appeared on television to proclaim: "The whole French people . . . are being prevented from living a normal existence by those elements, Reds and Anarchists, that are preventing students from studying, workers from working." But he also offered some concessions. The minimum wage was raised, and new elections were organized. The re-election of De Gaulle in late 1968, like the election of Richard Nixon in the United States, made it clear that many voters simply wanted a return to "normal existence." After most workers were appeased by better contracts, the French students lost their working-class allies and the forces of "law and order" reasserted themselves.

In eastern Europe, students also played a prominent role in the **Prague Spring** of 1968, the most ambitious movement for political reform in the Soviet sphere. In 1948 Czechoslovakia had been forced by Stalin's Red Army to give up its fledgling democracy (see Chapter 29). By the mid-1960s, discontent with the stifling conditions of Soviet-imposed communism was growing. Early in 1968 the pressure for change escalated as workers' strikes and students' protests forced the resignation of the hard-line communist leadership.

The new head of the Czechoslovak Communist Party, Alexander Dubček (doob-chek), promised "socialism with a human face," including freedom of speech and association as well as more liberal, market-oriented economic policies. The Czech public rallied to Dubček's cause, and students and teachers took advantage of the new atmosphere of intellectual freedom to discuss how economic justice and democratic freedoms could be achieved in their country.

The Soviet leadership saw the Prague Spring as a direct threat. Fearing that the movement toward liberalization would spread elsewhere, they ordered a half-million Soviet and Warsaw Pact troops into Czechoslovakia. Dubček was brought to Moscow and later replaced by a more compliant Czech Communist leader. There was no substantial resistance to the Soviet intervention. Reformers in Czechoslovakia,

• Prague Spring (1968) An attempt by political reformers in Czechoslovakia to reform the communist government and create "socialism with a human face." The Soviet Union invaded Czechoslovakia, ending this attempt at reform and reimposing communist orthodoxy.

as well as in Poland, Hungary, and the Soviet Union itself had been put on notice that no changes to the status quo would be condoned.

Mexico was another country where population growth had created a large school-age population with higher aspirations than their parents. But while Mexican society was changing rapidly, Mexican politics were not. The Party of Institutional Revolution (PRI), was the elitist, bureaucratic, and corrupt descendant of the old National Revolutionary Party (see Chapter 27). Since the PRI did not allow free elections, Mexican advocates of political change had no choice but to go to the streets.

The tensions of 1968 began when riot police used excessive force to break up a fight between two student groups. Over a hundred thousand students, with support from many of their teachers and parents, went on strike, marching through the city shouting "*¡Mexico, Libertad!* ("Mexico, Liberty!"). The timing of the protests was particularly awkward for the Mexican government. The Summer Olympic Games were to be held in Mexico City in October, and the government wanted to project a positive image to the worldwide television audience. Rather than risk being embarrassed by the strikes and protests, the government decided to crack down.

The result was the **Tlatelolco Massacre.** About ten thousand people, many of them students, had gathered to protest the closing of the National University; when shooting broke out, three hundred people were killed. The government said the protestors fired first, a contention that was contradicted by the many eyewitnesses watching from apartments lining the square. But the Mexican government had recovered the initiative, and the Olympic Games went on as planned; most of the world knew little about the bloodshed at Tlatelolco (tlah-tel-OHL-koh).

In spite of their passion and commitment, student protestors in the United States, France, Czechoslovakia, and Mexico were unable to radically change the status quo. In the longer view of history, however, the cultural contributions of this generation are unmistakable. In music and the visual arts, a new emphasis on global influences inspired tremendous creativity. Many of the student leaders of the 1960s became involved in social movements in the coming decades, bringing their idealism and activism to such fields as educational reform, environmental sustainability, and gender equality.

● **Tlatelolco Massacre** (1968)   Massacre that occurred when ten thousand university students, faculty, and other supporters gathered in Tlatelolco Plaza to protest the closing of the Mexican National University; government forces opened fire and killed three hundred people.

Death and Dictatorship in Latin America, 1967–1975

After his failed sojourn to Central Africa, Che Guevara was still looking for a place where a small group of guerillas could provide the spark for revolution. In 1967 he headed for Bolivia, convinced that its corrupt government would fall swiftly once the oppressed indigenous population rose against it. But Guevara's forces did not attract the level of local support he expected. Having long been exploited by Spanish-speaking outsiders, most indigenous Andeans were wary even of those who claimed to be fighting on their behalf. Wandering in the frigid mountains, short on rations, Che's rebel band lost their morale. In September 1967, Guevara was captured and executed by Bolivian soldiers as an agent of the CIA stood by.

The death of Che Guevara took place at a time when dictatorship was a rising political force across Latin America, with authoritarian governments justifying repression in the name of anticommunism. Chile's relatively strong tradition of democratic governance came under assault after 1970, when an alliance of center-left and left-wing parties led by the Marxist **Salvador Allende** (uh-YEN-day) (1908–1973) won a bitterly contested election. Allende's effort to build a socialist economy was strongly opposed by Chilean businessmen and landowners, and his nationalization of the copper mines alarmed American economic interests. In the fall of 1973, with the backing of the United States, the military staged a coup. Salvador Allende committed suicide as a force commanded by General Augusto Pinochet (ah-GOOS-toh pin-oh-CHET) stormed the Presidential Palace in Santiago. Pinochet rewarded his American allies by instituting free-market economic policies and inviting foreign investment in the Chilean economy. But economic liberalism was not matched by political openness, as Pinochet dismantled the institutions of Chilean democracy. Thousands of students and union leaders were, like the couple Che had once met on the open road, were jailed or killed.

In the mid-1970s military governments dominated the South American political landscape. In Argentina thousands of students vanished, their mothers holding silent vigils for months and years for these *desaparecidos* (deh-say-pah-re-see-dohs) ("disappeared ones"), not knowing that in many cases their sons and daughters had been killed, some drugged and pushed out of airplanes over the open sea. In Brazil as well, military authorities used anticommunism to institute harsh limitations on freedom of speech and freedom of association. Successive administrations in Washington, ever fearful that the Soviet Union would take advantage of insurrections for its own purposes following the Cuban example, were generally supportive of the right-wing regimes that dominated this dark period in Latin American history.

Détente and Challenges to Bipolarity

Relations between the United States and the Soviet Union were particularly strained during the early 1960s at the time of the Cuban Revolution and the Cuban Missile Crisis. Images from the time include that of the Soviet premier Nikita Khrushchev banging his shoe on a table at the United Nations while angrily denouncing American imperialism, and that of President John F. Kennedy pledging to put American astronauts on the moon before the end of the decade. In 1957 the Soviets had launched *Sputnik* (spuht-nick), the first artificial satellite to orbit the earth. In response America developed the Apollo space program, accomplishing the first manned mission to the moon in 1969. Indeed, increasing technological capacity was one side benefit of the Cold War as each side poured huge resources into applied scientific research.

By the mid-1960s, however, a state of reluctant coexistence between the superpowers, called **détente** (day-tahnt), was becoming the norm. Both the United States and the U.S.S.R. faced increasing challenges, both domestic and foreign. While the United States was dealing with the deep social rifts related to the Civil Rights Movement and increasing opposition to the Vietnam War, in the Soviet Union poor living standards were the issue. The Soviet people had guaranteed employment, universal education, and health care, but they faced persistent shortages of consumer goods, and those that were available were often of shoddy quality. Moscow was looking for some breathing space in which to develop its domestic economy.

In theory, the division between East and West, between capitalism and communism, was absolute. In reality, both the United States and the U.S.S.R. were having increasing difficulty controlling their respective blocs. After 1960 relations between Moscow and Beijing had become even more strained as tension, and even occasional armed confrontation, marked the long Chinese/Soviet border. It was this Sino-Soviet split that gave Richard Nixon a chance to make diplomatic headway with the People's Republic of China. The Western alliance was also not subject to complete American domination. In 1957, the Treaty of Rome laid the foundation for what would become the European Economic Community. While shielded from Soviet aggression by the North Atlantic Treaty Organization and the still powerful American military presence, in the 1960s and early 1970s western European leaders were beginning to come out from under the economic and political umbrella of the United States.

Because of these domestic and international factors, leaders in both Washington and Moscow decided that the Cold War division of the world was, if not permanent, at least likely to remain for the foreseeable future. In the resulting spirit of détente they began to soften some of their rhetoric and seek a way to live together. The greatest achievement was the Strategic Arms Limitation Treaty (SALT) of 1972, which froze the number of ballistic missiles in the possession of the United States and the Soviet Union. The specter of nuclear war, much in evidence ten years earlier, never disappeared, but in the mid-1970s it began to recede.

Chapter Review

 Download the MP3 audio file of the Chapter Review and listen to it on the go.

Long after his death, Che Guevara remains an iconic figure. Staring out from millions of tee-shirts and posters, his youthful image evokes romantic qualities: idealism, self-sacrifice, and a restless yearning to transform the world. Whether the real Ernesto Guevara, medical student turned revolutionary, is worthy of such latter-day worship remains an open question. What is beyond dispute is that the bitter divisions of the Cold War made the realization of global justice and equality all the more difficult to achieve.

What were the implications of successful revolutions in China and Cuba for the Cold War rivalry of the United States and the Soviet Union?

The establishment of the People's Republic of China in 1949 by the Chinese Communist Party under Mao Zedong added to the global power and prestige of communism and intensified fears in the United States and elsewhere of Soviet domination. In reality, however, Mao resisted Soviet models of development, and Sino-Soviet relations deteriorated. The Cuban Revolution in 1959 gave the Soviet Union another opportunity to expand its sphere of influence, but the Cuban Missile Crisis of 1961 showed just how dangerous the Soviet military alliance with Cuba was to the global balance of power, as both of the superpowers sought a face-saving compromise. More generally, the United States and the Soviet Union stayed within their own spheres of influence.

How were democratization and decolonization movements in the mid-twentieth century affected by the Cold War?

In many regions, such as Central Africa and Southeast Asia, decolonization took place in a political environment filled with Cold War tensions. The leaders who had gathered at the Bandung Conference pledged to create a world in which formerly colonized societies would maintain their nonalignment in the East/West power struggle. The difficulty of doing so was confirmed by the long war in Vietnam. Meanwhile, the United States and the Soviet Union undercut struggles for national independence, democracy, and social reform in countries from Guatemala to Hungary and from Congo to Poland.

What was the role of youth in the global upheavals of 1965–1974?

The "sixties" brought to the fore the cultural influence of the generation born during and just after World War II. In China, students responded enthusiastically to Mao Zedong's call for a Great Proletarian Cultural Revolution. Violence and disorder spread with the influence of the Red Guards. In many other parts of the world, students, while also politically active, organized against the established authorities. In 1968, student activists took to the streets of cities like Chicago, Paris, Prague, and Mexico City demanding change. Though the global youth movement of the 1960s certainly had long-term influence, the political aspirations of student activists were not achieved. In the United States, France, Czechoslovakia, Mexico, and elsewhere, leaders representing traditional institutions reasserted control. By 1974 the youth revolution had largely run its course. In the age of détente, the Cold War status quo of global division remained.

For Further Reference

Gaddis, John Lewis. *The Cold War: A New History*. New York: Penguin, 2005.

Guevara, Ernesto. *The Motorcycle Diaries: Notes on a Latin American Journey*. Edited and translated by Alexandra Keeble. Melbourne: Ocean Press, 2003.

Hart, Joseph, ed. *Che: The Life, Death and Afterlife of a Revolutionary*. New York: Thunder's Mouth Press, 2003.

Hunt, Michael. *The World Transformed: 1945 to the Present*. New York: Bedford/St. Martin's, 2004.

Jeffrey, Robin, ed. *Asia: The Winning of Independence*. London: Macmillan, 1981.

Kurlansky, Mark. *1968: The Year That Rocked the World*. New York: Random House, 2005.

McMahon, Robert J. *The Cold War: A Very Short Introduction*. New York: Oxford University Press, 2003.

Prashad, Vijay. *The Darker Nations: A People's History of the Third World*. New York: New Press, 2007.

Spence, Jonathan. *Mao Zedong*. New York: Viking Penguin, 1999.

Westad, Odd Arne. *The Global Cold War: Third World Interventions and the Making of Our Times*. New York: Cambridge University Press, 2007.

WEB RESOURCES

Pronunciation Guide

Interactive Maps

MAP 30.1 China and Taiwan

MAP 30.2 Cold War Confrontations

MAP 30.3 Decolonization

Primary Sources

Chapter Objectives

ACE Multiple-Choice Quiz

Flashcards

Websites

Che Guevara
(http://www.cheguevaralinks.com/).   Links to a wealth of information on the Argentinean revolutionary.

Decolonization
(http://www.casahistoria.net/decolonisation.htm). Texts, documents, and case studies from around the world, especially designed for student use.

Cold War Studies
(http://www.fas.harvard.edu/~hpcws/links.htm). A web portal maintained by the Harvard Project on Cold War Studies with links to archival publications, including declassified government documents, and lists of links to other Cold War sites.

Film

The Motorcycle Diaries. A 2004 feature film directed by Walter Salles that re-creates the motorcycle journey of Ernesto Guevara and Alberto Granado across South America.

Toward a New World Order, 1975–2000

Throughout the 1950s **Nelson Mandela** (b. 1918) had campaigned for racial justice and democracy as a member of the African National Congress (ANC). Forced underground in 1961 when the South African government banned the ANC, Mandela then traveled across Africa seeking support for the creation of a guerilla army. After returning to South Africa, he was captured and, in 1964, tried and sentenced to life in prison.

Finally, in early 1990, after decades of repression and violence, South Africa's white leaders responded to international calls for Mandela's release. A few hours after he walked through the prison gates, he spoke before a large crowd in Cape Town and before a global television audience:

(© David Tunley/Corbis)

Today, the majority of South Africans, black and white, recognize that apartheid has no future. . . . Negotiations on the dismantling of apartheid will have to address the overwhelming demand of our people for a democratic, nonracial, and unitary South Africa. There must be an end to white monopoly on political power and a fundamental restructuring of our political and economic systems to ensure that the inequalities of apartheid are addressed and our society thoroughly democratized. . . . I wish to quote my own words during my trial in 1964. They are as true today as they were then: "I have fought against white domination and I have fought against black domination. I have cherished the ideal of a democratic and free society in which all persons live together in harmony and with equal opportunities. It is an ideal which I hope to live for and to achieve. But if needs be, it is an ideal for which I am prepared to die."[1]

NELSON MANDELA

CL   This icon will direct you to interactive activities and study materials on the *Voyages* website: www.cengage.com/history/hansen/voyages1e

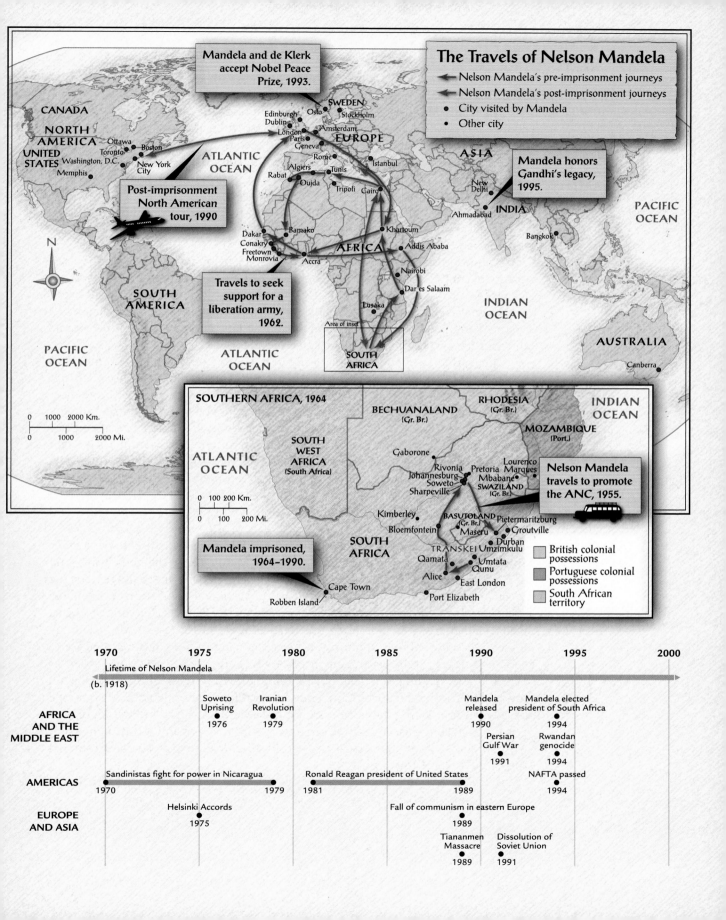

The Travels of Nelson Mandela

← Nelson Mandela's pre-imprisonment journeys
← Nelson Mandela's post-imprisonment journeys
• City visited by Mandela
• Other city

Mandela and de Klerk accept Nobel Peace Prize, 1993.

Mandela honors Gandhi's legacy, 1995.

Post-imprisonment North American tour, 1990

Travels to seek support for a liberation army, 1962.

Nelson Mandela travels to promote the ANC, 1955.

Mandela imprisoned, 1964–1990.

CANADA
NORTH AMERICA
UNITED STATES
Ottawa
Toronto   Boston
Washington, D.C.
New York City
Memphis

ATLANTIC OCEAN

SWEDEN
Edinburgh   Oslo   Stockholm
Dublin
London   Amsterdam
Paris   EUROPE
Geneva
Rome
Algiers   Istanbul
Rabat   Tunis
Oujda   Tripoli   Cairo

ASIA
New Delhi
Ahmadabad   INDIA
Bangkok

PACIFIC OCEAN

Dakar   Bamako   Khartoum
Conakry
Freetown   AFRICA   Addis Ababa
Monrovia
Accra   Nairobi
Dar es Salaam
Lusaka

INDIAN OCEAN

SOUTH AMERICA

PACIFIC OCEAN

ATLANTIC OCEAN

Area of inset
SOUTH AFRICA

AUSTRALIA
Canberra

N

0   1000   2000 Km.
0   1000   2000 Mi.

SOUTHERN AFRICA, 1964

RHODESIA (Gr. Br.)
BECHUANALAND (Gr. Br.)
INDIAN OCEAN

SOUTH WEST AFRICA (South Africa)

MOZAMBIQUE (Port.)

ATLANTIC OCEAN

Gaborone
Rivonia   Lourenco Marques
Johannesburg   Pretoria
Soweto   Mbabane
Sharpeville   SWAZILAND (Gr. Br.)

Kimberley   Pietermaritzburg
Bloemfontein   BASUTOLAND (Gr. Br.)   Groutville
Maseru   Durban
TRANSKEI   Umzimkulu
SOUTH AFRICA   Qamata   Umtata
Alice   Qunu
East London
Port Elizabeth

Cape Town
Robben Island

0   100   200 Km.
0   100   200 Mi.

British colonial possessions
Portuguese colonial possessions
South African territory

● **Nelson Mandela**
(b. 1918) South African
leader of the African
National Congress and
opponent of apartheid.
Sentenced to life in
prison in 1964; released
in 1990. After winning
the Nobel Peace Prize
in 1993, he became the
country's first democratically elected president in
1994.

None of Mandela's many journeys before and after his imprisonment were as significant as his short walk through those prison gates.

As a youth, Mandela received an early education in the history of his own Tembu
people and in the protocols of the chief's court while also attending an English-
language primary school. There a teacher assigned him the "proper" English name
of Nelson; before that, he was called Rolihlahla ("pulling the branch of a tree," or
"troublemaker"). He lived up to his African name at the all-black Methodist college
he attended when he became embroiled in student politics and was expelled after
leading a protest against the bad cafeteria food. In 1940 he headed for Johannesburg and earned a law degree through a correspondence course (since blacks were
not allowed to attend law school).

Mandela combined his practice of law with a passion for politics, taking a leadership role in the African National Congress, the party that had, since 1912, worked
for racial equality in South Africa (see Chapters 27 and 29). When their nonviolent
campaign was met with police brutality and escalating repression, Mandela was set
on the path that led to his imprisonment and his later triumph. In 1994 he became
the country's first democratically elected president.

The world had changed dramatically in the period of Mandela's confinement.
In 1964 Cold War tensions dominated international affairs. But with the collapse of
the Soviet Union in the early 1990s, new possibilities emerged. Hopes for democracy spread not only across Russia and the former Soviet sphere but also in many
other parts of the world, like South Africa, where Cold War alliances had empowered authoritarian regimes (see Chapter 30). Latin America, for example, was swept
by a wave of democratization in the last decade of the twentieth century. Capturing
the optimism of the time, President George H. W. Bush of the United States spoke of
a "new world order." With the stalemate of the Cold War broken, he said in 1991,
the path lay open to "a world in which freedom and respect for human rights find
a home among all nations."

Still, myriad challenges remained unresolved. Russia's transition to democracy
and capitalism was a difficult one, peace in the Middle East remained elusive, and
democratic elections in South Africa did not instantly or automatically remove the
social and economic inequalities of apartheid. The liberal association between free
trade and democratic politics was contradicted by the People's Republic of China,
where market-driven economic reforms created the world's fastest-growing economy
under the control of the communist government. Some critics of the United States
equated "globalization" with "Americanization" and saw the "new world order" as
a means of expanding American power. Among them were Islamist activists, who,
inspired by the Iranian Revolution, joined the struggle against what they saw as the
decadent West. While the last decade of the twentieth century therefore offered
hope, and in some places genuine progress toward freedom and security, the "new
world order" did not offer a clear and agreed-upon road map as humanity entered
the twenty-first century.

Focus Questions

🚐 **What were the major causes of the collapse of the Soviet Union?**

🚐 **How successful were free markets and political reforms in bringing stability and democracy to different world regions?**

🚐 **At the end of the twentieth century, in what ways were major conflicts in the Middle East still unresolved?**

🚐 **What were the major effects of economic globalization?**

⬤ The Late Cold War and the Collapse of the Soviet Union, 1975–1991

As the last U.S. forces pulled out of Vietnam in 1975, the country was divided and weary of war. Seeing an opportunity for greater influence, Soviet leaders expanded their navy and increased their global support for communist rebel movements. In 1981, however, the United States returned to an aggressively anti-Soviet foreign policy. Soon it was the Soviets who were unable to follow through on their military and strategic commitments. While the United States brought pressure on the Soviet regime with increased military spending, eastern Europeans were moving from simmering discontent toward outright rebellion against Soviet over-rule. After 1985 a new Soviet leader, Mikhail Gorbachev, began a series of reforms, but it was too little, too late. In 1989 the Berlin Wall fell, and in 1991 the Soviet Union was dissolved.

In the 1990s Germany was reunified while Poland and the Czech Republic seemed well on their way to becoming stable democracies. But it proved difficult to replace totalitarianism with democratic institutions in Russia and the Central Asian nations that emerged from the Soviet collapse. Russia's authoritarian political traditions proved persistent, and sharp inequalities accompanied the introduction of capitalist markets.

The United States in the Post-Vietnam Era, 1975–1990

U.S. society in the late 1970s was exhausted by the misadventure of the Vietnam War and the resignation in 1974 of President Nixon in the Watergate scandal. Then in 1979 at Three Mile Island the worst nuclear accident in U.S. history caused many to doubt the nation's technological capacity. At the same time, a steep rise in oil prices engineered by the Organization of Petroleum

Exporting Countries (OPEC) shocked Americans into an awareness of how much their high standard of living depended on cheap energy from foreign nations. *Stagflation* was a term coined to describe the combination of slow growth and inflation that afflicted the U.S. economy in the 1970s.

The people of the United States felt a deep anger and a sense of powerlessness after Iranian revolutionaries seized American hostages in late 1979 and a rescue attempt the following spring failed to free them. In the 1980 presidential campaign, Republican **Ronald Reagan** (1911–2004) promised that under his leadership American power and confidence would be restored. His sweeping victory brought a brash, nationalistic, and sternly anticommunist tone to American foreign policy. Liberals and moderates were alarmed, especially when huge tax cuts combined with sharp increases in military spending sent the budget into deficit. Still, after a harsh recession in 1981–1982, economic recovery provided the popular support Reagan needed for re-election in 1984, promising that it was "morning in America."

Many western Europeans were alarmed by Reagan's refusal to go along with the diplomatic language of détente (see Chapter 30). European protestors attended huge peace rallies, while their leaders, rejecting Reagan's description of the Soviet Union as an "evil empire," continued to use the language of peaceful coexistence. An exception was Reagan's close ally and fellow conservative, the British prime minister Margaret Thatcher. Reagan's harsh tone was offset by a sense of pragmatism, however, and in 1986 he agreed to meet with his Soviet counterpart in neutral Iceland. More progress was made at this summit meeting on arms limitation than most had expected. Still, Reagan kept the heat on the Soviets, traveling to Germany in 1987 and giving a speech that could be heard in both East and West Berlin, demanding, "Mr. Gorbachev, tear down this wall!" Few guessed that in just a few years the Berlin Wall would indeed come down.

From Leonid Brezhnev to Mikhail Gorbachev

The period from 1964 to 1982, when Leonid Brezhnev led the Soviet Union, was a time of relative stability for many Soviet citizens. While their standard of living was low, they had guaranteed employment and education and basic health care. They might never own a car, but they would probably be able to take an annual vacation on the Black Sea. While they had no freedom of speech, religion, or assembly, old-age pensions ensured that they would not suffer too badly at the end of their lives.

Increasing détente with the United States also provided some stability. The **Helsinki Accords** (1975) committed western Europe and the United States to recognize the borders of the communist bloc countries in return for a Soviet pledge to respect basic human rights. The accords emboldened some Soviet and eastern European dissidents to speak out, among them the physicist Andrei Sakharov (1921–1989), the man most responsible for the development of the Soviet hydrogen bomb. In 1975, Sakharov won the Nobel Peace Prize for his writings in defense of civil rights and democracy. In response, Brezhnev cut off Sakharov's communications with the outside world. The Soviet promise to protect basic human rights meant nothing in practice.

A large gap existed, however, between the Soviet Union's global ambitions and the resources generated by its inefficient economy. Brezhnev worsened the problem when, sensing a lack of resolve in the United States after withdrawal from Vietnam, he took on major new military commitments, such as expanding his country's nuclear submarine program and its Indian Ocean fleet. When the Reagan

---

• **Ronald Reagan** (1911–2004)   Fortieth president of the United States. A staunchly anti-communist Republican, he used harsh rhetoric toward the Soviet Union and increased American military spending but compromised when negotiating arms limitations agreements.

• **Helsinki Accords** A 1975 agreement made during the Cold War that gave recognition to the borders of communist bloc countries in eastern Europe in return for a Soviet promise, never fulfilled, to respect basic human rights.

administration stepped up military spending in the 1980s, an already overstretched Soviet Union could not keep pace.

War in Afghanistan took an especially heavy toll on Brezhnev's regime. After a communist government seized power in the capital of Kabul in 1978 with the help of Soviet Special Forces, the Soviet military faced years of tough resistance from guerilla fighters known as *mujahaddin* (moo-jah-ha-DEEN), some of whom aspired to create an Islamic state. Supplied with arms and intelligence by the United States and Pakistan, the mujahaddin wore down the Soviet forces, using their knowledge of the terrain and the sympathy of the local population to offset superior Soviet technology. The Soviet people soon grew tired of the war in Afghanistan, suggesting parallels with the experience of the United States in Vietnam.

When Brezhnev died in 1982, he left a difficult situation to the aging party functionaries who replaced him. Then in 1985 came a startling change when **Mikhail Gorbachev** (b. 1931) consolidated power. Knowing that real reform would be necessary to save the Soviet system, Gorbachev withdrew from Afghanistan and reached out to President Reagan, introducing policies of "restructuring" and "openness." *Perestroika,* "restructuring," brought substantial economic changes and the end of the massive economic centralization. While the state would still dominate, managers and workers would now use market incentives rather than bureaucratic command to raise production. *Glasnost,* "openness," allowed formerly taboo subjects to be discussed. Gorbachev's new policy was tested in 1986, when Soviet officials tried to cover up the extent of the Chernobyl disaster, the worst nuclear accident in history. Both the Soviet people and their European neighbors were enraged, and Gorbachev promised that the old cycle of cover-ups and lies would be replaced by honesty and openness.

While perestroika and glasnost did lead to reform and greater openness, they also produced dissatisfaction and instability. Gorbachev's attempt to combine the Marxist-Leninist tradition with market reforms and political transparency was a halfway measure, and it became clear in the later 1980s that the Soviet people wanted more fundamental change. Meanwhile, with Moscow having loosened its grip on power, the forces of repressed nationalism exploded in various Soviet republics, such as Georgia in the Caucasus Mountains and Lithuania on the Baltic. The Soviet Union began to break apart. Gorbachev had little choice but to agree to a treaty giving the republics of the U.S.S.R. their de facto independence as part of a commonwealth led from Moscow (see Map 31.1).

This proposal being too much for hard-line conservatives in the Communist Party, in the summer of 1991 they led a coup d'état in a desperate attempt to return to the Soviet status quo. But the people were against them. Huge crowds rallied to protect the newly elected government of the Russian Republic, and Gorbachev accepted the reality that the Communist Party could no longer dominate. He had tried but failed to find a middle ground between reform and revolution, and his political career was over.

● Mikhail Gorbachev (b. 1931)   Leader of the Soviet Union from 1985 to 1991 who introduced "openness" to Soviet politics and "restructuring" to the Soviet economy. Unable to control calls for even greater changes, Gorbachev presided over the collapse of the Soviet Union.

CL **Primary Source:** The Last Heir of Lenin Explains His Reform Plans: Perestroika and Glasnost *Read President Gorbachev's analysis of the Soviet Union's decline and his prescriptions for reform.*

Revolution in Eastern Europe

The suppression of the Hungarian uprising in 1956 and of the Prague Spring in 1968 had shown the force that was necessary to keep eastern Europe in Moscow's orbit (see Chapter 30). By the mid-1980s, however, the Soviet Union was losing its ability to intervene in the affairs of eastern Europe. In Poland, for example, grievances with communism had a religious basis, as the country's many practicing Roman Catholics despised the

MAP 31.1

The Dissolution of the Soviet Union   In the 1990s, the collapse of the Soviet Union led to the creation of new states across eastern Europe, the Caucasus Mountains, and Central Asia, regions that in the nineteenth century had been part of the Russian Empire. The Baltic states of Estonia, Latvia, and Lithuania emerged as thriving democracies. Conflict was endemic in the Caucasus, however, where Russia battled separatists in Chechnya, and Armenia and Azerbaijan fought for control of territory. The new nations of former Soviet Central Asia were dominated by strong-armed dictators.

atheism of their rulers. Catholicism remained a touchpoint for Polish nationalism and a historical connection with the West. The surprise announcement in 1978 that the Polish cardinal Karol Wojtyla would become Pope John Paul II powerfully affirmed that historic connection.

In 1980 public discontent with the communist regime took organizational form with the rise of **Solidarity,** a trade union formed by shipyard workers. Facing mounting popular pressure, the government was forced to recognize Solidarity, the first independent trade union in the Soviet bloc. In a direct challenge to the authority of the Communist Party, nearly a third of Poland's population joined the Solidarity movement. Faced with increasing domestic unrest, the government agreed to an election in 1989. Though the communists tried to stack the deck in their own favor, the result was a massive victory for Solidarity and the election of its leader Lech Walesa to the position of president.

● **Solidarity** Polish trade union created in 1980 that organized opposition to communist rule. In 1989, Solidarity leader Lech Walesa was elected president of Poland as the communists lost their hold on power.

Interactive Map

In Czechoslovakia the young rebels of the Prague Spring of 1968, now adults, began pushing for a new constitution. They had an additional grievance: the terrible environmental destruction caused by the communist regime's industrial policies. Unaccountable to public opinion, the communists had not matched western European progress in seeking to protect their nation's air, water, and forests. Though the police cracked down, Czech authorities were unable to keep control of events, and this time no Soviet forces arrived to keep them in power. The fall of communism in Czechoslovakia proceeded so smoothly and peacefully that it has been called the "Velvet Revolution."

In Romania in 1989, the transition to democracy was more sudden and violent. Here the dictator Nicolae Ceauşescu (chow-shehs-koo) had ruled with an iron fist, building massive palaces while his people went hungry and promoting family members to increase his personal control. Isolated in his palace, Ceauşescu did not realize the depth of public anger for the violence his security forces had used to suppress earlier protests. His subordinates organized a large public rally in the capital of Bucharest to reaffirm his position, but when the dictator stepped forward to receive the accolades of the crowd, he was loudly jeered. Television showed Ceauşescu's confusion as he heard, for the first time, his people's true opinion of him. His own security officials turned on him, and he was hastily tried and executed.

The most evocative image of the fall of communism in eastern Europe was the destruction of the Berlin Wall. Since 1961 the wall had been a concrete symbol of the Cold War divide, but in 1989, as part of the larger wave of revolution in central Europe, huge crowds of East Berliners streamed toward it. The next year the communist government of East Germany relented and opened the gates, allowing tearful reunions of long-separated families. Soon after, the Berlin Wall was dismantled, in a festival of constructive mayhem, by euphoric Germans. The Cold War was truly over.

Post-Soviet Struggles for Democracy and Prosperity

The final stage in the dissolution of the Soviet Union came in 1991. When hard-line communists attempted a coup d'état, the people rose against them, rallied by the newly elected president of the Russian Federation, **Boris Yeltsin** (1931–2007). (See the feature "Visual Evidence: Tanks and Protests in Moscow and Beijing.")

With input from American economic advisers, who argued that only a rapid and wholesale conversion to free markets could bring prosperity to the new Russia, Yeltsin instituted bold economic reforms. Huge fortunes were made as state assets were auctioned off. But the new money was concentrated in the hands of a small elite, some of whom behaved more like gangsters than corporate executives. As for the working class, they now had access to many consumer products but usually lacked the means to purchase them. The old securities of the Soviet system—free education and health care, guaranteed employment, old-age pensions—were disappearing while the market system had yet to boost productivity and wages. Russia simply did not have the institutional capacity, civic traditions, and managerial expertise to shift so rapidly to a capitalist system. By the end of the 1990s, life expectancy and fertility rates were in decline, and the population was shrinking. Senior citizens, including World War II veterans, were often hungry and cold.

Yeltsin's problems were compounded by unrest in the southern Caucasus region, long a troubled frontier zone of the Russian Empire, where a separatist movement organized by Muslim guerillas developed in Chechnya (CHECH-nee-yah).

● **Boris Yeltsin** (1931–2007)　First president of the Russian Federation, from 1991 to 1999. Rallied the people of Moscow to defend their elected government during the attempted communist coup of 1991, but his presidency was marred by financial scandals and war in Chechnya.

TANKS AND PROTESTS IN MOSCOW AND BEIJING

Among the many striking images associated with the late Cold War period are these very different representations of the role that tanks played in political protests in Beijing in 1989 and Moscow in 1991. The Chinese image shows the repression of democracy, the Russian one its triumph.

As China opened up to the world in the 1980s, it was undertaking a much more successful economic restructuring than Mikhail Gorbachev's perestroika, but its leaders had done virtually nothing to emulate his program of glasnost, or "openness." By 1989 some Chinese, especially students in the capital city

From April to August 1989, large crowds assembled in Beijing's Tiananmen Square to protest corruption and advocate democracy. Under the giant banner of Chairman Mao that dominates the square, some students erected a facsimile of the Statue of Liberty. Some communist officials were sympathetic to the protests and urged dialogue. Chairman Deng Xiaoping rejected their advice and sent in the People's Army to dislodge the protestors. Estimates on the number of those killed range from the hundreds to the thousands.

(AP Photo/Jeff Widener)

Taken with a long-range lens from a Beijing hotel room, this photograph of a lone individual trying to stop a line of surging tanks (which eventually went around him) summed up both the heroism and futility of the Tiananmen protests. He has never been identified. In 1989, *Time* magazine declared the "Unknown Rebel" to be one of the one hundred most influential people of the twentieth century.

QUESTION FOR ANALYSIS

How does the manner in which the photographer has framed each of the shots affect the viewer's reactions?

of Beijing, thought it was time for a change. They were inspired by a visit from Gorbachev but also by ideals of democracy they associated with the United States.

By this time it was becoming clear that fundamental changes were likely to occur in the Soviet Union. Gorbachev was in danger of losing central control as nationalists began discussing separation from the U.S.S.R. After first resisting that trend, he then agreed to a compromise that would enhance the power of the individual republics, reversing the old domination from Moscow. In the summer of 1991 a group of Communist Party officials and army officers, understanding that the Soviet Union stood on the brink of dissolution, launched the August Coup to restore central authority.

Boris Yeltsin, elected president of the Russian Republic, stands on top of a tank, rallying the people of Moscow in defense of their new democratic institutions. The commander of the tank brigade had declared his loyalty to the Russian Republic and had refused to join Soviet forces against it. Contrary to the wishes of the coup plotters, this image was shown on state television and became a rallying point for further defense of democracy.

In the background is the Russian "white house," the parliament of the Russian Republic. The authority of this elected body was part of the shift away from centralized Soviet control toward newly empowered governmental institutions within the republic. After declaring a state of emergency, the coup leaders had the building shelled.

(AP Photo)

The coup plotters were unable to muster enough military strength to overcome this resistance, which would have required a level of violence and death that was intolerable to most military commanders. Gorbachev regained his authority and declared the orders of the coup leaders null and void. It was not much of a victory, however, as the Soviet state quickly unraveled around him.

Though Yeltsin used massive military force against them, he was not able to suppress the uprising. When the ailing Yeltsin resigned in 1999, he handed power to a former intelligence officer named Vladimir Putin (b. 1952).

Unlike the unpredictable and fun-loving Yeltsin, Putin was stern and disciplined. Anxious to embrace an authority figure who promised a return to order, Russian voters returned Putin to office in 2000. Putin reined in the excesses of capitalism by restoring state authority over much of the economy and of the media, using control of oil revenues and television to build a substantial popular base of power. He crushed the Chechnya rebellion, stood up to the United States in global forums, and restored order to the Russian Republic. Some feared, however, that stability was being achieved at the expense of democracy and civil rights.

The former Central Asian republics of the U.S.S.R. faced an equally difficult transition to democracy and market economics. Strategically located on the borderlands between China, Russia, and the Muslim world, these newly independent nations had plentiful natural resources, especially oil and gas. The potential for democracy, however, was limited because, unlike in eastern Europe, regime change came from the top down rather than through popular mobilization. In places like Kazakhstan and Uzbekistan, independence was overseen by former communist officials who paid lip service to democracy while keeping a tight rein on power and resources.

In general, the transition to liberal governance and market economics was smoother in eastern Europe than in Russia or Central Asia. Hungary, the Czech Republic, and Poland all showed clear signs of political and economic progress in the 1990s, with a blossoming of the free associations that characterize civil society. The reunification of Germany, however, was a difficult process. The citizens of East Germany were much poorer than those in the West and usually lacked the job skills that would make them competitive in a modern economy. The first decade after the fall of the Berlin Wall brought freedom and opportunity to eastern Germany, but also unemployment and insecurity.

Though it is still too soon to assess its full implications, the fall of the Soviet Union was clearly a momentous turning point in modern history. It marked not only the failure of the world's longest experiment with communism but also the breakup of the formerly great Russian Empire.

The Late Cold War in Africa and Latin America: Crisis and Opportunity

Political crises had afflicted many parts of Africa and Latin America during the late stages of the Cold War (1975–1990) as the United States and Soviet Union maneuvered for influence. With the end of the Cold War, however, opportunities arose to heal political divisions and bring greater democracy. In Central America, violence in the 1980s between leftist insurgents and military regimes aligned with Washington gave way in the 1990s to elections and new hope for democracy and stability. Likewise in southern Africa, warfare in the 1980s gave way to elections and the promise of a brighter future after the collapse of communism. But civil war and genocide in Central Africa demonstrated that the destructive legacies of colonialism and superpower intervention were still powerful.

The Late Stages of the Cold War in Central America

Events in Chile in 1973 were a preview of things to come in late Cold War Latin America. That year a group of Chilean military officers, with U.S. backing, launched a successful coup against President Salvador Allende, the leader of a left-wing coalition hostile to American mining interests (see Chapter 30). The new military dictator, General Augusto Pinochet, denounced communism, protected U.S. investments, and brought down Chile's once-powerful labor unions. American economic advisers then remade Chile's economy along free-market lines, reforms that Pinochet carried out through authoritarian means. As elsewhere in Latin America during the Cold War, dictators like Pinochet were supported by the U.S. government because of their anticommunist credentials.

In the 1980s the main battleground between leftist rebels and military forces backed by the United States was Central America. Nicaragua, for example, had long been ruled by the Somoza family, anticommunist dictators aligned with American economic interests. Resistance to the Somoza dictatorship was organized by the rebel Sandinista National Liberation Front. When a major earthquake occurred in 1972, the Somoza family and its friends in government stole millions of the dollars of relief aid sent to Nicaragua by international donors, pushing many Nicaraguans toward sympathy with the rebels. In 1979 the Sandinistas ousted the Somoza family and formed a new government.

After Ronald Reagan took office in 1981, the U.S. government, alarmed at the close ties between the Sandinistas and Fidel Castro's communist regime in Cuba,

◢ Sandinistas

The Sandinistas were victorious in 1979, but their control over Nicaragua was then challenged by U.S.-backed *contra* rebels. The Sandinistas modeled themselves on Cuban revolutionary heroes; the soldier on the right wears a red-starred beret like that of Che Guevara. (© Jean Louis Atlan/Sygma/Corbis)

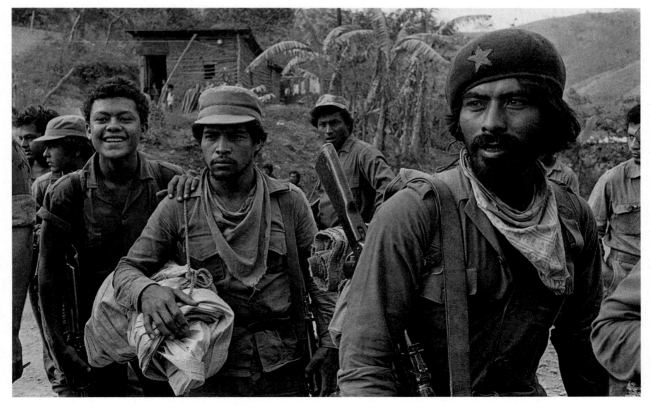

threw its support behind an anti-Sandinista insurgents known as *Contras,* led by military men associated with the previous regime. Faced with this dire threat, the Sandinistas retracted some of their earlier promises of expanded civil liberties. Like Fidel Castro twenty years earlier, they justified dictatorship in the name of saving the revolution.

Harsh conflict characterized Nicaragua throughout the 1980s. In the United States, the Reagan administration's support for the Contras against the Sandinistas was politically divisive; in the Iran-Contra scandal, officials evaded congressional oversight and illegally sold arms to Iran to gain funds for the Nicaraguan rebels. But the decline of Soviet power brought new possibilities for a negotiated settlement. Since Cuba's economy was undercut when Gorbachev phased out Soviet subsidies, Cuba could not continue to aid the Sandinistas. Then, as the Soviet threat receded, U.S. leaders no longer saw the Contras as necessary allies but rather as an embarrassment. Free elections were held in Nicaragua in 1989. The defeated Sandinistas adhered to the rules of democracy by peacefully handing over power and vowing to return via ballots rather than bullets. It was a major step forward for Nicaraguan democracy.

Guatemalan society was also marred by violence in the 1980s, most of it inflicted by paramilitary death squads aligned with the right-wing government. Their targets were communities suspected of sympathy or collusion with rebel armies, and hundreds of thousands of Guatemalans, mostly indigenous Maya people, were killed. Often the killers were children kidnapped by the army from Maya villages and forced into service. As many as a million refugees were displaced, fleeing from the mountains to the cities or across the border into Mexico. Guatemalan leaders either denied their connection to the death squads or justified the violence as necessary to defeat communism. Four decades after Che Guevara had witnessed the destruction of Guatemalan democracy (see Chapter 30), the position of the country's poor was worse than ever.

The end of the Cold War caused the United States to bring greater pressure on the Guatemalan government and military to work toward a solution. But it took until 1996 for the United Nations to broker a peace deal. The rebels agreed to lay down their arms in exchange for land, and for the first time since 1952 Guatemalans went to the polls to vote in free elections. Wounds from the years of violence remained deep, however, and a government panel was set up to investigate paramilitary atrocities.

Elsewhere in Latin America the trend was also toward democracy. In Chile, prodemocracy activists removed General Pinochet from power. In Argentina, the turning point was defeat in the brief Falklands War against Great Britain in 1982, when the incompetence of the Argentine generals brought about irresistible calls for political change. Shortly following Argentina's democratic transition, in 1985 Brazil felt the winds of change as elections swept the military from political power.

Entering the 1980s, Mexicans had also faced a severe deficiency of democracy. The problem had never been military governments or Cold War alignments, but rather the monopoly power of the Party of Institutional Revolution (PRI), which constrained Mexican political freedom and bound the country to incompetence and corruption (see Chapter 30). Finally, in 1989, a conservative opposition party won gubernatorial elections in the state of Baja California, the first time the PRI had lost control of a statehouse since the 1920s. The stage was then set for more open electoral competition at the national level. In 2000 the election of Vicente Fox of the National Action Party (PAN) finally ended the PRI monopoly on Mexican presidential politics.

The Congolese Conflict and Rwandan Genocide

In Africa, the big Cold War prize won by the United States was the former Belgian Congo. America's ally Joseph Mobutu (see Chapter 30) changed his name to Mobutu Sese Seko and took dictatorial control over the vast nation he rechristened Zaire. In return for facilitating Western access to Zaire's strategic minerals and for allowing American use of his military bases, he received large sums of aid supplied by American taxpayers that mostly disappeared into Mobutu's private accounts. In fact, his regime was so corrupt that political scientists developed a new term to describe it: *kleptocracy,* or "government by theft."

With the fall of the Soviet Union and the release of Nelson Mandela, the United States began to see its affiliation with Mobutu Sese Seko as an embarrassment, and in 1990 Congress cut direct aid to Zaire and supported efforts to democratize the country. Those efforts failed for two reasons. First, the political opponents of Mobutu were themselves bitterly divided. As in the early days of the Congo, most politicians represented regions and ethnic groups rather than ideas or policies. Second, a destabilizing shock wave hit the Congo in the wake of one of the most tragic incidents of the last decade of the twentieth century: the Rwandan genocide.

The Rwandan genocide is often presented as having "tribal" or "ethnic" roots, but that is not quite accurate. All Rwandans, Hutu as well as Tutsi, speak the same language, participate in the same culture, and mostly share a common Roman Catholic faith. As colonial rulers, however, the Belgians had sharply differentiated the two groups. Colonial officials favored the Tutsi, giving their children preferred access to European education. These policies generated resentments that surfaced at independence in 1960, when previously disenfranchised Hutu took power and expelled many Tutsi from the country. By the 1980s these Tutsi exiles had organized a rebel army in neighboring Uganda.

The tense situation exploded in early 1994, when a plane carrying the Rwandan president was shot from the sky. His death triggered extremist Hutu leaders to unleash genocidal attacks, primarily on Tutsi but also on moderate Hutu who had worked for peace. Within a few months nearly a million people were brutally slaughtered, many cut with machetes, while another million fled to neighboring countries. The United Nations peacekeeping force that had been stationed in Rwanda lacked sufficient support from the United States and France to effectively intervene.

As a Tutsi army entered the country and established a new government, many of the Hutu extremists who had perpetrated the horrible violence fled to refugee camps in neighboring Zaire. By this time Mobutu was old and sick and no longer able to hold the country together. As in the early 1960s, Zaire (which restored the name Congo in 1997) fractured along ethnic and regional lines. As the twentieth century ended, the alternative to Mobutu's authoritarian rule was not freedom but a state verging on anarchy, with multiple militias preying on helpless civilians with a violence reminiscent of the days of King Leopold (see Chapter 26). Neighboring African countries compounded the problem by sending in armies to back either the government or various rebel factions.

Although the "new world order" of democracy and civil rights did not arrive in Zaire, after 1995 Rwanda did make strides toward restoring peace and civility. It was further south that the dream of African democracy rising from the ashes of Cold War conflict came closer to fulfillment.

South African Liberation

For many years little hopeful news reached Nelson Mandela in prison. Successive National Party governments became more and more extreme in their definition and application of apartheid, as the government oversaw a "Bantu education" system that prepared blacks only for the most menial jobs. Residential segregation was strictly enforced: the pass law system made it illegal for blacks to be in "white" areas unless they could prove they were there for employment. Meanwhile, white South Africans enjoyed a First World standard of living.

To complete the racial separation, the South African government developed what it called the system of **Bantustans.** Spokesmen for apartheid argued that the Tswana, Zulu, Xhosa, and other peoples did not belong to a common South Africa but to "tribal" enclaves (Bantustans) where they should seek their rights. The Bantustan system was developed on the foundation of the old "native reserves," where inadequate access to land had long forced blacks to take whatever work they could get in white-controlled cities and mines. According to apartheid, these impoverished and scattered territories would form the basis for independent "nations." In reality, the Bantustans were simply a device to divide Africans and deprive them of any hope for rights in a unified South Africa.

While many ANC leaders languished in jail and others left South Africa to seek foreign allies for their cause, in the 1970s a new generation of leaders emerged. The Black Consciousness Movement was led by Steve Biko, who argued that black South Africans faced not only the external challenge of apartheid but also an inner challenge to surmount the psychological damage it caused. The first step toward liberation, Biko said, was for blacks to eliminate their own sense of inferiority.

Many black South African youths heeded his call. In 1976 the assertiveness of this new generation became clear in the **Soweto Uprising,** in which black students launched a large, well-coordinated protest against their inferior education. When marchers refused an order to disband, police fired into the crowd, killing dozens of children. As protests spread across the country, apartheid authorities responded with their usual harsh tactics. But this time resistance endured. Black consciousness stayed alive in the Soweto generation even after 1977, when Steve Biko's jailers beat him to death.

By 1983 black trade unions, church groups, and student organizations had formed a nationwide United Democratic Front. Many black children boycotted the apartheid schools, instead growing up on the increasingly violent streets. Some in the resistance movement were willing to take extreme action, especially against blacks accused of collaborating with apartheid: accused traitors sometimes had tires put around their necks and set ablaze. Nelson Mandela's own wife, Winnie Mandela, was implicated in the violence. In 1986 the government declared a state of emergency and sent the army into the black townships to restore order.

Outside South Africa, many argued that economic sanctions should be used to force the government into meaningful negotiations. College students in the United States and Britain played an important role in the divestment movement, demanding that their institutions sell off investments in companies that did business in South Africa. In 1986 the U.S. Congress passed a comprehensive sanction bill limiting trade with and investment in South Africa. President Reagan, viewing the South

• **Bantustans** Term used by apartheid planners for "tribal regions" in which Africans, denied citizenship in a common South Africa, were expected to live when not working for whites. They were not internationally recognized and were later reabsorbed into democratic South Africa.

• **Soweto Uprising** (1976) Youth demonstrations in South Africa that were met with police violence. The Soweto Uprising brought a new generation of activists, inspired by Steve Biko's Black Consciousness Movement, to the forefront of resistance to apartheid.

🔳 **Soweto Uprising**   In 1976 schoolchildren in South Africa protested the compulsory teaching of the Dutch-based Afrikaans language in their schools. When police fired into the crowd, made up mostly of teenagers, hundreds were killed and thousands injured. The Soweto generation played a central role in bringing down apartheid over the next fifteen years.   (Bettman/Corbis)

African government as an ally against communism, vetoed the bill. Responding to popular pressure, Congress overrode that veto to impose harsh penalties on the apartheid regime.

Feeling the pressure, the South African government offered to release Mandela if he renounced the ANC and all political activity. His daughter Zindzi read his response at a packed soccer stadium: "I will remain a member of the African National Congress until the day I die. . . . Your freedom and mine cannot be separated. I will return."[2] Then, as violence spread and sanctions undermined an already weak economy, the decline of the Soviet Union changed the global context of apartheid. The South African government's argument that Mandela and the ANC represented a front for a Soviet-backed communist state being no longer credible, in 1990 South African president F. W. de Klerk granted Mandela an unconditional release and began serious negotiations.

Many dangers had to be overcome before elections were held in 1994. Some white extremists threatened violence, and some African politicians used appeals to ethnicity to try to secure their own bases of power. But in the end the transition to democracy was more peaceful than anyone could have dreamed ten years earlier.

Truth, Justice, and Human Rights

When gross human rights violations have been committed, how do democratizing societies balance their quest for peace and reconciliation with the need for accountability and justice? This was a pressing issue in South Africa, where a Truth and Reconciliation Commission (TRC) met from 1995 to 1998. The TRC offered the possibility of amnesty to those who gave honest testimony about violent acts they committed in support of or in opposition to apartheid.

The TRC had its critics. For example, the widow and family of Steven Biko were outraged when the commission gave his murderers amnesty, complaining that there could be no true "reconciliation" without a real judicial process. For many in the world community, however, the TRC offered a model of how a society might move forward from a difficult past without becoming mired in vengeance and retribution.

Guatemala's Historical Clarification Commission was structured in a similar way, with a mandate "to preserve the memory of the victims, to foster a culture of mutual respect and observance of human rights and to strengthen the democratic process." As in South Africa, some Guatemalans felt their commission had helped the country put its brutal past behind it, while others would have preferred a more punitive process that punished more human rights violators.

A different model is the use of national or international courts to pursue charges of "crimes against humanity." That model was applied by the International Criminal Tribunal of the Rwandan Genocide and the Special Tribunal for Cambodia. The Cambodian tribunal will hold to account leaders of the Khmer Rouge government, who, from 1975 to 1979, implemented an extreme form of communism that resulted in more than one million deaths.

Like Pol Pot, the Khmer Rouge leader, and Augusto Pinochet, the former Chilean dictator, former Serbian leader Slobodan Milosović died before his prosecution for war crimes was completed. In 2008, however, former Serbian general Radovan Karadžić was captured and deported to the Netherlands to face charges for atrocities he allegedly committed during the dissolution of Yugoslavia in the 1990s. The Netherlands has long been home to international legal organizations, and in 2002 the International Criminal Court (ICC) was added to their number. The idea was to regularize the prosecution of crimes against humanity, but the status of the ICC declined when the United States and the People's Republic of China did not recognize its authority.

Thus far there has been no attempt to create an international equivalent to South Africa's Truth and Reconciliation Commission. Yet the model stands as a useful alternative for situations where forgiveness rather than retribution is the path most likely to balance the need for justice with the requirements of peace.

CL Primary Source:
The Rivonia Trial Speech to the Court
Read how Nelson Mandela defended himself against charges of treason before an all-white South African court in 1964.

Mandela was easily elected president, and the ANC became the dominant political force in the new South Africa.

True to the words he had spoken at his trial in 1964, Mandela emphasized the inclusiveness of his government. South Africa, christened the "rainbow nation," had a new flag, a new sense of self-identity, a multiracial Olympic team, and one of the world's most democratic constitutions. A Truth and Reconciliation Commission was charged with bringing to light the abuses that had occurred under apartheid, offering amnesty to those who acknowledged politically motivated crimes. (See the feature "World History in Today's World: Truth, Justice, and Human Rights.")

But if this was the story of a new dawn for South Africans, it was also clear that the legacies of racism would take a long time to overcome, especially deeply rooted inequalities in education and income. A severe crime wave and the rapid spread of HIV/AIDS posed difficult challenges for the Mandela administration. But at least all South Africans were empowered to help in finding solutions.

Enduring Challenges in the Middle East

Throughout the twentieth century the Middle East had been one of the most politically unsettled regions in the world, its tensions magnified by the area's strategic importance as a source of the fossil fuels demanded by the global economy. Local ethnic and religious rivalries combined with the involvement of external powers to create a combustible situation.

The Iranian Revolution of 1979 was of great historical import. For the first time in the postcolonial era, a state would be ruled under a constitution derived explicitly from Islamic law and tradition. Iran provided inspiration to **Islamists** (also referred to as Muslim fundamentalists) throughout the Middle East and across the Muslim world. The path toward a just society, Islamists argued, was not through absorption of Western influences and modernity but through a return to the guiding precepts of their religion. It was an explicit rejection of the secular ideologies that had dominated nineteenth- and twentieth-century global political discourse.

The rise to power of the Islamists in Iran, and their increasing influence elsewhere, accelerated existing conflicts in the Middle East. Regimes founded on the principles of secular Arab nationalism, such as Egypt, Syria, Iraq, and Jordan, were threatened by the popular appeal of this new ideology. The Iranian Revolution also provided inspiration and support for Islamist revolutionaries in Afghanistan.

Meanwhile the Israeli-Palestinian conflict endured. In spite of occasional signs of progress toward compromise, the late twentieth century saw no resolution to this problem. But it seemed impossible that any meaningful "new world order" could be constructed without one.

• **Islamists** Muslims who believe that laws and constitutions should be guided by Islamic principles and that religious authorities should be directly involved in governance.

CL Primary Source: Islamic Government *Learn why the future leader of Iran called for the establishment of new governments along conservative religious lines.*

Iran and Iraq

In the 1950s the power of the shah in Iran had been confirmed and augmented through American intervention (see Chapter 30). The shah used oil money flowing into Iran to modernize the country while his secret police kept a tight rein on the political opposition, especially as dissent increased in the 1970s. Opposition to the shah came from many directions: students, workers, and increasingly well-organized religious leaders who accused him of promoting decadent Western values and serving as a tool of U.S. power.

With riots and demonstrations spreading, the shah fled to the United States early in 1979. At the same time, Iran's most revered religious leader, the **Ayatollah Khomeini** (1902–1989), returned from exile in Paris. Khomeini had an organizational advantage over other political contenders because his authority was recognized by most of the ninety thousand members of the Shi'ite *ulama* (oo-leh-MAH), or community of religious scholars. Some of these scholars argued that while the ulama should advise political authorities on proper Islamic practice, they should not themselves wield governmental power. But Khomeini envisioned a tighter connection between religious and governmental authority. Though the radicals who seized the American Embassy in Teheran and held its employees hostage were motivated more by nationalism than by religion, they responded to Khomeini's assessment of the United States as "the great Satan."

Under Iran's new constitution, adopted in a 1979 referendum, the president and parliament were subject to strict oversight by a council of Islamic legal experts. A Ministry of Islamic Guidance was formed to supervise conformity with the new legal system, and vigilante groups patrolled the streets enforcing regulations on

• **Ayatollah Khomeini** (1902–1989) Shi'ite cleric who led the Islamic Revolution in Iran in 1979 and became Supreme Leader of the Islamic Republic of Iran.

Islamic dress. The schools, which had been primarily secular under the shah, now emphasized religious education.

After Iraq invaded Iran, a surge of nationalism further consolidated support for Khomeini's government. The political divide between the two countries also had religious overtones. While the vast majority of Iranians are Shi'ites, in Iraq under Saddam Hussein a Sunni minority ruled over a Shi'ite majority, as they had done since the days of the Ottoman Empire (see Chapter 17). During eight years of brutal fighting (1980–1988), echoing World War I in the use of heavily entrenched positions, as many as a million people died; Iranian civilians and soldiers also suffered terribly when the Iraqi army illegally used chemical weapons.

As the war dragged on, Iran's economic problems became acute. Starved of investment capital, the economy foundered. By the 1990s employment prospects for Iran's growing population of graduates were bleak, and dissatisfaction with the regime was growing. Even with the election of a moderate reformist candidate as president in 1997, ultimate power still rested with the religious leaders who had inherited Khomeini's authority after his death in 1989.

After reaching a stalemate with Iran, Saddam Hussein turned his expansionist ambitions toward Kuwait, a small, oil-rich state on the Persian Gulf. Hussein considered Kuwait part of Iraq's rightful patrimony, taken away from Baghdad's control by the British in 1919, and accused the Kuwaitis of using slanted pumps to reach below Iraqi soil and steal its oil. Guessing that the United States would not oppose him for fear of empowering Iran, Hussein sent his troops into Kuwait in the summer of 1990.

Though the United States had supplied Iraq with military aid during the war with Iran, President George H. W. Bush reacted to Hussein's gambit by forging an international coalition against him. In the past, Hussein might have tried to counterbalance the United States by seeking an alliance with the Soviet Union, but that option no longer existed. Early in 1991 the **Persian Gulf War** began with the devastating bombing of Baghdad by the United States, while troops from many

● **Persian Gulf War**
(1991) War that occurred when an international coalition led by the United States expelled Iraqi forces from Kuwait. Iraq was not invaded, and Saddam Hussein remained in power.

🔲 **Kuwait Oil Fields**
In 1991, near the end of the Persian Gulf War, retreating Iraqi soldiers set fire to Kuwait's oil fields, causing significant environmental damage. That damage was compounded when the Iraqis purposely dumped hundreds of millions of barrels of oil into the Gulf. (Nicolas Kamm/ AFP/Getty Images)

countries swiftly liberated Kuwait. Hussein's army melted away under the onslaught, many killed by aerial bombardment. The path to Baghdad was open, but the Bush administration calculated that removing Hussein was too risky given the delicate Middle Eastern balance of power. As the Americans withdrew, Hussein brutally crushed a rebellion in the largely Shi'ite south.

Hussein's regime, though left intact, was subjected to harsh United Nations sanctions intended to force further disarmament. The burden of sanctions, however, fell on the common people rather than the governing elite, and officials in the West grew skeptical about Hussein's disarmament reports. Consequently, some in Washington began to reconsider the wisdom of having left the regime in power. The "new world order" promised by President George H. W. Bush in the wake of the successful invasion of Iraq had yet to emerge.

Afghanistan and Al-Qaeda

Beginning in 1993, the administration of a new U.S. president, William Jefferson Clinton (b. 1946), was increasingly concerned about Afghanistan. In the aftermath of the Soviet withdrawal, Afghanistan had come under the control of an Islamist group known as the Taliban that imposed a legal system even harsher than that of neighboring Iran. Women especially suffered; education for girls was eliminated completely. Joining the Afghani mujahaddin were other Muslims who entered the fight against the Soviets in the 1980s inspired by the call to holy war. After the Soviet withdrawal, many of them returned home to places like Egypt and Saudi Arabia determined to bring Islamic revolution to their own societies. Others found refuge under the Taliban.

The most notorious was **Osama bin Laden** (b. 1957), a member of a rich and powerful Saudi family. Though formerly allied with the United States against the Soviets, Osama bin Laden saw the Americans as the leading power in a global system where the West played on Arab and Muslim disunity to prop up illegitimate and exploitative regimes in return for a flow of cheap oil. Bin Laden and his followers in al-Qaeda (el–ka-aye-dah) were willing to use terrorism to advance their cause, as shown by attacks on American embassies in the East African nations of Kenya and Tanzania in 1998. In retaliation, the Clinton administration bombed southeastern Afghanistan in an unsuccessful attempt to kill Osama bin Laden and destroy al-Qaeda's base of operations.

The link between extreme versions of Islamist theology and international terrorism had been made. While only a minority of the world's Muslims believed in the establishment of Islamic states or condoned violence against civilians in the name of jihad, some were proud to see someone standing up to the forces they blamed for their social, political, and economic ills. The unresolved Israeli-Palestinian issue added fuel to those flames.

• **Osama bin Laden** (b. 1957) Saudi Arabian leader of the Islamist group al-Qaeda whose goal is to replace existing governments of Muslim countries with a purified caliphate.

CL **Primary Source:** Declaration of Jihad Against Americans Occupying the Land of the Two Holy Mosques *Read a speech given by Osama bin Laden to his followers in Afghanistan, and soon published worldwide.*

The Israeli-Palestinian Conflict

A vicious cycle of violence rocked Israel and the occupied Palestinian territories in the 1970s and 1980s. Israel kept the territories it had occupied during the Six-Day War of 1967 (see Chapter 30), arguing that continued control of these territories, especially on the West Bank of the Jordan River and in Gaza, was necessary to ensure security. Some Israelis, however, believed that these lands, as part of the ancient Hebrew kingdom, should be permanently annexed. The conservative Likud (lih-kood) Party, in power for much of the period after 1977, sponsored the construction of Jewish settlements on Palestinian land as a first step toward permanent control. With half of the land on the West Bank given over to planned settlement, return of the territory to its Arab inhabitants began to seem almost impossible (see Map 31.2).

The Palestine Liberation Organization (PLO), an umbrella organization of resistance groups under the leadership of Yasir Arafat (1929–2004), felt justified in using any means to resist the Israeli occupation, including terrorist attacks on civilians. In 1982, Israel invaded Lebanon to root out the bases from which they faced constant attacks and to drive out the PLO, which had its headquarters in Beirut. Israel paid a high price for this action, as the international community was horrified by the savage attacks on Palestinian refugee camps by Lebanese militias allied with Israel. Support for Islamist organizations grew in both Lebanon, with the increasing influence of Hezbollah ("Party of God"), and in Palestine, where Hamas (the "Islamic Resistance Movement") arose as an alternative to the secular PLO.

Violence flared in Palestine in 1987 with the beginning of the first *intifada*, "ceaseless struggle," against the Israeli occupation of Gaza and the West Bank. The Israelis responded to this mass uprising with new security regulations that severely hampered Palestinian mobility. Even as the intifada and the harsh Israeli response increased tensions on the ground, however, diplomatic initiatives were bearing some fruit.

In 1991, under European and American sponsorship, Israeli and Palestinian diplomats met to discuss possibilities for compromise, and in 1993 the Oslo Accords laid out a mutually agreed-upon "road map" for peace based on the idea of two separate and secure nations living side by side. President Clinton then invited Yasir Arafat (yah-seer ahr-ah-fat) and the Israeli prime minister Yitzhak Rabin (yit-shak rah-BEEN) to Washington, where the two men, formerly implacable enemies, shook hands

■ Hope for Middle East Peace This 1993 handshake between Israeli prime minister Yitzhak Rabin and Yasser Arafat, chairman of the Palestine Liberation Organization, gave the world hope for a Middle East peace. However, negotiations for an Israeli-PLO peace accord, mediated by U.S. president Bill Clinton, proved unsuccessful. Some Israelis and their allies regarded Arafat as nothing more than a terrorist, and Rabin was later assassinated by an Israeli extremist for his role in the negotiations. (© Reuters/Corbis)

Map labels and annotations:

BULGARIA · Black Sea · RUSSIA · KAZAKHSTAN · UZBEKISTAN

Soviet occupation, 1979–1989
U.S. aid to rebels, 1980s
International and Northern Alliance
forces defeat Taliban, 2001

CHINA · GEORGIA · ARMENIA · AZERBAIJAN · Caspian Sea · TURKMENISTAN

Ankara · TURKEY

Mazar e Sharif · Kabul · AFGHANISTAN · Islamabad

U.S. troops, 1958, 1983–1984

Tigris R. · Euphrates R. · CYPRUS · Crete · SYRIA · Kirkuk · Tikrit · Tehran · Herat

Mediterranean Sea · LEBANON · Damascus · Fallujah · Baghdad · IRAN

U.S. arms sales, 1955–1978:
$20.8 billion
Shah overthrown, 1979
American hostages taken,
1979–1981

Kandahar · Quetta · PAKISTAN · Indus R.

Principal center of al-Qaeda
activity, 2004–

ISRAEL · Tel Aviv · Amman · IRAQ · JORDAN · Basra

Cairo · LIBYA · EGYPT · KUWAIT · Kuwait · Persian Gulf · INDIA · Karachi

U.S. and allies launch
First U.S.-Iraq War, 1991

U.S. arms sales, 1980s,
during Iran-Iraq War
Iraq invades Kuwait, 1990
Second U.S.-Iraq War, 2003

Manama · BAHRAIN · QATAR · Doha · Dubayy · Abu Dhabi · Muscat · Strait of Hormuz

Riyadh · SAUDI ARABIA · UNITED ARAB EMIRATES

Aswan Dam · Red Sea · Tropic of Cancer · Nile R.

Al-Qaeda headquarters,
1992–1996

SUDAN · Mecca · OMAN · Arabian Sea

Oil embargo, 1973
Source of 17% of U.S. oil imports
in 1975
Largest buyer of U.S. arms, 1978

ERITREA · Sana · YEMEN · Mukalla · Aden · Gulf of Aden · Socotra (Yemen)

Bombing of USS *Cole*
by al-Qaeda, 2000

DJIBOUTI · Djibouti · ETHIOPIA · SOMALIA

U.S. troops assist in relief of
famine, 1992–1993.
U.S. troops withdrawn, 1994.
U.S.-backed Ethiopian invasion
removes Islamist government,
2006

INDIAN OCEAN · Mogadishu

Members of the Organization of
Petroleum Exporting Countries
(OPEC)

Oil fields

0   250   500 Km.
0   250   500 Mi.

Arab-Israeli Conflict inset legend:

Jewish state after UN partition
of Palestine, 1947

Israel after War of 1948–1949

Area controlled by Israel after
Six-Day War, 1967

Israeli-occupied area after
Yom Kippur War, 1973

By Egyptian-Israeli agreements of 1975 and
1979, Israel withdrew from the Sinai in 1982.
In 1981 Israel annexed the Golan Heights.
Through negotiations between Israel and
the PLO, Jericho and the Gaza Strip were
placed under Palestinian self-rule, and Israeli
troops were withdrawn in 1994. In 1994
Israel and Jordan signed an agreement
opening their borders and normalizing their
relations.

LEBANON · Beirut · Damascus · SYRIA · GOLAN HEIGHTS · Haifa · Sea of Galilee · Jordan R.

Mediterranean Sea · Tel Aviv · ISRAEL · Jerusalem · WEST BANK · Amman · Dead Sea · Gaza · JORDAN

EGYPT · Cairo · Suez · Port Said · Suez Canal · Nile R. · SINAI PENINSULA · Elath · Gulf of Suez · Gulf of Aqaba · SAUDI ARABIA · Sharm el-Sheikh · Red Sea

ARAB-ISRAELI CONFLICT

MAP 31.2

Middle East Oil and the Arab-Israeli Conflict   Not all Arabs and Arab states benefit from Middle Eastern oil reserves, which are highly concentrated in Arabia and the Persian Gulf. Farther west, Israel, born into a state of war when attacked by its Arab neighbors in 1948, ruled over significant Palestinian populations after taking the West Bank from Jordan and the Gaza Strip from Egypt during the Six-Day War in 1967. Whatever their other disagreements, Arabs have been unified in their denunciation of the Israeli occupation of the West Bank.

Interactive Map

before a worldwide television audience. As in South Africa, the post–Cold War climate seemed to provide the possibility of a new beginning. Talks continued even after an Israeli opponent of negotiations assassinated Prime Minister Rabin in 1995.

The climax of the Israeli-Palestinian negotiations came in 2000 when Clinton hosted Arafat and another Israeli prime minister, Ehud Barak, for direct negotiations. Barak made a better offer than the Palestinians had ever received, promising to return 90 percent of the West Bank to control of a new Palestinian state. Arafat refused the deal, refusing to compromise on the right of Palestinian refugees to return to lands within Israel from which they had fled in 1948. Entering the twenty-first century, no way had been found out of this impasse.

The Economics of Globalization

With the fall of the Soviet Union and the Second World socialist economy, the post–World War II process of globalization took a huge leap forward. With a few exceptions (such as Cuba and North Korea, where state-dominated models continued under communist regimes), free trade led to unprecedented growth and international economic integration. Some Asian economies surged, with Taiwan, South Korea, and Singapore, the so-called "Asian Tigers," leading the way. Overcoming the disruptions of the Cultural Revolution (see Chapter 30), the People's Republic of China became the world's fastest-growing economy by adopting market principles. Likewise India embraced the market, purging old socialist and bureaucratic institutions to achieve stunning rates of growth (see Chapter 32).

The global position of western Europe was consolidated when the European Economic Community (see Chapter 30) was transformed into the European Union (EU). By the late 1990s the EU, expanding into the former Soviet sphere, represented a market larger than that of the United States. Along with China and the United States, the European Union constituted one of the three major centers of the global economy. At the same time, some pointed to the increasing inequality of economic globalization. Both within nations and between them, the benefits of economic growth were not equally shared, and an increasing gap emerged between the global haves and have-nots.

Japan and the "Asian Tigers" Japan rose quickly from the battering it took in 1945. Under occupation by the United States, Japanese leaders renounced militarism and accepted a democratic constitution drafted for them by American lawyers. The energy and drive that had earlier gone into empire building was now focused on domestic growth. Fukuzawa Yûkichi (see Chapter 24) would have been proud as Japanese products came to surpass those of Europe and the United States in both quality and price.

Several factors facilitated Japanese economic success. American military protection relieved the country of the financial burden of military spending, and close collaboration between the government bureaucracy and large corporations brought planning and coordination to the national economy. Japanese employees, famous for their work ethic, were also willing to accept policies that favored savings and investment over consumption. Both old corporations, like Mitsui, and new ones, like

Sony, developed organizational structures that emphasized long-term loyalty between employer and employee, leading to relatively harmonious labor relations and an absence of strikes.

This system worked much better for men than for women, however. Company loyalty extended beyond work hours, and male employees were usually expected to participate in activities such as golf outings and drinking parties from which women were excluded, except as ornaments and hostesses. Many Japanese housewives lived frustrated lives, raising children while rarely seeing their husbands.

In the 1970s, Japanese success was marked by a rapid increase in automobile exports, especially to the United States. Japanese inroads first came at the lower end of the market, targeting consumers of inexpensive yet well-built cars. Meanwhile, manufacturers in the United States had become complacent, building large vehicles of indifferent quality. After oil prices surged in 1973, demand for the more fuel-efficient Japanese models skyrocketed.

At the same time, the rising price of oil revealed vulnerabilities in the Japanese economy. In addition to being dependent on energy and food imports, Japan was subject to competition from other Asian nations that began to follow the same industrial export strategy with lower labor costs. It responded to the challenge by moving away from heavy industry and emphasizing knowledge-intensive sectors such as computers and telecommunications. Backed by large government subsidies for research and development, and coordinating their efforts with the Ministry for International Trade and Industry, Japanese corporations in the 1980s increasingly focused on such high-profit activities while relocating many of their factories to countries with lower labor costs.

Then, even as American executives studied the Japanese model for business success, the bubble burst. In 1989 the Tokyo Stock Exchange collapsed. Real estate speculation, political corruption, and a crisis in banking caused by bad loans were to blame. To reignite the economy, the government began to emphasize leisure and consumption over savings, hoping that Japanese workers would help the country spend its way out of the crisis. While the Japanese economy stabilized in the 1990s, the major sectors of Asian growth were now elsewhere.

The South Korean government self-consciously emulated the export-oriented industrial model of Japan, including close coordination between the state administration and the emerging Korean *chaebols,* economic conglomerates such as Hyundai. The South Korean government was fiercely anticommunist, led by authoritarian personalities with close ties to the military, and student and worker protests were often met with fatal force by paramilitary police. Then in 1988, with South Korea preparing to host the Summer Olympics and the power of the Soviet Union fading, liberal political reforms were finally instituted, with a peaceful transfer of power between political parties in 1992. The liberal political equation of rule of law, democratic process, and free markets had been achieved.

Taiwan was another Asian country characterized by economic growth and authoritarian government. The island's Guomindang government (see Chapter 30) was dominated by exiles from the mainland who controlled the bureaucracy, the military, and the economy. As in South Korea, popular discontent was growing during the 1980s, especially among those who had been born on the island. By 1988, as part of the general trend toward democratization, free elections had laid the foundation of Taiwanese democracy. Meanwhile, the economy blossomed.

By the 1980s Taiwan, along with South Korea, Singapore, and British-ruled Hong Kong, was counted as one of the "little dragons" of the Asian economy, adding high technology to its existing industrial infrastructure. South Korea became a leader in telecommunications technology, while Taiwan became a major supplier of microchips for the expanding market in home computers. Some analysts began to speak of "Confucian capitalism" as an alternative to the Western model, based on group consensus and hierarchy rather than individualism and class conflict. But no generalizations about Asian capitalism could be made without taking into account the transformation of the People's Republic of China.

Deng Xiaoping's China and Its Imitators

At the start of the nineteenth century China produced about one-third of the world's industrial output. When Mao took power in 1949, after a century and a half of European economic dominance, that percentage had shrunk to less than 3 percent. The country's astonishing economic growth in the last two decades of the twentieth century meant restoring its historical role as the major global center of manufacturing.

That turnabout was closely associated with the policies of **Deng Xiaoping** (1904–1997), one of the pragmatic "experts" who had opposed the excesses of the Great Leap Forward and the Cultural Revolution. After Mao's death and the defeat of the "Gang of Four" (see Chapter 30), Deng put China on a completely new economic path by adopting market incentives. The first step was to allow peasant farmers to use their own plots for private production. Food production surged, increasing state revenues and supporting a larger urban population. Deng was a hero to tens of millions of Chinese farming families, many of whom could afford small luxuries for the first time. When asked how he, a lifelong communist, could justify adopting capitalist market principles, Deng replied: "It does not matter whether the cat is black or white, as long as she catches mice."

The second stage in Deng's reforms was to provide legal and institutional mechanisms for the development of the industrial sector. In the southern region of Guangzhou, near the British-controlled territory of Hong Kong, Deng's administration set up special economic zones where foreign investors were invited to build manufacturing plants. In an embrace of international capitalism unthinkable under Mao, many multinational corporations moved their manufacturing operations to Guangzhou to take advantage of China's cheap labor.

Chinese banks also made funds available to local investors with connections to the Communist Party. The Red Army itself became a major economic power, controlling one of the world's largest shipping lines. As manufacturing spread from Guangzhou throughout eastern and central China, a vast flow of commodities crossed the Pacific destined for American markets. A huge construction boom also hit China's expanding urban areas, attracting millions of rural migrants willing to work for low pay in dangerous conditions. The city of Shanghai became a glittering cosmopolitan center as billboards and traffic jams replaced bicycles and moralistic party posters.

Although Deng Xiaoping resigned from his posts in 1987, he remained a dominant power behind the scenes until his death in 1997. During that period both the costs and benefits of his policies became more and more apparent. A great success was the return of Hong Kong from British to Chinese control. Communist leaders promised that the people of Hong Kong would retain their accustomed civil liberties such as rights of free speech and assembly, but some were suspicious that Beijing would impose its system of open markets and closed politics.

● **Deng Xiaoping**
(1904–1997) Chinese Communist Party leader who brought dramatic economic reforms after the death of Mao Zedong.

The big test to Deng's legacy came in 1989. Student activists, yearning for political change to match the economic transformation of their country, organized the largest antigovernment rally in China's long history, erecting a replica of the Statue of Liberty in the heart of Beijing to symbolize their yearning for freedom. This student-led prodemocracy movement ended with the **Tiananmen Massacre,** when communist authorities sent tanks and troops to clear the square, killing hundreds, perhaps thousands, of student activists and arresting many more. The Chinese Communist Party was taking no chances of losing its political monopoly, perhaps thinking of what had happened in the Soviet Union when its leaders had given in to pressure for reform.

China's economic transformation also created other challenges. Environmental problems multiplied. The gap between the rich and the poor increased dramatically, as did imbalances between wealthier coastal regions and China's interior. As corruption became widespread, rural protests increased among the same peasant population that Mao had made the center of his revolution. Still, whatever their social, political, and environmental byproducts, the economic policies of Deng Xiaoping had raised China to the status of a great power in world affairs. Many Chinese felt that China had returned to its proper historical role after two centuries of humiliation by the Western powers and Japan.

China's comparative advantage in the world economy was its political stability combined with low cost labor. By the 1990s other Asian countries were also able to build up export-oriented manufacturing centers. American consumers hardly even noticed that much of their clothing and other commodities were now produced in places like Thailand, Malaysia, Indonesia, and Vietnam. For much of the twentieth century, nationalist leaders in such places had dreamed of catching up with the West through industrialization. Now it seemed that they, like China, were moving toward that goal.

The nature of the global economy, however, had shifted. Industry had been overtaken by marketing, financial services, and other "knowledge industries" as the highest value-producing activities. Chinese leaders seemed aware of this fact as they worked to develop and borrow high technology as part the country's economic mix. But for many Asian workers, especially in Southeast Asia, industrialization brought little benefit. Young women with few skills other than manual dexterity made up much of the industrial workforce, and child labor was all too common. As global consumers demanded ever-cheaper products, wages fell in China, Southeast Asia, and other industrial economies.

• Tiananmen Massacre Massacre in a public square in Beijing, where, in 1989, students and workers demanded freedom and democracy. On order from the Communist Party, the Chinese military cleared Tiananmen Square with tanks and gunfire.

The European Union

Beginning in the 1980s, western European leaders, especially in France and Germany, began to discuss ways to deepen the level of cooperation already in place throughout the European Economic Community. A European Parliament, with little real authority but great symbolic importance, was elected. Negotiations were also begun to open borders, to create a single internal market free of all tariffs, and to move toward a common European currency. While these negotiations were taking place, the Soviet Union began to dissolve and talk turned to the possibility of incorporating new members from what had been the socialist Eastern bloc.

In 1992 the Treaty on European Union was signed at the Dutch city of Maastricht. It set a date of January 1, 1999, for the introduction of the euro (the EU's currency), limited the amount of public debt that a nation could hold to be

🌐 **MAP 31.3**

The European Union The European Union (EU) developed from the more limited European Economic Community, dominated by France and the Federal Republic of Germany and to which the United Kingdom, Ireland, Denmark, Spain, Portugal, and Greece were added in the 1970s and 1980s. The collapse of the Soviet Union led to a dramatic EU expansion into eastern Germany, central and southeastern Europe, and the Nordic and Baltic countries. Turkey's application for membership has proved controversial, while Russia has resisted the inclusion of Georgia and Ukraine.

admitted to the union, and created a European Central Bank to control monetary policy. Now with a clear timeline toward a common flag and common citizenship, some complained that a European "superstate" run by faceless bureaucrats in Brussels would undermine national sovereignty. Great Britain, Denmark, and Sweden all rejected the euro, refusing to surrender control of their own currencies. But the other basic provisions of the Maastricht Treaty were approved (see Map 31.3).

With an internal market larger than that of the United States, and members who represented complementary economic and human resources, the European Union was a major success, accounting for over 18 percent of global exports by century's end. While each member country benefited from the new relationship, growth rates were especially high in poorer, more agricultural countries: Ireland, Spain, Greece, and Portugal. Spain, Greece, and Portugal, all of which had suffered from authoritarian governments, became modern democracies with significantly more educated populations. Ireland was dubbed the "Celtic Tiger" for its transformation from a largely agricultural society to one based on strong educational foundations and a modern knowledge economy with prowess in high technology.

The European Union arose partly in reaction to the United States. Many Europeans saw the frenetic pace of American society as a threat to their own more leisurely mode of life and to their long-established policies of generous social benefits. In the 1990s, politicians such as Tony Blair in Great Britain and Gerhard Schroeder in Germany, leaders of traditionally socialist parties, advocated a "third way" to economic growth and social stability. Rejecting both the relatively unfettered capitalism of the United States and the inefficiencies of state socialism, they advocated a combination of market incentives and social investment. In France, the government reflected popular feeling when it took advantage of globalization while avoiding a "new world order" of cultural Americanization. (See the feature "Movement of Ideas: Jihad vs. McWorld.")

In spite of such occasional notes of defensiveness, on balance the European Union represented optimism and growth. In 2000 negotiations were under way to bring former Soviet satellites such as Poland, the Czech Republic, and Hungary into the EU, and the possibility of Turkish membership was also being discussed. To some, the idea of bringing predominantly Muslim Turkey into the European Union exceeded the limits of what could be defined as "European," though Turkey's connection with Europe had deep roots (see Chapter 28).

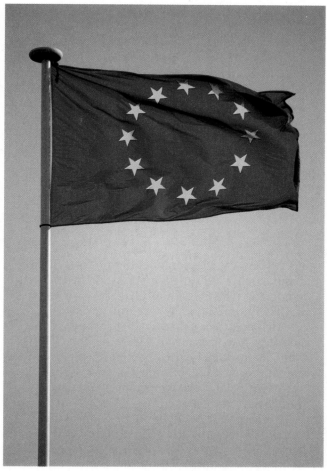

Flag of the European Union
During the 1990s, the flag of the European Union was often flown alongside the national flags of member nations. The twelve stars represent the peoples of Europe regardless of nationality; the circle symbolizes the union of these peoples to achieve a common purpose. (Chris Cheadle/Photographer's Choice RF/Getty Images)

Structural Adjustment and Free Trade in the Third World

As we have seen, the "new world order" based on democracy and free markets had a mixed record in the 1990s. The challenge across much of the world, especially in Africa and Latin America, was to balance the social needs of the population, such as spending on health and education, with economic liberalization policies that required steep cuts in government spending.

During the 1980s many Third World governments had become so indebted that to remain solvent they required loans from the International Monetary Fund

Jihad vs. McWorld

For half a century, all discussions of the global balance of power had been based on Cold War bipolarity. In the 1990s, lively debates took place over what "new world order" would replace that old one. One optimistic author trumpeted the fall of the Soviet Union as "the end point of mankind's ideological evolution and the universalization of Western liberal democracy as the final form of human government."* Another, more pessimistic observer predicted a looming "clash of civilizations."†

As part of this dialogue, Benjamin Barber has explained a complex scenario in which "globalism," which he labels "McWorld," and reactions against those forces, which he calls "Jihad," exist in critical balance with one another. Barber claims that across the world (including the United States) "McWorld" threatens local autonomy. Fearful of globalization, people rally around ethnic or religious differences for self-protection. According to Barber, neither "McWorld" nor "Jihad" is conducive to democracy.

Source: Benjamin Berber, "Jihad vs. McWorld," *The Atlantic Monthly*, March 1992.

Just beyond the horizon of current events lie two possible political futures—both bleak, neither democratic. The first is a retribalization of large swaths of humankind by war and bloodshed . . . in which culture is pitted against culture, people against people, tribe against tribe—a Jihad in the name of a hundred narrowly conceived faiths against every kind of interdependence, every kind of artificial social cooperation and civic mutuality.

The second is being borne in on us by the onrush of economic and ecological forces that demand integration and uniformity and that mesmerize the world with fast music, fast computers, and fast food—with MTV, Macintosh, and McDonald's, pressing nations into one commercially homogenous global network: one McWorld tied together by technology, ecology, communications, and commerce. The planet is falling precipitantly apart AND coming reluctantly together at the very same moment. . . .

Four imperatives make up the dynamic of McWorld:

THE MARKET IMPERATIVE. All national economies are now vulnerable to the inroads of larger, transnational markets within which trade is free, currencies are convertible, access to banking is open, and contracts are enforceable under law. . . . [S]uch markets are eroding national sovereignty—international banks, trade associations, transnational lobbies like OPEC and Greenpeace, world news services like CNN and the BBC, and multinational corporations that increasingly lack a meaningful national identity—that neither reflect nor respect nationhood as an organizing or regulative principle.

THE RESOURCE IMPERATIVE. Every nation, it turns out, needs something another nation has; some nations have almost nothing they need.

THE INFORMATION-TECHNOLOGY IMPERATIVE. Scientific progress embodies and depends on open communication, a common discourse rooted in rationality, collaboration, and an easy and regular flow and exchange of information. . . .

THE ECOLOGICAL IMPERATIVE. We know well enough that . . . Brazilian farmers want to be part of the twentieth century and are burning down tropical rain forests to clear a little land to plough . . . upsetting the delicate oxygen balance and in effect puncturing our global lungs. Yet this ecological consciousness has meant not only greater awareness but

*Francis Fukuyama, "The End of History?" *The National Interest*, Summer 1989.
† Samuel Huntington, "The Clash of Civilizations?" *Foreign Affairs*, Summer 1993.

also greater inequality, as modernized nations try to slam the door behind them, saying to developing nations, "The world cannot afford your modernization; ours has wrung it dry!"

The movement toward McWorld is in competition with forces of global breakdown, national dissolution, and centrifugal corruption. These forces, working in the opposite direction, are the essence of what I call Jihad.

. . . The passing of communism has torn away the thin veneer of internationalism . . . to reveal ethnic prejudices that are not only ugly and deepseated but increasingly murderous. Europe's old scourge, anti-Semitism, is back with a vengeance, but it is only one of many antagonisms. It appears all too easy to throw the historical gears into reverse and pass from a Communist dictatorship back into a tribal state.

Among the tribes, religion is also a battlefield. . . . [T]he new expressions of religious fundamentalism are fractious and pulverizing, never integrating. This is religion as the Crusaders knew it: a battle to the death for souls that if not saved will be forever lost.

The atmospherics of Jihad have resulted in a breakdown of civility in the name of identity, of comity in the name of community. International relations have sometimes taken on the aspect of gang war—cultural turf battles featuring tribal factions that were supposed to be sublimated as integral parts of large national, economic, postcolonial, and constitutional entities.

McWorld does manage to look pretty seductive in a world obsessed with Jihad. It delivers peace, prosperity, and relative unity—if at the cost of independence, community, and identity (which is generally based on difference). The primary political values required by the global market are order and tranquility. . . .

Jihad delivers a different set of virtues: a vibrant local identity, a sense of community, solidarity among kinsmen, neighbors, and countrymen, narrowly conceived. But it also guarantees parochialism and is grounded in exclusion. Solidarity is secured through war against outsiders. And solidarity often means obedience to a hierarchy in governance, fanaticism in beliefs, and the obliteration of individual selves in the name of the group. . . .

QUESTIONS FOR ANALYSIS

▶ How does Barber argue that increasing globalization leads to the development and expansion of the movements he labels as "Jihad"?

▶ In the world today, which forces seem stronger, those of "Jihad" or those of "McWorld"?

• **structural adjustment**
Economic policy imposed by the International Monetary Fund and World Bank on debtor nations, requiring significant cuts in government spending and reduced economic intervention in markets to create conditions for long-term growth.

(IMF) or the World Bank, two institutions that had been set up at Bretton Woods after the Second World War to guarantee global economic stability (see Chapter 29). In what they called a **structural adjustment** program, economists from the IMF and World Bank insisted that before they loaned money or invested in development projects, the recipient governments had to slash spending. Only when state expenditures represented a smaller part of overall economic activity, they argued, could developing countries reach sustainable levels of growth.

In Mexico, structural adjustment meant cutting government subsidies on the price of maize meal. In the long run, economists argued, the "magic of the market" would align production and consumption and lead to greater prosperity. In the short run it meant a sharp rise in the price of tortillas and thus more hungry children. When the East African nation of Tanzania accepted an IMF loan in 1987, it was forced to lay off thousands of teachers to help balance its books, suspending the country's goal to provide universal primary education. Still, advocates of structural adjustment argued that, in the long term, free markets were the only way to create abundance for the people of countries like Mexico and Tanzania.

The economics of liberal free trade also guided the development and passage, in 1994, of the North American Free Trade Association (NAFTA), uniting Canada, the United States, and Mexico in a market even larger than that of the European Union. NAFTA was controversial. In the United States, some commentators worried that the removal of tariffs on Mexican imports would mean the loss of high-paying industrial jobs as manufacturers seeking to pay lower wages moved south of the border. In Mexico, farmers worried that they would be ruined by open competition with U.S. corn farmers, who were heavily subsidized by their government. Then even as previously high-wage industrial jobs moved south, rural Mexicans would flee north because of falling crop prices.

In the southern state of Chiapas, a group of rebels calling themselves Zapatistas (after the great Mexican revolutionary; see Chapter 27) declared "war on the Mexican state" in 1994, with NAFTA as one of their principal grievances. The Zapatistas were part of a global movement of people hoping to reassert collective welfare against the free-market onslaught and locally based cultural and political forces against the wave of globalization. Such efforts would continue into the twenty-first century, but for better or worse, capitalism, with local and regional variations, was now the only game being played in the global economy.

Chapter Review

The world changed in dramatic ways during Nelson Mandela's decades of incarceration. When he walked free in 1990, the Cold War, at its height when he was convicted of treason in 1964, was coming to an end. New possibilities for democracy marked the emerging "new world order," a trend shown by the election of Nelson Mandela as president of South Africa in 1994. The high hopes of that period were only partially fulfilled, however. Global society entered the twenty-first century with no solution to enduring issues such as the Israeli-Palestinian conflict and with new challenges, such as economic globalization, still to be resolved.

What were the major causes of the collapse of the Soviet Union?

The collapse of the Soviet Union in the late 1980s was completely unexpected, yet in retrospect the weaknesses that brought it down are apparent. An upsurge in international commitments and military spending in the 1970s was not matched by equivalent advances in economic productivity, and in the renewed arms race of the 1980s the Soviets could not keep pace with the United States. The invasion of Afghanistan put tremendous strains on Soviet society. The long-suppressed nationalism of non-Russian minorities within the U.S.S.R. and of captive peoples in its eastern European satellites was ready to boil over at a moment's notice. Ironically, it was Mikhail Gorbachev's reform policies that doomed the Soviet Union. Once "restructuring" and "openness" came to Russia, calls for more radical change cascaded throughout the Soviet sphere and Gorbachev was unwilling to use force to stop them.

KEY TERMS

Nelson Mandela (908)

Ronald Reagan (912)

Helsinki Accords (912)

Mikhail Gorbachev (913)

Solidarity (914)

Boris Yeltsin (915)

Bantustans (922)

Soweto Uprising (922)

Islamists (925)

Ayatollah Khomeini (925)

Persian Gulf War (926)

Osama bin Laden (927)

Deng Xiaoping (932)

Tiananmen Massacre (933)

structural adjustment (938)

How successful were free markets and political reforms in bringing stability and democracy to different world regions?

The new nations formed from the old Soviet Union, and the eastern European ones liberated from Moscow's control, had a mixed record of democratization. European nations like Poland, which were liberated through an authentic popular movement, were more successful than the Central Asian ones where authoritarian rulers controlled the process of independence. Globally, the disappearance of Soviet sponsorship for left-wing insurgencies in Africa, Asia, and Latin America created new opportunities for democratization, especially when the United States withdrew its support from authoritarian, anticommunist regimes and backed international efforts at conciliation and democracy. In other areas, such as the Congo, historical legacies of division were so strong that the weakening of authoritarianism brought instability and civil war rather than freedom and democracy.

At the end of the twentieth century, in what ways were major conflicts in the Middle East still unresolved?

Progress toward a "new world order" was most difficult in the Middle East. Although the Israeli occupation of the West Bank and Gaza was explained as a security measure, Israelis began to build permanent settlements, further angering Arab nationalists in Palestine and elsewhere. The international coalition that ousted Saddam Hussein from Kuwait in 1991 overcame some of the divisions within the Islamic world, but only temporarily. Some Arabs became disenchanted with secular nationalism and turned to religion for their political ideals.

What were the major effects of economic globalization?

The economic forces of globalization were relentless. The economies of Japan and the "Asian Tigers" grew at unprecedented rates, and free-market reforms in the People's Republic of China made it, in the 1990s, the world's fastest-growing industrial economy. Both Europe, through the European Union, and the United States, through the North American Free Trade Association, expanded their free trade zones in response to globalization. Both the EU and NAFTA had their critics. Some worried about the potential loss of sovereign decision-making power in their nations when, for example, the euro was adopted as a common currency, and some worried over the possible movement of industrial jobs to low-wage markets like Mexico.

While citizens of wealthy nations debated the pros and cons of globalization, the transition to the new market regime was even more difficult for developing countries. Structural adjustment promised long-term benefits, but in the short term the deregulation of markets often had a negative impact on people's lives. Globalization also affected world culture in ways that left many people uneasy. Entering the twenty-first century, the political, social, cultural, and environmental consequences of globalization would be at the top of the world's agenda.

For Further Reference

Barber, Benjamin. *Jihad vs. McWorld: How Globalism and Tribalism Are Reshaping the World*. New York: Times Book, 1995.

Garthoff, Raymond. *The Great Transition: American-Soviet Relations at the End of the Cold War*. Washington, D.C.: Brookings, 1994.

Hoffman, David. *The Oligarchs: Wealth and Power in the New Russia*. New York: Public Affairs, 2002.

Kagan, Robert. *Of Paradise and Power: America and Europe in the New World Order*. New York: Knopf, 2003.

Kenney, Padaric. *A Carnival of Revolution: Central Europe, 1989*. Princeton: Princeton University Press, 2002.

Kepel, Gilles. *The War for Muslim Minds: Islam and the West*. Cambridge, Mass.: Harvard University Press, 2004.

Mandela, Nelson. *Long Walk to Freedom: The Autobiography of Nelson Mandela*. Boston: Little Brown, 1996.

Marti, Michael. *China and the Legacy of Deng Xiaoping: From Communist Revolution to Capitalist Evolution*. Washington, D.C.: Potomac, 2002.

Smith, Charles D. *Palestine and the Arab-Israeli Conflict*. 6th ed. New York: Bedford/St. Martin's, 2006.

Smith, Peter H. *Democracy in Latin America: Political Change in Comparative Context*. New York: Oxford University Press, 2005.

WEB RESOURCES

Pronunciation Guide

Interactive Maps

MAP 31.1 The Dissolution of the Soviet Union

MAP 31.2 Middle East Oil and the Arab-Israeli Conflict

MAP 31.3 The European Union

Primary Sources

Chapter Objectives

ACE Multiple-Choice Quiz

Flashcards

Websites

The Globalization Website
(http://www.sociology.emory.edu/globalization/ generallinks.html).   From Tufts University, useful links to websites dealing with all aspects of globalization.

Making the History of 1989
(http://chnm.gmu.edu/1989/).   Information on the fall of communism in Europe, including an introductory essay, primary sources, scholar interviews, teaching modules, and case studies.

The Mandela Page
(http://www.anc.org.za/people/mandela/).   Hosted by South Africa's ruling African National Congress party, with links to documents, speeches, photographs, and extensive extracts from the great anti-apartheid leader's stirring autobiography, *Long Walk to Freedom*.

CHAPTER
32

Voyage into the Twenty-First Century

Filmmaker **Mira Nair** (b. 1957) grew up with a variety of cross-cultural influences. Although her family was from the Punjab in India's northwest, she was raised in the different language and culture of the far eastern state of Orissa. She listened to the Beatles and also to the soundtracks from "Bollywood," the Indian film industry centered in Bombay (now called Mumbai). As a student she experienced boarding school in the tranquil foothills of the Himalayas, frequent visits to the bustling streets of Kolkata (Calcutta), and, finally, studies focused on photography and film at Harvard University. Nair now lives a tri-continental life, with a home and office in New York City, a film institute in Kampala, Uganda, and frequent trips to India. While her work deals with global influences, her emphasis is on the local and personal:

(Courtesy Mira Nair)

MIRA NAIR

[In] this post 9/11 world, where the schisms of the world are being cemented into huge walls between one belief and way of life and another, now more than ever we need cinema to reveal our tiny local worlds in all their glorious particularity. In my limited experience, it's when I've made a film that's done full-blown justice to the truths and idiosyncrasies of the specifically local, that it crosses over to become surprisingly universal. . . .

I've seen that the Indian films' influence—specifically that unabashed emotional directness, the freewheeling use of music, that emphasis on elemental motivations and values—is a thread

 This icon will direct you to interactive activities and study materials on the *Voyages* website: **www.cengage.com/history/hansen/voyages1e**

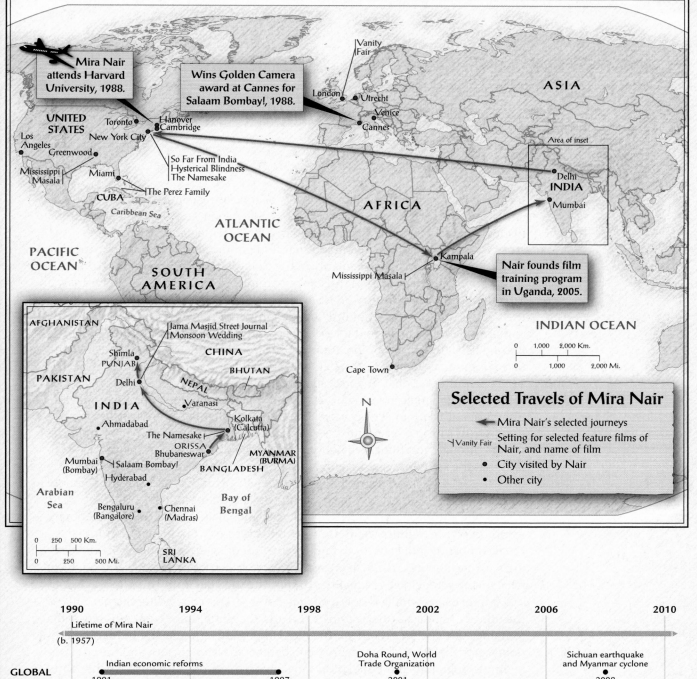

Mira Nair attends Harvard University, 1988.

Wins Golden Camera award at Cannes for Salaam Bombay!, 1988.

Nair founds film training program in Uganda, 2005.

ASIA

Vanity Fair

London · Utrecht
· Venice
· Cannes

Area of inset

· Delhi
INDIA
· Mumbai

UNITED STATES
Toronto ·
Hanover
Cambridge
New York City
Los Angeles
Greenwood

So Far From India
Hysterical Blindness
The Namesake

Mississippi Masala
Miami

The Perez Family

CUBA

Caribbean Sea

ATLANTIC OCEAN

PACIFIC OCEAN

SOUTH AMERICA

AFRICA

Kampala

Mississippi Masala

Cape Town

INDIAN OCEAN

0   1,000   2,000 Km.
0   1,000   2,000 Mi.

Selected Travels of Mira Nair

← Mira Nair's selected journeys

⊢Vanity Fair Setting for selected feature films of Nair, and name of film

· City visited by Nair

· Other city

AFGHANISTAN

Jama Masjid Street Journal
Monsoon Wedding

Shimla ·
PUNJAB
Delhi ·

CHINA

BHUTAN

NEPAL

PAKISTAN

INDIA

Ahmadabad ·

The Namesake

Mumbai (Bombay) ·
Salaam Bombay!
Hyderabad ·

Varanasi ·

Kolkata (Calcutta)

ORISSA
Bhubaneswar ·

MYANMAR (BURMA)

BANGLADESH

Arabian Sea

Bengaluru (Bangalore) ·
· Chennai (Madras)

Bay of Bengal

0   250   500 Km.
0   250   500 Mi.

SRI LANKA

N

1990   1994   1998   2002   2006   2010

Lifetime of Mira Nair
(b. 1957)

GLOBAL

Indian economic reforms
1991   1997

Doha Round, World Trade Organization
2001

Sichuan earthquake and Myanmar cyclone
2008

Kyoto Protocol
1997

September 11 terrorist attacks
2001

Invasion of Iraq
2003

Muhammad Yusuf, Nobel Peace Prize
2006

Wangari Maathai, Nobel Peace Prize
2004

Union of South American Nations (Unasur)
2008

running consistently through every one of my films; even when exploring foreign worlds, I have taken the bones and flesh of those societies and tried to infuse them with the spirit of where I'm from. . . . I find myself applying an Eastern gaze to Western contexts now, and enjoying the reversal.[1]

● **Mira Nair** (b. 1957) Influential New York–based Indian filmmaker and cultural critic, director of *Monsoon Wedding, My Own Country, Salaam Bombay!, Mississippi Masala, The Namesake, Hysterical Blindness, Vanity Fair,* and other films.

If current trends continue, there will likely be increasing commercial and aesthetic cross-fertilization between Hollywood and Bollywood and other global cultural institutions, even as each retains distinctive local elements.

As with cultural influences, economic and political influences are also moving in multiple directions. The bipolarity of the Cold War was followed in the 1990s by the rise of the United States as the sole remaining superpower. In what one analyst calls the twenty-first-century "post-American world," however, the global role of the United States is offset not only by the growth of the European Union and the continuing economic importance of Japan, but also by the rapid development of Brazil, Russia, India, and China, countries that are using their human capacities and natural resources to benefit from globalization.

When international financial markets collapsed in the autumn of 2008, with global capital markets freezing up as a result, the interrelationship of national and international economies was more forcefully highlighted than ever before. Nations across Europe, Asia, and the Americas struggled to stabilize their financial sectors through additional regulation of their economies, and in the process realized that the solution would require greater international coordination. Watching from the sidelines were those billion people left behind by globalization—those who, according to the World Bank, subsist on less than $1 a day.

To one author, India expresses the hopes and challenges of the contemporary world: "No other country matters more to the future of our planet than India. . . . From combating global terror to finding cures for dangerous pandemics, from dealing with the energy crisis to averting the worse scenarios of global warming, from rebalancing stark global inequalities to spurring the vital innovation to create jobs and improve lives—India is now a pivotal player."[2] This concluding chapter will use the films of Mira Nair (meer-uh nah-eer) and the situation of contemporary India to frame a discussion of some of the most important issues facing humanity: economic globalization; global security and democratization; health and the environment; demography and population movement; questions of identity; gender and human rights; and global culture.

Our survey of world history has given us some tools for assessing trends in each of these areas, especially for connecting local developments with broader patterns. Still, we cannot fully understand the most recent past because we cannot see far enough ahead to draw conclusions with the confidence that comes with evidence. Inevitably, then, our conclusions in this final chapter can be only tentative.

Focus Questions

✈ How is globalization affecting the world economy and global security?

✈ What are the most important environmental and demographic trends of the twenty-first century?

✈ To what extent is the world moving forward in gender equality, human rights, and democracy?

●Economic Globalization

The members of the upwardly mobile middle-class Indian family at the heart of Mira Nair's *Monsoon Wedding* (2001) are enthusiastic participants in global consumer culture. Late-model cars clog their New Delhi driveway, the latest electronics fill their home, and cell phones interrupt their conversations. Aditi Verma is conflicted about her engagement. Working as a television journalist, she is used to an independent lifestyle, including a torrid romance with a married producer that comes close to derailing her marriage. The marriage itself, in true Indian fashion, will be anything but private. Hundreds of people, including family flying in from Europe and the United States, will attend the lavish wedding ceremony and banquet. After the family surmounts some obstacles, including confronting a sexually abusive uncle, the marriage finally takes place, a riotous celebration of Punjabi music and culture.

A parallel love story in *Monsoon Wedding* follows the relationship of Dubey, the Vermas' wedding contactor, and Alice, one of their servants. A restless entrepreneur, Dubey shares a modest apartment with his mother, who constantly plies him with stock tips while he arranges deals on his cell phone. The happy, if modest, marriage of Dubey and Alice shows that even those without much education or family connections can find a path to success in India's newly globalized, consumer-focused economy. At multiple levels of society, then, *Monsoon Wedding* presents a positive portrait of twenty-first-century globalization in India.

In 1991 India's finance minister, **Manmohan Singh** (b. 1932), implemented a set of economic reforms that lowered business taxes and relaxed government regulations. Further reforms occurred in 1997 after the Soviet Union collapsed and the world moved toward free markets (see Chapter 31). The results were truly impressive. Annual economic growth rates surged toward 10 percent, and India's steel, chemical, automotive, and pharmaceutical industries, once bound by state regulation, made major strides in national, regional, and global markets. Middle-class families no longer had to spend years on a waiting list to buy a car; now they could choose from multiple models both foreign and domestic and use credit for their purchases. At the same time, India became a major player in the software industry, especially in the late 1990s, when concerns about a possibly devastating "millennium virus"

●**Manmohan Singh** Finance minister (1991–1996) and prime minister of India (from 2004) whose liberal reforms lessened government regulation of the economy, leading to rapid economic growth.

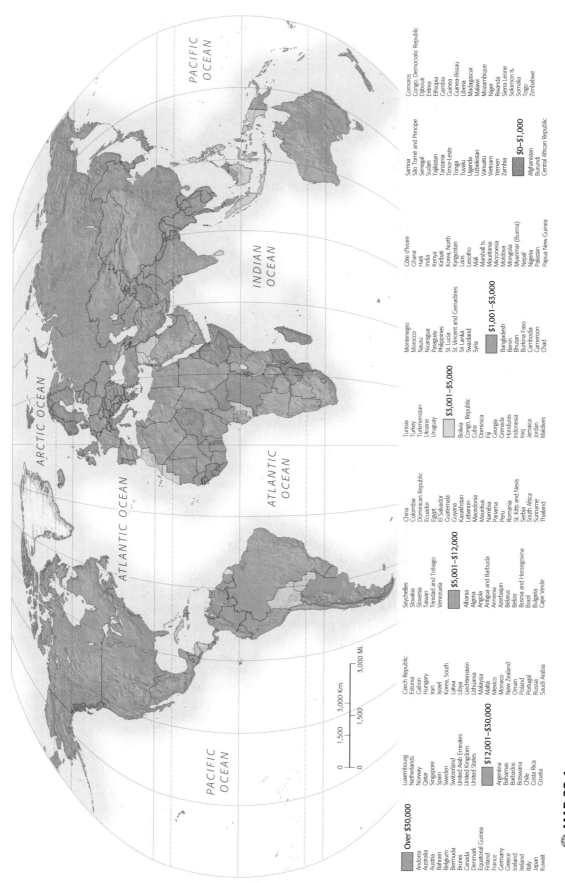

MAP 32.1

Per Capita Income In spite of recent surges in the economies of countries such as India, China, and Russia, the global economy is still dominated by the United States, western Europe, Canada, Australia, and Japan. Per capita income gives only a rough estimate of people's quality of life, however. The United Nations Development Program (UNDP) uses a Human Development Report that takes account of a variety of factors in addition to income—such as education, health care, environmental standards, and gender equality—in its rankings. According to the UNDP, the island nation of Iceland ranks first in human development, Canada fourth, Japan eighth, France tenth, and the United States twelfth.[3]

PACIFIC OCEAN

ARCTIC OCEAN

ATLANTIC OCEAN

INDIAN OCEAN

ATLANTIC OCEAN

PACIFIC OCEAN

0   1,500   3,000 Km.
0   1,500   3,000 Mi.

Over $30,000
Andorra
Australia
Austria
Bahrain
Belgium
Bermuda
Brunei
Canada
Denmark
Equatorial Guinea
Finland
France
Germany
Greece
Iceland
Ireland
Italy
Japan
Kuwait
Luxembourg
Netherlands
Norway
Qatar
Singapore
Spain
Sweden
Switzerland
United Arab Emirates
United Kingdom
United States

$12,001–$30,000
Argentina
Bahamas
Barbados
Botswana
Chile
Costa Rica
Croatia
Czech Republic
Estonia
Gabon
Hungary
Iran
Israel
Korea, South
Latvia
Libya
Liechtenstein
Lithuania
Malaysia
Malta
Mexico
Monaco
New Zealand
Oman
Poland
Portugal
Russia
Saudi Arabia
Seychelles
Slovakia
Slovenia
Taiwan
Trinidad and Tobago
Venezuela

$5,001–$12,000
Albania
Algeria
Angola
Antigua and Barbuda
Armenia
Azerbaijan
Belarus
Belize
Bosnia and Herzegovina
Brazil
Bulgaria
Cape Verde
China
Colombia
Dominican Republic
Ecuador
Egypt
El Salvador
Guatemala
Guyana
Kazakhstan
Lebanon
Macedonia
Mauritius
Namibia
Panama
Peru
Romania
St. Kitts and Nevis
Serbia
South Africa
Suriname
Thailand
Tunisia
Turkey
Turkmenistan
Ukraine
Uruguay

$3,001–$5,000
Bolivia
Congo, Republic
Cuba
Dominica
Fiji
Georgia
Grenada
Honduras
Indonesia
Iraq
Jamaica
Jordan
Maldives
Montenegro
Morocco
Nauru
Nicaragua
Paraguay
Philippines
St. Lucia
St. Vincent and Grenadines
Sri Lanka
Swaziland
Syria

$1,001–$3,000
Bangladesh
Benin
Bhutan
Burkina Faso
Cambodia
Cameroon
Chad
Côte d'Ivoire
Ghana
Haiti
India
Kenya
Kiribati
Korea, North
Kyrgyzstan
Laos
Lesotho
Mali
Marshall Is.
Mauritania
Micronesia
Moldova
Mongolia
Myanmar (Burma)
Nepal
Nigeria
Pakistan
Papua New Guinea
Samoa
São Tomé and Príncipe
Senegal
Sudan
Tajikistan
Tanzania
Timor-Leste
Tonga
Tuvalu
Uganda
Uzbekistan
Vanuatu
Vietnam
Yemen
Zambia

$0–$1,000
Afghanistan
Burundi
Central African Republic
Comoros
Congo, Democratic Republic
Djibouti
Eritrea
Ethiopia
Gambia
Guinea
Guinea-Bissau
Liberia
Madagascar
Malawi
Mozambique
Niger
Rwanda
Sierra Leone
Solomon Is.
Somalia
Togo
Zimbabwe

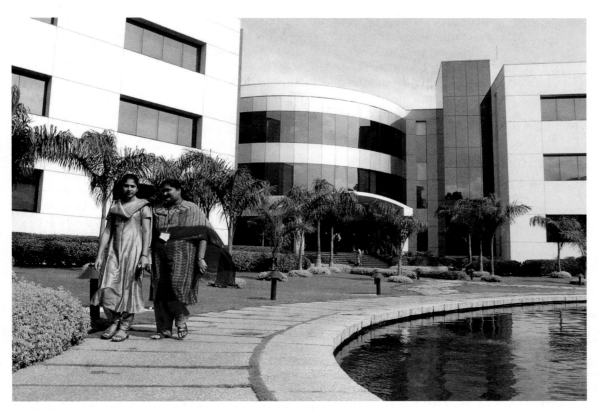

India's High-Technology Sector The southern Indian city of Bangalore is home to the headquarters of software giant Infosys Technologies, which reported over $3 billion in revenue for 2007. The beautiful Infosys campus, and the middle-class lifestyles of its employees, contrast sharply with the conditions faced by the hundreds of millions who have yet to share in the economic dynamism of the New India. (Dibyangshu Sarkar/AFP/Getty Images)

caused many Western companies to seek an inexpensive way to back up their electronic data. Indian firms like Infosys, based in the southern city of Bangalore, became major global players in software and the shining stars of India's new economy.

Such has been the good news for India, the world's largest democracy and one of its emerging economic centers. However, many have been left behind. Hundreds of millions of Indian citizens still live without access to clean water, let alone computers and other consumer products. Is it just a matter of time before those living in desperate poverty see an improvement, or is accelerating inequality a necessary outcome of economic globalization? Data from India, China, Brazil, the United States, and elsewhere show a strong correlation between global economic growth and rising inequality. Some in those countries have argued that, in their haste to liberalize their economies, governments have abandoned regulations to maintain the health and educational needs of their citizens. As one economist argues, "The ancient question of how market forces need to be tempered for the greater good of the economy and the society is now a global one (see Map 32.1)."[4]

Some energy-rich states have been able to control these inequalities by using income from natural resources for social investments such as roads, schools, and hospitals. Prime Minister Vladimir Putin of Russia and President Hugo Chávez of

Venezuela, both of whom challenge the orthodoxy of free-market economists, have been able to use the resources of their expanding energy sectors to provide more public services, such as roads and schools. In Africa, by contrast, wealth in energy-producing countries like Nigeria and Sudan has largely been monopolized by elites, bringing environmental degradation (in Nigeria) and empowering a government-backed genocide (in the Darfur region of Sudan).

India and China, lacking self-sufficiency in energy, have been aggressively pursuing access to African energy resources, extending lines of credit, technical assistance, and trade preferences to African petroleum-producing countries. Meanwhile, in 2008 the growth of India and China helped drive up petroleum prices, past $140 a barrel for the first time in history. While the United States and Brazil have both developed extensive ethanol programs as an alternative to expensive imported petroleum, the diversion of grain production to energy needs has had the unfortunate side effect of worsening world food shortages. In many regions people have had to eat less because of rising food prices resulting from high energy costs.

Global competition has also exposed many more people to the "creative destruction" inherent in capitalism. Rapid innovation renders old skills obsolete, and workers' wages are undercut when people in other countries will do the same work for less. **Outsourcing**—obtaining goods or services from an outside supplier—has entered the economic vocabulary, and here as well India has been a pioneer. Falling telecommunications prices combined with relatively low wages encouraged American firms to move customer service jobs to India. The same process is now affecting other service sectors. Thailand, for example, is building a reputation for its quality health facilities, which charge rates far below those of American health-care providers. (See the feature "Movement of Ideas: The World Is Flat.") While jobs have been outsourced to India and Thailand, talented entrepreneurs and highly educated professionals have left many of the poorer countries to seek opportunity in areas of global growth. This "brain drain" has made it even more difficult for many African nations—already deficient in transportation, communications, and educational infrastructure—to benefit from globalization.

The regional trading blocs that first arose during the 1990s, such as the North Atlantic Free Trade Association (NAFTA), have continued to be important (see Chapter 31). In all regional trade blocs, national interests have had to be balanced with regional goals, leading to controversy and tough bargaining. The United States, Canada, and Mexico all had complaints about NAFTA. The Mexican government, for example, worried that American agricultural subsidies, especially for corn, were making it impossible for their own farmers to compete, while union members in the United States thought that losing industrial jobs to Mexico was too high a price to pay for free trade. Similar concerns about the protection of national interests greeted the ratification of CAFTA—a free trade pact among the United States, the Dominican Republic, and Central American nations—in 2005.

The Common Market of the South, **Mercosur,** is a South American attempt to follow the path of the European Union. Originally founded by Brazil, Argentina, Uruguay, and Paraguay, Mercosur later expanded to twelve member nations. In May 2008, following the European example of using economic integration as a foundation for political cooperation, leaders of the twelve countries signed a treaty establishing the Union of South American Nations (Unasur). Implementation of the Unasur treaty was complicated by long-standing rivalries, however. Tension between Colombia, closely allied with the United States, and Venezuela, where President

outsourcing
Obtaining goods or services from an outside supplier. The term commonly refers to Western companies that contract work to providers in lower-wage markets, lowering their costs and increasing their competitiveness.

Mercosur
The Common Market of the South, a South American regional trade association that was the foundation for Unasur, the Union of South American Nations.

Hugo Chávez accused the United States of interfering in his country's internal affairs, divided Unasur from the start.

The European Union was clearly the most mature and successful of the regional blocs, even as it members haggled over the balance of power between national governments and the European Parliament, as well as over the protection of local interests against continental ones. Significant debates, for example, surrounded the adoption of the euro as a common currency after 1998. States that adopted the euro were willing to sacrifice some degree of national economic control for the trade advantages of a common European currency. (Denmark and the United Kingdom rejected the euro but stayed in the EU.) A significant setback on the road toward greater political integration came in 2008, when the people of Ireland voted against a proposed EU constitution, with many Irish fearful of losing national control over taxation policy and other important domestic decisions.

Even so, European Union membership expanded dramatically in the early twenty-first century, with twelve new countries added between 2004 and 2007 alone—Cyprus, Czech Republic, Estonia, Hungary, Latvia, Lithuania, Malta, Poland, Slovakia, Slovenia, Bulgaria, and Romania—many of them formerly part of the Soviet sphere. The new Balkan states formed from the breakup of Yugoslavia—Serbia, Croatia, Bosnia and Herzegovina, Montenegro, and Kosovo—all applied for EU membership, perhaps offering a path of economic cooperation to dampen continuing political and ethnic tensions. The controversy over Turkey's membership, which would bring the first Muslim-majority country into the union, tested the limits not only of Europe's integrated trade network but also of its identity (see the "World History in Today's World" feature in Chapter 23).

More ambitious than regional agreements was the attempt by members of the **World Trade Organization** (WTO), founded in 1995 by former signatories of the General Agreement on Tariffs and Trade (GATT) to establish rules of trade between member nations, primarily by lowering tariffs and opening markets. Organized opposition to the WTO began at once, and in 1999 critics of globalization traveled to Seattle to make their voices heard. The protestors, a loose alliance of environmentalists and campaigners for social justice, directed their anger not only at the WTO but also at multinational corporations, which, they argued, had the most to gain from the loosening of global trade restrictions. In particular, they objected to corporations avoiding labor protections and environmental regulations. Following the Seattle meeting, anticorporate activists formed a loosely organized confederation, the Global People's Network. Just as labor unions once arose in individual nations to counter-balance the power of industrialists, advocates of the Global People's Network argued for the need to have an international citizens' network to reduce the excesses of multinational corporate power.

The protests did not stop the World Trade Organization from beginning negotiations toward a comprehensive global trade pact at Doha, Qatar, in 2001. The importance of the Doha round of negotiations was magnified when the People's Republic of China, previously excluded from GATT because of perceived unfair trade practices, was accepted for WTO membership. Progress was slow, however, and the agreement remained unsigned. One controversial point was the insistence by member nations on retaining protective tariffs in the agricultural sector of their economies. When the U.S. Congress passed a farm bill in 2008 that continued subsidies and tariffs to protect American agriculture from global competition, it was clear that national politics restrained even the nation with the strongest rhetorical commitment to free trade from following through on the Doha initiatives. The European

• **World Trade Organization** (WTO) Membership organization founded in 1995 to establish rules for international trade, with an emphasis on lowering tariffs and other barriers to the free movement of goods.

CL **Primary Source:** Free Trade and the Decline of Democracy *Read a cogent critique by Ralph Nader, a consumer advocate and political activist, of international free trade agreements.*

The World Is Flat

It's a Flat World, After All" is an influential essay written by Thomas Friedman in 2005. Friedman, a *New York Times* columnist and Pulitzer Prize winner, portrays globalization as an opportunity for India, China, and other parts of the world; however, the technological and educational requirements for success in a "flat world," he argues, present a looming challenge for the United States of America.

Source: Thomas Friedman, "It's a Flat World After All," *New York Times*, April 3, 2005.

I encountered the flattening of the world quite by accident [when] . . . I interviewed Indian entrepreneurs who wanted to prepare my taxes from Bangalore, read my X-rays from Bangalore, trace my lost luggage from Bangalore and write my new software from Bangalore. . . . Nandan Nilekani, the Infosys C.E.O., was showing me his global video-conference room. . . . Infosys, he explained, could hold a virtual meeting of the key players from its entire global supply chain for any project at any time . . . its American designers could be on the screen speaking with their Indian software writers and their Asian manufacturers all at once. . . . Above the screen there were eight clocks that pretty well summed up the Infosys workday: 24/7/365. . . .

Nilekani explained, "[O]ver the last years . . . hundreds of millions of dollars were invested in putting broadband connectivity around the world. . . ." At the same time . . . there was an explosion of e-mail software, search engines like Google and proprietary software that can chop up any piece of work and send one part to Boston, one part to Bangalore and one part to Beijing, making it easy for anyone to do remote development. When all of these things suddenly came together around 2000, Nilekani said, they "'created a platform where intellectual work, intellectual capital, could be delivered from anywhere. It could be disaggregated, delivered, distributed, produced and put back together again—and this gave a whole new degree of freedom to the way we do work. . . ."

This has been building for a long time. Globalization 1.0 (1492 to 1800) shrank the world from a size large to a size medium, and the dynamic force in that era was countries globalizing for resources and imperial conquest. Globalization 2.0 (1800 to 2000) shrank the world from a size medium to a size small, and it was spearheaded by companies globalizing for markets and labor. Globalization 3.0 (which started around 2000) is shrinking the world from a size small to a size tiny and flattening the playing field at the same time. . . . But Globalization 3.0 [is] different in that Globalization 1.0 and 2.0 were driven primarily by European and American companies and countries. But going forward, this will be less and less true. Globalization 3.0 is going to be driven . . . by a much more diverse—non-Western, nonwhite—group of individuals. . . .

"Today, the most profound thing to me is the fact that a 14-year-old in Romania or Bangalore or the Soviet Union or Vietnam has all the information, all the tools, all the software easily available to apply knowledge however they want," said Marc Andreessen, a co-founder of Netscape and creator of the first commercial Internet browser. . . . "As bioscience becomes more computational and less about wet labs and as all the genomic data becomes easily available on the Internet, at some point you will be able to design vaccines on your laptop."

. . . [W]e are now in the process of connecting all the knowledge pools in the world together. We've tasted some of the downsides of that in the way that Osama bin Laden has connected terrorist knowledge pools together through his Qaeda network, not to mention the work of teenage hackers spinning off more and more lethal computer viruses that affect us all. But the upside is that by connecting all these knowledge pools we are on the cusp of an incredible new era of innovation. . . . Only 30 years ago, if you had a choice of being born a B student in Boston or a genius in Bangalore or Beijing, you probably would have chosen Boston, because a genius in Beijing or Bangalore could not really take advantage of his or her talent. They could not plug and play globally. Not anymore. Not when the world is flat, and anyone with smarts, access to Google and a cheap wireless laptop can join the innovation fray. . . . And be advised: the Indians and Chinese are not racing us to the bottom. They are racing us to the top. What China's leaders really want is that the next generation of underwear and airplane wings not just be "made in China" but also be "designed in China. . . ."

Rajesh Rao, a young Indian entrepreneur who started an electronic-game company from Bangalore [said], "We can't relax. . . . That is gone. There are dozens of people who are doing the same thing you are doing, and they are trying to do it better. . . . That is what is going to happen to so many jobs—they will go to that corner of the world where there is the least resistance and the most opportunity. If there is a skilled person in Timbuktu, he will get work if he knows how to access the rest of the world, which is quite easy today. . . ."

. . . There is no sugar-coating this: in a flat world, every individual is going to have to run a little faster if he or she wants to advance his or her standard of living. When I was growing up, my parents used to say to me, "Tom, finish your dinner—people in China are starving." But after sailing to the edges of the flat world for a year, I am now telling my own daughters, "Girls, finish your homework—people in China and India are starving for your jobs."

QUESTIONS FOR ANALYSIS

▶ What are the implications of Friedman's argument for college students in various parts of the world?

▶ How might the developing "flat earth" affect those hundreds of millions of people lacking in economic resources or access to education?

Union has also defended its farm subsidies, to the frustration of less developed countries seeking access to Western markets.

While defenders and opponents of free-market globalization engaged in spirited debate, a soft-spoken Bangladeshi banker named **Muhammad Yusuf** (b. 1940) was thinking of practical solutions to the problems of those left behind in the whirlwind of globalization. Yusuf's Grameen ("Village") Bank pioneered microfinance, lending small amounts of money to village women. The women proved to be trustworthy clients even when they had no collateral to secure the loans, and small investments often led to big returns as the women pooled their resources, energy, and ideas to start new enterprises. The Grameen Bank became a global model, and Yusuf (yuh-soof) won the Nobel Peace Prize in 2006.

The topic of microfinance was overshadowed when, in the autumn of 2008, a fall in global stock markets wiped out trillions of dollars of value. The crisis was precipitated by the collapse of the U.S. mortgage market, taking down some of the country's largest banks and brokerages. As the crisis spread, and as governments around the world struggled to put their own financial houses in order, it became clear that the existing mechanism of international regulation was insufficient. Even the European Union, with its tradition of shared financial planning, had difficulty organizing a common response. It seemed that the Bretton Woods institutions, designed to stabilize the global economy at the end of World War II (see Chapter 29), had become outmoded.

Whatever new international financial agreements may be reached, every nation will still face its own challenges in balancing economic growth and social equity. The social and political potential for progress exists in India, which has a mandate to extend the benefits of its new economy to hundreds of millions of people. If India can reform its state sector and make its operations more open and transparent, use the energies of its civil society, reinvigorate the tradition of social responsibility bequeathed by Mohandas K. Gandhi, harness private philanthropy, and invest in the education of its rural and urban poor, then it might make good on the optimism that lies at the heart of *Monsoon Wedding*.

● Global Security

The events of **September 11, 2001,** when terrorists flew planes into New York's World Trade Center and the Pentagon in Washington, reached deep into the world's consciousness. On that date al-Qaeda operatives (see Chapter 31) hijacked four airplanes in the United States and turned them into weapons of destruction. While two planes brought down both towers of the World Trade Center in New York, another caused extensive damage to the Pentagon, and the fourth plane, perhaps on its way to destroy the U.S. Capitol, fell in a Pennsylvania field. Thousands were killed, and international sympathy for the people of the United States was nearly universal.

As a resident of New York, Mira Nair was deeply affected and seized the opportunity to join in a remarkable international collaboration of eleven directors, each of whom made a short film of exactly eleven minutes, nine seconds, and one extra frame. For her contribution to *11"9'01,* Nair focused on the true story of Mrs. Hamdani, a Pakistani American who lost her son that day. Salman Hamdani was a young

● Muhammad Yusuf (b. 1940) Bangladeshi pioneer of microfinance whose Grameen ("Village") Bank gives small loans to the poor, usually women, to start small enterprises. His bank became a global model for microfinance, and in 2006 he was awarded the Nobel Peace Prize.

Primary Source: Selection from a Roundtable Discussion of Globalization and Its Impact on Arab Culture *An Arab intellectual discusses the challenges and opportunities of globalization for Arab culture.*

● September 11, 2001 Date of the al-Qaeda terrorist attacks on the United States in which two hijacked planes were used to destroy the two towers of the World Trade Center in New York City. Another hijacked plane crashed into the Pentagon, and a fourth fell in a Pennsylvania field.

paramedic who on that morning noticed smoke rising from Lower Manhattan and rushed to help, not pausing to tell his mother or anyone else where he was going; Nair shows his mother's devastating uncertainty when he failed to come home. Salman's remains were later salvaged from ground zero, where he had died rendering assistance to 9/11 victims.

Mrs. Hamdani's fear and pain were amplified by the suspicion of her neighbors. The film shows how previously friendly people on her block began to look at her strangely and turn away when she approached, wondering if her missing son had been involved in the attack. Indeed, the shock of 9/11 caused some Americans to suspect and stigmatize all Muslims, even citizens like Salman Hamdani who were doing their best to take advantage of the country's opportunities. Though not an overtly political filmmaker, Nair clearly was critiquing the racism that surfaced after 9/11.

The status of Muslims in India has also been affected by recent terrorist attacks. Suicide bombers from Pakistan have targeted Indian civilians as part of the ongoing dispute over the northern province of Kashmir, whose status has remained unresolved since partition in 1947 (see Chapter 30). In May 2008 a series of coordinated explosions in the city of Jaipur killed eighty people; Indian authorities suspected that local extremists carried out the bombings with aid from Islamist organizations in Pakistan. The terrorists focused the explosions on a Hindu temple and surrounding markets, perhaps intending to inflame tensions between Hindus and Muslims, and some in India have repeated the mistake of Mrs. Hamdani's neighbors by equating "Muslim" with "terrorist."

The people of India therefore paid close attention when President George W. Bush declared a "war on terror" and then invaded Taliban-controlled Afghanistan in October 2001 and Saddam Hussein's Iraq in April 2003. The invasion of Afghanistan took place against a background of nearly universal sympathy for the people of the United States and a broad global consensus behind a military response. Taliban leaders had given Osama bin Laden sanctuary and ideological support while imposing an extreme version of Muslim law on the Afghani people. Even regimes such as those of Iran, Russia, and China that were generally suspicious of American military expansion supported the move. An international military coalition, working with local anti-Taliban fighters in the Northern Alliance, quickly removed the Taliban from power.

The buildup to the U.S. invasion of Iraq, however, generated considerably more controversy. Unlike in 1991, when his father had assembled a broad international consensus and military coalition to evict Iraqi forces from Kuwait (see Chapter 31), George W. Bush failed to convince most of the world that there was a connection between the harsh, secular authoritarianism of Hussein and the radical Islamism of Osama bin Laden. While some Americans incorrectly believed that Iraq had been involved in the 9/11 attacks, others argued that Afghanistan should be the priority and that Iraq had no connection to al-Qaeda and represented no real threat to the United States. Many Americans, and even more members of the international community, were skeptical over the Bush administration's claims that the Hussein regime was amassing "weapons of mass destruction."

In 2002, United Nations weapons inspectors with access to Iraq had judged that earlier chemical, biological, and nuclear weapons programs were no longer active. U.S. and British intelligence services, however, produced more ambiguous reports on the status of weapons of mass destruction in Iraq, and some Western political leaders concluded that the U.N. inspectors were being deceived. With the support of

CL **Primary Source:** The Last Night *Read a list of instructions meant to be reviewed on September 10, 2001, by the terrorists who attacked the United States the next morning.*

British Prime Minister Tony Blair, President Bush presented a case that Iraq represented an imminent threat: "Facing clear evidence of peril, we cannot wait for the final proof—the smoking gun—that could come in the form of a mushroom cloud." Without United Nations sanction, Bush assembled a "coalition of the willing," invaded Iraq in April 2003, and removed Saddam Hussein from power. (See the feature "Visual Evidence: The Fall of Saddam Hussein.")

The Bush advisers who initiated the Iraq War explicitly rejected the moderate internationalism of the first Bush administration and argued for a more proactive and, if necessary, unilateral policy toward the Middle East. The "new world order" envisioned in the early 1990s by President George H. W. Bush could still be achieved, they argued, but only if the United States took a more aggressive role in bringing democracy to the Middle East. To them, 9/11 offered a rationale for achieving that goal. In their view, Iraq would swiftly become a model of democracy and free enterprise, an inspiration to the people of the Arab world and a bulwark against terrorism.

The reality of Iraq was much more complex. In removing the authoritarian power that previously held the country together, it seemed the United States and Britain had made the country and the region less rather than more secure. By the fifth anniversary of the invasion, over 130,000 U.S. troops were still in Iraq. Almost all the other partners in invasion and occupation had left, and even the British had begun drawing down their troops. Although the Shi'ite majority of the country had political control for the first time in over a thousand years, Iraq remained divided not just between Kurdish, Sunni, and Shi'ite interests but also between armed Shi'ite factions (see Map 32.2). The potential for stability and democracy now rested on hopes for incremental change, not the quick transformation that Bush and his advisers had promised.

While the U.S. government justified the "war on terror" by claiming to support democracy and human rights, it often had the opposite effect. Critics of Bush's policies worried that permanent damage was being done to constitutionally protected civil liberties through such policies as wiretapping without a warrant or court approval and the long-term detention of terrorism suspects without trial. Internationally, the United States seemed to be moving back to its Cold War tradition of supporting foreign governments based on their strategic usefulness rather than their democratic credentials. In 2006 it backed an Ethiopian invasion of Somalia to remove an Islamist government in Mogadishu, embroiling itself, as it had done during the Cold War, in an African conflict with complex ethnic and religious roots. Meanwhile, many governments, including those of Russia and China, borrowed the antiterror rhetoric of Washington to justify crackdowns on dissidents, especially in areas with large Muslim populations, such as the Caucasus region in the southern Russian Federation and China's western Xianjiang province.

The 9/11 terrorists showed the great damage that could be done by small, dedicated groups using minimal technology, while the Iraq War showed once again that sophisticated military forces could have difficulty containing and policing civil uprisings. A frightening realization was the potential for death and destruction that would follow if terrorists did gain access to more deadly biological, chemical, or nuclear weapons. Even if that danger were avoided, nuclear proliferation remained a difficult challenge to global security.

In Europe the threat of nuclear weapons seemed to have diminished after the fall of the Soviet Union. Still, there was reason to be worried that nuclear devices and technology in post-Soviet states might enter the global arms trade and find their way into the hands of extremist organizations or irresponsible governments.

🌐 **MAP 32.2**

Iraq in Transition   After the regime of Saddam Hussein, dominated by Iraq's Sunni Arab minority, fell to U.S.-led forces in 2003, some Sunnis took up arms against the U.S. coalition, independent Shia Arab militias, and the now Shi'ite-dominated Iraqi government itself. By 2007, however, violence abated as an increasing number of Sunni leaders rejected the terrorist tactics of the militants and as the U.S. increased its troop levels. The question remained whether the Iraqi government—with a Shi'ite prime minister, Kurdish president, and Sunni leader of Parliament—could effectively balance the complex regional, religious, and ethnic divisions of the country.

CL Interactive Map

Russian leaders bristled at the expansion of the North Atlantic Treaty Organization into former Soviet satellites such as Poland, pushing back Stalin's defensive buffer against attack from the West (see Chapter 29). The Russian response came with the invasion of independent Georgia in the summer of 2008. Vladimir Putin's resurgent Russia, like the Soviet Union and the tsarist empire before it, regarded the Caucasus Mountain region as part of its "near abroad," where Russian strategic interests must be paramount. The invasion was seemingly intended as a lesson not only to Georgia, but to Ukraine and other former Soviet republics looking west and contemplating membership in the North Atlantic Treaty Organization and the European Union.

   Russian anxiety over control of its borders had been heightened in 2007 when the United States announced plans to station antimissile defenses in eastern Europe, purportedly to contain a future Iranian nuclear threat but also with the capacity to shoot down Russian missiles. The nuclear threat was even more worrisome along the tense border between India and Pakistan. Both nations (along with Israel) have developed and tested such devices while refusing to sign the international Treaty on the Non-Proliferation of Nuclear Weapons. In 2007 the Bush administration, anxious to maintain strong relations with India, agreed to a compromise that would allow the transfer of civilian nuclear technology to New Delhi in spite of the potential conversion of that technology to military purposes. At the same time, the United States drew a firm line against Iran's nuclear program. While Teheran claimed merely to be advancing its civilian energy potential, President Bush argued that Iran was

THE FALL OF SADDAM HUSSEIN

During the 2003 invasion of Iraq, U.S. networks and the cable news stations used patriotic slogans and images in their coverage, often repeating the official terminology used by the Bush administration without critical comment. Featuring red, white, and blue flag motifs in their graphics, they referred to the "shock and awe" strategy of the war's initial phase, explained that the invasion was part of the "war on terror," and referred to the war as "Operation Iraqi Freedom."

Media coverage in the Arab world was quite different. Here the U.S. military was more likely to be presented as an army of occupation rather than as one of liberation, and reporters focused on civilian casu-alties and suffering. The contrast in coverage between U.S. media outlets and Arab ones was well captured by the Arab American documentary filmmaker Jehane Noujaim, who was working on a story about the Qatar-based Al Jazeera news network as the war began. Her film *Control Room* (2004) cuts between the version of the war presented by the U.S. Central Command and the sharply different portrayal by Al Jazeera. (In 2006 Al Jazeera launched an English-language service, making its voice widely heard across the world. Interested viewers in the United States could watch Al Jazeera only on YouTube, however, since the corporations that control the nation's major cable television systems refused to carry it.)

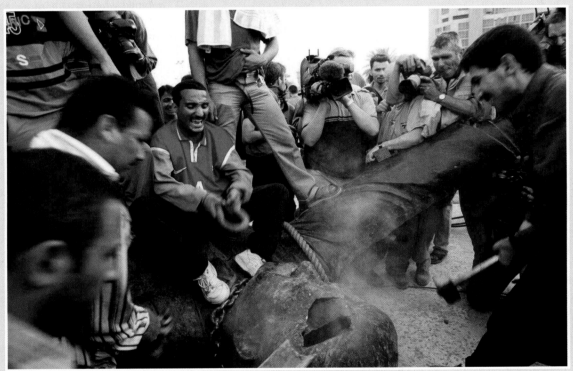

(Patrick Robert/Corbis)

Both print and media outlets in the United States concentrated on tightly framed images such as this one of enraged Iraqi citizens crushing the head of the fallen Saddam Hussein statue. The impression is of spontaneous mass action.

Before the statue fell, the crowd was throwing shoes and slippers at the hated image of the dictator, a grave insult in the Arab world.

In the rest of the world media coverage of the war was generally more subdued. Even media outlets in the United Kingdom, with coverage focusing on the southern part of Iraq occupied by British marines, offered a variety of viewpoints on the wisdom of Prime Minister Blair's strategy. CNN International used entirely different graphics and terminology to explain developments to its global audience from those used by CNN for its U.S. audience, again painting a less positive picture.

Many people clearly remember the image of an immense statue of the Iraqi dictator Saddam Hussein crashing to the ground on April 9, 2003. However, they are likely to recall the circumstances differently depending on where they lived and what type of media they were tuned in to.

(Facelly/Sipa)

In Europe and the Middle East television viewers were more likely to see the fall of the statue primarily as a U.S. military operation. The Iraqi crowd was actually quite small, and U.S. military personnel outnumber Iraqi civilians. The square was surrounded by American tanks.

Before the statue fell, a U.S. soldier climbed up and draped an American flag around Hussein's head. That flag was quickly taken down and replaced with an Iraqi one. The image of the stars and stripes in central Baghdad was used by those in the Arab media wishing to present the incident as an example of American imperialism.

QUESTION FOR ANALYSIS

Is it appropriate for journalists to challenge their government's version of events during times of war?

such a threat to world peace that it should not be allowed a civilian program that could be converted to military use. Using the same rationale, Israeli aircraft destroyed a Syrian nuclear power plant in 2007. A year earlier, the communist government of North Korea had snubbed international opinion by openly testing a nuclear bomb.

North Korean and Iranian scientists had made substantial strides after the chief of Pakistan's nuclear program shared his technology with them. South Asia has thus been a possible flashpoint for armed conflict between nuclear states and a focal point for the proliferation of nuclear technology beyond the relatively small club—the United States, France, the United Kingdom, Russia, Israel, Pakistan, India, China, and North Korea—already in possession of nuclear weapons. As of 2008, the Doomsday Clock (see Chapter 30) remained fixed at five minutes to midnight. Meanwhile, with so much attention fixed on terrorism and nuclear proliferation, insufficient progress has been made on other issues perhaps even more vital to long-term global security, including the health of the world's people and of the natural environment.

Health and the Environment

Global issues of health arise when we consider Mira Nair's film on the HIV/AIDS crisis, *My Own Country* (1998). The film was based on the memoir of Dr. Abraham Verghese, an Indian doctor whose family fled their home in Ethiopia to avoid civil strife. After completing his medical degree in India, Dr. Verghese began working as a Veterans Administration doctor in Johnson City, Tennessee. *My Own Country* shows the strains that affect this small town when a native son returns from the city, his body wracked with AIDS. The year was 1985, and in that era before the development of retroviral drug treatments, there was little medical help Dr. Verghese could offer. Yet simply by treating his patient with dignity and kindness, rather than the fear and homophobia such young men often encountered, the Indian doctor earned a reputation that spread across the region. Even though he faced prejudice and hostility for taking in patients who were ostracized in the community, Dr. Verghese persevered.

The presence of an Indian doctor in the rural United States is one of *My Own Country*'s global links. Small American towns must often look far afield to find appropriate doctors, and those trained in India are more likely than their American-trained counterparts to work as general practitioners for modest salaries. Another global dimension of the film is HIV/AIDS itself. When it was first diagnosed in the 1980s, the disease was associated with two particular groups, homosexual men in North America and Europe and intravenous drug users. Today, Africa has the largest number of AIDS victims, and there are more women than men among them. While medical advances have decreased suffering and extended life spans for those who can afford them, most of the world's HIV victims die without the benefit of any effective medical intervention. And while infection rates have stabilized in wealthier nations, many global health experts fear that India and China are now joining Africa as frontiers in the expansion of the disease.

It can be difficult to focus on HIV/AIDS in a country like India, where hundreds of millions lack access to the most basic health care and where older scourges like tuberculosis, polio, cholera, and malnutrition have yet to be effectively addressed. Yet if HIV were to spread as quickly in India as it did in South Africa in the 1990s (growing from 1 to 25 percent of the population between 1990 and 2005), the Indian health-care system would be overwhelmed and the economy would be battered. Unlike most epidemic diseases, which are deadliest for the very young and the very old, AIDS carries people away in the prime of their productive and reproductive lives, creating huge social and developmental costs.

HIV is just one of the viruses that have taken advantage of increased human mobility to spread quickly around the world. Virulent new strains of traditional killers like malaria, which until recently have remained confined to small geographic areas, now hop from continent to continent courtesy of mosquito hosts aboard jet airplanes. New strains of influenza, such as the avian flu virus from East Asia and the deadly Ebola (ee-BOH-lah) virus from Central Africa, have caused fear of uncontrollable global epidemics. Meanwhile, the worldwide use of antibiotics has led to the development of resistant strains of bacteria that make the suppression of diseases like tuberculosis more difficult. While viruses and bacteria do not recognize national borders, the global health-care system is insufficiently organized and funded to develop effective international interventions.

The threat to our health is being compounded by global climate change. Approximately 60,000 people are killed every year in natural disasters that scientists believe are related to increasing global temperatures, including a massive European heat wave in 2003, Hurricane Katrina in the United States in 2005, the huge cyclone that hit Myanmar in 2008, and unprecedented cycles of drought and flooding in many parts of Africa and Asia. Though climate change is not always a factor in natural disasters (the devastating Indian Ocean tsunami that claimed almost 250,000 casualties in 2004 was caused by an earthquake), many suspect that humans have been a principal cause of the increased tempo of such events in the early twenty-first century. Scientists predict that melting polar ice caps will soon present a tremendous health challenge in the world's highly populated coastal areas, especially Bangladesh, where fifty-five million people would be displaced by even a modest rise in sea levels.

Global climate change is also affecting the spread of infectious diseases. The director general of the World Health Organization, Dr. Margaret Chan, argues: "Many of the most important global killers are highly sensitive to climatic conditions. Malaria, diarrhea and malnutrition kill millions of people every year, most of them children. Without effective action to mitigate and adapt to climate change, the burden of these conditions will be greater, and they will be more difficult and more costly to control."[5] Violent monsoons and hurricanes generate conditions for the spread of water-borne disease, while warmer weather allows the spread of tropical diseases like malaria and dengue fever to formerly temperate regions. "No country can shield itself," Dr. Chan said, "from an invasion by a pathogen in an airplane passenger or an insect hiding in a cargo hold." Increasingly, anyone's health issue might become everyone's health issue.

The most significant international effort to address global warming is the **Kyoto Protocol,** an agreement adopted in 1997 under the United Nations Framework Agreement on Climate Change. For the first time, nations agreed to mandatory limits on emissions of the "greenhouse gases" that pump carbon dioxide into the atmosphere and contribute to increased temperatures. The effectiveness of the Kyoto (kee-oh-toh) Protocol was severely limited, however, by the refusal of the United States to ratify the treaty. The most contentious question was how to share the global burden. The largest contributors to global climate change historically have been the traditional industrial powers: Japan, the United States and Canada, and western

● **Kyoto Protocol** (1997) International agreement adopted in Kyoto, Japan, under the United Nations Framework Agreement on Climate Change in an effort to reduce greenhouse gas emissions linked to global warming. The Kyoto accords were not accepted by the United States.

■ **Global Warming**   Average temperatures in the Arctic are rising twice as fast as elsewhere in the world. The rapid melting of the polar ice cap is an outcome of global warming and also a further cause: in the future there will be less snow and ice in the Arctic to absorb the sun's heat and cool the planet. The peril faced by this polar bear mother and her cubs is immediate; the threat to humanity from rising sea levels is ominous.   (Jimmy Johnson/Getty Images)

Europe. Now the surging and largely unregulated Chinese and Indian economies threaten to offset progress elsewhere in the world. Major health problems accompany rapid industrialization in China, where most cancer deaths are attributable to pollution. The effects are not just local. A toxic cloud of coal smoke not only covers most of China but also drifts over neighboring countries and even across the Pacific Ocean.

China and India have argued that since most greenhouse gases are still produced in the United States and Europe, those countries should shoulder the largest burden in their reduction. Western governments, meanwhile, have argued that rapidly developing China and India should begin immediately to cut greenhouse gas emissions. In 2008, China became the world's largest producer of carbon dioxide emissions, much of it from coal-fired power stations. In fact, China brings on line two power stations every week. On the other hand, its per capita power consumption is only one-third that of the United States and western Europe, and its leaders say Chinese citizens have a right to a standard of living equivalent to that of the most developed nations. The goal of **sustainable development,** generating prosperity without poisoning the environment, is nowhere within reach.

● **sustainable development**
Economic growth that can be sustained without causing environmental damage.

Deforestation is magnifying the effect of the world's rising output of greenhouse gases. Tropical forests play a particularly important role in cleansing the atmosphere of carbon dioxide and replenishing it with oxygen. High prices and sustained demand for tropical hardwoods from Central Africa and Indonesia, however, have led lumber companies to fell vast areas of forest, sometimes bribing politicians to evade environmental regulations. In Brazil, rising grain prices give farmers an incentive to clear the forest for agriculture, especially when they can grow more sugar cane for ethanol. In 2008 the minister for the environment, Marina Silva, resigned when she lost a battle to stop government transportation projects that would hasten the extension of the country's agricultural frontier into the rainforest.

On environmental issues, as in other domains, India is both a source of worry and a source of hope. On the one hand, if the Indian economy can generate the millions of jobs necessary to lift its citizens into middle-class patterns of consumption, the environmental challenges of the subcontinent will grow many times more daunting. On the other hand, Indian scientists and entrepreneurs are already finding solutions in renewable energy sources such as wind power. The capital city of New Delhi has a sparkling, energy-efficient new subway system and has converted much of its public transportation to run on cleaner natural gas.

Personal choices and governmental policies, international agreements and local initiatives, the actions of rich nations, poor ones, and those on the rise: work is needed on every front to resolve the health and environmental challenges of our times. Meanwhile, rising population, urbanization, and global migration make the search for solutions all the more urgent.

Demography and Population Movement

India is a very crowded place, a realization that emerges from *Salaam Bombay!* (1988), the film with which Mira Nair first made her international reputation. It is a heartbreaking tale of the lives of the poor in India's largest city, with a cast made up largely of homeless children recruited and trained by Nair. Their presence gives an unmistakable authenticity to this story about "children who have never experienced childhood."[6]

We first meet the child protagonist Krishna as he returns to find that the circus at which he was employed has left without him. He had left his home village looking to bring back five hundred rupees to replace his brother's bicycle, which he had destroyed. Krishna does not know exactly where Bombay is located, but like so many in the countryside, he sees the big city as a land of opportunity. At the train station, the ticket seller leaves Krishna with the advice that he should return as a movie star. Alas, the glamor of Bollywood does not lie in Krishna's future. He takes up residence as a tea boy in a brothel. In this harsh world, those at the bottom band together to form a community and cherish opportunities for laughter and comradeship.

Krishna's story provides a context to discuss two more issues of great importance to India and the world: the size and composition of the world's population, and the movement of that population from villages into cities. India contains by far the largest youth population in the world, with over 600 million people (half the population) under the age of 25. By 2035 India is expected to surpass China as the most populous nation on earth, with 1.6 billion people. The move toward cities is a part of that growth. For the planet as a whole, demographers estimate that 2008 was the first year when the majority of humankind lived in cities.[7] India has yet to meet that benchmark, with only about 28 percent of its people living in urban environments. Yet unless more opportunities can be created in the countryside, the pressure driving migrants into the cities will increase, as will the already immense pressures on the urban infrastructure of transport, water, education, and sanitation. In the first decade of the twenty-first century, commercial television has spread to even remote hamlets, where portrayals of the urban "good life" in soap operas and commercials are increasing expectations among the young.

Expressed on a global scale, these trends are certainly alarming. Africa's population is even younger than India's, and the fertility of its women higher. While the population of wealthier countries grows old and in some cases (for example, Italy, Japan, and Russia) fertility rates are below the level needed to replace the current population, surging growth rates in Latin America, Africa, and much of Asia have created an enormous population of young people whose ambitions often far exceed their chances to fulfill them. For India and the planet, creating the sorts of educational opportunities that will tap the creativity and intelligence of these hundreds of millions of young people is a matter of urgent concern.

In the 1980s, leaders of the People's Republic of China adopted a radical solution to population growth. China's **One Child Policy** punishes parents who have a second child with heavy penalties and even prosecution, with enforcement being most strict in urban areas. Within a single generation the long Chinese tradition of extended families was largely replaced by small nuclear ones. Without siblings, the younger generation in China are accustomed to receiving the full attention and financial support of their parents, who usually focus on education. When the massive earthquake of 2008 toppled schools in the Sichuan province, many Chinese parents lost their only child.

At a global level, previously alarming predictions about the future effects of uncontrolled population growth have been replaced by an understanding that when people attain greater wealth and security they tend to have smaller families. Now population growth is slowing not just in richer countries but also across much of the world. Unfortunately, in much of Africa and elsewhere, high mortality from AIDS and other deadly diseases is partly accountable. Even so, there does appear to be a general leveling off and even decline in overall human fertility; if current trends hold, total global population will reach equilibrium sometime later in this century, perhaps at a level of nine billion people.

There is currently a demographic imbalance between world regions. On the one hand, countries like India have many underemployed young people of productive age; on the other, societies like Japan have aging populations and insufficient workers to support them. Through immigration, affluent societies such as the United States, Canada, Australia, Britain, and France are able to maintain a stable mix of working-age and senior citizens. Nations that reject immigration as a solution, such as Japan, will need to look to technological solutions (such as robotics) to help care for their graying populations. Even China is looking to a future where eventually there may not be enough workers to support the current working-age population when they retire. In 2008 the Communist Party openly discussed for the first time the possibility of relaxing its One Child Policy.

Of course, unequal distribution of wealth and resources, not simple demography, is the principal factor influencing global patterns of migration. People are

• **One Child Policy** In China, most parents are restricted by this policy to a single child to curb population growth. The policy has led to significant gender imbalance.

moving not only into cities but also across national borders. Not surprisingly, India is part of this wider trend in which people leave home, and often family, in search of higher wages. India sends not only doctors to Europe and the United States, but also construction workers and domestic servants to the Persian Gulf. The government of the southern state of Kerala, for example, relies heavily on remittances sent home by migrant workers from the United Arab Emirates. Migrant workers in the Gulf, as elsewhere, are often abused by unscrupulous employers, who subject them to unsafe conditions and withhold their pay.

Immigration policies are controversial all around the world. Since they are often willing to work for less, immigrants can drive down wages for native workers. In 2008, South African gangs killed twelve immigrants from other African countries, claiming that the outsiders were taking jobs that should go to local workers. In Italy, the government cracked down on illegal Roma (Gypsy) immigrants from southeastern Europe, claiming that they were responsible for an increase in crime. The Roma, like many recent immigrants, live apart from their host societies. In the United States, immigration from Latin America has shifted the cultural and linguistic balance of American society.

Many western Europeans are alarmed by Muslim immigration to their countries. In France in 2005, and then again in 2007, riots broke out in the suburbs of Paris, where many Arabs and Africans live. Conservatives called for the restoration of law and order and restrictions on further immigration; those with more liberal views cited racism as the cause of the riots and demanded greater educational and employment prospects for immigrant youth. The Netherlands, with a long-standing tradition of liberal immigration policies, was rocked in 2004 when Theo van Gogh, who had made a film critical of the treatment of women in Islam, was stabbed to death by a Dutch citizen of North African ancestry. In the United Kingdom, as in the United States, post-9/11 concerns with terrorism made some Britons suspicious of their Muslim neighbors, who, sensing the hostile atmosphere, clustered even more closely into separate ethnic and religious communities.

In the past, time and distance would usually have ensured the gradual assimilation of immigrants into host societies. Today, however, revolutions in transportation and communications make it possible for people to move great distances while remaining connected to familial and cultural networks on the other side of the globe. Mira Nair maintains homes on multiple continents and moves freely between them. Of course, mobility on that scale is an option only for those able to afford frequent transcontinental air travel. Still, the increasing movement of people and ideas has clearly sharpened questions of identity across the world, as people ponder the nature of the relationship between national, ethnic, racial, gender, religious, and other modes of self-identification.

Questions of Identity

Questions of identity—especially multiple, overlapping identities—are frequently at the heart of Mira Nair's films. In *Mississippi Masala* (1991), Jay Patel is unable to settle down and appreciate the success his family is having in the motel business in the rural American south. Though his origins lie in India, the home he longs for is in Uganda, the country from which his family had been expelled in

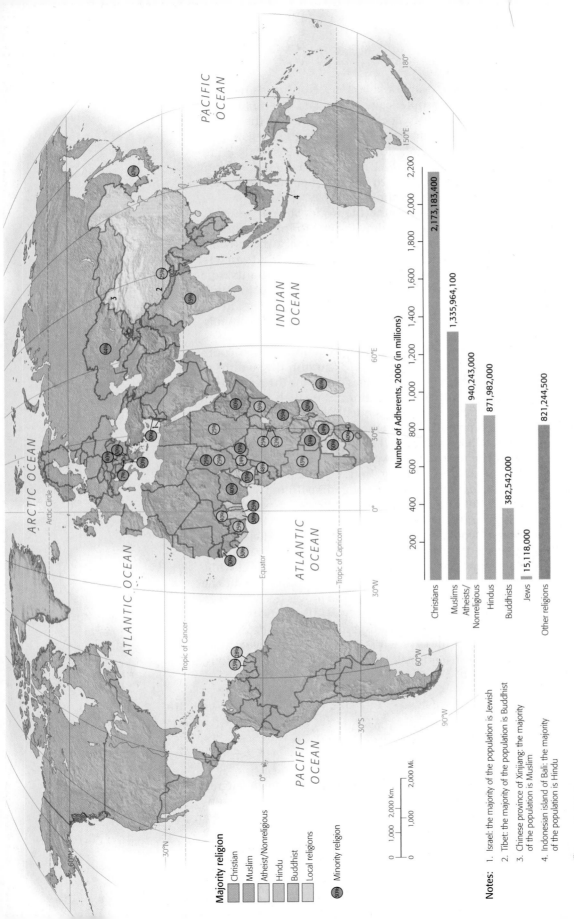

Majority religion
- Christian
- Muslim
- Atheist/Nonreligious
- Hindu
- Buddhist
- Local religions

50% Minority religion

Number of Adherents, 2006 (in millions)

Religion	Number
Christians	2,173,183,400
Muslims	1,335,964,100
Atheists/Nonreligious	940,243,000
Hindus	871,982,000
Buddhists	382,542,000
Jews	15,118,000
Other religions	821,244,500

Notes:
1. Israel: the majority of the population is Jewish
2. Tibet: the majority of the population is Buddhist
3. Chinese province of Xinjiang: the majority of the population is Muslim
4. Indonesian island of Bali: the majority of the population is Hindu

MAP 32.3

World Religions Christianity, Islam, Hinduism, and Buddhism are the four major world religions, with "atheists/nonreligious" forming a majority in Communist-ruled China. The religious map of Africa is especially complex. While Muslims predominate in the north and west, and Christians in the east and south, there is a great deal of mixing along the boundaries between them, and local religions are still strong in many areas. In much of Europe and Russia, where Christian majorities are indicated, secularism is also strong and rates of church attendance quite low. While Islam predominates in North Africa and the Middle East, the nation with the largest Muslim population in the world is Indonesia, in Southeast Asia.

 Interactive Map

the 1970s, along with the entire Ugandan Indian community, by the dictator Idi Amin. Self-identifying as an African, Patel writes letter after letter trying to have his property restored.

Meanwhile, his daughter Mina is developing a relationship with Demetrius, an African American carpet cleaner. Their relationship is frowned on by both the Indian and African American communities, even though both of them are "colored" in the eyes of the town's white population. In these circumstances, what does it mean to be "black," "Indian," "African," or "American"? The complexity of that question was recognized by the United States Census in 2000 when, for the first time, citizens were given the option to check more than one racial box.

On November 4, 2008 the election of Barack Hussein Obama as 44th president of the United States captured the world's attention and brought America's evolving identity conversation to the fore. The country's first African American leader, Obama's mother was from Kansas and his father from Kenya, and he was educated in settings as diverse as Honolulu, Jakarta (Indonesia), Los Angeles, and New York. After growing up in Hawaii as "Barry" Obama, he later stressed the black dimension of his identity by reclaiming his father's first name (which means "blessings" in Swahili) and by moving to Chicago to work as a community organizer on the city's heavily African American south side. As with the golf legend Tiger Woods, whose mother was from Thailand and whose black father had African, European, and Native American ancestry, complex global influences meant that Obama's identity could scarcely be captured by a single hyphen between "African" and "American."

In India as well, old categories have been realigned. South Asia has been called a *palimpsest*, a place where many cultural layers have built up on each other over time. All the migrants, invaders, and rulers that have come through India over the millennia have left their trace. One marker of that history is the hundreds of different languages spoken in India. Hindi, the most widely understood, is used by only 40 percent of the population. Though English is the language of the elite, fewer than 10 percent of all Indians understand it. What can hold this vast and diverse country together?

In the past two decades the **Bharatiya Janata Party** (BJP) has attempted to recast Hinduism as a unifying identity for India, countering the secular nationalism of the Congress Party. While in control of the federal government from 1998 to 2004, the BJP proved competent custodians of the Indian economy, but many Indians are uneasy about their use of Hinduism. Some groups within the BJP have long histories of promoting intolerance against minority groups, especially Muslims. Intercommunal violence in the western state of Gujarat in 2002 confirmed that such attitudes were present in the BJP leadership. That year fifty-eight Hindu nationalists were burned alive on a train heading for the contested site of a former Mughal mosque (see the "World History in Today's World" feature in Chapter 20). Hindu extremists, claiming that Muslims had set the fire, were actively aided by the BJP state government as they took vengeance, systematically raping Muslim women and dousing children with kerosene before setting them alight. Calm was restored, life returned to normal, and the BJP lost the next elections. Some worried, however, that the infusion of religion into politics was threatening India's secular democracy.

Issues of identity in India go far beyond religious differences (see Map 32.3). In fact, for most Indians until very recently, and still for many today, identities are intensely local, tied not to large, abstract concepts like "India" but rather to intimate networks of family, village, and caste. That local focus made sense for people whose

● **Bharatiya Janata Party** (BJP) Nationalist political party in India that emphasizes the country's Hindu identity, in contrast to the secular Congress Party. The BJP led the federal government from 1998 to 2004.

Studying World History

As you conclude your study of world history, you join millions of students around the world who are trying to make sense of the human past. Yet for many more students the study of history is restricted to their own nations or civilizations.

All societies relate the present to the past; in that sense historical consciousness is a universal and distinctively human trait. Modern historical scholarship, however, dates only from the nineteenth century, when nationalism was the dominant intellectual force in the world's most powerful societies. The study of history, usually divided along national lines, still reflects that heritage.

After the First World War, progressive historians in the United States, understanding that national history could not give students an adequate understanding of the world, promoted the study of "Western civilization" to connect the American experience to a history that was both deeper in time and broader in space. Courses in Western civilization focused primarily on America's European heritage and paid little attention to the histories of Africa, Asia, and Latin America.

To help correct that imbalance, a group of historians founded the World History Association in 1982, proposing that the deeper and broader historical foundations necessary to navigate the modern world must, by necessity, be global. Scholars from around the world constructed stories of the human past emphasizing global contexts, comparisons, and interconnections. In the past two decades books, articles, websites and other information resources to support world history have proliferated.

Challenges remain. Political and intellectual leaders frequently focus only on national history, and many historians and history teachers continue to emphasize narrow areas of specialization. Still, the quest for balanced and representative views of the human past is one of the most exciting intellectual puzzles facing historians today.

---

work and daily routines were not much different from those of their forebears. Now, however, increased mobility and accelerated connections with the larger world are creating more contexts where it makes sense for Indians to emphasize broader identities and imagine affiliations with people they may never meet. Television plays a powerful role. Before the 1990s few people had televisions and the government controlled all the programming. Now hundreds of millions of people watch domestic programs like soap operas and cricket matches, as well as imported channels like the Cable News Network (CNN) and the British Broadcasting Company (BBC).

Confusion over identity causes severe anxiety for Gogol Ganguli, the main character in Mira Nair's film *The Namesake* (2006), based on the novel by Jhumpa Lahiri. Gogol is the son of Indian immigrants to the United States. Named for a nineteenth-century Russian author for reasons known only to his father, Gogol spends his early life trying to piece together an identity from the cultural fragments around him, alternately rejecting and reconciling himself to his parents' Bengali traditions, while moving between Kolkata and New York. As so often in Nair's films, this intensely personal story points toward a broader thesis. Like Barack Obama, more and more people in the contemporary world find themselves with a complex menu of identities from which to choose. And like Obama, Gogol's solution, which makes him whole, is to embrace them all.

Meanwhile, the phrase *global citizen* has entered our vocabulary. In spite of all the markers that divide us each from the other, *human* is an increasingly relevant category on our ever-smaller planet. (See the feature "World History in Today's World: Studying World History.")

Gender, Human Rights, and Democracy

The theme of gender pervades Mira Nair's work. One of the saddest moments in her films occurs in *Salaam Bombay!* when a teenage girl named Solasaal arrives at the brothel where Krishna lives; the adults nickname her "Sweet Sixteen" and expect to make a big profit by selling her virginity. Solasaal's story is a grim reminder that brutal sexual abuse, and even child slavery, continue even while India moves forward.

In some respects, economic globalization and technological change have presented Indian women, at least those fortunate to receive advanced education, a world of new possibilities. It might seem that gender progress only needs a more general increase in living standards. Unfortunately, prosperity and technology have caused new problems even as they have eased others. In India, the **dowry system,** in which the bride brings gifts to the husband's household, has become a major problem. A girl's dowry has traditionally been one of the largest, if not the largest, expense faced by Indian parents. The poor have commonly turned to moneylenders for the resources needed to pay a dowry, at rates of interest that sometimes lead to lifelong indebtedness.

The dowry system is now more widespread than ever, and the greater availability of consumer goods has had an inflationary effect. The families of potential grooms demand ever-greater payments in return for marriage to their sons, including refrigerators, houses, cars, and even business capital. Newspapers abound in reports of young brides who fell down wells or died in kitchen fires, murdered by their in-laws after their dowry payments had been made. Officially there were 6,787 dowry murders in India in 2005; experts suspect that the actual number is much higher.

Because of the dowry system, for many Indians the birth of a girl is a kind of tragedy, ruining the family's financial prospects. One ancient tradition has been female infanticide, leading to a long-term gender imbalance in India favoring males. Now modern technology is making the process of selecting boys over girls more efficient. Across India, medical clinics advertise sonogram services, widely used across the world to check on the health, and anticipate the gender, of a fetus. In India, however, the results of the sonogram often determine whether the parents will abort the fetus. The use of modern technology has led to a sharp increase in the selective abortion of female fetuses, so that there are now only 927 young girls for every 1,000 young boys nationwide. The disparity is greatest in the north: in the Punjab there are fewer that 800 girls for every 1,000 boys.

In China as well, some parents, feeling that they need a male heir to carry on the family line, practice selective abortion using ultrasound technology. Here the traditional preference for boys has been magnified by the government's One Child Policy, since the birth of a girl means no male offspring. Demographers estimate that there are as many as seventy million more males than females in the country, an imbalance that makes it more and more difficult for young men to find brides. Even if a more balanced male-female birth ratio is achieved in the near future, tens of millions of Chinese men face a lifetime of bachelorhood.

While the problem of dowry slayings is an Indian one, and the One Child Policy is specific to China, the more general point is that overcoming powerful legacies of male dominance and rebalancing political, economic, and social power more evenly between men and women requires more than material prosperity, technological

• **dowry system**
Traditional Indian marriage system in which a bride brings substantial gifts to the household of her new husband. Though illegal, it has expanded as the country's wealth has grown, leading to chronic indebtedness and the frequent murder of young brides.

progress, or government intervention. Deeply seated cultural norms reproduce patriarchal relations in every society, and everywhere the path forward requires attention to local circumstances.

Connecting the local to the global is a hallmark of the work of **Wangari Maathai** (wahn-gah-ree mah-TIE), a Kenyan biologist and Nobel Peace Prize winner (2004). Dr. Maathai was the founder of the Green Belt Movement in Central Kenya. Alarmed by environmental degradation in the region of East Africa where she grew up, Dr. Maathai organized rural women into collectives to plant trees. The effort was successful and led to a global movement that now has affiliated organizations in several developing countries. Her success and international recognition did not come easily or without a fight, however. While planting trees may seem an innocuous act, and certainly not a politically charged one, in patriarchal Kenya it took great courage for partisans of the Green Belt Movement to organize for change.

• **Wangari Maathai** (b. 1940) Kenyan biologist, environmentalist, and human rights campaigner who founded the Green Belt Movement in Kenya, empowering rural women to plant trees and take leadership roles. Was awarded the Nobel Peace Prize in 2004.

■ **Wangari Maathai**   The Green Belt Movement led by Wangari Maathai stresses environmental renewal, women's empowerment, and human rights. Here Dr. Maathai (*right*) plants a tree in Nairobi's Uhuru Park with U.S. Senator Barack Obama, later elected president of the United States, who traveled to Kenya in 2006 to visit his father's homeland.   (AP Photo/Sayyid Azim)

These women, Maathai explains, have learned that "planting trees or fighting to save forests from being chopped down is part of a larger mission to create a society that respects democracy, decency, adherence to the rule of law, human rights, and the rights of women."[8] Reflecting on the path that led from environmental activism to a Nobel Peace Prize, Dr. Maathai emphasizes that the Green Belt Movement necessarily involved human rights and democracy-building efforts as well. She envisions peace as the stable top of an African stool, supported by the three stout legs of human rights, democracy, and protection of the environment.

Unfortunately, Africa's path toward democracy has not been smooth. In early 2008 disputed election results in Kenya led to widespread ethnic violence. The situation was even worse in Zimbabwe, where agents of the aged dictator Robert Mugabe falsified election results, used violence to suppress opposition parties, and made 700,000 people homeless in a slum clearance program called "Operation Drive Out Trash." Sudanese authorities evaded responsibility for arming the militias who killed thousands and made refugees of millions in Darfur, while Somalia remained a "failed state" without any effective government at all. The maturation of stable, multiparty democracies in countries like Tanzania, Ghana, and Botswana were hopeful exceptions to the continent's general lack of democracy.

In Asia as well, the mixed record of democratization of the 1990s (see Chapter 31) continued into the twenty-first century. Indonesia, the world's fourth most populous and largest Muslim-majority nation, successfully made the post–Cold War transition to democracy, with relatively clean elections and smooth transitions of power between parties. In Vietnam and the People's Republic of China, by contrast, communist parties kept their monopoly on power even as they transformed their societies through market economics. It remained to be seen whether economic growth would trigger political reform. The response to the Sichuan earthquake in 2008 offered a glimmer of hope, as Chinese citizens mobilized themselves independently from the government to provide aid to earthquake victims. Such civil autonomy, with citizens banding together in common cause, is a foundation of democracy long repressed by the Chinese Communist Party. On the other hand, there was no evidence of reform in China's harsh response to Tibetan protestors (see the "World History in Today's World" feature in Chapter 20).

The worst Asian case was the military dictatorship of Myanmar (Burma), ruled since 1962 by secretive generals without any restraint. The callousness of the generals shocked the world when they refused to allow international agencies to come to the aid of desperate victims of the catastrophic cyclone of 2008. Aung San Suu Kyi (awng san soo key), Myanmar's courageous human rights campaigner, remained under house arrest, having spent over twelve years in detention.

In today's world there is no lack of powerful women as role models, as Aung San Suu Kyi, Mira Nair, and Wangari Maathai all demonstrate. The issue is how to spread opportunity more equitably within and between societies. Education is key, not just to provide skills but also to promote empowerment. In Nair's film *Hysterical Blindness* (2002), the character of Debby is trapped in a narrow and stifling world; she has no idea how to escape from boredom and despair other than the futile hope that a man will come along and rescue her. Nair uses the recurrent image of a bridge to Manhattan seen from below to indicate the path to a wider and more hopeful world, though Debby never looks up to see it. In India, Kenya, Myanmar, and around the world, there is much to be done both to build and to cross such bridges.

⬤ Global Culture

When Mira Nair was growing up in India, the legacies of the British Empire were still strong. Like most educated Indians since the nineteenth century, she read the classics of English literature. One of the novels she most enjoyed as a teenager was William Thackeray's *Vanity Fair,* the story of a young woman using all her intelligence and guile to improve her station in class-bound early-nineteenth-century England. In Nair's version of *Vanity Fair,* the silk outfits of the aristocracy, the "oriental" furniture in their ornate homes, and their Indian servants remind the viewer that the British Empire had a profound effect on English domestic life. Nair hired a Bollywood choreographer, not someone from the West, for a scene in which Becky does a titillating dance for her love interest, asserting the legitimate contribution of Bollywood techniques in Western filmmaking.

Though the global film industry is vast and diverse, the two most influential players by far are Hollywood and Bollywood, and Mira Nair symbolizes the potential

⬛ **Bollywood Goes Global** This 2004 street scene from Kabul, Afghanistan, with a video shop in the foreground, shows the increasing international influence of India's massive film industry. The Islamist Taliban regime (1996–2001) banned Bollywood films, objecting to their romantic leading men and women, lavish sets, and boisterous singing and dancing. (AP Images)

for synergy between them. In fact, if current trends continue, the flow of technical, commercial, and artistic resources and talent between the U.S., European, and Indian film industries will increase dramatically in the not-too-distant future. Reliance Big Entertainment, a subsidiary of India's largest telecommunications company, has invested over $1 billion in Hollywood, while in 2008 American rapper Snoop Dogg was signed to perform "Singh Is King," the title song for a Bollywood movie.

Although globalization has been a mixed blessing, creating political confusion and economic anxiety for many people, the potential for cultural globalization still seems immense. Some equate globalization with Americanization, fearing that fast foods will replace local cuisines or that the global film industry will be homogenized through the dominance of Hollywood. But music and sport indicate that there is good reason to be optimistic.

The African experience shows the enduring cultural power of music. Even under colonialism, Africans adapted their music to new circumstances, instruments, and cultural influences. When transistor radios became available in the 1950s, African musicians responded to the Afro-Latin rhythms of the Cuban *mambo* and other American musical idioms that retained deep African roots. As they picked up guitars and trumpets, they reimported these musical styles and added their own modern voice to re-create global African music all over again. Listening to great masters of African popular music—such as Angelique Kidjo (Benin), Salif Keita (Mali), and the late Fela Anikulapo Kuti (Nigeria)—will leave little doubt that the creative power of African music has never been diminished. Standing on firm cultural ground, African musicians have borrowed what appealed to them.

Sport, especially football (or soccer), is another positive area. During the 1990s, one writer notes, "You could see globalization on the pitch. . . . Basque teams, under the stewardship of Welsh coaches, stocked up on Dutch and Turkish players; Moldavian squads imported Nigerians. Everywhere you looked, it suddenly seemed, national borders and national identities had been swept into the dustbin of soccer history." The internationalization of soccer does have some negative effects, as when Africa's best players sign with European teams, depriving their fellow citizens of a chance to watch them on home turf. Still, there is a net benefit, as "cultural alchemies . . . yielded wonderful new spectacles: The cynical, defensive-minded Italian style livened by an infusion of freewheeling Dutchmen and Brazilians; the English stiff-upper-lip style . . . tempered by a bit of continental flair, brought across the Channel in the form of French strikers."[9] As with film and music, global interaction unleashes untapped creative potential.

Mira Nair's commitment to increasing cultural connections is also clear from her sponsorship of the Maisha Film Makers Lab. Based in Kampala, Uganda, Maisha ("life" in Swahili) gives new screenwriters and film directors from East Africa and South Asia access to professional training and mentoring. The Maisha (mah-EE-sha) program's goal is to "unleash local voices from these regions . . . motivated by the belief that a film which explores the truths and idiosyncrasies of the specifically local often has the power to cross over and become significantly universal."[10] Artists like Mira Nair can help us make such connections between the local and the global.

Chapter Review

 Download the MP3 audio file of the Chapter Review and listen to it on the go.

The films of Mira Nair, though deeply personal, touch on universal themes. Serving as a bridge between Hollywood and Bollywood, Nair shows the creativity that often accompanies global cultural interaction. Globalization, while it has in many ways raised international stress and discord, has also given vast numbers of people a chance to discover the power and beauty of the world's cultural traditions. The optimistic view is that as the flow of world cultures increases, lives will be enriched, perhaps even helping lay foundations for peace.

How is globalization affecting the world economy and global security?

The increased pace of economic interchange and transfer of technologies in the twenty-first century has presented people across the world with new opportunities. As the emergence of the new India and the increased economic importance of Brazil, Russia, and China all show, globalization can result in rapid economic growth. The question remains, however, how equitably the benefits will be shared within societies and between nations. Meanwhile, terrorism has created uncertainty in international affairs, a landscape also altered by the emergence of China and the resurgence of Russia as great powers and by the growth of regional blocs like the European Union. These developments, combined with the extended war in Iraq, have resulted in the relative weakening of the United States as the main arbiter of international affairs, with unknown consequences for global security.

What are the most important environmental and demographic trends of the twenty-first century?

In the twenty-first century, the world's people became increasingly aware that the environmental damage caused by human activity, especially the release of the greenhouse gases that cause global warming, was a problem requiring global solutions. With every nation striving to maximize economic growth, however, remedies such as those proposed in the Kyoto Protocol remained hard to implement. Although most scientists no longer believe that it is simply the rising number of people that will place our planet at risk, economic and demographic imbalances still present a challenge. In some parts of the world, such as India and Africa, great numbers of young people seek access to education and opportunity, while in mature industrial countries graying populations might have insufficient workers to support them in old age. These trends, combined with faster telecommunications and better transportation, have led to an unprecedented movement of peoples. Most of the world's people now live in cities, which strain to provide them services, while in many countries tensions over immigration have increased.

To what extent is the world moving forward in gender equality, human rights, and democracy?

Disparities in education and income determine whether women experience globalization as an opportunity or a threat, though entrenched structures of male dominance everywhere hamper the drive toward gender equality. As in the 1990s following the collapse of the Soviet Union, the world's record on human rights and democracy has remained mixed. Democracy came to former military dictatorships like Brazil and Indonesia and former communist countries like Poland, but brutal dictators resisted change in places like Zimbabwe and Myanmar, and communist regimes in China and Vietnam were slow to match their free-market reforms with political openness. While many of the world's people have focused solely on ethnic and national interests and identities, a growing number have become aware of themselves as global citizens. Perhaps the best hope for the advancement of democracy, human rights, and gender equality lies with them.

 WEB RESOURCES

Pronunciation Guide

Interactive Maps

MAP 32.1 Per Capita Income

MAP 32.2 Iraq in Transition

MAP 32.3 World Religions

Primary Sources

Chapter Objectives

ACE Multiple-Choice Quiz

Flashcards

For Further Reference

Appiah, Kwame Anthony. *Cosmopolitanism: Ethics Is a World of Strangers*. New York: W.W. Norton, 2007.

Connelly, Matthew. *Fatal Misconception: The Struggle to Control World Population*. Cambridge, Mass.: Belknap Press, 2008.

Foer, Franklin. *How Soccer Explains the World: An Unlikely Theory of Globalization*. New York: HarperCollins, 2004.

Friedman, Thomas. *Hot, Flat and Crowded: Why We Need a Green Revolution*. New York: Farrar, Straus and Giroux, 2008.

Kamdar, Mira. *Planet India: How the Fastest Growing Democracy Is Changing America and the World*. New York: Scribner, 2007.

Luce, Edward. *In Spite of the Gods: The Strange Rise of Modern India*. London: Abacus, 2006.

Maathai, Wangari. *Unbowed: A Memoir*. New York: Knopf, 2006.

Muir, John Kenneth. *Mercy in Her Eyes: The Films of Mira Nair*. New York: Applause, 2006.

Obama, Barack. *Dreams From My Father: A Story of Race and Inheritance*. New York: Times Books, 1995.

Sen, Amartya. *Identity and Violence: The Illusion of Destiny*. New York: W.W. Norton, 2007.

Zakaria, Fareed. *The Post-American World*. New York: W.W. Norton, 2008.

Websites

British Broadcasting Company (http://www.bbc.co.uk/). Daily international news and useful background to contemporary events from one of the world's most respected news organizations. The BBC World Service, accessible from the website, broadcasts in thirty-two different languages.

Global Transformations Website (http://www.polity.co.uk/global/links.asp). Extensive links to global online information sources, by region and by topic.

Mira Nair (http://www.mirabaifilms.com/home.html). Mirabai Films is the director's official website.

Worldwatch Institute (http://www.worldwatch.org/). The official webpage of an organization dedicated to the cause of sustainability.

NOTES

Chapter 1

1. James C. Chatters, *Ancient Encounters: Kennewick Man and the First Americans* (New York: Simon and Schuster, 2001), pp. 20–21.
2. John Noble Wilford, "In Ancient Skulls from Ethiopia, Familiar Faces," *New York Times,* June 12, 2003, pp. A1, A8.
3. John Noble Wilford, "Report Reignites Feud over 'Little People' as Separate Species," *New York Times,* August 22, 2006, p. F2.
4. Thomas D. Dillehay, *The Settlement of the Americas: A New Prehistory* (New York: Basic Books, 2000), p. 167.
5. E. James Dixon, *Bones, Boats, and Bison* (Albuquerque: University of New Mexico Press, 1999), pp. 87 (Table 3.1); 108 (Table 4.1); 144–145 (Table 5.1).
6. Tom Koppel, *Lost World: Rewriting Prehistory—How New Science Is Tracing America's Ice Age Mariners* (New York: Atria Books, 2003), p. 110.
7. William H. Stiebing, *Ancient Near Eastern History and Culture* (New York: Longman, 2003), p. 13.

Chapter 2

1. Benjamin R. Foster, *The Epic of Gilgamesh* (New York: W. W. Norton, 2001), pp. 8–9 (Enkidu's encounter with Shamhat); 6–7 (description of Uruk); 11 (Enkidu's dream).
2. Martha T. Roth, *Law Collections from Mesopotamia and Asia Major* (Atlanta, Ga.: Scholars Press, 1997), pp. 76–81 (false accusation of murder); 121 (eye-for-an-eye clause).
3. Samuel Noah Kramer, *History Begins at Sumer: Thirty-nine Firsts in Recorded History* (Philadelphia: University of Pennsylvania Press, 1981), p. 58.
4. This book uses the chronology given in Douglas J. Brewer and Emily Teeter, *Egypt and the Egyptians* (New York: Cambridge University Press, 1999).
5. Anthony P. Sakovich, "Counting the Stones: How Many Blocks Comprise Khufu's Pyramid?" *KMT: A Modern Journal of Ancient Egypt* 13, no. 3 (Fall 2002): 53–57.
6. William H. Stiebing, Jr., *Ancient Near Eastern History and Culture* (New York: Longman, 2003), p. 127.
7. J. Pritchard, *Ancient Near Eastern Texts Relating to the Old Testament* (Princeton: Princeton University Press, 1955), p. 34.
8. Ann Hyland, "Chariots and Cavalry," in *The Seventy Great Inventions of the Ancient World,* ed. Brian M. Fagan (London: Thames & Hudson, 2004), p. 196.
9. Lionel Casson, *Travel in the Ancient World* (Baltimore: Johns Hopkins University Press, 1994), p. 39; for a recent critique of the nature of the text and its date, see also— Benjamin Sass, "Wenamun and His Levant—1075 BC or 925 BC?" *Ägypten und Levante* 12 (2001): 247–255.
10. William G. Dever, *Did God Have a Wife? Archaeology and Folk Religion in Ancient Israel* (Grand Rapids, Mich.: William B. Eerdmans, 2005), p. 13.
11. Ibid., pp. 64–69.
12. Stiebing, p. 240.
13. William G. Dever, *What Did the Biblical Writers Know and When Did They Know It? What Archaeology Can Tell Us About the Reality of Ancient Israel* (Grand Rapids, Mich.: William B. Eerdmans , 2001), p. 127.
14. Ibid., p. 118.

Chapter 3

1. "13th Major Rock Edict," in *Aśoka and the Decline of the Mauryas,* ed. Romila Thapar (Delhi: Oxford University Press, 1973), Appendix 5, pp. 255–256. Translation slightly modified.
2. Jonathan Mark Kenoyer, "Uncovering the Keys to the Lost Indus Cities," *Scientific American* 289, no.1 (July 2003): 67–75.
3. Jonathan Mark Kenoyer, *Ancient Cities of the Indus Valley Civilization* (Karachi: Oxford University Press, 1998), pp. 63 (the great bath); 70–71 (the writing system).
4. J. P. Mallory and D. Q. Adams, *Encyclopedia of Indo-European Culture* (Chicago: Fitzroy Dearborn Publishers, 1997), p. 306.
5. Richard H. Davis, "Introduction: A Brief History of Religions in India," in *Religions of Asia in Practice: An Anthology,* ed. Donald S. Lopez, Jr. (Princeton: Princeton University Press, 2002), pp. 19–30.
6. Wendy Doniger O'Flaherty, *The Rig Veda* (New York: Penguin Books, 1981), pp. 235, "Human Diversity: A Hymn to Soma" (about different occupations); 31, "The Hymn of Man."
7. J. W. McCrindle, *Ancient India as Described by Megasthenes and Arrian* (London: Trübner, 1877), pp. 68 (city's size); 87 (tasks of government officials and those who take care of foreigners); 40 (the philosophers); 105 (the Buddhists); 44 (caste rules about marriage); 43 (rank of government officials).
8. "11th Major Rock Edict," in *Aśoka and the Decline of the Mauryas,* Appendix 5, pp. 254–255 (gift of dharma); 256 (sending of envoys); 253 (meetings); 252 (officers of dharma); 253 (officials reporting to him).

Chapter 4

1. Martin Kern, *The Stele Inscriptions of Ch'in Shih-huang: Text and Ritual in Early Chinese Imperial Representation* (New Haven: American Oriental Society, 2000), pp. 18–23.
2. *The Analects of Confucius,* trans. Simon Leys (New York: W. W. Norton, 1997), p. 50.
3. *Chuang Tzu: Basic Writings,* trans. Burton Watson (New York: Columbia University Press, 1964), pp. 41 (Perfect Man); 45 (butterfly); 115 (talking skull).
4. *Tao Te Ching: The Classic Book of Integrity and the Way,* trans. Victor Mair (New York: Bantam Books, 1990), p. 54.
5. Kern, pp. 19–20 (superb and shining); 13 (way of filial piety); 17 (creating regulations).
6. Denis Twitchett and Michael Loewe, eds., *The Cambridge History of China,* vol. 1, *The Ch'in and Han Empires 221 B.C.–A.D. 220* (New York: Cambridge University Press, 1986), p. 61.

7. A. F. P. Hulsewé, *Remnants of Ch'in Law: An Annotated Translation of the Ch'in Legal and Administrative Rules of the Third Century B.C., Discovered in Yün-meng Prefecture, Hu-pei Province, in 1975* (Leiden: E. J. Brill, 1985), p. 205.
8. Hugh Scogin, "Between Heaven and Man: Contract and the State in Han Dynasty China," *Southern California Law Review* 63, no. 5 (1990): 1386.
9. Nancy Lee Swann, *Pan Chao: Foremost Woman Scholar of China* (New York: American Historical Association, 1932), pp. 84–85.

Chapter 5

1. http://www.pbs.org/wgbh/nova/maya/copa_transcript .html#08. For David Stuart's latest views about this text, see David Stuart, "The Beginnings of the Copán Dynasty: A Review of the Hieroglyphic and Historical Evidence," in *Understanding Early Classic Copán*, ed. Ellen E. Bell et al. (Philadelphia: University of Pennsylvania Museum of Archaeology and Anthropology, 2004), pp. 215–248; David Stuart, "'The Arrival of Strangers': Teotihuacan and Tollan in Classic Maya History," in *Mesoamerica's Classic Heritage: From Teotihuacan to the Aztecs*, ed. David Carrasco (Boulder: University Press of Colorado, 2000), pp. 465–513. To date, Professor Stuart has not published a full translation of this difficult text.
2. Scholars today use the word *Maya* to refer to the people and *Mayan* for the language they spoke.
3. Michael D. Coe, *The Maya*, 6th ed. (New York: Thames and Hudson, 1999), p. 196.
4. John Flenley and Paul Bahn, *The Enigmas of Easter Island: Island on the Edge* (New York: Oxford University Press, 2002), pp. 104 (the number of moai); 125–127 (van Tilburg's experiments).
5. K. R. Howe, *The Quest for Origins: Who First Discovered and Settled the Pacific Islands* (Honolulu: University of Hawai'i Press, 2003), p. 180.

Chapter 6

1. Herodotus, *The Histories*, trans. Aubrey De Sélincourt, further rev. ed. (New York: Penguin Books, 1954, 1996), pp. 188–189, Book III: passage 82 ("Constitutional Debate"); 57, I: 137 (truth-telling); 140, I: 57 (Zoroastrian burial practices); 399, VII: 83 (the Immortals); 193, III: 96 (melting of silver); 193, III: 97 (Ethiopian payments); 1, I: 0 (purpose of the book); 228–229, IV: 42 (circumnavigation of Africa by the Phoenicians with place names updated); 363, VI: 116 (casualties at Marathon); 402–403, VII: 99 (Artemisia as a commander).
2. M. Aperghis, "Population—Production—Taxation—Coinage: A Model for the Seleukid Economy," in *Hellenistic Economies*, ed. Z. H. Archibald et al. (London: Routledge, 2001), pp. 69–102, 77 (population estimate). Reference supplied by Christopher Tuplin (University of Liverpool).
3. Lionel Casson, *Travel in the Ancient World* (Baltimore: Johns Hopkins University Press, 1974), pp. 53–54; estimates speed of the couriers and translates Herodotus VIII: 98.
4. Richard N. Frye, *The Heritage of Persia* (New York: World Publishing Company, 1963), p. 85.

5. Josef Wiesehöfer, *Ancient Persia from 550 BC to 650 AD*, trans. Azizeh Azodi (New York: I. B. Tauris, 2001), pp. 63, citing Herodotus III: 89 (about the differences among three Achaemenid rulers); 69 (order from Persepolis); 197 (Ammianus Marcellinus about the Parthian cavalry); 165 (Shapur I's inscription).
6. M. Cary and E. H. Warmington, *The Ancient Explorers* (London: Methuen, 1929), pp. 47–48.
7. Aeschylus, *The Persians*, trans. Anthony J. Podlecki (Englewood Cliffs: Prentice-Hall, 1970), pp. 49–50; l. 251–255.
8. Email, dated June 23, 2005, from Kevin van Bladel, University of Southern California, summarizing the unpublished research of Shaul Shaked.

Chapter 7

1. Polybius, *The Rise of the Roman Empire*, trans. Ian Scott-Kilvert (New York: Penguin Books, 1979), pp. 41–43 (the importance of the Roman empire); 221–222 (Polybius's trip to the Alps); 227–228 (difficult conditions in the Alps); 427–428 (composition of Hannibal's army); 271 (appearance of the army); 332–333 (punishment in camp); 528–529 (meeting with Scipio Aemilianus).
2. Plutarch, *Roman Lives: A Selection of Eight Roman Lives*, trans. Robin Waterfield (New York: Oxford University Press, 1999), pp. 83, 115.
3. "Slavery," in *The Oxford Companion to Classical Civilization*, ed. Simon Hornblower and Antony Sparforth (New York: Oxford University Press, 1998), p. 671.
4. "Population, Roman," in *The Oxford Companion*, pp. 561–562.
5. Betty Radice, *The Letters of the Younger Pliny* (New York: Penguin, 1963), pp. 166–168 (about Pompeii); 126–127 (about his wife).
6. "Population, Roman," in *The Oxford Companion*, pp. 561–562.
7. Morton Smith, *Jesus the Magician* (New York: Harper and Row, 1978), p. 45. Chapter 4 of this book, "What the Outsiders Said—Evidence Outside the Gospels," provides an excellent introduction to non-gospel sources about Jesus. Only one nonchurch source from the first century refers to Jesus: the Jewish historian Josephus, writing sometime in 90 C.E., mentions "the brother of Jesus, the so-called Christ, James was his name." In addition to the sources discussed by Morton Smith, some scholars believe that the gospel of Thomas contains earlier versions of Jesus' sayings than those recorded in the canonical gospels, while others contend that they are later.
8. *Documents of the Christian Church*, ed. Henry Bettenson (New York: Oxford University Press, 1966), p. 35.
9. *Egeria: Diary of a Pilgrimage*, trans. George E. Gingras (New York: Newman Press, 1970), pp. 75–76.
10. Peter Brown, *Augustine of Hippo: A Biography* (London: Faber and Faber Limited, 2000), p. 430.

Chapter 8

1. Huili, *Da Ci'en si sanzang fashi zhuan* (Beijing: Zhonghua shuju, 2000), p. 20. In doing my translation, I consulted *A Biography of the Tripitaka Master of the Great Ci'en Monastery of the Great Tang Dynasty*, trans. Li Rongxi (San Francisco: Numata Center for Buddhist Translation and Research, 1995), pp. 31–32, which contains a full description of the meeting.
2. Richard H. Davis, "Introduction: A Brief History of Religions in India," in *Religions of Asia in Practice: An Anthology*, ed. Donald S. Lopez, Jr. (Princeton: Princeton University Press, 2002), p. 5.
3. Robert Kaplan, *The Nothing That Is: A Natural History of Zero* (New York: Oxford University Press, 1999), p. 41.
4. *A Biography of the Tripitaka Master*, p. 58.
5. *Si-yu-ki: Buddhist Records of the Western World Translated from the Chinese of Hiuen Tsiang (A.D. 629)*, trans. Samuel Beal (Delhi: Motilal Banarsidass, 1981; reprint of 1882 original), p. 82.
6. Anthony Reid, "Introduction: A Time and a Place," in *Southeast Asia in the Early Modern Era: Trade, Power, and Belief* (Ithaca: Cornell University Press, 1993), p. 3.
7. Valerie Hansen, *The Open Empire: A History of China to 1600* (New York: W.W. Norton, 2000), p. 159.
8. *Lives of the Nuns: Biographies of Chinese Buddhist Nuns from the Fourth to Sixth Centuries: A Translation of the Pi-ch'iu-ni chuan, compiled by Shih Pao-ch'ang*, trans. Kathryn Ann Tsai (Honolulu: University of Hawaii Press, 1994), pp. 20–21.
9. Hansen, p. 182.
10. Ilyon, *Samguk Yusa: The Legends and History of the Three Kingdoms of Ancient Korea*, trans. Tae-Hung Ha and Grafton K. Mintz (Seoul: Yonsei University Press, 1972), p. 188.

Chapter 9

1. Nabia Abbott, *Two Queens of Baghdad: Mother and Wife of Harun al-Rashid* (London: Al Saqi Books, 1986, reprint of 1946 original), p. 26; citing Jahiz (pseud.), *Kitab al-Mahasin wa Al-Addad*, ed. van Vloten (Leiden: E. J. Brill, 1898), pp. 232–233.
2. Charles Issawi, "The Area and Population of the Arab Empire: An Essay in Speculation," in *The Islamic Middle East, 700–1900: Studies in Economic and Social History*, ed. A. L. Udovitch (Princeton: Darwin Press, 1981), pp. 375–396; estimated population on p. 392.
3. Jacob Lassner, *The Topography of Baghdad in the Early Middle Ages* (Detroit: Wayne State University Press, 1970), p. 127, citing the Islamic writer Ya'qubi.
4. Lunde, Paul, and Caroline Stone, trans., *The Meadows of Gold: The Abbasids by Mas'udi* (New York: Kegan Paul International, 1989), p. 388. See an alternate translation in Dmitri Gutas, *Greek Thought, Arabic Culture: The Graeco-Arabic Translation Movement in Baghdad and Early Abbāsid Society (2nd–4th/8th–10th centuries)* (New York: Routledge, 1998), p. 30.

5. Richard W. Bulliet, *Conversion to Islam in the Medieval Period: An Essay in Quantitative History* (Cambridge, Mass.: Harvard University Press, 1979), p. 44, graph 5.
6. G. S. P. Freeman-Grenville, *The East African Coast: Select Documents from the First to the Earlier Nineteenth Century* (Oxford: Clarendon Press, 1962), excerpt #5, "Buzurg Ibn Shahriyar of Ramhormuz: A Tenth-Century Slaving Adventure," pp. 9–13.
7. Abbott, pp. 89–90. Compare *The History of al-Tabari*, Vol. XXX: *The Abbasid Caliphate in Equilibrium*, trans. and annotated by C. E. Bosworth (Albany: State University of New York Press, 1989), p. 42; romanizations changed for consistency.
8. *The Abbasid Caliphate in Equilibrium*, p. 45; also translated in Abbott, p. 92.
9. *The Travels of Ibn Jubayr*, trans. R. J. C. Broadhurst (London: Jonathan Cape, 1952): number of pilgrims, p. 191; prayers and weeping, 180; riot and plunder, 184; bazaar goods, 184–185; road from Baghdad to Mecca, 216; palace of the caliph, 236; Frankish captives, 313.

Chapter 10

1. Magnus Magnusson and Hermann Palsson, trans., *The Vinland Sagas: The Norse Discovery of America* (New York: Penguin Books, 1965), pp. 97–98.
2. Warren Treadgold, *A History of the Byzantine State and Society* (Stanford: Stanford University Press, 1997), pp. 196, 297.
3. Katherine Fischer Drew, *The Laws of the Salian Franks* (Philadelphia: University of Pennsylvania Press, 1991), p. 127.
4. http://www.fordham.edu/halsall/source/gregtours1.html. "The Incident of the Vase at Soissons," in *Readings in European History*, ed. J. H. Robinson (Boston: Ginn, 1905), pp. 51–55.
5. Patrick J. Geary, *Before France and Germany: The Creation and Transformation of the Merovingian World* (New York: Oxford University Press, 1988), p. 115.
6. Ibid., p. 130.
7. R. W. Southern, *Western Society and the Church in the Middle Ages* (Harmondsworth: Penguin, 1970), p. 65.
8. Paul Edward Dutton, *Charlemagne's Courtier: The Complete Einhard* (Orchard Park, N.Y.: Broadview Press, 1998), II: 25.
9. Magnusson and Palsson: *Warlock songs*, pp. 82–83; a ghost's instructions on burial, 89–90; a former slave proposes to Gudrid, 80; Erik the Red and his father leaving Norway, 49; first encounter with Skraelings, 65; Skraeling catapult, 99; Skraeling life, 102–103; reasons for leaving the Americas, 100.
10. James E. Montgomery, "Ibn Fadlan and the Rusiyyah," *Journal of Arabic and Islamic Studies* 3 (2000): 10.
11. Serge A. Zenkovsky, *Medieval Russia's Epics, Chronicles, and Tales* (New York: E. P. Dutton, 1974), pp. 67–68.

Chapter 11

1. Because of differences in the calendars, Islamic years often straddle two Western years. Although most sources give the year in both the Islamic calendar and the Western, this chapter, like Chapter 9, will give only the Western equivalent.

2. H. A. R. Gibb, trans., *The Travels of Ibn Battuta A.D. 1325–1354,* 4 vols. (London: Hakluyt Society, 1958–1994): departure from Tangier, I: 8; Mali griots, IV: 962; Taghaza and trading salt, IV: 947; inheritance in Mali, IV: 951; power of queens, IV: 963; Muslim practice, IV: 951; caravan leader and religious law, IV: 952; what was good, IV: 966; his divorce, I: 18; Ghazza, IV: 918; Damascus, I: 144; Mogadishu, II: 376; Kilwa, II: 379–380; Chinese ships, IV: 813–814.

3. David Lee Schoenbrun, *A Green Place, A Good Place: Agrarian Change, Gender, and Social Identity in the Great Lakes Region to the 15th Century* (Portsmouth, N.H.: Heinemann, 1998), p. 40.

4. Jan Vansina, *Paths in the Rainforest: Toward a History of Political Tradition in Equatorial Africa* (Madison: University of Wisconsin Press, 1990), pp. 31, 33.

5. Al-Bakri's *The Book of Routes and Realms,* as translated in *Corpus of Early Arabic Sources for West African History,* ed. N. Levtzion and J. F. P. Hopkins (New York: Cambridge University Press, 1981): Sijilmasa, pp. 65–66; Ghana, pp. 79–81.

6. Patricia and Fredrick McKissack, *The Royal Kingdoms of Ghana, Mali, and Songhay: Life in Medieval Africa* (New York: Henry Holt, 1994), p. 34.

7. D. T. Niane, *Sundiata: An Epic of Old Mali,* trans. G. D. Pickett (London: Longman, 1965).

8. D. T. Niane, "Mali and the Second Mandingo Expansion," in *General History of Africa* (California: Heinemann and UNESCO, 1984), p. 148, n. 62.

9. Ralph A. Austen, "The Trans-Saharan Slave Trade: A Tentative Census," in *The Uncommon Market: Essays in the Economic History of the Atlantic Slave Trade,* ed. Henry A. Gemery and Jan S. Hogendorn (New York: Academic Press, 1979), pp. 23–69; tables on pp. 31, 66.

10. Andrew M. Watson, "Back to Gold-and Silver," *Economic History Review* 20.1 (1967): 1–34, estimate in 30–31, n. 1.

11. Ross E. Dunn, *The Adventures of Ibn Battuta, a Muslim Traveler of the 14th Century* (Berkeley: University of California Press, 2005), p. 45.

12. J. N. Mattock, "Ibn Battuta's Use of Ibn Jubayr's Rihla," in *Proceedings of the Ninth Congress of the Union Européenne des arabisants et Islamisants,* ed. Rudolph Peters (Leiden: E. J. Brill, 1981), pp. 209–218, estimate on p. 211.

13. Michael W. Dols, *The Black Death in the Middle East* (Princeton: Princeton University Press, 1977), p. 215.

14. Peter Garlake, *Great Zimbabwe Described and Explained* (Harare: Zimbabwe Publishing House, 1982), p. 14.

15. P. S. Garlake, *Great Zimbabwe* (New York: Stein and Day, 1973): size of Elliptical Building, p. 27; estimate of number of laborers, 195; excavated horde, 131.

Chapter 12

1. Stephen Owen, "The Snares of Memory," in *Remembrances: The Experience of the Past in Classical Chinese Literature* (Cambridge: Harvard University Press, 1986): cartloads of books, p. 89; thirty years of calamity, 97; pawning clothes, 82; drinking game, 85; sacrificial vessels, 90.

2. *Women Writers of Traditional China: An Anthology of Poetry and Criticism,* ed. Kang-i Sun Chang and Haun Saussy (Stanford, Calif.: Stanford University Press, 1999), p. 98.

3. Valerie Hansen, *The Open Empire: A History of China to 1600* (New York: W. W. Norton, 2000), p. 266.

4. Tsien Tsuen-hsuin, *Chemistry and Chemical Technology, Part I: Paper and Printing,* vol. V:1 of *Science and Civilisation in China,* ed. Joseph Needham (New York: Cambridge University Press, 1985), pp. 201–202.

5. Patricia Buckley Ebrey, "The Women in Liu Kezhuang's Family," *Modern China* 10.4 (1984): 415–400, citation on 437.

6. Peter K. Bol, "The Sung Examination System and the Shih," *Asia Major,* 3d ser., 3.2 (1990): 149–171, statistic on 152.

7. Hansen, p. 295.

8. Ibid., p. 294.

9. Ellen Neskar, "Shrines to Local Former Worthies," in *Religions of China in Practice,* ed. Donald S. Lopez (Princeton: Princeton University Press, 1996).

10. Joseph Needham with Wang Ling, *Mathematics and the Sciences of the Heavens and the Earth,* vol. 3 of *Science and Civilisation in China,* ed. Joseph Needham (New York: Cambridge University Press, 1959), caption to fig. 226 facing p. 548.

11. Frederick Hirth and W. W. Rockhill, *Chau Ju-kua: His Work on the Chinese and Arab Trade in the Twelfth and Thirteenth Centuries, Entitled Chu-fan-chï* (St. Petersburg: Imperial Academy of Sciences, 1911): Vietnam, p. 46; Korea, 167; where the sun rises, 170; cedar planks, 171; Madagascar, 149.

Chapter 13

1. *The Letters of Abelard and Heloise,* trans. Betty Radice, rev. M. T. Clanchy (New York: Penguin Books, 2003), p. 3.

2. R. I. Moore, *The First European Revolution, c. 970–1215* (Oxford: Blackwell, 2000), p. 30, citing J. C. Russell.

3. Claudia Opitz, "Life in the Late Middle Ages," in *Silence of the Middle Ages,* ed. Chistiane Klapisch-Zuber, vol. 2 of A History of Women in the West (Cambridge, Mass.: Belknap Press of Harvard University Press, 1992), p. 296.

4. A. J. Minnis and A. B. Scott, *Medieval Literary Theory and Criticism, c. 1100–c. 1375* (Oxford: Clarendon Press, 1988), p. 99.

5. M. T. Clancy, *From Memory to Written Record,* 2d ed. (Oxford: Blackwell, 1993), pp. 120–121.

6. Joseph H. Lynch, *The Medieval Church: A Brief History* (London: Longman, 1992): inerrancy of the Roman Church, p. 146; Cistercians, 201; Franciscan followers, 232.

7. Robert the Monk's account, http://www.fordham.edu/halsall/source/urban2–5vers.html.

8. Francesco Gabrieli, *Arab Historians of the Crusades,* trans. E. J. Costello (London: Routledge and Kegan Paul, 1969), p. 100.
9. Thomas F. Madden, ed., *The Crusades: The Essential Readings* (Oxford: Blackwell, 2002), p. 109, n. 4; citing Robert of Clari, *The Conquest of Constantinople,* trans. Edgar Holmes McNeal (New York: Columbia University Press, 1936), p. 112.
10. Barbara H. Rosenwein, *A Short History of the Middle Ages* (Peterborough, Ont.: Broadview Press, 2002), p. 168.
11. Paul Freedman, "Spices and Late-Medieval European Ideas of Scarcity and Value," *Speculum* 80.4 (2005): 1209–1227.
12. Samuel K. Cohn, Jr., "The Black Death: End of a Paradigm," *American Historical Review* 107.3 (June 2002): 703–738: Avignon death statistics, p. 727; numbers of manuals, 707–708.

Chapter 14

1. Peter Jackson, trans., *The Mission of Friar William of Rubruck: His Journey to the Court of the Great Khan Möngke 1253–1255* (London: The Hakluyt Society, 1990): travel companions, pp. 70–71; division of labor, 90–91; khumis and open-air sleeping, 99; intense cold, 136; pick of horses, 140; description of Möngke, 178; drunk interpreter, 180; Hetum I's comments on William, Appendix V, 282; hunger, 141. Some changes made to avoid the use of brackets.
2. Joseph Fletcher, "The Mongols: Ecological and Social Perspectives," *Harvard Journal of Asiatic Studies* 46, no. 1 (1986): 1–56, explanation of tanistry on 17.
3. Ata-Malik Juvaini, *Genghis Khan: The History of the World Conqueror,* trans. J. A. Boyle (Seattle: University of Washington Press, 1958), p. 107.
4. André Wegener Sleeswyk, "The Liao and the Displacement of Ships in the Ming Dynasty," *The Mariner's Mirror* 81 (1996): 3–13.
5. Fei Xin, *Xingcha Shenglan: The Overall Survey of the Star Raft,* trans. J. V. G. Mills, rev. and ed. Roderich Ptak (Wiesbaden: Harrassowitz, 1996): size of ships and commodities at Mogadishu, p. 102.

Chapter 15

1. J. M. Cohen, trans., *The Four Voyages of Christopher Columbus* (New York: Penguin, 1969): description of Hispaniola, pp. 117–118; giving trifles, 35.
2. Michael E. Smith, *The Aztecs* (Malden, Mass.: Blackwell Publishing, 1996), p. 62, says four to six million.
3. Terence d'Altroy, *The Incas* (Malden, Mass.: Blackwell Publishing, 2002): mummies in Cuzco, p. 97 (citing Pedro Pizarro); human sacrifice statistics, 172; Inca insults, 226–227; population of the Inca empire, 48; storehouse of dried birds, 281.
4. Cassandra Fedele, "Oration to the University of Padua (1487)," in *The Renaissance in Europe: An Anthology,* ed. Peter Elmer et al. (New Haven: Yale University Press, in association with the Open University, 2000), pp. 52–56.
5. Peter Russell, *Prince Henry "the Navigator": A Life* (New Haven: Yale University Press, 2000), pp. 242–243, n. 8,

citing *Crónica dos Feitos na Conquista de Guiné,* II:145–148.
6. Stuart B. Schwartz, *Victors and Vanquished: Spanish and Nahua Views of the Conquest of Mexico* (New York: Bedford/St. Martin's, 2000): Spanish weapons and armor, p. 97; description of Tenochtitlan, 133.
7. Michael Wood, *Conquistadors* (Berkeley: University of California Press, 2000), p. 81, citing the *Florentine Codex.*
8. Alfred W. Crosby, *The Columbian Exchange: Biological and Cultural Consequences of 1492* (Westport, Conn.: Greenwood Press, 1972), p. 4, n.2, citing Christopher Columbus, *Journals and Other Documents on the Life and Voyages of Christopher Columbus,* trans. Samuel Eliot Morison (New York: The Heritage Press, 1963), pp. 72–73, 84.
9. Smith, p. 61; *Noble David Cook, Demographic Collapse: Indian Peru, 1520–1620* (Cambridge: Cambridge University Press, 1981), p. 94.

Chapter 16

1. *The Diary of Matthew Ricci,* in Matthew Ricci, *China in the Sixteenth Century,* trans. Louis Gallagher (New York: Random House, 1942, 1970), pp. 54–55.
2. E. Mungello, *The Great Encounter of China and the West, 1500–1800,* 2d ed. (Lanham, Md.: Rowman and Littlefield, 2005).
3. Michael Pearson, *The Indian Ocean* (London: Routledge, 2003), p. 121.
4. James D. Tracy, *The Political Economy of Merchant Empires* (New York: Cambridge University Press, 1991), p. 1.
5. Cited in John Reader, *Africa: A Biography of the Continent* (New York: Vintage, 1999), pp. 374–375.
6. Steven Warshaw and C. David Bromwell with A. J. Tudisco, *India Emerges* (Berkeley: Diablo Press, 1974), p. 60.
7. Matteo Ricci, *The True Meaning of the Lord of Heaven,* trans. Douglas Lancashire and Peter Hu Kuo-chen, S.J. (Paris: Institut Ricci-Centre d'études chinoises, 1985), p. 99.

Chapter 17

1. Sir John Chardin, *Travels in Persia, 1673–1677, an abridged English version of Voyages du chevalier Chardin en Perse, et autres lieux de l'Orient* (New York: Dover Press, 1988), p. 70. Spelling and usage have been modernized.
2. *The Turkish Letters of Ogier Ghiselin de Busbecq, Imperial Ambassador at Constantinople, 1554–1562,* trans. Edward S. Foster. New York: Oxford University Press.
3. Cited in Ronald W. Ferrier, *A Journey to Persia: Jean Chardin's Portrait of a Seventeenth Century Empire* (London: I. B. Tauris, 1996), p. 44.
4. William Shakespeare, *King Richard II,* Act 2, Scene 1.
5. Chardin, p. 8.

Chapter 18

1. Catalina de Erauso, *Lieutenant Nun: Memoir of a Basque Transvestite in the New World,* trans. Michele Stepto and Gabriel Stepto (Boston: Beacon Press, 1996), pp. 33–34.

Other quotations in the chapter from pages 4, 6, 16, 28–29, 39.

2. Quoted in Octavio Paz, *Sor Juana*, trans. Margaret Sayers Peden (Cambridge: Harvard University Press, 1988), p. 219.

3. Quoted in George Fredrickson, *White Supremacy: A Comparative Study in American and South African History* (New York: Oxford University Press, 1981), p. 100.

4. Octavio Paz, *The Labyrinth of Solitude* (New York: Grove Press, 1961), pp. 101–102.

Chapter 19

1. Olaudah Equiano, *The Interesting Narrative of the Life of Olaudah Equiano, or Gustavus Vassa, the African,* ed. Vincent Carretta, 2d ed. (New York: Penguin Putnam, 2003).

2. Quoted in David Northrup, *The Atlantic Slave Trade*, 2d ed. (Boston: Houghton Mifflin, 2001), p. 53.

3. *A Letter to a Member of Parliament, Concerning the Importance of Our Sugar-Colonies to Great Britain, by a Gentleman, Who Resided Many Years in the Island of Jamaica* (London: J. Taylor, 1745).

4. Quoted in *Equiano*, p. 83, spelling modernized.

5. Mark Kurlansky, *Cod: A Biography of the Fish That Changed the World* (New York: Penguin Books, 1997), p. 75.

Chapter 20

1. Xie Qinggao, *Hailu jiaoyi*, ed. An Jing (Beijing: Shangwu yingshugan, 2002).

2. Susan Mann, *Precious Records: Women in China's Long Eighteenth Century* (Stanford: Stanford University Press, 1997), p. 149.

3. J. L. Cranmer-Byng, ed., *An Embassy to China: Lord Macartney's Journal, 1793–1794* (Hamden, Conn.: Archon Books, 1963), p. 340.

4. Horace Walpole, speech quoted in *Cambridge History of India* (Cambridge: Cambridge University Press, 1929), vol. 5, p. 187.

5. Quoted in Francis Watson, *A Concise History of India* (London: Thames and Hudson, 1979), p. 131.

6. Xie, p. 63.

7. Conrad Totman, *Early Modern Japan* (Berkeley: University of California Press, 1993).

8. Quoted in Ryusaku Tsunoda et al., *Sources of the Japanese Tradition* (New York: Columbia University Press, 1958), pp. 399–400.

Chapter 21

1. J. C. Beaglehole, ed., *The Endeavour Journal of Joseph Banks,* 2d ed. (Sydney: Halsted Press, 1962), vol. 1, p. 252. Here as elsewhere, some revisions of Banks's punctuation and usage have been made.

2. Quoted in Patrick O'Brien, *Joseph Banks: A Life* (Chicago: University of Chicago Press, 1987), pp. 105 and 264.

3. Immanuel Kant, *The Critique of Pure Reason* (Garden City: Doubleday, 1966).

4. Sir Francis Bacon, *The Advancement of Learning* (London: Oxford University Press, 1960).

5. Alexander Pope, "Epitaph intended for Sir Isaac Newton."

6. Quoted in Richard Drayton, *Nature's Government: Science, Imperial Britain, and the 'Improvement' of the World* (New Haven: Yale University Press, 2000), p. 108.

7. Quoted in ibid., p. 55.

8. Quoted in ibid., p. 118.

9. Thomas Hobbes, *The Leviathan.*

10. Quoted in Moira Ferguson, ed., *First Feminists: British Women Writers, 1578–1799* (Bloomington: Indiana University Press, 1985), p. 86.

11. Kant, *Critique of Pure Reason.*

12. Quoted in Dava Sorbel and Willam J. H. Andrews, *The Illustrated Longitude: The True Story of a Lone Genius Who Solved the Greatest Scientific Problem of His Time* (New York: Walker & Co., 1998), p. 176.

13. Laura Hostetler, *Qing Colonial Enterprise: Ethnography and Cartography in Early Modern China* (Chicago: University of Chicago Press, 2001), p. 24.

14. Matthew H. Edney, *Mapping an Empire: The Geographical Construction of British India, 1765–1843* (Chicago: University of Chicago Press, 1990), p. 1.

15. Quoted in O'Brien, p. 94.

16. Ibid., p. 95.

Chapter 22

1. Simón Bolívar, "Oath Taken at Rome, 15 August 1805," trans. Frederick H. Fornoff, in *El Libertador: Writings of Simón Bolívar,* ed. David Bushnell (New York: Oxford University Press, 2003), pp. 113–144.

2. David Bushnell, *Simón Bolívar: Liberation and Disappointment* (New York: Pearson Longman, 2004).

3. Olympe de Gouges, *Écrits politiques, 1788–1791,* trans. Tracey Rizzo (Paris: Côtes Femmes, 1993), p. 209. Reprinted in Tracy Rizzo and Laura Mason, eds., The French Revolution: A Document Collection (Boston: Houghton Mifflin, 1999), p. 111.

4. Quoted in Bushnell, p. 77.

5. Ibid., p. 203.

6. Marie Jean Antoine Nicolas Caritat, Marquis de Condorcet, *The Future Progress of the Human Mind,* http://www.fordham.edu/halsall/mod/condorcet-progress.html.

Chapter 23

1. Alexander Herzen, *My Past and Thoughts,* trans. Constance Garnett (Berkeley: University of California Press, 1982), p. 313.

2. Quoted in *Edward Acton, Alexander Herzen and the Role of the Intellectual Revolutionary* (Cambridge: Cambridge University Press, 1979), p. 29.

3. Alexander Herzen, "An Open Letter to Jules Michelet," in *From the Other Shore and the Russian People and Socialism* (New York: George Braziller, 1956), pp. 189–190.

4. Herzen, *My Past and Thoughts*, p. 462.

5. Ibid., p. 414.

6. Friedrich Engels, *The Condition of the Working Class in England,* in *The Marx-Engels Reader,* ed. Richard C. Tucker, 2d ed. (New York: W.W. Norton, 1978), pp. 580–581.

7. John Stuart Mill, *On Liberty* (London: Longman, Roberts & Green, 1869), p. 5.
8. Herzen, *My Past and Thoughts,* pp. 333–334.
9. Quoted in Otto Pflanze, *Bismarck and the Development of Germany* (Princeton: Princeton University Press, 1990), vol. 1, p. 184.
10. Karl Marx and Friedrich Engels, *Manifesto of the Communist Party,* in *The Marx-Engels Reader,* ed. Richard C. Tucker, 2d ed. (New York: W.W. Norton, 1978), p. 500.
11. Ibid., p. 477.
12. Ibid., p. 474.
13. Ibid., pp. 476–477.
14. Herzen, *My Past and Thoughts,* p. 321.

Chapter 24

1. Fukuzawa Yûkichi, *The Autobiography of Yukichi Fukuzawa,* trans. Eiichi Kiyooka (New York: Columbia University Press, 1960), pp. 112–116.
2. Ibid., p. 277.
3. William H. McNeill and Mitsuko Iriye, *Modern Asia and Africa* (Oxford: Oxford University Press, 1971).
4. Franz Michael and Chang Chung-li, *The Taiping Rebellion: History and Documents* (Seattle: University of Washington Press, 1971), vol. 2, p. 314.
5. Jen Yu-Wen, *The Taiping Revolutionary Moment* (New Haven: Yale University Press, 1973), pp. 93–94.
6. Michael and Chang, vol. 3, p. 767.
7. Teng Ssu-yü and John K. Fairbank, *China's Response to the West: A Documentary Survey, 1839–1923* (Cambridge, Mass.: Harvard University Press, 1954), pp. 53–54.
8. Quoted in Patricia Buckley Ebrey, *Cambridge Illustrated History of China* (London: Cambridge University Press, 1996), p. 245.
9. Victor Purcell, *The Boxer Uprising: A Background Study* (New York: Cambridge University Press, 1963), p. 224.
10. Fukuzawa, p. 18.
11. Ibid., p. 164.
12. Ibid., p. 210.
13. Fukuzawa Yûkichi, *The Speeches of Fukuzawa: A Translation and Critical Study,* ed. Wayne Oxford (Tokyo: Hokuseido House, 1973), p. 93.
14. Fukuzawa, *Autobiography,* p. 190.
15. Fukuzawa Yûkichi, *Fukuzawa Yukichi on Japanese Women: Selected Works* (Tokyo: University of Tokyo Press, 1988), p. 138.
16. http://womenshistory.about.com/library/qu/blqutosh .htm?pid=2765&cob=home.
17. Quoted in Helen M. Hopper, *Fukuzawa Yûkichi: From Samurai to Capitalist* (New York: Pearson Longman, 2005), p. 120.
18. Stanley Wolpert, *India* (Berkeley: University of California Press, 1991), p. 51.
19. Quoted in Stanley A. Wolpert, *Tilak and Gokhale: Revolution and Reform in the Making of Modern India* (Berkeley: University of California Press, 1991, p. 191.

Chapter 25

1. Pauline Johnson-Tekahionwake, "A Cry from an Indian Wife," in *Flint and Feather: The Complete Poems of E. Pauline Johnson* (Tekahionwake) (Toronto: Hodder and Stoughton, 1969).
2. Cited in Thomas Bender, *A Nation Among Nations: America's Place in World History* (New York: Hill and Wang, 2006), p. 121.
3. *Aberdeen Saturday Pioneer,* December 20, 1890.

Chapter 26

1. King Khama of the Bangwato, quoted in Neil Parsons, *King Khama, Emperor Joe and the Great White Queen: Victorian Britain Through African Eyes* (Chicago: University of Chicago Press, 1998), p. 103.
2. W. E. B. Du Bois, *The Souls of Black Folk* (New York: Vintage, 1990).

Chapter 27

1. Louise Bryant, *Six Red Months in Moscow* (London: Heinemann, 1919), p. xx.

Chapter 28

1. Halide Edib, *Inside India* (New York: Oxford University Press, 2002).
2. Hashimoto Kingoro, "Address to Young Men," in *Sources of Japanese Tradition,* ed. William Theodore de Bary (New York: Columbia University Press, 1958), vol. 2, p. 289.
3. Ibid, p. 231.

Chapter 29

1. All quotations from Nancy Wake, *The White Mouse* (Melbourne: Australian Large Print, 1987).

Chapter 30

1. Ernesto Guevara, *The Motorcycle Diaries: Notes on a Latin American Journey,* ed. and trans. Alexandra Keeble (Melbourne: Ocean Press, 2003), pp. 75–78.
2. Quoted in David Sandison, *Che Guevara* (New York: St. Martin's Griffin, 1997), pp. 105 and 108.

Chapter 31

1. Nelson Mandela, *Nelson Mandela in His Own Words,* ed. Kader Asmal, David Chidester, and Wilmot James (New York: Little Brown, 2003), pp. 59–62.
2. Nelson Mandela, "I Will Return," ibid., pp. 46–47.

Chapter 32

1. Mira Nair, "Create the World You Know," Variety Cinema Militans Lecture delivered at the Netherlands Film Festival in Utrecht on September 29, 2002; http:// mirabaifilms.com/wordpress/?page_id=42.
2. Mira Kamdar, *Planet India: How the Fastest-Growing Democracy Is Transforming America and the World* (New York: Scribner, 2007), p. 4.

3. Caption data from http://hdr.undp.org/en/statistics. Map data from *The World Almanac and Book of Facts, 2008,* ed. C. Alan Joyce (World Almanac Books, 2008).

4. Robert Kuttner, "The Role of Governments in the Global Economy," in *Global Capitalism,* ed. Will Hutton and Anthony Giddens (New York: New Press, 2000), p. 163.

5. Dr. Margaret Chan, "Health in a Changing Environment," http://www.who.int/mediacentre/news/statements/2007/s11/en/index.html.

6. Mira Nair and Sooni Taraporevala, *Salaam Bombay!* (New York: Penguin Books, 1988), p. 7.

7. United Nations, *World Urbanization Prospects* (New York: United Nations, 2006).

8. *The Greenbelt Movement,* "Question and Answer Session with Prof. Wangari Maathai," http://www.greenbeltmovement.org/a.php?id=27.

9. Franklin Foer, *How Soccer Explains the World: An Unlikely Theory of Globalization* (New York: HarperCollins, 2004), pp. 2–3.

10. http://www.maishafilmlab.com/index.php.

TEXT CREDITS

pages 28, 30, 32, 35, 54: Excerpts from *The Epic of Gilgamesh,* translated by Benjmain R. Foster. Copyright © 2001 by W.W. Norton & Company. Used by permission of W.W. Norton & Company, Inc.

page 45: Excerpt from the *Book of the Dead* from James Pritchard, *Ancient Near Eastern Texts Relating to the Old Testament,* Third Edition With Supplement. Copyright © 1950, 1955, 1969, renewed 1978 by Princeton University Press. Reprinted by permission of Princeton University Press.

pages 60, 62, 81: Excerpts from *Aśoka and the Decline of the Mauryas,* ed. Romila Thapar, 1973, pp. 251–252, 253, 254–255, 255–256. Reprinted with permission of Oxford University Press, New Delhi.

page 68: From *The Rig Veda: An Anthology of One Hundred and Eight Hymns,* selected, translated, and annotated by Wendy Doniger O'Flaherty (Penguin Classics, 1981). Copyright © Wendy Doniger O'Flaherty, 1981. Reprinted with permission of Penguin Group/UK.

pages 80–81: From "The First Sermon of Buddha," from Walpola Rahula, *What the Buddha Taught,* Grove Atlantic, 1974, pp. 92–94. Copyright © 1959, 1974 by Wapola Rahula. Used by permission of Grove/Atlantic, Inc.

pages 88, 101: Excerpts from Martin Kern, *The Stele Inscriptions of Ch'in Shih-huang: Texts and Ritual in Early Chinese Imperial Representation,* American Oriental Society, 2000, pp. 18–23, 13, 17, 19–20. Reprinted with permission of the American Oriental Society, http://www.umich.edu/~aos/.

pages 96, 98–99: Excerpts from *The Analects of Confucius,* translated by Simon Leys. Copyright © 1997 by Pierre Ryckman. Used by permission of W.W. Norton & Company, Inc.

page 99: From *Records of the Grand Historian,* translated by by Burton Watson, 1993, pp. 233, 235. Copyright © 1993 Columbia University Press. Reprinted with permission of the pubisher.

pages 114, 116: Text from the *Nova* website for the program "Lost King of the Maya" located at http://www.pbs.org/wbgh/nova/maya/copa_transcript.html#08. From NOVA/WGBH Educational Foundation. Copyright © 2001 WGBH/Boston.

pages 128–129: Reprinted with permission of Simon & Schuster Adult Publishing Group, from *Popul Vuh: The Definitive Edition of the Mayan Book of the Dawn of Life and the Glories of Gods and Kings,* by Dennis Tedlock. Copyright © 1985, 1996 by Dennis Tedlock. All rights reserved.

pages 144, 149, 152, 156: From *The Histories* by Herodotus, translated by Aubrey de Selincourt, revised with introductory matter and notes by John Marincola (Penguin Classics 1954, second revised edition 1996). Translation copyright 1954 by Aubrey de Selincourt.

page 163: Reprinted with the permission of Simon & Schuster, Inc., from *The Persians* by Aeschylus, translated by Anthony J. Pedlecki. Copyright © 1970 by Prentice-Hall, Inc. All rights reserved.

pages 174, 176, 180, 181, 182: From *The Rise of the Roman Empire* by Polybius, translated by Ian Scott-Kilvert, selected with an introduction by F.W. Walbank (Penguin Classics, 1979). Copyright © Ian Scott-Kilvert, 1979. Reprinted with permission of Penguin Group/UK.

pages 186, 197: Excerpts from *The Letters of the Younger Pliny,* translated with an introduction by Betty Radice (Penguin Classics 1963, reprinted 1969). Copyright © Betty Radice, 1963, 1969. Reprinted with permission of Penguin Group/UK.

page 225: Figure 8.1 from Patricia Ebrey, Anne Walthall, and JamesPalais, *East Asia,* 2d ed. Copyright © 2009 by Wadsworth, a part of Cengage Learning, Inc. Reproduced by permission, www.cengage.com/permissions.

page 227: From V.H. Mair, *Tun-Huang Popular Narratives,* Cambridge University Press, 1983. Reprinted with permission of Cambridge University Press.

page 247: From N. Levtzion and J.F.P. Hopkins, *Corpus of Early Arabic Sources for West African History,* 1981, Cambridge University Press. Reprinted with permission of Cambridge University Press.

page 264: Table 9.1 adapted from Vincent J. Cornell, "Fruit of the Tree of Knowledge: The Relationship Between Faith and Practice in Islam." From John L. Esposito (ed.), *The Oxford History of Islam.* Copyright © 2001. Reprinted by permission of Oxford University Press.

pages 268, 270: From *The Vinland Sagas,* translated with an introduction by Magnus Magnusson and Hermann Palsson (Penguin Classics, 1965). Copyright © Magnus Magnusson and Hermann Palsson, 1965. Reprinted with permission of Penguin Group/UK.

pages 294–295: From James E. Montgomery, "Ibn Fadlan and the Rusiyyah," *Journal of Arabic and Islamic Studies,* 3 (2000), pp. 1–25. Reprinted with permission of Edinburgh University Press, www.euppublishing.com.

INDEX